Studies in Maritime Archaeology

Seán McGrail

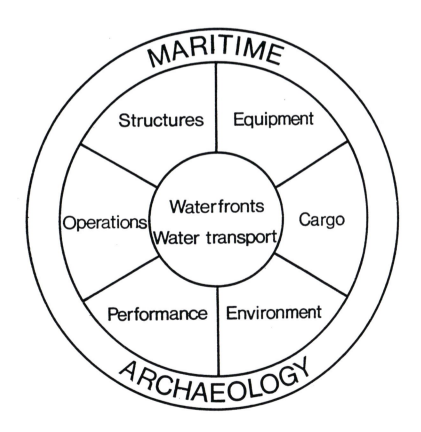

BAR British Series 256
1997

British Archaeological Reports are published by

John and Erica Hedges
7 Longworth Road
Oxford OX2 6RA
England
Tel/Fax +44 (0)1865 511560

All enquiries regarding the submission of manuscripts for future publication should be sent to the above address

BAR 256

Studies in Maritime Archaeology

© S McGrail

Volume Editor: Erica Hedges BA(Hons), MSt.

Printed in England by Biddles Ltd

ISBN 0 86054 903 8

All BAR titles available from:

Hadrian Books
122 Banbury Road
Oxford OX2 7BP
England

The current BAR catalogue with details of all titles in print, prices and means of payment, is available free from Hadrian Books

All volumes are distributed by Hadrian Books Ltd

CONTENTS

LIST OF TABLES

FOREWORD

by Dr Basil Greenhill

The first time I heard of Seán McGrail was in December, 1963. My wife, Ann Giffard, and I had hired a charming small house above a tributary creek of the river Torridge, just west of Bideford, where, on leave from the Diplomatic Service, we worked on a book about Devon settlers in Canada (Greenhill & Giffard, 1974). When we left to return to duty in London our landlord told us that the next occupant would be a Mrs. McGrail and her children, wife of a young Squadron Commander in the Fleet Air Arm of the Royal Navy, who was away at sea.

Seán was indeed then Commander of 849 Squadron, a seaman officer who also held a Merchant Ship Master's Certificate of Competence, who had turned to flying in the early 1950s and was a qualified pilot of both fighters and helicopters. This was a life which required great skill and precision, but gave little intellectual satisfaction. Not surprisingly, Seán left the navy and found a place at Bristol University as a mature student. There he took a First in Mathematics, History and Econometrics, as it proved an excellent foundation for what was to follow. The degree required the presentation of a dissertation on an historical theme and, working under the guidance of the medievalist, Maureen Barry (now Lady Merrison) Seán prepared a paper on Anglo Saxon Water Transport. In so doing, he became enthralled with the work of Ole Crumlin–Pedersen of the Danish National Museum, then a young naval architect, whose work on the development of vessels of the Viking period was to establish him by the 1990s as one of the world's leading maritime archaeologists.

Having, like Seán, changed my course in life, and been appointed Director of the National Maritime Museum, I had established close personal links with Ole Crumlin–Pedersen and, after the discovery and excavation (in which Ole took part) of the Graveney Boat, a contemporary of the period of the Viking expansion, in Kent in 1970, we at the Maritime Museum adopted a policy leading towards the setting up of a maritime archaeological research centre in Britain.

We began by advertising for a potential maritime archaeologist whose job would be to create and build up the Centre. This was a gamble. But fortunately for the future of the discipline in Britain the right number came up. Seán applied for the job and when challenged by the selection board as to why, gave the perfect reply, 'I wish to become the British Crumlin–Pedersen'.

Appointed, we told him to work for a Doctorate of Philosophy in Archaeology of the University of London. Working under David Wilson, later Director of the British Museum, his published thesis, 'Logboats of England and Wales' (McGrail, 1978) – has become one of the basic textbooks of maritime archaeology. Returning to full–time work at the National Maritime Museum he proceeded to build up a centre of multi–disciplinary research and study second only to that of the Danish National Museum at Roskilde near Copenhagen, as that centre then was. A number of excavations, international conferences, experimental work in specialist archaeological method and the problems of conservation of maritime archaeological material, and a formidable publication record gave the Centre, and the Museum, an international reputation. On a personal level, during these years Seán and I built up a close working association and friendship which has, to my great pleasure, continued ever since.

Unfortunately, several years after I had retired in the early 1980s, the Trustees of the Museum, for reasons for which no public explanation has ever been given, took the decision to close down academic work of this kind and the Centre was disbanded. Seán, however, was appointed Professor of Maritime Archaeology at the University of Oxford and was able to continue his own researches, work with students, and publication, in a new and stimulating environment, becoming a Doctor of Science of the university in the process. He continued at Oxford until his retirement in 1993. He was appointed Visiting Professor of Maritime Archaeology at Southampton University in 1991 and continues his work there at the time of publication of this book.

A recently published bibliography of Seán's work (Greenhill & Morrison, 1995) shows 98 books and papers published between 1974 and 1995. All are important to the development of the discipline of maritime archaeology but not all are easily accessible. This book comprises a selection, a cross–section of Sean's work, now made available to the growing body of students and researchers who are working in this field throughout the world.

Basil Greenhill
University of Exeter 1996

References

Greenhilll B. & Giffard A. 1974 *Westcountrymen in Prince Edward's Isle, Toronto University Paperbacks.*

McGrail S. *Logboats of England and Wales, British Archaeological Reports, Oxford, 1978.*

Greenhill B. & Morrison J. *The Archaeology of Boats & Ships, London, 1995.*

INTRODUCTION.

by Sean McGrail

This book contains a selection of my papers on Maritime Archaeology which were originally published, in a wide range of journals and books, between 1975 & 1995. The publication of this collection may be justified on two main grounds. First, students and practitioners of Maritime Archaeology generally approach that subject from one of two directions, archaeological or maritime: an integrated view, though very desirable, is rare. Archaeologists amongst these researchers will know of maritime–orientated papers in the *Oxford Journal of Archaeology*, the research reports of the CBA, the *Proceedings of the Prehistoric Society*, and similar media. On the other hand, these archaeologists may never have seen any of the *Maritime Monographs* formerly published at Greenwich, the publications of the Viking Ship Museum at Roskilde, Denmark, or the delightfully–named and elegantly–produced *Mariner's Mirror*: all these are archaeologically–orientated, at least some of the time. At the other end of the spectrum, many of those maritime archaeologists who are 'boat-buffs', divers or seafarers probably have a similarly partial, but opposite, view of the literature.

Moreover, several of the papers published here, first appeared in the National Maritime Museum's Archaeological Series, which was published for that museum by British Archaeological Reports between 1977 and 1987 : these eleven volumes are now out of print. Others were first printed in publications with only a limited distribution: for example *Atlantic Vision*, published in Dun Laoghaire, *Bullán*, published in Oxford, and *Studies in Mediterranean Archaeology*, published in Jonsered.

This selection of papers should therefore prove useful to those seeking to broaden their approach to Maritime Archaeology and to those who are, at present, frustrated in their pursuit of obscure references or rare copies of short–run publications. The text of each article or extract appears here as it was originally published, 'warts and all'. There are, however, minor changes to the illustrations: where there was duplication, figures have been deleted and a cross–reference substituted; and extra illustrations have been inserted where an extract from a book is not self–contained and needs an introduction.

Contents

The thirty–six articles have been grouped under eleven headings: an introductory section (1.0) centred on the question: what is Maritime Archaeology?; then three papers (2.0) on the fixed, as opposed to the floating, structures we deal with; two sections on the uses of ethnography (3.0) and on classification (4.0); a short section (5.0) on woodworking techniques; four section (6.0 – 9.0) dealing with logboats and plank boats; then a group of papers (10.0) on boat and ship operations; and finally, with the greatest number of papers, a section (11.0) on the currently contentious subject of experimental archaeology. Each section has an introductory commentary, and, within each section, papers are arranged in order of publication.

Clearly these eleven sections are not separated by watertight compartments. Several of the papers deal with a number of inter–related topics which cut across boundaries: for example, most of the papers on boats in sections 6.0 to 9.0 include details of woodworking techniques (also in 5.0); whilst experimental archaeology (11.0) perforce deals with logboats and plank boats (also in 6.0 to 9.0). These relationships are highlighted and cross–referenced in the introduction to each section.

There are other recognised topics which are discussed in several articles, but which are not formally grouped together here. These include:
Environmental studies – see papers 1.1, 1.3, 6.4, 7.1, 9.2 and 11.3
Quantitative methods – see papers 1.1, 1.3, & 6.1
Naval architecture – see papers 6.3, 10.2, & 11.1 to 11.8
Source criticism is essential in any discipline, but has seldom been discussed formally in the context of Maritime Archaeology. It is implicit in several papers in this collection, but for an introduction to this topic see, for example, McGrail (1981, 6–10; 1987, 2–3) and McGrail and Farrell (1979).

Coverage

In *time*, this collection of papers ranges from *c.* 40,000 BC to the late–medieval period. In *place*, the papers generally deal with, or are set within the context of, North West Europe, where most of my fieldwork has been done. However, the discussions on principles and theory (for example, in 2.2, 3.1, 4.1, 6.3, 8.2, and in Section 11.0) are generally intended to be universal in application. Furthermore, papers on seafaring and navigation (Section 10) describe methods and techniques which can be related to a wider context; and I have ventured into the Mediterranean in three papers – 10.5, on Bronze Age Seafaring; 10.2, a discussion on Ballast which was inspired by squabbles amongst Mediterranean pottery specialists; and 11.8, experimental archaeology in the context of the Athenian trireme, a 5th century BC oared warship.

As to the *types of water transport* dealt with – the choice closely reflects the range excavated: logboats (Section 6) and plank boats (Sections 7 to 9). However, paper 4.1 on Classification deals with all forms of water transport – floats, rafts and boats; and log rafts, bundle rafts and hide boats are specifically considered in papers 7.2 and 8.1.

Further Reading

References are given to other books and articles in the introduction to each section. Books covering a number of topics, which the reader might also wish to consult, include: Dr Basil Greenhill's *Archaeology of Boats and Ships* 2nd edition (1995); the first three volumes in Conway's History of the Ship – *Earliest Ships* (1996), Age of the Galley (1995) and *Cogs, Caravels & Galleons* (1994) ; and my own *Rafts, Boats & Ships* (1981), and *Ancient Boats in NW Europe* (1987). The index of the *International Journal for Nautical Archaeology* has entries under many, but not all, of the headings maritime archaeologists would wish to consult.

Acknowledgements

During the past twenty–five years I have benefited enormously from the advise, help and criticism of numerous colleagues. Amongst these I mention in particular: Maureen Barry (now Lady Merrison), whilst I was at the University of Bristol; Basil Greenhill, David Waters, Ted Wright, Harold Kimber, Owain Roberts and Arne–Emil Christensen, during my years at the National Maritime Museum, Greenwich; David Wilson, James Graham–Campbell and Roy Hodson, at the University of London; Barry Cunliffe and Andrew Sherratt, at the University of Oxford and my students in the Institute of Archaeology. I continue to have the friendship and guidance of many of these, and also of John Coates and Ole Crumlin–Pedersen, two naval architects who have, for many years, guided my mathematical enthusiasm for ideal models towards the practical concerns of boat 'design' and boatbuilding. Finally I wish to acknowledge the 'pre–academic' debts I owe to several, now nameless, petty officers who strove to convert me from landsman to seaman in my early years at sea.

The publishers and I are very grateful to the many holders of copyright who have readily given their permission for articles and extracts to be re–printed here. Specific attributions are listed overleaf.

Sean McGrail
Dept. of Archaeology
University of Southampton

1st August, 1996.

References

McGrail S. 1981 *Rafts, Boats & Ships*, HMSO/NMM.
McGrail S 1987 *Ancient Boats in NW Europe*, Longman.
McGrail S. & Farrell A. 1979 'Rowing: aspects of the ethnographic & iconographic evidence.' *Int. J. Nautical Archaeology*, 8, 155–166.

ACKNOWLEDGEMENT OF COPYRIGHT MATERIAL

The author and the publisher gratefully acknowledge permission to re-print articles in this volume from the following copyright holders.

Society of Antiquaries of London. Paper 1.2.
Paul Astroms Forlag, Jonsered, Sweden. Paper 10.5.
Editors, *Atlantic Vision*. Paper 10.3
Editor, *Bullán*. Paper 9.3.
Centre for Maritime Archaeology, Roskilde, Denmark. Papers 1.3, 11.4.
Council for British Archaeology. Papers 2.1, 8.1.
Historisk Museum, Bergen. Paper 2.3.

Institute of Archaeology, Oxford / Blackwell. Papers 10.1. 10.2. 11.5.
Editor, *Mariner's Mirror*. Paper 11.1.
Society for Medieval Archaeology. Paper 6.5.
National Maritime Museum. Papers 1.1, 2.2, 6.2.
Nautical Archaeology Society. Papers 3.1, 5.2, 7.3, 8.2, 9.1, 10.4, 11.6, 11.7.
Prehistoric Society. Papers 5.1, 7.2.
Royal Irish Academy / National Museum of Ireland. Paper 9.2.
Trireme Trust. Paper 11.8.
Editor, *World Archaeology*. Paper 4.1.

SECTION 1.0

MARITIME ARCHAEOLOGY

Introduction

This section begins with two papers primarily seeking to answer the question 'What is Maritime Archaeology?'. The first paper was originally presented to a National 'Maritime Museum seminar on Maritime Archaeology & Ethnography', held at the University of Bristol in March 1982. The second paper is an expanded version of a lecture given at the Society of Antiquaries in September 1988.

At the time of the Bristol seminar, the Archaeological Research Centre (ARC) at the National Maritime Museum, Greenwich was in the middle of its brief ten years' existence. It had been set up in 1976, by Basil Greenhill, Director of the NMM, as a research–orientated enlargement of the museum's Dept of the Archaeology of the Ship, itself started by Dr Greenhill three years earlier. It was to disappear in 1986, sunk almost without trace by Dr Greenhill's successor, Neil Cossons, as he moved towards the establishment of a research–free zone. The definition of Maritime Archaeology given to the Bristol seminar (Fig. 1.1.2) reflected ARC's primary concern at that time: the study of ancient boats & ships. By the time of the Antiquaries lecture, I had been at Oxford for two years and my definition was then a much broader one (Fig. 1.2.1), which included, not only water transport, but also the study of landing places, boatbuilding sites and all the other maritime structures found in the coastal zone and in the vicinity of rivers and lakes.

Archaeological Research

The flow diagram representing the process of archaeological research (Fig. 1.1.5) was based on one that, from *c.* 1975, had been displayed in the National Maritime Museum gallery dealing with ancient boats. I now prefer a slightly more complex diagram (see Fig. 11.8.1) which emphasises that research is a continuous process, not ending at the Publication stage, as it does in Fig. 1.1.5, but moving on through Re–assessment (self & by others) to a Research phase, thence back to Excavation, and so on around the circuit again (Fig. 11.8.1).

Problems in Maritime Archaeology

A number of problems , many of them peculiar to Britain, were highlighted in both the 1984 and the 1989 papers. A Not–easily solved one was the evident barrier between Maritime and 'Mainstream' Archaeology – surely a continuation of the age–old alienation between seamen & landsmen (Greenhill, 1995, 15–16). Today, generally speaking, Archaeology has more understanding of its maritime sub–discipline than it did a decade ago. For example: the Institute of Field Archaeologists has an active maritime section; cooperation between land–based & boat–based archaeologists is more evident, especially in the inter–tidal zone & in the coastal regions generally – as, for example, on the Welsh side of the Severn estuary; and several Archaeological Units have extended their spheres of interest below high water mark – Wessex Archaeology, for example.

Another concern, notably of the 1984 paper, was to establish research priorities. In the field of water transport it was suggested that priority should be given to:
(a)   Prehistoric boats
(b)   Vessels of the Romano–Celtic tradition, and
(c)   Rafts & non–plank boats.
During the intervening years there have been three important finds of prehistoric sewn–plank boats or fragments of boats see the introduction to Section 7.0 Furthermore, Blackfriars boat 1, the first vessel to be recognised as of the Romano–Celtic tradition, has been re–appraised; a ship of this tradition has been excavated in St. Peter Port Harbour, Guernsey; as has a boat from the Severn estuary margins at Barlands Farm, Gwent – see Section 8.0 On the other hand, no non–plank boats or rafts have been found, apart from logboats – an important one in this category being the Hasholme boat of c. 300 BC: see Section 6.

The vessels that have been excavated have been chance finds: it has not yet proved possible to mount a planned research excavation focused on a particular early boat type, apart, that is, from the Brigg 'raft' project (Section 7.0) which was a re–excavation. In Britain, a broad division, noted in these two papers, remains today: vessels found underwater are ships and are of relatively recent age; whereas, early vessels are found in the inter–tidal zone or on land, and they are boats. This may change.

The 1989 paper, in particular, highlighted the administrative, legal and financial differences between survey & excavation on land and similar work underwater: in such matters marine archaeology is at a disadvantage. During the past decade, administrative re–organisation has resulted in a somewhat more even–handed and a more heritage–orientated treatment of underwater archaeology. Governmental responsibility has been moved from the Dept. of Transport (Flinder & McGrail,

1990), via the Dept. of Environment to the Dept of National Heritage in England & to comparable (but more responsive) bodies in the other countries of the United Kingdom. For England this re-arrangement can only be a half-way house, since full parity will not be achieved until marine archaeology is under the same administration as land archaeology – ie within English Heritage.

Another step forward in recent times has been that the Royal Commissions on Historical Monuments are now responsible for compiling a record of wreck sites within territorial waters to the standards used for land sites. Furthermore, the Dept of National Heritage has increasingly made use of its Archaeological Diving Unit in a pro-active manner, thereby adding to the efficiency of historic wreck designation and the general management of important underwater sites. The ADU is also now tasked by the other countries within the United Kingdom.

Nevertheless, problems remain: there are three principal ones:

(a) To ensure (i) that every designated historic wreck site is surveyed &, where permitted, excavated to recognised standards; and (ii) that these sites are adequately published.

(b) To make the law on the disposal of underwater finds (McGrail, 1991) compatible with heritage management principles.

(c) To persuade the appropriate Government Department or Agency to assume responsibility for the stabilisation and *in situ* conservation of designated historic wreck sites, and to instigate research into these techniques (see Paper 9.1).

Training Maritime Archaeologists

The third paper in this Section was published in a *festschrift* for Ole Crumlin-Pedersen, excavator of the Skuldelev & many other wrecks, and *doyen* of medieval maritime archaeologists. There are now several universities in Europe, America and Australia with courses in Maritime Archaeology. In Britain the principal places for a post-graduate qualification are St. Andrews in Scotland and Southampton in England; there are other universities where a general introductory course may be taken at undergraduate level.

Paper 1.3 stresses that entry to the profession should not be restricted to archaeologists, and that naval architects, master mariners and others with a boatbuilding or seafaring background can contribute much to Maritime Archaeology, providing they are trained in archaeological theory and practice; archaeologists similarly need to learn about the maritime environment, the night sky, boatbuilding techniques and seafaring. This point was one of several I made in a public lecture at the Ashmolean Museum, Oxford on 14th May, 1993. Parker (1995, 93) has claimed that I argued then that 'maritime archaeologists should be master mariners'. I made no such point, either in that lecture or in paper 1.3. Nor did I state that today's Master Mariners could interpret wreck sites by using experience 'which is thought to be shared with ancient seafarers' (Parker, 1995, 93). Rather, in both lecture and paper, I urged that those who practise Maritime Archaeology should be trained in all aspects of this multi-disciplinary subject.

References

Flinder A. & McGrail S. 1990 'The UK Advisory Committee on historic wreck sites.' *Int. J. of Nautical Archaeology*, 18, 93–99.

Greenhill B. 1995 *The Archaeology of Boats and Ships*, Conway.

McGrail S. 1991 'Finds from maritime sites in Britain.' in Southworth E. (ed) *What's Mine is Yours*, Museum Archaeologist, 16, 23–29. Society of Museum Archaeologists.

Parker A.J. 1995 'Maritime cultures and wreck assemblages in the Graeco-Roman world.' *Int. J. of Nautical Archaeology*, 24, 87–95,

PAPER 1.1

MARITIME ARCHAEOLOGY PRESENT AND FUTURE

Introduction

The systematic study of ancient boats may be said to have started when Conrad Engelhardt published the Nydam find in 1865. Olsen and Crumlin–Pedersen gave a 20th century orientation to the subject with their preliminary publication of the Skuldelev finds in 1967, but it seems to me that we have almost exhausted the impetus given by their work and we now need to examine what we are attempting to do and perhaps reconsider how we might best achieve our aims.

The subject discussed at the Bristol seminar, or aspects of it, has been known by several names: Nautical Archaeology (IJNA); Naval Archaeology (Basch, 1972); Archaeology under water (Bass, 1966); Marine Archaeology (Blackman, 1973); Archaeology of the Boat (Greenhill, 1976); Archaeology of Water Transport (gallery at National Maritime Museum, Greenwich); and Maritime Archaeology (Institutes at Roskilde and St Andrews). All of these names include the word 'archaeology'; an admirable definition of which has recently been given by Gardin (1980, 5):
'... the sum of studies bearing on material objects which may throw some light, in conjunction with other data, on the history and way of life of ancient people...'
Historians investigate related matters by the study of contemporary documentary and iconographic evidence; whilst other scholars examine such matters from an ethnographic viewpoint. Archaeologists may also undertake these tasks, but our distinctive contribution to knowledge is the study of material excavated or surveyed by ourselves and others.

Of the adjectives used above to qualify 'archaeology', the most comprehensive is 'maritime'. But this would limit our studies to the sea and seafaring, whereas the inclusion of matters connected with inland waterways would make the subject internally cohesive and sufficiently differentiated at the margins to form an homogenous aspect or theme of Man's life: his interaction with, and use of, the waterways of the world. There is no one word which satisfactorily describes these activities, leaving 'Maritime Archaeology' as the least inadequate description, and I therefore recommend we use this term.

Keith Muckelroy also used 'Maritime Archaeology' to describe the subject he studied, and his book of that title includes a diagram (reproduced here as Fig. 1.1.1 defining this research area and showing its relationship to Archaeology under water and to Nautical Archaeology (which by implication he defined as the study of water transport). In Muckelroy's diagram, these three sets intersect: for example the study of the 'maritime technology' (=? building techniques)

of rafts, boats and ships found underwater (D) is common to all three topics. On the other hand, Muckelroy's definition does not permit the maritime archaeologist to study rafts, boats or ships found in graves (A), and his nautical archaeologist may not deal with material from drained sites (C) or non–boat remains from underwater sites (E). Muckelroy's preface states that his aim in writing this book was to establish a theoretical basis for scientific archaeological investigations under water; this limited aim caused him to bias his definition of Maritime Archaeology so that it was based on the location of the find–spot i.e. underwater.

My preferred definition (Fig. 1.1.2) is linked to Man's use of all types of waterways (lakes, rivers, seas) with its focus on the vehicles of that use, the rafts, boats and ships: how they were built, from the selection of the raw material to launching; and how they were used. Thus we seek answers to such questions as: how, when, where, why, and by whom was this raft/boat/ship built and used? The study of boat usage extends the domain of our subject way outside the confines of Boat Archaeology (*sensu strictu*) to the study of the distinctive range of maritime and inland waterway activities (McGrail, 1983A).

The evidence for these topics may come from any site, underwater, inter–tidal or on land, and is supplemented by relevant documentary and iconographic evidence. Ethnography, Naval Architecture, Botanical sciences and experimental Archaeology may throw further light on some of the questions raised by the excavated material.

Each find is set into its maritime context and then into its archaeological context so that its relevance to the body of general archaeological knowledge is made clear. Where possible, this archaeological data may then be related to an historical context. This possibility must not, however, be allowed to dominate research (Clarke, 1978, 11; Cunliffe, 1978, 345). The temptation to equate an archaeological entity (a boat find) with an historically documented one (e.g. the cog) is strong but such a relationship must be demonstrated and not assumed. However, if rigorous argument can establish a link between the two forms of evidence both disciplines benefit. Iconographic evidence may similarly be linked.

After the investigation of several finds, comparable in time and place, we may attempt to generalise to such matters as:

(a) The identification of 'boatyards' in the sense of an area where 'certain local practices' (Crumlin–Pedersen, 1977, 164) were used at a given period. As used here 'boatyard' has parallels with the term 'workshop' used in the study of medieval crafts, and (to a limited degree) with the use of 'axe factory' in prehistoric studies. Such a 'boatyard' has been provisionally identified in the middle reaches of the 12th century AD River Mersey, Lancashire (McGrail and Switsur, 1977).

(b) Main traditions of boatbuilding, possibly with regional and temporal variants. Four such traditions have been postulated by Crumlin–Pedersen (1978) for northern Europe in the medieval period: Nordic or Viking; Cog; Hulc; and 'Punt'; there may be others still to be recognised.

Relationships with Archaeology and other Disciplines

Maritime Archaeology is an integral part of the discipline of Archaeology (Fig. 1.1.3). Areas of interest common to maritime archaeology and 'mainstream' archaeology (defined as that practised by the majority of archaeologists) include tools and building techniques (mainly wood and metalworking, but also sewing, binding and basketry); landing places, harbours and other waterfront sites; and an array of cargo items, many of them having direct relevance to international trade. Aspects of waterborne operations are also relevant to both types of study: fishing and the choice of sea routes, to quote but two. Sea level changes are a mutual problem, and investigators of stone alignments and students of early methods of navigation are dealing with similar aspects of Man's knowledge and technical ability (McGrail, 1983B).

These overlapping interests are certainly recognised by the maritime archaeologist, but the awareness of the mainstream archaeologist is not so evident. Indeed, in some quarters there appears to be almost an antipathy to any form of maritime archaeology. Why is this? I offer three possible reasons:

(a) Many archaeologists avoid technological subjects.

(b) The general alienation of seaman and landsman. Basil Greenhill has frequently alluded to this antipathy and misunderstanding, and the reasons for it have been discussed by Lethbridge (1952, 23–34), among others.

(c) The identification of maritime archaeology solely with underwater work. Until relatively recently underwater excavation has not been pursued in a rigorous, disciplined manner and, as my colleague Martin Dean has pointed out to me, information about excavated material was more likely to be found in the saleroom catalogue than in a scholarly journal. In addition, late 16th to 18th century wreck sites have predominated amongst the finds made in the waters around Britain and Ireland and in most other regions apart from the Baltic and the Mediterranean. This imbalance is reflected in the fact that 61 out of 95 major papers in the first 11 volumes of the *International Journal for Nautical Archaeology* are about post–medieval finds. The traditional archaeologist remains unconvinced of the necessity for work in this period of plentiful documentary sources, and compares it unfavourably with the requirements of earlier periods: he tends to agree with Professor Peter Sawyer's remark that such work is 'an expensive way of telling us what we already know'.

Underwater work is certainly more expensive than land excavation: nevertheless, in certain spheres of research it may be the only way to recover information, and in any case there is much more to maritime archaeology than work under water. We must convince our mainstream colleagues of this by the breadth and the depth of our research. Perhaps we could also help them better to understand what we write by not overloading our papers and books with unnecessary saltwater idioms and technical terms when more widely understood words are available and can be used without loss of precision. If *cove* is synonymous with *groove*, let us use *groove*: the mainstream archaeologist will gain understanding and we will gain his active interest. The distinctive strake between the bottom and the side of a flat–bottomed boat has sometimes been called a *chine girder*, but such a term is probably incomprehensible to many; whereas, *transitional strake* is precise, functionally descriptive and readily understood, and has the added merit of having been used (ubergangsplanke) by Crumlin–Pedersen (1969, 27).

Until the *International Journal of Nautical Archaeology* attains a wider readership amongst mainstream archaeologists, its very existence means that they are not exposed to maritime influences, as important papers and book reviews which might be accepted by one of the national or regional journals are 'side tracked' into this specialist publication. Nevertheless, there are signs of increasing awareness of the maritime dimension as, for example, in certain British universities where aspects of maritime archaeology are taught to undergraduates. If this could be extended to post–graduate teaching and research the whole Archaeological discipline would benefit.

Maritime archaeology then feels itself to be an element of the archaeological discipline, but the discipline itself is not always aware of this relationship. This putative sub–discipline also has relationships with other disciplines as illustrated in Fig. 1.1.3. Unless the maritime archaeologist is truly a polymath, a boat excavation can only be successfully pursued and published with the co–operation of specialists in many, if not all, the fields there named. Whether Archaeology in general can claim to be a discipline and an archaeologist to be of professional standing, has been debated in the past. Some would have an archaeologist to be a technician or a jack of all trades and master of none: for such a view see Kay (1978); and for a counterview see McGrail (1978C). Be that as it may; our work must demonstrate our professionalism to others. There is no doubt, however, that he who would practise maritime archaeology must, in addition to his archaeological knowledge, be familiar with the sea, seamanship and navigation, have a good knowledge of wood science, naval architecture and boatbuilding, and be sufficiently familiar with aspects of the other disciplines mentioned in Fig. 1.1.3 that he can conduct a dialogue with specialists in those fields.

Problems in Maritime Archaeology

To the difficulties of establishing our identity and convincing others of our intellectual probity, professionalism and ability to increase knowledge of Man's past, must be added problems of strategy and tactics which are common to the whole of Archaeology but which are felt especially acutely in a sub–discipline attempting to establish itself. Table 1.1.1 shows how information is lost between antiquity and today due to a combination of natural, generally unavoidable, circumstances and human, generally avoidable, failings. Particular problem areas may be identified:

(a) How to expand our data base and where best to do so with limited resources that is, to identify the significant types of water transport in Group 4B and locate examples of them; and to extend our research to other aspects of maritime archaeology as defined in Fig. 1.1.2

(b) How to minimise the loss of information due to the destruction of exposed finds before recording can take place (Group 5B), and due to inadequate recording (Group 6B).

(c) How to minimise the loss of information due to non–publication (Group 7B) and to inadequate publication (Group 8B).

(d) How to handle the information efficiently.

Table 1.1.1 Information Loss

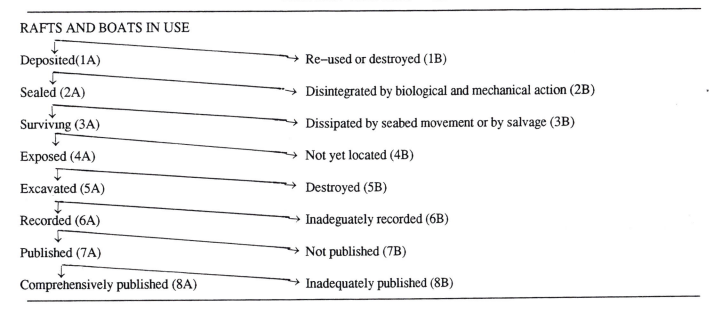

RAFTS AND BOATS IN USE

Deposited(1A) → Re–used or destroyed (1B)

Sealed (2A) → Disintegrated by biological and mechanical action (2B)

Surviving (3A) → Dissipated by seabed movement or by salvage (3B)

Exposed (4A) → Not yet located (4B)

Excavated (5A) → Destroyed (5B)

Recorded (6A) → Inadequately recorded (6B)

Published (7A) → Not published (7B)

Comprehensively published (8A) → Inadequately published (8B)

Research Priorities

Table 1.1.2 lists the numbers of plank boat finds from northern and western Europe, dated earlier than AD 1500 and assessed as important because of the quantity or quality of the remains, and as having been published to a minimum (but not very demanding) standard. Many logboat fragments have also been noted, but generally these are worse recorded than planked boats and most are undated: the priority here must be a systematic investigation, including dating, of the boats already in museums. Finds of other forms of water transport (boats of bark, reed and skin and the rafts) are very rare. The crude figures in Table 1.1.2 mask regional and functional differences, and there is undoubtedly much we do not know about 4th – 15th century maritime Europe. Nevertheless, this period is relatively well represented (5.55 finds per century). In addition, information is available from documentary and iconographic sources, and Crumlin–Pedersen (1978, 1981), Detlev Ellmers (1972, 1979) and others have identified the broad trends and are tackling some of the outstanding problems. This is not the case in the prehistoric period (1st century BC and earlier): not only are there absolutely and

relatively fewer finds, but none of them is of seagoing vessels in a period when Man undoubtedly did make sea voyages. Furthermore, excavation and recording techniques can now be used which were not available when these five boats were first excavated. Thus the relative increase in knowledge to be gained from an additional prehistoric find would be immense.

Ten of the eleven finds from the early centuries AD are thought to be members of a single tradition – Romano–Celtic. I have argued elsewhere (1981, 38) that these boats are a key to the understanding of the boats and ships of the later medieval period, but for one reason or another fewer than half these finds have been comprehensively published. Further finds are needed to extend the data base.

Gillmer (1982) has questioned whether attention should be given to early rafts and non–planked boats on the grounds that these were not the forms of water transport which were developed into the ships of the later medieval period. The counter to this argument is that studies of development are second–stage projects; our primary job as archaeologists is to seek to understand what happened at a particular time in all its aspects, regardless of whether some manifestations apparently proved to be dead–ends in the long run.

Thus our research must be extended into the fields of navigation, seamanship, building sites, landing places and the other aspects of maritime archaeology given in Fig. 1.1.2 And there are three groups of water transport where highly advantageous returns will accrue if we can locate and record further examples:

a.   Prehistoric plank boats
b.   Romano–Celtic plank boats
c.   Boats of skin, reed or bark and all rafts, from any period.

In addition, boats already in museums, especially the numerous logboats, should be re–examined, dated and re–published where necessary.

Table 1.1.2 Plank boat finds from northern and western Europe

Period	Finds	Finds per century
2000BC to BC/AD	5	0.25
1st to 3rd century AD	11	3.66
4th to 7th century AD	10	2.50
8th to 12 century	40	8.00
13th to 15th century	19	6.33

Source: see Appendix 1

Note: There are no finds earlier than the Ferriby boats of c. 1500 bc.

Inadequate Recording

The loss of information due to the destruction of finds before recording (Group 5B in Table 1.1.1 is a problem common to the whole archaeological discipline: it may be minimised by making the public more archaeologically aware. Boat finds in Group 6B pose a different problem. Archaeological objects are frequently excavated and recorded by non–specialists, in the sense that graves are not excavated solely by grave–diggers, undertakers or osteologists, nor pots exclusively by potters. Nevertheless, I believe that, until maritime awareness and capabilities become more widely diffused, it may be argued that, at the very least, water transport should be recorded, if not excavated, by a maritime specialist. My reasoning is based on knowledge of several recent boat finds and may be summarised:

a.   boats are the most complex structure liable to be excavated
b.   boats are not at present understood by the majority of archaeologists and the right questions may not be asked during recording: thus information will be lost if the remains are not lifted, or are lifted and allowed to dry out.

The decision whether to lift or re–bury boat remains must be taken in the light of the resources available to lift, conserve and display or store them, and in relation to their research value as defined above, and in the light of any local or regional factors. On–site recording by non–maritime archaeologists could be appropriate for remains which are to be lifted providing that the timbers are kept wet and , comprehensively photographed, and that a specialist is allowed to examine the remains on site, supervise the lifting and undertake the post–excavation research. On the other hand, finds which are not to be lifted *must* be recorded on site by a specialist, who must be allowed to sample diagnostic parts for further examination.

Adequate recording has been defined by Crumlin–Pedersen (1982, 73) as the minimum information 'a competent model builder would need to build a model of the structure so that it is correct in all detail' Correctness of detail is essential for, as Crumlin–Pedersen also pointed out, the elements of a boat find when joined together define the form of the hull, the underwater shape of which largely determines performance – capacity, speed, stability, etc. A difference of a few degrees in the bevel angle along the edges of clinker–laid planking could lead to significantly different reconstruction. This plank edge angle is also significant in the flush–laid style of shell boatbuilding (as in the Classical tradition). Unless planks are hollowed in cross section it is impossible to obtain a hull with a curved transverse section without such a bevel on one or other of adjoining strakes, yet such details are only infrequently published. Details of construction are also most important for classification studies and in attempts to identify regional traditions and local 'boatyards' (Fenwick, 1972, 178; Arnold, 1977, 293): yet characteristic features, such as the caulking details of some of the Roman–Celtic boats, are not always noted in published reports. A further example may be taken from outside Europe – the Cheops boat. Although Crumlin–Pedersen (1977, 173) has commended the published records of this boat (Abubakr and Mustafa, 1971), I doubt whether they truly reach the standard he has set: for example no details are given of how the planking was fastened and made watertight: no detailed model could be made from this publication. In passing, we may also note that models could of fragmentary remains); not even James Hornell escapes this criticism.

Recording standards may be improved by the use of attribute lists which should ensure that no feature is missed and that the right questions are asked about the state of each attribute. Provisional lists are available for logboats (McGrail, 1978A, 140–2, 331–7; 1978B, 45; McGrail and Switsur, 1979, 113–) and for open planked boats (McGrail and Denford, 1982, 48–65). At Greenwich, Gillian Hutchinson is currently expanding the sections dealing with planking and other elements, whilst the scheme used by Eric McKee (1983) to describe the shape of modern boats can probably be adapted to archaeological needs. The two published attribute lists are interim statements based on a limited number of finds: they need to be tested on material from outside Britain and modified in the light of experience – for example, new features added or existing features partitioned into more useful states. Feature lists engender a systematic approach to the recording and description of a find, with appropriate quantification, and in that sense are not new: Olsen and Crumlin–Pedersen's (1967, 96–152) structured descriptions of the five Skuldelev boats are attribute lists translated into prose.

The majority of these attributes can only be adequately assessed during post–excavation work in the laboratory. If, however, a find is not to be lifted, as many attributes as possible should be noted on site and standard methods of recording should be supplemented by detailed photography, and by stereo–photogrammetry if at all possible. In addition to their role as an *aide-memoire*, attribute lists have other advantages (McGrail and Denford, 1982, 46), not least that they can form the basis of an automated data storage and retrieval system (see below).

Inadequate Publication

Excavators of boats not yet published (Group 7B) can be encouraged to publish, if necessary by withdrawal of permission for further excavation, as suggested by the CBA and DOE working party on the *Publication of Archaeological Excavations* (1982, para 4.4). The inadequately published finds (Group 8B) are more of a problem in that it may now be too late to recover the information which could make the reports adequate. Such reports are often the direct consequence of inadequate work at the recording, analytical and synthesis stages. Two aspects may be highlighted for further discussion (a) Interpretation: the process of theoretically transforming excavated evidence into a reconstruction – from data to theory. (b) Presentation: the method of presenting data (excavated and deduced) so that it is of maximum use to the user.

Interpretation methods Figure 1.1.4 shows two quite different reconstructions made from the same minuscule stone fragments. It serves to focus attention on two points of great importance in maritime archaeology:

(a) Enthusiastic reconstruction can outrun and overstretch the evidence. In certain cases it may be

wise to conclude that, in the present state of knowledge, a full reconstruction is not possible.

(b) There may be several equally–valid hypotheses for the reconstruction of a boat find. In the select category of finds for which there is only one hypothesis may be placed the 24 logboats from south Britain reconstructed out of a total of 179 noted (McGrail, 1978A). Sufficient details had been recorded, and the boats were of sufficiently simple form, that each could be reconstructed in only one way. Attempts to reconstruct a typical Greek trireme may also result in a single solution: this is because the plentiful documentary and iconographic evidence imposes severe constraints on the design (Coates, 1983). In other cases, with lesser evidence, two or more reconstructions may be expected, each one compatible with the excavated evidence. For an example see the various Ferriby boat reconstruction drawings by John Coates (1977, figs. 2, 3, 4).

As performance depends on the reconstructed full form of the boat and on the structural strength of the various elements it is essential that the logical steps taken to convert the on–site and post–excavation data into a reconstruction drawing or lines and construction plans, be well documented so that others may judge the validity of this transformation. In particular, all logical possibilities should be enumerated at each step in the argument and reasons given why certain solutions are preferred and others discarded. The problem of demonstrating the validity of an interpretation is a general weakness in Archaeology: Clarke (1973, 15) emphasised its importance to the establishment of archaeological integrity; whilst the main theme of Gardin's (1980) work on archaeological theory is that much archaeological reasoning is non–rigorous and clearly inadequate.

It is usually possible to display such arguments clearly in symbolic forms or flow diagrams, but perhaps our readership is not quite ready for this. Such aids to clear thinking and orderly presentation of facts are, however, of great value when planning a research project and at almost every stage during the work, in particular during the preparation of the report: although they may not appear in the report they should form its invisible skeleton. The minimum requirement for clear presentation of interpretative arguments is that observed facts (including 'as found' and post–excavation drawings) should be clearly separated from theories and hypotheses (including reconstruction drawings); and the two elements must be linked by succinct, logical discussion. The Brigg 'raft' report (McGrail, 1981B) was intended to fulfil these precepts as far as practicable: others must rule on its success or otherwise. On reflection I think that this report would have been improved by the inclusion of one flow diagram summarising the logical steps and listing the phases of the research which are distinct yet related by feedback. Such a diagram would have been similar to Fig. 1.1.5, but would have dealt specifically with the Brigg research rather than the general procedure illustrated here.

Presentation of data

The basic data recorded on site and in the post–excavation laboratory must be readily available so that conclusions may be validated. Yet to include it all, especially in the detailed form I have recommended above, in the published report would lead to over–long and therefore unread and expensive reports. This is a general problem in the Archaeological discipline: see, for example, Lavell (1981); Alcock (1977–8); and the report by the CBA/DOe working party on *Publication of Archaeological Excavations* (1982). The generally agreed solution is that synthesis reports should be published, supported where necessary by microfiche inserts. This published report would be based upon the *site archive*, consisting of the finds, environmental and other samples, and on–site records (object cards, context cards, site logs, plans, photographs, etc) and the post–excavation *research archive* consisting of detailed drawings and photographs, measurements, analyses of data and samples, computer lists, etc. These two archives would be indexed and made available for examination by others, and to support the assertions made in the published summary or synthesis report.

As it stands, the Brigg 'raft' report is almost self–contained, albeit supported by archives at Greenwich. If it were to be published in the synthesis form recommended above, John Coates' paper on the safe carrying capacity of the reconstructed boat (1981, 261–9) could be transferred entirely to the research archive and his results quoted in a general paper bringing together all conclusions about the 'raft'. Nineteen other specialist reports in this publication could be similarly treated or published in specialist journals. Some of the illustrations could also be transferred to one of the two archives although the majority of explanatory diagrams would be retained; illustrations copied from other publications could be replaced by a reference. The result of applying such principles throughout the book would be to reduce the text from 138 to c. 57 pages and the pages with illustrations from 136 to c. 60. In these formative years of Maritime Archaeology such drastic pruning could be counter-productive. In contrast to an established subject, maritime technical information and knowledge are not widespread and post–excavation techniques are not well known, and there is thus a need to publish them in full. Nevertheless, if we do permit ourselves the 'luxury' of traditional reports for the present, a critical approach to their preparation and presentation is essential if we are to comply within the requirements of a scientific discipline. Whether a traditional or synthesis type of report is published it is essential that maximum use can be made of tabulated and diagrammatic information and the report must be tailored to the *user* and not just the reader.

Data Storage and Retrieval

If standard rules can be evolved for describing a boat find, based, I suggest, on internationally agreed attribute lists, then comparisons between finds become possible, and data about similar finds may be validly pooled. Objective classifications of features by attribute states may be achieved by reference to published drawings of standard structural detail (e.g. the methods of plank fastening illustrated by Eric McKee in Greenhill, 1976, 26), thereby also minimising language translation problems. Such sets of ordered archive material, located in many centres, would in effect constitute an international data bank, the individual parts of which could (in theory, but very inefficiently) be interrogated by correspondence or by personal visit. International data banks have been criticised, but they can work – indeed they must be made to work if progress is to be made in maritime archaeology which is international by nature. Universal data banks are obviously impracticable but when planned for a specific purpose they can be successful: boats in northern and western Europe up to c. AD 1300 seem to be such a specialised and well defined topic.

Data banks can be manually operated, but only a machine system can store and systematically investigate the amount of data generated by the detailed recording of the boat finds of northern and western Europe. Computerised data systems from preliminary planning stage, through excavation and post–excavation research, to archive preparation and publication must be the aim (Booth, 1983). Such a system would have the following advantages

a. Preparation of the system requires clear logical thinking and the definition of categories and attributes. Use of the system necessitates systematic processing of the data: the fact that aspects have not been recorded is noticed; anomalies and ambiguities have to be eliminated; and rigorous logic used.

b. Large quantities of data can be processed.

c. Attributes and their states can be changed, re–ordered, expanded, replaced, redefined, etc.

d. Derived attributes such as Length/Beam or Beam/Draft (and more complex ones) can readily be calculated and used to interpret function, and estimate performance, and for comparison with data from other finds. Such attributes can be stored in the units in which they are measured or as a ratio, rather than having to be stored as members of high/medium/low group differentiated almost arbitrarily, as in a manual system. The machine may then search for 'natural' groupings which may be used until change in input data suggests better ones.

e. Data can be sorted and analysed systematically; statistical analyses and pattern–searching techniques may be used; selected data and –analyses can be printed out in a variety of combinations. If all the putative members of the Romano–Celtic tradition of boat building had been comprehensively recorded, a computer could soon clarify whether this was a valid polythetic grouping and identify which attributes defined any sub–groups. We were reminded at the seminar that quality of output is only as good as quality of input; but the methods chosen to analyse the data can also influence the output: this is one reason why the correlations produced and the patterns suggested by the computer must be compared with the primary data; and an attempt must be made to understand the causes behind the patterns revealed.

f. Multiple or even random access to the data is possible. It has been suggested (Crumlin–Pedersen, 1977B) that the *International Journal for Nautical Archaeology* is a data bank with the index giving the points of entry: but the number of access points is limited, data may be missed and redundant data generated. Comprehensive catalogues have also been suggested as repositories of data. It may well be that, for example, Ellmer's catalogue (1972, 271–341) contains all available information about medieval cargo boats, but short of reading every entry and making lists, comprehensive information on a particular attribute or group of attributes, is not readily retrievable, as it would indeed be if this catalogue information were to be systematically computerised. Retrievable information would then not be limited to single features (moss) or even additive combinations (moss and treenails), but could be negative (moss without treenails) or of more complexity (clinker without clenched nails but with moss or hair).

Maritime archaeologists need to up–date their techniques especially in the areas of recording, data storage and retrieval, and publication. The corollary of this is that more time must be spent on fewer, but important, projects. Quality rather than quantity of research and publication must be our aim.

Acknowledgements

This paper has been improved by discussion with my colleagues in the Archaeological Research Centre at Greenwich, in particular Gillian Hutchinson, Ben Booth and Dr Richard Clarke read an earlier draft and made several useful suggestions. The illustrations are copyright, National Maritime Museum.

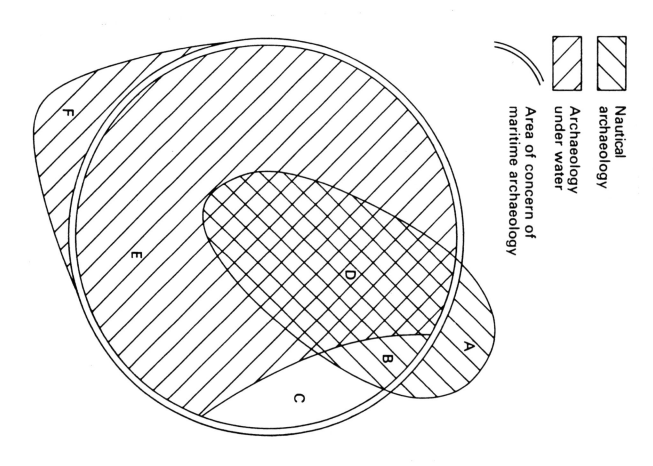

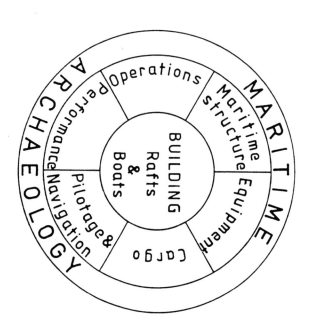

Figure 1.1.1 Muckelroy's maritime archaeology and its relationship to nautical archaeology under water. A = Finds in graves B = Finds on beaches C = Finds on drained sites D = Rafts and boats found underwater E = other finds from underwater F = Submerged land sites

Figure 1.1.2 The scope of maritime archaeology.
Building: tools and techniques from choice of raw materials to in-service repairs.
Maritime Structures: building sites, landing places and harbours, boat sheds, slipways, causeways, fish weirs, etc.
Equipment: anchors, bailers, guns, oars, mast, sail, rigging, rudders, compasses, etc. and crew's personal equipment.
Cargo: goods; international, coastal and river trade.
Pilotage and Navigation: methods, instruments, (e.g. sounding lead and astrolabe), charts, pilotage handbooks, lighthouses etc.
Performance: stability, load/draft/freeboard, speeds under oar and sail, windward performance, leeway, steering, etc.
Operations: seamanship; use of landing places; loading/stowage/unloading; fishing and other functional uses; sea routes; contemporary environment including former climate, sea levels, coastlines; tidal regimes and river courses etc.

Legend:
Nautical archaeology
Archaeology under water
Area of concern of maritime archaeology

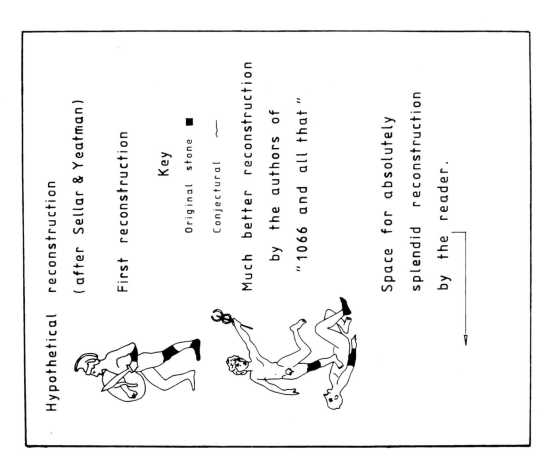

Figure 1.1.4   Hypothetical reconstructions – adapted from a drawing by J. Reynolds on p. 91 of *And now all this* by W.C. Sellar and R.J. Yateman (1944).

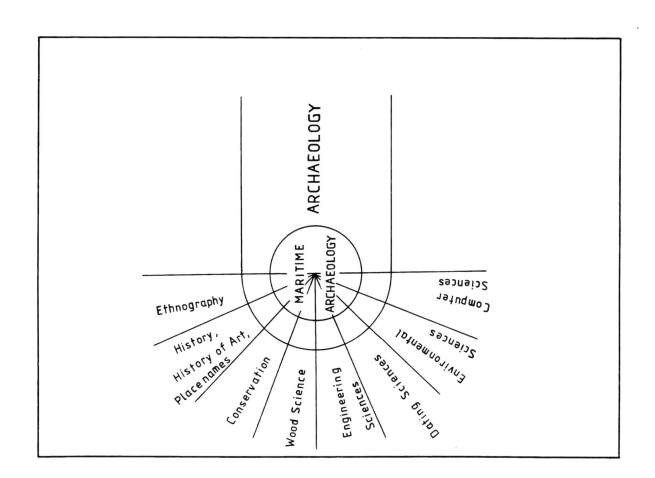

Figure 1.1.3   The relationship of maritime archaeology to Archaeology and other disciplines.

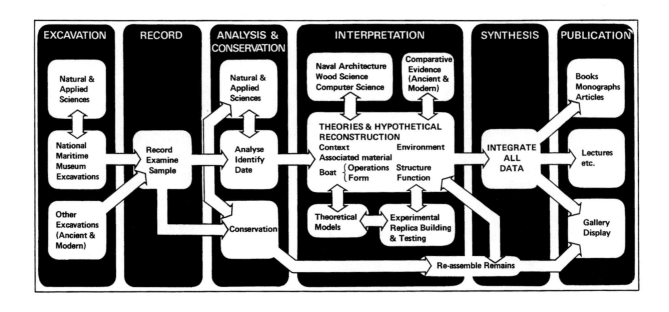

Figure 1.1.5   Flow diagram of research procedure used in the Archaeological Research Centre, National Maritime Museum, Greenwich

APPENDIX

Finds enumerated in Table 1.1.2

2000BC to BC/AD – 5

Brigg 'raft'
(McGrail,1981.B)
Ferriby 1, 2, 3
Hjortspring (Rosenberg, 1937)

1st to 3rd century AD – 11

Bevaix
Blackfriars 1
County Hall
Druten
New Guy's House
Pommeroeul 1, 2
Yverdon
Zwammerdam 2. 4.

4th to 7th century AD – 10

Barset
Gretstedbro
Halsnøy
Hasnaes 1
Kvalsund 1, 2
Nydam 2

Snape
Sutton Hoo 1, 2

8th to 12th century AD – 40

Årby (Arbman, 1940)
Askekarr
Baumgarth
Danzig–Ohra 1, 2, 3
Egnersund
Ellinga
Eltang
Falsterbo
Frevenburg 1, 2
Galtaback
Gokstad 1, 2, 3, 4
Graveney
Hasnaes 2
Hedeby
Klastad
Ladby (Thorvildsen, 1957)
Lynaes
New Fresh Wharf
(Marsden, 1979)
Oseberg
Ralswick 1, 2, 3, 4
Sjøvoll
Skuldelev 1, 2, 3, 5, 6
Stettin
Tune
Utrecht 1, 2, 4

13th to 15 century AD – 19

Bergen (Herteig, 1975)
Blackfriars 3
Bremen Cog
Elbing
Flevoland K73/74, N5, MZ22 (Reinders, 1979)
Grace Dieu
Kalmar 1, 2, 3, 4, 5 (Akerlund, 1951)
Kentmere 1
Kolding
Kollerup
Kyholm
N E Polder M.107 (Reinders, 1979)
Vej by

Note Where no reference is given, details may be found in Crumlin–Pedersen, 1981, Ellmers, 1972 or McGrail, 1981 A.

References

Abubakr A. M. and Mustafa A. Y. 1971 'Funerary boat of Khufu.' *Agyptischen Baufors chung und Altertumskunde*, 12, 1–16.

Akerlund H. 1951 *Fartygsfynden i den forna hamnen i Kalmar*, Stockholm.

Alcock L. 1977–8 'Excavation and publication: some comments.' *Proceedings of the Society of Antiquaries, Scotland*, 109, 1–6.

Arbman H. 1940 'Der Arby–fund.' *Acta Archaeologica* 11, 43–102.

Arnold B. 1977 'Some remarks on caulking in Celtic boat construction and its evolution in areas lying northwest of the Alpine arc.' *IJNA*, 293–297.

Arnold B. 1978 'Gallo–Roman boat finds in Switzerland.' in Taylor J du P. and Cleere H. (ed), *Roman Shipping and Trade*, 31–5. CBA Research Report 24.

Basch L. 1972 'Ancient wrecks and the archaeology of ships.' *IJNA* 1, 1–58.

Bass G. F. 1966 *Archaeology under Water*, Penguin.

Blackman D. J. (ed) 1973 *Marine Archaeology*, Butterworth.

Booth B. K. W. 1983 'Museum based Archaeology – an approach to data management.' *Institute of Archaeology Bulletin*, 19.

Clarke D. L. 1978 *Analytical Archaeology*, 2nd edition, Methuen.

Coates J. 1983. 'A Greek Trireme Project.' *Mariners Mirror*, 69, 89–90.

Coates J. F. 1977 'Hypothetical reconstructions and the Naval Architect.' in McGrail S. (ed) 1977, 215–226.

Crumlin–Pedersen O. 1969 *Das Haithabuschiff* Ausgrabungen in Haithabu, Bericht 3, Neumunster.

Crumlin–Pedersen O. 1977A 'Some principles for the recording and presentation of ancient boat structures.' in McGrail S. (ed) 1977, 163–200.

Crumlin–Pedersen O. 1977B 'Comment' in McGrail S (ed) 1977, 158.

Crumlin–Pedersen O. 1978 'Ships of the Vikings.' in Anderson T. and Sandred K. I. (ed) *The Vikings*, 32–41, Uppsala.

Crumlin–Pedersen O. 1981 'Skibe pa havbunden', 'Handels og søfartsmuseets Arbog*, 28–65.

Crumlin–Pedersen O. 1982 'Comment' in McGrail, S, (ed), 1982, 73.

Cunliffe B. 1978 *Iron Age Communities in Britain*, 2nd edition, R.K.P.

Ellmers D. 1972 *Fruhmittelalterliche Handelsschiffahrt in Mittel und Nordeuropa*, Neumunster.

Ellmers D. 1979, 'Cog of Bremen and related boats.' in McGrail S (ed) *Medieval Ships and Harbours in N Europe*, NMM Archaeological Series 5, British Archaeological Reports, Oxford, S66, 1–15.

Engelhardt C. 1865 *Nydam Mosefund*, Copenhagen

Fenwick V. H. 1972 'Thoughts on the recording of old ships.' *IJNA* 1, 177–180.

Gardin J–C 1980 *Archaeological constructs*, Cambridge University Press.

Gilimer T. 1982 'Review of Rafts Boats and Ships.' *IJNA* 11, 265–6.

Greenhill B. 1976 *Archaeology of the Boat*, A & C Black.

Herteig A. E. 1975 'Excavation of Bryggen, Bergen, Norway.' in Bruce–Mitford R. (ed) *Recent archaeological excavation in Europe*, 65–89.

Kay H. F. 1978 'Review of Sources and Techniques in Boat Archaeology.' *IJNA* 7, 89–90.

Lavell C. 1981 'Publication: an obligation.' *Bull. Institute of Archaeology*, 18, 91–125.

Lethbridge T. C. 1952 *Boats and Boatmen*, Thames and Hudson.

McGrail S. (ed) 1977 *Sources and Techniques in Boat Archaeology*, NMM Archaeological Series 1, British Achaeological Reports, Oxford, S29.

McGrail S. 1978A, *Logboats of England and Wales*, NMM Archaeological Series 2, British Archaeological Reports, Oxford, 51.

McGrail S. 1978B 'Medieval logboat from Giggleswick Tarn, Yorkshire.' in Annis P. (ed) *Ingrid and other Studies*, NMM Monograph 36, 25–46.

McGrail S. 1978C 'Letter to Editor.', *IJNA* 7, 347–8.

McGrail S 1981A *Rafts, Boats and Ships*, HMSO.

McGrail S. 1981B (ed) *Brigg 'raft'*, NMM Archaeological Series 6, British Archaeological Reports, Oxford, 89.

McGrail S. (ed) 1982, *Woodworking Techniques before 1500*, NMM Archaeological Series 7, British Achaeological Reports, Oxford, S129.

McGrail S. 1983A 'Interpretation of archaeological evidence for maritime structures.' in Annis P. (ed) *Sea Studies*, National Maritime Museum, Greenwich, 33–46.

McGrail S. 1983B "Cross–channel' seamanship and navigation in the late 1st Millennium BC.' *Oxford Journal of Archaeology*, 3, 299–337.

McGrail S. and Denford G. 1982 'Boatbuilding techniques, technological change and attribute analysis.' in McGrail, (ed), 1982, 25–72.

McGrail S. and Switsur R. 1979 'Medieval logboats of the R. Mersey.' in McGrail S. (ed) 1979, 93–115.

McKee E. 1983 *Working Boats*, Conway, London.

Marsden P. 1979 'Medieval ships of London.' in McGrail S. (ed) *Medieval Ships and Harbours*, 83–92, NMM Archaeological Series 5, British Archaeological Reports, Oxford, S66.

Milne G. and Hobley B. (ed) 1981 *Waterfront Archaeology in Britain and Northern Europe*, CBA Research Report 41.

Muckelroy K. 1978 *Maritime Archaeology*, Cambridge University Press.

Olsen O. and Crumlin–Pedersen O. 1967 'Skuldelev Ships I.' *Acta Archaeologica* 38, 73–174, (Copenhagen).

Reinders R. 1979 'Medieval ships: recent finds in the Netherlands.' in McGrail, S, (ed), *Medieval Ships and Harbours*, 35–44, NMM Archaeologic Series 5, Britsh Archaeological Reports, Oxford, S66.

Rosenberg G. 1937 *Hjortspringfundet*, Kφbenhaven.

Thorvildsen K. 1957, *Ladby–Skibet*, Kφbenhaven.

Note IJNA = Int. J. of Nautical Archaeology

Reprinted, with permission, from:

McGrail, S (ed) *Aspects of Maritime Archaeology and Ethnography*: 11–40. NMM Greenwich (1984)

PAPER 1.2

MARITIME ARCHAEOLOGY IN BRITAIN[1]

The Introduction to The Institute of Field Archaeologists' Code of Conduct states that: 'Archaeology is the study of the nature and the past behaviour of Man in his environmental setting'. One of the principal environments Man has used is the maritime one, and for convenience of exposition the term 'maritime' is taken here to include inland waters, lakes, rivers and estuaries, as well as the seas and oceans. This usage is not only for convenience but also because there is continuity between the sea and inland waters: they are physically connected, and often the same vessels and the same men use them.

'Maritime Archaeology' thus means the study of the nature and the past behaviour of Man in his use of those special environments associated with lakes, rivers and seas (Fig. 1.2.1). This topic is part of the archaeological discipline, yet is sufficently differentiated from other sub–disciplines to form a readily recognizable and distinctive aspect or theme of Man's life: his interaction with, and use of, the waters of the world. Overseas trade routes, navigational techniques, changes in sea levels and in coastlines, fishing equipment, causeways, landing places and harbours are studied, as well

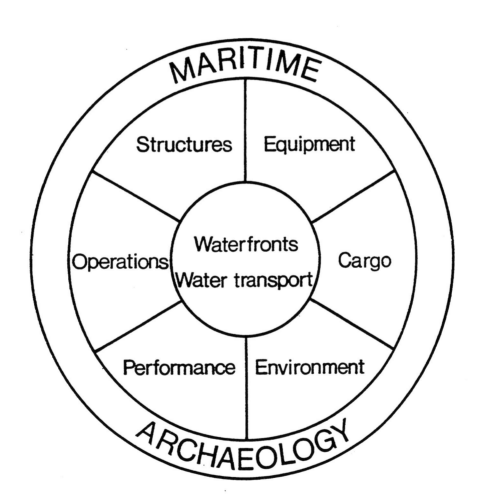

Figure 1.2.1 A diagram to illustrate the scope of maritime archaeology. 'Waterfronts' include: landing places, harbours, causeways, fish weirs and other maritime structures. 'Water Transport' includes: floats, rafts, boats and ships.
Copyright: Institute of Archaeology, Oxford

---

1 This is a slightly expanded version of a paper read to the Society of Antiquaries on 27 September 1988.

as the structure and the performance of rafts, boats and ships. The evidence for this may come from land as well as from underwater; the subject is defined by the research targets set and not by the techniques used.

In late 1971, the Chairman of the Trustees of the National Maritime Museum, Lord Runciman, and the Director, Basil Greenhill, prepared a paper entitled, 'The National Maritime Museum and new problems in archaeology'. They noted that these problems had arisen firstly because of increasing interest in what was then known as 'boat archaeology', for example, the Viking Age excavations at Skuldelev in Denmark; secondly because archaeological material was being increasingly recovered from shipwrecks due to improvements in diving techniques and the explosion of interest in amateur diving; and thirdly because of the increasing disturbance of the coastal environment by such activities as dredging, draining and land reclamation.

Some of the problems Runciman and Greenhill highlighted seventeen years ago are still problems today. These include:
(a)   the inadequacy of legislation
(b)   the lack of interest in shipwrecks displayed by those bodies mainly concerned with general archaeology, that is the non–maritime archaeological and museum establishment
(c)   the insufficiency of archaeological and conservation resources for the maritime task
(d)   the splitting–up of site archives, as finds from large shipwrecks are dispersed to specialist museums and into private ownership.

In addition, Runciman and Greenhill came to a simple yet profound conclusion: maritime archaeology (in Britain) falls almost fortuitously into two parts, boats and ships. Boats are mainly found on land, are relatively small, have few contents, and mostly date from before c. AD 1500. Ships (on the other hand) are mainly found under water in the form of wrecks, are larger, usually contain objects of general, rather than specifically maritime interest and mostly date from after 1500.

Lord Runciman and Dr Greenhill were not drawing any theoretical distinctions here but reporting the scene as they found it. Their observation was true in 1971 and, by and large, it remains true in Britain and in British waters today. A comparable division has recently been recognized in reports published by the Royal Netherlands Academy of Arts and Sciences[2]. The authors find that there have been, and are, great differences between the way the Dutch state deals with boats found on land and in the drained polders on the one hand, and the underwater investigation of shipwrecks on the other.

The division of maritime archaeology into early boats on land sites and later ships underwater, highlighted by Runciman and Greenhill, may not always remain so: early boats and ships may in future be found in the seas off the British coast.[3] Nevertheless, it is most important to recognize that this division exists now, if the recent history of maritime archaeology and the problems it faces today are to be understood. The aim of this paper is to describe some of the achievements and discuss some of the problems of maritime archaeology in Britain. There will be more emphasis on the latter topic since the achievements may be studied in detail in relevant publications, but the problems are seldom discussed in academic journals.

Achievements

Knowledge of the past
During the past twenty–five or so years our knowledge of Britain's maritime past has increased markedly, especially in the environmental, economic and technological spheres. This has been mainly, but not entirely, in the medieval, Roman and prehistoric periods, and primarily from excavations on land or in the inter–tidal zone rather than from underwater. Examples of such excavations include those of boats from land or inter–tidal sites at Ferriby, Brigg, Hasholme, Sutton Hoo and Graveney, and the underwater excavation of Bronze Age sites off Dover and off Salcombe (pioneering work by Keith Muckelroy, subsequently progressed by Martin Dean). Much has also been learned from the excavation of an impressive range of maritime sites: the prehistoric landing places at Ferriby, Brigg and Hasholme in Humberside; the causeways of the Somerset Levels; the overseas trading sites at Mount Batten in Plymouth Sound, Hengistbury in Christchurch Harbour and Redcliff on the Humber; and the waterfronts and harbours of Roman and medieval London, and medieval Newcastle, Hartlepool, Hull, Bristol, Reading, Exeter and Southampton, to name but a few.[4] It should now be possible

2 J. R. Brujin, G. W. Muller and H. H. van Regtern, Norms in the Study of Dutch Shipwrecks Royal Netherlands Academy of Arts and Sciences (Amsterdam, 1986) R. Reinders, Maritime Archaeological Heritage: Responsibility and Management Rijksdienst voor Ijsselmeer–polders Werkdocument 1 (1986).

3 See, for example, K. Muckelroy, 'Two Bronze Age cargoes in British waters', Antiquity 54 (1980), 100–9. M. Dean, 'Evidence for possible prehistoric and Roman wrecks in British waters', Int. J. Naut. Archaeol. Underwater Explor. 13 (1984), 78–80.
4 E. V. Wright, North Ferriby Boats, National Maritime Museum Monograph 23, (London, 1976). S. McGrail, Brigg 'raft' and her prehistoric environment, Brit. Archaeol. Rep. 89 (Oxford 1981). M. Millett and S. McGrail, 'Archaeology of the Hasholme logboat', Archaeol. J. 144 (1987), 69–155. R.L.S. Bruce–Mitford, Sutton Hoo Ship Burial I (London, 1975). V Fenwick, Graveney Boat, Brit. Archeol. Rep. 53 (Oxford 1978). K.Muckeloroy, 'Middle Bronze Age trade between Britainand Europe: a maritime perspective', Proc. Prehist. soc. 47 (1981), 275–97. B. Cunliffe, Mount Batten, Plymouth, Oxford Univ. Comm. Archaeol. Monographs 26 (Oxford 1988). B. Cunliffe, Hengistbury Head, Dorset, I, Oxford Univ. Comm. Archaeol. Monograph 13 (Oxford, 1987). D. Crowther, S. Willis and J Creigthon, (forthcoming) 'Topography and archaeology of Redcliff', in D.R. Crowther and S. Ellis (eds.), Humber and its Environs in History and Prehistory, University of Hull. J.M. Coles, Somerset Levels Papers 1–14 (1975–88). G. Milne and B. Hobley, Waterfront Archaeology in Britain and Northern Europe, CBA Res. Rep. 41 (London, 1981). A.E. Herteig, Conference on Waterfront Archaeology in North European Towns No. 2, Historisk Museum, Bergen (Bergen, 1985).

for both archaeologists and historians to compile a more balanced picture of prehistoric and medieval Britain, by including the maritime dimension.

The potential of underwater work on post–medieval sites has been strikingly demonstrated by the work of the Mary Rose Trust in locating and excavating to commendably high standards Henry VIII's *Mary Rose*, and raising the remains (Fig 1.1.2).

Conservation

A second area of achievement is an the field of conservation. Starting from a relatively low point, the conservation of material from wet sites has, if anything, outstripped progress made in other aspects of conservation. It is not yet known whether the polyethylene glycol method in its variant forms will conserve waterlogged wood in all stages of degradation for evermore, but the signs are good; and freeze–drying is being used on an ever increasing scale. There has also been progress in the conservation of metals, but perhaps with not quite the same degree of success, and more research is necessary on the stabilization of iron. The main problem in the field of conservation of materials from wet environments is to establish the best criteria for selecting which artefacts and structures should be conserved out of the vast numbers that are excavated from both land and underwater sites.

Legislative and organizational progress

The past fifteen years have also seen progress in legislative and organizational matters. The passing of the Wrecks Act of 1973; the consequent establishment of the Runciman Committee to advise the Secretary of State for Trade (and latterly of Transport) on the designation of historic wreck sites and related matters; and, more recently, the setting up of the Department of Transport's archaeological diving unit at St Andrews University, have been significant steps forward. This progress may not have been as fast or as far as some would like: this question will be considered further below, p. 32.

At about the time the Wrecks Act was passed, an Archaeological Research Centre was established at the National Maritime Museum. This centre made a significant contribution to maritime archaeology both on land and, increasingly from 1980, underwater, and also under took experimental research, until it was disbanded in 1986.

In the same year, 1973, an Institute of Maritime Archaeology was established at the University of St Andrews aimed especially at underwater work, both at sea and inland. Under different name, the Scottish Institute of Maritime Studies, and with a different status but with similar aims, this Institute continues to educate and train underwater archaeologists.

In the early 1970s also, extensive excavation of London's waterfront began, and there are now a series of reports on investigations from the Roman period onwards. Arising from these excavations, and others in Britain and elsewhere, came a series of conferences on waterfront archaeology. The subjects dealt with at these conferences considerably overlap the topics studied at the series of symposia on boat and ship

archaeology which had been established in 1976 as an outcome of a conference at Greenwich. There would be undoubted benefits if these groups, with so much in common, were to combine, at least for their conferences.

The Council for Nautical Archaeology (CNA) was set up in 1967 and gave birth to the *International Journal of Nautical Archaeology and Underwater Exploration (I.J.N.A.)* in 1972, and to the Nautical Archaeology Society in 1980. Subsequently the CNA became a specialist section of the Council for British Archaeology. The Nautical Archaeology Society has a membership of amateurs and professionals, qualified and unqualified, full–time and part–time, and one of its principal achievements has been to make divers more aware of the necessity for training before they investigate the underwater heritage. The *I.J.N.A.* has become the main vehicle for the publication of underwater work – mainly classical Mediterranean and post–medieval sites, but with some papers on land–based excavations and research. The establishment and the continuing prosperity of this journal is very much an achievement, but, unwittingly, it has created a problem for maritime archaeologists in a world dominated by period or regional societies and publications. It is difficult to decide whether to publish in this specialist journal, which generally speaking is little read by mainstream archaeologists, or to publish in a period or regional journal where the non–maritime world may more readily be also been influenced.

Archaeologists were late in setting up a professional organization, but the Institute of Field Archaeologists was finally established in December 1982 with a code of conduct similar in intention to those of other professions such as arehitects and engineers. A Maritime Affairs Group has recently been formed as a sub–group of the Institute, aiming to press for high professional standards underwater, and incidentally to demonstrate the 'respectability' of underwater work to land–based (possibly 'land–biased'?) archaeologists.

There are other groups that might be mentioned, such as the long–established Society for Nautical Research which publishes the *Mariner's Mirror*, a highly regarded historical journal. As in other areas of the historical and archaeological disciplines, the maritime societies and institutions are many and varied.

Educational achievements

The certification scheme recently introduced by the Nautical Archaeology Society is designed to lead divers, with little or no knowledge of archaeology or of working purposefully underwater, from a theoretical introduction, through lectures on techniques and fieldwork, to the completion of an examined project. The scheme is in its early days, but has attracted a useful number of candidates.

At a more specialized level, theoretical and sometimes practical courses on aspects of maritime archaeology are given to undergraduates at several universities, whilst at three of them, St Andrews, Bangor and Oxford, it is possible to work for a higher degree. However, there remains much work to be done by the universities to ensure that all students of archaeology and history understand the potential and the problems of maritime archaeology.

Allocation of resources

The gains in our knowledge of the past have very much depended on an increased allocation of resources to maritime archaeology. A variety of methods have been used to achieve this. Some maritime projects, especially those that are land–based, where costs are generally lower than under water, have been financed and controlled by a single institution, as for example the National Maritime Museum's excavation, conservation and publication of the prehistoric Brigg 'raft'. In other circumstances, two institutions with complementary facilities have worked together, as in the cooperation between the British Museum and the National Maritime Museum in the Graveney boat project (and also in the underwater excavation of the collection of bronze artefacts off Salcombe and in Langdon Bay, Dover). Furthermore, the Society of Antiquaries has joined the British Museum, Greenwich and others to finance the important excavations at Sutton Hoo.

A recent boat excavation involved cooperation between a landowner, a water board, an archaeological unit and a regional museum. This was the excavation and recovery (in advance of river bank stabilization) of a nineteenth–century wooden barge from the River Usk at Tredunnoc (fig 1.2.3) and involved the Glamorgan/Gwent Archaeological Trust and Newport Museum. Apart from the intrinsically valuable information obtained about an almost unknown boat type and about a poorly documented embankment of the River Usk, this project has also demonstrated that, with maritime advice, a land–based archaeological unit can effectively deal with a boat on an inland site.[5] The Glamorgan/Gwent Trust has further emphasized its commitment to maritime archaeology by excavating prehistoric sites in the inter–tidal zone of the Severn Estuary. It is to be hoped that this example may lead other units to consider involvement, should similar maritime opportunities present themselves. Perhaps coastal units should extend their interests to the limits of territorial waters?

An example of a non–institutional project may also be mentioned: the recovery of a small logboat from a former course of the River Lee at Clapton, Hackney. Here archaeologists, working in their own time, have not only recorded this chance find, but have also built a replica and used it.[6]

It seems then to be the case that, in general, there are sufficient resources to cope with important but small–scale maritime sites. There is an abrupt change of scale however in the size of resources required to control and finance the excavation, conservation, display and publication of a ship, and, as mentioned above, in Britain and in British waters the difference between the excavation of a small boat and that of

a ship generally means the difference between land and underwater excavation. The vast resources required and the long time–scale involved in such underwater projects have not been fully appreciated by many of the groups which have applied to the Department of Transport for a licence to investigate designated sites. There are two or three groups to which these strictures do not apply, for example the Mary Rose Trust. The Trust's key to the successful achievement of nearly all its aims lies in its early recognition of the vast job that lay ahead if the project was to be undertaken to high professional standards. The finance required to date is astronomically unbelievable to any university archaeologist, but by hard work and diligent fund–raising from a wide range of sources the Trust is now in the happy position of having no debts and being able to meet its running expenses from income generated by its museum and its Ship Hall.

The Mary Rose Trust's achievements in this respect can perhaps be best paralleled on land by the achievements of the Museum of London in its amassing of resources for the London waterfront excavations. That Museum's Department of Urban Archaeology and Department of Greater London Archaeology have excavated several sites along the Thames, revealing much about the maritime aspects of Roman and medieval London. They have dug to a time–scale agreed with developers and received finance from several sources, including government funded bodies, local authorities and commercial firms. The difficulties that the Museum of London, and similar organizations elsewhere, had to face in this type of excavation led to discussions between the British Property Federation and the Standing Conference of Archaeological Unit Managers (SCAUM). These discussions resolved some of the problems and have led to the adoption of a voluntary National Code of Practice by many urban archaeologists and developers. Under this code, before any digging or development is undertaken, an archaeological implications report should be prepared and form the basis of an agreement between the two parties which should result in cost effective working on both sides, with as beneficial an outcome for archaeology as can be obtained in present circumstances and under existing legislation.

On land then, maritime archaeology, although it may seem to some to be peripheral, does fit into the mainstream, and its problems are similar. Fieldwork is undertaken by single organizations or, increasingly, by cooperation between several organizations with multiple–source funding. There are, however, fundamentally different problems with the underwater aspects of maritime archaeology.

Problems and some Solutions

There are three main problem areas in underwater archaeology in Britain:

(a)   Particular problems due to the nature of the environment within which the fieldwork is undertaken

(b)   the generally poor perception of underwater archaeology by decision makers and resource allocators.

---

5 S. Parry and S. McGrail, 'Tredunnoc boat', Int. J. Naut. Archaeol Underwater Explorer 18 (1989), 43–49.

6 P.R.V. Marsden (ed), 'A Late Saxon logboat from Clapton, London Borough of Hackney', Int. J. Naut. Archaeol. Underwater Explor. 18 (1989), 89–111.

(c)   problems due to inadequate resources.

Particular problems

The very fact of working under water means that, whatever way the output of an excavation is measured, comparable work will cost more under water than on land. The requirement for boats and other specialist equipment, the generally slower work rate and the restrictions imposed by the weather and tidal flows all combine to increase relative costs. Good organization can reduce these effects, but they cannot be avoided entirely. Against these extra costs however, must be set the remarkable range of information obtainable from certain underwater sites that, can rarely, if ever, be obtained from land sites.

A second specialist problem is the degradation of sites by man and by nature. There is a long history of salvaging wrecks for commercial gain, and there are firms which specialize in the clearance dredging of harbours and channels, or dredging for materials which can be used in the construction industry. In these circumstances the maritime heritage can quickly be lost. The solution here may lie in persuading those who licence or organize salvage and dredging, and those groups or federations which undertake these activities to consider adopting an appropriate version of the property developers' Code of Practice. By these means, archaeologists with appropriate experience could be drawn into the discussions early in the planning stage, leading to an active participation in the operation with the aim of recovering the maximum archaeological information from the site within the constraints of current legislation.

From the moment of deposition all wrecks are subject to natural decay by biological, chemical and physical processes, although if a site is quickly covered by sediments and remains so, this degradation is slowed down, and a wreck may then achieve a near stability with its environment. As soon as such a site is disturbed the rate of degradation is markedly increased. An underwater site which is not being worked archaeologicallly or commercially and which is evidently well protected by sedimentation may nevertheless become exposed to degradation as the indirect results of human action, such as the building of a bridge or a tidal barrier, or the diversion of a river. Such processes disturb the waterflow and can remove protective sediments from underwater sites. A possible solution here is for the organizations representing archaeologists (IFA), county administrations (ACAO) and the regional units (SCAUM), to press for an archaeological input into such plans at a very early stage.

When an underwater site is backfilled after partial excavation there is inevitably some disruption of the equilibrium that previously existed. If a site if badly backfilled or otherwise inadequately protected it may be effectively destroyed by natural processes in a relatively short time. Sites which have been designated historic wreck sites, and those that have the potential to become so designated, may need physical protection, so that this natural degradation is reduced or indeed eliminated. The way ahead here is for the Department of Transport, the protector of designated wreck sites, to

commission research into these problems by one of the several establishments involved in oceanography or marine science. Another important outcome of this research, should it be successful (and Dutch, Canadian and Danish experience suggests that it should be) is that the Advisory Committee would then be able to recommend with confidence that important sites should be preserved until appropriate resources and techniques become available, rather than excavated.

One of the main bodies of legislation which affect underwater work on historic wreck sites, the 1894 Merchant Shipping Act, can lead to the auction and dispersal of finds, and some see this as a problem only encountered in underwater archaeology. However, this situation does have some parallels in the disposal of excavated objects from land sites. Small finds from land sites, that is portable antiquities, unlike monumental antiquities, cannot be protected under existing legislation in England and Wales . The owner of a find on land (except for finds of gold and silver declared treasure trove) can dispose of it as he wishes. It is mainly the climate of public opinion generated by a hundred years or so of archaeological endeavour that prevents as wide a dispersal of finds from land excavation as now takes place from underwater sites. The general answer to this underwater problem must lie in the education of public opinion, and of politicians.

A related problem is that chance finds from both land and underwater sites often go unreported and therefore unrecorded, and the information is thus lost. In theory, finds from under water should be reported to the Receiver of Wreck when they are brought ashore. But individual Receivers are unlikely to have the knowledge to identify historic artefacts or to recognize false descriptions, and for this and other reasons the present scheme is patently unsatisfactory. The answer to both the land and the sea problems would seem to lie in new legislation which would oblige those who make chance finds of archaeological importance on land or under water to report them and make them available for recording by an authorized unit.

Poor perceptions of archaeology under water

The second series of problems is mainly due to the poor standing underwater archaeology has (or has had until recently); with those who make decisions and allot resources within the archaeological establishment. The treasure–hunting activities of a few members of the under water fraternity are taken to represent the achievements and the philosophy of the many, and the whole activity of underwater archaeology written off as irresponsible and unworthy of support. The fact that, in British waters, the great majority of finds are post–medieval in date also makes it difficult for underwater archaeology to be 'respectable'. Until recently many mainstream archaeologists did not consider industrial archaeology to be a serious discipline, or if it was, it was not really part of archaeology and was of no concern to them. Indeed there are still archaeologists today who doubt the value of medieval archaeology in this they echo the beliefs of certain medieval historians who consider archaeology to be 'an expensive way of telling us what we already know'.

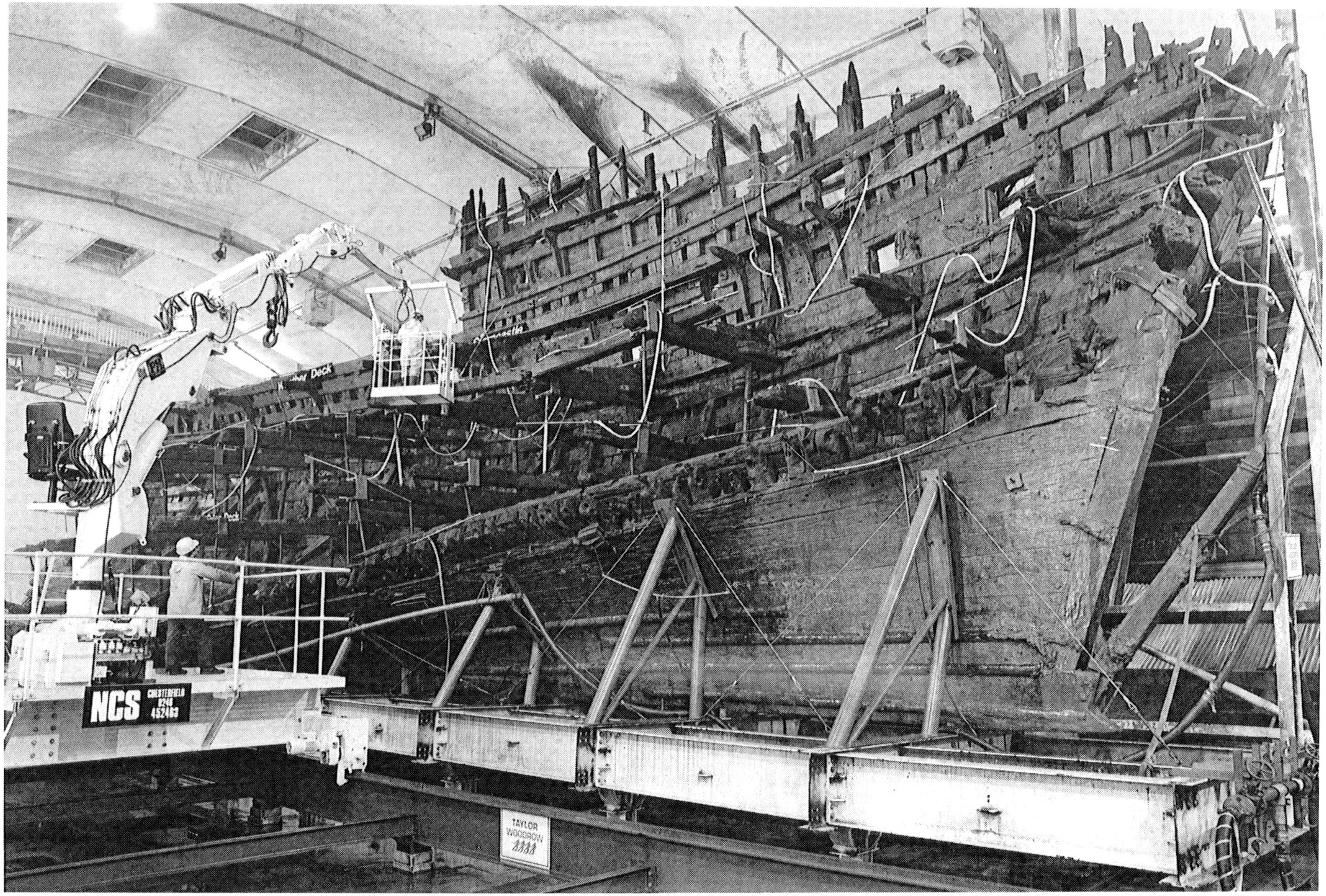

Figure 1.2.2 The *Mary Rose* inside the Ship Hall in the Naval Base at Portsmouth. She is under passive conservation whilst timbers which were excavated before recovery are replaced.

Photograph: Mary Rose Trust

Figure 1.2.3: A nineteenth–century barge in the bed of the River Usk at Tredunnoc near Newport, Gwent, during excavations behind a temporary embankment. Photograph: Glamorgan/Gwent Archaeological Trust

Underwater archaeology, being only very recently on the scene, is misunderstood even more by this type of person.

Such antagonism or antipathy to underwater archaeology is worldwide. John Roper has referred, in a Council of Europe debate, to the lack of recognition in most academic circles of underwater archaeology as a valid scientific discipline.[7]. Professor George Bass recently claimed that 'the study of the origins and development of seafaring has not yet been accepted as a valid (archaeological) concern'[8]. There is no doubt that this lack of esteem for maritime matters is compounded by the centuries old alienation between landsmen and seamen, as Basil Greenhill has pointed out[9]. Seafarers formed, and to a degree still do form, a separate community with unusual skills, which were used in an environment unknown to the landsman. Seamen also had their own special vocabulary, much of which was unintelligible to those unfamiliar with the sea and ships and seafaring. Regrettably, aspects of this division persist.

The answer to the problem of the poor perception of underwater archaeology would seem to lie mainly with the underwater archaeologist. He must demonstrate his 'respectability' by the clarity of his research design, by the standards of his work, by the rigour of his arguments, and by his publication record. He must convince the unconverted, land–based archaeologists (and indeed the general public) of the importance of the maritime dimension of archaeology, and of the continuity of research interests on land and in the sea. Harbours, with their associated facilities, and ships are interdependent: waterfronts cannot be understood without consideration of the boats and the boatmen that used them. Indeed, many of the finds made underwater, as Runciman and Greenhill pointed out, are artefacts for use on land, and they shed more light on land–based industries and life in general than they do on maritime activities. In a sense, the maritime archaeologist must aim to eliminate his specialization, whether on land or under water: that is, the long term aim must be to make the maritime dimension as familiar to *all* archaeologists as it is to specialists at present – as equally it should be to *all* historians.

Inadequate resources
This consideration leads naturally onto the third and last group of problems: those resulting from lack of resources in underwater archaeology. Such a state is due, to a degree, to generally poor perceptions of the value of work under water. Until relatively recently, few professional archaeologists were involved in underwater research and fieldwork, which was often left to people who, although well motivated, did not have the knowledge, the experience or the leadership to achieve archaeologically worthwhile results. The result has been a poor excavation record and an even worse record of

publication – as Martin Dean of the A.D.U. once said, 'too often the only published material available from an [underwater] site is in the saleroom catalogue'. Bass reviewing the worldwide underwater scene some five years ago, commented on its 'vast potential power not yet fulfilled'.[10] In British waters, and probably worldwide, this is still true today: the lack of resources in men and materials has led (with some remarkable exceptions) to poor achievements.

Other aspects of the relative poverty of underwater archaeology are that there are virtually no systematic area surveys of underwater sites; and there is no central, or even regional, collation of information about the sites that are known or suspected (except for an experimental scheme in the Isle of Wight and some local initiatives elsewhere). The result is that we have few data on which to base assessments of the archaeological potential of British coastal and estuarine waters.

A further telling point, reflecting the depressed nature if underwater work in this country, is that, although standards of fieldwork and professional techniques have improved, there has been virtually no theoretical work published in this field since Keith Muckelroy's death in 1980.

In general then, it can be seen that, in relation to archaeology on land, archaeology underwater is very much a poor relation. There are two main ways by which this imbalance can be corrected: firstly, methods by which underwater archaeology can help itself, principally through the Department of Transport's Archaeological Diving Unit; and secondly, methods which require a significant readjustment of the framework within which underwater archaeology operates and which should ensure that archaeology under water and archaeology on land are dealt with on reasonably equal terms.

The Department of Transport
The Department of Transport's Archaeological Diving Unit was set up to provide information which would enable the Department's Advisory Committee (the Runciman Committee) to reach soundly based conclusions. There is one permanent member of the Unit, Martin Dean, and two part–time members; they are all professional diving archaeologists. The ADU's task is to investigate and report on wreck sites proposed for designation or already designated; to report on the capabilities and advise on the standards of work of licencees working on designated historic wreck sites; and to report on the capabilities of applicants for new licences. This system has worked well in the first three years of operations. However, it is now clear from ADU reports that what once was only suspected is undoubtedly true: the standard of archaeolagical work on designated sites is generally very low; and sites which could well be of great importance are not reported to the Department and thus cannot be designated. There are several things the Department of Transport could do to improve the present situation. Two of them have been mentioned earlier:

7 J. Roper, 'Statement in report of the Committee on Culture and Education, Council of Europe,' <u>Underwater Cultural Heritage</u> (Strsbourg, 1978), 7.

8 G. Bass, 'Marine Archaeology: a misunderstood science', <u>Ocean Yearbook</u> 2 (Chicago, 1980), 137–52.

9 B. Greenhill ' The Wooden World' (talk on Radio 3) <u>The Listener</u> 22 January 1987.

10 G. Bass, 'The promise of underwater archaeology in reptrospect', <u>Museum</u> 35.1 (1983), 5–8.

(i) research into methods of physically protecting underwater sites

(ii) active support for new legislation on portable finds.

There are two other areas for improvement. Firstly, the Department should initiate discussions with the IFA, the ACAO and the unit managers and with representatives of salvaging and dredging interests, aiming to develop a Code of Practice which would lead to co–operation between underwater archaeologists and those who plan, quite legally, to exploit the maritime heritage in one way or another. Secondly, the Department should increase the role of its Archaeological Diving Unit in at least five ways. The ADU is already involved in some of these areas in a minor way; this involvement must now be increased:

(a) with the full backing of the Department of Transport the Unit should do all within its power to see that nominated archaeological directors of designated sites fully understand the duties the Department expects of them, that these directors plan the archaeological work to be undertaken and do indeed actively direct on site: no more absentee directors, no working by correspondence. Particular importance should be placed on the preparation of a research design, and directors must be encouraged to assume responsibility for post–excavation research and publication. The corollary of this must be that the Department should refuse licences to sub–standard applicants.

(b) The ADU should be tasked to advise licencees and their colleagues of the documentation required before, during and after an archaeological investigation, differentiating between a press hand–out, a popular report for Diver magazine, a seasonal report to the Department Transport, and the authoritative and comprehensive report that is required when the site is published.

(c) The Unit should also encourage members of diving teams to undertake training courses on archaeological techniques such as those run by the Nautical Archaeology Society, and, wherever possible, to work on a training excavation on land. Any that are suitably qualified should be encouraged to join the Institute of Field Archaeologists. Martin Dean's recently *Guidelines on Acceptable Standards in Underwater Archaeology* contains much that the apprentice archaeological diver needs to know, and should have a significant effect on standards, providing it gets to those at the sharp end.[11]

(d) The ADU should be allowed to liaise with county archaeologists, unit managers, area museum services, museum archaeologists and conservators and their professional organizations, so that the Unit can better advise licencees of designated sites on available facilities, on Sites and Monuments Records and on the disposal of small finds, in the best interests of their future as a source of knowledge. The aim should be for the ADU to act as a link between designated sites and the sources of advice and help which are available around the country, but which licencees may not know of, or which they feel unable to approach.

(e) Finally, the ADU should be allowed to increase its fieldwork so that it can investigate potentially important sites which might otherwise not be considered by the Advisory Committee. Copies of all declarations to the Receiver of Wreck should be automatically sent to the Unit so that they can be evaluated and, if considered to be of importance, reported to the national and regional Sites and Monuments Records. After consideration by the Advisory Committee, the sites such finds come from may then be investigated to determine whether they should be recommended for designation. It is also highly desirable that the ADU should survey an area for wrecks, thus beginning the systematic survey of British waters and the compilation of a national inventory which is so sorely needed. Such survey work might best be undertaken in conjunction with Marine Archaeological Surveys (MAS) which, on a very limited budget, and during weekends and holidays, has undertaken area surveys using remote sensing equipment. The Department of Transport should consider issuing a trial contract to MAS (or to similar organizations if there are any) so that, in conjunction with the Archaeological Diving Unit, the possibilities of systematic surveys of areas with a high density of wreck sites can de demonstrated. Consideration should also be given to tasking ADU/MAS jointly to develop methods of detecting early underwater sites in shallow waters such as in Mounts Bay or Christchurch Harbour. For foreshore and inter–tidal work the ADU could cooperate with such agencies as the Nature Conservancy Council which has begun a fieldwalking survey of the 5,000 miles of Britain's coastline.

Financial and legislative changes

The second group of solutions to the problems of maritime archaeology in its underwater form may require more time to implement as they necessitate changing the financial and legislative of an earlier framework within which underwater archaeology operates.

The Department of Transport should make funds available so that, on the recommendation of the Advisory Committee, grants may be made, as on land, to groups undertaking archaeologically important work on historic wreck sites. One major condition to be fulfilled before such grants could be awarded would be that the group had a professional underwater archaeologist as director.

Extra funds should also be made available, possibly jointly by the Department of Transport, the Museums and Galleries Commission and the Royal Commission for Historical Monuments, to set up a regionally based service for the reporting, recording, conservation and acquisition of underwater finds. Such a comprehensive scheme would need

---

11 Obtainable from: Scottish Institute of Maritime Studies, University of St Andrews, Fife KY16 9AJ.

some central coordination which an enhanced and expanded ADU might be able to give.

Finally, the Department of Transport should discuss with the Department of Education and Science, the British Academy, the IFA and possibly others, how the post–graduate training underwater archaeologists can best be undertaken.

Many of the heritage related tasks at present undertaken by the Department of Transport, and most of the additional ones recommended above, are peripheral to the main thrust of that Department's work – the Department would be the first to admit this. On the other hand, the Department of Environment and its agent, English Heritage, and their equivalents in Wales and Scotland, have wide experience in the administration and control of the public side of archaeology. There is clearly a case for dealing with all archaeological sites in a similar manner, be they on land, inter–tidal or underwater, and the appropriate body for this is the Department of Environment and its equivalents. Such a change in responsibilities could well become the occasion for a radical review of the laws affecting the underwater heritage.

Conclusions

Maritime archaeology has made great strides in Britain in the past 25 years and is now poised to make an even greater contribution to our knowledge of the past. This paper has highlighted some of its strengths and weaknesses – the principal problems being in the underwater aspects of the sub–discipline. Measures to tackle some of these problems can be taken now. The maritime education of mainstream archaeologists and historians, of politicians and of the general public can be started at once; universities can begin to widen their teaching to include Maritime Archaeology in all its forms; and discussion can now begin to produce a developers' Code of Practice for maritime sites. The improvement of standards in underwater archaeology will take longer and will require the Department of Transport to provide extra resources for its Archaeological Diving Unit; yet the gains in the protection of Britain's maritime heritage and in our knowledge of the past will be immense.

In the longer term the future lies with the Department of Environment. English Heritage has already dipped its collective toe in the water: it, and its counterparts in Wales and Scotland, should now take the plunge.

Acknowledgements

I am grateful to Professor Barry Cunliffe, Professor Martin Carver and Dr Basil Greenhill for their criticism of an earlier draft.

Reprinted, with permission, from:

Antiquaries Journal, 68: 10–22 (1989).

PAPER 1.3

TRAINING MARITIME ARCHAEOLOGISTS

In an address given to the York Conference on Medieval Archaeology, Ole Crumlin–Pedersen (1992) described how maritime archaeology had emerged as a recognisable field of study from the convergence of archaeological investigations into boats, waterfronts, wetlands and remains under water. Ole himself came to medieval maritime archaeology, in which he is now pre–eminent, from two of these study areas: from underwater investigations, by reason of his diving experience; and from boats, due to his training'as a naval architect. Others of his generation have approached the subject from a seafaring background or from general archaeological or historical studies. Like Ole, many of these do not have a first degree in archaeology, and some have no degree at all. Such 'non–professionalism' or 'non–exclusiveness' is common when a new discipline is evolving, or an established subject is being revitalised, or, as in this case, when aspects of several disciplines converge.

There comes a time, however, when the practitioners of newly established studies perceive the need to formalise the training of new entrants: perhaps to define the subject and give it coherence and professional standards; or to ensure that the experience of the pioneers is handed on in a structured way; or to attract students who would respond to an academic challenge; or to spread 'the word' to a wider, but not necessarily participating, constituency. Maritime Archaeology appears to be in that position today. A philosophy or 'raison d'etre' for the subject is beginning to emerge, and formalised training courses have been, or are being, established in several countries (see the Appendix).

In this paper I plan to discuss the academic training of maritime archaeologists and I shall argue that there are certain topics which cannot be omitted from any syllabus. By advocating an academic training with a core of essential studies, I am not suggesting that , in future, no–one could become a maririme archaeologist without an 'approved' degree. Whatever may be decided about the academic training best–suited to maritime archaeologists there must remain an avenue by which others (for example, naval architects like Ole, or ancient mariners, like myself) can become recognised as professionals. There is a parallel here in the regulation of a British professional association, the Institute of Field Archaeologists, for which a degree in archaeology is a basic requirement of membership, but alternative routes exist for those with other qualifications or, indeed, without formal academic training at all. Nevertheless, it is a premise of this paper that the core training, that which distinguishes the study of maritime archaeology from other subjects, should be encapsulated in an academic syllabus. For those on the non–academic, or parallel academic, routes, such a syllabus will be

a goal which they can aim to achieve through a combination of experience and further study.

This paper is undoubtely theoretical in nature, but it is based on practical experience in the field and on the foreshore, and also in the 'blackboard jungle'. I look forward to Ole Crumlin's 'robust criticism' in due course.

Maritime Archaeology

It is first necessary to define 'maritime archaeology', because that term does not mean the same to everyone. To some it appears to mean archaeology underwater or the archaeology of shipwrecks, whilst others see it solely as the study of boats and ships.[1] The definition used in this paper is wider than any of these: the study of Man's encounter or interaction with the waters of the world – ocean, seas, rivers and lakes. This research area includes the study of landing places and harbours as well as the study of the building, operation and performance of rafts, boats and ships (Fig 1.2.1). It also includes the study of anchors and fishing gear; overseas colonisations and trade routes; changes in past climates, in sea levels and in coastlines; and early seamanship and navigational techniques.[2] As this is an archaeological subject it is necessarily focused on material remains, nevertheless, it blends with the study of maritime history and also with maritime ethnography.

The evidence for these maritime studies comes not only from underwater – as with the Viking Age wrecks from Skuldelev[3], and from the inter–tidal sites – as, for example, the mid–2nd MBC stitched boats from N.Ferriby in the Humber estuary, England[4], but also from inland sites such as the 4th century AD boats from Nydam, Denmark[5] and the medieval waterfronts of Bergen[6], London[7] and Dublin[8]. Further evidence comes from historical accounts and illustrations as well as research in laboratories, workshops and, indeed, afloat.

A characteristic feature of Maritime Archaeology is that it necessarily has a worldwide perspective: the waters of the world connect rather than divide communities and it is possible, for example, to travel by boat from the Swiss lakes to the upper reaches of the Yellow River in China, or from

---

2 McGrail 1981, 23; 1984; 1985, 16–17 and 1–2; 1989, 10.

3 Olsen and Crumlin–Pedersen 1967.

4 Wrigth, 1990.

5 Crumline–Pedersen and Rieck 1993.

6 Christenses 1985.

7 Milne and Hobley 1981.

8 McGrail 1993A.

L.Victoria in E. Africa to the foothills of the Ural Mountains. Maritime Archaeology is also markedly inter–disciplinary and the sciences are used as much as, if not more than, the humanities. Furthermore, it is a constituent part of the discipline of Archaeology and thus is not hampered by boundaries at its margins, but overlaps, surrounds, and is surrounded by, other aspects of Archaeology. The discipline itself is seamless, without barriers – academic or otherwise – at low water mark, high water mark, river bank or lake margin.

Academic Training

From this it follows that maritime archaeologists need a firm grounding in Archaeology. Those starting *ab initio* and with academic aptitude would be best advised to start with a first degree which included archaeological theory, methods and techniques; others may be able to acquire this expertise in the field. In the final year of this degree it may be possible to take aspects of martime archaeology as special subjects (see the appendix). It will, howevere, be in a second–level (Master's) degree that maritime archaeologists will get their special training. Those who converge on the subject with a related qualification from another discipline – naval architect, master mariner, maritime historian, geomorphologist or oceanographer, for example – will need to master aspects of this post–graduate training as well as the essence of Archaeology.

The specialist master's degree should consist of two main elements: taught courses involving a range of disciplines; and practical experince of boat building and seafaring and work on inter–tidal and underwater sites. The value of the degree will much depend on the right balance being struck between intellectual quality and practical achievement. Some of the specialist courses, those concerning the natural world and the night sky for example, will deal with topics that were common knowledge at he beginning of this century but which are now little known, at least in Europe. Other courses may be technical in nature: hull structures, hydrostatics, sailing theory, sea–level changes, the properties of materials and so on. Nowadays archaeologists and historians are not generally noted for their understanding of technology.[9], but technical studies cannot be an optional extra for maritime archaeologists: seafaring and boatbuilding are central to their research. Waters (1993) has emphasised that the study of ship–handling, navigation and hydrography is as exacting as is the study of the classics or mathematics, and he has argued that, in order to understand how early ships were sailed, the 'landsman scholar' must first study seamanship. As Greenhill (1993) has pointed out, this echoes the advice that Pericles gave his fellows Athenians in the late–5th century BC: *Seamanship just like anything else, is an art. It is not something that can be picked up and studied in one's spare time; indeed it allows no spare time for anything else*[10].

Without training in a range of techincal subjects, those who seeks to inform may, in fact, misinform. See, for example:

Humphreys, and McGrail and Farrel on rowing techniques; Ballard, Johnstone, and Farrar on the earliest evidence for boats in northern Europe; and McGrail, and Bettess[11] on the identification of ancient units of measurement. These three examples – others could be quoted – demonstrate that multidisciplinary training, especially in the sciences, is essential for maritime archaeologists.

An M.Sc. degree in Maritime Archaeology

The foregoing discussion concerning the nature of maritime archaeology suggests the general pattern of a Master's degree syllabus. Several of the topics will be extensions, in breadth and in depth, of courses taken in a first degree in Archaeology. Others, of a more specialised nature, will be new to most students.

Much of the general archaeological knowledge and expertise gained on a first degree course will continue to be of use, especially source criticism, dating techniques, research methods, quantitative methods, excavation techniques, and the history of cultures and civilisations. Other subjects need to be studied in greater detail:
– Environmental studies to include: aspects of oceanography and coastal and riverine geomorphology; site formation in the maritime zone; sea levels, currents, tides, winds and the weather generally.
– Material studies to include the essentials of wood science and the sources of raw materials.
– Studies of tools and techniques to be focused on boatbuilding and its ancillary trades, such as the manufacture of nails, cordage and sails.
– Studies of settlement/discovery and trade/exchange to be focused on overseas routes, landing sites and harbours and associated overland routes, cargo handling and stowage.
– And the maritime aspects of conservation, curatorial studies and experimental archaeology should be explored.
New Subjects may be grouped under four headings:
a. Technical studies. An introduction to seamanship, navigation, boatbuilding, nautical astronomy and naval architecture.
b. Infrastructure studies. An introduction to the legal, administrative and institutional structures within which maritime archaeologists operate, nationally and internationally.
c. Historical studies. The history of seafaring and of rafts, boats, ships and harbours, both regionally and worldwide.
d. Practical work. Experience of boatmanship and of boat building; and of work in inter–tidal sites and/or underwater.

---

9 Lambert 1992; Greenhill 1993.
10 Thucydides, bbok 11, chapter 11 cited from Warner 1954, 94.

11 Humphreys 1978; McGrail and Farrell 1979; Ballard 1920, 216; Johnstone 1988, xxi; Farrar 1990, 15; McGrail 1196, 62; Bettess 1991.

A Maritime Institute?

The requirement for practical training within the proposed degree syllabus, may be met by the association of a university department with a maritime research unit, as in Denmark where the Dept. of Prehistoric and Classical Archaeology of the University of Copenhagen cooperates with the three research institutions at Roskilde[12]. Alternatively, where a university is already strongly involved in maritime research, most, if not all, training can be intra–mural. The University of Southampton is an example of this: The Dept. of Archaeology undertakes research amd teaching in several aspects of maritime archaeology and has recently established a lectureship in that subject. Furthermore, this department has managerial responsibility for Henry's V medieval warship, a designated historic wreck in the nearby R. Hamble. With the agreement of the Dept. of National Heritage, this wreck could in future be used by maritime archaeologists under training for non–intrusive surveys and for research into the best methods of preserving wrecks in high–energy environments.[13]

Moreover, within the University of Southampton there are Deaprtments of Law, Oceanography and Geography with strong maritime interests, and a Dept. of Ship Science with wind tunnel and towing tank facilities. Furthermore, the Faculty of Engineering trains engineer officers of the Royal Navy. Here, in Southampton, I suggest is the basis for a Maritime Institute which would integrate the maritime research ineterests of several university departments and also those of nearby institutions such as the Mary Rose Trust, the Royal Navy Museum, the Hampshire and Wight Trust for Maritime Archaeology and the Marine Unit of the Royal Commission for Historic Monuments.

Members of such Maritime Institute would have to be 'action men as well as philosophers'. They would undertake research, teach post–graduate students, and give a significant proportion of their time to explaining their work to lay public. Those involved in teaching maritime archaeology would emphasise the 'oneness' of Achaeology but would also initiate debate about the special problem areas in the maritime sub–discipline, including the tangled state of legislation affecting marine sites. Other problems to be tackled might include: how to establish criteria for deciding which wrecks should be designated 'historic' and preserved as national monuments, and which should be excavated; how to evaluate marine sites before they are commercially developed; and how best to make historic sites underwater 'open to visitors'.

There would also be practical problems: how to extract maximum information from an inter–tidal site, such as that in the R.Hamble, with the minimum of intrusive excavation[14]; what is the best way of backfilling an excavated, but unlifted wreck; and how to pinpoint the sites of premedieval wrecks in tidal waters. In the fullness of time, such an Institute might take on the building of reconstructions of important boat–finds and undertake sea trials.

A Maritime Institute with such a research programme, together with the research of the other, non–archaeological, constituent elements, would have both the intellectual climate and the practical approach which should lead to a lively and informative course of instruction for would–be maritime archaeologists. The syllabus I have outlined above is undeniably based towards the scientific and technical, whereas the ultimate aim of Archaeology is said to be the study of Man in his environmental setting[15]. There is not a contradiction here for archaeological research is mainly done through material and environmental remains: if these are interpreted incorrectly or incompletely, deductions and conclusions will be wrong or, at best, inadequate. The study of an array of scientific and technical subjects (not to the exclusion of the humanities) as proposed in this paper will enable future maritime archaeologists to interpret their evidence comprehensively and thus more fully understand Man in his maritime environment.

Appendix

Univerisity degrees which include aspects of Maritime Archaeology.

This appendix is based on response to Elisha Linder's proposal to form an association for those involved in teaching Maritime Archaeology – see IJNA (1992) 21, 356 – and additonal information from Professor George Bass.

A   Undergradute degrees
1.   Univ. College of N.Wales, Bangor. BA in History with Nautical Archaeology in the School of History and Welsh History.
2.   Univ. of Bristol. 3rd year subject in Dept. of Classics and Archaeology.
3.   Univ of Leiden. 3rd year subject in Centre for Archaeology.
4.   Univ. of Paris (1. Sorbonne). 3rd year subject in Dept. of History of Art and Archaeology.
5.   Univ of Southampton. 3rd year subject in Dept. of Archaeology.
6.   Univ of Stockholm. 3rd year subject in Dept. of Archaeology.

B.   Post Graduate degrees.
1.   Univ. of Bilkent, Ankara. Dept. of Archaeology and History of Art, in association with Univ. of Texas (A & M).
2.   Univ. of Bristol. Maritime Archaeology and History in Dept. of Classics and Archaeology.
3.   Univ of E. Carolina. Dept. of Maritime History and Underwater Research.
4.   Univ of Copenhagen. Inst. of Archaeology and Ethnology in conjunction with Centre for Maritime Archaeology, Roskilde.
5.   Univ. of Curtin, W. Australia, in association with the Western Australian Maritime Museum.
6.   Univ. of Haifa. Centre for Maritime Studies.

---

12 Crumlin–Pedersen 1993.

13 Clarke et al 1993; McGrail 1993B.

14 McGrail 1993B.

---

15 McGrail 1989, 10.

37

7. Univ of Paris (1. Sorbonne). Dept. of History of Art and Archaeeology in association with Musee de la Marine.
8. Univ of St. Andrews. Scottish Institute of Maritime Studies.
9. Univ. of Southampton. Dept. of Archaeology.
10. Univ. of Stockholm. Dept. of Archaeology in cooperation with the National Maritime Museum.
11. Univ. of Texas (A & M). Inst. of Nautical Archaeology.
12. Univ. of Texas (Austin). Dept. of Classics in association with the Univ. of Texas (A & M).

References

Cederlund C.O. 1990 'Maritime Musuems and University Education.' *Proc. 7th Congress of Maritime Museums*, 247–257.

Crumlin–Pedersen O. 1993 'Centre for Maritime Archaeology.' *IJNA* 22, 293.

Illsley J.S. 1992' Degree of BA in History with Nautical Studies.' *IJNA* 21, 79–80.

Jeffrey W. and Amess J. (ed) 1983. *Proc 2nd Southern Hemisphere Conference on Maritime Archaeology.* Adelaide.

Linder E. 1973 'Centre for Maritime Studies.' *IJNA* 2, 198–9.

Martin C. 1984 'Graduate courses in Maritime Studies.' *MM* 70, 95.

Bibliography

Abbreviations
IJNA. Int. J. Nautical Archaeology
MM. Mariner's Mirror

Ballard G.A. 1920 'Sculptures of Deir el–Bahri II.' *MM* 6, 212–217.

Bettess F. 1991 'Anglo–Saxon foot.' *Medieval Archaeology*, 35,44–50.

Christensen A.E. 1985 'Boat–finds from Bryggen.' *Bryggen Papers* 1, 47–280, Bergen University Press.

Clarke R. *et al* 1993 'Recent work on the R. Hamble wreck near Bursledon, Hampshire.' *IJNA* 22, 21–44.

Crumlin–Pedersen O. 1992 'Maritime Studies in Medieval Archaeology in M. Carver.' (ed) *Maritime Studies, Ports and Ships*, York, Medieval Europe, 1992.

Crumlin–Pedersen O. 1993 'Centre for Maritime Archaeology in Denmark.' *IJNA* 22, 293.

Crumlin–Pedersen O. and Rieck F. 1993 'Nydam ships.' in J. Coles *et al* (eds), *Spirit of Enquiry*, 39–45.

Farrar A. 1990 'Marsala Wreck.' *Ships and Boat International*, March, 1990, 15.

Greenhill B. 1993 'Seamanship, Scholarship and Maritime History.' *MM* 79, 478–9.

Humphreys S. 1978 'Artists' mistakes.' *IJNA* 7, 78–9.

Johnstone P. 1988 *Seacraft of Prehistory*. 2nd edition. Introduction.

Lambert A. 1992 'Review.' *MM* 78, 103–4.

McGrail S. 1981 'Medieval boats, ships and landing places.' in G. Milne and B. Hobley (eds) 17–23.

McGrail S. 1984 'Maritime Archaeology – present and future.' in S.McGrail (ed) *Aspects of Maritime Archaeology and Ethnography*, 11–40. Greenwhich: National Maritime Museum.

McGrail S. 1985 'Early landing places.' in A.E. Herteig (ed). *Conference on Waterfront Archaeology*, 12–18. Bergen: Historisk Museum.

McGrail S. 1987. *Ancient Boats in NW Europe*. London: Longman.

McGrail S. 1989 'Maritime Archaeology in Britain.' *Antiquaries Journal*, 69, 10–22.

McGrail S. 1992 'Boat and ship archaeology at Roskilde – ISBSA 6.' *IJNA* 21, 61–4.

McGrail S. 1993A *Medieval Boat and ship timbers from Dublin. Dublin*, Royal Irish Academy.

McGrail S. 1993B 'Future of the Designated Wreck site in the R.Hamble.' *IJNA* 22, 45–51.

McGrail S. and Farrell A.W. 1979 'Rowing: aspects of the ethnographic and icnongraphic evidence.' *IJNA* 8, 155–166.

Milne G. and Hobley B. 1981 *Waterfront Archaeology in Britain and Northern Europe*, CBA Research Report 41.

Olsen O. and Crumlin–Pedersen O. 1967 'Skuldelev Ships II.' *Acta Archaeologica*, 38, 73–174. Copenhagen.

Warner R. 1954. *Thucydides: The Peloponnesian War*, London: Penguin Books.

Wright C.W. and E.V. 1993 'Submerged boat at N.Ferriby.' *Antiquity*, 13, 349–354.

Wright E.V. 1990 *Ferriby Boats*. London, Routledge.

Reprinted, with permission, from:

Olsen O., Masden J.S. and Rieck F. (eds) *Shipshape*, 329–334, Viking Ship Museum, Roskilde (1995).

SECTION 2.0

MARITIME STRUCTURES

Introduction

Two of the papers in this Section were given at conferences on waterfront archaeology, whilst paper 2.2 was first published in a *festschrift* for Basil Greenhill, a polymath in maritime studies, and Director of the National Maritime Museum, Greenwich from 1968 to 1983. The theme linking all three is the use of ethnographic analogy to interpret the vestigial remains excavated from "waterfront" sites in harbours, on river banks and lakesides, and in their immediate vicinity. Maritime structures are the fixed, in contradistinction to the floating, structures of Maritime Archaeology. They are usually sited where water transport has an interface with the land, and generally – comprise the shore–based facilities needed by boats and ships.

Formal & informal sites.

Maritime structures are also mentioned in Papers 7.1,7.2, 8.1, 9.2, 10.1, and 10.4. Most of these papers are concerned with informal landing places which have few, if any, man–made facilities. Formal harbours (see Hutchinson, 1994) are unknown in North and North West Europe, apart from areas under Roman influence, until around the 9th century AD. Paper 9.2 includes a summary description of the port of Dublin as it changed to a more formal harbour between the 10th and 13th centuries, but still with informal landing places in use at the end of this period. This simultaneous use of two types of site can still be seen today in many parts of the world, for example India, (Blue *et al*, forthcoming); similarly, informal landing places must have continued to be widely used in earlier times, alongside grand harbours.

Beach landing places may be reinforced with wooden hurdles or other materials where there is a danger that boats will get stuck. Such wooden "hards" have been excavated at the prehistoric site of North Ferriby in the Humber Estuary (Paper 2.2), and at the medieval site of Graveney in the Thames estuary (Fenwick, 1978), whilst a gravel hard was exposed at the prehistoric site of Hengistbury Head in Christchurch harbour. (Cunliffe, 1990).

The identification of specific maritime structures.

Attempts are made in Paper 2.2, especially in Table 2.2.1, to identify the characteristic features of a range of maritime structures as an aid to the identification of excavated remains. As far as I am aware, there has been no criticism of this

information, which suggests that this paper has never been consulted by archaeologists excavating "waterfront!" sites ! Some of these archaeologists (see, for example Paper 2.3 on Runnymede) have a strong tendency to identify the structures they encounter as wharfs, jetties and bridges (with which they themselves are familiar) rather than the less–prestigious, and relatively unknown, bank reinforcement, causeway or hard. For a recent example, see the interpretation of remains found in the Eton rowing lake at Dorney, S. Bucks. as a Bronze Age Thames bridge (Allen & Welsh, 1996).

Wharfs, jetties and bridges may well be excavated in a Roman or medieval context; and it is a truism that the first use of some particular object or structure often proves to be earlier than the date proposed by previous investigators. Nevertheless, I suggest that bank reinforcements, causeways and hards should be the first structures to be considered when interpreting prehistoric remain in a maritime or riverine environment.

A major concern of people living on a flood plain is to prevent the river deviating from its usual channel or overflowing its banks – hence bank reinforcements. Jetties are only needed when boats have to be operated in the deeper water nearer mid–channel; prehistoric boats were not of the type or size that needed to be used in this way. When boats have to be loaded and unloaded on a soft, unconsolidated foreshore, a hard is built for the boat and a causeway for people and animals. In tidal conditions there may be two types of causeway: (a) short ones leading to boats beached on the foreshore; or (b) longer ones that cross a river or creek from one foreshore to another. These causeways are seldom useable at all states of the tide, but at or near low water: they may be compared and contrasted with fords in non–tidal contexts. Where part of a foreshore is firm and a causeway is not needed, the position and alignment of the useable foreshore (a "natural causeway") may need to be marked by a series of posts so that a boat may be approached, or the crossing used, at times other than when the foreshore is fully exposed.

The Nydam boat

In paper 2.2 some enigmatic timbers found in and around the 4th century AD boat Nydam 2, are tentatively identified as equipment used in the construction of fish weirs or in other fishing operations. Again, this hypothesis has neither been challenged nor supported. The Nydam boat, as now displayed in Schloss Gotorf, Schleswig Holstein, has recently been re–examined by a team from the Institute of Maritime Archaeology, Roskilde, and further excavations have been undertaken at the Nydam site (Rieck, 1994). Reports are now being prepared at Roskilde on these activities, and it may be that they will include comment on the function of these unusual timbers.

References

Allen T. and Welsh K. 1996 'Eton rowing lake.' *Current Archaeology*, 148: 124–127.

Blue L. Kentley E. & McGrail S. forthcoming 'Archaeology, ethnography and India's maritime past.' *Proceedings of the 1996 Lyon Conference on the Indian Ocean.*

Cunliffe B. 1990 'Hengistbury Head: a prehistoric haven.' in McGrail S. (ed) *Maritime Celts, Frisians & Saxons*, 27–31. CBA Research Report 71.

Hutchinson G. 1994 *Medieval Ships and Shipping*. Ch.6. Leicester University Press.

Rieck F. 1994 'Iron Age boats from Hjortspring & Nydam – new investigations.' in Westerdahl C. (ed) *Crossroads in Ancient Shipbuilding* 45–54. Oxbow Monograph 40.

PAPER 2.1

MEDIEVAL BOATS, SHIPS, AND LANDING PLACES

Types of water transport

Apart from personal flotation aids such as the inflated skins and sealed pots described by Hornell (1972, 1–20), there appear to be nine basic types of ancient water transports, some of them with hybrid forms. These types may be divided into two main groups:

Non–watertight rafts made of reed bundles, bark bundles, inflated skins, or logs/bamboos. They may be 'boat–shaped' or otherwise.

Watertight boats made of waterproofed reed, bark, skin or bitumen over a wooden skeleton, logs, or planks.

In the region of northern Europe considered at this conference, reed and bark boats and rafts made of bark or of skins have not been excavated and there are no surviving traditions which might indicate their earlier existence. Until a year or so ago a similar statement might have beenmade about reed rafts, but Breandán O Riordáin recently drew my attention to such a craft in the ethnographic collection of the National Museum of Ireland (Fig 2.1.1). This raft (*cliath thulca*) was made for the National Museum after the design of reed rafts known to have been used on the river Suck in southern Co. Roscommon in recent times (Delaney 1976, 24–8) These earlier rafts were poled as well as rowed, and the superstructure was of wickerwork rather than the timber shown in Fig (2.1.1). Such craft could obviously be made wherever suitable reeds grew and so it is advisable to keep an open mind about the possible use of reed rafts in medieval Europe.

European log rafts have been published by Ellmers (1972, 106, 112–6) and by Eskerod (1956, 59–61). Skin boats, represented in recent times by the currach and the coracle, have not yet been excavated, but there is documentary and iconographic evidence for their medieval use (Hornell 1972, 111–47; Severin 1978; Johnstone 1980). Until recently, logboats (= dugout canoes) were generally believed to be of prehistoric date but there is now a considerable body of evidence for their medieval use (McGrail 1978, 251–3; McGrail & Switsur, 1979a). Of the 24 reliably dated British logboats, for example) fourteen are from the 3rd to the 14th centuries AD. Planked boats appear to have reached a dominant position in north–western Europe at an early date, and medieval examples have been excavated from many sites.

Urban archaeologists may find some or all of these types of water transport associated with their excavations of medieval

waterfronts; planked boats and ships will undoubtedly be the most numerous.

Boat and ship archaeology

Boat and ship finds are almost always incomplete and therefore the archaeologist has to evolve conjectural reconstructions of the original vessel, so that he may attempt to answer questions about her performance. What could she have carried? What was her draft? Could she have come alongside this waterfront at high–water or low–water, or have to lie off? Could she have crossed the North Sea direct? How stable was he? To answer such questions the nautical specialist must evaluate the reconstruction(s) by eye, by calculation, by tank test, or by full scale replica to deduce operational capabilities. In addition, a knowledge of the prevailing regional weather and the tidal regime in a particular harbour is required, and the strength and resilience of the ship's structure and her methods of propulsion and steering must be established. Waterline shape is an important factor in the assessment of a ship's performance, but what was the medieval waterline? The best solution here, perhaps, is to use several values for freeboard and draft in the calculations. For this and other reasons (not least that several reconstructed forms may be compatible with the surviving remains) the nautical archaeologist may be unable to give a precise answer to some of the foregoing questions, but rather several answers, each valid for different sets of assumptions.

In the past, boat and ship remains have seldom been well recorded or dated, and there are at present few regions and periods with a sufficient number of well documented finds to support the identification of specific local types, although broader classifications may be possible (see below). Furthermore, it is often impossible to equate excavated remains with type–names from documentary sources, as historians and others would wish. Attempts have sometimes been made to equate a particular feature of boat building (such as the use of moss caulking or of treenail plank fastenings) with a unique time and place. But this may be unwarranted because of widespread use. For example, moss caulking was used on the Bronze Age Ferriby boats (Wright 1976), on post–medieval Dutch boats (Reinders 1979), and in intermediate periods; treenail plank fastenings were used on two of the 10th/11th Skuldelev ships (Olsen & Crumlin–Pedersen 1967, 100, 111) and on the 12th/13th century Norwegian Sjøvollen ship (Christensen 1968a, 140), as

Figure 2.1.1   A reed raft (*Cliath thulca*) being rowed by Patrick Gately, the builder, on the river Suck, Co Roscommon, Ireland, in 1962 (Photograph: National Museum of Ireland)

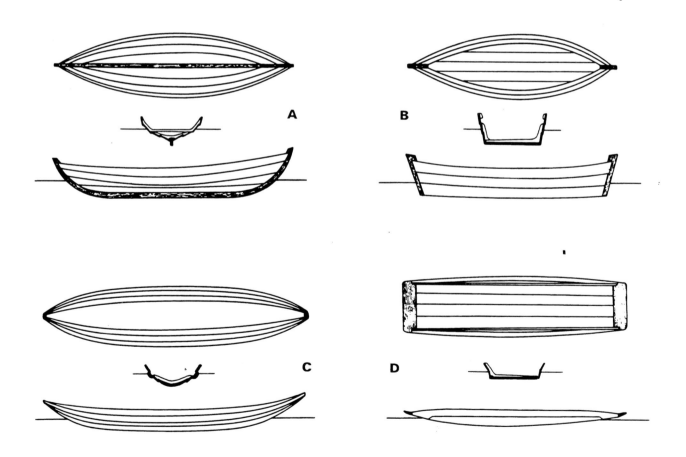

Figure 2.1.2   Basic characteristics of four medieval boatbuilding traditions in north–west Europe: (A) Nordic or Viking; (B) cog; (C) hulk; (D) punt or barge (drawing after Crumlin–Pedersen)

Figure 2.1.3 The 13th century seal of Winchelsea, depicting a late form of the Viking tradition of shipbuilding. (Photograph: National Maritime Museum)

Figure 2.1.4 A seal of Elbing (Elblag) Poland, dated *c* AD 1350: a late form of cog (Photograph: National Maritime Museum)

well as on 9th/ 10th century ships in the East Baltic (Crumlin–Pedersen 1969). Identification of a boat's origins and any link with a documented type–name is probably best pursued by systematic feature analysis and dating of the boat find, together with a similar analysis of the documentary references and iconographic representations. If successful, this investigation should reveal groups of characteristic features which may be tentatively identified with a named type, or, at a more detailed level, with particular regional or temporal variants (McGrail & Switsur 1979b). Diagnostic features, a sub–set of the characteristics, should then enable future finds to be allocated to these types.

Analysis of form and structure has proceeded sufficiently far in certain areas for some general boat and shipbuilding traditions to be identified. Thus, Crumlin–Pedersen (1978) has listed the common features of Viking warships and cargo ships, and the general characteristics of the Rhine barges of late Roman times are beginning to be understood (Marsden 1976; de Weerd 1978; de Boe 1978; Arnold 1978). Using this sort of evidence Crumlin–Pedersen (1978) has postulated that four types of indigenous planked boats were in use in north–western Europe from the beginning of the medieval period (Fig 2.1.2). In response to changing economic and military requirements, first one and then another was developed in size to become the principal ship of the day.

Thus, the period *c* AD 800–1200 was dominated by the Nordic or *Viking* shipbuilding tradition. For excavated examples, see Olsen & Crumlin–Pedersen (1967) and Christensen (1968b); representations of developed versions of this type can be seen (Fig 2.1.3) on 13th century town seals (Ewe 1972). The *cog*, a flat–bottomed, high–volume, cargo

carrier (Fig 2.1.4), possibly originating in the Netherlands, became the most important sea–going ship in the 13th and 14th centuries (Crumlin–Pedersen 1965; Ellmers 1976, 25–9; Ellmers 1979; Crumlin–Pedersen 1979). Documentary sources indicate that, subsequently, another tradition from the Frisian region came to dominate sea commerce in the 14th and 15th centuries. This was the *hulk*, whose characteristics are thought to be a banana shape with the planking not terminating at conventional stem and stern posts but on a horizontal line (Fig 2.1.5). No example has been excavated, but see Greenhill (1976, 283–5) for a summary of other evidence. Co–existent with these three sea–going types, Crumlin–Pedersen believes there was widesdespread use of a *punt* or barge type (Fig 2.1.6) on rivers and estuaries and in harbours.

Crumlin–Pedersen's thesis is a useful working hypothesis, though other traditions of boat and shipbuilding may remain to be identified. As the dominant ship type changed during the medieval period, so did the type of landing place required. In addition, as high–value, high–density goods gave way to low–density, mass–consumption goods, and with a general increase in the volume of trade, the sea–going ship was developed in size (Fig 2.1.7) with an increasing requirement for harbours with waterfronts. Defence requirements, the collection of custom dues, and warehouse methods of marketing probably reinforced this trend towards formal landing places.

Figure 2.1.5 Seal of New Shoreham of *c* AD 1295. The incription links the depicted ship with the former name of the town, Hulkesmoth. [This replaces an angel coin of Henry VIII in the original publication].

Landing Places

There is documentary and archaeological evidence that, at least until the 11th century, boats and ships – especially in tidal regions – did not need formal harbour facilities to discharge and take on cargo. For example, the marked wear on the keel and the lower planking of Skudelev ship 3 shows that she was frequently run ashore on sand or shingle beaches, not just settling down with a falling tide (Olsen & Crumlin–Pedersen 1967,130–2; Crumlin–Pedersen 1978,40). The 10th century Graveney boat's keel-plank is smooth underneath, apparently without significant wear from its original profile, but this is probably due to being berthed on mud banks (McKee 1978, 94). Where vessels might experience difficulty getting off mud, as at Graveney, simple hard–standings of parallel timbers are known to have been used, with stakes to hold the vessels upright and to check them at high–water (Fenwick 1978b, 181–5). Suitable strands or beaches of mud, sand or shingle were available on rivers and estuaries near towns, and coastal sites could have been used where there was protection, natural or artificial, from the prevailing winds. In tidal conditions relatively light–draft vessels such as the Skuldelev ships, the Graveney boat, and other medieval barge types could be run well up the foreshore before grounding; for a longer stay they might then be dragged, or moved by tackle or beach capstan, clear of the water. Not all vessels can be beached, however, for the strains on taking the ground may be considerable. An alternative is to anchor off a landing place or moor to posts in shallow water, and this would often be the best course of action in non–tidal areas. From such berths ships could be unloaded and loaded by men wading through the water, or on to carts driven into

the water (Fig 2.1.7). Vessels moored further of offshore could be unloaded by lighter or barge.

Similar informal sites were chosen for boat–building (Fig 2.1.9) in the open or under a simple shelter, with ready access to the water possibly via an elementary slipway. Such sites may leave insignificant structural remains to be excavated.

The 12th and 13th century ship of the Viking or Nordic tradition was probably beached only in unusual circumstances, and this was probably true of the cogs and hulks of the 13th century and later. Anchoring or mooring to posts would be possible, but coming alongside a waterfront with sufficient depth of water would save transshipment of goods and thus might be preferred. In favourable conditions sail may be used until close to a waterfront; otherwise the ship can be towed from a boat, smaller ones may be manoeuvred by oar. When within range the vessel may be warped alongside the waterfront by manpower, or by ship or shore–based windlass. The precise action would often be determined by the state and relative strengths of wind and tide. A flat–bottomed ship such as the cog would settle on an even keel when alongside waterfronts which dried at low water.

When estimating how many ships could use a section of waterfront it should be noted that if any ship exceeded 30m overall length they were the exception until later in the medieval period. It is relevant that Drake's *Golden Hind*, which circumnavigated the world in 1577–80, is thought to have been only 60ft (18.3m) from stem to stern and 75ft (22.9m) overall (Laird Clowes 1932, 67). Viking merchant ship Skuldelev 1 is *c* 16.5m in overall length, with a maximum beam of c 4 6m, and her loaded draft is estimated at 1.5m(Olsen & Crumlin–Pedersen 1967, 109). If a similar length/breadth ratio Is used, the 14th century Bergen ship with a beam of *c* 9m would be *c* 30m overall. The cog excavated from the river Weser at Bremen in 1962 is *c* 23.5m by 7.5m (Crumlin–Pedersen 1978, 38): a significant difference from the Viking ships is her depth (Fig. 2.1.7E) from midship sheerline to bottom of keel being almost 5m compared with *c* 1.9m for Skuldelev 1. Her operational draft remains to be calculated, but at full load it can scarcely have been less than 3m. The Roman Age barges so far excavated are estimated to have been 20–27m in length, with two (Zwammerdam 6 and Kapel Avezaath) possibly being 34–35m. Their maximum beams were generally 3m, and none can have drawn more than about 1m. The medieval Egernsund boat (Fig2.1.6), of similar form, was about 7m by 2m with a draft of less than 0.5m.

The Viking tradition of ship had, until the late 12th century, a side rudder, which extended to well below the keel and was also a potential obstruction to starboard. However, this type of rudder can easily and quickly be rotated to a position level with the keel and still be used albeit not so effectively. Fenders could be used to protect vulnerable parts of the ship when going alongside a waterfront, or to allow ships to berth alongside waterfronts with front braces. Floating pontoons or rafts could be similarly used, with gangplanks spanning the gap.

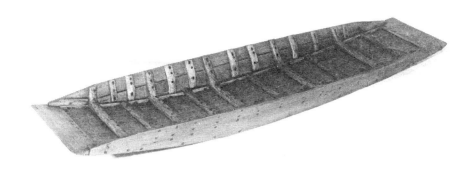

Figure 2.1.6   A model of the conjectural reconstruction of the punt–type of boat from Egernsund on the Flensburg Fjord, Denmark, dated to *c* AD 1090 (Photograph: O Crumlin–Pedersen)

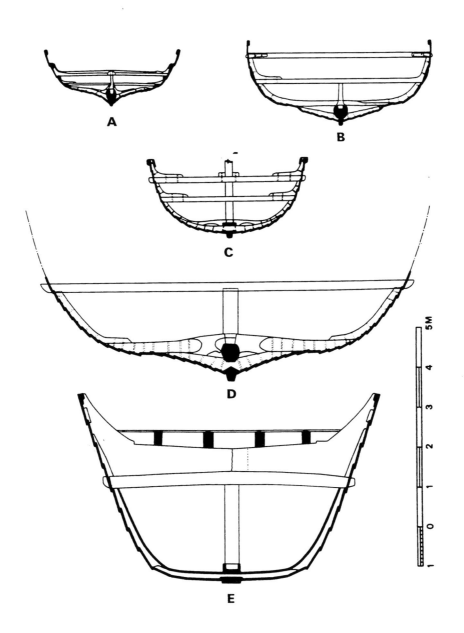

Figure 2.1.7   Transverse sections of he Bergen Cog (E) and four ships in the Viking tradition: (A) Skuldelev 3; (B) Skuldelev 1; (C) Galtaback; (D) Bergen;

Figure 2.1.8   The coasting ketch *Charlotte* discharging cargo on the beach at St Ives, Cornwall *c* 1908 (Photograph: Gillis
Collection)

Figure 2.1.9   A small schooner being built in 1977 at Brigus, Newfoundland. Similar stocks and shores could have been used in medieval Europe, leaving little remains to be found by excavation (Photograph: Basil Greenhill)

But ships are not restricted to berthing parallel to a waterfront: they may berth bow or stern first, and this position could be compatible with a front–braced structure. Having the stern to a waterfront is well documented in medieval illustrations, with either anchor or mooring post to hold the bow.

Tides present special problems to waterfront operations, although inland river sites with fluctuating depths of water also experience them to a degree. Deeply laden ships may only be able to approach and come alongside at or near times of high–water. In general terms, during a 12 hour period, a ship will move down relative to the quayside until low water and then back to high–water position again; this tidal range varies nowadays in Britain from 2m to 13m. Such vertical movement poses problems of how best a ship can be unloaded and loaded; however, near the times of high water and low water there are periods of 2–3 hours when height changes relatively slowly. In modern times intermediate stagings and stairs are sometimes used to facilitate cargo handling at low water. Such facilities may be detectable during excavation, as may steps at which small boats could berth at all states of the tide.

Changes in relative sea level have not been uniform within throughout north–western Europe and therefore the precise state in antiquity at a particular port needs to be established before the problems of tides and depths of water can be further investigated.

Co–operation between urban and nautical archaeologists

Medieval builders of waterfronts and boats worked with wood and used similar tools: their methods of selecting and converting timber and the joints they used were also probably similar or related. Thus, much may be learned from an integrated study of the material surviving from these trades and from other woodworking crafts (McGrail 1979a). One possible outcome of this research could be the ability to date boats, ships, and other wooden structures by phases of technological change. It may also prove possible to determine the origin of ships, should significant regional differences in woodworking techniques become evident.

A further area of joint study must be that of sea levels and tidal ranges. Although the general trend of change through the medieval period may be known, the precise effects at a particular waterfront are determined by local conditions and there is much work to be done here.

Technical terms must also be agreed. The various forms of scarf joint are not always known by the same name, for example, and even such terms as *jetty* and *dock* may need to be clarified.

The urban archaeologist needs to be aware of the range of water transport (including exotic types) which may be found and of the possibility of finding boatbuilding sites and informal landing places on river strands and estuary beaches. The possibility of identifying beacons, leading marks, and transits, which may have guided medieval seamen to a harbour entrance, should not be overlooked. Nautical archaeologists, who in the past may have concentrated too much on the identification of shipbuilding methods, now need to investigate boat and ship operations in greater detail, including operations in harbours and at landing places. If nautical and urban archaeologists are to exploit their own material to the full, they must explore the potential and understand the limitations of the other sub–discipline. In this way the waterfronts will be peopled with shipwrights and seamen as well as carpenters and merchants, and from this co-operation should evolve a greater understanding of medieval economic life and technology.

References

Arnold B. 1978 'Gallo-Roman boat finds in Switzerland.' in du Plat Taylor and Cleer 1978, 31–35.

Christensen A. E. 1968A 'Sjiφvollen Ship.' *Viking*, 32, 131–153.

Christensen A. E. 1968B *Boats of the North*, Olso.

Crumlin-Pedersen O. 1965 'Cog-Kogge-Kaage.' *Handels og Sjφfartamuseet Pa Kronberg* Arbog, 81–144.

Crumlin-Pedersen O. 1969 'Das Haithabuschiff.' *Ausgrabungen in Haithabu*, 3, Neumunster.

Crumlin-Pedersen O. 1978 'Ships of the Vikings.' in Anderson T. & Sandred K. I. *The Vikings*, 32–41, Uppsala.

Crumlin-Pedersen O. 1979 'Danish Cog-finds.' in McGrail, 1979b, 17–34.

de Boe G. 1978 'Roman boats from a small river harbour at Pommeroeul, Belgium.' in du Plat Taylor and Cleere 1978, 22–30.

Delaney J. 1976 'Fieldwork in south Roscommon.' in C. O. Danochair (ed) *Folk and Farm* 15–29, Dublin.

de Weerd M. D. 1978 'Ships of the Roman period at Zwammerdam.' in du Plat Taylor and Cleere 1978, 15–21.

du Plat Taylor J. and Cleere H. 1978 *Roman shipping and trade: Britain and the Rhine Provinces*, C.B.A. Research Report No. 24.

Ellmers D. 1972 *Frumittelalterliche Handelsschiffahrt in Mittel und Nordeuropa*, NeumUnster.

Ellmers D. 1976 *Kogge, Kahn und Kunststoffboot*, Bremerhaven.

Ellmers D. 1979 'The Cog of Bremen and related boats.' in McGrail, 1979b, 1–15.

Eskeröd A. 1956 'Early Nordic Arotic Boats.' *Arctica*, (1956): 57–87, Uppsala.

Ewe H. 1972 *Schiffe auf Siegeln*, Rostock.

Fenwick V. H. (ed) 1978A *The Graveney Boat*. NMM Archaeological Series No. 3, British Archaeological Reports, Oxford 53.

Fenwick V. H. 1978B 'The Site at Graveney and its possible use as a landing place.' in Fenwick, 1978A, 179–192.

Greenhill B. 1976 *Archaeology of the Boat*, London.

Hornell J. 1972 *Water Transport*, Newton Abbot.

Johnstone P. 1980 *Seacraft of Prehistory*, London.

Laird-Clowes G. S. 1932 *Sailing Ships*, London.

McGrail S. 1978, *Logboats of England and Wales*, NMM Greenwich Archaeological Series 2 British Archaeological Reports, Oxford 51.

McGrail S. 1979A 'Prehistoric boats, timber and woodworking technology.' *Proceedings of the Prehistoric Society*, 45, 159–163.

McGrail S. (ed) 1979B *Medieval Ships and Harbours*, NMM Greenwich Archaeological Series No. 5, British Archaeological Reports, Oxford S.66.

McGrail S. and Switsur R. 1979A 'Medieval logboats.' *Medieval Archaeology*, 23, 22

McGrail S. and Switsur R. 1979b 'Logboats of the River Mersey.' in McGrail (ed), 1979B 93–115.

McKee E. 1978 'Draughtsman's Notes.' in Fenwick, 1978A, 49–104.

Marsden P. V. 1976 'A boat of the Roman period found at Bruges, Belgium in 1899 and related types.' *IJNA*, 5, 23–55.

Olsen O. and Crumlin-Pedersen O. 1967 'Skuldelev Ships.' *Acta Archaeologica*, 38, 73–174.

Reindeers R. 1979 'Medieval ships: recent finds in the Netherlands.' in McGrail, 1979B 35–43.

Severin T. 1978 *The Brendan Voyage*, London.

Wright E. V. 1976 *The North Ferriby boats*, NMM Greenwich Monograph 23.

Reprinted with permission from :

Milne G. and Hobley B. (ed). *Waterfront archaeology in Britain and Northern Europe*, 17–23. CBA Research Report 41. (1981).

PAPER 2.2

THE INTERPRETATION OF ARCHAEOLOGICAL EVIDENCE FOR MARITIME STRUCTURES

Archaeological Interpretation

The function of an excavated object or structure and its relationship to the people who made and used it are often not self-evident but have to be established by reasoning. The aids to interpretation which the archaeologist may draw upon in this phase of research include: the on-site record of the object and associated material; post-excavation examination and recording; laboratory examination of samples from the object and from its environmental context; numerical calculations; attribute analysis and pattern searching techniques; comparison with other excavated objects and structures; information from iconographic and documentary sources, and from ethnographic and folk-life studies; small-scale model building; and experiments with full-scale replicas. By critical use of these sources much may be learned about how the object or structure was probably made and used. In conjunction with similar information about related objects and structures, inferences may then be drawn about the technological capabilities and the economic life of an ancient community, and, indirectly and with less certainty, about the social, political and spiritual aspects.

Ethnographic analogies

Archaeologists have generally tended to undervalue ethnographic and folk-life observations or have used them uncritically as an aid to understanding excavated material (Spriggs, 1977). Maritime students of archaeology, on the other hand, have been fortunate that Basil Greenhill's involvement with both archaeology and ethnography has demonstrated (notably in the display *The Development of the Boat* at the National Maritime Museum and in his book *Archaeology of the Boat*) how the latter can illuminate the archaeological record. This paper is offered to him as a small return for his help and guidance during my time at Greenwich.

A useful distinction may be made between the terms anthropology and ethnography. I take the latter term to include descriptive, primary data about material culture in non-industrial, generally illiterate, small-scale societies. This source is useful in the technological interpretation of the excavated material and in making deductions about the economic life of ancient communities. On the other hand, *social anthropology* is more concerned with relationships in these societies and thus may be of value to the archaeologist when dealing with the social, political and religious spheres. This link between archaeology and anthropology (in the sense defined above) has sometimes been doubted (see, for example Leach, 1977, 161). However the link between ethnography and archaeology appears to be stronger, and the discussion in this paper is concentrated on this area of interaction between the two disciplines.

Recognition of how an artifact or structure was made and used depends upon the interpreter's awareness of possibilities as well as on insight and reasoning. Ethnographic studies enable the archaeologist to escape the bounds of his own culture and to become aware of technologies other than his own. Where cultural continuity between prehistory and the recent past, or even the present, can be demonstrated, e.g. boatbuilding in certain parts of Norway (fide Christensen, 1977A), ethnographic, evidence can be especially useful. The problems are greater when analogies are used cross-culturally, but the more similar in environmental, technological and economic terms the two cultures can be shown to be, the greater is the likelihood that ethnographic studies will be of some relevance to archaeological material.

Although similarities of raw material, form, constructional techniques, and so on, may be demonstrated in a particular comparison of excavated and ethnographic evidence, a simple 1 to 1 relationship between artifact and function does not necessarily follow. Even within one culture an artifact may have several different functions: thus a paddle may be used to propel a boat, to steer, or to avoid an underwater obstacle (with the added complication that in certain parts of the world paddle-shaped artifacts are used to dig, to shovel, to beat washing and to stir butter, etc.). Conversely, a single function may be satisfied in several ways: thus withy stitches, wooden treenails, or iron nails may be used to fasten boat planking. Finally, there is no certainty that knowledge of the original use of an excavated artifact will have survived: the precise prehistoric use may not be included in any of the ethnographic data it is now possible to record.

Thus ethnographic analogues do not provide one certain identification, rather a range of possibilities for the archaeologist to combine with information about the context of the excavated object or structure and its spatial relationship to other artifacts, conclusions from the natural sciences, ergonomics, documentary evidence, and so on. As Graham Clark (1953, 357) said some 30 years ago, 'Comparative ethnography can prompt the right questions; only archaeology in conjunction with the various natural sciences ... can give the right answers' – with the rider that in the present state of knowledge no answers may be possible, and any answer will be probabilistic rather than be definitive.

Many early ethnographers and their predecessors, the travellers and missionaries, appear to have overlooked maritime matters, especially the technological aspects, and boatbuilding, and boat use did not become available until the mid–20th century (McGrail, 1978, 26). Today, the maritime ethnographer aims to record artifacts in such a way that from his data an authentic model or replica could be built and used, and so that theoretical calculations of a boat's performance can be made and compared with his field observations. If progress is to be made in the areas of common interest to Archaeology and Ethnography, integrated studies are essential. This is one of the principal reasons for the recent appointment of an ethnographer to the Archaeological Research Centre at Greenwich.

Evidence for Maritime Structures

The zone within which there is the greatest probability of encountering direct evidence of early maritime structures and activities may be defined as the sum of:

a) the region either side of the land/sea interface, from seaward of the position of Mean Low Water Springs (MLWS) to inland of Mean High Water Springs (MHWS) – this includes the tidal waters of estuaries.

b) an equivalent area along the non–tidal reaches of rivers and around other inland waterways. This is not generally thought of as maritime, but some of the artifacts and structures used there are similar to those of the maritime zone (in the strict sense) and therefore the area is included.

This definition is related to sea level and to river courses, and these have varied over time. Thus, in relation to today's sea level, the defined zone will be biased landward where the sea level is now relatively lower than in earlier times, and seaward where it is now higher.

In river valleys the zone will include all the long term meanders since the Upper Pleistocene.

Using several forms of evidence, much of it ethnographic, general descriptions may be compiled of the major types of maritime structure to be found in this zone. Within each type constructional details vary, but certain characteristics are common and these may be regarded as diagnostic features which differentiate one type of structure from the remainder. This paper does not aim to be a comprehensive review of all fixed maritime structures: canals, crannogs and fish ponds have been omitted because at present it appears impossible to generalise about them: salt pans because they have recently been dealt with elsewhere (de Brisay, 1975); and tidal mills and water wheels because they require lengthier treatment than is possible here. The information set out below (and summarised in Table 2.2.1) about a dozen or so structures may be of value to the archaeologist attempting to interpret remains excavated in the maritime zone. The archaeological discussion is restricted to the prehistoric and early medieval periods of northern and western Europe and generally excludes consideration of these regions directly and strongly influenced by the classical civilisations.

Boatbuilding sites

There is much ethnographic evidence for the use of informal, ad hoc boatbuilding sites, in the open or under an elementary shelter, close to a timber supply and with ready access to the water (Hornell, 1948, 47; Edwards, 1965, plates, 6, 7; Longstaff, 1930, 260; Eskerod, 1970, 74 6). Even today, in countries with a generally industrialised economy and technology including permanent shipyards, local communities continue to use temporary, informal boatbuilding sites: this has been noted for instance in Canada (McGrail, 1981B, fig. 23) Portugal (Filguieras, 1977, figs. 9.3, 9.13), Sweden (Ellmers, 1972, fig. 102; Hasslof, 1972, figs. 9, 10, 11), Finland (Johnstone, 1980, figs. 5.5 to 5.7) and Ireland (Johnstone 1980, figs. 10.13, 10.15, 10.16). Prehistoric and early medieval sites were probably similarly informal. Such sites will leave little for the archaeologist to excavate: one example may be quoted. Excavations at the Viking Age site at Paviken in Gotland (Lundstrom, 1971/2; Ellmers, 1972, fig. 132) revealed evidence for boatbuilding or repair – over 2000 used and unused clench nails and a special tool for loosening them – but no evidence for the stocks or shores which would be needed during construction. On other sites of greater potential it may prove possible to detect a pattern of vertical holes where stocks or keel blocks had been held in place by short stakes, with an arrangement of angled holes on both sides for shores (see for example Fenwick, 1978, fig. 10.1.4; Hornell, plate XXXVIB) and the possibility of shallow vertical holes outside these to support a light shelter.

From the late Medieval period however, when ships of some size were built, permanent sites of greater complexity were used. Such sites should leave significant traces – for parallel evidence see, for example, the early 20th century shipyard at Norrenabb, Sweden described by Nilsson (1972 figs. 4, 5, 6), with its complex of buildings and facilities.

Landing places

Away from technically advanced and economically complex societies 20th century boatmen use informal landing places. Examples may be quoted from the Indian Ocean (Hornell, 1946, 234/5, Frontispiece, plate XA, XIII; Hourani, 1963, 92–7); Poland (Smolarek, 1981, 56); Germany (Rudolph, 1974; Ellmers, 1981, 88); California (Casson, 1971, 361); Ecuador (Edwards, 1965, fig. 11b); and Britain (McGrail, 1981B, fig. 22; Finch 1976, 85). Technique have been evolved for landing and launching boats through surf on open beaches (*Seamanship Manual* 1, 1926, 246–252) but beaches in natural harbours or estuaries, protected from the prevailing wind and swell are preferred wherever available. Boats of suitable form and structure are operated directly from these places: after beaching they may be man–handled further inland on portable rollers or even oars (Finch 1976, 85). In tidal waters boats may be allowed to take the ground gradually on a falling tide; or they may be held off the foreshore at anchor or fastened to mooring posts, or mooring stones (for examples of the latter see Ellmers, 1972, figs. 1054). Similar methods may be used in tidal rivers: Beaudouin (1970, 75) has recorded how boats on the lower reaches of the R. Adour in S.W. France are secured by rope to

Table 2.2.1 Characteristic features of some maritime structures

	Boatbuilding Sites	Landing Places	Hard	Boatshelter or House	Causeway	Wharfs or Jetties	Blockages (other than by wrecks)	Fish Weirs
Environment	Above MHWS. Relatively near a timber supply	Around shoreline. River banks, especially near a confluence	Above MHWS	Above MWHS	Across wet land or tidal foreshore	In relatively deep water at some state of the tide	Below MLWS. In water deep enough to be used by watercraft	a) Between MLWS and MHWS. b) Across rivers or in non-tidal waters
Orientation	Area feature with longer axis approximately at right angles to shoreline	Area feature	Area feature with longer axis at approx right angle to shoreline	Area feature with longer axis at approx right angle to shoreline	Linear feature at an angle to shoreline	Wharfs parallel to shoreline Jetties at right angles	Linear feature At approx right angles to across a shipping route	a) Linear features. At an angle to shoreline, in direction of ebb b) At right angles from river bank or shoreline
Structural remains	Vertical posts holding stocks in position. Angled holes for shores	Stone alignments delineating clear area	Horiz. poles, hurdles or planks held in position by vertical timbers	Open-ended building. Walls may be curved in plan. No central roof supports	Horizontal hurdles, planks or stones held in position by vertical timbers. Stone. Hard packed sand or gravel	Stone structure. Wooden structure on piles	Parallel rows of vertical stakes	Vertical (or near) posts 50cm–2m apart. Posts linked by wattle–work or hurdles. Traps at intervals or at apex of V
Associated remains	Hard. Metal and wood–working tools. Nails and other fastenings. Wood waste	Hard Slipway. Causeway Clusters of artifacts. Anchors, mooring stones or posts	Vertical stakes to hold boat. Cause–way. Slip	Slip. Boat equipment. Repair materials and tools	Bridge. Landing site Hard	Market. Warehouse	Floating timbers linking rows of stakes	Stabilised by sole–plates, angled posts and/or boulders and/or brushwood bundles

Notes:
1. See text and references for details
2. MHWS; shoreline etc refer to ancient environment
3. Associated Remains entries give a range of possibilities
4. Some entries based on a very few finds therefore liable to be altered in light of future work

of a post, with a row of stakes on each side restraining them against the tidal current. On the non–tidal reaches of rivers particularly attractive 'landing sites may be formed where a relatively slow river joins a faster one. Deposition forms a gradually shelving beach between the two rivers, just upstream of the confluence, where boats may easily make a landing.

By analogy we would expect to find similar informality in ancient Europe (outside the influence of the Classical civilisations) until sometime in the Medieval period when a relatively high state of technology was achieved, with economic and commercial complexity. Flemming's survey (1980, 164 5) of the landing places of the pre–classical eastern Mediterranean lends support to this hypothesis. On the other hand Needham and Longley (1980, 418) have argued that the linear wooden feature excavated near a Late Bronze Age riverside settlement at Runnymede Bridge is the remains of a 'wharf against which craft might moor' but *a priory* this seems unlikely to be the principal use of this structure. From other considerations it seems more probable that it was erected to stabilise the river bank and prevent erosion next to the settlement (McGrail, forthcoming).

It is doubtful whether there would have been any advantage in taking the known indigenous boats from pre–historic northern and western Europe alongside a wharf, although a landing stage extension to a causeway (see below) might have been useful when riverine or estuarine deposition prevented large boats from coming close inshore. Logboats, skin boats and the Hjortspring, Ferriby and Brigg sewn plank boats could all be successfully operated from river banks or protected beaches; indeed the Ferriby and Brigg craft were excavated from precisely such contexts (Wright, 1976; McGrail, 1981A). Sewn boats of 1st/2nd century AD were certainly used off beaches in the Indian Ocean (*Periplus of the Erthyraean Sea*, Chs. 15,16, 36 see Huntingford, 1980); as indeed they were in the 19th and 20th centuries (Folkard, 1870, 310; Hornell, 1946, 236).

Turning to the Medieval period, we may note the informal use of landing places shown on the 1lth century AD Bayeaux tapestry where there are scenes with one boat being beached, another coming to anchor in the shallows, and others fastened to a mooring post (Stenton, 1957, figs. 36, 39, 45). In a review of medieval wrecks in Danish waters, Crumlin–Pedersen (1981) has noted that many of them have been found lying off 'beach market places'. The medieval wrecks from Skuldelev (Olsen and Crumlin–Pedersen, 1967, 108–9, 117–8, 130, 144–5) and Utrecht boat 1 (Ellmers, 1972, 138), among others, have wear on their keels or bottom plankings consistent with them having taken the ground on sand or gravel beaches. The wear pattern on transverse holes through the lower stems of other medieval finds (Kentmere 1, Graveney, Nydam 2 for example) indicate that these boats were probably pulled up the beach by rope.

Archaeological evidence for these informal landing places may be minimal, however single mooring posts were found with the 13th/14th century Kentmere boat 1 and the undated Walthamstow logboat (McGrail, 1978), and several oak posts, *c.* 10cm in diameter, were used to retain the late–9th century AD Graveney boat in position at a tidal river landing place (Fenwick, 1978, 181–5). Comparable methods were also used to restrain two undated Irish logboats (McGrail, 1978, 90). The site of a landing place may also be indicated by parallel rows of stones on the foreshore at right angles to the water, or cleared areas on an otherwise stony beach, as noted by Rolfson (1974, 136) in south–west Norway. Anchors and other items of boat's equipment, and otherwise inexplicable clusters of artifacts on the shoreline may also suggest former use as a landing place.

Slipways where boats can be more readily dragged in and out of the water may be found associated with landing sites. Lundström (1971/2) excavated two trenches 20m long and 0.5m deep sloping down the shore at the Viking Age site of Paviken, Gotland, which he interpreted as slips; re–used boat planking seems to have performed a similar function at the late 8th century site at New Fresh Wharf, London (Marsden, 1981, 11). The declivity or slope of a slip is an important feature because on a steep slipway severe strains can be imposed on the boat as she enters the waters and there may be stability problems. Modern slips have a slope of *c.* 1 in 20 (*c.*3°), but slips in the classical Mediterranean have been recorded with slopes between 1 in 4 (15°) and 1 in 14 (4°) – see Flemming, 1980, 169.

Hards

On soft beaches, when it is required to leave a boat temporarily out of water, simple hardstandings of horizontal hurdles or poles and other light timbers may be constructed to prevent the hull sinking into the mud. For a recent example in France see Beaudouin (1970, 75). On tidal sites these hards are generally sited above all but the highest of high waters so that the boat is normally aground yet may be floated off on a spring tide. Slipways may lead from a hard into the water, although temporary rollers or oars may also be used.

There is increasing archaeological evidence for hards. Part of the Neolithic Baker site in the Somerset Levels has been interpreted as a hard or platform of brushwood with a slip leading to a lower level (Coles, 1980, 8–15), and a light timber hard dated to the Roman period has been recorded at Bentumersial on the R. Ems (Ellmers, 1975, 336). The 9th century Graveney boat was found pulled up on to a hard mainly of willow (*Salix* sp.) (Fenwick, 1978, 181–5), and a similar structure has recently been excavated near the medieval waterfront at Norwich (Ayres, 1981, 279). It is possible that the undated logboat from Deeping Fen, Lincs. was also lying on a hard (McGrail, 1978, 185).

Boat shelters and boat houses

When not in use, especially for long periods, boats need protection from extremes of temperature and the effects of high winds. This may be simply achieved by pulling the boat well above high water mark, turning her over, and possibly covering her with boughs or brushwood (McGrail, 1978, 90; Rudolph, 1974, 16). On the other hand, special boat houses are built in some of the Pacific islands (Haddon and Hornell,

1936–7; Folkard, 1870, 283, 293). Such buildings generally have open ends and are orientated with their longer axis at right angles to the foreshore; they may be connected to the water by a slip of paving stones, logs or hard packed sand and earth (Rolfson 1974, 138–148). Generally speaking in pre–industrial societies boats are not built in boat houses but repairs and refits may be undertaken there.

Medieval structures interpreted as boat houses have been excavated in south west Norway (Rolfson, 1974) and at L'Anse aux Meadows, Canada (Christensen, 1977B). The Norwegian structures had outward curving side walls of turf on stone; the end facing the sea was open and the rear wall either open or of wood. There were no interior roof supporting timbers except close to the walls; the roofs were deduced to have been made of timbers covered with birchbark and turf. Whole and fragmented boat nails were found inside these houses suggesting that repairs has been carried out.

Early boat houses are also known from Iceland, Greenland and Denmark (Christensen, 1977B, 122) and Ellmers (1972, fig. 103; 1974, 138) has noted a 7th century German boat house at Hessens, Wilhelmshaven with an 11m wooden slipway.

Causeways

Causeways are linear structures slightly raised above their surroundings and used to cross wet or marshy ground. They may be of wood or stone or hard packed and consolidated sand, gravel or similar materials. Causeways leading to rivers give dry–shod access across marshy ground to ferry or ford. In tidal regions they lead down the foreshore to landing places and their lower sections are submerged at high water. Where causeways are used to cross a tidal inlet or river they may only be useable dry–shod for a period either side of low water, as for example in Bosham harbour, Sussex and the R. Deben near Sutton Hoo, Suffolk: the term 'hard' may be used on 20th century maps and charts for such causeways.

Causeways of logs and brushwood are thought to have been described by Homer, and Reed (1975) has argued convincingly that, in c. 10 BC, Nero Drussus built an embanked causeway across marshy ground between Bonn and Boulogne. In Britain, Neolithic and Bronze Age wooden causeways have been excavated on the Somerset Levels where they are known as 'trackways' (Coles, 1975–81), and there are Iron Age examples at Glastonbury, the earlier structure being of horizontal hurdlework, the later of planking and gravel (Ellmers, 1972, 140). At Brigg in south Humberside there seems to have been a long tradition for the use of causeways. Large holes through the Brigg 'raft' (650 bc) have been interpreted as indications of secondary use of the bottom of this boat as part of a causeway giving access to the estuarine channel of the prehistoric R. Ancholme (McGrail, 1981A, 249–250). It is possible that the lower end of this structure may have been afloat at high water acting as a simple landing stage. At a slightly earlier date, a causeway of transverse timbers lying upon longitudinally–laid tree-boles and branches (known in academic papers as the

Brigg track, but locally as the 'causey') gave dry–shod access to the river some 120m south of the position of the 'raft' (Smith, 1981, 143; McGrail 1981A, 277). The existence of a medieval causeway at Brigg has been deduced from placename evidence by Professor K. Cameron (McGrail, 1981A, 271).

Other medieval causeways are known from 8th/9th century excavations at Kaupang, Norway where they were built of stone and horizontal wooden poles. A stone structure in the 11th/12th century layers at Bryggen, Bergen is also considered to be one (Ellmers, 1972, 140–1), and the Colchester Archaeological Trust has recently excavated a 6th century causeway connecting Mersea Island to the Essex mainland (Hillam,.1981, 37). Causeways are sometimes mentioned in medieval documents: for example, an early 13th century causeway across Higham Marsh, Kent (Thornhill, 1977, 123).

It is possible that causeway remains may be misinterpreted as those of a collapsed or vestigial bridge. Clear evidence that the structure spanned a water channel is needed to support a bridge interpretation. Bridge foundations may be expected to be generally deeper and more substantial than the infrastructure of a causeway.

Wharfs and jetties

Evidence from Ancient Egypt, the Phoenician Era and the Classical Worlds (Shaw 1972; Muckleroy 1978,75–84; Flemming, 1980) indicates that formal harbour facilities (where boats may lie afloat alongside a structure from which they can be directly manned and their cargo loaded and discharged) became necessary when settlement became concentrated in cities with complex economic organizations and technological specialisation. Larger vessels of greater draft were then required to satisfy increasing demand at these focal points for low density, mass consumption goods. Defence requirements, the centralisation of political authority, the collection of custom dues, the requirement to accumulate stocks in warehouses and the silting of natural landing places which forced vessels to beach increasingly farther away from where their cargo was required, led to the construction of harbours which incorporated the deep water berths necessary for bigger vessels.

The first stage of development in the eastern Mediterranean appears to have been the construction of breakwaters to protect landing places from prevailing winds and swell; subsequently formal waterfronts were constructed, and beacons and lighthouses were built (Flemming, 1980, 168–175). The ability to bring waterborne goods close to the market place minimised handling and thus made these major constructions viable. Nevertheless widespread use of informal landing places continued in the less developed regions as is also the case today: see, for example, Edwards, 1965, fig. 11b and Hornell, 1946, plate XIIIB, where boats are beached rather than brought alongside nearby wharfs or jetties.

In northern and western Europe this economic and technological take–off point seems to have been reached in the 10th to 12th century AD. There is widespread archaeological evidence from this period for the construction of wharfs and jetties with deep water berths for the first time since the Roman Empire (Milne and Hobley, 1981, 7, 13–14, 19–22, 56, 824).

A *wharf* may be defined as a stone structure, or a wooden one supported on piles, alongside which vessels can lie. It is generally parallel to the shoreline and may either be in continuous contact with the land or off-set slightly from it and connected to it by two or more approach structures. A jetty is similarly constructed but it projects at right angles from the shoreline or from a wharf.

Milne and Hobley (1981) describe many waterfront structures but not all are jetties or wharfs; these may best be identified by consideration of the pattern of the surviving remains, the size of timbers used, the stratigraohic context, and environmental evidence. The depth of water generally alongside the structures has to be established where appropriate, some estimate of the tidal range obtained; without evidence for water of sufficient depth for loaded cargo vessels to come alongside at some state of the tide, linear structures parallel to the shoreline may more readily be interpreted as bank reinforcement, flood defences or walls built to enclose and gain land (see next section). Milne (1981, 36) has noted that 20th century timber piles in tidal regions decay most readily around the contemporary level of Mean High Water Neaps (MHWN). It thus seems reasonable to deduce, as Milne has proposed,that where there are repairs or replacement timbers at a consistent level in an excavated waterfront structure this level was probably near the contemporary MHWN. Such observations may contribute towards a demonstration that a particular structure was indeed in relatively deeper water and therefore probably a wharf or jetty.

Flood defences and sea walls built to gain land

Some linear waterfront structures are built today without the intention of providing a deep water berth but rather to consolidate a river bank or a seashore, or to gain new ground by enclosing the marshy or inter-tidal margins of a river or other waterway: both functions may be combined in one structure. Sand, gravel or pebble foreshores may also require stabilisation against lateral movement: in recent times this has been done by building wooden groynes generally at right angles to the shoreline.

The methods used to consolidate a waterfront, and to build flood defences and sea walls, for which there is archaeological evidence, may be summarised;
a) Closely-set piles in single or double rows, sometimes with interwoven hurdles.
b) Hurdies or bundles of poles, sometimes in conjunction with stones.
c) Horizontal logs laid on top of one another or against a sloping bank, sometimes held in place by vertical posts.

d) Earthen banks (sometimes stone-faced).

See Ellmers (1972, 139), and Needham and Longley (1980, 425).

Obstructions to waterways and harbour defences

Thirteenth century chronicles relate that Danes of the previous two centuries used underwater obstructions to block bays and channels against Slav seaborne raids (Crumlin–Pedersen 1973, 31), and Crumlin–Pedersen has investigated several underwater sites with linear structures of wood and stone which appear to date from this period. Ships could also be used to block channels as at the well – known site of Skuldelev in the Roskilde Fjord, Denmark where five Viking Age ships were sunk in a group (Olson and Crumlin–Pedersen, 1967). Landing places may also need protection as at the Viking Age site of Haithabu (Hedeby) where there was a multiple palisade to seaward (Ellmers, 1974, 138; Ellmers, 1972, fig. 123); there may have been similar defences around Birka, Sweden (Crumlin–Pedersen, 1973, 32). Fords may be made difficult to use: during his second invasion of Britain in 54 BC Caesar found that the Britons had obstructed a ford across the Thames by driving stakes into the river bed and banks (Handford, 1951, 137).

A section of an 11th century blockage across one entrance to Hefnaes Bay on the south west coast of Fyn has been investigated in some detail (Crumlin–Pedersen, 1973). The remains are in shallow water and consist of two elements: vertical piles; and horizontal timbers of a distinctive shape (Figs2.2.1 and 2.2.2). The vertical piles, in two parallel rows, were 2.8m–3.6m in length of which *c.* 1.5m had been driven into the seabed, and had double–fluked and pointed lower ends. The rows were *c.* 1.7m–1.9m apart and the piles at 1m–1.4m intervals. The horizontal timbers had been fashioned from half of a split log, and were 3.6m–3.9m in length and 8–14cm thick, with vertical rectangular holes cut through the timbers near their expanded ends. Both types of timber from Hasnaes were beech (*Fagus* sp.), but another fragment of a horizontal timber recovered from nearby Slivsφ was of oak (*Quercus* sp.). Crumlin–Pedersen deduced that the distinctively–shaped timbers were fitted across the rows of piles, parallel to the axis of the channel (Fig. 2.2.3); they would have been awash and thus would damage a ship at or near the waterline.

Stakes defending a ford may be in an irregular pattern in fresh water shallows or in tidal waters which are shallow at low water. Landing place defences are in relatively deepwater and may have a curved alignment. Channel obstructions are in water deep enough to allow the passage of boats and they are generally aligned at right angles to the shoreline.

Fish Weirs and Stake Nets

When 'fixed engines' (Went, 1964, 191) are used for fishing there may be significant structural remains to be excavated. Weirs and stake nets may be used in freshwater rivers, tidal estuaries and the sea shallows, and in a paper discussing the

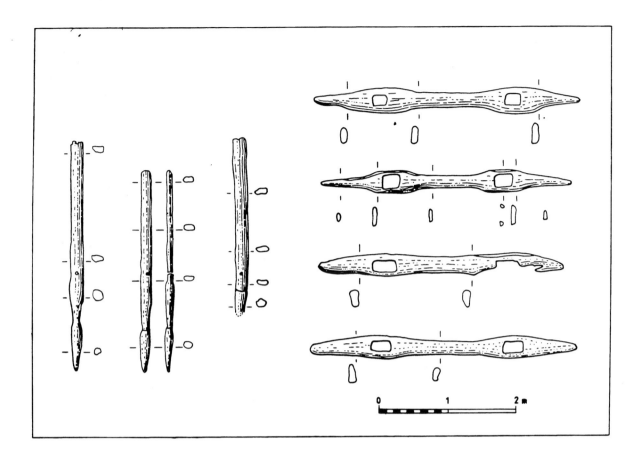

Figure 2.2.1 Piles and floating timbers from an 11th century underwater blockage at one entrance to Helnaes Bay, south west coast of Fin, Denmark. After Crumlin–Pedersen, 1973.

methods used to capture salmon, Went (1964) has described several different versions of these structures.

In the stake net method of trapping fish, baskets or nets (vertical or bag–shaped) are streamed between a series of stakes in the sea or (partly) across a river (Wheeler, 1979 fig. 3; *Salmon fisheries of Scotland*, fig. 4; Burdon, 1954, fig. 10, Jenkins, 1974B, 41–3; Hojrup, 1974, figs. 2 and 3; Davis, 1958, 25). The pattern of stake holes which would be left by such structures could be similar to those of bird trapping devices sometimes used on foreshores as well as inland. There is little or no tide in eastern Danish waters between Jutland and Fyn and so stake net structures used there have a gangway fastened to the stakes so that the nets can be tended without a boat (Hojrup, 1974). Where the bottom is too hard for stakes, nets are erected between stakes fastened to timber boxes fixed with ballast (Hojrup, 1974, figs. 4 and 5): such structures may leave no trace.

The general principle of fish weir operations is that a barrier is built across a known fish route, and this deflects the fish to an opening where there is a trap from which they are subsequently taken (fig.2.2.4) The method has widespread use in continental Europe (Clark 1952, 43–4), Wales (Jenkins, 1974A, 7), Scotland (*Salmon fisheries of Scotland*),Lamu East Africa (Prins, 1965, 137), Singapore (Burdon, 1954), China (Needham, 1971, 147) and Virginia (Davis, 1956, 2) for example. The barrier is often V–shaped with the long axis of

the V almost parallel to the fish route: in tidal waters the apex is generally to seaward and near low water mark, and fish are trapped on ebb (falling) tides; in a non–tidal river, weirs designed to catch salmon face downstream, whereas stake nets erected to catch eels, face upstream, and take them as they migrate seawards (Went, 1964, 215; Wheeler, 1979, 61).

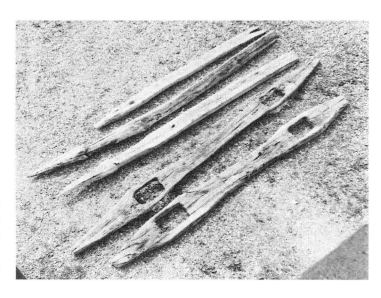

Figure 2.2.2 Piles and floating timbers from Helnaes. Photo: O. Crumlin–Pedersen

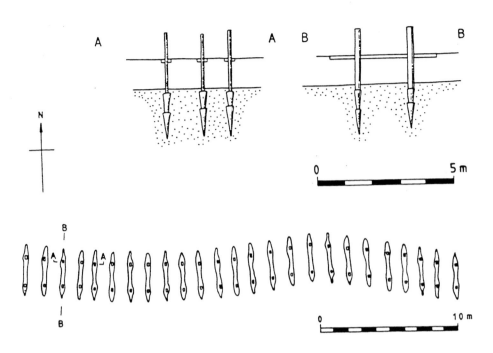

Figure 2.2.3 Reconstruction plan and sections of part of the Helnaes blockage. After Crumlin–Pedersen, 1973

Weir barriers are generally made of wattle screens driven into the sea or river bed, or wattlework may be woven between the stakes *in situ*. In the latter case the stakes are typically 10cm in diameter and spaced *c.* 60cm apart. Stakes of this size may be driven five or more feet into a mud and clay foreshore at low water by the use of a dropping 56lb (25kg) weight (Edmund Eglinton, personal communication). The arms of the weir may be up to 400m in length with wattlework 2–3m in height and the structure may be stabilised by stones. or by baskets of rocks attached to the downstream side. In tidal waters the wattlework tapers from 2–3m in deep water to 1m or less inshore (Davis, 1958, 254). On some Welsh weirs layers of brushwood and matting are placed alongside the arms near the apex to retain water around the trap during Spring tides (Jenkins, 1974B, 37). In recent times the wattlework has sometimes been replaced by nets which deflect the fish but do not enmesh them. Weirs of loose stones are also known, one in Doonbeg Bay, Ireland, having walls 600m in length (Went, 1964, 204); others are used in Queensland, Australia (Davis, 1958, 2).

The opening at the apex of these V–shaped weirs is closed by a basket or a net which may be emptied from a boat or from a platform erected between four stout posts (Fig. 2.2.4). At low water springs, however, some traps may (nearly) dry out and it may then be possible to approach them on foot (Collard, 1902) or even with carts.

A fish weir was still in use at Seasalter near Graveney, Kent, in the early 20th century on the south side of the Thames Estuary (Collard, 1902, 79 81) and the stumps of the posts can be seen at low water today in a complex pattern of interlocking and replaced V–shaped structures orientated downstream. Collard reported that these posts were of oak (*Quercus* sp.) and they varied in height above ground from 1ft (30cm) inshore to 6ft (1.83m) near the trap

Irish fish weirs are known to have been used from the 11th century (Went, 1964, 203) and possibly earlier in the Hiberno–Norse period, and Welsh ones are known from the 15th century (Jenkins, 1974A, 7). The Domesday book has several references to fish weirs on the main rivers (Darby, 1977, 279–285), and sea weirs – fences with nets along the shore – are also mentioned at Southwold and an unidentified site, 'Riseburc'. Two medieval weirs have recently been excavated at Colwick near Nottingham (possibly the site of a Domesday fishery) in a former bed of the R. Trent (Losco–Bradley and Salisbury 1980 and 1981). The 9th century weir was built of wattle hurdles, some 50 to 90cm in height, held between a double row of vertical posts, 7–14cm in diameter, which were originally c. 2.4m long with 1m buried in the river bed. These verticals were supported by angled posts whose heels were held in place by boulders. The 11th/12th century weir was complex in plan, but generally V–shaped and c. 100m in length. This complexity may be due to the replacement of a damaged arm or possibly two weirs interlocked there – both are known ethnographically. The vertical posts, some 10–15cm in diameter, were c. 50cm apart and were linked by vertical hurdles which were stabilised at the base by bound bundles of brushwood embedded in clay. Near the apex to the weir were found wattle stakes and horizontal wattlework which the excavators consider may have been part of a platform above the trap.

Figure 2.2.4 The head of a 19th century Irish V–shaped fish weir. Photo: Went, 1964, Plate XXXVC

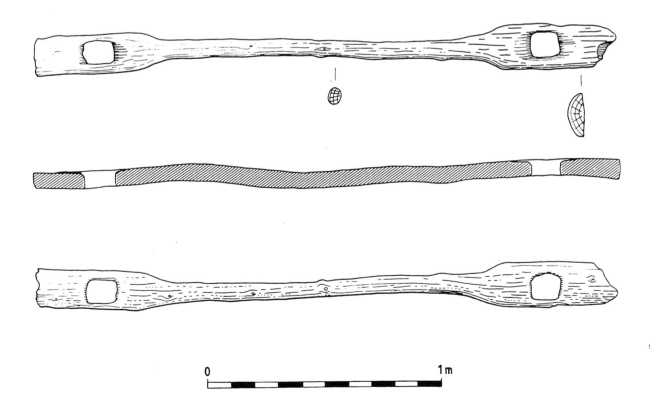

0   1 m

Figure 2.2.5 Oak timber found by T.E. Porter in association with the remains of a fishweir near Seasalter, Kent

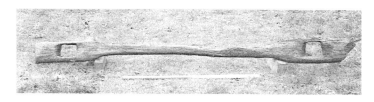

Figure 2.2.6   Oak timber from Seasalter. 2 metre ranging pole. Photo: National Maritime Museum

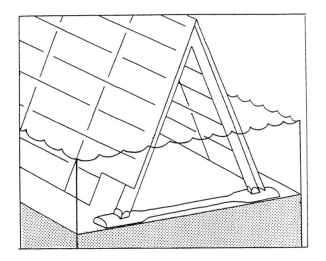

Figure 2.2.7   Digram showing the use of a disctinctively-shaped timber (see Figs 5 & 6) as a sole–plate in a 20th century fishweir near Seasalter, Kent. Drawing: National Maritime Museum.

Interpretation of Material from Two Maritime Sites

Finds from North Ferriby

In several seasons of excavation at N. Ferriby, Humberside, E.V. Wright (1947, 1976, 1978) recovered the remains of three sewn plank boats of the 2nd millenium BC from the tidal foreshore of the R. Humber. In the vicinity of these finds, and also one mile to the west at Melton, he and C.W. Wright noted traces of horizontal wickerwork hurdles (Figs 2.2.8 and 2.2.9) and one group of cleft oak (*Quercus* sp.) poles; in amongst these remains and nearby were small vertical posts. The excavator interpreted these fragmentary remains as evidence for trackways, generally orientated north/south across the foreshore. (Notes deposited at National Maritime Museum).

In 1978 the National Maritime Museum laid out a 60m x 20m rectangular area on the foreshore at Ferriby with the seaward baseline running east/west just to the north of the three boat trenches which are still recognisable at low water. Within this area of inter–tidal zone individual 1m x 2m rectangles were excavated during 1978–80. Some of these were on the site of exposures of wood identified by E.V. Wright; others were dug in an attempt to define the limits of deposited material. No indisputable evidence for wickerwork hurdles was found in these recent excavations, but, some 30–40cm below the

present day surface of the estuarine clay, short lengths of oak (*Quercus* sp.) roundwood, with some willow (*Salix* sp.) and birch (*Betula* sp) of 3–5cm diameter have been excavated; these horizontal sticks were generally on a north/south alignment, with some lying east/west (Figs. 2.2.10, 2.2.11, 2.2.12) There were also a few vertical sticks with worked points extending down some 5–10cm into the clay, and samples from three of these have been dated by A.E.R.E. Harwell:

HAR–2759: 3150 ± 80 bp (*c.* 1200 bc)
HAR–3682 :3540 ± 100 bp (*c.* 1590 bc)
HAR–4204: 3420 ± 90 bp (*c.* 1470 bc)

Thus these sticks are from the same general period as the three Ferriby boats. However, no sticks or hurdles were found associated with the boats when they were excavated, thus the possibility that the boats and these light wooden structures were precisely contemporary cannot be confirmed [This final sentence is wrong: wooden structures **were** found with Ferriby boat 2 – note added to 1997 publication.]

The general pattern of light timbers so far excavated is consistent with this being the vestigial remains of horizontal wickerwork held in place by short vertical stakes. E.V. Wright's earlier finds of hurdles (which no longer survive) in this vicinity give some support to this interpretation. Such a structure could either be a hard, inland of the boat landing place, or a causeway giving dry– shod access to the lower foreshore where boats were beached. Interpretation may become clearer when the extent of the remains has been defined.

Objects found with the Nydam boats

Nydam boat 2 was discovered in August 1863 during Engelhardt's archaeological investigations of the peat bog at Nydam, 5Onderborg, Slesvig (Engelhardt, 1866). This oak (*Quercus* sp.) rowing boat, *c.* 24m in length, has been dated to the end of the 4th century AD by the style of nine *fibulae* (brooches of safety–pin form) found in the bottom of the boat. When found, the boat had fallen apart and was not re–assembled and measured until some 4–5 months after excavation. In 1877 the boat was dismantled and again re–assembled; and in 1925 and again in 1941 she was moved to new locations; she reached her present site in the Schleswig–Holstein Landesmuseum in 1948.

Some parts of the boat were not recovered during excavation, and other parts were damaged or subsequently rotted, thus a significant proportion of the boat now on display is of modern timber (Engelhardt, 1866, 30 ϕrsnes, 1970, XV). Three theoretical reconstructions of the boat's original form have been made (Engelhardt, 1866; Shetelig and Johannesen, 1930; Åkerlund, 1963); only Åkerlund's drawings makes allowance for the considerable shrinkage that must have taken place, *c.* 14% in the tangential plane of each timber. Åkerlund's reconstruction drawings are probably as accurate as can now be expected: they give the boat a broader beam and a more rounded transverse section than earlier reconstructions.

From his drawings Åkerlund (1963,63) deduced that the boat would lack longitudinal strength in a seaway, and he therefore examined the objects which had been found with the boat to see

Figure 2.2.8　Wickerwork found by E.V. Wright on the foreshore at N. Ferriby, Humberside in 1937. Scale: folded two foot ruler. Photo: National Maritime Museum.

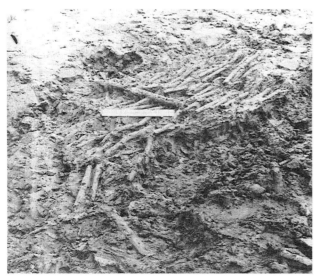

Figure 2.2.9　Oblique view of the wickerwork shown in Figure 8. Photo: National Maritime Museum

2 (Ferriby) 1/78　no.5

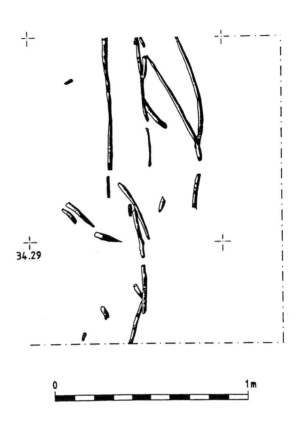

34.29

0   1m

Figure 2.2.10　Plan of some of the wooden remains excavated on the foreshore at North Ferriby in 1978. Drawing: National Maritime Museum

Figure 2.2.11　Light timbers exposed during excavation at North Ferriby in 1980. Note the modern eel traps exposed at low water. Photo: National Maritime Museum

Figure 2.2.12 Further light timbers exposed at North Ferriby in 1980. Photo: National Maritime Museum.

whether any could have been used to form a hogging truss or other strengthening arrangement which would lessen the risk of the seams springing. Two groups of timbers had indeed been found in this boat and in and around boat 3 (the pine (*Pinus* sp.) boat), for which Engelhardt (1866, 34) could find no obvious use. These enigmatic timbers were, firstly, several bundles of spars *c.* 3ft (91cm) long; and 1 in (2.54cm) diameter with a perforation near each end (Fig. 2.2.13A); and, secondly, timbers of a distinctive waisted shape, 41–62 in. (1.04–1.57m) in length, with holes through the enlarged ends (Fig. 2.2.13B). None of the first group appear to have survived and Engelhardt did not identify the timber species or give other details about them. Several examples of the second group of timbers are now with the boat in the Schleswig–Holsteinische Landesmuseum at Schloss Gottorp: two of these objects are of pine (*Pinus* sp.) and one of oak (*Quercus* sp.) (Åkerlund, 1963, 64). Åkerlund (1963. figs, 48, 49) postulated that these timbers had been used with ropes of walrus or seal skin to construct a dismountable longitudinal bracing for the boat (Fig.2.2.14) This interpretation is ingenious but unconvincing. It is by no means certain that the Nydam boat needed strengthening longitudinally. As Crumlin–Pedersen (1977, 20) has pointed out in another context, the combination of rib and crossbeam at about 1m intervals and thickened top strake contribute substantially to longitudinal strength. Though Nydam boat 2 may not have had the theoretically desirable resistance to hogging and sagging forces required by modern standards, she would have been operable in at least moderate sea states. The fact that there are no signs of hogging truss fittings in any of the boats and ships in this northern clinker–built tradition found to date, further emphasises the unlikeliness of Åkerlund's proposals.

Engelhardt deduced that the three Nydam boats had been deposited in what was then an inlet of the Alssund with access to the open sea. Subsequent measurements of relative heights above sea level and consideration of other topographical features has led later scholars to consider that at the time of deposition the Nydam area was a bog in an enclosed basin (ϕrsnes, 1970, IX–X) or possibly an inland body of water in the process of becoming a bog. The boats had been holed and many of the objects found with and near them had been damaged. It is now generally held in Scandinavia that these were votive offerings of war booty, deposited during the 3rd to 5th century AD in a lake or bog, in four groups, possibly centred on the three boats and one other spot, (ϕrsnes, 1970, XIII–XV).

Not all the artifacts deposited at Nydam were nautical or military: there were also woodworking tools and items of personal, domestic and economic use (Engelhardt, 1866, 37–8, 62–5, 74–80).Thus the two puzzling groups of objects (Figs. 2.2.13B and 2.2.13A) need not necessarily have been part of a boat's structure. Indeed, objects similar to the light spars (Fig 2.2.13A) but with notches rather than holes near the ends (Fig 2.2.15) were found by Engelhardt during excavation of other Danish bog sites at Thoresbjerg (1863, plate 18, fig.7–10) where the spars were found 'by the hundreds' spread over the finds layer.

Figure 2.2.13A One of the spars found in Nydam boat 2. After Engelhardt, 1866, Nydam plate III fig. 23

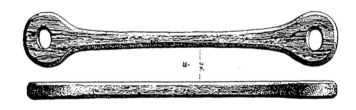

Figure 2.2.13B One of the timbers of distinctive shape found with Nydam boat 2. After Engelhardt, 1866, Nydam, plate IV fig. 26

Long wooden objects with a waisted central portion and pierced by relatively large holes, and thus generally similar in form to the Nydam second group of timbers (Fig. 2.2.13B), have been found associated with a 20th century fish weir at Seasalter in the R. Thames (Figs.2.2.5 and 2.2.6) and with an

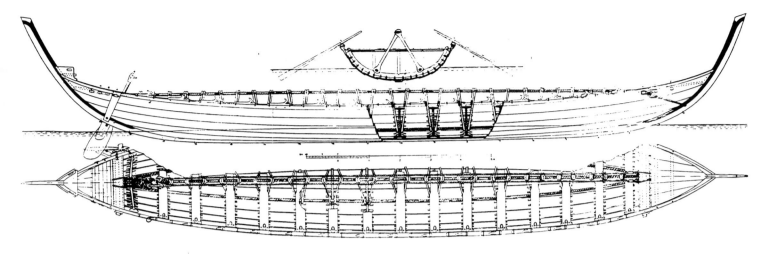

Figure 2.2.14 Åkerlund's reconstruction drawing of Nydam boat 2 showing his method of using the timbers shown in Fig 13B to support a hogging truss. After Åkerlund, 1963, Plate IV

underwater blockage in Helnaes in Denmark (Figs. 2.2.1 and 2.2.2). Timbers of similar form to those from Helnaes were used in medieval wooden bridges near Tretower, Mecklenburg and in Ober Ukersee (Crumlin–Pedersen, 1973, 45), and a similar, but smaller timber of this general shape has been used in the present century in Lough Swilly, Co. Donegal, at one end of the floatable framework of a 'loop' hand–fishing net (Went, 1956). This L. Swilly timber (Fig. 2.2.16) with rectangular holes c. 4in x 3in (10 x 7.;cm) near the ends, one of which is pointed so that it can be pressed into the seabed to maintain the frame at right angles to the flow of water. When a fish swims into the net the frame is allowed to float horizontally.

The characteristic form of the Seasalter, Helnaes and Swilly artifacts has three distinct properties:
a) It can be used to link two other timbers approximately at right angles to itself, thereby forming a stable structure in the case of the Seasalter fish weir and the Swilly frame net, and providing restraining guidelines for the Helnaes timbers.
b) It gives the lightest weight consistent with function: an advantage during transport and assembly.
c) The waisted portion makes the timbers easier to handle.

In addition, the ability of objects of beech, oak and pine to float at or near the surface of the water is essential to the function of the Helnaes and Swilly objects.

These four properties are general ones which could be used in other contexts and therefore it seems likely that there are, or have been, uses of wooden objects with this characteristic shape other than those described in this paper. The Nydam waisted timbers (Fig. 2.2.13B) are not precisely similar to any of the three quoted analogues, and it remains a possibility that timbers with a different function, yet with a form more readily comparable with the Nydam timbers, remain to be discovered in the ethnographic record. Nevertheless, within the limited range of parallels available at present, tentative conclusions may be drawn. The Nydam waisted timbers (Fig. 2.2.13B) do not have the pointed ends of the blockage timbers or of the frame net, (Fig, 2.2.16); thus, as a point is essential to the function of these two artifacts, it seems unlikely that the Nydam timbers had either of these uses. The possibility remains, therefore, that these Nydam timbers (Fig. 2.2.13B) were used as sole plates in a fish weir or in a stake–net system. The holes through the ends of the timbers were probably originally circular and stakes of c. 10cm diameter could have been driven through them to form A frames which would support wickerwork hurdles or nets.

The other enigmatic Nydam timbers (Fig 2.2.13A) may have been parts of the frame of a hand–fishing net (Davis, 1958, 145–9) similar to those marked C and F in Figure 2.2.16; or they may have been used to hold open the ends of a seine or draft fishing net, as suggested to me by Dr Went. Figure 2.2 17 shows the end of such a net being held open by slim poles some 3ft (91cm) long with holes at either end.

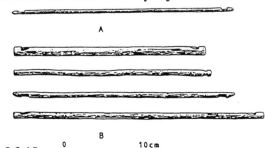

Figure 2.2.15
     (A) A spar from the Thorsbjerg Moss excavation. After Engelhardt, 1863, plate 18, fig. 26
     (B) Spars from the Vimose excavation. After Engelhardt, 1869, plate 19 figs 7–10.

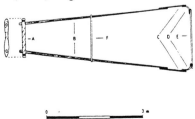

Figure 2.2.16 The wooden frame of a Lough Swilly 'loop' net. Note the distinctively shaped timber at A. After Went, 1956, fig. 1

Fishing equipment would not be inappropriate in the Nydam's assemblages: 'wickerwork mats' were found in the bottom of boats 2 and 3 (Engelhardt, 1866, 37); details were not recorded and the 'mats' do not survive, but their use in fish weir barriers seems at least as likely as the use by rowers postulated by Åkerlund (1963, 57). In addition, Engelhardt (1866, 65) noted that knotted and plaited fabrics, cords and strings of bast were frequently found at Nydam, and boat 3 contained (or had nearby) a net fastened to a pole (1866, 38, 65, plate XIV, fig. 14): nets on poles are used in fish weirs (Fig. 2.32.4) and in hand–fishing nets (Fig. 2.32.16). This Nydam net seems to have had a mesh of 2 ½ to 3in (6–7.5cm) sides, which would be suitable for catching fish of 3 to 8 lbs (1.3 to 3.6 kg) (Went, 1964, 231).

As reconstructed the Nydam boat has rowing positions along most of her length, leaving little space for other activities or the carriage of cargo. One of her main roles thus must have been that of transporting people, either as ferry in which (some of the) passengers were also oarsmen (as in the 20th century Scandinavian church boats) or as warboat or despatch vessel. The evidence considered in this paper suggest, however, that at least for some of her time afloat she may have been associated with some form of fishing activity, possibly in the erection of a fish weir or stake–net system, or in tending their traps.

The confiscation and subsequent destruction of the boat and her fishing equipment could have been an appropriate action after some dispute: indeed such action has modern parallels.

Figure 2.2.17 Hauling in a draft or seine fishing net. Note the spars used to hold open ends. After Went, 1964, fig. 22

Acknowledgements

I am most grateful to Mr. T. E. Porter who drew my attention to the Seasalter weirs, and told me about their former use and allowed me to examine the recovered timber. I am also grateful to Dr. A.J. Went for discussion and advice about fish weirs, and to Anne McGrail, Veryan Heal, Arne Emil Christensen and Ole Crumlin–Pedersen who read and commented on an early draft; and to E.V. Wright and Eric Kentley who criticised sections of that draft. Fig. 2.2.7 was drawn by Chris Gregson, and Johnathan Hunn re–drew figs. 1, 3, 5, 13, 15, 16 ind 17 for publication.

References

Åkerlund H. 1963 *Nydamskeppen* Goteborg.

Ayres B. 'Norwich.' *Current Archaeology* 80, 278–280.

Beaudouin F. 1970 *Les Bateaux de l'Adour* Bayonne.

Bourdon T.W. 1954 'Fishing methods of Singapore'. *JMBRAS*, 27 pt.2., 5–76.

Casson L. 1971 *Ships and seamanship in the Ancient World*, Princeton.

Christensen A.E. 1977A 'Comment.' in McGrail S. (ed) *Sources and Techniques in Boat Archaeology*, 112, NMM Greenwhich Archaeology Series 1. British Archaeological Reports, Oxford S29.

Christended A.E.. 1977B 'Test excavation of the boat-sheds.' in Ingstad, A.S., (ed) *Discovery of a Norse Settlement in America*, 109–127.

Clarke J.G.D. 1952 *Prehsitoric Europe – the Economic Basis*, Meuthen.

Clarke J.G.D. 1953 'Archaeological theories and interpretations.' in Kroeber A.L. (ed) *Anthropology Today*, 343–360, Chicago.

Coles J.M. 1975–81 *Somerset Levels Papers*.

Collard A.O. 1902 *Oysters and Dredgers of Whitstable*, London

Crumlin–Pedersen O. 1973 'Helnaes-spaerringen.' *Fynske Minder*, 29–48.

Crumlin–Pedersen O. 1981 'Sjibe pa havbunden.' *Handels–og Sj fartmuseets*, Årbog, 198, 28–65.

Darby H.C. 1977 *Domesday England*, Cambridge.

Davis F.M. 1958 *An account of the fishing of England and Wales*. Fishery Investigation Series II vol XXI No 8, HMSO 4th Edition.

de Brisay K.W. 1975 (ed) *Salt, the study of an ancient industry*, Colchester.

Edwards C.R. 1965 *Aboriginal Watercraft on the Pacific coast of South America*, Universiyy of California Press.

Ellmers D. 1972 *Frumittelalterliche Handelsschiffahrt in Mittel und Nordeuropa*, Neumunster.

Ellmers D. 1975 'Nautical Archaeology in Germany.' *IJNA* 4, 335–343.

Ellmers D. 1981 'Post–Roman waterfront installations on the Rhine.' in Milne and Hobley, 1981, 88–95.

Engelhardt C. 1863 *Thorsbjerg Mosefund* Copenhagen.

Engelhardt C. 1865 *Nydam Mosefund*, Copehangen.

Engelhardt C. 1866 *Denmark in the Early Iron Age* London.

Engelhardt C. 1869 *Vimose Fundet* Copenhagen.

Eskerod A. 1970 *Båtar från Ekstock till Tralare*, Lund.

Fenwick V. 1978 *Graveney Boat* NMM Greenwhich Archaeological Series 3., British Archaeological Reports, Oxford 53.

Filguiera O.L. 1977 'The Xavega boat.' in McGrail S. (ed) *Sources and Techniques in Boat Archaeology*, 77–111. NMM Greenwich Archaeology Series 1, British Archaeological Reports, Oxford, S29.

Finch R. 1976 *Sailing crafts of the British Isles*

Flemming N.C. 1980 'Structures under water.' in Muckleroy, K. (ed) *Archaeology under water* 164–175. McGraw-Hill.

Folkard H.C. 1870 *Sailing boat* 4th edition. Reprinted 1973 Wakefield.

Haddon A.C. and Hornell J. 1936–7, *Canoes of Oceania*, vols 1 and 2. Hawaii.

Handsford S.A. 1951 (ed) Ceasar: *The conquest of Gaul* Penguin.

Hasslöf O. 1972 'Main principles in the technology of shipbuilding.' in Hasslöf *et al*, 1972, 27–72.

Hasslöf O. Henningsen H. and Christenden A.E. 1972 (ed) *Ships and Shipyards, Sailors and Fishermen*, Copenhagen.

Hillam J. 1981 'An English tree–ring chronology.' *Medieval Archaeology*, 25, 31–44.

Højrup O. 1974 'En alegard pa Klippergrund.' in *Studier tillagnade Albert Eskerod*, 143–155.

Hourani G.F. 1963 *Arab Seafaring* Beirut.

Hornell J. 1946 *Water Transport* Cambridge. Reprinted 1970 Newton Abbot.

Hornell J. 1948 'Making and spreading of dugout canoes.' *Mariner's Mirror*, 36, 46–52.

Huntingford G.W.B. 1980 (ed) *Periplus of Erytharean Sea*, Halkyut Society 2nd Series No 151.

Jenkins J.G. 1974A 'Fisherweirs and traps.' *Folk Life*, 12, 5–9.

Jenkins J.G. 1974B *Nets and Coracles* Newton Abbot.

Johnstone P. 1980 *Seacrafts of Prehistory* R.K.P.

Leach E. 1977 'A view from the bridge.' in Spriggs 1977 161–176.

Longstaff, F.V., 1930, 'British Columbia Indian Cedar dugout canoes' *Mariner's Mirror*, 16, 259–62.

Losco–Bradley, P.M., and Salisbury, C.R., 1979, 'A medieval fishweir at Colwick, Notts.' *Trans. Thoroton Soc.*, 83, 15–22.

Lundström, P., 1971,–2, 'Klinknaglarna vittnesbörd', *Sjöhistorisk Arsbok*, 81–8.

McGrail, S., 1978, *Logboats of England and Wales*, NMM Greenwich Archaeological Series 2. BAR (Oxford) 51.

McGrail, S., 1981A, *Brigg 'raft' and her prehistoric environment* NMM Greenwich Archaeological Series 6. BAR (Oxford) 89.

McGrail, S., 1981B, 'Medieval boats, ships and landing places' in Milne and Hobley, 1981, 17–23.

McGrail, S., forthcoming. Interpretation of the Runnymead timber structures.

Marsden, P., 1981, 'Ear;y shipping and the waterfronts of London' in Milne and Hobley, 1981, 10–16.

Milne, G., 1981, 'Medieval riverfront reclamation in London' in Milne amd Hobley, 1981, 32–6.

Milne, G., and Hobley, B., (ed) *Waterfront Archaeology in Britain and Northern Europe* CBA Research Report 41.

Muckleroy, K., 1978, *Maritime Archeology*, Cambridge University Press.

Needham, J., 1971, *Science and Civilisation in China*, vol 4, part 3, Cambridge.

Needham, S., and Longley, D., 1980, 'Runnymead Bridge, Egham: a Late Bronze Age Riverside Settlement, in Barret, J., and Bradley, R., (ed) *Settlement and Society in the British Later Bronze Age*. BAR (Oxford) 83, 397–436.

Nilsson N., 1972, 'Shipyards and Shipbuilding at a wharf in southern Sweden' in Hasslof *et al*, 1972, 260–329.

Olsen, O., and Crumlin–Pedersen, O., 1967, 'Skuldelev Ships' *Acta Archaeologica*, 38, 73–174.

φrsnes, M., 1970 (ed) *Mosefund 2: Nydam Mosefund* (includes Engelhardt, 1865).

Prins, A.H.J., 1965, *Sailing from Lamu*, Assen.

Reed, N., 1975, 'Drusus and the Classis Britannica', *Historia*, 24, 315–23.

Rolfson, P., 1974, *Batnaust pa Jaerkysten* Stavanger.

Rudolph, W., 1974, *Inshore fishing craft of the southern Baltic* NMM Greenwich Monograph 14.

Salisbury, C., 1980, 'The Trent, the story of a river' *Current Archaeology*, 74, 88–91.

Salisbury, C., 1981, 'An Anglo–Saxon fish weir at Colwick, Noots.' *Trans Thoroton Society* 85, 26–36.

Shaw, J.W., 1972, 'Greek and Roman harbour works', in Bass, G.F. (ed) *History of Seafaring*, 87–112, Thames and Hudson.

Shetelig, H, and Johannesen,F., 1930, 'Das Nydhamschiff', *Acta Archaeologica* 1, 1–30.

Smith, A.G., *et al*, 1981, 'Environmental evidence from pollen analysis and stratigraphy', in McGrail, 1981A, 135–145.

Smolarek, P., 1981, 'Ships and ports in Pomorze' in Milne and Hobley, 1981, 51–60.

Spriggs, M., 1977, *Archaeology and Anthropology* BAR (Oxford) S19.

Stenton, F., 1957, *Bayeux Tapestry*

Thornhill, P., 1977, 'A lower Thames ford and the Campaigns of 54 BC and AD 43' *Archaeolgia Cantiana*, 92, 119–128.

Went, A.E.J., 1956, 'Swilly' 'loop' 'net for salmon', *J. Roy. Soc. Antiquaries Ireland*, 86, 215–7.

Went, A.E.J, 1964, 'Pursuit of Salmon in Ireland' *Proc. Roy. Irish Academy* 63, 191–244.

Wheeler, A., 1979, *Tidal Thames*, London.

Wright, E.V., and C.W., 1947, 'Prehistoric boats from N. Ferriby' *PPS* 13, 114–38.

Wright, E.V., 1976, *North Ferriby Boats*, NMM Greenich Monograph 23.

Wright, E.V., 1978, 'Artifacts from the boat–site at North Ferriby', *PPS*, 44, 187–202.

Abbreviations

JMBRAS: Journal of the Malayan Branch of the Royal Asiatic Society.

IJNA: International Journal of Nautical Archaeology.

PPS: Proccedings of the Prehistoric Society.

Reprinted with permission from:

Annis, P. (ed) *Sea Studies*: 33–46, NMM Greenich (1983)

PAPER 2.3

EARLY LANDING PLACES

Waterfronts and Landing Places

The late medieval harbours of Northern and Western Europe with their wharf, jetties, warehouses and cranes; moles and breakwaters; lighthouses, beacons and leading marks were preceded by the widespread use of informal landing sites (boat places). Evidence from the Mediterranean (Shaw, 1972; Muckelroy 1978, 75–84; Fleming 1980) indicates that the factors which encourage the change from informal landing place to formal harbour include:

a Transformation of certain waterside settlements into densely populated towns with complex economic organisation and technological specialisation.

b Defence requirements and the collection of custom dues.

c Increasing demand at these focal points for low density, mass consumption, imported goods. This demand could be best satisfied by vessels of larger capacity and greater draft which could not be efficiently loaded and unloaded at informal landing places. The silting of lower reaches of rivers exacerbated this problem.

Deep water berths alongside waterfronts facilitated cargo handling for these larger vessels, and breakwaters increased their protection from wind and swell in the open sector.

The remains of the major waterfront structures associated with harbours are generally readily recognised and several medieval examples have been excavated. On the other hand, informal landing places have rarely been located. This paper will therefore review the evidence for regularly–used landing places, and attempt to enumerate their characteristic features as an aid to the identification of archaeological remains. Factors which influence the choice of such sites will also be discussed: this may help in the prediction of where to look for early landing places. The discussion will generally be limited to those parts of Northern and Western Europe outside the direct influence of Classical technology.

The critical 'take–off' point, when formal harbours with waterfront structures became the optimum solution to a range of interacting problems, was reached earlier in some regions than others: on present evidence the earliest waterfronts seem to have been built in the 9th century AD; and most economic regions seem to have had at least one such site by the 12th century AD. Nevertheless, away from the main population centres, during and after this changeover period, boats, and indeed ships, of suitable form and structure continued to be operated from the foreshore, taking the ground on a falling tide,

Figure 2.3.1 Imme Gram, a modern replica of the Viking Age Ladby boat, using an infromal landing place in Vejle Fjord, Denmark. Photo: O. Crumlin–Pedersen

Figure 2.3.2   A 1:100 scale model of what the landing place at Graveney, N Kent, was probably like in the early 10th century AD. Photo: National Maritime Museum

anchoring or fastening to mooring posts or stones on the sea bed. Such landing places continued to be used in Northern and Western Europe in the present century and indeed, the practice is worldwide (McGrail 1983A, 34). Sometimes light landing stages are used at the end of a causewayed approach to the waterside, and simple hardstanding (hards) may be constructed on soft mud margins, but often there are no fixed structures – see, for example Fig 2.3.1 where a Danish replica of the 10th century Ladby boat is beached in the shallows awaiting the loading of horses. Such a scene with a wide variety of cargo, would have been familiar throughout medieval Europe and indeed later in rural areas. Beach operations are not limited to small boats: the coasting ketch *Charlotte* which operated from the beaches of SW England supplying local communities in the early years of this century (McGrail 1981A, fig 22), had a cargo capacity (dwt) of 80–100 tons (Fig 2.1.8) and Eglinton (1982) has described his early life in 20th century vessels of similar capacity carrying loads of stones to isolated mud landing places on the N Somerset coast.

From earlier times we have beach operation scenes on the Bayeux tapestry, both Norman and Anglo Saxon. The small 10th/11th century cargo vessel, Skuldelev 3, shows signs of having been operated from sand or shingle beaches (McGrail,1981A, 22); and the 9th/10th Graveney boat (Fenwick, 1978) was excavated from a landing place on the muddy inter–tidal margin of a tributary of the R Thames where she had been berthed on a hard (mainly of willow, *Salix* sp) for repair and/or unloading (Fig 2.3.2). 'Wattle mats' interpreted as hards have been excavated from a Late Saxon waterside site at Norwich (Ayers 1981, 278–9); and fragments of late 8th century boat planking appear to have been used as a hard at New Fresh Wharf on the R Thames foreshore (Marsden 1979).

The three mid 2nd millenium BC boats from N Ferriby (Wright 1976) and the mid 1st millenium boat from Brigg (McGrail 1981B) were operated from the foreshore of the Humber estuary. Investigations in 1937 on the N. Ferriby foreshore revealed fragmented light timbers (Fig 2.2.9), now lost, which may have been the remains of a hard or a causeway leading to the landing place, a!though the possibility that this was a collapsed fish weir should not be overlooked. In 1963 a hard–standing of alder (*Alnus* sp) poles was found (1) under Ferriby boat 3; and other light timbers dated by radio carbon (HAR–2759, 3682, 4204) to the general period of the Ferriby boats have been located in recent excavations on the foreshore (McGrail 1983A, 41–43).

The Runnymede 'waterfront'

Thus the limited amount of archaeological evidence supplemented by analogies from 20th century cultures (see McGrail 1983A, 34 for examples from the Indian Ocean, Poland, Germany, California and Ecuador), suggests that, until the spread of Classical civilisation, landing places in Northern and Western Europe were informal ones. Yet Needham and Longley (1980 and 1981) have argued that the Late Bronze Age settlement site (9th/8th century BC) near the R.Thames at Runnymede (some 30 miles upstream from London) had a 'timber waterfront' with a 'wharf against which craft might moor' and possibly with a 'jetty' extending from the 'wharf' into the river. This would be the earliest known example of a waterfront structure in Northern and Western Europe; however, there are reasons for suggesting that this hypothesis may not be supported by the evidence. Firstly, Needham and Longley's 'wharf' (1980, 397–9; 1981, fig 47) 47) has the form of a series of arcs and any boat longer than *c* 2m would be unable to lie securely alongside (although such boats could theoretically moor bow or stern–to). Secondly the excavators (1980, 418–22) conclude that this 'wharf' would dry out in summer and would only be usable by boats in times of 'typical low flood' which they equate with winter high water levels – a distinct limitation to regular boat operations. And thirdly there would be little or no advantage in taking any of the boats for which we have evidence in NW Europe in the prehistoric period, alongside a wharf (if one had existed): logboats, skin boats and the Ferriby, Brigg and Hjortspring planked boats could have been operated from the river margins with more regularity and efficiency. People and goods could have been readily moved to and from these boats moored or aground in the shallows or on the foreshore. If further environmental work shows the Late Bronze Age riverbed to have had gravel margins (as it has today) there would probably have been no necessity to build a hard. The outlying stakes and the loose structure of poles and withies noted by Needham and Longley (1980, 420) may then possibly be interpreted as the remains of a fish weir or similar structure. On the other hand, if the riverbed was soft mud, these objects may have been the remains of a hard.

The settlement at Runnymede was probably at a confluence where a tributary entered the eastward flowing Thames from the north, or even on an island. There was thus undoubtedly a landing place there, but probably of the informal type and the precise site has not yet been identified. On present evidence the main linear wooden structure seems best interpreted, not as an 'impressive wharf' with 'a permanent fleet of river craft' alongside (1980,421) but as an early example of one, or two, protective revetment(s) ('structural consolidation' 1980, 422) to stabilise the river bank and prevent erosion next to the settlement. It is noteworthy that the settlement was evidently severely flooded late in the occupation which may have led to the abandonment of the site (1980, 401).

Figure 2.3.3   Modern beach capstan in use on the Baltic coast of Germany (DDR). Photo: Wolfgang Rudolph

Landing places characteristics

If one accepts the thesis outlined above that there was little, if any, fixed structure at an early landing place, it follows that prehistoric and early medieval landing places in Northern and Western Europe may be difficult to recognise archaeologically, except on the few occasions when boats are found beached. There may, however, be indirect evidence, and if a waterside site is found to have two or more of the following characteristics of the appropriate period there must be a strong presumption that a regularly–used, early landing place has been located:

1 Hard, slipway or causeway

2 A cleared area on an otherwise stony foreshore, possibly marked by parallel rows of stones at right–angles to the shoreline (Rolfson 1974, 136)

3 The remains of isolated mooring posts or stones

4 Anchors (often difficult to date accurately) or other items of boat's equipment

5 Remains of beach capstans. See fig 2.3.3 for a modern example

6 Artifact clusters near the shoreline, the position of which is otherwise inexplicable

Location of landing places

Inland

Where a relatively fast river joins a slower one deposition frequently creates a gradually shelving beach where boats may easily be put ashore. Unless defence was paramount, settlement near such landing place would be preferred to sites on stretches of the river with poor or no landing places. When a waterside settlement had access to a settled hinterland it could well become an inland trading place. This would especially be the case with a site near the head of a tidal estuary (which might also be near the lowest fordable point) when decreasing depths of water could force a change to boats of less draught (or a shift to land transport) and thus the site would become a natural break point for river traffic. Landing places may also be found where tracks lead to unfordable waterways and ferries have to be used. Medieval sites of this type are known and prehistoric examples are at N Ferriby and Brigg in Humberside, where environmental evidence and the structure, form and size of the excavated boats indicate these sites were landing places for ferries.

Coastal

Sheltered landing places can generally be found in estuaries, river mouths and bays (see the section below on international maritime trade), but landing places on open coasts unprotected from wind and swell by offshore islands or by the arms of a bay may be used by fishermen and traders when sites with greater shelters are not available; or by raiders when secrecy is paramount. Landing and launching through the surf off such places may be difficult but techniques are well–known (see, for example, *Admiralty Seamanship Manual 1* (1926) 246–52).

Landing places are often close to settlements, but they are also needed in remote, uninhabited locations or near temporary and seasonal settlements (see, for example, the paper on King φystein's harbour at Agdenes by Kalle Sognnes in this volume). Thus, fishermen may operate from a forward base much nearer the fishing grounds than where they live, as recently practised in Shetland (Sandison 1954). The requirements of defence, revenue collection and pilotage may lead to the establishment of landing places in sheltered positions near a river mouth or the entrance to a bay, fjord or natural harbour, but far from permanent settlements. Landing places may also be found on either side of headlands,

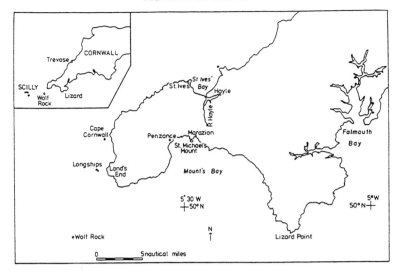

Figure 2.3.4   S W England: a portage overland from Mounts Bay to St Ives Bay would obviate the difficult passage around Lands End. Drawing: National Maritime Museum

especially where there is access to drinking water: coastal vessels would wait here for a fair wind and/or tidal stream so that they could round the point.

International Maritime Trade

MacKnight's study (1973) of trade within the Indonesian archipelago shows (*inter alia*) that before the advent of western cultural ideas there was undoubtedly real and regulated maritime trade, although some artifacts and raw materials might be exchanged for ceremonial or non–economic reasons. And a principal outcome of this trade was the creation of emporia ('ports of trade' – Polanyi 1963; 'gateway communities' – Hirth 1978). Documentary evidence

indicates a similar situation in early medieval Europe (Hodges 1982) and, although ceremonial gifts may have been relatively more common in the prehistoric period, maritime trade, regulated to a degree by political authority, undoubtedly took place between the early analogues of emporia on the northern and western seaboard of pre–Roman Europe.

Theoretical analysis suggest that there are three main viewpoints influencing the choice of landing place for such trade: the seaman, the trader and the political authority (two of these roles may be combined) each with different ideas as to what constitutes the ideal landing place (McGrail 1983C, 311–313).

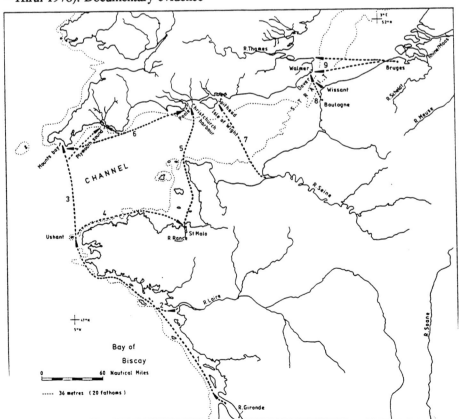

Figure 2.3.5   The Channel between the Continent and Britain. The suggested 1st century BC cross–Channel routes are numbered 3, 5, 7, 8, & 9. Drawing: National Maritime Museum

The seaman's ideal landing place is sheltered from the predominant wind and swell; it must have a readily identifiable landfall nearby and the approaches to it must be defined by landmarks and seamarks; it should be usable almost regardless of wind direction or tidal state; and there should be access to drinking water. Such sites are to be found within natural harbours such as estuaries, especially where they have wide, uncluttered approaches with a short fetch (open water) and an open sector away from the predominant wind.

The trader, on the other hand, requires a landing place immediately adjacent to the emporium for the regional economy, which may lie well inland. The third party in this international maritime trade (political authority) requires the landing place to be near the coast, ie as near as possible to the common 'frontier', in a readily defined area where traders and seamen can be segregated, protected and supervised, and tolls imposed. Landing places on coastal promontories, peninsulas or rivers are thus suitable from the political viewpoint.

These three somewhat different sets of requirements may best be met by:

a) The use of landing places within natural harbours, on an island, on a well-defined promontory, or at a river confluence, where such harbours are fed by a river system giving access to the regional emporium (if one exists) and to other settlements. For example: a site on Christchurch Harbour, Dorset; or a site on the island of Birka in L Malar, Sweden; or a site between the R Itchen and R Test in Southampton Water.

or b) landing places within archipelagoes or in the lee of skerries, with access by water to other coastal sites or to a hinterland. For example: Bergen in W Norway.

or c) landing places at protected sites near the base of an isthmus where river travel and land portages obviate a long or difficult sea passage. For example: sites at Hedeby and Lubeck at the base of the Jutland peninsula where portages can connect the North Sea and the Baltic; St Michael's Mount, off SW Cornwall. Peacock (1978, 49) has suggested that, in the Roman world, overland portages cost at least 22.6 times as much per mile as transport by sea. If part of the overland journey could be done by river then relative costs would be reduced to c 5 times that of sea transport, but costs due to multiple handling would be increased. When Peacock's figures are used to compare a coastal voyage from a landfall at the Lizard around Land's End to a position 5nm north of Hayle (Fig 2.3.4) with a journey which includes an overland portage from St Michael's Mount, the latter costs over 2½ times as much as the sea voyage. However, the passage around Land's End, even when the notorious Scilly Isles are left well to the westward, can be difficult and may indeed be impossible for several consecutive days until there is a favourable wind shift. Thus portage might not only be more reliable but could even be cheaper if the costs of delays due to foul winds are counted.

The documentary and archaeological evidence for international trade across the English Channel (La Macnhe) in the late 1st millenium BC may be examined in the light of the foregoing analysis (McGrail 1983C). Five main cross-Channel routes (Fig 2.3.5) may be suggested, and the location of the settlement sites (emporia) in their terminal areas may be tentatively identified (Table 2.3.1), but the location of the landing places associated with these international trading settlements is much more difficult to determine. Nevertheless, with the exception of the West Pas de Calais region (where Wissant and Boulogne may have been more important militarily than commercially), each terminal area listed in Table 2.3.1 has stretches of coastline in the vicinity of the emporia with landing places which could have satisfied the seaman, the trader and the political authority. As more data becomes available on the early sea levels and geomorphology in these terminal areas it may become possible to suggest the most likely sites for landing places associated with known emporia. Early use of the major rivers in France and the Rhineland for trade is reasonably well documented (McGrail 1983C) but there is little direct evidence that the middle and upper reaches of British rivers were similarly used in this period. Further investigation of the former courses, gradients, depths and speed of the rivers feeding British natural harbours is necessary before we can be certain that they could have been regularly used for inland transport.

Future Research

Other regions and periods with evidence for maritime trade may be similarly investigated to identify the areas within which individual landing places were probably located. Only systematic fieldwork, much of it apparently unproductive, over a lengthy period, together with chance finds or the by-products of settlement excavations, will enable the precise location of such early landing places to be determined.

Investigation of early landing places is an element of Maritime Archaeology which may be defined as the study of Man's use of all types of waterways (lakes, rivers and seas): the study of how early rafts, boats and ships were built and how they were used (McGrail 1983B). Research into uses of water transport extends the domain of the subject (Fig 1.2.1) well outside the bounds of what has been called 'boat archaeology' to include such topics as navigation and seamanship; speed, stability, freeboard and cargo capacity; sea levels, tidal patterns and coastal geomorphology; methods of loading and operational equipment; and the whole range of maritime structures (McGrail 1983A, 34–41). Waterfront archaeology has also expanded from its original base and seems now to be converging with maritime archaeology. In the past it has been viewed in a landlubberly fashion as a mere extension, or a special case of urban archaeology. But many of those working in specialist field have come to realise that the 'hintersea' is as important to waterfront studies as the hinterland and, if we may judge by the proceedings of the first waterfront conference (Milne and Hobley 1981) and, with even greater clarity, by the coverage of this present volume, waterfront archaeology is now very similar, but not-precisely identical, to maritime archaeology.

This convergence of the two specialisations is to be welcomed as it should lead to wider yet more detailed knowledge of the maritime aspects of early cultures. An essential prerequisite to future research is an improved understanding of ancient geomorphology, sea levels and weather. Quantified data on former weather patterns, on coastlines and river courses, and on general sea levels and specific tidal ranges experienced at particular times and places, should facilitate the prediction of where early landing places are likely to have been, and also enable the vestigial remains of bridges, causeways, jetties, wharfs, revetments, fish weirs and other maritime structures to be distinguished from one another with greater confidence.

Table 2.3.1   Possible cross–channel routes in the 1st millemiun BC (1)

	Continental		British	
Route	Terminal Area	Emporia	Terminal Area	Emporia
Rhine/Thames	Rhine estaury or thereabouts	Domburg? Colijnsplaat? Bruges?	Thames, Stour (Kent) Blackwater and Colne estuaries	Thanet? Canterbury? Colchester?
Strait of Dover	W Pas de Calais	Wissant? (2) Boulogne? (2)	Thames and Stour (Kent) estuaries	Thanet? Canterbury?
Seine/Spithead	Seine estuary	?	Solent and adjacent waters	Isle of Wight?
Mid–Channel	Rance estuary	Alet/St Malo?	Christchurch Harbour and Poole Harbour	Hengistbury Head Green Is? Hamworthy
West Channel	Loire and Gironde estuaries	Nantes? Bordeaux?	Plymouth Sound and Mounts Bay (3)	Mount Batten Mt St Michael?

Notes: 1 See McGrail, 1983C for details

2 Limited access inland by water

3 Possible portage to Hayle in St Ives Bay, N Cornwall (see Fig 2.3.4)

Acknowledgement

This paper has benefited considerably from criticism of an early draft by my colleagues in the Archaeological Research Centre at Greenwich. Fig 2.3.4 was kindly drawn by Eric Kentley.

Footnote 1. The statement in McGrail 1983A, 43 (Paper 2.2), that no hard was found under any Ferriby boat, is wrong.

Bibliography

Ayers,B,1981 Norwich, *Current Archaeology*, 80, 278–280

Eglinton, E, 1982 *Last of the sailing coasters*, HMSO, London.

Fenwick, V, 1978 The site at Graveney and its possible use as a landing place, in Fenwick, V (ed) *Graveney boat*, 179–192 NMM Greenwich Archaeological Series 3. BAR (Oxford) 53

Flemming, N C, 1980 Structures under water, in Muckelroy, K (ed) *Archaeology under water*, 164–175. McGraw–Hill. London

Hirth, K G, 1978 Inter–regional trade and the formation of prehistoric gateway communities, *American Antiquity*, 43, 35–45

Hodges, R, 1982 Evolution of gateway communities, in Renfrew,C, and Shennan,S, (eds) *Ranking, resources and exchange*,117–123 Cambridge University Press

McGrail, S, 1981A Medieval boats, ships and landing places, in Milne,G and Hobley,B 1981, 17–23

McGrail, S, 1981B *Brigg 'raft' and her prehistoric environment*, NMM Greenwich Archaeological Series. BAR (Oxford) 89

McGrail, S, 1983A Interpretation of archaeological evidence for maritime structures in Annis,P, (ed) *Sea Studies*, 33–46, NMM Greenwich

McGrail, S, 1983B Maritime Archaeology present and future in McGrail,S, (ed) *Aspects of Maritime Archaeology & Ethnography*, NMM Greenwich

McGrail, S, 1983C Cross–Channel seamanship and navigation in the late 1st millenium BC, *Oxford Journal of Archaeology*, 2, 299–337.

MacKnight, C C, 1963 Nature of early maritime trade, *World Archaeology*, 5, 198–208.

70

Marsden, P, 1979, Medieval ships of London, in McGrail, S, (ed) *Medieval Ships and Harbours*, 83–92, NMM Greenwich Archaeological Series 5.BAR (Oxford) S66.

Milne, G, & Hobley, B, (eds) 1981 *Waterfront Archaeology in Britain and Northern Europe*, CBA Research Report 41.

Muckleroy, K, 1978, *Maritime Archaeology*, Cambridge University Press.

Needham, S, & Longley, D, 1980 Runnymede bridge, Egham: a late bronze age riverside settlement, in Barrett, J, & Bradley, R, (eds), *British Later Bronze Age*, 397–436, BAR, (Oxford) 83 vol 2.

Needham, S, & Longley, D, 1981 Runnymede Bridge, in Milne, G, & Hobley, B, 1981, 48–50.

Peacock, D P S, 1978 The Rhine and the problem of Gaulish wine in Roman Britain, in Taylor, J du P, and Cleere, H, (eds), *Roman shipping and trade*, 49–51 CBA Research Report 24.

Polany, K, 1963 Ports of trade in early societies, *Journal Economic History* 23, 30–45.

Rolfson, P, 1974 *Båtnaust pa Joerkysten*, Stavenger.

Sandinson, C, 1954 *The Sixareen*, Lerwick.

Shaw, J W, 1972 Greek and Roman harbour works, in Bass, G F, (ed) *History of seafaring*, 87–112, Thames and Hudson.

Wright, E V, 1976 *North Ferriby boats*, NMM Greenwich Monograph 23.

Reprinted with permission from:

Herteig, A.E. (ed) *Confernece on Waterfront Archaeology No 2* 12–18. Bergen (1985).

SECTION 3.0

ETHNOGRAPHIC STUDIES

Introduction

The one paper in this Section was written on the occasion of Eric McKee's untimely death in 1983. McKee brought to the post–excavation recording of the medieval Graveney boat (Fenwick, 1978), the talents he had used to record 20th century working boats, thereby setting high standards for maritime archaeologists to follow. His *Working Boats of Britain* (1983) is essential reading for archaeologists who want to learn about the fundamentals of boatbuilding and use. Greenhill (1995) presents many examples ethnographic boat studies, whilst Eglinton's two books (1982; 1990) give much information about sailing in British coastal waters earlier this century.

Ethnographic analogy is used to interpret maritime structures in paper 2.2, and it is used extensively in the hypothetical reconstruction of boats as a prelude to the experimental work discussed in Section 11. I have also discussed elsewhere, the logic behind the use of ethnographic evidence when tackling archaeological problems (McGrail, 1981: 5–10; 1987: 1–3; 1996). Examples of such use may be found in McGrail (1978:26–93) and in McGrail & Farrell (1979). Blue *et al.*(forthcoming A) includes a discussion of the ways ethnographic & ethno–archaeological studies are of value to Archaeology. A description of the *patia*, a 20th century Indian fishing boat with reverse clinker planking is given in Blue *et al.*(forthcoming B). A knowledge of the *patia*'s structure may, in time, help archaeologists understand how the medieval *hulc* was built (Greenhill, 1995: 250–255).

References.

Blue, L. Kentley, E. and McGrail, S. forthcoming A. Archaeology, ethnography and India's maritime past. *Proceedings* of the 1996 Lyon Conference on the Indian Ocean.

Blue, L. Kentley, E. and McGrail, S. forthcoming B. The *patia* fishing boat of Orissa: a case study in ethno–archaeology. *South Asian Studies.*

Eglinton, E. 1982 *Last of the Sailing Coasters.* HMSO.

Eglinton, E. 1990. *The Mary Fletcher.* University of Exeter Press.

Fenwick, V. (ed) 1978. *Graveney Boat.* BAR Oxford. 53.

Greenhill, B. 1995. *Archaeology of Boats & Ships.* Conway.

McGrail, S. 1978. *Logboats of England & Wales.* BAR Oxford. 51

McGrail, S. 1981. *Rafts, Boats & Ships.* HMSO.

McGrail, S. 1987. *Ancient Boats in NW Europe.* Longman.

McGrail, S. 1996. Study of boats with stitched planking. in Ray, H.P. & Salles, J–F. (ed) *Tradition & Archaeology*: 225–238. Manohar. New Delhi.

McGrail, S. & Farrell, A. 1979. Rowing: aspects of the ethnographic & iconographic evidence. *Int. J. Nautical Archaeology.* 8: 155–166.

PAPER 3.1

BOAT ETHNOGRAPHY AND MARITIME ARCHAEOLOGY

Ethnography can be of great value to archaeologists as one of the sources to be used in the interpretation of excavated material. Ethnographic studies can make the archaeologist aware of a range of solutions to general problems such as are found in house building, boatbuilding and other technologies. Using such ethnographic analogies and other forms of evidence the archaeologist can then propose hypothetical reconstructions of incomplete objects or structures, suggest the possible function of enigmatical structural elements, and describe in some detail how an object or structure was made and used.

The maritime archaeologist deals with a range of structures (McGrail, 1983: 34–41), but one of his principal concerns is the interpretation of the incomplete remains of boats and other forms of water transport. When he turns for analogies to the ethnographic literature on boats he finds a veritable *pot–pourri*, good in parts. Crumlin–Pedersen (1982: 73) has defined the adequate recording of a boat find as that standard of recording which contains the information 'a competent model builder would need to build a model of the structure so that it is correct in all details'. For an ethnographic report to be 'adequate', to this definition must be added (a) the recording of the function of all fittings, and (b) a detailed description of the uses and operational performance of the boat. Such 'adequate' reports are rare: even the wide–ranging reports published by James Hornell and summarized in *Water Transport* (1946) are seldom up to this standard.

In recent years, however, the standard of ethnographic report has improved, especially in Scandinavian and N. American publications: see for example, Faerøyvik and Christensen (1979), Crumlin–Pedersen (1980); Crumlin–Pedersen and Madsen(1980); Hansen and Madsen(1981); Petersen (n.d.); Arima (1975); Zimmerly (1979) and Taylor (1980). In Britain, Eric McKee has made his mark by his ethnographic research published in the *Mariners Mirror* (1970; 1971; 1976a; 1977a), the French journal *Le Petit Peroquet* (1975) a National Maritime Museum monograph (1972), and in his recent masterly *Working boats of Britain* (1983). With systematic descriptions and detailed drawings and diagrams McKee has documented both the general traditions of recent British wooden boatbuilding, and specific types such as the Somerset *flatner* and the Dorset *lerret*. In his first monograph *Clenched lap or clinker* (1972) McKee described the building of a small clinker–built boat. By including cut–out drawings which the reader could make into a cardboard half–model McKee more than fulfilled Crumlin–Pedersen's criteria for 'adequate recording'. This model–making also revealed to not a few archaeologists, the problem of producing a three–dimensional object from two–dimensional material.

In *Working boats of Britain* McKee not only published the results of his fieldwork, recording wooden boats still to be found in use around the coasts of Britain, but he also examined the factors (operating environment, function, propulsion method, available materials and techniques, and hydrodynamics) which influence the choice of boat shape, and considered how such shapes may be realised in practical terms. In addition he presented a scheme for classifying boat shapes which, with minor modification, can also be used to describe archaeological finds. This book is undoubtedly a mine to be worked by those dealing with the building and use of early wooden boats. Where else could be found in one volume an informed discussion on the difference between *boat* and *ship*; authoritative definitions of deadwood knee, false stem, and zoned discontinuous framing; the optimum position for a barge's towing post; factors affecting sailing performance; rowing geometry data; the difference between a structure and a mechanism; explanation of racking and torsion stresses; and a classification of beaches in relation to practicability of boat operations and degree of exposure to the predominant wind? The text is terse and technological terms are not avoided, but reference to the glossaries published elsewhere by McKee (1972; 1976b) and study of the many fact–packed diagrammatic drawings in this book help to fill–out the succinct discussion.

The topics which McKee discusses in *Working boats* must be appreciated by anyone attempting to study how ancient boats were built and used. McKee's standard oarsman may be bigger or smaller than the Viking Age oarsman, his boatbuilders may use different woodworking techniques and have a wider range of tools than the builders of the Ferriby boats, and the 20th century coastline, sea level and climate may be different from those of the Bronze Age or even the Medieval period, but McKee's principles and his fieldworking and analytical methods can be used with profit by maritime archaeologists. And if due allowance can be made for differences in the main technological and environmental parameters, then some of McKee's findings can be applied to archaeological problems.

In addition to pure ethnographic work, McKee has himself applied his ethnographic knowledge and practical experience to archaeological matters such as a glossary of boat–building terms (1977b; 1977e) and the tentative interpretation of the development of boatbuilding in NW Europe (1976b; 1977d); but his major contribution to archaeology have been his work on the Graveney boat (1978), his involvement in experimental archaeology (1974), and his evaluation of hypothetical reconstructions of incomplete boat finds using the criteria of practical boatbuilding and operations afloat (1977c; 1978;

1984). The meticulous methods he used to record the Graveney boat timbers after excavation, and the sea trials programme he evolved for the Greenwich *faering* replica have become standard procedures.

Eric McKee's publications fully bear out the importance of ethnographic boat studies to maritime archaeology. They should be read and re-read by all involved in this field of research.

References

Arima, E. Y., 1975, *Contextual study of the Caribou Eskimo Kayak*, Canadian Ethnology Service Paper No.25, Ottawa.

Crumlin-Pedersen, O., (ed) 1980, *Nordlansbaden*, Working Paper No. 12. National Museum of Denmark.

Crumlin-Pedersen, O., 1982, 'Comment' in McGrail, S. (ed.) *Woodworking techniques before AD 1500*: 73. NMM Greenwich Archaeological Series 7. BAR (Oxford) S129.

Crumlin-Pedersen, O. & Madsen, J. S., (eds) 1980 *Umiaq'en fra Peary Land*. Roskilde.

Faerøyvik, B. & O. & Christensen, A. E., 1979, *Inshore craft of Norway*. Conway Maritime Press.

Hansen, K. & Madsen, J. S., 1981, *Barkbade*. Roskilde.

Hornell, J., 1946, *Water Transport*. Cambridge (republished 1970 Newton Abbot).

McGrail S. 1983, The interpretation of archaeological evidence for maritime structures in Annis, P. (ed.) *Sea Studies*: 33–46. NMM Greenwich Monograph.

McKee, E., 1970, Flatners, *Mariners Mirror* 70: 232–4.

McKee, E., 1971, Weston-super-Mare Flatner, *Mariners Mirror* 57: 25–39.

McKee, E., 1972, *Clenched lap or Clinker*. NMM Greenwich.

McKee, E., 1974, *Building and trials of the replica of an ancient boat*: the Gokstad *faering* part 2: the sea trials. NMM Greenwich Monograph 11B.

McKee, E., 1975, Le lerret de Chesil Bank, *Le Petit Peroquet* 17: 29–41.

McKee, E. 1976a, Traditional British boatbuilding methods *Mariners Mirror* 62: 3–14.

McKee, E. 1976b, Identification of timbers from old ships of north-western European origin. *IJNA* 5: 3–12.

McKee, E., 1977a, Lerrets of Chesil Bank. *Mariners Mirror* 63: 39–50.

McKee, E., 1977b, 'A glossary of Boat Archaeology terms', in McGrail, S. (ed.), *Sources and Techniques in Boat Archaeology*: 9–13, NMM Greenwich Archaeology Series 1. BAR (Oxford) S29.

McKee, E., 1977c, Hypothotical reconstructions in Boat Archaeology, in McGrail, S. (ed.), *Sources and Techniques in Boat Archaeology*: 205–214. NMM Greenwich Archaeology Series I . BAR (Oxford) S29.

McKee, E., 1977d, Rejoinder to McGrail's 'A comment'. *IJNA*, 6: 252–3.

McKee, E., 1977e, A glossary for nautical archaeologists. *IJNA* 6: 253–5.

McKee, E., 1978, 'Set of drawings of parts of the hull and draughtsman's notes', 'Reconstructing the hull', 'Model planks'; 'Drawing the replica'; 'Tentative sequence for building the replica' in Fenwick, V. (ed) *Graveney boat*, 49–104, 265–302, 307–310. NMM Greenwich Archaeological Series 3. BAR (Oxford) 53.

McKee, E., 1983, *Working boats of Britain*. Conway Maritime Press.

McKee, E., 1984, Techniques of the reconstruction, in Coates, J., and McGrail, S. (eds), *The Greek Trireme of the 5th century BC*. NMM Greenwich Monograph.

Petersen, H. C. n.d., *Instruction in Kayak builduing Roskilde*.

Taylor, J. G., 1980, *Canoe construction in a Cree Cultural tradition*, Canadian Ethnology Service Paper No. 64. Ottawa.

Zimmerly, D. W., 1979, *Hooper Bay Kayak construction*, Canadian Ethnology Service Paper No. 53. Ottawa.

Reprinted with permission from:

International Journal for Nautical Archaeology, 13: 149–150 (1984).

SECTION 4.0

CLASSIFICATION STUDIES

Introduction

Classification schemes are essential in Maritime Archaeology if only because of the wide variety of materials & techniques that have been used to build rafts, boats & ships. They enable some order to be imposed on an apparently chaotic set of data, and thus scholars around the world can be certain that they are talking about similar structures, forms and techniques; patterns can be recognised; and fundamental shifts in technology may be identified. Such schemes are, however, an approximation, a best–fit to reality; they cannot precisely match the endless variety actually known, otherwise they would be unwieldy and overwhelm one of their main advantages – simplicity. Furthermore, classification cannot remain static: as fresh evidence emerges and new ways of analysing the data are evolved, schemes must be re–examined and revised where necessary.

The scheme proposed in Paper 4.1 (which, as far as I am aware, has never been criticised, although it has been quoted) deals only with the very early stages of the classification of water transport, merely separating out the major groups 'floats', 'rafts and boats', with some refinement of the boat group. Further stages in this classification (beyond the lowest level shown on Fig. 4.1.1) could include the consideration of a wide range of characteristics, leading to the identification of natural groupings. In this way, boatbuilding traditions such as the vessels of Viking Age NW Europe, or the vessels of the eastern Mediterranean in the Iron Age, might be defined. An example of this extended procedure, though not formally presented, is given in Paper 8.2 where it is argued that the characteristic features of a Romano–Celtic tradition can be identified.

Classification is also dealt with, implicitly or explicitly, in Papers 6.1, 9.2, and 10.5. A case for the identification of a group of medieval logboats in the R. Mersey region has been made by McGrail and Switsur (1979); and another medieval grouping has been tentatively identified in the R. Lea (a tributary of the R. Thames) by McGrail(1989).

References.

McGrail, S. 1989. Clapton logboat – boatbuilding characteristics. *Int. J. Nautical Archaeology*, 18: 103.

McGrail, S. & Switsur, R. 1979. Medieval logboats of the R. Mersey. in McGrail, S. (ed) *Medieval Ships & Harbours in Northern Europe*: 93–115. BAR Oxford S66.

PAPER 4.1

TOWARDS A CLASSIFICATION OF WATER TRANSPORT

Even a cursory glance through the pages of James Hornell's *Water Transport* (1946) will reveal something of the wide range of objects Man has used, and continues to use, in his exploitation of lake, river and sea. During the past 100 years several attempts have been made to classify this varied material as an aid to further archaeological and ethnographic study: that these were not entirely successful is due, in part at least, to problems of definition and methodology. Nautical terms are not always precisely defined: take, for example, the problem of distinguishing clearly between a boat and a ship (for a useful discussion of this question see McKee (1983: 14–16). And regional names for specific craft have often been used loosely: the S. American type–name *balsa* has been applied to a boat principally built of hide and also to rafts of logs and rafts of reed bundles (Hornell 1946: 150,41,81); *coracle* is the general name for Welsh hide–on–frame boats, but it has been applied to any boat of circular form; *canoe* can similarly be a specific boat or a general boat shape, and has indeed been applied to rafts (Hornell 1946: plate Vll). Secondly, early attempts at classification were seldom systematic and most authors were diverted from this goal by forays, which frequently proved sterile, into the field of 'evolution' or 'development', seeking to demonstrate, sometimes with cladograms, genetic relationships between types of water transport: for example, that plank boats developed from logboats, or outrigger canoes from rafts.

The aim of this present paper is to review previous work and then to attempt to devise a general classification scheme for boats and small ships, to identify what may be termed primary classes each composed of individual members with internal cohesion – relatively similar to other members of their class – and external isolation – relatively dissimilar to members of other classes (Hodson 1980: 4). Such a scheme should be capable of being summarised in a dendogram, with no implications of genetic descent. If this can be achieved then each of these polythetic classes should convey the same image to all users of the scheme, and newly observed units of water transport may readily be allocated to one of these classes by reference to key, diagnostic attributes.

Early classification schemes

As in many other fields General Pitt–Rivers was an early contributor to the study of worldwide water transport (Lane–Fox 1875). Basing his scheme on the 'constructive arts of existing savages' (1875: 401) he recognised the following main types by name, but not by explicit definition: the R. Euphrate logboats (dugouts); plank boats; bark canoes; skin

boats; rafts. The General did not state the basis for this differentiation but it was evidently based on material and form, and (when differentiating rafts from boats) structural attributes.

Suder's paper published in 1930 was a landmark in water transport studies. Although bedevilled by ideas of 'evolution' (as the title *Von einbaum und floss zum schiff*, might suggest) this work presented a wealth of well–documented and illustrated archaeological and ethnographic data, with distribution maps. Suder recognised the following main groups:

> A wide variety of *floats*.
> Log, reed, bark and buoyed *rafts*.
> Log, bark, skin, basket and plank *boats*.

In addition, Suder had a class of 'round boats' which, unlike the other groups which were based on attributes similar to those used by Pitt–Rivers, was evidently defined only by form: at this level of classification this criterion seems inadequate.

Subsequent workers in this field(Hornell 1946; Eskerod 1956; Needham 1971; Doran 1973; Greenhill 1976; Phillips–Burt 1979) have followed Suder to a greater or lesser extent, although none of them included Suder's class of bark rafts. Other authors (Rudolph 1966, 1974a; Marsden 1976; Christenden 1977; Crumlin–Pedersen 1978; Ellmers 1984; Prins, forthcoming) have dealt with classification at a less–general level, attempting to define sub–groups, principally in the plank boat field.

Recent work

The latest general scheme is one proposed by McGrail (1981a). This scheme uses Suder's *float* and *raft* classes, but modifies his classification of *boats* by adding a reed class and omitting the round and basket classes. Basket boats (see Hornell 1946: fig. 12 for an example) were assigned to the skin boat class (1981a: 5,57) because they were considered to have a continuous water proofing envelope of resin and dung or ground bamboo outside their wooden (woven, plaited or twilled) basketry: this was taken to be analogous to skin boats with their hide cover outside a wooden framework. This assignment now seems doubtfully valid as on most, if not all, basket boats the dung mixture is not spread over the entire surface but used to caulk the interstices only (Nishimura 1931: 36; Hornell 1946: 110).

A reed boat class was defined as 'bound bundles of reed lashed together (coiled basketry) to produce a hollow form, and waterproofed with bitumen' (1981a: 5). A fuller description would read: bound bundles of reed, grass or straw lashed together by coiled basketry or similar techniques to produce a hollow form which is strengthened with a light framework and then waterproofed with bitumen. Reed boats are readily distinguishable from reed *rafts* which are not made watertight, and may be distinguished from other boats because the reed boat's shape is determined by *coiled* reed, grass or straw basketry or a similar technique, rather than by shaped hide or wood or by a *woven* wooden basketry. There is intermittent documentary evidence for the use of such reed boats in Arabia from the reign of Sargon of Akkad, c. 2300 BC (Anderson 1978: 49), through the time of Moses (Exodus 2, 3) and the 1st century AD (Strabo 16.5.15), to reports of the 19th century *tarada* (Layard 1853: 552). Twentieth century examples of reed boats from the same region are, firstly, the *quffa* (McGrail 1981a: plate 26; Hornell 1946; plates IVB and XVIIB) which appears to be similar in construction to the boats Hamilton noted on the R.Euphrates in the early 18th century(Hornell 1946: 104–5);and, secondly, the elongated *jillabie* (Heyerdaht 1978: 35) and *zaima* (Thesiger 1978: 128, fig. 45).

Kentley (1984) has recently criticised McGrail's boat classification scheme and has proposed that:

(a) basket boats should become a primary class sub-divided into coiled basketry (which would include McGrail's reed boats), and woven or twilled basketry.

(b) *piroga* (extended logboats) should become a primary class.

(c) *skin boats* should be sub-divided into 'shaped frame' and 'lath frame'.

The third proposal is certainly worthy of consideration but may not be directly relevant to the identification of primary classes. Extended logboats are something of a hybrid as, when only a few (one or two?) strakes are added to the sides (the *oruwa* of Sri Lanka – Hornell 1943) the boat is still clearly a sub-class of logboats; whereas when several strakes are added, as in many Oceanic types (for example, those from the Gilbert Is. – Haddon and Hornell 1936: fig. 245), the logboat base may scarcely be recognisable and the boat may best be classified as a plank boat; the 13th/14th century AD Kentmere boat 1 (Wilson 1966) which has five strakes added to an obvious logboat base may be thought to be intermediate. Buoyed rafts (see, for example, that from the R. Swat, Pakistan – McGrail 1981a: plate 3) present similar classification problems they may be thought of as a sub-set of the log raft class with extra buoyancy from floats, or as floats linked together by a light framework and therefore a primary type in their own right. The netted gourd rafts of S. America (Edwards 1965: 59) are equally difficult to classify.

A new approach

Kentley's suggestion that Suder's basket boat class should be re-instated has much in its favour. Consideration of this proposal, with its emphasis on structure, and evaluation of earlier classification schemes suggests that a new approach to water transport classification may be required, one in which structural considerations take precedence over choice of raw materials, and in which the attributes identify, whenever possible, choices which have cultural significance. The

following principles are advanced as a basis for a general classification scheme for boats.

(a) The identification of classes primarily by the *material* used can lead to confusion when it is possible to use other materials to build what is essentially the same boat e.g.

(i) curachs made of tarred flannel or canvas instead of hide are still called 'skin' boats.

(ii) boats and rafts of grass, straw, bark or even light poles (ambatch) bundles are structurally the same as those built of reed bundles.

In addition, boats of the same materials may be built by quite different construction methods (see below). And, although the selection of one material from among several substitutes may be a cultural choice, the availability of raw material is an environmentally related attribute.

(b) The *form* or shape required of a unit of water transport will vary with desired function, although the range of possible shapes in any one case may be constrained by the nature of the raw materials. Thus there can be different forms of hide–on–frame boats e.g. round or elongated. But this distinction is principally functional and not generally determined by cultural choice.

(c) Emphasis on *structural* differences may reveal culturally–determined principles. How a boat is conceived or reified as a three–dimensional object is probably determined by culture. Thus the method used by the builder to translate idea into artifact (the 'design' of the boat) and thereby obtain the structural form he requires, is a fundamental attribute.

It has been recognised for some years that there are two distinct ways of conceiving and building planked boats: the *shell* sequence in which the form is defined by a watertight envelope or shell of planking, and into which a strengthening timber framework is subsequently inserted; and the *skeleton* sequence in which the form is defined by a timber framework or skeleton, which is subsequently waterproofed by an enveloping layer of split planking moulded to the shape of the framework. (Greenhill 1976: 60). This distinction may also be applied to boats built of materials other than planks: for example, whereas certain cultures (e.g. Irish and Aleut) have thought of, and built boats as a wooden, or bone plank framework around which a waterproofing envelope of hide, or waterproofed flannel or canvas was wrapped (Hornell 1946: 111–80), the builders of the S. American *pelota* (Hornell 1941; 1946: 150–4), and certain N. American (Adney and Chapelle 1964: 219–20) and Mongol (Sinor 1961: 158) boatbuilders thought of, and built their boats as a watertight shell of hide (a leather bag), which was sometimes but not always reinforced by inserted framework. Again, whereas many cultures (Australian, C. African, N. and S. American) conceive their boats as a shell of bark, possibly with inserted framing (Greenhill 1976: figs 77 and 78; McGrail 1981a: 78, plate 6; Roth 1899; Hornell 1946: 183), there is some evidence from the Sweden and Siberia that boats were built there by sewing or lashing bark to a pre erected used frame. A 1934 find from the R. Viskan near Byslatt, Istorp Soke, Vastergotland and now in Goteborg Museum (Humbla and von Post 1937: 11; Eskerod 1956: 71; Johnstone 1980: – 24; Ellmers 1972: No. 318; Hansen and Madsen 1981: 4–5) consists of a sheet of elm or beech bark *c.* 3.5 m x 0.7 m with fragments of three hazel ribs and juniper lashings. Pollen analysis indicates a date between

700 BC and AD 1000. Holes through the bark suggest that this boat was built by lashing the bark to a framework of ribs and other timbers. Several reports of late 19th century/early 20th century Swedish bark boats state that the bark was sewn or lashed to a wooden framework (Eskerod 1956: 71; Westerdahl 1982). When describing the boats of the R. Kuntenai region (S. British Columbia and Washington and Idaho) and those of the R. Amur region (E. Sibeda) Brindley (1919: 106) states that they had a wooden frame, 'of ribs and horizontal slats on which strips of bark are sewn.

Thus there are two approaches to building boats of planks, hide and bark. On the other hand shell–built bundle boats (e.g. of reed) seem improbable, as an outer waterproofing layer *has* to be applied to the framework of bundles to turn this form of construction into a boat – and this is the skeleton sequence.

(d) Other structural differences may be seen in the choice of techniques the builder makes when converting his material into a boat. Analysis becomes overcomplex if we consider such initial processes as felling a tree, obtaining a hide, cutting a reed, etc. Thus (if we disregard modern boatbuilding materials such as metal, GRP and cement and the inflatables) the principle materials from which boats have been built may be listed as: logs, reeds, hides, clay, tar and bone/antler. Adapting the concepts devised by Rudolph (1974*b*: 11) and McKee (1972– 2; 1983: 44) three main techniques may be identified, which boatbuilders use to convert these materials into a boat:

(i) *Reduction* (or subtractive technique). The raw material is reduced in volume as in the hollowing of a log to make a logboat or in the fashioning of a log to make a keel.
Note: Stone masons have an analogous approach.

(ii) *Construction* (or additive technique). The junction of several smaller parts (some of which may have been obtained by reduction techniques, e g. planks or bark). Examples are:
Binding reeds to make bundles and linking the bundles together as in the coiled basketry method of building a *quffa* (Hornell 1946: 101–8).
Production of frameworks by weaving, twilling, plaiting or fastening light timbers or layer of split bamboo as in the framework of Arctic skinboats, Vietnamese basket boats or Irish curachs (Nishimura 1931;Hornell 1946; 109–11; Hornell 1936–8).
The junction of planks by fastenings of sewing, lashing, wood or metal as in edge–fastened plank boats.
Note: Potters who make coil–built pottery and tinkers and tailors use analogous methods.

(iii) *Transformation* (or moulding technique). Altering the shape of the material without addition or subtraction, as in the expansion of a Satakunta logboat (Johnstone, 1980, figs 5.5 and 5.6) or the inflation of a skin float or the bending of a plank to a new shape.
Note: Potters who throw pots and blacksmiths and founders use analogous methods.
One or more of these techniques may be used to make the form–determining watertight envelope of shell–built boats. The corresponding 'design' element in skeleton built boats, from the inner framework, does not appear to show much variation – all three techniques are used except in reed boats where there is only construction and transformation. Thus classification of skeleton–built boats by the techniques used to make the *outer*

waterproofing elements (as for the shell–built boats) is considered to be analytically more rewarding at this level of classification.
(e) The use of boat type names – either genuine or regional ones (*mtepe*) – or those commonly used by Europeans (*dhow*; *junk*; *prahu*) – in a classification scheme may lead to confusion. For example, Layard's 19th century *tarada* reed boat is very different from the 20th century *tarada* described by Thesiger (1978: figs 9, 15) which is a planked boat: the common link may be the use of bitumen (tar) as an essential *waterproofing* on the 19th century reed boat and as an optional *paying* or preservative on the 20th century plank boat. As a second example we may note Hornell's use (1946: 106) of the name *quffa* to describe the 5th century B.C. Arabian boats noted by Herodotus (1.194); but these prehistoric craft had a hide on woven wood framework construction, whereas the 20th century *quffa* is a reed boat built by the coiled basketry technique. Neutral, structurally–related descriptions are therefore to be preferred for class labels. If these cannot be devised then the use of specific names of well–documented regional types may be an acceptable alternative.

A proposed scheme

A method of defining primary classes of boats which would undoubtedly be rigorous would be to record the many individual traits of a large representative sample and then to search for clusters of attributes (McGrail 1984: 22). This is clearly impracticable in present circumstances: there are no comprehensive glossaries or attribute lists (although provisional ones for limited ranges of logboats and plank boats have been published – McGrail 1978*a*: 140–2, 331–7; 1978*b*: 45; McGrail and Switsur 1979: 113–5; McGrail and Denford 1982: 48–65); few units of water transport are recorded in the detail such analytical procedures would require; and the international co–operation necessary to undertake this task is not yet evident. It is intended in this paper therefore to use the principles described in the previous section in an attempt to identify primary Classifcation classes, using attributes which are considered to be culturally diagnostic.

Although floats (personal aids to flotation with the man partly immersed in water) and rafts (not intended to be watertight) have undoubtedly made a significant contribution to Man's use of inland and inshore waters – see for example, Hornell (1946: 14,5; 1942; 1945), the scheme presented here will deal principally with boats. Rafts can indeed be used on almost all rivers and lakes but their use at sea is restricted to the zones of warmer waters, probably between latitudes of 40°N and 40°S. This environmentally–related factor apart, the choice between boat and raft is mainly a culturally related one: whether to invest in a low level technology, often relatively short–life, wash–through raft; or in a relatively dry boat which requires greater investment of materials and effort and the use of higher level technology but generally has a life measurable in years and possibly decades.

The analytical method used in this paper may not be the theoretical optimum, especially in view of the doubtful accuracy and incompleteness of many ethnographical boat reports (McGrail 1984: 21), but its use may well hasten the time when more comprehensive methods become appropriate, as the resulting discussion should clarify the questions to be asked of boats and thus lead the way to the compilation of realistic attribute lists. A subsidiary outcome of the general recognition of primary classes could be especially important to prehistoric archaeology. Knowledge of water transport used before the 1st century AD in northern and western Europe is very limited (McGrail 1984: 18–19): there is even less information outside this region. If primary classes can be identified from the range of water transport known ever to have been used and if we can define the techniques, tools and materials needed to build them, then it should prove possible to indicate the earliest periods in which these types of water transport could have been used by analogy with the known states of technology in the various regions of the world (see McGrail 1981*a*: table 1 for an attempt to do this). The scheme, shown diagrammatically in Fig. 4.1.1 and tabulated in in Table 4.1.1, results in 14 classes of boat (C1 to C14), distinguished by the states of two attributes: shell or skeleton; and principal techniques.

C1 *Shell–by reduction*

Basic logboats hollowed from a single log, such as the medieval ones from Llyn Llangorse (McGrail 1978a: 233–6, figs 29 and 69) and Kew (McGrail 1978*a*: 226–9, figs 27 and 68) and the 20th century boat from the White Nile depicted by Hornell (1946: plate XXVIIA) are members of this class.

C2 *Shell–built by construction*

No examples known.

C3 *Shell–built by transformation*

Pottery boats such as the *tigari* from Bengal (Hornell 1946: fig. 9) are members of this class (but see C6). Shell–built single hide boats could be members of this class if the hide was not cut to shape (seeC5).

C4 *Shell–built by reduction and construction*

Extended logboats such as the medieval Kentmere 1 (McGrail 1981*a*: plate 16) are built by adding washstrakes (planks reduced from logs) to a hollowed log.

Basic logboats which have a fitted transom added (e.g. the prehistoric boats from Brigg & Poole), or those with transverse strengthening timbers across the ends (e.g. the medieval boats (C1 to C14), from Warrington and from Giggleswick) – see McGrail 1978*a* and *b* and McGrail and Switsur 1979 – are also in this class.

As are shell–built plank boats where the planking is not bent to shape (transformed) The Brigg 'raft' (McGrail 1981*b*) of *c*. 650 bc and the three Ferriby boats of c. 1500 bc (Wright 1976) are probably in this class. The so–called 'raft' was a flat-bottomed, square sided boat and thus the planking did not have to be bent to shape: in the Ferriby boats shape was achieved by hollowing (reducing) the planking. Some of the simple 20th century plank boats from the S. Baltic rivers described by Rudolph (1974a: 5–15) e.g. the Warnemunde *prahm*, the Dievenow *knutrkahn* and the Pomeranian *konger* are also in

this class; as are the tub–boats of Japan and China (Hornell 1946: fig. 11 and plate XVIII).

C5 *Shell–built by reduction and transformation*

Expanded logboats are built by reducing a log and then deforming it to the required shape after heat treatment. Such boats are known from Finland, Estonia, India, Burma, Siam, British Columbia, Tierra del Fuego, Guianas, Brazil, Amazon Basin (McGrail 1978*a*: 38–9). Those that are also extended should be in C7.

The simple bark boats of Australia (Hornell 1946: 182–6; Birdsell 1977) and of S. America and Central Africa (Hornell 1946: 183–6) are made from a one–piece bark shell obtained by reduction from a log or tree. The bark is transformed (sometimes after heat treatment) into the required shape and the ends fastened (McGrail 198 la: 65–6).

The S. American *pelota* (Hornell 1941) and the simple hide boats of the Mongols seen in use by the mid–13th century traveller Iohannes de Plano Carpini (Sinor 1961: 158;Serruys 1981: were made from a single hide, cut to shape (reduced) and then moulded to shape by the cargo carried or sometimes by an inserted light framework. The bull boats of the N. American Indians may also have been of this class, but the two principle recorders of these craft (Adney and Chapelle 1964: 219–20; Hornell 1946: 148–50) differ in their interpretation of the function of the elementary framework.

C6 *Shell–built by transformation and construction*

If they exist, boats built of coiled pottery, rather than thrown pottery, would be in this class.

C7 *Shell–built by reduction, transformation and construction*

Logboats which have been expanded and then extended (for example,20th century boats from Satakunta, Finland – Johnstone 1980: figs 5.5 to 5.7) are in this class.

Shell–built plank boats in which the planking is stressed and bent (transformed) into the required curved shapes (rather than hewn as in C4) are also in this class: they include the 9th/ 10th century AD Graveney boat and all boats built in the Viking tradition (McGrail 1981a: 31–6). Medterranean boats of the Classical period (Casson 1971: 201–13) were generally similar. Many of the plank boats in the Indian sub continent today are built in this manner (Greenhill 1976: 50–6).

The more complex Australian bark boats and the majority of those recently built in N. America (Greenhill 1976: figs 77–8) and S. America (McGrail 1981a: 77–8, plate 6) were built from several sheets of bark sewn together and moulded to shape: the inserted framework strengthened this bark shell and held it in shape.

The temporary or emergency hide boats of the N. American Malecites were built of two or more skins in a similar manner to the American bark boats (Adney and Chapelle 1964: 219–20) and thus are also members of this class.

Table 4.1.1 Classification Scheme derived from three key attributes

Attribute		States	
1.	Buoyancy derivation	1.1	From the flotation characteristic of individual elements: the materials must have a specific density of less than 1. Such a craft is a raft though some may superficially resemble a boat in shape – see for example the Lobito Bay raft (Greenhill 1976, fig. 43) or the ambatch 'canoe' raft from Kenya (Hornell 1946, plate VIIIA).
		1.2	From the floation characterisitcs of the whole vessel: due to the displacement of water by a hollowed form with a continous watertight outer surface – the specific density of the material is not restricted. Such a craft is a boat
2.	Fundamental Conception of Boat (applied here only to craft in class 1.2	2.1	Shell building sequence i.e. primarily as a watertight shell into which framing may subsequently be insterted.
		2.2	Skeleton building sequence i.e. primarily as a framework which is subsequently covered by a waterproofing envelope.
3.	Principal technique (apllied to classes 2.1 and 2.2)	3.1	Reduction (subtractive) technique
		3.2	Construction (additive) technique
		3.3	Transfromation (moulding) technique
		3.4	Reduction and Construction techniques
		3.5	Reduction and Transformation techniques
		3.6	Construction and Transformation techniques
		3.7	Reduction, Construction and Transformation techniques

The wooden basketry of the Vietnamese boats described by Nishimura (1931: 36–43), Hornell (1946: 109–11) and Cairo (1972) are built from split bamboo (reduction) which is woven and thus pre–stressed (addition and transformation). As the resin and dung mixture is generally only applied as a caulking to the interstices of this closely woven basketry (rather than applied overall as a waterproofing envelope) the boat belongs in this class – but see C12.

C8 *Skeleton built with waterproofng envelope made by reduction, transformation and construction*
The planking of many skeleton–built boats (but see C11) is fashioned by reduction and then forced into shape (transformed) around the framework. In northern and western Europe this technique does not seem to have been used until the 14th century (McGrail 1981a: 42–3) although aspects of it may be seen in some of the boats of the Romano–Celtic tradition and possibly in the cogs of N. Europe (McGrail 1981a: 22–4, 36–8, 42–3): these boats, and such vessels as the 1st century B.C. Madrague de Giens and later Mediterranean craft are probably best identified, at a lower level of classification, as hybrid types. From the 14th century the use of this skeleton sequence became increasingly common in Europe, especially for the larger boats and ships (Greenhill 1976: 60–88,268–301).

The hide waterprooftng envelope of the British and Irish *coracles and curachs* (Hornell 1936–8), the *umiak kayak,*

biadara and *baidarka* of the northern circum–polar lands (Johnstone 1980: fig. 4.12; Hornell 1946: plate XXIVB; McGrail 1981a: 27) the *parisil* of S. India (Kentley 1984) and others from Manchuria, Korea and Tibet are made by cutting hides to shape (reduction), fastening them together and moulding them to the pre–erected wooden framework. The boats Herodotus (1.194) saw on the river at Babylon in the 5th century BC were probably built in a similar manner. Waterproofed flannel or canvas has replaced hide on recent Irish, otherwise their characteristics appear to be retained from earlier times.

Certain bark boats in Sweden (Hansen and Madsen 1981: 4–5; Westerdahl 1982) and in E. Siberia and NW America (Brindley 1919: 106) seen to have, or to have had, a bark envelope produced by reduction and construction, and then moulded to pre–erected wooden or bone framework: they are therefore to be classified here.

C9 *Skeleton–built with waterproofing envelope made by transformation and construction*
None known.

C10 *Skeleton–built with waterproofing envelope made by reduction and transformation*
Single hide and single bark boats built on a frame, if they exist, would be in this class.

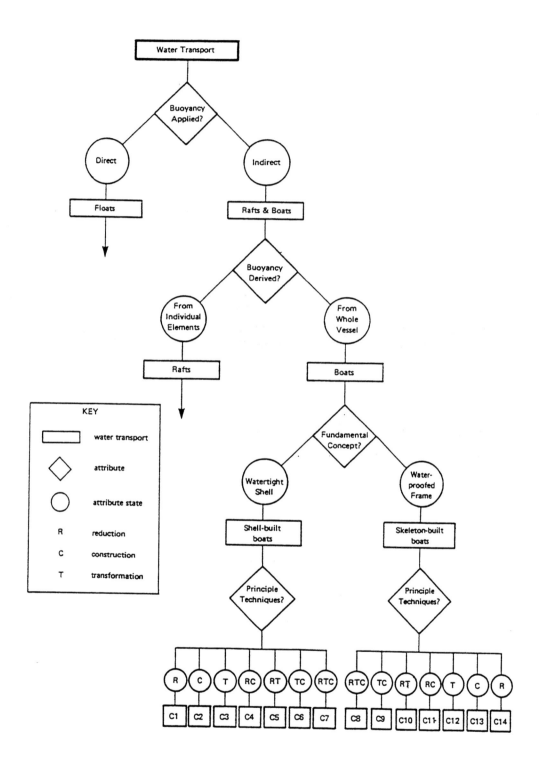

Figure 4.1.1 A classification scheme for water transport – mainly boats. Drawing: National Maritime Museum

C 11 *Skeleton–built with waterproofing envelope made by reduction and construction*

Skeleton–built boats whose planking is not transformed by bending into the required shape would be in this class – some of the 2nd–4th century AD Romano–Celtic flat–bottomed barge–like boats (McGrail 1981 a: 23–4) of the R. Rhine may have been built in this way — publication of further details is awaited.

C 12 *Skeleton–built with waterproofing envelope made by transformation*

The reed bundle, coiled basketry framework of the boats of Sargon, (Anderson 1978: 49) Moses (Exodus 2, 3) and Strabo (16.1.15), the 19th century *tarada* (Layard 1853: 552) and the modern *quffa* (McGrail 1981a: plate 26), *zaima* (Thesiger 1978: 128, fig. 45) and *jillabie* (Heyerdahl 1978: 35) are covered with bitumen which is transformed from a solid mass into a waterproofing envelope. Similar boats built of materials other than reed would be in this class.

Any woven wooden basket boats (possibly some of those from Vietnam) which are given a complete waterproofing envelope would be in this class rather than in C7. As also would skeleton–built boats of other materials with a complete waterproofing envelope.

C 13 *Skeleton–built with waterproofing envelope made by construction*

None known.

C 14 *Skeleton–built with waterproofing envelope made by reduction*

None known.

Discussion

It is argued above that boats should be classified using two attributes:

(a) the builder's concept of his boat either as a watertight shell or as a waterproofed frame and

(b) the combination of techniques (reduction, construction and transformation) the builder chooses to make the boat's outer envelope.

This results in 14 theoretical classes C1–C14, as illustrated in Fig. 4.1.1 Five of the seven shell–built classes are known to have members and a sixth may have members. Of the seven skeleton–built classes, two are known to have members: two others may have members but structural information at present available does not permit this being more than a possibility. All the classes with certain and with doubtful members are listed in Table 4.1.1.

Table 4.1.2 Proposed boat classes with their members listed by traditional type names

Class	Attributes		Traditional Type Name
	Concepts	Techniques	
C1	Shell	R	Basic logboats
C3	Shell	T	Pottery boats (some)
C4	Shell	RC	Extended logboats
			Unstressed plank boats (some)
C5	Shell	RT	Expanded logboats
			Basic bark boats
			Basic hide boats
(C6)	Shell	(TC)	Possibly some pottery boats
C7	Shell	RTC	Logboats expanded and extended
			Stressed plank boats (some)
			Complex bark boats (some)
			Complex hide boats (some)
			Basket boats (some)
C8	Skeleton	RTC	Stressed plank boats (some)
			Complex hide boats (some)
			Complex bark boats (some)
(C10)	Skeleton	(RC)	Possibly some basic bark boats
			Possibly some basic hide boats
(C11)	Skeleton	(RC)	Possibly some unstressed plank boats
C12	Skeleton	T	Bundle (reed) boats
			Possibly some basket boats

Notes	1	Unlisted classes have no known members
	2	Items in parenthesis are doubtful
	3	Traditional type names are defined in the text by reference to specific, reasonably well–documented examples
	4	R = reduction T = transformation C = construction

It seems unlikely that members of classes C9, C13 and C14 (skeleton) and C2 (shell) exist, as such constructions are difficult to conceive, even theoretically. Nevertheless, future research, especially rigorous recording of building methods, may result in the identification of members of these empty classes, and may reveal additional members of known classes, or indeed suggest re–allocation of existing members.

Boats which have in the past been classified as an homogenous group and given a single type (e.g. bark boats or plank boats) appear in Table 4.1.2, in several classes. This may be more clearly seen in Table 4.1.3 which is a re–arrangement of the data in Table 4.1.2.

Logboats are all shell construction and may be built using four different combinations of techniques depending upon whether they are to be basic, extended, expanded or expanded and extended logboats – the complexity and the range of achievable shape increasing in that sequence.

Plank boats may be built in shell or skeleton sequence, the class determinant then being whether or not the planking is hewn and bent to shape or only hewn to shape – significantly different approaches to boatbuilding.

Table 4.1.3 Traditionally–named boat types classified on two structural attributes

| Traditional Type Name | Attributes | | Class |
	Concept	Techniques	
Logboats	Shell	R	C1
	Shell	RC	C4
	Shell	RT	C5
	Shell	RTC	C7
Plank boats	Shell	RC	C4
	Shell	RTC	C7
	Skeleton	RTC	C8
	Skeleton	(RC)	(C11)
Bark boats	Shell	RT	C5
	Shell	RTC	C7
	Skeleton	RTC	C8
	Skeleton	(RT)	(C10)
Hide boats	Shell	RT	C5
	Shell	RTC	C7
	Skeleton	RTC	C8
	Skeleton	(RT)	(C10)
Bundle (reed) boats	Skeleton	T	C12
Pottery boats	Shell	T	C3
	Shell	(TC)	(C6)
Basket boats	Shell	RTC	C7
	Skeleton	(T)	(C12)

Note: Items in parenthesis are doubtful

Bark and hide boats feature in the same classes, two shell and one skeleton, with a further possible skeleton class. The difference between the two groups of techniques (RT or RTC) is whether the design requires a single hide or bark, or several to be used: this is more a question of size than a significant structural difference. The choice of shell or skeleton for hide and bark boats, whilst an important conceptual difference, may also be related to size in that the difficulties of visualising the shape of larger boats and indeed stabilising the hull during construction would seem to increase significantly with size – although this may be merely 20th century lack of knowledge and expertise. On the other hand, such considerations, plus the requirement to give large, plank–built, sea–going ships sufficient strength to withstand the stresses imposed in a sea way (McGrail 1981*a*: 42–3) undoubtedly influenced the widespread change from shell sequence to skeleton sequence in later Medieval Europe.

Bundle boats by their nature need to have their coiled basketry framework waterproofed, most readily done by the transformation of some mastic–like substance (e.g. tar). Other materials, such as hide, might be used but this seems an overcomplex solution and one which, as far as is known, has not been tried – the *quffa* covered with skins which Layard (1849: 380) mentions, and which Hornell (1946: 104) believes had a reed bundle frame, was in all probability a hide boat with a woven wooden basketry frame. It seems unlikely therefore, that bundle boats of reed, grass or similar materials could be represented in any other class but C12.

The known pottery boats (C3) are said to be made by throwing (Hornell 1946: 98) but it is conceivable that some could be made by coil techniques and therefore may be in class C6.

Basket boats, like bundle boats, appear to have a very restricted distribution – within Indo China – and the existing documentation appears to indicate that they are mostly, if not all, built with the techniques of class C7, that is, the closely woven split bamboo shell is virtually watertight and therefore requires only caulking rather than waterproofing. On the other hand, any basket boats with a complete covering of dung mix, etc. would be conceptually the same as class C 12.

Individual boat–types which are well defned may be identified by extension of the proposed C8 classification scheme (not shown in Fig. 4.1.1) Thus a group of Irish skin boats generally known as *curachs* and a group of Arctic skin boats generally known as *umiaks* are both in class C8. They may best be distinguished from one another by identifying the states of certain structural attributes: an example would be the distinction proposed by Christensen (1977: 275), and incorporated in Kentley's scheme (1984, fig. 1) as a cross–sectional, shape–determining attribute. Sub–groups may be further recognised by other structural considerations (woodworking techniques, methods of fastening) and by the answers to questions about function and form and by distributions in time and space.

The attribute analysis approach used in this paper readily lends itself to the identification of clusters. This should be a long–term aim of boat classification studies. It is important, however, that, before patterns are searched for and before any cultural significance is deduced, the classification scheme proposed here be subjected to further criticism and, wherever possible, doubtful records about boatbuilding techniques and sequences be verified or amended.

Acknowledgment

I am very grateful to my colleague Eric Kentley whose recent paper (1984) stimulated me to re–think my ideas about the classification of boats, and who has criticised earlier drafts of this present paper. I am also indebted to him for several specific examples of general boat classes. Janet Storey has three times turned my manuscript into typescipt, and for this I am most grateful.

References

Adney, E. T. and Chapelle, H. I. 1964. *Bark Canoes and Skin Boats of North America*. Smithsonian Institution, Washington.

Anderson, B. W. 1978. *Living World of the Old Testament*. 3rd edition.

Birdsell, J. H. 1977. Recalibration of a paradigm for the first peopling of Greater Australia. In Allen, J. et al. (eds) *Sunda and Sahul*, pp. 1 1 3–68. Academic Press.

Brindley, H. H. 1919–20. Notes on the boats of Siberia. *The Mariner's Mirror* 5: 66–72, 101–7, 130–42,184–7;6: 15–18, 187.

Cairo, R. 1972. A note on S. Vietnamese basket boats. *The Mariner's Mirror* 58: 135–53.

Casson, L. 1971. *Ships and Seamanship in the Ancient World* . Princeton.

Christensen, A. E. 1977. Ancient boatbuilding – a provisional classification. In McGrail, S. (ed.) *Sources and Techniques in Boat Archaeology*, pp. 269–80. NMM Greenwich Archaeological Series 1. British Archaeological Reports (Oxford). S29.

Crumlin–Pederson, O. 1978. The Ships of the Vikings. In Anderson, T. and Sandred, K. 1. (eds) McGrail, S. *The Vikings*. Uppsala, pp. 32–41.

Doran, E. 1973. *Nao, Junk and Vaka*. Texas A. & M. University.

Edwards, C. R. 1965. *Aboriginal Watercratt on the Pacific coast of South America. Ibero–Americana* 47. University of California.

Ellmers, D. 1972. *Fruhmittelalterliche Handelsschiffahot in Mittel und Nordeuropa*. Neumunster

Ellmers, D. 1984. Punt, barge or pram – is there one tradition or several? In McGrail, S. (ed.) *Maritime Aspects of Maritime Archaeology and Ethnography*. NMM (Greenwich).

Eskeröd, A. 1956. Early Nordic Arctic boats. *Arctica*. 1956: 57–87. (Studia Ethnographica Upsaliensia).

Greenhill, B. 1976. *Archaeology of the Boat*. London: A. & C. Black.

Haddon, A. C. & Hornell, J. 1936. *Canoes of Oceania*. 1. 1937. *Canoes of Oceania*. 2. 1938. *Canoes of Oceania*. 3. Honolulu.

Hansen, K. and Madsen, J. S. 1981. *Barkbåde*. Roskilde.

Heyerdahl, T. 1978. *Early Man and the Ocean*. London: Allen & Unwin.

Hodson, F. R. 1980. Cultures as types? Some elements of classification theory. *Bulletin of the Institute of Archaeology*. 17: 1–10.

Hornell, J. 1936–8. British coracles and the curraghs of Ireland. *The Mariner's Mirror*. 22: 5–41, 261–304; 23: 74–83, 148–75; 24; 5–39.

Hornell, J. 1941. Pelota or hide – balsa of South America. *Man*. 41: 1–4.

Hornell, J. 1942. Floats; a study in primitive water transport. *Journal of the Royal Anthropological Institute*. 72: 33–44.

Hornell, J. 1943. Fishing and coastal craft of Ceylon. *The Mariner's Mirror*. 29: 40–53.

Hornell, J. 1945. Floats and buoyed rafts in military operations. *Antiquity*. 19: 72–9.

Hornell, J. 1946. *Water Transport*. Cambridge. Reprinted Newton Abbott 1970.

Humbla,P.and van Post,L. 1937. *Galtabacksbaten och Tidigt Batbyggeri i Norden*.

Johnstone, P 1980. *Seacraft of Prehistory*. Routledge & Kegan Paul.

Kentley, E. 1984. Skin boats and basket boats: a note on the classification of water transport. *International Journal of Nautical Archaeology*. 13: 81–3.

Lane–Fox, A. 1875. On early modes of navigation. *Journal of the Royal Anthropological Institute*. 4: 399–437.

Layard,A. H. 1849. *Nineveh and its Remains*.2.

Layard, A. H. 1853. *Discoveries in the Ruins of Nineveh and Babylon* .

McGrail, S. 1978*a*. *Logboats of England and Wales*. National Maritime Museum (Greenwich) Archaeological Series 2. British Archaeological Reports (Oxford) 51.

McGrail, S. 1978*b*. Medieval logboat from Giggleswick Tarn,Yorkshire. In Annis,P. (ed.) *Ingrid and other Studies*. National Maritime Museum (Greenwich). Monograph 36: 25–46.

McGrail, S. 1981*a*. *Rafts, Boats and Ships*. HMSO.

McGrail, S. 1981*b*. *Brigg 'raft'*. British Archaeological Reports (Oxford) 89. National Maritime Museum (Greenwich) Archaeological Series 6.

McGrail, S. 1984. Maritime archaeology – present and future. In McGrail, S. (ed.). *Aspects of Maritime Archaeology and Ethnography*. National Maritime Museum (Greenwich).

McGrail. S. and Denford, G. 1982. Boat building techniques, technological change and attribute analysis. In McGrail, S. (ed) *Woodworking Techniques before AD 1500*. 25–72. NMM (Greenwich) Archaeological Series 7. British Archaeological Reports (Oxford) S 129.

McGrail, S. and Switsur, R. 1979. Medieval logboats of the River Mersey. In McGrail, S. (ed.) *Medieval Ships and Harbours*, 93–115. British Archaeological Reports (Oxford) S66. National Maritime Museum (Greenwich) Archaeological Series 5.

McKee E. 1972. *Clenched Lap or Clinker*. National Maritime Museum (Greenwich).

McKee, E. 1983. *Working Boats of Britain*. Conway Maritime Press.

Marsden, P. 1976. A boat of the Roman period found at Bruges, Belgium in 1899 and related finds. *International Journal of Nautical Archaeology*. 5: 23–55.

Needham, J. 1971. *Science and Civilisation in China*. 4: part 3. Cambridge.

Nishimura, S. 1931. Skinboats. *Ancient Ships of Japan* . 5, 6, 7, 8. Tokyo.

Phillips–Burt, D. 1979. *Building of Boats*. Stanford Maritime.

Prins, A.H.J. Forthcoming. *Sewn Boats*. National Maritime Museum (Greenwich).

Roth,H. L. 1899 *Aboriginies of Tasmania*. 2nd ed. Halifax.

Rudolph, W. 1966. *Handbuch der Volkstumlichen Boote im ostlichen Neider–Deutschland*. Berlin.

Rudolph, W. 1974*a*. *Inshore Fishing Craft of the Southern Baltic from Holstein to Curania*. National Maritime Museum (Greenwich). Monograph 14.

Rudolph, W. 1974*b*. *Boats, Rafts and Ships*. London: Adlard Coles.

Serruys, H. 1981. Hun–t'o: tulum, floats and containers in Mongolia and Central Asia. *Bulletin of the School of African and Oriental Studies*. 44: 105–19.

Sinor, D. 1961. On water–transport in Central Eurasia. *Ural–Altaische Jahrbdcher*. 3: 156–79.

Suder, H. 1930. *Vom Einbaum und Floss zum Schiff*. Berlin: Mittler.

Thesiger, W. 1978. *Marsh Arabs*. Harmondsworth: Penguin.

Reprinted with permission from:

World Archaeology, 16: 289–303 (1985)

SECTION 5.0

WOODWORKING TECHNIQUES

Introduction

The first of the two papers in this Section puts the case for using *all* forms of evidence, including that from boats, in studies of woodworking techniques, rather than dealing exclusively with land–based material, as was current practice in the 1970s. It is equally a plea that boatbuilding techniques should not be studied in isolation. The interchange of views that took place as a result of this paper, led to a conference on 'Woodworking Techniques before AD 1500', which was held at Greenwich in 1980 (McGrail, 1982). At that time, Professor John Coles and his select band of waterlogged wood specialists were regarded as 'fringe' by most archaeologists. Nowadays, wetland studies seem to be well integrated into the discipline; on the other hand, there still seems to be resistance to the assimilation of boat–related studies.

That conference in 1980 could have marked the beginning of synthetic studies in woodworking techniques; but it did not. There is, for example, no study of British Bronze Age woodworking which includes data from the Ferriby, Brigg, and Caldicot boats, all of which have been published in detail (see Section 7). These nautical studies also include such useful information as the sizes of Bronze Age oaks, but this data has never been used in environmental publications, as far as I am aware. At a recent Oxford conference on the British Bronze Age, one speaker regretted the lack of evidence for ropes; however, prehistoric ropes of yew and of willow, from c 1 inch to over 3 inches in size (girth; the diameter would be c 10 to 25 mm.) are well–documented in boat publications. There is an urgent need for comprehensive studies of ancient woodworking & boatbuilding techniques.

A suggestion that the chronology of technological change should be investigated was made in one of the papers presented at the 1980 conference (McGrail & Denford, 1982). The second paper in this Section is an attempt to do that for early boatbuilding techniques in Britain & Ireland. Much of the new data in that paper came from the Hasholme logboat which had recently been dated by dendrochronolgy to within a few years of 300 BC (Section 6; Papers 8.1, 11.5). The paper, as published here, incorporates ammendments made in 1987 in *IJNA*, 17:158; it is still, by & large, up to date but will undoubtedly need to bo ammended when the mid–2nd. millennium BC boat from Dover is published (Section 6). Subsequent to the conference, Switsur (1989) published a list of calibrated radiocarbon dates for many early British boats.

To–date, only three British boat finds have been dated by dendrochronology, the Hasholme & Clapton logboats & the Goldcliff plank boat fragments (Sections 6 & 7). It has not proved possible to date other prehistoric British boat finds by this technique: although site chronologies exist for the Ferriby, Brigg & Caldicot finds, they cannot yet be matched with dated sequences elsewhere. Curators are sometimes reluctant to allow dendro–samples to be taken, however, if maximum information is to be obtained from an excavated boat, dendrological examination (including dating where possible) must be undertaken (Morgan *et al*, 1981): the best time to sample the timbers is after post–excavation recording and before conservation.

References.

McGrail, S. 1982. (ed). *Woodworkinq Techniques before AD 1500*. BAR Oxford S.129.

McGrail, S. & Denford, G. 1982. Woodworking techniques, technological change and attribute analysis. in McGrail (ed) 1982: 25–72.

Morgan, R.A., Hillam, J., Coles, J.M. & McGrail, S. 1981. Reconciling tree–ring sampling with conservation. *Antiquity*, 55: 90–5.

Switsur, R, 1989. Early English Boats. *Radiocarbon*, 31: 1010–1018.

PAPER 5.1

PREHISTORIC BOATS, TIMBER, AND WOODWORKING TECHNOLOGY

The recent paper by Coles *et al.* (1978) on the use and character of prehistoric timber is a most timely reminder that the study of wooden artifacts can make a significant contribution to our understanding of early man. This potential may never be realised, however, unless full records are compiled on site whilst the artifacts are maintained in a stable state by 'passive' conservation techniques, and samples of the timber are recovered for post–excavation research. In the past much information has been irretrievably lost because these actions were not taken. It is also necessary to be cautious before accepting that wooden artifacts excavated or found before, say, 1960 are necessarily from the period ascribed to them. Not all simple artifacts are prehistoric.

1. Boats

Until relatively recently all British and Irish logboats (= dugout canoes) were generally assumed to be prehistoric, and Wilson (1966, 85) was almost a lone voice when he suggested that some of the British boats could be post–Roman. Wilson's thesis has in fact been confirmed by several recent radiocarbon determinations, many of them obtained by Switsur of the Godwin Laboratory, Cambridge using samples collected by McGrail in the course of his examination of all accessible surviving logboats in England and Wales (McGrail 1978a). Of the 24 dates now available for British logboats, 14 are Romano–British or Medieval, ranging up to *c.* ad 1335 for the Giggleswick Tarn logboat (Q–1245: 615 bp + 40)

The ten prehistoric dates are listed in Table 5.1.1.

Table 5.1.1 Radiocarbon Dates for Prehistoric Logboats from Britain

Laboratory reference number	Logboat (Catalogue Number)		bp	Date bc	±
SRR–326	Locharbriggs		3754	1804	125
Q–288	Branthwaite	(19)	3520	1570	100
BM–213	Chapel Flat Dyke	(28)	3450	1500	150
Q–80	Appleby	(5)	3050	1100	80
Q–79	Short Ferry	(126)	2796	846	100
Q–78	Brigg	(22)	2784	834	100
Q–357	Shapwick	(124)	2305	355	120
Q–821	Poole	(112)	2245	295	50
Birm–132	Holme Pierrpont I	(57)	2180	230	110
SRR–403	Loch Arthur (Lotus)		2051	101	80

Note: Catalogue numbers refer to the catalogue published by McGrail (1978a)

There are problems in establishing whether wooden remains, especially fragmentary ones, are indeed from boats (McGrail 1978a 18–19), and the remains from Branthwaite, Cumberland, and Chapel Flat Dyke, Yorkshire are by no means indisputably logboats.

The special nature of boats and their find–sites means that only rarely can they be dated from their context or by association (McGrail 1978b, 239). And the study of the form and structure of early boats is at too early a stage to attempt precise dating

by morphology or from technological considerations. Thus dating the materials used in the construction of the boat is frequently the only reliable method, and this means radiocarbon dating until dendrochronology becomes practicable. In the past, however, dates have sometimes been attributed to boats on very slender evidence. The oft–quoted mesolithic date for the logboat from Perth may be unreliable, for Geikie (1879, 1) did not visit the site until a 'number of years' after it had been found, and by then the find had been laid aside on a bank for a long time. The identification of its stratigraphic position on which its date depends was thus not from an in situ examination by Geikie but from the memory of the manager of the Friarton brickworks.

Dating evidence for some of the other finds in Coles et al's catalogue (1978,34–42) may also be questioned.

Eccles, Lancashire. This logboat is also known as Barton (11) and the remains are in Manchester University Museum. It is one of the boats recently dated by Switsur to the medieval period: Q–1396: 920 bp ± 65 = *c.* ad 1030. Eight other logboats from the same stretch of the Rivers Mersey and Irwell are also now known to be from the 11th and 12th centuries ad (McGrail and Switsur, forthcoming).

Glastonbury, Somerset. The first Glastonbury (50) logboat (now in the Tribunal, Glastonbury) was found in a ditch 'a few fields distant' from Glastonbury Lake Village (Bulleid 1893, 121; Bulleid 1906,52) and thus cannot be dated to the Iron Age by association as Fox (1926, 150) attempted to do. The second logboat (51), which is now lost, was excavated from peat in the sub–structure of the village (Bulleid 1906,52; Bulleid and Gray 1911,333) and thus its date may be related to that of the village.

Holme–Pierrepont, Nottinghamshire. Three logboats (now re–buried) were found during gravel extraction from an abandoned meander of the River Trent. Boat 1 (57) has been dated by radiocarbon to c. 230 bc (Table 1), but with these conditions of deposition and recovery it would be imprudent to assume a similar date for Boats 2 and 3 without further evidence.

Maudlin, Norfolk. This (now lost) logboat is also known as Magdalen Bend (91). It was found in a layer of peat where a Roman road was reported to be on the peat (Marshall 1878–9). It may therefore be considered pre–Roman, but not necessarily Neolithic.

Short Ferry, Lincolnshire. With a date of *c.* 846 bc (Table 1) this logboat (126) may be assigned to the Bronze Age.

Planked boats and other wooden artifacts

Four prehistoric British planked boats are known: the three Ferriby boats (Wright 1976, 1978); and the Brigg 'raft' (McGrail 1975). The latter has several radiocarbon dates around 600 bc (McGrail and Switsur 1975; and subsequent unpublished work by Switsur) and may be considered securely dated. On the other hand, as Wright (1976) has pointed out, there are problems in interpreting the dates available for the Ferriby boats: on present evidence they are best ascribed to the period 1776–960 bc. Dendrochronological work now being undertaken by Hillam at Sheffield and further radiocarbon dating by Switsur at Cambridge may give more precise dates and help decide whether the three boats were contemporary. Caution must be exercised, however, when considering Wright's recent suggestion (1978, 190) that, 'it is a fair assumption that they (wooden objects found in the North Ferriby estuarine clay in which the boats were also found) are all of Bronze Age date'; and his conclusion (1978, 201) that the non–boat wooden objects from the estuarine clay 'belong firmly to the Bronze Age'. Excavations by the National Maritime Museum's Archaeological Research Centre in 1978 and early 1979, based on an exposure identified by E. V. Wright, have indeed revealed fragments of what was probably a trackway or possibly a hard standing in the vicinity of Ferriby boat 2, with one C14 date in the mid–2nd millennium bc. Nevertheless, this strand at North Ferriby has had long use as a boat–place, extending on place–name evidence into the Viking Age and even to recent times, and it is possible today to recover undoubtedly 20th–century artifacts 'sealed at least in part' (Wright 1978, 190) in the estuarine clays. As I know my colleague E. V. Wright is well aware, positive evidence is required before wooden artifacts in this type of context can be given a firm date.

2. Timber and Woodworking technology

Few logboats have been rigorously examined before they dried–out, shrank and split, and the 1974 recovery of part of the Brigg 'raft' was a re–excavation of a site first exposed in 1888. Thus, apart from E. V. Wright's records of the Ferriby boats, the source material for information about selection of timber and woodworking technology is unpromising. Nevertheless some estimates and deductions can be made.

Of the six undoubted logboats from England and Wales, only two (Brigg and Poole) can be hypothetically reconstructed using the criteria I have postulated (McGrail 1978a, 127). Thus only limited data is available from the other four. Table 5.1.2 lists some properties of these six boats and their parent logs.

All six logs were of oak (*Quercus* sp). Of the ones made from, or possibly made from, a whole log, the Appleby, Short Ferry and Brigg boats had fitted transoms across open sterns (the butt–end of the log). There is a possibility therefore that these logs had a rot known as brittle heart (a disease prevalent in modern oaks of any great size) in the worked–away centre of the lower bole. On the other hand Holme Pierrepont 1, which was made from a whole log, evidently has an integral stem and the log from which it was made cannot therefore have had brittle heart rot.

The approximate age at felling may be determined by some future dendrochronological examination of the surviving boats: for the present, the diameter of the ideal logs or the maximum beam of the boat may be some guide to the relative ages of the logs. After felling, the logs for Shapwick and Poole (and possibly Short Ferry) were split longitudinally and one half used for the boat. Brigg and Holme Pierrepont I were built from whole logs. 90.8 per cent of the Brigg log and 93.6 per cent of the Poole log was worked–away externally and internally during the boatbuilding. Some sapwood is reported to have been left on the Short Ferry boat.

Table 5.1.2 Data for six Prehistoric Logboats and their Parent Logs

| Logboat | Approximate date bc | Boat remains | | Whole or half log used | Parent log[2] | |
		Length	Max. beam		Volume	Max. diameter
Appleby	1100	7.50m+	1.46	N.K.	–	–
Short Ferry	846	*c* 7.5m	0.94m	Half(?)	–	–
Brigg	834	14.78m	1.37m	Whole	37.95m³	1.90m
Shapwick	355	*c* 6.15m	*c* 0.70m	Half	–	–
Poole[1]	295	10.01m	1.52m	Half	16.76m³	1.72m
Holme Pierrepont I	230	6.40m+	*c* 0.90m	Whole	–	–

Notes:
1. The data for Poole include an allowance for the shrinkage the boat experienced before it was recorded. The calculation which is based on measurements of elliptical holes is described in McGrail 1978a, 123–8.

2. To estimate the size of the parent log, the minimum radii to circumscribe the boat at both ends was calculated, taking into account the position in the boat of the log's pith. An allowance of 0.10 m was then added for sapwood and bark and the volume of the log calculated using the length of the boat. The parent log was obviously longer and a reasonable assumption might be that the tree would be felled *c.* 0.70 m above the ground. Details of the assumed taper of the log are given in the appropriate catalogue entry in McGrail 1978a: 143–306.

The lengths of these prehistoric logs varied from over 6 m to over 14 m, but this is too small a sample necessarily to be representative of the prehistoric period. We may note with due caution, however, that the oak (*Quercus* sp) logs of six well–documented medieval boats had a mean length of only 4m ± 0.05.

The remains of four of these logboats (Brigg no longer survives, and Holme Pierrepont 1 cannot yet be examined) are now in such a condition that they reveal little evidence of the tools used or the sequence of boatbuilding–but for the latter, some comparative ethnographic evidence is available (McGrail 1978as 26–36). We can, however, appreciate some of the prehistoric technology: Dovetailed joints and treenails were used to attach fittings to the boats. Repairs were made in the Bronze Age by sewing or treenailing on patches or by the use of flat dovetailed–shaped clamps (fig 5.1.1, 5.1.2); iron–nailed, lead patches were used in the third century bc (Fig 5.1.3). Logboats have a great tendency to split along the medullary rays at the ends and this was combatted by fastening transverse strengthening timbers, some of them fashioned from natural crooks selected so that they fitted the curve of the end of the boat. Transoms (vertical boards) were fitted across open ends, let into transverse grooves in the bottom (Fig 5.1.4) and made watertight with mosses or other caulking. The bottom of the boat could be given a uniform thickness by the use of gauges (Fig 5.1.4) radially orientated holes bored to a pre–determined depth in the part of the log which was to become the bottom of the boat. Rectangular or half–rounded ends and transverse sections could be given to the boat; false stems, oculi and other non–functional features were sometimes incorporated. There is no sign that after hollowing these oak (*Quercus* sp.) logs were expanded to give greater beam and hence stability, as was recently practised in Europe and elsewhere with timber other than oak. However, there is some evidence that lateral stability may have been improved by pairing two logboats or by fastening external horizontal timbers at the waterline on both sides of single logboats. There is no evidence that the boats were propelled other than by paddle or pole.

Examination of the timber from the Ferriby boats and the Brigg 'raft' is not yet finished, but Wright (1976,22, fig. 8) has published a diagram showing that one element of the Ferriby boat 2 oak (*Quercus* sp.) keel–plank had a minimum diameter of 1.10 m over a length of 6.38 m. Planks for all four boats were fashioned from logs which had been split longitudinatly into halves, giving a maximum of two planks per log. The parent trees must have been straight–grained, forest–grown oaks with few branches on their lower boles. The standard of woodworking achieved by these: Bronze Age boatwrights may be gauged from the intricate method used to interlock the planking of the Ferriby boats (Wright 1976,8–19, figs. 4, 5) and by the precision with which the side strake was fashioned with a curve in two planes to meet two of the bottom planks.

3. Dating technological change

The date of first and last appearance of certain woodworking techniques may be noted thus defining their apparent floruit. This has been attempted for the logboats of England and Wales using the few reliably–dated boats which have such features as a half–rounded transverse section, a transverse groove and fitted–transom, or a particular type of repair. We can say, for example, that, on present evidence, dovetailed joints were used on these logboats from *c.* 1100 bc to well into the medieval period. Dovetailed timbers are in fact known to have been used in other contexts from ancient Egypt through to modern times, and to trace technological change it is therefore necessary to partition such general features as dovetails into several well–defined types. In this way any changes with time may be revealed.

Figure 5.1.1 The after end of the logboat from Appleby, Lincolnshire. Note the vertical holes through the bottom of the boat on either side of a split. A two stranded birch (*Betula* sp) rope, wedged with oak (*Quercus* sp) slips had been used to bind the split together, (Scale centimetric; National Maritime Museum)

To make this analysis worthwhile the evidence from the prehistoric planked boats must be integrated with that from the logboats and as more prehistoric dates become available this analytical technique may enable the characteristic boatbuilding technology used in a certain region during a defined period to be identified. But boatbuilding techniques cannot be understood in isolation: the analysis must be extended to the woodworking technology used in the manufacture of other wooden artifacts discussed by Coles *et al.* (1978). Boats (though pouibly not logboats) and wheels may be deposited far from their region of origin and thus the use of evidence from tracks, coffins and other artifacts which in general would not be expected to travel far, should provide a necessary control as well as enlarging the data base.

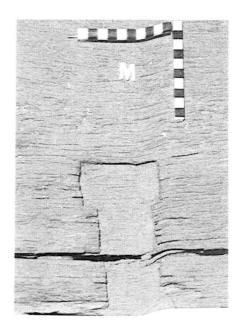

Figure 5.1.2 A second method of repair on the Appleby logboat. A flat clamp had been inserted inot this double–dovetail shape cut across a longitudinal split (Scale centimetric; National Maritime Museum)

Figure 5.1.3 The stern of the Holme Pierrpont I logboat. A lead patch (*c* 300 x 90 x 5 mm) had been nailed across a split using round–headed nails with square shanks. A wooden wedge had been insterted into a split radiating from the pith of the log probabaly to tighten the boat against a conjectural strengthening timber fitted into the transverse groove in the upper surface of the end (Nottingham Museums)

Figure 5.1.4 The stern of the Poole logboat from above. A vertical slot had been cut to receive a separate transom board which was caulked with animal hide. The hole to the right is one of three vertical holes through the bottom of the boat. These were probably used to gauge the thickness of the bottom; this aftermost one may subsequently have been used a a drain hole (Poole Museums)

References

Bulleid, A., 1893. 'Ancient canoe found near Glastonbury', *Somerset and Dorset Notes and Queries* 3, 12I.

Bulleid, A., 1906. 'Prehistoric boat found at Shapwick, 1906', *Proceedings of thc Somersetshire Archaeological and Natural History Society* 52, 51–54.

Bulleid, A, Gray, H. St G., 1911. *Glastonbury Lake–Village* Vol. I, Glastonbury.

Coles, J. M., Heal, S. V. E. and Orme, B. J., 1978. 'Use and character of wood in Prehistoric Britain and Ireland', *PPS* 44, 1–45.

Fox, C., 1926. 'Dugout canoe from South Wales', *Antiq. J..* 6, 121–151.

Geikie, J., I 879. 'Discovery of an ancient canoe in the old alluvium of the Tay at Perth', *Scottish Naturalist* 5, 1–7.

McGrail, S., 1975. 'Brigg "raft" re–excavated', *Lincolnshire History and Archaeology 10, 5–13.*

McGrail, S., 1978a. *Logboats of England and Wales.* Brit. Archaeol. Rep. 51. National Maritime Museum Archaeological Series No. 2.

McGrail, S., 1978b. 'Dating ancient wooden boats'. In J. Fletcher (ed.), *Dendrochronology in Europe.* Brit.Archeol. Rep. S51. National Maritime Museum Archaeological Series No. 4, 239–258.

McGrail, S. and Switsur, R., 1975. 'Early British boats and their chronology'. *Internat. J. Nautical Archaeol.*4, 191–200.

McGrail, S. and Switsur, R., forthcoming. 'Medieval logboats of the River Mersey' to be published by Brit. Archeol. Rep. (Oxford) in the proceedings of the Bremerhaven Symposium on Boat Archaeology.

Marshall, W., 1878–9. 'On an ancient canoe found imbedded in the fen–peat near Magdalen Bend on the River Ouse in the County of Norfolk', *Cambridge Antiquarian Communications* 4, 195–206.

Wilson, D. M., 1966. 'A medieval boat from Kentmere, Westmorland', *Medieval Archaeology* 10, 81–88.

Wright, E. V., 1976. *North Ferriby boats.* National Maritime Museum Monograph No. 23, Greenwich.

Wright, E. V., 1978. 'Artifacts from the boat–site at North Ferriby, Humberside, England', *PPS* 44, 187–202.

Reprinted with permission from

Proceedings of the Prehistoric Society, 45: 159–163 (1979).

PAPER 5.2

EARLY BOATBUILDING TECHNIQUES IN BRITAIN AND IRELAND – DATING TECHNOLOGICAL CHANGE

The Hasholme boat (Fig 5.2.1) of *c* 300 BC is a complex logboat displaying a wide range of boatbuilding techniques, including a bow extension, a fitted transom at the stern, washstrakes in the fore part, and treenail fastenings locked by wooden keys or cotters (McGrail & Millett, 1985; 1986; Millett & McGrail, 1987). Date ranges for the use of selected boatbuilding techniques have been published by McGrail (1978*a*, 332–3, 1978*b*, 41), McGrail and Swistur (1979, 109) and McGrail and Denford (1982, table 3.2). The Hasholme data has recently been integrated with the information in those earlier publications, and the results are here presented in two tables: Table 5.2.1 lists techniques specific to logboats; Table 5.2.2 lists techniques used in plank boats and in logboats.

Table 5.2.1 Date Ranges of Selected Logboat Features

Feature[1]	Earliest date[2]	Latest date[3]
Conversion from whole log	834 bc±100 Brigg 1	ad 1335±40 Giggleswick Tarn
Conversion from half log	846 bc±100 Short Ferry (probably)[4] 355 bc±120 Shapwick	ad 1190±60 Warrington 1
Rectangular or flared transverse section	1100 bc±80 Appleby	ad 1335±40 Giggleswick Tarn
Half–rounded transverse section	1550 bc±150 Chapel Flat Dyke (possibly)[5] 834 bc±100 Brigg 1	ad 1190±60 Warrington 1
Composite bow	332 to 277 BC Hasholme[6]	–
Transom fitted at stern	110 bc±80 Appleby	295 bc±50 Poole 332 to 277 BC Hasholme
Transverse strengthening fittings ar ends	846 bc±100 Short Ferry (probably), 332 to 277 BC Hasholme	ad 1335±40 Giggleswick Tarn
'Steps' at one end	230 bc±110 Holme Pierrpont 1	ad 814±60 Lyn Llangorse
'False' stem	295 bc±50 Poole	ad 1300±120 Kentmere 1
Beak with hole	ad 814±60 Lyn Llangorse	ad 1190±60 Warrington 1
Ridges across bottom	834 bc±100 Brigg 1	ad 1190±60 Warrington 1
Treenails in thickness gauges	1100 bc±80 Appleby	ad 1300±120 Kentmere 1
Washstrakes	332 to 277 BC Hasholme	ad 1300±120 Kentmere 1
Fitted ribs	ad 990±70 Stanley Ferry	ad 1300±120 Kentmere 1
Stabilisers at waterline	ad 900±70 Stanley Fery (probably)	ad 1300±120 Kentmere 1
Rubbing strake at sheer	ad 1335±40 Giggleswick Tarn	–

Notes

1. See McGrail & Denford (1982, 42–3) on the problems of accurately defining features

2. See McGrail (1978a, 103–109; 1978c, 239–258) on the problems of dating boat finds

3. Dates in the third column are the latest known before <u>c</u> AD 1450. Some of these techniques continued to be used in the post–medieval period

4. Where a fitting has not survived and its fromer presence is deduced, the date is followed by (probably)

5. It is not certain that the remains from Chapel Flat Dyke are those of a boat

6. Dates give 'ad' or 'bc' are radiocarbon dates. The Hasholme date (BC) is from dendrochronology

7. Further details of the boat named may be found in McGrail (1978a, 1987, 56–87)

Table 5.2.2 Date ranges of selected wooden boatbuilding techniques[1]

Feature	Earliest date	Latest date
Plank converted from half log	*c* 1500 bc Ferriby 1	Late 12th century AD Wood Quay Dublin (pine planks)
Radially oriented planks	Late 9th century AD Graveney	*c* AD 1416 *Grace Dieu*
Fastenings:		
Sewing	*c* 1500 bc Ferriby 1	*c* 650 Brigg 2
treenails	1100bc±80 Appleby (probably) 332–277 BC Hasholme	*c* AD 1416 *Grace Dieu*
treenials locked by keys	332–277 BC Hasholme	–
treenails locked by wedges	Late–9th century AD Graveney	*c* AD 1400 Blackfriars 3
draw–tongue joints (mortice & tenon)	Late–3rd century AD County Hall`	–
iron nails	230 bc±110 Holme Pierrepont I	*c* AD 1416 *Grace Dieu*
hooked nails	3rd century AD Blackfriars 1	–
nails clenched over roves	6th century AD Sutton Hoo 2	*c* AD 1416 *Grace Dieu*
Caulking		
moss	*c* 1500 bc Ferriby I	*c* AD 1416 *Grace Dieu*
hide	295bc±50 Poole	–
hair	Late 9th century AD Graveney	–
wood	3rd century AD Blackfriars 1	–
oakum	*c* AD 1416 *Grace Dieu*	–
Repair		
sewn	1100 bc±80 Appleby	–
cleat	834 bc±100 Brigg 1	–
treenailed wooden block	332 to 277 BC Hasholme	–
nailed lead sheet	230 bc±110 Holme Pierrepont I	ad 1300±120 Kentmere 1
nailed board	late 6th century AD Sutton Hoo 2	late 12 century AD Wood Quay, Dublin
Cleat and transverse timber	*c*1500 bc Ferriby I	322 to 277 BC Hasholme
Scarfs		
thorugh–splayed on edge	late 6th century AD Sutton Hoo (probably)	*c* AD 1416 *Grace Dieu*
stop–splayed on edge	late 9th century AD Graveney	–
stop–spayed on face	late 3rd century AD County Hall	–
edge–halfed	*c* 1500 bc Ferriby 1	late 9th century AD Graveney
Other joints		
interlocked	*c* 1500 bc Ferriby 1	–
edge half lap	*c* 1500 bc Ferriby 1	332 to 227 BC Hasholme
edge splayed–up	*c* 650 bc Brigg 2	ad 1300±120 Kentmere 1
butted	*c* 650 bc Brigg 2	late 3rd century AD County Hall
dovetails	1100 bc±80 Appleby[2] 846 bc±100 Short Ferry	ad 1335±40 Giggleswick Tarn
Oculi	834 bc±100 Brigg 1	332 to 277 BC Hasholme

Notes: 1. See Table 1, notes 1–4 and 6

           2. The Appleby 'dovetail' is I–shaped

           3. Further details of the boats named may be found in McGrail (1987)

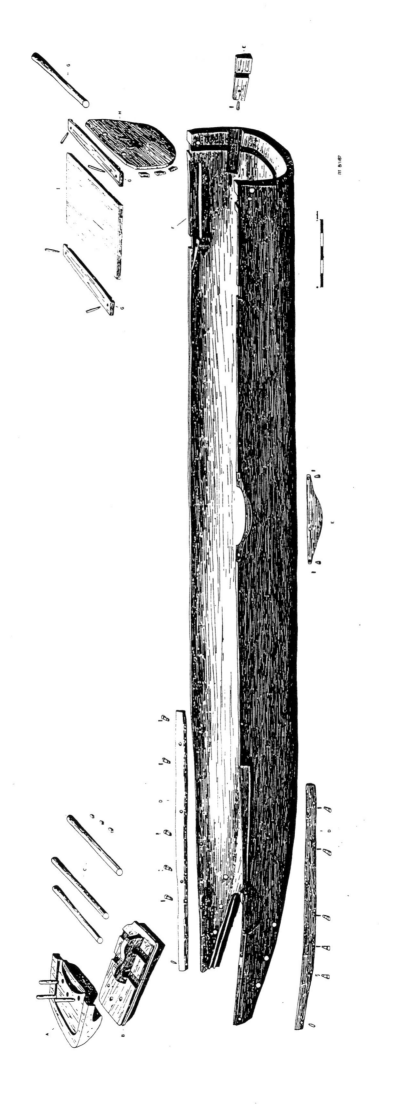

Figure 5.2.1 An 'exploded' diagram of the theoretically reconstructed Hasholme boat: A, upper bow with treenails; B, lower bow; C, transverse timbers with wedges; D, washstrakes with treenails and keys; E, repairs with treenails and keys; F, shelves for decking; G, beam ties; H, transom with wedges; I, steering platform or deck.

References

McGrail, S 1978*a*, *Logboats of England and Wales* NNM. Archaeological Series 2. BAR (Oxford), p. 51.

McGrail, S., 1978*b*, Medieval logboat from Giggleswick Tarn, Yorkshire, in Annis, P. (ed.) *Ingrid and other Studies* NNM. Monograph 36, pp. 25–46.

McGrail, S.,1978*c*, Dating ancient wooden boats in Fletcher,J. (ed) *Dendrochronology in Europe* NNM Archaeological Series 4 BAR (Oxford) S. 51, pp.239–58.

McGrail, S., 1987, *Ancient boats in N W Europe*. Longman.

McGrail, S. & Denford, G.,1982, Boatbuilding techniques, technological change and attribute analysis, in McGrail, S. (ed.) *Woodworking techniques before 1500* NNM. Archaeological Series 7. BAR (Oxford) S. 129, pp. 25–72.

McGrail, S. & Millett, M., 1985, The Hasholme logboat. *Antiquity* 59, 117–20.

McGrail, S. & Millett, M., 1986, Recovering the Hasholme logboat. *Current Archaeology* 99, 112–3.

McGrail, S. & Switsur, R., 1979, Medieval logboats of the River Mersey, in McGrail, S. (ed.) *Medieval Ships and Harbours in N Europe* NNM. Archaeological Series 5. BAR (Oxford) S. 66, pp. 93–115.

Millett, M. & McGrail, S., 1987, The archaeology of the Hasholme logboat. *Archaeological Journal* (in press).

Reprinted with permission from:

International Journal for Nautical Archaeology 16: 343–6 (1987); 17: 158 (1988).

SECTION 6.0

LOGBOATS

Introduction

Logboats (sometimes called dugout canoes) are boats built by hollowing out a single log. Nowadays such boats often have additional fittings, but, on ancient logboats, these seldom survive to be excavated (the Hasholme logboat see Paper 11.5 – is a rare exception) and archaeologists have to interpret the pattern of holes where timbers were formerly fastened to the boat.

Logboats are inherently limited in stability (a function of the beam measurement at the waterline) and in capacity by the dimensions of their parent log. These constraints may be eased by using one or more of the following techniques (McGrail, 1978: 38–55):
(i). *Extend* – add planking (washstrakes) to increase the height of the sides.
(ii). *Pair*.– join two similar hulls together, side by side.
(iii). *Expand* – after heat treatment, force out the sides of the boat.
(iv). *Outrigger/stabilisers* – add timber floats either on the end of an outrigger, or fastened to the hull at the waterline.

In general (i) increases capacity, whilst the others enhance stability. There are often difficulties in establishing whether these techniques had been used on an excavated logboat.

This Section includes a selection of papers concerning the prehistoric and medieval logboats of Britain. Two of the papers (6.3 & 6.4) are taken from my University of London thesis (published as McGrail, 1978): they deal with the naval architectural & wood science aspects of logboats, but much of the discussion in both papers is also relevant to plank boats. Naval architectural matters are also considered in Paper 10.2, in Section 11 and in McGrail (1987: Ch. 3 & 11); a detailed presentation may be found in Rawson & Tupper (1983/4). One of the appendices to Paper 6.3 is a glossary; glossaries with a wider range of terms may be found in Greenhill (1995) and in McGrail(1987). A discussion of Wood Science as applied to boats generally may be found in McGrail (1987: Ch.4). The size of early logs is mentioned in Papers 6.3 & 6.4, and also in Papers 5.1, 11.5 & 11.6.

Paper 6.1, a preliminary discussion of aspects of my thesis, was first presented at the initial meeting of the grandly-named 'International Symposia for Boat & Ship Archaeology'

(ISBSA), at Greenwich in September, 1976. This academic gathering has prospered, and triennial meetings have been held at Bremerhaven, Stockholm, Lisbon, Amsterdam, Roskilde and Tatihou. ISBSA 8 will be at Gdansk in September 1997.

Papers 6.2 & 6.5 are detailed studies of logboats which had previously been only summarily described in my thesis. The Giggleswick Tarn paper was written for a festschrift presented to David Waters, former Fleet Air Arm pilot, distinguished historian of the navigational sciences, and an outstanding mentor to National Maritime Museum curatorial staff in the 1970s. The research presented in that paper is an example of the teamwork formerly undertaken in the Archaeological Research Centre at Greenwich: the re-assembly, re-assessment and conservation of a very fragmented boat (McGrail & O'Connor, 1979). Such work ceased when the ARC was disbanded in 1985/6.

Crumlin–Pedersen (1991:261) has listed the 10th to 13th century AD Stanley Ferry boat, described in Paper 6.5, amongst logboats he considers to have been expanded. It is true that this boat was found with ribs fitted, and the other two British logboats Crumlin–Pedersen mentions – Walton & Smallburgh – have patterns of holes which suggest they may also have had ribs. Nevertheless, having fitted ribs is only one of nine criteria which Crumlin–Pedersen (1991: 254) suggests should be used when examining logboats for signs of expansion, and none of these boats fully matches these requirements. For example,all three logboats have sides and bottoms up to 60 mm thick; Crumlin–Pedersen quotes no figures, but I doubt very much whether oak logboats (even of 'green' oak) of this thickness can be successfully expanded. Furthermore, the Stanley Ferry logboat has flared sides which meet the bottom in a chine (Fig. 6.5.2) and the ribs conform to that shape: such an angular transverse section is incompatible with expansion (Crumlin–Pedersen, 1991: 254). Under the heading '(c) Fittings', Paper 6.5 lists four reasons unconnected with expansion, why logboats may be fitted with ribs; in the case of the Stanley Ferry boat, ribs were probably fitted to support crossbeams used as thwarts by passengers, a role for this boat echoed in the site name.

Logboats are also dealt with in Papers 5.1, 7.2, 8.1, 11.5 & 11.6; and in Ch 6 of McGrail (1987).

References.

Crumlin–Pedersen, O. 1991. *Badgrave og Gravbade pa Slusegard.* Slusegardgravpladsen III. Jysk Arkaeologisk Selskabs Skrifter XIV.3. Aarhus.

Greenhill, B. 1995. *Archaeology of Boats & Ships.* Conway.

McGrail, S. 1978. *Logboats of England & Wales.* BAR Oxford. 51

McGrail, S. 1987. *Ancient Boats in NW Europe.* Longman.

McGrail, S. & O'Connor, S. 1979. Giggleswick Tarn logboat. *Yorkshire Archaeological J.* 51: 41–49.

Rawson, K.J. & Tupper, E.C. 1983/4. *Basic Ship Theory.* 3rd Edition. Two volumes. Longman.

Note: The following reference contains tables of calibrated radiocarbon dates for British logboats:

Switsur, R, 1989, 'Early English Boats', *Radiocarbon*, 31: 1010–1018.

PAPER 6.1

SEARCHING FOR PATTERN AMONG THE LOGBOATS OF ENGLAND AND WALES

The requirement

The fragmented, distorted, and ephemeral nature of boat finds produces problems which, whilst not unknown in other branches of Archaeology, are presented to the boat archaeologist in an acute form. The search for pattern – the recognition and interpretation of regularities (Hodson, 1971:30) amongst this assorted jumble of evidence may thus degenerate into the formulation of hypotheses based on Inadequate foundations, and over confident attempts to equate finds with known historical types. Real progress can only be made if we stick to the scientific method, of which quantification is an essential aspect. By *quantification* I mean something more than the use of numerical methods: I mean the recording of hard fact, and the use of clearly defined, objective methods to analyse and to synthesise this evidence. In this wider sense I hope we shall see references to quantification in all the themes of this Symposium.

The general case for quantification in archaeology has been well summarised by Doran and Hodson (1975: 3–7, 93). It is especially relevant to boat archaeology where we are investigating not only the form but also the funetion and capabilities of our finds, for these latter qualities can only be fully evaluated by the quantitative methods of the naval architect. Form and function are inextricably linked in our study, and this is to our great advantage I believe, because thereby we can achieve a greater understanding of man the boatbuilder and boatuser. The use of quantification, in its broadest sense, at all stages of research should ensure that terms are defined, that reasoning is made explicit, and that assumptions, abstractions, and methods can be critically appraised by other workers who, if they are convinced by this demonstration can then have full confidence in the published results. Quantification also has the following advantages:

(i) A full, objective record of evidence is obtained which can be used by subsequent workers .
(ii) A great quantity of data can be validly summarised.
(iii) Selected information can be displayed in easily comprehended ways tables, diagrams, curves, etc.
(iv) Numerical methods, and computational aids, can be used on the data to investigate hypotheses rigorously.

By advocating the use of numerical methods I do not mean that all archaeologists must necessarily understand the finer points of mathematical theory, but I do believe that they must become aware of the capabilities and limitations of these procedures, and thus use them wisely. An understanding of the use of confidence limits applied to radiocarbon dates is already common place among archaeologists, and indeed, as Spaulding has observed (1971: 15), all archaeologists use implicit mathematical reasoning even though they may be unaware of the fact; what is now required is that this reasoning be extended and made explicit.

Nor does my advocacy of these methods imply that I have no confidenee in the work of those who have the apparently intuitive ability to compare and classify artifacts, a facility which is often the fruit of long years of experience. But I believe that the onus is upon them to demonstrate the reasoning behind this ability, and to define their terms, so that others can follow. Authority is not enough; the man with vision must demonstrate by quantification .

An example of the use of quantitative methods

a) *The Survey*. I will illustrate some methods of quantification by describing aspects of my recent study of the logboats of England and Wales.Here I will not mention the several false starts I made, but I will simply describe the method I finally decided was the best, and ask you to evaluate it against my definition – or your own definition – of quantitative procedures.

During the three years of this investigation, there were no new logboat finds in England and Wales, and so the research was partly based on other people' s data, although in a surprisingly large number of cases I recorded for the first time by measured drawing, logboats which had been excavated up to 50 years ago. My first step was to trace all documentary evidence for the finds, whether published or otherwise, in learned journal, daily newspaper or on museum record cards. Particular emphasis was placed on tracing the earliest drawing or table of measurements, and on establishing evidence from which to judge whether the logboat had been recorded before or after significant shrinkage had taken place. When duplicates had been eliminated I had records of 172 unexpanded logboats. The evidence for each one was summarised on a standard Basic Data record form from which I was able to formulate questions to be answered during my survey of those 67 logboats which survive in various stages of degredation.

Outwitting those few museum curators whose aim seemed to be to keep their logboats hidden, preferably filled with other artifacts, I measured or remeasured 61 of these 67: the other six being inaccessible. The present state of those I measured was compared with their earliest recorded state , and these details were noted on a second standard form, on which were also recorded the features and fittings still detectable, and the characteristics of the parent tree – species, position of pith,

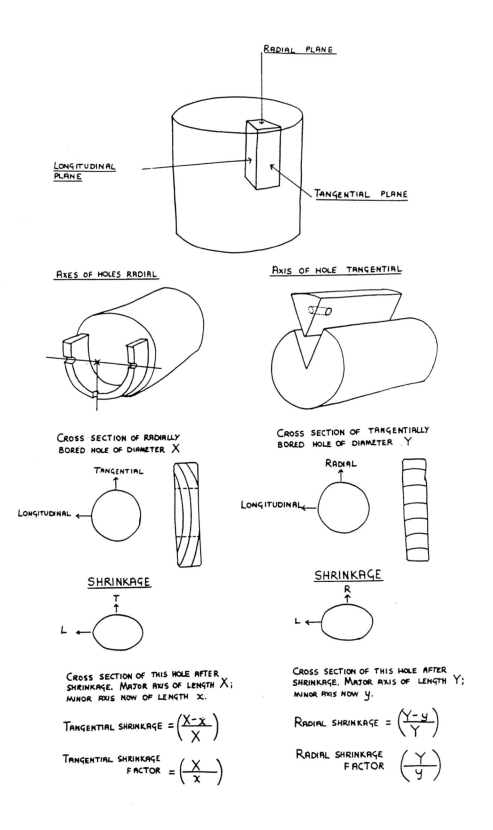

Figure 6.1.1 The calculation of tangential and radial shrinking factors. National Maritime Museum

orientation of butt–details which had seldom been recorded previously. I also attempted to trace any conservation treatment from museum records – but, in general, logboats are badly catalogued, and conservation records are almost non existent.

A fair drawing at 1:10 scale was then compiled, based on the earliest reliable drawing; to it were added, where applicable, features identified during the survey but which had not previously been recorded. At this stage I considered I had assembled the objective data.

b) *Interpretation*. An attempt was then made to interpret features such as ridges, holes, and so on, using evidence from the Continent and Ireland where logboats which are more nearly complete have been excavated, and using ethnographic parallels where these were valid. In the event, several features remained unidentified. The next and crucial step was to estimate how much each boat had shrunk between the time it was in use and the time it was first reliably recorded. A mean shrinkage ratio was calculated from two sets of measurements, for those finds where these could validly be made:

(i) The first method was by comparing the lengths of the major and minor axes of the now elliptical cross section of holes in the logboats. It was assumed that the holes were circular when bored, and thus this com parison would be a measure of shrinkage. Wood shrinks differentially, the relative measurements for oak (*Quercus* Sp.) being approximately 1 in the longitudinal plane, 12 in the radial plane, and 25 in the tangential plane. Longitudinal shrinkage is relatively insignificant, whilst tangential shrinkage is approximately twice radial shrinkage. This differential shrinkage over a period of time thus distorts a round hole into an elliptical one (Fig 6.1.1).The vast majority of holes measured had been bored radially into the log and thus had one axis of their cross section in the longitudinal plane of the parent tree and one in the tangential plane. The longitudinal axis of the cross section of the hole experiences negligible shrinkage and thus remains very close to the original diameter of the hole when bored. However, the timber shrinks significantly along the other axis and thus the ratio of major to minor axis is a measure of tangential shrinkage. Two boats in the survey (Kentmere and Llandrindod Wells) have radially split planking associated, and the ratio of major to minor axis of holes in these planks is a measure of radial shrinkage. Oak (*Quercus* Sp.) dried from the green state to a moisture content of 12%, shrinks c. 7.5% tangential and 4% radially, (Farmer, 1972:147). However when waterlogged wood is allowed to dry, it shrinks significantly more than this, the amount evidently being dependent on the degree of waterlogging, and on the degree of drying allowed to take place. Locally this shrinkage may also be effected by the run of the grain, the orientation of the hole, the presence or absence and the orientation of a treenail in the hole, and the timber species of both

treenail and logboat. Thus the ratio major/minor axis of the cross section of bored holes varies not only from logboat to logboat but also between holes in the same boat, (but only in four boats was this range significantly great). The mean tangential shrinkage ratio for 123 holes measured in 31 log boats was 1.27, This is equivalent to (.27/1.27) = 21% shrinkage. The radial shrinkage ratio based on only 2 boats was 1. 09 = 8% shrinkage. These values are comparable with measurements made on the timber from the WASA where the tangential shrinkage was calculated, by methods unspecified, to be 16% to 24%, and the radial 8% to 12% (Barkman, 1975:68).

(ii) The second method of estimating shrinkage was by comparing corresponding dimensions recorded at widely separated times, preferably the scantlings near the time of excavation compared with equivalent measurements taken in 1972/5. Akerlund (1963, 155) used a somewhat similar method during his re–examination of the Nydam boat when he compared Engelhardt's 1863 measurements of the "circumference of the planking amidships" with Johannessen' s 1929 measurements, and estimated the shrinkage between these two dates to be 9%. As the Nydam boat had been excavated for 4 months before Engelhardt took his measurements, Akerlund concluded that 13% to 14% would be a reasonable estimate of Nydam' s tangential (?) shrinkage between excavation and 1929. When this comparison method is applied to logboats the principal difficulty is to ensure that the corresponding measurements are taken at exactly the same part of the structure. An additional difficulty is that although many logboats have shrunk uniformly, maintaining a similar shape but of reduced dimensions, some have split along the bottom allowing the sides to open out, whilst others have reacted to the stresses of shrinkage by forcing the sides closer together at the sheer. In these abberant cases comparison of depths and of sheer breadths are invalid; but where the bottom is sound, comparison of breadths across the bottom may be made. A logboat' s overall shrinkage pattern can be complex, and it is sometimes difficult to decide whether a particular comparison ratio is a measure of tangential or radial shrinkage or an intermediate figure. Nevertheless, both in individual cases and as an overall mean, these estimates of shrinkage based on scantling comparisons, generally supported tne estimates based on elliptical hole measurements. Seventy–five main scantlings comparison gave a mean tangential shrinkage ratio of 1. 22.

c) *Hypothetical Reconstruction*. The logboats selected for hypothetical reconstruction were those for which the evidence reached a minimum standard, deflned as:

(i) full length recorded
(ii) original sheer line recorded over a significant length
(iii) representative transverse sections recorded.

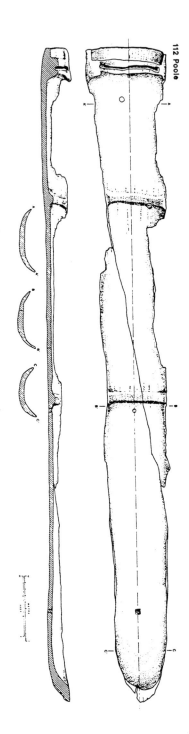

Figure 6.1.2 The remains of the Poole logboat recorded in August 1974. National Maritime Museum

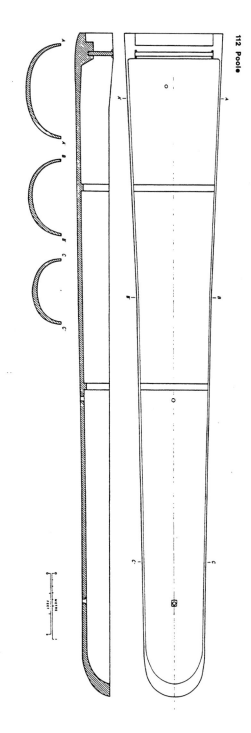

Figure 6.1.3 The hypothetical reconstruction of the Poole logboat, after an allowance has been made for shrinkage. National Maritime Museum

These are strict criteria, and only 24 boats reached this standard. The criteria are so rigorous that although there may be variant fittings, reconstruction of the hull is limited to one possibility for each find, whereas in general a unique solution to the problem of deciding the full form of a fragmented find is unattainable, and multiple hypotheses are to be expected (McGrail, 1976:25). Relaxation of these criteria could result in two or more equally plausible hypothetical reconstructions which could have significantly different hydrodynamic characteristics.

The evidence for each of the 24 logboats chosen for reconstruction was assessed to determine whether the definitive drawing was pre or post shrinkage. The original recorded measurements were used for 13 boats which were deduced to have been recorded before there was any significant shrinkage. But where the drawing was assessed as post shrinkage, a shrinkage factor was used to restore the logboat to its original size: seven boats were reconstructed using their individual shrinkage factor calculated from elliptical hole measurements; shrinkage factors calculated from comparisons of scantlings were used for two, where there were no holes to be measured; and the overall mean shrinkage factor was used to reconstruct two others for which no individual estimate could be made. In these calculations both tangential and radial factors were used as appropriate to the particular form of the logboat and its relationship to its parent tree. The general effect of using these factors to compensate for shrinkage is that, whilst the length of the boat remains substantially the same, the breadth and depth become 10% to 20% greater (Figs 6.1.2 and 6.1.3). This effect has also been noted by Ellmers (1973:33).

d) *Parameters*. Given that the reconstructed logboat is an accurate representation of the original – and this depends on the sequence of recording and interpretation described above – there are still a number of critical parameters which have to be given a value before estimates of capacity and performance can be attempted. The reasoning behind my choice of specific value will be given in the full publication of the research; in this present paper I list them to make my assumptions explicit and so that they may possibly provoke discussion.

(i) The specific density of wood was taken to be that equivalent to 25% moisture content. Thus oak (*Quercus* Sp.) weighs 800 kg/m³ and ash (Fraxinus Sp.) 700 kg/m³.

(ii) The average crewmember was taken to weight 60 kg (short and lean), and to have his centre of gravity at 1.1 m when standing, at .45 m when kneeling, and at .4 m when sitting. A case can in fact be made for the centre of gravity being at the point of pivot i.e. feet, knees, or backside; the values used in my calculations are therefore a worst case, and calculated metacentric heights may thus be pessimistic ones.

(iii) Cargo was chosen to give a range of density: stone at 2500 kg/m³, corn at 680 kg/m³, and turf or peat at 435 kg/m³. It was assumed that 80% of the hollowed-out volume of the logboat was available for cargo, and that the load could extend above the sheerline where stability considerations allowed this.

(iv) Logboats carrying cargo were generally given a crew of one man, standing so that he could pole and also to give the worst stability condition. But the four longest ones (>8.5 m) were given more crew as they obviously required two or more men to manoeuvre them successfully.

(v) Freeboard requirements were taken to be:

Standard = .15 m

Minimum = that at which the sheer would be awash at 10° heel.

(vi) It was assumed that logboats would not be used with a negative transverse metacentric height (GM), but that the bare minimum of a positive m (.001 m) would be acceptable. (GM is a measure of initial stability see fig. 16.5 in the paper by Coates in this volume).

e) *Calculations*. After three of these reconstructed boats had been analysed by hand computation and a limited array of hydrostatic curves plotted, this laborious task was kindly undertaken by Dr. Ewan Corlett, and Mr. Jones and Mr Hamilton-Smith of Burness, Corlett and Partners, produced definitive hydrostatic curves using a programmable desk calculator (Fig. 6.1.4)

From the survey information and from the hydrostatics it was then possible to analyse each of the 24 reconstructed logboats as a log, as a boat, and as a load carrier. The following information could then be tabulated for each one.

(i) The diameter, girth and the volume of the parent log (minimum size).

(ii) The scantlings, the volume and weight of timber, and the volume of the " hollow" of the reconstructed logboat.

(iii) The results of load/draft/stability calculations at four standard states:

> a. carrying the maximum number of men
> b. draft restricted to .3 m, and carrying men and some high density cargo.
> c. standard draft, equivalent to .15 m free board, carrying loads of varying density.
> d. maximum draft, equivalent to minimum density freeboard, carrying loads of varying density.

(iv) Coefficients which attempted to evaluate the conversion of the parent log into a boat: log conversion; load

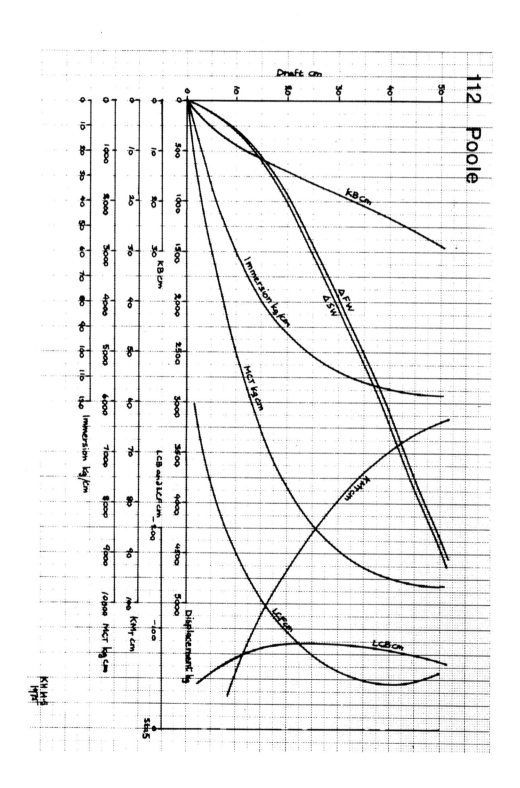

Figure 6.1.4 The hydrostatic curves for the Poole logboat reconstruction, compiled by Burness, Corlett and Partners. National Maritime Museum

space. A coefficient which measured the ability of the logboat to carry loads in the restricted draft state. Five coefficients devised to measure the ability of the logboat to carry a range of cargo at standard draft in a stable condition – that is, with a positive metacentric height. One coefficient to be representative of the logboat's ability to carry cargo at maximum draft. Three coefficients to measure the logboat's ability to carry men. Ten naval architectural coefficients: block (Cm); prismatic (Cp); volumetric (Cv); waterplane (Cwp); slenderness; symmetry; position of maximum beam; draft/length of waterline; maximum beam/draft. These 22 coefficients will be defined, and the reasons for choosing them will be given, when the full research is published. Some in fact, proved to be redundant, and these will not be used in future surveys.

The naval architectural coefficients are well known and can be interpreted, in so far as they apply to a logboat form: some permit estimates of propulsion effort to be made. The other coefficients are experimental and they can only be interpreted in relation to the 24 boats analysed. Thus we may say that, on the evidence of one of these coefficients (Table 6.1.1, column 2), the Brigg logboat was very good at carrying high density loads when compared with the other 23 boats, and twice as good as the Banks logboat (per unit volume of log); but we do not yet know how Brigg compares with the general capabilities of prehistoric and medieval logboats. A greater number of logboats than the 172 in this survey must be investigated before we can obtain a sample which could be more representative of the original logboat population – a more objective functional classification may then result.

The results I obtained are obviously dependent on the values assigned to the parameters and, although the effect of varying some of them was calculated for two or three logboats, no systematic sensitivity analysis was undertaken due to the relatively great computational effort required. Neither large angle nor dynamical stability were investigated, only initial stability, as without this latter characteristic the other measures of stability are irrelevant. Transverse initial stability was investigated in detail for each boat, and sufficient longitudinal initial stability calculations were undertaken to show that in general these 24 boats would be trimmed by the stern which in many cases would bring the sheerline approximately horizontal. The initial stability requirement in the transverse plane was sufficiently stringent in fact to modify the apparent carrying ability of the 24 logboats, in one way or another. Thus, when the three ratios in Table 6.1.1 were calculated for each boat, significant differences in performance became apparent, and these suggest the provisional functional classification shown in Table 6.1.2.

The three unplaced boats in Table 2 had relatively poor performance in all three roles; high density cargo, bulky loads, and men. My hypothetical reconstruction of the Giggleswick Tarn logboat was principally based on measurements recorded at about the time of discovery (O'Callaghan, 1864). The major part of this ash (*Fraxinus* Sp.) boat has fortunately survived, albeit in 196 separate fragments, which are undergoing conservation treatment here at Greenwich. After conservation it is hoped that it can be reassembled and reliable estimates made of its original size and form. Provisional shrinkage

calculations indicate that its beam should be *c.* .7 m rather than the 2 ft. (.61 m) given in the 1864 record and used in my hypothetical reconstruction. A beam of this order would give a more stable logboat, and future work may show Giggleswick Tarn to have been a more useful boat than it appears to be from my calculations based on the 19th century record.

Giggleswick Tarn logboat (Fig. 6.1.5) is unusual because it is fitted at sheer level with external longitudinal timbers. These were called "auxiliary gunwales" for "heightening the sides" by Sheppard (1910:42), leading subsequent authors to describe them as washstrakes; it is more probable that they are stabilisers. The hydrostatic properties of this boat were investigated both with and without these stabilisers. They improve the transverse initial stability at the deep drafts where they are immersed, and this effect is more marked when the stabilisers are aligned with the longer axis of their cross section horizontal rather than vertical. This is as one would expect, the water plane area, and especially the beam, being increased more quickly with very little change in displacement (see, for example, Rawson and Tupper, 1976:97). It is probable that these fittings would also have a beneficial effect at light draft when subjected to heel, as large angle stability would be increased as the stabilisers entered the water. Constructionally, these timbers must have given longitudinal strength to the boat at sheer level (See Paper 6.2)

It is also possible that the two Preston boats have been hypothetically reconstructed incorrectly. There is not one clear, unambiguous, early account or drawing of either of them, and a composite solution, not using a shrinkage factor, was used as a basis for the hydrostatic curves and my subsequent calculations. The resulting poor theoretical performance may indicate that the composite solutions were unsoundly based, and that the logboats had in fact been recorded post shrinkage. If the recorded scantlings were to be modified by the general mean shrinkage factor of 1.27, the resulting hypothetical reconstructions might be more useful and possibly more authentic. This work remains to be done.

f) *The results of the investigation.* After this sequence of recording, interpretation and reconstruction, and calculation, it became possible to compile a standard inventory entry for each of the 24 boats. This consisted of details of the logboat's history and its conservation; the earliest reliable measured drawing; a description of the boat, its features, and its parent log; an estimate of the logboat's shrinkage; an interpretation of some of its features; a hypothetical reconstruction drawing, and a coded description of its shape; specification of its carrying ability in four defined states; tabulation of 22 coefficients; and a general description of the logboat's probable use and performance. Inventory entries were also compiled for the remaining 148 boats in the survey in as much detail as the evidence warranted.

g) *Conclusions derived from the Logboat Survey.*

(i) Quantification is essential if worthwhile results, ones that can be sustained on rational grounds, are to be obtained. The methods, the selection of data, the parameters, the supporting evidence, and the

Table 6.1.1 Coefficient measuring ability to carry various types of load at standard draft, in a stable condition

Logboats	Ability to carry high density cargo measured by: Deadweight/Volume of log	Ability to carry bulky cargo measured by: Volume of cargo/Volume of log	Ability to carry men measured by: No of crew members/Volume of log
Baddiley Mere	184	.308	.960
Banks	147	.440	1.198
Barton	119	.183	.542
Blae Tarn	40	1.429	.420
Brigg	282	.356	.738
Clifton 1	75	.251	.933
Clifton 2	89	.331	.955
Ellesmere	113	.169	.273
Giggleswick Tarn	95*	.059*	zero
Gastonbury 1	96	.181	.401
Hardham 1	88	.329	1.228
Hardham 2	103	.293	.976
Hulton Abbey	112	.469	.754
Hylton 2	168	.274	1.395
Irlam	35	.578	.878
Kew	229	.212	.363
Llyn Llangrose	73	.191	.559
Oakmere	42	.978	1.042
Poole	101	.675	1.074
Preston 1	60*	zero	zero
Preston 2	60	.093	.297
Thornaby	111	.238	.351
Walton	163	.320	1.026
Warrington 2	63	.462	1.410

* = Crewman cannot stand, but sits at sheer level so that the logboat may remain stable

Notes   1. When displacement was used instead of Volume of Log in the denominator of these three ratios, generally similar sequences of relative ability were obtained
2. The first and third ratios can be made dimesionless by multiplication by a constant factor

discussion are then clearly exposed for others to criticise.

(ii) To facilitate co–operation between research workers in this field and to avoid duplication of effort, future logboat finds should be recorded and analysed to agreed standards, and the data made available to all. A standard terminology is an essential prerequisite.

(iii) All feasible attributes/characteristics/features should be recorded even though some may not seem immediately relevant to current problems; subsequent workers will thus be able to use this information should the logboat not survive or should it only survive in a degraded state. It may be thought impossible to record everything, but Doran and Hodson are surely correct when they state (1975:101) that this problem can be solved by a clear definition of the term attribute, by eliminating redundant attributes, and by the use of common sense in not going out of the way to seek obscurity.

(iv) Current research methods including quantification can usefully be applied to old finds, providing the drawings and other documentation are critically assessed and compared with any surviving remains. Certain earlier archaeologists were not rigorous in their methods of recording; there are, for example, drawings of logboats which include elements of reconstruction without this being stated (McGrail, 1976:25).

(v) At present the number of logboats investigated by rigorous methods is small, and therefore the results of these investigations are necessarily relative and tentative.

(vi) Nevertheless even this small sample generates much data, there are many repetitive caleulations to be done, and it would also be desirable to investigate the effects of varying the several parameters used in the caleulations. There is thus a requirement for aids to computation.

(vii) Classification as attempted by Fox (1926), Graham (1966), and others based solely on morphology is inadequate. In a recent important publication Ellmers (1973), inter alia, attempts to define five logboat types differentiated primarily by the form of their transverse sections, and secondly by the shape of the ends, (Ellmers, 1973:35–40). This is of limited value, especially as it is based on a small sample of finds, and three of the types, (b), (d) and (e) appear to have only one member. Ellmers does discuss the function of some of the boats and gives estimates of their deadweight tonnage, but his methods of calculation are not given, and it is not clear whether he took stability into account although he does refer (1973:24) to some work on this by Timmermann (1956, 1957/8). Quantification could help Ellmers to make his case much more forcibly.

Table 6.1.2 Provisional functional classification of 24 logboats

All–round performance, 1st rate (relatively good in all three roles: men, bulky loads, high density cargo)	Banks, Hylton 2, Poole, Walton
High density cargo carriers, 1st rate	Baddiley Mere, Brigg, Kew
High density cargo carriers, 2nd rate	Barton, Ellesmere, Glastonbury 1, Thornaby
Personnel carriers, 1st rate	Clifton 1, Clifton 2, Hardham 1, Hardham 2
Personnel carriers, 2nd rate	Llyn Llangorse
Bulky cargo carriers, 1st rate	Blae Tarn, Hulton Abbey, Irlam
Bulky cargo and personell carriers, 1st rate	Oakmere, Warrington 2
Unplaced (relatively poor in all three roles)	Giggleswick Tarn, Preston 1, Preston 2

Notes   None of the 24 logboats analysed had anything reliably associated with it which might have helped to determine its specific use. Nor did the types of site at which they were found suggest any differentiation of function.

Estimates of performance, such as the ability to carry various loads, can be used to compare and contrast logboats and thus assign probable functions to them. Provenance, date, associated material, the techniques of building and repair, and the additional fittings incorporated in each boat should also be recorded. Only when this range of data is available from a large sample of logboats can comprehensive classification schemes be attempted. A dating programme is an essential complementary investigation, (McGrail and Switsur, 1975). (viii) Ethnographic accounts of logboats are generally unsatisfactory. There are notable exceptions, but in general they tend to concentrate on form; where building methods are described there is undue prominence given to methods of expansion. Notes and Queries on Anthropology prepared by a Committee of the Royal Anthropological Institute, has a section dealing with travel and transport by water (6th edition, 1971:300–8) which enumerates what should be recorded. There is good advice here, but one would wish to see more emphasis placed on recording the detatls of construction, on elucidating the function of the features described, and on describing operational techniques such as any specialisation of use, freeboard requirements and loading strategies, apparent stability etc. The aim should be to record the boat ashore and in use in sufficient detail to enable draft, load, and stability caleulations to be made for operational states actually used.

More general application of these conslusions

If we extend these conclusions, especially (vi), from the logboat survey to a consideration of plank boats, we can appreciate more clearly the magnitude of our problems in boat archaeology. Compared with a simple logboat, each plank boat find will, in general, have more attributes (I used 90 attributes in my logboat survey), and will thus generate more data; there will be more caleulations to undertake and more parameters to vary; probably there will be several equally plausible hypothetical reconstructions; and the complexities of sail will need to be investigated. Aids to computation and power assisted data storage systems may be desirable when investigating 24 logboats; when investigating plank boats (probably in far greater numbers) these aids are essential, and only electronic computers have the necessary accuracy, capacity and speed. With these aids the following tasks can be achieved:

a) A data bank can be constituted, in which the data can be rapidly updated, and retrieved on demand. Some forms of graphical input and output are possible, in addition to numerical ones.

b) The data can be sorted and analysed systematically; statistical analyses can be carried out, and selected data can be printed out in a variety of formats

c) Repetitive caleulations can be done rapidly and accurately, and the effects of varying the parameters can be investigated.

d) Variant forms of hypothetical reconstructions can be investigated and a series of calculations and simulations undertaken – possibly in conjunetion with tank testing of small scale models.

e) Seriation, and classification by objective pattern recognition techniques can be attempted, where there are too many variables for these to be done by other means. Discussion of the application of these techniques to archaeological problems, may be found in Hodson, Kendall and Tautu (1971), Doran and Hodson (1975), and in the proceedings of the annual conference at the Computer Centre, University of Birmingham (Anon, 1974–1976).

Figure 6.1.5 The Giggleswick Tarn temporarily reassembled, with one of the longitudinal timbers in the foreground. National Maritime Museum

It may be appropriate to emphasise at this point that detailed classification of plank boats is as premature as that of logboats, if not more so. The data base of adequately recorded finds is too small to justify anything but the most tentative and limited classification (McGrail 1976:27). As well as requiring a large sample of finds, future classification studies should be based on an array of attributes and not on a single characteristic. Concepts such as *Shell* and *Skeleton* build (Hasslof, 1963), and the recently published *Edge—joined* and *Non—edged joined* classifications (Greenhill, 1976:60–88) are invaluable: they clarify some previously muddled ideas, and enable us to recognize distinctive approaches to boatbuilding. But they are two amongst many, and although they may be very significant characteristics, their full diagnostic value will only be revealed when we have comprehensive records.

If we are to make full use of quantitative methods we must aim at recording and analysing boat finds in such a way that we can recognise clusterings of attributes which identify:

(a) functional types e.g. the coastal trader, the river boat, the ferry, the raider, the ocean voyager, the high density cargo carrier (these are not mutually exclusive).

(b) widespread traditions, e.g. "Viking" or "Celtic" – if such existed.

(c) particular "boatyards" – what Crumlin–Pedersen calls " a certain local practice at a given time and place".

And we should look for those connected series which show progression from one set of attributes to another, orderings which may help to trace the development of the planked boat through time and space. I submit that these aims can only be attained by classification studies based upon many attributes.

A plan future for the future

I propose the following action:

a. The compilation of a provisional list of attributes to be tested internationally on a variety of boat finds, and on modern wooden boats.

b. All future boat finds to be quantitatively recorded to an agreed standard, using an agreed list of attributes.

c. Old boat finds to be critically re–examined and, where necessary, re–recorded to the agreed standards.

d. Documentary, iconographic, and ethnographic evidence to be similarly treated, as far as the methods are applicable.

e. The data from a, b, c, and d to be published in a standardised form and also to be stored in a computer data bank. This data bank would be the basis for all future studies, possibly by the methods outlined in Part 3 of this paper.

Doran and Hodson (1975:319–20) have enumerated objections to the idea of a data bank in archaeology; especially significant, and one with much support, is that voiced by those who prefer the idea of an individual scholar collecting and recording his own data, analysing and synthesising this data, and storing the information in his own files, for publication in the manner he considers appropriate, at the time he determines. A data bank, on the other hand, would hold pooled data which would be accessible to all. This may be an innovation but I suggest that therein lles the only way to real progress in boat archaeology; the only way we can handle and investigate in a systematic manner the inereasing quantity of data. There are many practical problems (Doran and Hodson, 1975:320–22; Scholtz and Chenhall, 1976) but these are not insoluble. Universal archaeological data banks may never be practicable, but there is general agreement (Scholtz and Chenhall, 1976:94–5; Doran and Hodson, 1975:326–7) that data banks can be successful when they are planned for a specific limited purpose. The specialised and well defined topic of boat archaeology is, I suggest, a suitable subject for a data bank

Acknowledgement

I wish to thank Professor F R. Hodson, Professor K. G. Rawson, and Professor D. M. Wilson who kindly read and commented on an earlier draft of this paper.

References

Anon,, 1971, *Notes and Queries on Anthropology*, 6th edition, prepared by a Committee of the Royal Anthropological Institute, London.

Anon., 1974–6, *Computer Applications in Archaeology*, University of Birmingham.

Åkerlund, H., 1963, *Nvdamskeppen*, Göteborg.

Barkman, L., 1975, 'Preservation of the warship Wasa' in Oddy, W. A., (ed), *Problems in the Conservation of Waterlogged Wood*: 65–105, Greenwich, N. M. M. M. + R. No. 16.

Doran, J. E., and Hodson, F. R., 1975, *Mathematics and Computers in Archaeology*, Edinburgh.

Ellmers, D., 1973, "Kultbarken, Fähren Fischerboote Vorgeschichtliche Einbäume in Niedersachsen". *Die Kunde*, N. S. 24: 23–62.

Farmer, R. H., 1972, *Handbook of Hardwoods*, H.M.S.O., London.

Fox, C., 1926, "Dugout canoe from South Wales with notes on chronology, typology, and distribution of monoxylous craft in England and Wales", *Antiquaries Journal*, 6:121–151.

Graham, J. M., 1966, *Dugout Canoes of the British Isles*. Unpublished dissertation for the degree B,A., University College, Cardiff.

Greenhill, B, 1976, *Archaeology of the Boat*, London.

Hasslöf, O., 1963, "Wrecks, Archives and Living Tradition" *Mariner's Mirror* 49: 162–177.

Hodson, F. R., 1971, "Numerical typology and prehistoric archaeology" in Hodson, F. R., Kendall, D G., and Tautu, P (ed) 1971:30–45

Hodson, F. R., Kendall, D. G., and Tautu, P., 1971 (ed) *Mathematics in the Archaeological and Historical Sciences*, Edinburgh.

McGrail, S., 1976, "Problems in Irish Nautical Archaeology", *Irish Archaeological Research Forum*, 3(i):21–31.

McGrail, S., and Switsur, R., 1975, "Early British boats and their chronology" *International Journal of Nautical Archaeology*, 4:191–200.

O'Callaghan, X., 1864, "On an ancient canoe discovered at Giggleswick" *Journal of the British Archaeological Association*, 20:195–6.

Rawson, K. J., and Tupper, E. C., 1976, *Basic Ship Theory*, 2 volumes, London.

Scholtz, S., and Chenhall, R. G., "Archaeological data banks in theory and practice", *American Antiquity*, 41 :89–96.

Sheppard, T, 1910, 'Prehistoric boat from Brigg', *Transactions of the East Riding Antiquarian Society*, 17:33–60.

Spaulding, A. C., 1971, "Some elements of quantitative archaeology" in Hodson, F. R, *et.al.* (ed) 1971:3–16.

Timmermatm, G., 1956, "Vom Einbaum zum Wikingerschifft" *Schiff und Hafen* 8: 130–8.

Timmermatm, G., 1957/8, "Zur Typologie der Einbaume", *Offa*, 16: 109–112.

Reprinted from:

McGrail, S (ed) *Sources and Techniques in Boat Archaeology*: 115–135. British Archaeological Reports. S29 (1977).

PAPER 6.2

A MEDIEVAL LOGBOAT FROM GIGGLESWICK TARN, YORKSHIRE

Introduction

T Tindall Wildridge, writing in 1888, some 25 years after the Giggleswick Tarn logboat had been found, described a drawing of the boat and commented: '.... it is here presented to show how great are the difficulties in judging the original appearance of these vessels, and especially how great they will be in the future, when time's relentless tooth has further gnawed the relics'. (Wildridge, 1888:134). This present paper, written after 90 years of 'time's relentless tooth', is an attempt to tackle the difficulties described by Wildridge. It attempts to establish from the surviving fragmentary remains (Fig 6.2.1), and from the meagre 19th–century records, the most probable original form of the boat, and hence deduce its performance. Some of the techniques used to build the boat, and the possible function of the fittings are also discussed.

David Waters has long been a distinguished practitioner of the art of applying scientific methods to historical problems. This paper is offered in gratitude to him for his encouragement and guidance during the past six years.

Figure 6.2.1 The Giggleswick Tarn logboat in fragments in 1974

Figure 6.2.2 The Giggleswick Tarn boat in 1883, supported by an internal framework of modern timber. Leeds City Museum

Giggleswick One-tree Boat, shewing its present condition, August, 1888.

Figure 6.2.3 A sketch of the boat by the Secretary of the Leeds Philosophical Society. Leeds City Museum

History of the find

This logboat was found by Joseph Taylor on the 25 May 1863, whilst he was draining a field on land which had formerly been Giggleswick Tarn, in Craven, Yorkshire (NGR: SD 8073 6459). The tarn or lake had itself been drained in the early 19th-century. The boat was at first thought to be a mere log and was damaged during its extraction (O'Callaghan, 1864: 196); subsequently it shrank and split as it was allowed to dry out (Brayshaw, 1887: 10). The landowner, William Hartley, gave the boat to the Leeds Philosophical and Literary Society, who displayed it for a time on top of one of their ethnological cases (O'Callaghan,1864:195). This Society transferred its collection to the City of Leeds in 1921, to form the basis of the present Leeds City Museum.

O'Callaghan (1864) and Brayshaw (1887) both recorded the main dimensions of the boat, but neither published a measured drawing. O'Callaghan (1864:195) did, however, publish an amateurish sketch of the boat, and Brayshaw (1887:11) published a photograph (Fig 6.2.2), taken in 1883. Wildridge (1888:132-4) quoted Brayshaw's description of the Giggleswick Tarn boat, and added a comment from the Secretary of the Leeds Philosophical Society that, at that time, one of the fittings was lying loose in the bottom of the boat, another had been fastened on by modern nails, and a wooden framework had been inserted to hold the boat together. Wildridge re-published Brayshaw's photograph of 1883, together with a sketch of the boat dated August 1888 (Fig 6.2.3).

The boat became known to a wider audience when Sheppard (1910:42) mentioned it in his publication on the Brigg logboat, then in Hull Museum. Sheppard's particular interest in the Giggleswick boat was that it had what he called 'auxiliary gunwales' for 'heightening the sides': this description led subsequent authors to claim that this logboat had been fitted with washstrakes, making it unique among British logboats. Neither Sheppard nor later authors appear to have inspected the remains.

In February 1974, during my survey of the logboats of England and Wales (McGrail, 1977), I examined this logboat in the reserve collection of Leeds City Museum. The boat was then in a large packing case in innumerable fragments, some of them wrapped in the *News Chronicle* for 1st May 1940. The internal structure of the timber had become degraded as it dried over the years from its waterlogged state, and it was evident that at some stage, external conservation with a sticky tarry substance had been attempted. The remains proved of sufficient interest to warrant further study, and Miss Elizabeth Pirie, Keeper of Archaeology at the Leeds City Museum kindly agreed to this. Subsequently the boat was loaned to the National Maritime Museum for conservation, re-assembly, and further research: its temporary acquisition number is ARC 1974/6L.

The first stage of research in 1974-6

The 45 major, and the many minor, fragments of this boat were temporarily re-assembled at Greenwich for examination, and a measured drawing was compiled in 1975, 112 years after the boat had been found. Using the methods outlined in McGrail(1977:117-131), and discussed in detail in McGrail(1978B),a standard catalogue description of the boat was compiled; a hypothetical reconstruction of the boat was drawn; and stability/displacement/weight calculations made in an attempt to deduce what the boat could have carried and what her performance would have been in several standard conditions of load and draft. Some of these methods are experimental when applied to logboats, and until they are applied to a larger body of data than has been attempted to date, the deductions made are necessarily tentative, and assessments of loads, stability and speeds are measures of relative performance. These procedures have, so far, been applied to only 24 logboats from England and Wales; as the data base is enlarged and as analytical techniques are improved, we may converge towards an assessment of each boat's absolute performance.

In making a hypothetical reconstruction of a logboat find not recently excavated, the basic problems are to identify the earliest reliable measured drawing, and to determine whether that drawing was compiled before or after shrinkage. Shrinkage of waterlogged wood during drying can be considerable: although the length of a logboat remains approximately constant, the depth and breadth can be 10% to 25% less after drying out than when in use (McGrail, 1978B: Ch.7). The earliest measured drawing of the Giggleswick boat was not compiled until 1975, and thus was post shrinkage. However, this drawing could only be provisional as the precise form of the boat could not be established until the fragments had been fitted together permanently. In my assessment of this boat (1978B: catalogue entry No. 49), I therefore concluded that a tentative reconstruction could be based on the measurements recorded by O'Callaghan (1864), which were the earliest available, and on the general form and the features revealed by my examination in 1975-6. The provisional loading and stability calculations based on this reconstruction, showed the boat to have a poor performance, mainly because of inadequate transverse stability. When indices, intended to measure this reconstructed boat's performance, were compared with those from the other 23 logboats, without exception they proved to be amongst the worst. It was clear that a more accurate assessment of this logboat would have to wait until the fragmented remains could be precisely re-assembled.

Research in 1977

Conservation and re-assembly

The catalogue of English and Welsh logboats was finalised on 1st September 1976, and it was not until after that date that it proved possible to clean and stabilise the individual fragments of the boat and then to re-assemble them this task being principally undertaken by Sonia O'Connor of the Museum's Archaeological Research Centre. Although most of the

Figure 6.2.4 The fragmented boat re–assembled in 1977

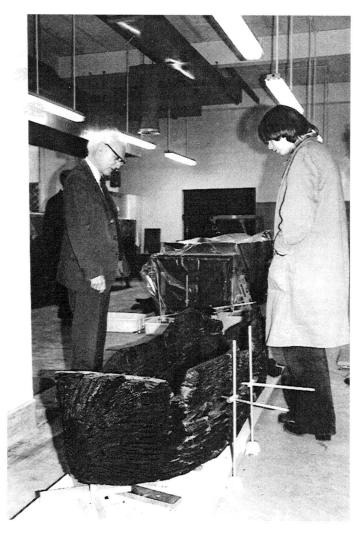

Figure 6.2.5 David Waters and Sonia O'Connor examining the logboat

fragments could be re-assembled, leaving but few gaps in the boat (Figs. 6.2.4 and 6.2.5), not all adjacent parts could be fitted flush, due most probably to distortion of certain pieces during the early stages of drying out in the 19th-century. However, these few misfits leave gaps which are never wider than c 20 mm, and they do not materially affect the form of the boat, which is determined by continuous sections of flush fitting fragments. The associated transverse and longitudinal fittings cannot now be fastened to the boat because of differential shrinkage and distortion.

Drawing and measuring the remains
The boat was drawn at 1:10 scale (Fig 6.2.6), and the fittings re-examined and re-drawn where necessary. The principal differences between the drawing published here (Fig 6.2.6) and the provisional drawing published in McGrail (1978B); are that the ends are now rotated upwards, and the narrower end in plan is twisted from the centreline.

The scantlings of the boat as now re-assembled are closer to the measurements published by Brayshaw (1887), than those published by O'Callaghan (1864). In particular, the length overall is now 2.45 m, compared with 8 ft 2 in (2.49 m) recorded by Brayshaw, and 8 ft 5 in (2.57 m) recorded by O'Callaghan. The maximum breadth is now .63 m compared with the 2 ft (.61 m) recorded by both O'Callaghan and Brayshaw. The general impression is that Brayshaw's measurements were reasonably accurate but post shrinkage; whereas O'Callaghan's measurements appear doubtfully accurate, although they were evidently made relatively soon after the discovery of the boat, as he read his paper to the Leeds Congress of the British Archaeological Association on 15 October 1863.

Dating
Brayshaw (1887: 10) stated that this boat was 'evidently of Celtic or British workmanship', and he referred to the owner as an 'old savage'. But this is mere prejudice; as with most logboat finds, there are only two ways of dating the Giggleswick boat: by dendrochronology and by radiocarbon assay (McGrail,1978A). The former method is dependent on the existence of a master chronology and has not so far been applied to logboats, although many would appear to be suitable. In any case, this boat is of ash (*Fraxinus* Sp), and most dendrochronological work has been directed towards the production of oak (*Quercus* Sp) chronologies. Dating logboats by radiocarbon has, on the other hand, made recent progress. Dr. Roy Switsur of the Godwin Laboratory, University of Cambridge, has processed samples from 40 logboats taken during the 1972-5 survey (McGrail & Switsur,1975), and several dates are now available. The date for a sample taken from a position nearest the outside of the parent log of the Giggleswick Tarn boat is: Q-1245: 615 BP ± 40 = c 1335 ad.

Several other medieval dates have been obtained by Dr. Switsur, indicating the relatively late use of logboats in England and Wales. The Giggleswick date is, so far, the latest radiocarbon date for a logboat in Europe, although there is documentary evidence for the use of logboats in Ireland and in Scotland in the 17th and 18th-centuries; and in Sweden, Denmark, Finland, Estonia, Albania and Austria, logboats are known to have been built and used in the present century. The 14th-century date for the Giggleswick boat is close to the date for the Kentmere boat (D-71: 650 BP ± 120 = c 1300 ad). Both boats were found on former lake sites, only some 25 miles (40 km) apart, and the boats have certain similarities in boatbuilding techniques (see below), although the Kentmere boat is, in fact, a five strake, extended logboat – a hybrid log/plank boat (Wilson,1966).

Description of the remains
During the re-assembly of the remains each fragment of the boat was examined by Sonia O'Connor and by me, and other members of the Archaeological Research Centre examined certain features. The description given below is thus the result of teamwork.

Raw material
The boat was built from a whole ash (*Fraxinus* Sp) log (Fig 6.2.7); the fittings were also of ash. It is difficult to identify the butt end of the log, but it is probably the broader end of the boat. There is now a near-horizontal longitudinal hole through this end, close to the pith (Fig 6.2.8), and Brayshaw (1887:11) noted that, when the boat was found, this hole was 'plugged up woth a conical piece of wood' – this 'plug' does not appear to have survived. The grain and growth ring pattern around this area are confused and it may be that the hole marks a forking in the main bole, possibly in the buttress of the root system; or it may have been an area of heart rot. O'Callaghan (1864) does not mention the hole or 'plug': there is thus the possibility that this 'plug' was inserted during early conservation work.

Form and size
The transverse section of the boat is rectangular or sub-rectangular, the breadth/depth ratio n being c 1.33 to 1. The sides taper in plan and in elevation towards the narrower end, so that the boat generally conforms to the log shape. The broader end is rounded in plan, whilst the other end is a rounded point (these terms are defined in McGrail, 1978B: Fig 205); both ends are rounded in elevation. The main scantlings of the boat as re-assembled are:

length overall	= 2.45m
maximum beam	= .63m
external height bow	= .46m
external height stem	= .47m
mean thickness of sides	= 50mm
mean thickness of bottom	= 70mm

The full original length of the boat appears to have survived, and the original top edge is present in many places; the remains therefore fulfil my criteria (1977:120) for a hypothetical reconstruction to be attempted.

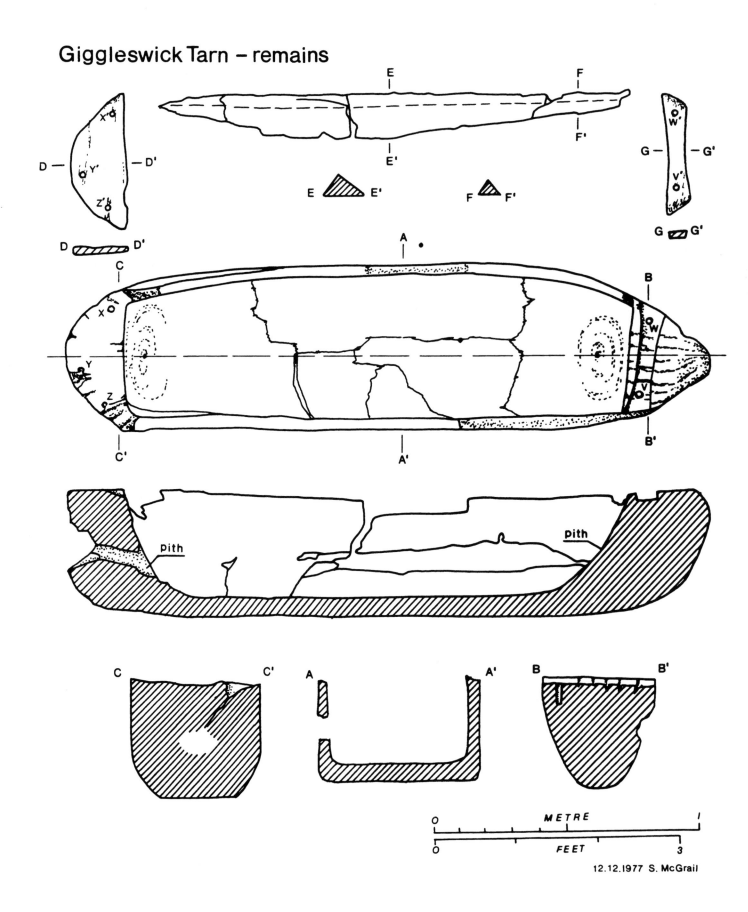

Giggleswick Tarn – remains

METRE

FEET

12.12.1977 S. McGrail

Figure 6.2.6 A measured drawing of the Giggleswick Tarn logboat, 1977

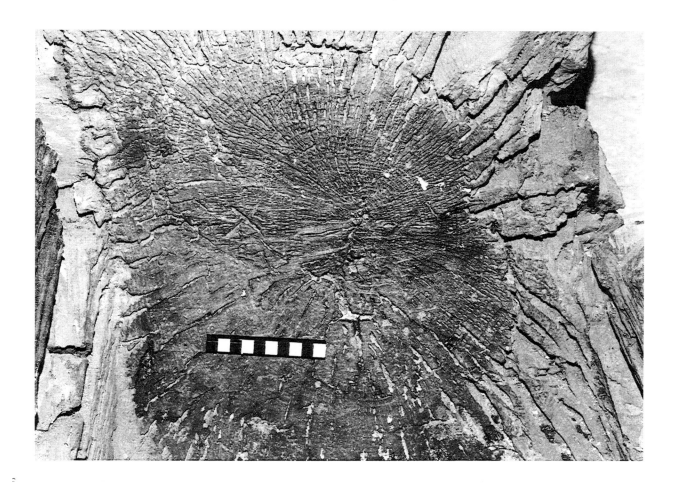

Figure 6.2.7 The interior of the bow showing the pith of the log, growth rings, and tool marks. Scale centimetric

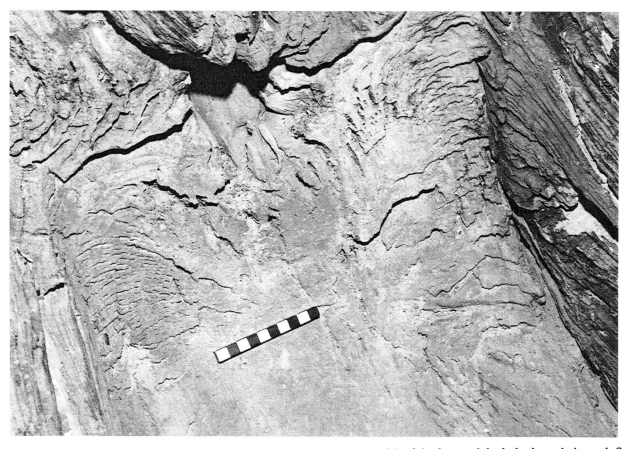

Figure 6.2.8 The interior of the stern showing the confused area around the pith of the log, and the hole through the end. Scale centimetric

Fittings and other features

In the top surface of the broader end are three vertical holes which are now too broken and distorted to be measured (Fig. 6.2.9). In a transverse groove at the other end are two vertical holes, one of which is now 80 mm deep with a maximum diameter of 23.1 mm (Figs 6.2.10 and 6.2.11)). On the inner face of the boat's narrower end, tool marks, measuring 50 and 80 mm can be seen (Fig 6.2.7). In one side, at the junction of side and bottom, is a worked depression; this may not be original and is more likely to have been made to take some of the modern internal supporting framework which can be seen in Fig 6.2.2. Another depression worked in the bottom of the boat at the broader end (Fig 6.2.8) had a modern support timber in it when the boat was examined in 1974: it is possible that this or a similar timber held in place the conical 'plug' referred to by Brayshaw (1887:11).

The surface of the wood is now cracked and corrugated (Fig 6.2.4), as is usual with dried–out waterlogged timber, but there is no reason to suppose that the workmanship and finish imparted to the boat were not of the high standard evident on the majority of ancient boat finds when they are examined before they dry out – see, for example, the Bronze Age Ferriby boats (Wright, 1976), and the Brigg 'raft' (McGrail,1975). Terms used by O'Callaghan such as 'roughly formed', and 'very rudely fashioned' are inappropriate. Indeed, the timber described by O'Callaghan. (1864: 196) as, 'A piece of roughly made plank, fastened over the taffrail', is in fact a well–fashioned timber from a radially split ash (*Fraxinus* Sp) board, nicely worked to fit the broader end of the boat (Fig 6.2.12). It was fastened there by three vertical treenails, also of

ash (*Fraxinus* Sp), of original diameter *c* 23 mm, and some 110 mm in length. The timber which fits across the other end of the boat also displays fine workmanship (Fig. 6.2.13): it has splayed ends of double dovetail shape and was fastened by two vertical treenails into the *c* 30 mm deep groove across that end of the boat so that the upper surface was flush.

Two other timbers, also of ash (*Fraxinus* Sp) were found associated with the boat (Fig 6.2.4). O'Callaghan (1864:196) recorded that these were ' triangular piece(s) of timber, fastened by wooden pins to the outer side of the gunwale, running near its whole length', and that ' their upper flat surfaces (were) flush with the gunwale'. The sketch published by O'Callaghan is a poor one; the general form is inaccurate, and the transverse groove at the narrower end is not shown and its associated timber is incorrectly placed. One of the longitudinal timbers is shown fastened to the side near the top edge of the boat, but this adds little to our knowledge. Brayshaw (1887: 11) also recorded that these two long timbers had formerly been treenailed to the sides of the boat, and the photograph he published, which Wildridge (1888: 134) stated was taken in 1883, shows one such timber fastened near the boat's top edge, (Fig. 6.2.2). The drawing published by Wildridge (1888) and dated August 1888, shows the same timber, by then clearly broken, fastened to the boat in a similar position (Fig. 6.2.3). By this date, the timber was fastened by modern iron nails (Wildridge, 1888:134), and as Brayshaw's 1883 photograph shows the boat to be very similar to its state in 1888, including the use of modern internal supports, it seems probable that these modern iron nails were already in use when the 1883 photograph (Fig. 6.2.2) was taken.

Figure 6.2.9 A near vertical view of the stern, showing the distorted nature of the three holes, X, Y, Z,. Scale centimetric

Figure 6.2.10 A near vertical view of the bow, showing holes set in the double dovetail shaped transverse groove. Scale centimetric

Figure 6.2.11 A horizontal view of the bow. Scale centimetric

These timbers are now distorted as well as fragmented (Fig. 6.2.4). It is difficult to find a representative cross section, but it is probable that they were originally of triangular section, as recorded by O'Callaghan (1864:196). Their cross section near the centre now measures c .10 m x .13 m x .16 m; either the .10 m or the .13 m side would need to be vertical next to the boat's side to give a horizontal surface flush with the top edge of the boat. Using a shrinkage factor (see section 4.6.1 below), the pre–shrinkage dimensions of the timbers' cross sections are estimated to have been c .11 m x .15 m x .19 m. Using the Brayshaw photograph of 1883 (Fig. 6.2.2) as a guide, Sonia O'Connor was able to position one of the longitudinal timbers by matching a 19th–century iron nail driven into the timber with a faint trace of a nail hole through a broken part of the boat's side. In this position the timber is orientated with the longer side of its cross section (now .13 m), horizontal and flush with the top edge of the boat. Brayshaw (1887: 10–11) gave the 'breadth including two "washboards"', as 3 ft (.91 m), and the breadth with one "washboard" missing as 2 ft 6 in (.76 m): we may therefore conclude that the horizontal dimensions of each longitudinal timber, as fastened to the sides of the boat in 1883, was c 6 in (.15 m). This tends to confirm that in 1883 the shorter side (.10 m, formerly .11 m) of the timber's cross section was against the boat's side, with the longer side (.13 m, formerly .15 m) horizontal and flush with the top edge.

The orientation of the timbers in 1883 is an indication of how they may have been orientated in antiquity, but it is not proof. The only holes that can now be detected in the timbers are less than 11 mm in diameter, and they have modern iron nails or nail fragments in them, which are probably the ones reported by Wildridge (1888:134). On comparative evidence, treenail holes would be expected to have been 15 to 25 mm in diameter (see below). Detailed examination of the boat has also failed to reveal the holes by which these timbers were treenailed, although the sides survive to a great extent up to the original top edge. Possibly these holes have closed somewhat and been distorted during the drying–out period, so that they are no longer detectable in the cracked and corrugated timber.

This is the case on the Kentmere boat where the nail holes, reported by the excavator (Wilson,1966), to be around the ends of the boat, can no longer be detected. But the Kentmere fastenings were of metal: the Giggleswick treenails would be expected to be of greater diameter and thus their holes less likely to be hidden by shrinkage. An alternative explanation is that the Giggleswick Tarn timbers were fastened to the boat only at their ends. The timbers now measure c 1.8 m in length: they are broken at both ends and could conceivably have been over 2.05 m originally. Timbers of this length would extend to the thick ends of the boat, where there are now gaps or broken sections on both sides and at both ends. It is conceivable that these missing sections are where the timbers were originally fastened by treenails.

Interpretation of the remains

The ends
The broader end is the stern, and it was probably also used as a seat.

Treenails
Loose fragments of two treenails, which probably fastened fittings to the boat, were examined. They are fashioned from ash (*Fraxinus* Sp) timber at some distance from the pith, and are generally parallel sided with a maximum breadth varying from c 18.5 mm to 20.5 mm. Two other fragments remain in holes in the ends of the boat, and there is another fragment in a small detached piece of timber which cannot yet be positioned. Treenails from other logboats examined during the 1972–5 survey varied in maximum diameter from c 18 mm to 25 mm; as in the Giggleswick boat, none of them showed signs of having been split and wedged as was recently the practice, but this evidence may have been lost.

Thickness of bottom
The thickness of the bottom now is uneven, being c 50 mm near the centreline and varying from 60 to 100 mm near the sides. Brayshaw (1887) stated that the bottom was 3 in (75 mm) thick, whilst O'Callaghan (1864: 196) implied that it was 5 in (c 130 mm), but this can scarcely have been representative. Of the 31 boats whose bottom thickness could be measured in the 1972–5 survey, only six were generally thicker than Giggleswick Tarn.

Thickness gauges – holes bored in the outside of the parent log to a pre determined depth and plugged with treenails when the boat was finished – were used in recent logboat building as an aid to obtaining the required bottom thickness. There is no sign of them in this boat.

External longitudinal timbers
There is widespread archaeological and ethnographic evidence from Scandinavia to South America and the Philippines for the use of external longitudinal timbers fastened directly, or close, to the sides of logboats (McGrail, 1978B: Ch 3). Their function varies, depending on their relationship to the waterline. When at the waterline – as, for example, on the Kentmere boat – they enhance initial transverse stability by increasing the waterplane area, especially the beam, with little change in displacement. Above the waterline they may act as rubbing strakes to minimise damage to the boat, or as spray deflectors offsetting a low freeboard. In this position they could also act as stabilisers at large angles of heel when one became immersed, or when the boat was at such a deep draft that both were partly immersed. From the 19th–century descriptions by O'Callaghan (1864), Brayshaw (1887) and Wildridge (1888), we must conclude that the Giggleswick Tarn timbers were fastened at or near the top edge, as rubbing strakes or spray deflectors, and as stabilisers at deep drafts. Rubbing strakes would be a luxury in waters without formal landing places, but the triangular cross section of these timbers would effectively deflect spray. A more important consideration may have been that timbers in this position give longitudinal strength to the boat. On the debit side however, they raise the hull's centre of gravity and thus, when not immersed, they have a de–stabilising effect. When immersed they increase the wetted surface area and thus increase drag; when above the waterline they increase air resistance.

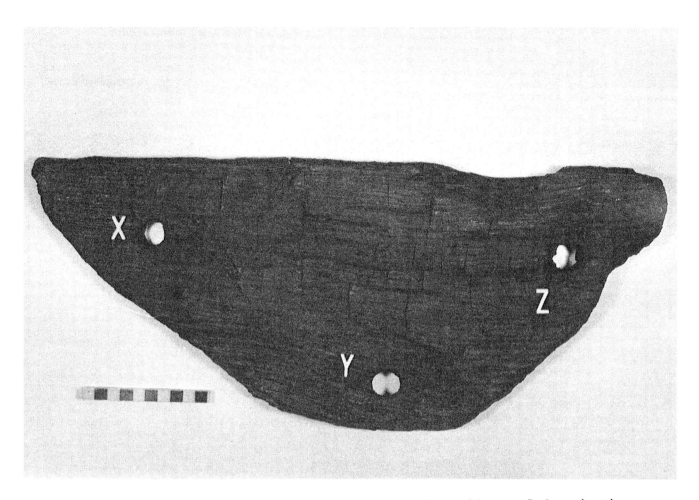

Figure 6.2.12 The D–shaped timber which was fastened across the top of the stern. Scale centimetric

Figure 6.2.13 The transverse timber fashioned to fit the double dovetail shaped groove across the bow. Scale centimetric

Two logboats found in Scotland may have had similar fittings to the Giggleswick Tarn boat, but neither was well recorded, and there appear to be no surviving remains. The logboat recovered from Loch Dowalton, Wigtownshire, had planks fastened to the top edge by treenails, and projecting a few inches outboard (Stuart,1864–5 :118, plate Xl fig 1). A similar fitting was reported by Munro (1882:208–9) on the Loch Buston logboat, which had a 'sort of gunwale' treenailed near the top edge from 'within a few feet of the stem till it projected a little beyond the stem'.

Transverse strengthening timbers at the ends

The two fittings, which were fastened to the top of the boat ends, were there to give transverse strength where there is a great tendency for logboats to split. Additionally, the timber at the stem of the boat (Fig 6.2.12) could have been used as a seat. There are many instances of these fittings, in a variety of forms, not only from Britain, but also from continental Europe. They have sometimes been found associated with fitted–transoms, when a transverse timber is essential to hold the sides of the open stern together. In many cases these fittings have not survived, and their former presence has been deduced from fragmentary remains or from a pattern of fastening holes. It is fortunate that the Giggleswick Tarn fittings survive, for otherwise the pattern of vertical treenail holes at the ends (Figs 6.2.9 and 6.2.10) might have been interpreted as the attachment points for joining two logboats together as a pair. Such an interpretation has been advanced for comparable patterns of holes by Paret (1930: 100–3) for several finds from the R Oder in Silesia; by Humbla (1937: 15) for a logboat from Ockelbo, Sweden; and by Ellmers (1973:50–6), who followed Paret's interpretation and identified an Oder type of paired logboat. In all these cases the fittings do not appear to have survived, and a simpler and more convincing explanation of the pattern of holes would be as attachment points for transverse strengthening timbers such as that fitted in the groove across the bow of the Giggleswick Tarn boat (Fig 6.2.13).

Morphology

Using the code given in McGrail (1978B:Ch.8), the morphological description of the Giggleswick Tarn boat is: 224: 221:324. This is a modification of the code adduced before the fragments were precisely re–assembled. Thus, this boat is a variant member of the canoe form defined in McGrail (1978B), with a rectangular instead of a rounded transverse section. It most closely resembles the logboats from Llyn Llangorse and from Walton.

Analysis

Shrinkage calculations

The drawing compiled in 1977 (Fig. 6.2.6) is the earliest reliable drawing of this boat, but it is post shrinkage. An estimate of shrinkage must therefore be made, so that the original dimensions of the boat can be calculated. The cross section of the one hole (W) in the boat which can now be measured accurately, is elliptical in plan (Fig. 6.2.10) with a major to minor axis ratio of 1 to 1.11; this is a measure of shrinkage in the tangential plane . The two transverse timbers are fashioned from radially cut boards, and holes in them are also now elliptical due to differential shrinkage. The three

holes (XYZ') in the D–shaped timber (Fig. 6.2.12) have shrinkage indices ranging from 1.06 to 1.24, with a mean of 1.13: this is a measure of the radial shrinkage of that timber. The holes in the dovetailed timber (Fig. 6.2.13) are also now elliptical but with their greater dimension now in the radial plane rather than, as would be expected, in the longitudinal plane of the board. The hole (W) in the boat has a major axis of 23.1 mm, and the mean of the major axes in the three holes (X'Y'Z') in the D–shaped timber, is 23.0 mm. It seems probable, therefore, that the holes bored into the dovetailed timber were also originally 23 mm in diameter. These holes now measure 19.2 to 20.2 mm in the timber's longitudinal plane, and 20.8 mm to 22.0 mm in the radial plane. The reason for this anomalous shrinkage is not understood, but it may be due to the fitting having partly dried out with treenails still in position, in such a way that normal shrinkage was prevented. Experimental work is now being undertaken in the Archaeological Research Centre to attempt to find a reason for this type of shrinkage.

In addition to estimating shrinkage from elliptical hole measurements, comparison of scantlings may be used. The distance ZX (Fig 6.2.6) is in the boat's tangential plane: the corresponding distance Z'X' on the D–shaped timber is in the board's longitudinal plane: the ratio Z'X'/ZX, a measure of the boat's tangential shrinkage, is 1.07 to 1. Radial shrinkage is normally less than tangential, but here the mean radial shrinkage factor for the D–shaped timber (1.13) is greater than the tangential shrinkage factor for the boat (1.07) and, thus, this board's shrinkage is unusual. Other measurable distances at the stern of the boat are in planes other than radial, tangential, or longitudinal, and thus cannot be used to estimate shrinkage directly. Comparable calculations cannot be attempted for the bow because of the anomalous shrinkage of the dovetailed timber.

It is considered that the best estimate of a mean tangential shrinkage factor for this boat is the weighted mean of the index for the hole W (1.11 with a loading of 3), and the comparison index for Z'X'/ZX (1.07). The shrinkage factor used is thus 1.10. This logboat is made from ash (*Fraxinus* Sp), and thus no comparison can be made with shrinkage factors from other logboats in the 1972–5 survey, which were for oak (*Quercus* Sp).

Hypothetical reconstruction

Using this shrinkage factor of 1.10, the principal dimensions of the reconstructed logboat become:

length overall	= 2.45 m(as at present)
maximum beam	= .69 m
external height bow	= .51 m
external height stern	= .52 m
mean thickness of sides	= 53 mm
mean thickness of bottom	= 74 mm

The maximum cross section of the longitudinal timbers becomes c .11 x .15 x .19 m, and they are considered to be 2.05 m in length.

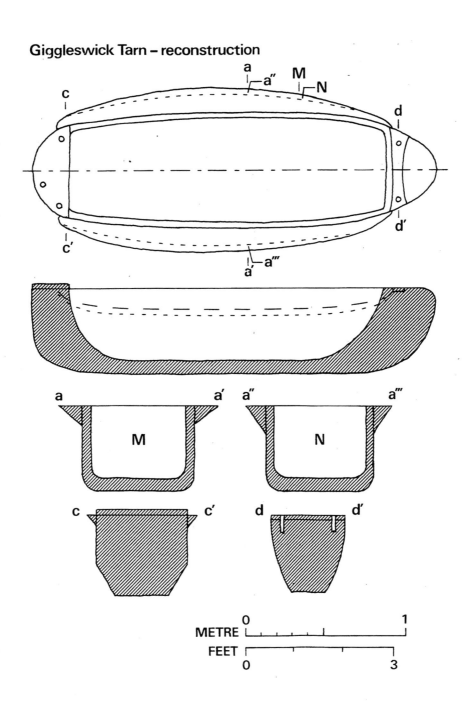

Giggleswick Tarn – reconstruction

Figure 6.2.14 A reconstruction drawing of the Giggleswick Tarn boat, 1977.

M: the longitudinal timbers are orientated with the longer side of their cross section jutting out from the top edge of the boat
N: this longer dimension is vertical against the side of the boat

From these scantlings the hypothetical reconstruction in Fig. 6.2.14 was drawn. Two different alignments of the longitudinal timbers are shown.

Using the methods explained in McGrail (1978B) the following can then be calculated:

      hull weight   274 kg
      volume of wood .391 m³
      volume of ho110w .309 m³
      crew space   1 man standing and 2 kneeling

Stability, displacement and weight calculation

A lines plan with 11 transverse sections was drawn, based on this reconstruction drawing. Using an HP97 desk calculator and programs written by John Watson of Burness, Corlett and Partners, hydrostatic curves were then calculated from the lines plan data. Further programs enabled stability, displacement and weight calculations to be made for the four standard states of Maximum Men, Restricted Draft, Standard Freeboard, and Minimum Freeboard. Finally, 25 coefficients were calculated: these are designed to describe the parent log and the form of the boat, and to assess the boat's performance in carrying several standard loads.

Two sets of calculations were undertaken: one with the longitudinal timbers positioned so that the greater dimension of their cross section was horizontal (Fig 6.2.14M); and one with this dimension vertical (Fig 6.2.14N) These calculations show that the boat can carry the following loads in a condition of initial transverse stability (i.e. with positive metacentric height (GM_T))

State A   Maximum men.

    load   1 man kneeling
    draft   .26 m   freeboard .26 m
    GM_T .012 m   displacement 336 kg

State B Restricted draft

    load   1 man kneeling and 57 kg equipment
    draft   .30 m   freeboard .22 m
    GM_T 033 m   displacement 393 kg

State C Standard freeboard

    (i) with longitudinal timbers "horizontal" (Fig. 14M)
    load   1 man sitting and 154 kg stone to .33 m below sheerline
    draft   .37m   freeboard   .15 m
    GM_T .023m   displacement 490 kg

    (ii) with longitudinal timbers "vertical" (Fig.14N)
    load   1 man standing and 164 kg stone to .32 m below sheerline
    draft   .37m   freeboard   .15 m
    GM_T .007m displacement   500kg

State D Minimum freeboard

    (i) with longitudinal timbers "horizontal" (Fig 14M)

    load 1 man standing and 289 kg stone to .24 m below sheerline
    draft   .46m   freeboard   .06 m
    GM_T .097m   displacement   625 kg

or   load 1 man standing and 2 kneeling and 169 kg equipment
    draft   .46m   freeboard   .06 m
    GM_T .035m   displacement   625 kg

    (ii) with longitudinal timbers 'vertical' (Fig.14N)

    load 1 man standing and 294 kg stone to .24 m below sheerline
    draft   .46m   freeboard   .06m
    GM_T .097m   displacement   630kg

or   load 1 man standing and 2 kneeling and 174 kg equipment
    draft   .46m   freeboard   .06m
    GM_T .036m   displacement   630kg

Description of the reconstructed boat

The parent log
O'Callaghan(1864:196) thought that the log boat was made from pine (*Pinus* Sp),whilst Brayshaw(1887:10) described it as oak (*Quercus* Sp). It is in fact ash (*Fraxinus* Sp), as are all the fittings and the one treenail which has been identified. The use of ash (*Fraxinus* Sp) for a logboat is unique in England and Wales, but it is known to have been so used in recent times in Sweden (Eskerod,1956:62). Oak (*Quercus* Sp) is the predominant species in the archaeological record and, although there may be differential survival because of oak's greater durability, there are several reasons why oak is very suitable for logboats (McGrail,1978B:Ch.7). Ash is, however, comparable with oak for straightness of grain, density and therefore strength, and workability: but it is not so durable, and it generally does not achieve the oak's length and diameter of bole.

A whole log was used for the Giggleswick boat, the pith being nearly central at the bow, but lower down at the stern where there is an area of confused growth rings at this the butt end of the log. All sapwood appears to have been removed. The deduced size of the parent log of the Giggleswick Tarn boat is: diameter 1.10 m at .5 m from the butt end, tapering to .96 m at 2 m; the girth was 3.46 m; the volume of timber was *c* 2.04 m³. There are no comparable figures for other ash logs, but when compared with the parent oaks of 23 logboats from England and Wales, this ash log is the eighth smallest in diameter and the second smallest for volume.

Conversion of the timber

The rectangular transverse section giwn to the boat fits the general pattern found in the English and Welsh survey: boats made from half a longitudinally split log generally had semi–rounded sections (13 out of 21); whereas boats of rectangular or flared sections were made from a whole log (14 out of 18). Best use was thus made of the chosen timber.

Giggleswick Tarn's log conversion coefficient is .193, which means that 80.7% of the log was worked away. This puts it second to the boat from Hulton Abbey which, of those logboats reconstructed, had the least amount of timber (80.2%) worked away.

Size

The length of the Giggleswick Tarn boat, 2.45 m, places it in the lowest group (2 to 2.99 m of those 76 boats in the survey whose lengths could be assessed. 50% of these boats had lengths within the range 2.77 m to 4.65 m. The boat's maximum breadth of .69 m also places it in the lowest group. The modal set here is .73 m to .99 m, with 67% (16 out of 24 boats).

Boatbuilding techniques

The position and function of the two transwrse timbers is clear, but this is not the case with the two longitudinal timbers. To give the boat improved stability at standard freeboard, these timbers would need to have been fitted so that their upper surface was some .15 m below the boat's top edge. The 19th–century reports, sketchy though they are, indicate that these timbers were in fact flush with the top edge: this cannot be contradicted by the evidence now surviving, and it is supported to a degree by reports of two Scots logboats with longitudinal timbers in a similar position.

Calculations show the boat to have a relatively poor performance at drafts when these longitudinal timbers are not immersed, and relatively mediocre performance when the timbers are only slightly immersed. On present evidence it would seem therefore, that this boat was built to be operated at drafts approaching the maximum, (top edge awash at a 10° heel); or that the builder was concerned to give the boat additional longitudinal strength. With these longitudinal timbers at top edge level, and with transverse timbers across the top surfaces of the ends, the boat is enclosed in a box girdle – an effective precaution against splitting. In addition, these longitudinal timbers could act as spray deflectors or possibly as rubbing strakes.

Whatever their purpose, these longitudinal fittings are characteristic features of this boat, as are the transverse members. Other distinctive features are: the use of treenails to fasten fittings; the dovetail shape used across the bow end to enhance transverse strength; and the generally rectangular transverse section. Too few logboats have to date undergone detailed examination to allow classification by boatbuilding techniques, but it is possible to list provisional date ranges for the earliest and latest appearance of distinctive features in British logboat building, using the few radiocarbon dates available (McGrail, 1978B:Ch 11). Four features of the Giggleswick boat (dated c 1335 ad) also appear on the Kentmere boat (dated c 1300 ad). These are:

(i) rectangular or flared transverse section (Fig. 6.2.6) – earliest appearance c 9th century bc

(ii) treenails to fasten fittings (Figs. 6.2.12 and 6.2.13), – probable earliest appearances, c 4th century bc

(iii) external longitudinal fittings (Fig 6.2.4) – possible earliest appearance, c 9th century bc

(iv) transverse strengthening fittings at the ends (Figs 6.2.9, 6.2.10 and 6.2.11) – probable earliest appearance, c 3rd century bc

Thus, the *floruit* of these four features is conflrmed as extending from a date in the first millenium bc to the 14th century ad. The date range for the use of dovetail shaped fittings (Fig. 6.2.13) which previously was from 12th century bc to 9th century bc, is now extended to the 14th century ad by the Giggleswick Tarn boat.

Function

There are many documentary references to the recent use of logboats, in Europe and elsewhere, as ferries, and for fishing, fowling and the collection of reeds. It may be presumed that these were also their roles in antiquity. Artifacts found associated with logboats, and the nature of the site where the logboat was found, may however indicate a more precise function. The Giggleswick boat's find spot was formerly a tarn or lake (Fig. 15) with a stream leading to the R Ribble (Wildridge, 1888:134). But, without further details of the local environment and economy in antiquity, this cannot suggest any particular use for the boat. There were no associated finds.

I have argued elsewhere (1977:12&8) that the value of certain coefficients may indicate that a logboat was built with one of three roles in mind: personnel carrier, high density cargo carrier, or bulky low density cargo carrier. These coefficients must be calculated for each boat at standard conditions (for example, with at least one man standing) so that comparisons can be made. If the Giggleswick Tarn boat's longitudinal timbers were orientated in antiquity as they seem to have been in 1883 (Fig. 6.2.14M), then they would not be immersed at standard draft, and in this condition initial transverse stability is insufficient to permit a man to stand in the boat. Thus, coefficients calculated for this state are not truly comparable with those for other boats. Transverse stability is, however, sufficient to permit a man to sit on the stern, and the boat appears to have been built with this in mind. At this state the boat performs better at carrying high density cargo, rather than bulky low density cargo, or men. It is relatively only moderately good in this high density cargo role, and thus may be classified provisionally as a 2nd rate high density cargo carrier.

When the longitudinal timbers are orientated as in Fig. 6.2.14N, they are partly immersed at standard draft, and a man can now stand in a condition of initial transverse stability. The boat is now clearly a 2nd rate high density cargo carrier, in the same category as the logboats from Barton, Ellesmere,

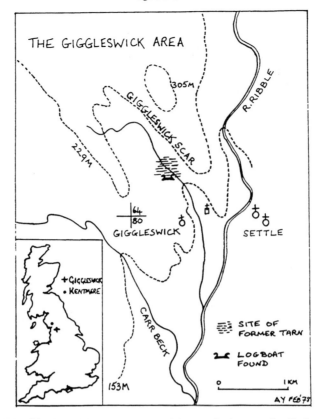

Figure 6.2.15 The Giggleswick area – base, with permission, on the Ordnance Survey

Glastonbury 1, and Thornaby (McGrail, 1978B: Ch 11). At deeper drafts, with the longitudinal timbers in either orientation, the boat maintains its relative position as a 2nd rate carrier of high density cargo.

Performance
The results of calculations listed in section above, show that the boat has a relatively poor performance before the longitudinal timbers begin to be immersed at drafts of .40 m (Fig. 6.2.14M), and .36 m (Fig. 6.2.14N).

The standard conditions for State A (maximum men) require that at least one man should stand in an unballasted boat. The best that the Giggleswick Tarn boat can achieve at light drafts without ballast, is one man kneeling. The theoretical full crew of one man standing and two kneeling can only be carried when the boat is ballasted at drafts approaching the maximum of .46 m (i.e. when the longitudinal timbers are well immersed). It is doubtful whether there would be sufficient space for the 169–174 kg ballast required by this theoretical assessment, in addition to the crew.

The boat has a poor to moderate performance in the restricted draft (.30 m) condition (State B), where transverse stability is insufficient to allow a man to stand or to sit on the stern: a stable state can only be achieved with one man kneeling and 57 kg ballast.

At standard draft (State C) with the longitudinal timbers as in Fig. 6.2.14M, the boat once again cannot attain a condition comparable to other logboats, as there is insufficient transverse stability to allow a man to stand. However, with the timbers as in Fig. 6.2.14N, when they are partly immersed, stability can

be achieved in standard conditions with a cargo of 164 kg stone, of bulk density 2,500 kg/m3. With any cargo of bulk density less than 1949 kg/m3, this stability could not be achieved. The boat is thus limited to carrying dense loads.

At deeper drafts (State D), as the longitudinal timbers become more effective as stabilisers, stability with a cargo of stone can be achieved with the longitudinal timbers orientated as in Fig. 6.2.14M; as well as in Fig. 6.2.14N. The critical bulk density (i.e. that density of cargo which results in zero metacentric height) here, is 832–846 kg/m3, and thus loads much less dense than stone can be carried, with transverse stability still maintained. However, there is no condition in which either turf (bulk density 435 kg/m3) or grain (680 kg/m^3) – the other two standard cargoes used in the 1972–5 research – can be carried, with a man standing in the boat.

If we were to assert that the stability requirement for a man to stand in the boat is too severe, and that this boat should be assessed with a man sitting on the stern, the relative performance is marginally improved. At State C (standard draft) with the longitudinal timbers orientated as in Fig. 6.2.14M, a man can sit on the stern providing 154 kg of stone is carried. Performance at other states is not affected by this relaxation of the standard criteria.

Propulsion
There is no evidence for the use of sail or oar on the remains of the Giggleswick Tarn boat, and it must be presumed that pole or paddle were used, however poling would not be possible in certain states because limited transverse stability would not permit a man to stand in the boat. A paddler seated on the stern would probably have been the usual mode of propulsion. In the

survey of English and Welsh logboats, sound evidence for rowing was found in only one case: the logboat from Banks, Martin Mere, Lancashire (Brodrick,1902:17–8), although there are modern examples of rowing logboats from France, Spain, Albania, Austria and Sweden, and a number of excavated finds in Scotland and Ireland have a combination of thwart, pivot and foot timber, which indicate that they were probably propelled by oar (McGrail, 1978B:Ch 3).

Speed and manoeuvrability

With the longitudinal timbers as in Fig. 6.2.14N the Giggleswick boat has slow to medium relative speed potential, and low relative paddle power, with moderate to poor manoeuvrability. These terms are defined in McGrail (1978B). With the timbers as in Fig. 6.2.14M, the boat is in a non–standard state as the man cannot stand but has to sit on the stern for stability reasons. In this condition the boat's speed and manoeuvrability are similar to the Fig. 14N case.

General classification

I have elsewhere (1978B:Ch 8) proposed that logboats should be described under six headings: date; function; form; propulsion and speed potential; region; and size (as indicated by deadweight tonnage at standard freeboard, and length overall). As more research is undertaken in this field it may become possible to add boatbuilding techniques to the description. The logboat from Giggleswick Tarn may therefore be described:

A 14th century, 2.45 m, 2nd rate high density cargo carrier when operated at deep draft, and when operated at standard draft with the longitudinal timbers orientated as in Fig. 6.2.14N (i.e. with the longer dimension of their cross section vertical against the side of the boat). In other conditions the boat has a poor relative performance. The boat is of variant canoe form and was propelled by paddle (and possibly by pole in certain circumstances) at relatively poor speeds, with a deadweight capability of 224 kg at standard draft (providing the longitudinal timbers are as in Fig 6.2.14N).

The significance of the Giggleswick Tarn boat

The Giggleswick Tarn logboat was once thought to be one of the very few examples of an excavated logboat with washstrakes. The longitudinal timbers associated with the boat are not washstrakes however, but spray deflectors/ rubbing strakes, and stabilisers at deep drafts. They also strengthen the boat and, in conjunction with the transverse fittings, enclose the boat in a box girdle and thus prevent longitudinal splitting. In the 1972–5 survey it was found that, in general, the logboats of England and Wales were lacking in transverse stability rather than in freeboard. Thus, longitudinal timbers as former fittings would often seem to be a wiser interpretation of a series of horizontal holes through both sides of a logboat, than would washstrakes. The Giggleswick boat thus does not lose importance by the identification of these timbers as spray deflectors and longitudinal strengthening fittings which would also improve transverse stability at deep draft, but rather gains in significance. The two transverse fittings are also significant, for they provide valuable comparative evidence for the interpretation of similar patterns of fastening holes on logboats whose fittings have not survived. They provide transverse strength where it is most needed, and were probably an essential fitting on many logboats. For this reason, where fittings do not survive, this interpretation is to be preferred to the more complex interpretation as fastening positions for fittings to join a pair of logboats.

The fact that this boat is of ash (*Fraxinus* Sp) is unusual and therefore important, for it reminds us that the sample of logboats surviving to be excavated is not necessarily representative of the ancient logboat population. Other boats made of timber less durable than oak (*Quercus* Sp) may not have survived.

The location of the boat in time and space is also significant. The 14th–century date emphasises that not all logboats are prehistoric, as has often been assumed in the past, and the find spot (Fig. 6.2.15) throws an interesting light on the use of lakes in the highland zone, and their economic importance to local communities.

Notes: 1.Dates 'bc' and 'ad' are in radiocarbon years.

2.Illustrations are National Maritime Museum copyright, except where stated otherwise.

APPENDIX

Giggleswick Tarn logboat coefficients

Coefficients	Longitudinal timbers as in Fig. 6.2.14M	Longitudinal timbers as in Fig. 6.2.14N
1. Crew capacity	.111	.111
2. Manpower	2.976 (k)	2.976 (k)
3. Men (C)	.490 (k)	.490 (k)
4. Volumetric	.0234 (k)	.0234 (k)
5. Restricted	draft 58.820 (k)	58.820 (k)
6. Critical bulk density (C)	1085 (s)	1949
7. Deadweight	.437 (s)	.448
8. High Density Cargo (C)	104.901 (s)	109.804
9. Cargo Volume	.290 (s)	.168
10. Bulky low density (C)	.070 (s)	.041
11. Midships	.987 (s)	.990
12. Block	.783 (s)	.777
13. Prismatic	.794 (s)	.785
14. Waterplane	.846 (s)	.834
15. Slenderness	3.551 (s)	3.451
16. Symmetry	.919	.919
17. Station of Maximum beam	–	–
18. Length/Draft	6.622 (s)	6.622
19. Beam/Draft	1.865 (s)	1.919
20. High Density (D)	171.078	173.529
21. Log conversion	.193	.193
22. Load space	.151	.151
23. Bulky (D)	.170	.170
24. Men (D)	1.470 (including ballast)	1.471 (including ballast)
25. C.B.D. (D)	832	846

Legend   k = man kneeling

s = man sitting on stern

(in other cases the man is standing as is the standard requirement)

Note: Three coefficients (23, 24, 25) have been added to the list published in McGrail (1978B). These three, in conjunction with coefficient 20, assess the logboat at State D (minimum freeboard).

References

Brayshaw, T.,1887, 'British Canoe' *Collectanea Giggleswickiana*. No.9 in the 'Stackhouse' Series of Local Tracts.

Brodrick, H.,1902, 'Martin Mere', *Transactions of the Southport Society of Natural Science*, 8th report,13th session: 5–18

Ellmers, D.,1973, 'Kultbarken, Fähren, Fischerboote Vorgeschichtliche Einbaüme in Niedersachsen',*DieKunde*, NS24: 23–62

Eskeröd, A.,1956, 'Early Nordic Arctic Boats' *Arctica*, 1956: 57–87. (Studia Ethnographica Upsaliensia) Upsala.

Humbla, P., and von Post, L,1937, *Galtabäcksbaten och Tidigt Båtbyggen* i Norden, Goteborg

McGrail, S.,1975, 'Brigg "raft" re–excavated', *Lincolnshire History and Archaeology*, 10:5–13

McGrail, S.,1977, 'Searching for pattern among the logboats of England and Wales' in McGrail, S (ed), *Sources and Techniques in Boat Archaeology*, British Archaeological Reports S29. National Maritime Museum Archaeological Series No.1: 115–135

McGrail, S.,1978A, 'Dating ancient boats' in Fletcher, J. (ed) *Proceedings of the 1977 Dendrochronology Symposium* (in press)

McGrail, S.,1978B, *The logboats of England and Wales* (in press)

McGrail, S., & Switsur, R.,1975, 'Early British boats and their chronology'. *International Journal of Nautical Archaeology*, 4:191–200.

Munro, R.,1882, *Ancient Scottish Lake Dwellings or Crannogs*, Edinburgh

O'Callaghan, X.,1864, 'On an ancient canoe discovered at Giggleswick', *Journal of the British Archaeological Association*, 20: 195–6

Paret, O.,1930, 'Die Einbaüme im Federseeried und im übrigen Europa', *Prahistorische Zeitschrift*, 21 :76–116

Sheppard, T., 1910, 'Prehistoric boat from Brigg', *Transaction of the East Riding Antiquarian Society*, 17:33–60

Stuart, J.,1864–5, 'Notices of a group of artificial island in the Loch of Dowalton, *Wigtownshire'*, *Proceedings of the Society of Antiquaries of Scotland*, 6: 114–178

Wildridge, T.T.,1888, 'Ancient one–tree boats of Northumbria' in Wildridge, T.T. (ed) *Northumbria*: 123–137

Wilson, D.M.,1966, 'A medieval boat from Kentmere, Westmorland', *Medieval Archaeology*, 10:81–8

Wright, E.V.,1976, *The North Ferriby boats*. National Maritime Museum Monograph No.23

Reprinted with permission from:

Annis, P (ed) *Ingrid and other studies*: 25–46. NMM Greenwich Monograph 36. (1978).

PAPER 6.3

ASPECTS OF NAVAL ARCHITECTURE

Archaeology and Naval Architecture

The purpose of this chapter is to extract from the body of naval architectural knowledge what is relevant to logboats operated on inland and estuarine waters. This is not an easy task, for logboats are made of wood, are generally small and propelled by hand, and have an unusual form determined to a great extent by the parent log: whereas today's naval architects deal, in general, wlth ships and large boats operating at sea, and propelled by mechanical means, or by sail. In addition, although much structural work has been done on the design of metal vessels, there has been little, if any, on wooden boats.

Naval Architecture as a scitentific discipline cannot be said to have influenced ship–design until the 17th century, and possibly not until the 19th century, in any appreciable way. As Rawson and Tupper (1976:1) point out, however, there must have been earlier equivalents to naval architects, the intelligent craftsmen who, by trlal and error methods and by observing the effects of varying certain factors, could reject sub–optimal methods and materials and perfect those which gave their boats destrable characteristics. This empirical approach is still an essential aspect of Naval Architecture, which is an art and craft as well as a science. Inevitably too, with the numerous variables with which the naval architect has to contend (not least that boats and ships operate at the interface of two media: water and air), any design is a compromise, and theory must be confirmed by practical trials, the naval architect seeking feed–back to his drawing–board, his computer and his test–tank, from the actual performance of the built ship (Coates, 1977: 225–6). This problem is intensified in the present enquiry by the difficulty of resolving the fragmented, sometimes uncertain character of the excavated data, with the apparently precise and exact methods of calculation used in a scientific enquiry. For all these reasons, therefore, theoretical evaluations of logboats must in due course be tested by practical trials.

Some areas of great importance to naval architects wlll not be considered here: seakeeping; flooding and collision; complex structural design; launching and docking; powering, as these are not relevant to logboats. Instead, I shall consider:

(i) the 'ideal' logboat and the aims of a logboat designer/builder,

(ii) which forms and fittings give desirable characteristics,

(iii) the effects on performance of choosing various forms or fittings for the logboat.

Definitions of terms and symbols used will be found in Appendix 1 and 2.

The Ideal logboat

The naval architect's job, ln brief, is to design a boat which will meet certain specifications of performance and of safety. Logboat performance and safety requirements may be measured under several heads:

Performance   (i) speed (minimise resistance and maximise propulsive force)
            (ii) payload (maximise displacement volume and minimise hull–weight)
            (iii) manoeuvrability

Safety   (iv) structural strength and durabililty, and watertightness

            (v) stability

Which characteristlos are to be emphasised ln a particular design wlll depend to a great extent on the role the boat is to fuifill and its operating environment.Thus, speed and manoeuvrabllity may be emphasised ln a boat for raiding, whilst payload and stability may be the characteristics most required in a fishing boat. Even when the design requirement is clear the design achieved will be a compromise, as some of these characteristics are incompatible to a degree: for example, the maximum payload theoretically obtainable from a given log is probably unattainable if maximum structural strength is also requlred. In addition, there are practical constraints placed on the logboat builder by the tool–kit available to him, by the current state of technology, and by the shape of the log.

How desirable characteristics may be attained

We may consider how a given log may be best converted into a logboat with the individual characteristics described above bearing in mind that it is the form of the underbody of the boat (that is, below the loaded waterline) which principally determines the boat's performance.

Speed may be increased by increasing the propulsive force, and by reducing the drag or resistance which has to be overcome by that force. Neglecting resistance caused by waves and spray, and resistance induced by heel, total resistance to motion is made up of the following elements, which may be studied separately although there is some interaction:

(i) skin–friction
(ii) wave–making
(ii) viscous pressure (eddy)
(iv) appendage
(v) air

For a logboat operating at low speeds in relation to its length, skin–friction is of most significance although, with certain forms, eddymaklng resistance will play a part, and appendage resistance may be taken into account where there are such fittings as stabilisers. Skin–friction resistance varies directly as the wetted or immersed surface area of the boat. Any abrupt changes in form will increase vortex–shedding (eddy–making) and thus increase resistance; conversely wave–making will decrease with increased length, thereby reducing total resistance. The way that certain design variables affect resistance to motion and propulsive force available is considered below.

Length: In general, because skin–friction is such a major part of the total resistance of a logboat, a longer boat will be more resistful than a shorter one of the same transverse section.

Transverse sections: Half–rounded, square and rectangular sections are compared in Appendix 3, where it is shown that a rectangular sectlon has 9%, and a half–rounded section 23%, less frictional resistance than a square transverse section. Viscous pressure resistance will be greater at the oversharp turn of the bilge in the square and rectangular forms, thus inereasing their total resistance somewhat; whereas with the rounded form, water is able to flow along the diagonals, resulting ln less eddy resistance. In sum, then, the half–rounded section is least resistful, and thus is of potentially greater speed.

The shape in plan: A ' boat–shaped' plan with the maximum beam near the midships station will give the least abrupt changes to the waterflow and thus tend to reduce resistance. Having the maximum beam right aft, as happens when the logboat builder makes maximum use of the tapered log, will increase resistance.

The ends: Blunt ends are resistful, whereas rounded ends with smooth changes in section have less drag. At the bow there is marked interference with the streamlines ahead of a blunt end; at the stern an area of negative pressure is created, with resultant reverse flow and increased drag.

Propulsive force: Obtaining the maximum length of boat from the given log will ensure (subject to stability considerations) that maximum paddlers can be carried: the maximum propulsive force will thus be available. This advantage must be balanced empirically against the increased skin–friction due to length and to increased draft.

Payload

Payload depends on the internal dimensions of the boat, the space occupied by the crew, and the reserve of buoyancy. For a given propulsive force, i. e. crew, this payload potential can be increased by reducing the weight of the boat, and by inercasing the displacement volume. The actual payload which may be carried will depend on the bulk density of the load and on stability considerations.

For a given log, displacement volume can be increased by allowing the boat to take the natural taper of the log (thereby taking advantage of the wide buttend) and by having vertical or inclined ends, whlch may however, have other disadvantages. In Appendix 3 it is shown that a log of rectangular transverse section has 13% less payload potential than one of square form, whereas a log of half–rounded section has 21% less payload than one of square form. This may be taken as an approximation to the relative capabilities of logboats of these forms.

The weight of the boat may be reduced by using a low density species of timber, and by making the hull of the boat as thin as possible. These choices may, however, be incompatible with requirements for strength and durability.

Manoeuvrability

Logboats are inherently long, narrow and relatively shallow. A high ratio Lwl/Bx results in good directional stability and thus the boat is more difficult to manoeuvre. Conversely, a high ratio Lwl/T will mean inereased manoeuvrabillty, as the relatively shallow draft will produce less lateral resistance to turning. Thus, a beamy, shallow boat will be the most manoeuvrable.

Strength, durability and watertightness

Strength and durablllty may be inereased by the right choice of timber species, by leaving more timber at the ends of the boat, and by having thicker sides and bottom: these may, however, have undestrable side effects, such as raising the centre of gravity.

Watertightness is an integral virtue of the logboat design, and may be enhanced by inereasing the loaded displacement volume and hence improving freeboard, and by the addition of washstrakes. Heart rot in a log (see Paper 6.4) may mean that at least one end of the boat (the butt end of the log) must be open, with a resulting diminution in watertightness which the fitting of a transom may only partly rectify.

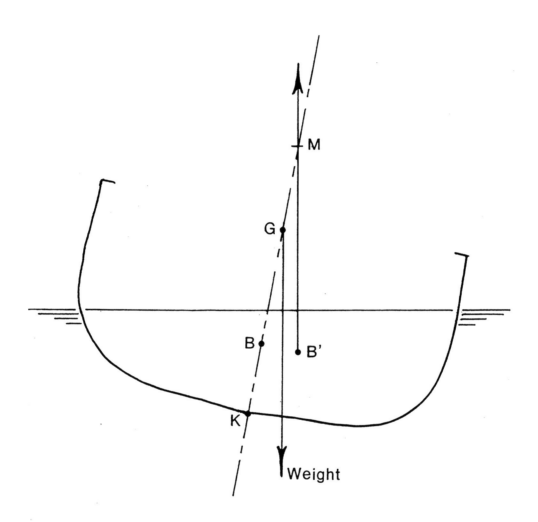

B – Centre of Buoyancy
B' – Centre of Buoyancy when heeled
K – Datum point
G – Centre of Gravity
M – Metacentre
$\overline{GM}$ – Metacentric Height

Figure 6.3.1 Diagram illustrating terms used when discussing transverse stability

Stability

Free surface effects are not considered in this evaluation.

In general, in the conditions in which a basic logboat may be expected to operate, longitudinal stability will be no great problem, providing the load is distributed evenly, without excessive loading at the ends to cause hogging, or amidship to cause sagging. If the maximum size boat has been obtained from a tapered log, it will be heavier at the butt end, probably the stern, and will trim naturally by this end. This will result in the top edge or sheerline of the boat becoming horizontal, or nearly so, when afloat.

On the other hand, given the relative narrowness of a log, transverse stability is a critical problem in logboat design. For stable initial equilibrium a boat must have a positive metacentric height; that is M, (the point of intersection of the buoyancy or righting force with the vertical axis) must be higher than G, the centre of gravity of the loaded boat, for infinitely small angular displacements from the vertical (Fig. 6.3.1). In this condition, any tendency for the boat to heel from the upright will automatically be opposed by the buoyancy force; a measure of this righting moment is the distance GM_t = metacentric height. A large GM_t means a strong righting moment and results in a *stiff ship*; the opposite condition is known as tender. There are other stability concepts – large angle stability, and dynamical stability – but initial stability is fundamental and *sine qua non*; this is, therefore, the one considered here.

There are many variables which influence stability and most of them interact and are interdependent. In general therefore, it is not possible to alter one parameter without consequential changes in another, nevertheless general guidance may be given (Rawson and Tupper, 1976:124–7). There are two basic ways to increase the value GM_t, and thus improve stability: one is to raise the position of M by increasing the distance BM; and the other is to lower the position of G.

(i) Increasing BM_t

$BM_t = It/\nabla LB^3/LBT = KB^2/T$ ($10 \leq K \leq 15$) – for a rectangular section

Thus, length (L) does not influence transverse BM, but beam (B) increases it according to its square; and draft (T) increases it as its inverse. In general then, for most forms of cross–section, increased beam and reduced draft, especially the former, improve transverse stability. In other words, increasing beam at the expense of displacement increases BM_t; and if G, the centre of gravity, remains the same or lower, then initial stability, measured by GM_t, will be increased.

In Appendix 3 it is shown that a rectangular section has a GM_t 37 times, and a half–rounded section a GMt 70 times, as great as that of a boat of square form; with corresponding relative values for initial transverse stability. The square and rectangular forms will, however, be more highly damped than the half–rounded form in any roll that may develop.

(ii) Lowering G

The centre of gravity of the boat may be lowered by making the bottom relatively thick and the sides thin. Similarly, crewmen kneeling will produce a lower G than when they are standing. In critical cases, standing may not be possible, unless there is a compensating reduction in the height of G by using ballast. In such conditions it will not be practicable to carry bulky, low–density loads which would have the effect of raising G beyond the critical point where it coincides with M, and GM_t is reduced to zero.

Effects of varying certain features amidships

Having examined how certain desirable characteristics may best be obtained, we may now turn the problem around and attempt to describe the effect of varying certain design features. It must be emphasised that the factors are complex and inter–related, and to date have received little study in so far as they are incorporated in logboat design. In general, then, absolute statements and quantification cannot be made, but it is possible to discuss the general effect these variables have on performance.

Half log or whole log

A whole log, or one half of a log split longitudinally may be used to build a logboat, with the following results:

Whole log   (i) more depth, and therefore more freeboard for a given displacement.
(ii) maximum use of the log achieved by using a rounded transverse section with tumblehome.

Half log   (i) a half–rounded transverse section will make maximum use of the half log,
(ii) greater beam obtainable, and greater (B/T) means that transverse stability will be greater.
(iii) more appropriate to shallow waters .
(iv) with relatively light draft, manoeuvrability is greater.

General form of the hull

Three representative forms are considered here: other forms are best considered as combinations of the individual features discussed subsequently.

Log–shaped: A boat made from a whole log will have a rounded transverse section with tumblehome and will taper from the butt end. This form makes maximum use of the log to obtain maximum displacement and hence payload, and has the stability and resistance advantages associated with rounded transverse sections. Maximum use of the log would lead logically to blunt ends which are resistful. Having the maximum beam at or near the stern is also resistful.

A boat made from half a split–log would have a half–rounded transverse sectlon, otherwise the above considerations apply.

Punt–shaped with flared sides: With a half log the maximum possible beam can be achieved, albeit at the top edge or sheerline. Transverse stability and payload (measured by tonnes per metre immersion) increase with increasing draft. The ends are resistful, and the transverse section is more resistful that a half–rounded section. The outward sloping sides and ends may be more easily damaged than vertical ones but they also result in a drier boat in a lop, and thus less freeboard will be required. From a given log, a broader, and hence more stable, boat is obtained by using a flared transverse section rather than a rectangular one.

'Boat' –shaped: 'Boat'–shaped here means having the maximum beam near the midships station, and having a sheerline higher at the ends than amidships. More of the log is worked away than in other designs (*ceteris paribus*), and thus, for a given log, displacement and hence payload are the least. However, there are gains in speed, stability and manoeuvrability, and the sheer at the ends could extend the conditions within which the boat could be operated.

The shape of the ends

Rounded or rounded–point (spoon–shaped) ends will give the least reslstance, and blunt ends the most. A spoonshaped bow can be more readily operated off a rlver bank, and when underway it will ride over obstructions and thus deflect blows whereas a blunt bow would absorb the full force of collision. Blunt ends on the other hand, give the maximum load space, but they produce short end–grain, unless the ends are thick. The punt–end has been discussed above. A fitted–transom stern is structurally sound; it provides transverse strength without the extra thickness and hence weight, implicit with other designs, and it overcomes the problem of short end–grain at the stern. For maximum strength and watertightness it must be combined with a beam–tie. A transom stern will, however, cause more drag than a rounded stern.

Thick ends required for structural reasons may be turned to good effect by using them as seats or as fishing platforms.

The transverse section

In Appendix 3, half–rounded, rectangular, and square transverse sections are compared, with the following results. The square section has least stability and is most resistful; but has the best payload. The rectangular section has 37 times the stability, 9% less resistance, but 13% less payload than the square form. The half–rounded section has 70 times the stability, 23% less resistance, but 21% less payload than the square form. These comparisons of resistance are based solely on wetted surface area, and as the sharp turn of the bilge of both square and rectangular forms will induce eddies, their total resistance will be further increased

A variant form of transverse section is one with tumblehome where maximum use is made of a whole log. This will give the maximum depth of boat out of any given log and this form will (*ceteris paribus*) have the maximum freeboard. The flared transverse section has been discussed above.

Overall dimensions varied with constant displacement

Keeping a constant dlsplacement volume we may investigate the effect on speed, manoeuvrability and stability when a logboat' s principal dimensions are varied by small increments.

Length and beam: To maintain constant displacement and draft, the length must be decreased in the same ratio as the beam is increased (Rawson and Tupper, 1976:97) and vice versa. An increased beam under these conditions means a boat with more transverse initial stability. Thus, the shorter, beamier logboat will have more initial stability. A reduced (L/B) means a more manoeuvrable boat, but it will have a reduced power/drag ratio, if relatively fewer crew are carried.

Draft: To maintain constant displacement and length the draft must be decreased in the same ratio as the beam is increased. (Rawson and Tupper, 1976:97). There will be no appreciable effect on resistance; manoeuvrability will be increased due to reduced (L/B), offset to a degree by reduced draft. Inereased beam will again mean an inherently more stable boat.

Overall dimensions varied in proportion to displacement.

Length: If beam and draft are kept constant, and length is increased in proportion to displacement, there is no change in GM_t, and initial stability as measured by GMt will only be affected if the transverse centre of gravity alters. Increased (L/B) will mean less manoeuvrabillty. Inereased length will mean that the boat is more resistful but it may also permit more crew to be carried to propel the boat. Thus, a longer boat (beam and draft constant) will carry more, but will be less manoeuvrable; there will probably be no appreciable change in transverse stability, or in power/drag ratio.

Beam: If length and draft are kept constant, and beam inereased in proportion to displacement, there will be an inerease in BM_t proportional to the square of the increase in beam. With a virtually unchanged KGt and KBt there will thus be an improvement in transverse initial stability. Reduced (L/B), will mean greater manoeuvrability. There will be more wetted area and therefore the boat will be more resistful. Increased beam may mean room to carry more crew .

Thus, a beamier boat (length and draft constant) will carry more, will have greater manoeuvrability and be more stable, but wlll probably be capable of a lower maximum speed, unless the ability to carry extra crew compensates for the increased resistance.

Draft: If length and beam are kept constant and draft is inereased in proportton to dlsplacement, initial stability will be reduced. Increased draft will mean that it will be not so readily manoeuvrable, and that there will be more drag due to the increased wetted area.

Thus, a logboat drawing more water (beam and length constant) will carry more, will not be so readily manoeuvrable, will be capable of lower maximum speeds and have reduced initial stability.

Paired logboats

Joining two logboats together laterally produces a more stable platform. The effective beam is increased, and thus KMt is increased, the amount of increase depending on the spacing of the two boats. If the load can still be carried *within* the boats, the increase in KMt will be directly reflected in increased metacentric height. Even if the load has now to be carried on a platform at the level of the top edge, with a consequential increase in KG, it is probable that there will be a net gain in metacentric height.

As there will now be a greater wetted area with no increase in length, the configuration will be more resistful than a single boat. However, the space available for crew will be greater and thus propulsive force may be increased. Any toe–in or toe–out will increase the drag, and even when the boats are parallel, there will be interaction effects. With an effectively smaller (L/B), manoeuvrability will be improved; but controllability – abiliy to maintain a desired course – may be less.

External longitudinal timbers

Structurally, these fittings will provide a measure of longitudinal strength and act as a rubbing strake. If near the top edge, they may also act as a spray deflector in a lop and thus offset a low freeboard. In addition, they will introduce appendage drag and will have other hydrostatic and hydrodynamic effects, the nature and extent of which will depend on their position on the boat's side.

At the loaded waterline, the increased beam, with an imperceptible increase in displacement, will means that BM$_t$ will be increased with a resulting increase in initial stability when compared to the boat without these fittings. This effect will be greater the broader and less deep the timbers are – although there will be an appreciable effect even when these dimensions are equal. There will be virtually no increase in displacement or payload. Manoeuvrability may be improved slightly, due to decreased (L/B). But as there will be an increase in wetted surface area, drag will be increased.

Thus, these timbers or *firs* would be fitted at the waterline to improve stability whilst keeping displacement virtually constant.

At the top edge, being above the waterplane, initial stability, manoeuvrability, displacement, and resistance will not be affected except by the relatively small amount KG has increased. These timbers will become effective at large angles of heel when one of them becomes immersed, at which point transverse stability will be increased. This improvement will be limited, as an increased angle of heel will result in the deck–edge being immersed. If the boat were to be operated at the deep drafts where these timbers were continuously immersed, they would have the effects on initial stability noted above.

Longitudinal timbers fitted between top edge and waterline, which thus became effective at lower angles of heel, would have the advantages described above, without the immediate limitation of deck–edge immersion. There may be a position close to but not touching the water surface when – as with an – outrigger boomed out from the hull –the timber is subjected to dynamic lift, thus improving payload.

Expansion and extension

Expansion increases the beam of a basic logboat, and may also give it sheer with consequent reduced freeboard amidships. Increased beam means improved initial stability, and this is the prime reason for expanding logboats.

Extension by one strake – as we are limited to in this work – can restore any freeboard lost by expansion, and may provide the basis for those improvements which can be incorporated in multi–part boats

References

Coates, J.F., 1977. hypothetical reconstructions and the Naval Architect in McGrail, S. (ed) *Sources and Techniques in Boat Archaeology*: 215–226. BAR S29, Oxford.

Jane, F.W., 1970. *Structure of Wood*. 2nd Edition

McKee, E., 1976. Identification of timbers from old ships of NW European origin. *Int. J. Nautical Archaeology*, 5: 3–12.

Rawson, K.J. and Tupper, E.C., 1976. *Basic Ship Theory* 2 volumes. 2nd edition (3rd edition, 1983 & 1984).

Rendle, B.J., 1971 *Growth and Structure of Wood* HMSO

APPENDIX 1

Glossary

This Glossary of logboat terms is based principally on the Glossary published by Basil Greenhill in *Archaeology of the Boat*, 1976. Eric McKee and Richard Clarke have helped me formulate several definitions, and the following works have also been consulted: McKee (1976:10–12); Rawson and Idwelght Tupper (1976); Rendle (1971); Jane (1970). The numbers after some terms refer to the corresponding positions on fig 6.3.2.

auger	tool to bore holes
batten	flexible length of wood used for less important structures
batten seam	*seam* masked by a batten which primarily retains *caulking*, but may take fastenings
baulk	a tree trunk which has been roughly squared.
beak (1)	projection from the *bows* of a boat.
beam (crossbeam)	transverse strengthening member in the main body of the boat; may also be used as a *thwart*.
beam–tie (2)	transverse strengthening member at the ends of a logboat, may be in the form of a *crook*.
bevel	surface which has been angled to make a fit with another
bilge (12)	area between the sides and the bottom of a boat.
blind fastening	one in which the point of the nail does not protrude through the timber.
blind hole	one which does not pierce the timber.
bottom boards	lengths of timber laid over the bottom of a boat as flooring
bole	main stem or trunk of a tree.
bow	fore–end of a boat (see diagram).
bulkhead (9)	a transverse partition extending from (near) *top edge*, which divides the boat into compartments.
butt (end)	base of the main trunk of a tree.
buttresses	above ground swelling of *bole*; beginning of root system.
caulk	to insert material between two members *after* they have been assembled, and thus make the junction water tight (see *luting*).
clamp	a device for holding elements of a boat together (temporarily).
cleat	a short piece of wood or a projection to which other fittings may be fastened.
clench (rivet)	to deform the end of a fastening so that it will not draw out – usually done over a *rove*.
clinker–built	a form of boat–building in which the *strakes* are placed so that they partly overlap one another – usually upper strake outboard of lower strake or of logboat *top edge*.
construction plan	a scale drawing of a boat with longitudinal section, horizontal plan, and several transverse sections. The position and

	nature of the *scarfs*, and other important constructional details and scantlings may also be given.
crook	a curved piece of wood which has grown into a shape useful for boat building.
deadweight	in this text: weight of crew, equipment and cargo.
density, bulk	mass per unit volume of an homogenous, bulk cargo.
density, critical bulk	that bulk density which, in standard conditions, reduces GM_t to zero.
depth, internal	vertical distance from the *top edge* to the inside bottom of the boat, normally at the station of maximum beam (see diagram).
double–ended	a boat which is (nearly) symmetrical about the midships transverse plane.
draft (draught)	vertical distance from the lowest point of the hull to the waterline (see diagram).
faying	fitting closely, in contact.
feather edge	tapering to nothing.
fibre saturation point	a theoretical stage in wood–water relations when all the water (free water) has been removed from the cell cavities, but none from the cell walls. For most timbers this is at a moisture content of 25%to to 30%.
flare	the transverse section of a boat inereases in breadth towards the *top edge*.
floor	a transverse member – often a *crook* – extending from turn of *bilge* to turn of bilge (see *frame*)
frame	a transverse member made up of more than one piece of timber, usually extending from *sheer* to *sheer* and set against the planking (see *rib* and *timber*).
freeboard	vertical distance from the *top edge* to the waterline (see diagram).
grommet	strand(s) of animal or vegetable fibre laid up in the form of a ring.
height, external	vertical distance from the *top edge* to the lowest part of the hull, normally at the *station* of maximum beam (see diagram).
knee	a naturally grown *crook* used as a bracket between two members set at about right–angles to each other.
land	that part of a *strake* which is overlapped by the strake immediately above it.
lines	the inter–relation of sections in different planes which show the shape of a boat's hull. They usually consist of (a) sheerplan with longitudinal sections b) half breadth plan with waterlines or horizontal sections (c) body plan with transverse sections. Diagonal lines, longitudinal section lines on the half–breadth plan, and waterlines on the sheer plan, enable the three plans to be related to each other and checked for

fairness. Lines converted to numbers are known as a Table of Offsets.

logboat ,basic a monoxylous waterborne craft; a boat made from a single log, without expansion or extension.

logboat, expanded a basic logboat enlarged by forcing the sides apart.

logboat, extended a basic or expanded logboat with the height of the sides inceased by the addition of *washstrakes*.

luting traditionally, luting is a plastic substance such as paint used between two adjacent members of a boat's structure. In this text the term is used to describe any material inserted between two members *before* they are assembled (see *caulk*).

mast step fitting with a mortice to locate the heel of a mast.

mean shrinkage factor see *shrinkage factor*.

metacentric height distance from the metacentre to the centre of gravity of a loaded boat (see Fig. 6.3.1).

moisture content the weight of water in a specimen of wood expressed as a percentage of the weight of oven-dry wood. Thus, the figure can be greater than 100% O

outrigger framework of boom(s) and float(s) projecting from the side(s) of a boat.

painter light head rope by which a boat is made fast; mooring rope.

plank a component of a *strake* that is not all in one piece.

planking, radial the plane of the plank's surfaces are at right-angles to the growth rings, i. e. parallel to the *rays* (such planking is normally split from the log).

planking, tangential the plane of the plank's surfaces are tangential to the growth rings, i. e. at right-angles to the *rays*.

rays thin vertical sheets of parenchyma cells, one or more cells wide, radially disposed in the wood such that their longer axes are in the horizontal and radial plane.

rib (6) a simple form of frame. This term is preferred to frame in the logboat context.

ridge (7) (8) a transverse length of timber a few cms high, left proud of the inside of the hull, extending across the bottom of the boat, and sometimes from (near) *top edge* to (near) top edge.

rocker the underside of the boat rises towards the ends, in the longitudinal plane.

rove (roove) a washer-like piece of metal, which is forced over the point of a nail before it is *clenched*.

scarf (scarph, scarve) a tapered or wedge shaped joint between pieces of similar section at the join.

seam juncture of two members required to be watertight.

sheer (sheer line) the curve of the upper edge of the hull; for *basic* logboats, *top edge* (s) may be preferable .

shrinkage index the ratio of the pre-shrinkage to post shrinkage dimensions of a hole or other feature in a boat. It may be tangential or radial.

shrinkage factor the arithmetic mean of several shrinkage indices from one boat. Mulitplication by this factor will convert shrunken dimensions to the best estimate of the pre-shrinkage scantlings.

shrouds ropes leading from the mast head to the sides of the boat to support the mast athwartships.

Spanish windlass a simple rope and rod device for forcing two elements closer together, and holding them there.

stabilisers (firs) (14) external longitudinal timbers fastened to the boat's side at, or close to, the loaded waterline, to enhance transverse stability.

stays ropes leading from the masthead forward and aft, to support the mast.

stern after-end of a boat (see diagram). '

Stockholm tar a blackish semi-liquid prepared by the destructive distillation of various trees of the *Pinaceae* family

strake a single *plank* or combination of planks which stretches from one end of a boat to the other.

strake, rubbing (13) an additional strake or length of timber fastened external to the boat's side for protection against chafing and bumping.

stretcher athwartships *timber* or fittintg against which a rower braces his feet.

thickness gauges (11) holes bored to pre-set depths into a log which is to be hollowed, to obtain the required thickness of bottom (and sides).

thole a pin projecting upwards at *sheer* level to provide a pivot for an oar.

thwart a transverse member used as a seat (see *beam*).

timber an element of a frame. Often also used to refer generally to any piece of wood used in boatbuilding.

timber, foot see *stretcher*.

top edge (5) the highest surface of a *basic* logboat (see *sheer*)

transom (10) athwartship *bulkhead*; in this text it is normally applied to a fitted bulkhead at the stern.

treenail (trenail, trunnel) wooden peg or through-fastening used to join two members. It may be secured at each or either end by the insertion of a wedge.

tumblehome the transverse section of a boat deereases in breadth, as the sides approach the *top edge*, (opposite of *flare*).

washstrake (3) an additional *strake* normally fitted to keep out spray and water; in this text it is applied to any strake fitted to a *basic* or *expanded* logboat.

References

Jane, F.W., 1970. *Structure of Wood* 2nd edition.
McKee, E., 1976. Identification of timbers from old ships of NW European origin *Int. J. of Nautical Archaeology*, 5:3–12.
Rawson, K.J. and Tupper, E.C., 1976. *Basic Ship Theory*, 2 volumes.
Rendle, B.J., 1971. *Growth and Structure of Wood*. HMSO.

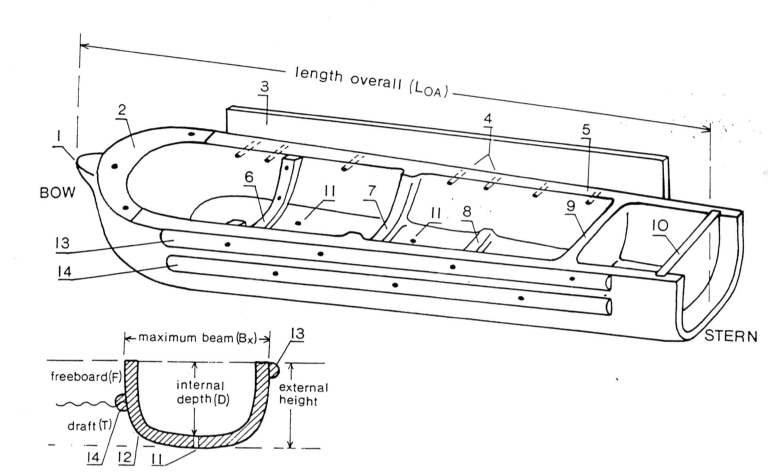

1   Beak
2   Grown timbers treenailed on to give transverse strength to the boat at the ends
3   Washstrake nailed overlapped to the boat
4   Iron nails
5   Sheer line or top edge
6   Fitted rib treenailed to the boat
7   Ridge left in solid from sheer to sheer
8   Ridge left in solid across the bottom

9   Bulkhead left in the solid
10 Fitted transom in groove
11 Thickness gauges
12 Turn of the bilge
13 Rubbing strake treenailed to the boat near sheer
14 Stabilising timber treenailed to the boat at water-line

Figure 6.3.2 Diagram explaining some terms used. Drawing: National Maritime Museum

APPENDIX 2

Symbols used in the text
(after Rawson and Tupper, 1976)

F	freeboard (m)	V_l	volume of log (m³)
T	draft (m)	V_h	volume of logboat's hollow (m³)
D	internal depth of boat (m)	V_w	volume of wood in boat (m³)
L_{oa}	length overall (m)	V_{cc}	critical cargo volume (m³)
L_{wl}	length of waterline (m)		
B_x	maximum beam (m)	C_b	block coefficient
		C_m	maximum–beam section coefficient
		C_p	longitudinal prismatic coefficient
KB	distance 'keel' to centre of buoyancy (m)	C_∇	volumetric coefficient
KG	distance 'keel' to centre of gravity (m)	C_{wp}	fineness of waterplane coefficient
BM	distance centre of buoyancy to metacentre (m)	C_{cc}	crew capacity coefficient
		C_{mp}	manpower coefficient
KM_t	distance 'keel' to transverse metacentre (m)	C_{men}	men coefficient
GM_t	transverse metacentric height (m)	C_{rd}	restricted draft crew
I_t	transverse moment of inertia	C_{dwt}	deadweight coefficient
		C_{hd}	high–density cargo coefficient (at standard freeboard)

See Figure 6.3.1

		C_{cv}	cargo volume coefficient
Note: 'keel' is taken to be the lowest point of the hull.		C_{bc}	bulky low–density cargo coefficient
		$C_{l/b}$	slenderness coefficient
A_x	transverse area at station of Bx(m²)	C_{sy}	symmetry coefficient .
A_w	waterplane area (m²)	C_{mb}	position of Bx coefficient ;
S	wetted surface area (m²)	$C_{l/t}$	length/draft coefficient 1;
R_f	frictional resistance	$C_{b/t}$	beam/draft coefficient
		C_{hdm}	high–density cargo coefficient (at minimum freeboard)
W_{dwt}	deadweight (kg) ;	C_{log}	log conversion coefficient
W_{bh}	weight of bare hull (kg)	C_{space}	load space coefficient
Δ	displacement force (kg)	M	number of men carried
∇	displacement volume (m³)	M_x	theoretical maximum number of men
		C.B.D.	critical bulk density

APPENDIX 3

Theoretical comparison of three transverse sections

Three different forms of transverse section are analysed here, but as *solid* sections of a log, rather than the hollowed–out sections of a logboat. This theoretical analysis will thus not take several factors into account. Nevertheless, it is considered that this analysis of solid forms will give a good indication of the *relative* properties of hollowed forms.

Rectangular and half–rounded transverse sections are well represented in the logboat–finds of England and Wales, and

these forms are therefore analysed, together with a square section for comparison. The three sections are taken from a standard log of diameter B (no allowance being made for sapwood and bark); the half–rounded form is taken from a half log, and the other two from a whole log, as was generally found in the Survey. The square and half–rounded forms are the maximum obtainable; the rectangular form has been chosen so that (Beam/Depth) = <'3, which is a close approximation to the mean figure (1.69) for the reconstructed logboats with this form.

TRANSVERSE SECTIONS

Square	Half–rounded	Rectangular

1. *Hull weight* (i) This is proportional to the section area

$$W_{bh} = \frac{B}{\sqrt{2}} \cdot \frac{B}{\sqrt{2}} = \frac{B^2}{2}$$

$$W_{bh} = \frac{\tilde{\Pi}}{2} \cdot \frac{B^2}{4} = \frac{\tilde{\Pi} B^2}{8}$$

$$W_{bh} = \frac{B\sqrt{3}}{2} \cdot \frac{B}{2} = \frac{B^2 \sqrt{3}}{4}$$

2. *Maximum payload* (i) This is taken to be when the top edge is awash and is proportional to the area of the non–immersed section when floating without a load.

(ii) Using oak of density 0.8, Non–immersed area = 0.2 (section area)

$$W_{dwtx} = \frac{2}{10} \cdot \frac{B^2}{2} = \frac{B^2}{10}$$

$$W_{dwtx} = \frac{2}{10} \cdot \frac{\tilde{\Pi} B^2}{8}$$
$$= \frac{\tilde{\Pi} B^2}{40}$$

$$W_{dwtx} = \frac{2}{10} \cdot \frac{B^2 \sqrt{3}}{4}$$
$$= \frac{B^2 \sqrt{3}}{20}$$

3. *Friction resistance* (i) This is proportional to the wetted surface.

$$R_f = \frac{B}{\sqrt{2}} + \frac{4\sqrt{2}B}{5}$$
$$= \frac{13\sqrt{2}B}{10}$$

$$R_f = c \frac{19}{21} \cdot \frac{\tilde{\Pi} B}{2}$$
$$= \frac{19 \tilde{\Pi} B}{42}$$

$$R_f = \frac{\sqrt{3}B}{2} + \frac{4B}{5}$$
$$= \frac{(5\sqrt{3} + 8)B}{10}$$

4. *Transverse resistance* (i) KG is the height of the centre of gravity of the section.
(ii) KB is the height of the centre of gravity of the wetted section.
(iii) BM = I/$\triangledown$
(iv) GM$_t$ = KB + BM − KG = metacentric height.

$$\overline{KG} = \frac{B}{2\sqrt{2}} = \frac{\sqrt{2}\,B}{4} \qquad \overline{KG} = \underline{c}\,\frac{3}{5} \cdot \frac{B}{2} = \frac{3B}{10} \qquad \overline{KG} = \frac{B}{4}$$

$$\overline{BM} = \left(\frac{B}{\sqrt{2}}\right)^3 \frac{5}{12 \cdot 2B^2} \qquad \overline{BM} = (.989B)^3 \frac{10}{12\,\tilde{\Pi}\,B^2} \qquad \overline{BM} = \left(\frac{B\sqrt{3}}{2}\right)^3 \frac{5}{12B^2\sqrt{3}}$$

$$= \frac{5\sqrt{2}\,B}{96} \qquad\qquad = \frac{.967B}{1.2\,\tilde{\Pi}} \qquad\qquad = \frac{15B}{96}$$

$$\overline{KB} = \frac{\sqrt{2}\,B}{5} \qquad\qquad \overline{KB} = \underline{c}\,\frac{B}{4} \qquad\qquad \overline{KB} = \frac{B}{5}$$

$$\overline{GM}_t = \frac{\sqrt{2}\,B}{5} + \frac{5\sqrt{2}\,B - \sqrt{2}B}{96}\,\frac{}{4} \qquad \overline{GM}_t = \frac{B}{4} + \frac{.967B}{1.2\,\tilde{\Pi}} - \frac{3B}{10} \qquad \overline{GM}_t = \frac{B}{5} + \frac{15B}{96}\,\frac{B}{4}$$

$$= \underline{c}\,.0029B \qquad\qquad = .206B \qquad\qquad = \underline{c}\,.106B$$

Relative Abilities

These are compared in the order − square: half rounded: rectangular.

a) *Maximum payload* These are in the ratio:

$$\frac{1}{10} : \frac{\tilde{\Pi}}{40} : \frac{\sqrt{3}}{20} = \underline{c}\,4 : 3.1416 : 3.464 = \underline{1 : .785 : .866}$$

The square form can carry more than the rectangular form, which can carry more than the half−rounded form.

b) *Frictional resistance* These are in the ratio:

$$\frac{13\sqrt{2}}{10} : \frac{19\,\tilde{\Pi}}{42} : \frac{5\sqrt{3}+8}{10} = \underline{c}\,1.84 : 1.42 : 1.67 = \underline{1 : .772 : .908}$$

The square form has more resistance than the rectangular form, which has more resistance than the half−rounded form, i.e. the half−rounded form is potentially faster than the rectangular form, which is potentially faster than the sqaure form.

c) *Transverse stability* (measured by GM$_t$) These are in the ratio:

.0029 : .206 : .106 = *1 : 70 : 37*

The half−rounded form has better stability than the rectangular form, which has better stability than the square form.

Summary

Using the square form as a basis for comparison, these results are summarised below.

	Transverse Sections		
	Square	*Half-rounded*	*Rectangular*
Payload (see note)	Basis for comparison	21% or less	13% or less
Frictional resistance		23% or less	9% or less
Transverse stability		70 times more	37 times more

Aknowledgment

The general method of analysis was suggested to me by Professor K.G. Rawson.

Note: Ole Crumlin–Pedersen has subsequantly shown that, for *hollowed-out* forms of thickness:

half–rounded	constant thicknes = t
square	bottom = 2t, sides = t
rectangular	bottom = 2t, sides = t

both half–rounded and rectangular forms have 15% less payload than the sqaure form.

Reprinted from

McGrail, S., *Logboats of England and Wales*:94–102. British
Archaeological Report 51 (1978).

PAPER 6.4

ASPECTS OF WOOD SCIENCE

Timber suitable for logboats

The ideal tree for the hull of a basic, unexpanded logboat would have the following characteristics:

(i) Long straight bole of substantial girth and little taper, with straight grain and no recent branches low down.

(ii) The species of timber to be durable and resistant to fungal decay, yet relatively easy to work; strong to withstand damage, yet light weight to improve loadbearing capacity and to increase portability.

(iii) To be situated where it can easily and safely be felled, with ready access to a water–course.

TImber for ribs and other curved fittings needs to have its grain, and hence its greatest strength, following the required curve.

Table 6.4.1 which has been compiled from publications by the Forest Products Research Laboratory (*Handbook of Hardwoods*, 1956; *Handbook of Softwoods*, 1965; Farmer, 1972), tabulates various properties of modern samples of those species of timber known to have been used for logboats. It may be taken as a general guide to the properties of timber used in antiquity.

Oak (Quercus sp)

Of the species of timber available during the past 6000 years in north–west Europe, forest–grown oak (*Quercus* sp) appears to be nearest to the ideal for logboat hulls. In competition with other trees it will not grow as rapidly in girth as would a free–standing oak, but if left to grow for two centuries or more, it will achieve an impressive length of straight bole with reasonable girth and little taper. Shading by other trees will cause the death of the older branches which will fall off, their bases and snags becoming buried in the timber as the trunk increases in girth. Thus, the older, central wood of the lower bole will have some knots, but the outer, younger layers will give clear timber (Jane, 1970:198) Oak is durable, being In the second of five categories used by the Forest Products Research Laboratory (Farmer, 1972:148); and forest–grown oak, being slow–growing, requires less effort to work than timber from an isolated relatively fast–growing tree. Oak is also easier to work whilst it is still 'green', i. e. of a high moisture content, before the log has seasoned. There is evidence that, until relatively recently, timber for plank–boats was worked soon

after it was felled (McGrall, 1974.40), and what little ethnographic evidence there is indicates that logboats were similarly fashioned from ' green' logs. In the absence of experimental evidence it is not possible from present day standard tests of timber species, to decide whether oak (*Quercus* sp) could be successfully used to build an expanded logboat.

Free–standing oaks (and other specles) will grow crooked branches, some of them low down on the bole, and these 'crooks' will be best suited for the curved fittings required in logboats.

Size of modern oaks: To permit standard comparisons to be made, sizes of growing trees are often given as the girth measured at ' breast height' c 5 ft (1.52 m) from the highest point of the ground; this girth is easily converted into diameter of bole. For lengths of bole up to 15 m, Farmer (1972: 146) gives c 1.2 to 1.8 m as the present–day range for the diameter of mature European Oak grown under forest conditions. Alan Mitchell of the Forestry Commission (personal communicatlon) estimates that the bole diameter generally expected in England and Wales is c 2.4 m – but this includes free–standing oaks. Individual trees have been recorded with the following dlameter: Newland Oak, Forest of Dean, Gloucester c 4.27 m (Edlin, 1970:Plate Va); Pontfadog, Chirk c 5.12 m (Edlin, 1970:175); Bowthorpe Farm, Lincolnshire, c 3.78 m (Mitchell, 1974:356). Regrettably, the length of bole is seldom mentioned, but it appears that nowadays few, if any, oaks combine great girth with length of bole, as many of them are pollards, often of no greater bole length than 2.5 m. Unpollarded trees grow to greater heights, but these are nowadays generally of unexceptional girth.

Size of ancient oaks: Peck (1815:3) recorded that a fallen oak preserved in the peat of Hatfield Chase near the Yorkshire/Lincolnshire border, was 40 yd (36.58 m) long, and 4 yd (3.66 m) in diameter at one end, tapering to 2 yd (1.83 m) at the other; and MacCormick (1968:28) although giving no sizes, stated that numerous large, straight oak–boles had been found in the gravels of the R. Trent at Holme Pierrepont and elsewhere. The caption on the back of the original photograph of logboat Hylton 1, records that the oak log in the background was dredged from the R . Wear in 1880 and measured 32 ft (9.75 m) x 5 ft (1.52 m) in diameter (Whitcomb, 1968:299). According to Wildridge (1888:136), trees, of sufficient size to make a logboat similar to that found at Brigg, had been unearthed in several parts of the country, including one from South Kelsey, near Brigg. Wildridge also claimed that similar

Table 6.4.1 properties of modern samples of timber

Species	Length of bole	Diameter of bole	Grain	Density	Workability	Durability
1. Alder (*Alnus* sp)	6–12m	.3–1.2m	Straight	Medium	Good	Perishable
2. Ash (*Fraxinus* sp)	10–15m	.6–1.5m	Straight	Heavy	Moderate	Perishable
3. Aspen (*Populus* sp)	18–25m	.9–1.2m	Straight	Light	Moderate/Good	Perishable
4. Beech (*Fagus* sp)	10–15m	c 1.2m	Straight	Heavy	Moderate	Perishable
5. Chestnut (*Castenae Sativa*)	6m	c 1.5m	Straight	Medium	Moderate/Good	Durable
6. Elm (*Ulmus* sp)	12–18m	1–1.5m	Tendency to be cross	Medium	Moderate	Non-durable
7. Lime (*Tilia* sp)	15m	up to 1.2m	Straight	Medium	Moderate/Good	Moderate
8. Oak (*Quercus* sp)	up to 15m	1.2–1.8m	Straight	Heavy	Moderate	Non-durable
9. Pine (*Pinus Sylvestris*)	?	.6–.9m	Spiral is common	Medium	Moderate	Non-durable
10. Spruce (*Picea* sp)	?	.7–1.2m	?	Medium	Good	Non-durable

Notes:

1. Deatils of the classification system may be found in the Handbook of Hardwoods (1956) and the Handbook of Softwood (1965), published by H.M.S.O.
2. In general, increased strength goes with increased density (Farmer, 1972, 2)
3. The data is for modern samples grown under forest conditions

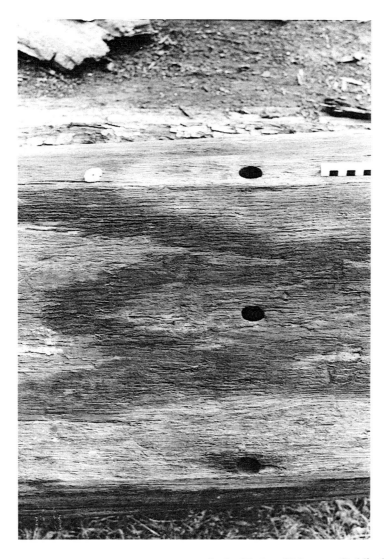

Figure 6.4.1 A vertical view inside a logboat from Lough Erne, now in the National Museum, Dublin. The holes piercing the dried-out timber are now elliptical. Photo: National Maritime Museum, Greenwich.

sized oaks were growing in his day at, for example, Canon Ashby, Northampton.

Estimates of the sizes of the parent logs of excavated material have some times been made, although the basis for the calculations is rarely stated. The following estimates are, however, well–documented and may therefore be taken to be reliable. Atkinson (1887:367) deduced that the smallest circumscribing circle for the stem of the 14.78 m long Brigg logboat was 5 ft 4 in (1.63 m) in diameter, and to this he added 6in (.15 m) for sapwood and bark, making a bole diameter of 1.78 m. Wright (1976:22 fig. 8) deduced that one element of the oak keel–plank of Bronze–Age Ferriby boat 2, came from a tree of minimum diameter 1.1 m over a length of 6.38 m. Fletcher (forthcoming) has calculated that the oak log from which some of the mid 10th–century A.D. Graveney boat split planking came, had a diameter of *c* 1 m: the longest length of plank here is *c* 3.87 m. The greatest breadth of oak plank recorded in the five Viking–Age ships from Skuldelev, Denmark, is.42 m (Olsen and Crumlin Pedersen, 1967:158). As experimental evidence (unpublished work by Egon Hansen at Moesgard, Denmark) indicates that the diameter of the parent log must be some 3. 33 times the breadth of split planking, a

parent log of *c* 1.4 m diameter at some point in its length, is indicated for this Skuldelev timber.

It therefore seems clear that oak logs which combined great length with great breadth were more readily available in the past than they are today.

Comparison with other species: Oak (*Quercus* sp) is durable and thus probably survives for excavation in greater quantity than other species. However, Alder (*Alnus* sp), Lime (*Tilia* sp), Pine (*Pinus* sp), Spruce (*Picea* sp), Elm (*Ulmus* sp), and Chestnut (*Castanea sativa*) are stated to have been used for excavated logboats; in addition, Beech (*Fagus* sp), Ash (*Fraxinus* sp) and Aspen (*Populus* sp) have been used for north–west European logboats in the past two or three centuries.

Table 6.4.1 demonstrates that oak (*Quercus* sp) is the best all–round choice for a logboat, as it is closer to the ideal requirement than other species. Its relatively high density – which gives it strength – means, however, that an oak logboat is not so easily portable as, for example, one made from aspen

(*Populus* sp). Furthermore, it is not certain that an oak logboat can be expanded.

Examination of the timber

In addition to the identification of the timber species, careful examination of a logboat can reveal important information about the parent log.

The orientation of the log

It may be difficult to identify by visual inspection, the butt end of a log after it has been fashioned into logboat shape, as the tree will probably have been felled above the point where the root system is evident. Grimes (1931:140) pointed out, however, that branch insertion in an oak tends to be horizontal or at an angle above the horizontal and thus the orientation of the log can be deduced if the direction of a knot or knot–hole relative to the log axis can be ascertained. Where there are several knots showing the same direction, the identIfication of the butt–end may be made with reasonable confidence.

Alternatively, or in addition, it is reasonable to assume that in a tapered boat, the broader end is the butt end of the log – the alternative would be perverse. This reasoning is independent of attempts to identify the stem of the boat.

Growth inerements show in a longitudinal section of the log as a series of cones with their apices pointing to the top of the tree (Jane, 1970:71–2). Thus a detailed dendrological examination would reveal log orientation with more precision, but this may have to be done in the laboratory.

The pith and growth rings

A (partial) cross–section of the parent log may be visible at the ends of the boat, or at a bulkhead left in the solid. The position of the pith may then be noted directly, if it has survived, or it may be deduced by estimating the centre of the growth–ring pattern, or the point of intersection of the medullary rays. As logboats which have been allowed to dry out may spllt along these rays, radial splits may also be used, with care, to indicate the pith position. The relationshlp of the top edges of the boat to the position of the pith will show whether the boat was made from a whole log or from one half of a logitudinally–split log.

Ellmers (1973A:4) reported that recent logboat–builders in Austria took care to have the side with densest growth rings at the bottom (or top) of their boats. Any such asymmetric growth may be detected during examination of the boat, but detailed measurements may have to be undertaken in the laboratory.

Sapwood and bark

If sapwood can be identified, then not only can a more accurate estimate of the diameter of the parent log be made, but dendrochronological dating of the felllng year also becomes practicable. Samples of modern British oak with more than 80 growth rings, have been shown to have 20 ± 5 sapwood rings, whilst Irish samples have 32 ± 9 (Bailie, 1973:10). Fletcher (forthcoming) has evolved a somewhat different allowance in which the number of sapwood rings varies with the mean thickness of the recent heartwood rings. Thus, using one of these formulae, the number of rings outwards from the sapwood/heartwood transition, and hence the thickness of the wood, can be estimated. To this, must be added the thickness of bark to obtain the diameter of the original tree; this girth is then comparable with current measurements of standing timber. Mitchell (personal communication) has suggested that empirical thickness estimates for mature oak would be 3 in (76 mm) for sapwood, and 1 in to 12 in (25–38 mm) for bark. This gives a range of 102 mm to 114 mm, and, as the bark estimate is something of a maximum, a standard allowance of 100 mm for sapwood and bark seems reasonable. It is of interest to note that, from the diagrams published by Wright (1976:22 fig. 8) and by Olsen and Crumlin–Pedersen (1967:153 fig. 62), it can be calculated that these authors used sapwood plus bark allowance of *c* 100 mm for a Ferriby parent log, and *c* 80 mm for a Skuldelev log.

Degeneration of trees

Heart rot

Large–sized and therefore over–mature, oaks tend to develop a rot known as *brittle heart* (Jane, 1970:228). This is most extensively developed at the butt–end and decreases with height. Atkinson (1887:367) quoted W. Stephenson, 'an authority on trees and timber', for the statement that the log from which the Brigg logboat was made was hollow at the heart, the hollow extending to the first lateral branches at the bow end of the boat. The precise relationship extent of rot and age or size of oak is not known, but Mitchell (personal communication) believes that this decay is well under–way, although invisible externally, in any substantial oak, and he has noted that almost all modern oaks greater than *c* 2 m in diameter are palpably hollow. It therefore follows that, assuming a similar medieval and prehistoric lifecycle for the oak, there must be a limit to the breadth of logboat which can be built with integral ends; for oaks of greater diameter than this will have a hollow or rotten core at least at one end. The introduction of a fitted–transom stem may have been a solution to this problem.

It has been suggested that the larger, hollow oaks might more easily be blown over and thus be readily to hand for the logboat builder. In fact this sort of tree retains good stability against wind until decay is well advanced, since it is the perimeter and the root hold which are important in this context. Eventually loss of vigour, and any root damage wlll reduce this stability.

Induced rot

Knapp (1924:103–4) has suggested that the Maoris of New Zealand induced a long crevice of decay to extend up the trunks of *totara* trees which were to be used for logboats, by notching a sapling some 2 m from the ground. Such damage to one side of a tree could well cause local decay, which might then spread vertically (Brazier, F.P.R.L., personal communication), but an otherwise healthy tree would, in time, cover this damage, and the tree would have to be wounded repeatedly for a significant hollow of decay to be maintained. The practicability of this method therefore remains questionable.

Conversion of timber

The easiest way to split an oak is radially, because its rays assists the cleaving. The first radial split would be into two half–logs, and with a large tree and a good split, each half could become a logboat. Tangential splitting to achieve a horizontal surface on the upper side of a felled oak log (section 3. 2.1.4) would probably be difficult, although the builders of an Ulster experimental logboat are reported to have achieved this with wedges.

Whether made from a whole log or half a log, a logboat in use would have tendencies to split along the rays: this would be especially so at the ends (see, for example, Rasmussen, 1953:17–8). Hence, the several methods evolved to fit transverse strengthening timbers near the ends, which would resist this tendency.

Degeneration of logs

Rot and the use of fire

The surface of wood that has been decayed by dry rot (wood–destroying fungi which break down the cellulose and related substances) typically shows cuboidal cracking as splits develop across and along the grain. In the advanced stages of decay, the timber becomes darker brown in colour and crumbles to dry powder when handled (Jane, 1970:230–2, fig. 120A). Excavated log–boats which are allowed to dry–out may be attacked by this fungi and the ensuing cuboidal cracking may be interpreted by the inexperienced eye as charcoal produced by the use of fire during the building of the boat. See, for example, Wilson (1851:32) and Geikie (1879:2). Similar misinterpretations may be made when examining waterlogged timber which has dried out: the biodegradation here causes cubical cracking on the surface.

van Zeist (1957:8) recorded that on the inside and outside of the Pesse logboat a 'thin layer of carbonised wood' could be seen. This may be more authentic, but ethnographic evidence shows that when fire was used as an aid to hollowing–out a logboat, the charred timber was subsequently removed by metal or shell tools . Thus, only after secondary use or in an unfinished boat, would one expect to find charcoal remains. Salmonsson' s logboat from Skane, Sweden, had a slightly carbonised layer in the *unfinished* part (1957:292).

Shrinkage of fresh wood

Wood is anisotropic material: that is, its properties vary according to the orientation of the axis of the cells. When wood is dried from the ' as felled' or ' green' state, to below its fibre saturation point (fsp), (equivalent to moisture contents of c

28% to 30%), it shrinks differentially: the relative shrinkages for fresh European oak (*Quercus* sp) being 1: *c* 12: c 25 in the longitudinal, radial, and tangential planes. This longitudinal shrinkage is less than 1% and may, for most purposes, be disregarded. The other measures of shrinkage are of significance: for example, when fresh oak is dried from the ' green' state to a moisture content of 12%, it shrinks *c* 7. 5% measured tangentially, and *c* 4% radially (Farmer, 1972:147). A circular hole bored, into a ' green' log other than in the longitudinal direction, will be distorted into an ellipse by this differential shrinkage, as the log dries (Fig.6.4.1).

A hole bored radially into a log will have one axis of its cross–section in the longitudinal plane of the parent tree and the other axis in the tangential plane. Shrinkage in the longitudinal plane during drying will be negligible, and this dimension will remain close to the original diameter of the hole when bored. Shrinkage in the tangential plane will, however, be significant, and thus the hole will become elliptical, the ratio of its major to minor axis being a measure of the tangential component of shrinkage. A hole bored tangentially into a fresh log will, after drying, similarly give a measure of the radial component of shrinkage.

Shrinkage of waterlogged wood.

Waterlogged wood has experienced chemical and biological degradation which has altered its normal structure, and thus shrinkage experienced during drying from the waterlogged state will be abnormally high and irreversible. Barkman (1975:68), for example, has calculated, by unspecified methods, that timber from the *Wasa* had a tangential shrinkage of 16–24%, and a radial shrinkage of 8–12%. This shrinkage might be thought to be some function of time buried, but it undoubtedly is related more directly to other factors which, determine the degree of waterlogging and breakdown of the cell structure, and which thus determine the shrinkage experienced on drying.

When a waterlogged logboat is allowed to dry out – providing it holds together – it will shrink in breadth and depth: that is the sides and the bottom will be drawn together, (See Stampfuss, 1961:305, for an example of this effect).

The shrinkage of waterlogged wood is thus greater and more complex than the shrinkage of fresh wood. Little work has been published in this field, but it is assumed here as a working hypothesis that, as with fresh wood, the longitudinal shrinkage is relatively insignificant, although de Jong (1977:28) has recently published experimental data which indicate that there may be an appreciable longitudinal shrinkage of small samples, when forced–dried.

Elliptical hole measurement: The precise effect of this differential shrinkage on a circular hole bored into a logboat which subsequently becomes waterlogged and after excavation is allowed to dry out (Fig 6.1.1) will depend on such factors as the exact orientation of the hole, the local run of the grain, the presence or absence (and if absent, the point in the waterlogging or the drying phases when it was lost), and the orientation of any treenail in that hole, and the timber species of both treenail and logboat. For example, an oak treenail inserted into a radially bored hole in an oak logboat so that the treenail's radial dimension (relative to its own parent tree) is aligned with the hole's tangential dimension, could constrain the tangential shrinkage of the hole. Holes in different parts of the boat may experience different degrees of waterlogging which on drying will result in different amounts of shrinkage. Thus, not only will different waterlogged boats show different shrinkages, but there may also be different shrinkage rates in different parts of the same boat. It is considered, however, that a reasonable estimate of the shrinkage a waterlogged and subsequently dried–out logboat has experienced between the time the hole was bored and the time the minor and major axes of the hole are measured, may be obtained by the ratio of these measurements, providing that:

> (i) the measurements are taken at right angles to the axis of the hole,

> (ii) both faces of the hole are measured, wherever possible,

> (iii) the mean of the individual ratios (indices) for all the holes in a boat is calculated; any ' wild' readings being noted, but not included in the calculatlon.

This mean may be called the shrinkage factor for a particular boat, and it can be used to estimate the boat's original dimensions.

Scantling comparison: An alternative method of estimating shrinkage may be used, elther as an independent check of estimates made from elliptical hole calculations, or in its own right when a logboat has no measurable holes. In his re–evaluation of the remains of the Nydam plank boat, Åkerlund (1963: 155) compared Englehardt's 1863 measurements of the "circumference of the planking amidships" with Johannessen's 1929 measurements, and calculated the shrinkage (orientatlon unspecified) between these two dates to be 9%. He concluded that, as the Nydam boat had been excavated for four months before Englehardt took his measurements, 13% to 14% would be a reasonable estimate of shrinkage between excavation and 1929. When this method is applied to dried–out logboats, today, scantlings may be compared with the earliest recorded scantlings. If the shrinkage factor, calculated as the mean of several comparison indices, is insignificant, then it may be deduced that the earlier measurements were recorded *after* shrinkage, and thus were not the original dimensions of the boat. A shrinkage factor comparable in magnitude with those calculated for elliptical holes would, on the other hand, indicate that the earlier recording had been *before* any significant shrinkage had taken place. In the absence of other shrinkage data, this shrinkage factor calculated from scantling comparisons may be used to deduce the original dimensions of a dried–out logboat which survives sufficiently well to be recorded in some details, but whose original recording consisted of a few measurements and no detailed drawing.

A principal difficulty in applying this method of shrinkage calculation is to ensure that corresponding measurements are taken at exactly the same part of the structure. Additionally, although many logboats appear to have shrunk uniformly, maintaining a similar shape but of reduced tangential and radial dimenslons some have split along the bottom allowing the sides to open out, whilst others have reacted to the stresses imposed by shrinkage by forcing the sides closer together at the sheer. In these latter cases comparisons of depths and sheer breadths are invalid; but where the bottom is sound, comparison of breadths across the bottom may be made.

Shrinkage factors: Shrinkage is usually taken to be a comparison of the reduction in dimension with the original dimension, and may be expressed as a percentage. More useful in the archaeological context is a ratlo which may be called the *shrinkage index*, defined as the original dimension compared with the shrunken dimension. In the case of an elliptical hole, this index is (major axis/minor axis). The mean of the individual shrinkage indices from the several holes in a boat may be called the *mean shrinkage factor*. Multiplication by this factor will convert a present day shrunken dimension to the best estimate of the original pre–shrinkage dimension.

References

Åkerlund, H., 1963. Nydamskeppen *Goteborg*

Atkinson, A., 1887 Notes on an ancient boat found at Brigg *Archaeologia* 50 (part 2): 361–370.

Baillie, M., 1973. Dendrochronology: an excercise in archaeological dating. In Scott, B.G. (ed) *Perspectives in Irish Archaeology*: 6–16. Belfast.

Barkman, L., 1975. Presrvation of the warship *Wasa* in Oddy, A., (ed) *Problems in the conservation of waterlogged wood*: 65–105 NMM Monograph 16. Greenwich.

deJong, J., 1977. Conservation of old waterlogged wood in McGrail, S., (ed) *Sources and Techniques in Boat Archaeology*: 23–44. BAR S29 Oxford

Edlin, H.L., 1972. *Trees, Woods and Man.*

Elmers, D., 1973A. Kultbarken, fahren, fischerboote, vorgeschichtliche einbaume in Niedersachen. *Die Kunde*, NS24: 23–62.

Farmer, R.H., 1973. *Handbook of Hardwoods* 2nd edition HMSO.

Fletcher, J., *et al*, 1978. Tree Ring Studies in Fenwick, V., (ed) *Graveney Boat*: 111–124. BAR 53. Oxford

Geikie,J., 1879. Discovery of an ancient canoe in the old alluvium of the Tay at Perth. *Scottish Naturalist* 5: 1–7.

Grimes, W.F., 1931. Two dug–out boats from Wales. *Antiquaries Journal* 11: 136–144.

Jane, F.W., 1970. *Structure of Wood* 2nd edition.

Knapp, E.V., 1924. Canoe–building tools of the Tasman Bay Maoris. *J. of the Polynesian Soc* 33: 103–113.

MacCormick, A.G., *et al*, 1968. Three dugout canoes and a wheel from Holme Pierrepont, Nottinghamshire *Trns Thoroton Soc.* 72: 14–31.

McGrail, S., 1974. *Building and trials of a replica of an ancient boat: the Gokstad faering* Part 1 NMM Monograph 11. Greenwich.

Mitchell, A.F., 1974. Estimating the age of big oaks in Morris, M.G. and Perring, F.H., (ed) in *British Oak*; 355–6. Botanical Society of the British Isles.

Olsen, O., and Crumlin–Pedersen, O., 1967. Skuldelev Ships II *Acta Archaeologica* 38: 73–174.

Peck, W., 1815. *Topographical Account of the Isle of Axholme* 1.

Rasmussen, H., 1953. Hasselo –Egen. *Kuml* 15–48.

Salmonsson, B., 1957. Decouverte d'une pirogue prehistorique en Scaine. *L'Anthropologie*, 61: 289–294.

Stampfuss, R., 1961. Der einbaum von Gartrop–Buhl. *Bonner Jahrbucher* (Koln) 161: 300–307.

vanZeist, W., 1957. De Mesolithische boot van Pesse *Nieuwe Drentse Volksalmanak*: 4–11. Assen.

Whitcomb, N.R., 1968. Two prehistoric dugout canoes from the R. Wear at Hylton near Sunderland, Co. Durham. *Archaeologica Aeliana*, 46: 297–301.

Wildridge, T.T., 1888. Ancient one–tree boats of Northumbria *Northumbria*: 123–137.

Wilson, D., 1851. *Archaeology and Prehistoric Annals of Scotland*.

Wright, E.V., 1976. *North Ferriby Boats* NMM Monograph 23. Greenwich.

Reprinted from:

McGrail, S., *Logboats of England and Wales*: 117–124. British Archaeological Reports 51 (1978).

PAPER 6.5

A MEDIEVAL LOGBOAT FROM THE RIVER CALDER AT STANLEY FERRY, WAKEFIELD, YORKSHIRE

History of the find

This logboat (dugout canoe) was found in the bed of the R. Calder (SE 3561 2305) during excavations for an aqueduct in August, 1838. It was aquired by the Yorkshire Philosophical Society in 1840 and for a time was displayed in their museum at York on top of a case of stone tools (Fig 6.5.1). During the period of my survey of the logboats of southern Britain[1] the fragmentary remains of this boat were under conservation by the North Western Museums Service and could not be examined – however, the documentary evidence then available was summarized in the published catalogue of English and Welsh logboats.[2]

During conservation the surviving timbers were consolidated with PVA in Acetone and IMS, and they were then re–assembled by pinning with brass rods, the missing areas being filled with expanded aluminium covered with a pigmented mixture of polyester resin and sawdust. Eleven ribs of new pinewood were fitted using metal screws through some of the original holes in the boat. The two parts of the reconstituted boat were mounted on cradles so that the boat was sandwiched between cradles and new ribs. The boat was returned to the Yorkshire Museum in 1976 and became available for examination.

Recording the boat

The plan and sections (Fig. 6.5.2) are of the boat as reconstituted; they attempt to differentiate between original wood and modern 'fill'. The transverse section (CD) was taken at a position thought to give the most representative form of the original boat. There are 29 easily visible holes through the boat's bottom and sides which appear to be original; 21 other possibly original holes, marked X on the drawing, are partly obscured by modern ribs. Removal of these ribs whilst maintaining the safety of the boat is a lengthy procedure and was attempted only once: should it in future prove necessary to remove ribs for other reasons, the holes revealed should be compared with Fig. 6.5.2. On the drawing the holes have been allocated either a letter (A to O) or, if interpreted as for treenails to fasten ribs, the letter R and a number. One original rib has survived, but because of distortion it is impossible to convey an accurate representation of its shape in a two–dimensional drawing.

The reconstituted boat.

There is no early measured drawing of this boat and the main evidence for the original condition are two photographs from the period 1891–1925 now held in the Yorkshire Museum. The reconstitution of the fragmented remains was thus a difficult task and the North Western Museum Service are to be congratulated in producing a displayable artefact, approximating in form to that evident in the early photographs (Fig 6.5.2) Nevertheless, some of this work inevitably had to be done subjectively and it is possible to question some of the detail. In places the boat has been given a rounded form where the bottom meets the sides: on the evidence of original wood this should be an angular junction with flared sides, as in the transverse section CD in Fig.6.5.2. The fragments of original wood generally now appear to be at or close to their relative positions in antiquity, but the side shown in the longitudinal section of Fig. 6.5.2 is not connected by original timber to the remainder of the boat and should probably have been re–assembled at a lower level to match the other side. It also seems likely that the fragment which forms the surviving end of the boat and which is also unconnected should be neither so prominent nor so high.

Interpretation

(a) *The log*
The log was oak (*Quercus* sp.) and the early photographs show it had at least two moderately large knots. The pith is not visible in the surviving remains but the position deduced from the growth rings visible on the end fragment is marked on Fig. 6.5.2, so a whole log rather than half a split log was used. If this end fragment were to be repositioned as I have suggested above, the pith position would be lowered. The maximum diameter of the original log cannot be estimated with precision but it must have been greater than Hodson's maximum inside beam measurement of 1.17 m + *c.* 0.12 m (thickness of two sides) + 0.10 m (sapwood and bark) = *c.*1.39 m. The length was greater than 5.41 m. When compared with parent logs of other logboats this log was well above average for girth and above average for length.[3]

(b) **The boat**
In a letter to the Yorkshire Museum dated 3rd April, 1840, H. Hodson of the Aire and Calder Navigation Office at Goole gave the surviving length of the boat as *c.*17 ft. 9 ins. (5.41 m), and the internal breadth as *c.* 3 ft. 10 ins. (1.17 m). As

1 S. McGrail, <u>Logboats of England and Wales</u> (National Maritime Museum Archaeological Series 2, BAR 51, Oxford, 1978)

2 Ibid., no. 132

3 Ibid., 309

Figure 6.5.1 Logboat from Stanley Ferry, near Wakefield, Yorks. Photographed in the Yorkshire Museum in the early 20th century. Photo: Yorkshire Museum, York.

reconstituted the remains are now 5.55 m in length with a maximum internal breadth of 0.84 m. If the end fragment were to be placed nearer the other original timbers as suggested above, the surviving length would be reduced to *c.*5.41 m: the original full length cannot now be determined. The difference between original and present maximum internal breadth may partly be explained by shrinkage: the mean shrinkage factor[4] calculated from eight holes is 1.23 which indicates an original internal breadth of *c.* 0.84 x 1.23 = 1.03 m. Hodson did not give a height for this boat, but the maximum external height where there is original wood is now 0.27 m (excluding the raised end) which suggests an original height of *c.* 0.33 m. The bottom would originally have been *c.*25 mm thick, and the sides at the top edge *c.*60 mm. With external measurements of length> 5.41 m, breadth 1.29 m and height amidships 0.33 m, this boat was above average for length and well above average for breadth but below average for height, when compared with other logboats.[5]

The surviving end need not have been the bow, for logboats with similar bow and stern are known, nevertheless it would be a suitable shape for one, albeit probably not protruding as much as now reconstituted: the form of the other end cannot now be determined. The transverse section of flat bottom with flared sides results in good cargo space: it also ensures good transverse stability for as the boat is heeled the righting arm is increased. Having the sides thicker than the bottom results in a relatively higher centre of gravity and thus tends to reduce stability, but this thick top edge adds to the boat's longitudinal strength.

(c) **Fittings**
The series of holes shown on Fig. 6.5.2 with an R identification are interpreted as for treenails to fasten ribs (R1 to R11). In the early photographs (Fing 6.5.1) two fitted ribs are shown approximately in the position of my R1 and R2 rows, but the first modern rib in the reconstituted boat appears to be too close to the end. The original ribs seem to have been fastened with up to four treenails through the bottom and one or two through each side. The one surviving rib, whidh is an oak crook (naturally curved timber), is now very distorted but it is probable that the portion to the right of EF on Fig. 6.5.2 would formerly have been horizontal, thus making it likely that the notch was a limber hole to allow free passage of bilge water along the bottom of the boat. As oak crooks with appropriate double curves were probably difficult to find it seems likely that the ribs were 'alternating half–ribs plus side timbers'[6] with the near–vertical arm of the L–shaped, grown timbers on alternate sides. Another possibility, that these were closely–paired, alternating half–ribs, seems less likely. Rib spacings are 320 and 450 mm between the first two pairs and then 480–500 mm for the remainder.

There are several reasons why ribs may be fitted to logboats:

(i) To help retain the shape of an expanded boat (sides forced apart).

(ii) To support washstrakes (extra planking to extend height of boat).

(iii) To support thwarts (crossbeams used as seats).

(iv) For use as footrests.

(v) An unnecessary copying of plank boat fittings.

Whether this boat was originally expanded cannot now be determined, but it seems unlikely as there is no oak logboat indisputably known to have been expanded.[7] In order to support washstrakes the ribs would have to extend above the top edge of the boat and there is no evidence for this in the

---

4 Ibid., 123–25
5 Ibid., 325–26, 350

6 Ibid., 59
7 Ibid., 40–41

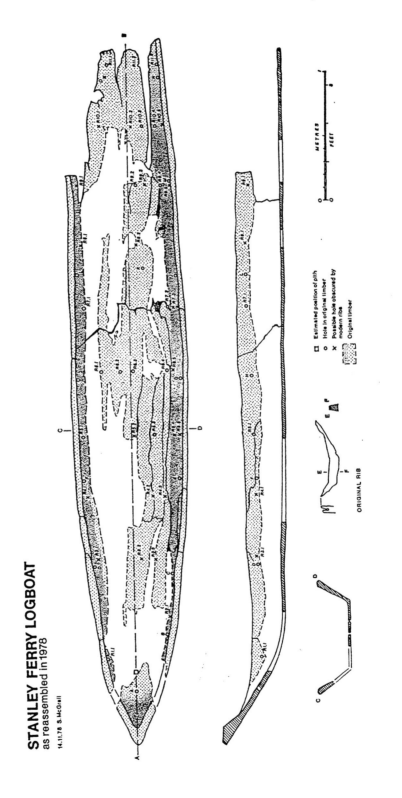

Figure 6.5.2 Measured drawing of the reconstituted Stanley Ferry logboat. Drawing: National Maritime Museum

Stanley Ferry logboat. None of the other reasons seems likely but thwarts for passengers to sit upon seems the least improbable: 500 mm between thwarts is too short for paddlers[x] but adequate for passengers. If this boat had indeed been used to carry passengers, crew with paddles or poles could have been stationed at bow and stern.

Holes A and K (and possibly O) through the bottom of the boat are interpreted as thickness gauges[9] used to indicate the required hull thickness when hollowing the log. There may have been similar holes in the now missing parts, and some of the holes used to fasten fittings may have had a previous use as thickness gauges.

The horizontal holes (B, C, E, G, J, M, N, and D, F, H, L) along each side of the boat, *c.* 70–110 mm down from the top edge, could be for treenails to fasten either washstrakes or stabilizers. These holes are spaced at an average of 800 mm over the central section reducing to 300–500 mm towards the surviving end: this is too wide for a waterproof joint between washstrake and hull.[10] On the other hand, in the southern British logboats so far analysed transverse stability is more of a problem than inadequate freeboard[11] and thus it may be argued that stabilizing timbers are more likely to have been fitted than washstrakes. The extra buoyancy provided by such stabilizers would compensate for the relatively low side height of the Stanley Ferry boat. With small half–logs treenailed along the sides at the waterline as stabilizers the boat would have had little freeboard, but ethnographic parallels indicate that this is often the case in logboat operations on inland waterways.[12]

The principal holes found in this boat had an average pre–shrinkage diameter of 20 mm: there could have been 75 or more of them originally. There are also many smaller diameter holes which were probably recent ones used to fasten metal supports when the boat was on display (Fig 6.5.1).

Date

Fragments of wood which could not be positioned during re–assembly were left untreated and some of these were subsequently dated by the Harwell Carbon 14/Tritium Measurements Laboratory: HAR 2835: 960 BP $\pm$ 70 = *c.* ad 990. It is unfortunate that samples with a known location in the log could not have been made available. Nevertheless it is likely that the samples provided were from near the outside of this logboat thus giving a *terminus post quem* for the felling of the tree and the building of the boat; an early 11th century A.D. date seems likely.

Significance of the find

This medieval oak logboat is important not least because she is the earliest–known logboat from Britain with direct evidence for fitted ribs. Her useful beam, flared transverse section and (probable) stabilizers mean that she would have had good stability. This and the fact that she may have had thwarts would make her suitable for use as a passenger ferry, a role echoed in the site name.

Aknowledgements

I am grateful to Elizabeth Hartley, Keeper of Archaeology at the Yorkshire Museum for facilities to examine this boat; to J. Atkinson for information about the conservation and re–assembly of the boat; to Eva Wilson who prepared Fig.6.5.2 from my measured drawing; and to Mary McGrail and April Whincop who helped with the measurement.

The Society is grateful to the National Maritime Museum for a publication grant received for this paper.

Reprinted with permission from:

Medieval Archaeology, 25: 160–164 (1981).

---

8 Ibid., 132

9 Ibid., 31–32

10 Ibid., 42

11 Ibid., 314

12 Ibid., 91

SECTION 7.0

PREHISTORIC PLANK BOATS

Papers 7.1 & 7.3 are specifically concerned with the Brigg 'raft', whilst 7.2 is more general in nature & considers the seafaring aspects of prehistoric trade between the Continent and Britain. The Brigg 'raft'– actually a flat–bottomed boat – is one of a handful of plank boats from 2nd & 1st millennium BC North West Europe. They are all sewn or stitched boats: one is from Denmark, the Hjortspring boat of c.350 BC (Rosenberg, 1937; Jensen, 1989; Rieck, 1994); the remainder are from southern Britain: the Ferriby boats from the northern foreshore of the Humber estuary (Wright, 1990); the large fragment from Caldicot on the Welsh side of the Severn estuary (Parry & McGrail, 1994); the Dover boat (Parfitt, 1993); the Brigg 'raft' from the R. Ancholme which was formerly a tidal creek of the Humber estuary (McGrail,1981); and the fragments from Goldcliff on the Severn foreshore, less than 10 miles from Caldicot (Bell, 1992). The first three of these British finds are dated to the mid–2nd millennium BC in calibrated radiocarbon years; Brigg is similarly dated to c. 800 BC, whilst the Goldcliff find is dated by dendrochronology to c. 1000 BC.

The Brigg 'raft'

The Brigg 'raft' was first exposed in 1888 by workmen digging for brick clay in a field between the Old and New Rivers Ancholme. The remains were re–excavated in 1974 by the National Maritime Museum, seeking to add to the body of data about prehistoric boats which, at that time, included only the Ferriby and Hjortspring boats. Paper 7.1 is an extract from one chapter in the report on that re–excavation. The problem of reconstruction, which is one of the topics considered in that paper, is taken further in Paper 11.3.

Paper 7.3 was written in response to a paper by Owain Roberts (1992) in which he concluded that the 'raft' was a round–bilged boat capable of short sea crossings, rather than a flat–bottomed ferry used on the middle reaches of a tidal creek. Roberts subsequently wrote a response (1995) to my rejection of his hypothesis.

Seagoing vessels.

In Paper 7.2 it is concluded that the known prehistoric plank boats were not truly seagoing craft, and it is suggested that the hide boat may well have been the workhorse of the seas off early NW Europe. No hide boat has, so far, been excavated, however, and the earliest documentary evidence for them is from the mid–1st millennium BC. For further discussion of this problem see McGrail (1996); for the capabilities of hide boats see Johnstone 1980/8: 26–44, 121–139); McGrail (1987: 173–191); and Greenhill (1995: 91–96).

The qualities considered to be needed by a seagoing vessel are listed in Table 7.2.1. These are the qualities against which the characteristics of known prehistoric plank boats, and of hypothetical early hide boats, were measured in Paper 7.2 to determine seagoing potential. Someone, possibly Peter Marsden, suggested to me that 'aesthetically–pleasing lines' should be added to this assessment table. As with sub–sonic fixed–wing aircraft, boats with eye–pleasing lines usually have good performance; to that extent this could be another desireable quality, although undoubtedly overlapping with some of the other characteristics in Table 7.2.1. A high Cargo / Crew ratio might also be a target to aim at in "designing" a seagoing cargo vessel; but the size of ship in which this would matter was not used in Atlantic Europe until Roman times and, in any case, it is difficult to estimate crew numbers from archaeological evidence alone.

References

Bell, M. 1992. Goldcliff, 1992. in Bell, M. (ed) Severn *Estuary Levels Research Committee Annual Report*: 15–30.

Greenhill, B. 1995. *Archaeology of Boats & Ships*. Conway.

Jensen, J. 1989. Hjortspring boat re constructed. *Antiquity*, 63: 531–5.

Johnstone, P. 1980/8. *Seacraft of Prehistory*. Routledge.

McGrail, S. 1981. *Brigg 'raft' and her Prehistoric Environment*. BAR Oxford. 89.

McGrail, S. 1987. *Ancient Boats in NW Europe*. Longman.

McGrail, S. 1996. Bronze Age in NW Europe. in Christensen, A.E. (ed) *Earliest Ships*: 24–38. Conway's History of the Ship. vol. 1.

Parfitt, K. Dover boat. *Curr. Archaeology*, 133: 4–8.

Parry, S. and McGrail, S. 1994. Bronze Age sewn boat fragment from Caldicot, Gwent, Wales. in Westerdahl, C. (ed) *Crossroads in Ancient Shipbuilding*, 21–28. Oxbow Monograph 40.

Rieck, F. 1994. Iron Age boats from Hjortspring & Nydam: new investigations. in Westerdahl, C. (ed) *Crossroads in Ancient Shipbuilding*: 45–54. Oxbow Monograph 40.

Roberts, O. 1992. Brigg 'raft' re–assessed as a round bilge Bronze Age boat. *Int. J. Nautical Archaeology*, 21: 245–258.

Roberts, O. 1995. A response. *Int. J. Nautical Archaeology*, 24: 159–160.

Rosenberg, G. 1937. *Hjortspring fundet*. Copenhagen.

Wright, E.V. 1990. *Ferriby Boats*. Routledge.

Note: The following reference contains a table of calibrated dates for the Ferriby boats and the Brigg 'raft':

Switsur, R. 1989. Early English Boats. *Radiocarbon*, 31: 1010–1018.

PAPER 7.1

THE BRIGG 'RAFT'

The Evidence

In this paper all surviving evidence about the 'raft' is evaluated, and the methods and sequence of construction are deduced. The possibility of hypothetically reconstructing the original craft is considered and her operational use is discussed; and the circumstances leading to deposition are investigated.

Individually, the two 1:12 scale models in Lincoln Museum add little to knowledge gained from other sources as they do not include such details as the strake fastenings or the cross sections of the planking. This is to be regretted for both models include the south eastern end of the 'raft', in particular the smaller, incomplete model shows precisely those cleats (17 to 110; 27 to 210; 37 to 310; 47 to 49 and 56 to 59) which were not encountered during the 1974 excavation. However something may be deduced when the differences between the two models are considered. The south eastern end of the 'raft' must first have been encountered as the clay diggers advanced across Island Carr from the east on a face aligned north/south. It seems probable that, when those parts of the 'raft' south east of a line from cleat 56 to 17 (Fig 7.1.1), had been exposed, they were recorded in sufficient detail for them to be modelled by Sam Coles with the (as yet unrecorded) timbers to the north west left in the form of modelled half–logs. It may be that at this stage the exposed planking was extracted: some of the planks (e.g. strake 2 south east of cleat 26) were sawn through; others were broken off. Parts of exposed cleats 510 (= G5) and 410 (= G4) were left in *situ* to the south–east.

When the full surviving length of the 'raft' had been revealed S. Coles must have realised that he had left insufficient timber to complete the model and thus a second one was made. This is clearly based on J. Thropp's drawing (Fig 7.1.2) having the curved north–easterly edge of strake 5, now known to be due to strake 6, and having the transverse timbers fill the holes through the cleats.

The 1888 photograph (Fig 7.1.3) published by the Rev. A. Hunt (1907/8), was taken by the Rev. A. M. Clay from the south–east, proably from within the area where planking had already been extracted. Many details are unclear, strake 6 cannot be identified for example, but we can see that the 'raft' was in a better condition when the photograph was taken than when re–exeavated 1974 (Figs 7.1.1, 7.1.4, 7.1.5). It is clear, however, that by the time of the 1888 photograph little, if any, of the moss, laths and stitches was *in situ* between the strakes. It can also be seen that the clay in many of the morticed holes through the cleats had been cleaned out, leaving only the insubstantial, fragmented transverse timbers. The subsequent continued exposure of the timbers to a fluctuating

environment, followed by backfilling with unsuitable materials resulted in the damage and degradation encountered in 1974. Nevertheless, the 'raft' *was* backfilled, and did survive to be re–excavated.

Apart from alerting us to the date of the finding of the 'raft' and its lengthy exposure, contemporary newspaper accounts add little to our knowledge. More significant are the references to a "pontoon bridge" in the title of Hunt's paper (1907/8); the phrase "floating ford" used on a pre–publication copy of the photograph accompanying this paper, now in Lincoln Museum; and the recognition by an anonymous reviewer in *Lincolnshire Notes and Queries*, 1889, 160, that the "raft" was really a boat.

Thropp's paper (1887) and measured drawing (Fig. 7.1.2) provide the most substantial account of the "raft's" form and structure, but these must be evaluated for internal consistency and in the light of the 1974 excavation to determine how much they may be relied upon for information about evidence available in 1888 but missing in 1974. Thropp is as accurate as can be expected on the position of the 'raft' in relation to the two rivers, and on the overall dimensions, 40 ft by 9 ft. The breadth given for the north western end of the boat is also similar to that found in 1974, and the general features of oak planking made watertight by moss and fastened by sewing over a longitudinal lath were also confirmed on re–excavation; as was the presence of some form of transverse timbers through morticed holes in the cleats projecting from the planking.

However, Thropp is at variance with the 1974 evidence on the following significant points:

(a) He failed to record the 6th strake evidently absorbing it into the 5th strake and giving the south western edge of the 'raft' (strake 1) a corresponding, but non–existant, bulge.

(b) He imposed an unjustifiable regularity on the spacing, length and height of the cleats; and a false symmetry in the breadths of strake 1 with 5, and strake 2 with 4.

(c) The cross section of the planking given by Thropp does not show the significant bevels on the inner edges, nor the relatively much thicker outer edges of strakes 1 and 5.

Thropp's evidence must therefore be used with caution in reconstructing the original form of the 'raft'. Its evident unreliability is to be much regretted, as it and its derivatives

Figure 7.1.1 Vertical photograph of 'raft' during excavation, 1974. North west is to the left. The white dots mark sewing holes. The circular black markers are targets for the photgrammetric photography. 2 metre ranging poles. The planks were numbered 1 to 6, from the bottom of this photograph. The rows of cleats were numbered 1 to 6 from the left of this photograph. Thus the cleat at the bottom left of this photograph became cleat 11; the cleat top left was 51; the cleat bottom right was 16. The detached cleats to the SE were known as G4 and G5, G4 being in line with plank 4

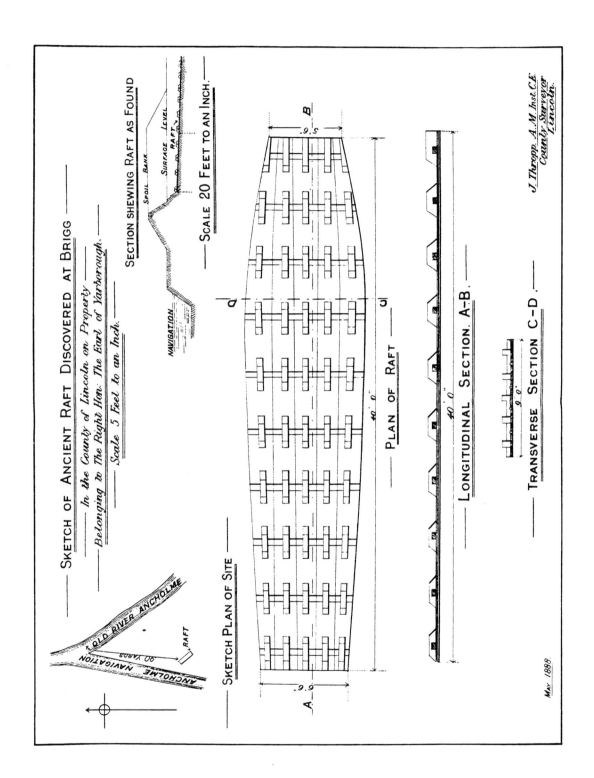

Figure 7.1.2 Thropp's drawing of the 'raft' done in May 1888. Photo: National Maritime Museum, Greenwich

THE VIKING PONTOON BRIDGE, OR RAFT.

Made to rise and fall with the tide; discovered in 1886 at Glanford-Brigg, North Lincolnshire. The only one ever found in England.

Figure 7.1.3 The 'raft' photographed from the south east by Rev. A.N. Claye in 1888 and published by Hunt (1907/8).

Figure 7.1.4 The NW end of the 'raft' taken from approximately the same position as Fig. 7.1.2. White dots mark sewing hole. 2 metre ranging poles. Strake 1 is on the left

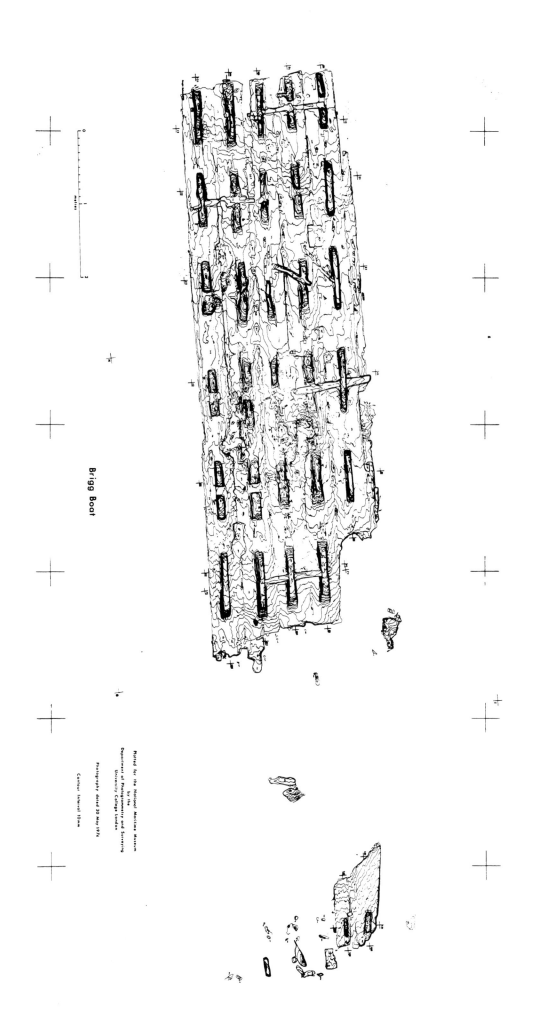

Figure 7.1.5 Photgrammetric contour plot from photography on 20th May 1974. North West is to the left

Brigg Boat

Plotted for the National Maritime Museum
by the
Department of Photogrammetry and Surveying
University College London

Photography dated 20 May 1974

Contour interval 10 mm

are the main source for the state of the south eastern end of the find.

Indirect evidence may be of value, however. Four main attributes of the Brigg 'raft' are relatively common in boat–building and something may be learned about the 'raft' by an examination of other boats. These attributes are:

(a) sewn planking

(b) the watertightness arrangements

(c) the flat–bottomed form

(d) certain woodworking techniques

Boats with one or more of these features are to be found widely dispersed in time and space, and thus it may be possible to make generalisations about missing aspects of the 'raft' with some measure of confidence in their practicability, but with no implication of connections through time or across space.

(a) **Sewn Planking**. Logboats from prehistoric Europe and 20th century Oceania and elsewhere have had planks sewn on (washstrakes) to give extra freeboard (McGrail, 1978A, 41–3). Sewing has also been used in repairs: the Brigg logboat; the Appleby logboat from the prehistoric R. Ancholm, (McGrail, 1978A, figs. 80, 81, 86); and the undated logboats from L. Laggan Scotland (McGrail, 1978A, fig. 115) and from Fiholm, Sweden (Lindqvist, 1924). Boats of sewn planks are known from the Bronze Age to modern times: the Egyptian Cheops boat of the mid–3rd millennium BC (McGrail, 1981); the 2nd millennium bc Ferriby boats (Wright, 1976) – (Fig 7.1.6); the Ljubljana boat dated by Müllner (1892) to the period 500–100 BC; the Danish Hjortspring boat (Rosenberg, 1937) of 350 to 300 BC; a boat from the R. Nin, Yugoslavia (Brusic, 1968) thought to be 1st to 3rd century AD; and the sewn boats of medieval, and indeed post–medieval, northern Europe and those of the 19th and 20th century in the Indian Ocean, Oceania and America (McGrail, 1981). Some of these examples are well–documented, but many are not. Professor Prins is undertaking an analysis of the sewing techniques used in certain boats, archaeological and ethnographic, claisifying them either as continuous stitching or single lashings, and identifying the type of stitch used: diagonal, paired, button–hole, knotted, looping and so on. Until his work is available not only are detailed descriptions lacking but there is not even an agreed terminology. Nevertheless certain boats can provide comparative evidence.

(b) **Watertightness arrangements** The sequence: absorbant material wooden lath/fastening, has been widely used to make boats watertight from the time of the prehistoric Ferriby boats and some of the Romano–Celtic barges to the 16th century AD Netherlands, 17th century sewn boats of the west coast of S. America and the 20th century *masula* of south eastern India (McGrail, 1981, Ch. 3, 4, 12), and even in a type of metal fastened boat, the *weidling* in recent use on Swiss lakes (Arnold, 1977, 296). The Polish *galar* (Fig. 7.1.7), still in use

on the R. Vistula, has a similar sequence: moss, juniper lath, turned nails, (Greenhill, personal communication).

(c) **The flat–bottomed form** of boat is also widely known in time and space. Developed and used for a particular function in a particular operating environment it is not to be thought of as "less valuable" or "more primitive" than craft of the round–hulled tradition. Contrary to popular opinion, a flat–bottomed craft can be propelled by sail and can be sea–going: see for example Filgueiras, 1980. Nevertheless, the design features of such a craft are especially useful in allowing a relatively good payload to be carried in inland/ inshore waters where the boat can be run ashore or allowed to take the ground on a falling tide. The Cog of 12th–13th century medieval Europe was a flat bottomed ship, the most advanced sea–going vessel of her time with complex design features. At the other end of the spectrum we find simple "box–like" forms of boat such as the *masseira* from Portugal, the *weidling* from Switzerland and the *galar* from the R. Vistula (Fig. 7.1.7). Any of these latter three would have been suitable for operations in the prehistoric R. Ancholme region.

A possible flat–bottomed boat or raft from the Brigg region was noted by the editor of de la Prynne's diary (1870, 65). He recorded that a "very primitive" raft "fastened together with wooden pegs" had been found at Greenhoe, Yaddlethorpe near Scunthorpe in the early 19th century. Parts of its were said to have been incorporated in nearby farm buildings; however, these timbers cannot now be traced.

(d) **Woodworking techniques**. In northern Europe many logboat finds and the major elements of almost all planked boat finds are oak (*Quercus* sp.). Oak's durability means that it is more likely to survive to be excavated than many other timber species and thus finds may be unrepresentative of the range of timber formerly used. Nevertheless there are sound reasons for preferring oak for boatbuilding to other northern European species (McGrail, 1974, 39): there was a strong preference for oak, wherever it was available,in the later medieval period and this preference probably extended back into earlier times. Similarly, there is a long history of choosing the precise timber to match an individual requirement: thus natural crooks were selected to fit curved portions of a boat, thereby ensuring maximum strength.

It is only in recent years that the archaeological value of wood has been significantly exploited and relatively accurate dating of such deposits become practicable (Coles *et al.*, 1978); thus the chronological development of woodworking techniques is as yet only poorly documented (McGrail, 1979). Nevertheless a start has been made in some areas: it is possible to say, for example, that the following techniques were used in logboat building during the British Bronze Age:

Transom fitted into a groove and made watertight.
Thickness gauges used to pre–determine thickness of timber.
Repairs by sewing, by double dovetail key and by means of a cleat–patch.
Possibly the use of treenails to fasten fittings to a boat.

Figure 7.1.6 An exposed portion of Ferriby boat 1 on the foreshore of the R, Humber at North Ferriby in 1946

Figure 7.1.7 Two views of a *galar* at Szezvcin, R. Vistula, Poland. Note the method of making the planking watertight on the upper photograph

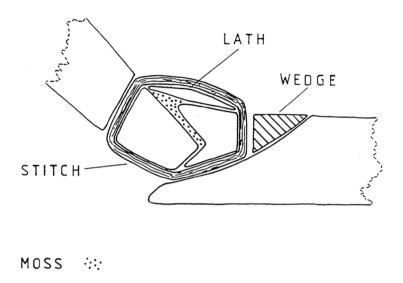

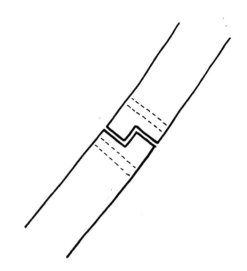

Figure 7.1.8 Method of fastening side strakes to outer bottom plank of the Ferriby boats; the join between outer bottom planks and the keel–plank is similar

Method of joining the Ferriby 1st and 2nd side strakes

After Wright, 1976, Figs 3 and 6

Furthermore, the Ferriby boats demonstrate British Bronze Age ability to fashion planking with cleats from half logs and with edges bevelled so that adjacent planks interlock in a form of "tongue and groove" work (Fig. 7.1.8). These boatbuilders also had the ability to produce strakes fashioned to a variable cross section so that they not only formed the transition between bottom and sides but also met the outer bottom plank and the keel–plank in different watertight joints. Halfed scarfs were used between elements of the keel–plank, and to join the second strake to the first (Fig.7.1.8). The fact that these techniques were used at N. Ferriby in the mid 2nd millennium bc does not mean that they were necessarily used 1000 years later even on a site only 12 miles away and in the same drainage area. This and other similar evidence does, however, provide some guide to the state of technology in Bronze Age Britain: the use of more complex techniques should therefore not be assumed.

Woodworking techniques used in the manufacture of other prehistoric artifacts–trackways, coffins, houses, etc. – could also provide evidence of the technological environment within which the Brigg 'raft' was built. However, there is no readily accessible single source for dated techniques, although the Somerset Levels project is accummulating a substantial body of data.

Building the ' raft '

(a) Choice of raw material

The boat was built entirely from organic materials: three species of timber and three different mosses. A sample of moss recovered from near strake 6 contained *Thuidium tamarixinum* and another unidentified moss, whilst samples from near strakes 3 and 4 were of *Drepanoeladus aduncus*: the former species was one of those used to caulk a split in the Brigg logboat (Atkinson, 1887, 365). Moss has been used as a boat caulking in a wide range of times and places: the logboat Holme Pierrepont 2 (MacCormick, 1968, 29); Viking Age boats of the eastern Baltic (McGrail, 1981, Ch. 4); and planked boats of the 16th century AD Netherlands (Reinders, 1979). Moss was also used to plug splits in house timbers at the mesolithic Star Carr site (Clark, 1954) and has been found during excavations at Roman Age Vindolanda and Viking Age York (Seaward & Williams, 1976). It has been claimed that a specific species of moss *Neckera complanata* was selected for Ferriby boat 3 (Seaward & Williams, 1976, 174) because of its caulking ability. However, all mosses are absorbent and can be moulded to fit gaps and, in the absence of quantitative data, it seems more appropriate to adopt the less demanding hypothesis that whatever species were available locally were used.

Dr. D. F. Cutler of the Jodrell Laboratory, Royal Botanic Gardens, Kew, identified wood samples from the various elements of the 'raft'. Light Hazel (*Corylus avellana*) stems or straight branches split in two were used for the longitudinal laths along the plank seams: the average diameter was *c.* 55 mm; lengths of individual pieces cannot now be determined. The worked post driven through the hole by cleat 26 was also a hazel stem. Willow (*Salix* sp.) withies were split and the two halves twined together to make the plank stitching. Willow is relatively lightweight (450 kg/m³) and easily worked, but from ethnographic experience and from the evidence of the prehistoric withy ropes excavated from Breiddin (Musson, personal communication) it seems probable that it was well–soaked and twisted along its length before being laid–up into 'thread' or 'rope'. These Brigg withies had a diameter of *c.* 10 mm; lengths used for sewing cannot now be determined.

Oak (*Quercus* sp.) was used for the planking and for the transverse timbers. These latter had a rectangular cross–section and had generally been worked from radial splits. It seems likely that each one extended across the 'raft' and thus individual lengths would have been 2. 27 m; thickness was 30 mm before shrinkage, with breadths up to 130–170 mm.

Hillam's dendrochronological examination reveals that three trees were used for the bottom paanking: tree 1/5, tree 3/4 and tree 2. Hillam also shows that fragment G5 was from tree 1/5, and G4 from tree 3/4. As G5 has a similar cross–section to strake 5 and was found almost in line with it, it becomes highly probable that strake 5 originally extended at least from cleat–unit 51 to cleat–unit 510 (= G5). Similarly, strake 4 probably included fragment G4. This hypothesis receives support from the fact that the girth deduced for G5's parent log is 2. 45 m indicating a natural increase in girth from the 2.01 m at cleat 55. It seems likely therefore that all five bottom strakes were of single half logs. Thropp's drawing and text do not contradict this.

These three oaks (trees 1/5, 3/4 and 2) were therefore at least 12. 2 m in length with the following approximate *pre* shrinkage girths: near the upper end (at cleat row 2): – 2.07 m; 5–6 m from the butt end (at cleat row 6): – 2.21 to 2.49 m; and at breast height (the forester's position for comparisons): – 2.70 m for tree 1/5, and 3. 03 m for trees 3/4 and 2 (assuming an inerease in breadth over the missing portions south east of cleat row 6 similar to the inerease between cleat rows 2 and 6). These measurements may be compared with the parent oak for Ferriby 2 keel–plank which had a girth of *c*. 3.45 m (Wright, 1976, 22, fig. 8). It has not proved possible to estimate the size of the corresponding parent oak for Ferriby 1 as much depends on the estimates of the extent and orientation of the curved end; however it must have been at least 2 m in girth. The oak from which the Brigg logboat was fashioned was 14.78 m in length with a girth near the butt of 5. 90 m and of 5. 40 m at 13. 5 m; the Poole logboat's oak was 10. 01 m in length with a lower girth of 5.40 m and 3.77 m at 9 m (McGrail, 1978A, 119, 170, 256, 309).

Strake 6 was from a different oak which could have been much less substantial, and it is possible that the transverse timbers came from the same tree, although this cannot now be verified. The now–missing ends and sides of the 'raft' (see below) could have been fashioned from this log or from the other half of strake 2's parent log.

The oaks slected for the Brigg 'raft' would have been standing forest oaks of straight grain, with few, if any, low branches. Knots were indeed found in all the strakes, especially tree 2, but many of the branches these represented had died back early on as the canopy closed and competition increased. The trees would also have been chosen for ease of access and extraction, and would ideally have had a damage–free felling area surrounding them.

It would not be necessary to wait for such trees to be brought down by natural effects or to be provided fortuitously by floods as driftwood. Indeed,the Brigg oaks of *c*. 170 years would not be near the end of their natural lifespan and it is unlikely that they would have developed heart rot which the parent oaks of the Poole and Brigg logboats probably had (McGrail, 1978A, 121). Trees such as those destined for the 'raft' can be felled with a simple toolkit, in a variety of ways – see for example Maori methods used in a Stone Age context (Best 1925, 42–54). Heal, in her paper on the wood–working tools that may have been used has suggested the use of fire. It is not possible to determine when the trees were felled but winter seems the most likely season (McGrail, 1974, 39). After felling, the head and branches would be removed leaving a substantial log. Hillam suggests that these logs would have been partly converted into planking on site, and it is true that by this means extraction from the forest may be simplified. Nevertheless, there are advantages in conversion close to the building site, and documented Maori methods (Best, 1925, 54–5) demonstrate the ingenious ways in which great logs can be moved over long distances, and if the building site is downstream of the forest logs may be floated there. Buckland's environmental evidence suggests that there was an oak forest not far from the 'raft's' findspot, however it is not possible to be precise about the relative positions of forest, boatbuilding 'yard', area of use, and deposition site except that it is probable that all were relatively close together.

(b) **Conversion of bottom planking**

Green (unseasoned) oak is easier to work than seasoned and has other advantages in boatbuilding (McGrail, 1974, 39–42). Soon after felling then, the logs destined for the 'raft' were split longitudinally into two halves, probably using wooden wedges. It may have been at this stage that a log was specifically chosen for strakes 1 and 5 which were to have thick planking along one edge. It may also have been during conversion (or during felling) that damage occurred to the lower section of tree 3/4, resulting in the relatively narrow breadth of strake between cleat–units 43 and G4, instead of the generally inereasing breadths from top (= north west end) towarfs the butt of all other surviving lengths of strakes. Such a restriction in available breadth of wood may, however, have been due to malformation or damage during growth.

After splitting, the bark and much of the sapwood were removed from each half log. The general increase in breadth of strake from the north west corresponding to the natural form of the tree, and the fact that some sapwood was left on in at least parts of each strake emphasise that the builders were seeking to make maximum use of the timber available to obtain the greatest breadth of planking. Damage or natural defects apart, the south–east end of each strake would have been potentially as broad, and most probably broader, than the breadths at cleat row 6 (i. e. halfway up the trunks) Thropp's drawing (Fig. 7.1.2) appears to show that, except for strake 3, these theoretical breadths were not used to the full, indeed strakes 1 and 5 are evidently significantly reduced in breadth towards the southeast end. The position given by Thropp for the cleats at this end of the raft is somewhat contradicted by the evidence from excavation, and unless log 1/5 had a natural bend near the butt end there is no way that the kinks shown by Thropp in strakes 1 and 5 southeast of cleat row 7 could be obtained from a single log. Nevertheless, examination of fragments G5 (= cleat–unit 510) and G4 (= 410) show that at these (butt) ends of trees 1/5 and 3/4 the strakes were some 150–200 mm narrower than they need have been if the theoretical amount of heartwood had indeed been available. This reduction in breadths cannot be attributed to a design requirement as such breadths could more economically have been obtained from the other (upper) ends of the logs. It thus seems likely that all three trees were damaged at their butt ends, with the damage extending further up the trunk of tree 3/4 in the half that became strake 4.

Breadth measurements between surviving edges and between opposing sewing holes on the same strake show that, in addition to the constant breadths between cleats 43 and 46, there were slight departures from the general rule of steadily increasing dimensions towards the south–east end. For example, breadth measurements between sewing holes increase relatively sharply at cleat–unit 33 and then increase less quickly to cleat–unit 36. This anomolous region on strake 3 corresponds with the region of approximately constant _ breadths on strake 4. These changes in breadths are only of the order of 20–30 mm greater or less than would be expected from a regularly tapering tree over a length of 2–3 m, but they are nevertheless significant. It seems likely, therefore, that the strakes did not have absolutely straight edges but a slight waviness. This would be consistent with the builder's aim to obtain the maximum breadth along the length of each strake: where there was natural damage, or when minor mistakes in woodworking led to a reduction in breadth, the adjacent strake was fashioned to match the contiguous defect.

A likely time. for such mistakes to occur would be during the working of the strake edge bevels, especially the thin ones. The Ferriby boats may have had similar wavy edges (Wright, personal communication) and such non–linearity may be seen on modern sewn boats from the R. Niger, Mali (Fig. 7.1.9).

In addition to generally increasing in breadth, by some 5 cm over a surviving length of *c.* 7 m, the strakes (including cleats) increase in height towards the south–eastern end: this again is related to the natural taper of the logs. But the cleats do not increase in height in the regular manner drawn by Thropp with the planking remaining a constant thickness (Fig. 7.1.2). In fact the planking increases in thickness from *c.* 2 cm at the north west to *c.* 5 cm at cleat row 6, whilst the cleats generally range in height from 12 to 13 cm.

The cleats are not evenly spaced along each strake (1. 25 m to 1. 31 m, centre to centre), they vary in individual length from 0.63 m to 1. 00 m, and the longitudinal position of the morticed hole through them is not standard. Builders of a recent Danish replica of the prehistoric Hjortspring boat, which also has cleats integral with the planking, found it difficult to fashion cleats so that the morticed holes were precisely in line with those on adjacent planks. They therefore cut oversize, blank cleats, and did not cut mortices until after the planking had been fastened (*Roar Linde* 71, p. 24). It seems possible therefore that the 'raft' builders fashioned blank cleats which were simlar but not identical to each other, and made them oversize so that there would be some latitude in spacing and in length of cleat to accommodate difficulties due to the position of knots and the vagaries of woodworking.

Figure 7.1.9 A dismantled sewn boat from the River Niger

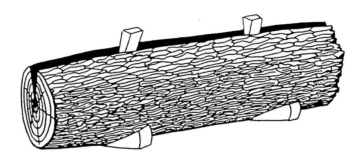

1

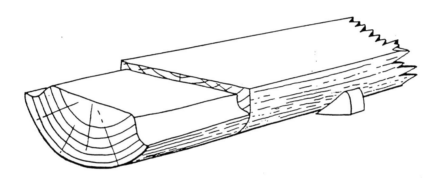

2

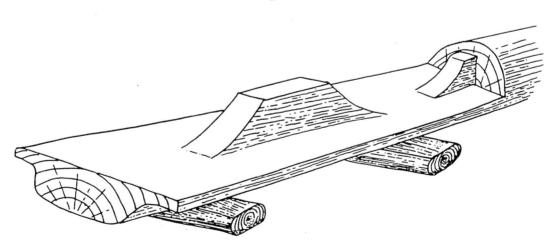

3

Figure 7.1.10 Conjectural building sequnce for the 'raft'

1. Log split
2. Undersurface with bevels worked
3. Upper surface with blank cleats fashioned

A construction sequence consistant with the foregoing discussion would be:

1. Half–log placed flat surface down, bark and outer sapwood removed.

2. Half–log chocked flat surface (pith side) uppermost, defective area trimmed, wedged surface made smooth and bevels cut along plank edges leaving sapwood only where essential (Fig. 7.1.10).

3. Half–log reversed. It would be possible to fashion the upper surface of the planking with the log on the ground; however, as access to the under surface would be required subsequently it is probable that the half–log was placed on "stocks" of short transverse logs at this stage (Fig 7.1.10). Plank worked away to leave oversize blank cleats, accepting deviations from the ideal interval.

(c) Fastening the bottom planking and making watertight

Thropp (1887, 96) states that, "moss caulking has been found in the joints [between the planks] " and as a further effort to make it, to some extent, watertight, the sides of each plank were pierced with 3/8 in. holes 2 or 3 inches apart, and the joints covered with straight pieces of wood, 2 in. diameter fastened by lashing, which was passed through the holes and over these round packing pieces." Figure 7.1.14 is a re–drawn enlargement of Thropp's cross section of the 'raft' shown in Figure 7.1.2. Even at this scale, details of the fastenings cannot be deduced.

On excavation in 1974 the planking was found to have shrunk away from adjacent strakes and anything connecting the planking to have been displaced or removed. Twisted willow stitch material was, however, found within most of the sewing holes. Moss was not found *in situ* but wads of it were found on, or in one case under, the planking. The "round packing pieces" had also been removed during the 1888 exposure but fragmented lengths of split hazel stems were found on top of the planking, sometimes associated with moss.

Thropp's diagram (Fig. 7.1.14) shows the planking (with very misleading cross sections) butting together at the edges. A shrinkage factor of *c.* 12% would indeed bring the original edges of adjacent planks, as found, into close proximity; the sewing holes would then be *c.* 35 to 45 mm apart. Thropp gives no indication of the relative disposition of these holes and any slight movement of individual planks after deposition could result in a misleading impression on excavation. However, in general, holes on adjacent planks seem to be disposed diagonally and not paired. This diagonal disposition is also noticeable in the repairs to cleat–unit 26 and to fragment G4; these must be their original relative positions.

A wide variety of sewing techniques have been used in early boatbuilding. They vary from simple, single lashings between paired holes (the method used in the Ferriby boats – see Wright, 1976, 16), to sewing with a continuous thread, as for example in the R. Nin sewn boats (Fig 7.1.15), or in the Ljubljana boat (Fig 7.1.16) as published by Mullner (1892). The drawing by the latter implies that some form of double stitching was used as the space between every pair of holes is crossed diagonally by stitching. Continuous stitching can be (and has been) used with paired holes or with diagonally disposed holes, but single lashings would seem to be logically restricted to paired holes. Evidence from the Cheops boat is little help in interpreting the Brigg material as Landström's reconstruction drawing shows there to be continuous stitching but *across* the planking rather than along the edges, and in any case the published work to date does not state what was found and what is conjectural. The evidence from Hjortspring, R. Nin and Ljubljana also does not make this distinction. In addition, as Professor Prins (personal communication) has pointed out, the evidence for the sewing of the Hjortspring boat is entirely from impressions in the resin paying and is as compatible with simple lashings as with continuous stitching.Modern sewn boats, for example the East African *Mtepe* (Hornell, 1941), have sewing patterns more complex than that evidently used in the Ljubljana boat,with the thread passing two or more times through every hole.

The most likely interpretation of the Brigg evidence is that the 'raft' planking was sewn with single stitching with a two–stranded thread of split willow threaded "continuously" through holes which were diagonally disposed to one another. The holes were bored almost vertically through the inner edges of planking, where the wood was *c.* 12 mm thick, some 20 mm from the edge (Fig. 7.1.17). Only one case was encountered where a replacement hole had had to be bored because the original one had broken; however, several holes near the centre of the 'raft' had been enlarged underneath – these are discussed further in the section below on Maintenance. Most holes were parallel sided, but some were hour–glass shaped, having been worked from top and bottom faces.

The stitching is potentially a most vulnerable aspect of any sewn boat, and boatbuilders ancient and modern have taken various measures to protect it, especially the outboard portions. This is especially important for boats operating off foreshore or river bank where they regularly take the ground and may also be dragged in and out of the water. Two well–documented methods of protection are: (a) to countersink the stitches as in Maori boats (Best, 1925, 72); and (b) to wedge the stitches within the sewing holes and cut off the external section so that each stitch becomes in effect a staple or 'dog', as in the *Mtepe* (Hornell, 1941, 61). In the Brigg 'raft' stitch protection is achieved by working the bevel along the inner strake edges which "lifts" the stitches some 15–30 mm above the bottom of the planking, and at the outer edges of strakes 1 and 5 by bringing the stitches through the thick edges (Fig. 7.1.17). The comparable technique used in the Ferriby boats is shown in Fig 7.1.8.

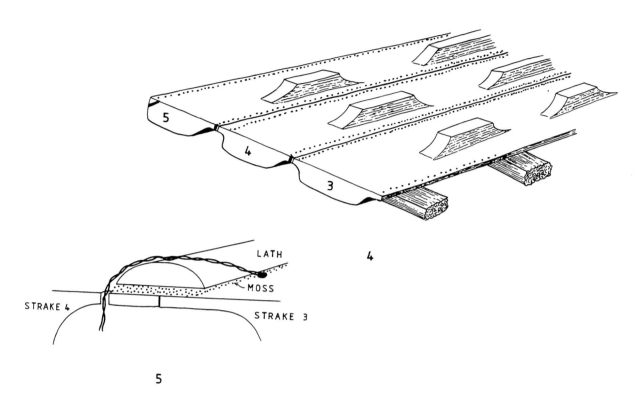

Figure 7.1.11 Conjectural building sequence:

4. Bottom strakes positioned and sewing holes bored
5. Strakes fastened by sewing over moss and longitudinal lath

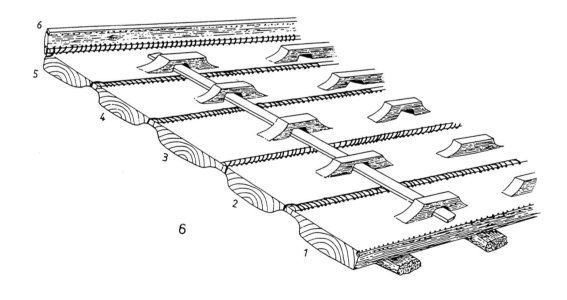

Figure 7.1.12 Conjectural building sequence:

6. Mortices cut thorough cleats and transverse timbers inserted. Lower side strakes (=strake 6) fastened to outer bottom strake (=strake 5)

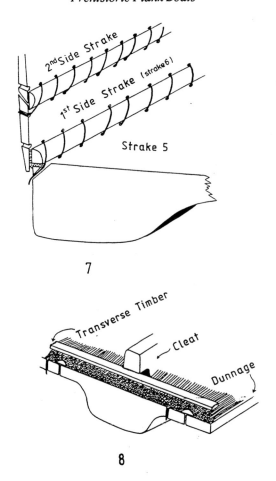

7

8

Figure 7.1.13 Conjectural building sequence

7. Second side strake fastened to lowest side strake
8. Dunnage inserted under transverse timbers

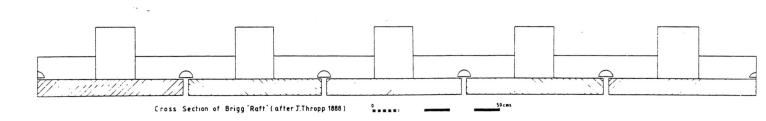

Cross Section of Brigg 'Raft' (after J.Thropp 1888)

Figure 7.1.14 Enlargement of Thropp's transverse section of the 'raft'. See Fig 7.1.2

178

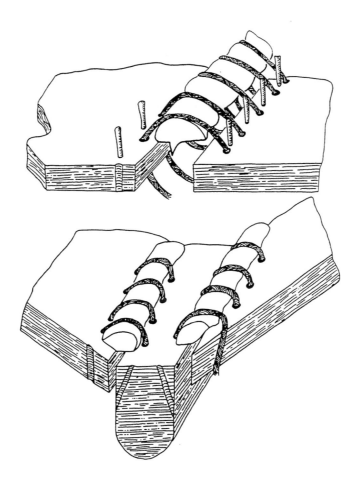

Figure 7.1.15 Method of fastening the planking of the River Nin boat of the 1st to 3rd centuries A.D. The stitching is wedged in the holes by treenails. After Brusic, 1968, fig 8

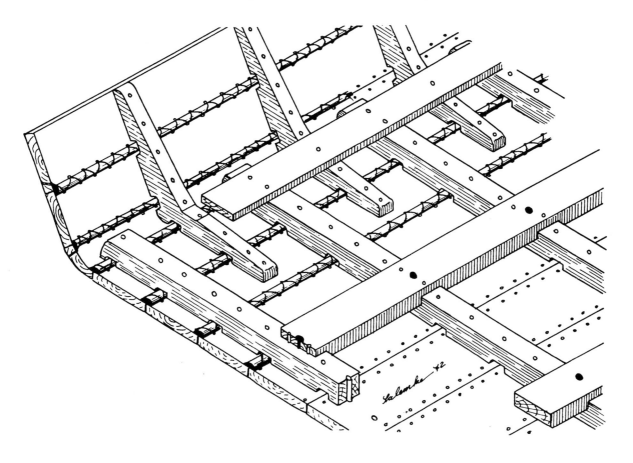

Figure 7.1.16 Constructional details of the 2nd half of the 1st millenium B.C. Ljubljana boat. After Müllner, 1892

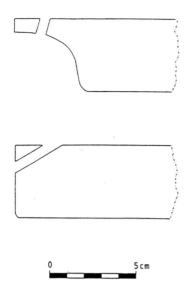

0   5 cm

Figure 7.1.17 Idealised sections of the 'raft's' edges: thin edge
above; thick edge below

Wedges also reduce leakage through the sewing holes and this
may have been their purpose in the repair to the Appleby
logboat (McGrail, 1978A, 148) dated *c.* 1100 bc (Q–80). The
sewing holes in the Hjortspring boat of c. 300 BC appear to
have been waterproofed with a resin as were those of the R.
Nin boat, and a paying of pine gum is known to have been
applied to sewn repairs to the logboats of recent Oregon
Indians (Folkard, 1870, 351). No wedges or traces of resin
were recovered on re–excavation of the Brigg 'raft', but in view
of the history of this find their use cannot be entirely ruled out.

Thropp's statement that moss and laths were used to make the
'raft' seams watertight was confirmed on re–excavation, but the
precise method used is not clear. Longitudinal laths and
absorbant materials such as moss have been used in antiquity
and ethnographically in a number of ways. The Ferriby boats
have a single lath inboard on top of moss (Fig. 7.1.8); Swiss
boats of the 1st–20th century recorded bv Arnold (1978) have
the lath outboard, below the absorbant material; and Maori
sewn boats had laths both inboard and outboard (Best, 1925,
77). Thropp's cross section (Fig. 7.1.14) although inaccurate in
several details, appears to show the use of inboard laths and
for lack of contrary evidence this must be the preferred solution
(Fig 7.1.11 detail).

Fig. 7.1.11 illustrates the fourth stage in the postulated
sequence for building the 'raft'. Holes were bored through the
edges of the strakes and, with the holes disposed diagonally,
the planks were fastened together with a continuous thread over
the watertight elements of moss and lath. In Oceania simple
leverage devices were used to tighten each stitch as the sewing
progressed: the Maori *tanekaha* (Best, 1925, 79) and the Cook
Is. *keke* (Buck, 1927; Fig. 112), for example, are both
Y–shaped crooks; the *Mtepe* stitches are also tightened by
lever (Hornell, 1941, 61). Wedges are used to hold each stitch
once it has been tightened; sometimes these are left in position
but more usually all but the final one are removed in
succession.

(d) Cleats and transverse timbers

Once the bottom planking had been fastened by sewing, the
relative position of the strakes was fixed. As the strakes were
to be linked in some manner by transverse timbers, morticed
holes would then be cut through the cleats so that they were in
line across each row; the lower surfaces of these holes would
also need to be on the same level (Fig. 7.1.12). Thus these
morticed holes would not necessarily be centrally positioned
within each cleat and, whilst some would be flush with the
upper surface of the planking, others would have a 'step'. This
indeed was found to be the case on post–excavation
examination.

One function of these cleats seems therefore to have been to
maintain the relative position of the strakes by means of
transverse timbers through the morticed holes. It is therefore
highly likely that there was one single timber through each row
of cleats: this is not contradicted by excavated evidence. Such
timbers are not akin to the timbers of recent skeleton–built
boats which determine the form of the hull and supply a great
part of the strength: the Brigg timbers can only have been in
position *after* the bottom of the 'raft' had been formed, and, as
far as can be determined, had no part to play in determining the
form of the sides. Nor can they be directly compared with the
timbers of shell–built boats where they are added after (some
of) the hull has been built, and reinforce the strength of the hull:
the Brigg timbers, if they were continuous, can only have been
fitted *before* the second side was added.

Thropp reported that the transverse timbers were "secured by
wedges driven in at the sides of the Raft, and also in the middle
rows of cleats": this evidently refers to strakes 1, 3 and 5.
Wedges were not found on re–excavation and the transverse
timbers had evidently been much disturbed in 1888. Thropp
described them as "rough branches of trees", and his drawing
(Fig. 7.1.14) shows them evidently fflling the morticed holes
through the cleats. It is possible that during deposition and
excavation the transverse timbers split along the rays and what
was found on re–excavation was a thin lamination of what had
formerly been a substantial timber. However, this is theorising,
and Thropp has been shown to be wrong in other aspects of his
report. It therefore seems advisable to assume that what was
found on re–excavation was what was deposited, but shrunken:
certainly the transverse timbers visible in the 1888 photograph
(Fig. 7.1.3) are as insubstantial as those found in 1974. The
fragmented timbers were, in fact, squared–off radial splits of
oak, the *pre*–shrinkage dimensions of which would have been
up to 30 mm thick and 130 mm–170 mm wide: they would
have occupied less than half the vertical dimension of the
morticed holes which would have been *c.* 70 mm
pre–shrinkage, but it seems likely that they would have filled
the mortice horizontally.

These timbers would thus have been up to *c.* 2. 27 m in length
and would have been placed in position after the planking had
been positioned and the mortices cut, but before the second side
had been added. It is theoretically possible that they could have
been present during the sewing of the bottom planking for,
being so thin, they could have been lifted within their mortices
to permit sewing to take place. However, it has been argued

above that mortices were not cut until the relative position of the strakes had been fixed by stitching and thus it seems likely that, on building (but not on re–assembly) the timbers were inserted after the sewing had been completed (Fig.7.1.12).

Such timbers, wedged as Thropp reported, would prevent the cleats and hence the planking from relative movement in the fore–and–aft direction. The The 'raft', evidently designed to operate off mudflats (see below), would be exposed to such relative, sliding movements especially if, as seems probable (see below) the ends of the bottom strakes did not turn up. Unless all five bottom strakes touched the ground simultaneously the momentum of those strakes still fully afloat would tend to stress the stitching: transverse timbers would minimise or even prevent such movement. Individual strakes would also experience varying vertical forces both on taking the ground and when underway: these would similarly impose stresses on the stitching, sometimes with rapid reversal of direction. Transverse timbers wedged firmly in some of their mortices would also tend to minimise the effect of these forces.

The Brigg 'raft' had ten transverse timbers in a length of *c.* 12.20 m whereas Ferriby boat 1 had *c.* 6 in a length of *c.* 15.35 m. However, Ferriby 1 probably required fewer, even though she was also operated off mud flats, as her upturned end would allow a smoother arrival and hence reduce shearing forces. On the other hand, Ferriby boat 2 had *c.* 18 transverse timbers in c. 11. 25 m, but the form of her ends is unknown. The Ferriby transverse timbers are stouter than those of the 'raft', being *c.* 5 x 4 cm, and they just about fill the morticed holes in the cleats; somewhat stouter ones might therefore seem to be even more appropriate to the Brigg 'raft'. Possible reasons may, however, be advanced for their thinness relative to the vertical dimensions of the mortice holes. Firstly, this would permit broken sewing to be repaired or moss caulking to be added in the immediate vicinity of the transverse timbers without having to dismantle one side of the boat so that the timbers could be removed. Secondly, these timbers may have been used to hold a dunnage of light timbers of brushwood in position, thereby protecting the inboard stitching from accidental damage (Figs. 7.1.13 [lower] and 7.1.18) and protecting the cargo from the inevitable bilge water. As Coates points out in his paper on the cargo capacity of the 'raft', such dunnage would also improve the transverse stability of the 'raft' by reducing the adverse free surface effects of this bilge water. Thirdly, the upper portions of some of the morticed holes could have been used as temporary lashing points: although cattle may have been thrown and hobbled, and sheep penned–in, it may have been advantageous to tie down goods in barrels or sacks.

In addition to their operational function, transverse timbers would be available to re–align the planking after any substantial dismantling (see below). They may therefore be thought of as constructional as well as structural.

The cleats thus had a role to play in minimising stitch wear by providing housings for the transverse timbers, but they were of equal importance in helping to maintain transverse stability by reducing free surface effects. Ten relatively large cleats on each strake formed a discontinuous longitudinal sill or dam thereby reducing the tendency for de–stabilising bilge water to move across the bottom of the 'raft' in response to a heel. In this respect the 'raft' is technically more advanced than Ferriby boat 1.

(e) The sides

The outer edges of strakes 1 and 5 are different from all other bottom strake edges being relatively thick with sewing holes leaving through the edge rather than underneath (Fig. 7.1.17) It is probable then that here is the transition from bottom to sides of the boat. This transition is a particular problem in flat–bottomed boat design and has been solved in different ways. The Ljubljana boat and the flat–bottomed Romano–Celtic craft have a transition strake of curved cross–section so that bottom is blended into side, the inboard parts of the transition strakes forming part of the bottom planking (Fig. 7.1.16). The strakes next to the outer bottom planks of the Ferriby boats, on the other hand, although hollowed out, do not so evidently form part of the bottom; they may be thought of as flared, lowest side strakes interlocking with the bottom planking along a waterproofed seam (Fig 7.1.8). Other early sewn boats, the Hjortspring find and the craft from the R. Nin, are round–hulled. It is permissable, however, to note that the 20th century Swiss *weidling* (which has been shown above to have some features comparable with, but by no means identical to, the Brigg 'raft' – (see Arnold, 1977) has a flared lowest side strake which overlaps the bottom planking. However, this boat is built in the skeleton sequence; that is the angle taken by the side planking is determined by the form of the previously fitted timbers. The Brigg 'raft' in common with the Ferriby boats, on the other hand, was shell built; that is the angle taken by the side planking was determined as the lowest side strake was fastened to the bottom plank and as subsequent strakes were fastened to each other: the angle at which the planking edges meet and the cross section of the planking being the determining factors.

Thropp states, "It is not a little difficult to prove satisfactorily whether the Raft had sides and, if so, in what manner they were connected with the floor. The tracing of grooving for the sides are very slight, but certainly in one or two boards it was observed". Grooving seems an inappropriate word for any feature of the remains found during re–excavation. Strake 6, unrecorded by Thropp, may be interpreted as part of the lowest side strake formerly fastened to strake 5. because of its position and its cross section (Fig 7.1.19) especially the bevel on its outer edge as found, and the hole's along both edges. It is assumed that this side strake fell outwards after deposition and that either then or during 1888 the transverse timber through cleats 44 and 54 became displaced and came to lie on top of it. A possible method of fastening strake 6 to strake 5 is shown in Fig. 7.1.12 with the side strake slightly overlapping the outer bottom strake and lying at about right angles to it. A flared side strake would be hydrostatically more desirable because of improved stability characteristics, but there is no evidence for such a flare. A quartered round lath, figured by Thropp (Fig. 7.1.14) but not found on re–excavation, is used with moss to make the seam watertight; the stitching is diagonal by analogy with the method deduced for the bottom planking.

Figure 7.1.18 Dunnage of brushwwod incorporated into one side of a 1:10 model of Feeriby boat 1

This side strake ends in a curve to the north west by cleat 52 comparable with that of Ferriby boat 1 but only in one plane. Strake 5 has holes through its outboard edge over the whole length excavated and so there must have been further side planking to the north west of strake 6, but how these two (or more) elements forming the lowest side–strake were joined to each other is not clear. As reconstructed in Fig. 7.1.12 and 7.1.13 the side strake extends above the upper surface of the bottom planking by *c.* 150 mm, bringing it to some 10–60 mm above the top of the cleats. It is assumed that a similar side strake was fastened to strake 1.

It might be argued that strake 6 did not simply collapse outwards after deposition, as has been assumed in the foregoing discussion, but collapsed inwards and then slid outwards, so that the edge found next to strake 5 would formerly have been the top edge of the lowest side strake. The bevel at C on Fig. 7.1.19 would, however, then be outboard and low down, to no apparent useful purpose: the possibility is therefore discounted.

Over the greater length of strake 6 as recovered, the upper edge has a bevel which has been worked along a ray in the timber (Fig. 7.1.19 lower). A second side strake may thus be postulated, fastened by sewing through holes along both sides of a bevelled overlap (Fig. 7.1.13), comparable with the Hjortspring boat; by analogy with the Brigg bottom strakes there may have been an internal lath associated with this seam. The short length of strake 6 found alongside cleat 55 and to the south east had a different cross section (Fig. 7.1.19 upper): This seems to imply that over this section of the boat (near amidships) the joint between first and second side strakes changed from an overlapping one to a butted one similar to the bottom strakes. This transition may have been achieved by forming the second side strake of two elements (or more) joined in some manner near this bevel change.

The breadth of the postulated second side strake can only be estimated, possibly it was similar to the lowest one, that is *c.* 170 mm, which with a 20 mm overlap with the lowest side strake would give an overall height of sides above the lower surface of the bottom planking of some 0. 34 m. Sides of this height would generally keep out the water when operating on such a waterway as the postulated estuarine arm of the Humber (see *Primary* use, below) and yet would not be a great obstruction when loading and unloading, even to walking animals. They would easily permit men to use a paddle, yet would retain any dunnage. The side height is further discussed in *Hypothetical Reconstruction*, below.

(f) The Ends

No indication of the form of the ends, their method of fastening, or indeed their precise position was found on re–excavation.

Thropp called the north west end the "fore end" and stated that at both ends, "the cleats were finished flush with the planking". On excavation, however, the planking was found to extend at least 20 or 30mm to the north west of the cleats in row 1. To the south east, fragments G4 and G5 were found to have been damaged during 1888 and thus it is not possible to verify or contradict Thropp's statement here. As the ends must be conjectural, further discussion of them is best left to the section on hypothetical reconstruction.

(g) Propulsion and Steering

No evidence for the methods of propulsion was found either in 1888 or 1974. Pivoted oars on a 5th century BC gold model from Durnberg are the first indication of rowing in northern Europe (Ellmers, 1978, 11), and the Broighter boat model of the 1st century BC (Farrell and Penney, 1975) and Caesar's statement about the boats of the Veneti (*de Bello Gallico*, III, 13) are the earliest evidence for indigenous sail. The use of sail or oar to propel the 'raft' is therefore discounted, for the present.

Paddles have been found generally throughout north and western Europe (not all are for nautical uses) including one from the mesolithic site of Star Carr (Clark, 1954). Although few others are well–dated, it seems safe to infer that paddles would have been available in mid–1st millenntum bc Humber side. There is no direct evidence for poling (colloquially "punting") until the Roman Age (Ellmers, 1978, 10) but as this requires only simple equipment (a pole, which may not be recognisable as such on excavation) and is in use world–wide, it seems likely that the Brigg 'raft' could also have been poled. Working a boat by means of a line held or pegged at both ends is practicable across a narrow waterway, but this seems unlikely to have been the case at Brigg.

No evidence for the steering arrangements has survived and it is doubtful if there were permanent fittings: the first evidence for specialised fittings in northern Europe appear to be those on the 1st century BC Broighter model. The 'raft' could have been controlled directionally by orders to the paddlers or polesmen, in addition to the efforts of specialised steersmen with freely held paddles near the stern.

(h) Maintenance

There is much ethnographic evidence for the annual or periodic dismantling of sewn boat for the stitching to be renewed. Indian Ocean: Hornell, 1941, 62; Hornell, 1946, 236; Hourani, 1963, 94; Folkard, 1870, 309. Oceania: Folkard, 1870, 291; Malinowski, 1978, 141; Best, 1925, 221. It would have been necessary to have access to the underside to re–sew the 'raft': this could be achieved by floating logs transversely underneath the craft and then letting the set–up dry out at an exceptionally high spring tide. Alternatively, the 'raft' may have been dismantled in shallow water and manhandled piecemeal above high water. Under the central lengths of strakes 2, 3 and 4 several of the holes are enlarged so that in section they resemble a truncated cone. The enlargement is not assymetric as would be caused by wear. A possibility is that during a period of maintenance jammed fragments of stitching had to be bored out before the strakes could be re–sewn. Sewing breaks experienced in between these major refits would have had to be repaired by *ad hoc* means including much use of moss. The various precautions taken to protect the stitching, described above, would reduce such repairs to a minimum.

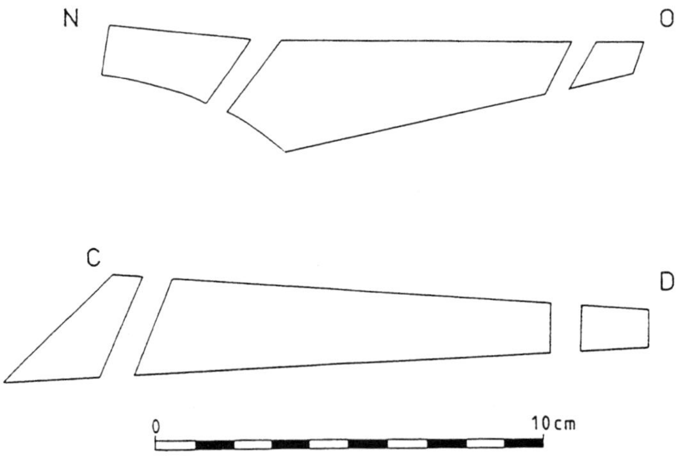

As the stabilising effect of the dunnage would be gradually neutralised as it absorbed water, it would be necessary to change it at intervals, possibly more often than annually, depending on the permiability of the wood species used.

Splits within the 'raft's' planking on strakes 2 and 4 had been repaired by sewing. Nothing but the holes and some fragmentary stitching within them has survived but it seems likely that moss and laths were also used as in the Ferriby repairs (Fig. 7.1.20) and the undated Fiholm boat. The Appleby logboat repair stitches were wedged but seem not to have had a lath associated; other splits in this boat were held together by double–dovetail flat keys (McGrail, 1978A, fig. 82 – see also Figs 5.1.1 and 5.1.2 in this present volume) so the repair technique here would seem to rely on binding the split when the wood was realatively dry and allowing expansion on re–immersion in water to "seal" it. In common with the repaired split on Ferriby boat 1 (Fig. 7.1.20,the two sections of repair on the 'raft' (by cleat 26 and by fragment G4) do not seem to have been countersunk into the under surface of the planking. The holes on one side of the split in cleat–unit 26 are, in fact, set into a fore and aft groove on the underside, but it does not seem possible to devise a pattern of stitching which would be countersunk over its vulnerable sections. These repairs would thus be in direct contact on grounding and subject to abrasion when the boats were dragged across the foreshore. However, incomplete evidence of the 'raft' repairs survived and it could be that these repair stitches had been wedged and the underneath, exposed portion cut away flush with the planking – a known ethnographic technique (Hornell, 1941). Arnold (1977, 296) has noted that splits in the planking of 20th century Swiss *weidling* boats often occur during building rather than when in use; it is possible that this was the case with the 'raft'.

Hypothetical Reconstruction

Individual reconstruction features have been discussed in preceding parts of this Paper, but there is insufficient surviving evidence to justify a full structural drawing. Structural aspects of the sides and especially the ends must remain conjectural, and the breadths of each strake and the precise position of each cleat between row 6 and row 10 cannot now be known. Never theless, if any estimate is to be made of the capabilities of the 'raft' it is necessary to attempt a hypothetical reconstruction of the original full form, that is the overall size and shape of the 'raft'. In this way, capacity, stability, freeboard and draft can be investigated. The maximum extent of the surviving part of the planking reported by Thropp is 40 ft by 9 ft *c.* 12.19 m x *c.* 2. 74 m), but this includes strake 6 in the breadth and some doubt must remain about the existance of further rows of cleats at either end. The original form of the north western half of the bottom may be taken to be as found on re–excavation with some allowance for shrinkage. Some indication of the sides has been obtained from the arguments set out above. The form of the south eastern end of the 'raft' is thus the most difficult to reconstruct.

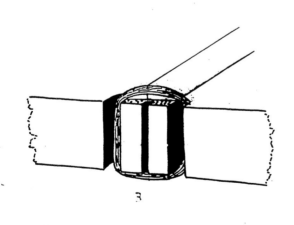

Figure 7.1.19 Idealised sections of strake 6. See Fig. 2.3.11. Edges O and D were next to strake 5 when found

Figure 7.1.20 Method of repairing a split in Ferriby boat 1. The stitch passes over moss and a lath lying on top of the split. After Wright, 1976,fig. 4

Although techniques such as the use of treenatis to fasten fittings and the fashioning of variable cross section planking were used in Britain before the mid–1st millennium bc (McGrail, 1979; Wright, 1976), it seems inappropriate to incorporate them into any reconstruction of the 'raft' as the evidence for woodworking techniques that has survived at Brigg indicates a tradition of two (not three)–dimensional planking, and there is no hint of fastenings other than by sewing.

It has been shown that the bottom was most probably made of five strakes each of one plank. Over the lengths surviving in 1974 these strakes increase in breadth from the north west in accordance with the natural form of the parent tree. The overall, post–shrinkage breadth of the 'raft' increases from *c.* 2.00 m at cleat–unit 1 to *c.* 2. 20 m at cleat–unit 5, an increase of some 20 cm. If this rate of increase were continued south eastward the overall breadth of row 10 would be *c.* 2. 40 m: Thropp states that it was 5 ft 6 in (1. 68 m): and it has been argued above that all three parent trees were damaged at their butt–ends (i. e. the south–east end of the 'raft').

Fragment G5, which has been shown above to be the south eastern end of strake 5, was found where it was deposited, apart from a slight translational displacement so that it overlapped G4. If this displacement is allowed for and the broken end of G5 extended to the length of an average cleat (0.80 m), and this position then joined to that of strake 5 extended to the presumed position of cleat 56 on the 1974 site plan (Fig. 7.1.5), it is seen that the outer edge of strake 5 is indeed brought back south westward but not so sharply as Thropp shows (Fig. 7.1.1). As we have no 1974 evidence for the position of the other corner of this end of the bottom, and Thropp's drawing is suspect, the best course of action seems to be to establish this position by symmetry with G5. Such a reconstruction results in a breadth at this end of the bottom of 1.71 m compared with the 5 ft 6 in (1.68 m) given by Thropp. An allowance for shrinkage increases 1.71 m to 1.75 m. The comparable pre–shrinkage breadth at the north western end is 2. 09 m, and 2. 27 m across the 'raft' between the 6th and 7th rows of cleats some 7.8 m from the north west end. The length of the bottom becomes 12. 20 m (shrinkage is insignificant in this plane) compared with Thropp's 40 ft (12.19 m).

The length/breadth ratio of the bottom (without ends) thus becomes *c.* 5.37 which is comparable with other early boats of this form: Romano–Celtic 'barges', 5. 9 to 8.1; medieval European 'punts', *c.* 5 (McGrail, 1981, Ch. 4); Mullner's estimate (1892) of the Ljubljana boat, *c.* 7. A National Maritime Museum reconstruction model of Ferriby boat 1, based on the excavated evidence with the minimum of conjecture, has a ratio of *c.* 7. 5.

There were at least two side strakes, as shown in Fig. 7.1.13 and discussed above, bringing the top edge of the sides to about 0. 34 m above the lower surface of the bottom strakes. The length/depth ratio thus becomes *c.* 36. This is almost twice the value for Romano–Celtic 'barges' (21. 5 to 28. 3), the medieval European 'punts' (*c.* 17) and the Ferriby model (*c.* 22). This could indicate that the hypothetical reconstruction should include a broader second side strake, or even a third side strake. A length/depth ratio of 22 would bring the overall side height to c. 0. 55 m above the lower surface of the bottom planking. Capacity and stability calculations by Coates also suggest that this greater side height would be more appropriate, especially when there was water in the bottom of the boat, a condition which is almost unavoidable. The minimum height of the sides is therefore taken to have been 0.34 m, with 0. 55 m as an alternative hypothesis.

The reason for the change in the method of fastening the second side strake over the midship region is unclear, but this need not affect the general form of the 'raft's' transverse section which, on the minimum hypothesis, was rectangular. The Ljubljana boat had knees to support her sides (Fig. 7.1.16) but there is no surviving evidence for such fittings on the Brigg remains, although such relatively thin sides (*c.* 25 mm) would appear to require some support over a length of 12 m – possibly the conjectural dunnage would provide this.

Open ends are known ethnographically and have been used in the hypothetical reconstruction of the Viking Age Egernsund 'ferry' (Crumlin–Pedersen, 1977, 175), and of an 18th century *courau* of the R. Adour (Beaudouin, 1970, 71), but these are only practicable where the ends are made to rise above the waterline by one means or another. There is no evidence for rising ends in the Brigg 'raft' remains and therefore the minimum solution to the problem of closing the ends is to have vertical, watertight transoms up to the height of 0.34 m postulated for the sides, with 0.55 m as an alternative. Coates has emphasised that strength would be required here to retain the ends of the strakes at a common level, thereby minimising destructive forces on the stitching. A thickness of 50 mm, twice that of the side planking, is therefore postulated. The precise method of fastening transoms to bottom and sides cannot be deduced, but it may have been a variant of the moss, lath, stitch technqiues used elsewhere on the 'raft', or the transoms may have been set into grooves.

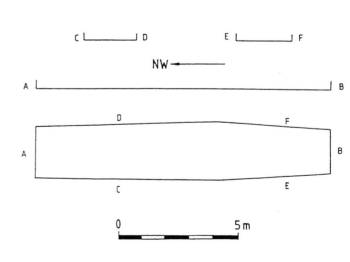

Figure 7.1.21 Outline hypothetical reconstruction drawing of the 'raft'. See Fig. 7.3.1 for a reconstruction model

185

Operational Performance

The resultant outline reconstruction drawing (Fig. 7.1.21) has a length overall of 12.30 m and a maximum beam of 2.32 m at 7.80 m from the north west end. This version, Alternative 1, has side and end heights of 0.34 m. Alternative 2 (not shown) is similar but has a height of 0. 55 m. Coates calculates that such a boat when empty displaces 1.47 tonnes (alternative 1) or 1.60 tonnes (alternative 2), and floats, with the waterline about level with the upper surface of the bottom planking. Coates' table shows that when various theoretical loads of men and animals are carried in a dry boat all result in a positive GM; that is, the 'raft' always has transverse stability. However, some of these loads are not practicable because of inadequate freeboard. Thus, although Load B of 50 men (or 10 men and 48 sheep) has a safe freeboard of 0.176 m in Alternative 1, Load D (100 sheep and 20 men) gives a freeboard of only 0. 059 m which would not be sufficient to prevent water coming over the lower side if four men were to move across the 'raft'. On the other hand, Load D in Alternative 2 results in a freeboard of 0.264 m which is sufficient to cope safely with such movement.

What would have been the minimum acceptable freeboard to the Brigg 'raft' boatmen is difficult to assess. Coates' 'movement of four men' test may be near the mark. On the other hand, the concept of an acceptable angle of heel with the top of the lower side awash, as used to assess logboats theoretically (McGrail, 1978A, 133) may also be applicable to planked boats, although a 5° heel would be more realistic than the 10° suggested for logboats. Until there is general agreement on the criteria to be used, comparisons between the theoretical performance of different boats will not be possible.

Coates also highlights the adverse effects of bilge water on the stability and loadcarrying capability of flat–bottomed craft such as the Brigg 'raft'. Unless the depth of bilge water is minimised and its potential to flow across the boat in response to a transverse disturbance is constrained, hydrostatic stability is reduced and in certain circumstances may be entirely lost. In assessing performance it is therefore more realistic to consider a 'raft' that is leaky (i. e. has bilge water) than one that is dry.

Using the standards for minimum acceptable freeboard suggested by Coates, if the depth of bilge water can be kept less that *c*. 0. 02 m, and its transverse movement restricted by 0. 05 m thickness of dunnage, a safe load of *c*. 5 tonnes can be carried in an Alternative 1 'raft'. If bilge water is allowed to increase to 0.10 m, however, dunnage of 0. 20 m would be necessary to control it, and in this state the 'raft' would no longer have the minimum safe freeboard. On the other hand, an Alternative 2 'raft', of height 0. 55 m, could safely carry a load of *c*. 5. 23 tonnes with this deeper bilge water. An Alternative 1 'raft' with 0.10 m of bilge water would only be safe if free surface effects could be virtually eliminated by longitudinal sills or dams; but even with these the safe load would only be *c*. 1.54 tonnes because of freeboard limitations.

The excavated evidence lends support to the hypothesis that *c*. 0.05 m of dunnage was used (Fig. 7.1.13); in addition, the lines of cleats along each bottom strake form discontinuous sills or dams which would reduce (but not eliminate) free surface effects. Thus a realistic assessment of the minimum reconstruction of the 'raft' is that Alternative 1 could carry a safe load of *c*. 2. 58 tonnes – the equivalent of *c*. 40 sheep and 10 men – providing the depth of bilge water was kept less than *c*. 0. 02 m. h similar conditions Alternative 2 could carry a load of *c*. 8.10 tonnes – the equivalent of *c*. 30 cattle and 20 men. In both cases, if the depth of bilge water were to increase to 0. 03 m the discontinuous sills of cleats could probably contain the potential increase in free surface effects; the safe loads would, however, be reduced by 0.274 tonnes to compensate for the increased bilge water.

A minimum crew of ten men is suggested: three paddling on each side, one in the bow, one at the stern and two men bailing. Additional crew might be needed to tend any animals, although on short crossings the bailing men could probably cope with this. Twenty–four men could usefully propel and steer the 'raft': there would be space for this number along the sides and at the ends, the only limitation being one of freeboard. Thus the maximum would be of the order of 30 men. The optimum number required on any one crossing would depend upon the relative importance given to security of animals, payload capability and speed, and upon what was considered to be the minimum acceptable freeboard and the maximum safe depth of bilge water.

Primary Use

The box–like form postulated for the Brigg 'raft' (Fig. 7.1.21) is a version of a form much used on inland waterways and in inshore waters (Fig 7.1.7). This form has maximum volume load capacity, adequate transverse stability, the ability to take the ground well on a falling tide, and is not complex to build. With a gently rising bottom at the ends (*not* postulated for the Brigg 'raft') such a boat can easily be run onto a rising beach or river bank – on sites with little gradient rising ends would not be so necessary. A true raft could have some of these features but it would not be watertight and, if made of oak (probably the only tree species of any great length and breadth of bole available to the Brigg boatbuilders) which has a relatively high specific density of *c*. 0. 8 when in use afloat, its payload by weight (= deadweight tonnage) would be correspondingly less. A watertight boat of oak – even with the low sides and ends postulated for the Brigg 'raft' – would not have these disadvantages. These sides would keep out the water in most conditions to be expected in the prehistoric Ancholme near the find–spot, would restrain loads from slipping overboard and retain the postulated dunnage, whilst not being a serious obstacle to loading and unloading.

Such a form is not suitable for open sea conditions nor is it a design for speed. But these qualities were not necessary for the function the "raft" was built to undertake in the particular environment of the 1st millennium bc Ancholme.

From Fletcher's geomorphological maps it can be seen that the Ancholme valley narrows in the vicinity of Brigg. Thus for travel between the two upland regions – the limestone Lincoln

Edge to the west and the chalk Lincolnshire Wolds to the east, both areas of good quality land (Gardiner, 1980, Fig. 1), there would be the minimum of ill–drained ground and estuarine water to cross. The Brigg 'raft' was the paddled or poled ferry at this nodal point, one of four Lincolnshire river sites where Gardiner (1980, 112) has found clustering of bronzes. Animals, goods and men could be embarked during the period of flood tide as the 'raft' lay on the mudflats on the edge of the estuarine channel where she had grounded at a previous high water. It is conceivable that, as appears to have happened at the North Ferriby site, (McGrail, 1979, 161) a "hard" of light timbers would be used to prevent the 'raft' settling into the mud, and even allow her to be dragged towards the channel at low water so that she would certainly become afloat at the next high water. At the destination the 'raft' would be run aground or onto a "hard" and held there until she dried out, or possibly until ready for a return passage. The tidal stream (the horizontal movement of water) might impose boat handling problems at Brigg; its precise speed would depend on the morphology of the Humber estuary and the junction with the Ancholme. Operating during the slack water period at about the time of high water would minimise these problems.

Crossings would be possible at other states of the tide, but, before embarking and after disembarkation, travellers and beasts would have to cross mudflats, possibly using trackways. On a rising (flood) tide the 'raft' would be gradually eased up the foreshore during loading and unloading; on a falling (ebb) tide the 'raft' could become stranded on the mud or the 'hard', so that a preferred method could be to hold the 'raft' in the shallows, with men and beasts wading to and from the foreshore.

Although east/west crossings seem the most likely use for the 'raft', it is not inconceivable that she might have been used for north/south passages with the tide. But this can only have been in sheltered waters for open water where the wind could work–up a sea would be hazardous to a craft of the form and structure postulated. And as her plank fastenings (Fig. 7.1.11) evidently result in a less watertight joint than that òf the Ferriby boats (Fig. 7.1.8), where the planking interlocks, the 'raft' is less likely to have been used in the lower reaches of an estuary.

During periods of inactivity the 'raft' could be hauled up the foreshore or moored in the main channel where she could be reached by a small boat. Constant use of mudflats or 'hards' would cause wear of the undersurface of the planking and this probably explains why no toolmarks were found during post–excavation examination. Stitch wear would be reduced by the "uplifting" of the exposed sewing, and by the constraints on individual strake movement imposed by the transverse timbers, and the postulated transom ends.

Providing stitch wear and failure is minimised by good design and building techniques, boats of sewn planking can be used in the most arduous conditions. For example: off open beaches in several regions of the Indian Ocean (Hornell, 1946, 234/5; *Periplus*, Ch. 15, 16, 36, see Huntingford, 1980; Hourani, 1963, 92–7; Wright and Churchill, 1965; McGrail, 1981, Ch. 5, 6, 7); and during the Somali campaign of 1904 the Royal Navy used native–manned *masula* sewn boats from Madras to disembark men, equipment and even camels through the surf: "they stood the knocking about better than the man–of–war boats, being made of solid wood sewed together, so that there was no special point of weakness .... " (*The Naval Annual*, 1905 ed. T. A. Brassey, p. 60–61). The *masula* is a "boat–shaped" craft designed to operate through surf, so this is no precise parallel for the Brigg 'raft', but it does serve to emphasise the practicability of sewing as a boatbuilding technique; the worldwide evidence for this method of fastening planking and its evident long use further emphasises that the sewn boats were not of inferior seaworthiness. Such boats leaked (as indeed do iron–fastened boats) and probably needed constant bailing. The early 20th century Lamu *mtepe* had two men bailing throughout the voyage (Hornell, 1941, 62) and Maori seamen carried caulking material in their sewn boats to check any leaks (Best, 1925, 39). No doubt the Brigg 'raftsmen' carried a good supply of moss as well as several bailers, for, as Coates points out, if bilge water is not kept to a minimum the 'raft' as reconstructed can become unstable. An east/west crossing of the Ancholme estuary would not be an overlong voyage, and if the 'raft' could be left to drain on the mudflats after each short crossing, or after a series of crossings, bilge water would not be accumulated to an unsafe depth.

Secondary Use

During re–excavation, four large holes were found through the planking near cleats 16, 26, G4 and G5. Through the one near 26 a hazel post of round wood had been driven into the underlying clay. A sample from this post has been dated to 2560 bp ± 50 (Q–1261) and is thus contemporary with the 'raft'. The Brigg trackway was held in position in a similar but not identical manner by vertical posts of 3 1/2 in diameter driven through morticed holes (Wylie, 1884); and comparable methods are known from the Somerset Levels (Coles et *al.*, Somerset Level Papers).

Thus it seems probable that at some stage the use of the 'raft' as a ferry became impracticable or uneconomic. This may have co–incided with the onset of falling sea–levels which increasingly left areas of soft, marshy ground to be crossed to gain access to the estuarine channel. She was therefore left on the mudflats of a quiet creek within an expanse of *Spartina*, probably above all but spring tides, and used as part of the approach trackway to the estuarine channel or possibly as a stage with the north western end on (relatively) dry ground and the south eastern end floating in the channel where boats could be manned. With the postulated dunnage still in position, the cleats need not have been too difficult an obstacle to movement to and from the river. To ensure that the 'raft' did not float away at Springs she was held in position by a few vertical posts – there may have been others through unrecovered parts of the 'raft'. The 'raft' would thus "rise and fall with the tide" as Hunt (1907/8) suggested. His description of the 'raft' as a "pontoon bridge" and as a "floating ford" may mean that the evidence for such a secondary use may have been more obvious in 1888.

It may have been during this re-use phase that the ends and the sides were dismantled as they were not needed in the raft's new role. Lack of maintenance would eventually lead to rotting stitches and lost wedges – the dunnage may have been removed or possibly drifted away on a high tide. As local sea level fell from the maximum c. 650 bc, the 'raft' would be only rarely, and then never, awash in estuarine waters. She settled into the *Spartina* bed to be covered in the next few years by non-marine sediments from upstream.

Note The Illustrations are copyright, National Maritime Museum.

References

Arnold, B., 1977. 'Some remarks on caulking in Celtic boat construction' *I. J. N. A.*, 6, 293–7.

Arnold, B., 1978. 'Gallo–Roman boat finds in Switzerland' in Taylor, J. du P., and Cleere H. (ed.) *Roman Shipping and Trade*, 31–6. CBA Research Report 24.

Atkinson, A., 1887. 'Notes on an ancient boat found at Brigg', *Archaeologia*, 50 (Pt. 2) 302–370.

Beaudouin, F., 1970, *Les bateaux de l'Adour*, Bayonne.

Best, E., 1925. *Maori Canoe*, Dominion Museum New Zealand Bulletin No. 7.

Brusíc, Z., 1968. 'Istrazivanje anticke luke kod Nina', *Diadora*, 4, 203–9.

Buck, P. H., 1927. *Material Culture of the Cook Islands*. Board of Maori Ethnological Research, Volume 1. New Zealand.

Clark, J. G. D., 1954. *Excavations at Star Carr*. Cambridge.

Coles, J. M., Heal, S. V. E. and Orme, B. J., 1978. 'Use and character of wood in prehistoric Britain and Ireland', *P. P. S.*, 44, 1–45.

Crumlin–Pedersen, O., 1977. 'Some principles for the recording and presentation of ancient boat structures' in McGrail (1977) 163–177.

de la Prynne, A., 1870. *Diary of Abraham de la Prynne*, Surtees Publication.

Ellmers, D., 1978. 'Shipping on the Rhine during the Roman period', in Taylor, J. du P., and Cleere, H., (ed) *Roman Shipping and Trade*, 1–14. CBA Research Report 24.

Farrell, A. W., and Penney, S., 1975. 'Broighter boat: a re-assessmentt *Irish Archaeological Research Forum* 2. 2, 15–26.

Filgueiras, O. L., 1980. *Decline of Portuguese Regional Boats*. NMM Greenwich Monograph 47.

Folkard, H. C., 1870. *Sailing boat*, 4th edition. Reprinted 1973, Wakefield.

Gardiner, J. P., 1980. 'Land and social status_a case study from eastern England' in Barrett, J., and Bradley, R., *British Later Bronze Age*. BAR (Oxford) 83, 101–114.

Greenhill, B., 1976. *Archaeology of the Boat*.

Hornell, J., 1941. 'Sea-going mtepe and dau of the Lamu Archipelago' *M. M.*, 27, 54–68.

Hornell, J., 1946. *Water Transport*, Cambridge. Reprinted 1970, Newton Abbot.

Hourani, G. F., 1963. *Arab Seafaring*, Beirut.

Hunt, A., 1907–8. 'Viking raft or Pontoon Bridge' *Saga Book of the Viking Club*, 5, 355–362.

Huntingford, G. W. B., 1980(ed.) *Periplus of the Erythraean Sea* Hakluyt Society 2nd series No. 151.

Landstrom, B., 1970. *Ships of the Pharaohs*.

Lindqvist, S., 1924. 'Baten fran, Fiholm Vastmanlandt, *Fornvannen*, 19, 224–5.

MacCormick, A. G., 1968. 'Three dugout canoes and a wheel from Holme Pierrepont, Nottinghamshire', *Trans. Thoroton Soc.* 72, 14–31.

McGrail, S., 1974. *Building and trials of the replica of an ancient boat: the Gokstad faering*, NMM Greenwhich Monograph 11 (part I).

McGrail, S., (ed.) 1977. *Sources and Techniques in Boat Archaeology*, BAR (Oxford) S29. NMM Greenwhich Archaeological Series 1.

McGrail, S., 1978A. *Logboats of England and Wales*, BAR (Oxford) 51 NMM Greenwhich Archaeological Series 2.

McGrail, S., 1979. 'Prehistoric boats, timber and woodworking technology' *P. P. S.*, 45, 159–163.

McGrail, S., 1981., *Rafts, Boats and Ships*, NMM Greenwich and HMSO.

Malinowski, B., 1978. *Argonauts of the Western Pacific*.

Mullner A., 1892. 'Ein schiff im Laibacher Moore,' *Argo*, 1, 1–7.

Reinders, R., 1979. 'Medieval ships: recent finds in the Netherlands' in: McGrail, S., (ed). *Medieval Ships and Harbours in Northern Europe*, 35–43, BAR (Oxford) S.66. NMM Greenwich Archaeological Series 5.

Rosenberg, G., 1937, *Hjortspring–fundet*, Copenhagen.

Seaward, M. R. D. and Williams, D., 1976. 'An interpretation of mosses found in recent archaeological excavations', *J. Archaeological Science*, 3, 173–7.

Thropp, J., 1887. 'An ancient raft found at Brigg, Lincolnshire' *Assoc. Architectural Societies Reports and Papers*, 19 part 1, 95–7.

Wright, E. V., 1976. *North Ferriby boats*, NMM Greenwich Monograph 23.

Wright, E. V. and Churchill, D. M., 1965 'Boats from North Ferriby, Yorkshire, England' *P. P. S.*, 31, 1–24.

Wylie, W. M., 1884. (A note by A. Atkinson on the Brigg Trackway) *Proc. Soc. Ant.*, N.S. 10, 110–115).

IJNA = International Journal of Nautical Archaeology.

MM = Mariner's Mirror.

PPS = Proceedings of the Prehistoric Society.

Proc. Soc. Ant. = Proceedings of the Society of Antiquaries.

Reprinted from:

McGrail, S. (ed) *Brigg 'raft' and her prehistoric environment*: 211–252. British Archaeological Reports 89 (1981).

PAPER 7.2

PREHISTORIC SEAFARING IN THE CHANNEL

In a paper entitled 'Middle Bronze Age trade between Britain and Europe: a maritime perspective', Keith Muckelroy (1981) described some of the evidence for prehistoric voyages across the Channel, including his own underwater excavations of the Bronze Age sites off Moor Sands, east of the Salcombe Estuary in Devon, and in Langdon Bay, east of Dover harbour. In this present article, I aim to build on Muckelroy's pioneering work, which was brought to a premature end by his death in 1980 at the early age of 29. In particular I shall consider the routes, the boats, the landing–places and the navigational techniques used on this cross–Channel traffic.

Maritime Archaeology is thought by some to be at the margin or periphery of the discipline rather than at the core; nevertheless the middle phase of many an ancient artefact's 'life' (production–distribution–consumption) included an overseas voyage and thus the problems raised here relate to an important element in prehistoric economic and social life, not without interest to the most landlubberly of archaeologists, especially those from the archipelago of islands off the north–west coast of Europe.

Oversea trade routes

There are no excavated examples of vessels wrecked whilst actually crossing the Channel in prehistoric times, although the Langdon Bay underwater finds may have come from such a wreck.[1] The evidence for early voyages must therefore come indirectly, and after appropriate source criticism, from the distribution patterns of artefacts and of those ideas which are archaeologically visible as 'monuments', as 'ritual' and as technological innovations. Although early prehistoric distribution patterns do not indicate clearly which overseas routes were used, distribution patterns from later prehistory (O'Connor 1980; Bradley 1984; 1990; Northover 1982; Tomalin 1984; 1988) suggest that the predominant routes used then were where, on nautical grounds, one would expect them to be:

    – mid–Channel routes linking the Normandy/Brittany region of France and the River Seine catchment area with the Wessex region of central southern England, via the Solent and the rivers at Christchurch and Poole

    – eastern routes connecting the Rhine region to the Thames region, each of these rivers having enormous catchment areas.

In the protohistoric period, from the first century BC onwards, there is literary confirmation of cross–Channel voyages in the writings of late Classical authors such as Caesar (*B.G.* III 8; IV 21–36– ,V 2.23) Pliny (*N.H.* IV 101 (xv); 102 (xvi)); Strabo (*Geog.* 4.1.14 4.2.1; 4.3.3–4; 4.4.1; 4.5.1–2) and Diodorus Siculus (V 21–3; 2.2–4; 38.5). This documentary evidence when combined with contemporary distribution patterns (Cunliffe 1982, 42–51; 1983; 1987; 1988a, 98–104, 145–9; 1991; Fitzpatrick 1985; McGrail 1983, 319–34) suggests that there were then four principal sea routes between the Continent and Britain with associated coastal passages (Fig 2.3.5).

    – the Rhine to the Thames
    – in the region of the Strait, at the shortest crossing
    – mid–Channel routes
    – from western Brittany to south–west Britain and to south–east Ireland, for vessels coming from the Loire and Garonne estuaries.

These Channel crossings linked the maritime trading networks of the Continental Atlantic coast and rivers to the indigenous networks in British and Irish waters. Portages between the upper reaches of French rivers (Cunliffe 1988b; 1991) linked maritime north–west Europe to the maritime networks of the central and eastern Mediterranean, whilst the Iberian coastal maritime route linked north–west Europe to the western Mediterranean (Fig. 7.2.1). This Iberian coastal route would not have been an easy one, especially when northward–bound, as the summer winds would have been generally from the north, whilst the current would have set southerly. In addition, there were several prominent headlands to be rounded, for example Cape St Vincent to the south–west of the Algarve, which could involve a delay of several days whilst awaiting a favourable combination of wind and tidal stream. On such coastal passages it would have been necessary to work the tides, possibly involving anchoring or lying hove–to during foul winds and streams. It would probably also have been necessary to anchor during non–moonlit nights, and much use may have had to be made of evening or early morning land breezes to work away from lee shores. The passage westwards from the Mediterranean to the Atlantic through the Strait at Gibraltar would also have been arduous, owing to the strong eastward–flowing currents in the Strait.

That this Atlantic coastal route was indeed used is suggested by extracts from a *Periplus* of the sixth century BC incorporated by Avienus in the fourth century AD into his *Ora Maritima* (Hawkes 1977, 19; Murphy 1977; McGrail 1990, 36) which describes what was evidently an established trade route along the western coast of Atlantic Europe and then along the northern shores of the Mediterranean to Massilia (Marseille).

Figure 7.2.1 The Atlantic coast of Europe and NW Africa. Drawing: Institute of Archaeology, Oxford

This route is described in stages: from Ireland/Britain to western Brittany; from western Brittany to Tartessus (a harbour in the Gulf of Cadiz); and from Tartessus through the Pillars of Hercules (Strait of Gibraltar) to Massilia, with a subsidiary route to Carthage. The text seems to suggest that Mediterranean merchants sailed to and from western Brittany, whilst the cross–Channel sections of these voyages were undertaken by the 'hardy and industrious peoples of the islands and coasts around Ushant' (Murphy 1977, 94–116). Pytheas also appears to have used this route in his late fourth century BC voyage of scientific and and commercial exploration of the northern seas (Hawkes 1977; 1984). The fact that a lighthouse was built at La Coruna in north–west Spain during the Roman period (Hague 1973) further supports these arguments for early use of this difficult coastal route.

One of Columbus' major achievements five hundred years ago was to connect European maritime trade networks to the indigenous American networks (McGrail 1992). A little later, in 1497–9, Vasco da Gama sailed around southern Africa and re–connected European networks to those of the Indian Ocean (they had formerly been connected via a canal or by an overland portage from the River Nile to the Red Sea). These Indian Ocean networks were already connected to the networks of south–east Asia. Maritime connections were completed

worldwide and the world encompassed by trade routes in 1519 to 1522 when Ferdinand Magellan and Sebastian del Cano, during their voyage of world circumnavigation, connected the American maritime trade networks to those of south–east Asia: this is probably the earliest examples of a commercial 'world system'. The establishment of individual maritime trading networks in the earlier prehistoric period and their interconnection during the later prehistoric period may thus be seen, as the first steps in a process which led to the European domination of world trade routes in the sixteenth to eighteenth centuries AD.

Boats used on the cross–Channel routes

Nowadays, in favourable conditions, people swim the Channel, and the Atlantic Ocean has been crossed by adventurers in the most unlikely vessels. Perhaps in prehistoric times there were similar adventurers with a 'Guinness Book of Records' attitude to the sea, and perhaps the Channel was crossed on occasions in what, by any standards, would be considered unseaworthy craft. Nevertheless, in an evaluation of early possibilities it is essential to identify those types of vessel which, without special preparations, could carry a reasonable load and have a good chance of making return crossings of the Channel in the conditions then prevailing. This is not to claim that prehistoric humans had a modern attitude to reliability and timekeeping, nor our twentieth century expectations of low–risk, minimum–delay sea travel – on the contrary, in earlier times, when there was unseasonal weather, voyages were postponed until conditions improved, although doubtless there were occasional bad–weather crossings. The vessels regularly used on prehistoric cross–Channel voyages must have had certain qualities which made them reliable and seaworthy in Channel conditions, and suitable to undertake the functions required of them, which may have included sea fishing as well as cross–Channel passages.

The principal desirable qualities required in a boat are listed in Table 7.2.1 under the headings of Safety and Performance. All these desirable characteristics, however, cannot be maximized in one boat: for high speed, for example, a boat should be long in proportion to its breadth and have the minimum wetted hull surface area. Such dimensional parameters impose constrictions on cargo capacity, transverse stability and seakindliness and thus these attributes cannot be maximized at the same time as speed. Every boat is thus a compromise: if some characteristics are maximized, less than optimum performance has to be accepted in other qualities.

Table 7.2.1 Desirable qualities in a seagoing vessel

Safety

    Seaworthiness   – buoyancy
                            – strength and durability

    Stability

Performance
    Cargo capacitiy
    Speed
    Manoeuvarbility and controllability
    Closeness to the wind and minimum leeway (if sail)
    Sea–kindliness and dryness

The most important qualities for an early sea–going boat which could be used as a ferry and for fishing are probably the safety attributes of seaworthiness and stability – without these the boat would capsize, be swamped, or otherwise founder. High ratings would also be desirable in the performance attributes of closeness to the wind (otherwise the crossings could prove long and, on occasions, impossible) and seakindliness (without this quality the hull and rigging could be overstrained and the crew excessively seasick). The potential speed, manoeuvrability and cargo capacity of such a vessel would be residual attributes constrained by the necessity to achieve the qualities with higher priority, although without a reasonable (undefined) capacity for cargo, passengers and/or fishing catch there would be little point in going to sea.

The use of sail. The identification of the attribute 'closeness to the wind' as an important one implies that the ideal prehistoric cross–Channel ferry/fishing boat should be sailed. The earliest direct evidence for the indigenous use of sail in Atlantic

Europe is from the first century BC: Caesar's description (*B.G.* III 13) of the leather sails of the boats of the Veneti of south and western Brittany; and the small gold model from Broighter (Fig. 7.2.2) near Limavady in the north of Ireland (Farrell & Penny 1975) which has a mast stepped near amidships. There is, however, indirect evidence for earlier use in the sixth century BC Massiliote *Periplus* incorporated into Avienus' *Ora Maritima* (Hawkes 1977; Murphy 1977) which refers to voyages between western Brittany and Ireland which take two days. The speed of *c.* 5 knots which this implies and the long distance involved means that sail was almost certainly used. Sail was used in Egypt before 3000 BC and in the eastern Mediterranean from around 2000 BC (Casson 1971, fig. 6; figs 34–36). As sail, like the wheel, is its own advertisement, there is thus a possibility that sail was used in the seas off north–west Europe before the mid–first millennium BC, but probably not earlier than, say, the mid–second millennium.

As a working hypothesis it may be suggested therefore that, in Neolithic times, cross–Channel voyages were undertaken in paddled or oared vessels, which were possibly restricted to the shortest crossing in the Strait. By the Iron Age, however, although some oared craft may have continued to be used across the Strait, the majority of voyages were under sail, but with oar power available for use in contrary or light wind conditions and when manoeuvring in inshore waters, i.e. a galley type of vessel. This use of sail would not only result in speedier and less arduous passages and higher cargo/crew ratios, but would also make the longer sea crossings in the western Channel a more practicable proposition.

Nowadays the predominant winds in the Channel are between south–west and north–west. They have probably been from that sector from 1000 BC and possibly much earlier (a summary of the environmental evidence for sea levels, coastlines, tidal regimes and weather patterns may be found in McGrail 1983, 303–7; 1987, 258–60). In the open sea, the wind would thus be more or less on the port beam of a vessel on a northward passage and on the starboard beam of a southbound vessel, i.e. at 80° to 100° to the intended track. This is as close as one would expect prehistoric sailing craft to achieve, bearing in mind that it has been estimated that Classical Mediterranean and north European Viking age vessels with a single square sail could achieve only *c.* 75° to 80° (McGrail 1987, 260–2); and that the best which Columbus, with a three–masted vessel, appears to have achieved on his Atlantic voyage was *c.* 70° to 75° (McGrail 1992). A wind at right angles to the intended track is nowadays known as 'soldier's wind' because the passage both ways can be made without tacking, and thus little nautical skill is needed. Indeed, for two–way voyages over relatively short distances such a beam wind is the best possible wind to have.

Logboats. In the lands bordering the Channel a dozen or so logboats ('dugout canoes') have been dated to pre–Roman times (Booth 1984; Bahn 1992). The dimensions of a simple basic logboat are however limited by the size of its parent log and thus its inherent stability, which is proportional to the cube of the waterline beam measurement, and its freeboard (height of the sides above the waterline) are generally insufficient to match the seaworthiness and stability criteria identified above

Figure 7.2.2 Small gold model boat of the 1st century BC from Broighter, Co. Derry, Ireland. Photo: National Museum of Ireland

as necessary attributes in a seagoing vessel. Furthermore, a basic logboat has insufficient stability to allow it to use sail other than in a light breeze from the stern sector.

On the other hand, there are many ethnographic examples, worldwide, of simple logboats which have been modified so that they gain the extra stability and freeboard they need to make them seaworthy. The hollowed parent log may be expanded in breadth after specialized treatment; a simple logboat may be fitted with stabilizing timbers along the sides at the waterline; or two such logboats may be paired side–by–side: such alternatives increase the waterline beam measurement and thereby enhance transverse stability (McGrail 1987, 66–73) which may then be sufficient to permit sail to be used. The freeboard (a measure of reserve buoyancy and thus of safety) of such stability–enhanced logboats may be increased by adding one or more strakes of planking to the sides.

There is, however, no indisputable evidence for such alterations and additions in the prehistoric logboats so far excavated in north–western France and southern Britain. Thus,

on present evidence, logboats are unlikely to have been used on cross–Channel voyages.

Plank boats. Apart from the Hjortspring boat of the mid–fourth century BC from the Baltic island of Als, all prehistoric plank boats known to date come from Britain: three, or possibly four, from the northern shore of the Humber estuary at North Ferriby (Wright 1990) dated to *c.* 1300 cal. BC (Switsur & Wright 1989); the so–called Brigg 'raft' – actually a flat–bottomed, boat of *c.* 800 cal. BC (Switsur & Wright 1989) from the River Ancholme, a tributary of the Humber (McGrail 1981b; 1985b); and a plank fragment (Fig. 7.2.3) dated to the period 1594–1454 cal. BC recently excavated from a waterlogged site near the River Nedern, a tributary of the Severn, at Caldicot Castle, Gwent (Parry & McGrail 1991). These boats were all built from oak planks fastened together by yew (*Taxus* sp.) lashings (Caldicot and Ferriby) or a by a continuous willow (*Salix* sp.) ' stitching' (Brigg).[2]

The Caldicot, Ferriby and Brigg boats were all narrow, relatively long, and flat–bottomed (Fig. 7.2.4), without stems or significant keels. The Brigg boat having a rectangular transverse section and squared ends, would have been used

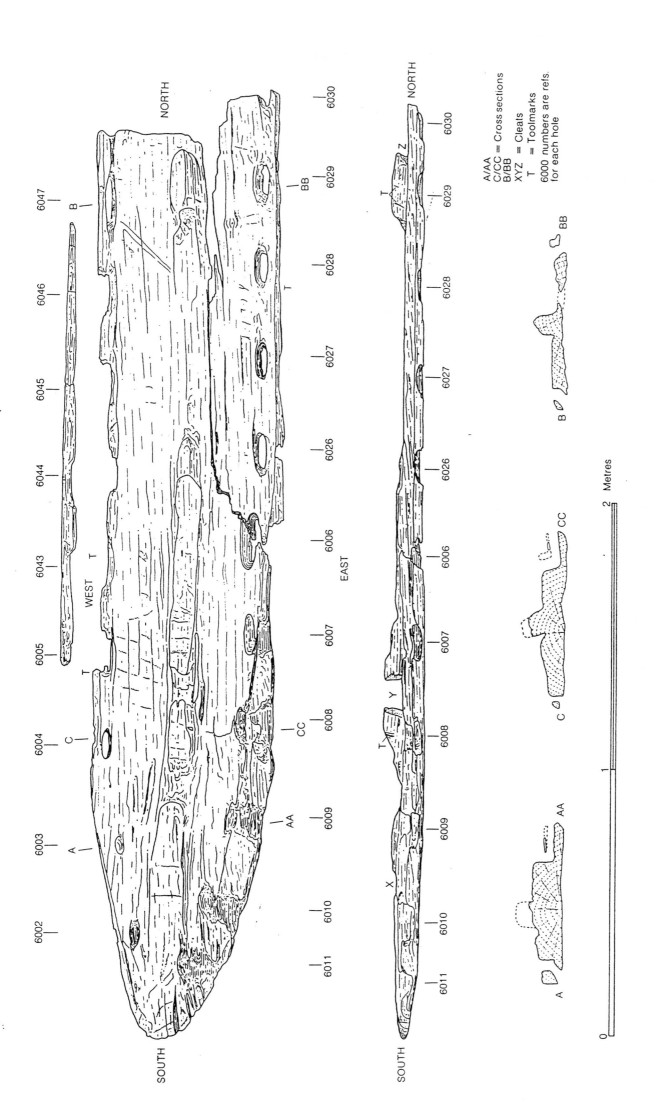

Figure 7.2.3 Plank fragment from Caldicot Castle, Gwent. Drawing: Institute of Archaeology, Oxford (based on G.G.A.T. drawings)

mainly for upstream work; the Caldicot and Ferriby boats probably carried goods and people along and across the tidal estuaries and associated rivers – it is unlikely that they were seagoing except on very rare occasions. This is not because they were sewn boats – there are several examples of seagoing sewn plank boats, worldwide, from the twentieth century and the recent past (McGrail 1981a, 29–30, 47–8, 51, 54–5, 58, 63–4, 69, 80–1) – but because their shape and structure did not allow them to meet the stability and seakindliness criteria postulated above. Moreover, there is no evidence that they had mast and sail, although this has recently been suggested (Wright, 1990, 110–3), or even oars: they were, in all probability, propelled by paddle and by poles in shallow water.

There is however a hint in the British archaeological record that there may have been an early tradition of planked boats with keel and stems which may have been more seaworthy than the boats of the Caldicot/Ferriby/Brigg tradition. One of the Bronze Age logboat-shaped coffins from Loose Howe, North Yorkshire, has a fitted pseudo–keel and a pseudo–stem (Elgee & Elgee 1949; McGrail 1978); and the Iron Age logboat from Poole has a stem similarly worked in the solid (McGrail 1978). These features are unnecessary and non–functional in a logboat and may well have been copied from a plank boat: such a boat, however, has not yet been found.

By the late Iron Age, there is definite evidence for sea–going plank boats: the sail–propelled Channel trading vessels of the Veneti described by Caesar (*B.G.* 3.13) and by Strabo (*Geog.* 4.4.1); and cargo ships depicted on two first century AD bronze coins (Fig. 7.2.5) of Cunobelin (Muckelroy *et al.* 1978; McGrail 1990, 43–4). These first century BC/first century AD descriptions and depictions may be forerunners of the second/third century AD seagoing ships of the Romano Celtic tradition excavated from Blackfriars, London (Marsden 1990), and from St Peter Port Harbour, Guernsey (Rule 1990): these two finds are the earliest remains of north–west European sailing ships which were indisputably seagoing.

Hide boats. Classical authors refer to the indigenous use of hide boats on inland waters and at sea off north–west Europe (Caesar *B.G.* 1.54; Pliny *N.H.* 7.206; Lucan *Pharsalia* 4, 130–8; Solinus *Polyhistor* 23). Pliny (4.104) quotes Timaeus' statement that the British used hide boats in the overseas tin trade during the third century BC; whilst the *Ora Maritima* of the fourth century AD is believed to include evidence for similar use in the sixth century BC. It seems very likely that the first century BC gold model from Broighter (Fig. 7.2.2) represents such a sail–powered, sea–going hide boat (McGrail 1987, 186–7).

Complex hide boats suitable for use at sea were technologically possible from Mesolithic times (McGrail 1990, 34). Hide boats are quickly built and readily repaired; they fit well into a crofter–style economy and can be operated from most types of shore using informal landing places, and they are excellent boats in a surf. Their resilient structure is lightweight, giving good freeboard even when loaded. In general, they are more seaworthy and seakindly and have more transverse stability than the equivalent plank boat. Their principal disadvantage is that, although they can be sailed in difficult conditions, their relatively light draft and good freeboard mean that they are more susceptible to leeway (drift downwind) than a keeled plank boat (McGrail 1987, 184–5). Apart from this drawback, the hide boat, up to 12m or so in length, appears to match the specification for a cross–Channel vessel outlined above and it may be that it was so used in the Bronze Age. Hide boats were certainly used later, that is in the Iron Age; and possibly they were used earlier, in the Neolithic.

The foregoing argument is based almost entirely on theoretical considerations: the case for a Bronze Age seagoing hide can only be taken further if and when one is excavated.

Landing places

Harbours with breakwaters, waterfronts and other man–made facilities were used in the Mediterranean from the early first millennium BC (Casson 1971, 361–70) and probably earlier, although away from the main commercial and naval ports, informal landing places, such as we find described in the *Odyssey*, continued to be used. Apart from a few important commercial sites of the Roman period, as for example London, landing places with few if any man–made facilities were the rule in north–west Europe until the eighth or ninth century AD when formal harbours began to be built in selected places (McGrail 1981c; 1985a).

Cross–Channel boats were beached at such informal landing places on a falling (ebb) tide, or they were anchored off the beach and their goods unloaded into smaller boats (logboats?) or horse drawn carts (Ellmers 1985, 25–30); or these goods were carried ashore by people wading. When there was a firm beach there need be no fixed structure (Fig. 2.1.8). On soft, muddy beaches where a beached boat might have difficulty in floating off as the tide rose, or where people and horses would find movement difficult, hards of gravel (as found at Hengistbury Head within Christchurch Harbour: Cunliffe 1990) or of light timber or hurdles (as found near the boat site at North Ferriby on the Humber foreshore: Wright 1990), would have been prepared. Similarly constructed causeways (colloquially labelled 'trackways', especially with reference to the Somerset Levels) may have connected such hards to firmer ground beyond High Water mark. Such sites may be difficult to locate precisely, but there would be certain characteristic features which may help to identify them (McGrail 1983b, 34–41).

Navigational techniques

In good weather, on the shortest Channel route across the Strait, either the Continental or British coast would have been visible all the time. In these circumstances visual pilotage techniques can be used – the seaman proceeds from one position, known by reference to landmarks (mountain peaks, cliffs, headlands, menhir, tumuli) and seamarks (shoals, reefs, races, etc.) to another position known by reference to similar features in the region of the destination (McGrail 1983a, 314–5).

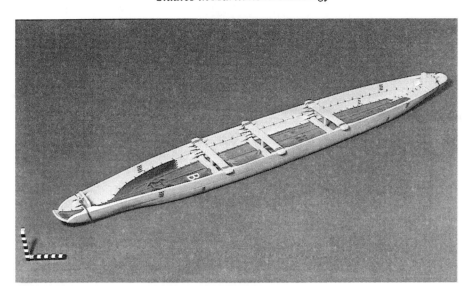

Figure 7.2.4 A 1:10 scale model of Ferriby boat 1: the parts coloured white are conjectural. Photo: National Maritime Museum, Greenwich

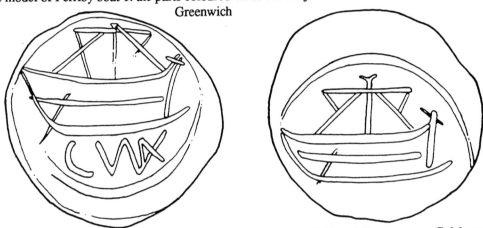

Figure 7.2.5 Drawing of 1st century AD Cunobelin bronze coins from Canterbury (left) and Sheepen near Colchester (right). Drawing: Institute of Archaeology, Oxford (based on C.A.T. photographs)

On the mid–Channel routes land would be out sight for between two and eight hours except in rare meteorological conditions of unusual refraction when land may be seen beyond the natural horizon. On the west Channel route from the vicinity of Ushant to a landfall at the Lizard there would have been a minimum of ten hours out of sight of land, even in midsummer. For such open sea voyages, deep sea navigational techniques were necessary, in addition to the skills of coastal pilotage (McGrail 1983a, 315–9).

The sounding lead can be used not only to measure depths of water and thus get warning of shoal water and hence the proximity of land, but also to sample the seabed, which can give some indication of position. Sounding leads have been found with Egyptian model boats of the second millennium BC, and Herodotus (2.5.2) was familiar with their use in the sixth century BC on board ships approaching the River Nile. Leads (Fig. 7.2.6), have been recovered from Mediterranean sites of the late centuries BC (Casson 1971, 246), but early ones have not yet been recognized in northern waters.

Apart from the use of the sounding lead, non–instrumental techniques were used for open-sea navigation throughout the world until the twelfth or thirteenth century AD. Some

indication of what these methods were can be found in such diverse sources as Homer, Caesar and the lives of early medieval sailor–saints such as St Brendan. Further light may be shed on the matter by a consideration of the non–instrumental methods used by recent navigators in the Pacific and the North Sea (McGrail 1983a).

Prehistoric navigators of the Channel probably used dead reckoning methods based on estimates of courses steered and speeds achieved, using every available clue from their environment (directions from the wind and swell; signs indicating a change in the weather, and so on), and from the heavens (Polaris, the sun, and some constellations for directions; time from the sun's change in azimuth and from the relative position of circumpolar constellations); and a knowledge, based on inherited wisdom and long experience, of speeds achieved and leeway (drift downwind) experienced by their boat in a wide range of conditions. Apart from the use of the magnetic compass and the chart, these dead reckoning techniques were the ones used by Columbus when he first crossed the Atlantic in 1492 (McGrail 1992).

Notes

1. The arguments for and against the Langdon Bay site being that of a wreck are to be published by Keith Muckelroy's successors in this Dover Harbour research project. When the distribution of bronzes is published it may become clear whether a boat was wrecked or whether the bronzes were dumped overboard by a crew seeking to keep their vessel afloat. It is understood that these bronzes weigh around 60 kg and thus could have been suitable ballast (possibly saleable ballast: McGrail 1989, 357) for a small boat. The actual traded goods on this voyage would then have been of lower density/higher stowage factor materials, such as wool, pottery, corn, or even people (McGrail 1989, table 1).

2. During Autumn 1992 there were further finds of early sewn plank boats in Britain: two fragments of planking at Goldcliff, Gwent, on the northern foreshore of the Severn estuary and substantial remains of a boat at Dover, Kent.

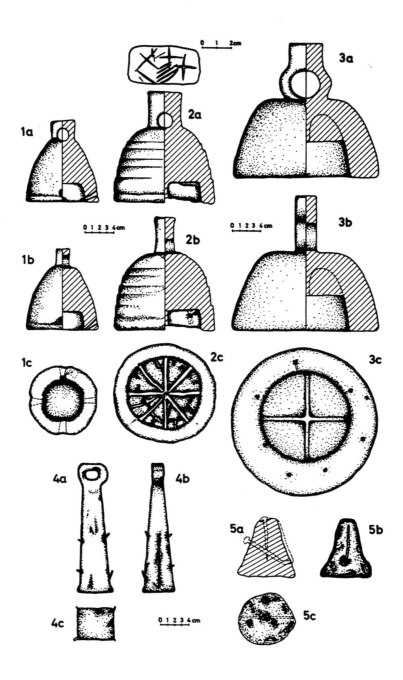

Figure 7.2.6 Sounding leads from the French Mediterranean coast. dated to the first half of the second century BC (nos 4 & 5) and to the middle of the first century AD (nos 1 & 2). Drawing after Fiori & Joncheray (1973)

References

Bahn, P.G., 1992. Paris in the Neolithic. *Newswarp* 11, 21.

Booth, B., 1984. Handlist of maritime radiocarbon dates. *International Journal of Nautical Archaeology* 13, 189–204

Bradley, R., 1984. *The Social Foundations of Prehistoric Britain: Themes and Variations in the Archaeology Power*. London & New York: Longman

Bradley, R., 1990. *The Passage of Arms*. Cambridge: Cambridge University Press

Casson, L., 1971. *Ships and Seamanship in the Ancient World*. Princeton: Princeton University Press. (2nd ed.1988)

Cunliffe, B., 1982. Britain, the Veneti and beyond. *Oxford Journal of Archaeology* 1, 39–68

Cunliffe, B., 1983. Ictis: is it here? *Oxford Journal of Archaeology* 2, 123–6.

Cunliffe, B., 1987. *Hengistbury Head, Dorset, 1*. Oxford: Oxford University Committee for Archaeology, Monograph 13

Cunliffe, B., 1988a. *Mount Batten, Plymouth*. Oxford: Oxford University Committee for Archaeology, Monograph 26

Cunliffe, B., 1988b. *Greeks, Romans and Barbarians*. London: Batsford

Cunliffe, B., 1990. Hengistbury Head: a late prehistoric haven, in *Maritime Celts, Frisians and Saxons*, ed. S. McGrail. London: Council for British Archaeology Research Report 71, 27–31

Cunliffe, B., 1991. *Iron Age Communities in Britain*. 3rd ed. London: Routledge.

Elgee,H.W.,& Elgee,F., 1949.An Early Bronze Age burial in a boat–shaped wooden coffin from north east Yorkshire. *Proceedings of the Prehistoric Society* 15, 87–106

Ellmers, D., 1985. Loading and unloading ships using a horse and cart standing in the water: the archaeological evidence, in *Conference on Waterfront Archaeology in North European Towns*, ed. A.E. Herteig. Bergen: Historisk Museum 25–30.

Fiori, P. & Joncheray, J.–P., 1973. Mobilier metallique provenant de fouilles sous marines. *Cahiers d 'Archeologie Subaquatique* 2, 86–9

Fitzpatrick, A.P., 1985. The distribution of Dressel 1 amphorae in north–west Europe. *Oxford Journal of Archaeology* 4(3), 305–40.

Farrell, A.W., & Penny, S., 1975. Broighter boat: a re assessment. *Irish Archaeological Research Forum* 2 (2), 15–26.

Hawkes, C.F.C., 1977. Pytheas: *Europe and the Greek Explorers*. Eighth J.N.L. Myres Memorial Lecture. Oxford.

Hawkes, C.F.C., 1984. Ictis disentangled and the British tin trade. *Oxford Journal of Archaeology* 3, 211–33

Hague D B . 1973. Lighthouses, in *Marine Archaeology* ed D.J. Blackman. London: Butterworth, 293–314

McGrail, S., 1978. *Logboats of England and Wales* Oxford British Archaeological Reports British Series 51

McGrail, S., 1981a. *Rafts, Boats and Ships*. London: H.M.S.O.

McGrail, S, 1981b *The Brigg 'Raft' and her Prehistoric Environment*. Oxford: British Archaeological Reports British Series 89

McGrail, S., 1981c. Medieval boats, ships and landing places, in *Waterfront Archaeology in Britain and Northern Europe*, eds G. Milne & B. Hobley. London: Council for British Archaeology Research Report 41, 17–23

McGrail, S., 1983a. Cross–Channel seamanship and navigation in the late 1st millennium BC. *Oxford Journal of Archaeology* 2, 299–337

McGrail, S., 1983b. Interpretation of archaeological evidence for maritime structures, in *Sea Studies*, ed. P. Annis. Greenwich: National Maritime Museum

McGrail, S., 1985a. Early landing places, in *Conference on Waterfront Archaeology in North European Towns*, ed A.E. Herteig. Bergen: Historisk Museum, 12–18

McGrail, S., 1985b. Brigg 'raft': problems in reconstruction and in the assessment of performance, in *Sewn Plank Boats*, eds. S. McGrail & E. Kentley. Oxford: British Archaeological Reports International Series S276, 165–94

McGrail, S., 1987. *Ancient Boats in North West Europe*. London: Longman

McGrail, S., 1989. The shipment of traded goods and of ballast in antiquity. *Oxford Journal of Archaeology* 8, 353–8

McGrail, S., 1990. Boats and boatmanship in the late prehistoric southern North Sea and Channel region, in *Maritime Celts, Frisians and Saxons*, ed. S. McGrail. London: Council for British Archaeology Research Report 71, 32–48.

McGrail, S., 1992. Ships, seamanship and navigation in the time of Columbus. *Medieval History* 2 & 3, 76–92

Marsden, P., 1990. A re–assessment of Blackfriars 1, in *Maritime Celts, Frisians and Saxons*, ed. S. McGrail. London: Council for British Archaeology Research Report 71, 66–74

Muckelroy, K., 1981. Middle Bronze Age trade between Britain and Europe: a maritime perspective. *Proceedings of the Prehistoric Society* 47, 275–97

Mukcelroy, K., Haselgrove, C., & Nash, D., 1978. A pre–Roman coin from Canterbury and the ship represented on it. *Proceedings of the Prehistoric Society* 44, 439–44

Murphy, J.P., 1977. *Rufus Festus Avienus' Ora Maritizna*. Chicago: Chicago University Press

Northover, P., 1982. Metallurgy of the Wilburton hoards. *Oxord Journal of Archaeology* 1, 68–109

O'Connor, B., 1980. *Cross–Channel Relations in the Later Bronze Age*. Oxford: British Archaeological Reports Internatioal Series S91

Parry, S., & McGrail, S., 1991. Prehistoric plank boat fragment and a hard from Caldicot Castle Lake, Gwent, Wales. *International Journal of Nautical Archaeology* 20, 321–4

Rule, M., 1990. Romano–Celtic ship excavated at St Peter Port, Guernsey, in *Maritime Celts, Frisians and Saxons*, ed. S. McGrail. London: Council for British Archaeology Research Report 71, 49–56

Switsur, V.R., & Wright, E.V., 1989. Radiocarbon dates and calibrated dates for the boats from North Ferriby, Humberside a reappraisal. *Archaeological Journal* 146, 58–67

Tomalin, D.J., 1984. The pottery: its character and implication for sea transport, in E. Greenfield, Excavations of the three round barrows at Puncknowle, Dorset, 1959. *Proceedings of the Dorset Natural History & Archaeological Society* 106, 63–76

Tomalin, D.J., 1988. Armorican vases à anses and their occurrence in southern Britain. *Proceedings of the Prehistoric Society* 54, 203–11

Wright, E.V., 1976. *North Ferriby Boats*. Greenwich: National Maritime Museum

Wright, E.V., 1990. *The Ferriby Boats*. London: Routledge

Reprinted with permission from:

Scarre, C., and Healy, F., (ed) *Trade and Exchange in Prehistoric Europe*: 199–210. Oxbow Monograph 33 (1993).

PAPER 7.3

THE BRIGG 'RAFT': A FLAT BOTTOMED BOAT

The remains of a stitched prehistoric plank boat, colloquially known as the Brigg 'raft', were first encountered in 1888 near the R. Ancholme, one mile (1.6km) to the NW of Brigg, S. Humberside (Thropp, 1887; Hunt, 1907/8). The boat was relocated and excavated by the National Maritime Museum in 1974, and the site was published as the sixth volume in the Museum's Archaeological Series (McGrail, 1981). In that report it was concluded that the so-called 'raft' was in fact a flat-bottomed boat, with a shape similar to that of a lidless box (Fig. 7.3.1), for which there are many ethnographic parallels (McGrail, 1985: 11.5–11.8), and also archaeological parallels, for example, the Romano–Celtic 'barges' from Zwammerdam, Netherlands (McGrail, 1987: fig 8.38). This interpretation of the boat's form was re-evaluated in 1984 in a paper given at a Greenwich conference on sewn plank boats, but no reason could be found to revise the hypothesis in any significant way. It was concluded that reconstruction as a flat bottomed ferry best fitted not only the surviving evidence, but also the context of the find and its technological environment (McGrail, 1985, 190, fig. 11.16). This was a minimum solution to the reconstruction problem: other solutions were theoretically possible but would involve more conjecture.

Figure 7.3.1 A 1:10 scale model of the preferred reconstruction of the Brigg 'raft' with side height 0.55m made by Kim Allen for the National Maritime Museum in 1984. (After McGrail, 1985). Scales in centimetres (Photo: National Maritime Museum, Greenwich)

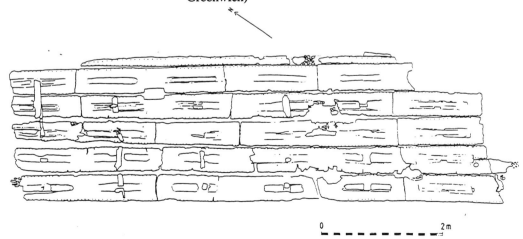

Figure 7.3.2 A composite plan of the north–west end of the 'raft' prepared after post–excavation recording by joining together plans of individual cleat units. (After McGrail, 1981). (Drawing: National Maritime Museum, Greenwich)

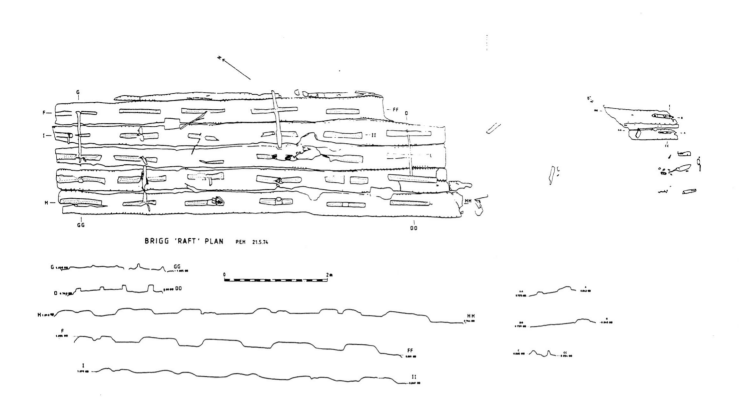

Figure 7.3.3 The on–site plan of the north–west end of the 'raft', with profiles (After McGrail, 1981). (Drawing: National Maritime Museum, Greenwich)

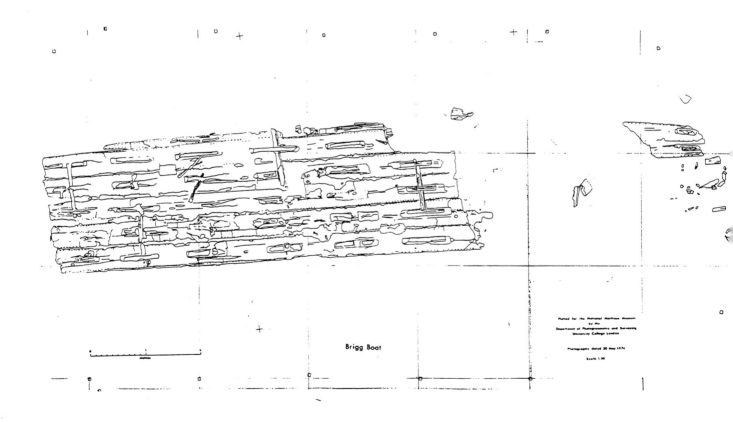

Figure 7.3.4 The photogrammetric detail plot of the north–west end of the 'raft' from photography on 20.5.74 (After McGrail, 1981) (Drawing: National Maritime Museum, Greenwich)

Figure 7.3.5 The 'raft' during excavation in May, 1974, photographed from the north–west end. The first bottom plank is to the right, the fifth bottom plank and the lowest side strake, to the left. (Photo: National Maritime Museum, Greenwich)

Owain Roberts has recently re–assessed this boat and concluded that it was 'a lean, round–bilged, stable, buoyant craft having a versatile operational capacity which would include coastal passage-making and short sea crossings'. (Roberts, 1992: 245, fig. 19). In his view, the Brigg 'raft' was not flat–bottomed but round–hulled. Roberts' argument is based mainly on his belief that the bottom planks, when found, were 'close together in the mniddle of the 'raft' and splayed at the left [i.e. north–west] end' (Roberts, 1992: 245, figs 1 & 5). As he rightly says, such an arrangement of the planking could best be interpreted as the springing apart of the end planking of a round hulled boat as the stitching broke or rotted after deposition.

The basis for Roberts' theory, and the only drawing of the boat quoted by him, is fig. 2.1.19 in (McGrail, 1981). reproduced here as Fig. 7.3.2. This drawing is, as its original caption stated, a 'composite plan of the 'raft' prepared after post–excavation recording by joining together plans of individual cleat–units', cleat–units being sections of planking as lifted. At first sight, some of the bottom planking on this drawing may appear to be splayed out at the north–west end. However, the post–excavation recording of this boat was undertaken some considerable time after excavation and, sad to say, by that time fragments of timber had been lost (McGrail, 1981: 60), especially from the north–west end which had been left exposed for nearly five months in 1888 (McGrail, 1975: 7) and, as a consequence, was found to be the most degraded part of the vessel when re–excavated 1974.

On site, the vessel was recorded in a number of ways: 1:10 plans with profiles (Fig. 7.3.3); stereo photogrammetric plans and profiles (Fig. 7.3.4), black and white (Fig. 7.3.5), and colour photography; and in detailed notes related to the cleat numbering system (McGrail, 1981: 29–46). In the post–excavation phase, individual cleat units of planking were recorded by orthogonal photography of upper, lower and end faces leading to conventional 1:10 plans with transverse and longitudinal sections (McGrail, 1981: 57–82, figs 2.1.4–2.1.14). It was these thirty measured drawings which were combined to produce the composite plan used by Roberts (Fig. 7.3.2). This composite plan is incomplete, however, as can be seen by comparison with the site plan (Fig. 7.3.3), the two photogrammetric drawings (for example, Fig. 7.3.4), and on–site photographs (Fig. 7.3.5). Although much was missing from both edges of the north–west end of the central bottom plank (plank 3) when re–excavated, the seams between the first and second bottom planks (on the right of Fig. 7.3.5 and towards the bottom of Figs 7.3.3 and 7.3.4), and between the fourth and fifth bottom planks (left on Fig 7.3.5, near the top of Figs 7.3.3 and 7.3.4) were almost complete: they showed no splaying but had a relatively constant gap along their length. South–east of cleat–row 3, the seams on either side of the central bottom plank were similar. The planking had shrunk across its breadth between deposition and excavation by 11 or 12% and, if an allowance is made for this, opposing plank edges butt together along their surviving lengths (McGrail, 1981: 228; 1985: 178).

Dendrological examination and the ring ray patterns recorded at every exposed cross section of each bottom plank and of the two detached fragments G4 and G5, show that the bottom of the vessel had been made from three trees at least 12.2 m in length, with girths of 2.07 m near their upper ends, 2.21–2.49 m at 5–6 m from the butt (lower) end, and 2.70–3.03 m at breast height, that is, *c*. 1 5 m from the butt (McGrail, 1981: 84,224; 1987: 39–40). The logs from these parent trees were converted into planks by first splitting them longitudinally into two halves. Planks 1 and 5 (outer bottom planks) were fashioned from one log; planks 3 and 4 from another; and plank 2 from a third. The builder's aim seems to have been to obtain the greatest possible breadth of planking, since the natural taper of the parent logs was retained and some sapwood was left on the edges of every plank. Furthermore, although these planks generally had straight edges, occasionally there was a gentle waviness: where there was natural damage or when a minor wood–working mistake led to a slight reduction plank breadth, the builder had fashioned the adjacent strake, to match the contiguous defect. These planks did not have curved edges: there were very minor and occasional 'waves' in otherwise straight edges. The Ferriby boats probably had similar wavy edges, and they may be seen on 20th–century stitched boats (McGrail, 1981: 225, fig. 4.1.10).

On the building site, the planks were positioned close alongside one another with their narrower ends (north–west end, as found) adjacent, thereby giving the boat an elongated trapezium shape in plan. This technique is widely used when building true rafts, as it results in an enhanced waterline shape with the narrower end being forward, leading to improved hydrodynamic characteristics. During felling or conversion, all three Brigg logs were significantly damaged near their butt ends, with the damage extending furthest up the bole of parent tree in the half that was to become plank 4. Thus the trapezium shape could not be maintained right to the after end of the bottom. The resultant modified trapezium shape may be seen in the small–scale model (Fig. 7.3.1), the outline reconstruction drawing, and also, to a degree, in Thropp's idealised 1888 drawing (McGrail, 1981: figs 4.1.23 & 1.1.4).

Discussion

It is not possible to interpret the Brigg 'raft', or indeed any boat–find, using only one element of the on–site and post–excavation record: all elements must be used for they are complementary to one another. For example, when the contrast between clay and wood is insufficient on black and white prints, colour photographs often resolve the matter. Moreover, whilst photogrammetry is generally more accurate than traditional planning, details on photogrammetric plots can sometimes be inaccurate due to difficulties in interpreting photographic images which are not always well–defined and clearly outlined; the archaeological planner, on the other hand, can himself clarify the details as he goes. On–site planning and photography, although essential, cannot replace post–excavation recording, not only because the under surfaces are seldom seen on site, but also because the detailed examination of fastenings and caulking, the direct measurement of bevel angles and the like, and the recording of 'shadows' of former fittings are only practicable in a laboratory or workshop. When reconstructing the Brigg 'raft' it was necessary to use all these sources of information, and also the 1888 measured drawing by the Lincolnshire County Surveyor, J. Thropp, and the photograph of the 'Viking pontoon bridge or raft' published by the Rev. A. Hunt in the early 20th century (Thropp, 1887; Hunt, 1907/8; McGrail, 1981: figs. 1.1.4 & 1.1.6).

The Brigg 'raft' did not have a round hull: she was flat–bottomed (McGrail, 1981: figs 4.1.11–4.1.14, 4.1.19, 4.1.21, 4.1.23). This bottom may, however, have been rockered, and the overall length of the boat, the height of sides, and the form of the ends are by no means certain (McGrail, 1985: 178, 184, 185). It is hoped that Owain Roberts' timely paper will lead to further informed debate on these points: a seminar at Greenwich could prove useful, after conservation is completed and before the timbers are re–assembled for display.

Although this boat was not the trader visualized by Owain Roberts, she undoubtedly played an important part in the everyday lives of the Late Bronze Age folk who lived *c*. 800 BC between the limestone Lincoln Edge to the west and the chalk Lincolnshire to the east. She was a poled or paddled ferry on the middle reaches of a tidal arm of the R. Humber, at a nodal point in the Ancholme valley. Her role may not have been spectacular – a commonplace river ferry – and she was not over–engineered for this function.

Nevertheless, this boat is not to be thought of as second rate; she undoubtedly matched the demands made on her and made a significant contribution to the economic and social well–being of that region, being able to carry a safe load of between 40 sheep with 10 men, and 30 cattle with 20 men, depending on the height of sides (0.34m or 0–55m) and the freeboard requirements.

Acknowledgment

This paper was written whilst I was Gaeste Professor at the National Museum of Denmark's Centre for Maritime Archaeology, Roskilde. I am grateful to Ole Crumlin–Pedersen for this invitation.

References

Hunt, A., 1907/8, Viking raft or pontoon bridge, *Saga Book of the Viking Club*, 5: 355–362.

McGrail, S., 1975, Brigg 'raft' re–excavated. *Lincolnshire History & Archaeology*, 10: 5–13.

McGrail, S. (Ed.), 1981, *Brigg "Raft" & her Prehistoric Enviroment*. B.A.R. (Oxford) 89.

McGrail, S., 1985, Brigg 'raft' – problems in reconstruction & in the assessment of performance. In McGrail, S. & Kentley, E. (Eds) *Sewn Plank Boats*. B.A.R. (Oxford) S.276: 165–194.

McGrail, S., 1987, *Ancient Boats in North West Europe*. Longman, London.

Roberts O. T. P., 1992, Brigg 'raft' reassessed as a round bilge Bronze Age boat. *IJNA*, 21: 245–258.

Thropp, J., 1887, An ancient raft found at Brigg, Lincolnshire. *Association of Architectural Societies Reports & Papers*, 19, Part 1: 95–97. [Not issued until 1889].

Reprinted with permission from:

International Journal for Nautical Archaeology, 23: 283–8 (1994)

SECTION 8.0

CELTIC BOATS AND SHIPS

It is difficult to define the *floruit* of Celtic culture in time and space (Green, 1995: 3–7): indeed, some scholars deny that Iron Age Europeans can be identified as Celts, and reserve the term 'Celtic' for a group of languages. Others see archaeological evidence in parts of Europe for cultural continuity from the middle of the second millennium BC through to Roman times, and use the term 'proto–Celtic' for the earlier centuries of this period. (Audouze & Buchsenschutz, 1991). Furthermore, a committed Celtic view sees Celtic cultural traits, identified in Roman times, continuing into the medieval period and beyond in Ireland, western Britain and Brittany, and possibly other parts of Atlantic Europe.

The academic arguments behind these differing schools of thought concern the precise relationship between material remains excavated in central and western Europe, ethnicity claimed and attributed, and language. If we turn from such matters to the history of technology, limited though the evidence is, I think that we can recognise a degree of continuity, in parts of Atlantic Europe, in the methods used to build plank boats and logboats from the 2nd millennium BC through to late Roman times (Sections 5, 6, 7 & 8). There is also a continuity in the use of hide boats, on inland waters and in the seas between NW France, Britain & Ireland, from the mid–1st millennium BC to the Medieval period, and even on to today in western Ireland and parts of Wales (McGrail, 1995: 264–265).

Celtic Boatbuilding.

Whether we are committed–Celts or anti–Celts in the culture / ethnicity / language debate, it is entirely permissable, as well as convenient, to refer to Celtic traditions of boatbuilding (plank, hide & log), providing that 'tradition' is understood here as an archaeological construct, a conceptual tool which helps us understand the past. A 'tradition' is an abstraction from reality, and its definition must be changed, on occasions, to absorb new information and reflect new concepts. In this sense, the 'Celtic boats and ships' of this Section are those vessels which, within their groupings of logboats, hide boats and plank boats, have many technological characteristics in common. There is a core period for these traditions of, say, 600 BC to 600 AD, with earlier and later 'tails', and the core region is western Europe.

Paper 8.1 brings together a range of evidence for this Celtic water transport, and discusses boatbuilding techniques and performance estimates. Navigational methods, trade routes, harbours and landing places are also considered. The table of

boatbuilding techniques used in late–prehistoric NW Europe (table 8.1.4) may be compared with tables 5.2.1 & 5.2.2 which give earliest & latest known dates for certain woodworking techniques.

Paper 8.2 concentrates on one sub–group of Celtic water transport – that of the plank boats and ships built in the early centuries AD and generally known as 'Romano–Celtic'. The antecedents of this tradition are unclear, although certain parallels may be drawn with aspects of NW European sewn plank boats (Section 7). What happened to this style of building after the 4th century AD is also unclear: Ellmers (1996) has attempted to demonstrate that Germanic peoples took over Romano–Celtic techniques to build their river and lake boats, but this argument is not entirely convincing. Other scholars see a connection between the Romano–Celtic tradition and the medieval Cog – for example, Runyan (1994: 47).

Celtic Innovation.

These Celtic wooden boatbuilders were evidently great innovators: they introduced to NW Europe the hooked iron nail and used it to fasten framing to planking; they probably were the first indigenous peoples to use sail in NW Europe, with a fore–&–aft sail as well as the square sail, and they were the first builders known to us who seem to have visualised their vessels in terms of the framing – they built their vessels frame–first (McGrail, 1996).

This third Celtic innovation was most important for the long term future of wooden ship building. Although frame–based methods seem to disappear from NW Europe after the 4th century AD, they susequently re–appear, in a somewhat different form, in the Mediterranean: a 6th century vessel from Tantura Lagoon, Israeli a 6th/7th century ship from the mouth of the R. Rhone; a 7th century wreck, Yassi Ada 2, from SW Turkey; and the nearby 11th century wreck from Serçe Limani (McGrail, 1997). It seems likely that this Mediterranean trend towards frame–orientated shipbuilding then spread westwards to Atlantic Europe (Bellabarba, 1993; 1996), which led, in due course, to the frame–based, 3–masted, square and lateen–rigged, ocean–going ships in which 15th/16th century Europeans sailed the seas of the world (McGrail,1996) and, eventually, to the fully skeleton–built ship with the shape of the entire hull determined by a pre–erected full framework (McGrail, 1987: 103–105; Greenhill,1995: 256–273).

References

Audouze, F. & Buchsenschutz, O. 1991. *Towns, Villages and Countryside of Celtic Europe*. Batsford.

Bellabarba, S. 1993. Ancient methods of designing hulls. *Mariner's Mirror*, 79: 174–292.

Bellabarba, S. 1996. Origins of the ancient methods of designing hulls: a hypothesis. *Mariner's Mirror*, 82: 259–268.

Ellmers, D. 1996. Celtic plank boats and ships, 500 BC – AD 1000. in Christensen, A.E. (ed) *Earliest Ships*. Conway's History of Ships. vol 1.

Green, M.J. 1995. (ed) *Celtic World*. Routledge.

Greenhill. B. 1995. *Archaeology of Boats and Ships*. London: Conway.

McGrail, S. 1987. *Ancient Boats in NW Europe*. Longman.

McGrail, S. 1995. *Celtic seafaring and transport*. in Green. 1995: 254– 284.

McGrail, S. 1996. The ship: carrier of goods, people and ideas. in Rice, E.E. (ed) *Sea and History*. Allan Sutton.

McGrail, S. 1997. Early frame–based methods of building wooden boats & ships. *Mariner's Mirror*, 83: 76–80.

Runyan, T.J. 1994. Cog as a warship. in Unger, R.W. (ed). *Cogs, Caravels & Galleons*: 47–58. Conway's History of the Ship. vol. 3.

PAPER 8.1

BOATS AND BOATMANSHIP IN THE LATE PREHISTORIC SOUTHERN NORTH SEA AND CHANNEL REGION

Water transport

Theoretical investigations, based upon:

(a) the identification of the materials, tools and techniques required to build the various forms of water transport and

(b) the determination of the earliest appearance in the archaeological record of these characteristics – albeit not in a nautical context

indicate that, by the end of the Neolithic, some 2000 years before the period under consideration, almost all the types of float, raft and boat known to Man could have been built in north–west Europe (Table 8.1.1). The only types of water transport which became, tecnnologically possible after the Neolithic, and are therefore not listed

(i) bundle boats – for which there is no known tradition outside Arabia

(ii) complex bark boats – for which there is no known tradition in north–west Europe, apart from some minor and late evidence from Finland

(iii) complex plank boats – of which there are indeed examples in the Bronze Age of north–west Europe (see below).

Floats and rafts

No matter how structurally seaworthy they might have been, floats and rafts are unlikely to have been used at sea in early north–west Europe because of the relatively cold sea temperature which, when combined with exposure to wind, can soon lead to hypothermia (McGrail, 1987:5). On the other hand it does seem likely that some of the floats and rafts listed in Table 8.1.1 were used on lakes and rivers in this region.

No ancient floats have survived but there is some evidence for rafts. The earliest excavated log rafts are the two from 2nd century AD Strasbourg noted by Ellmers (1972, 106, figs 83, 84), but there are 1st century BC references to their use on the River Rhine (Caesar *Bello Gallico*, 1.12, 6.35). Earlier use on this and similar rivers seems likely. Bundle rafts have not been excavated, but they have been used in the recent past on inland waters in Ireland and elsewhere (McGrail 1987, 163), and early use seems likely wherever reeds were available. Thus, the little evidence there is, suggests that, in the late Iron

Age, rafts of logs and of reed bundles and a variety of floats could have been used on inland waters in the lands bordering the southern North Sea and the Channel.

Boats

The evidence for boats is more promising, as there is evidence for logboats (dugout canoes), hide boats and plank boats from before, and actually in, the period under discussion.

Logboats

Logboats have been discovered in Britain, Ireland, France, Belgium, the Netherlands, Germany, and Denmark (Ellmers 1973, McGrail 1978; Rieck & Crumlin–Pedersen 1988), but only about half of the 60 or so that have been well documented are dated to the prehistoric period (Booth 1984; Rieck & Crumlin–Pedersen 1988). Of these, five are from the late Iron Age of the southern North Sea region: Hasholme, c 300 BC (Millett & McGrail 1987); Shapwick, 2305 ± 120 bp (Q–357); Poole, 2245+50 bp (Q–821); Holme Pierrepont 1, 2180 ± 110 bp (Birm–132); and Loch Arthur/Lotus, 2050 ± 80 bp (SRR–403). This is a very limited number on which to base conclusions; nevertheless it seems likely that, wherever there were sizeable trees, simple logboats would have been built and used on inland waters for hunting, fishing, fowling, and as ferries of men and of cargo. In some cases these logboats may have carried armed men, as seen in the Roos Carr, north Humberside, models (Sheppard 1901; 1902), recently dated to 2460 ± 70 bp (OXA–1718).

Simple logboats may be modified in several ways to give them the extra transverse stability and freeboard required to become usable at sea. The parent log, providing it is of a suitable timber species, may be *expanded*, normally after heat treatment, to give greater beam at the waterline and hence increased stability, (McGrail 1978, 38–41). Or logboats may be fitted with stabilisers (a sort of close–in outrigger) which also increases their effective beam (ibid, 51–4). At hird way of increasing stability is by pairing two logboats side–by side (ibid, 44–51). Additional freeboard may be obtained by extending logboats vertically by adding one or more strakes of planking to the sides of the basic boat (ibid, 41–3). There is, in fact, no evidence in any of the north–western European logboats dated to pre–Roman times of expansion, or of stabilisers, or of pairing. Thus it seems unlikely, on present evidence, that logboats were used at sea in prehistoric times.

Table 8.1.1 A theoretical assessment of the earliest technological stage that certain types of water transport could have been used in north–west Europe

Technological stage	Water transport	At sea or inland waters
Palaeolithic	log float	inland waters
	bundle float	inland waters
	hide float	inland waters
	simple log raft	inland waters
	simple hide–float raft	inland waters, but no known tradition
	simple bark boat	inland waters, but no known tradition
	simple hide boat	inland waters
Mesolithic	compex log raft	inland waters
	multiple hide–float raft	inland waters, but no known tradition
	bundle raft	inland waters
	simple log boat	inland waters
	multiple–hide boat	at sea and on inland waters
	basket boat	at sea and on inland waters, but no known tradition
Neolithic	pot float	inland waters, but no known tradition
	pot–float raft	inland waters, but no known tradition
	complex log boats	at sea and on inland waters
	simple plank boats	inland waters

Notes: 1. For definition of types see McGrail 1985c; 1987a, 4–11

2. For sources of technological evidence see McGrail, 1981, 12; 1987, 53–54, 85–7, 96–7, 171–2, 185–7, 191

It is generally agreed that comaprisons of theoretical cargo capacity are best made when boats (and not just logboats) are loaded to a waterline where 2/5 of the boat's height of sides is freeboard (McGrail 1987, 198–201; 1988, 38). The waterline (2/5 freeboard or 3/5 draft) is the one given for a fully loaded vessel in chapter 166 of the medieval Icelandic Law Code, *Grågås* (Morcken 1980). Table 8.1.2 gives comparative figures for two late Iron Age logbaots from Poole in Dorset and Hasholme, north Humberside. It can be seen that the Poole logboat, with a draft of only 0.30 m, could readily have used the natural harbour at Poole and the lower reaches of the rivers Frome, Piddle and Sherford, carrying nearly 1 tonne of cargo with a crew of four paddlers (McGrail 1978). The Hasholme logboat, operating in the River Humber, its creeks and tributaries, could have carried over 5 tonnes of cargo with a crew of five (McGrail 1988). Logboats could evidently make a significant contribution to economic and social life in the late Iron Age.

The Hasholme boat is a large and complex logboat and therefore may not be typical of those generally in use in the late prehistoric period (Millett & McGrail 1987). Nevertheless, the techniques used to build her illustrate the high standard of woodworking that Celts could achieve in a region which was not necessarily in the forefront of technology in those times. The boat measured 12.78 x 1.40 x 1.25 m and her parent log was *c* 800 years old and over 13 m in height, with a lower girth of at least 5.40 m (1.72 m or *c* 6 ft in diameter). Figure 5.2.1, an exploded diagram, shows that the Hasholme boat had a two–part bow as an extension to the main log. The lower bow was fastened to the log by a cleat and transverse timber assemblage showing affinities with the Ferriby sewn–plank boats of the 2nd millenium BC (Wright 1976; 1985) and that from Brigg of the mid 1st millenium BC (McGrail 1981b; 1985a). Washstrakes were fastened to the fore part of the main hull by treenails locked in position by keys or cotters (as were the repairs at the stern (Fig 8.1.1) and three large vertical treenails, 60mm in diameter, locked bottom, sides, washstrakes and bow elements together. At the stern she had a separate transom wedged in a groove, and three beam ties clamped the sides of the boat firmly against this transom, thus making the stern watertight. Also shown in Figure 5.2.1 is a hypothetical quarter deck for two steersmen using large paddles; it is thought that such a deck could have rested on the shelves found in the sternsheets (Fig 8.1.2).

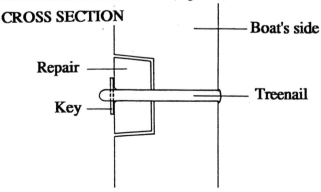

Figure 8.1.1 Diagram of repair to stern of Hasholme boat. (Drawing: Institute of Archaeology, Oxford)

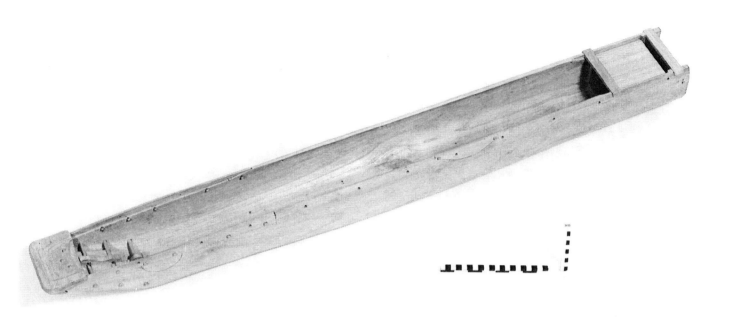

Figure 8.1.2 1:10 scale model of reconstructed Hasholme boat (Photo: Institute of Archaeology, Oxford)

Table 8.1.2 Theoretical load carrying performance of the logboats from Poole and Hasholme

Boat	Description	Draft (m)	Freeboard (m)	%[1]	Deadweight[2] (kg)	Deadweight[3] coefficient
Poole	Light displacement (862 kg)	0.19	0.31	38	–	–
Hasholme	Light displacement (4398 kg)	0.38	0.87	30	–	–
Poole	Maximum men (2 plus 16)	0.30	0.20	60	1080	0.56
Hasholme	Maximum men (2 plus 18)	0.46	0.79	37	1200	0.21
Poole	4 men plus 898 kg peat[4]	0.30	0.20	60	1102	0.55
Hasholme	5 men plus 5502 ks peat[4]	0.75	0.50	60	5802	0.57

Notes: 1. Ratio of draft to maximum height of sides expressed as a %. It is considered that the 60% values are best for comparison of boats as cargo carriers (see McGrail 1988)

2. Weight of cargo and crew

3. Deadweight/Displacement. A measure of ability of boats to carry cargo, in particular high density, low stowage factor, loads

4. Alternatively, materials of greater bulk density (eg grain, meat, timber, iron or stone) may be carried, resulting in increased stabililty

In several parts of the world today – for example, Pakistan (Greenhill 1971) or South America (Edwards (1977, 19) and others date to the 6th century BC, before 1965) – logboats are used in the same river systems as planked boats. Logboats fit into a different cultural context from planked boats, being usually found in peripheral regions; they are generally preferred to plank boats for economic reasons. Thus it is not surprising to find prehistoric logboats in the River Humber, where prehistoric planked boats were also used, and it seems reasonable to suppose that both types were similarly used in the lands bordering the southern North Sea and Channel in the late Iron Age.

Hide boats

The evidence for the use of hide boats (sometimes known as skin boats) in north–west Europe before the Iron Age is meagre: antler fragments from Husum, Schleswig–Holstein, of doubtful provenance (Ellmers 1984); a so–called boat grave at Dalgety, Fife (Watkins 1980); rock carvings in Scandinavia and northern Russia, including some which probably represent boats, though there are differing views on dating and on type of boat depicted (Marstrander 1963; Johnstone 1972; Coles & Harding 1979, 317); a small shale bowl from Caergwrle, Wales (Denford & Farrell 1980; Grcen *et al* 1980), which it is difficult to demonstrate represents a boat (except in a symbolic way) let alone to identify the type of boat; and some minute gold models from Nors, Denmark (Muller 1886) which do have a more obvious boat–like form and which Johnstone (1980,126) believes represent Bronze Age hide boats, but which Crumlin–Pedersen (this volume) has suggested may represent expanded logboats of 5th/6th century AD. This is not to imply that hide boats were not used, for they were technologically possible from the Mesolithic, but the evidence available at present is thin. However, in the Iron Age and the Roman period there is more substantial evidence, although no actual hide boat has yet been found, apart from a 'coracle–like vessel' with a human skeleton found near the River Ancholme at South Ferriby, South Humberside, and thought by Sheppard (1926) to be of Roman date – the remains no longer exist.

A small gold model from Broighter, County Derry, Ireland, dated to the 1st century BC (Farrell & Penny 1975) originally had nine rowing thwarts with associated oars in grommets on each side, and there are also three poles for propelling the boat in the shallows (Fig 7.2.2). A yard on a mast stepped through a hole in the central thwart indicates that this boat could also be sailed, probably using a square sail of aspect ratio between 0.75 and 1.38, depending on where on the mast the yard was positioned. She was steered by a steering oar over the quarter and had a four–hook grapnel anchor. From the general shape and the proportions of this model it seems likely that it represents a sea–going hide boat of the curach type.

There are several references by Roman authors (1st century BC – 3rd century AD) to the contemporary use of hide boats on inland waters, and at sea off north–west Europe (Ceasar, *Bello Civili*, 1.54: Pliny, 7.206; Lucan, *Pharsalia* 4, 130–8; Solinus, *Polyhistor*, 23). Two other refemeces arc important because they contain information from much earlier sources. Pliny (4,

104), writing in the 1st century AD and quoting from an early 3rd century BC history by Timaeus, states that Britons involved in the tin trade used boats with a withy framework covered with sewn hides (*vitilibus nasigiis corio circumsatis*; see also Pliny *Nat Hist* 34, 156). In his 4th century AD poem, *Ora Maritima*, Avienus preserved extracts from an early *periplus* which Hawkes and others date to the 6th century BC, before the time when the Cathaginians are known to have prevented Greek ships passing through the Strait of Gibraltar. *Periploi* were originally oral aids to coastal pilotage for mariners and traders, and the *Massaliote periplus* quoted by Avienus describes the main features of a voyage southbound along the western coast of Atlantic Europe and then along the northern shores of the Mediterranean to *Massilia* (Marseilles). There are undoubted difficulties in interpreting the names of people and places mentioned, difficulties increased by the apparent interpolation of extraneous matter – for example, Himilco of Carthage's description of a windless, tideless, seaweed–strewn sea (Murphy 1977, line 117–29, 380–9, 406–16). Nevertheless, the main elements of the description are clear, even if some details remain ambiguous. The information of relevance to the present discussion – those lines dealing with seafarers who lived in the vicinity of a headland *Oestrymnin* – may best be presented by paraphrasing and interpreting Murphy's translation (1977):

The hardy and industrious peoples of the islands and coasts of the lands around Ushant or Ouessant [ie the predecessors of the Veneti, Osismii and Coriosolites] were heavily involved in maritime trade, much of it in tin and lead. They used hide (*netisque cumbis*) on these oceanic voyages. [Lines 94–107]
From Ushant/Ouessant it is two–days' sail to Ireland [see Fig 8.1.3; a two–day voyage requires an average of *c* 5 kts made good – which is not impossible] and Albion [Britain] is sighted on this voyage. [Lines 108–112]
Merchants from Tartessus [a harbour in the Gulf of Cadiz, south–west Spain], from Carthage, and from the vicinity of the Pillars of Hercules [Strait of Gibraltar] sailed to the Ushant/Ouessant region to trade. [Lines 113–116]

Thus, from at least the early Iron Age, hide boats were used on sea–going trading voyages in the western Channel and the north Bay of Biscay region (Fig 8.1.3).

Caesar (*Bello Civili*, 1.54) states that British hide had keels, and this is sometimes thought to have been a mistake as 20th century Irish and Welsh curachs and coracles do not have them, and only certain types (eg those from County Kerry) have a central lath which is broader than other laths in the framework. However, Adomonnan in his 6th/7th century AD *Vita St Columbae* (Anderson & Anderson 1961) and other medieval authors (Marcus 1953–4, 315) refer to curachs with keels, and a late 17th century drawing by Captain Philips, now in the Pepys Library, Magdalene College, Cambridge, shows a large Irish sailing curach with prominent keel and stem (Fig 8.1.4). It seems very possible that Iron Age sea–going hide boats similarly had keels and stems.

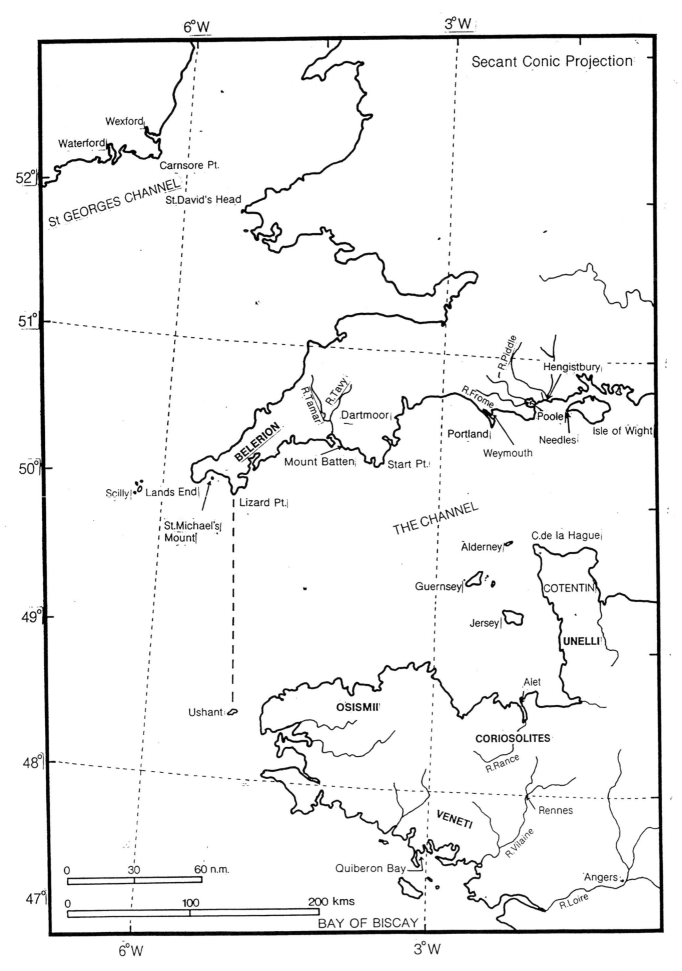

Figure 8.1.3 Map of region between south–east Ireland, south–west Britain and north–west France (Drawing: Institute of Archaeology, Oxford)

Figure 8.1.4 Captain's Phillips' late 17th century drawing of curachs (Photo: Pepys Library, Magdalene Colleg, Cambridge)

Philip's 'Wilde Irish' curach also had a woven wickerwork hull inside the hide (as has a 19th century Scottish curach now in Elgin Museum; Fenton 1976), and not the unwoven, fastened-lath framework of recent curachs. Descriptions by Ceasar (*Bello Civili*, 1.54), Lucan (*Pharsalia* 4, 136–8), Pliny (*Nat Hist* 7, 205–6; 34, 156) and Dio Cassius (48, 18–19) strongly suggests that the framework of early British and Irish hide boats also was a woven wickerwork. It seems likely that these boats, which were probably the most important type in prehistoric north–west European waters for explorations, trade and fishing, were similar in form to the 20th century Siberian *baidara* or the Inuit *umiac* (McGrail 1987, 173–87) of the circumpolar zone (themselves not unlike the Broighter model); and in size say, 11.0 x 1.75 x 0.60m. These late Iron Age hideboats were probably propelled by a single square sail, or by oars in foul winds, and steered by a steering oar over the quarter as we see on the Broighter model).

Hide boats fit well into an environment with exposed coasts, where there are a few large trees but a good supply of hides from land or sea animals, and where life can be sustained by animal husbandry and by sea fishing and hunting – a 'crofter' economy. They are quickly built, are cheap when compared to a plank boat of similar capacity, and are readily repaired. Hide boats can be operated from almost any shore from informal landing places, and are excellent surf boats. Their lightweight structure is buoyant, giving good freeboard even when loaded; thus in general terms they are more seaworthy and seakindly than equivalent plank boats. The woven framework is resilient and energy absorbent, yet it holds the shape of the boat and gives strength to the hull for least weight. Although Severin's *Brendan* may not have been an authentic replica of a prehistoric sea–going hide boat, her trials did demonstrate that such a boat had good seakeeping qualitites and was generally reliable (Severin 1978).

There are some disadvantages to these boats: the hide cover, which is relatively easily holed contributes little to strength, and thus boats are limited in length to *c* 12 m (or possibly 18 m; McGrail 1987, 184); thus they could never have been enlarged into ships. The lightness of the structure and consequent good freeboard also mean reduced resistance to leeway (despite having a protruding keel and the use of a steering oar), thus windward performance may not be as good as that of a comparable planked boat. Nevertheless, in certain physical environments and economic conditions, the hide boat has advantages and is preferred to the planked boat, and there is every reason to believe that they were widely used in the early southern North Sea and Channel region, both sea–going types and others more suitable for inland waters, even though in certain parts of that region the planked boat was also known and used (see below).

Table 8.1.3 Theoretical cargo capacities of the plank boats from North Ferrivy, Brigg and Hjortspring

Boat	Draft (m)	Freeboard (m)	%[1]	Deadweight[1] (kg)	Deadweight[1] coefficient
Ferriby 1	0.30	0.36	45	3000	0.54
	0.40	0.26	61	5500	0.52
Brigg 2	0.25[2]	0.09	74	1540	0.23
	0.46[3]	0.09	84	7160	0.57
Hjortspring	0.31	0.39	44	2110	0.80

Notes:
1. See notes 1, 2 and 3 in Table 8.1.2
2. Side height of 0.34m
3. Side height of 0.55m

Bronze Age planked boats

Despite the apparent dominance of hide boats as sea–going craft in the early Iron Age of the southern North Sea and Channel region, the future was to lie – as in the rest of the world – with the planked boat which, of all the boat types, was the one that could be successfully developed into a ship. There are five planked boats from north–west Europe dated to the Bronze Age: three finds from North Ferriby, North Humberside, dated to the 2nd millenium BC (Wright 1976; 1985); the planked boat from Brigg, South Humberside, of the mid 1st millenium BC (McGrail 1981b; 1985a); and the boat from Hjortspring, Als, southern Denmark, dated to *c* 350 BC (Rosenberg 1937). These boats were all sewn–plank boats, no iron fastenings were used, and they were all suitable for river and estuary work rather than open sea voyages, the Brigg 'raft' of box–like form being especially suited to upstream work. The Ferriby boats with their high length/breadth ratio (*c* 6:1) were evidently built with speed in mind, essential when crossing the tidal Humber estuary. Estimates of the cargo capacity of these three boats are given in Table 8.1.3, although these figures are not directly comparable as they have not been calculated at similar waterlines.

None of these boats had any evidence for sailing or rowing (the earliest evidence in north–west Europe of oared propulsion is on the small gold model from Durmberg of the 5th century BC; Ellmers 1978), and it must be assumed that they would have been propelled and steered, by paddles, which were indeed found with the Hjortspring boat.

The Brigg 'raft' is keel–less: Ferriby boat 1, on other hand, has a keel, in the sense that the central longitudinal member of the bottom is of greater scantlings than the remainder of the bottom planking, but it is not a very prominent one and may be best classified as a 'thin–plank' keel (McGrail 1987, 112–13). There are suggestions, however, that, in addition to the Ferriby/Brigg type of planked boat, there were also boats with prominent keels and stems in early Britain: the Bronze Age boat–shaped log coffin from Loose Howe, North Yorkshire (Elgee & Elgee 1949) has a pseudo–keel and stem; and the Iron Age logboat from Poole, Dorset has a pseudo–stem. Such features are non–functional on a logboat and thus must have been copied from a planked boat, or possibly a hide boat.

Early Iron Age planked boats

Table 8.1.4 attempts to summarise the range of boatbuilding techniques available to late prehistoric man in north–west Europe, based on the evidence from boat–shaped coffins, logboats, hide boats and planked boats. Thus, at the beginning of the period under review, some or all of these techniques could have been used to build the planked boats of the southern North Sea region. Whether there were in fact early Iron Age planked boats with these features remains to be demonstrated by excavation, and whether such hypothetical boats were used at sea, in addition to hide boats, or were restricted to lakes, rivers and estuaries, as were their only known Bronze Age predecessors, must remain an open question for the present.

Later Iron Age planked boats

The early Iron Age planked boat is therefore conjectural, but towards the end of the Iron Age, in the 1st century BC and the early 1st century AD, the sea–going plank boat becomes more tangible as there is documentary and iconographic (but not excavated) evidence for them in the Channel region.

The Veneti boats

Caesar (*Bello Gallico*, 3.13) and Strabo (4.4.1) have left descriptions of the sea–going boats of the Veneti, a sub–group of the Belgae of north–west France (Fig 8.1.3). These vessels were solidly built with high bow and stern, and bottoms that were flatter than those of the Roman ships, enabling them to sail closer inshore and to take the ground readily in tidal waters. These Celtic craft were more seaworthy than Caesar's ships, yet not so fast. Most, if not all, of these differences are to be expected when sail–propelled Channel trading vessels are compared with oared warships which, although they may have been built on the River Loire (*Bello Gallico*, 3.9) were undoubtedly to a Mediterranean specification. Other points made by Caesar and Strabo may be more diagnostic of the late Iron Age, Celtic boatbuilding tradition.

Table 8.1.4 Techniques available to the late prehistoric boatbuilder of north–west Europe

Shape	▪ flat–bottomed (Ferriby, Brigg) ▪ round–hulled (Hjortspring, Logboats)
Sequence	▪ shell (Ferriby, Brigg, Hjortspring) ▪ skeleton (Hideboats)
Ends	▪ with stems (Loose Howe, Poole) ▪ with stems plus protusion (Hjortspring) ▪ without stems (Ferriby, Brigg)
Keels	▪ with prominent keel (Loose Howe) ▪ without keel (Brigg, Hjortspring) ▪ with 'low profile' keel (Ferriby)
Planking	▪ overlapping but superficially flush–laid (Ferriby, Brigg, Hasholme) ▪ overlapping clinker–style (Hjortspring)
Caulking	▪ moss (Ferriby, Brigg, Hasholme) ▪ hide (Poole)
Fastenings	▪ sewn (Ferriby, Brigg, Hasholme) ▪ cleats with transverse timbers (Ferriby, Brigg, Hasholme) ▪ locked treenails (Hasholme) ▪ metal (Holme–Pierrepont 1)
Occuli	▪ boat's eyes (Logboats from Brigg, Loch Arthur, Hasholme and the Roos Carr model)

Sources: Wright 1976, 1985; McGrail 1981b; 1985a; Rosenberg 1937; Elgee 1949; McGrail 1978; Millett & McGrail 1987

The Veneti ships had oak planking – presumably (at least superficially) flush–laid, otherwise the difference from the Classical tradition would have been noted. This planking was caulked with what is usually translated as 'seaweed' but which may have been moss (E V Wright, pers comm) or even reeds (*harundines*) which Pliny (*Nat Hist*, 16.158), of the 1st century AD, tells us was used by the Belgae to caulk seams 'where it held better than glue and was more reliable than pitch'. The Veneti boats' thwartships timbers (*transtra* – which should probably be translated as 'frames' or 'floor timbers' rather than 'crossbeams') were *c* 1 ft or 0.30 m thick (*pedalibus in altitudinem*) and were fastened by iron nails (*ferreis digiti*), a thumb or 1 inch (25 mm) in diameter. Caesar tells us these ships were propelled by leather sails but he gives no description of mast, yard or standing and running rigging, except for a passing reference to ropes (*funes*) which fastened the yard to the mast. There is also no mention of the steering arrangements and so, perhaps, it may be concluded that it was by side rudder, generally similar to those used in Classical ships. Caesar does, on the other hand, tell us that the Veneti used iron chains with their anchors – these chains were probably forerunners to cables of organic material and similar to the 6.5 m iron chain found with a 1st century AD iron anchor at Bulbury, Dorset, some 2–3 miles up the River Shelford from Poole Harbour (Cunliffe 1972).

Caesar (*Bello Gallico*, 3.8) and Strabo (*Geog*, 4.4.1) also describe the seafaring activities of the Veneti, how they had numerous ships and exercised authority over coastal traffic by making 'almost all' pay tribute. In the theory and practice of seamanship they had no equal, and they regularly sailed to an emporium in Britain.

The distribution of Veneti gold coins (Galliou 1977) indicates that the Veneti, from their territory in Morbihan, were active up the River Loire beyond Angers, along the rivers Auine and Elorn, and as far as Rennes on the River Vilaine (Fig 8.1.3). On the other hand, they are not well documented in the archaeological record of Britain but, as Cunliffe (1982, 43–5) and Langouet (1984) have pointed out, the Coriosolites *are*, in both coins and pottery. The latest distribution maps of early amphorae finds (Galliou 1984; Fitzpatrick 1985) seem to reflect a coastal trade from the Garonne and the Loire to Ushant, with the possibility thence of a direct crossing Ushant/Lizard or a coastal route to Alet, the Coriosolites' emporium. Galliou (1977; 1984, 28) has pointed out the possibility an overland route between Quiberon Bay and Alet via the rivers Vilaine and Rance, with a portage between headwaters. Early amphorae have also been found in the Cotentin peninsula and the Channel Islands suggesting the involvements of the Unelli/Venelli in this cross Channel trade.

Although Caesar creates an impression of the unique maritime power of the Veneti, his statement that 'almost all' paid them tribute, implies that there were other Celts independently involved in trading voyages. In their fight against Caesar the Veneti were helped, not only by British auxiliaries, but also by most of the tribes of coastal Armorica and Belgic Gaul, from the Osismii near Ushant to the Manapii at the mouth of the Rhine, except for the Coriosolites of the Brittany Cote du Nord and the Venelli/Unelli of the Cotentin peninsula (*Bello Gallico*, 3.9). Documentary and archaeological evidence thus tend to suggest that, although the Veneti may have specialised in trading voyages along the Atlantic coast from the Loire to near Ushant and across the western Channel route to Britain (and possibly to Ireland as their predecessors had done in hide boats 500 years earlier), the Coriosolites and Venelli/Unelli used the mid Channel route, Mediterranean goods having been brought to Alet and the Cotentin peninsula for trans–shipment, despite the Veneti 'monopoly'.

Several attempts have been made to put flesh on the skeleton of Caesar's description of the Veneti vessels. Creston (1956; 1961) thought that they must have been like the early 20th century *sinagot* (*Le Yacht* 601 (14 9 89), 310–11) of the Gulf of Morbihan, whilst Beaudouin (1975, 104) saw similarities with a 19th century boat from Brest, the *lanveoc* (Paris 1882, pl 38). Others have seen aspects of Caesar's descriptions in the Romano–Celtic boats of the 2nd–3rd century AD, and there are more similarities here than in the earlier speculations (see papers by Rule, Arnold, Marsden and Lehmann in this volume).

The ponto

Johnstone (1980, 87–8) and, following him, Weatherhill (1985) have suggested further consideration should be given to the *ponto*, a view first expressed by Jal (1848, 1201) and then by de la Ronciere & Clerc–Rampel(1934, 2–3). Some six years after Caesar had first encountered the Veneti ships he mentions in his book on the Civil War (*Bello Civili* 3.29) *pontones quod est genus navium Gallicarum*, a 'kind of Gallic craft' known as a *ponto*, which was a *navis oneraria*, capable of transporting troops, and possibly horses. This *ponto* probably had a reputation as a reliable sailing ship for Antony left thirty of them at Lissus in north–west Greece so that Caesar might use them to pursue Pompey (*Bello Civili* 3.40).

Johnstone (1980, 87–8) has drawn attention to a *ponto* named and depicted on a mosaic from a cross–shaped floor in the *frigidarium* of the Maison des Muses at Althiburus (Mediena), Tunis, now in the Bardo Museum. This mosaic, dated to the second half of the 3rd century AD but probably copied from an earlier source, has illustrations of nearly 30 ships and boats named in Latin and sometimes in Greek (Dunbabin 1978, 24, 127, 136, pl 122). The ponto (Fig 8.1.5 & 8.1.6), which. is being towed by a boat of similar form, appears to be a ship of some size, with a relatively deep hull (length/depth = 3.36). The sheerline is generally parallel to the keel except at the ends where it rises sharply and, at the stern, curves forward. There appears to be a wale or rubbing strake below the sheer. She was propelled by a square sail (aspect ratio of *c* 1) on a mast stepped near amidships which is supported by shrouds. The yard, on which the sail is furled, has several lifts to the mast–head, and braces from the yard arms to the deck. Other rigging leads to a now–obliterated, sharply angled mast which probably had an artemon sail over the bows. There is a rudder on the port quarter which may be one of a pair.

Stem projections

This appears to be a representation of a ship 'high and dry' rather than afloat, thus the lowest part of the hull visible may be taken to be the keel which meets the curved stem in a projecting forefoot. Projections of various forms may be seen, for example, on the prehistoric Hjortspring boat (Rosenberg 1937); on late Bronze Age and early Iron Age Scandinavian rock carvings (Christensen 1972, 162); on 1st century BC coins of the Continental Atrebates (Fig 8.1.7); on British coins of the early 1st century AD (see below); on a bronze model river boat

from Blessey near the source of the River Seine (Johnstone 1980, fig 12.5); on several late 3rd century AD coins of Allectus (Marsden 1964; Dove 1971); and on an engraved stone from Loddekopinge, Sweden, tentatively dated to the 9th century AD (Rieck & Crumlin–Pedersen 1988, 131, 143) (Fig 8.1.8). They are also found in the Mediterranean region; on Minoan engravings of c 2000 BC (Casson 1971, fig 36); on the 7th century BC boat models and engravings from Italy (Bonino 1975); on the 3rd century BC Punic shipwreck from Marsala (Basch & Frost 1975); and on the 1st century BC Madrague de Giens wreck (Tchernia et al 1978); on 1st/2nd century mosaics at Ostia (Basch 1983, fig 1); on a mosaic of the 1st century AD at Magdala (Raban 1988); see also Casson (1971, figs 30, 137, 140, 145, 191). They have been known in the 20th century on boats of the Celebes (Hornell 1946, 210, fig 39); in Lake Victoria (Worthington 1933); Siberia (Brindley 1919/20); and in Oceania and the Indian Ocean (Hale 1980, 126). These projections are thus wide–ranging in time and space.

Only rarely do they represent rams, which are only practicable at the waterline of an oared fighting vessel. There are a number of other reasons why boats may such projections:

(i) for use when beaching bows first when the protrusion prevents the bows digging in,

(ii) to increase speed potential, by increasing the waterline length, by reducing resistance or drag due to the cancellation of the bow wave, and by fairing an otherwise blunt bow,

(iii) to improve windward performance by increasing the lateral plane area thus increasing resistance to leeway,

(iv) to improve steering characteristics (Mudie 1986, 53),

(v) in a short, steep sea it is said to be effective in keeping up a boat's head (Worthington 1933, 161) or

(vi) as a structural solution to the problem of making a strong, watertight joint between keel and stem by running the keel beyond the stem and supporting the latter by an external knee.

Ships on Celtic coins

The representation of boats with stem projections, nearest in time and place to Caesar's Veneti, are the on the 1st century BC Atrebates gold coin (Fig 8.1.7) and those on two bronze coins of Cunobelin (Figs 8.1.9 and 7.2.5). The Atrebatic depiction is stylistic and little more than the fact that this is a relatively deep boat with a bow projection can be deduced. The coins from Canterbury and Sheepen, which were issued by Cunobelin of the Trinovantes/Catuvellauni during the period 20–43 AD (van Arsdel 1989,408, cat no 1989–1,pl 51),show more details.

There are problems in interpreting representations on coins: the engraver is constrained by the shape and size of the coin; he

Figure 8.1.5 A *ponto* on 3rd century AD mosaic from Maison des Muses at Althiburus, Tunisia (Photo: Bardo Museum, Tunis)

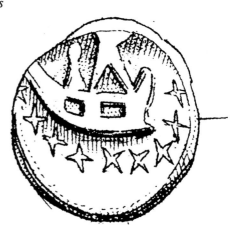

Figure 8.1.7 Drawing of ship on gold coin of 1st century BC Atrebates in Cabinet des Medailles, Paris (After Muret et Charbouillet 1889, pl 35, coin 8611)

may be drawing something from outside his own experience and the model he uses may be taken from another culture and/or another age; the representation may be stylised and details may be difficult to interpret; and boats are generally represented by a longitudinal elevation whereas transverse sections are needed if worthwhile estimates of performance are to be made. The difficulties here have been well described by Coates (1987). Even when it is certain that the representation is of a boat or ship, it is difficult to be certain about the precise type depicted. Marsden (this volume) has, for example, raised the question of whether the boats depicted on the two Cunobelin coins may be representations of Classical vessels in view of the fact that on the reverse of both coins there is a copy of a Classical motif, a standing winged Victory. However, there are other instances of Celtic and Classical art forms appearing on the same coin, for example, early 1st century AD silver coins of Verica of the Atrebates/Regni (van Arsdell 1989, 164, cat no 506–1) has a bull of Augustus on the obverse and a Celtic deity on the reverse (Andrew Burnett, pers comm).

Moreover, there is reason to believe that Cunobelin was indeed in the political, economic and geographic position as leader of the Trinovantes/ Catuvellauni to use his own ships in the cross–Channel trade, the main axis of which had, by this time, moved from the western and central Channel to the eastern crossings linking the Rhine mouth and Belgic Gaul with the Thames and the Essex Stour, Blackwater and Colne (Cunliffe 1982, 52–3; van Arsdell 1989, 393). Furthermore, it is not possible to suggest a Classical representation of a sailing vessel with the group of features shown on the Cunobelin coins from which they might have been copied. It seems not unreasonable,

then, to consider the alternative hypothesis that the engraver depicted a ship type that he knew, and that these are representations of a ship of the Trinovantes/ Catuvellauni during the period 20–43 AD Catuvellauni which Cunobelin recognised as a prime support to his political prestige which was based on cross–Channel trade, as suggested by Muckelroy *et al* (1978).

The ship on the Canterbury bronze coin (Fig 8.1.9) has a relatively deep hull (L/d = 3.2), comparable with that of the Althiburus *ponto*. The sheer line is generally parallel to the keel except at the ends where it rises, especially at the bows. She was propelled by a square sail (aspect ratio of c 0.70) on a mast stepped just forward of amidships, which is supported by forestay and backstay. The mast is cut short at the edge of this coin, but on the coin from Sheepen (Fig 7.2.5) there appears to be a feature at the mast head. The yard is depicted fore and aft, as is often the case on coins, and there appear to be braces from the yard–arms (or possibly these lines depict the sail). There is a transverse spar at the head of the fore stem (also on the Sheepen coin) which may represent a cleat for securing a bowline to the weather leach of the sail, thereby improving windward performance, or it may be a lead for an anchor cable; it seems too low to be the yard for an *artemom* sail.

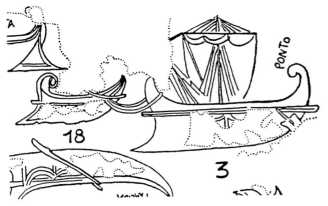

Figure 8.1.6 Drawing of the Althiburus *ponto* and tug (After Gauckler 1905, pls 9 and 10)

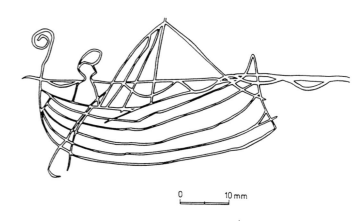

Figure 8.1.8 Drawing of 9th century engraving found at Löddeköppinge, Skane (After Rieck & Crumlin–Pedersen 1988, 143)

Figure 8.1.9 Early 1st century AD bronze coin of Cunobelin from Canterbury. Sclae 2:1 (Photo: Canterbury Archaeological Trust)

This appears to be a representation of a ship 'high and dry' rather than afloat, thus the lowest horizontal line is the keel which displays some rocker or longitudinal curvature. As in the Althiburus *ponto* the keel meets the fore stem (here straight rather than curved) in a projecting forefoot. The near–horizontal lines half–way down the hull may represent a wale, or possibly the waterline. A side rudder appears to be depicted to the left of the coin, ie, on the starboard quarter of the vessel.

The coin from the River Colne at Sheepen, near Colchester, was found by an anonymous metal detector and and is now in the British Museum (1981/12/34/1). The boat depicted is generally similar to that from Canterbury but is not from the same die as certain proportions and measurements are different: the L/d is 3.5; the yard/mast ratio is *c* 0.76 (compared with 0.64); the square sail would have had an aspect ratio of *c* 0.48; and the rise in sheer at the bow is not abrupt, being similar to the stern.

The ships depicted on these two coins, with their distinctive sheerline, were evidently designed to be seaworthy craft. Furthermore, the possibility that they were fitted with bowlines and with braces suggests that attempts had been made to make them weatherly, as does the projecting forefoot, for (as with the *ponto*) this was not a beaching aid. In (near) tide–less seas, as in the Mediterranean, beaching by running a boat ashore is often practicable, but in tidal zones, as in the Channel, an alternative and frequently better method is to let the boat or ship take the ground on a falling (ebb) tide and at about half–tide, thus avoiding being neaped (stranded above the high water mark). The rockered keel of the Cunobelin ships (in longitudinal section the keel has a slight rise away from midships) would have been a useful characteristic when beached, for it would facilitate re–floating on the rising (flood) tide. If these Cunobelin ships had a waterline beam in proportion to their depth of hull they would have been stable, seaworthy ships of good cargo capacity, but not outstanding for speed. These characteristics, together with their weatherliness

and their ability to operate from informal landing places, were necessary in cross–Channel trade; they also match aspects of Caesar's description of the Veneti craft.

The ponto, the Celtic coin ships and the boats *the Veneti*

Interpretation is obviously limited by the nature and quality of these representations; nevertheless it is possible to recognise that the Althiburus *ponto* and the Cunobelin ship have certain features in common:

(i) they both (and the Atrebates coin) have relatively deep hulls, suggesting a cargo carrying function,
(ii) the main mast is stepped near amidships in a position suitable for a square sail; the method of slinging the yards from their mid–points provides support for this hypothesis,
(iii) the *ponto* has braces; the Cunobelin ship probably has them,
(iv) the *ponto* has wales; the Cunobelin ship probably has them,
(v) both (and the Atrebates coin) have stem projections.

The differences may also be listed:

(i) whereas both sheerlines rise markedly at the ends, the *ponto*'s after post is incurving in stylus fashion (Casson 1971, 66–8),

(ii) neither ship has a high aspect ratio sail, but the *ponto*'s ratio is greater (1 compared with 0.70/0 50)

(iii) the *ponto*'s yard is supported by lifts,

(iv) the Cunobelin ship's sail may have had a bowline to taughten its leading edge when close to the wind,

(v) the *ponto* has an *artemon* as an auxiliary sail,

(vi) the *ponto* mast is supported by shrouds whereas the Cunobelin mast has stays. This may not be especially significant as shrouds and stays together on a representation hide detail and the two craftsmen may have chosen to omit one or the other for clarity,

(vii) both have side rudders but the *ponto* may have had two,

(viii) the *ponto* keel is straight and its stem is curved, whereas the Cunobelin ship has a rockered keel and a straight stem.

Caesar's and Strabo's descriptions undoubtedly refer to a type of Celtic sea–going cargo ship used in the Channel and the northern region of the Bay of Biscay in the 1st century BC. Whether this was the *ponto* subsequently mentioned by Caesar seems likely but is not certain. We cannot, however, precisely equate the 1st century BC *ponto* of Caesar with the 3rd (possibly 2nd) century AD *ponto* of Althiburus, for it is well–known for ship types to change over time, both in form and in function, although the same name continues in use – for example, the punt, the barge and the *hulc*. On the other hand,

Caesar was evidently impressed by the capabilities of the Veneti cargo ships and it is not unlikely that he requisitioned some for his own fleet. Such a vessel would need some modification for use in Mediterranean waters and it is likely that there would be some introduction of Classical techniques and practices. Gains in general shipbuilding knowledge and competence are also likely to have occurred with the passage of time. Thus an *artemon* sail and paired side rudders could have been fitted, as we see on the Althiburus *ponto*, to increase manceuvrability and improve steering. The introduction of the head sail would have necessitated the moving aft of the mainmast towards the centre of the waterline length. The use of an oared tug to tow the Althiburus *ponto* suggests not only the use of harbours rather than informal landing places, but also an increase in size of ship. Large ships require larger masts and yards and heavier yards require lifts to be fitted. Other changes in the rigging and the addition of an incurving stern suggest there may have been less requirement in the 2nd/3rd century Mediterranean to sail close–hauled and more time spent with a following wind and sea. The use of formal harbours where the cargo vessel could berth alongside a waterfront implies not only that a rockered keel was no longer essential but also that the *ponto* stem projection was not to assist in beaching but more probably to improve the hydro–dynamics of the hull.

The Celtic tradition of boat- and shipbuilding

As is often the case in a proto–historic period, there are problems in attempting to conflate archaeological and documentary evidence and to identify archaeological entities with historical facts. Nevertheless, there is sufficient overlap in the several forms of evidence considered above to advance as a working hypothesis that, in Caesar's descriptions of the Veneti craft and of the Gallic *ponto*, in the ships depicted on the Atrebates and Cunobelin coins, and in the *ponto* on the Althiburus mosaic, we can see different aspects of a boatbuilding tradition indigenous to the southern North sea and Channel region, which changed somewhat over time and was adapted for several functions, including use in the Mediterranean. A boat- or shipbuilding tradition is a broad concept and there is no requirement that all vessels built in that tradition, even at any one time, should be identical. Such variability may be due to differences in function or in operating environments, or to technological progress. In any one planked boat or ship tradition, for example, the Viking or the Classical, we may expect to find river barges, ferries and coastal fishing boats as well as fighting vessels and ocean–going cargo ships. A tradition is identified, and may be recognised, by a general continuity in time and space and by a set of diagnostic attributes which are more likely to be technological characteristics than morphological features. Shape has a relatively minor part to play in defining traditions as it is itself generally determmined by the function the vessel is to undertake and by the operating environment. Only in the case of an innovation in shape, or in the case of a tradition with a very limited range of functions and operating environments, may this other attribute make a significant contribution towards defining a specific tradition.

There is, to date, no excavated ship or boat of the 1st century BC southern North Sea and Channel region to give support to this working hypothesis or, alternatively, to cause it to be questioned. There are, however, a dozen or more boats of the 2nd/3rd century AD, from the Thames estuary, the Rhine region and Guernsey which have distinctive boatbuilding features generally known as Romano–Celtic or Gallo–Roman (du Plat Taylor & Cleere 1978; McGrail 1981a, 23–4; papers by Rule; Amold; Marsden; de Weerd; and Lehmann, this volume).

Some characteristics of these Romano–Celtic craft, the heavy floor timbers, the massive nails, and possibly the caulking (Arnold 1977), reflect aspects of Caesar's description of the Veneti ships. The majority of these vessels are river barges but two of them, St Peter Port, Guernsey and Blackfriars 1, London, are clearly estuary vessels and probably sea–going, although their lack of a prominent keel would have limited their operational performances. The mast steps of these two are approximately one–third the waterline length from the bow, an ideal position for a towing mast for bank towage, but not so for a mast with a square sail (McGrail 1987, 216–8). It may by that these two vessels were two–masted and the second mast step has not been found, but this seems unlikely. Another possibility is that they were dumb–lighters towed by larger ships or oared boats. An alternative hypothesis is that these vessels were fitted with a single fore–and–aft sail, such as a sprit or lugsail, which would need to be stepped forward of amidships. Ellmers (1969, pl 16; 1975, fig 8; 1978, fig 3) has suggested that representations of Romano–Celtic river boats of the 2nd/3rd century AD on a mosaic at Bad Kreuznach and on a gravestone from Junkerath depict leather lugsails with battens. It may thus be that Celtic lugsails began to be used in the 2nd century AD, replacing earlier square sails.

The working hypothesis formulated above may now be extended to include the evidence from the Rhine, Thames and Guernsey vessels of the 2nd–3rd centuries AD. The hypothesis then is that there was a tradition of plank boat and shipbuilding extending from before the 1st century BC to after thes 3rd century AD. The diagnostic attributes of this tradition may tentatively be identified as the use of a form of the skeleton sequence of building, with planking that was generally not edge–joined, but fastened to heavy floor timbers and side timbers by large iron nails clenched by turning the point through 180° so that the nails became J–shaped, and with a distinctive caulking between the strakes (see Rule; Arnold; Marsden; and Lehmann, this volume). The use of leather sails may also be a distinguishing feature. A stem projection may be typical of some of them but not characteristic of the entire tradition.

The majority of the Romano–Celtic vessels so far excavated have a flat–bottomed transverse section with hard chines; but this need not be a diagnostic attribute of the Celtic tradition, rather a requirement of their function as river barges. The exceptions are the Blackfriars 1 and St Peter Port wrecks which have bottoms which are flattish in the floors with rounded chines. Such a transverse section would indeed be flatter than those of Caesar's fighting ships and would ensure good cargo capacity, give the necessary transverse stability, and enable the vessels to sit upright on the beach for loading and unloading. The fact that these two vessels did not have prominent keels need not preclude other (as yet unknown) sea–going vessels of the Celtic tradition having them, and it can be seen from Table 8.4.1 that such a feature was within the technological inheritance of late prehistoric north–west Europe. A hull form with a prominent keel does not prevent a vessel taking the ground; Figure 2.1.8 shows a 100 ton ketch of round–hull form with prominent keel beached for cargo unloading at St Ives, Cornwall. The transverse sections of medieval cogs, which are also known to have been beached (Ellmers 1979, fig 1.6; Crumlin–Pedersen 1979, fig 2.12), are not unlike those of the Blackfriars 1 and St Peter Port vessels, except that the former have a more prominent keel.

The foregoing hypothetical description of the Celtic building tradition is based on three descriptive passages, four representations, and a dozen or so boat finds. When more evidence comes to light, especially wrecks from the period 200BC–AD500, it may become clearer whether this is indeed one tradition, what the distinctive characteristics are, how the tradition changed over time, and how it was adapted to build vessels for different functions and for use in different environments. Such studies should also increase our understanding of the early history of the medieval cog (Fliedner 1964; Crumlin–Pedersen 1965; Ellmers 1979): they may also throw some light on the early history of skeleton building.

Trade routes and navigation

The seaborne distribution of stone within the British Isles in the Neolithic period (Flanagan 1975; Cummins & Clough 1988, maps 1, 2, 3, 6, 9, 10, 11, 12, 16) and the cross–Channel metal trade in the Middle Bronze Age (Muckleroy 1981) indicate a long established seafaring tradition in Britain, Ireland and France. Their successors in the later Bronze Age and Early Iron Age were thus able to respond to the overseas demands for tin. Subsequently in the late Iron Age cross–Channel trade was in insular gold, iron and other metals, grain, cattle, hides, slaves and hunting dogs (Strabo, 4.5.2; Cunliffe 1988a, 98–104, 145–9) and the import of Mediterranean produced goods such as wine, figs, glass and pottery.

Four or five cross–Channel routes between the Continent and Britain may be identified from excavated and documentary evidence as having been used in the 1st century BC, and probably earlier (McGrail 1983a). It seems likely that the open sea route from Ireland to the Continent was from Carnsore Point, Wexford to the vicinity of Scilly (both lie approximately on longitude 6¼° W); and then from Lizard Point to the vicinity of Ushant (both on *c* 5¼° W), this leg also being the westernmost of the probable Britain/Continent routes (Figs 8.1.3 and 2.3.6). The likely maximum speed made good on these two legs can hardly have been more than 5 kts: at this speed and with the requirement to take departure from, say, Carnsore Point or Lizard Point in daylight and and to make a landfalll at Scilly or Ushant also in daylight, there would have been a period of at least 10 hours out of sight of land even in midsummer. Thus for such open sea voyages deep–sea

navigational techniques were necessary, in addition to the skills of coastal pilotage (McGrail 1983, 314–9).

As similar voyages – on the evidence of the *Massaliote Periplus* (see above) – were undertaken in the 6th century BC, Iron Age seamen must have been capable of ocean navigation from those times, or even earlier. Furthermore, it seems likely that such voyages were undertaken primarily by sail rather than under oars (although this method must remain a possibility). If this proposition is accepted, then the date for the earliest use of indigenous sail in the weaters of north–west Europe is put back to *c* 600 BC, half a millennium earlier than the Broighter boat model's mast and yard and the sails of the Veneti ships described by Caesar (*Bello Gallici* 3.13) and by Strabo (*Geog* 4.4.1).

Harbours and landing places

The sea routes discussed above are based on the evidence of Classical authors (McGrail 1983a) and on excavated sites and artefacts, leading to the identification of natural harbours with river access to the interior. Excavated evidence has shown that, by the late Bronze Age, sites within certain harbours, as for example at Mount Batten within Plymouth Sound (Cunliffe 1988b), had became the prehistoric equivalent of ports. But these were not ports with built–up waterfronts as were to be found in the Classical world at that time (Casson 1971, 361–70). The indigenous hide and (later) wooden boats and ships of the southern North Sea and Channel region (even those that were ocean–going) used informal landing places adjacent to the settlement, workshops and trading areas which comprised the 'port'. Here they were beached by taking the ground on a falling tide or they were anchored or moored in the shallows and their goods unloaded by wading men or into smaller boats (logboats?) or into horse–drawn carts (Ellmers 1985, 25–30), as still happens in certain parts of the world today (McGrail 1981c; 1985b).

With few, if any, fixed structures the precise sites of early landing places may be difficult to identify archaeologically but there are certain characteristics which may help in the search for them (McGrail 1983b, 34–41). One such landing place has recently been identified at Hengistbury Head within Christchurch Harbour by the recognition of a man–made gravel hard close to the site of a 1st century BC international trading place (Cunliffe, this volume).

In the late 4th century BC Pytheas sailed from Massalia to explore the northern sea and bring back commercial and navigational information (Hawkes 1977; 1984). Pytheas' subsequent book is now lost, but Strabo (*Geog, passim*) of the 1st century BC and Pliny (*Nat Hist* 4, 102–4) of the 1st century AD, quote from him and from Timaeus of the 3rd century BC, and from these several accounts it is deduced (Hawkes 1977; 1984) that Pytheas probably made a landfall at *Belerion* (Lands End in Cornwall), followed by a landing somewhere in the south–west peninsula, where he was told that tin, mined nearby, was taken by hide boat to *Mictis*, an island some six days' sail up the Channel (ie, to the east), where it was made available to foreign merchants. It is generally agreed that this emporium was probably on or near the Isle of Wight (*Vectis* in later times). The practice of using an island or a promontory as a mart or entrepot has been, and is, widespread: on such isolated and readily defended sites traders can be segregated, protected and supervised, justice dispensed and tolls imposed (McGrail 1983a, 311–3).

Diodorus (5.22.1–4) of the 1st century BC mentions an island *Ictis* connected at low water to the British mainland by a causeway where tin, mined in the *Belerion* peninsula, was brought in wagons for foreign merchants to buy and transport to the Mediterranean via Gaul. Sixteen or more places have been suggested for the location of *Ictis* (Maxwell 1972): the two considered most likely being the island of St Michael's Mount, Cornwall and the peninsula of Mount Batten on the eastern side of Plymouth Sound (Cunliffe 1983; 1988b; Hawkes 1984). A major difficulty is to establish whether either site in the 1st century BC would have been an island which dried at low water leaving a (natural) causeway to the mainland. St Michael's Mount has scarcely been investigated archaeologically, but there are a number of finds from Mount Batten which indicate that it was prominent in international seaborne trade from the 4th century BC until just before the Roman Conquest (Cunliffe 1988b). Access may readily be gained from Mount Batten by rivers Tavy and Tamar to tin and copper deposits on Dartmoor and around Callington. These minerals would thus almost certainly have been brought to Mount Batten by boats, although other material to be exported could have been brought by wagon. Wagons could also have been used to load and unload ships anchored or moored in the shallows off both Mount Batten and St Michael's Mount. An alternative interpretation of Diodorus' causeway might be that it was a hard of the Hengistbury type which dried at low tide, and on which boats were beached.

There are other natural havens on the south coast of Britain, for example in Poole Harbour and in Weymouth Bay (Cunliffe 1982, 46), with some evidence for use as international 'ports'. On the east coast recent excavations at the 1st century BC/AD site at Redcliff on the northern shores of the River Humber have also revealed evidence for international trade, although it is not yet clear whether this was by a direct or an indirect route (Crowther *et al* forthcoming). It seems likely that a similar site or sites remain to be found in the River Thames near the head of tidal waters. Excavations at Bordeaux on the River Gironde (Debord & Gauthier 1979) and at Alet near St Malo, Brittany (Langouet 1984) have revealed further evidence for an international trade which linked Atlantic north–west Europe, especially the southern North Sea and the Channel region, with the Mediterranean. There must be numerous smaller sites with landing places, associated with local coastal and river traffic, remaining to be discovered.

End note

1   The meaning of 'landfall' is sometimes misunderstood. In this paper it means the sighting and identification of a prominent coastal feature, usually when at some considerable distance from it.

References

Anderson A.O. & Anderson M. O. (eds), 1961 *Adomnan's life of St Columba.*

Arnold B. 1977 'Some remarks on caulking in Celtic boat construction and its evolution in areas north–west of the alpine arc.' *Int J Naut Archaeol* 6, 293–97.

Basch L. 1983 'Bow and stem appendages in the ancient Mediterranean.' *Mar Mirror* 69, 395–412.

Basch L. & Frost H. 1975 'Another Punic wreck in Sicily: its ram.' *Int J Naut Archaeol* 4, 201–28.

Beaudouin F. 1975 *Bateaux des cotes de France.*

Bonino M. 1975 'Picene ships of the 7th century BC engraved at Novilara (Pesaro, Italy).' *Int J Naut Archaeol* 4, 11–20.

Booth B. 1984 'Handlist of maritime radiocarbon dates.' *Int J Naut Archaeol* 13, 189–204.

Brindley H.H. 1919/20 'Notes on the boats of Siberia.' *Mar Mirror* 5, 66–72, 101–7, 130–42, 184–7; 6, 15–18, 187.

Casson L. 1971 *Ships and seamanship in the ancient world* (1986 ed).

Christensen A.E. 1972 *Boats of the North*

Coates J.F. 1987 'Interpretation of ancient ship representations.' *Mar Mirror* 73, 197.

Coles J.M. & Harding A. F. 1979 *The Bronze Age in Europe.*

Creston R.Y. 1956 'Considerations techniques sur la flotte des Venetes et des Romains.' *Annales de Bretagne* 63.

Creston R.Y. 1961 'Les navires des Venetes.' *Actes du 11c Congres International d'Archeologie Sous–marine* 369–80.

Crowther D., Willis S. and Creighton J. forthcoming 'Topography and archaeology of Redcliff.' in Crowther D.R. and Ellis S. (eds), *Humber and its environs in history and prehistory.*

Crumlin–Pedersen O. 1965 'Cog-kogge-Kaag.' *Handels og Sjφfartsmuseum pa Kronberg Arbog* 81–144.

Crumlin–Pedersen O. 1979 'Danish cog-finds.' in McGrail S. (ed), *Archaeology of medieval ships and harbours* BAR International Series 66, 17–34.

Cummins W.A. and Clough T.H.McK, 1988 *Stone axe studies volume 2* CBA Res Rep 67.

Cunliffe B.W. 1972 'Late Iron Age metalwork from Bulbury, Dorset.' *Antiq J* 52, 293–308.

Cunliffe B.W. 1982 'Britain, the Veneti and beyond.' *Oxford J Archael* 1, 39–68.

Cunliffe B.W. 1983 'Ictis: is it here?' *Oxford J Archaeol* 2, 123–6.

Cunliffe B.W. 1988a *Greeks, Romans and barbarians: spheres of interaction.*

Cunliffe B.W. 1988b *Mount Batten, Plymouth, Oxford Univ Comm Archaeol* 26.

de la Roncire C. and Clerc–Rampel G. 1934 *Histoire de la martne francaise.*

Debord P. and Gauthier M. 1979 'Bordeaux – la fouille de L'Ilot St Christoly.' *Dossier Aquitaine* 36–9.

Denford G.T. and Farrell A. W. 1980 'Caergwrle bowl.' *Intr J Naut Archaeol* 9, 183–92.

Dove C.E. 1971 'First British navy.' *Antiquity* 45, 15–20.

Dunbabin K.M.D. 1978 *Mosaics of Roman North Africa.*

du Plat Taylor J. and Cleere H. (eds), 1978 Roman *shipping and trade* CBA Res Rep 24.

Edwards C.R. 1965 'Aboriginal watercraft on the Pacific coast of South America.' *Iber–Americana* 4.

Elgee H.W. & Elgee F. 1949 'An Early Bronze Age burial in a boat-shaped wooden coffin from north–east Yorkshire.' *Proc Prehist Soc* 15, 87–106.

Ellmers D. 1969 'Keltischer Shiffbau.' *Jahrbuch des Romisch–Germanischen Zentralmaseums Mainz* 16, 73–122.

Ellmers D. 1972 *Fruhmtttelalterltche Handelsschzffahrt in Mittel und Nordeurope.*

Ellmers D. 1973 'Kultbarken, fahren, Fischerboote vorgeschichthche Einbaume in Niedersachsen.' *Die Kunde* ns 24, 23–62.

Ellmers D. 1975 'Antriebstechniken Germanischer.' Schiffe im 1 Jahrtausend N CHR.' *Deutsches Schiffahrtsarchiv* 1, 79–90.

Ellmers D. 1978 'Shipping on the Rhine during the Roman period.' in du Plat Taylor, Cleere (eds) 1978, 1–14

Ellmers D. 1979 'Cog of Bremen and related boats.' in McGrail S. (ed) *Archaeology of medieval ships and harbours* BAR International Series 66, 1–15.

Ellmers D. 1984 'Earliest evidence for skin boats in Palaeolithic Europe.' in McGrail S. (ed) *Aspects of maritime archaeology and ethnography* Nat Marit Mus Monog, 41–85.

Ellmers D. 1985 'Loading and unloading ships using a horse and cart standing in the water.' in Herteig (ed) 1985, 25–31.

Farrell A.W. and Penny S. 1975 'Broighter boat: a re–assessment.' *Irish Archaeol Res Forum* 2.2, 15–26.

Fenton A. 1976 'Curragh in Scotland.', *Scot Stud* 16, 61–81.

Fitzpatrick, A, 1985 'Distribution of Dressel 1 amphorae in north–west Europe.' *Oxford J Archaeol* 4, 305–40.

Flanagan L.N.W. 1975 'Ships and shipping in pre Viking Ireland.' *Cultura Maritima* 1, 3–8.

Fliedne S. 1964 *Die Bremer Kogge.*

Frost H. 1976 'Punic ship.' *Notizie Degli Scavi* 30, supplement.

Galliou P. 1977 'Les monnaies et les amphores.' in Problemes de navigation en Manche Occidentale a l'epoque romaine, *Caesarodanum* 12, 496–9.

Galliou P. 1984 'Days of wine and roses?' in MacReady and Thompson (eds) 1984, 24–36.

Gauckler P. 1905 'Un catalogue figure de la battellerie greco–romaine. La mosaique a Althiburus.' *Monuments et Memoires publies par l'Academie Inscriptions et Belles–Lettres.*

Green H.S., Smith A.H.V., Young B.R. and Harrison R.K. 1980 'Caergwrle bowl: its composition, geological source and archaeological significance.' *Rep Inst Geol Sci* 80.1, 26–30.

Greenhill B. 1971 *Boats and boatmen of Pakistan.*

Hale J.R. 1980 .Plank–built in the Bronze Age.' *Antiquity* 54, 118–27.

Hawkes C.F.C. 1977 *Pytheas* 8th J.L.Myres Memorial Lecture.

Hawkes C.F.C. 1984 'Ictis disentangled and the British tin trade.' *Oxford J Archaeol* 3, 211–33.

Herteig A.E. (ed) 1985 *Conference on waterfront archaeology* 2.

Hornell J. 1946 *Water transport* (republ 1970).

Jal A. 1848 *Glossaire Nautique.*

Johnstone P. 1972 'Bronze Age sea trial.' *Antiquity* 46, 269–74.

Johnstone P. 1980 *Seacraft of Prehistory* (2nd ed 1988).

Langouet L 1984 'Alet and the cross–Channel trade.' in Macready & Thompson (eds) 1984, 67–77.

McGrail S. 1978 *Logboats of England and Wales* British Archaeologocal Report British Series 51.

McGrail S. 1981a *Rafts, boats and ships.*

McGrail S. (ed) 1981b *Brigg 'raft' and her prehistoric environment* British Archaeological Report British Series 89.

McGrail S. 1981c 'Medieval boats, ships and landing places.' in Milne G. and Hobley B. (eds) *Waterfront archaeology in Britain and northern Europe* CBA Res Rep 41, 17–23.

McGrail S. 1983a 'Cross–channel seamanship and navigation in the late 1st millennium BC.' *Oxford J Archaeol* 2, 299–337.

McGrail S. 1983b 'Interpretation of archaeological evidence for maritime structures.' in Annis P. (ed) *Sea Studies* Nat Marit Mus Monog, 33–46.

McGrail S. 1985a 'Brigg 'raft' – problems in reconstruction and in the assessment of performance.' in McGrail S. and Kentley E. (eds) *Sewn plank boats* British Archaeological Reports International Series 276, 165–94.

McGrail S. 1985b 'Early landing places.' in Herteig (ed) 1985, 12–18.

McGrail S. 1985c 'Towards a classification of water transport.' *World Archaoel* 16, 289–303.

McGrail S. 1987 *Ancient boats in north–west Europe*

McGrail S. 1988 'Assessing the performance of an ancient boat – the Hasholme logboat *Oxford J Archaeol* 7, 35–46.

Macready S. and Thmpson F.H. 1984 *Cross–Channel trade between Gaul and Britain in the pre–Roamn Iron Age* Soc Antiq London Occas Pap n ser 4.

Marcus G.J. 1953–4 ' Factors in early Celtic navigation.' *Etudies Celtique* 6, 312–27.

Marsden P. 1964 'Warship on Roman coins *Mar Mirror* 50, 260.

Marstrander S. 1963 *Ostfolds Jorordbruksristninger*: Skjeberg 2 vols.

Maxwell I.S. 1972 'Location of Ictis.' *J Roy Inst Cornwall* 6, 293–319.

Millett M. and McGrail S. 1987 'Archaeology of the Hasholme logboat.' *Archaeol J* 144, 69–155.

Morcken R. 1980 *Langskip, Knarr og Kogge.*

Muckelroy K. 1981' Middle Bronze Age trade between Britain and Europe: a maritime perspective.' *Proc Prehist Soc* 47, 275–97.

Muckelroy K., Haselgrove C. and Nash D. 1978 'A pre–Roman coin from Canterbury and the ship represented on it.' *Proc Prehist Soc* 44, 439–44.

Mudie C. 1986 'Designing replica boats.' in Crumlin–Pedersen O. and Vinner M. (eds) *Sailing into the past* 38–59.

Muller S. 1886 'Votivfund fra Sten–ogBronzealderen.' *Aarboger for Nordisk Oldkyndighed og Historie.*

Muret and Charbouillet 1888 *Cabinet des Medailles a Paris.*

Murphy J.P. 1977 *Rufus Festus Avienus Ora Maritima.*

Paris F.E. 1882 *Souvenirs de marine conserves*.

Prins A.J.H. 1987 *Sewn boats*.

Raban A. 1988 'Boat from Migdal Nania and the anchorages of the Sea of Galilee from the time of Jesus.' *Int J Naut Archaeol* 17, 311–29.

Reick F. and Crumlin–Pedersen O. 1988 *Bφade fra Danmarks Oldtid*.

Rosenberg G. 1937 *Hjortspring fundet*.

Severin T. 1978 *Brendan voyage*.

Sheppard T. 1901 'Notes on the ancient model of a boat and warrior crew found at Roos in Holderness.' *Trans East Riding Antiq Soc* 9, 62–74.

Sheppard T. 1902' Additional notes on the Roos Carr images.'*Trans East Riding Antiq Soc* 10, 76–9.

Sheppard T. 1926 'Roman remains in north Lincolnshire.'*Trans East Riding Antiq Soc* 25, 170–4.

Tchernia A., Pomey P. and Hosnard A. 1978 'L'Epave Romain de la Madrague de Giens.' *Gallia*, 34th supple.

Watkins T. 1980 'Prehistoric coracle in Fife.' *Int J Naut Archaeol* 9, 277–86.

Weatherhill C. 1985 'Ships of the Veneti – a fresh look at the Iron Age tin ships, *Cornish Archaeol* 24, 163–9.

Worthington E.B. 1933 'Primitive craft of the central African lakes.' *Mar Mirror* 19, 146–63.

Wright E.V. 1976 *North Ferriby boats*, Nat Marit Mus Monog 23.

Wright E.V. 1985 'North Ferriby boats – a revised basis for reconstruction.' in McGrail and Kentley (eds) 1985, 105–44.

Reprinted with permission from:

McGrail S. (ed) *Maritime Celts, Frisians and Saxons* 32–48, CBA Research Report 71 (1990)

PAPER 8.2

ROMANO–CELTIC BOATS AND SHIPS: CHARACTERISTIC FEATURES

Introduction

The Romano–Celtic tradition of ship and boat building was first recoglused by Peter Marsden in his 1967 publication of the Blackfriars 1 ship. Subsequently, Detlev Elmers in 1969 set this vessel and the boat from New Guys House, London (Marsden, 1965) into their historical and archaeological context in his seminal publication *Keltischer Shiffbau*. Since that time, there have been further finds of similar boats in the Netherlands (de Weerd, 1978; 1988; Lehmann, 1978), Germany (Hockmann, 1982), Belgium (de Boe, 1977; Marsden, 1976), Northern France (Arnold, 1978), Switzerland (Arnold, 1992), Guernsey (Rule & Monaghan, 1993), and SE Wales (Nayling *et al.*, 1994). Marsden (1994: table 16, fig. 146) has recently published a list of these finds and a distribution map.

Marsden and Ellmers both recognised that this style of ship and boatbuilding was different from that of the early Mediterranean and from that of early northern Europe; as did Basch (1972: 41) in his important analytical paper on building techniques. Marsden drew attention to similarities between his two boat finds and Caesar's description of the boats of the Veneti (Marsden, 1967: 34–5), whilst Ellmers (1969) called this distinctive style of boatbuilding 'Celtic'. In more recent times, some of these unique finds have been described as 'Gallo–Roman' (Arnold, 1992; Rule & Monaghan, 1993), but 'Romano–Celtic' seems preferable, notwithstanding Parker's criticism (1991), as it more accurately describes the date and place of these finds. The 'Celtic' part of this binomial reflects their spatial distribution which is, by and large, in regions formerly occupied by Celtic-speaking peoples; and the 'Roman' element reflects the temporal distribution, 1st to 4th century AD, and acknowledges the possibility of Roman technological influence.

The time–span of these ships and boats, as known today, is very short – 250 to 300 years – and it may be that both earlier and later finds remain to be discovered. Earlier finds might point towards the prehistoric origins of the Romano–Celtic style of building, and later ones might suggest lines of development from that tradition in post–Roman times. Some scholars have seen parallels between these Romano–Celtic vessels and the prehistoric stitched plank boats of the 15th to 8th century BC, from Ferriby, Dover, Caldicot, Brigg & Goldcliff (Basch: 1972, 42; Arnold, 1977; Wright, 1990); whilst others believe that the medieval cog may be in some way descended from the Romano–Celtic tradition (Ellmers, 1994: 34; Runyan, 1994: 47). There is something to be said for both these suggestions, but, until further evidence is excavated, they must remain speculative.

Boatbuilding traditions

A boatbuilding tradition may be defined as 'the perceived style of building generally used in a certain region during a given time range'. As with all classification schemes, building traditions are an abstraction from reality. Not being mass–produced, finds are bound to be unique in some way or another and, in ultimate detail, each forms a class of its own. Only by simplifying complexities of structure and form, and ignoring particular dimensions and details can we claim that, for example, Skuldelev wreck 3 and wreck 6 (Olsen & Crumlin–Pedersen, 1967) are similar and therefore members of the same tradition. Moreover, for the purposes of such classification, these traditions must be given arbitrary start and stop dates, although it is clear that in many cases their earliest and latest phases merge into other traditions. If classification schemes are too complex, they run the risk of obscuring patterns; if too simple, the classifier may be tempted to drive them too far and drawn unwarranted conclusions. Furthermore, these schemes cannot be static – as further finds are excavated or fresh analytical tools become available, they may need to be revised to fit the facts.

Notwithstanding these drawbacks, classification schemes are useful in maritime studies both archaeological and ethnographical, because of the wide range of material and techniques that have been used in the past to build rafts boats and ships They have two main advantages:

(a) superficially disparate data can be ordered and thereby become more readily understandable;
(b) patterns can be recognised, significant similarities and differences highlighted, and a picture of groupings emerge.

Within one class of artefacts or structures (in this present paper, a particular boatbuilding tradition), it is not necessary that all members have all attributes (features, characteristics) in common. In *polythetic* groups, which are considered to be 'natural' by numerical taxonomists, each member shares with every member a large number of characteristics in common, but no one characteristic *has* to possessed by all members, although, of course, it may (Doran & Hodson, 1975: 160). In this respect, such groupings reflect an intuitive understanding of the real world.

The Romano–Celtic tradition

Although much detail is missing from the publications of some of the finds thought to be the Romano–Celtic tradition, it is possible to identify those characteristics which are generally present in these vessels. Such characteristics are the features by which we recognise, for example, that the Barland's Farm boat (Nayling *et al.*, 1994) is from the same tradition as Blackfriars 1 (Marsden, 1994): they are also the features by which we recognise that Nordic boats, such as Nydam 2 (Crumlin-Pedersen, 1990) are *not* members of this tradition.

In general terms, without precise definitions and with little attempt at quantification, the characteristic features of the Romano–Celtic tradition, as known at present, seem to be:

1. Built wlth non–edge fastened flush–laid planking.

2. Large nails, driven through treenails and clenched by turning the emerging point through 180 degrees ('hooked'), fasten planking to framework.

3. The framing consists of relatively massive and relatively closely–spaced groups of framing timbers including floors spanning bottom and bilges, asymmetric timbers spanning the bottom and one side, and side timbers. At any one station framing units may be composite, but individual timbers are not fastened together (McGrail, 1987: 141–146).

4. Hulls are either (a) flat–bottomed, keel–less and without stems, or (b) full–bodied with stems and a plank–keel.

5. The mast–step, towing and/or sailing, is placed well forward of amidships

Several of the boats and ships said to be Romano–Celtic have all these features, but some have one or two features missing or the evidence is unclear. Boats and ships in the latter categories are not thereby excluded from this tradition as it is a polythetic grouping. Furthermore, it is the *combination* of these general characteristics (or a significant number of them), and not individual features, that defines this group of vessels as 'Romano–Celtic', for each one of these characteristics, unless defined with extreme precision, may be found in other traditions. For example: 'built with non–edge flush–laid planking' appears in the Mediterranean in the 11th–century AD ship from Serçe Limani (Steffy, 1994: 85–91). Moreover, the second Romano–Celtic each one of characteristic listed above – 'large nails driven through treenails and clenched by turning the emerging point through 180 degrees ('hooked'),fasten planking to framework' – may be seen in Mediterranean ships of the 1st millennium BC: for example, in the 4th century BC Kyrenia ship (Steffy, 1994: 42–59). In this latter case, a subtle distinction may be made: in the Kyrenia ship these nails fastened framing to planking; whereas in the Romano–Celtic tradition, they fastened planking to framing, i.e., a different building sequence.

Skeleton–built, part–skeleton–built or bottom–built?

Those scholars who have investigated Romano–Celtic vessels in detail have found it difficult to describe their building sequence using the conventional terminology. For example,

Basch (1972: 41) concluded that the Blackfriars 1 ship was 'neither skeleton nor shell technique' Marsden (1994: 79) is also undecided for, although he considers Blackfriars 1 to be 'primarily skeleton–built', he qualifies this by saying that this ship was 'essentially skeleton–built at the sides but the bottom could have been in part shell–built'. In like manner, Margaret Rule believes that the St. Peter Port 1 ship was 'neither wholly skeleton–first, nor shell–first, but a step–wise alternation of the two' (1993: 28). Furthermore, Beat Arnold has concluded that the flat–bottomed Lake Neuchatel boats, Bevaix & Yverdon 1 & 2, were 'neither based upon the shell–first principle, nor upon skeleton construction but rather upon a bottom–based construction; in other words, the flat bottom constitutes a base for the entire construction' (1992: 120; 1991: 22–3).

Frame–orientated and plank–orientated approaches

The difficulties experienced by Basch, and Rule in classifying these finds stem from the use of the terms 'shell–built', 'shell–first', 'skeleton–built' and 'skeleton–first', which focuses their analysis onto the precise sequence of construction. These terms are undoubtedly useful archaeological constructs and analytical tools, but not concepts that ancient boat–builders had at the forefront of their minds. On the contrary, *they* had first to work out how to build the required shape of hull (Basch, 1972: 34; Pomey, 1994). Before drawings and models came into common use, boatbuilders had, in some way, to visualize the hull shape of the vessel about to be built. Archaeological and ethnographic evidence, worldwide, suggests that for keel boats this visualization may take two forms: primarily in terms of the planking; or primarily in terms of the framing.

A principal thesis of this paper is that these 'visualization' concepts are to be preferred to the 'sequence' concepts when analyzing and classifying early boat and ship structures (see also Pomey, 1994). The terms 'frame–orientated' and 'plank-oriented' have demonstrable advantages over 'skeleton first' and 'shell–first when describing hulls which do not fully conform to recent practice. 'Frame –oriented' does not imply that full skeleten (as known in the 19th century) was erected before any planking was undertaken: the framework may be extended as the building proceeds, possibly only just ahead of the next series of strakes; indeed, some frames may not be added until after the planking is completed. Furthermore, the framing timbers at any one station do not necessarily have the to be fastened together. The essential feature is that elements of the framing should define and determine the hull shape: in the Basch (1972) terminology, these framing elements are *active*. Correspondingly, 'plank–orientated' does not imply that the entire planking was completed before any framing was added; the framing (*passive*) may be built up in stages, keeping pace with, but *after* phases of planking: the planking defines and determines the hull shape (Basch, 1972; Pomey, 1994).

Romano–Celtic vessels with keels
In the frame–orientated approach to the building of a keeled vessel (keel or plank–keel), the initial shape of the hull is

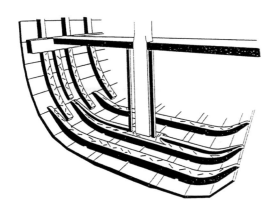

Figure 8.2.1 Reconstruction drawing of part of the hull of Blackfriars 1, near the mast–step. The two central bottom planks form the plank–keel (Drawing: Peter Marsden)

determined by the keel and posts, and then by other elements (not necessarily the entirety) of the framework or skeleton. The builder visualises the hull in terms of the framing. In the plank–orientated approach, the shape of the hull is initially determined (as in the frame–orientated approach) by keel and posts: after this the hull shape is determined by the planking. The builder visualises the hull in terms of the planking.

From Marsden's analysis of the structure of the round–hulled Blackfriars 1 ship (1994: 76 – 9), it is clear that the initial shape of her hull was determined by the posts and the

plank–keel (the two thicker, central planks – see Fig.8.2.1). As Marsden's building sequence diagram shows, her subsequent hull shape was also determined by framing elements; floors up to the fourth side strake, and, from the fifth to the ninth side strakes, by side timbers (1994: fig. 70). The builder of Blackfriars 1 was 'frame–orientated': this ship was 'frame–based'.

Rule's description of the lower hull of the St. Peter Port 1 ship (1993: 13–28) suggests that three small framing timbers at each end were fitted *after* the planking had been fastened (1993: 27, fig. 14, stages 13 and 15), and thus the shape of these six floors had to be made to conform to the planking, which, in the 'sequence' terminology, would introduce a 'shell–first' element into the building sequence. However, if the evidence is examined from the boatbuilder's view of how the shape of this rounded hull was determined, it is clear that these six timbers (which extend over only 2.5 m, that is approximately 10% of the overall length) had no influence on hull shape, for they were fitted after the run of the planking had been fixed and the lower hull of the shape determined by the posts, the plank–keel composed of three thicker central planks (Fig. 8.2.2) and some (all?) of the other 34 floor timbers. Other evidence (1993: fig. 14, stage 16) suggests that the shape of the upper hull was determined by side timbers. Like the builder of Blackfriars 1, the builder of St Peter Port 1 was 'frame–orientated': this ship was 'frame–based'.

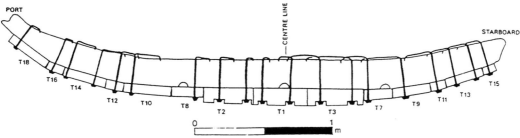

Figure 8.2.2 Reconstruction of the transverse section of the lower hull of the St Peter Port 1 ship, at the station by floor timber T42. Planks T2, T1 and T3 form the plank–keel (Drawing: Margaret Rule)

Romano–Celtic keel–less boats

The truly flat–bottomed boats in this Romano–Celtic tradition – those without keel – are difficult to analyse in terms of 'shell' and 'skeleton' sequence of building. It is possible to gain some insight, however, by once again asking how did the builder visualise his boat – was he plank– or frame–orientated?

As Arnold (1991) has suggested, the initial shape of such hulls comes from the shape of the bottom planking which is obtained by placing shaped planks of equal thickness, alongside one another. At this stage the floor timbers conform to the shape of the bottom planking and merely bind it together. The starting point for the side planking is also the bottom – the position in space of the outer edges of the bottom. The angle at which this side–planking lies to the bottom may, however, be determined in one of two ways: if the builder is frame–orientated, that angle will be determined by the uprising elements of the framing; on the other hand, if the builder is plank–orientated, that angle will be determined by a bevel worked on the outer

edges of the bottom, and/or on the lower edges of the lowest side strakes. In the special case of flat–bottomed boats with transition strakes (*iles*; chine–girders), the shape of the lowest part of the sides may be determined by the uprising element of this strake, as visualised by a plank–orientated builder; or this transition strake may be shaped to conform to the uprising elements of the framing by a frame–orientated builder. This analysis may be extended to higher side strakes.

It is suggested, then, that ancient builders visualised the shape of their flat–bottomed boats as a combination of two elements: initially bottom–based; and then either plank or frame determined. The 19th–century boat from Tredunnoc on the River Usk, SE Wales, may be quoted as an example of this dual approach. The hull of this flat–bottomed canal barge was initially bottom–based, but after the first side strake had been fitted, her builder adopted the frame–orientated approach, and the shape of the upper hull was determined by the knees (McGrail & Parry, 1991). The published data on those boats of

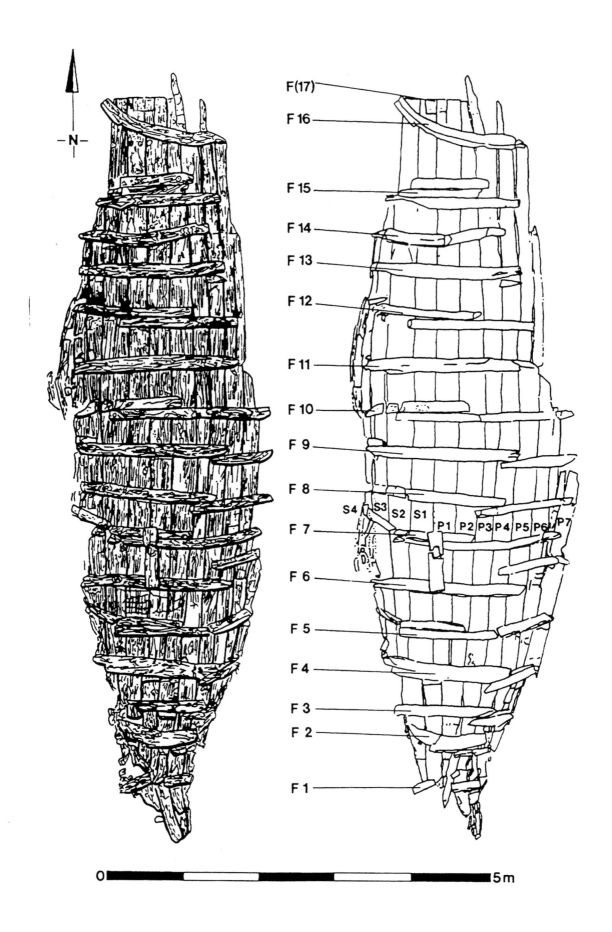

Figure 8.2.3 Plan of the Barland's Farm boat derived from photogrammetry and field drawings. Planks S1 and P1 from the plank–keel (Drawing: Glamorgan Gwent Archaeological Trust)

the Romano–Celtic tradition which are keel–less and have flat bottoms are, in most cases, not sufficiently detailed for their boatbuilders' orientation to be determined, but it may be that, like the builders of the flat-bottomed barge from Tredunnoc, they were frame–orientated. Perhaps the excavators of these boats would now publish their own analyses?

Vessels in other traditions

These visualisation concepts may also prove useful in the analysis of hull structures from other traditions. For example, the hull of the 4th–century BC Kyrenia ship (Steffy, 1994: 42–59) was visualized by her builder in terms of the planking, whilst the 11th century AD Serçe Limani ship (Steffy, 1994: 85–91) was visualized in terms of the framing. On the other hand, the builder of the 7th–century AD Yassi Ada ship 2, with a 'transitional' structure (Steffy 1994: 80–3), and the builder of the 20th–century South Vietnamese ship noted by Basch (1972: 31–4), both had a dual approach: in terms of the planking to the turn of the bilge, beyond that, in terms of the framing.

Certain 17th–century round–hulled Dutch ships were evidently built by temporarily clamping their flush–laid planking together, then inserting the framework and permanently fastening the planking to it (Maarleveld, 1994). It is difficult to describe these hulls in the 'sequence' terminology. However, in the 'shape visualization' terminology advocated in this paper, we can say that the builders of these vessels were clearly plank–orientated. Although this planking was not fastened together but was fastened to the framing, the shape of the hull was derived from the planking.

Functional sub–groups within the Romano–Celtic tradition

There are a number of technological differences between individual boats and ships of the Romano–Celtic tradition (McGrail, 1981a: 23–4). Such variability may be due to differences in function or in operating environment, or to changes over time, or it may indicate regional groupings. The evidence at present available suggests that there are two sub-groups within this tradition which differ in their operating environment. On theone hand, in sub–group A, are the lake, river and canal boats such as Bevaix, Zwammerdam and Pommeroeul (McGrail, 1981a: 23): and on the other hand there are the sea–going vessels of sub–group B, such as Blackfriars 1 and St. Peter Port 1 (Marsden, 1994; Rule and Monaghan, 1993).

These two sub–groups differ in four respects:

1. Hull shape in transverse section:
    Sub–group A is flat–bottomed with flared or vertical sides; sub–group B has a full form with rounded sides.

2. Builder's visualization of shape:
    A, a dual approach: first bottom–based and then probably frame– or possibly plank–orientated (the published evidence is not clear on this point); B is frame–orientated.

3. Structural elements:
    A is keel–less and without end posts; whereas B has both keel and posts. It may be relevant in this context to note that the prehistoric round–hulled Ferriby stitched boats had plank–keels (Wright, 1990), whereas the Brigg 'raft', of 'lidless box' shape was keel–less (McGrall, 1981b): possibly a pointer to the ongins of the two Romano–Celtic sub–groups?

4 Propulsion:
    A by paddle, pole, oar or tow, and possibly by sail in winds from the stem sector; B by oar and by a sailing rig (a lugsail?) which probably enabled them to sail 'by–and–large'.

The Barland's Farm boat

Post–excavation work on the 3rd–century AD Barland's Farm boat from SE Wales, is still underway (Nayling *et al*, 1994), but it is already clear that this boat has features which identify it as a member of the Romano–Celtic tradition (Fig. 8.2.3). Her builder was undoubtedly frame–orientated and she was frame–based: large iron nails fasten the planking to massive and closely–spaced framing; her mast step is about one–third her overall length from forward; and she has posts and a plank–keel. These last two features, and other characteritics, place her in sub–group B, with Blackfriars 1 and the St. Peter Port ship. She may not have been fully seagoing, but it seems likely that she was an estuary boat, capable of voyages between Wales and England in appropriate weather conditions, and of using the tides to go up and down the many rivers that entered the Severn Estuary.

Acknowledgments

This article is a revised version of a paper given to a seminar in the Centre for Maritime Archaeology at Roskilde, Denmark in September, 1994: it has benefited from discussion with Dr Ole Crumlin–Pedersen and other members of that seminar. I am also grateful to Dr John Coates and Dr Basil Greenhill for their criticism of a subsequent draft.

References

Amold B. 1977 'Some remarks on caulking in Celtic boat construction and its evolution in areas lying NW of the Alpine arc.' *IJNA* 6, 293–297.

Amold B. 1978 'Navigation.' *Archeologia* 118, 52–68.

Amold B. 1991 'Gallo–Roman boat of Bevaix and the bottom–based construction.' In Reinders R. and Paul K. (Eds) *Carvel Construction Techniques* 19–23. Oxbow Monograph, 12.

Amold B. 1992, *Batellerie gallo–romaine sur le lac de Neuchatel*. Two vols. Archeologie Neuchateloise, volumes 12 and 13.

Basch L. 1972' Ancient wrecks and the archaeology of ships.' *IJNA* 1, 1–58.

Crumlin–Pedersen O. 1990 'Boats and ships of the Angles and Jutes.' In McGrail S. (Ed.) *Maritime Celts, Frisians and Saxons* 98–116. CBA Research Report 71.

de Boe G. 1978 'Roman boats from a small river harbour at Pommeroeul Belgium.' In Taylor J du P. and Cleere H. (Eds) *Roman Shipping and Trade* 22–30. CBA Research Report, 24.

de Weerd M. 1978 'Ships of the Roman period from Zwammerdam.' In Taylor J. du P. and Cleere, H (Eds) *Roman Shipping and Trade* 15–21. CBA Research Report, 24.

de Weerd M. 1988 *Schepen voor Zwammerdam* Haarlem.

Doran J. E. and Hodson F.R. 1975 *Mathematics and Computers in Archaeology* Edinburgh University Press.

Ellmers D. 1969 'Keltischer Schiffbau.' *Jahrbuch des Romisch–Germanischen Zentralmuseums* 73–122. Mainz.

Ellmers D. 1994 'Cog as a cargo carrier.' In Unger R.W. (Ed.) *Cogs, Caravels and Galleons* 29–46. London: Conway.

Höchmann O. 1982 'Spatromische schiffsfunde in Mainz.' *Archaeol. Korrespond* 12, 231–50.

Lehman L.Th 1978 'A flat–bottomed Roman boat from Druten Netherlands.' *IJNA* 7, 259–268.

McGrail S. 1981a *Rafts, Boats and Ships*. HMSO.

McGrail S. 1981b *The Brigg 'Raft' and Her Prehistoric Environment*. BAR (Oxford) 89.

McGrail S. 1987 *Ancient Boats in NW Europe*. London: Longman.

McGrail S. and Parry S. 1991 'Flat–bottomed boat from the R.Usk at Tredunnoc, Gwent, Wales.' In Reinders R. and Paul K. (Eds) *Carvel Construction Techniques* 161–170. Oxbow Monograph, 12.

Maarleveld T.J. 1994 'Double Dutch solutions in Flush–Planked Shipbuilding: continuity and adaptation at the start of Modern History.' In Westerdahl C (ed) *Crossroads in Ancient Shipbuilding* 153–163. Oxbow Monograph, 40.

Marsden P. 1965 'Boat of the Roman period discovered on the site of New Guy's House Bermondsey, 1958.' *Transactions of the London and Middlesex Archaeological Society* 21, 118–131.

Marsden P.R.V. 1967 *Roman ship from Blackfriars, London*. London: Guildhall Museum.

Marsden P. 1976 'Boat of the Roman period found at Bruges, Belgium in 1899 and related types.' *IJNA* 5, 23–56.

Marsden P. 1994 *Ships of the Port of London: First to Eleventh Centuries AD*. English Heritage.

Nayling N., Maynard D. and McGrail S. 1994 'Barland's Farm, Magor, Gwent: a Romano–Celtic boat.' *Antiquity* 68, 596–603.

Olsen O. and Crumlin–Pedersen O. 1967 'Skuldelev Ships II.' *Acta Archaeologica* 38, 73–174. Copenhagen.

Parker A.J. 1991 'Review of 'Maritime Celts, Frisians and Saxons'.' *IJNA* 20, 363.

Pomey P. 1994 'Shell conception and skeleton process in ancient Mediterranean shipbuilding.' In Westerdahl C. (ed.) *Crossroads in Ancient Shipbuilding* 125–130. Oxbow Monograph, 40.

Rule M. and Monaghan J. 1993 *Gallo–Roman Trading Vessel from Guernsey*. Guernsey Museum Monograph, 5.

Runyan T.J. 1994 'Cog as a warship.' In Unger R.W. (ed.) *Cogs, Caravels and Galleons* 47–58. London: Conway.

Steffy J.R. 1994 *Wooden Shipbuilding and the Interpretation of Shipwrecks*. Texas A&M University Press.

Wright E. 1990 *The Ferriby Boats*. London: Routledge.

Reprinted with permission from:

International Journal for Nautical Archaeology, 24: 139–145 (1995)

SECTION 9.0

MEDIEVAL BOATS AND SHIPS

Thirty years ago, Ole Crumlin-Pedersen propounded the idea that there were three main types of medieval, seagoing, cargo ship in Atlantic and Baltic Europe: the Nordic ship; the Cog; and the Hulc – see Paper 2.1. Nothing has arisen since to change that hypothesis significantly: more Nordic vessels, especially post-Viking ones, have been excavated; the number of Cogs has significantly increased; and the *Hulc*, well-documented in port and custom accounts, remains archaeologically invisible. There is, however, more awareness today of the merging of types in the later medieval period, and the emergence of what are recognised as new types. Accounts, some detailed, some in outline, of vessels from these three traditions and their successors may be found in: Unger (1994: 11–58), Hutchinson (1994: 4–64), Greenhill (1995: 173–255), Friel (1995), and Christensen (1996: 72–88).

The Nordic tradition.

The three papers in this Section are based on my own fieldwork and thus deal only with vessels of the Nordic tradition. This tradition is sometimes referred to as 'Viking', but this style of building had its origins before the Viking period, and continued after it, and 'Nordic' (in Ireland, 'Norse') is a more apt term. The wreck in the R. Hamble, discussed in Paper 9.1, is a very late example of this shipbuilding tradition, with triple-thickness clinker planking and closely-spaced framing. After this time, generally speaking, only boats of this tradition were built.

Designated Wreck Sites

The R. Hamble wreck, probably that of Henry V's *Grace Dieu*, is a Designated Historic Wreck, one of 40 or so in United Kingdom waters. Although coming under different legislation, such sites have a comparable status to Historic Monument sites on land. Some of the problems connected with these marine sites have been discussed in the introduction to Section 1; a further problem – that of their physical protection and on-site conservation – is taken up in Paper 9.1. Although there is more

awareness of this problem today, the governmental bodies administrating ancient wresks legislation have not yet tackled it, nor have they fully accepted that they have responsibilities for managing such sites.

Re-used boat & ship timbers

Paper 9.3 describes some of the problems faced when interpreting the remains of wooden boats and ships re-used in medieval waterfront sites. The examples discussed are all in Ireland: several sites in Dublin (see below); a site in Cork city (Hurley, 1986); and one in Waterford (Hurley & Scully, 1997).

Paper 9.2 is taken from chapter 5 of my book dealing specifically with Dublin (McGrail, 1993). Six sites between Christchurch Cathedral and the R. Liffey were excavated between 1962 & 1981 (Fig. 9.3.2), and the ship & boat timbers and other nautical artifacts form only a small part of the material excavated – see the series of Monographs, *Medieval Dublin Excavations* published by the Royal Irish Academy. Paper 9.2 uses the evidence described in earlier chapters of my Dublin book to build up a picture of the boats and ships that used Dublin, as it changed from a harbour with informal landing places and anchorages to a port with formal waterfront structures, between the 10th and 13th centuries AD – see Section 2. Note that,in this paper and in 9.3, TG = Timber Group.

The opportunity to undertake further excavations in the vicinity of *dubh linn*, the 'black pool' east and south-east of Dublin Castle, or on the former strand west of Wood Quay has not yet arisen. A second proposal made in Ch. 6 of the Dublin book (not re-printed here), that further timbers should be dated by dendrochronology, is still under consideration. A third proposal, for a re-evaluation of the Dublin nautical evidence, must await publication of the Skuldelev & Lynaes excavations. The methods I used to estimate the size of the parent vessels of the Dublin timbers, and the typologies I devised for the constituent parts of boats and ships (keels, stems, planking and the like) await criticism.

References

Christensen A.E. 1996 *Earliest Ships* Conway's History of the Ship. vol 1.

Friel I. 1995 *Good Ship*. British Museum Press.

Greenhill B. 1995 *Archaeoloqy of Boats and Ships*. Conway.

Hurley M.F. 1986 'Excavations in medieval Cork: St Peter's market.' *J. Cork Historical and Archaeoloqical Soc* 91, 1–25.

Hurley M.F. and Scully O.M.B. (ed) 1997 *Late–Vikinq Age and Medieval Waterford*. Waterford Corporation.

Hutchinson G. 1994 *Medieval Ships and Shipping*. Leicester University Press.

McGrail S 1993 *Medieval Boat and Ship Timbers from Dublin*. Royal Irish Academy.

Unger R.W. 1994 *Cogs, Caravels & Galleons* Conway's History of the Ship. vol. 3.

PAPER 9.1

THE FUTURE OF THE DESIGNATED WRECK SITE IN THE R. HAMBLE

Importance of the wreck

The evidence reviewed by Ian Friel (*IJNA* 22: 16–17) and a radiocarbon date of AD 1225 to 1405 cal.(HAR–4249) show that the Designated Wreck in the R. Hamble at SU5014.1059 (Figs 9.1.1 and 9.1.2) is late–medieval in date and almost certainly the remains of Henry V's *Grace Dieu* (1418). Whether or not that identification is correct, this is an important vessel by any standards. This wreck is one of the very few known from a period of great change in the shipbuilding and rigging techniques used in Atlantic Europe. During the 14th and 15th centuries there was a change from a single–masted, square–rig to a three–masted rig with square and lateen sails. Furthermore, at about the same time, there was a change from a shell–first sequence of building, in which the hull shape and much of the strength came from the planking, to a sequence in which increasing reliance was placed on the framework for strength. By the late 15th/early 16th century the vessels of the oceanic explorers were evidently built in a skeleton sequence, on one or two master frames with ribbands, which led in due course to the fully pre–erected framework of the 17th century (Greenhill, 1976: 65, 72; McGrail, 1981: 42–43; 1987: 104; Greenhill, 1988: 67–76).

These technological changes are not well–documented and thus each wreck from the period 14th to 16th centuries is of great importance in helping us to see precisely when, how and where these changes took place, and possibly throw light on why there were such changes. There are sufficient well–recorded wrecks in northern waters from the period *c.* AD 800 to 1100 for the main characteristics of the Viking/Nordic tradition of shipbuilding to be documented. In the following centuries, up to *c.* AD 1400, aspects of its development can be traced in the few wrecks so far excavated (Crumlin–Pedersen, 1991; Åkerlund, 1951) also in some of the town seals of northern Europe (Ewe, 1972), and in the fragmented remains of ships re–used to build waterfront structures in Bergen (Christensen, 1985), Dublin (McGrail, forthcoming), London (Marsden, forthcoming) and elsewhere in northern Europe (Milne & Hobley, 1981).

The wreck in the R. Hamble is built of radially–split, clinker–laid strakes, edge–fastened by clench nails, with a caulking of moss and tar. These features are characteristic of the Viking/Nordic tradition and we may think of the R. Hamble wreck as a late example of this method of shipbuilding. Being a royal warship, however, she may not be entirely representative of the general type of Nordic ship, most of them merchantmen, being built at that time: this is almost certainly true of her size. Table 1 shows that her overall length of 40 m

Table 9.1.1 Estimated dimensions and cargo capacity of selected medieval vessels

Vessel	Type	Date (AD approx)	Length (m)	Max breadth (m)	Depth of hold (m)	Approx cargo capacity (tonns)
1. Skuldelev 1	Nordic	1000	16.3	4.5	2.1	24
2. Hedeby 3	Nordic	1060	*c* 25	5.7	2.5	40
3. Lynaes	Nordic	1150	*c* 25	6.0	2.5	60
4. Dublin (TG.6/9)	Nordic	1200	*c* 25	6.5	2.5	60
5. Bergen Great Ship	Nordic	1240	*c* 30	9.5	3.7	155
6. Bremen Cog	Cog	1380	22.7	7.6	4.3	120
7. R. Hamble	Nordic	1418(?)	*c* 40	*c* 15	*c* 6.5(?)	1400
8. *Santa Maria*	Nao	1492	23.6	7.97	4.7	106

Source for 1, 2, 3, 5, 6: Crumlin–Pedersen, 1991, 77–80, fig. 10; sources for 4: McGrail, forthcoming; sources for 7: Anderson 1934a; Prynne, 1968; Friel (IJNA 22, 3–19); source for 8: Martinez–Hidlago, 1966.
The dimensions and tonnage of the R. Hamble wreck are generally comparable with those of the other vessels, but not precisely so, as a different basis for estimates has been used.

and estimated maximum breadth of 15m were both much greater than the largest of those earlier vessels in this tradition which it has proved possible to reconstruct theoretically. The dimensions of two non–Nordic vessels, the late 14th–century Bremen Cog and Columbus' late 15th–century *Santa Maria*, are also much less than those estimated for the Hamble wreck. As the R. Hamble wreck's depth of hold is likely to have been significantly greater than the 4.3 m of the Bremen Cog, the volume of her hold, a medieval measure of size, was almost certainly of a different order of magnitude from the other vessels listed in Table 9.1.1.

Table 9.1.1 also lists the approximate cargo capacity (tons burden) of these seven ships. The capacity of the ships in the Nordic tradition (Nos 1 to 5) and the Bremen Cog have been estimated by standard methods (Crumlin–Pedersen, 1991), and the method used for *Santa Maria* is similar: the tonnage measurements here are therefore generally comparable. On the other hand, the tonnage given for the R. Hamble wreck is that documented for *Grace Dieu* (Friel, *IJNA* 22: 16–17). In their estimates of the tonnage of the R. Hamble wreck, Anderson (1934a: 161) and Prynne (1968: 123) used a late 16th century shipbuilder's rule which requires the depth of hold to be known as well as keel length and maximum breadth of hull. Whereas the original length and breadth of this wreck can be estimated with some certainty, the depth of hold is much more difficult, and only by assuming this to have been *c.* 21 ft (6.5 m) can Anderson and Prynne have arrived at their estimate of *c.* 1400 tons (which coincidentally turns out to be the same as that documented for *Grace Dieu*).

Nevertheless such an estimate appears not unreasonable in view of the size and form of the remains. These cargo capacities thus emphasise the great difference in size between the R. Hamble wreck/*Grace Dieu* and the other vessels in Table 9.1.1. The drawing Prynne (1968) used to illustrate his lecture to the Society for Nautical Research strikingly shows how these estimates place the R. Hamble wreck in the same league for size as two skeleton–built warships of the 17th century, *Wasa* and *Sovereign of the Seas*.

Characteristics of the R. Hamble

Due to the difficulties of excavation and recording inherent in the R. Hamble site, any attempt to summarize what is known about the wreck cannot be entirely accurate. Both Anderson (1934a: 162) and Prynne (1973: 233) subsequently had doubts about the observations they made and the drawings they compiled in 1933 and 1936, and the experience on site of the National Maritime Museum's team confirms that their misgivings were justified. Nevertheless, an attempt will be made here to present the main characteristics of the wreck and, in the next section, details of its structure.

The Designated Wreck is that of a large ship, by medieval standards, with her planking fastened in an elaborate form of clinker. This planking (appears to be generally of three thicknesses (Fig. 9.1.3) however Anderson (1938: 113) noted that in one section it may have been only two planks thick. The mid–15th–century wreck from Aber Wrac'h, NW Brittany, is built generally of a single layer of clinker planking: however, in the preliminary publication of the site by L'Hour and Veyrat (1989:fig. 13) the wreck appears to have double thickness planking in the vicinity of her cross–beams. By analogy, it cannot be known with certainty whether the R. Hamble wreck has generally three thicknesses of planking or only two, until much more planking has been excavated and carefully recorded.

The Hamble planking is also said, on the basis of hearsay, to be '... made up of pieces not more than 6 or 7 ft (*c.* 1.8 to 2.2 m) long' (Anderson, 1934a: 165). Without detailed recording of many examples of all layers of planking it cannot be certain whether such short planks are the general rule or not.

Prynne (1938: 282; 1968: 124; 1973: 231) has stated that at least some, and possibly all, of this small planking was fastened together by nails driven from inboard and clenched outboard, and Anderson (1934a: 160) has claimed that there is 'some evidence for this practice'. Only the impressions of nail heads and roves and traces of shanks survive on the timbers so far examined, both on site and in museums, but it seems clear from this evidence that round–headed nails were driven from outboard through the planking and clenched inboard over rectangular roves. This is the usual practice in North European clinker construction, although during repairs, or other special circumstances, some nails may be clenched outboard. Once again, only detailed examination of many more examples *in situ* can clarify which method was generally used in the R. Hamble wreck.

Prynne (1968: 124; 1973: 231)has also tackled the difficult question, evidently overlooked by other workers in this field, of how and when the wreck's triple–thickness strakes were built up. In a shell–built, clinker–planked *boat* it is generally the practice nowadays to scarf individual planks together before fitting an entire strake as one unit to the keel or to the strakes already place. Whether this method is practicable in a large shell–built *ship* is not – to my knowledge – a question which has up to now been asked, but a definitive answer in the affirmative seems doubtful. In the case of a large shell–built ship with multiple–thickness planking, it seems likely that such composite strakes were assembled on the hull, both thickness–wise, as Prynne (1968; 1973) has suggested, and also lengthwise.

The method of assembly outlined by Prynne (1968: 124; 1973: 231) requires the inner planking of each strake to be first fastened to 'master frames or moulds which had already been set–up': that is, in contradiction to his statements elsewhere, Prynne suggested here that this ship was built in the skeleton sequence – a dilemma which Anderson (1934b: 5) also faced. It is, however, unnecessary to postulate the skeleton sequence of building in order to explain how the wreck's triple–thickness planking may have been assembled. The following method is generally compatible with the excavated evidence and with the *shell* sequence of building:

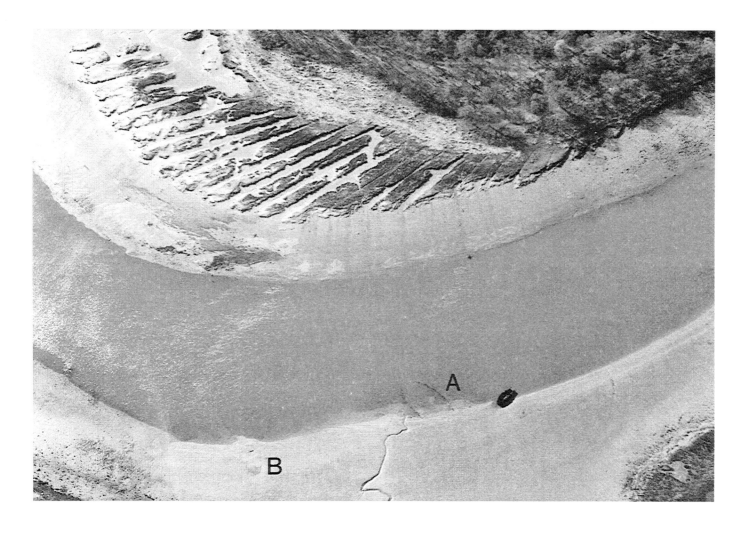

Figure 9.1.1 Vertical air photograph, taken in April 1979, showing the R. Hamble wreck (A) and the possible second wreck (B). The parallel lines on the far bank of the river are said to be where invasion landing craft, belonging to the shore base HMS *Cricket*, were moored during the Spring of 1944. Photo: RCHM(E)

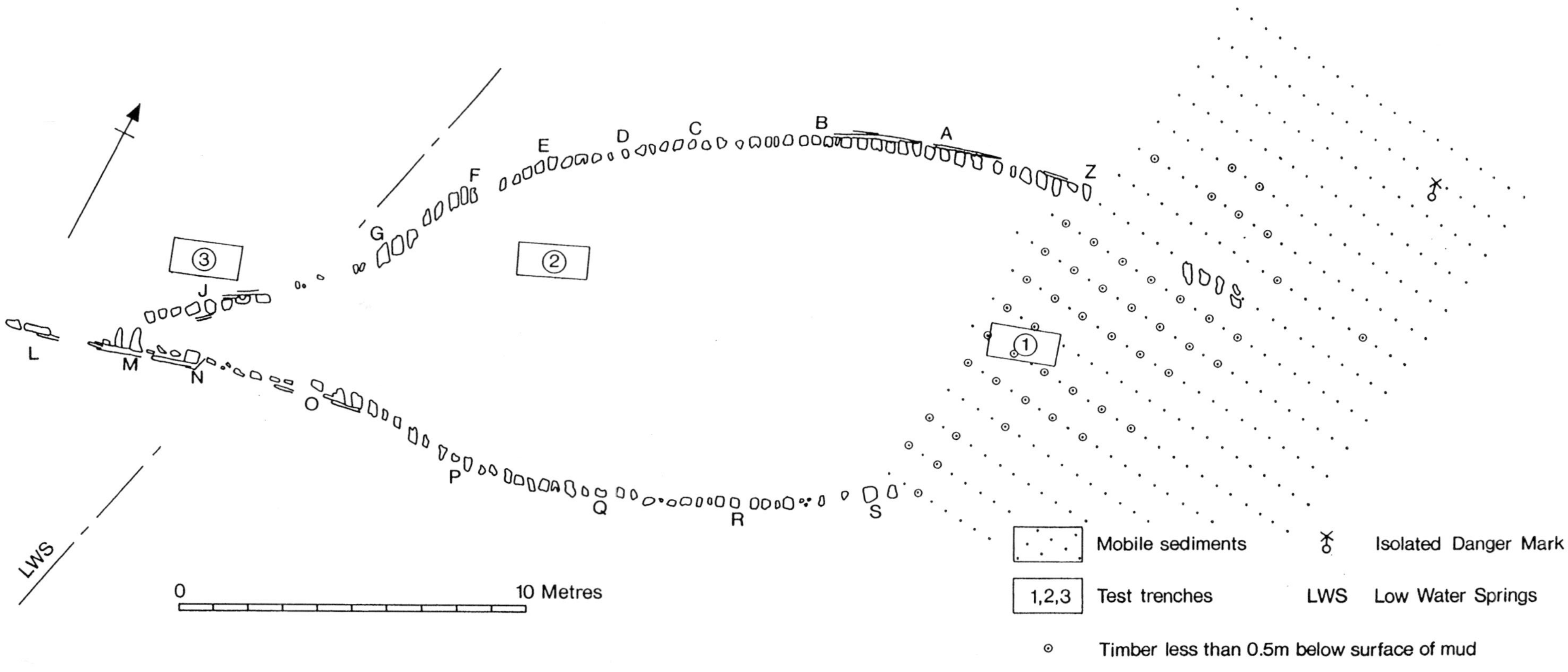
LWS
L
M
N
J
3
O
G
F
E
D
C
B
A
Z
2
1
P
Q
R
S
0
10 Metres
Mobile sediments
Isolated Danger Mark
1,2,3
Test trenches
LWS
Low Water Springs
Timber less than 0.5m below surface of mud

Figure 9.1.2 Plan of the wreck site in the R. Humble, compiled from above water, under water, and probe surveys. Drawing: National Maritime Museum, Greenwich

Fasten the outer plank to the middle plank along lower and upper edges by occasional small nails, some used as spikes, some clenched by turning the point along the inboard face of the middle plank. Prynne (1968: 124; 1973:231; 1976:290) has described nails in the wreck's planking which were smaller than the clench nails, with 1/4 inch (22mm) diameter round heads which were counter–sunk within the planking. He thought that they were used to fasten the middle layer of planking to the strake below (1973: 231) or the middle layer to the inner layer (1968: 124). Recent examination of planking removed from the wreck earlier this century (Clarke, *IJNA* 22: 26–31), whilst not conclusive, suggest that these small nails were used to fasten the outer planks to the middle planks.

– Fasten the lower edges of these two planks (outer and middle) to the upper edge of the three planks in the strake below using large clench nails spaced at 0.15 to 0.20 m.

– Position the inner plank on top of the strake below and fasten the outer, middle and inner planks together along the mid–line of the strake by clench nails spaced at 0.45 to 0.75 m.

– Subsequently, fit framing timbers; then nail all three thicknesses of planking to the framework.

Anderson and Prynne also tried to determine how the shape of the hull was obtained. Anderson (1934b: 5) considered that 'there must have been some sort of framework to give the planking its shape'; whilst Prynne believed that they used 'moulds built–up on the keel, made to the shape of sections of the ship' (1968: 124) or 'master frames not too far apart' (1973: 231). These suggestions imply that the R. Hamble wreck must have been built in the skeleton sequence, an implication which contradicts Anderson's (1934a: 160, 166; 1934b: 5) and Prynne's (1938: 282; 1973: 231) demonstration that she was shell–built from the fact that the planking was fastened before at least some of the frames were fitted and from the direction in which some of the frame elements were scarfed to each other.

In the skeleton sequence of building, the hull shape comes from the pre–erected skeleton to which the planking is made to conform. In the pure shell sequence the shape comes from the planking itself; the set of a strake and hence the developing shape of the hulk is determined by the run of the upper edge of the strake already in position and by the bevel angle cut on the outer side of that edge or, for hollow curves, by the bevel angle worked on the lower inboard edge of the strake being fitted (McGrail, 1987: fig. 8.3). Some scholars believe that hull shape in this shell sequence can be achieved 'by eye'; others that building aids were used (McGrail, 1987: 98–103).

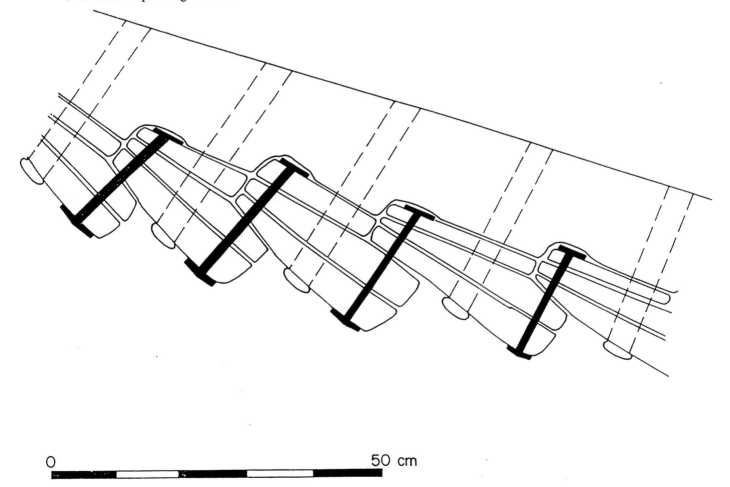

0   50 cm

Figure 9.1.3 Diagram to show the idealised form of the wreck's triple thickness planking. Drawing: National Maritime Museum, Greenwich

For a large complex ship such as the R. Hamble wreck, where building 'by eye' would seem to be impracticable, there are, in the absence of drawings or models, two main possibilities for building aids: the ship's shape was known as a set of plank breadths and bevel angles at a series of stations along the length of the vessel – such information may be stored encoded on a boatbuilder's level, a boatbuilding aid used from at least the 17th century in Norway (McGrail, 1987: 100–102); alternatively, moulds (wooden templates of transverse profile of the ship) may have been used, amidships and at key stations where the hull shape was rapidly changing. A third possibility is that a combination of these two types of building aid may have been used. (McGrail, 1987: 102).

The limited evidence from the R. Hamble wreck does not allow us, at present, to decide precisely how the hull shape was obtained. The possibility must, however, be borne in mind that, at this late stage in–the Nordic clinker–built tradition, although the R. Hamble ship had edge–fastened planking, her general shape may have been obtained, as Prynne and Anderson appear to suggest, from an elementary skeleton of keel, stems and a few frames of light scantlings erected before planking began: such a framework could be temporary or permanent. Whether this technique was used can now only be investigated by further excavation.

Details of the wreck's structure

The foregoing discussion and reports quoted therein show that the R. Hamble wreck had multiple thickness clinker planking, caulked with moss and tar, and fastened by iron nails, more than 0.22 m in length, with 20 mm square–section shanks and domed heads some 60 to 70 mm in diameter, which were clenched inboard over *c.* 50 x 70 mm rectangular roves. Framing timbers averaged *c.* 0.28 m sided and *c.* 0.20 moulded and were closely spaced at *c.* 0.40 m centre to centre. They were fastened to the planking by oak treenails of *c.* 38 mm diameter, with domed heads outboard. Where the framing did not closely fit the planking, wedges were driven in.

Other structural features of this wreck include:

– futtock timbers scarfed to the floor timbers

– a keel of *c.* 130 ft (40 m) length

– a keelson, 0.55m sided and 0.16m moulded, with a simple mast–step *c.* 0.58 x 0.29 m and *c.* 0.20 m deep

– ceiling planking some 30 to 40 mm thick

– stringers of various sizes

– crossbeams with protruding heads (Anderson, 1934a: fig. 9; Prynne, 1938; figs 9 and 10) – similar in form to those of the mid–15th century Aber Wrac'h wreck (L' Hour & Veyret, 1989: figs 12 and 13); see also the crossbeams in the 12th–century Kalmar 1 (Åkerlund, 1951), the late 14th–century Bremen Cog (Ellmers,

1979: fig. 1.6), and the 13th/14th century finds from Bergen – 90357, 90359, 90395, 90438 in Christenden (1985)

– ballast around the mast–step was large rounded flints.

Structural details not yet known or needing clarification

In order to understand the R. Hamble wreck, fully and determine her place in the development of European shipbuilding techniques, the following information is needed:

– detailed plan and sections of the entire remains

– answers to general questions: how was timber selected? What was the sequence of building and how was the shape of the hull obtained? How was the planking shaped, assembled and fastened?

– specific problems to be investigated:

Planking

– entirely triple–thickness?

– ring/ray diagrams and other details of parent logs

– samples for dendrochronological examination

– direction clench nails were driven

– distribution and purpose of 'small nails'

– distribution and purpose of mid–plank clench nails

– sample any surviving fastenings

– position and gradients of plank scarfs

– lengths of individual planks

Framing

– are all floors and futtocks scarfed or are some connected by projecting dowels?

– ring/ray diagrams and other details of parent logs

– samples for dendrochronological examination

– are inboard ends of treenails wedged?

– are floors fastened to keel/keelson?

– evidence for any framing erected before planking?

Other fittings

– details of the following timbers, their scarfs and their fastenings: keel, keelson, mast–steps, stems, deadwoods, stringers, ceiling planking, knees, crossbeams and any other elements that survive

Ballast – details and sample.

Future work on the site

The indisputable importance of the remains of he R. Hamble ship to the history of European shipbuilding more than justifies its designation as an Historic Wreck. The minimum work to be done on site in the future is the regular monitoring of the visible remains to ensure that they are not deteriorating or sustaining damage. The major part of the site is exposed for only a few days each year, and the western part of the wreck including the presumed sternpost seldom, if ever, dries. The majority of the timbers in the intertidal zone are protected by silts: only 0.10 to 0.15 m of the framing projects above the the present riverbed and the planking is generally not visible. In the past few years, this natural protection has increased as soft mobile silts have extended from the eastern river bank out towards the mainstream channel (Clarke *et al.*, *IJNA* 22: figs 16 and 17). Only in one short section of the wreck – on the presumed port quarter of the vessel, by datum point J (Clarke *et al.*, *IJNA* 22: figs 16 and 17) – has the wreck been undercut by the river, and, on a recent inspection by the Heritage Department's Diving Unit, the depth of this undercutting appears to have been reduced by silting from *c.* 0.50 m to *c.* 0–32 m.

Should future monitoring reveal either deterioration of the visible timbers or reduction in the natural protection, corrective measures must be taken. The National Maritime Museum's experiments (Clarke *et al.*, *IJNA* 22: 37–43) did not conclusively demonstrate that protective sedimentation could be artificially induced and more research is required here to establish the best methods of protection (this point is returned to below, in the section on excavation). Deterioration of the timbers which could not be halted might necessitate excavation.

Apart from monitoring work, future research on site could take one of three forms which, in order of increasing intrusiveness, are: remote–sensing survey; partial excavation; or total excavation.

Remote–sensing survey

This would cause virtually no disturbance to the site and should be undertaken not only on the Designated Site but also on the site of the possible second wreck *c.* 60 m to the SSW (Clarke *et al*, *IJNA* 22: 24). The aim of such surveys would be to produce a plan and, if possible, profiles of the Designated Wreck and its detached timbers, and to determine whether more active intervention into the second site would be justified.

Excavation

Only the bottom part of the hull, a metre or so above the keel, now survives and it is doubtful if any contemporary artefacts are now associated with the wreck, apart from ballast. If the entire hull, as it is now, were to be excavated and lifted, the maximum historically–valuable information could be obtained and the displayed remains would be of great interest to maritime archaeologists and historians. Such a display would, on the other hand, have little attraction for the general public as the scant remains could give little idea of the original size and appearance of the ship. It is doubtful, therefore, whether the resources required to lift, conserve and display this wreck could be justified in terms of the enlightenment of non–specialists, nor could the research value by itself justify such a vast sum.

An alternative strategy would be to remove the overburden archaeologically from the wreck and to plan the site; trench and record under the wreck in selected places; lift selected parts of the structure; and finally backfill the site. In this way, the costs of lifting, conservation and display would be largely avoided yet near–maximum technological information about the wreck could be obtained. The only viable way to undertake such an area excavation would be within a cofferdam, excavating either in air or within filtered water, as suggested by Martin Dean (Clarke *et al.*, *IJNA* 22: 37). Public information displays about the wreck could include timbers lifted from the wreck and small–scale models of the hull structure based on the excavation findings.

A less ambitious plan would be to undertake limited excavation within trenches designed to throw light on specific problems. Many of the research questions posed above could be investigated by exploratory trenches along one side of the ship, a longitudinal trench along the middle–line and one or more transverse trenches. The most effective way of tackling this type of excavation would be to excavate when the site is under water and to survey as much as possible of the areas excavated, in air at low water. Selected parts of the structure could be lifted for detailed examination, dendrochronological dating and public display.

Whether to undertake a full area excavation or part–excavation by selected trenches can be determined by comparing the information which would probably be gained with the resources needed in both cases. It seems likely that, in absolute terms, more information would be gained by area excavation within a cofferdam, but this would also be the more expensive option. The precise trade–off between costs and information for each of these methods needs to be evaluated after wide discussions. The author's subjective assessment, at this time and for this particular wreck, is that the extra costs of cofferdam excavation would not be commensurate with the additional information gained. Selective trench excavation could, on the other hand, put us a long way towards the goal of fully understanding this wreck site, at a fraction of the cost.

Whether to excavate at all or to restrict future site activities to survey cannot be decided solely by the depth of one's purse and on a cost/benefit analysis. Or, more accurately, cost/benefit assessments must include consideration of how excavation will affect those remains which are not lifted. Any intrusive work on the site will in theory disturb the near–equilibrium state established between the ship and her environment. It must be acknowledged, however, that notwithstanding the action–packed excavations undertaken in 1933 and 1936 (Anderson, 1934a; 1938) the exposed timbers are still very sound judged both by visual examination and by moisture content and chemical analysis of samples (Clarke *et al.*, *IJNA* 22: 43).

Fewer timbers would be exposed for less time and thus be less likely to be degraded, if partial excavation of the wreck were to be undertaken rather than an area excavation. Furthermore, there would be less to backfill after excavation and it is the quality of backfilling that will determine the long–term future of the site. Only limited research into this problem has so far been undertaken and it does not seem possible in the present state of knowledge to recommend a best method. The Department of National Heritage and the equivalent bodies in Scotland and Wales are responsible for the implementation of the Protection of Wrecks Act, 1973 and their present policy is, quite rightly, directed towards protection from unauthorized excavation. In the longer term, many designated underwater sites are liable, by their very nature and by their position in high energy environments, to be threatened by degradation and deterioration due to natural forces, especially after excavations which have not included full recovery of the wreck structure.It would be most appropriate, therefore, for these heritage bodies to take the lead in tackling this problem and to sponsor research into the best methods of backfilling and protecting underwater sites.

Conclusion

Some information about medieval shipbuilding in northern Europe has been gained, over the years, from the important wreck site in the R. Hamble, but several fundamental questions remain unanswered. At present the remains are in a good condition and are reasonably well protected by the natural environment: it is essential that the regular monitoring of wreck and context should continue. Remote–sensing survey of this site and of the possible second wreck *c.* 60 m SSW (fig 9.1.1.) should also be undertaken when resources become available.

The University of Southampton now undertakes teaching and research in the field of maritime archaeology. Furthermore, the University owns the R. Hamble wreck and, in an exchange of letters with the Ministry of Defence on the occasion of the transfer to the University of the Crown's right, title and interest, the University agreed to 'use its best endeavour at all times as far as possible to protect and preserve this wreck' (MOD letters DC 22(1)51956/69 of 2 and 30 January 1970). It would thus be most appropriate for the University of Southampton to become licensee of the Designated Site and to undertake regular periodic monitoring. Remote–sensing surveys of the R. Hamble within, say, 100 m of the Designated Wreck should also be undertaken. In the medium term, the University should give serious consideration to a research orientated excavation and, after a cost–benefit analysis on the lines discussed above, should decide which method of excavation would give the best return of information, consistent with minimum hazarding of the remains.

A prerequisite of any such excavation must be the availability of proven methods of safely backfilling partly–excavated underwater sites. Research into these matters would be best co–ordinated by the Department of National Heritage, as the problem is potentially relevant to all designated underwater sites.

References

Åkerlund H 1951 *Fartygsfynen i den forna hammen i Kalmar* Stockholm.

Anderson R.C. 1934a 'Burlesdon ship.' *Mariner's Mirror* 20, 158–70.

Anderson R.C. 1934b 'Wreck in th R. Hamble.' *Antiquaries Journal* 14, 1–6.

Anderson R.C. 1938 'Burlesdon ship.' *Mariner's Mirror* 24, 112–13.

Brock E.P.L. 1876 'Discovery of an ancient warship near Botley.' *Journal of the British Archaeological Association* 32, 70–1.

Christensen A.E. 1985 'Boat finds from Bryggen.' *Bryggen Papers* 1, 47–278.

Crumlin–Pedersen O. 1991 'Ship types and sizes AD 800 to 1400.' *Aspects of Maritime Scandinavia AD 200 to 1200* edited by O. Crumlin–Pedersen, 69–82. Viking Ship Museum, Roskilde.

Ellmers D. 1979 'Cog of Bremen and related boats.' *Medieval Ships and Harbours in N Europe* edited by S. McGrail 1–15. BAR Oxford S66.

Ewe H. 1972 *Shiffe auf siegeln*. Rostock

Greenhill B. 1976 *Archaeology of the Boat* London

Greenhill B. 1988 *Evolution of the Wooden Ship*. London.

L'Hour M. and Veyrat E. 1989 'Mid–15th century clinker boat off the north coast of France, the Aber Wrac'h wreck.' *IJNA* 18, 285–98.

McGrail S. 1981 *Rafts, Boats and Ships*. HMSO.

McGrail S. 1987 *Ancient Boats in NW Europe*. London.

McGrail S. forthcoming *Medieval Boat and Ship Timbers from Dublin*. Royal Irish Academy, Dublin.

Marsden P. forthcoming *ancient Shipping of the Port of London*. English Heritage.

Martinez–Hidalgo J.M. 1966 *Columbus' ships*. Barre, Massachusetts.

Milne G and Hobley B. 1981 *Waterfront Archaeology in Britain and N Europe*. CBA Research Report 41.

Prynne M.W. 1938 'Medieval man–of–war.' *Royal Engineers' Journal* 52, 273–88.

Prynne M.W. 1968 'Henry V's *Grace Dieu*.' *Mariner's Mirror* 54, 115–28.

Prynne M. 1973 'Some general considerations applying to the examination of the remains of old ships.' *IJNA* 2, 227–33.

Prynne M. 1976 'Cawfott–nails and Calafati.' *Mariner's Mirror* 61, 289–90.

Reprinted with permission from:

International Journal for Nautical Archaeology, 22: 45–51. (1993).

PAPER 9.2

THE BOATS AND SHIPS OF TENTH TO THIRTEENTH CENTURY DUBLIN

Dublin as a port

The boats and ships timbers from medieval Dublin range in date from the early tenth century (the High Street and Fishamble Street sites) to the mid–thirteenth century (the Wood Quay site). Dublin had been founded in the mid–ninth century as a Viking settlement on high ground to the west of the confluence of the R. Poddle with the R. Liffey, and separated from the latter by an intertidal zone of mainly salt–marsh (Mitchell 1987). By the early tenth century it had become an important commercial centre, especially in the overseas trade with Bristol (Sherborne 1965), Chester and certain Welsh ports.

The earliest post–Roman harbours in north–west Europe with waterfront structures alongside which vessels could berth were built in the ninth century (Hodges 1982, 97–8; McGrail 1981c; 1985). These early formal harbours were few in number, however, and there are no special reasons for thinking that Dublin was in the forefront of such developments: it is more likely that Dublin, like her main trading partners in Britain and Scandinavia, continued to use informal landing places in the ninth century and for some centuries afterwards. The environmental evidence (Mitchell 1987) and such archaeological evidence as there is suggest that boats and ships arriving in and working out of Dublin in the tenth and eleventh centuries used a natural harbour or haven out of the main stream, in the R. Poddle to the east of the Viking town (Fig. 9.2.1) These vessels would have anchored in this *dubh linn* or 'black pool' ('black' because of its relative depth?), or they would have been beached on an adjacent strand, below the eastern end of the 18m (50ft) ridge on which Dublin Castle now stands, by taking the ground on a falling tide. Beach operations are not limited to small boats (Fig 2.1.8; McGrail 1987, 267), and ships of the size known to have been used in the tenth and eleventh centuries could have been readily operated from firm beaches or from man–made hards built upon soft mud on the margins of the Poddle natural harbour. Vessels at anchor in the pool could have been unloaded into smaller craft or possibly into horse–drawn carts or onto pack animals (Ellmers 1985).

Wallace (1981) has described the tenth– and eleventh–century embankment of the R. Liffey, first by three successive clay banks with post and–wattle structures, and then, *c* 1 1 00, by a stone wall (Fig 9.2.2). These were erected to constrain the river and prevent flooding, to allow the town to expand to the north, and to provide town defences, and should not be seen as waterfronts against which ships could berth.

The twelfth century was to bring change. The invasion in 1169/1170 led by the Norman Richard de Clare (Strongbow) was the first direct English intrusion into Irish affairs and abruptly altered the political and social scene in the south and east of Ireland. As a result, Hiberno–Norse (i.e. post–Viking) Dublin became Anglo–Norman Dublin: In a charter of 1171–2, Henry II granted the city to the 'men of Bristol', and the Hiberno–Norse were banished to Oxmanstown, to the north of the R. Liffey (Wallace 1987, 281).

In 1192 Prince John confirmed the 1171–2 charter and encouraged the citizens of Dublin to take in more land from the intertidal salt–marsh north of the city. Further permission for expansion was given in 1202 (Wallace 1981, 113–14). The archaeological reality, corresponding to these pronouncements is a fourth wattle–and–daub bank of *c.*1200, followed from *c.*1210 by a succession of four wooden revetments (Fig. 9.2.2); ship timbers (TG3) were incorporated into the second of these (no. 1A). The first three revetments (1, 1A and 2) were all front–braced and unlikely to have been designed as wharfs. With the back–braced fourth revetfnent (no. 3), dated to the late thirteenth century, the possibility arises that ships in the R. Liffey mav have been able to berth alongside. This possibi)ity becomes more likely with the building of the stone quay waterfront in *c.* 1300 or in the first decade of the fourteenth century (Wallace 1981, 114–16). It may also have been at this time that a slipway for fishing boats (*fyssche slyppe*) was built near the northern end of what is now Fishamble Street (Wallace 1981, 116). Other vessels may have been berthed on the foreshore of the R. Liffey to the west of what is now Wood Quay, which formerly had the placename *Strand* (Fig. 9.2.1B).

In the wake of these significant chages in political allegiance, in the size of Dublin and in civic engineering projects came a general increase in overseas trading and intensification of the trade with Britain (Sherborne 1965) and with France from Rouen to Bayonne (Doherty 1980). Seafaring became of such importance to Dublin that when King John authorised the mayor and city council to have a common seal in 1229 they chose to depict a ship on the obverse (Strickland 1923; Fig. 9.2.3).

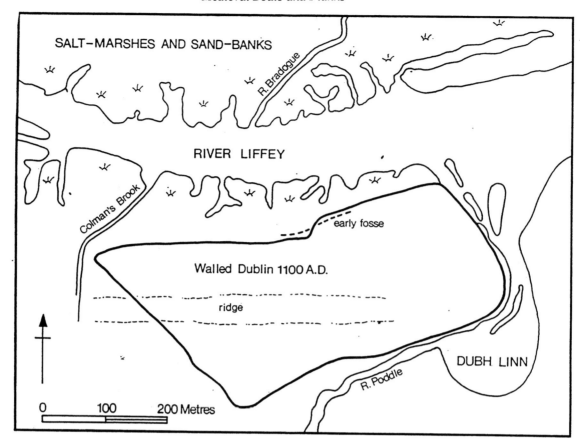

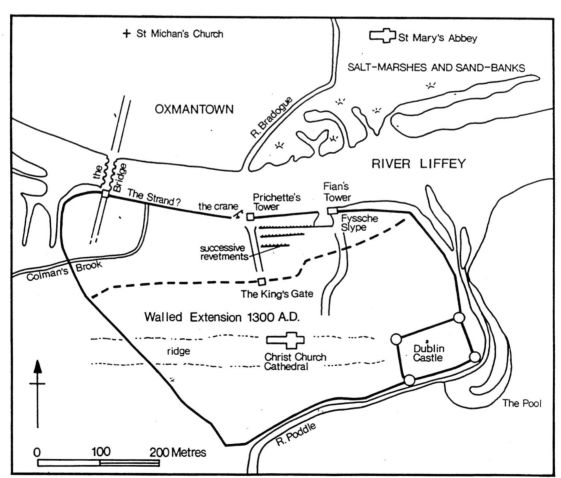

Figure 9.2.1   A. Conjectural map of Dublin *c* 1100 (after Mitchell 1987, fig. 2a, and maps published by the Ordnance Survey, 1977 and 1978)

B. Conjectural map of Dublin *c* 1300 (after Mitchell 1987, fig. 2b, and maps published by the Ordnance Survey, 1977 and 1978)

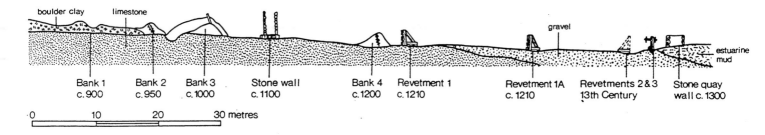

Figure 9.2.2 Schematic section of Dublin's waterfront, 900–1300 (after Wallace 1981, fig. 107)

Two questions arise from a consideration of these events: after the Anglo–Norman take–over, was there a change in the type and build of the vessels using the port of Dublin, and was there a change in the methods of berthing these vessels? To answer these questions it is necessary first to compare the Dublin boats and ships with those known elsewhere in north–west Europe in the Viking Age and later, and secondly to consider whether the types of vessel using Dublin in the late twelfth and thirteenth centuries would have necessitated a change from an informal harbour or haven to one with formal structures. A supplementary question must first be tackled: were the parent boats and ships of the Dublin timbers in the mainstream of the Viking/Norse tradition or were they a regional variant?

Viking Age

The characteristic attributes of the (mainstream) Viking tradition of boat and shipbuilding in the tenth and eleventh centuries may be summarised under four main headings: selection and conversion of timber; form; structure; and propulsion and steering. The evidence is drawn mainly from Olsen and Crumlin–Pedersen 1967; Nicolaysen 1882; Christensen 1959; 1968b; 1972; and Crumlin–Pedersen 1981; 1983b; 1986a; 1986b.

Selection and conversion of timber. Oak (*Quercus* sp.) was used whenever it was available; where it was not, as in most of Norway, pine (*Pinus* sp.) was used. Pine and ash (*Fraxinus* sp.) were also used for planking even though oak was available, when particular lengths and breadths were required. The timber was chosen to match the job in hand; for example, logs and limbs with curving grain, or natural crooks, were chosen for curved structural elements. Oak logs were converted into planking by splitting them into half then half again, and so on, to produce radial planks. Pine logs were converted into planks from half–logs. Keels, stems, framing timbers and so on were obtained by reducing a log or a half–log to the required shape following the natural run of the grain wherever possible.

Form. Viking Age vessels had (near) symmetrical ends ('double–ended') in plan, elevation and section, with a post at bow and stern. In longitudinal section, there was a smooth transition between keel and stem, and a distinctive sheerline, curving upwards to high ends. In transverse section these vessels had a generally rounded bottom with flared sides.

Structure (Fig 9.2.4). These vessels were essentially 'open boats'. They were built in the shell sequence–planking before framing (Fig. 9.2.5). Strakes, consisting of several relatively thin planks joined in vertical scarfs, were laid overlapping in clinker fashion and fastened by iron nails clenched by deforming the point over a rove (Fig.9.2.6). The scarf between keel and stems was a vertical one similar in form to the plank scarfs. The floor timbers were symmetrically placed about the middle line of the vessel and were spaced more or less evenly throughout the length, with bulkheads near the ends. Above each floor timber were crossbeams and knees, and the hull was further reinforced by stringers and by side timbers. Framing timbers were fastened to the planking by treenails, wedged inboard.

Propulsion and steering. Oars in boats were used against tholes to which they were loosely connected by grommets. In large boats and in oared ships oars were pivoted through oarports in one of the upper strakes. The style of rowing in boats was two oars/sit/pull (McGrail and Farrell 1979): that is each man pulled two oars from a sitting position. In fighting ships such as Skuldelev 2, each man pulled one oar from a sitting position. Oars in the ends were also used for manoeuvring in some cargo vessels – large boats such as Skuldelev 3 (Fig 9.2.4) and small ships such as Skuldelev 1 – and the rowing style used here was probably similar to that used in fighting ships. Large boats and ships were propelled by a loose–footed single square sail set on a pole mast stepped near midship. The aspect ratio of the sail is uncertain but was probably *c*.1, i.e. the sail was as broad as it was deep. Details of the standing and running rigging are also not clear but the simple rig shown in Fig. 9.2.4 seems to be the most likely. Small oared boats probably had no rudder, but large boats and ships were steered by a side rudder, generally fitted to the

Figure 9.2.3 The thirteenth–century seal of Dublin (see Brindley 1913 and Strickland 1923). Photo: National Museum of Ireland

starboard quarter, which was rotated around a boss projecting from the ship's side.

Variants

Crumlin–Pedersen (1969; 1983a; 1984; 1988) has demonstrated that there was probably an eastern Baltic or Slav variant tradition, differing in some details from the mainstream tradition: the clinker planking was fastened by small treenails (Fig. 9.2.7) rather than clenched iron nails, and the caulking was of moss rather than animal hair. It also seems that masts in vessels of this regional tradition were stepped in a transverse floor timber rather than in a longitudinal keelson, and that keels had a cross–section with a low (M/S) ratio, i.e. they were broader than they were high. Several of the vessels thought to be of this regional tradition are neither well recorded nor well published and thus, although there does seem to have been a variant tradition in the eastern Baltic, more evidence is required before the diagnostic features can be defined with certainty. Others have argued that there was a distinctive form of boatbuilding in southern England, extending from the ninth to the fourteenth century, which can be distinguished from the generality of boats and ships in the Viking tradition (Fenwick 1978; Cameron 1982; Goodburn 1986). Some of the features of the ninth/tenth–century Graveney boat (Fenwick 1978) are certainly different from corresponding features in the mainstream Viking tradition: the general shape; the keel's cross–section; the heavy, closely spaced floor timbers; the apparent absence of crossbeams; and the form of the sternpost with its pronounced heel. However, most, if not all, of these differences seem to suggest a specialised function and a specialised operating environment: a local modification to the mainstream Viking tradition rather than a distinctive and separate tradition.

Post–Viking traditions

Crumlin–Pedersen (1978) has identified three main traditions of sea–going vessels in post–Viking north–west Europe: the Norse ship, the cog, and the *hulc* (Fig 2.1.2). The second and third of these traditions are of very limited use in this study of the medieval Dublin ships and boats as only two timbers may

have come from such vessels. Descriptions of cog and *hulc* characteristics may be found in McGrail (1981a, 36–40), Crumlin–Pedersen (1965; 1979b; 1983b; 1984), Ellmers (1972; 1976; 1979), Greenhill (1976; 1989) and Hoekstra (1975).

The Norse tradition of shipbuilding, as discussed here, is considered to be the continuation into post–Viking times (twelfth to fourteenth century) of the Viking tradition: it is the evolution of one tradition over time. The evidence comes from representational evidence such as murals in the thirteenth–century church at Sikjon, Telemark, Norway, and fourteenth–century ones at Skamstrup, Zealand, Denmark (Crumlin–Pedersen 1983b), and twelfth– to fourteenth–century town seals from Ireland, England and France (see, for example, Fig 9.2.3), and from several ship finds typified by the mid–twelfth century Lynaes ship (Crumlin–Pedersen 1979a; 1981; 1983a; 1984; 1986a). The medieval English word for this sort of cargo ship appears to have been *ceol* or *keel* (McCusker 1966, 288–9).

The largest Norse vessels were bigger than their Viking predecessors, as evidenced by the ability to carry a boat on board (thirteenth–century Sandwich seal) and by the use of a windlass to weigh anchor (thirteenth–century Winchelsea and Pevensey seals) and to hoist and lower the yard, but they appear to have retained the general shape of the Viking Age ship (Ewe 1972). Certain changes in structure can be deduced from the iconographic evidence: for example, the addition of castles forward and aft (twelfth–century seal of Dunwich, thirteenth–century seals of Dublin (Fig 9.2.3) and Winchelsea; and crossbeams which protruded through the sides (thirteenth–century Winchelsea). There is also documentary evidence for the use of mast crutches or mykes. The Lynaes ship has, to date, been published only in an abbreviated form, but from published cross–sections it can be seen that floor timbers, which in the Viking Age had extended over the breadth of the bottom from bilge to bilge, were replaced by two timbers: a short floor timber over which was a much longer timber (*bitte*), which combined the functions of a lower

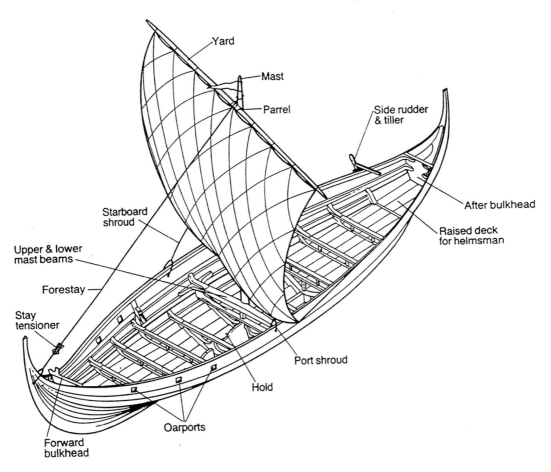

Figure 9.2.4 Reconstruction drawing of Skuledev 3. After Crumlin–Pedersen

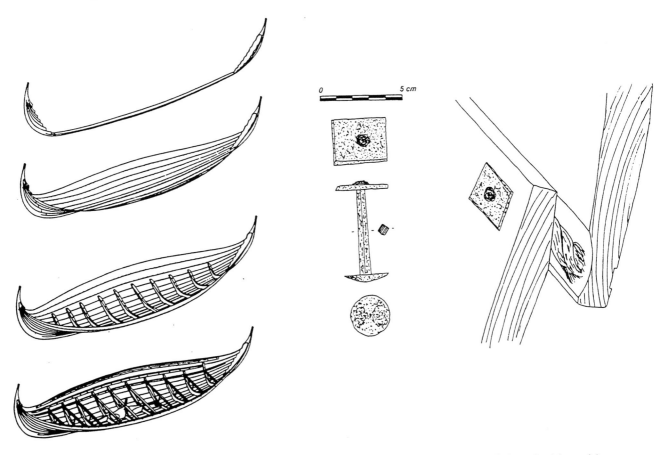

Figure 9.2.5 Shell–first or plank–before–framing method of boatbuilding. After Crumlin-Pedersen

Figure 9.2.6 Method of fastening clinker planking with clenched nails. After Christensen

243

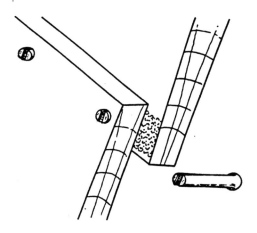

Figure 9.2.7 Clinker planking fastened by treenails (after Crumlin–Pedersen 1988, fig. 21)

crossbeam and two side timbers. The ships depicted on the thirteenth–century Winchelsea seal and on an early fourteenth–century seal of Poole, and several others (Ewe 1972), appear to be decked so that the crew could eat, sleep and shelter below decks. The Lynaes ship had sufficient height of sides (2.5m amidships) for her also to have been decked, although Crumlin–Pedersen (pers. comm.) believes her to have been open with only half–decks fore and aft.

Although there were evidently significant advances in rigging, a single square sail remained standard until topsails were set in the late fourteenth century (Sandahl 1958): a second mast does not seem to have appeared in north–west Europe until the early fifteenth century (Friel 1983). Bowlines may be seen on the seal of Yarmouth (1300), and bowsprits are on this seal and on the thirteenth–century seal of Poole – both are important when sailing close–hauled. The area of usable sail may be varied by reefing and unreefing, and reef points are seen on the thirteenth–century seals of Dublin (Fig 9.2.3) and Bergen, and on the fourteenth–century seal of Rye (Ewe 1972).

The single side rudder, but of greater size, seems to have continued in use on the Norse ship until the early fourteenth century when the 1325 seal of Poole depicts a centre–line rudder. The earliest appearance of this type of rudder is in fact on the late twelfth–century fonts at Winchester and Zedelgem near Bruges, but these vessels appear to be in the *hulc* tradition. As the early fourteenth–century seals of Faversham and Winchelsea depict ships with side rudders it may be that the median rudder on the Poole seal was rare and that the side rudder continued in general use on Norse ships until they were superseded by the *cog* and the *hulk*.

Shipbuilding in Dublin

Before reviewing the evidence from the Dublin ship and boat timbers and comparing it with the Viking and Norse evidence described above, it is first necessary to establish whether these timbers came from boats and ships built in Dublin. This is a widespread problem in maritime archaeology, for ships are designed to travel and may be wrecked or dismantled and reused many miles from their port of origin. Furthermore, although most *boats* may spend their whole lives within a few miles of where they were built, medieval ships sometimes towed or carried boats on board on overseas voyages, and thus boats too may enter the archaeologicai record far from their home base as Crumlin–Pedersen (1985) has pointed out. Notwithstanding these undoubted difficulties, it seems reasonably certain that the great majority of the Dublin timbers were parts of boats and ships built in the Dublin region: there is both: direct and indirect evidence to support this contention.

The direct evidence is that the dendrochronological pattern of samples from TG9C/D best match the Dublin master chronology (Baillie 1978; 1982, 239). Thus the large ship represented by TG9C/D must have been built from oak grown in the Dublin region and it seems highly likely that she was built in this region, if not in Dublin itself. The planking in TG9A and 9B has similar features to TG9C and 9D and is complementary in shape, and thus must have come from the same ship; there is a strong possibility that TG6 is also from this one large ship.

The late eleventh–century warship Skuldelev 2 was also built of oak from the Dublin region (Bonde and Crumlin–Pedersen 1990), and it seems more likely that she was built here than that she was built in Denmark of oak imported from Ireland (although this must remain a theoretical possibility).

Furthermore, there is documentary evidence that ships were built in Dublin in the early thirteenth century: in 1222 Henry III ordered the men of Dublin (and of Waterford, Drogheda and Limerick) to build galleys (PRO 1875, Calendar of Documents relating to Ireland – G. D. Kelleher, pers. comm.); and in 1233, and again in 1241, the men of Dublin were told to build and maintain a great galley (*magna galia*) for the king's service (Strickland 1923; Wallace 1981; Murphy 1974).

This evidence for shipbuilding in or close to Dublin in the eleventh and the thirteenth centuries reinforces the argument that the ship represented by TG9 planking was built there in the late twelfth century. This argument cannot.be directly extended to the ships and boats represented by timbers other than those in TG9 and TG6; nevertheless. on balance, it seems reasonable to conclude that the majority of the Dublin timbers were from boats and ships dismantled and reused close to the site where they were built. The fact that certain timbers were unfinished, having no fastening holes (e. g. T366), further supports the argument for a boat – and shipbuilding 'yard' in medieval Dublin.

The dismantling of these ships and boats must have taken place in Dublin, and was probably undertaken by shipwrights who would have the skills and the tools to dismantle them in a way that would economically produce reusable timbers rather than just firewood: see Lundstrom (1971/2) for an example of a specialist tool required to remove clenched nails (McGrail 1987, 158–9). Moreover, there is evidence in the Dublin ships themselves that timbers from other dismantled ships had been used to build them Furthermore, several of these Dublin timbers may have had an intermediate use between being part of a ship and becoming part of a waterfront: see the catalogue entries for T54, T55, T292 and T293. The predecessors of these Dublin shipwrights who dismantled boats and ships in the early thirteenth century could have built them in the late twelfth century.

Boats, and indeed small ships, can be built on a site with very little infrastructure, possibly only some simple stocks (baulks of timber) temporarily set up in a cleared area on or near the shore (McGrail 1981c; 1983; 1985). The evidence for this activity that would remain to be excavated would thus be minimal. On the other hand, the large ships for which there is evidence in Dublin would require more complex and possibly more permanent stocks and other facilities, parts of which might be recognisable on excavation. In addition to woodworking and metalworking tools, there could be wood, metal, tar and cattle hair, and rope waste. The only example of such finds from recent Dublin excavations (apart from tools) is a pot sherd, associated with TG3.2/3.3, which had a tarry deposit on its inner face. On examination, the deposit proved to be wood tar with rosin, which was shown by gas liquid chromatography (BM 6170/1) to be similar to the tar used in the caulking in TG3 seams. Some future excavations below Dublin Castle near the margins of the 'black pool', or near the former strand to the west of Wood Quay (Fig. 9.2.1B), might reveal more substantial evidence for shipbuilding.

The characteristic features of the Dublin timbers

Selection of timber

The Dublin timbers, including the treenail wedges, are almost all of oak (*Quercus* sp.); the exceptions are two, possibly three, planks of pine (*Pinus* sp.) (T340, T341, and possibly T387); one knee/breasthook (T366), which has been tentatively identified as of alder (*Alnus* sp.); one treenail of holly (*Ilex* sp.) in the possible mast step (T54), but this was probably fitted during an intermediate use of this timber (all other treenails examined were of willow (*Salix* sp.)); the yew (*Taxus* sp.) rope (T362); and plugs of birch (*Betula* sp.) in former nail holes in plank T93.

Figure 9.2.8 The parent trees of straight and curved timbers. Drawing: Insititute of Archaeology, Oxford

The trees selected for the keels, most of the planking and the flattest of the floors were all straight–grained, relatively slow–grown oaks with few knots: these must have been forest–grown, where competition would have resulted in long straight boles. Relatively fast–grown oak (that is, where the growth ring breadths exceed 3mm) was only found in parrel rib T220, the possible cleat T363, the stem T364 and frame T368. Spiral grain, which can be difficult to work, was found in the possible mast step T54 and side timber T274.

The evidence for size of parent tree may well be biased as some of the fragmented and broken timbers were originally longer and broader than when measured. From surviving evidence, however, it appears that none of the keels came from an exceptionally tall tree, and the parent trees of the largest oak planks, T282 and T288, need have been only 6m and 5m in length of bole. The largest pine bole, the parent of plank T340, was at least 6m in length. The largest oaks would have had a girth in the range 3.14–4.29m (1–1.36m in diameter), whilst the largest pine would have been 1m in girth a (0.32m in diameter) or greater. The largest floor timber (T55) came from a tree of relatively small girth (possibly 1.57m), as did the keels.

The parent trees of other timbers were evidently chosen not so much for length or breadth as for a natural curvature or some other characteristic which matched the job in hand. Thus bulkheads (T187, T351), knees (T218, T352 and T380), floors (T368 and T372), the possible beam with knee (T225). *mykes* (T51 and T58), breasthooks (T366 and T367), parrels (T356 and T360). and stems (T52, T224 and T364) were fashioned from 'crooks' (curved limbs) or from a natural fork, or from the junction of bole and stem (Fig. 9.2.8). Furthermore, the curving ends of strakes, both single planks, as in Timber Groups 6, 9B and 9C/D, or as multiple end planks (T219, T279, T353, T359, T384, T392), had a natural run of grain which generally matched their curvature: in this way maximum strength was obtained. Some of the shapes required could have come from forks in forest–grown oaks, but the more curved shapes would have been more readily found in fringe or isolated oaks. Available timber did not always entirely match the required curvature and some timbers were worked across the grain, as can be seen on, for example, the large floor T55, where the very ends had begun to split where they had been worked across the grain, and on floor timbers T222 and T368, which had broken along the cross–grain line. Stems T357 and T53 similarly had some short grain, as did the mykes T51 and T58.

Conversion of timber

It seems likely, but cannot be demonstrated, that the Dublin timbers were converted to shape soon after their parent logs were felled; that is, they were worked 'green' (McGrail 1987, 27–8). Sapwood was found on one plank and may have been present, though undetected, on others. Sapwood, and occasionally bark, was also found on some non–plank timbers where a particular dimension was required, often on a curve. These included knees T218 (and bark), T268, T378 (and bark), and T380 (and bark): breasthooks T366 (and bark) and T367; *mykes* T51 and T58; parrels T356 and T360; frame T372; and possible mast step T54. On Skuldelev 3 Crumlin Pedersen (1986b, 139) found sapwood only on the very tip of the stem; bark was found on elements of the fourteenth–century Vejby cog (*ibid.*, 147).

The Dublin oak planking, stems (T52, T224 and T364) and treenail wedges and the willow treenails were all fashioned from radial segments of their parent logs or limbs. In theory, 32 radial planks might be obtained from a single log: in practical trials Crumlin–Pedersen (1986b) has found sixteen to be the maximum. The remaining Dublin timbers were worked either from whole logs, limbs or crooks (that is, the pith was still visible in the finished timber), or they were worked from a log which had first been split into halves or even into quarters. Examples of these categories include:

whole logs, limbs, crooks: floor T55; light frame T372; keels T56, T361 and T381; knee T218; breasthook T366; parrels T356 and T360; and the possible beam with knee T225;

half–logs: floors T275, T278, T280 and T379; keel T382; knee T352; side timber T274; stem T53; and pine planking T340, T341 and T387;

quarter–logs: possible mast step T54; and the possible stem T224.

Framing timbers T368 and T379, bulkhead T351, breasthook T367 and *myke* T58 all now show a half–log in their cross–section, and *myke* T51 shows a near–quarter–log. Whether large forked timbers or crooks can be successfully the split into halves and indeed into quarters to produce such timbers has not been reported in any published boatbuilding

experiment: the alternative of possibility is that they were worked down from a whole crook or fork.

Crumlin–Pedersen (1986b, 139) has estimated that, in Skuldelev 3, 52% of the timbers (by number) were radially split planks, 24% were fashioned from a whole log, 8% from a half–log and 16% from a quarter–log. As no Dublin boat or ship can be fully reconstructed, comparable data are not available.

Oak planking was fashioned from radial segments because oak readily splits along the line of the rays and because oaks grow to such a size that reasonable breadths of planking can be obtained even from one–third of the diameter. Moreover, oak boards which are split radially are not only stronger but have fewer knots, and when drying out from the green state they are more stable, shrink less in breadth and are not so liable to warp, check or split; in addition, they are more resistant to fungal infection than tangentially converted boards. Furthermore, such clove boards have two distinct advantages when used in clinker planking: (a) thickness changes in reaction to changing relative humidity, although greater as a percentage than shrinkage in breadth, are small in absolute terms and are cushioned by the caulking and resisted by the clenched nails; (b) these nails are driven into a radially converted plank at right angles to the plane of weakness, whereas nails in a tangentially orientated plank would be driven parallel to this radial plane and thus have a greater tendency to split the plank (McGrail 1987, 28–32).

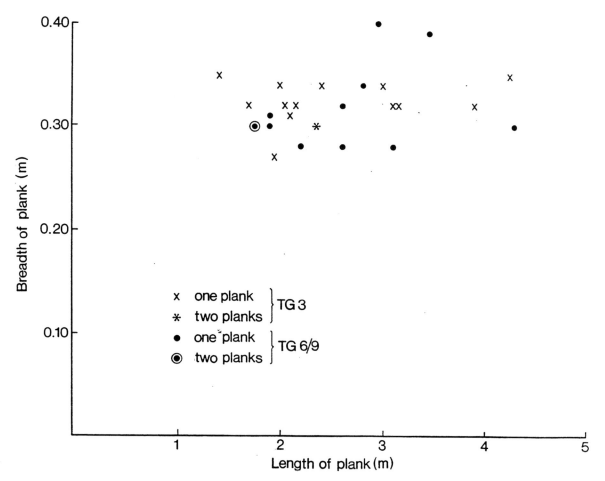

Figure 9.2.9 Graph showing the relationship of plank length to plank breadth in Dublin TG3 and TG6/9. Drawing: Institute of Archaeology, Oxford

Figure 9.2.6 is a plot of length against breadth of those individual planks TG3, 6 and 9 which were undamaged, whilst Fig. 9.2.7 is a similar plot for the radially split oak planking from Skuldelev 3 (Crumlin–Pedersen 1986a, 220, fig. 11; 1986b, 146, fig. 7). Crumlin–Pedersen suggests that the Skuldelev distribution shows that three distinct logs were used for this planking (1986a, 220) although this hypothesis does not yet appear to have been confirmed by dendrological examination. No such clear pattern emerges from the Dublin data for any one of the Timber Groups, probably because there are relatively few points in the plot.

The mean and standard deviation data are not available for the Skuldelev3 planking, nor for that of Lynaes, and so the Dublin planking is best compared with them by giving the range of lengths and breadths, as shown in Table 9.2.1.

Most of the Dublin oak planks were worked to a lenticular shape in cross–section, but the waterline strakes in TG6/9 were given a bulging cross–section over the central part of the ship, directly comparable with similarly placed planking in the Lynaes ship and also with certain planks from Bergen (Christenden 1985, 112, fig. 6.19).

Pine planks were used widely in regions where oak was not readily available, for example in medieval Norway, and also elsewhere when breadth, length and relative lightness of plank was required, as for example in the top strakes of small boats, as in TG10. Furthermore, the natural plane of cleavage of pine is across the diameter, resulting in two planks from each bole.

Table 9.2.1 Sizes of oak planks from Skuldelev 3, Lynaes and Dublin TG3 and TG6/9 (Crumlin–Pedersen 1986a; 1986b)

	Date	*Length (m)*	*Breadth (m)*
Skuldelev 3	Early eleventh century	2.5–5.5	0.25–0.36
Lynaes	Mid–twelfth century	1.5–4.5	0.18–0.30
TG6 and TG9	1180–1225	1.7–4.3	0.21–0.41
TG3	1230–75	1.4–4.2	0.28–0.36

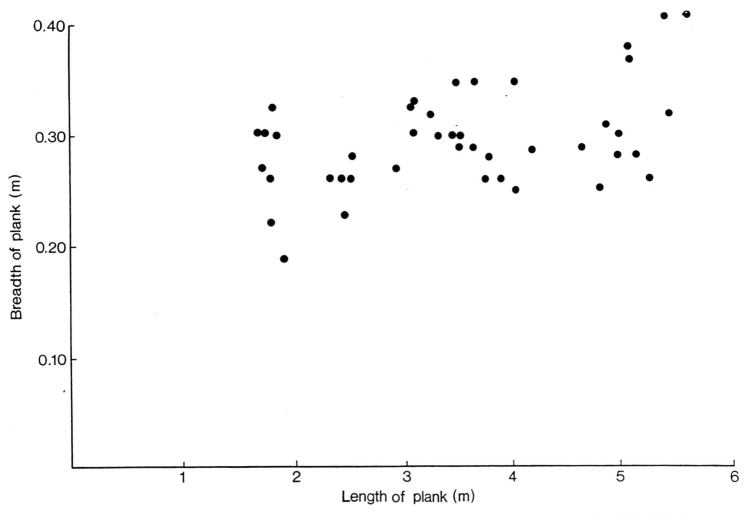

Figure 9.2.10 Graph showing the relationship of plank length to plank breadth in a hypothetical reconstruction of Skuledev 3 as built (after Crumlin–Pedersen 1986a, fig. 11)

For the non–plank timbers there is no comparable division by type, for framing timbers and keels were fashioned from whole (T55, T56, T361, T372, T381) or half–logs (T275, T278, T280, T368, T379, T382). Tha aim of the medieval shipbuilder was to select the log, limb or crook most appropriate to the form of timber required and then work away excess timber so that the necessary strength was there without excess mass: the first stage in this reduction process must often have been to split the log (or limb or crook if this is indeed practicable) logitudinally into two halves.

Joints

apart from a morticed joint in the stock of rudder T369, the only woodworking joints in the Dublin timbers, as in Norse shuipbuilding in general, were scarfs and bevelled overlaps. Caulking of tarred animals hair was found in all these joints.

Scarfs

Scarfs were found in two places: where individual planks were extended to form strakes, and where keels were joined to stems, either directly or through an intermediate timber. There were two types of plank scarf: short scarfs with gradients in the range of 21–37% found in the late eleventh–century boat planking, and longer scarfs in the ship planking of the late twelfth/early thirteenth century with gradients between 8% and 17%. The keel/stem scarf evidence is not so impressive or clear owing to ends missing from both keels and stems and to distortion, the sum total being: T56, from a ship or large ship of *c.* 1180–1225, gradients of 40% amd 46%; T381, a keel with a notched scarf, from a large boat of *c.* 995–1000, 23%; and T357, a stem from an eleventh/twelfth–century boat similar to the Gokstad *faering*, 39%. Thus, although boat keel T381 has a shortish scarf similar to those in its contemporary boat planking, ship keel T56 and boat stem T357 have very short scarfs in contradistinction to their near–contemporary ship planking. In comparison the plank scarfs of the eleventh–century Skuldelev boats are all short ones in the range 25–35%, whilst keel/stem scarfs are in the range 17–62% for boats 1 and 5 (Olsen and Crumlin–Pedersen 1967). These are all relatively short, as are the keel/stem scarfs of ninth–century Gokstad and Oseberg ships and boats and fifteenth–century Bergen stem B92384. The unusual scarfs are thus the long ones in the Dublin ship planking, for which there are, as yet, no published parallels from medieval times, although there are parallels from recent boatbuilding – twentieth–century woodworkers are recommended to use long scarfs of 8–14% gradient (McGrail 1987, 115).

Bevelled overlaps.

Bevelled overlaps were used to join together strakes at the seams and the garboard strake to the keel; they were also found, usually as back bevels, where the ends of strakes were joined to stems. The strake overlaps are discussed in detail above: in general the hood ends of strakes have not survived in sufficiently good condition for details to be recorded, but there are specially shaped ends to the strakes of TG9B and 9C/D.

Fastenings

Iron nails. These were used as fastenings in three ways in the Dublin timbers

(a)   clenched over roves: in the strake seams; at the head of framing timbers in the boat represented by TG10 timbers; to reinforce a potential split in such timbers as stem T53 and parrel T356; and in some plank repair patches (Fig. 9.3.1);

(b)   clenched by turning through 90°: in some plank repair patches;

(c)   spikes: in some plank repairs; to reinforce a plank scarf T86/T88; and in some plank fastenings to keels and stems where it was not possible to clench–fasten because of the thickness of the timber (T56, T52, T53).

These nails were all dome–headed; most shanks were round in section but, in special circumstances, nails with rectangular shanks were used. The special nails with points under their heads in the planking of TG9 are discussed above. Roves were four–sided, generally diamond– shaped.

There were two main sizes of nails.

(a)   Larger ones: heads 30–40mm, shanks 9–12mm, and roves *c.*30–50mm. These were used to fasten the majority of ship planking at the seams and to fasten breasthook T367 to the planking.

(b)   Smaller ones: heads 16–21mm, shanks 6–8mm, and roves *c.*20–25mm. These were used to fasten the boat planking in TG10, to fasten end planking of ships and boats to stems, to fasten bulkheads T351 and probably T187 to boat planking, and probably to fasten garboard strakes to keels of boats and ships (T56, T361, T381–3).

Treenails. These were all of willow (*Salix* sp.) with oak wedges. They were used to fasten framing timbers to the planking in boats and ships, and thole stringers to the boat planking in TG10. Exceptionally, they appear to have been used to fasten multiple end plank T279 to adjacent planking. It is also possible that they were used to fasten rigging fittings to planking (T107, T229/230, T310, T340, T341).
There were two sizes of treenail.

(a) Larger ones: heads *c.*40mm and shanks 28–38mm. These were used to fasten fittings to ship planking in TG3, TG6 and TG9. Fittings with holes for such treenails include floor timbers T55, T222, T277, T278 and T280: side timbers T274, T289, and T290; knee T352; and the possible cleat T363.

(b) Smaller ones: heads *c.*28mm and shanks 18–25mm. These were used to fasten fittings to the boat planking in TG10, T1–23, T147, T255–6, T264–6, and T387. Fittings with them include bulkhead T187; floor timbers T275, T372 and T379; knee T378; and multiple end plank T279. A Dublin timber of doubtful function, T221, has holes 29mm and 39mm in diameter. The possibility that this might be a treenail gauge is slightly strengthened as these sizes correspond to the upper and lower limits for the larger treenails. On the other hand, this may just reflect the fact that similar tools were used to bore treenail holes in this timber as were used in many other Dublin timbers.

Framing patterns
Framing patterns may be summarised as follows.

(i) **TG10, a late eleventh–century boat**. Framing timbers of c.60mm siding were spaced at intervals of 0.98 ± 0.09m (*n* = 6). These framing timbers were probably floor timbers, knees and crossbeams (thwarts), with semi–bulkheads at the ends, similar to the arrangements in Gokstad 2, the *seksaering*

(ii) **TG9, a late twelfth–century large ship**. Framing timbers of 0.14–0.22m siding were spaced at intervals of 0.48–0.61m towards the ends. In the midship region there were framing timbers of 0.2m siding spaced at intervals of 0.41m. These framing timbers may have consisted of floor timbers plus knees with side timbers on the upper planking in between the floors, as in the Skuldelev finds, but it seems more likely that there were floor timbers and knees at every station (without side timbers), similar to the arrangements thought to have been in the Lynaes ship. Whatever the arrangements, it seems likely that, although there were probably regularly spaced crossbeams in the ends, there were few if any crossbeams in the region of the hold.

(iii) **TG6, a late twelfth–century large ship**, possibly the same one as TG9. Framing timbers of 0.14–0.22m siding were spaced at intervals of 0.41–0.67m towards the bow. The framing arrangements were probably as in TG9.

(iv) **TG3, a large ship of the thirteenth century**. Framing timbers of 0.18–0.22m siding were spaced at intervals of 0.52–0.62m over the midship region. These framing timbers were probably similar to those in the Lynaes ship. There would have been few crossbeams in the region of the hold.

Apart from the lowest two strakes surviving in TG3, all strakes in these timber groups have gaps in what would otherwise be a regular treenailing pattern: that is, in TG3.1, five out of thirteen framing timbers are not fastened to at least one strake; in TG3.2, three out of fourteen; in TG9A, three out of seven; in TG9B, two out of eight; in TG9C/D, five out of nine; and in TG6, four out of twelve framing timbers. In no case does there appear to be any pattern which might suggest that such gaps were in strakes with only framing units of floors and knees at *c*. lm spacing or where there were only side frames at a similar spacing: the overall impression is one of framing units covering all surviving strakes at *c*.0.5m spacing, with haphazardly distributed gaps in a regular treenailing pattern.

It should prove possible to interpret the framing evidence in the large ships represented by Dublin TG3 and TG6/9 with more confidence when the Lynaes ship is published in detail. Moreover, the number and position of crossbeams in the Dublin large ships cannot at present be estimated. That there are few signs of fastening positions for lodging knees in this planking might be because there were few, if any, upper crossbeams in the region of the hold. However, it would normally be expected that there would be crossbeams towards the ends, away from the hold, but in this planking (TG6, TG9B, and TG9C/D) there is also minimal evidence there for lodging knees and no evidence that crossbeams protruded through the sides – as is seen, for example, on the late twelfth–century seal of Winchelsea (Fig. 2.1.3) and is known from the Bergen timbers (Christensen 1985, 59–83). An alternative possibility is that any crossbeams or bulkheads in the ends of the Dublin large ships were fastened in a way that did not use lodging knees.

The evidence from the Dublin floor timbers, albeit from different timber groups, complements that from the planking, which is mainly from above the waterline, by giving an indication of the treenailing pattern in the lowest strakes. Floor timber T55 from TG2 was fastened to the 2nd to 7th strakes but not to the garboard strakes or the keel. Floor timber T222 from TG4 was also not fastened to keel or garboard, but was fastened to alternate strakes, 3rd, 5th, 7th and 9th. The other nine floor timbers which provide evidence on this matter are all from TG7: T275 was not fastened to keel or garboards but, like T55, was fastened to the remaining strakes. There is no further evidence on keel and garboard fastenings as the other eight floor timbers are fragmentary: four of them (T252, T280, T292 and T293) were fastened to all strakes for which evidence survives, whereas T245, T277 and T278 were fastened to alternate strakes. Floor timber T223 in TG4 was fragment and poorly documented, but appears to have been fastened by two treenails to each of the five strakes it covered – two treenails were also used to fasten knees in the Klåstad ship to one particular strake (Christensen and Leiro 1976) Thus there does not seem to be one single pattern in the way the Dublin floor timbers were fastened to the lower strakes.

Building sequence
To the evidence for the shell building sequence (Fig. 9.2.5) which comes from the planking – clenched strake fastenings and scarf fastenings under the deduced position of framing timbers – may be added the evidence from some of the floor timbers (e.g. T278 and T280) where there are clear impressions of roves on their outboard faces.

Tool marks and decorative mouldings
The only tool mark found on the planking was that of a bit within treenail holes. In addition, marks made by a 70mm straight–edged blade were noted on floor timber T55 and on bulkhead T351, and gouge marks were detected in the V–shaped decoration cut on this bulkhead.

Scribed lines cut by a knife were found on plank T124, marking the position of a framing timber; on planks T91, T124, T228 and T333, marking the beginning of scarfs; on plank T93 to mark the limit of a repair patch: on plank T219 to mark the overlap; on floor timbers T252 and T293 and on breasthook T367 to mark where notches ('joggles') were to be cut: and on keel T361, as guide–lines for nails for the starboard strake.

A considerable number of woodworking and ironworking tools have been found in Viking and later contexts: many of these could have been used in boat- and shipbuilding (see, for example, Olsen and Crumlin-Pedersen 1967, 154–62; McGrail 1974, 45–7; Christensen 1985, 209–13; 1986; McGrail 1987 149–58). An exhibition catalogue, Viking and medieval Dublin (1973), published by the National Museum of Ireland contains descriptions and illustrations of several woodworking and metalworking tools.

Simulated planking was carved on stems T357 and T364 and on the multiple end planks. In addition two of the multiple end planks (T353 and T359) had simple decorative mouldings. A V-shaped decorative groove was cut on one of the faces of bulkhead T351, and a decorative groove was also cut on both side of and parallel to the inner curve of knee T352. The tenth-century possible stem T386 was decorated more finely than any other ship or boat timber from Dublin (see Lang 1988, fig. 11). Lang (1988, 9) describes this decoration as 'purely Scandinavian'. As this decoration was done before the possible stem was reused as a threshold, the boat from which this stem came was either built in Scandinavia and brought to Dublin on board a ship (or towed) or built (or at least decorated) in the Dublin region by Scandinavian craftsmen. One floor timber, T278, had the edges of its upper face bevelled, as were the lower outer edges of a handful of planks (T65, T107, T217 and T282). Such bevels – and the decorative mouldings – give the impression of a little extra pride in craftsmanship. There may have been other examples which were not noticed owing to the poor state of some of the timbers when examined.

Repairs
Minor leaks through plank seams were staunched by adding extra nails: plank scarfs were reinforced by spikes; and treenail fastenings tightened by driving a nail or a wedge into the head. Elsewhere, loosened treenails were replaced by another one nearby: in some cases new and old treenail holes merged, not only in the planking but also in knee T218, stem T384, two side timbers T290 and T292, and floor timber T55.

Splits and loose knots in planking were repaired by nailing on patches: these were mostly outboard, but some were inboard in positions where framing timbers would have had to be removed before such repairs were undertaken. In some of these repairs, for example those on planks T333 and T341, the nails fastening the patch were clenched by turning their points through 90° along the face of the plank rather than by deforming the point over a rove as was invariably the case in plank fastenings.

Splits, or possible incipient splits, in stem T53 and parrel T356 were consolidated by driving a nail through the timber across the split and clench-fastening it over a rove.

Propulsion and steering
Small boats were propelled by paddles (T355 and T367). The oar fragment from Dublin (T377), with a blade breadth of 0.1m, would have been used in a large boat. The planking with oarports (T50 of A.D. 1180–1225, and T217 of A.D. 1160–1200) probably came from large boats or small ships where rowing was ancillary to sail. The parent vessel of T217 was rowed in the conventional manner (sit/pull) with standard rowing geometry; the oarsmen in T50's parent vessel, on the other hand, may have stood to use their oars.

Although no masts were excavated, the Dublin timbers show evidence for masts of girths from 0.45m, appropriate to a large boat or small ship, to 2.70m which would have been fitted in ships or, more probably, in large ships. Two- to five-inch (0.05–0.12m) ropes were used for rigging, and for mooring and towing. Anchor cables, on the other hand, may have been up to 10 inches (0.25m) in circumference.

Windward ability, as measured by garboard deadrise angles and (M_2/S_2) ratios on floor timbers and keels, was comparable with the Skuldelev ships, and indeed may well have been generally better. There is no clear indication of significant improvements over time in the Dublin material.

There is minimal evidence for the steering arrangements – only T369 the tiller and upper stock of a small boat rudder: this is of conventional Viking/Norse design except for the apparent use of a morticed joint .

Dublin boats and ships

Table 9.2.2 presents an estimate of the size of boats and ships represented in the Dublin timbers. It is not possible to give accurate estimates of numbers of vessels for two reasons: (i) the wide, and sometimes overlapping, ranges of dates for the groups of timbers; and (ii) the general (e.g. TG7), rather than specific, contexts available for some of the timbers. Although timbers within a timber group were deposited at the same time, unless they were found articulated they are not necessarily from the same vessel: this is clearly so in the case of, for example, two timbers from the Fishamble Street site; the boat stem T357, similar to that of the Gokstad *faering* (Gokstad 3) was found 'directly on top' of bulkhead T351, similar to that from the large boat Skuldelev 3. Conversely, timbers which were deposited in separate sections of the Dublin sites but within a similar date range *may* have come from the same vessel: this is thought, for example, to have been the case with the planking from TG6 and that from TG9.

Each entry in Table 9.2.2 relates to timbers identified as being from a particular size of vessel (boat, large boat, small ship etc.) which were excavated from the same general context: thus they probably represent one vessel. but they may represent two or more.
The evidence may conveniently be grouped together in five periods.

Early to mid-tenth century (A.D. 905–75)
From this period there are the remains of a small boat the size of the Årby boat (Arbman 1940); two boats; one or more large boats; and a small ship similar in form to Skuldelev 5 but bigger in size, though not as large as Skuldelev 1.

Table 9.2.2 Boats and ships represented by the Dublin timbers

Phase[a]	Site	Vessel	Timbers
1 Early to mid–tenth century (905–75)	High St	Boat	Floor 368
	Fishamble St	Small boat	Floor 372
	Fishamble St	Boat	Keel 383
	Fishamble St	Large boat(s)	Keel 361; plank 384
	Fishamble St	Small ship	Keel 382
2 Tenth/eleventh century (955–1040)	Fishamble St	Small boat	Knee 378
	Fishamble St	Boat(s)	Floor 379; planks 388–92
	Fishamble St	Large boat	Keel 381
	Fishamble St	Small ship	Knees 352, 380
3 Eleventh/twelth century (1055–1125)[b]	Fishamble St	Small boat	Stem 357
	Fishamble St	Boat(s)	Plank TG10 (330–50); plank 387; breasthook/knee 366
	Fishamble St	Large boat(s)	Bulkhead 351; oar 377
	WQ.TG7	Boat(s)	Planks 255–6; 264–6; 279
	WQ.TG7	Large boat(s) or small ship(s)	Framing 245, 252, 263 274–8, 280, 289, 290, 292 293
	WQ.TG7	Ship	Planks 282–8
	John's Lane	Ship	Planks 353, 359
4 Twelth/thirteenth century (1160–1125)[c]	WQ.TG1	Boat	Planks TG1 (1–30)
	WQ.TG4	Large boat	Bulkhead 187
	WQ.TG2	Large boat(s) or small ship(s)	Side timber 57; mast step(?) 54; stems 52 and 53
	WQ.TG2	Large boat or small ship	Planks TG2 (31–50)
	WQ.TG4	Small ship(s)	Planks 147, 167, 217, 219; floors 222 and 223
	WQ.TG4	Ship(s)	Knee 218; parrel 220A; parrel rib 220
	WQ.TG2	Ship(s) or large ship(s)	Keel 56; *mykes* 51 and 58
	WQ.TG1	Ship or large ship	Stringer 30A
	WQ.TG2	Large ship	Floor 55
	WQ.TG6 and 9	Large ship	Planks TG6 and 9 (226–39 and 297–329)
5 Thirteenth century (1230–75)	WQ.TG3	Large ship	Planks TG3 (59–146)

Notes: a. timbers from phases 1, 2 and 3 may be attributed to the Hiberno–Norse period in Dublin, and those from phases 4 and 5 to the early Anglo–Norman period (i.e. post–1169)

        b. Brasethook T367, Parrel T360 and stem fragment T364 may also be from this period

        c. Two timbers ffrom TG6, crossbeam (?) T224 and stem(?) T225, are not included as they appear to come from outside the Viking/Norse tradition

Tenth/eleventh century (A.D. 955–1040)

There are remains from a small boat the size of the Arby boat; one or more boats; a large boat similar in form to Skuldelev 5 but probably smaller in size than Skuldelev 3; and a small ship.

Eleventh/twelfth century (A. D. 1055–1125)

In TG10 from the Fishamble Street site there is good evidence for a boat or boats similar in form and structure to the mid–ninth–century Gokstad 2, the *seksaering* (see Johannessen 1940). The oak and pine planks (T330–50) are similar to their counterparts in the Norwegian boat (Fig. 9.3.4). The broken treenail holes in the two pine strakes (T340 and T341) – 13–17mm in diameter, spaced at intervals of 0.17–0.26m – correspond with holes in the pine top strakes of Gokstad 2, which are where a *c.*2.9m board was fastened on each side to take three pairs of tholes (oar pivots). The holes in T340 and T341 extend over a length of 3.3m, and so the timbers fastened there could also have taken three pairs of tholes. The spacing of the six sets a of framing timbers estimated for the TG10 planking 0.94–1. 1m, is close to that of the six framing units in Gokstad 2, 0.92–0.97m. The clenched nail on pine plank T341 is probably where the head of a side timber was fastened, also as in Gokstad 2.

Pine plank T387 and breasthook/knee T366 may also have come from this or a similar boat. It thus seems reasonable to conclude that all these timbers are the remains of a six–oared boat similar in form and structure to Gokstad 2. From this same site, Fishamble Street, another boat or boats is represented by the planking T255–6, T264–6, and T279; a small boat similar to Gokstad 3 by the stem T357; and a large boat similar to Skuldelev 3 by bulkhead T351 and possibly by the oar T377.

TG7 timbers (from Wood Quay), which came from a large boat the size of Skuldelev 3 (Fig. 9.2.4) include four floor timbers (T263, T275, T292 and T293) and two side timbers (T274 and T290). Two other floor timbers (T245 and T252) may have come from a large boat or small ship. Timbers from small ships the size of Skuldelev 1 include three floor timbers (T277, T278 and T280), a side timber (T289) and a knee (T276).

Planks T282–8 from Wood Quay, TG7, came from a ship, as probably did plank T359 from John's Lane.

There are three other important timbers from the Fishamble Street site which may be from this period but, as they are only dated to the general period of this site (early tenth to early twelfth century), they have not been included in Table 30. Breasthook T367 was probably used as a seat in the stern of a large boat or possibly a small ship. The parrel T360 is from a small ship; and the stem fragment T364 was probably broken off the tip of a ship's stem.

Twelfth/thirteenth century (A.D. 1160–1225)
The planks in TG1 were from a boat, whilst those in TG2 were from a large boat or possibly a small ship. The low bulkhead T187 was from a large boat similar in size to Skuldelev 3. The possible mast step T54, stems T52 and T53 and side timber T57 came from a large boat(s) or a small ship(s).

Planking in TG4 and floors T222 and T223 came from a small ship(s); whilst the knee T218, parrel T220A and parrel rib T220 came from ships.

Keel T56 and mykcs T51 and T58 of TG2 and stringer (?) T30A of TG1 came from ships or large ships. T56 has a similar form to the keel of Skuldelev 1 but its scantlings indicate that it comes from a much larger ship.

Floor timber T55 in TG2 is the largest timber in the Dublin assemblages and must have come from a large ship comparable in size with the Lynaes ship (Fig. 9.3.5). Planking in TG6 (T226–39) and TG9 (T297–329) came from large

ships; it has been argued above that they were from the same ship, which had a double–ended form and was of a size comparable with the Lynaes ship.

There is also a possibility that in this period vessels not in the Viking/Norse tradition were using the port of Dublin: a flat–bottomed barge, punt or praam type of boat is possibly represented by T225, the crossbeam with knee – such a vessel may have been similar to the Egernsund find (Crumlin–Pedersen 1981, 36–77) (see Fig. 2.1.6).

Thirteenth century (A.D. 1230–75)
The planking in TG3 (T59– 146) came from the midship region of a large ship comparable with Lynaes in size. This large ship, and indeed those of the preceding period, are unlikely to have been *galleys*, a type of large ships frequently mentioned in accounts of thirteenth–century shipbuilding in Britain and Ireland (Whitwell and Johnson 1926; Johnson 1927; Anderson 1928; Tinniswood 1949), for such vessels were royal ships, propelled by oar as well as by sail, which, although they may have carried some goods, were principally warships. There is no evidence for rowing in the Dublin large ships and their form seems more appropriate to a cargo vessel than a galley.

Dublin shipbuilding and the Viking/Norse tradition

During the Viking period and up to the mid–twelfth century (the first three phases in Table 9.2.2) the evidence is thus overwhelmingly that the Dublin ships and boats were in the mainstream of the Viking tradition, in their sequence of building, in their form and structure, and in their method of propulsion (and probably also steering). The planking and associated fittings in TG10 (T330–50), for example, are almost identical to those of the Gokstad *seksaering*, even to the extent of using pine top strakes; and the principal Viking methods of closing the ends (i.e. joining the planking to the stems) are also used in Dublin – back–bevelled planking fastened to a type A stem, winged stems (type C), and multiple end planks; even the occasional use of treenails as plank fastenings, as in the Skuldelev boats, is found in Dublin. The Dublin woodworking techniques are in the mainstream, with little, if any, sign of regional variations.

The chronological groupings shown in Table 9.2.2 cannot be rigid owing to the overlapping date ranges; nevertheless, the timbers in the fourth and fifth phases may generally be attributed to the early Anglo–Norman period. i.e. post–1169. The timbers from these two phases show no marked change in techniques from the preceding Hiberno–Norse phase – rather the principal change is in size of vessel. From the Hiberno–Norse period there is insubstantial evidence for vessels bigger than small ships, i.e. bigger than, say, Skuldelev 3 in size: only some planking in TG7 (T282–8) and one plank (T359) from the John's Lane site. In contrast, from the late twelfth and thirteenth centuries (Anglo–Norman) there is ample evidence for ships, and indeed large ships in addition to smaller craft.

From the Dublin viewpoint these changes seem to be the result of a natural process of development rather than a sudden shift in technology: the sequence of building and the double–ended form are retained, but the planking becomes thicker, the fastenings bigger, the scarfs longer and the framing correspondingly greater in length and cross–section, and masts are of correspondingly greater girth. Other ships and boats of the post–Viking/Norse tradition are not yet well published and so it is difficult to judge these developments in Dublin against an international backcloth, although it is clear that the Dublin ship represented by TG6/9 planking has some affinities with the Lynaes ship in the bulging cross–section of the waterline planking and in her general structure and framing pattern. Whether some of the other Dublin changes – longer plank scarfs, bigger nails and treenails and so on – were only regional or corresponded to changes elsewhere will not become clear until the Scandinavian finds are published in detail. Of these features, perhaps lipped plank scarfs, nails with points under their heads and nail shanks of square cross–section and the technique of clenching nails by turning may be regional attributes, but in the present state of research this must remain only conjecture.

Of developments known outside the Viking/Norse tradition from the twelfth century and later there is little sign in the Dublin material: no evidence for a median rudder, or for a second mast, or for the proto–skeleton sequence of building. The little evidence there is suggests that flat–bottomed punt/barge/*praam* types may have been introduced as lighters (T225); and timber T226, the possible stem, may also be from a non–Norse tradition.

Changes in ship performance in the twelfth century

The introduction of a composite parrel with ribs (T220) and trucks in ship performance in the the late twelfth/early thirteenth century may indicate a change in the size of twelfth century masts and yards rather than a more weatherly performance; nor is it possible to detect any improvements here from changes in the underwater shape deduced from the cross–section of keels and floor timbers. On the other hand, the development from Hiberno–Norse boats and small ships to Anglo Norman ships and large ships undoubtedly resulted in increased cargo capacity. Crumlin–Pedersen (1989, 424, fig. 10) has estimated that the Lynaes ship could have carried 60 tonnes of cargo, whereas his estimate for Skuldelev 1 (small ship) at the same relative draft (3/5 height of sides amidships) is only 24 tonnes, and for Skuldelev 3 (large boat), 5 tonnes (Crumlin–Pedersen 1986a, 226). The Dublin tonnages would have similarly been increased. The increase in capacity may also be measured by the length of the cargo hold in relation to the length overall (McGrail 1987, 203, table 11.6): this ratio is 0.338 for Skuldelev 1, whereas it is 0.56 for Lynaes 1 and was probably similar for the Dublin ships.

Changes in berthing arrangements in the twelfth century

Dublin bank 4 and front–braced revetments 1 and 1A (Fig. 9.2.2) were built during the first 30 or 40 years of the Anglo–Norman period. They were unlikely to have been designed as wharfs alongside which ships could berth, but were

most probably built (as were banks 1–3 and the stone wall) to restrain the R. Liffey to a more clearly defined channel and so reduce the risk of Dublin being flooded, and also to enclose part of the intertidal salt–marsh so that the city could expand northwards.

Large ships such as Lynaes, Dublin TG6/9 and Dublin TG3 may still be operated from tidal beaches. The minimum depth of water that a loaded Lynaes size of large ship would need to float is c.1.5m (i.e. 3/5 of 2.5m) and so, providing there was that depth (even if only at spring tides) in the R. Liffey and in the Poddle mouth, the Poddle pool, *dubh linn*, could have continued to be used after 1169, as it had been in Hiberno–Norse times, by beached and anchored vessels. However, with the additional capacity of these large ships, double– or even treble–handling of cargo would become increasingly unattractive, and the advantages of a waterfront berth where cargo handling aids could be used and warehousing built would become very apparent. There may also have been an addltional impetus for change as the R. Poddle mouth silted and ships, and indeed boats, had to be unloaded and loaded further away from the city. Silting did indeed become such a problem in later years that by 1306 *great ships* could no longer reach Dublin fully laden and had to be partly offloaded (e.g. 13 out of 20 tuns of wine) at Dalkey Island, south of the R. Liffey mouth (Mills 1914, 316–17).

Back–braced revetment 3 (Fig. 9.2.2) of the late thirteenth century is the first one that could conveniently be used by vessels and may have been built not only to constrain the R. Liffey but also to provide a wharf alongside which large ships could be berthed, and upon which derricks, sheer legs and other cargo handling devices (see, for example, the hoisting spar in Herteig 1981, fig 88; Elimers 1981, 95) could be erected and wharehouses built. The stone quay probably built in the period 1300– 10 (Wallace 1981, 117) served a similar purpose and provided comparable facilities, but in a more substantial and enduring way. Whether the large ships represented by the Dublin timbers listed in the fourth (1160–1225) and fifth (1230–75) phases in Table 9.2.2 did indeed berth alongside revetment 3 cannot be known with certainty, not least because of the wide date ranges for the revetments and for the ships' timbers, but it remains a strong possibility. On the other hand, it seems likely that smaller vessels, which could be economically loaded and unloaded by informal means, continued to use the R. Liffey strand or the pool in the R. Poddle (Fig 9.2.1B).

References

Anderson R.C. 1928 'Enlgish galleys in 1295.' *Mariner's Mirror* 14, 220–41.

Arbman H. 1940 'Der Arby–fund.' *Acta Archaeologica* 11, 43–102.

Baillie M.G.L. 1978 'Dating of some ships' timbers from Wood Quay, Dublin.' In J Fletcher (ed.) *Dendrochronology in Europe*, 259–62. B.A.R. International Series S.51 Oxford.

Baillie M. 1982 *Tree–ring dating and archaeology*. London. Croom Helm.

Bass G. 1972 *History of Seafaring*, London, Thames & Hudson.

Bonde N. and Crumlin–Pedersen O. 1990 'The dating of wreck 2 from Skuldelev, Denmark', *Newswarp*. 7, 3–6.

Cameron P.N. 1982 'Saxons, sail and sea.' *Int. J. Nautical Archaeol*. 11, 319–32.

Christensen A.-E. 1959 'Faeringen fra Gokstad.' *Viking* 23, 57–69.

Christensen A.-E. 1968b *Boats of the north*. Oslo. Norske Samlaget.

Christensen A.-E. 1972 'Scandinavian ships from earliest times to the Vikings.' In G.F. Bass (ed.) *History of seafaring*, 159–80. London. Thames and Hudson.

Christensen A.-E. 1979 'Viking Age rigging.' In S. McGrail (ed.), *Archaeology of medieval ships and harbours*, 183–94. B.A.R. International Series S.66. Oxford.

Christensen A.-E. 1985 'Boat finds from Bryggen.' *Bryggen Papers* 1, 47–280. Oslo University Press.

Christensen, A.-E. 1988 'Ship graffiti and models.' In P. Wallace (ed.), *Miscellanea 1*, 13–26. Medieval Dublin Excavations 1962–81, Ser. B, vol. 2. Dublin. Royal Irish Academy.

Christensen A.-E. and Leiro, G. 1976 *Klåstadskipet*. Vestfoldminne. Tønsbergs Aktietrykkeri.

Crumlin–Pedersen O. 1965 'Cog–kogge–Kaag.' *Handels og Sjøfartsmuseet på Kronberg Årbog*, 81 – 144. Helsingør.

Crumlin–Pedersen O. 1966 'Two Danish side rudders.' *Mariner's Mirror* 52, 251–61.

Crumlin–Pedersen O. 1969 *Das Haithabaschiff*. Ausgrabungen in Haithabu, Bericht 3. Nemünster. Schleswig–Holsteinisches Landesmuseum.

Crumlin–Pedersen O. 1972 'Kaellingen og Kløften.' *Handels og Sjøfartsmuseet pa Kronbarg Arbog*, 64–80. Helsingør.

Crumlin–Pedersen O. 1977 *From Viking ship to Victory*. Greenwich. National Maritime Museum.

Crumlin–Pedersen O. 1978 'Ships of the Vikings.' In T. Andersson and K.I. Sandred (eds), *The Vikings*, 32–41. University of Uppsala.

Crumlin–Pedersen O. 1979a 'Lynaesskibet og Roskilde Søvej.' In F.A. Birkebaek (ed) *13 Bidrag til Roskilde by og egn's historie*, 64–77. Roskilde Museum.

Crumlin–Pedersen O. 1979b 'Danish cog–finds.' In S. McGrail (ed.), *Archaeology of medieval ships and harbours*, 17–34. B.A.R. International Series S.66. Oxford.

Crumlin–Pedersen O. 1981 'Skibe på Havbunden.' *Handels og Sjøfartsmuseewts Årbog*, 28–65 Helsingør.

Crumlin–Pedersen O. 1983a 'Schiffe und Seehandelsrouten im Ostseeraum 1050–1350.' *Lübecker Schriften zur Archäologie und Kulturgeschichte 7*, 229–37.

Crumlin–Pedersen O. 1983b *From Viking ship to Hanseatic cog*. Third Paul Johnstone lecture Greenwich. National Maritime Museum.

Crumlin–Pedersen O. 1984 'Der Seetransport: die Schiffe von Haithabu.' *Archäologische und naturwissenschaftliche Untersuchungen an Siedlungen im deutschen Kustengebiet 2*, 241–8 Acta Humaniora. Weinheim.

Crumlin–Pedersen O. 1985 'Ship finds and ship blockages A.D. 800–1200.' In K. Kristiansen (ed.), *Archaeological formation processes*, 215–28. Copenhagen. Nationalmuseet .

Crumlin–Pedersen O. 1986a 'Aspects of Viking Age shipbuilding.' *J. Danish Archaeol. 5*. 209–28.

Crumlin–Pedersen O. 1986b 'Aspects of wood technology in medieval shipbuilding.' In O. Crumlin–Pedersen and M. Vinner (eds), *Sailing into the past, 138–49*. Roskilde The Viking Ship Museum.

Crumlin–Pedersen O. 1988 'Schiffe und Schiffahrtswege im Ostseeraum während des 9–12 Jahrhunderts.' In M. Müller–Wille (ed.), *Oldenburg, Wolin, Staraja Ladoga. Norgorod, Kiev*, 530–63. Bericht der Romisch–Germanischen Kommission 69. Mainz P. van Zabern.

Crumlin–Pedersen O. 1989 'Schiffstypen aus der frühgeschichtlichen Seeschiffahrt in den nordeuropäischen Gewässern.' *Untersuchungen zu Handel und Verkehr der vor– und J frühgeschichitlichen Zeit in Mittel– und Nord–europa 5*, 405–30.

Doherty C. 1980 'Exchange and trade in early medieval Ireland.' *J.R. Soc. Antiq. Ir.* 110, 67–89.

Ellmers D. 1972 *Frühmittelalterliche Handelsschiffahrt in Mittel– und Nordeuropa*. Neumunster. Karl Wachholtz.

Ellmers D. 1976 *Kogge, Kahn und Kunststoffboot*. Bremerhaven. Deutschen Schiffahrtsmuseum.

Ellmers D. 1979 'Cog of Bremen and related boats.' In S. McGrail (ed.), *Archaeology of medieval ships and harbours*, 1–15. B.A.R. International Series S.66. Oxford.

Ellmers D. 1981 'Post–Roman waterfront installations on the Rhine.' In G. Milne and B. Hobley (eds), *Waterfront archaeology in Britain and northern Europe*, 88–95. C.B.A. Research Report 41. London. Council for British Archaeology.

Ellmers D. 1985 'Loading and unloading ships using a horse and cart, standing in the water.' In A.E. Herteig (ed.), *Conference on waterfront archaeology in northern European towns*, vol. 2, 25–30. Bergen. Historisk Museum.

Ewe H. 1972 *Schiffe auf Siegeln*. Rostock. V.E.B. Hinstorff.

Fenwick V.H. (ed.) 1978 *The Graveney boat*. B.A.R. British Series. 53. Oxford.

Friel I. 1983 'England and the advent of the 3–masted ship.' *Int. Congress of Maritime Museums*, 4th Conference Proceedings, 130–8. Paris. Musees de la Marine.

Goodburn D.M. 1986 'Do we have evidence of a Saxon boatbuilding tradition?' *Int. J. Nautical Archaeol*. 15, 39–47.

Greenhill B. 1976 *Archaeology of the boat*. London. A. and C. Black.

Greenhill B. 1989 *Evolution of the wooden ship*. London. Batsford.

Herteig A.E. 1981 'Medieval harbour of Bergen.' In G. Milne and B. Hobley (eds). *Waterfront archaeology in Britain and northern Europe*, 80–7. C.B.A. Research Report 41. London. Council for British Archaeology.

Hodges R. 1982 *Dark Age economics*. London. Duckworth.

Hoekstra T.J. 1975 'Utrecht.' *Int. J. Nautical Archaeol*. 4, 390–2.

Johannessen F. 1940 'Båtene fra Gokstadskibet.' *Viking* 4, 125–30.

Johnson C. 1927 'London shipbuilding AD 1295.' *Antiq. J.* 7, 424–37.

Lang J.T. 1988 *Viking Age decorated wood* Medieval Dublin Excavations 1962–81, Ser B, vol. 1. Dublin. Royal Irish Academy.

Lundström P 1971/2 'Klinknaglarnas vittnesbörd.' *Sjöhistorisk Årsbok*, 81–8. Stockholm.

McCusker J.J. 1966 'Wine prise and medieval mercantile shipping.' *Speculum* 41, 279–96

McGrail S. 1974 *Building and trials of a replica of an ancient boat*. National Maritime Museum . Monograph 11A. Greenwich.

McGrail, S. 1981a *Rafts, boats and ships*. London. H.M.S.O.

McGrail, S. 1981c 'Medieval boats, ships and landing places.' In G. Milne and B. Hobley (eds), *Waterfront archaeology in Britain and northern Europe*, 17–23. C.B.A. Research Report 41. London. Council for British Archaeology.

McGrail S. 1983 'Interpretation of archaeological evidence for maritime structures.' In P. Annis (ed.), *Sea studies*, 33–46. Greenwich. National Maritime Museum.

McGrail S. 1985 'Early landing places.' In A.E. Herteig (ed.), *Conference on waterfront archaeology in northern European towns*, 12–18. Bergen. Historisk Museum.

McGrail S. 1987 *Ancient boats in N. W. Europe*. London. Longman.

McGrail S. and Farrell A. 1979 'Rowing: aspects of the ethnographic and iconographic evidence.' *Int. J. Nautical Archaeol.* 8, 155–66.

Mills, J. (ed.) 1914 *Calendar of justiciary rolls of Ireland*, vol. 2, 1305–7. London.

Mitchell G.F. 1987 *Archaeology and environrnent in early Dublin*. Medieval Dublin Excavations 1962–81, Ser. C, vol. 1. Dublin. Royal Irish Academy.

Murphy P.J. 1974 'Medieval Irish ships and trade.' *Cultura Maritima* 1, 13–15.

Nicolaysen N . 1882 *Viking ship discovered at Gokstad in Norway*. Kristiania. Cammermeyer.

NMI 1973 *Viking and medieval Dublin*, National Museum excavations 1962–73. Catalogue of exhibition (reprinted 1976). Dublin. National Museum of Ireland.

Olsen O. and Crumlin–Pedersen O. 1967 'Skuldelev Ships II.' *Acta Archaeologica* 38, 73– 174.

Sandahl B. 1958 *Middle English sea terms, vol. 2. Masts, spars and sails*. Studia Anglistica Upsaliensia 20. University of Uppsala.

Sherborne J.W. 1965 *Port of Bristol in the Middie Ages*. Bristol. Historical Association.

Strickland W.G. 1923 'Ancient official seals of the city of Dublin.' *J. R. Soc. Antiq Ir.* 53, 121–31.

Tinniswood J.T. 1949 'English galleys 1272–1377.' *Mariner's Mirror* 35, 276–315.

Wallace P.F. 1981 'Dublin's waterfront at Wood Quay: 900–1317.' In G. Milne and B Hobley (eds), *Waterfront archaeology in Britain and northern Europe*, 109–18. C.B.A. Research Report 41. London. Council for British Archaeology.

Wallace P.F. 1987 'The layout of the later Viking Age Dublin – inferences for its regulation and problems of continuity.' In J.E. Knirk (ed.), *Proceedings of the Tenth Viking Congress*, 271–85. Oslo. Universitetets Oldsaksamlings Skrifter.

Whitwell R.J and Johnson , C. 1926 'The Newcastle galley.' *Archaeologia Seliana*, 4th series,. 2, 142–96.

Reprinted with permission from

McGrail, S. *Medieval Boats and Ship Timbers from Dublin*: 81–100. Royal Irish Academy. (1993).

PAPER 9.3

SHIPS TIMBERS FROM WOOD QUAY, DUBLIN AND OTHER MEDIEVAL SITES IN IRELAND

During the 12th to 14th centuries AD there were three main types of sea–going ships in Northwest Europe (Fig 2.1.2) – the cog, the hulc and the Nordic ship (Crumlin–Pedersen, 1978). Each of these traditions of shipbuildings had its roots in earlier times and each was to contribute something to the development, in the 15th century, of the skeleton–built, 3–masted ship in which Europeans first sailed all the seas of the world between *c* 1480 and *c* 1530 (Greenhill, 1989, 67–76).

The Nordic ship

This tradition is sometimes known as 'Viking', but it had its origins well before the Viking Age, in the 4th century AD and even earlier, and it extended beyond the Viking Age (say 800 to 1100 AD) into high medieval times. Within this tradition there were not only warships and cargo ships but also small ferries and fishing boats. These boats and ships had a distinctive shape in plan and in profile and their main structural characteristic lay in the way their overlapping planking was fastened together (fig.9.3.1): by iron nails clenched by distorting the point over a rove (washer) – an early form of rivet (McGrail, 1993, 84–5). From its origins in Scandinavia, this style of shipbuilding spread to the South Baltic, the northern isles, Ireland, Britain and the European Atlantic coasts. Although after the 15th century *ships* were not built in this tradition, *boats* continued to be built and used, indeed into our own times, in West Norway, Shetland and Orkney.

The Cog tradition

The origins of this tradition are, at present, obscure, but they possibly lie in late–Roman times in the region of the Rhine estuary and the nearby Frisian islands (Crumlin–Pedersen 1965, 1979B, 1983B). Thirteenth and 14th century cogs, large and small, have been found in the Netherlands, North Germany, Denmark and Sweden. In 1960 an almost complete Cog hull, dated 1380 AD, was excavated from the river Weser at Bremen (Ellmers, 1979). The distinctive features of this type of shipbuilding are firstly the specialised shape, with its relatively flat bottom and its full cross–section; and secondly, the way the overlapping side planking was fastened together by nails which were clenched by turning the point through 180°, back into the planking. The bottom was flat mainly so that cogs could take the ground on a falling (ebb) tide and be unloaded into boats or into carts and waggons. The full form, together with great height of sides, meant that these cogs could carry relatively large amounts of cargo ('tuns burden').

The Hulc tradition

During the 14th century hulcs are frequently mentioned in documents referring to overseas trade, especially westwards and southwards from the Rhine estuary. The origins of this tradition are also obscure and no convincing example has yet been excavated. There are, however, representations of *hulcs* on town seals (fig 2.1.5) and on fonts in Winchester and Zedelgem, Belgium, and from these we can speculate that the *hulc's* distinguishing features were: a more curvaceous shape than either the cog or the Nordic ship; and distinctive ends where the planking did not terminate at stempost and sternpost but at a horizontal deck, well above the waterline (Greenhill, 1976, 1989).

Irish nautical timbers

In Ireland, so far, we have no medieval ship finds, although the Viking longship of *c* 1075 AD known as Skuldelev 2, excavated in 1960 from Roskilde Fjord, Denmark and now on display in the Viking Ship Museum there, was built of oak which dendrochronological examination has shown came from the Dublin region (Bonde & Crumlin–Pedersen, 1990) . But we do have in Ireland an ever–increasing number of timbers from *dismantled* boats and ships, which had been re–used in medieval times to build waterfronts and other structures, or had simply been discarded (Wallace, 1981; 1992; Hurley, 1986; Scully, forthcoming). These timbers come from the 11th to 13th century Arundel Square site in Waterford, the 13th century Cornmarket Street site in Cork, and from several Dublin sites dated from the 10th to the 13th century (Fig. 9.3.2): – High Street, Christchurch Place, Winetavern Street, Fishamble Street, John's Lane and principally Wood Quay (Wallace,1981; 1992; Mitchell,1987,5–6) . In Britain there have been comparable finds of re–used nautical timbers in Perth, Newcastle, Grimsby and London, and there is a notable collection of similar timbers from the Bryggen site at Bergen, Norway (Christensen, 1985).

All the nautical timbers excavated from Dublin, Waterford and Cork have proved to be from the Nordic tradition, with two exceptions which are further considered below. The principal timbers found were planking, keels, stems and framework timbers such as floors, knees and crossbeams; there were also examples of spar crutches (*mykes*), oars, paddles, a rudder and elements of rigging (McGrail, 1993). None of these timbers were joined together in the form of a boat or ship, although from the Wood Quay site in Dublin (Fig. 9.2.3) there were several large groups of planking joined together but flattened out for use in the waterfront structures (McGrail, 1993, 38–9)

Two of the more interesting problems which had to be tackled during post–excavation research on these nautical timbers were:

(a)   how to identify which timbers came from the same parent ship or boat

(b)   whether there was a valid method of deducing the size of those parent ships and boats.

Boat or Ship?

A subsidiary problem had first to be tackled: how to define the terms 'ship' and 'boat', for in the English language these words are not defined precisely, yet if the maritime specialist is to communicate ideas about the past in terms that most people can understand these words have to be used.

At the extremes of size it is clear that a small vessel is a boat and a large vessel a ship, but the dividing line between 'boat' and 'ship' is fuzzy. Consideration of work by Muller–Wille (1968–9) on early medieval boat graves, and by Crumlin–Pedersen (1981; 1985) on Danish Viking Age boat finds led to the proposal that the term *ship* should be applied to any vessel whose length was greater than 20m and *boat* to one whose length was less than 12m. *Small boats* were then defined as being less than 7m and *large ships* as greater than 24m. The difficult ones to classify proved to be those of intermediate length, 12 to 20m. The solution to this problem seemed to be to decide which of this group were *large boats* and which *small ships* after consideration of such factors as their general structure (open boat or decked) and their function (rivercraft, coastal vessel, ocean–going and so on). These definitions of boats and ships are given in Table 9.3.1.

Table 9.3.1 Size of Nordic boat and ship defined in relation to their overall length

Length overall (m)	Size of vessel
less than 7	small boat
7 to 12	boat
12 to 20	large boat/small ship (Note 1)
20 to 24	ship
greater than 24	large ship

Source: McGrail 1993, 19–21.

Note: 1. Whether large boat or small ship depends upon hull structure and upon operational role

Timbers belonging to the same parent vessel

When re–used ship timbers are excavated fastened together as they had been in their primary use, we know they are all from the same parent vessel. Timbers which are found close together but not fastened are, on the other hand, not necessarily from the same vessel. Conversely, timbers which were indeed from the same vessel may be excavated from different parts of a site.

Christensen (1985) working on the re–used ships' timbers from Bergen, recognised timbers from the same parent vessel by the decorative linear patterns which had been worked along their length. There were only four examples of such mouldings in the Dublin timbers and these were only simple single grooves and therefore not diagnostic.

Comparison of timber species, timber thicknesses and breadths, the sizes of iron nails used to fasten the planking together, and the treenails (wooden pegs or dowels) used to fasten planking to the framework, and the spacing between these fastenings, led to more useful results:

(a)   Six much–repaired 11th century planks (Timber Group 10), which were excavated separately, proved to be very similar, on these criteria, and therefore they probably came from the same vessel (Dublin 10).

(b)   Three separate groups of late 12th century/early 13th century planking (Timber Group 9A, 9B, 9C) see Fig. 9.3.3, probably came from the starboard side of one vessel, whilst a fourth group of planking (Timber Group 6) came from the port bow of the same vessel, which we may call Dublin 69.

(c)   Two further groups of 13th century planking (Timber Group 3A and 3B) probably came from opposite sides of yet another vessel (Dublin 3).

Size of parent vessel

The first step in working out what sizes of parent vessel are represented in these Irish re–used timbers was to calculate the massiveness – as represented by the cross sectional area – of the various types of timbers (keels, stems, framing etc.) in excavated Nordic ships and boats, most of them from Scandinavia. These well–documented vessels could be classified as small boats, boats, large boats, small ships, ships or large ships, using the criteria of overall length defined in Table 9.3.1. A correlation was found, as expected, between size of vessel and the massiveness of its timbers. It was then possible to say, for example, that keels with a cross–section area (CSA) of not more than 110 units came from a boat, with a CSA between 127 and 224 units from a large boat or small ship, CSA greater than 272 from a ship, and CSA greater than 348 from a large ship. Ranges of cross section area were similarly established for other types of timber.

Figure 9.3.1 Clenched nails from Dublin planking B + D from large ships; A from a ship; C + E from boats. Drawing: Institute of Archaeology, Oxford

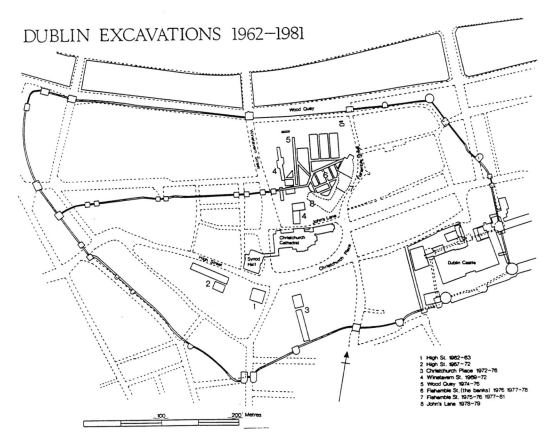

Figure 9.3.2 Dublin excavations 1962–81. Drawing: Institute of Archaeology, Oxford

259

Figure 9.3.3 Planking from Wood Quay timber group 9 during excavation. Scale measures 1m. Photo: National Maritime Museum, Greenwich

Furthermore, it was found that planking could be divided into two groups representing boats on the one hand and ships on the other. Planking from Nordic ships was found to be not longer or broader, generally speaking, than planking from boats, but significantly thicker: greater than 30mm compared with 15 to 20mm. There were also significant differences in the fastenings used: iron nails had head diameters of greater than 30mm (ship) and less than 21mm (boat), and shank diameters of greater than 10mm and less than 8mm; whilst treenail diameters were greater than 28mm and less than 20mm.

Using this criteria it was possible to suggest the size of vessel from which the re–used boat timbers in Dublin, Waterford and Cork had come. In certain cases it was possible to give more specific information by detailed comparisons with well–documented ship and boat finds. Thus the group of 11th century planking known as Timber Group 10 (above) came from a boat the form and size of the 9th century Gokstad boat 2, a *seksering* or 6–oared boat (Johannessen 1940). This similarity was remarkably close, even down to the choice of pine for the top strake of planking when all other planks were oak, in both cases.(Fig. 9.3.4).

The four groups of late–12th century or early 13th century planking known as Timber Group 6 and Timber Group 9 (above) came from a large ship (Dublin 69) which had several features in common with the mid– 11th century Hedeby 3 cargo ship and the mid–12th century Lynaes cargo ship

(Crumlin–Pedersen,1981,1983,1984,1986).This similarity is clearly seen, for example, in the bulging cross–section of all three ships' planking near the waterline. Dublin large ship 69 was probably similar in size to the Lynaes ship (25 x 6.4 x 2.5 m) which Crumlin–Pedersen (1989, 424, fig. 10) has calculated would have carried c60 tons of cargo. In comparison, it is relevant to note that most ships in the Ireland/Bristol trade in the 14th and 15th century were 20 to 30 tons burden (O' Neil, 1987, 108).

Further evidence that sizeable ships used the port of Dublin comes from Wood Quay floor timber (T55), part of the framework of a large ship. Timber T.55 is slightly longer, and has a somewhat bigger cross–section, than the equivalent timber in the Lynaes ship (McGrail, 1993, fig. 16) and thus must have come from a ship of similar or even greater cargo capacity (Fig. 9.3.5)

From the limited Cork and Waterford material there is evidence for boats and large boats, but, so far, not for ships. In contrast, in the much greater volume of Dublin material (nearly 400 nautical timbers) there is evidence for every size of vessel from small boats under oars to large ships under sail. The one clear development seen in the Dublin timbers between the 10th and the 13th century is the increase in size of vessel. From Hiberno–Norse Dublin there is insubstantial evidence for vessels bigger than small ships; whilst from *c* 1170 AD onwards, in Anglo–Norman Dublin, there is ample evidence for ships and indeed large ships, as well as the smaller craft. Otherwise, boat and shipbuilding techniques remained more or less the same throughout the 400 year period, comparable with near–contemporary methods in Scandinavia.

Non–Nordic vessels

From Dublin and from Waterford there are single timbers which cannot be identified as Nordic in style. They are more readily interpreted as floor timbers with an integral knee as used in medieval lighters and river barges (fig. 2.1.6), such as the 12th century *praam* from Egernsund, Denmark (Crumlin–Pedersen, 1981, 36–7). These vessels, of little draft even when loaded, would have been used to unload ships at anchor off Dublin and off Waterford and to move cargo upstream where the deeply–laden ships could not go.

Dublin–built ships and boats or ships and boats dismantled in Dublin?

Ships may be dismantled and re–used many miles from the place they were built; and boats were sometimes carried or towed by medieval ships. Nautical timbers may therefore enter the archaeological record far from their home port. In the case of the Dublin nautical timbers, however, there are good reasons for believing that the parents ship and boats were actually built in Dublin.

Firstly, the dendrochronological pattern of wood samples from the late 12th/ 13th century Timber Group 9 groups of planking best matches the Dublin master oak chronology (Baillie,1982,239) . Thus this large ship was built from oaks grown in the Dublin region. It seems very probable therefore that this ship was built in that region, if not in Dublin itself. Furthermore there is some artifactual and documentary evidence that ships were being built in Dublin in the early 13th century (McGrail, 1993, 86–87).

On balance then, it seems not unreasonable to conclude that the majority of the Dublin nautical timbers were from boats and ships which had been dismantled and re–used close to the site where, some 20 or so years earlier, they had been built (Fig. 9.2.3)

Footnote
Further information on the medieval excavations in Dublin may be found in volumes in the series, Medieval Dublin Excavations, published by the Royal Irish Academy and the National Museum of Ireland.

Figure 9.3.4 The 9th century boat Gokstad 2 in the Viking Ship Hall, Bigdøy, Oslo. Photo: *Universitets Oldaskamling*, Oslo

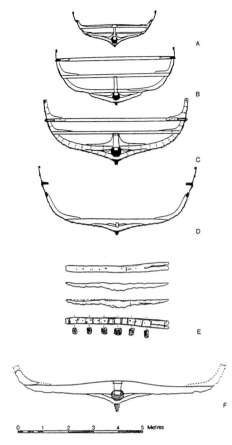

Figure 9.3.5 Dublin floor timber T55 (E) compared in size with the transverse sections of five Viking/Nordic vessels: A. Skuldelev 2; B. Skuldelev 1; C. Hedeby 3; D. Lynaes; F. Bergen 'big ship'. Drawing: Institute of Archaeology, Oxford

References

Baillie M. 1982 *Tree ring dating & archaeology* (London, 1982).

Bonde N. & Crumlin–Pedersen O. 'The dating of Wreck 2 from Skuldelev, Denmark', *Newswarp7*, (1990), pp. 3–6.

Christensen A–E. 'Boat finds from Bryggen' *Bryggen Papers* 1, (Oslo, 1985), 47–280.

Crumlin–Pedersen O. 'Skibe på Havbunden' *Handels og Sjøfartsmuseets Årbog*, (Heslingør 1981), 28–65.

Crumlin–Pedersen O. 'Schiffe und Seehandelsrouten im Ostseeraum' 1050–1350, *Lübecker Schriften zur Archäeologie und Kulturgeschichte 7*, (1983), 229–237.

Crumlin–Pedersen O. 'Der seertransport: die Schiffe von Haithabu.' *Archäeologische und naturwissenschaftliche Unter–suchungen an Siedlungen im deutchen Küstengebiet 2*, (1984), 241–8. Acta Humaniora Weinheim.

Crumlin–Pedersen O. 'Ship finds and ship blockages. AD 800 to 1200' in K Kristiansen (ed.), *Archaeological formation processes*, 215–228 (Copenhagen, 1985).

Crumlin–Pedersen O. 'Aspects of Viking Age shipbuilding'. *Journal of Danish Archaeology* 5, (1986), 209–228.

Crumlin–Pedersen O. 'Schiffstypen aus der fruh–geschichtlichen Seeschiffahrt in den nordeuropaischen Gewässern.' *Untersuchungen zu Handel und Verkher vorund früh–geschichtlichen Zeit in Mittel–und Nord–europa* 5 (1989) 405–430.

Ellmers D. 1979, 'Cog of Bremen and related boats', in S. McGrail (ed.) *Archaeology of medieval ships and harbours* (Oxford, 1979), 1–15.

Greenhill B. *Archaeology of the boat* (London,1976).

Greenhill B. *Evolution of the wooden ship* (London, 1989).

Hurley M.F 'Excavations in Medieval Cork: St Peter's Market.' *Journal of the Cork Historical and Archaeological Society.* 91, (1986), 1–25.

Johannesen F. 'Båtene fra Goksradskibet.' *Viking* 4, 1940, 125–130.

McGrail S. *Medieval boat and ship timbers from Dublin* (Dublin, 1993).

Mitchell G.F. *Archaeology and environment in early Dublin* (Dublin, 1987).

Müller-Wille M. 1968-9, 'Bestattung im boot.', *Offa* 25/6 1968-9, 7–203.

O'Neill T. 1987, *Merchants and Mariners in Medieval Ireland.* (Dublin, 1987) .

Wallace P.F. 1981, 'Dublin's waterfront at Wood Quay: 900–1317.' in G. Milne & B. Hobley (eds.), *Waterfront Archaeology in Britain and N. Europe* (CBA Research Report 4 1, 1981), 109–118.

Wallace P.F. *VikingAge buildings of Dublin* (Dublin,1992).

Reprinted with permission from:

Bullán 1: 49–61. Oxford (1994).

SECTION 10.0

SEAFARING AND NAVIGATION

The seafaring knowledge and navigational skills needed in the Cross–Channel trade in the late–1st millennium BC are discussed in Paper 10.1. In fact, the core elements of these skills and knowledge are independent of environmental context and of type of vessel used. The problems of working a vessel, of determining her position, and of taking her in safety from one place to another, without instruments other than the sounding lead, are universal ones, and the solutions evolved in different times and places are remarkably similar (Taylor, 1971: 3–88; McGrail, 1987: Ch. 13 & 14).

For non–instrumental (sometimes known as environmental) navigation in the ancient Mediterranean, see McGrail (1996); in proto–historic Atlantic Europe, see Papers 7.2 & 8.1; ; in early medieval NW Europe, see Paper 10.3; in the Viking period, see Schnall (1996) and Vebaek & Thirslund (1992); in Indian waters, see Arunachalam (1996); and in Oceania, see Irwin (1992), Lewis (1994), and Finney (1994).

For early developments in instrumental navigation see: Taylor (1971: 89–279) – generally; Waters (1978) – in the context of 16th and 17th century England; and Tibbetts (1971) and Fatimi (1996) – for Arab navigation. For Columbus' navigational techniques in 1492–3, see Waters (1992) and McGrail (1992). Although Needham has long advocated the primacy of the Chinese in instrumental navigation (Ronan, 1986: 164–180), Fatimi has recently traced the Arab use of the Kamal, to measure the altitude (angular height) of stars, back to the 10th century AD.

How early seafarers could become aware of land out of sight, over the horizon, is discussed in Paper 10.4; the carriage of ballast in Paper 10.2; whilst Paper 10.5 considers, in a Mediterranean context, such archaeological problems as the origins of a particular ship and the route taken on her final voyage, and the earliest known use of sail. Remarks by Westerdahl (1995, 41–43) on the reasons for the late use of sail in northern European waters (late–8th century AD) may throw light on the relatively late use of sail in the Mediterranean when compared with Egypt.

References

Arunachalam B. 1996 'Traditional sea & sky wisdom of Indian seamen & their practical applications.' in Ray, H.P. & Salles. J–F. (ed) *Tradition & Archaeology*, 261–282. Manohar. New Delhi.

Fatimi S.Q. 1996 'History of the development of the kamal.' in Ray, H.P. & Salles, J–F. (ed) *Tradition and Archaeology* 283–292. Manohar. New Delhi.

Finney B. 1994 *Voyage of Rediscovery*. University of California Press.

Irwin G. 1992 *Prehistoric Exploration and Colonisation of the Pacific*. CUP.

Lewis D. 1994 *We, the Navigators*. 2nd Edition. University of Hawaii Press.

McGrail S. 1987 *Ancient Boats in NW Europe*. Longman.

McGrail S. 1992. 'Columbus' trans–Atlantic voyage in 1492–3. *Medieval History*, 23: 353–355.

McGrail S. 1996. 'Navigational techniques in Homer's Odyssey.' *Tropis*, 4: 311–320.

Ronan C.A. 1986 *Shorter Science and Civilisation in China*. CUP.

Schnall U. 1996 'Early shiphandling & navigation in Northern Europe.' in Christensen A.E. (ed) *Earliest Ships* 120–128. Conway's History of the Ship. vol. 1.

Taylor E.G.R. 1971 *Haven–finding Art*. Hollis & Carter.

Tibbetts G.R. 1971 *Arab Navigation in the Indian Ocean before the coming of the Portuguese*. Royal Asiatic Soc.

Vebaek C.L. 1992 *Viking Compass*. Denmark.

Waters D. 1978. *Art of Naviqation in England in Elizabethan & early Stuart Times*. 3 vols. Greenwich.

Waters D. 1992 'Columbus' Portuguese inheritance.' *Mariner's Mirror*, 78: 385–406.

Westerdahl C. 1995 'Society & sail.' in Crumlin–Pedersen, O. & Thye, B.M. (ed) *Ship as a Symbol*, 41–50. National Museum, Copenhagen.

PAPER 10.1

CROSS CHANNEL SEAMANSHIP AND NAVIGATION IN THE LATE FIRST MILLENIUM BC

Any enquiry into the maritime aspects of prehistoric contacts across the English Channel (la Manche) has to tackle three main questions:

(1) what sorts of boats were used?

(2) How were these boats handled (seamanship)?

(3) How did seamen find their way (navigation)?

The Boats

The evidence for the types of water–transport in use in later prehistoric northern and western Europe has been summarised by McGrail (1981, 16–25). Excavated remains are of logboats and plank boats more suitable for inland waterways and sheltered estuaries than for sea crossings. However, a boat-representation on a coin excavated from Canterbury, Kent, and two boat finds from the river Thames dated to the early centuries A.D. may give a pointer towards the type of sea craft in use in the Channel in the late first millenium. The Blackfriars 1 and New Guy House finds (Marsden, 1976) appear to be members of an indigenous boatbuilding tradition first identified by Ellmers (1969) and recently called Romano–Celtic (McGrail, 1981, 22–4), and some similarities with Caesar's (*BG* III.13) and Strabo's (*Geog* 4.4.1) descriptions of the plank boats of the Veneti have been noted. The early first century A.D. coin (possibly of Cunobelin) shows a deep–sided boat with mast, yard, stays and possibly braces, which has a sheerline echoing Caesar's description (Muckelroy *et al.* 1978 – see Figs 7.2.5 and 8.1.9).

Of the Celtic seagoing skin boats described by several Latin authors (for example: Pliny, *Nat. Hist.* IV.104) there are no known remains, although the small gold model from Broighter, Co. Derry (Fig 7.1.2) of the first century B.C., may represent this type of craft (Farrell and Penny, 1975).

Sail was used in Arabian waters from *c.* 3000 B.C. (McGrail, 1981, 44–5) and in the Mediterranean from at least 2000 (Casson, 1971, 31, but the earliest evidence for indigeneous sail in northern and western Europe is from first century B.C.: the mast and yard on the Broighter model, and Caesar's description of the boats of the Veneti. Rowing is feasible in moderate seas and in fact may be preferred in light winds and necessary in foul (contrary) winds; but little evidence has survived.

In order to investigate the problems of indigenous cross–Channel operations it is necessary to define a standard cargo–carrying boat with the general characteristics of form and propulsion suggested by the scanty evidence: I deduce this to have been a planked, open boat, some 7 to 12 m in length, propelled by a single square sail, with a few oars or sweeps for use inshore in calms and in foul winds and streams. This boat would have had a good sheer (upcurving) at the bow and stern as a reserve of buoyancy and to protect her from bow and quartering seas. Her transverse sections would have been full with rounded bilges and flared sides to give good cargo space with a flattish bottom to allow her to take the ground easily. She would have been broad in relation to her length to give her stability, and sufficiently deep–sided to have safe freeboard. Skin boats may also be built to this general specification although without much sheer (*cf Brendan*, Severin, 1978).

Early twentieth–century decked fishing boats would not put to sea in winds above Force 6 (see Beaufort scale in Heaton, 1970, 171–2), therefore I assume that the prudent limit for a prehistoric open boat would be Force 5, that is up to a fresh breeze of *c.* 20 kts, although a skin boat may have been able to cope with Force 6 winds (*c.* 25 kts) because of better seakeeping qualities.

Severin's experimental skin boat *Brendan* (1978, 290) could sail to within 6 points (*c.*67° of the wind but had a leeway (drift downwind) equivalent to 2 points (c. 22°) and therefore made no headway in these conditions. The performance of replicas of Viking boats with single square sails (Binns, 1980, 165, 168) suggests that 6 points was also their limit in the best of weather, with a 1 point (11¼°) leeway. *Brendan* had a foresail as well as a mainsail and the Viking replicas had modern rigging which improved their windward performance. In addition, the form of boat postulated above for the prehistoric period would have a performance inferior to that of the Viking hull form. I therefore assume that the indigenous, prehistoric open boat could not sail closer to the wind than 7 points, a sector of 157½° centred on the wind (Fig. 10.1.1) with a 1 point leeway for a planked boat (Fig. 10.1.2) and 2 point leeway for a skin boat. Although maximum speed in ideal conditions might be as much as 7 kts for a boat of 7.m waterline length, on 9 kts for one of 12 m, classical documentary evidence and the performance of recent boats and experimental replicas lead to the conclusion that, on a typical cross–Channel voyage, the

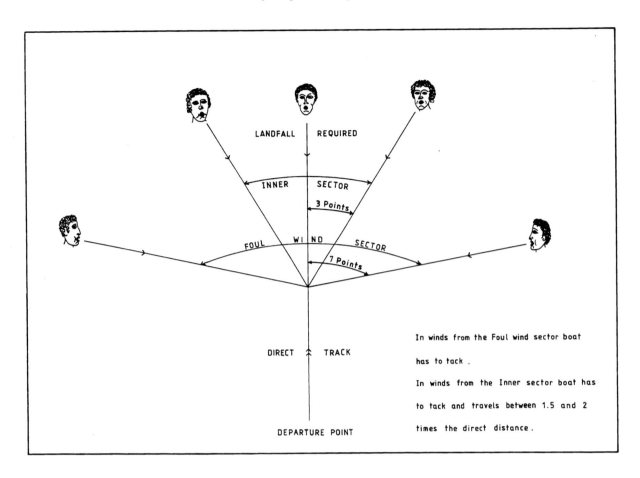

Figure 10.1.1 Diagram showing a foul wind sector of 14 points for the postulated first–millennium boat, with an inner sector of 6 points, where 1 point = 11¼°. Winds blowing from directions outside the foul wind sector are 'fair'; with such winds a boat could sail along the direct track between Departure and Landfall (discounting leeway and drift – see Fig. 10.1.2. Not to scale

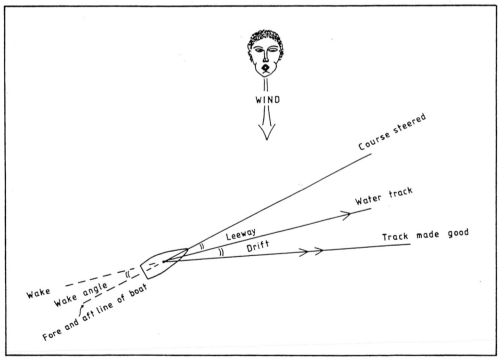

Figure 10.1.2 Diagram, not to scale, showing leeway due to winds as an angular displacement from the course steered. With the wind blowing from a stern sector 5 points either side of the boat's fore and aft line, leeway would be negligible. Drift due to current and tidal stream (here acting in the *same* direction as the wind) is shown as an angular displacement from the track through the water; this gives the track made good over the seabed. If the combined effect of current and stream were *opposed* to the wind, drift would cancel out some or all of the leeway.

Dead reckoning (DR) positions would be on the 'course steered' vector, and estimated positions (EP) on the 'track made good' vector

average speed made good towards the destination would have been *c.* 2½kts, giving an average 24–hour day sail of 60 nautical miles (n.m.): with generally fair winds the average speed could have been 5 kts. Average speeds on coastal routes may have been somewhat less, as such voyages can often include periods at anchor during foul tidal streams and winds (see Greenhill, 1978, 200 for a 19th–century example), and during overcast nights; or periods underway but making little headway with fair winds but foul stream (see description of Caesar's cross–Channel voyages below).

Seamanship and navigation

It is necessary to define these terms before the second and third questions posed above can be tackled since navigation, for example, may have a meaning akin to 'seafaring' rather than the technical sense used in this paper.

Seamanship: The art and science of working a vessel so that a voyage is conducted safely and efficiently. This term includes *navigation*.

Navigation: The art and science of determining a vessel's position and of taking her in safety from one place to another. This term includes *pilotage*.

Pilotage: The art and science of conducting a vessel within waters restricted by the proximity of land and which are generally shallow.

Navigation is now regarded primarily as a science, but has not always been so. It is pertinent to note that two important works on the history of navigation (Taylor, 1971; Waters, 1978) include in their titles the 'haven–finding art' and 'art of navigation': where art implies personal skills. Even as late as the sixteenth century the methods used were inexact although generally adequate, and relied to a great degree on handed–on experience, local knowledge and detailed observation of natural phenomena (Waters, 1978, 3–38). The bulk of early 19th–century navigation was similar, see for example, Binns (1980, 79–80), and late 19th–century innumerate fishermen found their way to distant fishing grounds and back with minimum instrumental aids (Olsen, 1885; see also Greenhill, 1978, 199–205 and Kemp, 1976, 123–4). Polynesian methods of navigation used in this century were similarly based (Lewis, 1972) and may truly be described as environmental rather than instrumental. It is probable that navigation in prehistoric Europe was generally of this nature.

It is important to note in this context that late 20th–century expectations of accuracy and time-keeping are unprecedentally high, and expectation of risk, delay and indeed loss, correspondingly low. This was not so in antiquity, as may be seen for example, in Sidonius's description of the fifth–century Saxon seaman's almost casual attitude to the dangers of shipwreck (*Ep.* VII.6.13). In addition, modern man is generally only a superficial observer of such natural phenomena as the weather sequences, the tides, movements of stars and planets, and the habits of birds and fish. By contrast, in earlier times, survival could depend upon perceptive

interpretation of these observations, and such a body of orally–transmitted knowledge was an important aspect of a culture. Early navigators were of necessity masters of techniques which their modern counterparts need not attempt to use except in conditions of equipment–failure or shipwreck.

The Channel and Bay of Biscay environment

Environmental changes

The shape and character of the coastline (partly determined by mean sea–level), the depth of water and nature of the sea–bed, the position of shoals, reefs, banks and bars, the tidal–stream regimes, the general weather sequences and the direction of the predominant winds are all of immediate concern to the seaman. Yet how different from present conditions these were in late prehistoric times is difficult to quantify. We may take Christchurch Harbour as an example of one aspect of this problem. Cunliffe (1978, 11) has estimated that, in the last 200 years, erosion has removed some 150 m of land from the seaward side of Hengistbury Head; but earlier erosion–rates are unknown. Eastward drift in the Channel has eroded material in a long shingle spit across the entrance to this harbour (Chatwin, 1960); whilst, inside, the Stour and the Avon have deposited alluvium and marsh has formed. The long–term rate of the these depositions is also unknown and thus the shape of the harbour entrance and the position of the shoreline within the harbour some 2000 years ago cannot be determined with precision. At Dover where more environnental work has been done, pre–Roman and post–Roman spits have been recognised (Rigold, 1969, fig. 1): yet even here the details of the shoreline at any one time are not known.

In addition to changes caused by natural forces, recent drainage and other engineering works have considerably affected landing–places: for example, until the late nineteenth century St. Malo was an island in the estuary of the river Rance connected to the mainland by a causeway, whilst Alet (1½ n.m. to the south and now part of St. Malo) was a peninsula until 1965 (Belin, 1764, chart 44; Purdy, 1842, 219; Langouët, 1977, 38).

Weather has a slgnificant effect on boat operations and navigation, but ancient weather patterns are difficult to define except in the most general terms. However, Lamb (1981) has argued that after 1000 B.C. there was a decisive shift in the climate of the north–western European seaboard towards colder, wetter conditions, so that the weather in *c.* 300 B.C. would have been comparable with today.

Lamb (1981, 205) also considers that the global sea–level may have dropped by *c.* 1.5 m to 2 m between 1000 and 300 B.C., but assessment of local sea–level is complicated by the isostatic sinking of the land in SE Britain associated with the warping of the earth's crust in the N Sea basin, and by sediment consolidation, uplift and subsidence. The latest estimate taking these global and local effects into account is that along the southern coast of England there has been a general rise in sea–level, but at a diminishing rate, from *c.* 7000 B.C. to the present day (Devoy, 1982, 85 fig. 9; Heyworth and Kidson, 1982, 94 fig. 2). Thus in the late first millenium mean sea-level was lower than today, but within today's tidal range.

In cetrain parts of the region under discussion the evidence may be sufficient to allow the theoretical reconstruction of the late first- millenium coastline with varying degrees of confidence: see Devoy (1982, 67 fig 2); Hawkes (1977B, maps 8 and 10); du Plat Taylor and Cleere (1978, frontispiece); Cunliffe (1980, 41 fig. 18, 44 fig. 19); Thoen (1978, 242 map 3); and Ryckaert (1980, 76 fig. 1). Other areas on both sides of the Channel lack detailed treatment of sea-level and river-gradient changes, coastal erosion and deposition; and in these regions it may be difficult to be precise about boat operations as the features of a harbour or landing-place are determined by local conditions.

In the light of thepreceding discussion I shall assume that in the late first millenium B.C. Channel Bay region:

> a) Execpt where there is evidence to the contrary, coastlines were generally as they are now, with a slightly lower mean sea-level.

> b) There was less silting of estuaries, and spits and bars across their entrances were not so prominent.

> c) The climate was generally as it is now.

> d) The tidal regime was generally as it is today.

The environmental conditions in the Channel and Bay of Biscay may then be ascertained from charts and Admiralty Pilot handbooks, supplementd by person experience. The handbooks contain descriptions of the weather and meteorological statistics for the sea areas they cover, together with pilotage instructions for coastal passages between the major, and many of the minor, ports. Where available, 19th- and early 20th- century editions have been used, but certain data are only in recent editions. The weather statistics are only available for a limited number of reporting stations: for example, the Channel winds are averaged and summarised in one wind rose. In additions the data are simple mean values and there are, for example, no statistics giving the probability of having three consecutive days with a SW wind of Force 1-5. Notwithstanding these deficiencies it is considered that the data can be used to make valid comparisons between routes.

The Channel and the Bay of Biscay
The northern part of the Bay of Biscay and the English Channel, towards the edge of the Continental shelf, are to leeward of the predominant SW wind, in the path of Atlantic depression, and downstream of the North Atlantic current. The Bay and the Channel absorb much of this energy and, in particular, the wedge-shaped Channel narrowing from the west restricts the movement of a large body of water, and thus funnels and intensifies these natural elements, and strong tidal streams of complex pattern are generated. Thus passages within this region can present a wide variety of problems to the seaman, both inshore and in more open waters.

These sea areas lie within the 100-fathom (c. 200m) line and are thus relatively shallow. The nature of the sea-bed – mud, sands, gravels, and stones of different colour and size – varies in different areas, and these characteristics (including smell) obtained from a sounding-lead sample, combined with the depth of water, may be used when nearing land to determine an approximate position or to identify the entrance to an estuary or channel.

The weather is variable, seasonal changes being not so noticeable as in other parts of the world, and actual weather can differ considerably from seasonal means. Forecasting the weather for short periods ahead without instruments is practicable, especially the sequences of a depression with its high cloud forewarning. Although timing is difficult, simple observations of the clouds, wind, sea and air mass and the behaviour of sea birds provide useful indications of future weather (see, for example, *Reids Nautical Almanac* 1983, 714/5; Slade and Greenhill, 1974, 24).

The predominant winds and the resultant swell are from between SW and NW throughout the year, and the general set of the surface current in the Channel is north-easterly, although averaging only 6 n.m./ day, with a maximum of 36 n.m./day in strong SW winds. Thus there is a general tendency for cross-Channel traffic to be set towards the NE, that is up-Channel, if insuffficient allowance is made for displacement caused by wind and current. In the Bay of Biscay, on the other hand, whilst predominant winds are still from the westerly sectors, the inshore current tends to be parallel to the coast in a SE direction from Ushant.

Superimposed on these horizontal movements of the sea caused by predominant winds are the regular ebbs and flows of the tidal stream generated by astronomical forces and modified by topography and locally by weather. In mid-Channel the set of this stream is NE/SW at speeds of 1-3 kts, depending primarily on the phases of the moon: the streams are weaker in the Bay away from the entrance to the Channel. During each tidal cycle the mid-Channel stream flows NE for c. 6¼ hrs, then SW for c. 6¼ hrs (Fig. 10.1.3) resulting in a theoretical net horizontal movement of zero in a 12½ hr period. Cross-Channel boats, however, will generally experience some net displacement when they traverse areas with differing streams.

Local conditions

In the open water between Ushant and Scilly the set of the tidal stream traces out an ellipse, so that for about half the cycle it is generally N and S rather than E and W. There is a similar circulation inshore in the Bay, with a SE/NW alignment. The stream pattern is modified generally in inshore waters where sets are at an angle to the mid-Channel alignments, and the times of flow-reversal (slack water) are altered. The rates of tidal stream also vary inshore, and speeds up to 10 kts can be experienced in narrow channels such as that to the east of Alderney. Favourable tidal streams with more than a certain depth of water are always desirable and often essential when leaving or approaching landing-places (Greenhill, 1978, 199–205; Eglinton, 1982, 1–29): thus the the times of flow-reversal and of high and low water (not necessarily the

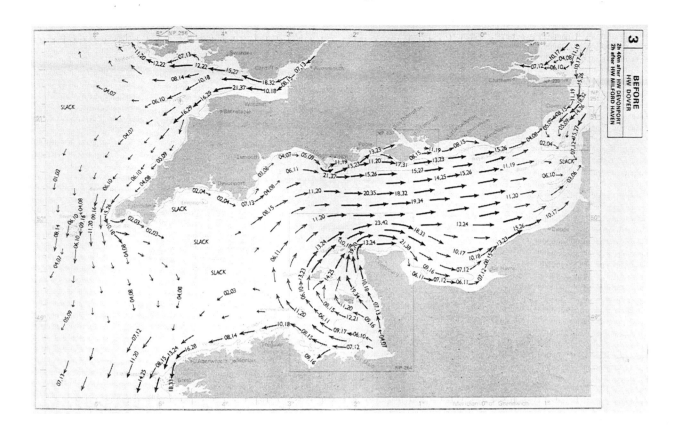

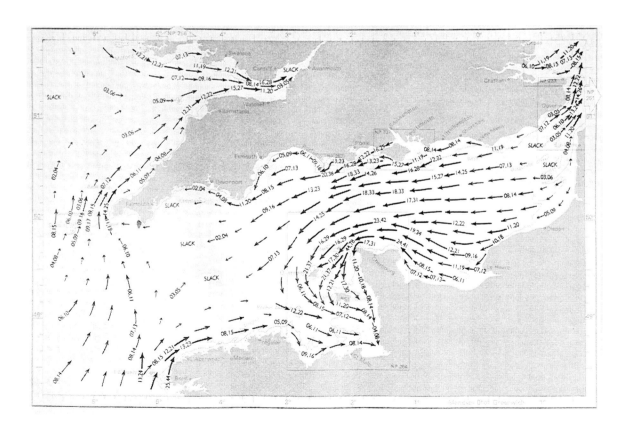

Figure 10.1.3 The charts show tidal streams in the Channel and adjacent waters at *c* 3 hours before (upper) and 3 hours after (lower) datum, which in this case is the time of high water at Dover. The arrows indicate direction of flow and are graded for rate of stream, so that a thick arrow means a strong stream. The figures against some arrows give rates at neap and spring tides e.g. 07,12 = a mean neap rate of 0.7 kts and a mean spring rate of 1.2 kts. Source: *Tidal Stream Atlas*, 1973 (NP.250). Hydrographic Dept. Taunton

same) need to be known with some precision. Local knowledge is also required to estimate the variations that persistent strong winds impose on the tidal regime, and to identify contra–flows in estuaries so that progress may be made against an unfavourable stream.

The sequence of high and low water at landing–places and generally in inshore water is linked to the tidal stream–pattern and to the age and bearing of the moon, the chief arbiter of tides (Waters, 1978, 31): in the pre–literate era this complex relationship had to be learned by observation and by rote for each landing–place. The tidal range (the vertical distance from high water to low water) at individual landing–places had also to be learned, as this determines the depth of water in the approach channel and, together with the slope of the beach, influences the decision to beach or to moor a boat, and also determines how and when she will be loaded and unloaded.

The wind's strength and direction are also modified by local effects near the coast: thus in the lee of a headland there will be an area of light winds, then an area of turbulent winds and seas. Furthermore land and sea breezes, caused by unequal heating and cooling of land and sea, will modify the general wind pattern. Because of the retarding effect of the land, W and SW gales (which generally predominate) are less severe and last half as long in the eastern Channel than in the western Channel and Bay of Biscay. On the other hand, sea fogs are more common in the west and in the Bay.

Seasonal variations in weather

Cloud cover in the Channel and Bay is generally between 5/8 and 6/8, with only slight improvement in summer (June to August). In the period between late autumn and the end of spring the whole area may be overcast for several successive days, making celestial observations impossible. However, NW winds bring clearer periods generally, and in the southern part of the Bay cloud generally may be less than 4/8 in summer. Although rain may be heavier in summer, it falls more often and lasts longer in winter (December to February) with a probability of 66% compared with a summer probability of 33%.

The sea temperature, even in summer, is too low for free–flooding rafts to be used, and makes conditions unpleasant in an open boat which in a moderate or rough sea will inevitably take water over the sides or ends. Lower air and sea temperatures in winter, combined with exposure to wind and wetness from rain or sea water, soon make a man numb: such conditions were the main cause of wartime deaths in open boats (Miles, 1971–2).

Gales of force 7 and above are eight times more frequent in winter than in summer, and almost twice as frequent in autumn (September to November) than in spring (March to May). These gales are predominantly from the W and SW and generate a swell from that direction, but in February and March N and NE gales may prevail. Rough seas induced by these storms have a probability of 22% in winter compared with 8% in summer.

The sailing season

There are thus several reasons against operating open boats in the Channel and Bay from mid–November to mid–March. This season was also avoided in the classical Mediterranean (Casson, 1971, 270) and in medieval Scandinavia (Ross and McLough 1977, 147). Winter sailing was undertaken in 19th–century British coastal waters, but voyages consisted of broken passages with many long waits for brief periods of settled weather (Greenhill, 1978, 201–4).

In summer, cloud cover may make observation of sun, moon and stars difficult but generally not impossible. A further conclusion is that routes across the eastern Channel are not only shorter but have marginally better weather than in the west.

Evidence and methodolgy

Ancient scientific knowledge

For this period of essentially non–instrumental pilotage and navigation little artifactual evidence is to be expected, although sounding–leads with a cavity to sample the sea bed (with which Herodotus, 2.5.2, was familiar) have been recovered from several Classical wreck sites (Casson, 1971, 246; Fiori and Joncheray, 1973), and a find from the Antikythera wreck, excavated in 1901, has been identified as an instrument of *c.* 80 B.C. which indicated the movements of the sun, moon and principal stars (Price, 1959).

The documentary evidence is more rewarding, although again mainly confined to the Mediterranean world. Classical authors (for example, Pliny, *NH* Bk. 2) indicate that celestial observations were used to estimate time and direction, and to obtain a form of latitude on land (Taylor, 1971, 3–64).

Vitruvius (I.3–10) enjoined first–century architects to study astronomy so that they might 'learn the direction points, the orders of the heavens, the equinoxes and and solstices and the movement of the stars' and 'to understand how clocks and sundials work': seamen also needed this knowledge. The influence of the moon's phases on the tides was also known (Strabo, *Geog.* 1.3.11 and 3.5.8–9), as were the Mediterranean sea conditions to be expected from certain weather sequences; and the directions from which prevailing winds blew were used as reference bearings (Taylor, 1971, 14–20).

Turning to northern and western Europe we find that knowledge of the sun's movements, and possibly those of the moon and stars, is evidenced in Neolithic and Bronze Age Britain and France by the alignment of certain megalithic structures (Heggie, 1981, 222–3); direct application to sea navigation or tidal prediction seems unlikely (Wood,1978, 184–8); nevertheless the knowledge would have been useful at sea. The Celtic world certainly had a working knowledge of astronomy (Caesar, *BG* VI 14) with particular emphasis on the moon (Piggott, 1974, 104–5): such learning could have been used in direction–finding and in tidal prediction.

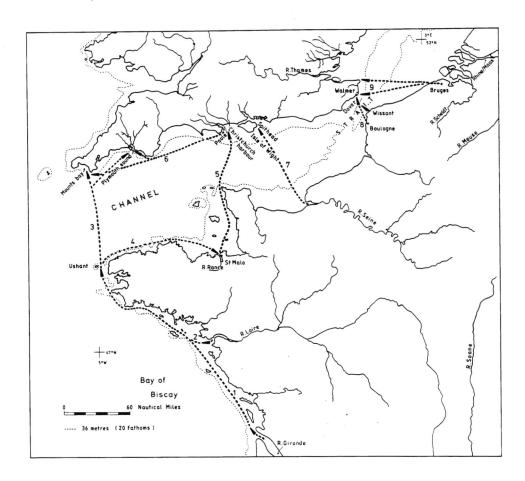

Figure 10.1.4 The nine routes described in the text (see also Table 10.1.1). The routes shown are approximate and not precise tracks

Sea Routes

Classical authors mention the Continental departure–points of cross–Channel sea routes (but see Cunliffe, 1982, 42, for a cautionary note), and excavated evidence of coins and traded goods may be used to suggest the location of some of the British terminals for this traffic (Fig. 10.1.4). The evidence for five such routes (3, 5, 7, 8, 9) and four intermediate coastal routes (1, 2, 4, 6) is summarised in Table 10.1.1.

The ability to undertake coastal and cross–Channel voyages implies knowledge and technical capabilities of at least a minimum standard in seamanship, pilotage and navigation. Some indication of what these skills and techniques were may be obtained from cross–cultural comparisons with maritime peoples of roughly similar technology and scientific attainment. An attempt may also be made to evaluate these Mediterranean routes by comparing the following characteristics for outward and inward legs:

    a) Time taken at 2½ kts and at 5 kts. Navigational and weather–forecasting problems may be expected to be greater the longer the voyage.

b) Distance out of sight of land. In good visibility high ground can be sighted from a considerable distance to seaward. Table 10.1.2 lists typical distances from sea level. In theory another 2.57 n.m. should be added to these distances to allow for the height of the observer, but as some time is required to distinguish a headland (without a beacon or lighthouse) from the horizon the tabled figures are probably the best estimate of visibility distance in good weather. The proportion of a voyage spent out of sight of land is some measure of the time when navigational methods, rather than pilotage, have to be used. Poor visibility and darkness decrease the distances given in Table 10.1.2, and an estimate of the effect of the latter can be made for typical summer passages at 2½ kts and 5 kts.

c) Theoretical displacement, during passages out of sight of land, due to current and tidal stream (assuming departure on ebb tide).

d) Probability of having a foul wind on a typical day in the summer months. If the wind is from a direction less than 7 points (c. 80°) away from the direct track between departure point and destination, the standard indigenous cargo–boat defined above will have to

Table 10.1.1 Bay of Biscay and Channel Routes in the Late 1st Millenium BC

Routes	References	Remarks
1. R. Gironde to W Brittany	Strabo, *Geog.* 4.1.14; 4.2.1; 4.5.2 Peacock, 1971, fig. 36 Cunliffe, 1982, 42–3	May link with Route 3 or with Routes 4 and 5
2. R. Loire to W Brittany	Strabo, *Georg.* 4.1.14; 4.2.1; 4.5.2 Peacock, 1971, fig. 36 Cunliffe, 1982, 42–3	May link with Route 3 or with Routes 4 and 5
3. W Brittany to Cornwall/Devon	Cunliffe, 1978A, 73 Cunliffe, 1983 Cunliffe, 1982, 48, 51 Clarke, 1971, 153 Strabo, *Geog.* 4.4.1 Ceasar, *B.G.* III.8 Diodorus, V.21.3; V.22.22–4 André, 1976–8, 153	Routes 4, 5 and 6 may be an alternative to Route 3
4. W Brittany to NE Brittany	Cunliffe, 1982, 42–3	Note 1
5. NE Brittany to Dorset	Cunliffe, 1982, 42–5, figs. 8, 9, and 10 Diodorus, V.38.5	Note 1
6. Dorset to Devon/Cornwall	Cunliffe, 1982, 47–51, figs. 13 and 14 Cunliffe, 1983 Pliny, *Nat, History*, IV 102 (xvi)	
7. R Seine to Britain	Strabo, *Geog.* 4.1.14; 4.3.3–4; 4.5.2	
8. NW France to Kent	Ceasar, *B.G.* IV, 21–36; V.2–23 Pliny *Nat, History*, IV 102 (xv) Diodorus, V.21.3	
9. Rhine to Britain	Strabo, *Geog.* 4.3.3–4; 4.5.1–2 Pliny, *Nat History*, IV, 101 (xv) Peacock, 1971, fig. 36 Cunliffe, 1978B, 158, fig. 10.19	

Note: 1. West Brittany to Poole/Portsmouth is a theoretical alternative to Routes 4 and 5

tack (Fig. 10.1.1). With a wind blowing directly opposed to the required track, at least twice the direct distance has to be covered; with a wind some 3 points off the direct track the distance to be covered because of tacking is at least 1.5 times the direct distance. For route comparison the probability is estimated of having a foul wind a) in a sector 7 points either side of the direct route, and b) in an inner sector 3 points either side of the direct route.

e) Unusual aspects of the route, for instance difficult legs, as through the Channel Islands or along the Brittany coast.

Landing places

Even though excavation may clearly indicate that a coastal settlement, such as the one on the southern side of Christchurch Harbour, NW of Hengistbury Head, was involved in this cross–Channel trade, the associated landing–place or places may be difficult to recognise (McGrail, 1983). Outside the Classical world, formal waterfront structures do not seem to have been built until about the tenth century, and even today boats are beached on open coasts or in natural harbours and on river banks, or as at Christchurch they are allowed to take the ground on a falling tide, or held off the foreshore at anchor, or secured to mooring posts (see Eglinton, 1982 for such operations in the early twentieth century). Thus, rather than coherent structures, we may expect to find the remains of individual mooring posts or anchors of stone or iron and other items of boat's equipment. Clusters of artifacts which are otherwise inexplicable may also indicate a regularly–used landing–place, as also may parallel rows of stones at right to angles to the shoreline, or cleared areas on an otherwise stony strand as known in recent times in Norway, Shetland and the outer Hebrides.

The seaman, the trader and the political authority may each have different views on what constitutes the ideal landing–place for international trade. The seaman requires one with nearby natural features (headlands, etc.) which make a good landfall and can readily be distinguished. The approach must be well–defined and usable, almost regardless of wind direction, and the landing–place itself should have an aspect such that it is sheltered from the predominant wind and swell. A moderately sloping beach of sand, shingle or mud where the boat can easily take the ground is also to be preferred, and small tidal range is advantageous; but landing–places with steep rock beaches and great tidal ranges can also be used, albeit with more difficulty. Landing–places on open coasts unprotected by off–shore islands or by the arms of a bay are exposed to wind and swell; techniques for landing and launching through surf off such places are well known (see, for example, *Seamanship Manual* 1, 1926, 246 52), but these places are only used when sites with greater protection are not available or when secrecy is paramount. Natural habours, such as at Christchurch and the many others along the southern English coast between Beachy Head and the Lizard (Fig. 10.1.5), and estuaries such as the Humber, generally provide the best landing–places from the seaman's viewpoint, especially where they have uncluttered approaches. Where otherwise good landing–places have a sector exposed to rough seas and dangerous ground swell, alternative places protected from this open sector may be found nearby.

The trader requires a landing–place close to a settlement (seasonal or permanent) where he can find shelter, food and water, where he and his goods will be safe and where he can meet buyers and possibly assemble a return cargo. Such a site has been called a 'port of trade' (Polyani, 1963) or a 'gateway community' (Hirth, 1978). This site should ideally be at the centre (if one exists) of the regional economy or with good access to it. The natural economic and political centres for many regions lie away from the coast and in these cases the trader's ideal site would be inland, up a river and possibly at a ford as at Dublin, London and Bristol in the early medieval period.

The political authority requires a well–defined, possibly defended, site, preferably near the coast (i e as near the common 'frontier' as practicable), where traders can be segregated, protected and supervised, justice dispensed and tolls imposed. Settlements in the coastal zone on promontories or islands are suitable locations for these activities.

The seaman's and the political authority's requirements may be satisfied by a landing–place within an estuary or natural harbour, on a well–defined promontory or island. The trader's requirement for access to the economically and politically dominant regional centres may be met by choosing natural harbours fed by important river systems. A break in a cross–Channel voyage at a site within a natural harbour is almost inevitable for trans–shipment of goods from seagoing craft to boats of less draft suitable for inland waterways, and because the seaman's knowledge of pilotage may not extend far upriver. Where these rivers cross political boundaries further controls including tolls may be imposed, as in late first millennium France (Strabo, *Geog.*, 4.3.2), and the pilot may be changed.

Table 10.1.2 Theoretical Visibility Distances from Seaward

Headland height	Distance
30m (100 ft)	11.5nm
61m (200 ft)	16.2nm
152m (500 ft)	27.7nm

Source: <u>Inman's Nautical Tables</u>, 1920, 12.

Note: Theoretical visibility distance is approxiamtely equal to: $1.1 \sqrt{h}$ nautical miles, where h = height of land in feet

There are difficulties in comparing landing–places objectively, as the precise sites may be unknown; the geomorphology and other environmental features may be different today; and it may not be possible to quantify local effects on the wind, sea and swell. Nevertheless, it is considered that sufficient reliable information exists to make assessments of the relative ease and reliability of boat operations in the vicinity of sites which

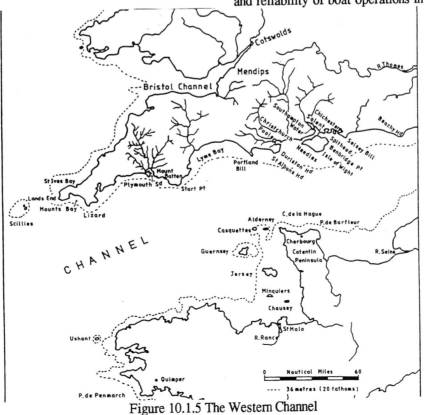

Figure 10.1.5 The Western Channel

273

have been suggested as late prehistoric landing–places, by comparing the following features:

a) Summer probability of not leaving because of no wind, winds stronger than Force 5, and foul winds within safe departure sector(s).

b) Summer probability of not being able to approach the landing–place because of no wind, winds stronger than Force 5, and foul winds within safe approach sector(s).

c) Sea state. Wave height generated by wind is proportional (*inter alia*) to $\sqrt{F}$ (to a maximum of 300 n.m.) – where F is the distance of open water to windward of the landing–place or estuary entrance. A measure of this effect has been obtained by multiplying the square root of the average fetch in the exposed sector for each landing–place by the probability of having a wind from this sector.

d) Approach and departure characteristics. For example Purdy (1842, 219) recognised St. Malo/Alet as the 'best harbour on the coast' yet the approach required much skill and local knowledge as it was encumbered by numerous islets and rocks. The presence or absence of prominent headlands or other natural landfalls may also be compared.

Analytical Units

In the analyses which underlie the remaining sections of this paper, modern units of measurement are used, and no attempt is made to establish the ancient units for direction, distance and speed.

Courses, tracks and bearings are given in points, there being 32 points in the azimuth plane nowadays, each one equal to $11\frac{1}{4}°$ This points system is used today for such variables as wind and swell: it was widely used for courses and bearings until the nineteenth century. This broad unit – rather than the degree – is appropriate to the standard of course–holding expected, especially when it is remembered that when sailing to windward (on the wind) a boat is steered so as to keep the trim of sail appropriate to a fluctuating wind velocity.

Linear distances are given in *nautical* miles (n.m.), and the *Knot* (kt) of one nautical mile per hour is used for speed. Nautical and meteorological data are available in these units which are derived units in the S I system. Depths and heights, on the other hand, are given in metres (m), as is the practice today.

The analytical use of these units and such concepts as tracks, courses, currents, tidal streams and leeway does not imply that these were explicitly understood by the ancient seaman. It seems probable, for example, that current and tidal stream (and possibly leeway also) were not thought of separately but rather as one entity, which varied in a complex way with the phases of the moon and also with the prevailing wind, and which had an effect which was very apparent in inshore waters but which could also displace a boat (frequently in a NE direction) when crossing the Channel. The seaman noted the effects of wind and sea on his boat and took action to allow for them, without necessarily having an analytical understanding of the causes.

Pilotage and Navigation

Outbound Pilotage
When preparing for a cross–Channel coastal voyage the seaman would intuitively compare actual wind, sea and tide, and the conditions to be expected in the next day or so, with those generally prevailing on the intended route at that time of year. With this information he could estimate the course to be steered and the time required for the crossing as deviations from the course generally used and the time usually taken. He would thus form a mental picture which he would revise during the voyage in the light of further observations of natural phenomena (see Slade and Greenhill, 1974, 27 on the planning of early 20th century voyages, very little of which was committed to paper).

He would most probably leave on a daylight ebb (outflowing) tide using channels appropriate to the wind direction, and steering by reference to landmarks and visible shoals and reefs. Oars could be used to clear a windbound landing–place when offshore winds were known to be favourable.

Once clear of land, the pilot would check the wind, sea and swell against a known directional relationship such as a transit between two headlands, the bearing of an island, the genral trend of the coast, or in relation to a back bearing (in Oceania fires were lit ashore for this – Lewis, 1972, 61), and work his way to windward in foul wind conditions. Before losing sight of land he would 'take departure' by estimating his position relative to some prominent landmark – this would be the first datum point on his mental chart. With a fair wind the pilot would then set a course which would allow for his estimate of the set of the tidal stream and current and any leeway. With a foul wind the boat would be brought as close to the wind as prudence allowed, and an estimate made of the displacement caused by current, stream and leeway: with due regard to the likelihood of a shift in such a wind, and the number and lengths of tacks required to make the landfall could then be assessed. It would be essential to plan to make the landfall in daylight or bright moonlight. Other things being equal it would also be prudent to aim to make a landfall slightly to windward or uptide of the destination, thus having a less arduous leg for the final approach.

Inbound Pilotage
Early warning of land may be given by orographic cloud or by the flight of sea birds at dawn and dusk. A good landfall is made when the pilot recognises the silhouette and characteristics of the coast as it becomes visible at a range when the boat is still clear of inshore hazards. If due to thick weather land is not sighted until close inshore, details such as colour and composition of the cliffs may enable the precise

position to be recognised: thus the cliffs to the west of Dover are smooth and white with dark patches of grey, whilst those to the east are marked with vertical strata of flint (Purdy, 1842, 46). With the position of the boat relative to the destination established, the mental chart is now re-orientated if necessary and a safe course set for the landing-place, or the boat held off to await the flood (ingoing) stream. In poor visibility lead and line are used to obtain warning of shallows and hence the nearness of land and to note the nature of the bottom so that safe channels may be recognised. 'Small blacke sande' on the sounding lead told the early 16th century Spanish mariner that he had the Lizard peninsula abeam at a safe distance, whereas 'white sande and white soft wormes' in shallow water warned that the Lizard was 'very nigh' (Waters, 1978, 19). Reflected wave patterns or the sound of surf breaking in the shallows (Greenhill 1978, 201) or even the smell of sheep give directions when close inshore. At night or in poor visibility fires may be lit onshore as leading marks. Thomas (1981) has suggested that such a beacon may have been sited on Gt. Ganilly island, Scilly, in the late first millennium; see also Eglinton (1982, 1–2) for a recent example.

Leading marks, especially transits, are of great use when approaching a harbour entrance or individual landing-place where there are stable channels: the boat can thereby be kept on a safe track. Prehistoric barrows on the coasts and islands of western Sweden are known to have been used in recent times as sailing marks (Westerdahl, 1980, 324): similar use in earlier times seems probable. Whether the site of any barrow visible from sea-level in the Channel was chosen so that it would be a useful landmark from seaward may now be impossible to determine, but should be borne in mind when surveying a coastal area. A large coastal barrow or group of barrows would certainly assist the pilot to recognise that part of the coast, and a transit bearing, with the edges of two barrows in line for example, might be available as a leading mark to indicate a safe line of approach.

Coastal passages

On coastal passages the seaman would establish his position relative to natural landmarks and seamarks. Should visual contact be lost through poor weather, or by heading across the arms of a bay, or because of having to haul out to seaward to avoid some hazard, he would use his mental chart to record estimated position until he could close the coast and regain his visual bearings. On such a passage it would be necessary to work the tides possibly including anchoring or lying hove-to during foul streams (Eglinton, 1982, 12–13; Greenhill, 1978, 200). It would also probably be necessary to anchor during non-moonlight nights.

Navigation

Once out of sight of land the navigator has to rely on his mental chart and his assessments of tracks and speeds made good relative to the sea bed(Fig.10.1.2): these are the essentials of dead reckoning navigation (Oatley, 1974), more accurately called, navigation by estimated position (EP). Of the cross-Channel routes listed in Table 10.1.3, the Ushant to Cornwall passage has a 52 n.m. section out of sight of land; river Seine to Spithead, 35 n.m.; Bruges to Kent, 30 n.m.; and

river Rance to Dorset, 10 n.m. These are minimum theoretical distances which would be considerably increased in poor visibility. At 2½ kts none of these four passages can be undertaken entirely in daylight, and darkness also inevitably increases the out-of-sight distances. Thus 80 n.m. of EP navigation (equivalent to 32 hours at 2½ kts) could be necessary on the Ushant to Cornwall route, with figures for other routes being correspondingly less.

Direction relative to the swell

Over a short period of time, wind and sea maintain a fairly constant direction, but swell (the sea motion originated by predominant wind and which persists after that wind had died down) gives a more certain indication of direction for longer periods, although less pronounced in summer than winter. In the Bay of Biscay the swell comes from between W and NW, and in the Channel generally SW to W, although a moderate NE swell may sometimes be encountered in the Strait. Oceanic navigators placed great reliance on swell direction to give them their bearings. Lewis (1972, 90) found, for example, that one navigator was able to steer by swell direction through several wind changes and make a good landfall after covering over 45 n.m. in overcast conditions.

The predominant swell has to be differentiated from wave motion, from any lesser swells, and from wave diffraction patterns from islands or promontories. When not visually recognisable it can be identified by feel, the navigator lying on the deck to analyse the boat's motion, the testicles being the finest sensor (Lewis, 1972, 86–92) Walton (1974, 10) has noted that in recent times Shetland fishermen were also able to detect and use the underlying swell ('Mother Wave') in a confused sea. Such ability was probably more widespread in earlier times, but atrophied with the advent of instrumental aids.

Direction from celestial observations

Oceanic navigators were so familiar with the night sky and the sun's daily and seasonal movements that in those lower latitudes one glimpse of the sun, and more especially a star or constellation, in an otherwise overcast sky enabled them to establish their bearings, and they could steer accurate courses in relation to rising and setting stars (Lewis, 1972, 52–4) The obliquity of celestial motion in higher latitude rules out such precise use in the Bay and the Channel region; nevertheless the fixed direction (South) of the sun's zenith (noon) position may be determined with reasonable accuracy when visible, as there is a period of little change in azimuth and altitude at that time. At dawn and dusk East and West may similarly be identified, providing the seasonal directions of sunrise and sunset (amplitude) have been established before the voyage, relative to a known bearing ashore: in summer the sun's amplitude vanes by less than 3° over any 6 day period. With more diffficulty, the Channel navigator may be able to maintain his direction at other times of the day by reference to the changing altitude and azimuth of the sun (a feature of bird navigation): the Oceanic navigator did this by 'delicate judgements' as distinct from scientific measurement.

The moon and stars move or appear to move in relation to the earth, but the celestial pole or null point (near *Polaris* nowadays) maintains a fixed direction and is identlfiable without instruments in clear night skies. This null point was know from early Classical times (Homer, *Odyssey* V.271–6) although the star then nearest the pole was *Kochab* rather than *Polaris* (Taylor 1971, 9–12): its use in NW Europe in the late first millennium seems likely.

A course could thus be maintained by keeping the swell, or the celestial pole (or for shorter periods the wind or sun) on one of eight relative bearings: ahead, astern or on bow, beam or quarter of the boat. It may be that further division was possible down to 16 relative bearing sectors each of 22½°, but finer accuracy seems unlikely. The prudent navigator uses all directional aids available to him, cross–checking one with the other. Thus at morning twilight the sun's azimuth, the bearing of the predominant swell, and the relative wind could be checked against the direction of the celestial pole.

Leeway and Drift Allowance
To determine the track actually sailed over the sea–bed and thus to know the bearing at any one time of the point of departure or of the destination, each course steered has to be modified by the angular amount of leeway experienced due to the wind, and by the angular dlsplacement due to current and tidal stream (Fig. 10.1.2). Leeway is negligible when the wind is from a sector some 5 points either side of dead astern; otherwise it may be estimated by wake angle. Drift allowance depends on the navigator's evaluation of the changing state of the tidal stream since taking departure: an alternatlve method is to assume that, on cross Channel voyages, these displacements cancel out during each period of 12½ hours, leaving a slight NE drift due to current. This latter method is not valid when the boat passes through radically different tidal systems, but this is generally not the case on the legs out of sight of land of the five routes discussed here.

Distance estimation
In order to obtain a mental fix of his position, the navigator now has to establish how far he has travelled along this track (bearing from his departure point) which he has estimated by applying leeway and drift to the course steered. Distance travelled is determined by speed and time: both are difficult to estimate without aids, and it seems unlikely that any of the known Classical devices for time measurment were used at sea. However, at any one season of the year the ratio of daylight to darkness could be deduced from measurements on land, and thus sunrise, noon and sunset could become 'fixed' points in time; and some measure of the passage of time during daylight could be obtained from the sun's change in azimuth, providing it could be noted relative to a 'fixed' bearing such as the swell direction.

In several maritime societies distances have been expressed in units of a *day's sail* (Casson, 1971, 281–96; Morken 1968; Gelsinger, 1970; Taylor, 1971, 50–2, 79, 126) implicit in this is the concept of a 'standard' speed to be expected from the 'usual' sort of boat in 'normal' wind and sea conditions.Where landfalls can be seen from departure points the experience to establish such a standard may soon be acquired; on longer routes average performance could take longer to establish and might not be so accurate. Estimates of actual speeds achieved

may then be expressed in relation to this standard. Such estimates of speed may be made in a number of wavs. Lewis (1972, 119) found that the Oceanic navigators used a multitude of indications including spray turbulence and wind pressure. Another method is to note (when it can be seen) the position of the second bow wave created by the boat. In deep water wave length is related to speed (Kay, 1971, 142); this relationship is non–linear, $\lambda = 0.558 \, (\text{speed})^2$, but the further aft the second bow wave is, the faster is the boat moving. Yet again a dutchman's log (foam bubbles or an object thrown overboard) may be timed between bow and stern (Greenhill, 1978, 195); or the time to make a passage between known coastal marks may be noted: in both cases a standard phrase might be chanted to give a measure of elapsed time. Such usage is not recorded, but chants were used to keep Classical (Morrison and Williams, 1966, 196) and Saxon (Colgrove, 1927, 26) oarsmen synchronised. Another timing mechanism might be the pulse or heartbeat. By such means, an experienced seaman learnt what speeds his boat achieved on different courses in various combinations of wind, sea and swell: the speeds being estimated relative to the 'standard' speed.

Estimated Position
Thus knowing his track (course(s) steered relative to celestial pole, swell or some other 'fixed' bearing, amended for leeway and drift) and the distance(s) sailed (as a relative speed), the navigator can mark his estimated position on his mental chart, at the 'fixed' times of sunrise, noon and sunset, and possibly at intermediate times. As his appreciation develops of how his boat's progress is deviating from the 'norm' for this route, the navigator will be able to decide whether to adjust his course to regain the direct track (if the wind will allow this) or to adjust his estimate of arrival time at destination and the tidal streams and depths of water to be expected inshore.

Other navigational possibilities
Changes in the angular height (altitude) of the celestial pole, or of other heavenly bodies on the meridian, indicate a change in latitude, that is a displacement N or S. This was certainly measured on land using a *gnomon* in the Classical world (Strabo, 1.4.4, for example); and also at sea by approximate measurement against mast and yard (Lucan, *Bel. Civ.* 8.177–81). However such techniques were probably not of practical use on the relatively short Channel crossings.

Lewis (1972, 120) has denied that 20th century Oceanic navigators have any 'sixth sense' to help them find their bearing in overcast conditions. Yet recent research at the University of New York and at M.I.T. indicates that bees, salmon, dolphins and pigeons use the earth's magnetism to find their way (*Sunday Times*, 2.11.1982), and Baker (1980) has shown that in a significant number of instances humans, possibly using magnetic orientation, can point out the direction of their home–base after being taken blindfolded to an unknown position on land. Baker, *et al.* (1983) have also shown that some humans have ferric iron in their sinus complex. There thus remains a possibility that man has or has had the capability of establishing his bearings by 'following his nose'.

The Channel Seaman

Greenhill (1978, 199–205) has described the pilotage and navigational expertise possessed by masters of early 20th–century merchant schooners. These skills were similar to those of Chaucer's 14th–Century shipman who could reckon tides, tidal streams, the phases of the moon, and his tracks and distances; he knew well the harbours and havens from Gotland to Cape Finistere, and the creeks of Brittany and Spain (*Canter Tales* – Prologue: see Karkeek, 1884, 455 or translated by Coghill, 1951, 35–6). The Channel seaman of the late first millennium B.C. would have required similar knowledge and skills. In inshore waters as a pilot he would need to be familiar with stretches of coastline on both sides of the Channel; off–shore soundings and the nature of the sea bottom. He would also have to have a detailed knowledge of the main landing places (and their alternatives), their safe channels and sailing marks, their hazards in various states of tide and weather; and the times of high and low water and slack stream in relation to the moon's phases.

As a navigator out of sight of land, he would use a mental chart which had 'marked' on it the bearing and distance between point of departure and landfall for each cross–Channel route he used. Distance would probably be in units of a standard day's sail. Direction, might be given relative to the celestial pole e.g. 'the required landfall is ahead when the pole is fine on the port bow'; or relative to some known alignement on the coast near

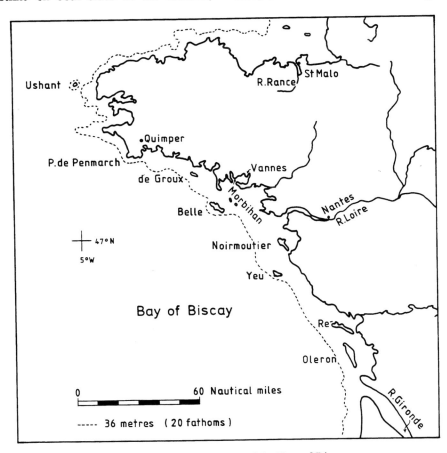

Figure 10.1.6 Northern part of the Bay of Biscay

the point of departure. Or it might be given relative to the swell for a number of standard weather conditions; for instance 'in summer the requied landfall is ahead when the predominant swell is just aft of the port beam'. On passage the seaman observed and interpreteted natural phenomena and then amended his mental chart to allow for the conditions actually experienced when they differed from the norm.

The apprentice Channel navigator/pilot of late prehistoric period had much to learn, but stereotyped phrases and rules of thumb could have assisted his memory. Like many illiterate people, the Celts paid great attention to memory training for transmission of culture (Chadwick, 1970, 45–7; Ross, 1970, 125/6) and the oral teaching of the Gauls included such subjects as the motion of the stars (Caesar, *BG*, VI, 14). The modern equivalent of learning by rote may be seen in empirircal rules

such as Buys–Ballot's Law for ascertaining the direction of the centre of a depression, the 'twelfths' rule for establishing the height of tide, and tables giving drift for various speeds of ship and stream (Waters, 1978, 576). Well–tested sea lore is incorporated in verbal aids to memory such as weather–forecast rhymes, the Beaufort scale for wind strengths, the shanty *Spanish Ladies* which lists the main headlands between Dodman and Dungeness (*Mariner's Mirror* 5, 159–60), the jingle giving times of ebb and flow at points between London and King's Lynn (*Mariner's Mirror* 3, 319) and in the *Fisherman's Catechism*, questions and model answers about courses and distances to various fishing grounds from Grimsby (Olsen, 1885, 178–91).

The Channel seaman also had to know his boat: her best point of sail, how close to the wind she would sail, speed achieved and leeway experienced in various sea states and in various loaded conditions; for these characteristics helped him estimate his position on his mental chart. This fact may go some way towards explaining why many seamen were (and are) reluctant to alter their traditional form of boat to one with unproven characteristics.

Bay of Biscay and Channel Routes

Routes 1 and 2; River Gironde and River Loire to Ushant (Figs 10.1.4, 5, 6)

Evidence
Strabo states that the two of the four usual routes for Britain were from the mouths of the Gironde and the Loire. These sea-passsages probably started from near *Burdigalia* (Bordeaux) and *Corbilo* (Nantes?), which were emporia within sheltered estuaries. Amphorae from a wreck off Bell Ile provide some artifactual evidence for the use of these routes. Intermediate landing–places at Vannes in the Morbihan (with its 20 m–tall Grand Menhir Brisé as a pilotage aid, see Merritt and Thom, 1980) and near Quimper have been suggested by Cunliffe, possibly for overland portage to the river Rance. On sea–passages to Britain boats pass the westernmost part of Brittany near Ushant (Ile d'Ouessant, *Axanthos* of Pliny, NH, IV, 103), and then follow Route 3 to Cornwall and Devon; or round this headland and follow Routes 4 and 5 to Dorset via the Rance.

Outbound
Both estuaries are encumbered by rocks and shoals and are generally open to the west with maximum fetch and with only c. 30% chance of a fair wind for leaving to the NW. From the Gironde the route is generally NW to a landfall near Pte de Penmarc'h, the northern limit of the Bay of Biscay (Golfe de Gascogne), thence a more arduous leg coastwise to Ushant: a boat can be never more than 25 n.m. from land on this route. Alternatively a NNW route closer inshore may be taken, passing E of Ile d'Yeu, to seaward of the Loire estuary, and NE of Belle Ile. From the Loire to Pte de Penmarc'h the route is generally WNW. The islands near these routes may be hazards or aids to pilotage, depending upon the weather encountered, especially visibility. On the inshore routes local knowledge of the channels is essential as there are strong tidal streams (e.g. in the Raz de Sein) and there can be heavy onshore swells. There is a 47% chance of having a fair wind. At 2½ kts the voyage to the vicinity of Ushant from the Gironde takes 4 and a sixth days and from the Loire, 2 ½ days. Working the tides would be essential on this coastal passage and night sailing would only be possible in clear moonlight: otherwise periods of up to 8 hours of darkness and 4 to 5 hours of foul streams could be spent at anchor or hove–to. On the other hand, a route well clear of land should allow 24 hour sailing, but estimation of position would be more difficult.

Ushant has a fearsome reputation in sea lore: the Pilot urges 'the greatest caution' and advises a wide berth. However, there are inshore channels to the east of Ushant (e.g. Chenal du Four) which are more sheltered from the predominant wind and

swell, but with strong tidal streams of up to 9 kts, steep seas and poor visibility. The probability of a fair wind for this passage of Ushant in summer is *c.* 46%: local knowledge would be essential and the passage would only be undertaken in daylight with a northerly tidal stream.

Return.
The return journey would face similar conditions off the rocky leeshore of W Brittany. However, the probability of a fair wind is 83% for the route, and over 75% for entering the estuaries. The latter are open to a moderate westerly swell.

Route 3: Ushant to Mounts Bay and Plymouth Sound

Evidence
Caesar states that the Veneti sailed to Britain, and Strabo that they used an emporium there. Diodorus describes how tin was mined near Belerium Promontory (Lands End) which was four days' sail from the Continent: this estimate of time is compatible with a passage from the Loire. The tin was then taken to *Ictis* (possibly St. Michael's Mount in Mounts Bay or Mount Batten in Plymouth Sound – see Cunliffe, 1983) by wagon at low water, and merchants transported it to Gaul. Finds in Cornwall and at Mount Batten indicate contact with NW France. Cunliffe prefers an indirect route (overland from Vannes or Quimper to Alet/St. Malo, then by Routes 5 and 6) but this direct route from Ushant to Mounts Bay/Plymouth Sound remains a possibility.

Outbound
From Ushant (see Routes 1 and 2) this route is generally N to a landfall at the Lizard. Hawkes (1977A, 31) quoting Dion (1966), believes that the current near the entrance to the Channel 'must always have drawn navigation to pursue it, up north along the British west coast . . .'. It is true that a 2nd/1st–century B.C. Mediterranean type of anchor–stock has been found off Porth Felen near Aberdaron, N Wales (Boon, 1977), and there are other indications of a Wales/Brittany trade–route (André, 1976–8); but these could well have been intentional voyages and not just the results of a north–flowing current. Such a surface current does exist (Rennell's), setting NW from the Bay towards Scilly, but it flows only intermittently at a rate of 1–1½ kt, and is generally only experienced in winter after strong gales (*Biscay Pilot*, 1970, 28). The general trend in the Channel is for wind and current to set a boat up–Channel rather than into the Irish Sea, although in certain circumstances the latter can happen.

The probability of fair wind for this route in summer is 66%. At 2½ kts it would take *c.* 1½ days to Mounts Bay and 2 days to Plymouth Sound. Because of constraints both on passing Ushant and making a Lizard landfall in daylight, up to 80% of the Ushant/Lizard leg could be out of sight of land, even in clear weather; thus for *c.* 32 hrs navigational methods would be needed.

As well as being near the souorce of tin, Mounts Bay gives acces to a 7 km overland portage to St Ives Bay at Hayle: this could be used to avoid rounding Lands End (Fig 2.3.5). Plymouth Sound is the entrance to the Tamar estuary and

Mount Batten is on a promontory at the confluence of the Plym and Tamar, with sheltered landing–places in the Catterwater to the N and E. Clark (1971, 155) considers Mount Batten inconvenient of access by land, but the rivers St Germans, Tavy, Lynher, Plym and especially the Tamar give access to hinterland by boat (Fig 10.1.5). Although Plymouth Sound is further from Ushant, it is less exposed (measured by fetch and wind probability) than Mounts Bay, and has a *c.* 65% probability of fair winds for arrival and departure compared with *c.* 56% for Mounts Bay.

Return

The return journey would face similar conditions except that the current and predominant wind and swell would be on the starboard bow. Other things being equal, a landfall on the Brittany coast is more likely than leaving Ushant to the E. The probability of a fair wind on passage is *c.* 58% and thus greater than when northbound. Ushant is discussed in Routes 1 and 2.

Route 4: Ushant to River Rance (Figs 10.1.4, 5)

Evidence

The distribution of amphorae and documentary reference to Venetic traders leads Cunliffe to postulate an overland route between SW and NE Brittany; however, a sea route from the south around Ushant and eastwards to the River Rance is also a possibility.

Outbound

Rounding Ushant on an inshore passage is difficult, with great likelyhood of high sea states even in summer, and the probability of fair wind is only *c.* 45%. The route is then generally E along the inhospitable coast of Brittany, then SE to the Rance. The tidal streams are fast – up to twice the speed of those on the opposite English coast – and in places they have an onshore component which can set a boat onto off–lying plateaux of rocks. The probability of a fair wind on passage is 89%. At 2½ kts it would take *c.* 2¼ days, but as with other coastal passages (Route 1 and 2) there may be long periods when no headway is made.

Along this coast the times of local high and low water differ markedly from slack water, and the tidal range is considerable, being generally 6–11 m, but reaching a maximum of 12m in the Baie de St Michael. The Baie de St Malo has numerous rocks and shoals and local knowledge is required: the probability of a fair wind for arrival in the river Rance is 63%. The 19th century landing–place was to the E of St Malo island (Purdy, 1842, 220): this or the Rade de Solidor, S of the Alet peninsula, may have been the landing–place for the Late Iron Age site noted by Cunliffe (1982, 43, 45). The river Rance gives some access to the hinterland.

Return

There is a probability of only 39% for a fair wind when leaving the Rance on a NW heading and there is a relatively high fetch factor in this sector. For the passage to Ushant, the probability of a fair wind is only 31%, the lowest for any of the routes. This return passage is thus more arduous and uncertain than the outbound leg.

Route 5: River Rance to Christchurch and Poole *(Figs. 10.1.4, 5)*

Evidence

Distribution–patterns of amphorae and other potsherds and coins suggest a route from NE Brittany via the Channel Islands to the Christchurch/Poole region. Hawkes (1977B, 145) has interpreted a passage in Diodorus (V.38.5) about the tin trade as a reference to this route. Cunliffe has suggested that the Brittany landing–place would have been in the vicinity of Alet/St Malo in the Rance estuary (1982, 43, 45), and has drawn attention to a possible open–beach site at Nacqueville, W of Cherbourg (1982, 45).

Outbound

The probability of a fair wind for leaving the Rance on a NE heading is 63%, but high sea states may be encountered when the wind is NW. The first half of the route is a coastal passage via the Channel Islands, then there is an open sea crossing from Cap de la Hague or from Casquettes. The overall time at 2½ kts is *c.*2¼ days, but as noted in other coastal routes (1, 2 and 4) this could be an underestimate. Up to 40 n.m. of the open sea leg of *c.* 60 n.m. could be out of sight of land, although with good visibility on a clear night this could be reduced to *c.* 10 n.m.

The Channel Islands occupy a large part of the bight between Ile de Bréhat and Cap de la Hague and present problems to the pilot: off–lying shoals and extensive reefs; a great tidal range (7–10 m) and strong and erratic tidal streams (the race of Alderney flows at up to 10 kts); heavy on–shore swells; and winds which can vary considerably over a short distance. Thus there would be a significant chance of a broken passage with waits for daylight or fair tidal streams. Apart from this inter island route (for which there is excavated evidence) there are three main ways to transit the islands:

> a) Head NW from the Rance, when wind and stream permit, and pass well to the W of Guernsey and W of Casquettes before altering to the NE.

> b) Head N, keeping W of the extensive reef Plateau des Minquiers but passing between Jersey and Guernsey, then through the race of Alderney on a favourable tide.

> c) Head NE to pass between the mainland and the Iles Chaussey, or between these islands and the Minquiers, and then northward along the Cotentin coast to the race of Alderney. There are strong and erratic streams on this route, but at high water with local knowledge and in daylight both the Passage de la Déroute and the Déroute de Terre are practicable.

Passage through the Alderney race could only be attempted in daylight with a north flowing stream. Departure would subsequently be taken from C de la Hague. The probability for a fair wind on this generally northerly route is *c.* 72%.

There are several distinctive promontories and headlands between Portland and Needles any one of which could be a readily recognizable landfall; the nearest one to the west (in the direction of the predominant wind) is Durlston Head. The probability of a fair wind for the approach to Christchurch is 60% and 46% for Poole. Both harbours have rocks and shoals on the approach which were porobably there in the prehistoric period and more prominent in times of lower sea–level. The sandbanks and bars which now lie across both entrances may, however, have been formed in more recent times, created by the generally easterly longhsore drift. with a less–impeded route the tidal streams would not have been as strong as they are today, although still a hazard especially with an onshore wind and an ebb (outflowing) tide.

Like most places between Selsey Bill and St Alban's Head, Poole and Christchurch have an unusual tidal pattern with a double high water. At Poole for example there is very little range of tide at neaps and only *c.* 2m at springs, and the tide stands around high water for over 3½ hours; thus there is effectively HW for 14 hours out of 24, a distinct advantage in boat operations and cargo handling. Both Poole and Christchurch harbours give access by river to a hinterland. From Christchurch the tributaries of the Avon and Stour are especially wide–ranging, and with a portage from the Wiltshire Wylye to the Somerset Frome there is theoretical access to the Bristol Channel and the Mendip and Cotswold regions. Whether inland river journeys were indeed possible is difficult to decide: much depends on the former course, seasonal depths and speeds of particular rivers which would have had steeper gradients in times of lower sea–level. Travel upstream may involve towing heavily–laden boats (or sailing with a near following wind). Such use of inland waterways is documented for France (Strabo *Geog.* 4.1.14, 4.3.2,; Diodorus V.26.3) and in other parts of the Roman Empire (Johnstone, 1980, 156–68),but not for Britain. The only boat find from this region, dated to the period under discussion, is the Poole logboat of *c.* 295bc (Q–821). Her ability to carry *c.* 1700kg with a draft of only 0.37m would have made her very useful within Poole harbour and the lower river reaches. However, she was somewhat unhandy, being 11m in length and having a definite bow and stern (thus not paddleable with the stern leading) and was probably unsuitable for upriver work (McGrail, 1978, 254–7); smaller logboats or skinboats would have been required on the Sherford, Corfe, Frome and Piddle. The fact that the Poole logboat has a 'stem' carved in the solid log indicates that her builders were familiar with planked boats which may also have been used on these rivers.

Return
The probability of a fair wind for leaving Poole is 65% and Christchurch 61%: their fetch factors are relatively low. A fair wind on passage has a probability of only 52% and as there is a probability of only 40% for arrival at the river Rance from the NE, there is more uncertainty on the return than the outbound passage, the section through the Channel Islands being equally arduous in both directions.

Regular use of a landing place near Nacqueville (Cunliffe, 1982, 45) seems unlikley, as it is in an exposed position and has no obvious acces to the hinterland.

Route 6: Christchurch and Poole to Plymouth Sound and Mounts Bay (Figs 10.1.4, and 2.3.5)

Evidence
The distribution–pattern of amphorae and the natural sources of materials excavated at Hengistbury suggests to Cunliffe that there was a coastal route between the Hengistbury area and Devon (Mount Batten) and Cornwall (Mounts Bay). Pliny quotes Timaeus's statement that tin (known in S Britain only from Devon and Cornwall – see Hawkes, 1977A, 24 map 7) could be found on the island *Mictis*: this could have been St Michael's Mount or Mount Batten; on the other hand, as *Mictis* is said to be 6 days' sail 'inwards' (up–Channel?), this could refer to a landing–place up to 360 n.m. to the east. The Isle of Wight (*Vectis*) is *c.* 180 n.m. from Lands End: this would take 3 days at 2½ kts, or possibly 6 days if sailing in daylight only.

Outbound
Leaving Poole and Christchurch is discussed in Route 4. The route is generally westerly along the southern coast of England, with a fair wind probability of only 32%. Distance may be saved by cutting across bays, when land is never more than 23 n.m. away. At 2½ kts it would take *c.* 1 and two thirds days to Plymouth Sound and *c.* 2½ days to Mounts Bay: as with other coastal routes (1, 2, 4 and southern part of 5) passage time may in fact have been longer. The tidal streams are generally parallel to the coast with onshore sets in bays (especially Lyme Bay) and off Start Point and the Lizard. From the Lizard to Mounts Bay the streams become more elliptical. There are races off St Alban's Head and Portland Bill which may be avoided by opening from the coast or by passing close inshore to the north of the races thereby saving distance. It could be necessary to anchor east of Start Point or of the Lizard to await a fair wind for Plymouth Sound or Mounts Bay. The approaches to these two places are discussed in Route 3.

Return
The return journey is less arduous as a fair wind has a probability of 86%. Arrival at Poole and Christchurch is discussed in Route 5.

Route 7: R Seine to Spithead (Figs. 10.1.4, 5)

Evidence
Strabo states that boats leave the mouth of the Seine for Britain which is less than a day's sail away – 60 n.m. at 2½ kts. The Seine landing–place is not mentioned, but by analogy with *Corbilo* on the Loire and *Burdigala* on the Gironde it seems likely that it would have been some miles up the estuary. The destination in Britain is not clear, although there is a possible hint that it is *Cantium* (S Foreland) in Kent (4.3.3); but this is 115 n.m. away. The nearest points to the River Seine are in fact between Beachy Head and the Isle of Wight. There are a number of natural harbours similar to Poole and Christchurch betwen Selsey Bill and the Solent, all of which could provide

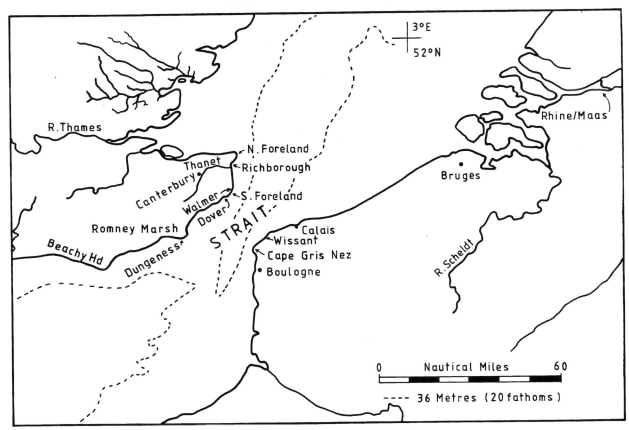

Figure 10.1.7 Strait of Dover

good landing–places though not all give access by river to a hinterland. By the second century A.D. there was a *magnus portus* north of the Isle of Wight (Rivet and Smith, 1979, 116) with access inland via the Solent and Southampton water. I assume for the purposes of this paper that the destination for the late first–millennium voyages was also in this general area; with an entrance via Spithead.

Outbound

The Seine has many shifting banks and shoals and during the higher tidal ranges a tidal bore runs. In the estuary there are 2–hour stands and double high waters. During the up–Channel (easterly) phases of the tidal stream the set is from P de Barfleur directly into the estuary, which could set a vessel towards the shore N of Le Havre. The probability of a fair wind for leaving is 68%. The route for Spithead is generally NW with open sea once clear of the estuary. The fair wind probability on route is 55%. At 2½ kts it would take *c*. 1½ days; at 4 kts it would take 21 hours – 'less than a day'. Land would generally be out of sight for *c*. 45 n.m. of this 85 n.m. passage, say 18 hrs, although on a moonlight night with good visibility this could be reduced to *c*. 35 n.m.

The entrance to Spithead is between Bembridge Point and Selsey Bill, and the latter would make a good lanfall. A fair wind to make Spithead has a probability of 60%. The tidal streams in this region are non–standard and there are sands and spits on the approach. Southampton Water gives access via the rivers Meon, Hamble, Itchen and Test to the region bordered by the New Forest, Salisbury Plain, Hampshire Downs and the South Downs. Other natural harbours in this region have only

short rivers flowing into them, although Chichester harbour gives access to Chichester and beyond.

Return

A fair wind for leaving Spithead has a probability of 61%; on route it is 68%; and approaching the Seine, 66%. The river Seine, like Spithead, has a low fetch factor. The cliffs N of the Seine estuary are of chalk and make a good landfall as they are easily recognisable in good visibility.

Route 8: Boulogne and Wissant to Dover and Walmer (Figs 10.1.4, 10.1.7)

Evidence

Diodorus tells us that at the Strait, 'where the sea has its outlet', it is *c*.100 stadia (10 n.m.) across to *Cantium* promontory (S Foreland) and that this is shortest distance from the Continent. The shortest distance (between C Gris Nez and S Foreland) is now *c*. 18 n.m. Caesar states that the shortest crossing was from the lands of the Morini. Hawkes (1977B, 151) believes that Caesar's crossing in 55 B.C. was from Wissant (NE of C Gris Nez) for the main body and Ambleteuse *ulterior portus* for the cavalry: the landfall is thought to have been near Dover. In 54 B.C. Caesar took the 'most convenient' passage of *c*. 30 Roman miles (24 n.m.) from *Itius* which Hawkes (1977B, 157) believes was Boulogne (the *Gesoriacum* of Pliny). Hawkes also considers that Caesar's course was N from there and that he was not heading for Dover. However, Caesar's text is consistent with him aiming to make a landfall at S Foreland, and as he had noted (*BG* V.13) that almost all ships from Gaul

281

approached *Cantium*, it would have been prudent for him to do likewise.

The probability then is that vessels from NE France used landing–places a few miles NE or S of Cap Gris Nez. They aimed to make a landfall at or near S Foreland (*Cantium*) and then headed northwards to the east of the Goodwin Sands for landing–places on the east Kent coast (e.g. Walmer or Richborough) or passed E or W of Thanet (N Foreland) for the river Thames.

Outbound. Boulogne has a fair weather probability of 64%, whilst for Wissant this is only 40%; their fetch factors are relatively low.

The routes to a landfall at S Foreland are northerly with a fair wind probability of *c*. 54%. In daylight or on a clear moonlit night a boat need never be out of sight of land, but with poor visibility up to 80% of the voyage could be out of sight. At 2½ kts the passage takes 1/3 to 3/8 day, but speed made good would depend very much on the phase of the tidal stream which on these short crossings will almost always have a net effect. Whilst daylight crossings might be preferred, night crossings could be chosen because of favourable tidal streams: it would be prudent, however, to plan to make a landfall in daylight. The tidal streams in the Strait are generally parallel to the coasts and can run up to 3 kts at springs. As they are slightly asymmetric, they are often more favourable to the southerly passage. In mid–Channel there are banks lying in the direction of the stream; however, bearings of landmarks on both side of the Channel may be used to keep clear of them.

S Foreland is readily identified, as are the chalk cliffs which begin just E of Dover. The Foreland may be rounded at ½ n.m. distance, and the chalk cliffs continue almost as far as Walmer which is thus recognised. The Goodwin Sands, E of Walmer, dry out and are a grave hazard in foul weather, but there is a channel to the west through the Downs and the Gull Stream to N Foreland and the Thames, or in former times via the Wantsum Channel, W of Thanet. Dover is more exposed than Walmer (27% compared with 7%) but has a higher probability of a fair wind for arrival – 65% compared with 47%. Neither landing–place gives access to the hinterland by water, although there is a small stream at Dover; but via the river Stour there is access to Canterbury and the Weald, and by the Thames and its tributaries access to a vast region of SE England.

Return. The probabilities of fair winds for leaving Dover and Walmer are 67% and 52%, with *c* 67% on route. C Gris Nez is a landfall for both Boulogne and Wissant; the latter may be recognised by its position between this Cape and C Blanc Nez, south of chalk cliffs. There are dark red cliffs from Boulogne with off–lying banks and shoals. The fair wind probability for arrival at either landing–place is *c*. 65%. Neither landing–place gives water access to the hinterland, although there is a small river at Boulogne.

Caesar's voyages
Caesar gives times and places (albeit not precisely) for his two voyages to Britain, and he mentions tidal streams and wind directions: its is therefore possible to analyse this route in greater detail than the others. In 55 B.C., on or about 27 August, Caesar left (?) Wissant 'at about the third watch'. This watch would have been from 2359 to 0230 and we may approximate at 0100. We may assume he 'worked the tides' using the NE tidal stream which begins in the C Gris Nez region some two hours before high water at Dover. For the next six hours his vessels would be affected by NE/N stream of 1½ to 2 kts in addition to their speed under sail. By sunrise (*c*. 0500) he would be 6 to 8 n.m. from the Kent coast and could identify S Foreland. The stream would continue to be favourable until *c*. 0800 and then a period of slack water. Caesar arrived at Dover at the fourth hour (*c*. 0830 to 0940), just about the time of low water (0900). He remained anchored there until the ninth hour (*c*. 1420–1530) when he sailed with a favourable wind and tide. Slack water at Dover was between 1500 and 1600 with the stream turning again to NE. A West to SSW wind (probability 29%) helped him clear the land, and with fair stream and wind he rounded S Foreland, passed to the E of the Goodwin Sands and made the 7 Roman miles (5.6 n.m.) to the beach landing–place at (?) Walmer by, say 1800, around the time of high water but before sunset (*c*. 1900). His transports took the ground on a falling tide allowing his men to disembark. Subsquently the longships were hauled up the beach, but evidently not above high–water mark of spring tides which at the end of August (possibly in conjunction with an onshore gale – probability only 11%) overwhelmed some of them and also damaged some of the anchored transports.

On the return voyage, some time before the autumnal equinox and thus possibly around 15 September, Caesar sailed 'a little after midnight' – this was probably some 4½ hours after high water when he would be able to make most use of S and SW tidal streams. Two of his ships were carried south of their destination (Wissant), and thus it seems likely that he arrived off C Gris Nez whilst there was still a SW tidal stream, that is before 0600: this would have been *c*. 1½ hours before high water at Boulogne and shortly after sunrise (*c*. 0550), so he would be able to identify his landfall. Thus this passage possibly took *c*. 7 hours compared with 8 hours for the outward journey. This ties in with Purdy's observation (1842, 244) that 'Dover to Calais is always found shorter (than reverse) because the tide is more favourable'.

In 54 B.C., probably on 6 July, with a different type of transport, Caesar left Boulogne at 'about sunset' (*c*. 2100), bound for Walmer. A departure some two hours before high water at Dover would enable him to work the tides. A slight SW wind failed at about midnight; the stream then carried him NNE until sunrise (*c*. 0350), which was also about the time of slack water, when he sighted Kent to port. At 5 kts with a fair wind and tidal stream he would have been *c*. 15 n.m. NNW of Boulogne when the wind failed. A further four hours drifting with a 2 kts stream would bring him to a position *c*. 6 n.m. ESE of S Foreland. Under oars, Caesar's fleet then passed south of the Goodwin Sands and made the 7 n.m. Walmer by midday at an average speed of 1 knot, with the tidal stream on their starboard beam for the first five hours then, after slack water, on their port beam. The overall average speed Boulogne to Walmer was *c*. 1.8 kts.

Table 10.1.3 Comparative statistics for nine cross-Channel routes in Summer

	Route See note	Leave 1st place % 1	Leave 1st place √Fx% 2	Distance n.m. 3	Time at 2½ kts Days 3	Time at 2½ kts Hrs	Time at 5 kts Days	Time at 5 kts Hrs	Displacement n.m. 4	Outbound Route % Outer 5	Outbound Route % Inner 6	OOSL n.m. 7	Arrive 2nd Place % 8	Leave 2nd Place 1	Leave 2nd Place √Fx% 2	Return Route %Outer 5	Return Route %Inner 6	Arrive 1st Place % 8
1	R Gironde to Ushant	67	17x46	250	4	4	2	2	–	53	25	–	°52	°33	17x50	17	4	25
2	R Loire to Ushant	71	17x52	150	2	12	1	6	–	54	22	–	°52	°33	17x50	17	4	30
3A	Ushant to Mounts Bay	54°	17x50	95	1	14	0	19	16–17NE	34	14	52–80	43	45	17x31¾	43	15	41°
3B	Ushant to Plymouth Sound	54°	17x50	120	2	0	1	0	16–12NE	34	14	52–80	37	34	10x29½	43	15	41°
4	Ushant to R Rance	55'°	17x50	130	2	4	1	2	–	11	4	–	37	61	12x40+ 6x9½	69	35	68'°
5A	R Rance to Christchurch	37''	12x40+ 6x9½	130	2	4	1	2	3–7NE	28	11	10–40	40	39	8x15¾	48	21	60''
5B	R Rance to Poole	37''	12x40+ 6x9½	130	2	4	1	2	3–7NE	28	11	10–40	54	35	9x8	48	21	''60
6A	Christchurch to Plymouth Sound	39	8x15¾	100	1	16	0	20	–	68	37	–	37	34	10x29½	14	3	40
6B	Christchurch to Mounts Bay	39	8x15¾	155	2	14	1	7	–	68	37	–	43	45	17x31¾	14	3	40
6C	Poole to Plymouth Sound	35	9x8	100	1	16	0	20	–	68	37	–	37	34	10x29½	14	3	54
6D	Poole to Mounts Bay	35	9x8	155	2	14	1	7	–	68	37	–	43	45	17x31¾	14	3	54
7	R Seine to Spithead	32	10x18¾	85	1	10	0	17	6–7NNE	45	18	35–45	40	39	8½x22½	32	8	34
8A	Wissant to Dover	40	8½x13½	18	0	7	0	3½	8NE 10SW	47	18	0–16	35	33	11x22	31	10	36
8B	Wissant to Walmer	40	8½x13½	20	0	8	0	4	8NE 10SW	47	18	0–18	53	48	5x11½	31	10	36
8C	Boulogne to Dover	36	17x7	24	0	9½	0	4¾	8NE 10SW	45	18	0–22	35	33	11x22	36	9	34
8D	Boulogne to Walmer	36	17x7	27	0	11	0	5½	8NE 10SW	45	18	0–24	53	48	5x11½	36	9	34
9A	Bruges to Dover	33	9½x23¾	65	1	2	0	13½	3–7NNE	50	24	30–40	35	33	11x22	35	16	32
9B	Bruges to Walmer	33	9½x23¾	68	1	3	0	13	3–7NNE	53	19	30–40	53	48	5x11½	32	12	32

Notes to Table 10.1.3

1. Probability of not leaving due to no wind, winds stronger than force 5, and foul winds within safe departure sector, on any one day in Summer.
2. Square root of average fetch in open sector(s) multiplied by probability of wind from that sector: this is some measure of sea state and swell.
3. Times and distances are for one leg (either outbound or return). Average speeds achieved on coastal voyages may have been less that 2½ kts due to broken passages because of darkness and foul streams.
4. Theoretical displacement due to current and net tidal streams on typical voyage departing on ebb tide. Not estimated for coastal voyages.
5. Probability of wind on passage being within 7 points of direct track thereby causing boat to tack (see Fig 10.1.1).
6. Probability of wind on passage being within 3 points of direct track thereby causing boat to sail 1.5 to 2 times direct distance (see Fig. 10.1.1).
7. Theoretical distance out of sight of land, and maximum distance out of sight of land in good visibility when subject to contraints of departing and arriving in daylight and no visual contact with land during night. Not estimated for coastal voyages.
8. Probability of not being able to approach landing–place due to no wind, winds stronger than force 5, and foul winds within safe approach sector, on any one day in Summer.
9. For routes passing Ushant   } using mean of
10. For routes rounding Ushant   } probabilities calculated
                                               } as in 5 and 6
11. To and from NE via W coast of Contentin

Caesar returned to Boulogne in mid–September, leaving Walmer in a 'complete calm' at the beginning of the second watch (2100) and arriving at dawn (*c.* 0530) which was also around the time of high water. To use the tidal stream he would leave some 4½ hours after high water at Dover and could have been carried some 12 n.m. before the stream turned. At this time (*c.* 0300) without wind he would be *c.* 9 n.m WNW of C Gris Nez with a foul stream to come and unable to steer. The calm must therefore have changed to a fair wind (probability 64%) some time after leaving Walmer. The average speed overall was 3kts.

The traders whom Julius Caesar questioned before his voyage in 55 knew the 'coast and the regions opposite Gaul', but were unfamiliar with the interior and claimed not to know any 'harbours (*portus*) suitable for a number of large ships'. If by *portus* was meant a formal harbour on Classical lines none can have existed at that time in Britain; the best to be expected was a beach landing-place as at Walmer or one on a river as at Dover or Richborough. Caesar has sometimes been criticised for his poor seamanship. In fact his seamanship was generally sound: for he chose the best times for departure and made best use of winds and streams so that he made a landfall, three out of four times, at the optimum time soon after sunrise, and arrived off his landing place, again on three out of four occasions, near the time of local high water and before the tide had begun to ebb. his late arrival at Walmer in 54 B.C. and the majority of other misadventures (e.g. transport failing to join him) were inbuilt hazards of cross-Channel sailing. His only major error appears to have been to underestimates the combined effect of a spring tide and an onshore gale in 55 B.C.: this is surprising in view of his experiences the previous year off the Venetic coast where the tidal range is greater and the conditions more arduous. The delay of 25 days at Boulogne due to a NW wind in late June is also difficult to explain as there is only 15% chance on any one day of such a wind, and only a 4% chance of Force 6 and above, and the fetch factor is low. There may have been non-maritime reasons. These apart, Caesar seems to have been a competent seaman or had an efficient subordinate. The traders whom Caesar consulted may well have given him local pilotage information or, more probably, they themselves acted as pilots.

Route 9: R Rhine to Dover and Walmer (Figs 10.1.4 and 10.1.7)

Evidence
Strabo states that one of the four main sea–routes to Britain began on the Morinic coast south of the Rhine's mouth. He does not explicitly state that the river was used to bring goods from the south to the coast; but Peacock's distribution–map of Dressel 1A and 1B amphorae gives some support to this possibility; and in the Late Roman period the archaeological evidence for the use of the Rhine is more definite: for trade see Peacock, 1978, fig. 44; Fulford, 1978, fig. 4; for river–boats see de Weerd (1978) and Hockmann (1982, 245, fig. 7). Strabo also states that *Cantium* (S Foreland) was directly opposite the Rhine mouth and that it was visible from there; but S Foreland is *c.* 90 n.m. away and could only be seen in most unusual atmospheric conditions.

As Pliny tells us that the Rhine had three mouths and as Strabo emphasises its marshy nature, we may deduce that there was a complex estuary there with islands, shifting banks and channels, possibly similar to the Rhone (Strabo 4.1.8); and it is relevant to note in this context that Narbonne and Massilia were situated well clear of the Rhone delta. The Belgian (Morinic) coast has been altered considerably in the past 2000 years through changes of sea level, natural build–up and flooding of sand dunes, and reclamation land. Recent work has demonstrated that during the Dunkirk 1 transgression, in the last four centuries B.C., Bruges, south of the Scheldt/Rhine estuary, was close to or on the coastline in a tidal inlet or bay (Ryckaert, 1980; Thoen, 1978). The boat fragments found there in 1899 (Marsden, 1976) and recently dated to the second or third century A.D. (HAR–472) lends support to the hypothesis that, in the late first millenium B.C., Bruges or a nearby site was a landing place for cross–Channel voyages, bearing a similar relation to the Rhine as Massilia and Narbonne bore to the Rhone. The British destinations for this trade were probably up the Thames and the river Stour in Kent and the Blackwater/Colne estuary in Essex (see the Dressel 1B distribution in Cunliffe, 1978B, 158), with the N Foreland as a landfall. However, to allow comparison with other routes I shall assume that Walmer or Dover were the initial landing places.

Outbound
Assuming a similar coastline alignement as today there would be a fair wind probability for leaving Bruges of 67%; the fetch factor is low/moderate, similar in magnitude to Dover. The route for a land–fall at either N or S Foreland is generally westerly with a fair wind probability of *c* 49%. At 2½ kts it would take 1 and one eighth to 1 and one twelfth days. The distance out of sight of land could be up to 40 n.m. in good visibility, that is *c.* 16 hours of navigation. The tidal streams are at the meeting of the Channel and N Sea systems, but generally run parallel to the coast. The approaches to Dover and Walmer via S Foreland are discussed in Route 8. N Foreland is the NE point of Thanet and has chalk cliffs some 37 m high. A landfall here should keep a vessel north of the Goodwin Sands and allow a safe approach to Walmer or Richborough, or to the entrances to the Stour and the Thames.

Return
The probability of a fair wind for the return voyage is *c* 67% and 68% on approach to the postulated landing–place near Bruges.

Comparisons of routes

The problem facing the seaman on the coastal routes considered in this paper (see Table 10.1.1, Routes 1, 2, 4 and 6) are somewhat different from those experienced on the cross–Channel routes (3, 5, 7, 8 and 9): thus the two groups are best compared separately. A relative measure of the difficulties generally experienced within these two groups may be obtained by summing the assessments given in Table 10.1.3. The following values were first calculated for each sub–route from the data in that table.

(a) the mean value of eight foul–wind probabilities

(b) the length of the direct route as a percentage of the longest route

(c) the mean of the fetch/wind factor for both ends of the routes as a percentage of the greatest

(d) (for cross–Channel routes only) the mean of the out–of–sight–of–land distances as a percentage of length of direct route.

Table 10.1.4 Relative order of merit for regular, safe passage

1. Cross Channel

	Route		Relative Reliability Factor	Reliability Groups
8B	Wissant	Walmer	100	1.1 Strait of Dover
8A	Wissant	Dover	98.4	
8D	Boulogne	Walmer	98	
8C	Boulogne	Dover	97	
9B	Bruges	Walmer	73	1.21 Rhine/Thames
9A	Bruges	Dover	72.6	1.22 Seine/Spithead
7	R Seine	Spithead	71	
5B	R Rance	Poole	63.5	1.3 Mid–Channel
5A	R Rance	Christchurch	63	
3B	Ushant	Plymouth	47	1.4 W Channel
3A	Ushant	Mounts Bay	43	

2. Coastal

	Route		Relative Reliability Factor	Reliability Groups
6C	Poole	Plymouth	100	2.1 Wessex/Devon
6A	Christchurch	Plymouth	99	
6D	Poole	Mounts Bay	81	2.2 Wessex/Cornwall
6B	Christchurch	Mounts Bay	80.5	
4	Ushant	R Rance	62	2.31 N Brittany
2	R Loire	Ushant	53	2.32 N Biscay
1	R Gironde	Ushant	36	

<u>Note</u>: Routes 5A and 5B are partly coastal through the Channel Islands

Each of these percentage values (say X%) is some measure of operational *difficulty*: the sum of the complementary (100–X) percentages may therefore be taken to represent *reliability* of operations (relative reliability factor). This factor is shown in Table 10.1.4 for each sub–route as a percentage of greatest value in (1) the cross–Channel routes, and (2) the coastal routes. The sub–route with the highest factor has the best chance of regular and safe passages, outward and return in the summer months.

The 18 sub–routes, ordered by relative reliability factor, fall into natural divisions as indicated in the last column of Table 10.1.4 Of the cross–Channel routes, the short ones used by Caesar to cross the Strait probably had least commercial value because of limited river access inland on the French side, although there was good access in Britain via the Thames. The passages from the Rhine and the Seine (9 and 7) were evidently the most reliable commerical sea routes, given that Continental goods could readily be brought to these rivers and that imports to Britain could be distributed, and exports assembled, in the

Needles/Selsey Bill region for Route 7, and in the Thames/Stour region for Route 9.

The difficulties encountered on the southern section of Route 5, in the vicinity of the Channel Islands, give this mid–Channel route a relatively low position in Table 10.1.4; nevertheless there is archaeological evidence for voyages between NW France and the Channel Islands (Cunliffe, 1982, 45) and the entire route is practicable, although it may have taken longer than Table 10.1.3 suggests. As there is only limited access inland via the river Rance, Mediterreanean exports would have had to be brought there either by Routes 1, 2 and 4 (R. Gironde or R. Loire to R.Rance via Ushant), or by the southern portions of Routes 1 and 2 followed by an overland portage across Brittany to the river Rance, as proposed by Cunliffe (1982, 42–3). Route 4, along the N Brittany coast from Ushant, is assessed as relatively low for reliability, as are the northern parts of Routes 1 and 2 thus the overland portage route may have been preferred to the sea passage around Ushant, at least at the begining and the end of the sailing season. At the British and of Route 5 there is good access to the Wessex hinterland

(and possibly further afield by portage). Import distribution and the assembly of exports via Route 6, the Wessex/SW Britain coastal route, would have been relatively reliable, although the westbound leg probably took longer than Table 10.1.3 indicates.

The N Biscay/W Channel routes (Gironde/Loire to SW Britain Routes 1, 2 and − 3), have the lowest reliability factors: nevertheless they would have been practicable in summer. The Gironde and the Loire both provided routes from the Mediterranean to NW Europe, which although they included overland portages, may have been more reliable and taken less time than the long coastal routes thruogh the Strait of Gribaltar mentioned by Peacock (1978, 49).

Future research

The nautical and environmental evidence for the period under discussion is sparse: direct evidence for the sea–going boats of the late first millennium is needed, as are geomorphological data on the coastlines of Britain and France. Evidence for trade is more plentiful but patchy: promontory and island sites such as St Malo, Alet, Mont St Michel, St Michael's Mount; Mount Batten and Green Island in Poole Harbour especiall,y need further investigation and publication. Theoretical reconstruction of the prehistoric coastline may suggest other sites, for example in the area between the Needles and Selsey Bill. There is an urgent requirement to update distribution–maps of early amphorae and other well–provenanced finds, especially for NW France.

Such research–programmes may reveal the evidence for weather, coastlines, landing places and boat types different from those proposed in this paper, and they may suggest additional sea–routes. Thus some of the parameters on which the relative assessments in Table 10.1.4 are based could be changed; nevertheless the method of analysis, or a modification of it, should remain useful.

Aknowledgements

This paper has benefited considerably from criticism of an earlier draft by Professor Barry Cunliffe, Institute of Archaeology, University of Oxford, and by colleagues at the National Maritime Museum: Dr Basil Greenhill, Director; David Waters, former Deputy Director and Head of Navigation and Astronomy; Eric McKee, formerly Caird Research Fellow; and Owain Roberts, boatbuilder and seaman. I am also grateful to Christopher Terrell, Curator of Hydrography at the National Maritime Museum, for access to charts and pilots, and to Alan Stimson, Curator of Navigation, for advice and discussion. Figs 10.1.1, 2 and 10.1.4–7 were redrawn by Jonathan Hunn from the author's originals. The illustrations are copyright, National Maritime Museum.

References

Adlard Coles K. 1965 N. *Brittany harbours and anchorages*, London, Adlard Coles.

Adlard Coles K. and Black A.N. 1970: *N. Biscay Pilot*. London, Adlard Coles.

André P. 1976–8: 'Un lingot de cuivre en Bretagne' *Bull. Board Celtic Studies* 27, 148–53.

Baker R.R. 1981 'Goal orientation by blindfolding humans after long–distance displacement: possible involvement of a magnetic sense.' *Science* 31, 555–7.

Baker R.R., Mather I.G. and Kennaugh J.H. 1983 'Magnetic bones in the human sinuses.' *Nature* 301, 78–80.

Barnes R.S.K. 1974 *Estuarine Biology*. London, Arnold.

Bellin J.N. 1764 *Le Petit Atlas Maritime* 5th volume. Paris.

Binns A. 1980 *Viking Voyages*. London, Heinemann.

Boon G.C. 1977 'Greco–Roman Anchor–stock from N Wales.' *Antiquaries J.* 57, 10–30.

Casson L. 1971 *Ships and seamanship in the Ancient World.* Princeton.

Chadwick N. 1970 *The Celts*. Harmondsworth, Penguin.

Chatwin, C.P. 1960 *Hampshire Basin and adjoining areas* 3rd edition, London, Inst. of Geological Sciences.

Clarke P.J. 1971' Neolithic, Bronze and Iron Age and Romano–British finds from Mount Batten, Plymouth 1832–1939.' *Proc. Devon. Arch. Soc.* 29, 137–61.

Coghill N. 1951 *Canterbury Tales*. Harmondsworth, Penguin.

Colgrove B. 1927 'Life of Bishop Wilfred.' London.

Cunliffe B. 1978A *Hengistbury Head*. London, Elek.

Cunliffe B 1978B: *Iron Age Communities in Britain* 2nd Edition. London, RKP.

Cunliffe B W 1980 'Evolution of Romney Marsh: a perliminary statement.' in Thompson F.H. (ed) *Archaeology and Coastal Change*. London, Soc. of Antiquaries, Occ. Papers NSI, 37–55.

Cunliffe B. 1982 'Britain, the Veneti and beyond.' *Oxford Journal of Archaeology* 1, 39–68.

Cunliffe B 1983 'Ictis: is it there?' *Oxford Journal of Archaeology* I 2, 123–6.

Devoy R.J. 1982: 'Analysis of the geological evidence for Holocene sea–level movements in SE England.' *Proceedings Geologists' Association* 93, 65–90.

De Weerd M.D. 1978 'Ships of the Roman period at Zwammerdam. In du Plat Taylor, J. and Cleere, H. (eds), 15–21.

Dion R. 1966 'Pythéas explorateur.' *Revue de Philologie, de Litt. et d'Histoire ancienne* 92, 191–216.

Du Plat Taylor J. and Cleere H. 1978 (eds): *Roman shipping and trade* (London, CBA Research Report 24).

Eglinton E. 1982 *Last of the sailing coasters*. London, HMSO.

Ellmers D. 1969 'Keltischer Schiffbau.' *Jarbruch des Römisch–Germanischen Zentralmuseums Mainz* 16, 73–122.

Farrell A.W. and Penny S. 1975 'Broighter boat: a reasessment.' *Irish Archaeological Research Forum* 2.2, 15–26.

Fiori P. and Joncharay J–P. 1973 'Mobilier métallique provenant de fouilles sous marines.' *Cahiers D'Archeologie Subaquatique* 2, 86–9.

Fulford M. 1978 'Interpretation of Britain's late Roman trade.' In du Plat Taylor, J. and Cleere, H. (eds) 59–69.

Gelsinger B.E. 1970 'Norse 'Day's Sailing'. *Mariners Mirror* 56, 107–9.

Greenhill B 1978 *Merchant Schooners* vol 1, 3rd edition. London, HMSO.

Hawkes C.F.C. 1977A *Pytheas* 8th J.L. Myres Memorial Lecture. Oxford.

Hawkes C. 1977B 'Britain and Julius Ceasar. Mortimer Wheeler Archaeological Lecture, 1975.' *Proceedings British Academy*, 63, 125–92.

Heaton P. 1970 *Sailing*. Harmondsworth, Penguin.

Heggie D.C. 1981 *Megalithic Science*. London, Thames and Hudson.

Heyworth A. and Kidson C. 1982: 'Sea level changes in southwest England and in Wales. *Proceedings Geologists' Association* 93, 91–111.

Hirth K.G. 1978 'Inter–regional trade and the formation of prehistoric gateway communities.' *American Antiquity* 43, 35–45.

Hobbs J.S. 1859 *British Channel Pilot* (London, Wilson) Reprinted 1972. Truro, Bradford Barton.

Höckmann O. 1982 'Spätrömische schiffsfunde in Mainz.' *Archäologisches Korrespondenzblatt* 12, 231–50.

Johnstone P. 1980 *Seacraft of Prehistory*. London, RKP.

Karkeek P.Q. 1884 *Chaucer's Schipman*. Reprinted from publications of Chaucer Society.

Kay H.F. 1971 *Science of Yatchs, Wind and Water*. Henley on Thames, Foulis.

Kemp P 1976 *Oxford Companion to Ships and the Sea*. Oxford University Press.

Lamb H.H. 1981 'Late Bronze Age Climate.' in McGrail (ed) *Brigg 'raft'*. Oxford, British Archaeological Reports 89, 205–7.

Langouët L. 1977 '4th–century Gallo–Romano site at Alet.' In Johnston D.E. (ed) *Saxon Shore*. CBA Research Report 18, 38–45.

Lewis D. 1970 'Polynesian and Micronesian Navigation Techniques *J Inst of Navigation* 23, 432–47.

Lewis D. 1972 *We the Navigators*. Canberra, National University Press.

McGrail S. 1978 *Logboats of England and Wales*. Oxford, British Archaeological Reports 51.

McGrail S. 1981 *Rafts, Boats and Ships*. London, HMSO.

McGrail S. 1983 'Interpretation of archaoelogical evidence for maritime structures.' In Annis P (ed) *Sea Studies*. Greenwich, National Maritime Museum, 33–46.

Marsden P. 1976 'A boat of the Roman period found at Bruges, Belgium, in 1899 and related finds.' *International Journal of Nautical Archaeology* 5, 23–55.

Marsden P. 1980 *Roman London*. London, Thames and Hudson.

Merrit R.L. and Thoms A.S. 1980 'Le Grand Menhir Brisé.' *Archaeological Journal* 137, 27–39.

Miles S. 1971–2 'Shipwrecks and survival.' *Proceedings Royal Society*. Edinburgh, 73, (B.Biology), 97–103.

Morken R. 1968 'Norse nautical units and distance measurements.' *Mariner's Mirror* 54, 393–401.

Morrison J.S. and Williams R.T. 1966 *Greek Oared Ships*. Cambridge, University Press.

Mukleroy K, Haselgrove C and Nash D. 1978 'A pre–Roman coin from Canterbury and the ship repesented on it.' *Proc Prehistoric Soci.* 44, 439–44.

Oatley K. 1974 'Mental maps for navigation.' *New Scientist* (19.12.1974) 863–6.

Olsen O.T. 1885 *Fisherman's Seamanship*. Grimsby.

Peacock D.P.S. 1971 ' Roman amphorae in pre–Roman Britain in Hill, D and Jesson M. (eds) *Iron Age and its Hill Forts* 161–79, Southampton.

Peacock D.P.S. 1978 'The Rhine and the problem of Gaulish wine in Britain.' in du Plat Taylor J. and Cleere H. (eds), 49–51.

Piggot S. 1974 *The Druids*. Harmondsworth, Penguin.

Piggot S. 1979 'SW–England – NW Europe.' *Proceedings Devon Archaeological Society* 37, 10–21.

Polyani K. 1963 'Ports of trade in early societies.' *Journal Economic History* 23, 30–45.

Purdy J. 1842 *New Sailing Directory for the English Channel*, 9th edition. London, Laurie.

Price D.J. de S. 1959 'ancient Greek Computer.' *Scientific American*, June, 60–7.

Rigold S.E. 1969 'Roman haven of Dover.' *Archaeological Journal* 126, 78–100.

Rivet A.L.F. and Smith C. 1979 *Place–names of Roman Britain*. London, Batsford.

Ross A. 1970 *Everyday Life of the Pagan Celts*. London, Batsford.

Ross J.B. and Mclaughlin M.M. (ed) 1977 *Portable Medieval Reader*, 144–9. Harmondsworth, Penguin.

Ryckaert M. 1980 'Resultaten van het historisch–geografisch onderzoek in de Belgische kustvlakte. In Verhuist A. and Gottschalk M.K.F. (eds) *Transgressies en occupatiegeschiedenis in de kustgebieden van Nederland en België*, 75–92. Gent, Centre belge d'histoire rurale.

Severin T. 1978 *Brendan Voyage*. London, Hutchinson.

Slade W.J. and Greenhill B. 1974 *West Country Coasting Ketches*. Greenwich, Conway.

Taylor E.G.R. 1971 *Haven–fnding art*. London, Hollis and Carter.

Thoen H. 1978 *De Belgische Kustviakte in de Romeinse Tijd*. Paleis der Academien, Brussel.

Thomas C. 1981 'Lord of Goonhilly'. *Nat. Trust Studies for 1980*. London.

Walton K. 1974 'A Geographer's view of the sea.' *Scottish Geographical Magazine* 90, 4–13.

Waters D 1978 *Art of Navigation in England in Elizabethian and Early Stuart Times*. Greenwich, National Maritime Museum.

Westerdahl C. 1980 'On oral traditions and place names.' *International Journal of Nautical Archaeology* 9, 311–29.

Wood J.E. 1978 *Sun, Moon and Standing Stones*. Oxford University Press.

Admiralty Pilots

Channel	Pt.1	1931	12th edition
Channel	Pt.2	1938	10th edition
Channel	NP27	1977	1st edition
Bay of Biscay	NP22	1970	5th edition
North Sea	Pt.4	1934	9th edition
North Sea (West)	NP54	1973	1st edition
North Sea (East)	NP55	1977	1st edition
Dover Strait	NP28	1971	1st edition

See also Purdy, 1842; Hobbs, 1859; Adlard Coles, 1965; 1970.

Reprinted with permission from *Oxford Journal of Archaeology* 2, 299–337. (1983).

PAPER 10.2

THE SHIPMENT OF TRADED GOODS AND OF BALLAST IN ANTIQUITY

The question whether Greek decorated pottery was a valuable and profitable trade commodity or merely saleable ballast or a space–filler has recently been considered by Boardman (1988a, b) and by Gill (1987, 1988a and b). Boardman (1988a) has pointed out the difficulties in estimating the value of goods shipped overseas and the profits to be made from them. He believes, however, that the relative value of pottery may be measured by calculating its price per unit of weight (40 kg.) and per unit of volume (144 litres = 0.144 m³), and then comparing these prices with those similarly calculated for wine, oil, wheat, barley and other traded goods.

Merchants will undoubtely have been influenced in their choice of goods to be traded by the strength of overseas demand for particular products and by the relative profts to be made. The purpose of this note is to suggest that matters which were primarily the concern of the ship's Master must have determined the nature and quantity of goods actually carried. I shall assume that Masters did not also act as merchants or shippers (although this may sometimes have been the case) and that, although they must have had some interest in the profitability of each voyage they made, their main aim was the safe and timely arrival of the ship at the next destination. I shall further assume that we are dealing with patterns of trade which involve loading, unloading and re–loading at several ports ('tramp' voyages) rather than regular traffic on one 'shipping lane', although the main principles of cargo stowage also apply there.

The volume and weight of cargo which a ship may safely carry depends upon several factors, the principal one being the design of the hull and the chosen operating conditions, especially freeboard. In this note the volume of usable carge space is taken to be that of the hold; ship's stores are not considered, although in antiquity it is likely that they took up a significant proportion of available space. Nor is deck cargo considered, but the effects of its use can readily be deduced.

Stability

The underwater geometry of the hull determines the position of the metacentre, a theoretical point which has an important bearing on a ship's transverse stability (McGrail 1987, 15). The metacentric height GM (the vertical distance between M, the metacentre, and G, the centre of mass of the loaded vessel) is some measure of this stability (Fig. 10.2.1). Thus a positive GM ensures that, when a ship is displaced from the vertical, there will be sufficient righting moment from the buoyancy force (acting through B') to return the ship upright. If GM is large (i.e. with a dense cargo, low in the hold), a ship

will quickly return upright and is said to be *stiff*; excessive stiffness means that a ship is no longer seakindly and this has adverse effects on ship and crew. If there is a small GM, the vessel will only slowly return upright and is said to be *tender*, or in the worst cases *crank*. If there is a negative GM (i.e. cargo is loaded so that the centre of mass lies *above* the metacentre) the ship will be unstable and, when displaced slightly from the vertical, will continue to roll into a position of permanent heel known as *loll*. Without a knowledge of naval architecture, a seaman can recognise from her motion in a seaway the sort of stability his boat or ship has, and we may assume that the experienced mariner of ancient times would have evolved rules of thumb for loading cargo, so that the extreme conditions of metacentric height were avoided. By loading goods of different densities in particular parts of the hold (taking care to avoid shearing stresses in the hull and hogging or sagging damage), he would fix the position of the centre of mass G so that, in our terms, there was a positive GM but not an excessive one.

Freeboard

The total volume of cargo that can be loaded is limited by the capacity of the hold. The total weight of cargo that can be loaded is determined by safety requirements, in particular the necessity to have an adequate freeboard. Freeboard is the vertical distance between the highest watertight deck (or top of sides in an open boat) and the water–line (Fig. 10.2.1). As cargo is loaded, draft is increased and freeboard decreased. Should a vessel be loaded to a waterline where freeboard is less than the safe minimum she may founder after shipping water. Reduced freeboard means deeper draft which may result in a ship not being able to enter harbour at certain states of the tide or even lead to a ship running aground. Deeper draft also increases the resistance of the hull to motion and thus decreases speed potential, although there will be an increased resistance to leeway. With excessive freeboard (light draft), on the other hand, problems of ship–handling and steering can arise, and the power to carry sail may be reduced.

The choice of freeboard is thus a key factor in determining the safety of a ship and her operational performance, and, as it also influences the underwater characteristics of the hull, it has an effect on stability (see above). What was considered to be a safe freeboard in ancient times is conjectural, and what may have been considered safe in Summer in the Mediterranean would not necessarily have been thought safe in the North Sea in the Spring (cf. the 20th century Plimsoll lines). Lacking precise information from antiquity it seems not unreasonable to use, for analytical and comparative purposes, the safe

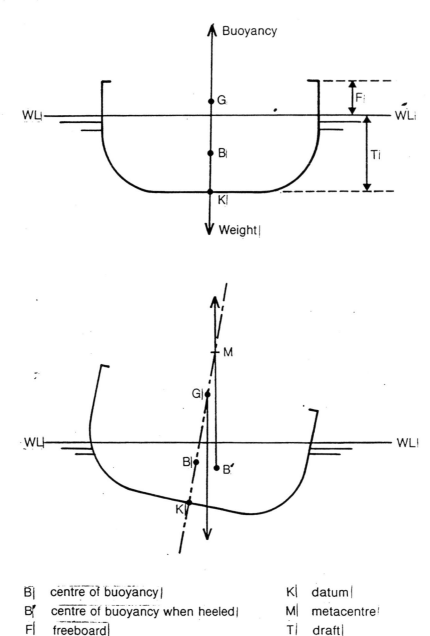

B	centre of buoyancy	K	datum
B'	centre of buoyancy when heeled	M	metacentre
F	freeboard	T	draft
G	centre of mass	WL	waterline

Figure 10.2.1 Diagrams to illustrate transverse stability. Upper: vessel floating in equilibrium. Lower: vessel heeled through a small angle

freeboard defined in a Medieval Icelandic law as that which equals 2/5 of the height of sides of the vessel (McGrail 1988, 38).

Stowage factors

A Master has to ensure that his ship is loaded in a manner that meets the requirements of these two interacting factors – hull design and operational freeboard – if he is to make a safe voyage. He has to arrange that his cargo is of such a mix and loaded in such a sequence that the resultant centre of mass (in magnitude and position) leads to an adequate metacentric height and a safe freeboard. Furthermore, particular consignments have to be readily accessible for offloading at the

Table 10.2.1 Stowage Factors (m³/tonne)

Tin ingots	0.22 to	0.28
Lead pigs	0.22	0.31
Lead ingots	0.28	0.33
Iron pigs	0.28	0.33
Iron ore	0.33	0.42
Lead ore	0.36	0.39
Marble blocks	0.42	0.47
Granite slabs	0.45	0.50
Marble slabs	0.50	0.56
Sand	0.53	0.56
Ivory	0.84	0.98
Iron scrap	0.98	–
Water	1.00	–
Oak	1.00	1.31
Wheat	1.18	1.34
Wheat in bags	1.34	1.50
Barley	1.36	1.50
Hides, baled and dry	1.39	1.67
Elm	1.39	1.78
Barley in bags	1.45	1.67
Pine	1.52	1.84
Ivory in cases	1.53	1.67
Wine in casks	1.62	1.78
Wine in cases	1.67	1.95
Olive oil in casks	1.67	1.73
Earthenware in crates	1.70	2.13
Tiles	2.13	2.27
Peat or turf, dry	2.30	–
Tiles in crates	2.41	–
Hides, dry	2.79	4.18
Hay in bales	3.34	4.46
Porcelain in crates/ cases/baskets/tubs	3.34	5.57
Wool in bales	5.55	6.00

Figures are for bulk stowage, except where noted. These stowage factors apply to the relatively large and obstruction–free holds of modern vessels: factors for vessels in antiquity would probably have been at the higher end of the given ranges. Sources: Lewis 1962; Thmas 1983.

next port. Loading cargo is thus not a simple problem. It is not just the volume of the constituent elements of the cargo, nor its weight, which are of concern, but the relationship of weight to volume i.e. density. And not just specific density, but *cargo density* which takes into account the volume and weight of any containers (sacks, barrels, amphorae etc.); any dunnage used to protect cargo and ship; and the volume of space lost in the interstices between individual containers, or between individual grains or other units if it is a bulk cargo. The inverse of cargo density is known as the *stowage factor* which is generally given as a range of values to allow for variations in these stowage parameters. Stowage factors are used nowadays to convert known weights of cargo into stowed volumes and thus the position of the centre of mass may be calculated. A ship's Master in antiquity would have had to make analogous estimates based on experience and inherited rules of thumb.

Table 10.2.1 gives stowage factors for some 20th century goods, and analogies with goods traded and containers used in former times may be drawn. The figures are based on those in Thomas (1983) and in Lewis (1962): the latter work was 'compiled from experience', as cargo stowage is something of an art.

Ballast and Goods of Low Stowage Factor

When a potential cargo contains materials with a high stowage factor (i e low cargo density) the Master will generally have to consider embarking a compensating consignment of materials of a low stowage factor. His aim wouid be, from his experience, to compile a mix of cargo that should result in a safe freeboard and a reasonable metacentric height for the next leg of the voyage. It may be that in achieving this aim the Master cannot safely use the entire volume of the hold. Materials with a low stowage factor effectively lower the centre of mass of the whole cargo, and if the Master is able to embark low stowage goods (tin ingots, lead pigs, iron bars, granite, millstones, or marble, for example) rather than untradeable ballast such as rubble, stone, gravel, shingle or sand (Falconer 1780, 28) he will not only achieve a balanced, safe mix of cargo but will also be able to earn income from all consignments. In this sense cargo with a low stowage factor may be described as 'saleable ballast'. If a Master has to load unsaleable ballast it may well be discharged into the harbour at the next port if a high density/low stowage factory consignment of cargo becomes available for the subsequent voyage.

Buckland and Saddler (forthcoming) have drawn attention to the information on trade routes which may be obtained from petrological identification of ballast excavated from wrecks or from harbour sites. They have noted, however, that the off–loading and re–loading of ballast can lead to re–cycling and thus ballast may not necessarily indicate direct contact between the place of origin and the place of deposition, but may be the result of a complex trade pattern. That ballast was used in the early Mediterranean we know, for example, from the underwater sites of Cape Gelidonya (Bass 1967), Kyrenia (Katzev 1972) and Serçe Liman (Bass and van Doorninck

1978). The men who worked ballast in Roman harbours were known as *saburrarii* (Laures 1986).

There may, however, be a requirement for ballast to be carried permanently in a vessel to improve performance, ship handling and sailing balance, regardless of the type of cargo embarked. Such ballast may be disposed symmetrically, if loaded mainly to improve stability, or asymmetrically if loaded to adjust the vessel's trim. In a small boat ballast may be moved several times during one voyage, trimming the boat fore and aft or athwartships to achieve optimum sailing trim for varying conditions of relative wind, but this is generally impracticable in a ship. Permanent ballast is usually set in dunnage (e.g. sand, hopleaves or even moss) to protect the ship's structure. Should ballast (or indeed low stowage factor cargo) shift from its stowed position the ship can take on a dangerous list which may lead to disaster.

The possibility exists then, that in antiquity part–cargoes of stone or heavy metals such as iron, lead, copper or tin remained in a ship as ballast or as compensatory low stowage factor materials for some considerable time, and were not unloaded for sale or exchange until another consignment of low stowage factor could be obtained. It may be, for example, that the 352 bronzes weighing *c*.60 kg., excavated from the underwater site of Langdon Bay, Dover (Muckelroy 1981; Needham, personal communication), were in fact ballast, assembled over a period of time and from different ports.

Greek Decorated Pottery

The relatively high stowage factor of pottery (earthenware, *c*. 2; porcelain, *c*. 4.5) and its delicate nature necessitating special handling and stowage, mean that it is unlikely to have been used as ballast in antiquity. It is possible, on the other hand, that on specific voyages but not necessarily as a general rule small amounts were consigned as 'space fillers', subject to the constraints discussed above. Whether a shipper decided to offer a substantial consignment of pottery rather than some other goods to a ship's Master for transport overseas and what quantity was offered would be determined principally by the relative profit to be made. Whether these offered goods were indeed embarked would be determined by the Master after consideration of the stowage problems discussed in this note.

Aknowledgements

I am grateful to Owain Roberts and to Dr A.E. Lieber who commented on an earlier draft. I am also grateful to Alison Wilkins who re–drew figure 10.2.1. The illustrations are copyright, Institute of Archaeology, Oxford.

References

Bass G F. 1967 'C. Gelidonya: a Bronze Age shipwreck.' *Trans. American Philosophical Soc.* NS57 pt. 8.

Bass G.F. and Van Doorninck F.H. 1978 'Serçe Liman Shipwreck.' *Int. J. Nautical Archaeology* 7, 119–132.

Boardman J. 1988a 'Trade in Greek decorated pottery.' *Oxford J. of Archaeology* 7, 27–33.

Boardman J. 1988b 'Trade figures.' *Oxford J. Archaeology* 7, 371–373.

Buckland P. and Sadler JP. (forthcoming) 'Ballast and building stone: a discussion.' In Parsons. D. (ed) *Quarrying and Stone Supply: from Roman Britain to the end of the Middle Ages.* Leicester University Press.

Falconer W. 1780 *An Univeral Dictionary of the Marine* Cadell, London. Reprinted *c*. 1974 David and Charles, Newton Abbot.

Gill D.W.J. 1987 'The date of the Porticello shipwreck.' *Int. J. of Nautical Archaeology* 16, 31–33.

Gill D.W.J. 1988a: 'Trade in Greek decorated pottery: some corrections.' *Oxford J. of Archaeology* 7, 369–370.

Gill D.W.J. 1988b 'Expressions of wealth: Greek art and society.' *Antiquity* 62, 735–743.

Katzev M.L. 1972 'Kyrenia ship.' In Bass G.F. (ed.), *History of Seafaring*, 50–52.

Laures F.F 1986 'Roman maritime trades.' *Int. J. of Nautical Archaeology* 15, 166–7.

Lewis G.P. 1962 *Handy guide to Stowage.* Imray, Laurie, Norie and Wilson, London.

McGrail S. 1987 *Ancient boat in NW Europe.* Longman.

McGrail S. 1988 'Assessing thc performance of an ancient boat – Hasholme logboat.' *Oxford J. of Archaeology* 7, 35–46.

Muckelroy K. 1981: 'Middle Bronze Age tradc between Britain and Europe: a maritime perspective.' *Proc. Prehistoric Soc.* 47, 275–297.

Thomas O.O., Agnew J. and Cole K.L,. 1983: *Thomas' Stowage* 7th edition. Glasgow.

PAPER 10.3

PILOTAGE AND NAVIGATION IN THE TIMES OF ST. BRENDAN

Introduction

The 9th century text, *The Voyage of St. Brendan* (O'Meara, 1978) describes a 6th century Saint who was also a boatbuilder and a seaman of note, but it is his achievements as a navigator I wish to examine in this paper. By navigator I do not mean just a seafarer but one with the technical competence to determine a vessel's position at sea, and to take her safely from one place to another. *Pilotage* is included in the term *navigation* and may be defined as: the art and science of conducting a vessel within waters restricted by the proximity of land and which are generally shallow. Navigation is now rightly regarded as a science, but it has not always been so: until relatively recently it was largely an art, in the sense of the use of personal skills, and achievement depended on handed–on experience, local knowledge and detailed observation and interpretation of natural phenomena (Waters, 1978, 3–38).

Needham (1971, 555) has identified three stages in the development of navigational techniques:

1. Non–instrumental
2. Quantitative
3. Mathematical

The third phase, mathematical or scientific navigation, did not begin until the 17th century. The second stage may be said to have started in N.W. Europe with the use of the mariners' compass in the late–12th century, although it was not until the 15th century that such navigational aids as the sandglass, traverse tables, astrolabes, quadrants and *rutters*, (written sailing directions or pilots) became relatively commonplace in the northern seas. Thus, in prehistoric and medieval times, navigation was essentially non–instrumental, the only instrument for which there is any evidence being the sounding lead. Boat users in N.W. Europe were not all equally affected by the introduction of quantitative and mathematical techniques, and aspects of non–instrumental navigation continued therefore to be used in boats and small ships into the l9th and even 20th centuries (Olsen, 1885; Kemp, 1976, 123–4; Greenhill, 1978, 199–205; Binns, 1980, 79–80). Polynesian navigators of the mid–20th century used comparable methods (Lewis, 1972) which have been described as *environrnental* rather than instrumental.

Early navigational knowledge

In the Mediterranean, seamen of Classical and earlier times used stars for steering and orientation at night, and even to obtain an approximation of movement in a N/S direction (equivalent to change of latitude) by measurement against mast and yard; and distances were estimated in terms of a day's sail. The influence of the moon on the tides was known, as were the sea conditions associated with specific weather sequences, and the directions from which predominant winds blew were used as reference bearings to produce a wind–rose (McGrail, 1983).

There is little direct information on the contemporary state of scientific knowledge in N.W. Europe, but some conclusions may be drawn from the archacological evidence and from descriptions by the Romans of their barbaric neighbours.

The alignment of certain megalithic structures in Britain, France and Scandinavia suggests Neolithic and Bronze Age knowledge of the sun's movements and possibly those of the moon and stars (Heggie, 1981, 222–3; Ellmers, 1981) and such knowledge would have been useful at sea. In the Iron Age, the Celts had a good working knowledge of astronomy (Caesar, *BG*, 6.14) with particular emphasis on the moon (Piggott, 1974, 104–5): such learning could have had direct application to direction finding at sea and to tidal prediction. Like many illiterate peoples, the Celts (and probably their predecessors) paid great attention to memory training for transmission of learning and culture (Chadwick, 1970, 45–7; Ross, 1970, 125–6) and the oral teaching of the Gauls, for example, included the motion of the stars (Caesar, *BG*, 6.14). Stereotyped phrases and rules of thumb about the motions of the heavenly bodies, the ebb and flow of the tides, the weather sequences, descriptions of coastal landscapes and the "directions and distances" between key landfalls could have been memorised and used empirically. Recent equivalents are known (McGrail, 1983, 319).

We may get some idea of the capabilities of early medieval navigators by considering Brendan's achievements, some of the problems he encountered and some of the techniques he used, as set out in the *Navigatio*.

Achievements

a. Inter–island voyages, generally in sight of land and therefore *pilotage* techniques used (*passim*).

b. Probably longer range voyages (e.g. in Ch. 21) out of sight of land and therefore *navigational* techniques had to be used.

c. Places previously visited were re–located (Ch. 26)

d. Return to 'home–port' after wide travels (Ch. 28)

Problems encountered

     e. Bearings lost–in fog–Ch. 1.

     f. Bearings lost, possibly when sky obscured – Ch. 6.

     g. Delayed due to weather (Ch. 16).

     h. Making landfall in fog – Ch. 28.

     i. Search for suitable landing places – (*passim*).

Techniques used

     j. Oral sailing directions (Ch. 1).

     k. Forecast weather (Ch 16).

     l. Use of landward–flying seabirds (Ch. 18).

     m. Use of a specialised pilot (Ch. 18).

Apart from the *Navigatio's* somewhat ambiguous evidence for voyages out of sight of land (and it may refer to the 9th century when the Latin version was first written down rather than the 6th century of St. Brendan) the earliest documented voyages out of sight of land in N.W. European waters are the late–8th century ones from Ireland to some of the northern islands, possibly including Iceland, as described by the early–9th century Irish monk Dicuil. (Taylor, 1971, 69–70; O' Meara 1978, XI). Many of the earlier sea voyages in N.W. European waters could have been undertaken at short crossing points where prominent headlands on both sides were visible from a point in mid–channel, and thus pilotage techniques used. However, there is evidence that Celts of the late–prehistoric period did undertake voyages out of sight of land between France and Britain (McGrail, 1983), and it therefore seems possible that similar long range voyages were made at about the same time in the seas to the north of Ireland and west of Scotland and that navigational techniques were used there at an earlier date then historical sources might suggest.

Although the *Navigatio* and similar documents add to our knowledge of early medieval navigational techniques it is, in sum, very little. It might seem therefore that an attempt to establish how Brendan found his way and kept his reckoning was doomed to failure because of lack of evidence. However, another line of approach appears to be both valid and fruitful: by identifying the basic problems, which, in general, are not specific to region, culture or time, it is possible to make reasoned suggestions about early navigational and pilotage techniques from an examination of how seamen of recent, pre–industrialised societies tackled analogous problems. This is not to claim that ancient and modern concepts were the same, rather that similar methods may have been used by seamen from roughly the same technological background when faced with essentially the same problems.

Early methods of pilotage and navigation

In the light of all the forms of evidence – archaeological, documentary and ethnographic analogy – suggestions can be made as to the probable methods of pilotage and navigation used by 6th century seamen.

Leaving harbour

Preparation for a voyage would have included an evaluation of the actual wind, known sea and tide, a forecast of the weather to be expected, and a comparison of these with the conditions generally prevailing on the intended route at that time of the year. With this information the 6th century seaman could estimate the course to be steered and the time required for his voyage as deviations from the course generally used and the time usually taken. He would thus form a mental picture (a 'chart') of his forthcoming passage, which he would revise during the voyage in the light of further observations of natural phenomena.

He would probably leave with a fair wind on an ebb (outfowing) tide, steering by reference to landmarks and visible shoals and reefs. The sounding lead would be used when in doubt about the depth of water and to recognise safe channels.

Coastal and inter–island passages

On coastal passages the seaman would frequently establish his position relative to prominent natural landmarks and seamarks. Should visual contact be lost with the land he would record his estimated position on his "mental chart" until he could close the coast and regain his bearings. On such a passage it would be necessary to work the tides, possibly including anchoring or lying hove–to during foul streams (Eglinton, 1982, 12–13; Greenhill, 1978, 200), and it could prove necessary to wait for a fair wind before being able to round headlands. Alfred's account of Ohthere's 9th century voyages along the Norwegian coast contains references to such events (Lund, 1984). It would also probably be necessary to anchor during non–moonlight nights – but see Marcus (1980, 116) on 13th century pilots who could find their way in Norwegian fjords by star–light.

Open Sea Voyages

Taking departure

Once clear of land the direction of wind, sea and swell would be checked against a known relationship such as a transit between two headlands, the bearing of an island, the general trend of the coast, or in relation to a back bearing. Before losing sight of land the 6th century seaman would 'take departure' by estimating his position relative to some prominent landmark – this would bocome a datum point on his "mental chart". In good visibility high ground can be kept in sight for a considerable distance: for example, a 30m high headland can be seen out to 11 n.m.; and a 305m headland out to *c*. 36 n.m.

With a fair wind the seaman would then set a course which would allow for his estimate of the set of the tidal stream and current and any leeway. With a foul wind the boat would be brought to the heading on which the boat was known to make the most ground to windward, and an estimate made of the displacement caused by current, stream and leeway.

Navigational techniques

Once out of sight of land methods other than pilotage have to be used. The navigator has to rely on his assessments of tracks and speeds made good relative to the last known position or relative to his destination. Courses steered and speeds achieved relative to the water give a dead reckoning (DR) position. When angular allowance is also made for leeway and drift an estimated position (EP) is obtained which, if the allowances are reasonable, gives the track made good.
This navigational problem may be resolved into two parts:

> (a) how to estimate directions such-as courses, leeway and drift; and

> (b) how to estimate speeds or distances.

Direction from the celestial pole

The moon and stars appear to move, in relation to the Earth, but the celestial pole or null point (near *Polaris* nowadays) maintains a fixed direction and is readily identifiable without instruments in a clear night sky. This null point was known from at least early Classical times (Homer *Odyssey* V. 271–6) although the star then nearest the pole was *Kochab* rather than *Polaris* (Taylor, 1971, 9–12, 43). The Anglo–Saxon 9th century AD vocabulary included two phrases for the pole star, *scip steorra* and *lad steorra* which indicate its use at sea, and there are other references in early medieval literature which testify to its navigational importance (Ellmers, 1981; Marcus, 1980, 108). It thus seems likely, though not demonstrable, that the celestial pole was similarly used in Brendan's time.

With one point fixed, in this case North, it is practicable to identify South, East and West, and also possible to recognise the half–cardinal points: NE, SE, SW and NW.

Direction from other celestial bodies

Polynesian navigators were able to establish their bearings and steer accurate courses by reference to single stars or constellations (Lewis, 1972, 52–4). The obliquity of celestial motion in higher latitudes rules out such precision in N.W. European waters, except when using the pole star, nevertheless directional information can be obtained. In daytime the fixed direction (South) of the sun's zenith (noon) position may be determined with reasonable accuracy when visible, as there is a period of very little change in azimuth and altitude at that time. At dawn and dusk East and West may be approximately identified, providing the seasonal directions of sunrise and sunset (amplitude) have been established before the voyage,

relative to a known bearing. On East/West voyages in N.W. European waters in the March to September sailing season, the sun's amplitude changes by less than 1°/day, whilst on N/S passages the change could be *c.* 5°/day. Thus on a five day voyage the maximum change in bearing of sunrise and sunset from the bearing known before leaving land would be 25° (*c* 2pts). With more difficulty, the navigator may be able to maintain his direction at other times of the day by reference to the changing altitude and azimuth of the sun: the Polynesian navigator did this by 'delicate judgment' as distinct from scientific measurement (Lewis, 1972).

Direction relative to wind and swell

When the sky is obscured and celestial bodies cannot be seen, bearings may be related to the wind or swell. Wind and sea maintain a fairly constant direction for only a relatively short time in N.W. European waters, unlike areas where there are seasonal trade winds. However, winds from different directions may be recognised by the weather accompanying them: thus a warm wet wind comes from the SW and a cold wet wind from the N.W. Bearings can thus be established in relation to the wind blowing at any one time, and the Vikings are known to have used such a "wind rose" (Taylor, 1971, 8).

Swell (the sea motion originated by a strong predominant wind), on the other hand, gives a more certain indication of direction for longer periods, although the effect is less pronounced in summer than winter. Polynesian navigators placed great reliance on swell direction to give them their bearings, and were able to distinguish the predominant swell, from any lesser swells, from wave motion, and from wave diffraction–patterns due to islands or promontories. Shetland fishermen in the recent past are known to have been similarly capable of recognising the underlying SW swell ('Mother Wave') in a confused sea (March, 1970, 39; Binns, 1980, 20–1). Such an ability may well have been widespread in early N.W. Europe, but atrophied with the advent of instrumental aids.

Leeway and drift allowance

Leeway is negligible when the wind is from a sector some 4 points either side of dead astern; otherwise it may be estimated by wake angle. Drift allowance depends on the navigator's evaluation of the changing state of the tidal stream since taking departure and of any current. An alternative method is to assume that, in general, tidal stream displacements cancel out during each period of 12½ hours, leaving a slight drift due to current, but this is not valid when the boat passes through radically different tidal systems.

Distance estimation

In order to obtain a "mental fix" of his position, the navigator has to establish how far he has travelled along his track (bearing from departure point) which he has estimated by applying leeway and drift to the courses steered. Distance travelled is determined by speed and time; both are difficult to estimate without aids. However, at any one season of the year the ratio of daylight to darkness can be deduced from measurements on land, and thus sunrise, noon and sunset measurement could become 'fixed' points in time. Some measure of the passage of time during daylight could be obtained from the sun's change in azimuth, providing it could be noted relative to a 'fixed' bearing such as swell direction. At night an estimate of lapsed time since sunset may be made by noting the position of the circumpolar constellations.

In several maritime societies (for example, the Classical Mediterranean and Viking Age Scandinavia) distances have been expressed in units of a day's sail (Casson, 1971, 281–96; Morken, 1968; Gelsinger, 1970; Taylor, 1971, 50–2, 79, 126). Implicit in this is the concept of a 'standard' speed to be expected from the 'usual' sort of boat in fair wind and sea conditions. There are several possible methods of estimating actual speeds achieved, measured in relation to this 'standard' speed. Lewis (1972, 119) found that Polynesian navigators used a multitude of indications including spray turbulence and wind pressure. Another method is to use a dutchman's log; foam bubbles or an object thrown overboard may be timed between bow and stern (Greenhill, 1978, 195); or the time to make a passage between two known coastal marks may be noted: in both cases a standard phrase may be chanted to give a measure of elapsed time. Such usage is not recorded, but chants are known to have been used to keep Classical (Morrison and Williams, 1968, 196) and Saxon (Colgrove, 1927, 26) oarsmen synchronised. Another timing mechanism might be the pulse or heartbeat. By such means. an experienced seaman established what speeds his boat could achieve on different courses in various combinations of wind, sea and swell, the speeds being estimated relative to a 'standard' speed.

Estimated position

Thus knowing his track (course steered relative to some heavenly body, the wind or swell, amended for leeway and drift) and the distance sailed along it (in terms of a relative speed or as a fraction of a "day's sail"), the navigator can "mark" his estimated position on his "mental chart" at noon, sunrise and sunset as a measure of his progress since the last EP or as an estimated bearing and distance from departure point or destination.

Inbound pilotage

Early warning of land, the 'expanded' target of David Lewis (1972), may be given by orographic cloud, the flight of seabirds at dawn and dusk, and other adventitious aids (Binns, 1980, 79; Marcus, 1980, 114–5). Lead and line may be used to obtain warning of shallows and hence the nearess of land and to note the nature of the bottton so that safe channels may be recognised. Reflected wave patterns or the sound of surf breaking in the shallows or even the smell of sheep may indicate the heading on which land lies. Shore sighting birds – as used by Noah, in Viking times (*Landnambok*. Jones, 1964, 118), and in the waters off Ceylon in Classical times (Pliny *NH*

6.24.83). Colour changes of the water also give an indication of position as for example when approaching the mouth of a large river.

A good landfall is made when the pilot recognises the coastal landscape as it becomes visible at a range when the boat is still clear of inshore hazards. The position of the boat relative to the destination may then be established and a safe course set for the landing place. Leading marks especially transits (two objects in line) are of great use when approaching the entrance to a bay or estuary or an individual landing place. Prehistoric barrows are known to have been used as sailing marks in recent times in Swedish waters (Westerdahl, 1980. 324): similar use in earlier times seems possible. Certain medieval churches may have been sited for similar reasons, as sugggested by Binns (1980) for the Humber region.

Landfall on an unfamiliar coast

Providing the general track followed since leaving the last firm position is known, a seaman in sight of unfamiliar land is not lost although he may not know his position until he has obtained more information e.g. investigating the colour and composition of the cliffs, the nature of the beach material, etc. He can orientate himself and estimate a course to destination or back to his point of departure by observing the direction of the celestial pole (North) or the noon sun (South). By landing or anchoring in sheltered water, and waiting for clear weather he may be able to observe the celestial pole with greater accuracy and thus obtain some measure of the distance he has travelled north or south of his departure point by estimating the altitude (angular elevation) of the celestial pole (or of the noon sun if direct vision could be avoided) possibly against the ship's mast, or by using such a simple device as the Arab *Kamal*, a tablet and knotted string (Taylor, 1971, 128–9, fig. XI; Severin, 1982, 92–3). Other possible measuring standards include finger breadths, or palms/fist/finger spans at arms length (Taylor, 1971, 49); a stick calibrated in the sun's apparent radius (Marcus, 1953, 120); or the use ashore of a *Gnomon* or sundial to measure the ratio of index mark to shadow (as known in the Classical world – see Strabo 1.4.4 and 2.5.8). Southward deviation in the Northern hemisphere is indicated by decreased pole altitude and increased sun's meridian altitude. Change of latitude (N/S movement) is also indicated by changes in the azimuth (bearing) of sunrise and sunset which draw nearer to due East or West (i.e. at right angles to the N/S line) with southerly movement. As with the other indicators, such changes would be appreciated by the seaman as a difference from the data known for a standard site, probably the departure point or "home port".

New lands were indeed encountered by unplanned storm drifts as suggested in the *Navigatio*: see, for example, the Vikings' "discovery" of Iceland (Foote and Wilson, 1970, 52), Greenland and America (Taylor, 1971, 74, 79–80). In meteorological conditions of refraction theoretical visibility distances from sea level can be significantly increased and previously unknown lands seen. The flight path of migrating birds can indicate the direction of new lands and this may have been the way 8th century Irishmen were led to Iceland and other northern islands as recorded by Dicuil (Taylor, 1971, 76). Other clues to new land may be given by cloud and swell: orographic cloud may be seen over land well out of sight; and an abrupt change in a swell pattern may indicate that a boat has entered the "shadow" of a distant, previously unknown, island which is distorting the predominant swell.

Conclusions

Archaeological and documentary evidence suggest that the main problems of pilotage and non–instrumental navigation were solved to an acceptable degree of accuracy in the seas between France and Britain (and ..elsewhere) well before the 6th century AD. This is not to claim that prehistoric man or even medieval man used modern analytical concepts, nor that he achieved 20th century standards of accuracy and timekeeping; indeed it was not until very recent times that our present–day expectations of low risk, minimum delay sea travel were realised.

These early non–instrumental techniques were refined and improved by succeeding generations of seamen in N.W. European waters, but the indications are that there were no significant alterations or additions until late–medieval times. Brendan and his contemporaries in the 6th century AD thus used techniques inherited from their predecessors, which would have not have been unfamiliar eight centuries later – or indeed 1400 years later in some parts of the world.

A 4th century AD description of the capabilities of an Indian Ocean navigator reads:

'he knew the course of the stars and readily orientated himself; he also had a deep knowledge of the value of signs, whether regular, accidental or abnormal, of good and bad weather. He distinguished the regions of the ocean by the fish, by the colour of the water, by the nature of the bottom, by the birds, the mountains, and other indications." (Needham, 1971, 555; Taylor, 1971, 85).

The 13th century Norwegian seaman (Taylor, 1971, 81–4) depicted in the *Konungs Skuggsja* was familiar with finding his direction from the stars and could divide the horizon into a wind rose of 8 "points". He knew the weather sequences to be expected, had a good knowledge of the movements of whales, fish, walrus, seals and sea–ice, and could calculate the tides in relation to the moon's phases. Chaucer's 14th century shipman (Coghill, 1961, 35–6) could also reckon tides, tidal streams, phases of the moon, and his tracks and distances; he knew well the harbours and havens from Gotland to C. Finisterre and the creeks of Brittany and Spain. With slight modification these descriptions could well apply to Brendan and his contemporaries.

In coastal waters, in any age, the seaman using non–instrumental techniques has to be familiar with the details of the coastline, offshore soundings and the nature of the sea bottom, safe channels to the main landing places, their sailing marks and hazards, and the times of high and low water and slack streams in relation to the moon's phases. As a navigator out of sight of land he has to set the best course he can make relative to the wind, keep his "reckoning" and adjust his course where possible to allow for deviation from the norm, to make a good landfall, his aim being at any one moment to know his position with an accuracy which will allow him to approach his destination on as constant a bearing as the elements will allow.

References

Binns A.L. (1980) *Viking Voyagers*. Heinemann.

Casson L. (1971) *Ships and Seamanship in the Ancient World*. Princeton.

Chadwick N. (1970) *The Celts*. Penguin.

Coghill N. (1951) *Canterbury Tales*. Harmondsworth.

Colgrove B. (1927) *Life of Bishop Wilfrid*.

Eglinton E. (1982) *Last of the sailing coasters*. HMSO.

Ellmers D. (1981) 'Der Nachtsprung an eine hinter dem Horizont liegende Gegenküste.' *Deutsches Schiffahrtsarchiv* 4, 154–167.

Foote P.C. and Wilson D.M. (1970) *Viking Achievement*.

Gelinsger B.E. (1970) 'Norse "Days Sailing.'', *Mariners Mirror* 56, 107–9.

Greenhill B. (1978) *Merchant Schooners* Vol. 1, 3rd edition HMSO.

Heggie D.C. (1981) *Megalithic Science*. Thames and Hudson.

Jones G. (1974) *Norse Atlantic Saga*.

Kemp P. (1976) *Oxford Companion to Ships and the Sea*. O.U.P.

Lewis D. (1972) *We the Navigators*. Canberra Nat. University Press.

Lund N. (ed) (1984) *Two Voyagers at the Court of King Alfred*. York.

McGrail S. (1983) 'Cross–channel seamanship and navigation in the late 1st millennium BC.' *Oxford J. of Archaeology* 2, 299–337.

March E.J. (1970) *Inshore Craft of Britain*. 2vols. Newton Abbot.

Marcus G.J. (1980) *Conquest of N. Atlantic*. Boydell Press.

Morken R (1968) 'Norse nautical units and distances measurements.' *Mariner's Mirror* 54, 393–401.

Morrison J.S. and Williams R.T. (1968) *Greek Oared Ships, 900–322 BC*.Cambridge.

Needham J. (1971) *Science and Civilisation in China* 4 pt. 3. Cambridge.

Olsen O.T. (1885) *Fisherman's Seamanship*. Grimsby.

O'Meara J.J. (1978) *Voyage of St. Brendan*. Dolmen. Dublin.

Piggott S. (1974) *The Druids*. Harmondsworth.

Ross A. (1970) *Everyday life of the Pagan Celts*. Batsford.

Severin T. (1978) *Brendan Voyage*. Hutchinson.

Severin T. (1982) *Sinbad Voyage*. Hutchinson.

Taylor E.G.R. (1971) *Haven–finding art*. Hollis and Carter.

Waters D. (1978) *Art of Navigation in England in Elizabethan and Early Stuart Times*. NMM Greenwich.

Westerdahl C. (1980) 'On oral traditions and place names.' *IJNA* 9, 311–329.

Reprinted with permission from:

deCourcy–Ireland J. and Sheehy D.C. (ed) *Atlantic Vision*: 25–35. Dun Laoghaire. (1989).

PAPER 10.4

EARLY SEA VOYAGES

This paper summarizes the sparse evidence for the earliest known open sea voyages in the western Mediterranean, north America, south–east Asia/Australia, and Oceania. In the absence of direct evidence, ethnographic and archaeological analogies are used: to deduce how overseas lands may first have been detected; to suggest which navigational techniques were used in inshore waters and in open sea conditions; to infer what sort of water transport was available for these early migratory voyages.

The evidence for the earliest sea voyages is indirect rather than direct; four examples may be given, drawn from different regions of the world.

(a) Technological affinities between the stone tools of Spain and southern France and those of north–west Africa (Roe, 1980, 77) raise the possibility that, 500,000 to 300,000 years ago, man crossed the Mediterranean by the shortest sea route from Africa to Gibraltar (Sherratt, 1980, 438) where, at the lowest sea–levels, there would have been a channel 6 miles wide (Clark & Piggott, 1976, 41).

(b) A series of radiocarbon dates from southern Australia and other evidence show that the maritime colonization of Greater Australia (a land mass which, because of lower sea–levels, included New Guinea and adjacent islands) from mainland Asia (which included western Indonesia) probably took place before 40,000 BP (Mulvaney, 1975; Clark, 1977, 454; Allen *et al.*, 1977; Bailey, 1980; Thorne, 1980; Habgood, 1986; van Andel, 1989).

(c) The Oceanic islands were also peopled from south–east Asia and Indonesia; Melanesia,before 3000 BC; Micronesia, from the mid 2nd millennium BC; Polynesia, from the 2nd millennium BC to the 11th century AD (Shulter, 1975; Clark, 1977: 488; Irwin, 1980; Bellwood,1978; Irwin *et al*, 1990).

(d) The American continent was populated from north–eastern Siberia across what is now the Bering Strait to what is now Alaska, but there are differing views as to when this migration began. A long–held view is that it began in post–glacial times, from *c.* 12,000 BP; others have suggested that it was some time in the period between 20,000 and 12,000BP; a more radical view, based on recently published dates from sites in Chile and Brazil, is that man must have been in northern America as early as 40,000 BP (Guidon & Delibrias, 1986; Bray, 1986; Bray *et al.*,

1989: 1–5). Study of the teeth of Amerinds and of East Asians, and study of language groupings within the Amerind population have suggested that there were two further major migrations from Asia to America after the earliest one and that these were post–glacial (Bray, 1986).

Beringia, a land corridor with tundra vegetation, some 1000 km wide connecting the ice–free parts of Siberia and Alaska, was inundated by rising sea–levels, and the Bering Strait formed in *c.* 12,000 BP (Klein, 1980, 87; Street, 1980, 56; van Andel, 1989). Thus any migrations before this date could have been overland, whereas after 12,000 BP some form of water transport would have been necessary. Furthermore, whatever the date of the first migration, glacial or post–glacial water transport would probably have been needed from the earliest times to facilitate hunting and fishing and movement along the coastlands of Alaska and British Columbia southwards to warmer latitudes.

The evidence for these early voyages is not corroborated by correspondingly early finds of water transport. Apart from simple logboats, the earliest dated to *c.* 6,500 BC (McGrail, 1987, 86) no float, raft or boat has been identified which can be reliably dated to earlier than the Cheops boat from Egypt of *c.* 2500 BC (Lipke, 1984) and the earliest iconographic evidence for any form of water transport is from the 4th millennium BC. Nor is there evidence how these early seamen became aware of new overseas lands, and how they navigated to them. The aim of this paper is to suggest that by using archaeological and ethnographic analogy it is possible to shed some light on these problems.

Detecting new lands

Previously unknown lands may be seen from a boat when some miles away from, but still in sight of, the home coastline. Such sightings may be made at considerable distances, especially when there are prominent headlands or high ground near one or both coasts (Table 10.4.1). These theoretical distances can be significantly extended in certain meteorological conditions.

The position of new lands may also be inferred, even when not in sight, when smoke from naturally occurring fires can be seen (Habgood, 1986), from the presence of orographic cloud, from the flight line of migrating bird, by the otherwise inexplicable deflection of a predominant swell, and by colour changes in the water (McGrail, 1983; 1987, 279–80).

Pilotage and navigational techniques

It seems likely that the earliest sea voyages were coastal ones or across channels where land was always in sight, or from island to island in archipelagos. In such conditions pilotage techniques are used: landmarks and seamarks are noted and the seaman progresses from one position, known relative to the land, to another known position (McGrail, 1983). In such visual conditions the varying effects on the boat of wind, tidal streams and currents can be appreciated and allowed for. By these means, in conditions of good visibility, considerable stretches of water can be crossed. However, when night falls, or if the weather changes so that there is poor visibility, pilotage techniques may become inadequate, and *navigational* techniques appropriate to voyages out of sight of land become essential.

Table 10.4.1 Theoretical visibility distances from sea-level

Height of land		Distances
m	*(ft)*	*(nautical miles)*
15	(50)	8.1
30	(100)	11.5
61	(200)	16.2
152	(500)	25.7
305	(1000)	36.3

Source: Inman's Nautical Tables, 1920:12

An approximation is given by: distance (n.m.)=1.1 √height (ft).

In meteorological conditions of refraction high ground may be seen at more than the theoretical distance; in poor visibility the distance is much less.

From the mastehad, visibility is increased by the corresponding amount taken from the table: thus for a height of eye of 7.6m (25ft) visibility is increased by 5.7 n.m.

Early pilots and navigators had no instruments other than the sounding pole (known from 2nd–millennium BC Egypt) and the sounding lead and line (described by Herodotus, 2.5.2 in the 6th century BC). The methods they evidently evolved to find their way across open sea may be called 'environmental navigation'. That is, they used every possible clue they could observe from natural phenomena to find their way across the trackless sea. The problem they faced, of how to navigate when out of sight of land, may be resolved into two elements:

> (a) how to estimate directions such as courses steered and leeway (movement downwind due to the wind) and drift (movement due to currents and tidal streams) experienced; and

> (b) how to estimate speeds or distances.

At night when the sky is clear, direction in the northern hemisphere can be related to the celestial pole (near *Polaris* nowadays) about which the heavens appear to rotate. In daylight, the directions can be related to the noon position of the sun and, with less precision, to the direction of sunrise and sunset. At other times of day the navigator may be able to maintain his directions, but with more difficulty, by reference to the altitude and azimuth of the sun, and at night by reference to circumpolar constellations – as did early 20th–century Polynesian navigators, in the low latitudes of Oceania (Lewis, 1972).

When the sky is obscured, direction can be related to the wind (especially relatively steady 'trade' winds) or to the swell (undulation of the sea surface) which maintains a near–constant direction for much longer than the wind which causes it. The navigators of Oceania placed much reliance on swell for establishing their bearings (Lewis, 1972, 90), and Shetland fishermen in the early 20th century used similar methods (Walton, 1974; Binns, 1980, 20–1).

Distance travelled is determined by speed and time; both are difficult to estimate without aids. However, with practice a seaman can estimate his speed, probably expressed as faster or slower than usual, using spray turbulence and wind pressure; or an object thrown overboard may be 'timed' from bow to stern – the timing being done by repeateadly chanting a standard phrase.

In several maritime cultures distances have been expressed in units of a day's sail (Casson 1971, 281–96; Morcken, 1968; Gelsinger, 1970; Taylor, 1971, 50–2, 79, 126): implicit in this the concept of a 'standard' speed to be expected from the usual sort of boat in fair wind–and–sea conditions. Once this standard is established speeds or distances travelled on a particular voyage may be estimated as deviations from the norm.

Thus knowing the direction he has sailed, with an estimated allowance for leeway and drift due to wind and sea and the distance he has covered the navigator can 'mark his position' on his 'mental chart' as an estimated position relative to his departure point. (McGrail, 1983; 1987, 276–84). If he is on a repeat voyage, he will also 'plot' his position relative to his intended destination. If he is on a voyage of exploration, he needs to note such information so that he can, if necessary, return to his home base. Should the voyage extend beyond daylight hours, the prudent navigator must try to ensure that he makes a landfall (sights land) in daylight so that he has ample warning of inshore and coastal hazards.

Weather forecasting ability was also needed by these early navigators so that they could choose the best season for embarking on a lengthy sea–crossing and also so that, *en route*, they could make allowances for the future effects on the boat of wind and other weather–induced variables. At certain seasons in many parts of the world forecasting the weather without instruments is practicable even for lengthy periods. In other regions, only short term forecasts may be possible and timing may be difficult. Nevertheless, simple observations of the clouds, wind, sea and air mass and the behaviour of sea birds provide useful indications of future weather – see, for example, Slade & Greenhill (1974, 24). Such weather lore can be encapsulated in verbal aids to memory, often in rhyme form (McGrail, 1983, 305, 319).

Types of water transport

In the absence of artefactual evidence it is suggested that something may be learned about the types of water transport used in Palaeolithic and Neolithic times by using the following procedure.

(a) Identify the primary units of water transport which together comprise the full range used by man.

(b) Establish the materials, the techniques and the tool–kit needed to build these float, rafts and boats.

(c) Deduce in general terms the earliest technological stage when each primary unit could have been built, by analogy with the tools, technology and materials known to have been used in the manufacture of other artefacts which have survived.

(d) Identify those variants of the primary units of water transport which could have been sea–going: these will not necessarily be of the simplest construction.

If we follow this procedure we may then say that in a Palaeolithic stage of technology, for example, such a type of raft or such a type of boat *may* have been used. Whether these were indeed built at a particular time and place would depend upon the local availability of raw materials, whether the idea of applying these tools and techniques to water transport had arisen; whether the idea had been conceived of forming floating structures by fastening together individual units of buoyant material. In addition, before such craft could have been used purposefully, methods of steering and propulsion would have had to be devised. The earliest evidence for such devices is iconographic and is from Egypt and Arabia and dated to the late 4th millennium BC (McGrail, 1981, 49–50).

Floats, rafts and boats

Floats are individual buoyancy aids with the man partly immersed in the water. A raft's buoyancy is derived from the flotation characteristics of its individual elements; whereas a boat's buoyancy comes from the flotation characteristics of a hollowed vessel, due to the displacement of water by a continuous water–tight outer surface. Floats and rafts are generally classified by the principal raw material used, e.g. hide float; log raft. Boats may be similarly classified, although other schemes are possible, such as that based on the building sequence and on the techniques the boatbuilder uses to convert his raw material (logs, reeds, hide, clay, tar, bone/antler, etc.) into a boat (McGrail, 1985). In this present paper, traditional binomial–types names are used, and the primary units of water transport may be listed as:

floats – bundle floats, hide floats, log floats, pottery floats;
rafts – bundle rafts, float rafts, log rafts;
boats – bundle boats, hide boats, log boats, pottery boats, tub boats, basket boats, bark boats, plank boats.

Pottery boats (Hornell, 1946: fig. 9; Strabo, 1 7. 1.4) and tub boats (Hornell, 1946: fig. 11) being small and directionally unstable have little, if any, sea–going potential on a purposeful voyage and are therefore not considered in detail in this paper. Floats are considered only briefly as their use at sea is also very limited. The technological evidence evaluated, and the names of technological stages (e.g. Upper Palaeolithic) are taken mostly from European contexts and this should be borne in mind when considering any application to early technologies in other parts of the world.

Bundle rafts and boats. Bundle rafts may be defined as: two or more bound bundles of reed, grass, straw, bark or light poles, lashed together by coiled basketry or similar techniques. The bundles are often arranged to form a hollowed shape, but rafts with a generally flat upper surface are also known (McGrail, 1987, 163–72). Bundle *boats* are made by binding and lashing together bundles of reeds to make an elongated or round, hollowed form which is strengthened with a light framework; the bundles are then waterproofed externally with some mastic–like substance. Such boats are today known only on the inland waters of Arabia where the two main types are called the *zaima* (elongated) and the *quffa* (round). They may, however, remain to be recognized in other regions with a readily available supply of resin, tar, creosote, pitch, asphalt bitumen.

Bundle rafts have been used recently in coastal waters off South America (Edwards, 1965, 1–3; Hornell, 1946, 41–2), Corfu (Johnstone, 1973, 6), Sardinia (Johnstone, 1980, 12) and Tasmania (Jones, 1976; Birdsell, 1977), and they may have been used for coastal voyages from Egypt to Palestine in the 8th century BC (Isaiah, 18:1–2). Pliny (*NH* 6.24.82), quoting Eratosthenes, states that reed craft were used before the 1st century AD for coastal voyages from the River Ganges to Ceylon, and Heyerdahl (1978, 28–34) in his experimental reed–bundle rafts, *RA* 1 and 2, has shown that, in certain circumstances, one–way, trans–oceanic voyages may be made in this type of craft, the main problem being how to delay the decay and the waterlogging of the bundles (McGrail, 1987, 169). In general, rafts of all types are only usable as sea between latitudes 40°N and 40°S where temperatures are suitable for flow–through water transport. In colder waters men soon succumb to the chilling effects of sea and wind (McGrail, 1987, 5).

Technological assessment of these craft suggests that bundle rafts could probably not have been built before the Mesolithic stage in north–west Europe; and that bundle *boats* could not have been built before the Bronze Age (McGrail, 1987, tables 9.3, 9.4).

Hide boats. A simple hide boat consists of a single hide shaped into the form of a leather bag which may be reinforced by an inserted frame work. More complex, and hence seaworthy, boats have several hides fastened together and moulded around a pre–erected framework. Hide boats may be circular or elliptical in shape, but 20th–century sea–going ones (e.g. curach, umiak, biadara) are generally 'boat–shaped'. The hides and the material for sewing and lashing are taken from a wide range of land and sea animals, and frameworks of withies or other light timbers, bamboo and whale bone are known (McGrail, 1987, 173–87).

Off western Ireland hide boats are today used for coastal fishing and inter–island work. In the Arctic waters of North America, Greenland and Siberia they are used for sea–fishing, the hunting of seals and walruses and for coastal voyages (Brindley, 1919: 131–6). Early sea–going voyages in the Irish Sea and the Channel were described by Classical authors and in several medieval British, Irish and Anglo–Saxon chronicles (Hornell, 1946: 5–41). Severin's experimental hide boat *Brendan* was generally built by pre–industrial techniques and proved to have considerable stability, and, despite the continuously varying stresses she experienced in rough seas, she was in good shape at the end of her trans–Atlantic voyage (Severin, 1978).

Technological evidence (McGrail, 1987, tables 10.6, 10.7, 10.8) suggests that the frame–less single–hide boat could have been built in the Upper Palaeolithic. Framed single–hide boats with lashed framework could also have been built in the Upper Palaeolithic; in the Mesolithic, if of woven basketry; the Neolithic, if fastened with treenails; and in the Bronze Age, if metal fastenings were used. The light timbers or bones required in this framework would have been available from the Upper Palaeolithic. Multi–hide boats would have been possible from the Mesolithic – and it is considered that open sea voyages of discovery and settlement would have needed such a complex boat.

Float rafts. These rafts are made from individual floats of hide, gourds, kelp bladders or pots, linked together by a framework of light poles. They are widely used on rivers (Hornell, 1946, 22, 26, 37; Worcester, 1966, 120), but offshore use is known in Oceania employing kelp bladders (Hornell, 1946, 39) and in South America where multi–hide floats are used (Hornell, 1946,33; Edwards, 1965, 18–9). These South American float rafts can remain at sea for 2 or 3 days (Edwards, 1965, 19) and are successfully operated through surf.

Technological assessment (McGrall, 1987, table 10.10 and 10.11) suggests that rafts with single–hide floats may have been possible from the Upper Palaeolithic, and rafts with multi–hlde floats from the Mesolithic. Rafts buoyed by pots could have been in use from the Neolithic or Mesolithic. The sea–going capabilities of rafts of gourds and pots are unknown, but the other types can be so used within the zone 40°S to 40°N.

Log rafts. A simple log raft consists of two or more logs or tree limbs fastened together by lashings or by wooden or metal fastenings to form a rigid structure. Sea–going performance may be achieved by: adding extra layers of log to give the raft more structure above the loaded waterline; arranging the logs so that they form a hollowed boat shape; adding shaped bow and stern pieces. Such improved rafts remain 'wash–through' but their hollow form gives freeboard (height of side above waterline) and creates a relatively secure space for equipment

and cargo, and their boat shape is hydrodynamically advantageous.

Log rafts have had widespread use on inland waters wherever there were trees of a buoyant species. In addition they have been used for inter–island traffic in Oceania and in the coastal waters of South America, Formosa and India (Hornell, 1946, 61–8, 76–80; Edwards, 1965, 64–80). There is no direct evidence for early transoceanic voyages by log raft, but Heyerdahl (1978, 188–213) has demonstrated in certain circumstances, such voyages are practicable, but within the zone 40°S to 40°N.

Technological assessment (McGrail, 1987, tables 5.1 and 5.2) indicates that simple log rafts of light poles could have been built in the Upper Palaeolithic. Substantial rafts could not have been built until the Mesolithic in north–west Europe when trees of some size became available. In lower latitudes, where substantial trees were common from earlier times, sea–going log rafts could have been built in the Palaeolithic.

Logboats. Logboats are hollowed logs, shaped externally to improve their operational capabilities. Such basic logboats have their beam measurements limited to the breadth of the parent log. Hence, unless they are built from trees of enormous size, such as the redwood of British Columbia and the north–west United States, their inherent stability is inadequate or, at best, marginal for sea–going. They may, however, have their effective breadth at the waterline, and hence their stability, increased in one of four ways:

(a) *expansion* – the sides of the boat are forced apart (not all timber species can be so treated);

(b) *pairing* – two logboats are linked side–by side;

(c) *stabilisers* – longitudinal timbers are fastened to each side of the boat at the waterline;

(d) *outriggers* – longitudinal timbers (floats) are boomed out from the boat's side or sides.

Sea–going capabilities may be further enhanced by fitting washstrakes (extra planking) to the logboat's sides thereby increasing the freeboard (height of sides above waterline).

Technological assessment (McGrail, 1987, tables 6.4 to 6.6) suggests that, although suitable Mesolithic tools and techniques to build simple logboats may have been available from the Upper or even Middle Palaeolithic, there are unlikely to have been suitable logs in north–west Europe until the Mesolithic, although these existed in lower latitudes. Sea–going logboats with two boats paired or fitted with stabilisers, outriggers and wash strakes may have been possible in the Neolithic, and expansion may have been practised from the Bronze Age.

Basket boats. Basket boats are known in Indo–China where there are sea–going craft as well as boats suitable only for inland waters (Nishimura, 1931, 36 43; Hornell, 1946, 109–11; Cairo, 1972; Needham, 1971, 385). The basic boat consists of a closely inter–woven basketry of split bamboo on a framework of light bamboo poles. The interstices in the basketry are caulked with a resin and dung mix; alternatively, bark or nut husk may be mixed with the resin. Technological assessment suggests that such boats may have been built in the Neolithic or possibly in the Mesolithic.

Bark boats. A simple bark boat can be made from from a single sheet of bark from certain tree species, with two or three light timbers set transversely to stop the bark curling, and the ends blocked with clay or grass–tempered mud (McGrail, 1987, 89 90). Better shapes and hence improved performance can be obtained by moulding the bark sheet after heat treatment and binding or skewering the upturned ends. Complex bark boats are built from several sheets of bark sewn together with waterproofed seams. This bark shell is then reinforced by a light framework. Such complex boats have a beam–measurement greater than that of a single bark and their stability may then be adequate for sea–going. Open sea voyages in such multi–bark boats are known in Australian waters and off the coasts of North and South America (Edwards, 1972; 9, 10, 35; Adney & Chapelle, 1964, 96, 98,; Edwards, 1965, 21).

Technological assessment (McGrail, 1987, tables 7.5 to 7.7) suggests that the tools and techniques to build a basic bark boat were available from the upper Paleolithic. Sizeable trees from which a large sheet of bark could be taken were not available in north–west europe until the Mesolithic, but they were available earlier in lower latitudes. Moulded bark boats may not have been practicable until the Neolithic, and it may not have been until the Bronze Age that the bark boat of more than one sheet became a possibility. Thus sea–going bark boats are unlikely before the Bronze Age.

Plank boats. The plank boat was the most adavanced from of early water transport. It was readily adaptable for use in a variety of functions and in a range of environments, and it proved to be the only type which could be developed in size to become a ship. A technological assessment suggests that the earliest period for building plank boats would be the Bronze Age or possibly the Neolithic. The Bronze Age is indeed the period from which we have direct evidence of plank boats: the mid 3rd–millenium BC Cheops boats from Egypt (Lipke, 1984); the mid 2nd–millenium boats from Ferriby, North Humberside (Wright, 1976, 1990) and from Caldicot, Gwent (Parry & McGrail, unpublished); the 1st millenium BC boat from Brigg, South Humberside (McGrail, 1981); and the two sea–going vessels of the mid 2nd–millenium BC from Cape Gelydonia and Ulu Burun in the eastern Mediterrean (Bass, 1967; 1989).

Early migrations

A synthesis of the foregoing technological analysis, as set out in Table 10.4.2, can be used to suggest the types of water transport which may have been available for the four early migrations described at the beginning of this paper.

Oceania
There appears to be no historical or surviving tradition of hide boats or basket boats in Oceania. The latter are, however, used today in south–east Asia in the general area whence the

---

Table 10.4.2 Theoretical earliest technological stages for the building of sea–going rafts and boats

Technological stage	*Types of water transport*[1]
Lower & Middle Palaeolithic	Log floats[2]
Upper Palaeolithic	Bundle floats[2]
	Hide floats[2]
	Log ratfs[3,4]
	Float rafts[3]
Mesolithic	Bundle rafts[3]
	Hide boats (multi–hide)
	Basket boats[5]
Neolithic	Pot floats[2]
	Log boats (with extra stability)
Bronze Age	Bundle boats[5]
	Bark boats (multi–bark)
	Plank boats

1.	Sea–going versions are not necessarily of the simplest construction
2.	Floats could have been used at sea only for short voyages in latitudes between c 40°N and 40°S
3.	Rafts are unlikley to have been used at sea north of c 40°N and south of c 40°S
4.	Not until the Mesolithic in northern regions
5.	Of limited distribution

Neolithic migrants came, so the possibility that sea–going basket boats were used for some of the Oceanic voyages should not be overlooked. Float rafts might also have been used (McGrail, 1981, 68) but the other two types of craft which were technologically possible in the Neolithic period – log rafts and complex log–boats with features giving them extra stability – seem more likely. Sea–going log rafts were seen at the time of first European contact in the late 16th to early 19th centuries AD, and the many types of plank boats which were then encountered were evidently developed from a logboat base – all were extended by the addition of washstrakes; some were paired, and others had outriggers (McGrail, 1981, 68–73).

Australia
Log rafts and float rafts could theoretically have been used on the Upper Palaeolithic voyages to greater Australia. Although neither type was found in use in Australia on first European contact in the 17th/18th century AD, Birdsell (1977, 142–3) has pointed out that bamboo, and other timbers known to be used for log rafts, are found along the migration routes from south–east Asia to Australia. In the present state of knowledge log rafts thus seem most likely to have been used on the open sea legs of this migration.

America

Rafts are most unlikely to have been used for Upper Paleolithic sea–going voyages in the high latitudes of north-east Asia and north–west America as the air and sea temperatures would have been too cold. On the other hand, simple log rafts made of any light timber to hand, and bundle rafts could have been used to cross rivers, and possibly bays, and perhaps to circumnavigate headlands encountered on a land route southwards from Alaska along the coast of British Columbia to the vicinity of California where the climate would have permitted the use of sea–going rafts. Such a land–based coastal route from Alaska seems more likely than it did 15 years ago as it is now believed that the ice–sheets, which were formerly thought to have blocked southwards movement for several millenia, were less extensive in time and space (Bray et al., 1989, 2).Today, northerly and north–westerly flowing warm currents known as the Japan stream (*kuro siwo*) and the Kamtchatka current favourably affect the coastal climate of the north–west of the American continent so that, for example, the temperature of the sea on the shore of the Bering Strait is c. 15°F higher than that of the waters of the Asiatic shore, and the American coast is ice–free from April whereas the coast of Asia has ice until July (Bedford, 1920, 183–7). Conditions were generally different in the Upper Palaeolithic period, but if there was a comparable current from south–east Asia in those times, an overland coastal route southwards would probably have been practicable.

The simple hide boat that it was theoretically possible to build in the Upper Palaeolithic (McGrail, 1987, table 10.7), would have been unsuitable for sea voyages, but could have been used instead of, or in addition to, the rafts for river crossings. On the other hand, although simple bark boats could also in theory have been built in those times (McGrail, 1987, table 4.5) it is unlikely that the trees available in sub–Arctic north–west America would have supplied sufficiently large sheets of bark.

For the migrations in early post–Glacial times complex sea–going hide boats with a framework and made of several hides seem most likely to have been used (Table10.4.2).
When future research reveals definitive dates for the migrations from Asia to America and for man's subsequent progress southwards, and as knowledge of the ancient environment increases, it should prove possible to deduce with more confidence what types of water transport were used.

Western Mediterranean

A hypothetical crossing of the Mediterranean some 500,000 to 300,000 years ago poses several problems. At such an early date only log floats seem technologically possible (Table 10.4.2). The sea and air temperature would have permitted such use, but whether controlled drifting by a group of people would have been practicable is an open question. Swimming the Strait of Gibraltar (possibly assisted by log floats) remains an alternative; whether man could swim at this time is impossible to say, but see Johnstone (1988, 3–4) for further discussion.

Acknowledgement

This is a revised and extended version of a paper read at the World Archaeological Congress, Southampton in 1986.

References

Adney E. T. & Chapelle H. 1. 1964 *Bark Canoes and Skin Boats of North America* Washington: Smithsonian Institution.

Allen J. Golson J. & Jones R. (eds.) 1977 *Sunda and Sahul: Prehistoric Studies in South East Asia, Melanesia & Australia* London: Academic Press.

Bailey G. N. 1980 'Holocene Australia.' In *Sherratt*, 1980: 333–341.

Bass G. F. 1967 'Cape Gelydonia a Bronze Age Shipwreck.' *Transactions of the American Philosophical Society*, 57. 8.

Bass G. F. 1989 'Construction of a seagoing vessel of the late Bronze Age.' *Tropis* 1: 25–35. Athens: Hellenic Trust for the Preservation of Nautical Traditions.

Bedford F. 1920 *Sailor's Pocket Book*, 10th edition. Glasgow: Brown, Son & Ferguson.

Bellwood P. 1978 *The Polynesians*. London, Thames & Hudson (2nd edition, 1987).

Binns A. 1980 *Viking Voyagers*. London, Heinemann.

Birdsell J. H. 1977 .Recalibration of a paradigm for the first peopling of Greater Australia.' in Allen J. *et al* (eds) [see above], 113–168. London, Academic Press.

Bray W. 1986 'Finding 'the earliest Americans.' *Nature*, 321: 126.

Bray W. M. Swanson E. H. & Farrington I. S. 1990, *The Ancient Americas*, 2nd edition. Oxford, Phaidon.

Brindley H. H. 1919–20 'Notes on the boats of Siberia.' *Mariner's Mirror*, 5, 66–72; 101–7; 130–142; 184–7; 6, 15–18; 187.

Cairo R. 1972 . 'A note on S. Vietnamese basket boats.' *Mariner's Mirror*, 58 135–153.

Casson L. 1971 *Ships and Seamanship in the Ancient World* Princeton. Princeton University Press.

Clark G. 1977 *World Prehistory*, 3rd edition. Cambridge, Cambridge University Press.

Clark G. & Piggott S. 1976 *Prehistoric Societie*. London, Penguin.

Devoy R. J. 1982 'Analysis of the geological evidence for Holocene sea–level movements in S. E. England.' *Proceedings of the Geologists Association*, 93, 65–90.

Edwards C. R. 1965 *Aboriginal Watercraft on the Pacific Coast of South America*. Berkeley and Los Angeles, University of California, Ibero–Americana, 47.

Edwards R. 1972 *Aboriginal Bark Canoes of the Murray Valley*, South Australia Museum.

Gelsinger B. E. 1970 'Norse Day's Sailing.' *Mariner's Mirror*, 56, 107–109.

Guidon N. & Delibrias G. 1986 'C14 dates point to Man in the Americas 32,000 years ago.' *Nature*, 321, 769–771.

Habgood P. J. 1986 *Aboriginal migrations: they came to a land down under*. Paper read at the Warld Archaeological Congress, Southampton.

Heyerdahl T. 1978, *Early Man and the Ocean*, London. Allen & Unwin.

Hornel; J. 1946 *Water Transport*. Cambridge, Cambridge University Press. (Reprinted 1970, Newton Abbot, David & Charles).

Irwin G. J. 1980 .Prehistory of Oceania: colonisation and cultural change.' In *Sherratt*, 1980,: 324–332.

Irvin G., Buckler S. & Quirke P. 1990 'Voyaging by canoe and computer: experiments in the settlement of the Pacific Ocean.' *Antiquity*, 64 34–50.

Johnstone P. 1973 'Stern first in the Stone Age?' *IJNA*, 2, 3–11.

Johnstone P. 1988 *Seacraft of Prehistory*. 2nd edition. London, Routledge.

Jones R. 1976 'Tasmania: aquatic machines and off–shore islands.' in Sievking G. Longworth, I. H. & Wilson K. E. (eds) *Problems in Economic and Social Archaeology*, 235–263. London, Duckworth.

Klein R. 1980, 'Later Pleistocene hunters.' In *Sherratt* 1980, 87–95.

Lewis D. 1972 *We the Navigators*. Canberra, National University Press.

Lipke D. 1984 *Royal Ship of Cheops*. Oxford, British Archaeological Reports, S225.

McGrail S. 1978 *Logboats of England and Wales*. Oxford, British Archaeological Reports, 51.

McGrail S. 1981 *Rafts, Boats and Ships*. London, HMSO.

McGrail S. 1983 'Cross–channel seamanship and navigation in the late 1st millennium BC.' *Oxford Journal of Archaeology*, 2, 299–337.

McGrail S. 1985 'Towards a classification of water transport.' *World Archaeology*, 16: 289–303.

McGrail S. 1987 *Ancient Boats in NW Europe*. Harlow, Longman.

Morcken R. 1968 'Norse nautical units and distance measurements.' *Mariner's Mirror*, 54: 393–401.

Mulvaney J. 1975 *Prehistory of Australia*. London, Penguin.

Needham J. 1971 *Science and Civilisation in China*. 4. 3. Cambridge, Cambridge University Press.

Nishimura S. 1931 *Skinboats. Ancient Ships of Japan* vols. 5–8. Tokyo, Japanese Society of Naval Architects.

Roe D. 1980 'The handaxe makers.' in *Sherratt*, 71–78.

Severin T. 1978 *The Brendan Voyage*. London, Hutchinson.

Sherratt A. 1980 *Cambridge Encyclopaedia of Archaeology*. Cambridge, Cambridge University Press.

Shutler R. & Shutler M. E.,1975. *Oceanic Prehistory*. California, University of California.

Slade W. J. & Greenhill B. 1974 *West Country Coasting Ketches*. Greenwich, Conway.

Street F. A. 1980 'Ice Age environments.' in *Sherratt*, 52–56.

Taylor E. G. R. 1971 *Haven finding art*. London, Hollis & Carter.

Thorne A. 1980 'The arrival of Man in Australia.' in *Sherratt*, 96–100.

van Andel T. H. 1989 'Late Quarternary sea–level changes and Archaeology.' *Antiquity*, 63, 733–745.

Walton K. 1974 'A Geographer's view of the sea.' *Scottish Geographical Magazine*, 90, 4 13.

Worcester G. R. G. 1966 *Sail and Sweep in China*. London, HMSO.

Wright E. V. 1976 *North Ferriby boats*. Greenwich, National Maritime Museum, Monograph 23.

Wright E. V. 1990 *N. Ferriby Boats: Seacraft of Prehistory*. London, Routledge.

Reprinted with permission from:

International Journal of Nautical Archaeology, 20: 85–93. (1991).

PAPER 10.5

BRONZE AGE SEAFARING IN THE MEDITERREAN: A VIEW FROM N W EUROPE

Introduction

This paper is based on impromptu remarks made in response to, or in extension of, topics dealt with by speakers at the Conference. There is thus no single theme running through what follows rather a series of observations from the viewpoint of a maritime archaeologist whose main work has been in the prehistoric and early medieval periods of NW Europe, which are offered for consideration in the context of the early Meditenanean.

The identification of wrecks

It can be difficult to deduce a ship's last port of call and her intended destination from the remains of hull and cargo found on the sea bed. There are, on the other hand, two proven, though not always practicable, ways of investigating where an ancient ship was built: by dendrochronological examination; and by classification

Dendrochronological timber analysis

Ancient timber has its fingerprint or signature (to use words in frequent use at the Conference) implicit in the pattern of its growth rings and this can reveal the timber's region of origin (Fletcher 1978; Ward 1987). The five Viking Age wrecks which were excavated from Roskilde Fjord, Denmark by Olaf Olsen and Ole Crumlin–Pedersen (1967) were long assumed to have been built within Scandinavia. However, recent dendrochronological analysis has not only dated the ships to the 11th century AD but has also revealed that the tree ring pattern of one of them (Skuldelev 2 the *circa* 18m warship) is compatible with the master oak chronology for Dublin; (Crumlin–Pedersen p.c.). Thus, if this ship was not actually built in Dublin, she was built from timber exported from that region.

The Bronze Age Mediterrean differs in several ways from medieval northern Europe, for example, different timber species were used in shipbuilding, and past Mediterrenean climates may not have imposed such readily recognisable signatures on growth ring patterns as in northern Europe. Nevertheless, promising steps have been taken towards the establishment of chronologies for southern Europe (Kuniholm and Striker 1987; Bucholz 1988), and if future research can establish long chronologies in the Mediterranean basin, it should prove possible to recognise the source of timber excavated from ancient wrecks.

Classification studies

Clues to where a ship was built may also lie within the hull structure: each ship has the signature or fingerprint of her master builder (McGrail & Denford 1982; McGrail 1985; 1987, 4–11). In the Bronze Age (and indeed until much later) in both northern and southern Europe, boats and ships were individually built, and were not standard units built to a fixed pattern. These vessels were built by individual master builders each of whom, although not working within an overall tradition, inevitably imparted an individuality to the boats and ships he built in terms of his selection of raw materials and in the precise woodworking techniques he used (McGrail & Denford 1982).

In the prehistoric Mediterranean two main traditions of boat and ship building can be recognised: the sewn–plank tradition (McGrail & Kentley 1985); and the tradition well described by Bass and his colleagues in their publications of the early wrecks they have excavated (Bass 1967; 1989; Bass and van Doorninck 1982; Steffy 1984; 1985; van Doorninck 1976.) The diagnostic features of this latter tradition appear to be: firstly the shell sequence of building (hull planking erected before framing fitted); and secondly, the use of wooden draw–tongue joints ("mortice and tenon") to fasten the flush–laid planking. This latter characteristic clearly distinguishes this tradition not only from the sewn plank tradition but also from the later traditions of NW Europe: the Romano–Celtic tradition in which the flush–laid planking was generally not edge–fastened; and the Norse tradition in which iron nails were used to clench–fasten clinker planking (McGrail 1981a, 22–4, 30–4). This Mediterranean way of building boats and ships is usually known as the "Classical tradition", but on the evidence of the Ulu Burun wreck; (Bass 1989), it is a tradition which began before 1400 BC (and probably much earlier, as the techniques used to build the Cheops ship – Lipke, 1983 – may be considered to foreshadow the Mediterranean tradition); and at the other end of the timescale, it lasted into the Byzantine period (van Doorninck 1976; Bass & van Doorninck 1982) or even later.

Drawing on ethnographic parallels (Hornell 1946) and on the comparative situation in medieval NW Europe (Crumlin–Pedersen 1969; 1983), it seems most unlikely that this Mediterranean tradition was homogeneous; rather that there were both regional variants and developments over time. Some of the later changes have been documented (van Doorninck 1967); it is now necessary to look also for spatial differences. This can best be done by the detailed recording of every ancient Mediiterranean ship–find, from the criteria evidently used to select raw materials to the precise details of plank fastenings and other woodworking techniques. Analysis of this data should lead to the recognition of key features, diagnostic of variant groupings within the main tradition (McGrail 1984). In theory it might thereby prove possible (given sufficient documentation) to recognise an individual master builder or a particular "shipyard"; in practice the best that can be expected in the foreseeable future is the identification of the main regional sub –traditions.

The shipment of high density cargo and ballast

Copper ingots of ox–hide and of bun form have been excavated not only from the wrecks off Ulu Burun and Cape Gelidonya (Bass, this volume) but also from many land sites (Gale, this volume), indicating widespread transport by sea. Can any pattern be detected in the contexts of the many land finds which might suggest that these ingots had a special value so that, for exarmple, ingots of Cyprus copper would be welcomed in Sardinia, which had its own copper sources? Does the evident near–standardisation of the ox–hide shape over time and space mean that these particular ingots had a symbolic value (possibly encapsulated in the inscriptions) greater than their value as raw material, so that they could be an element in elite gift exchanges? A parallel may be drawn here with the Neolithic stone axe "trade" in Britain: stone axes (like copper ingots) undoubtedly had uses but at the same time they may have possessed symbolic importance, as some were undoubtedly deposited with considerable formality (Bradley & Edmonds 1988, 182-3).

Other sea–transported goods mentioned at the Conference were almost certainly prestige items for gift or exchange, or luxury goods exported in response to elite demand: unlike ingots, these items appear mostly to be of low relative–density and to have a high stowage–factor. Such objects take up a relatively large volume of the ship's cargo space in relation to their weight (especially when the packaging and protection that precious and breakable items require is taken into account) thereby raising the overall Centre of Gravity of the cargo and thus reducing ship stability (McGrail 1989). Although the human body has a relative density of near unity, passengers such as envoys or merchants and their clerks, may also be considered to have a high stowage–factor, for such people need to have a relatively large volume of space allotted to them where they may eat, sleep and generally live. Similar considerations apply to the transport of slaves.

The main aim of a ship's Master, ancient or modern is the safe and timely arrival of his ship at the next destination. One of the principal concerns of a Bronze Age Master was thus the safety of his ship. How can this concept of safety be measured? I suggest in the main by the criteria of freeboard and stability. If a ship has insufficient freeboard she may founder after shipping water; with insufficient stability a ship displaced from the vertical forces will continue to roll into a position of list or permanent heel (known as loll) or in an extreme case she will capsize. It is sometimes not recognised that too much freeboard and too much stability can also lead to shiphandling problems, if not to disaster: with excessive freeboard, probems in steering and in the power to carry sail may arise and there may be excessive leeway; with excessive stability (i.e. with a

large righting moment as might occur with a dense cargo low in the hold) a ship loses her seakindliness, with adverse effects on hull, rigging and crew. A Master must thus aim to embark that mix of cargo in volume and in weight which results in his ship having sufficient, but not too much, freeboard and stabilitiy.

As the problem of insufficient stability is potentially the most dangerous and as (unlike freeboard problems) it is not always readily obvious when a loaded ship is in this unstable condition cargo ships generally have a permanent ballast of some high density, easily obtainable, substance, such as the pebbles and small stones found in the Ulu Burun wreck (Bass 1989). However, when a Master has to carry large quantities of luxury or prestige items or passengers or slaves, all of which have high stowage–factors (as discussed above) he may need to embark either extra ballast or (better from an economic point of view) some "tradeable ballast" of high density, low stowage–factor goods to bring his ship's stability into the optimum range for a safe voyage. Copper and lead ingots obviously fit into the "tradeable ballast" category, and a Master in these circumstances would welcome such a consignment provided it was made available for embarkation early in the loading process, and providing that it could be stowed securely in the hold – a problem which seems to have been solved in the angled stowage system adopted in the Ulu Burun ship.

Consignments of tradeable ballast might well be destined for off–loading at a particular port as items of trade or exchange or as gifts. On the other hand, it is possible that, in certain circumstances, consignments of ingots remained in a ship as compensatory, low stowage–factor material for some considerable time and were not unloaded until another consignment of low stowage–factor material could be obtained, or until the cargo to be embarked had no (or only a small proportion of) high stowage–factor, luxury or prestige items, when the permanent ballast by itself would give the ship the required stability.

Assessment of performance

A question posed at the Conference was whether the Master of the ship wrecked at Ulu Burun may not have embarked an excessive amount of high density materials, that is permanent ballast and low stowage–factor cargo (" saleable ballast"), thereby leading inevitably to disaster. This is one of the problems that will undoubtedly be addressed in the post–excavation research. If the original form and structure of the ship can be theoretically reconstructed, and if the embarked position of ballast, cargo consignments, ship's exquipment. and personal possessions can be deduced, then freeboard and draft can be estimated and stability calculated as, for example, undertaken by Åkerlund (1963) for the 4th century AD Nydam boat from Als, Denmark; by McKee and Corlett (Fenwick 1978) for the 10th/11th century AD Graveney boat from Kent, England; by Coates (McGrail 1981) for the 7th century BC sewn plank boat from Brigg, S. Humberside, England; and recently by Steffy (1989) for the Kyrenia ship.

This sort of research can also lead to estimates of performance for other loaded conditons and estimates of speeds achievable;

and may possibly give some idea of how close to the wind a ship could sail (McGrail 1986). Such theoretical investigations are an essential and very cost effective method of assessing performance *before* embarking on the much more expensive course of building a full–size model of an ancient ship based on theoretical reconstruction drawings. Furthermore, if these theoretical calculations suggest that the ancient ship may have had a poor performance, the excavated evidence and the process of producing the reconstruction drawing may be re-examined to see whether other interpretations of the evidence are possible. If this proves to be the case the calculations can readily be re–worked using revised data; whereas if these calculations are bypassed and such mistakes do not become obvious until after a full–size model has been built, re–building the model to fit the revised interpretation can be very expensive indeed.

The key to accurate assessment of performance is in the production of valid reconstruction drawings, and when the excavated evidence is incomplete, disarticulated and distorted, as are most ship wrecks, the problems of compiling an authentic drawing are indeed formidable (Crumlin–Pedersen & Viner 1986). In some cases the surviving evidence may not justify a complete reconstruction drawing; in others there may be two or more reconstructions, each compatible with the evidence; in a few cases it may become clear that there is a unique solution to a reconstruction problem and that a single authentic full–scale model ("replica") could be built.

It is essential that rigorous standards obtain in this hypothetical reconstruction process otherwise it is not possible to make valid deductions about the performance of an ancient ship. For example, variations in beam measurement at the waterline have a great influence on stability: if a small error is made in deducing this measurement, the error in the deduced metacentric height (a measure of stability) will be magnified. Thus, for example, if the waterline beam of the reconstruction is 10% more than the beam the ancient vessel actually had, the stability of the reconstruction will be more than 20% greater than the original (McGrail 1987, 15, 16). Small errors in a reconstruction drawing may thus lead to wrong conclusions being drawn about an ancient vessel's performance. For many years, the 4th century AD Nydam boat from Schleswig Holstein was said to be unstable unless a large amount of ballast was carried. However, Åkerlund's re–assessment (1963) suggested that, because of shrinkage, the excavated timbers had been re–assembled to give a beam measurement less than that of the original boat: a slight theoretical increase of the beam at the water–line resulted in a stable hypothetical reconstruction without ballast.

Early evidence for sail

The earliest evidence for sail anywhere in the world is from the Near East: a clay model of *c.* 3400 BC from Eridu in S. Mesopotamia (Bass 1972, 12) may represent a boat with a mast step; more convincing is the painting of a boat with a rectangular sail on an Egyptian, late–Gerzean vase of *circa* 3100 BC (Bass 1972, 13). Tomb paintings and models from later centuries depict Egyptian sailing craft on the Nile and at sea (Casson 1971, 18–22, figs. 16–19).

Not until *circa* 2000 BC, however, is there evidence for sail in the islands of the eastern Mediterranean: ships on Minoan seals with mast, rigging and sail (Casson, 1971 33, figs. 34–6). It has been well said that, 'a ship is her own advertisement': thus it might be expected that if early Egyptian sailing ships operated in the eastern Mediterranean, as seems likely, they would have stimulated the early adoption of sail by seamen from Cyprus, Crete and the Aegean islands.

However, the change from oared propulsion to sail is not necessarily immediately stimulated by an awareness of its practicability. A hull shape suitable for efficient rowing is not the best one for efficient sailing; and the stresses that sailing imposes on the hull mean that the structure of a sea–going oared boat has to be modified to take sail. In addition, the advantages of sail over oar only become significant in the carriage of large volumes of goods over relatively long distances. Oared boats can satisfy the small–scale, short range requirements for fishing and local trade appropriate to relatively self–sufficient and (in relation to the Near Eastern civilisations) relatively under–developed economies that were evidently the norm in the Early Bronze Age of the eastern Mediterrean. Moreover, piracy and voyages of exploration may also be undertaken, given the right circumstances, in oared boats.

It may be that the apparently late adoption of a sail in these island civilisations only reflects the lack, or non–recognition, of evidence. On the other hand, it may be that sail was indeed not adopted until the end of the 3rd millennium BC because it was not until then that these people had evolved economically and politically to the point where it became worthwhile to build large vessels of different form and structure from their oared craft, and capable of being sailed. Furthermore, it is unlikely that representations of these sailing vessels would appear on seals until they represented a significant element in the economy.

The choice between open–sea and coastal passages

It is difficult, if not impossible, in the absence of other evidence, to deduce from the distribution of finds of traded commodities and raw materials, or even from the cargo of wrecked ships, whether Bronze Age goods were transported at sea by direct routes involving an open–sea passage or longer coastal routes, generally in sight of land. There are, however, two occasions in the Odyssey when we get glimpses of seafarers making the choice between a coastal passage and an open sea voyage. Menelaus, Nestor and Diomedes, returning from Troy to Greece, paused at Lesbos and discussed whether to make the direct passage across the Aegean to the southern end of the island of Euboea, or to take the longer, coastal and inter–island route east of Chios and through the southern Sporodes and Cyclades (Odyssey, 3). The second event is mentioned in Odysseus' account of how, after returning from Troy, he sailed first to Egypt and thence to Phoenicia. We are told that in a northerly wind, a ship bound for Libya from the Levant, "took the central route and ran down the lee side [ie south] of Crete" (Odyssey, 14). The first leg of this voyage would have been across open sea until the southern coast of Crete was sighted; the second leg was another open sea passage from a known position south of Crete to a landfall in Libya. As this was the central route, the alternatives to it must have been: either a coastal passage southwards from the Levant to the Nile region and thence westwards along the N. African coast; or a coastal passage northwards then westwards along the coast of Asia Minor, and then an inter–island passage to Crete, followed by the open–sea voyage to Libya.

When both coastal and open sea voyages were possible, the choice of which to take on any specific occasion must have been determined after consideration of a number of important factors: the ship's performance; the Master's seamanship; and the environmental conditions expected.

The ship: For an open sea voyage the ship must not only have been structurally suitable for the conditions but she must also have been equipped to sustain life at sea, in terms of shelter, food and water, for the necessary period of time. It would also be highly desirable that she should be able to make some progress, not necessarily very great, against the wind, with minimum leeway, and thus be able to cope with an unexpected shift in the wind.

The Master: The Master must have had the ability to get the best out of his ship in any adverse conditions encountered on an open–sea voyage, when he would be unable to seek shelter in a haven. He must also have been used to navigating out of sight of land. Nestor's ships took a "long day" to sail direct from Lesbos to Euboea and they arrived at Geraestus in the night (Odyssey, 3). Although they could check their position when the island of Psyria was visible to port, they must have been out of sight of land for some of this crossing. Homer also noted that a passage from Crete to Egypt with a fair wind, generally took four days and nights (Odyssey. 14) ("though some say three" – Strabo 10.4.5) and for most of that time a ship would have been out of sight of land. On such passages the Master would need navigational techniques additional to those used on coastal voyages (McGrail 1983).

The Environment: The weather to be expected would also have to be taken into account whan deciding which route to take. In particular, it would be necessary to estimate the strength and direction of wind and currents in relation to each other and to the ship's intended track on each of the alternative routes, coastal or open sea.

Superimposed on these three factors, for the Master of a cargo ship, would be constraints imposed by the very nature of his trade. If the ship had cargo for only one destination then there may well have been a choice of routes, open–sea or coastal. On the other hand, if she had a cargo of several consignments for different destinations it could be that only the coastal route would be appropriate, and the ship would have to await suitable weather conditions, regardless of the ship's performance or the Master's ability.

It is generally thought that direct voyages from Egypt to Crete were not undertaken in the Bronze Age, although there were direct voyages from Crete to Egypt. This may have been. as suggested at the Conference, because of the prevailing north–westerly and a generally south–easterly flowing current. On the other hand, this direct route to Crete may not have been used because the trading pattern was such that the Crete to Egypt route was not one leg of a "shuttle service" or "trunk route", but rather part of a "tramp route" which linked Egypt, the Levant, Asia Minor, Greece and Crete and their respective hinterlands. The apparent anti–clockwise nature of this "tramp route" may have been determined on the one hand by economic and political factors or, on the other hand, by a combination of such factors as the operational performance of Bronze Age ships, the standards of Bronze Age seamanship and navigation, and the velocities of predominant winds and currents. Which were the prime reasons can only be determined by further research.

Evidence in Homer may not be of direct use in this research as it is not clear whether in all circumstances he was recording inherited knowledge of Bronze Age techniques and achievements rather than those of his own time. It cannot therefore be taken as certain that the open–sea voyages and star navigation described in the Odyssey were actually undertaken in Bronze Age; it remains possible that these were not achieved until the Early Iron Age. Documentation from literate Bronze Age societies such as those of Egypt or Crete may throw light on this problem.

Further research is also needed into past Mediterranean climates and weather patterns and into sea currents and sea levels, all of which are, at present, difficult to define except in broad terms. For recent research into such matters for the eastern Mediterranean see Mantzourani and Theodorou (in press). The Bronze Age seaman's knowledge and competence are also difficult to assess, although attempts may be made using analogous evidence based on the seamaship and non–instrumlental navigation practised in recent times by seafarers from relatively simple maritime societies such as those of Oceania (McGrail, 1983).

Of the two examples of Bronze Age Mediterranean ships so far excavated, that from Ulu Burun seems likely to have been able to sustain life at sea for several days and thus not have been limited to coastal voyages for this reason alone. Her abilities sailing into wind and the leeway generated will not become clear until the hull is fully excavated and much post–excavation research undertaken. There is clearly scope for further research into all these matters, preferably by an inter–disciplinary group.

Landing Places

Informal landing places without fixed structures are known throughout the world today. Boats, and indeed small ships, may be operated either directly from the beach or from shallow waters close inshore, at anchor, or fastened to mooring posts or stones (McGrail 1987, 267–273). It seems lilkely that similar sites were used in the Bronze Age Mediterranean (see for example Odyssey Ch. 1, 3, 4, 5, 12 and 13), but they may not have been immediately adjacent to a settlement, and may be difficult to recognise today. Nevertheless, it is possible to suggest, in general terms, the sort of locations where early landing places are likely to be found.

z

Inland

— At the confluence of a relatively fast river with a slower one.

— Where a river leaves or enters a lake.

— Near the lowest fordable point of a river.

— At the head of a deep water inlet.

Coastal

— Within sheltered havens such as estuaries, river mouths and bays.

— In a sheltered position close to, but not actually in, the delta of a river which has many, often–changing channels.

— On either side of a headland in sheltered places with access to drinking water, where vessels can wait for a fair wind to enable them to round the point.

— Near the entrance to a channel or strait with a strong outflowing current, where a vessel may wait for a favourable wind to offset the current.

— On coastal sites protected by an island chain from the predominant wind.

— On islands or well defined promontory sites where foreign traders and seamen may readily be segregated and supervised and tolls imposed.

— On sites which dominate restricted waters eg a narrow channel, whence controls and tolls can be imposed on through traffic.

References

Åkerlund H. I963 *Nydamskeppen.* Goteborg.

Bass G.F. 1967 'Cape Gelidonya, a Bronze Age Shipwreck.' *Transactions of the American Philosophical Society,* 57, part 8.

Bass G.F. 1972 (Ed). *A History of Seafaring.* London.

Bass G.F. 1989 'Construction of a sea–going vessel of the Late Bronze Age. *Hellenic Trust for preservation of Nautical Traditions,* Athens.

Bass G F. & F.H. van Doorninck *et al* 1982 *Yassi Ada* Vol 1. A&M University Press, Texas.

Bradley R. & M. Edmonds 1988 'Fieldwork at Great Langdale, Cumbria.' *Antiquaries Journal* 68, 181–209.

Bucholz H–G. 1988 'Archaoloaische Holzfunde aus Tamassos, Zypem.' *Acta Praehistorica et Archaeologica* 20, 75–157.

Casson L. 1971 *Ships & Seamanship in the Ancient World* Princeton, (2n edition, 1986).

Crumlin–Pedersen O. 1969 *Das Haithabuschiff.* Neumunster.

Crumlin–Pedersen O. 1983 *From Viking Ships to Hanseatic Cogs.* 3rd Paul Johnstone Lecture. NMM Greenwich.

Crumlin–Pedersen O. & M. Viner (eds) 1986 *Sailing into the past.* Viking Ship Museum, Roskilde.

Fenwick V.H. (ed) 1978 *Graveney Boat.* BAR 53, Oxford.

Fletcher J. (ed) 1978 *Dendrochronology in Europe.* BAR 51, Oxford.

Homer *The Odyssey* translated by E.V. Rieu. 1946, Penguin Classics.

Hornell J. 1946 *Water Transport.*Cambridge, (Republished 1970, Newton Abbot.

Kuniholm P.I. and Striker C.L. 1987: .Dendrochronological investigations in the Aegean and adjacent areas', *Journal of Field Archaeology* 14, 385–398.

McGrail S. 1981a *Rafts, Boats & Ships.* HMSO, London.

Mcgrail S. 1981b: *Brigg 'raft'.* BAR 89, Oxford.

McGrail S. 1983 'Cross–Channel Seamanship and navigation in the late 1st millennium BC.' *Oxford Journal of Archaeology* 2, 299–337.

McGrail S. 1984: 'Maritime Archaeology – present and future.' In S. McGrail (ed), *Aspects of Maritime Archaeology & Enthnography,* 11–40. NMM Greenwich.

McGrail S. 1985 'Towards a classification of water transport.' *World Archaeology* 16, 289–303.

McGrail S. 1986 'Experimental boat archaelogy – some methodological considerations.' In O. Crumlin–Pendersen & M. Viner (eds), 8–17.

McGrail S. 1987: *Ancient boats in NW Europe: the archaeology of water trausport to AD 1500.* Longman.

McGrail S. 1989: 'Shipment of traded goods and of ballast in Andquity.' *Oxford Journal of Archaeology* 8, 353–8.

McGrail S. and Denford G. 1982 'Boatbuilding techniques, technological change and attribute analysis.' In S. McGrail (ed), *Woodworking Techniques before 1500.* BAR 127, 25–72, Oxford.

McGrail S. and Kentley E. (eds.) 1985: *Sewn Plank Boats.* BAR S276, Oxford.

Mantzourani E.K. & A.J. Theodorou in press 'An attempt to delineate the sea–routes Crete and Cyprus during the Bronze Age.' *Proceedings of the 1989 conference at Larnaka.*

Olsen O. and Crumlin–Pedersen O. 1967 'Skuldelev Ships II.' *Acta Archaeologica* 38, 73–174

Steffy J.R. 1984 'Structural philosophy and technology – clues from shipwrecks.' In J. Coates & S. McGrail (eds), *Greek trireme of the 5th century BC,* 23–38 NMM Greenwich.

Steffy J.R 1985: 'Kyrenia ship.' *American J. of Archaeology* 89, 71–101.

Steffy J.R. 1989: 'The role of three dimensional research in the Kyrenia ship reconstruction.' *TROPIS* 1, 249–262. Hellenic Institution for preservation of Nautical Tradition.

van Doorninck F.H. 1976 '4th century wreck at Yassi Ada.' *Int. Journal of Nautical Archaeology* 5, 115–131.

Ward R.G.W. (ed.) 1987 *Applications of Tree–ring Studies.* BAR 333, Oxford.

Reprinted with permission from:

Gale N.H. (ed) *Bronze Age Trade in the Mediterrean*: 83–91.
Studies in Mediterrean Archaeology 90, Sweden (1991).

SECTION 11.0

EXPERIMENTAL ARCHAEOLOGY AND THE ESTIMATION OF PERFORMANCE

Experimental archaeology is one of a number of scientific ways of investigating ancient boats & ships. Using all available evidence, an authentic reconstruction is designed, built and tested, so that deductions can be made about the original vessel or class of vessels: how a particular vessel, or a typical vessel, was probably built, propelled, steered and used, and the likely sort of operational performance she had. Other methods of estimating aspects of performance include: building models for ship tank and wind tunnel trials; the use of computers, including computer aided design; and the use of hydrostatic curves and speed indices. These alternative methods may be used during preparatory work in the design of a full–size reconstruction. On the other hand, these methods of assessment may of themselves be sufficient and make an actual reconstruction unnecessary. They are usually far less demanding in resources than experimental work. (McGrail, 1987: 192–203).

Hypothetical reconstructions

A crucial stage which must precede each one of these evaluations is the reconstruction, as a scale model or drawing, of the form and structure of the ancient vessel being investigated, together with her propulsion outfit and her steering arrangements. Even though the scientific methods and the experimental techniques used may be unchallanageable, the sources which archaeologists and historians draw on are far from perfect, and an element of uncertainty will be associated with every reconstruction. It is sometimes possible to reduce or redistribute this uncertainty by specifying more than one reconstruction, perhaps a minimum and a maximum solution to the problem, but uncertainty cannot be eliminated. All reconstructions are therefore hypotheses which not only need to be tested for their practicability during subsequent experimental work or by other kinds of assessment, but also need to be tested by other workers not involved in the project, against the sources of evidence, and against independent evidence if such exists. By analogy, a full–scale reconstruction in the form of a boat or ship may be thought of as a 'floating hypothesis' (McGrail, 1992; Coates *et.al.* 1995).

All the papers in this Section are concerned, in one way or another, with this reconstruction phase, either from a theoretical standpoint, seeking to define valid principles and methods (Papers 11.1, 11.2, 11.4, 11.7 & 11.8), or as a step towards evaluating the performance of a particular ancient boat (Papers 11.3, 11.5, 11.6). Performance estimates are also made in Papers 6.2, 7.2, 7.3 & 8.1.

The first paper (11.1) in this Section was written after I had worked, in 1972/3, with Harold Kimber, a master shipwright from coastal Somerset, and Eric McKee, a marine engineer and recorder of boats – see Paper 3.1. We built and tested a reconstruction of a 9th century AD *faering*, the 4–oared boat from the Gokstad burial mound (McGrail & McKee, 1974). The final paper (11.8) was written, by invitation, as a critical commentary on the work of the Trireme Trust in designing, building and testing a reconstruction of a typical 4th century BC Athenian trireme (Morrison & Coates, 1986; Shaw, 1993).

These two projects, the *faering* & the trireme, illustrate two different approaches to experimental boat archaeology; in one, the reconstruction is of a *specific* boat; in the other, it is of a *representative* member of a class of vessel. Which approach is used in a given project is determined by the sort of evidence available. The *faering* reconstruction was based mainly on excavated evidence from one particular boat; the trireme reconstruction was based mainly on documentary and iconographic evidence concerning a class of vessel. Both methods are valid ways of finding out more about the past; what we can learn from any one individual reconstruction will depend on:

    (a). the quality of the evidence;

    (b). the rigour of the interpretation of that evidence, the building of the full scale reconstruction, and the subsequent trials; and

    (c). the clarity of publication and criticism (Coates *et.al,*1995: 295).

Three Scandinavian scholars, two of them closely associated with the 'specific' approach to experimental boat archaeology as practised at Roskilde, Denmark, have recently criticised the 'representative' approach, claiming that physical remains are the only basis for formulating hypotheses about ancient vessels (Westerdahl, 1992; 1993; Crumlin–Pedersen, 1995; 1996; Bill,1996). On the contrary, it is not just excavated evidence that is relevent to archaeology. Nautical reconstructions are no different, in principle, from other forms of archaeological reconstruction in which *all* forms of evidence are used, after being subject to source criticism.

In fact,the Roskilde–based Danish group which built full size reconstructions of the 10th / 11th century boats, Skuldelev 3 & 5, *did* use all available forms of evidence iconographic, documentary, ethnographic analogy, and scientific theory – when they reconstructed the vessels that their incomplete, fragmented and distorted excavated wrecks represented. This is especially so for the sailing rig, for which the excavated evidence is vestigial (Crumlin–Pedersen, 1996). I have no doubt that this group were rigorous in their source criticism when they devised models and drawings of each reconstructions, & in the building and trials of the full size vessels. They have demonstrated the way to undertake an experimental project based on a specific boat–find, and when these experiments are published much will undoubtedly be added to our knowledge of the use & performance of Nordic boats and ships.

Both types of experiment (specific & representative) are valid ways of investigating the past. Furthermore, both types result in the building of a 'floating hypothesis'. How much confidence can be placed in individual reconstructions depends, not on whether they are 'specific' or 'representative', but on an objective appraisal of each project.

It might be suggested that the 'representative' approach is a second–best solution, inferior to the 'specific' reconstruction. In fact, in relation to the available evidence, the 'representative' reconstruction can be the best solution. I say 'can be' and not 'is' because there is great scope for the imagination in that type of project, and such projects may attract 'fringe freaks'. Furthermore, there is a danger that 'representative' projects may be pursued when there is little, if any, ancient evidence and thus become mere ethnographic speculation. As in any seientific work, vigilance and outside criticism is essential.

There are, however, comparable problems when dealing with excavated remains of a specific boat. Indeed, since no complete remains of an ancient vessel has yet been found, or is likely to be, all 'specific' reconstructions are necessarily also "representative" in parts, usually the upperworks and the propulsion system.

With minimum remains, no "specific" reconstruction is possible – see, for example, Fig.1.1.4. When a large portion of the remains survive, hovever, reconstruction may be attempted, but there can be different opinions about where to draw the line between 'possible' and 'not possible' to reconstruct. In my survey of the logboats of southern Britain (McGrail, 1978: 127) I used the following criteria to determine whether or not reconstruction was justified:

>   (i). full length, or almost full length, recorded.

>   (ii). original sheerline recorded over significant lengths.

>   (iii). representative transverse sections recorded.

These relatively strict criteria meant that only 24 out of 179 logboats could be reconstructed; they also meant that there was virtually only one possible hull for each boat, although several alternative fittings could be proposed to explain vestigial features. A different, perhaps more imaginative, approach would have permitted the apparently valid reconstruction of many more of these boats.

In general, there is more uncertainty in the 'specific' reconstruction process than its three Scandinavian proponants admit. Nevertheless, I believe that there can be a high confidence factor in the particular case of the Skuldelev wrecks. Correspondingly, I do not think that there is as much certainty about the reconstruction of a representative trireme as some of the Trireme Trust's publications might suggest: although, here again, I believe that their reconstruction is probably as near the original as it is possible to get with the information at present available.

Both groups have undertaken their projects with rigour and have used scientific methodology; and both have sought to deal with facts and not imagination. The one major difference I can see between these two groups is that, whereas the trireme folk concede the validity of the 'specific" approach in the Skuldelev context, the Nordic folk do not agree that the 'representative' approach can also be valid when, as has been argued for the trireme, documented high performance places physical constraints on the design which greatly limit the range of otherwise possible alternative reconstructions.

Scale Models at Sea

In recent reports on experiments with half–scale reconstructions of the 6th/7th century Sutton Hoo boat & the 9th/10th century Graveney boat, the Giffords (1995; 1996) have sought to draw conclusions about the sailing characteristics and performance of Anglo–Saxon ships. This claim may be examined from archaeological and methodological viewpoints.

There is no direct evidence for the use of mast and sail in either of these boats (Bruce–Mitford, 1975; Fenwick, 1978), and neither excavator has unequivocally claimed that these vessels were so fitted. Although the Celts and other indigenous people in NW Europe used the sail from Roman times and even earlier (Section 8), the Scandinavian/Saxon peoples appear, on present evidence, not to have used sails until c. 800 AD (Westerdahl, 1995: 42–3). The Giffords, however, argue for earlier use of sail on three main grounds:

>   (i). *Shape.* The Sutton Hoo boat has a midship section and waterline shape generally associated with sailing vessels. This view may be contrasted with those of Christensen (1996: 79): '[Sutton Hoo] has a hull form better suited to rowing than sailing'. See also Westerdahl (1995: 42).

>   (ii). *Performance.* The Sutton Hoo boat is so suited to sailing that it is difficult to believe that she was not intended for that purpose. Such an argument from hindsight cannot constitute proof.

>   (iii). *Structural.* Extra framing on the quarter, projection of the posts beyond the planking, and closely–spaced (*sic*) framing are all more appropriate to a sailing vessel than an oared vessel. Comparison with the oared boat from Nydam (Akerlund, 1963), for example, provides a counter–argument.

Westerdahl (1995: 41–3) has stressed that there was a long history of rowing in northern waters in pre–Roman times, and argued that there were factors in Scandinavian/Saxon society which predisposed them to continue in this way, even when they were aware of the sail. An oared Sutton Hoo boat would not be out of place in such a context. The Graveney boat was built when sail was commonplace. Nevertheless, her characteristics and her deduced role within the Thames estuary suggest that we should consider the possibility that she primarily used the tides, with oars or sweeps for secondary propulsion.

The Giffords make the valid point that speeds achieved by a scale model may readily be converted to speeds achievable by a similar full–size boat. However, scale models can mislead on other aspect of performance. Since the crew remain full size, difficulties arise if one attempts, for example, to use a scaled–down model to investigate rowing. It is impossible to achieve the appropriate rowing geometry for oarsmen in relation to height above the waterline, the position of oar pivots, the length of oar, its angle and gearing. Furthermore, if oarsmen are to be stationed at an optimum distance apart, the rowing section of the boat may have to be stretched in relation to the ends; the position of the framing may not then accord with a true scaling–down, with consequent effects on the hull structure.

Launching, recovering, loading, & unloading, & steering the boat, and handling the sailing rig may all be correspondingly affected by disparities of scale. Such problems made Binns (1980: 106–7) comment, after his voyage in the two–thirds model of the Gokstad ship, *Odin's Raven,* that 'scaling....should be avoided as far as possible when building replica ships and one should use originals of the size one can manage to build and crew'.

Full size reconstructions are thus to be preferred. On the other hand, scale models undoubtedly have the virtue of significantly reducing the costs of an experiment. Furthermore, when understanding is slight, as it is at present in the case of the performance of early Medieval boats & ships, experiments using scale models can lead to a worthwhile expansion of knowledge, limited though this may be in comparison with what might be obtained from a full size reconstruction (Coates *et. al.*,1995: 295–6).

References

Åkerlund H. 1963 *Nydamskeppen.* Goteborg.

Bill J. 1996 'A Review.' *Int. J. Nautical Archaeology* 25, 72.

Binns A. 1980 *Viking Voyagers.* Heinemann.

Bruce–Mitford R. 1975 *Sutton Hoo Ship Burial.* Vol.1, British Museum.

Cederlund C.O. 1993 (ed) *Arby Boat.* Stockholm Monographs 2.

Christensen A.E. 1996 'Proto–Viking, Viking and Norse craft.'in Christensen A.E. (ed) *Earliest Ships,* 72–88. Conway's History of the Ship, Vol.1.

Coates J. *et al.* 1995 'Experimental boat & ship archaeology: principles and methods.' *Int. J. Nautical Archaeology,* 24, 293–301.

Crumlin–Pedersen O. 1995 'Experimental archaeology and ships – bridging the arts and sciences.' *Int. J. Nautical Archaeology* 24, 303–5.

Crumlin–Pedersen O. 1996 'Problems of reconstruction and the estimation of performance.' in Christensen A.E. (ed) *Earliest Ships,* 110–119. Conway's History of the Ship. Vol.1.

Fenwick V. 1978 (ed) *Graveney Boat.* BAR Oxford 53.

Gifford E & J. 1995. 'Sailing characteristics of Saxon ships as derived from half–scale working models with special reference to the Sutton Hoo ship.' *Int. J. Nautical Archaeology* 24, 121–131.

Gifford E. & J. 1996 'Sailing performance of Anglo–Saxon ships as derived from the building & trials of half–scale models of the Sutton Hoo & Graveney ship finds.' *Mariner's Mirror,* 82, 131–153.

McGrail S. 1978 *Logboats of England & Wales.* BAR Oxford 51

McGrail S. 1987 *Ancient Boats in NW Europe.* Longman.

McGrail S. 1992 'Replicas, reconstructions & floating hypotheses.' *Int. J. Nautical Archaeology,* 21, 353–355.

McGrail S. & McKee E. 1974. *Building & trials of a replica of an ancient boat: Gokstad faering.* NMM Greenwich Monograph 11. Two parts.

Morrison J. & Coates J. 1986 *Athenian Trireme.* CUP.

Shaw T. 1993 *Trireme Project.* Oxbow Monograph 31.

Westerdahl C. 1992 'A review.' *Int. J. Nautical Archaeology,* 21, 84–85.

Westerdahl C. 1993 'Trireme – an experimental form?' *Int. J. Nautical Archaeology,* 22, 205–207.

Westerdahl C 1995. 'Society & Sail.' in Crumlin–Pedersen O. & Thye B.M. (eds) *Ship as Symbol,* 41–50. National Museum, Copenhagen.

PAPER 11.1

MODELS, REPLICAS AND EXPERIMENTS IN NAUTICAL ARCHAEOLOGY

In asking whether Paul Johnstone had proved his point in his trials of a Bronze Age boat replica (Johnstone, 1972), John Coles (Coles, 1973) has drawn attention to the necessity for thorough scientific planning if worthwhile results are to be obtained from any form of experimental archaeology. Valid conclusions can only be drawn if the experiment is based on rigorous theory and if full consideration is given to all the variables. David Clarke places the building of replicas – 'material hardware analogues' – at a low level in his hierarchy of models, much inferior to the all–powerful, fully comprehensive mathematical and systems models, and he allows them only elementary predictive capacity (Clarke, 1972, 10; 13). Nevertheless, the construction and operation of a full scale replica of a boat may often be the only way that the archaeologist can become aware of the full array of factors involved, and of possible solutions to the problems encountered. The practical experiment may enable him subsequently to set up a more general, abstract model.

In some respects an archaeological experiment is similar to excavation in that the archaeologist poses questions or advances hypotheses which the experiment or excavation is designed to answer or test. Only infrequently can excavation or experiment give a deterministic answer: more often, probabilities will emerge, some possibilities or hypotheses may be eliminated, and the most probable solution or a limited range of solutions may be obtained. Some archaeological experiments may be repeatable in similar or varied conditions, and thus the original findings may be confirmed or extended. But where a boat is to be reproduced and extensive trials carried out, economic considerations may mean that for all practical purposes the experiment is not repeatable. It is thus especially important in nautical archaeology that all aspects of the experiment be subjected to critical examination, including a form of cost/benefit analysis, so that maximum value can be obtained, and reliable, archaeologically valuable results derived.

As Coles has pointed out (Coles, 1966, 1), there are two main phases in an archaeological experiment: the reproduction of the original object, and its subsequent use. The first phase can reveal information on the technical processes involved, the choice of raw material and tools, and how the technique might have been passed on to a subsequent generation. Marks or features of the structure not previously understood or possibly dismissed as peripheral, may be shown to be significant characteristics. Analysis of the original artifact and the synthesis of other relevant evidence may enable missing or damaged parts to be reconstructed in their most probable form. And estimates of the pre–historic cost in terms of raw material and manpower may be made, and may be compared with related ethnographical data.

If the experiment is to be complete, it is essential that the replica be put to use; it must not become a museum exhibit or a national monument, but rather a tool for further research, a true working replica. This phase of the experiment should reveal the potentials and the limitations of the original artifact under standard test conditions, and also under the most probable conditions of its original use. Hypotheses are here put to practical test – in her natural element a boat replica may soon bolster or refute an armchair theory. Life expectancy may also be studied, as may the effects of the environment on the replica with over a long period, and the results of these studies can provide clues to help in the interpretation and identification of excavated material. It is important, however, that the replica, with its power to focus the mind and create a feeling of authenticity, should not be confused with the original. The replica is a hypothesis in material form; it may be valid, but it may be proved wrong as more evidence comes to light or as improved analytical and experimental techniques are evolved.

Johnstone's Bronze Age replica is one of the latest in a long line of bost replicas, but few if any of the earlier ones could be claimed as successful archaeological experiments. From the Gokstad ship replica of 1893, to the current British replicas of the *Mayflower*, *Nonsuch* and *Golden Hind*, all have been influenced by a mixture of motives such as national prestige, commercial success, and historic nostalgia. Such considerations have often overshadowed the claims of research, and few have been published in sufficient detail for their authenticity and scientific value to be established. Possibly Heyerdahl's rafts and some of the latest Danish replicas may not for fully deserve these structures.

In an attempt to put boat replica building on to a firm academic basis, the National Maritime Museum has recently built a replica of the *faering* from Gokstad. This four–oared boat was the smallest of the three found inside the Gokstad ship when she was excavated from her burial mound on the west side of Oslo fjord in 1880 (Nicolaysen, 1882). She was chosen for the experiment because she has many of the distinctive characteristics of the ninth–century Viking ships, because she has distinguished twentieth–century descendants in the Oselver boats of SW. Norway and in the fourerns of Shetland, and because she – or at least her reconstruction of the 1940's – is available for study in the Bygdøy Viking Ship Hall. The building of this replica cannot be daimed to be an ideal archaeological evidence experiment for it was the Museum's first venture into this field, assumptions were made which were later proved wrong, and some of the logical reasoning and analysis which might have preceded the experiment was done as the boat was being built and often with hindsight. For these reasons, and also because of doubts about the authenticity of some of the Bygdøy reconstruction, the full potential of information cannot be gathered from this experiment. Nevertheless there have been some extremely valuable results: new light has been thrown on several aspects of ninth–century boat–building techniques; a range of sea trials has been established which it is planned to use with a future replica of the Graveney boat; and perhaps, above all, invaluable experience has been gained in the general theory and practice of replica building and in the setting up of archaeological experiments. Some of the conclusions reached are set out below.

Choice of experiment

The experiment chosen must be one which poses significant questions which have a reasonable chance of being answered, and there must be sufficient archaeological and documentary evidence for the most probable form of the original boat to be deduced. The boat chosen as the subject of the experiment may be either a specific one, or a synthesis of the characteristic features of a well defined boat type. There are, however, difficulties with both these sources of action. If a specific boat replica is to be built, the builder must find the right supply of timber to fit the given design, whereas his predecessor in antiquity (indeed up to modern times) would have built his boat from the stock of wood immediately available to him – a very different approach and one which may result in the modern product having different characteristics from the ancient one. On the other hand a replica of a synthesis of characteristic traits may be equally difficult, for there will be subjective views of which traits are relevant, and the result may be something which behaves catastrophically at sea. The reasons for choosing one of these courses of action rather than the other must be clearly stated so that their validity may be judged.

Choice of replica maker

The builder should be someone who can to a great extent divorce himself from his own traditons. He must be able to visualize a range of possible solutions to the problems of replica building, and not impose – even unwittingly – his own culture's solution. He must not build a 'better' boat by incorporating modern features and materials. He should in fact try to adopt the attitude of mind of the original craftsman: if he is building a replica of the Sutton Hoo ship for example, he must 'think Saxon'. It is a moot point whether he must be experienced in boatbuilding. A modern professional may be difficult to guide into the ancient idiom: during the *faering* experiment significant differences emerged between recent British clinker boatbuilding practice and the probable techniques used in ninth–century Scandinavia; and Odd Johnson, while building the skin boat for Paul Johnstone, did not always use the probable Bronze Age methods (Johnstone, 1972, 270). On the other hand, although a team of enthusiastic volunteers may be brought to think and work Saxon, they may be difficult to find and to keep together, and their lack of

boatbuilding experience may result in their missing some solutions to their problems, and in their misinterpretation of some evidence. The optimum choice is probably a blend of technical competence and of archaeological awareness, an archaeologist and a woodworker – preferably a boatbuilder – working together on the project.

Choice of environment

It is not possible to build a replica of a ninth–century boat in a modern boatyard and remain uninfluenced by contemporary boatbuilding techniques. The effects of the twentieth–century environment must be neutralized as far as possible, and more appropriate surroundings used. Boat–building in the ninth–century idiom, for example, should probably be on an open river bank. The right setting allows the various aspects of the work to interact authentically with each other and with the environment. It is not suggested that absolute accuracy is required in reproducing an ancient environment, but the significant features must be there, otherwise the experiment will be invalidated.

Choice of construction methods

The techniques to be used should be determined by analysis of the construction of the boat to be reproduced, supplemented by historical evidence and valid ethnographical comparisons. It is important that all possible materials, tools and techniques be considered before the most probable solutions are chosen. The 'obvious' solution may not be the right one, and where there is doubt, variant solutions should be investigated. In certain cases small scale models may be an intermediate step in resolving some of the problems encountered. Clarke has pointed out the distortion which can be introduced into an experiment by scale effects (Clarke, 1972, 13), and the experimenter must be aware of these when he draws condusions.

Criteria must be established by which to judge whether some departure from authentic methods may be allowed for reasons of economy of time or effort, or because they have only an insignificant effect on the main research problem. Did the use of an electric drill to make holes affect the performance or the durability of the Kalnes Bronze Age boat replica? May a power saw be used to fell a tree which is subsequently to be split and worked by ninth–century methods? Is there a significant difference between axes of the Iron Age and of the present day? The answers to these points will be determined by the aims of the experiment. For example, the last question might be answered 'Yes' if we are interested in detailed evaluation of man–hours, but probably 'No' if our experiment is designed to answer only more general questions.

Building a replica of a specific boat raises the difficult problem of how to 'translate' the original into a replica. By the act of copying we may introduce an artificial element into our work. It is generally agreed that before the age of accurate measurements and scale drawings, craftsmen had an ideal model in view or in their mind as they began to work. The craftsman may have wanted to repeat a known design or to modify one: to make 'a pair of shoes like the old ones', or to build 'a boat like the one you built for Ola last year, but two feet longer and with rather more beam aft' (Christensen, 1972, 237). If we are to build a replica in the ancient idiom may it not be wisest to use the ancient methods of reproduction if these can be established? Did the builder of the original *faering* have another boat close by, or could he copy or modify a previous design entirely in his mind? Did the Viking boatbuilder build by eye, or did he have methods of recording the essential features of a boat – the passive mould, the boat ell, or the boat level? (Basch, 1972, 34ff; Christensen, 1973, 141ff). If archaeological or historical evidence can answer these questions then that method should be used by the modern replica builder.

Choice of trial programmes

The trials should evaluate the boat in a range of uses, and under varied conditions. There should be tests of strength, capacity, stability and other design features, and trials to evaluate the boat in her operational uses under representative environmental conditions, with varying payload, and different methods of propulsion and steering. There should also be in longer–term trials to determine the effects of repeated use, and the wear to be experienced over a specified period.

Conclusions

Experimental archacology, or the construction and testing of 'material hardware analogues', can increase our knowledge of past technologies and economies, and thus it is a valid and valuable archaeological technique. This paper has put forward principles which it is believed are applicable to experimental nautical archaeology. Their use should ensure more 'value for money' in this often expensive work.

Aknowledgments

I wish to acknowledge Professor David Wilson's valuable comments on the first draft of this paper.

References

Basch L. 1972 'Ancient Wrecks and the Archaeology of Ships.' *International Journal of Nautical Archaeology* 1, 1–58.

Christensen A. E. 1972 'Boatbuilding Tools and the Process of Learning.' in O. Hasslof (ed.), *Ships and Shipyards, Sailors and Fishermen* 235–259 (Copenhagen).

Christensen A. E. 1973 'Lucien Basch: Ancient Wrecks and the Archaeology of Ships.' A comment.' *International Journal of Nautical Archaeology* 2, 137–145.

Clarke D. L. 1972 'Models and Paradigms in Archaeology.' in D. L. Clarke (ed.), *Models in Archaeology* 1–60.

Coles J. M. 1966 'Experimental Archaeology.' *Proceedings of the Society of Antiquaries of Scotland* XCIX, 1–20.

Coles J. M. 1973 'Kalnes Bronze Age Boat" *Antiquity* XLVII, 60.

Johnstone P. 1972 'Bronze Age Sea Trial.' *Antiquity* XLVI, 269–274.

Johnstone P.1973 'Kalnes Bronze Age Boat,' *Antiquity* XLVII, 60–61.

Nicolaysen N. 1882 *Langskibet fra Gokstad ved Sandefjord* (Christiania) reprinted 1971 (Farnborough).

Reprinted with permission from:

Mariner's Mirror, 61: 3–8 (1975).

PAPER 11.2

ASPECTS OF EXPERIMENTAL BOAT ARCHAEOLOGY

I very much regret that it proved impossible for Alan Hinks to present a paper at this Symposium on 'Sources and Techniques in Boat Archaeology'. He is chairman of J. . Hinks and Son, the North Devon shipbuilders (Farr 1976, 17, 18), and unexpectedly has to carry out sea trials on a recently completed ship. We would have learned much from his experience of commercially building replicas of ancient boats. I hope that one day we may hear him at another forum – possibly on site in his boatyard, as recommended in another context by Hasslöf (1972). I felt it impossible to invite others to prepare a paper on this topic at short notice, and therefore I reluctantly undertook this task myself.

Boat Replicas

Later in this Symposium Timothy Severin will describe the building of his skin boat *Brendan* and how he sailed her this year from Ireland to Iceland. *Brendan* is the latest in a long line of boat replicas, though not all could be classified as archaeological experiments. Paul Johnstone of the BBC "Chronicle" programme, who but for his untimely death would have presented a paper at this Symposium, had traced details of a replica trireme built for Napoleon III in 1861 (Eveillard, n.d. 233); this is possibly the earliest replica of which we have records. Johnstone himself was involved in the building and filming of several experimental craft: firstly Atkinson's Stonehenge experiment in 1954, when a replica bluestone was transported by a multiple "dugout" (Atkinson, 1960: 113–4); secondly the building of a tarred canvas curragh and its trial crossing of the Irish Sea in the 1960s; and more recently he worked with Professor Marstrander on his Bronze Age skin boat experiment (Johnstone, 1972; Marstrander, 1976).

A not so well publicised replica is that of the Nydam boat shown in Fig. 11.2.1 (Åkerlund, 1963:45–7). Paul Johnstone noted in a summary of his projected paper that this was the first boat replica trial to be recorded in film and he wondered whether this film could now be traced.

A better known replica is *Viking*, Captain Magnus Andersen's 1893 replica of the Gokstad ship, (Fig. 11.2.2) which he sailed from Bergen to Newfoundland in 28 days (Andersen, 1895). *Viking* was built as close to the original form as possible, with

Figure 11.2.1 A replica of the Nydam boat built in 1935 for use in a German film. H Åkerlund

321

Figure 11.2.2 *Viking* Magnus Andersen's 1893 replica of the Gokstad ship. Norsk Sjøfartsmuseum, Oslo

Figure 11.2.3 *Viking* in the North Sea, with a foresail in addition to her square mainsail. Magnus Andersen

Figure 11.2.4 *Hugin* the 1949 Danish replica of the Gokstad ship. Danish Tourist Board

Figure 11.2.5 The Danish National Museum's Norland *Ottring*

the ribs lashed to cleats on the planking, and therefore Andersen's account of her voyage is of great importance for the understanding of the sea worthiness and the sea keeping qualities of this form of hull. But there are doubts about what can be learned from her performance under sail. Her square mainsail was similar in shape and material to those used in late 19th century Norway: that is it was made of hemp or flax, and of high aspect ratio, tall and narrow. Christensen (1968: 39) considers however, that Viking Age sails were probably twice as wide as they were tall, that is of low aspect ratio, and the consensus of opinion is that they were made of *wadmal*, a coarse woollen cloth, possibly strengthened by strips of linen or leather (Haasum, 1974:113). Furthermore, *Viking* sometimes carried a top sail, and sometimes a foresail (Fig. 11.2.3). Thus great care must be taken in drawing any conclusions about the sailing capabilities of Viking Age ships from this replica's performance.

Another replica of the Gokstad ship, *Hugin*, (Fig. 11.2.4) was built in 1949 and sailed from Denmark to Kent (Røjel, 1949). The English language account of this replica does not give sufficient information for us to judge her value as an archaeological experiment, although one interesting fact is recorded: 20th century Danes, 2 metres tall, could not easily row in the space between adjacent rowing stations. One may conclude from this that Viking Age oarsmen were not as tall as their 20th century descendents, or that rowing styles have changed. The remains of this replica can still be seen on the beach at Pegwell Bay, Kent.

There has recently been inereasing Danish interest in building boat replicas: Egon Hansen (1974) has recorded six built since 1963. Apart from three notes by Crumlin–Pedersen (1966: 256–8; 1969; 1970:9, 18) describing aspects of the *Imme Gramme* replica of the Ladby ship, there is no readily accessible publication giving details of these experiments. Crumlin–Pedersen (1975: 130) has stated that these replicas have not 'been rigged and sailed properly, nor have they been subjected to serious trials'. Nevertheless it would be of great value if he could give an authoritative summary of past Scandinavian experience with boat replicas so that future research workers can learn from it. Possibly the forthcoming report on his current work evaluating the problems of sailing a Norland *Ottring* (Fig. 11.2.5) with a single square sail, could become the occasion for a comprehensive paper.

The Greenwich Faering Replica

The National Maritime Museum's direct experience of experimental boat archaeology is limited to the building and trials of a replica of the *faering* from Gokstad (Figs. 11.2.6, 7; 11.2.9, 10, 11). This was not an ideal experiment (McGrail, 1975A, 5), but we learned much from it, and gained valuable experience in the theory and practice of replica building. As with the 1893 Gokstad replica,there are problems in attempting to use our experimental results to draw conclusions about Viking Age seamanship. Some of these difficulties have been considered elsewhere (McGrail, 1974: 34), but I would like to discuss further aspects here, to illustrate some of the problems inherent in boat replica work.

Fig. 11.2.7 shows the forward inclined frame fitted to the Greenwich *faering*, with two holes piercing it. The dimensions of these holes had been scaled up from Christensen's 1:10 drawing (Fig. 11.2.6) and their longest dimension was *c.* 6 cm that is, about three fingers breadth. The function of these holes was not clear to us until we operated the boat from the beach, when it became natural to attempt to use them as handholes when hauling the boat into and out of the water. Inaccurate scaling meant that they were in fact too small, although those on the original faering in Oslo could be so used. When building his *faering* replica, Egon Hansen of the Prehistoric Museum, Moesgård, Aarhus, Denmark obviously appreciated this use (Fig. 11.2.8), although his handholes are somewhat bigger than those on the original *faering*.

Christensen's construction plan for the *faering* (Fig. 11.2.6) shows an oar, reconstructed from a fragment, which is *c.* 3.29 m (10ft.9in.) long. It is now next to impossible to say which of the fragmented oar remains belonged to which boat, and it may be that Christensen based his drawing on fragments from the larger, 6–oared boats, also found in the Gokstad ship (Christensen, personal communication). In static trials at Greenwich an oar of this length seemed to be too long for the *faering*, and Harold Kimber, the master boatbuilder in charge of building the Greenwich replica, made two oars of length *c* 2.52 m (8ft. 3in.), calculated as twice the beam of the boat at the tholes. This pair was used in the rowing trials together with 20th century pairs of oars of 2.46 m and 3.05 m length (McKee, 1974: 18). In retrospect, it might have been wiser and more in keeping with experimental methods for us to have done more research in the Bygd#y archives before building the replica, or to have used a pair of 3.29 m long oars, and attempted to find a rowing technique and an operating environment suitable to them. The fact that we also experienced difficulties during our trials when using 20th century rowing methods in the seemingly inadequate distance between the thwarts (.95 m = 3ft. 1½in.), emphasises the latter point.

McKee (1974: 13–17) has described some of the problems encountered in evaluating the steering arrangements of the *faering*. It may not have been sufficiently emphasised however that the effectiveness of the side rudder probably depends to a marked degree on the shape of the rudder boss (Fig. 11.2.9), and the fit of the rudder to that boss. There are obviously great difficulties in getting the precise three dimensional shape from Christensen's drawings, as can be seen by comparing the Greenwich boss (Fig. 11.2.9) with the drawing (Fig. 11.2.6).Furthermore, at the time of the Greenwich experiment it was not appreciated that the inboard surface of the original rudder may have been dished to match the shape of the boss. The surviving evidence is not unambiguous and the depression on the inside of the *faering* rudder may be due to wear in use or pressure damage in the ground (Christensen, personal communication), but if the depression is intentionai it would effect the rudder efficiency. In addition, we did not persist in our attempts to find the best method of binding the rudder by withy thongs through the boss to the aft inclined frame (McKee, 1974: 14), but used hemp rope Ior the recorded trials. With these doubts and discrepancies it is not possible to draw

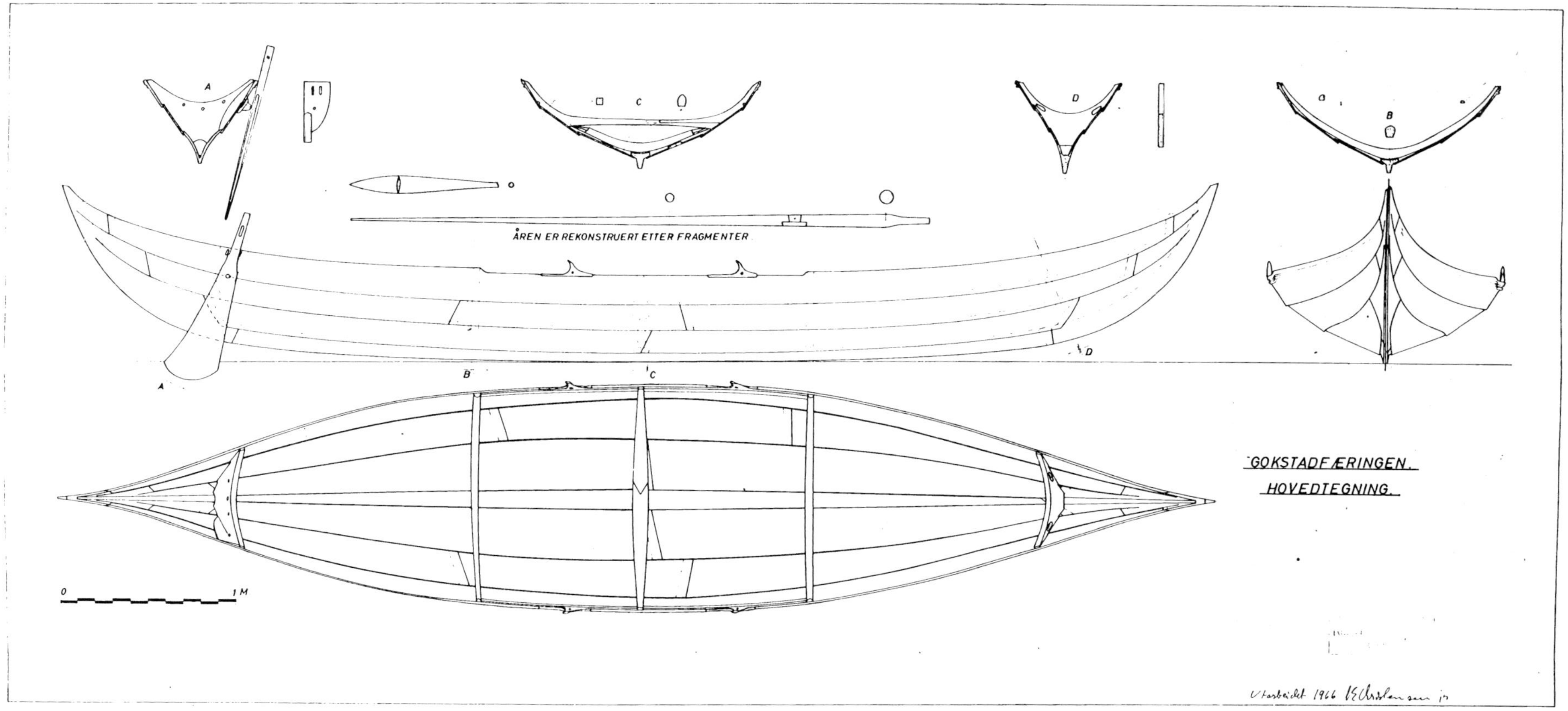
A
B
C
D
ÅREN ER REKONSTRUERT ETTER FRAGMENTER
GOKSTADFÆRINGEN.
HOVEDTEGNING.
0
1 M

Figure 11.2.6 The Gokstad *faering* construction plan by Arne Emil Christensen. Universitetets Oldsaksamling, Oslo

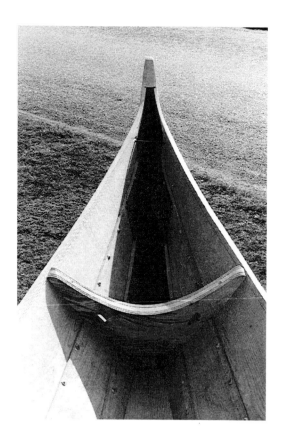

Figure 11.2.7 The fore stem and the forward inclined frame of the Greenwich *faering* replica. National Maritime Museum

Figure 11.2.8 A similar view of the *faering* replica built by Egon Hansen at Mosegård. National Maritime Museum

Figure 11.2.9 The rudder boss on the Greenwich *faering* replica. National Maritime Museum

conclusions from the Greenwich experiment about the efficiency of the original *faering*'s steering gear. Nor need we yet consider McKeets tentative hypothesis (1974: 26), that since the steering gear of the Greenwich *faering* is only

effective for small angles of helm, this may have been 'a significant obstacle to the development' in Viking times 'of a sailing boat that could change tacks'. More research and experimental work are required.

Long term uses of boat replicas

During 1975 and 1976 Eric McKee sailed the *faering* replica with a single square sail (Fig. 11.2.11) to gain some understanding of the problems of handling a small boat with this type of rig. Further trials in the Spring of 1977 will be the final ones in the first series. Would a further series of trials be productive? We are planning longer term trials to assess wear in use and other effects. But is there more we can get from replicas such as this one, which represent a heavy investment? Time and money may be justified by the knowledge gained during the building and the trials. We may also gain an additional return by using the replica as a test vehicle to learn the art of sailing with a single square sail; or to evaluate a prototype trials programme; or to act as a control by providing feedback to theoretical models used in the naval architectural evaluations. But can a boat replica be archaeologically useful right to the end of her life? I have elsewhere suggested (McGrail, 1974, 37) – possibly lightheartedly – that the *faering* replica might be interred in a burial mound to be excavated in future years on the lines of the experimental earth works at Overton Down (Jewell and Dimbleby, 1966) and

Figure 11.2.10 The Greenwich *faering* replica under oars. National Maritime Museum

Figure 11.2.11 The Greenwich *faering* replica under sail. Basil Greenhill

Wareham (Evans and Limbrey, 1974). There would be problems of finance and logistics, of continuity and repeatability – but is this suggestion worth considering seriously? Would boat archaeologists and others gain sufficient to justify the effort? If not, are there better ways of using a boat replica in the long term, to the greater gain of Archaeology? I believe that questions such as these should be asked as part of the cost benefit analysis that must precede any decision to build a boat replica.

The principles and methods of experimental boat archaeology

The theory of archaeological experiments expounded by John Coles in the preceding paper generally applies to boat replicas. Elsewhere (1975A) I have discussed procedures which may ensure maximum archaeological value from a boat replica experiment. These include the choice of a worthwhile subject for the experiment; the selection of the project team; the choice of the environmental conditions for building and testing the replica; the choice of tools and of constructional methods and the way to "translate" the original into a replica; the design of a trials programme; and finally the necessity to record the experiment in detail, including the reasoning behind decisions to adopt or reject particular courses of action, so that others can assess the validity of the experiment.

Since 1974 the National Maritime Museum has been planning the building of a replica of the Graveney Boat, a mid 10th century A.D. cargo boat whose fragmentary remains were excavated by the National Maritime Museum and the British Museum in 1970 (Fenwick, 1978). This preliminary planning has led me to believe that greater emphasis should be placed on the early stages of an experiment. In general there will be several possible solutions to the problem of hypothetically reconstructing the full original form of an incomplete boat find: some of these solutions may vary only be cause of minor differences in fittings and "trimmings", but others may have significantly different hydrostatic and hydrodynamic characteristics, and operational capabilities. I believe that these variants should be thoroughly investigated in a variety of ways *before* a decision is taken which version the replica builder is to use in his practical experiment. Thus, by small scale model building, by naval architectural calculations and the plotting of hydrostatic curves, by computer simulation, and by tank tests, these theoretical alternatives can be evaluated for practicability of building, for stability and load carrying effectiveness, and for performance with different methods of propulsion under a range of operational and environmental conditions. These are experiments which can be repeated using many different values of the parameters, and they can be repeated by others. These theoretical models can be 'dismantled' and 'rebuilt' many times before we need crystallise our ideas on the version to be built as a full size replica, which will have only limited adaptability once its main design parameters are established. Much should be learned during these theoretical evaluations: negative findings and the rejection of hypotheses can give valuable insight, often as valuable as positive information; inconsistancies in reasoning may be highlighted and directives reformulated accordingly;

and the criteria by which to choose a preferred solution should be clarified. In certain cases this form of analysis may show that it is not yet the time to proceed to the full size replica phase – the decision possibly being deferred until more evidence becomes available.

There must however be controls for these theoretical investigations, and indeed as John Coates points out (This volume) naval architects prefer to have practical confirmation of calculated assessments, especially those of speed and of sailing performance. There should be feedback to theoretical models from both the building and the trials phases of a boat replica experiment, enabling the theoretical models to be amended, for example, by the addition of new variables whose existence was not suspected until the practical work revealed them. The first boat replica investigated by these methods will undoubtedly take longer to build than anticipated, and there will be much discussion whilst the theoretical and practical aspects are synchronised and made consistant, but future experiments should benefit from the refined analytical techniques which emerge.

Haasum (1974), has used some of the interdiseiplinary techniques I have described above in a theoretical investigation of Viking ships under sail. Her work has been criticised by Crumlin–Pedersen (1975, 130) because of her uneritical use of sources and methods. Whilst agreeing that this criticism may be well founded, I would nevertheless applaud Haasum for her pioneering spirit in attempting to use hydrodynamic and aerodynamic analysis to gain insight into the possible capabilities of ships of the Viking Age. There is a place for this type of theoretical assessment in any study of an ancient boat, providing that the data is sound. Additionally, there is a requirement to validate the theoretical model by practical trials, but this may have been beyond the resources available to Haasum.

The National Maritime Museum will probably use this intermediate stage of theoretical model building to investigate not only the Graveney boat but also the Brigg 'Raft' (McGrail, 1975b) and the Kentmere boat (Wilson, 1966). E.V. Wright and John Coates are now evaluating several alternative hypothetical rereconstructions of Ferriby boat 1, (Wright, 1976) and it is conceivable that they too may use these theoretical procedures to explore their reconstructions. I believe that time spent on this stage of any research programme will be of tremendous benefit not only because of the knowledge immediately gained, but also in the ultimate value of the full size replica, should it be decided to build one.

Acknowledgement I am grateful to Arne Emil Christensen for discussions on aspects of this paper.

References

Andersen M. 1895 *Vikingefaerden*, Kristiania .
Atkinson R.J.C. 1960 *Stonehenge*, London.
Åkerlund, H., 1963 Nydamskeppen, Goteborg.
Christensen A.E. 1968 *Boats of the North*, Oslo.

Crumlin–Pedersen O. 1966 'Two Danish Side Rudders.' *Mariner's Mirror*, 52, 251–261.

Crumlin–Pedersen O. 1969 'Kopi af et Vikingeskib.' *Skalk* 1969 (2), 26–27.

Crumlin–Pedersen O. 1970 'Viking Ships of Roskilde.' in National Maritime Museum Monograph No. 1 *Aspects of the History of Wooden Shipbuilding*, 7–23, Greenwich.

Crumlin–Pedersen O. 1975 'Viking Seamanship Questioned.' *Mariner's Mirror* 61, 127–131.

Evans J.G. and Limbrey S. 1974 'Experimental Earthwork on Morden Bog', Wareham, Dorset, England 1963–1972.' *Proceedings of the Prehistoric Society*, 40, 170–202.

Eveillard E., n.d. 'Navigation de plaisance.' fascicle No. 70 in Lacroix E. (ed) *Nouvelle technologie des arts et metiers* Volume 4, tome 7. Paris.

Farr G. 1976 *Shipbuilding in North Devon*, National Maritime Museum Monograph No. 22, Greenwich.

Fenwick V.H. (ed), 1978 *Graveney Boat*. BAR 53, Oxford

Haasum S. 1974 *Vikingatidens Segling och Navigation*, University of Stockholm, Theses and Papers in North European Archaeology 4. Stockholm.

Hansen E.H. 1974 Unpublished paper on archaeological replica building. Moesgaard .

Hasslof O. 1972. 'Concept of Living Tradition.' in Hasslof O. *et al* (ed) *Ships and Shipyards, Sailors and Fishermen*, 20–26, Copenhagen.

Jewell P.A. and Dimbleby G.W. (eds) 1966 'Experimental Earthwork on Overton Down, Wiltshire, England: the first four years.' *Proceedings of the Prehistoric Society*, 32, 313–42.

Johnstone P. 1972 'Bronze Age sea trial.' *Antiquity* 46, 269–274.

McGrail S. 1974 *Building and trials of a replica of an ancient boat: the Gokstad faering*, Part 1. National Maritime Museum Monograph No. 11. Greenwich.

McGrail, S., 1975A 'Models, Replicas and Experiments in Nautical Archaeology.' *Mariner's Mirror*, 61, 3–8.

McGrail S. 1975B 'Brigg Raft re–excavated.' *Lincolnshire History and Archaeology*, 10, 5–13.

McKee E. 1974 *Building and trials of a replica of an ancient boat: the Gokstad faering*, Part 2, National Maritime Museum Monograph No. 11, Greenwich.

Marstrander S. 1976 'Building a hide boat. An archaeological experiment.' *International Journal of Nautical Archaeology*, 5, 13–22.

Røjel J. 1949. *1949, Cruise of the Viking Ship Hugin.* Copenhagen.

Wilson D.M. 1966. 'Medieval boat from Kentmere, Westmorland.' *Medieval Archaeology*, 10, 81–88.

Wright E.V. 1976 *North Ferriby Boats*, National Maritime Museum Monograph No. 23, Greenwich.

Reprinted with permission from:

McGrail s. (ed) *Sources and Techniques in Boat Archaeology*, 245–258, BAR S29, Oxford 1977.

PAPER 11.3

THE BRIGG 'RAFT' – PROBLEMS IN RECONSTRUCTION AND IN THE ASSESSMENT OF PERFORMANCE

History and description of the find

The remains of the flat–bottomed plank boat known as the Brigg'raft' were first encountered in 1888 by workmen digging for clay in a field adjacent to a brickyard between the Old and New Rivers Ancholme one mile (*c.* 1.5km) to the NW of Brigg, then in Lincolnshire and now in South Humberside (Fig.11.3.1). The flat appearance of the remains led to the find being called a raft. A measured drawing (Fig. 7.1.1) and a brief description were published by Thropp (1887) the County Surveyor.Part of the remains was "taken up as well as could be done" (Thropp,1887, 95) and the remainder was covered with soil (Hunt, 1907/8) whilst clay digging continued around the find spot. A fragment of planking in Lincoln Museum appears to be all that now survives of that portion of the 'raft' lifted in 1888. The site was subsequently used as a municipal rubbish tip and in the 1950's more fill was added to produce a surface suitable for the Glanford Boat Club's boats when hoisted out.

The buried remains were re–located by the National Maritime Museum in 1973 and excavated in 1974 (McGrail, 1975; 1981A). When a vertical photograph of the 1974 excavation (Fig. 11.3.2) is compared with Thropp's 1888 drawing (Fig. 7.1.1), it can be seen that the Victorian clay diggers removed almost half of the remains they had uncovered, and much of what they re–buried shrank and split and was damaged in other ways during the time the 'raft' remained exposed between mid–February and late–June or early–July, 1888.

In addition to recording technological detatls of the boat which had not been noted in the 19th century the 1974 excavation revealed part of a side strake as well as the remains of the five lengths of bottom planking recorded by Thropp, all of them in a water logged and internally degraded condition. The remains were lifted and brought to the National Maritime Museum at Greenwich for post excavation recording and conservation. The lengthy task of conserving this waterlogged wood by immersion in hot Polyethylene Glycol is now almost completed and it is intended to exhibit the re–assembled remains in the near future to complement the explanatory small–scale models now on display in the Archaeological Gallery at Greenwich.

The 'raft' has the following principal constructional features:

a. Oak (*Quercus* sp) planking sewn with willow (*Salix* sp) stitches, and seams made watertight by a moss caulking capped by longitudinal laths of hazel (*Coryllus avelana*).

b. Transverse timbers of oak pass through holes in cleats which are integral parts of the bottom planks (Fig. 11.3.3).

c. There are no hewn curves in the surviving structure, except for those forming the underside edges of each strake, and no evidence that timbers were bent to achieve the desired overall shape of the boat.

Some of these features are similar to those used in the building of the Ferriby boats which are 1000yrs older and which were excavated from the R. Humber foreshore (Fig. 11.3.1) only 12 miles (19km) north of Brigg (Wright, this volume). However, the details of the plank fastenings are different, and the Ferriby boats are shaped by hewing at the ends.

The reconstruction problem

This is not a 'raft' but a *boat* (defined as a form of water transport in which buoyancy is derived from the displacement of water by a hollowed form with a continuous watertight outer surface). But this is a boat which, by the time she was excavated in 1974, had shrunk and become distorted in shape, and lost her ends, most of her sides and part of the bottom (Fig. 11.3.2). The excavated evidence is thus incomplete: for example, although we know that her planking was fastened using sewing techniques we do not directly know the sewing pattern that was used, as the stitches survived only *within* the holes (Fig. 11.3.3). If we are to attempt to reconstruct, albeit in a theoretical way, the full form and structure of the original boat as she was *c.* 2800yrs ago it is necessary to interpret the surviving remains in the light of all available evidence and try to "fill in" the missing pieces and "iron out" the distorted ones.

The evidence

In addition to the evidence of size and shape and of boatbuilding techniques directly obtainable from the excavated timbers, indirect evidence is available. For example: holes through the upper edge of the fragmentary side strake indicate that there was a second (non surviving) side strake (McGrail, 1981A 90–4, 239–40).

The boat may be set into her spatial and temporal contexts using environmental evidence excavated from the site and dating evidence. Suffice to note here that the environmental evidence suggests that the Brigg boat was used in a shallow

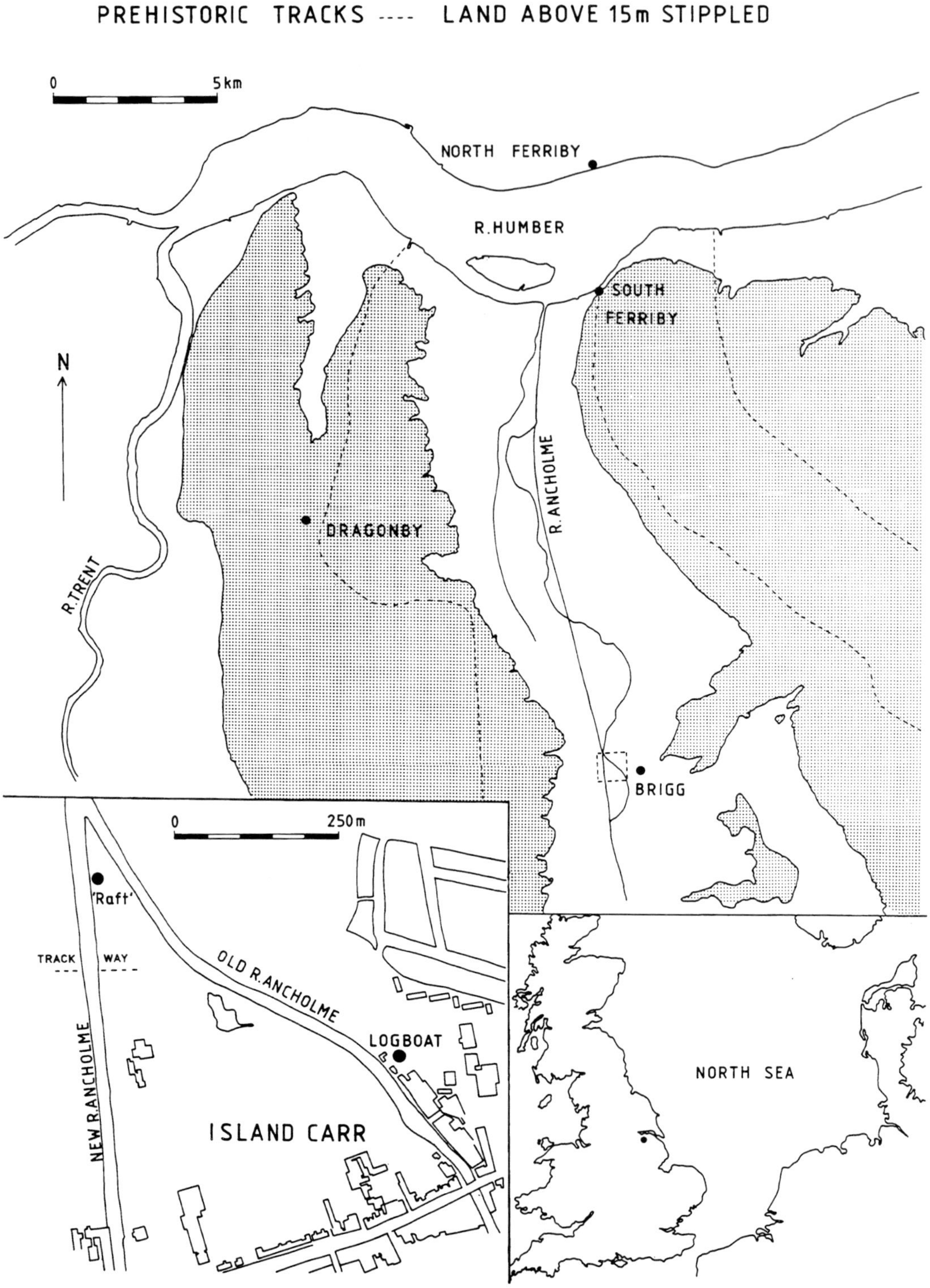

PREHISTORIC TRACKS ---- LAND ABOVE 15m STIPPLED

Figure 11.3.1 Map of the Brigg region. Drawing: National Maritime Museum, Greenwich

Figure 11.3.2 The 'raft' during excavation 1974. NW is at the bottom of the page. The white dots mark sewing holes. The fragmented side strake is towards the left of the picture; the outlying plank fragments towards the top. 2m ranging pole. Photo: National Maritime Museum, Greenwich

Figure 11.3.3 The 4th cleat on the 5th bottom plank. Part of the fragmented side strake is in the foreground. The transverse timber passing through cleat 54 became displaced over the side strake before 1974. White arrows point to some of the sewing holes; the triangle points to the NW. Scales centimetric. Photo: National Maritime Museum, Greenwich.

southerly arm of the Humber estuary where there was brackish water and tidal mud flats with reeds. The dating evidence from 13 radio–carbon assays is that the boat was in use in c. 650 bc, which Switsur (1981) has estimated as equivalent to c. 800BC. Dendrochronological dating was also attempted but the 160yrs floating chronology obtained cannot be related to the few fixed oak chronologies at present available (Hillam, 1981). This dendrochronological examination did, however, reveal additional information about the selection and conversion of timber.

Comparative evidence is also available from several sources, contemporary and non–contemporary, which can be used with caution to suggest solutions to some of the reconstruction problems (McGrail, 1983, 33–4). This may be conveniently discussed under four headings:

Other boat finds
There are only five other European prehistoric sewn plank boat finds:

Three Ferriby boats of the mid–2nd millennium BC (Wright, 1976; this volume). Boats 1 and 2 are now at Greenwich; boat 3 is in Hull.

The boat from Hjortspring, Als, Denmark of c. 350BC (Rosenberg, 1937) now in the National Museum, Copenhagen.

The boat from Ljubljana, Yugoslavia (formerly Laibach, Austria) dated to the period 500 to 100BC (Müllner, 1892). This boat no longer exists.

Although timber from one of the two boat finds near the ancient Adriatic harbour of Enona – now Nin near Zadar, Yugoslavia – is dated by radio–carbon assay to the 3rd or 4th century bc, their excavator has argued from stratigraphic evidence that these boats are 1st century AD (Brusic, this volume).

A number of prehistoric logboats have sewn repairs; for example, the Brigg logboat (not to be confused with the 'raft') dated c. 834 bc, and that from Appleby, Lincolnshire (Figs. 5.1.1, 2) of c. 1100bc (McGrail, 1978). The sewing techniques used in these logboat repairs and in the fastenings of the boats may provide analogies when considering the incomplete evidence from the Brigg 'raft'. Equally, these boats and other contemporary ones, provide evidence of an array of woodworking techniques.

If we restrict consideration to the prehistoric plank boats and logboats of Britain, the principle boatbuilding techniques in use in the period from the mid–2nd millennium bc to the late 1st millennium bc may be listed as:

a. Planks fastened and made watertight by a combination of caulking, longitudinal lath and stitching. The Ferriby boatbuilders used single stitches (individual lashings) whereas other builders seem to

Figure 11.3.4 Box–like boat fitted with a pen: typical of boats used to transport cattle on the rivers of northern Europe in the early 20th century. Photo: National Maritime Museum, Greenwich

Figure 11.3.5 A 20th century *galar* on the R. Vistula at Szezvcin, Poland. Note the method of making the planking watertight. Photo: National Maritime Museum.

have used continuous sewing. The outboard part of the stitch was so arranged that, in general, it did not have direct contact with the foreshore when beaching.

b. Planks converted from half-logs and with worked bevel edges.

c. Planks linked by means of transverse timbers through cleats.

d. Shapes fashioned by hewing.

e. Halved scarfs and dovetail joints.

f. Transom (vertical transverse board) fitted into groove and made watertight, to close an end of a boat.

g. Repairs by sewing, by double-dovetail key, by wooden cleat patches and by inset block or graving piece. Lead repair patches were also used, but the first evidence for this is not until after the date of the Brigg 'raft' – on Holme-Pierrepoint logboat 1 of *c.* 230 bc (McGrail, 1978).

h. Treenails to fasten together structural elements of a boat. Holes and treenails survived with the Appleby logboat but no associated fittings; thus these holes may have been thickness gauges and the treenails may have been plugs rather than fastenings. However, treenails were used to fasten together the multi-part, extended bow of the Hasholme logboat of the late-1st millennium bc (Millett and McGrail, 1985).

i. The stem carved in the solid bow of the Poole logboat of *c.* 295 bc (McGrail, 1978) suggests that plank boats with stems were known in southern Britain during the late prehistoric period; indeed this possibility (and that of keels) may be projected back to the Early Bronze Age if we accept that the shape of one of the log coffins from Loose Howe, N.E. Yorkshire (Elgee, 1949) was based on a boat proto-type.

We must critically examine such evidence, however, before using it in relation to the Brigg 'raft' material. The fact that these techniques were used somewhere in Britain before *c.* 200 bc does not necessarily mean that they were used by the builders of the 'raft'.

Nevertheless this list of techniques does provide some guide to the state of technology in Bronze Age and Early Iron Age southern Britain, and it would seem prudent not to use techniques outside this range in any reconstruction of the Brigg 'raft'.

General Woodworking techniques

It is also theoretically possible to use analogies from roughly contemporary examples of woodworking in trades other than boatbuilding – trackways (causeways), houses, coffins, etc. However, in general the chronological changes in these techniques are poorly documented in Britain and there is little

readily-accessible data, although significant progress is now being made to this end by Orme and Coles (1983; 1985).

Experimental boat archaeology

The building and trials of an authentic replica of an ancient boat can increase our knowledge of past technologies and thus be of use in theoretical reconstruction projects (McGrail, 1985). Although there have been some spectacular replicas built of medieval boats (Crumlin-Pedersen, 1984), there is little published work on the experimental building of boats using pre-historic technology. Of these few sources two may provide information of use in a Brigg 'raft' reconstruction: an experiment in fastening oak planking using yew (*Taxus* sp) withies (Wright, 1984); and the experimental building of a Hjortspring boat replica (*Roar Linde* 71).

Ethnographic evidence

Ethnographic studies enable an archaeologist to escape the bounds of his own culture and become aware of technologies other than his own. They can thus be of great use in the interpretation of archaeological evidence, especially when the latter is incomplete. Such ethnographic analogies do not provide one certain solution to a reconstruction problem, rather a range of possibilities for the archaeologist to consider in conjunction with other information about the excavated material (McGrail, 1983). There are a number of examples of recent sewn plank boats – several of them described in this volume – from which we can learn about the range and variety of sewing techniques. There are also many examples of boats with (near) flat bottoms and even box-like forms (Fig. 11.3.4 – 7) which the Brigg 'raft' may well have been akin to in shape.

Reconstruction

With some boat finds insufficient evidence survives on which to base a theoretical reconstruction, however there appears to be sufficient evidence for the Brigg 'raft' to justify such research (McGrail, 1981A, 243 – 5).

Conversion of Raw materials

Examination of cross sections of planking (Fig. 11.3.8) shows that the strakes were fashioned from oak half-logs. Dendrochronological measurements by Jennifer Hillam have revealed, among other things, that two of the five bottom planks (numbers 1 and 5) were halves of the same log. Planks 3 and 4 were similarly from another log, plank 2 was from a third log, and the fragmentary side strake (plank 6) probably from a fourth. The larger of these logs were *c.* 170yrs old. Hillam (1981) has also shown that two plank fragments, found some 3 to 4m SE of the main part of the boat (Fig. 11.3.2), were from the same logs as planks 4 and 5. As these fragments had similar cross sections to planks 4 and 5 and were found almost in line with them, it is highly probable that planks 4 and 5 were scarfless, each a single plank some 12.20m in length (McGrail 1981A, 94-8, 222-3). Table 11.3.1 gives the deduced *post*-shrinkage sizes of the parent logs from which these planks came. Girths at breast height of the *pre*-shrinkage logs would have been between 2.70m and 3.03m.

Figure 11.3.6 an 18th century *komiega* on the R. Vistula at Gdansk, Poland. Such boats brought grain downstream, the oars at bow and stern being for steering and manoeuvring rather than propulsion. Photo: Town Library, Gdansk

Figure 11.3.7 an 18th century box–like passenger ferry in the port of Gdansk. The boat was worked along a fixed line. Photo: Town Library, Gdansk

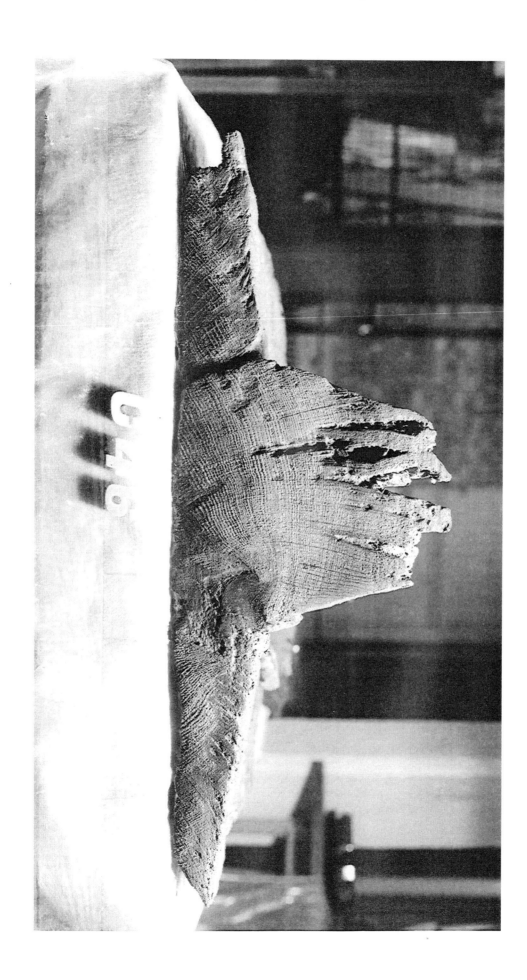

Figure 11.3.8 A section cut through one of the cleats of the 4th bottom plank. Note the medullary rays and growth rings. Photo: National Maritime Museum, Greenwich

Table 11.3.1 Deduced sizes of the parent trees of the Brigg bottom planking

Tree	Bottom Plank	Diameter of Tree by Ring pattern (m)	Diameter of Tree by Ray projection (m)	Approximate Girth (m)
1/5	1	at cleat 14: 0.64	at cleat 12: 0.60 at cleat 16: 0.62–0.64	1.88 2.01
2	2	at cleat 26: 0.72	at cleat 22: (C) at cleat 26: 0.68–0.74	(C) 2.26
3/4	3	at cleat 36: 0.72 to 0.80	at cleat 32: 0.54–0.60 at cleat 36: 0.68–0.70	1.88 2.26
3/4	4	at cleat 46: 0.60 to 0.74	at cleat 42: 0.60 at cleat 46: 0.64–0.68	1.88 2.10
1/5	5	at cleat 55: 0.66 to 0.70	at cleat 52: 0.60 at cleat 55: 0.60–0.70	1.88 2.01

Notes:
A. No allowance made for shrinkage: the pre–shrinkage diameters and girths would have been some 10–12% greater
B. 0.10m has been added to heartwood radii to allow for sapwood and bark
C. No estimate possible

The edges of the strakes were broken and incomplete when excavated but examination revealed regularities in their cross sections (Fig. 11.3.9): inner edges are relatively thin, whilst the outer edges of the two outer bottom planks are relatively thick to provide a seating for the side strakes. The sewing holes, *c.* 1cm diameter, were bored vertically through inner edges of the planking where the wood was at least 12mm thick, some 20mm from the edge, at intervals of *c.* 5.5cm (Fig. 11.3.9). On the outboard edges of the outer bottom plank the sewing holes were bored at an angle so that they emerge through the sides (McGrail, 1981A, fig.4.1.19). In both cases the stitching did not come into direct contact with the ground.

Overall size and shape
The remains as excavated in 1974 had shrunk from their dimensions when built. This shrinkage is insignificant in the longitudinal plane of the planks when compared with that in the radial and tangential planes. Some measure of this shrinkage may be obtained from the ratio of major to minor axis of now eliptical holes (McGrail, 1978, 123–5). Measurement of 170 sewing holes, which are deduced to have been originally bored circular, now eliptical (Fig 11.3.10) indicates that the Brigg 'raft' had shrunk by *c.* 11% across the breadth of each plank. When this shrinkage is allowed for the planks as excavated become broader and opposing edges butt together. The overall dimensions of the boat's bottom then become 12.20 x *c.* 2.27m, giving an L/B ratio of 5.37:1 which is comparable with other

boats of this form (Ferriby, *c.* 7.5; Ljubljana, *c.* 7; Romano–Celtic 'barges', 5.9 to 8.1 – see McGratl, 1981A, 244).

The shape of the bottom (Fig. 11.3.11) was not quite rectangular but generally broadened from the NW end with the natural increase in breadth of each log towards its butt (lower end) – compare the 17th and 18th century flat–bottomed boats *komiega* and *galar* of the R. Vistula, Poland as described by Smolarek (1981, fig.61). However, the Brigg 'raft' had a, possibly unintentional, decreasing breadth close to her SE end: this may well have been because of a reduction in the breadth of some of the available planking, possibly due to damage sustained by the logs at their butt ends during felling or conversion (McGrail,1981A, 224; Heal, 1981, 253–4).

The surviving side strake is insufficiently long to act as a "control" in determining whether the bottom had any longitudinal curvature (rocker). The fragmented SE ends of bottom planks 4 and 5 were found lying on a gentle slope up to the SE, rather than up to the NW as were the main runs of planking (McGratl, 1981A, fig.1.2.1). It was deduced that this change of slope was not due to a built–in rocker but rather the result of the boat settling on a slightly uneven surface during deposition: thus the minimum hypothesis that the boat had a flat bottom was used.

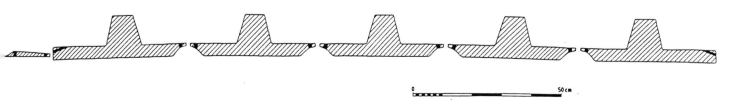

Figure 11.3.9 Idealised diagram of a representative transverse section of the 'raft' as excavated. Note the position of the sticth holes. Drawing: National Maritime Museum, Greenwich

Figure 11.3.10 Part of the side strake with a hole which has shrunk to an elliptical shape. The triangle points to the NW and also indicates the longitudinal axis of the strake's parent tree. Scale centimetric. Photo: National Maritime Museum, Greenwich

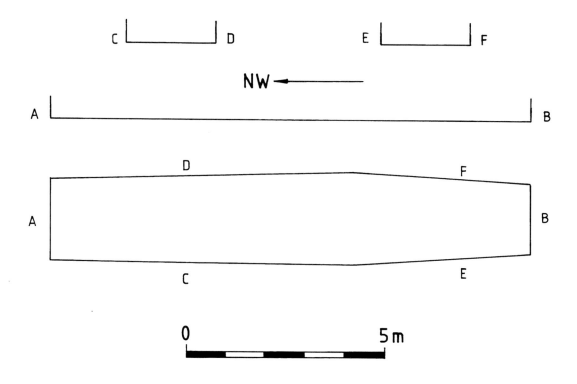

Figure 11.3.11 An outline reconstruction of the 'raft' with a side height of 55cm. Drawing: National Maritime Museum, Greenwich

Figure 11.3.12 Part of bottom plank No2 showing the sewing holes on either side of a split. Photo: National Maritime Museum, Greenwich

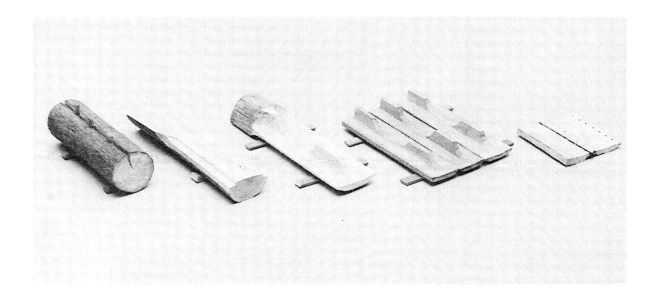

Figure 11.3.13 Small scale models depicting stages in building the bottom of the 'raft'. Photo: National Maritime Museum, Greenwich

Fastenings

Due to the deteriorated condition of the sewing, the pattern of plank fastenings was not readily apparent when re–excavated in 1974. It was noticeable, however, that the sewing holes on adjacent planks were disposed diagonally to one another (Fig. 11.3.3) and not opposite pairs: this was true not only of adjacent planks, which might have been displaced relative to one another during deposition, but also of sewing holes on either side of longitudinal splits in Plank 2 (Fig. 11.3.12) and fragment G4 (McGrail, 1981A, figs. 2.1.6, 2.1.10, 2.3.8).

Most of the sewing patterns used in recent plank boats (e.g. the *mtepe* – see Hornell, 1941) are more complex than the evidence for Brigg suggests, for fragments of only one thread of two–stranded split willow (*Salix* sp) were found within the sewing holes. On the other hand some of the other boats excavated seem to have had a simple sewing pattern and all except those from Ferriby appear to have had continuous stitching rather than lashings. Consideration of all available evidence (McGrail 1981A, 228–234) suggests that the 'raft' planking was sewn with a continuous thread in a zig–zag or helical pattern similar to that in Nin boat 1 (Brusic, 1968). Wedges, as found with the Nin boat and others, would seem to be essential to jam the stitches in helical sewing, but none were found with the Brigg 'raft', nor were there any traces of resin which might have been used as it evidently was in the Hjortspring boat (Rosenberg, 1937) – but evidence for these features may have been lost during the 1888 exposure.

Moss caulking held in the seams by longitudinal laths was noted in 1888, but the precise method used was not recorded. The sequence of caulking/wooden lath/fastening has been widely used to make plank seams watertight, sometimes with the lath and caulking inboard (as in the Ferriby boats), sometimes outboard as in Swiss boats of the 1st – 20th centuries AD recorded by Arnold (1978), and sometimes on both sides as in Maori sewn boats (Best, 1925, 77). Moss was not found *in situ* during the 1974 excavation but small wads of it were found on, and in one case under, the planking. Fragmentary lengths of split hazel laths were found on top of the planking, sometimes associated with the moss. The balance of evidence seems to be that the laths and caulking were originally positioned only inboard, held in place by the stitching.

Transverse timbers

The remains of the transverse timbers were fragmentary and shrunken but it was possible to identify them as squared off, radially–split oak. In the absence of contrary evidence I assume that these timbers were single–piece and extended across the breadth of the boat, each one through the mortices in five cleats. When the estimated near–radial shrinkage of 11% is applied to the remains of the transverse timbers it is seen that, before shrinkage, they would have filled the morticed holes in the fore and aft direction. In general the tangential component of shrinkage is greater than the radial component – in fresh oak it is about twice as great: the corresponding ratio for waterlogged wood is not known but may be assumed to be of a similar order. However, an allowance for tangential shrinkage even as great as 22% does not give the transverse timbers a pre–shrinkage thickness which would fill the

mortices in height. Milne (1982, 10) has noted, however, that in waterlogged wood, "the thinner the timber, the greater the shrinkage" (without precise quantification) and the state of the timbers supports this viewpoint. Tangential shrinkages of waterlogged wood greater than 22% are indeed known (McGrail, 1978) and thus the Brigg transverse timbers may have originally almost filled the cleat mortices, the gap being taken up by wedges – as found in the Ferriby boats (Wright, 1976); or possibly dunnage was laid under the timbers thereby raising them to the top of the morticed holes. A dunnage of light timbers would not only protect the inboard plank fastenings, but would also reduce the adverse free surface effects of bilge water (McGrail, 1981A, 236–237, figs.4.1.14 and 4.1.20).

These transverse timbers were not crossbeams or floor timbers as known in later boats, but they did reinforce the plank fastenings against vertical and horizontal movement when afloat and thus minimise stitch breakages. They were also probably used to align the planking during re–building after periodic dismantling (McGrail, 1981A, 236–8).

The sides

A 5m length of a relatively narrow sixth plank, not recorded in 1888, was excavated in 1974. Because of its position, alongside one of the outer bottom planks, and its cross section (McGrail, 1981A, figs.2.3.11 and 4.1.21) which was quite different from that of the bottom planks, this is interpreted as part of the lowest side strake which had fallen outwards during deposition (McGrail, 1981A, 90–4, 239–40). A similar strake is deduced to have been fastened to the thick outer edge of the other outer bottom plank. Flared side strakes would be desirable because of improved stability, but there is no evidence of such angling out of the sides and therefore the minimum hypothesis of vertical sides is preferred. There are sewing holes along the upper edge of the surviving lower side strake, therefore there was at least one more strake, the breadth of which, however, is conjectural. If it were of similar breadth to the lowest side strake, the total height of the sides measured from the lower surface of the bottom planking would be *c.* 34cm resulting in a L/D ratio of *c.* 36 to 1 which would be roughly twice the value for Romano–Celtic barges (21.5 to 28.3) – see McGrail, 1981B, 24), certain medieval 'punts' (*c.* 17) see McGrail, 1981B, 40) and a reconstruction model of Ferriby boat 1 (*c.* 22), all of them long, narrow boats like Brigg. The 'raft may therefore have had a broader second side strake or even a third. A L/D ratio of 22 to 1 would require an overall side height of *c.* 55cm and this is proposed as an alternative hypothesis to 34cm.

Capacity and stability calculations by John Coates (1981), suggest that this greater side height would be more appropriate, especially when there was free–surface water in the bottom of the boat. Such a side height of 55cm would not be a significant obstruction when loading and unloading animals; and would still allow the crew to use paddles over the sides and ends for propulsion and steering.

Most, if not all, ethnographic and excavated boats of this general form have knees or similar fittings to support the sides – see for example the Ljubljana boat from Yugoslavia

(McGrail, 1981A, fig.4.1.17). There is no surviving evidence for such fittings or for cross beams on the Brigg remains, but such relatively thin (2.5cm) strakes would appear to need some support over the length of 12m., although it has proved possible to build a 1:10 model without them. Possibly the conjectural dunnage would have provided some support to the sides. An alternative hypothesis is that moveable hurdles extended across the boat to pen animals (c.f. Fig. 11.3.4) could also have given transverse support to the hull.

The ends

On re–excavation in 1974 there was no indication of the form of the ends, the method of fastening them to sides and bottom, or indeed their precise position. There appear to be four principal ways of closing the ends of a planked boat to form a watertight shell:

a. By curving the side planking of a stemless boat until the strakes meet in a bevel – no ancient boat finds with this stem solution are known.

b. By running the bottom planking up, clear of the water–line to end on a horizontal plane, as in the 11th century Egernsund find– – see Fig. 2.1.6 (Crumlin–Pedersen, 1977, 8) and the 20th century *weidling* of the R. Aar, Switzerland (McGrail, 1981A fig.4.1.7). Analytically the Ferriby boats may be considered as a variant within this classification as the ends of their plank–keels were hewn to give an upturning curve, which terminated above the waterline.

c. The bottom and side planking terminate as a transom, as in the *galar* of the R. Vistula (Fig. 11.3.5).

d. By running bottom and side planking onto a post or stem.

Boats with beam–keels almost invariably have stems or, in recent times, a stem terminating in a transom above the waterline (McKee, 1983, 79), but those with plank–keels (such as the Ferriby boats and boats in the cog tradition (McGrail, 1981B)), and keel–less boats (such as Bevaix (Arnold, 1975) and Egernsund) may have any type of end, and may have technologically different ends at bow and stern.

There is no suggestion in the keel–less Brigg remains that the boat had stems; nor that the side strakes met on the centre line; nor that the bottom planking had been made to rise above the waterline at the ends. The minimum solution, compatible with the recovered boatbuilding evidence, is therefore that the "raft" had two transom ends. Angled transoms used as ramps (as for example at one end of the Polish *galar*) would have been operationally useful and thus a ramp bow could be an alternative hypothesis. Such transoms may have been fastened by a variant of the Brigg moss/lath/stitch technique or they may have been set into a transverse groove as in some Bronze Age logboats (McGrail, 1978).

The original Brigg "raft"

Bringing together all evidence for the building of the "raft" we can say that, with some certainty, we know what raw materials were used and the sequence of building (Fig. 11.3.13).

a. Oak logs were split longitudinally into two halves; damaged areas were cleaned up.

b. The inner face of each half log was levelled and fashioned with bevels along the edges.

c. Each partly–worked half–log was rotated onto its inner face, bark and most of the sapwood removed, and the upper surface of the plank fashioned leaving cleat blanks at intervals.

d. The bottom planking was positioned on stocks and sewing holes were bored.

e. The planking was fastened by willow sewing over moss caulking and longitudinal laths of hazel.

f. Mortices were cut through the cleats and oak transverse timbers inserted. Dunnage may have been inserted and the timbers wedged within their mortices.

g. The side strakes (Fig. 7.1.13) and ends were fastened in position.

With fair certainty we can also deduce the overall shape and dimensions of the boat (Fig. 11.3.11). With the sides and ends we are on less firm ground, but variant solutions can be suggested compatible both with the surviving evidence and the boat's "technological environment". A model of the minimum solution with a side height of 55cm is shown in Fig. 11.3.13.

Operational performance

One of the main reasons for undertaking the theoretical reconstruction of a boat is so that performance can be assessed – to see what could have safely been carried and in what conditions, and thus throw light on Bronze Age economic activities (McGrail, 1985). John Coates' assessments of the "raft's" performance are shown in Table 11.3.2. These are estimates of freeboard and metacentric height (a measure of transverse stability) when carrying selected conjectural loads (others could have been postulated) in a dry–bilge condition i.e. without allowing for the adverse effects of free–surface water due to leaking seams. All these loads result in a positive metacentric height (GM_t) and may therefore be assessed as stable, but some have "inadequate freeboard" (e.g. 5.9cm or even 12.2cm) by present day standards. But what was the minimum freeboard acceptable to the Bronze Age boatman using this Brigg "raft" on the upper reaches of the Humber estuary? John Coates (1981) has suggested that such a craft should have sufficient freeboard to allow four men to move across the boat from one side to the other without water being shipped over the lower side. Another possible criterion is related to the angle of heel experienced when the lower side is awash (McGrail, 1978, 133). Other criteria may be chosen, but

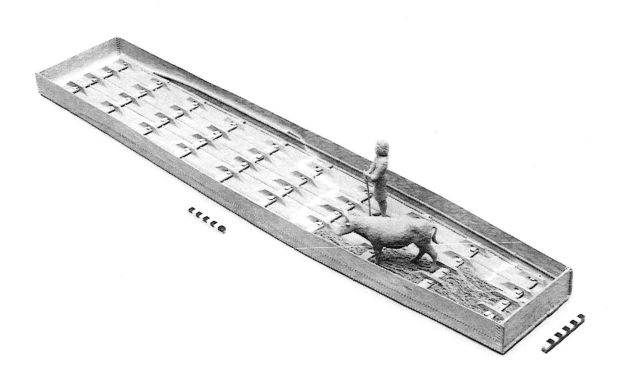

Figure 11.3.14 A 1:10 scale model of the minimum solution Brigg 'raft' reconstruction, with a side height of 55cm. The model was made by Kim Allen. Photo: National Maritime Museum, Greenwich

Table 11.3.2 Displacement, transverse stability (GM$_t$) and freeboard of two hypothetical reconstructions

Load	*Alternative 1. Side and end height 0.34m*			*Alternative 2. Side and end height 0.55m*		
	Displacement (tonnes)	*GM$_t$ (m)*	*Freeboard (m)*	*Displacement (tonnes)*	*GM$_t$ (m)*	*Freeboard (m)*
A. Zero	1.47	7.87	0.286	1.60	7.23	0.491
B. 50 men, standing solidly	4.49	1.85	0.176	4.62	1.76	0.381
C. 75 men, standing solidly	5.99	1.13	0.122	6.12	1.06	0.323
D. 100 sheep and 20 men, all standing solidly	7.69	1.05	0.059	7.82	1.03	0.264
E. 50 cattle and 25 men, all standing solidly	13.95	0.17	(sinks)	14.08	0.17	0.037

Source: Coates, 1981

until there is general agreement on which criterion to use, comparisons between the theoretical performance of different boats will not be possible.

Other parameters also need to be standardised, for example: the height and weight of the average crewman; and the types of load and their specific or bulk densities. At my suggestion John Coates used the following weights in his Brigg calculations:

Crewman of 60kg
Sheep of 50kg
Cow of 225kg

The figure of 60kg was chosen on the assumption that a Bronze Age crewman would be a short, lean, wiry person; however, different weights (which may include equipment) have been used by other investigators:

50kg Sutton Hoo boat 2 – Corlett in NMM Greenwich display.

70kg Greek Trireme – Foley et al, 1982.

72kg Hjortspring – Rosenberg, 1937.

80kg Gokstad 1 – Christensen, 1975.

At present there are no readily available estimates of the size and weight of prehistoric animals. The weights used in the Brigg calculations are therefore questionable. I am indebted to Peter Reynolds of the Iron Age Experimental Farm at Butser, Hampshire for the information that 20th century breeds which may be akin to prehistoric animals have the following weight ranges:

Dexter cattle 400 to 500kg
Shetland sheep 45 to 65kg
Soay sheep 25 to 45kg

If these weights, and the corresponding spaces occupied by individual animals, were used in stability/free–board calculations significantly different performance figures would be obtained for some of the roles listed in Table 11.3.2. Further research into prehistoric vital statistics is thus required before agreed, reliable data can be used in performance calculations.

Conclusions

The direct, indirect and analogous evidence is sufficient to formulate several hypothetical reconstructions of the Brigg "raft" differing in details. There undoubtedly remains uncertainty about the precise form of the ends and sides, but the minimum solution reconstruction offered in this paper is firmly based on the surviving evidence, and is not anachronistic but compatible with the find's "technological" environvment.

When further, well–dated evidence for prehistoric boat–building is obtained it may well be necessary to re–assess the reconstructions described in this paper. We may therefore look forward to future work on this topic.

More research is also required into the parameters upon which performance calculations are based. And international agreement on the criteria to be used when comparing the performance of different boat finds is essential if progress is to be made in this field.

Note 1. *Dating*. The following convention is used:

bc, ad = dates in radiocarbon years

BC, AD = dates in calendar years.

As a general guide, 100 to 300 years has to be added to radiocarbon dates in the 1st millennium bc to obtain an approximation of the calendar date (BC).

Acknowledgements

I am most grateful to Dr Jerzy Litwin for making available to me Figs. 11.3.6, 7; and to my colleagues Veryan Heal, Dr Eric Kentley and Dr Richard Clarke for their constructive criticism of an early draft of this paper.

References

Arnold B. 1975 'Gallo–Roman boat from Bay of Bevaix, L. Neuchâtel, Switzerland.' *IJNA* 4, 123–6.

Arnold B. 1978 'Gallo–Roman boat finds in Switzerland.' in Taylor J. du P. and Cleere H. (eds) *Roman Shipping and Trade*, 31–6. CBA Research Report 24.

Best E. 1925 *Maori Canoe*, Dominion Museum New Zealand Bulletin No.7.

Brusic Z. 1968 'Istrazivanje anticke luke kod Nina.' *Diadora*, 4, 203–9.

Coates J. 1981 'Safe carrying capacity of the hypothetical reconstruction.', in McGrail S. (ed) 1981A 261–9.

Christensen A.E. 1975 'The famous Viking longship.' in Almgren B. *The Viking* 247–282. Nordbook Gothenburg.

Crumlin–Pedersen O. 1977 *Traeskibto*. Council of the Danish Timber Trade.

Crumlin–Pedersen O. 1984 'Experimental boat archaeology in Denmark.' in McGrail S. (ed) *Aspects of Maritime Archaeology and Ethnography*, 97–122. NMM, Greenwich.

Elgee H.W. and F. 1949 'An early Bronze Age burial in a boat–shaped wooden coffin from N.E. Yorkshire.' *P.P.S.*, 15, 87–106.

Foley V. Soedal W. and Doyle J. 1982 'Trireme displacement estimates.' *I.J.N.A.* 11, 305–318.

Heal S.V.E. 1981 'Tools useable in the construction of the "raft".' in McGrail S. (ed) 1981, 253–260.

Hillam J. 1981 'Tree–ring analysis.' in McGrail S. (ed) 1981A, 103–116.

Hornell J. 1941 'Sea–going *mtepe* and *dau* of the Lamu archipelago.' *M.M.* 27, 54–68.

Hunt A. 1907–8 'Viking raft or Pontoon Bridge.' *Saga Book of the Viking Club* 5, 355–362.

McGrail S. 1975 'Brigg "raft" re–excavated.' *Lincs. History and Archaeology*, 10, 5–13.

McGrail S. 1978 *Logboats of England and Wales*, NMM Greenwich Archaeological Series No.2. BAR (Oxford) 51.

McGrail S. 1981A (ed) *Brigg "raft" and her Prehistoric Environment.* NMM Greenwich Archaeological Series No.6. BAR (Oxford) 89.

McGrail S. 1981B *Rafts, Boats and Ships.* HMSO.

McGrail S. 1983 'Interpretation of archaeological evidence for maritime structures.' in Annis P. (ed) *Sea Studies*, 33–46. NMM Greenwich.

McGrail S. 1985 'Experimental boat archaeology — some methodological considerations.' in Crumlin–Pedersen O. and Viner M. (eds) *Sailing into the Past.* Roskilde, Denmark.

McKee E. 1983 *Working boats of Britain.* Conway Maritime Press.

Millett M. and McGrail S. 1985 'Hasholme logboat.' *Antiquity* 59, 117–120.

Milne G. 1982 'Recording timberwork on the London Waterfront.' in McGrail S. (ed) *Woodworking Techniques before AD 1500 7–23.* NMM Greenwich Archaeological Series No.7. BAR (Oxford) S.129.

Müllner, A., 1892 'Ein schiff im Laibacher Moore,' *Argo* 1, 1–7.

Orme B.J. and Coles J.M. 1983, 1985 'Prehistoric Woodworking from the Somerset Levels.' in *Somerset Levels Papers* 9, 19–43; 11, 7–50.

Rosenberg G. 1937 *Hjortspring–fundet.* Copenhagen.

Smolarek P. 1981 'Types of Vistula Ships in the 17th and 18th centuries.' *Transport Museums* 8, 85–116.

Switsur V.R. 1981 'Radiocarbon dating.' in McGrail S. (ed.) 1981A 117–121.

Thropp J. 1877 'An ancient raft found at Brigg, Lincolnshire.' *Assoc. Architectural Societies Reports and Papers*, 19 part 1, 95–7.

Wright E.V. 1976 *N. Ferriby Boats*, NMM, Greenwich. Monograph 23.

Wright E.V. 1984 'Practical experiments in boat stitching.' in McGrail, S. (ed) *Aspects of Maritime Archaeology and Ethnography*, 58–84. NMM, Greenwich.

Note IJNA = Int. J. Nautical Archaeology
MM = Mariner's Mirror
PPS = Proc. Prehistoric Society

Reprinted from:

McGrail S. and Kentley E. (eds) *Sewn Plank Boats*: 165–194. British Archaeological Reports, S276. (1985).

PAPER 11.4

EXPERIMENTAL BOAT ARCHAEOLOGY – SOME METHODOLOGICAL CONSIDERATIONS

"Those who fall in love with practice without science are like a sailor who steers a ship without a helm or compass, and who never can be certain whither he is going."
Leonardo da Vinci

An experienced boatbuilder, seaman or naval architect can look at a boat or examine lines plans and constructional drawings and, for those forms, and rigs within his experience, assess capacity and likely performance. Such assessments cannot readily be applied to the evidence for ancient boats (be this excavated remains, iconographic representations or documentary descriptions) for three main reasons:

a. boat–finds are incomplete and distorted; as are early written descriptions

b. diagrammatic, decorative or votive representations with unknown conventions are not working drawings.

c. the investigator may be confronted with unfamiliar shapes and features.

As in all branches of archaeology (see for example Rahtz, 1982 on the problems of reconstructing timber buildings from archaeological evidence) it is necessary to transform the partial and often distorted excavated evidence into models – theoretical, diagrammatic, mathematical or three–dimensional analogues – which represent the (several) most likely form(s) and structure of the original artifact: and which, if successfully tested, may enable us to deduce function and performance. This logical activity, which proceeds backwards in time from present–day observation of the evidence towards the reality in antiquity has been called extracting filters and unscrambling the evidence by Muckelroy (1978, 165–9). For a boat–find the aim of such work (in a theoretical way and not with actual timbers) is to re–assemble the excavated remains and to add missing elements. In some cases insufficient evidence may survive to define the full form of the ancient boat. In other cases there may be a unique solution to this reconstruction problem (see the Greek trireme described by Coates in this volume); for others again, several versions (Fig. 11.4.1, 2, 3) may arise (Coates, 1977, 216). When such hypothetical reconstructions can be made, our knowledge of technology, trade and seafaring in former times may be extended by deductions made about:

a. building techniques

b. the uses to which the boat might have been put

c. the likely performance she may have attained.

Figure 11.4.1 Ferriby boat 1 during excavation from an intertidal site in the river Humber in 1946. The oak planks are sewn together with yew lashings. Radiocarbon analyses indicate a date in the mid–2nd millemium BC

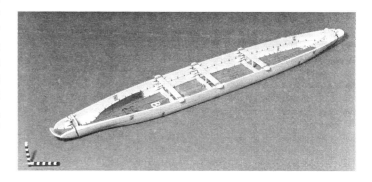

Figure 11.4.2 A 1:10 scale model of the ' minimum – solution' reconstruction of Ferriby boat 1. The dark colour indicate those parts excavated: the remainder is conjectural

347

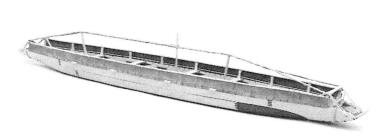

Figure 11.4.3 A more complex reconstruction model of Feriby boat 1, incorporating a third strake of hide and a hogging truss

These estimates of performance may be made by hand calculations, computer work, small–scale models, or by the building and trials of a full–scale replica.

Such an investigation into a boat's performance is in the spirit of scientific enquiry, an important aspect of which is the formulation of hypotheses (models) based on observable data, which are then tested by repeatable experiment. The results of such an experiment may refute or reinforce the hypothesis or suggest how it may be modified. Such a process is iterative and one part, the test of the hypothesis, cannot be divorced from the other, the formulation of the hypothesis. Yet, in the archaeological discipline, it is the test by replica building which is most frequently highlighted and has been given the name of experimental archaeology.

Without the less–spectacular process of hypothesis formulation or model building, experimental archaeology cannot be undertaken: and if it is undertaken after inadequate or ill–based hypothetical reconstruction any conclusions must be invalid. In his exposition of model building methods David Clarke demonstrated that the building and trials of a replica is only one of several methods available to the scientifically–orientated research worker and one that may be least effective in cost/benefit terms (1972, 10–13). Clarke, in fact, placed the building of replicas, 'material hardware analogues', at a low level in his hierarchy of models, roughly equivalent to ethnographic analogies; and much inferior to mathematical and systems models, and he allowed them only elementary predictive capacity.

Although we may not have such a low opinion of replica building as David Clarke, I believe that many of us now accept that, in the past, much experimental work in Maritime Archaeology has been of slight consequence when measured by the standards of authenticity and cost/benefit. It is also true that some of the information being sought by these full scale experiments was already available by ethnographic analogy or in documentary sources. Furthemore, small scale model and experiments could well have been more cost effective than those at full scale, and simple mathematical assessments could

have gone a long way towards answering questions about performance or (equally valuably) have eliminated certain hypotheses because they were impracticable. The physical laws of nature as manifest in assessment of displacement, freeboard and draught, strength and stability, apply to all floating vessels and thus can be validly used to assess hypothetical reconstructions. These methods, and small–scale model building (and possibly tank and wind–tunnel tests), are more appropriate than full–scale replica building in the early stages of an investigation into the performance of an ancient boat find.

Table 11.4.1 Levels of experimental research

---

1. A simulation – a copy which represents the original form; used primarily for display and first–level education, and possibly also for publicity and fund raising.
2. Building a copy using authentic materials and methods.
3. Testing the functions of an authentic copy.

Table 11.4.2 Experimental boat replica experiments classified by aim.

A. To establish by a comprehensive experiment, using authentic methods and materials, how an ancient boat or raft was built and used, and to estimate performance.

B. To establish how *part* of a boat or raft was built (i.e. making watertight joints), using authentic methods and materials.

C. To establish (with authentic methods and materials) how *part* of a boat or raft (e.g. rudder or sail) was built and used, and to estimate effects on performance: this may include trials of the particular part installed in a hull of known capabilities.

D. To undertake A, B or C in a *less–than–comprehensive manner* (e.g. to accept a hypothetical reconstruction generated elsewhere or to use construction drawings produced by others) and/or in a *less–than–authentic* manner (e.g. use of un–authentic raw materials) to gain experience in the theory and practice of experimental boat archaeology.

E. To undertake A, B or C in a *less–than–comprehensive* and/or *less–than–authentic* manner to investigate aspects of building (e.g. effectiveness of authentic tools or the production of authentic caulking); or to investigate certain aspects of use (e.g. loading and carriage of horses, stability, speed, or non–instrumental navigation). Experimental workers with such an aim would plan to be authentic in all aspects they considered would affect the functions being tested; other aspects need not be authentic.

However, some of the models and techniques used by the naval architect require to be calibrated for use in unfamiliar areas of research. Naval architectural methods of calculating such aspects of performance as speed, windward ability, or movement in a seaway, while based on established theories do rely on some idealisation of the phenomena concerned. Assessment of the factors responsilble for the difference between prediction and outcome is essentially empirical and as the methods of assessment and the supporting experimental work have generally been evolved to deal with metal ships driven by mechanical means, they need not necessarily apply unmodified to wooden boats propelled by oar or sail. In the particular cases of speed and sailing naval architects prefer to have practical confirmation of calculated assessments, due to the theoretical unpredictability of the formation of vortices and the consequent energy loss (Coates, 1977, 224–6).

Thus, after feasibility studies of various hypotheses have been undertaken, the building of a full size replica of an ancient boat may be the only way that we can quantify the full array of variables involved and thus enable naval architectural models to be calibrated and performance to be accurately assessed. In addition, certain questions about ancient building techniques may only be answerable by full–scale replica building, although this need not always require an entire boat to be built, merely a portion.

In certain circumstances therefore, especially in the early stages of establishing standard procedures in Maritime Archaeology, the building and trials of a full–size replica boat may be justifiable and, indeed, essential, if the full range of information from an excavation is to be obtained. Nevertheless, for many projects small–scale experiments and naval architectural assessments should suffice. It is, for example, questionable whether a full–scale replica need be built of each one of the five Skuldelev boats: one or two authentic, problem–orientated replica projects set up on a sound theoretical basis should enable the investigators to evaluate the other finds by means which are less demanding in resources.

Experimental Research

Coles (1977; 1979, 36–42) has suggested that there are three levels of research in experimental archaeology; level 3 contributing more to our understanding of the past than level 2, which itself contributes more than level 1: see Table 11.4.1.

Experiments to date in boat archaeology, when considered by their published reports, do not readily fit into these categories, unless they are all assigned to level 1. A more useful classification may result from an analysis of the aims of these experiments. Where these aims are not explicitly defined by those involved they may be deduced from the published achievements of the experiments. Such an analysis suggests the classification by aim shown in Table 11.4.2

Examples of experiments with these aims include:

Class A. Heyerdahl's log raft and reed raft replicas (1978) Ellmers Husum skin boat replica (1984) .

Johnstone's Kalnes skin boat replica (1978, 204–13). Severin's skin boat and sewn plank replicas (1978, 1982).
Napoleon III's trireme (Lehmann, 1982).
Whether all these experiments achieved the aim they set themselves or I have allotted to them is questionable. They all involve non–specific replicas based on general features interpreted from iconographic and documentary evidence, supplemented by ethnograpllic analogies and naval architectural knowledge. In certain cases, one may question whether all possible interpretations of such evidence may have been considered; whether the replicas are in all respects consistant with the technology of the period and area under investigation; and whether the limited evidence available will bear the weight of deductions made by the experimentors.

Class B. Wright's experiment to reproduce a watertight joint, as used in the prehistoric sewn–plank Ferriby boats (1984).

Class C. Heyerdahl's work on *guares* (centreboards) (1978, 204–13). Roberts' work on square sails (1984).

Class D. The Greenwich *faering* (Fig. 11.2.10) experiment (McGrail and McKee, 1974).

Class E. Many Scandinavian replicas (Crumlin–Pedersen, 1984) may be in this class (or in D), as may Doran's work on Formosan sailing rafts (1978), and David Lewis's (1972) work on Oceanic methods of navigation. Building a plastic logboat, ballasted to investigate speed and stability could be a further example.

To be valid, class A experiments would have to conform to the sequence listed in Table 11.4.3; classes B to E would have to conform in as much as their defined aim required.

Table 11.4.3 Sequence of action in a class A boat replica experiment

---

1. Establishment of hypothetical reconstruction(s) firmly bassed on evidence. This may need to be reviewed when the excavated material is re–assembled after conservation.

2. Rigorous testing of such reconstruction(s) by:
   a. calculations and simulations
   b. small–scale models (possibly   elimination of
      including tank and wind   some (or all)
      tunnel tests)   reconstructions
   c. outside critiscisn
   Some, or even most, projects may finish here (without a publication).

3. Building a full–scale replica of selected hypothetical reconstruction(s) by authentic means.

4. Trials to evaluate performance measured against some generally agreed standards.

5. Publication.

Note: There should be feedback to earlier phases at all stages of this sequence

---

Experimental Results

The results from boat replica experiments to date are generally disappointing when measured by their contribution to knowledge of ancient technology and seafaring, rather than by their gains in self–education, social benefit or national prestige. Non–specific replicas such as *Kon Tiki*, *Ra* 1 and 2, *Brendan* and *Sohar* have demonstrated the seaworthiness of rafts and boats built in these particular ways and have indicated the length of hull life to be expected in ocean conditions. *Ra* and *Kon Tiki* have also demonstrated the practicability of one–way drift voyages. Thus these replicas have contributed something to our *general* knowledge of early technology and seafaring, but how this should be applied to *specific* questions about prehistoric and medieval times is not at all clear.

When we turn to the experimental building and use of replicas of specific boat–finds we find that, although something has been learnt about aspects of building, only very generalised conclusions about performance have emerged As students of seafaring in antiquity we seek answers to questions about cargo capacity, reliability, typical speeds over the ground, closeness to wind, numbers in crew, etc. so that quantitative assessments can be made of early maritime trade and seafaring, and so that changes over time can be objectively documented. In fact, the only real guidance we get so far on such matters comes not from experimental replicas but from theoretical assessments by naval architects, for example Ewan Corlett (1978) on the Graveney boat (Figs. 11.4.5, 6) O. Crumlin–Pedersen (i.p.) on Skuldelev 1 and 3; and John Coates on the prehistoric boats Ferriby 1 (1978) and Brigg 2 (1981) – see figures 11.3.2, 11.3.14. All these were done by hand or by computer assisted calculation from reconstruction lines, plans, drawings or small–scale models.

Research Design

If future boat replica experiments are to be made more productive than they have formerly been it is essential that research programmes be thought out clearly, from the identification of the aims of the project and the selection of the model to be copied, to the publication of a comprehensive report. The main points to be considered may be listed under eight headings:

Motives. Aims of project to be defined–class A to E (see Table 11.4.2)

Model. Choice of model to be copied – general or specific. Establishment and evaluation of hypothetical reconstruction(s): some projects may end at this stage (see Table 11.4.3).

Money. Resources to be quantified.

Management/Men. Choice of project management. and of project team, especially the input of boatbuilding, seamanship and archaeological expertise. Until a reservoir of experience is established there may be difficulties in blending these inputs.

Map reference. Where to build.

Materials. Choice of raw materials and tools.

Methods. Choice of building methods, of trials programme (short term and long term) and of methods of publication.

I have elsewhere discussed aspects of such a research design (1975; 1977B): suffice in this present paper to highlight seven further points

a. Iterative Research None of the eight main points listed above is independent of the others, and there will be an iterative process throughout the planning phase: thus, for example, the fourth to eighth points must become compatible with the first three; and should it be found that only a limited range of ttimber is available, the aims of the project may have to be re–formulated.

b. Aims The class of research, and hence the aims of the experimental phase of the project, is probably best established by listing the questions to which answers are sought and then matching costs against resources. The classification A, B, C, D or E (Table 11.4.2) will determine not only how comprehensive the programme is to be and the degree of authenticity required, but also the range of validity of the experimental results and their potential relevance to knowledge of early boatbuilding and seamanship. It is unlikely that a project will remain consistant and logical within itself unless aims are clear. Aims may need to be revised as problems are solved (or become insoluble) and as resources ebb and flow.

c. Authentic materials Obtaining timber of the correct species and dimensions is a special problem. Not just that the budget may not allow purchase, but that trees of the size formerly used, and curved limbs may not be readily obtainable nowadays. Thus laminations and additional scarf joints may be unavoidable, but if contrived with a proper understanding of the material properties of wood need not compromise functional authenticity.

d. Building aids If an authentic copy is to be obtained then building aids, be they moulds, paper patterns, boat ells or levels or direct measurements, have to be used. I can see no way round this superficial dilemma until much more experience in replica building has been acquired. 'Building by eye' – if this is indeed possible – should be a separate experiment in which mistakes do not matter, and indeed the builders should profit from them.

e. Ancient Units Measurements used in the experiment should be present–day ones i.e. metric. The establishment of ancient units of measurements, if undertaken at all, should be a separate research project. Natural units of measurements, such as the *thumb* and the *foot* and the *ell*, do appear to be deeply ingrained in many cultures and it has to be recognised that such approximate units would probably have been

Figure 11.4.4 The 9/10th century Graveney boat excavation in 1970. Ole Crumlin–Pedersen in the right foreground

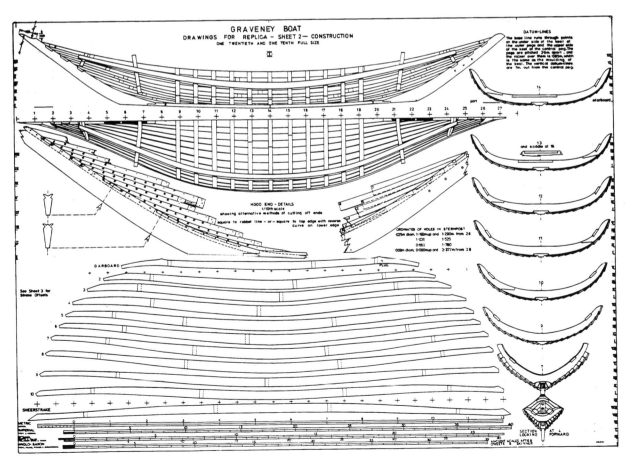

figure 11.4.5 Construction drawings for a replica of the Graveney boat, by Eric McKee

used to determine key measurements of the original boat, and that timber scantlings would have been chosen from simple multiples or fractions of them. Nevertheless, by definition they vary from man to man, and even when standardised in later times they varied regionally. The investigation of such local standards may be a by-product of a boat replica experiment, but should not intrude into the main task of producing an authentic copy.

f. Time taken and Manpower calculation The time taken to build a replica and the knowledge of past technologies, economies and manpower used will bear little relationship to the time taken in former times. In an experiment there are inevitably periods of stagnation and indeed regression: much learning and re-learning is involved. This lengthening of the time scale may introduce a degree of unauthenticity into the experiment in that, for example, timber may not be used until some considerable time after it has been felled.

g. Publication The publication of a class A archaeological experiment will be the final phase of a project which began with the examination of excavated evidence, or possibly at an even earlier stage (Figs 1.1.5 and 11.8.1). To enable others to judge the authenticity of the replica, both excavated and comparative evidence should be published alongside the hypothetical reconstruction(s), and the publication should document the logical steps taken to transform evidence into reconstruction. The testing of the hypothetical reconstructions and the trials programme used by the replica should also be documented so that the validity of the trial results can be evaluated. Lectures and museum displays can further disseminate information about the boat; the experimental theory and the research design and execution thereby become subject to criticism which should stimulate further consideration of both theoretical and practical aspects of the project.

Conclusions

Experimental archaeology or the construction and testing of replicas of ancient boats can increase our knowledge of past technologies, economies and seafaring and thus it is a valid and valuable archaeological technique provided that it is problem orientated and that it is preceded by a stage of theoretical model building and rigorous evaluation of the hypothetical reconstructions generated.

Some classes of experiment may be repeatable in similar conditions or modified in the light of experience gained, and thus the original findings confirmed or changed. But Class A experiments in particular are expensive in resources, and economic considerations may mean that for all practical purposes the experiment is not repeatable. It is thus especially important that such experiments be well chosen and planned,

rigorously undertaken and subjected to critical appraisal from all angles and at all phases.

By such cost-benefit analysis we can ensure maximum value for money and reliable and scientifically valuable results should be obtained. Projects tackled in this manner build up a wealth of expertise both in experimental work *per se* and in aspects of ancient technology and seafaring. As Coles (1979, 40) and Crumlin-Pedersen (1984) have pointed out, this is a 'reservoir of experience' which at present is usually dispersed at the end of each project. Maritime archaeology would benefit if a permanent group comparable with the land archaeological groups working at Lejre in Denmark and at Little Butser and West Stow in Britain, could be formed to foster boat archaeological experiments and to ensure that expertise was handed on.

Acknowledgements

Several of the ideas in this paper were formulated in discussions with John Coates and I am indebted to him for this. I am also grateful to him and to Gillian Hutchinson for their criticism of an earlier draft.

The illustrations are copyright, National Maritime Museum.

References

Clarke D.L. 1972 'Models and paradigms in Archaeology.' in Clarke D.L. (ed) *Models in Archaeology*, 1–60.

Coates, J.F. 1977 'Hypothetical reconstructions and the Naval Architect.' in McGrail S. (ed) 1977A, 215–226.

Coates J.F. 1978 'Information published in the Archaeological Gallery, National Maritime Museum, Greenwich.'

Coates J.F. 1981 'Safe carrying capacity of the hypothetical reconstruction.' in McGrail S. (ed) *Brigg raft*, 261–9. British Archaeological Reports Oxford 89. NMM Archaeological Series No 6.

Coles J.M. 1977 'Experimental Archaeology – theory and principles.' in McGrail S. (ed), 1977A, 233–244.

Coles J. 1979 *Experimental Archaeology*, Academic Press.

Corlett E. 1978 'Appreciation of the lines.' in Fenwick V. (ed) *Graveney Boat*, 303–6, British Archaeological Reports. Oxford 53. NMM Archaeological Series No. 3.

Crumlin-Pedersen O.1984 'Experimental Boat Archaeology in Denmark.' in McGrail S (ed) 1984.

Crumlin-Pedersen O. i.p. 'Cargo Ships of Northern Europe AD 800– 1300.' in *Proceedings of the 2nd Waterfront Archaeology Conference*, Bergen 1983.

Doran E. 1978 'Seaworthiness of Sailing Rafts.' *Anthropological Journal of Canada* 16,17–22.

Ellmers D. 1984 'Earliest evidence for skin boats in Late Palaeolithic Europe.' in McGrail S. (ed) 1984.

Heyerdahl T. 1978 *Early Man and the Ocean*. Allen and Unwin.

Johnstone P. 1972 'Bronze Age Sea Trial.' *Antiquity* 46, 269–274.

Lehmann L. Th. 1982 'A trireme's tragedy.' *International Journal of Nautical Archaeology* 11, 145–151.

Lewis D. 1972 *We the Navigators*. Canberra National University Press.

McGrail S. 1975 'Models, replicas and experiments in Nautical Archaeology.' *Mariner's Mirror* 61, 3–8. London.

McGrail S. (ed) 1977A *Sources and Techniques in Boat Archaeology*, British Archaeological Reports, Oxford S29, National Maritime Museum Greenwich, Archaeological Series 1.

McGrail S. 1977B 'Aspects of Experimental Archaeology.' in McGrail S. (ed) 1977A, 245–258.

McGrail S. (ed) 1984 *Aspects of Maritime Archeology and Ethnography*, National Maritime Museum, Greenwich.

McGrail S. and McKee E. 1974, *Building and Trials of the Replica of an ancient boat: the Gokstad faering*, National Maritime Museum, Greenwich, Maritime Monograph 11.

Muckelmoy K. 1978 *Maritime Archaeology*, CUP, Cambridge.

Rahtz P. A. 1982 'Architectural reconstruction of timber buildings from archaeological evidence.' *Vernacalar Architecture* 13, 39–41. London.

Roberts O. 1984 'Viking sailing performance.' in McGrail S. (ed) 1984.

Severin T. 1978 *The Brendan Voyage*, Hutchinson, London

Severin T 1982 *The Sindbad Voyage*, Hutchinson, London.

Wright E. V. 1984 'Practical experiments in boat stitching.' in McGrail S. (ed) 1984.

Reprinted with permission from:

Crumlin–Pedersen O. and Vinner M. (ed) *Sailing into the Past*: 8–17. Viking Ship Museum, Roskilde. (1986).

354

PAPER 11.5

ASSESSING THE PERFORMANCE OF AN ANCIENT BOAT –
THE HASHOLME LOGBOAT

Methods of Assessment

The value of performance estimates (that is, stability and trim, cargo capacity and speed) is directly related to the quality of the data used and the appropriateness of the assessment techniques (McGrail 1986, 8–9). Boat–finds are almost always incomplete and may frequently be shrunken and distorted: thus, as a first step towards performance assessment, the original form and structure have to be theoretically reconstructed, and the details of the propulsion outfit deduced. An authentic reconstruction drawing may be defined as one that is firmly based on the excavated evidence and one that incorporates hypothetical additions only after rigorous argument. Once such a drawing is available, the performance of an ancient boat may be assessed in several ways:

a. By eye. General assessments by an experienced seaman, boatbuilder or naval architect.

b. Using simple coefficients. As performance is related to shape, such coeffficients as L/B, C_m or C_b can give some idea of a boat's capabilities.

c. Using hydrostatic curves (Fig. 11.5.1). The boat's transverse section areas and underwater volumes are calculated, and curves are plotted relating key features of the underwater geometry of the hull to various waterlines whIch are identified by draft (distance between lowest point of hull and the waterline). From this set of curves deductions may be made about performance. (McGrail 1987, 12–15).

d. Small–scale models. Models may be tested in tanks and, if fitted with sails, in wind tunnels to evaluate performance by empirical means.

e. Computer work. An effective way of investigating certain aspects of performance, esspecially when there are alternative reconstructions to be investigated.

f. Building a full–scale replica and undertaking trials. An expensive and lengthy process if authenticity is to be achieved and scientifically valuable results obtained. An essential prelude must be to evaluate possibilities using methods (a) to (e).

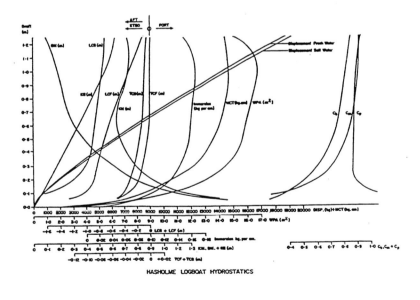

HASHOLME LOGBOAT HYDROSTATICS

BM)	
KM)	see Fig. 2
KB)	
LCB	longitudinal centre of buoyancy
TCB	transverse centre of buoyancy
LCF	longitudinal centre of flotation

TCF	transverse centre of flotation
MCT	moment to change trim
WPA	waterplane area
C_b	block coefficient
C_m	midships coefficient
C_p	prismatic coefficient

Figure 11.5.1 Hydrostatics for the Hasholme logboat. Compiled by Keith Hamilton–Smith of Burness, Corlett & Partners

Of these six methods, the use of hydrostatic curves seems to be the most cost effective in assessing a boat's stability, trim and cargo capacity at varying drafts. Speed potential may best be estimated using a number of simple coefficients (Toby 1986; McGrail 1987, 195–8). In the rare cases when authentic replicas are built, practical results of trials (method f.) may profitably be compared with theoretical assessments (method a. to e.). In this way 20th century methods of assessment may be calibrated for use with data from ancient boats

Use of Hydrostatic Curves

Stability. There are several stability concepts (Rawson and Tupper 1976–7), but initial static stability is fundamental and *sine qua non*. The transverse metacentric height (GM_t) for a particular condition is a measure of this stability, as it gives an indication of the size of the righting moment generated when a boat is heeled through a small angle. From Fig. 11.5.2 it can be seen that: $GM_t = KM_t - KG_t$.

KG_t can be calculated for a boat carrying a particular load; and KM_t can be read off the hydrostatic curve (Fig. 11.5.1) at the appropriate draft (McGrail 1987, 15); and thus the GM_t is obtained.

Trim. The movement of the centre of buoyancy and the centre of flotation as the draft varies, may be read off the appropriate curve (Fig 11.5.1; LCB and TCB for buoyancy; LCF and TCF for flotation), and thus the effects on trim (difference between drafts at bow and at stern) may be estimated. The curve MCT enables estimates to be made of the effects on trim of adding or subtracting load at various stations. (McGrail 1987, 14).

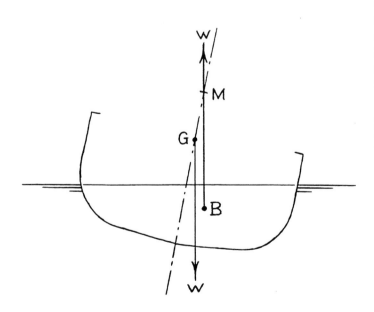

Figure 11.5.2 Diagram illustrating Transverse Stability.
Drawing: John Coates

Carrying capacity. The payload a boat can carry may be determined by displacement/draft/stability calculations, taking

into account the space available for cargo and the reserve of buoyancy available beyond that at light displacement, i.e. without crew, cargo or equipment. (McGrail 1987, 20–22). Before such calculation can be attempted, certain parameters must be evaluated:

bulk density of the cargo.
the number in the crew, their station in the boat and their average weight.
the operational drafts of the boat.

Cargo. If elements of cargo were excavated with the boat or if there is other evidence to indicate what was generally being traded in that region at about that time, then a representative cargo may be used in the calculations. Otherwise an indication of the boat's capabilities as a cargo carrier may best be obtained by using a variety of cargoes with a range of bulk densities (McGrail 1978, 132). For example:

Iron ore or Stone with a bulk density of $c.2500$ Kg/m³.
Oak timber with a bulk density of $c.800$ Kg/m³.
Grain or Meat with a bulk density of $c.680$ Kg/m³.
Peat (dry) with a bulk density of $c.435$ Kg/m³.

Crew. Failing direct evidence, ethnographic evidence may be used to estimate the minimum number of crew necessary to work the boat and to determine their stations in the boat. In recent publications different authors have used weights for the average ancient man varying from 50 to 72 kg (McGrail 1987, 201). Until authoritative guidance becomes available from analysis of excavated skeletons, a standard weight of 60 kg, including paddle or oar, seems reasonable. As an alternative to taking the crew's effective centre of gravity (C of G) to be coincident with their bodily C of G, it may be argued that standing crewmen would in fact shift their balance to oppose any heel of the boat, and thus their C of G would be at their feet. If this is accepted KG_t becomes less, and hence transverse stability is improved, as measured by the increased metacentric height (GM_t).

Draft. Several attempts have been made (eg. Coates 1981, 263; McGrail 1978, 91, 132–3; 1987, 199) to define the loaded waterline of an ancient boat in terms of operational roles, such as:

a. shallow water operations–draft limited to, say, 30 cm.

b. the draft when carrying the maximum number of men.

c. a standard freeboard (distance from waterline to top of sides) taking into account safety considerations, say 15 cm.

d. a minimum freeboard as a function of transverse stability.

It is now clear that larger boats may be penalised when using some of these criteria to assess performance: some boats, for example, cannot float at the arbitrarily required chosen restricted draft; and some can only achieve the stability appropriate at deeper drafts by carrying ballast. This seems to be not a true reflection of reality in antiquity, rather a faulty analysis. A more promising method, one which still allows comparisons to be made between boats and one which may be closer to reality, is to assess the boat loaded to waterlines (ie. drafts) at defined fractions of the total depth of the hull. This method is an extension of the ideas expressed in Ch. 166 of the medieval Icelandic Law Code Grågås, where it is stated that a cargo vessel is fully loaded when 2/5 of her sides is freeboard[1] (Morcken 1980, 178).

Draft (T) is the complement of freeboard (F), and their sum equals the height of the sides. To obtain a range of performance assessments for a particular boat we may undertake draft/displacement/stability calculations when the boat is empty (light displacement); when carrying a full crew; and at the following drafts: $((T+F)/2) = 50\%$ height of sides; $(3(T+F)/5) = 60\%$ height of sides; $(2(T+F)/3) = 67\%$ height of sides; $(3(T+F)/4) = 75\%$ height of sides.

For the present it may be best to use the Grågås ratio, with the waterline at 60% height of sides $(3(T+F)/5)$, for comparisons between boats.

Assessing Speed Potential For displacement craft it is found empirically that resistance to motion (Drag) increases markedly when the speed–length ratio $V/\sqrt{L} \triangleq .34$ (Marchaj 1964, 248–254), where V = speed in knots, L = waterline length in feet.

A disproportionate increase in power is then required to overcome this drag and thus the speed equivalent to a ratio of 1.40 may be taken to be the theoretical maximum speed for a displacement boat. It should be noted, however, that, for certain forms of boat whose volumetric coefficient (Cv) is less than 2×10^{-3}, this displacement "trap" may be avoided and higher speeds attained, providing the appropriate propulsive power is available (McGrail and Corlett, 1977). At the lower speed ranges, say where $V/\sqrt{L} < 1.1$, three other coefficients (Fig. 11.5.1) may be used to assess speed potential[2]:

Block coefficient $(C_b) < 0.65$
Midship coefficient $(C_m) < 0.85$
Prismatic coefficient $(C_p) < 0.75$
These indicate good speed potential (McGrail 1987, 196–8).

The Hasholme logboat
The assessment methods based on hydrostatic curves and speed–related coefficients, described above, may be used to investigate the performance of the Hasholme boat, a logboat of some complexity dated dendrochronologically to 322 to 277 BC (Millett and McGrail 1987; McGrail forthcoming). The remains of this boat were encountered, in July 1984, by a machine laying field drains at Hasholme Hall near Holme on Spalding Moor, N Humberside (SE 822326), where there had

formerly been a tidal stretch of a tributary of the River Humber. The boat was excavated (Fig. 11.5.3) by a team from the University of Durham, the National Maritime Museum and the East Riding Archaeological Society. Subsequently the boat was transported to Greenwich where the timbers were cleaned, the main hull rotated to the vertical through c.40° and, after many of the detached and fragmented pieces had been re–assembled, the boat was recorded (Fig. 11.5.4). The Hasholme boat is now in Hull where she will be conserved and then displayed.

A reconstruction drawing (Fig. 11.5.5) was compiled based on the recorded evidence – this process is fully discussed in Millett and McGrail (1987). The dimensions of the reconstructed boat are, 12.78m overall length, 1.40m maximum beam (near the stern), and 1.25m maximum depth (also by the stern). From this reconstruction drawing a lines plan and sections and hydrostatic curves (Fig. 11.5.1) were prepared by Keith Hamilton–Smith of Burness, Corlett and Partners, and these curves were subsequently used to assess the boat's performance within a range of drafts 0.38 to 0.94m These drafts were based on the following operational roles:

Role   A. Light displacement (no crew, cargo or equipment)

       B. Maximum Men (20) – see Fig. 11.5.6

       C. Loaded to a waterline equivalent to a draft of $(T+F)/2 = 50\%$ height of sides

       D. Loaded to a (Grågås) waterline equivalent to a draft of $3(T+F)/5 = 60\%$ height of sides.

       E. Loaded to a waterline equivalent to a draft of $2(T+F)/3 = 67\%$ height of sides

       F. Loaded to a waterline equivalent to a draft of $3(T+F)/4 = 75\%$ height of sides

Trim. Inspection of the hydrostatic curves shows that in Role A (light displacement) the boat floats at a draft of 0.38m with the centre of buoyancy 24cm above the lowest point of the boat, 2.5cm to starboard of the middle line, and 88cm aft of the midship station. This shift to starboard is due to the asymmetric shape of the boat near the stern, the lower port side being not so full as the starboard side (Fig. 11.5.4, 5), probably due to asymmetry in the parent log. The centre of buoyancy is aft of midships because the boat conforms generally to the shape of the parent log with the butt end, and hence greater dimensions, aft: thus the boat floats trimmed by the stern with the sheerline (top edge of the sides) near horizontal. The waterplane at this draft has an area of 15.2m² with the centre of flotation also displaced to starboard and aft.

As the draft is increased to 0.94m (Role F), by adding men and cargo, the centre of buoyancy rises by 28cm and the waterplane area increases to 16.6m². The centre of buoyancy and the centre of flotation move nearer the middle line and nearer the midship station.

---

1 In Ancient Boats in NW Europe the ratio of freeboard to height of sides is correctly given as 2/5 on p.13, but on p. 199 it has been mis–printed at 2/3.

2 On p. 197 of Ancient Boats in NW Europe the values of C_b and C_m indicating good speed potential have been transposed.

Figure 11.5.3 A near–vertical view of the Hasholme logboat during excavation. Photo: National Maritime Museum, Greenwich

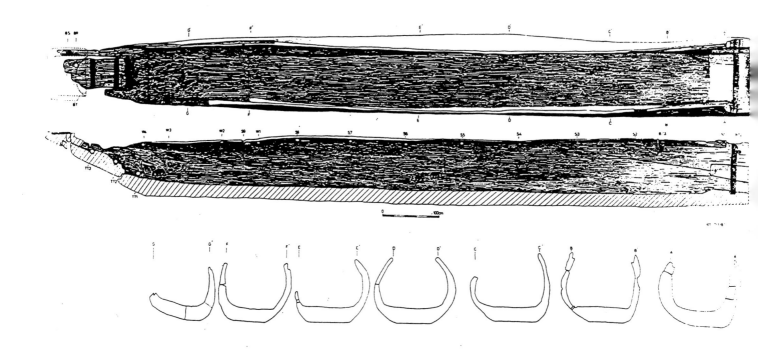

Figure 11.5.4 The Hasholme logboat as re–assembled in Autumn 1985. Drawing: National Maritime Museum, Greenwich

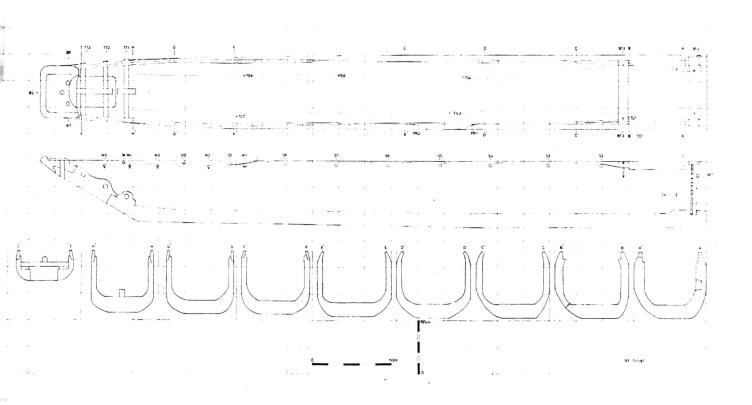

Figure 11.5.5 Reconstruction plan and sections of the Hasholme boat. See also Fig. 5.2.1. Drawing: National Maritime Museum, Greenwich

Figure 11.5.6 Reconstruction drawing of the Hasholme boat underway with a crew of 18 paddlers and 2 steersmen. In rock—strewn or shoal waters a further crewman may have been stationed on the bow platform to steer the boat clear of such hazards. Drawing: National Maritime Museum, Greenwich

Carrying capacity and Stability. The results of draft/displacement/stability calculations are tabulated in Table 11.5.1. It was assumed that the cargo in roles C to F was homogenous and that it occupied 80% of the length of the hollowed volume of the boat. The crew for these cargo—carrying roles was taken to be three paddlers standing on the bottom of the boat, forward, and two steersmen/paddlers standing on the raised deck near the stern.

With a full crew of 18 paddlers and 2 steersmen (Role B) the Hasholme boat requires a minimum of 0.46m of water: she has reasonable transverse stability with a metacentric height of

29cm (or 6cm if the effective C of G of the men is taken to be their actual C of G).

With a crew of five she is stable carrying a range of materials (from stone/iron with a bulk density of 2500 kg/m³ to peat of bulk density 435 kg/m³) down to a draft of 0.75m (equivalent to 60% of height of sides). At this (Grågås) draft she has metacentric height of between 3cm and 1mm, when carrying a homogenous load of a low density material such as peat.

At drafts deeper than 0.75m she cannot carry homogenous loads of low density materials such as peat, as transverse stability is inadequate as indicated by a negative GM_t. Peat *could* be carried at these drafts if ballast was substituted for part of the load. Alternatively, homogenous loads of grain, meat, timber, iron or stone could be carried, as the greater bulk density of these materials would result in the C of G of the load being lower and thus the metacentric height would be adequate e.g. in the case of grain or meat it would be between 9cm and 6cm at a draft of 0.83m (Role E: 67% height of sides); and between 4cm and 2cm at a draft of 0.94m (Role F: 75% height of sides).

If the boat were to be operated at drafts greater than *c*. 1m (that is with only 0.25m or less of freeboard) she would have to be loaded with denser materials such as timber or even iron ore or stone in order to remain stable.

Table 11.5.1 Theoretical load carrying performance and stability of the Hasholme logboat

Role[1]	Draft (m)	Freeboard (m)	$(100T/T+F)^2$	Description	Wt of load (kg)	Ht of Cargo (m)[3]	GM_t1 (m)[4]	GM_t2 (m)[4]
A	0.38	0.87	30%	Light displacement (4398 kg)	–	–	–	–
B	0.46	0.79	37%	Max. men (20)	1200	–	0.060	0.290
C	0.63	0.62	50%	5 men & 3502 kg peat[5]	3802	–0.30	0.110	0.150
D	0.75	0.50	60%[6]	5 men & 5502 kg peat[5]	5802	+0.18	0.001[7]	0.030
E	0.83	0.42	67%	5 men & 6802 kg grain or meat[8]	7102	–0.06	0.060	0.080
F	0.94	0.31	75%	5 men & 8602 kg grain or meat[8]	8902	+0.18	0.020	0.040

Notes:
1. Roles A & B are defined by the load carried; roles C to F are defined as set drafts
2. Draft (T) as a % of the maximum height of sides (where F = freeboard)
3. Relative to sheerline
4. Metacentric height – a measure of transverse stability. GM_t1 is based on the asumption that the crew's effective C of G coincides with their bodily C of G (ie 1.1 m above their feet). GM_t2 assumes that this C of G is at their feet
5. Alternative materials of greater bulk density (e.g. grain, meat, timber, iron or stone may be carried, resulting in a lower height of cargo and therefore increased GM_t
6. As defined in the Grågås medieval Icelandic law code
7. The very minimum of stransverse stability
8. Alternatively, material of greater bulk density may be carried – see note 5

Speed potential. The Hasholme boat would have been propelled by paddles, or by poles in shallow water. Over the range of operational drafts the waterline length is *c*.41ft (12.5m). The boat thus has a theoretical maximum achievable speed of *c*.9kts (ie 1.4√41). However, as can be seen from the values of the coefficient in Table 11.5.2 her underwater shape is such that she could only achieve a fraction of this theoretical speed no matter how much propulsive power was available. The Block coefficient (C_b) ranges from 0.70 to 0.80; the Midships coefficient (C_m) from 0.80 to 0.90; and the Prismatic coefficient (C_p) from 0.88 to 0.89. Except for C_m at drafts less than *c*.0.60m, the values of all these coefficients suggest a resistance–generating form. This is further emphasised by the values for the Volumetric coefficient (C_v) which are greater than the critical value of 2.0 x 10^{-3}.The boat's full form can also be appreciated from the reconstruction drawing (Fig. 11.5.5) – a high resistance form, accentuated by the unfaired, vertical, transom stern. Even with a full crew of paddlers (Role B and Fig. 11.5.6) it is unlikely that the Hasholme boat could be operated at V/√L > 0.5 (similar to a modern cargo vessel) although 0.75 might be achieved in a 'sprint'. This suggests a maximum speed of *c*.3kts, possibly up to 5kts in a short burst.

Table 11.5.2 Speed assessment coefficients for the Hasholme logboat

Role	Draft (m)	C_b	C_m	C_p	C_v $(x10^{-3})$
B	0.46	0.70	0.80	0.88	3.0
C	0.63	0.75	0.86	0.88	4.4
D	0.75	0.78	0.88	0.88	5.5
E	0.83	0.79	0.89	0.89	6.1
F	0.94	0.80	0.90	0.89	7.0

Note: See Table 11.5.1 for definitions of roles and see appendix for definition of coefficients

Summary of performance

The Hasholme boat as reconstructed is a good load carrier of men or of a range of cargo, able, for example, to carry a payload of over 5.5 tonnes in only 75cm of water. She has a useful, though not exceptional, speed potential. As she had no stabilisers added at the waterline, or other features to improve her natural stability, it is unlikley that she would have been used at sea, rather on inland waters and possibly also in the middle reaches of esatuaries in relatively calm conditions.

Aknowledgements

I am grateful to John Coates and Owain Roberts who commented on an earlier draft of this paper, and to Rosemary Trestini, who re-drew Figs. 11.5.4, 5 and to Alison Wilkins who re-drew Fig. 11.5.6.

Appendix Symbols used in the text

A. underwater cross section area at station of maximum beam ie. stern of Hasholme boat. (m^2)

B. maximum beam at waterline (m)

$C_b, \nabla/BLT$)

$C_m. A/BT$)

$C_p \nabla/AL$) note: $C_p = C_b/C_m$

$Cv\nabla/L^3$

F. freeboard at station of maximum beam (m).

GM_t)

KG_t) see Fig. 11.5.2

KM_t)

L. waterline length (m) [except in ratio $(V/\sqrt{L})$ – see text]

T. draft at station of maximum beam (m).

V. speed in knots.

∇ displacement volume (m^3)

References

Coates J. 1981 'Safe carrying capacity of the hypothetical reconstruction.' in McGrail S. (ed.) *Brigg raft and her prehistoric environment* NNM Archaeological Series 6, Oxford, Britlsh Archaeological Reports 89, 261–9.

McGrail S. 1978 *Logboats of England and Wales.*, NMM Archaeolgoical Series 2, Oxford, British Archaeological Reports 51.

McGrail S. 1986 'Experimental boat archaeology – some methodological considerations.' in Crumlin–Pedersen O. and Viner M. (eds) *Sailing into the Past*, Roskilde 8–17.

McGrail S. 1987 *Ancient boats in NW Europe* London, Longman.

McGrail S. forthcoming: 'Early boatbuilding techniques in Britain and Ireland – dating technological change.' *International Journal of Nautical Archaeology* 16.4.

Marchaj C.A. 1964 *Sailing Theory and Practice*, London, Adlard Coles.

Millett M. and McGrail S. 1987 'The Archaeology of the Hasholme logboat.' *Archaeological Journal*, 144, 69–125.

Morcken R. 1980 *Langskip, Knarr og Kogge*, Bergen.

Rawson K.J. and Tupper E.C. 1976–7; *Basic Ship Theory* 2 vols, London, Longman.

Toby A.S. 1986 'World's first warships; tubs or ocean greyhounds?' *International Journal of Nautical Archaeology*, 15.4, 339–346.

Reprinted with permission from:

Oxford Journal of Archaeology, 7: 35–46. (1988).

PAPER 11.6

THE THEORETICAL PERFORMANCE OF A HYPOTHETICAL RECONSTRUCTION OF THE CLAPTON LOGBOAT

Introduction

The Clapton logboat was discovered by chance in October 1987, near the River Lea in the London borough of Hackney. The remains, about two thirds of the original boat, were recorded and subsequently a hypothetical reconstruction drawing was compiled by 'removing' distortions in the boat as found and by 'filling–in' missing parts (Marsden, 1989: figs. 3 and 8). From this reconstruction drawing, supplemented by observations, members of the charity group Marine Archaeological Surveys and students from the Institute of Archaeology, University College, London, led by Damian Goodburn, built a full–size boat, measuring 3.75 x 0.68 x 0.39 m (Goodburn & Redknap, 1988). Preliminary trials were subsequently undertaken in mid–1988 on a pond next to the building site, followed in 1989 by further informal trials on the middle Thames.

A cost–effective way of evaluating the performance of an ancient boat is to undertake theoretical calculations using hydrostatic curves derived from drawing(s) of hypothetical reconstruction(s), as a prelude to the study of the feasibility and the potential research value of a full–size model (McGrail, 1986). In this way, before any of the costs of building an authentic replica are incurred, answers can be given to questions about performance or, equally valuably, certain

hypothetical reconstructions may be eliminated because they are impracticable.

Plans and sections of *Ravensbourne*, the fullsize model of the Clapton logboat, were made available to me by Damian Goodburn in mid–1989, and from these drawings a set of hydrostatic curves (Fig. 11.6.1) was prepared by Keith Hamilton–Smith of Burness, Corlett & Partners. Using these curves, the freeboard, draft and metacentric height of this boat have been calculated at various loaded conditions, (Table 11.6.1), as undertaken, for example, when assessing the performance of the Iron Age logboat from Hasholme (McGrail, 1988).

Performance

Carrying capacity and stability
Using the space parameters given in McGrail (1978, 131–132) it can be shown that theoretically there is room in the *Ravensbourne* logboat for four crewmen. However, calculations show that, with one man sitting on the stern and one on the midships bulkhead, and one man kneeling in each of

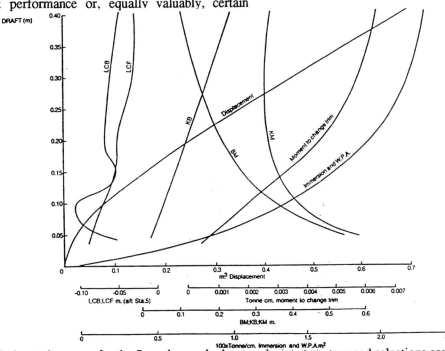

Figure 11.6.1 Hydrostatic curves for the *Ravesbourne* logboat as depicted in plans and selections compiled by Damian Goodburn. LCB, longitudinal centre of buoyancy; LCF, longitudinal centre of floatation; KB, distance from datum (lowest point) to the centre of buoyancy; BM, distance from centre of buoyancy to the metacentre; WPA, waterplane area; KM, distance from datum to metacentre. Publication drawing by Alison Wilkins from an original by Keith Hamilton–Smith.

Table 11.6.1 The Clapton logboat – capacity and stability

Role[a]	Load[b]	Displacement (kg)	Draft (m)	Freeboard (m)	Draft/Height of sides (%)	Metacentric[c] Height (GM_t) (m)	GM_t/Beam (%)
1 Light displacement	–	242	0.20	0.19	51	–	–
2 Maximum men	1 man sit, 2 men kneel	422	0.28	0.11	72	0.020	3
3 2 men + cargo (A)	1 man sit, 1 man kneel, 60 kg peat	422	0.28	0.11	72	0.070	10
4 1Man + cargo (A)	1 man stand, 60 kg peat	362	0.25	0.14	64	0.060	9
5 1 Man + cargo (B)	1 man sit, 60 kg peat	362	0.25	0.14	64	0.120	18
6 Standard draft (A)	1 man stand, 11 kg peat	313	0.23	0.16	60	0.005[d]	1
7 Standard draft (B)	1 man sit, 11 kg peat	313	0.23	0.16	60	0.080	12
8 1 Man + cargo (C)	1 man stand 133 kg peat	435	0.29	0.10	75	0.050	7
9 1 Man + cargo (D)	1 man sit, 133 kg peat	435	0.29	0.10	75	0.110	16
10 2 Men + cargo (B)	1 man sit, 1 man kneel, 73 kg peat	435	0.29	0.10	75	0.080	12

Notes:

a. Roles 1 to 5 are defined by the load carried; roles 6 to 10 are defined at set drafts (i.e. 60% and 75% of height of sides).

b. As an alternative to peat, materials of greater bulk density (lower stowage factor) i.e grain, meat, timber, iron or stone, cuold be carried, resulting in a lower height of cargo and thus a greater GM_t. A medieval crewman is taken to weigh 60Kg.

c. Metacentric height is a measure of transverse stability (McGrail, 1987, 12–16). In the calculations on which this table is based, it is assumed that the crew's effective centre of gravity coincided with their bodily centre of gravity (i.e. 1.10m above feet, 0.45m above knees, or 0.40m above seat). If it were assumed that the crew's effective centre of gravity was at their feet, knees or seat, as it would be if they remained upright when the boat rolled, the GM_t would be increased and hence there would be greater stability.

d. This is a barely positive GM_t.

the two compartments, the boat would be transversely unstable. Even if one of the crew were to kneel on the bottom of the boat rather than sit on the stern (a configuration which might be difficult to achieve, but which would give the lowest overall Centre of Gravity for a crew of four) the boat would still not be stable. In addition, the boat would be operating at a (draft/hull) ratio of 80%, with a freeboard of only 80 mm. For these reasons a four–man crew is considered to be impracticable.

As further calculations show that with a man sitting on the stern the boat is generally trimmed by the stern (i.e. draft aft is greater than forward) to an uncomfortable degree, the maximum number of men this boat could carry is taken to be three (Table 11.6.1, role 2), with one paddler sitting on the central bulkhead and one kneeling on the bottom of the boat within each compartment. The metacentric height (GM$_T$ – a measure of stability) in this role is a bare 20 mm and the boat would be slow to recover ('tender') when displaced from the vertical. However, as these calculations are done for the worst centre of gravity case [see footnote ") to Table 11.6.1], it is considered that, in this role, the   t would have a not unreasonable stability in calm waters.

With a 2–man crew, one sitting amidships and another kneeling in one of the compartments, a cargo of a relatively light material such as peat (or any other material of greater cargo density) can be carried in the other compartment. Role 3 in Table 11.6.1 has a 60 kg load with a freeboard of 110 mm which is considered the minimum acceptable – with such a freeboard it would require a roll of only 20° to put the top edge of the boat under water. In both roles there is adequate metacentric height (70 mm and 80 mm).

The size and form of the boat suggest that a one–man crew would most frequently be used if cargo is to be carried, and calculations show that that in this role the boat is indeed most effective. Roles 4, 5, 8 and 9 in Table 11.6.1 demonstrate one man standing in one compartment or sitting on the bulkhead amidships, with either 60 kg or 133kg of peat distributed between the two compartments. The metacentric height varies from 60 mm to 120 mm which is adequate for this size of vessel; indeed in Role 5 with a metacentric height of 120 mm, and Role 9 with a metacentric height of 110 mm, the boat would probably return upright relatively quickly and might be considered as 'stiff' (with excessive stability). Roles 8 and 9, with heavier loads than Roles 4 and 5, have a freeboard of only 100 mm, i.e. the minimum acceptable.

Roles 6 and 7 in Table 11.6.1 have one man, and that amount of cargo (11 kg) which would give a draft of 60% the height of the sides. This is 'standard draft' which may be used to compare the form of different boats (McGrail, 1987, 13). In Role 6, with the man standing on the bottom of the boat to paddle or to pole, the metacentric height is only 5mm, the barest of positive values, equal to only 1% of the boat's beam. This would be a very tender condition, and the crewman would probably have to constantly adjust his balance, similar in some ways to a bicyclist's instinctive reactions. On the other hand, these calculations are based not only on the worst centre of gravity, but also on a load of peat, and an equal weight of any material with a greater bulk density (e.g. grain, meat, timber, iron or stone) would produce a greater metacentric height and thus improve transverse stability and make the boat less tender.

Speed potential Table 11.6.2 shows values of several coefficients which may be used to assess the speed potential of the Clapton logboat in the Maximum Men role i e. when propelled by three paddlers (Role 2 in Table 11.6.1. None of these values suggests a high speed potential in absolute terms, rather a reasonable speed for this type of boat.

For displacement craft it has been found empirically that resistance to motion increases markedly when the speed/length ratio

$(V/\sqrt{L}) = c\ 1.34$
V = speed in knots
L = waterline in length and feet

A speed equivalent to a ratio of 1.40 is thus taken to be the theoretical maximum speed. For the Clapton logboat this is:

$1.4\sqrt{12.14} = 4.8$ kts

It is unlikely that a boat with the relatively full form of the Clapton logboat could be operated at

$(V\ \sqrt{L}) > 0.75$

which would suggest an actual maximum attainable speed of *c* 2.5 kts providing the appropriate paddle power was there.

Table 11.6.2 Speed assessment coefficients for the Clapton Logboat with a crew of three paddlers

Role	Draft	Cb	Cm	Cp	C_∇	Slenderness
2 Maximum Men	0.28	0.63	0.85	0.74	8.33 x 10⁻³	5.69

Definitions of these coefficients may be found in McGrail 1987, 196–7.

Conclusion

The foregoing analysis suggests that *Ravensbourne*, the full size model of the Clapton logboat, should carry useful cargo loads of up to 133 kg with a 1 or 2–man crew, in less than 0.30 m of water. She has a reasonable, though not exceptional, speed potential of *c.* 2.5kts when paddled by a 3–man crew.

Strictly speaking, deductions made about performance from the data given in Tables 11.6.1 and 11.6.2 apply only to the boat portrayed in the plans and sections that were analysed. If these drawings are an accurate representation of the full–size model *Ravensbourne*, then the forecasts in these tables are also applicable to her. Furthermore, if this full–size model (itself based on a hypothetical reconstruction drawing) is an authentic replica of the original form of the Clapton logboat, then the data in Table 11.6.1 will be a 'forecast' of the performance of this 10th– to 11th–century AD logboat. Thus, whether or not these calculations tell us anything about medieval times depends upon a series of identities:

The analysed ≡ *Ravensbourne*
   drawing

Ravensbourne ≡ Hypothetical ≡ Original
              reconstruction   Clapton
              drawing   logboat

If rigorous fully–documented trials can now be undertaken in the *Ravensbourne* full–size model, it should prove possible to compare theoretical forecasts with practical results, and thereby assess the usefulness of theoretical assessments. It is understood that trials are planned for 1990.

Acknowledgement

I am grateful to Keith Hamilton–Smith, naval architect, who kindly calculated the hydrostatics for *Ravensbourne* and plotted the curves shown in Fig. 11.6.1 and to Dr John Coates for his criticism of an earlier draft.

References

Goodburn D. & Redknap M. 1988 'Replicas and wrecks from the Thames area.' *London Archaeologist*, 6(1), 7–10; 19–22.

McGrail S. 1978 *Logboats of England and Wales*, British Archaeological Reports 51, Oxford.

McGrail S. 1986 'Experimental boat arehaeology – some methodological considerations.' in *Sailing into the Past*, O. Crumlin–Pedersen and M. Viner (eds), 8–17, Roskilde.

McGrail S. 1987 *Ancient boats in N W. Europe*, London.

McGrail S. 1988 'Assessing the performance of an ancient boat – the Hasholme logboat.' *Oxford Journal of Archaeology*, 7, 35–46.

Marsden M. (ed) 1989 'A late Saxon logboat from Clapton, London borough of Hackney.' *IJNA*, 18, 89–111.

Reprinted with permission from

International Journal of Nautical Archaeology, 19: 93–99. (1990).

PAPER 11.7

REPLICAS, RECONSTRUCTIONS AND FLOATING HYPOTHESIS

In a review of Frank Welsh's *Building the Trireme*, Christer Westerdahl (1992) has questioned whether a 'scientifically based reconstruction' can be made of a ship type for which there is documentary, iconographic and comparative evidence, but no physical remains. There are indeed problems in attempting such an undertaking; but there are comparable, although not identical, problems in building a 'replica' of an excavated vessel, such as that of the 3rd/4th century BC Kyrenia ship, which Westerdahl evidently considers can be more readily justified than can a 'reconstruction' of a 5th century BC Athenian trireme.

These replica/reconstruction projects are examples of the two general classes of research in experimental boat archaeology:

(i) Copies or 'replicas' are built of specific ancient boats, using excavated remains as the primary evidence. In addition to the Kyrenia ships other examples of this class are the Danish replicas of Skuldelev 3 and 5, and the German replicas of the Bremen cog.

(ii) 'Reconstructions' or 'simulations' are built of some ancient type, known primarily from written and iconographic sources. In addition to the trireme, other examples may be found in the published work of Heyerdahl (1978) and of Severin (1978, 1982, 1985, 1987).

There is no intrinsic reason why either of these two methods should be better than the other: they are both valid research techniques and entirely reasonable ways of investigating the past, providing that in each case the research is undertaken with scientific rigour and appropriate techniques. Which of the two methods is used is determined by the nature of the surviving evidence.

The authenticity of the vessels designed and built by both these methods and what, if anything, they can tell us about the past depends, as with all archaeological experiments, on:

(a) The quality of the data (excavated, documentary, etc.)

(b) The rigour of the arguments for transforming those data into a hypothesis or hypotheses of the full form and structure of the original vessel (in scale drawings or models).

(c) The appropriateness of the techniques used to turn such a hypothesis into a full-scale vessel, in effect a 'floating hypothesis'.

(d) The rigour, relevance and effectiveness of the trials programme to measure and otherwise evaluate performance and operational limitations.

(e) The full and widespread publication of the expriment so that it can be critically appraised.

It is impossible to assess many of the boat archaeological experiments that have been undertaken because they have not been adequately published. The Kyrenia ship replica is certainly based on a 'well executed and well published excavation of the highest scientific standards' as Westerdahl (1992, 85) has argued, but the way that this excavated evidence (incomplete, fragmented, distorted and leaving much to be deduced) was transformed into a complete ship Kyrenia 2 and how her sea trials were undertaken have not yet been published in the necessary detail. The reason why Kyrenia 2 has received 'far less attention' to quote Westerdahl again, is that no one outside the experimental team is able to judge the authenticity of this replica or the value of the trials and their relevance to the study of 4th/3rd century BC boat-building and seafaring. Some of the well-known replicas from northern Europe may be similarly 'in limbo' owing to less-than-comprehensive publication.

Whatever may be the faults of the Trireme Trust, it cannot be accused of inadequate publication: to the books listed by Westerdahl (1992, 84) may be added Coates (1988/9; 1989; 1990; 1991) and Coates & Morrison (1987). Moreover, detailed building drawings are available (Morrison ;& Coates, 1986: 228). Anyone who has studied these publications and drawings can assess the Trireme Trust's claims that their experiment was valid, their reconstruction authentic and that their trials throw light upon nautical affairs in the 5th century BC Aegean. Furthermore, conferences were organized by the Trust at Greenwich before building (Coates & McGrail, 1984) and at Oxford after three seasons of trials (Shaw, 1993), at which the principal exponents of the Trireme hypothesis were criticized and questioned about their sources and techniques.

It is right that projects claiming to be involved in experimental archaeology should be criticized; if only because to date we have learned little about early boat-building and seafaring from the many replicas reconstructions that have been built: a cost-effectiveness of almost zero. It is questionable whether most of them can be considered as scientific experiments which is what they should be if there are to be worthwhile results (McGrail, 1990). Many of these projects appear to be aimed at 'learning about oneself' rather than learning about the past, or were motivated by national prestige, historic nostalgia or commercial success – such aims may be fine in themselves, but the related projects cannot claim to be archaeological experiments unless they have an over–riding archaeological aim (McGrail, 1986).

Hypotheses must be investigated and tested by experiment, a process which lies at the foundation of all sciences. As Westerdahl states (1992, 84), 'we never know what we should have known beforehand'. And after testing, the research must be published so that it may be criticized. The Trireme Trust's arguments, both evidential and physical, are, as is proper, open to criticism and with hindsight it is possible to suggest that certain theoretical and practical aspects of their research might have been tackled in a different way: for example, more emphasis might have been placed on evaluating several hypotheses by theoretical and other means before the Trust became committed to one hypothesis, and perhaps more time given to sailing trials. Nevertheless, I consider that the Trust's approach to research, building and trials has been rigorous and that they have undertaken an extremely valuable archaeological experiment. This is my view; others who have read the Trust's publication or taken part in the trials may come to different conclusions, but it is upon such detailed evaluations of the Trust's arguments and practices that criticism should be based, not on any general belief that physical remains are the only basis for formulating hypotheses about ancient ships.

The Trireme Trust is now, I understand, reevaluating its hypotheses concerning certain particulars of the 5th century BC Athenian trireme, and in due course will present a reappraisal for public discussion. Perhaps builders of other replicas and reconstructions could now follow the Trust's example and publish their experiments in full. Only by widespread discussion of actual experiments will this important aspect of maritime archaeology realize its proper potential.

References

Coates J. 1988/9 'Trireme project – design and trials.' *Transactions of the Institute of Engineering & Shipbuilding in Scotland*, 132, 76–84.

Coates J. 1989 Trireme sails again.' *Scientific American*, 260.4, 96–103

Coates J. 1990 'Research and engineering aspects of reconstructing the ancient Greek Trireme warship.' Paper read to the Society of Naval Architects and Marine engineers in San Francisco.

Coates J. 1991 'The 1990 sea trials of the reconstructed Greek trireme *Olympias*, *IJNA* 20, 70–1.

Coates J. & McGrail S. (eds) 1984 *Greek trireme of the 5th century BC*, Greenwich, National Maritime Museum.

Coates J. & Morrison J. 1987 'Authenticity in the replica *Trieres*, *Antiquity*, 61, 87–90.

Hayerdhal T. 1978 *Early Man and the Ocean*, London, Allen & Unwin.

McGrail S. 1986 'Experimental boat archaeology – some methodological considerations,' in Crumlin–Pedersen, O. and Vinner M. (eds) *Sailing into the Past*, 8–17, Roskilde: Viking Ship Museum.

McGrail S. 1990 'review of Throckmorton, P. (ed) *History from the Sea*, *IJNA* 19, 167–8.

Morrison J. S. & Coates J. F. 1986 *Athenian Trireme*, Cambridge University Press.

Severin T. 1978 *Brenadan Voyage*, London, Hutchinson.

Severin T. 1982 *Sinbad Voyage*, London, Hutchinson.

Severin T. 1985 *Jason Voyage*, London, Hutchinson.

Severin T. 1987 *Ulyses Voyage* London, Hutchinson.

Shaw T. 1993 *Trireme Project*, Oxbow Monograph 31.

Westerdhal C. 1992 'Review of Welsh, F. 1988 *Building the Trireme*.' *IJNA* 21, 84–5.

Reprinted with permission from:

International Journal of Nautical Archaeology 21, 353–355. (1992).

PAPER 11.8

EXPERIMENTAL ARCHAEOLOGY AND THE TRIREME

Archaeology has been defined by the Institute of Field Archaeologists as "the study of the nature and past behaviour of Man in his enviromental setting". In undertaking this research, archaeologists use a variety of techniques, many of them interdisciplinary, and they have evolved procedures for the discovery and excavation of sites: the recording and analysis of finds and structures; and the formulation and testing of theories, which lead to interpretation and synthesis, and finally to publication by book, lecture and museum display. As the flow diagram in Fig. 11.8.1 shows, this is a never–ending procedure since publication leads not only to evaluation and criticism by others but also to re–assessment by the author: thus other projects, both theoretical and practical are born; and, in this way, progress is made.

One of the techniques that can be used in the hypothesis testing phase of such a research programme is Experimental Archaeology. In the nautical context this is usually taken to be the building and testing of a vessel which is variously described as a 'replica', a 'simulation, an 'exact copy' or a 'reconstruction' of some ancient boat or ship. I believe that such research vessels, or 'material hardware analogues' as David Clarke called them (1972, 10, 13). are in fact hypotheses – three–dimensional hypotheses. 'They are not statements of facts, but floating theories. In other words, such a vessel is a full–size model of a hypothetical reconstruction of the form and structure of some ancient boat.

The theory behind an archaeological experiment is that, by such means, we can learn more than is immediately or superficially obvious from the direct evidence – be this excavated, documentary, iconographic, or a combinatioln of these – that is, we can learn more about how ancient ships or boats were built, how they were used, and what sort of performance they had: speeds, cargo capacity, stability, closeness to the wind, etc.

The value of an archaeological experiment that is, what it can tell us, if anything, about ancient times, principally depends upon three factors:

A.   Quality of the data.

B.   Rigour of the hypothesis–building process – Theory.

C.   Appropriate evaluation of the hypothesis – Practice.

In the several scores of boat building projects which claim to have been undertaken in the spirit of experimental archaeology, the Trireme project is just about unique, in that the Trireme Trust has fully published its research and therefore assessments can be made of the Trust's claim that the Trireme experiment does tell us something new about nautical matters in 5th century BC Greece. First of all the Trust has published detailed descriptions of the data used – corresponding to (A) above; secondly, the Trust has published arguments for its hypothetical reconstructions (Fig. 11.8.2) as in (B); and thirdly the Trust has published the methods it has used to build the full size floating hypothesis *Olympias* and has described how trials were undertaken as in (C). The data, the methods, the arguments and the conclusions are there for all to see and to criticise (Coates & McGrail. 1984, Morrison & Coates, 1986; 1989, Coates, 1988/9; 1989; 1990; 1991; Coates and Morrison 1987, Coates, Platis & Shaw, 1990) an opportunity which has been notably seized. for example, by Lucien Basch (1987) and by Alec Tilley (1990).

This is not the case with most other replica projects. The information published to date about them is insufficient, in my opinion, for their rescarch programme to be evaluated, and thus observers are not in a position to judge the validity of these experiments and cannot identify what, if anything, the trials tell us about early boat–building and seafaring.

In addition to the books and articles published by the Trireme Trust, the conference held at Oxford in 1991 gave participants the chance to question the principal exponents of the project's sources and techniques. That conference allowed judgements to be made on the quality of the data, the rigour of the hypothesis–building process, and the appropriateness of the methods used during the building and trials of *Olympias*. In my opinion this project has been a valid archaeological experiment: a model for others to follow. With hindsight one can see that certain aspects might have been tackled in a different manner, but this was inevitable as the Trireme project was, in many ways, pioneering work. The Trust's publications and my experience of the 1990 trials lead me to believe that, in all aspects of research, building and trials, the Trust's approach has been rigorous.

In this paper I offer some comments, in the light of the 1991 conference, on the theory and practice of experimental work in general and the Trireme project in particular, in the hope that they may be of value to the Trust as it pauses to reflect on its achievements and considers what remains to be done.

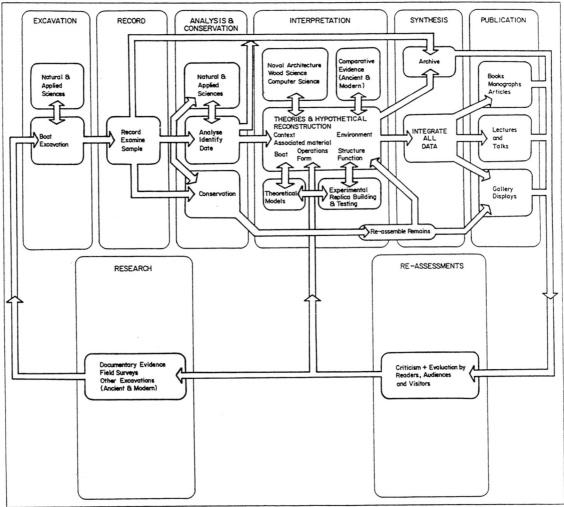

Figure 11.8.1 A diagram to illustrate the process of archaeological research. Drawing: Institute of Archaeology, Oxford

Hypothesis building

Unless the data for an ancient ship and the assumptions that have to be made in the absence of contemporary information are validated by rigorous challenge and counterchallenge, the formulation of useful hypotheses – i.e. the design of hypothetical reconstructions – is impossible. This is not to say that there must be only one hypothesis: different assumptions (when there is no definite guidance from the ancient evidence) can lead to different hypotheses, different reconstruction drawings or different models. Such variant solutions are entirely proper providing they are compatible with the evidence, and providing that they fit readily into what might be called the "technological environment" of the appropriate time and place.

However, different reconstructions almost always mean different performance assessments, and such structural or dimensional differences need not be very great to have a significant effect on performance. For example, the three reconstruction drawings of the 4th century AD Nydam 2 boat, compiled by Engelhardt (1863), Johannessen (1949) and Åkerlund (1961), have slightly different beam measurements at the waterline (Fig. 11.8.3). Now, in simple terms, transverse stability is proportional to the cube of the vessel's beam at the waterline, and if 'replicas' were to be based on these drawings, each would have a different transverse stability and therefore

different performance. Indeed, Åkerlund calculated that the one with the least beam would only be stable if a large amount of ballast were carried: whereas, Åkerlund's own reconstruction based on the same primary data but with a greater waterline beam measurement, would not need ballast to be stable. As Nydam boat 2 is one of the very few boat finds from 4th/5th century AD NW Europe, conclusions about the performance of Migration period boats depend very much on which of these three hypotheses is chosen. In fact, Åkerlunds' arguments for a broader beam, based on deduced shrinkage of the Nydam boat's planking, seem to me to be irrefutable (although his argument for a hogging truss is not convincing) and I follow Åkerlund in concluding that Nydam boat 2 was a reasonably stable boat.

A vital region where assumptions have to be made and therefore where there is scope for several solutions is in the design of the sailing rig of hypothetical reconstructions. No sail has survived from ancient times, no complete yard or mast has survived which can be attributed to a specific vessel, and the iconographic and documentary evidence from anywhere in the world is not so detailed as to permit us to define any rig precisely, in terms of sail size, shape and material and standing and running rigging. Thus it is to be expected that the rig of any 'replica', whether of a Classical Greek or of a Viking Age vessel, although possibly constrained within certain broad parameters, would have some variability in points of detail. In

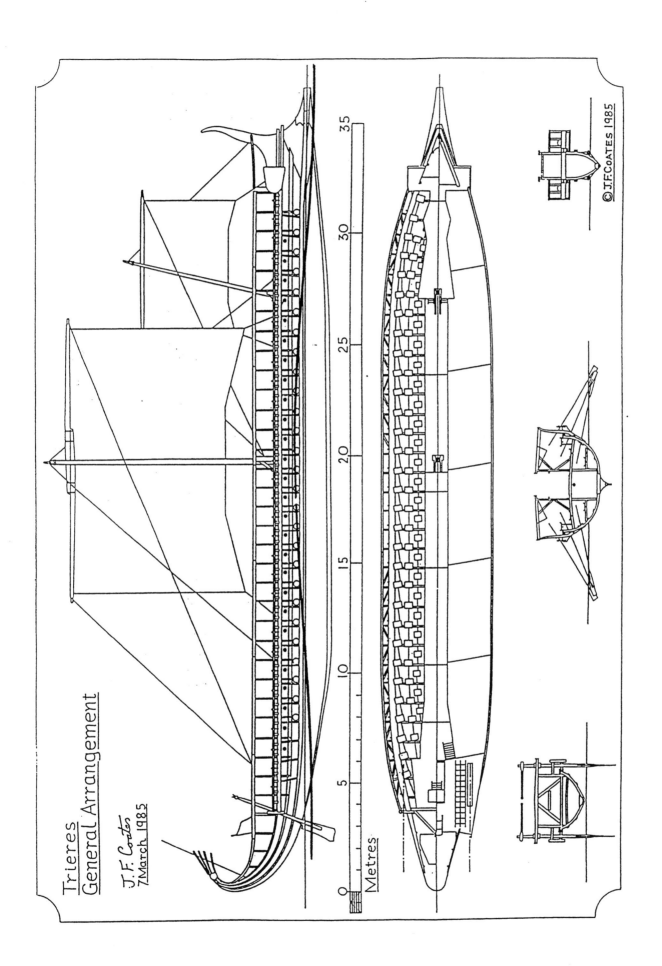

Figure 11.8.2 Plan, elevation and cross–section of *Olympias*. The elevation shows the contour of a wave of amplitude 1/40 of the length of the ship. Drawing: Trireme Trust

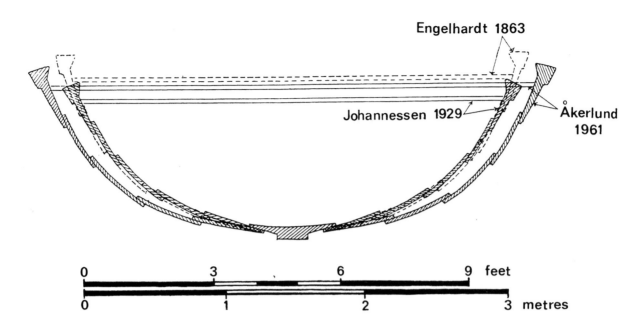

Figure 11.8.3 Hypothetical reconstruction of Nydam Boat 2 by Engelhardt in 1863, Johanessen in 1929 and Åkerlund in 1961.
Photo: National Maritime Museum, Greenwich

the light of further reflection, it may thus prove possible to propose alterations or additions to *Olympias*' rig.

The process of hypothesis building – theoretical reconstructions on paper or in the form of a small–scale model of the vessel which is the subject of the project – is most important, for practice without theory is futile. In other words, there is no value in proceeding to the building and testing of a 'replica' or floating hypothesis, unless the approach to theoretical reconstruction has been rigorous and the resultant hypothesis (or the several hypotheses) which have emerged from the process are in as authentic a form as possible.

The usual form of the problem to be tackled in this research phase may be illustrated by reference to the Hasholme logboat of *c.* 300 BC (Millet and McGrail 1987, McGrail 1988). We are concerned here with establishing a rigorous method of transforming the incomplete remains depicted in Figure 11.5.3 into a hypothetical reconstruction drawing such as that given in Figure 11.5.5, or into a small–scale model such as shown in Figure 8.1.2. Once a valid transformation has been made, the drawing or model can then be used to build a replica or floating hypothesis or as a basis for other methods of assessing aspects of performance (see below).

In the case of the Trireme project, however, there are no excavated remains to form the kernel or nucleus of the reconstruction. Instead, the data are mostly in documentary and iconographic form, with some indirect evidence from archaeological remains. In this case then, the problem has been to formulate a hypothetical reconstruction which it is thought would achieve those aspects of performance that are documented, whilst meeting the constraints imposed by the other evidence – overall dimensions, length of oars and so on, as described by John Morrison (Morrison and Coates 1986).

As with the Hasholme logboat research, the hypothetical reconstruction drawings produced by John Coates from data supplied by John Morrison (Coates 1985ff, unpublished) may be used as a basis for deductions about the past. However, the outcome to be expected from these two types of archaeological experiment (Hasholme and Trireme) differ somewhat. From a Hasholme replica experiment we might expect to learn about the performance of a large Iron Age logboat when used in various roles: manoeuvrability, capacity as a cargo carrier, as a ferry or as a boat of war; sprint and cruise speeds and distances achievable during a long day. In the trireme experiment, on the other hand, certain aspects of performance are already known, in fact they have been used as parameters in the design of *Olympias*. The outcome of the Trireme project, what new information we gain about the past, must therefore be in such fields as: the details of ship building techniques; steering methods; sailing techniques; command and control in battle; the precise details of the ramming manoeuvre; and other operational matters which are not adequately documented in the ancient sources.

Performance estimates by theoretical means

Some of this new information about the past is only obtainable by building a 'replica' or floating hypothesis, but much light may be shed on certain aspects of performance by relatively cheap, theoretical means. Five methods may be considered either as alternatives to replica building and sea trials, or, for exceptionally important projects, as one stage in a research programme progressing towards a replica.

a) By eye. An experienced seaman, boatbuilder or naval architect may be able to make general assessments of performance by examining a reconstruction drawing or model.

b) The use of Coefficients. Coefficients based on the boat's underwater form may be used to assess qualities such as speed. For example, a long, narrow boat suggests high speed potential. There are other more complex ratios such as the block and volumetric coeffients which give more refined assessments of speed potential, and there is a simple calculation which tells us the maximum theoretical speed of a boat (McGrail 1987, 195–8)

c) The use of hydrostatic curves (Fig 11.5.1). Curves can be plotted using the underwater geometry of the hull, (McGrail 1987, 12–16) and from them we can see for example, that at a given draft a boat will have a certain displacement; or that if the boat is loaded with a given weight of cargo and/ or men she will have a corresponding draft. These curves can thus be used to estimate such data as cargo capacity and transverse stability at different waterlines (McGrail 1987, 20–2).

d) Computer work. This is not cheap but can be a cost effective method of investigating performance and can be especially useful when there are alternative reconstructions to be investigated. Indeed there are some computer programs which will directly calculate the information incorporated in hydrostatic curves, thus greatly facilitating the estimation of loading and stability (Marsden 1991).

e) Small–scale models may be built for towing tank tests to evaluate such aspects of performance as wave and eddy making resistance at different speeds as is done for new designs of yachts and of tankers. It is also possible to use wind tunnels to investigate aspects of sail performance.

Building a full–scale model

The most spectacular method of assessing performance (and additionally learning something about ancient boatbuilding techniques) is by building a full–scale floating hypothesis and undertakmg trials. However, with significant exceptions, much of this type of experimental work undertaken to date has been of slight consequence when measured by the standards of authenticity and cost–benefit. What has been learned about the maritime past has been minimal when compared with the resources deployed. In many cases hydrostatic curve investigations, small–scale model building and testing, and computer modelling, would have been more cost–effective than the full–scale replica or floating hypothesis work actually undertaken. It seems to me to be essential to go through these simple and relatively inexpensive methods of assessing aspects of performance even if the ultimate aim is, if resources permit, to build a 'replica'.

Experimental archaeology, in its most advanced form of the floating hypothesis, has several disadvantages: it is indeed expensive if undertaken rigorously: and it seems to attract

those who have neither the ability nor the time to publish. But, above all, for a project of any size and complexity it is difficult, if not impossible, to modify the floating hypothesis in any significant way if sea trials indicate that this is necessary. Nevertheless, there are undoubtedly projects of much importance where the only way to gain detailed information is to proceed to the floating hypothesis phase, and build a replica/reconstruction. This may also be the only way that it is possible to demonstrate, in a form that everyone can readily recognise, what the shape, the structure and the rowing arrangements of an ancient boat were like.

The future – *Olympias* 2

If I understand correctly the hypothesis–building arguments advanced by the Trust, the conclusion they reached at the end of this phase of their experiment was that the interacting constraints imposed by the ancient evidence and by naval architectural requirements were so tight that, as regards the fundamental aspects – hull form and construction, displacement and the oar system – only one hypothesis was possible: the hypothetical reconstruction designed by John Coates, which became the floating hypothesis *Olympias* 1 (Fig. 11.8.2).

The Trust are now contemplating a change of design which, in effect, would necessitate the building of another vessel on the grounds that *Olympias* cannot quite achieve the documented performance of certain 5th century BC triremes (see for example Chapters 10 and 12 below). It is undoubtedly true that, under oars, at the higher speeds, say above 5 knots, the lowest level of oarsmen in *Olympias*, the thalamians, contribute little effective power (Chapter 10). It is also agreed that there are physical obstructions at thalamian level which intrude on the space oarsmen need to give of their best. The argument for a change in design is that if such physical constraints can be removed, the thalamians as a group will become much more effective and thus the target speeds will be achieved.

The archaeological assessment of whether proposed changes to the design are valid – be they structural or in terms of measurement units (the interscalmium) – must not be based on whether they are likely to increase speed without having adverse side effects e.g. on stability: that is the prerogative of the naval architect. The archaeological assessment must be based on whether these proposed changes accord with known evidence and do not cause other constraints to be exceeded.

The possibility that such a re–design would allow 6ft 6in (1.98) Americans to man thalamian oars effectively, is also irrelevant to an archaeological assessment. If this proves to be a spin–off result due to structural changes argued on other grounas, then this will be a bonus. On the other hand, perhaps there should be an explicit constraint included in the parameters for the revised design (the new hypothetical reconstruction) which acknowledged that 5th century BC Athenian males averaged only 5ft 6in (1.68m) in height with, on present evidence, little dispersion about this mean figure (Musgrave, J.H., personal communication). There would have had to be compelling reasons indeed for 5th century Greek shipwrights to build an oared vessel with much more than the minimum space needed by oarsmen 5ft 6in in height.

Given that these theoretical points can be satisfactorily answered and that the archaeological response is that the proposals are compatible with the known evidence and do not cause other constraints to be exceeded, then the question arises whether this revised hypothetical reconstruction (or perhaps several such reconstructions) of a 5th century Athenian trireme, needs be turned into a floating hypothesis, i.e. the question is whether a second trireme has to be built and tested. The considered answer to this question maybe: "Yes, there are compelling reasons for proceeding to Phase 3 of the research design; the value of the knowledge gained by building another 'replica' will be commensurate with the resources invested and there is no other way of acquiring this knowledge". That might well be the answer. Nevertheless I would urge the Trust to consider preliminary evaluation of the redesign by all available theoretical and model–building means, and to publish their findings for wide discussion before they reach the decision whether to build, and precisely what to build.

References

Åkerlund H. 1963 *Nydamskeppen* Göteberg.

Basch L. 1987 Review article *Mariners' Mirror* 73, 93–105.

Clarke D. 1972 'Models and paradigms in Archaeology', in Clarke D.L. (ed) *Models in Archaeology* 1–60, Cambridge.

Coates J. F. 1985ff: .Reconstruction Drawings of the Trieres'. Unpublished, but available from the Trireme Trust.

Coates J. F. 1988/9 'Trireme Project – design & trials.' *Trans. Inst. Engineers and Shipbuilders in Scotland* 132, 76–84.

Coates J. F. 1989 'Trireme sails again.' *Scientifc American* 260, 4, 96–103.

Coates J.F. 1990 *Research and Engineering aspects of reconstructing the ancient Greek Trireme warship.* Paper read to the Society of Naval Architects and Marine Engineers in San Francisco.

Coates J.F. 1991 'The 1990 sea trials of the reconstructed Greek trireme *Olympias*. *Int. J. Nautical Archaeology* 20, 70–1.

Coates J F. & McGrail S. (eds) 1984 *The Greek trireme of the 5th century BC.* Greenwich, National Maritime Museum.

Coates J.F. and Morrison J.S. 1987 'Authenticity in the replica Athenian trieres.' *Antiquity* 61, 87–90.

Coates J. F. Platis S. K. and Shaw J.T. 1990 *The Trireme Trials 1988.* Oxford: Oxbow

Engelhardt C. 1865 *Nydam Mosefund.* Copenhagen.

Marsden P. 1991 *Shipping and the Port of London from Roman times to the 13th century AD.* Unpublished thesis submitted to the University of Oxford for the degree of D. Phil.

McGrail S. 1987 *Ancient boats in NW Europe.* London, Longman.

McGrail S. 1988 'Assessing the performance of an ancient boat: the Hasholme logboat.' *Oxford J. of Archaeology* 7, 35–46.

Millet M. and McGrail S. 1987 'The archaeology of the Hasholme logboat,' *Archaeological Journal*, 144, 69–125.

Morrison J.S. & Coates J.F. 1986 *The Athenian trireme Cambridge*, CUP.

Morrison J.S. and Coates J.F. 1989 *An Athenian trireme reconstructed.* Oxford, BAR S.486.

Shetelig H. and Johannessen F. 1930. Das Nydamschiff. *Acta Archaeologica* 1, 1–30.

Tilley A.F. 1990 Review, *Int. J. Nautical Archaeology* 19, 169.

Reprinted withpermission from:

Shaw T (ed) *Trireme project,*: 4–10. Oxbow Monograph 31. (1993)

OET
OCCUPATIONAL ENGLISH TEST

NURSING

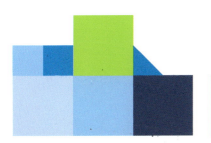

Official OET Practice Book 1

Contents

An overview of OET

About OET

OET is an international English language test that assesses the language proficiency of healthcare professionals seeking to register and practise in an English-speaking environment. It provides a validated, reliable assessment of all four language skills – listening, reading, writing and speaking – with the emphasis on communication in healthcare professional settings.

OET tests candidates from the following 12 health professions: Dentistry, Dietetics, Medicine, Nursing, Occupational Therapy, Optometry, Pharmacy, Physiotherapy, Podiatry, Radiography, Speech Pathology and Veterinary Science.

Candidates are encouraged to prepare thoroughly for their OET test.

Language proficiency and test taking skills

For more information about OET including the latest test dates and a complete list of test locations and preparation providers, as well as access to our free test preparation package Start for Success, visit the OET website: **www.occupationalenglishtest.org**

About the test

OET assesses listening, reading, writing and speaking.

There is a separate sub-test for each skill area. The Listening and Reading sub-tests are designed to assess the ability to understand spoken and written English in contexts related to general health and medicine. The sub-tests for Listening and Reading are common to all professions.

The Writing and Speaking sub-tests are specific to each profession and are designed to assess the ability to use English appropriately in the relevant professional context.

Sub-test (duration)	Content	Shows candidates can:
Listening (45 minutes)	3 tasks Common to all 12 professions	follow and understand a range of health-related spoken materials such as patient consultations and lectures.
Reading (60 minutes)	3 tasks Common to all 12 professions	read and understand different types of text on health-related subjects.
Writing (45 minutes)	1 task Specific to each profession	write a letter in a clear and accurate way which is relevant for the reader.
Speaking (20 minutes)	2 tasks Specific to each profession	effectively communicate in a real-life context through the use of role plays.

Listening subtest

The Listening sub-test consists of three parts, and a total of 42 question items. You will hear each recording once and are expected to write your answers while listening. All three parts take 45 minutes to complete. The Listening sub-test has the following structure:

Part A – consultation extracts

Part A assesses your ability to identify specific information during a consultation. You will listen to two five-minute health professional-patient consultations and you will complete the health professional's notes using the information you hear.

Part B – short workplace extracts

Part B assesses your ability to identify the detail, gist, opinion or purpose of short extracts from the healthcare workplace. You will listen to six one-minute extracts (e.g. team briefings, handovers, or health professional-patient dialogues) and you will answer one multiple-choice question for each extract.

Part C – presentation extracts

Part C assesses your ability to follow a recorded presentation or interview on a range of accessible healthcare topics. You will listen to two different five-minute extracts and you will answer six multiple-choice questions for each extract.

Reading subtest

The Reading sub-test consists of three parts, with a total of 42 question items. You are given 60 minutes to complete all three parts (15 minutes for Part A and 45 minutes for Part B and Part C). The Reading sub-test has the following structure:

Part A – expeditious reading task

Part A assesses your ability to locate specific information from four short texts in a quick and efficient manner. The four short texts relate to a single healthcare topic, and you must answer 20 questions in the allocated time period. The 20 questions consist of matching, sentence completion and short answer questions.

Part B and Part C – careful reading tasks

Part B assesses your ability to identify the detail, gist or purpose of six short texts sourced from the healthcare workplace (100-150 words each). The texts might consist of extracts from policy documents, hospital guidelines, manuals or internal communications, such as email or memos. For each text, there is one three-option multiple-choice question.

Part C assesses your ability to identify detailed meaning and opinion in two texts on a topic of interest to healthcare professionals (800 words each). For each text, you must answer eight four-option multiple choice questions.

Writing subtest

The Writing sub-test consists of one profession specific task based on a typical workplace situation. The writing test takes 45 minutes to complete - 40 minutes to write your letter and 5 minutes at the start to read the case notes on which to base your writing. The Writing sub-test has the following structure:

The task is to write a letter, usually a referral letter but sometimes a different type of letter such as a letter of transfer or discharge, or a letter to advise or inform a patient, carer, or group.

Along with the task instructions, you will receive stimulus material (case notes and/or other related documentation) which includes information to use in your response.

Speaking subtest

The Speaking sub-test consists of two profession specific role-plays and is delivered individually. It takes around 20 minutes to complete. In each role-play, you take your professional role (for example, as a nurse or as a pharmacist) while the interlocutor plays a patient, a client, or a patient's relative or carer. For veterinary science, the interlocutor is the owner or carer of the animal. The Speaking sub-test has the following structure:

In each Speaking test, your identity and profession are checked by the interlocutor and there is a short warm-up conversation about your professional background. Then the role-plays are introduced one by one and you have 3 minutes to prepare for each. The role-plays take about five minutes each.

You receive information for each role-play on a card that you keep while you do the role-play. The card explains the situation and what you are required to do. You may write notes on the card if you want. If you have any questions about the content of the role-play or how a role-play works, you can ask them during the preparation time.

The role-plays are based on typical workplace situations and reflect the demands made on a health professional in those situations. The interlocutor follows a script so that the Speaking test structure is similar for each candidate. The interlocutor also has detailed information to use in each role-play. Different role-plays are used for different candidates at the same test administration.

How the test is scored

You will receive your results in the form of a score on a scale from 0 to 500 for each of the four sub-tests:

OET Results table - effective from 9 September 2018 test date

OET results to August 2018	OET score from September 2018	OET band descriptors	IELTS equivalent band score
A	500 490 480 470 460 450	Can communicate very fluently and effectively with patients and health professionals using appropriate register, tone and lexis. Shows complete understanding of any kind of written or spoken language.	8.0 - 9.0
B	440 430 420 410 400 390 380 370 360 350	Can communicate effectively with patients and health professionals using appropriate register, tone and lexis, with only occasional inaccuracies and hesitations. Shows good understanding in a range of clinical contexts.	7.0 – 7.5
C+	340 330 320 310 300		6.5
C	290 280 270 260 250 240 230 220 210 200	Can maintain the interaction in a relevant healthcare environment despite occasional errors and lapses, and follow standard spoken language normally encountered in his/her field of specialisation.	5.5 – 6.0
D	190 180 170 160 150 140 130 120 110 100	Can maintain some interaction and understand straightforward factual information in his/her field of specialisation, but may ask for clarification. Frequent errors, inaccuracies and mis-or overuse of technical language can cause strain in communication.	Less than 5.5
E	90 80 70 60 50 40 30 20 10 0	Can manage simple interaction on familiar topics and understand the main point in short, simple messages, provided he/she can ask for clarification. High density of errors and mis- or overuse of technical language can cause significant strain and breakdowns in communication.	

Test takers guide to OET

Listening

Part A

Remember, in **Part A** you listen to a recording of 2 consultations between a health professional and a patient (dialogue). You take notes while you listen. This part of the test usually lasts around 15 minutes. Before you attempt the Practice Test, consider some important tips below.

Do

» Use the sub-headings to guide you .

» Give specific rather than general information from the recording.

Don't

» Jump ahead or back: the gaps follow the sequence of the recording.

» Write full sentences: a word or short phrase is sufficient.

» Don't waste valuable time using an eraser to correct a mistake if you make one. Simply cross out any words you don't want the person marking your paper to accept; this takes a lot less time and you will not be penalised.

Part B

Remember, in **Part B** you listen to six recorded extracts from the healthcare workplace. You answer one multiple-choice question for each extract. This part of the test usually lasts around 10 minutes.

Do

» Read the contextual information for each extract to understand the interaction you will hear.

» Read through each question carefully.

» Mark your answers on this Question Paper by filling in the circle using a 2B pencil.

Don't

» Select your answer until you have heard the whole extract.

» Fill in more than one circle on the Question Paper as the scanner will not be able to recognise your answer and you will not receive any marks for that question.

Part C

Remember, in **Part C** you listen to 2 recordings of a recorded presentation or interview on a health-related issue. You will answer six multiple-choice questions for each recording while you listen. This part of the test usually lasts around 15 minutes. Before you attempt the Practice Test, consider some important tips below.

Do

» Read through each question carefully.

» Mark your answers on this Question Paper by filling in the circle using a 2B pencil.

Don't

» Wait for key words in the question or answer options to be said in the recording. The speaker(s) will often use synonyms of the words you read.

» Fill in more than one circle on the Question Paper as the scanner will not be able to recognise your answer and you will not receive any marks for that question.

General

» Have a spare pen or pencil ready just in case.

» Stay relaxed and receptive – ready to listen.

» Focus on listening and understanding then recording your answer.

» Demonstrate that you have understood the recording (as well as heard it).

» Take a sample test under test conditions beforehand so you know what it feels like.

» Don't be distracted by what is going on around you (e.g., sneezing, a nervous candidate at the next desk)

» When the recording starts, use the time allowed to look through the questions carefully, scanning the headings and questions so you know what to listen out for.

» Use common abbreviations and symbols.

» Write clearly; don't make it difficult for the assessor to read your responses as you may not get all the marks you could.

» Don't lose your place during the test; remain focused on each question.

Checking at the end

» Think twice about going back to change something – it may be better to leave what you wrote the first time if you are not sure.

» Don't leave any blanks; have a guess at the answer.

Developing your listening skills

» You should practise listening to English delivered at natural speed in a variety of voices and contexts. Learners who do this regularly are more confident at extracting key information and gist meaning, even when they are not able to decode every single word or phrase. Make sure you are exposed to speakers of different ages and backgrounds, and to the language of different contexts (e.g., informal discussions, formal lectures, etc.).

» Although it is useful to practise exam techniques by using exam materials and course books, you should also use real-life sources to develop your listening skills. You can find a variety of authentic sources for free on the internet, particularly in the form of training videos and professional development talks.

» Practise dealing with listening texts in a variety of ways. For example, you can listen to a text once for the gist, and produce a summary of the main ideas or attitudes expressed by the speakers. You can then listen to the same text a second time in order to retrieve specific information or to focus on useful language.

» At a high level in OET Listening, it is not enough to be able to pick out particular words or specific details. You need to be able to understand the overall meaning of what the speakers are saying. It is important to practise following a speaker's line of argument and identifying his/her opinion or attitude.

What to expect in the test

» The instructions for each task are given on the question paper, and you will also hear them on the recording. They give you information about the topic and the speakers, and tell you about the type of task you have to do.

» There is a pause before each section to give you time to read through and think about the questions. Use the time to familiarise yourself with the task and start to predict what you are likely to hear.

» Use the task on the paper to guide you through the recording as you answer the questions.

Reading

Part A

Remember, in **Part A** you locate specific information from four short texts related to a single healthcare topic. You have 15 minutes to answer 20 questions. Before you attempt the Practice Test, consider some important tips below.

Do

» Keep the Text Booklet open in front of you so that you can see all the texts and the answer booklet at the same time. You need to be able to move between the different texts quickly and easily.

» Use the headings and layout of the short texts to get a quick initial idea of the type of information they contain and how they are organised. This will help you select which text you need for each section of the test.

» For short answer and sentence completion questions, use the statement to find out what type of information you need and decide which of the short texts is likely to contain that information. Then navigate to the relevant part of the text.

» Use correct spelling: incorrectly spelt answers do not receive any marks. You may use either British or American spelling variations (e.g. anemia and anaemia are both acceptable).

Don't

» The answers for Part A need to be consistent with the information of the texts. It is not a good strategy to use your professional background knowledge to answer Part A and avoid skimming and scanning the text.

» Use words with similar meaning to words in the texts. These words are known as synonyms.

» Waste valuable time using an eraser to correct a mistake if you make one. You may, for example, accidentally include an extra word or write the wrong word in the wrong space. Simply cross out any words you don't want the assessor marking your paper to accept; this takes a lot less time and you will not be penalised.

» Begin Part A by simply reading all texts from beginning to end as this will waste valuable time. Use the questions to guide you to which text to read first.

Part B

Remember, in **Part B** you answer one multiple-choice question about six short texts sourced from the healthcare workplace. The combined time for Parts B and C is 45 minutes. Before you attempt the Practice Test, consider some important tips below.

Do

» Read the contextual information for each text to help you understand the purpose and audience of the content.

» Read each answer option carefully and scan the text for evidence to support this option being correct or incorrect.

» Manage your time carefully. You should aim to spend the majority of the 45 minutes on Part C.

» Mark your answers on this Question Paper by filling in the circle using a 2B pencil.

Don't

» Read each text before reading the questions. You need to be efficient with your time: read the answer options and then focus on the text.

» Be distracted by unfamiliar vocabulary. Use the surrounding words to approximate the meaning and continue to search for the answer. Questions can often be answered without understanding all the vocabulary.

» Fill in more than one circle on the Question Paper as the scanner will not be able to recognise your answer and you will not receive any marks for that question.

Part C

Remember, in **Part C** you answer eight multiple-choice questions on each of two texts which are about a topic of interest to healthcare professionals. The combined time for Parts B and C is 45 minutes. Before you attempt the Practice Test, consider some important points below.

Do

» There are no thematic links between the two texts. Focus on one text at a time rather than moving backwards and forwards between them.

» Manage your time carefully. Allow enough time for both Part C texts as the reading skills it requires are quite considered and detailed.

» Read each question carefully, looking out for key words.

» Consider each of the options and explain to yourself what makes each one right or wrong.

» If you are unsure about a question, consider moving on and coming back to it later.

» Mark your answers on this Question Paper by filling in the circle using a 2B pencil.

Don't

» Get stuck on one question – keep going and come back to it at the end when you have answered all other questions. Marks are not deducted for incorrect answers.

» Fill in more than one circle on the Question Paper as the scanner will not be able to recognise your answer and you will not receive any marks for that question.

General

» Have a spare pen and pencil ready just in case.

» Bring and use a soft (2B) pencil. Remember you cannot use a pen to answer the multiple-choice questions for Parts B and C. It is a good idea to bring one or two extra 2B pencils as spares or a small pencil sharpener.

» Note how the text is organised (e.g., with sub-headings, tables/diagrams etc.).

» Write on the texts if it helps you (e.g., underlining key words and phrases etc.) but don't make it more difficult for you to read by adding too many marks.

» When checking at the end, don't make any last-minute changes unless you are sure.

Developing your reading skills

» You should practise reading a variety of text types in English so that you become familiar with a wide range of language and organisational features. Candidates who do this regularly are more confident at understanding the overall function and message of texts and at following a line of argument in a text.

» Although it is useful to practise exam techniques by using exam materials and course books, you should also use real-life sources to develop your reading skills. Following up on your own professional or personal interests is a good way to increase your exposure to different types of texts.

» Practise dealing with texts in a variety of ways. For example, you could read a text once for the gist, and produce a summary of the main ideas or attitudes expressed by the writers. You could then read the same text a second time in order to retrieve specific information or to focus on useful language.

» At a high level in OET Reading, it is not enough to be able to pick out particular words or specific details. You need to be able to understand the overall meaning of the text. It is important to practise following a writer's line of argument as well as identifying specific pieces of information.

» Take the sample test under test conditions beforehand so you know what it feels like. For Part A, set yourself a strict time limit of 15 minutes. For Part B, set your timer for 45 minutes.

What to expect in the test

» The instructions for each task are given on the question paper. They give you information about the topic and the texts, and tell you about the type of task you have to do.

» You will complete the Reading sub-test in two parts. First you will be given the Text Booklet and the Answer Booklet for Part A. When the 15 minutes for Part A have finished, these will be collected from you. You will then be given the Text Booklet for Parts B & C.

» You will not be able to go back to Part A, even if you finish Parts B & C early. Leave yourself enough time in each Part to check your answers.

» You may write your answers in either **pen** or **pencil** for Part A.

Writing

Do

» Take time to understand the task requirements.

» Use your own words to paraphrase or summarise longer pieces of information from the case notes.

» Make sure you understand the situation described in the case notes.

» Think about how best to organise your letter before you start writing.

» Use the space provided to plan your letter (though a draft is not compulsory).

» Use the five minutes' reading time effectively to understand the task set

- What is your role?
- Who is your audience (the intended reader)?
- What is the current situation?
- How urgent is the current situation?
- What is the main point you must communicate to the reader?
- What supporting information is necessary to give to the reader?
- What background information is useful to the reader?
- What information is unnecessary for the reader? Why is it unnecessary?

» Explain the current situation at the start of the letter (e.g., perhaps an emergency situation).

» Use the names and address given.

» Set out the names, address, date and other information to start the letter clearly.

» As you write, indicate each new paragraph clearly, perhaps by leaving a blank line.

Don't

» Include everything from the case notes – select information relevant to the task.

» Simply copy chunks of text from the case notes.

» Write notes or numbered points.

General

» Have a spare pen and pencil ready, just in case.

» Fill in the cover pages for the task booklet and the answer booklet correctly.

» Fill in your personal information on the answer sheet correctly.

» Take a sample test under test conditions beforehand so you know what it feels like.

» Practise writing clearly if you have poor handwriting.

» Write clearly and legibly.

Checking at the end

» Make sure your letter communicates what you intend.

» Make sure you meet the basic task requirements:

- length of the body of the text approximately 180–200 words
- full sentences, not note form
- appropriate letter format.

» Check for any simple grammar and spelling errors that you may have made.

» If a page is messy, use clear marks (e.g., arrows, numbers) to show the sequence in which the parts of your text should be read.

» Cross out clearly anything you do not want the assessors to read.

Speaking

Do

Candidates should use the prompts/notes on the role-play card to guide them through the role-play:

» What is your role?

» What role is your interlocutor playing – patient, parent/son/daughter, carer?

» Where is the conversation taking place?

» What is the current situation?

» How urgent is the situation?

» What background information are you given about the patient and the situation?

» What are you required to do?

» What is the main purpose of the conversation (e.g., explain, find out, reassure, persuade etc.)?

» What other elements of the situation do you know about (e.g., the patient appears nervous or angry, you don't have much time etc.)?

» What information do you need to give the patient (remember, though, this is not a test of your professional skills)?

Don't

» Rely on scripted or rehearsed phrases during the test. Many of these phrases will not be appropriate for certain role-plays.

» Speak about topics not related to the role-play. Your focus should be on what's on your role-play card.

Information about role-play cards

Candidates will have an opportunity to read through the role-play card before starting each role-play. Both role-play cards are laid out in a similar way. At the top of the role-play card is information about the setting (i.e. where the conversation is taking place). Candidates receive information on each role-play card, which he/she keeps while doing the role-play. Candidates may write notes on the role-play card if they want to.

The role-play card explains the situation and what candidates are required to do. If candidates have any questions about the content of the role-play or how a role-play works, they may ask for clarification before starting.

The top paragraph contains background information about the patient and his/her situation. It will be made clear if the interlocutor is taking on the role of the patient or somebody talking on behalf of the patient (i.e., the patient's carer, parent, etc.). The bottom half of the role-play card contains information to assist candidates in what they need to mention during the role-play. Each role-play card contains approximately 100-150 words (prompts/notes to guide candidates during the role-play).

The Speaking sub-test is in three parts:

1. Warm-up conversation (this is not assessed)

» format of the test explained

» candidate helped to relax

» questions asked about areas of professional interest, previous work experience, future plans, etc.

2. First role-play (assessed)

» candidate handed role-play card

» candidate has 2-3 minutes to prepare

» candidate can ask questions to clarify before role-play starts

» role-play is conducted (approximately 5 minutes)

3. Second role-play (assessed)

» above procedure is repeated using a different role-play

Using the Speaking practice tests

» Copy the role-play.

» Ask a friend or colleague to play the role of the patient (or patient's carer, etc.).

» Take the role of the health professional.

» Ask another friend or colleague to observe the role-play and give you feedback on your performance.

» Read the information on the role-play card carefully.

» You have to deal with the case details as outlined on the role-play card by asking and answering questions put to you by the patient or client.

» Speak as naturally as possible.

» Remember it is important to be interested in the welfare of the patient and to reassure the patient or relation of the patient that the treatment being proposed is appropriate.

» Keep to the time limit of 5 minutes (approximate) for each role-play.

» Ask the friend or colleague who observed for comments and feedback.

NURSING

PRACTICE TEST

1

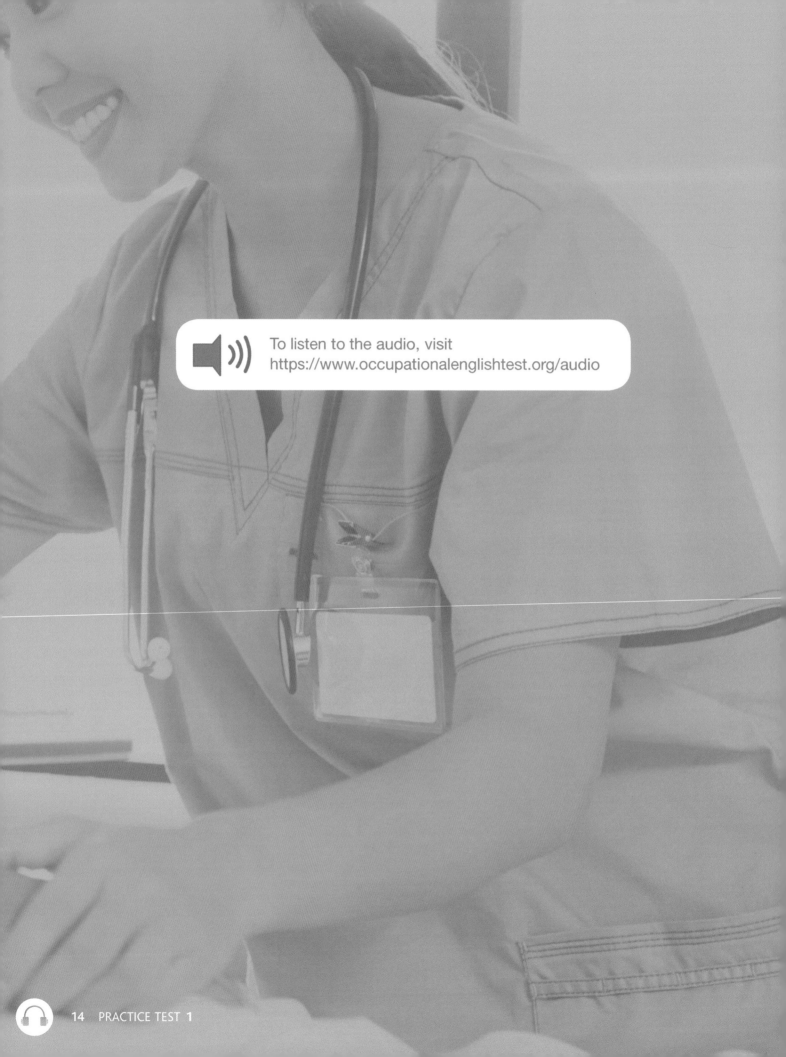

To listen to the audio, visit
https://www.occupationalenglishtest.org/audio

OCCUPATIONAL ENGLISH TEST

LISTENING SUB-TEST – QUESTION PAPER

CANDIDATE NUMBER:

LAST NAME:

FIRST NAME:

MIDDLE NAMES:

PROFESSION:

VENUE:

TEST DATE:

Candidate details and photo will be printed here.

Passport Photo

CANDIDATE SIGNATURE: _____

TIME: APPROXIMATELY **40 MINUTES**

INSTRUCTIONS TO CANDIDATES

DO NOT open this question paper until you are told to do so.

One mark will be granted for each correct answer.

Answer **ALL** questions. Marks are **NOT** deducted for incorrect answers.

At the end of the test, you will have two minutes to check your answers.

At the end of the test, hand in this **Question Paper.**

You must not remove OET material from the test room.

HOW TO ANSWER THE QUESTIONS

Part A: Write your answers on this **Question Paper** by filling in the blanks. **Example: Patient:** _____Ray Sands_____

Part B & Part C: Mark your answers on this **Question Paper** by filling in the circle using a 2B pencil. **Example:** Ⓐ
Ⓑ
Ⓒ

 SAMPLE

Occupational English Test

Listening Test

This test has three parts. In each part you'll hear a number of different extracts. At the start of each extract, you'll hear this sound: --beep—

You'll have time to read the questions before you hear each extract and you'll hear each extract **ONCE ONLY**. Complete your answers as you listen.

At the end of the test you'll have two minutes to check your answers.

Part A

In this part of the test, you'll hear two different extracts. In each extract, a health professional is talking to a patient.

For **questions 1-24**, complete the notes with information you hear.

Now, look at the notes for extract one.

Extract 1: Questions 1-12

You hear an obstetrician talking to a patient called Melissa Gordon. For **questions 1-12**, complete the notes with a word or short phrase.

You now have 30 seconds to look at the notes.

Patient	Melissa Gordon

- works as a **(1)**

Medical history

- has occasional **(2)**

- is allergic to **(3)**

- has a **(4)** _____ diet

- non-smoker

- this will be her second child

- needed **(5)** _____ treatment before first pregnancy

- first baby presented as **(6)** _____

  - **(7)** _____ required during intervention

- after giving birth, had problems with **(8)**

  - helped by midwife

Baby's father

- family history of **(9)** _____

- child from previous marriage has **(10)** _____

Points raised

- not keen on amniocentesis

- enquired about the possibility of **(11)** _____ testing

- provided her with a leaflet on preparing **(12)** _____ for new baby

Extract 2: Questions 13-24

You hear a GP talking to a new patient called Mike Royce. For **questions 13-24**, complete the notes with a word or short phrase.

You now have thirty seconds to look at the notes.

Patient

Mike Royce

New patient transferring from another practice

Description of initial symptoms

- severe left knee pain in **(13)** _____ area

- worsened after an accident at work

- developed **(14)** _____ on back of knee (described as trigger points.)

Impact on daily life

- unable to **(15)** _____ while working (house painter)

- problems climbing ladders

Initial treatment

- exercise programme including
  - stretching exercises
  - rest

- **(16)** _____ for pain

Developments in condition

- GP suspected **(17)** _____

- prescribed hospital-based rehabilitation

- temporary improvement noted

Current condition	• muscular problem diagnosed by **(18)** _____
	– was performing treatment on **(19)** _____
	• experiencing insomnia and **(20)** _____
	• suspects **(21)** _____ (own research)
	• has recorded experiences in **(22)** _____
	• beginning to experience pain in both **(23)** _____

Suggested course of action

    • recommend referral to **(24)** _____

That is the end of Part A. Now look at Part B.

Part B

In this part of the test, you'll hear six different extracts. In each extract, you'll hear people talking in a different healthcare setting.

For **questions 25-30**, choose the answer (**A**, **B** or **C**) which fits best according to what you hear. You'll have time to read each question before you listen. Complete your answers as you listen.

Now look at question 25.

25. You hear a dietitian talking to a patient.

What is she doing?

A correcting the patient's misconception about obesity

B describing the link between obesity and other diseases

C stressing the need for a positive strategy aimed at weight loss

26. You hear members of a hospital committee discussing problems in the X-ray department.

The problems are due to a delay in

A buying a replacement machine.

B getting approval for a repair to a machine.

C identifying a problem with a particular machine.

27. You hear a senior nurse giving feedback to a trainee after a training exercise.

The trainee accepts that he failed to

A locate the CPR board quickly enough.

B deal with the CPR board on his own.

C install the CPR board correctly.

28. You hear a trainee nurse asking his senior colleague about the use of anti-embolism socks (AES) for a patient.

The patient isn't wearing the socks because

(A) she's suffering from arterial disease in her legs.

(B) there is sensory loss in her legs.

(C) her legs are too swollen.

29. You hear a vet talking about her involvement in the management of the practice where she works.

How does she feel about her role?

(A) She accepts that it's become surprisingly complex.

(B) She wishes her boss took more interest in the finances.

(C) She values the greater understanding it gives her of her work.

30. You hear a physiotherapist giving a presentation about a study she's been involved in.

She suggests that her findings are of particular interest because of

(A) the age of the subjects.

(B) the type of disorder involved.

(C) the length of time covered by the study.

That is the end of Part B. Now look at Part C.

Part C

In this part of the test, you'll hear two different extracts. In each extract, you'll hear health professionals talking about aspects of their work.

For **questions 31-42**, choose the answer (**A, B** or **C**) which fits best according to what you hear. Complete your answers as you listen.

Now look at extract one.

Extract 1: Questions 31-36

You hear a sports physiotherapist called Chris Maloney giving a presentation in which he describes treating a high jumper with a knee injury.

You now have 90 seconds to read **questions 31-36**.

31.   When Chris first met the patient, he found out that

      (**A**)   she was considering retirement from her sport.

      (**B**)   her state of mind had aggravated the pain in her knee.

      (**C**)   she had ignored professional advice previously offered to her.

32.   During his assessment of the patient's knee, Chris decided that

      (**A**)   her body type wasn't naturally suited to her sport.

      (**B**)   the pain she felt was mainly located in one place.

      (**C**)   some key muscles weren't strong enough.

33.   In the first stage of his treatment, Chris

      (**A**)   was careful to explain his methods in detail.

      (**B**)   soon discovered what was causing the problem.

      (**C**)   used evidence from MRI scans to inform his approach.

34.   Why did Chris decide against the practice known as 'taping'?

      (**A**)   The patient was reluctant to use it.

      (**B**)   It might give a false sense of security.

      (**C**)   The treatment was succeeding without it.

35. In the patient's gym work, Chris's main concern was to ensure that she

(A) tried out a wide range of fitness exercises.

(B) focussed on applying the correct techniques.

(C) was capable of managing her own training regime.

36. Why was the patient's run-up technique changed?

(A) to enable her to gain more speed before take off

(B) to reduce the stress placed on her take-off leg

(C) to reinforce the break from her old mindset

Now look at extract two.

Extract 2: Questions 37-42

You hear a clinical psychiatrist called Dr Anthony Gibbens giving a presentation about the value of individual patients' experiences and 'stories' in medicine.

You now have 90 seconds to read **questions 37-42**.

37. What impressed Dr Gibbens about the case study that was sent to him?

(A) where it was originally published

(B) how controversial its contents were

(C) his colleague's reasons for sending it to him

38. Dr Gibbens has noticed that people who read his books

(A) gain insights into their mental health problems.

(B) see an improvement in personal relationships.

(C) benefit from a subtle change in behaviour.

39. What disadvantage of doctors using patients' stories does Dr Gibbens identify?

  (A) evidence-based research being disregarded

  (B) patients being encouraged to self-diagnose

  (C) a tendency to jump to conclusions

40. In Dr Gibbens' opinion, why should patients' stories inform medical practice?

  (A) They provide an insight not gained from numbers alone.

  (B) They prove useful when testing new theories.

  (C) They are more accessible than statistics.

41. How does Dr Gibbens feel about randomised medical trials?

  (A) He questions the reliability of the method.

  (B) He is suspicious of the way data are selected for them.

  (C) He is doubtful of their value when used independently.

42. When talking about the use of narratives in medicine in the future, Dr Gibbens reveals

  (A) his determination that they should be used to inform research.

  (B) his commitment to making them more widely accepted.

  (C) his optimism that they will be published more widely.

That is the end of Part C.

You now have two minutes to check your answers.

END OF THE LISTENING TEST

OCCUPATIONAL ENGLISH TEST

READING SUB-TEST – TEXT BOOKLET: PART A

CANDIDATE NUMBER:

LAST NAME:

FIRST NAME:

MIDDLE NAMES:

Candidate details and photo will be printed here.

PROFESSION:

VENUE:

TEST DATE:

Passport Photo

CANDIDATE SIGNATURE: _____

INSTRUCTIONS TO CANDIDATES

You must **NOT** remove OET material from the test room.

The use of feeding tubes in paediatrics: Texts

Text A

Paediatric nasogastric tube use

Nasogastric is the most common route for enteral feeding. It is particularly useful in the short term, and when it is necessary to avoid a surgical procedure to insert a gastrostomy device. However, in the long term, gastrostomy feeding may be more suitable.

Issues associated with paediatric nasogastric tube feeding include:

- The procedure for inserting the tube is traumatic for the majority of children.
- The tube is very noticeable.
- Patients are likely to pull out the tube making regular re-insertion necessary.
- Aspiration, if the tube is incorrectly placed.
- Increased risk of gastro-esophageal reflux with prolonged use.
- Damage to the skin on the face.

Text B

Inserting the nasogastric tube

All tubes must be radio opaque throughout their length and have externally visible markings.

1. Wide bore:

   - for short-term use only.
   - should be changed every seven days.
   - range of sizes for paediatric use is 6 Fr to 10 Fr.

2. Fine bore:

   - for long-term use.
   - should be changed every 30 days.

In general, tube sizes of 6 Fr are used for standard feeds, and 7-10 Fr for higher density and fibre feeds. Tubes come in a range of lengths, usually 55cm, 75cm or 85cm.

Wash and dry hands thoroughly. Place all the equipment needed on a clean tray.

- Find the most appropriate position for the child, depending on age and/or ability to co-operate. Older children may be able to sit upright with head support. Younger children may sit on a parent's lap. Infants may be wrapped in a sheet or blanket.
- Check the tube is intact then stretch it to remove any shape retained from being packaged.
- Measure from the tip of the nose to the bottom of the ear lobe, then from the ear lobe to xiphisternum. The length of tube can be marked with indelible pen or a note taken of the measurement marks on the tube (for neonates: measure from the nose to ear and then to the halfway point between xiphisternum and umbilicus).
- Lubricate the end of the tube using a water-based lubricant.
- Gently pass the tube into the child's nostril, advancing it along the floor of the nasopharynx to the oropharynx. Ask the child to swallow a little water, or offer a younger child their soother, to assist passage of the tube down the oesophagus. Never advance the tube against resistance.
- If the child shows signs of breathlessness or severe coughing, remove the tube immediately.
- Lightly secure the tube with tape until the position has been checked.

Text C

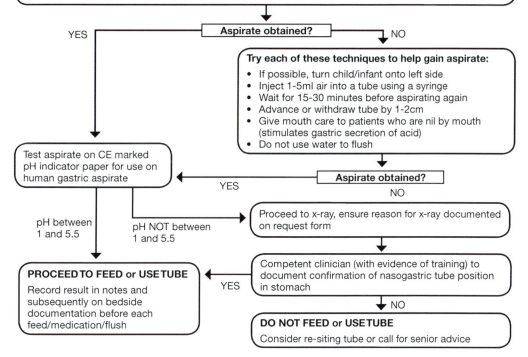

- Estimate NEX measurement (Place exit port of tube at tio of nose. Extend tube to earlobe, and then to xiphistemum)
- Insert fully radio-opaque nasogastric tube for feeding (follow manufacturer's instructions for insertion)
- Confirm and document secured NEX measurement
- Aspirate with a syringe using gentle suction

Aspirate obtained?

YES ← | → NO

Try each of these techniques to help gain aspirate:

- If possible, turn child/infant onto left side
- Inject 1-5ml air into a tube using a syringe
- Wait for 15-30 minutes before aspirating again
- Advance or withdraw tube by 1-2cm
- Give mouth care to patients who are nil by mouth (stimulates gastric secretion of acid)
- Do not use water to flush

Aspirate obtained?

YES ← | → NO

Test aspirate on CE marked pH indicator paper for use on human gastric aspirate

pH between 1 and 5.5

pH NOT between 1 and 5.5 → Proceed to x-ray, ensure reason for x-ray documented on request form

Competent clinician (with evidence of training) to document confirmation of nasogastric tube position in stomach

YES → **PROCEED TO FEED or USE TUBE**
Record result in notes and subsequently on bedside documentation before each feed/medication/flush

NO → **DO NOT FEED or USE TUBE**
Consider re-siting tube or call for senior advice

A pH of between 1 and 5.5 is reliable confirmation that the tube is not in the lung, however, it does not confirm gastric placement. If this is any concern, the patient should proceed to x-ray in order to confirm tube position.

Where pH readings fall between 5 and 6 it is recommended that a second competent person checks the reading or retests.

Text D

Administering feeds/fluid via a feeding tube

Feeds are ordered through a referral to the dietitian.

When feeding directly into the small bowel, feeds must be delivered continuously via a feeding pump. The small bowel cannot hold large volumes of feed.

Feed bottles must be changed every six hours, or every four hours for expressed breast milk.

Under no circumstances should the feed be decanted from the container in which it is sent up from the special feeds unit.

All feeds should be monitored and recorded hourly using a fluid balance chart.

If oral feeding is appropriate, this must also be recorded.

The child should be measured and weighed before feeding commences and then twice weekly.

The use of this feeding method should be re-assessed, evaluated and recorded daily.

END OF PART A
THIS TEXT BOOKLET WILL BE COLLECTED

READING SUB-TEST – QUESTION PAPER: PART A

CANDIDATE NUMBER:	
LAST NAME:	
FIRST NAME:	
MIDDLE NAMES:	**Passport Photo**
PROFESSION:	Candidate details and photo will be printed here.
VENUE:	
TEST DATE:	

CANDIDATE DECLARATION

By signing this, you agree not to disclose or use in any way (other than to take the test) or assist any other person to disclose or use any OET test or sub-test content. If you cheat or assist in any cheating, use any unfair practice, break any of the rules or regulations, or ignore any advice or information, you may be disqualified and your results may not be issued at the sole discretion of CBLA. CBLA also reserves its right to take further disciplinary action against you and to pursue any other remedies permitted by law. If a candidate is suspected of and investigated for malpractice, their personal details and details of the investigation may be passed to a third party where required.

CANDIDATE SIGNATURE: _____

TIME: 15 MINUTES

INSTRUCTIONS TO CANDIDATES

DO NOT open this **Question Paper** or the **Text Booklet** until you are told to do so.

Write your answers on the spaces provided on this **Question Paper.**

You must answer the questions within the 15-minute time limit.

One mark will be granted for each correct answer.

Answer **ALL** questions. Marks are **NOT** deducted for incorrect answers.

At the end of the 15 minutes, hand in this **Question Paper** and the **Text Booklet.**

DO NOT remove OET material from the test room.

www.occupationalenglishtest.org

© Cambridge Boxhill Language Assessment – ABN 51 988 559 414

[CANDIDATE NO.] READING QUESTION PAPER PART A 01/04

Part A

TIME: 15 minutes

- Look at the four texts, **A-D**, in the separate **Text Booklet**.

- For each question, **1-20**, look through the texts, **A-D**, to find the relevant information.

- Write your answers on the spaces provided in this **Question Paper**.

- Answer all the questions within the 15-minute time limit.

- Your answers should be correctly spelt.

The use of feeding tubes in paediatrics: Questions

Questions 1-7

For each question, **1-7**, decide which text (**A**, **B**, **C** or **D**) the information comes from. You may use any letter more than once.

In which text can you find information about

1	the risks of feeding a child via a nasogastric tube?	_____
2	calculating the length of tube that will be required for a patient?	_____
3	when alternative forms of feeding may be more appropriate than nasogastric?	_____
4	who to consult over a patient's liquid food requirements?	_____
5	the outward appearance of the tubes?	_____
6	knowing when it is safe to go ahead with the use of a tube for feeding?	_____
7	how regularly different kinds of tubes need replacing?	_____

Questions 8-15

Answer each of the questions, **8-15**, with a word or short phrase from one of the texts. Each answer may include words, numbers or both.

8   What type of tube should you use for patients who need nasogastric feeding for an extended period?

_____

9   What should you apply to a feeding tube to make it easier to insert?

_____

10   What should you use to keep the tube in place temporarily?

_____

11   What equipment should you use initially to aspirate a feeding tube?

_____

12   If initial aspiration of the feeding tube is unsuccessful, how long should you wait before trying again?

_____

13   How should you position a patient during a second attempt to obtain aspirate?

_____

14   If aspirate exceeds pH 5.5, where should you take the patient to confirm the position of the tube?

_____

15   What device allows for the delivery of feeds via the small bowel?

_____

Questions 16-20

Complete each of the sentences, **16-20**, with a word or short phrase from one of the texts. Each answer may include words, numbers or both.

16   If a feeding tube isn't straight when you unwrap it, you should

_____ it.

17   Patients are more likely to experience _____ if they need long-term feeding via a tube.

18   If you need to give the patient a standard liquid feed, the tube to use is

_____ in size.

19   You must take out the feeding tube at once if the patient is coughing badly or is

experiencing _____ .

20   If a child is receiving _____ via a feeding tube, you should replace the feed bottle after four hours.

END OF PART A

THIS QUESTION PAPER WILL BE COLLECTED

READING SUB-TEST – QUESTION PAPER: PARTS B & C

CANDIDATE NUMBER:

LAST NAME:

FIRST NAME:

MIDDLE NAMES: Candidate details and photo will be printed here.

PROFESSION:

VENUE:

TEST DATE:

Passport Photo

CANDIDATE DECLARATION

By signing this, you agree not to disclose or use in any way (other than to take the test) or assist any other person to disclose or use any OET test or sub-test content. If you cheat or assist in any cheating, use any unfair practice, break any of the rules or regulations, or ignore any advice or information, you may be disqualified and your results may not be issued at the sole discretion of CBLA. CBLA also reserves its right to take further disciplinary action against you and to pursue any other remedies permitted by law. If a candidate is suspected of and investigated for malpractice, their personal details and details of the investigation may be passed to a third party where required.

CANDIDATE SIGNATURE: _____

TIME: 45 MINUTES

INSTRUCTIONS TO CANDIDATES

DO NOT open this **Question Paper** until you are told to do so.

One mark will be granted for each correct answer.

Answer **ALL** questions. Marks are **NOT** deducted for incorrect answers.

At the end of the test, hand in this **Question Paper**.

HOW TO ANSWER THE QUESTIONS:

Mark your answers on this **Question Paper** by filling in the circle using a 2B pencil. **Example:** Ⓐ
Ⓑ
Ⓒ

Part B

In this part of the test, there are six short extracts relating to the work of health professionals. For **questions 1-6**, choose answer (**A**, **B** or **C**) which you think fits best according to the text.

1. If vaccines have been stored incorrectly,

    A   this should be reported.

    B   staff should dispose of them securely.

    C   they should be sent back to the supplier.

Manual extract: effective cold chain
The cold chain is the system of transporting and storing vaccines within the temperature range of +2°C to +8°C from the place of manufacture to the point of administration. Maintenance of the cold chain is essential for maintaining vaccine potency and, in turn, vaccine effectiveness.
Purpose-built vaccine refrigerators (PBVR) are the preferred means of storage for vaccines. Domestic refrigerators are not designed for the special temperature needs of vaccine storage.
Despite best practices, cold chain breaches sometimes occur. Do not discard or use any vaccines exposed to temperatures below +2°C or above +8°C without obtaining further advice. Isolate vaccines and contact the state or territory public health bodies for advice on the National Immunisation Program vaccines and the manufacturer for privately purchased vaccines.

2. According to the extract, prior to making a home visit, nurses must

(A)   record the time they leave the practice.

(B)   refill their bag with necessary items.

(C)   communicate their intentions to others.

Nurse home visit guidelines

When the nurse is ready to depart, he/she must advise a minimum of two staff members that he/she is commencing home visits, with one staff member responsible for logging the nurse's movements. More than one person must be made aware of the nurse's movements; failure to do so could result in the breakdown of communication and increased risk to the nurse and/or practice.

On return to the practice, the nurse will immediately advise staff members of his/her return. This time will be documented on the patient visit list, and then scanned and filed by administration staff. The nurse will then attend to any specimens, cold chain requirements, restocking of the nurse kit and biohazardous waste.

3.   What is being described in this section of the guidelines?

(A)   changes in procedures

(B)   best practice procedures

(C)   exceptions to the procedures

Guidelines for dealing with hospital waste
All biological waste must be carefully stored and disposed of safely. Contaminated materials such as blood bags, dirty dressings and disposable needles are also potentially hazardous and must be treated accordingly. If biological waste and contaminated materials are not disposed of properly, staff and members of the community could be exposed to infectious material and become infected. It is essential for the hospital to have protocols for dealing with biological waste and contaminated materials. All staff must be familiar with them and follow them. The disposal of biohazardous materials is time-consuming and expensive, so it is important to separate out non-contaminated waste such as paper, packaging and non-sterile materials. Make separate disposal containers available where waste is created so that staff can sort the waste as it is being discarded.

4. When is it acceptable for a health professional to pass on confidential information given by a patient?

  (A) if non-disclosure could adversely affect those involved

  (B) if the patient's treatment might otherwise be compromised

  (C) if the health professional would otherwise be breaking the law

Extract from guidelines: Patient Confidentiality
Where a patient objects to information being shared with other health professionals involved in their care, you should explain how disclosure would benefit the continuity and quality of care. If their decision has implications for the proposed treatment, it will be necessary to inform the patient of this. Ultimately if they refuse, you must respect their decision, even if it means that for reasons of safety you must limit your treatment options. You should record their decision within their clinical notes.
It may be in the public interest to disclose information received in confidence without consent, for example, information about a serious crime. It is important that confidentiality may only be broken in this way in exceptional circumstances and then only after careful consideration. This means you can justify your actions and point out the possible harm to the patient or other interested parties if you hadn't disclosed the information. Theft, fraud or damage to property would generally not warrant a breach of confidence.

5. The purpose of the email to practitioners about infection control obligations is to

(A) act as a reminder of their obligations.

(B) respond to a specific query they have raised.

(C) announce a change in regulations affecting them.

Email from Dental Board of Australia

Dear Practitioner,

You may be aware of the recent media and public interest in standards of infection control in dental practice. As regulators of the profession, we are concerned that there has been doubt among registered dental practitioners about these essential standards.

Registered dental practitioners must comply with the National Board's Guidelines on infection control. The guidelines list the reference material that you must have access to and comply with, including the National Health and Medical Research Council's (NHMRC) Guidelines for the prevention and control of infection in healthcare.

We believe that most dental practitioners consistently comply with these guidelines and implement appropriate infection control protocols. However, the consequences for non-compliance with appropriate infection control measures will be significant for you and also for your patients and the community.

6.   The results of the study described in the memo may explain why

  (A)   superior communication skills may protect women from dementia.

  (B)   female dementia sufferers have better verbal skills.

  (C)   mild dementia in women can remain undiagnosed.

Memo to staff: Women and Dementia

Please read this extract from a recent research paper

Women's superior verbal skills could work against them when it comes to recognizing Alzheimer's disease. A new study looked at more than 1300 men and women divided into three groups: one group comprised patients with amnestic mild cognitive impairment; the second group included patients with Alzheimer's dementia; and the final group included healthy controls. The researchers measured glucose metabolic rates with PET scans. Participants were then given immediate and delayed verbal recall tests.

Women with either no, mild or moderate problems performed better than men on the verbal memory tests. There was no difference in those with advanced Alzheimer's.

Because verbal memory scores are used for diagnosing Alzheimer's, some women may be further along in their disease before they are diagnosed. This suggests the need to have an increased index of suspicion when evaluating women with memory problems.

Part C

In this part of the test, there are two texts about different aspects of healthcare. For **questions 7-22**, choose the answer (**A**, **B**, **C** or **D**) which you think fits best according to the text.

Text 1: Asbestosis

Asbestos is a naturally occurring mineral that has been linked to human lung disease. It has been used in a huge number of products due to its high tensile strength, relative resistance to acid and temperature, and its varying textures and degrees of flexibility. It does not evaporate, dissolve, burn or undergo significant reactions with other chemicals. Because of the widespread use of asbestos, its fibres are **ubiquitous** in the environment. Building insulation materials manufactured since 1975 should no longer contain asbestos; however, products made or stockpiled before this time remain in many homes. Indoor air may become contaminated with fibres released from building materials, especially if they are damaged or crumbling.

One of the three types of asbestos-related diseases is asbestosis, a process of lung tissue scarring caused by asbestos fibres. The symptoms of asbestosis usually include slowly progressing shortness of breath and cough, often 20 to 40 years after exposure. Breathlessness advances throughout the disease, even without further asbestos inhalation. This fact is highlighted in the case of a 67-year-old retired plumber. He was on ramipril to treat his hypertension and developed a persistent dry cough, which his doctor presumed to be an ACE inhibitor induced cough. The ramipril was changed to losartan. The patient had never smoked and did not have a history of asthma or COPD. His cough worsened and he complained of breathlessness on exertion. In view of this history and the fact that he was a non-smoker, he was referred for a chest X-ray and to the local respiratory physician. His doctor was surprised to learn that the patient had asbestosis, diagnosed by a high-resolution CT scan. The patient then began legal proceedings to claim compensation as he had worked in a dockyard 25 years previously, during which time he was exposed to asbestos.

There are two major groups of asbestos fibres, the amphibole and chrysotile fibres. The amphiboles are much more likely to cause cancer of the lining of the lung (mesothelioma) and scarring of the lining of the lung (pleural fibrosis). Either group of fibres can cause disease of the lung, such as asbestosis. The risk of developing asbestos-related lung cancer varies between fibre types. Studies of groups of patients exposed to chrysotile fibres show only a moderate increase in risk. On the other hand, exposure to amphibole fibres or to both types of fibres increases the risk of lung cancer two-fold. Although the Occupational Safety and Health Administration (OSHA) has a standard for workplace exposure to asbestos (0.2 fibres/millilitre of air), there is debate over what constitutes a safe level of exposure. While some believe asbestos-related disease is a 'threshold phenomenon', which requires a certain level of exposure for disease to occur, others believe there is no safe level of asbestos.

Depending on their shape and size, asbestos fibres deposit in different areas of the lung. Fibres less than 3mm easily move into the lung tissue and the lining surrounding the lung. Long fibres, greater than 5mm cannot be completely broken down by scavenger cells (macrophages) and become lodged in the lung tissue, causing inflammation. Substances damaging to the lungs are then released by cells that are responding to the foreign asbestos material. The persistence of these long fibres in the lung tissue and the resulting inflammation seem to initiate the process of cancer formation. As inflammation and damage to tissue around the asbestos fibres continues, the resulting scarring can extend from the small airways to the larger airways and the tiny air sacs (alveoli) at the end of the airways.

There is no cure for asbestosis. Treatments focus on a patient's ability to breathe. Medications like bronchodilators, aspirin and antibiotics are often prescribed and such treatments as oxygen therapy and postural drainage may be recommended. If symptoms are so severe that medications don't work, surgery may be recommended to remove scar tissue. Patients with asbestosis, like others with chronic lung disease, are at a higher risk of serious infections that take advantage of diseased or scarred lung tissue, so prevention and rapid treatment is vital. Flu and pneumococcal vaccinations are a part of routine care for these patients. Patients with progressive disease may be given corticosteroids and cyclophosphamide with limited improvement.

Chrysotile is the only form of asbestos that is currently in production today. Despite their association with lung cancer, chrysotile products are still used in 60 countries, according to the industry-sponsored Asbestos Institute. Although the asbestos industry proclaims the 'safety' of chrysotile fibres, which are now imbedded in less friable and 'dusty' products, little is known about the long term effects of these products because of the long delay in the development of disease. In spite of their potential health risks, the durability and cheapness of these products continue to attract commercial applications. Asbestosis remains a significant clinical problem even after marked reductions in on-the-job exposure to asbestos. Again, **this** is due to the long period of time between exposure and the onset of disease.

7. The writer suggests that the potential for harm from asbestos is increased by

    Ⓐ a change in the method of manufacture.

    Ⓑ the way it reacts with other substances.

    Ⓒ the fact that it is used so extensively.

    Ⓓ its presence in recently constructed buildings.

8. The word '**ubiquitous**' in paragraph one suggests that asbestos fibres

    Ⓐ can be found everywhere.

    Ⓑ may last for a long time.

    Ⓒ have an unchanging nature.

    Ⓓ are a natural substance.

9. The case study of the 67-year-old man is given to show that

    Ⓐ smoking is unrelated to a diagnosis of asbestosis.

    Ⓑ doctors should be able to diagnose asbestosis earlier.

    Ⓒ the time from exposure to disease may cause delayed diagnosis.

    Ⓓ patients must provide full employment history details to their doctors.

10. In the third paragraph, the writer highlights the disagreement about

    Ⓐ the relative safety of the two types of asbestos fibres.

    Ⓑ the impact of types of fibres on disease development.

    Ⓒ the results of studies into the levels of risk of fibre types.

    Ⓓ the degree of contact with asbestos fibres considered harmful.

11. In the fourth paragraph, the writer points out that longer asbestos fibres

   (A) can travel as far as the alveoli.

   (B) tend to remain in the pulmonary tissue.

   (C) release substances causing inflammation.

   (D) mount a defence against the body's macrophages.

12. What is highlighted as an important component of patient management?

   (A) the use of corticosteroids

   (B) infection control

   (C) early intervention

   (D) excision of scarred tissue

13. The writer states that products made from chrysotile

   (A) have restricted application.

   (B) may pose a future health threat.

   (C) enjoy approval by the regulatory bodies.

   (D) are safer than earlier asbestos-containing products.

14. In the final paragraph, the word 'this' refers to

   (A) the interval from asbestos exposure to disease.

   (B) the decreased use of asbestos in workplaces.

   (C) asbestosis as an ongoing medical issue.

   (D) occupational exposure to asbestos.

Text 2: Medication non-compliance

A US doctor gives his views on a new program

An important component of a patient's history and physical examination is the question of 'medication compliance,' the term used by physicians to designate whether, or not, a patient is taking his or her medications. Many a hospital chart bears the notorious comment 'Patient has a history of non-compliance.' Now, under a new experimental program in Philadelphia, USA, patients are being paid to take their medications. The concept makes sense in theory - failure to comply is one of the most common reasons that patients are readmitted to hospital shortly after being discharged.

Compliant patients take their medications because they want to live as long as possible; some simply do so because they're responsible, conscientious individuals by nature. But the hustle and bustle of daily life and employment often get in the way of taking medications, especially those that are timed inconveniently or in frequent doses, even for such well-intentioned patients. For the elderly and the mentally or physically impaired, US insurance companies will often pay for a daily visit by a nurse, to ensure a patient gets at least one set of the most vital pills. But other patients are left to fend for themselves, and it is not uncommon these days for patients to be taking a considerable number of vital pills daily.

Some patients have not been properly educated about the importance of their medications in layman's terms. They have told me, for instance, that they don't have high blood pressure because they were once prescribed a high blood pressure pill – in essence, they view an antihypertensive as an antibiotic that can be used as short-term treatment for a short-term problem. Others have told me that they never had a heart attack because they were taken to the cardiac catheterization lab and 'fixed.' As physicians we are responsible for making sure patients understand their own medical history and their own medications.

Not uncommonly patients will say, 'I googled it the other day, and there was a long list of side effects.' But a simple conversation with the patient at this juncture can easily change their perspective. As with many things in medicine, it's all about risks versus benefits – that's what we as physicians are trained to analyse. And patients can rest assured that we'll monitor them closely for side effects and address any that are unpleasant, either by treating them or by trying a different medication.

But to return to the program in Philadelphia, my firm belief is that if patients don't have strong enough incentives to take their medications so they can live longer, healthier lives, then the long-term benefits of providing a financial incentive are likely to be minimal. At the outset, the rewards may be substantial enough to elicit a response. But one isolated system or patient study is not an accurate depiction of the real-life scenario: patients will have to be taking these medications for decades.

Although a simple financial incentives program has its appeal, its complications abound. What's worse, it seems to be saying to society: as physicians, we tell our patients that not only do we work to care for them, but we'll now pay them to take better care of themselves. And by the way, for all you medication-compliant patients out there, you can have the inherent reward of a longer, healthier life, but we're not going to bother sending you money. This seems like some sort of implied punishment.

But more generally, what advice can be given to doctors with non-compliant patients? Dr John Steiner has written a paper on the matter: 'Be compassionate,' he urges doctors. 'Understand what a complicated balancing act it is for patients.' He's surely right **on that score**. Doctors and patients need to work together to figure out what is reasonable and realistic, prioritizing which measures are most important. For one patient, taking the diabetes pills might be more crucial than trying to quit smoking. For another, treating depression is more critical than treating cholesterol. 'Improving compliance is a team sport,' Dr Steiner adds. 'Input from nurses, care managers, social workers and pharmacists is critical.'

When discussing the complicated nuances of compliance with my students, I give the example of my grandmother. A thrifty, no-nonsense woman, she routinely sliced all the cholesterol and heart disease pills her doctor prescribed in half, taking only half the dose. If I questioned this, she'd wave me off with, 'What do those doctors know, anyway?' Sadly, she died suddenly, aged 87, most likely of a massive heart attack. Had she taken her medicines at the appropriate doses, she might have survived it. But then maybe she'd have died a more painful death from some other ailment. Her biggest fear had always been ending up dependent in a nursing home, and by luck or design, she was able to avoid that. Perhaps there was some wisdom in her 'non-compliance.'

Text 2: Questions 15-22

15. In the first paragraph, what is the writer's attitude towards the new programme?

   Ⓐ He doubts that it is correctly named.

   Ⓑ He appreciates the reasons behind it.

   Ⓒ He is sceptical about whether it can work.

   Ⓓ He is more enthusiastic than some other doctors.

16. In the second paragraph, the writer suggests that one category of non-compliance is

   Ⓐ elderly patients who are given occasional assistance.

   Ⓑ patients who are over-prescribed with a certain drug.

   Ⓒ busy working people who mean to be compliant.

   Ⓓ people who are by nature wary of taking pills.

17. What problem with some patients is described in the third paragraph?

   Ⓐ They forget which prescribed medication is for which of their conditions.

   Ⓑ They fail to recognise that some medical conditions require ongoing treatment.

   Ⓒ They don't understand their treatment even when it's explained in simple terms.

   Ⓓ They believe that taking some prescribed pills means they don't need to take others.

18. What does the writer say about side effects to medication?

   Ⓐ Doctors need to have better plans in place if they develop.

   Ⓑ There is too much misleading information about them online.

   Ⓒ Fear of them can waste a lot of unnecessary consultation time.

   Ⓓ Patients need to be informed about the likelihood of them occurring.

19. In the fifth paragraph, what is the writer's reservation about the Philadelphia program?

(A) the long-term feasibility of the central idea

(B) the size of the financial incentives offered

(C) the types of medication that were targeted

(D) the particular sample chosen to participate

20. What objection to the program does the writer make in the sixth paragraph?

(A) It will be counter-productive.

(B) It will place heavy demands on doctors.

(C) It sends the wrong message to patients.

(D) It is a simplistic idea that falls down on its details.

21. The expression '**on that score**' in the seventh paragraph refers to

(A) a complex solution to patients' problems.

(B) a co-operative attitude amongst medical staff.

(C) a realistic assessment of why something happens.

(D) a recommended response to the concerns of patients.

22. The writer suggests that his grandmother

(A) may ultimately have benefited from her non-compliance.

(B) would have appreciated closer medical supervision.

(C) might have underestimated how ill she was.

(D) should have followed her doctor's advice.

END OF READING TEST
THIS BOOKLET WILL BE COLLECTED

WRITING SUB-TEST – TEST BOOKLET

CANDIDATE NUMBER:

LAST NAME:

FIRST NAME:

MIDDLE NAMES:

PROFESSION: Candidate details and photo will be printed here.

VENUE:

TEST DATE:

Passport Photo

CANDIDATE DECLARATION

By signing this, you agree not to disclose or use in any way (other than to take the test) or assist any other person to disclose or use any OET test or sub-test content. If you cheat or assist in any cheating, use any unfair practice, break any of the rules or regulations, or ignore any advice or information, you may be disqualified and your results may not be issued at the sole discretion of CBLA. CBLA also reserves its right to take further disciplinary action against you and to pursue any other remedies permitted by law. If a candidate is suspected of and investigated for malpractice, their personal details and details of the investigation may be passed to a third party where required.

CANDIDATE SIGNATURE: _____

INSTRUCTIONS TO CANDIDATES

You must write your answer for the Writing sub-test in the **Writing Answer Booklet.**

You must **NOT** remove OET material from the test room.

OCCUPATIONAL ENGLISH TEST

WRITING SUB-TEST: NURSING

TIME ALLOWED: **READING TIME:**   5 MINUTES
WRITING TIME: 40 MINUTES

Read the case notes below and complete the writing task which follows.

Notes:

You are a registered nurse working at Newtown Community Hospital. Your patient, Ms Mary Bell, is being discharged today.

Patient:	Mary Bell (Ms)
Age:	66 Years
Marital status:	Single
Family:	Nil
First admitted:	24 June 2017, Newtown Community Hospital
Discharge:	15 July 2017
Diagnosis:	Unstable diabetes mellitus.
	Small infected (left) foot ulcer.
Medical history:	Non-insulin-dependent diabetes mellitus – 15 years.
Medications:	Glibenclamide (Glimel) 5mg daily.
	Metformin (Diabex) 850mg t.d.s.
	Amoxycillin/clavulanate (Augmentin Duo Forte) 875/125mg orally, b.d.

Social/family background: Retired at 65 from managerial position 2016.

Lives alone in own four-bedroom home.

Income: small pension – much lower than pre-retirement income.

Reports no relatives or close friends.

Reports no outside interests.

Since retirement alcohol intake has increased and dietary quality has decreased.

Periodic problems with self-administration of hypoglycaemic medication.

Nursing management and progress:

Medical hypoglycaemic agent (glibenclamide) to continue.

Antibiotic therapy (Augmentin Duo Forte) for review at completion of current course.

Ulcer daily saline dressing, monitor wound margins, observe for signs of complications, review healing progress, etc.

Discharge plan:
Monitor medication compliance, blood sugar levels, alcohol intake, diet.

Encourage moderate exercise programme.

Suggest establishment of income-producing activity.

Encourage establishment of social activities.

Prepare a letter to the community nurse, emphasising the need for an overall life-style plan, and suggesting involvement of community social worker service.

Writing Task:

Using the information given in the case notes, write a letter of discharge to Ms Jane Rudik, the community nurse at Newtown Community Health Centre, informing her about the patient's condition and her medical and social needs. Address your letter to Ms Jane Rudik, Community Nurse, Newtown Community Health Centre, Newtown.

In your answer:

- **Expand the relevant notes into complete sentences**
- **Do <u>not</u> use note form**
- **Use letter format**

The body of the letter should be approximately 180–200 words.

WRITING SUB-TEST – ANSWER BOOKLET

CANDIDATE NUMBER:	
LAST NAME:	
FIRST NAME:	
MIDDLE NAMES:	Passport Photo
PROFESSION:	Candidate details and photo will be printed here.
VENUE:	
TEST DATE:	

CANDIDATE DECLARATION

By signing this, you agree not to disclose or use in any way (other than to take the test) or assist any other person to disclose or use any OET test or sub-test content. If you cheat or assist in any cheating, use any unfair practice, break any of the rules or regulations, or ignore any advice or information, you may be disqualified and your results may not be issued at the sole discretion of CBLA. CBLA also reserves its right to take further disciplinary action against you and to pursue any other remedies permitted by law. If a candidate is suspected of and investigated for malpractice, their personal details and details of the investigation may be passed to a third party where required.

CANDIDATE SIGNATURE: _____

TIME ALLOWED
READING TIME: 5 MINUTES
WRITING TIME: 40 MINUTES

INSTRUCTIONS TO CANDIDATES

1. **Reading time: 5 minutes**
   During this time you may study the writing task and notes. You **MUST NOT** write, highlight, underline or make any notes.

2. **Writing time: 40 minutes**

3. Use the back page for notes and rough draft only. Notes and rough draft will **NOT** be marked.

   Please write your answer clearly on page 1 and page 2.

   Cross out anything you **DO NOT** want the examiner to consider.

4. You must write your answer for the Writing sub-test in this **Answer Booklet** using **pen or pencil**.

5. You must **NOT** remove OET material from the test room.

Please record your answer on this page.

(Only answers on Page 1 and Page 2 will be marked.)

_____
_____
_____
_____
_____
_____
_____
_____
_____
_____
_____
_____
_____
_____
_____
_____
_____
_____
_____
_____
_____
_____
_____
_____
_____
_____
_____
_____
_____
_____
_____
_____
_____
_____
_____

OET Writing sub-test – Answer booklet   1

Please record your answer on this page.

(Only answers on Page 1 and Page 2 will be marked.)

_____

_____

_____

_____

_____

_____

_____

_____

_____

_____

_____

_____

_____

_____

_____

_____

_____

_____

_____

_____

_____

_____

_____

_____

_____

_____

_____

_____

_____

_____

_____

_____

OET Writing sub-test – Answer booklet   2

Space for notes and rough draft. Only your answers on Page 1 and Page 2 will be marked.

SPEAKING SUB-TEST

CANDIDATE NUMBER:	
LAST NAME:	
FIRST NAME:	
MIDDLE NAMES:	Your details and photo will be printed here.
PROFESSION:	**Passport Photo**
VENUE:	
TEST DATE:	

CANDIDATE DECLARATION

By signing this, you agree not to disclose or use in any way (other than to take the test) or assist any other person to disclose or use any OET test or sub-test content. If you cheat or assist in any cheating, use any unfair practice, break any of the rules or regulations, or ignore any advice or information, you may be disqualified and your results may not be issued at the sole discretion of CBLA. CBLA also reserves its right to take further disciplinary action against you and to pursue any other remedies permitted by law. If a candidate is suspected of and investigated for malpractice, their personal details and details of the investigation may be passed to a third party where required.

CANDIDATE SIGNATURE: _____

INSTRUCTION TO CANDIDATES

Please confirm with the Interlocutor that your roleplay card number and colour match the Interlocutor card before you begin.

Interlocutor to complete only

ID No: _____   Passport: ☐   National ID: ☐   Alternative ID approved: ☐

Speaking sub-test:

ID document sighted? ☐   Photo match? ☐   Signature match? ☐   Did not attend? ☐

Interlocutor name: _____

Interlocutor signature: _____

ROLEPLAYER CARD NO. 1	**NURSING**

SETTING	Hospital Casualty Ward
PATIENT	You are in hospital following a road accident. You are not seriously injured, but have lost blood and have been told that you need a blood transfusion. You have no idea what the procedure will involve. You are anxious about the procedure and the danger of receiving infected blood. You have read that patients have contracted HIV through blood transfusions.
TASK	• You are anxious and upset. Express your fear of contracting HIV. Respond to the nurse's reassurances accordingly.
	• Seek an explanation from the nurse about the procedure and the risks involved.
	• Eventually agree to have the transfusion.

Sample role-play

OET Sample role-play

CANDIDATE CARD NO. 1	**NURSING**

SETTING	Hospital Casualty Ward
NURSE	The patient is in hospital following a road accident. The patient's condition is stable but he/she has lost blood and needs a blood transfusion. The patient does not understand what will happen. The patient is anxious about the procedure.
TASK	• Find out about the patient's concerns.
	• Reassure the patient that the possibility of infection is very small (as care is taken to screen donors and test donated blood for possible infection).
	• Explain the procedure for a blood transfusion (e.g., sterile conditions, new syringes, nurses watch closely, etc.).
	• Stress that the patient really needs the transfusion in order to recover fully.

Sample role-play

ROLEPLAYER CARD NO. 2	**NURSING**

SETTING — Community Health Centre

PARENT — Your six-year-old son has just cut a finger on his right hand with a kitchen knife that was left on the kitchen bench. The finger won't stop bleeding, and you are panicking about it. Your child is afraid of doctors and you have to weigh this consideration against your concern about his finger. You are also worried about possible scarring.

TASK

- Outline what happened. Explain that the cut looks deep to you, your child is in pain and you are very worried. Shouldn't your son have stitches?
- Convey your anxiety and uncertainty to the nurse. Ask how long the finger will take to heal and if it will be scarred for a long time. Ask when your son, who is right-handed, will be able to use this hand properly again.
- Ask the nurse what to do about your son's finger.
- If the question of your responsibility for the injury comes up, be defensive. You're a busy person and can't spend every minute of your day watching him.

© Cambridge Boxhill Language Assessment

Sample role-play

CANDIDATE CARD NO. 2	**NURSING**

SETTING — Community Health Centre

NURSE — This parent's six-year-old son has cut his finger, which is bleeding freely. You examine the cut, which is not too serious, and you don't think he needs stitches.

TASK

- Find out how the cut happened.

- Reassure the parent. Answer his/her questions about length of time for healing, any scarring, whether stitches are necessary, etc.

- Explain how to clean, apply antiseptic, and dress the cut suitably. Point out the need to keep the finger clean and dry.

- Warn the parent about keeping sharp implements out of reach. Be tactful in giving advice.

© Cambridge Boxhill Language Assessment

Sample role-play

Listening sub-test

ANSWER KEY – Parts A, B & C

LISTENING SUB-TEST – ANSWER KEY

PART A: QUESTIONS 1-12

1. (computer) programmer

2. asthma (attacks)

3. penicillin

4. vegetarian

5. fertility

6. breech

7. forceps / forcipes

8. breastfeeding

9. epilepsy

10. Down syndrome / DS / DNS / Down's (syndrome)

11. CVS / chronic vill(o)us sampling

12. sibling(s) / brothers and/or sisters

PART A: QUESTIONS 13-24

13. medial meniscus OR medial

14. (very tender/tender/painful) bumps

15. squat (properly) / bend (his) knee

16. (used) ice pack(s)

17. tendonitis

18. (hospital) physio(therapist) / physio(therapist) (in the hospital)

19. hamstring(s)

20. (constant) anxiety

21. fibromyalgia

22. (a pain/pain) diary

23. (his) shoulders and elbows / (his) elbows and shoulders

24. rheumatologist

PART B: QUESTIONS 25-30

25. A correcting patient's misconception about obesity
26. B getting approval for a repair to a machine.
27. A locate the CPR board quickly enough.
28. B there is sensory loss in her legs.
29. C She values the greater understanding it gives her of her work.
30. A the age of the subjects.

PART C: QUESTIONS 31-36

31. A she was considering retirement from her sport.
32. C some key muscles weren't strong enough.
33. B soon discovered what was causing the problem.
34. C The treatment was succeeding without it.
35. B focussed on applying the correct techniques.
36. B to reduce the stress placed on her take-off leg

PART C: QUESTIONS 37-42

37. A where it was originally published
38. A gain insights into their mental health problems.
39. C a tendency to jump to conclusions
40. A They provide an insight not gained from numbers alone.
41. C He is doubtful of their value when used independently.
42. B his commitment to making them more widely accepted.

—

END OF KEY

Listening sub-test

Audio Script – Practice test 1

This test has three parts. In each part you'll hear a number of different extracts. At the start of each extract, you'll hear this sound: ---***---.

You'll have time to read the questions before you hear each extract and you'll hear each extract ONCE only. Complete your answers as you listen.

At the end of the test, you'll have two minutes to check your answers.

Part A. In this part of the test, you'll hear two different extracts. In each extract, a health professional is talking to a patient. For questions 1 to 24, complete the notes with information you hear. Now, look at the notes for extract one.

PAUSE: 5 SECONDS

Extract one. Questions 1 to 12.

You hear an obstetrician talking to a patient called Melissa Gordon. For questions 1 to 12, complete the notes with a word or short phrase. You now have thirty seconds to look at the notes.

PAUSE: 30 SECONDS

---***---

M: So, this first meeting, Mrs Gordon, is mainly a chance for you and I to get to know each other. I'll ask you about your medical history and this is also an opportunity for you to ask me any questions that you've got at this point.

F: *Sure.*

M: So, some background. What kind of work do you do?

F: *I have a job at an engineering company. I'm a computer programmer. I currently do four days a week, but I hope to reduce that to three after my maternity leave.*

M: Ahh, excellent. So tell me about your medical health? Do you have any conditions I should know about?

F: *Well err, I have asthma attacks but they don't happen often. I lost about ten kilos and that's certainly helped. I have an inhaler but I hardly ever use it. Oh, I should also let you know that I come out in terrible hives if I take penicillin, but not other things - I'm fine if I eat nuts, for example. I have a fairly healthy lifestyle. I'm a vegetarian and I've never smoked.*

M: Good.

F: *I'm afraid I don't go to the gym or anything, but I walk to work and err... generally keep active.*

M: Ahh that's good. So is this your first pregnancy?

F: *No, I have a daughter called Ella – she's three now.*

M: Ahh...and did everything go smoothly that time?

F: *There were no major problems during the pregnancy itself. But it took me quite a time to fall pregnant - the first time. After having various tests, I was given some fertility drugs. Ohh what were they called? It's on the tip of my tongue. Ahm, never mind. It'll come back to me. This time, though, I didn't need any help.*

M: It's no problem. What about labour last time around?

F: *That was a nightmare…though everything - thank goodness - worked out in the end. It was a breech birth. It looked as if I might have to have a caesarean, and I really didn't want that. I was pleased I managed without an epidural too. They had to use forceps to get Ella out but I didn't need any stitches, so that was OK. Unfortunately, though, I had some difficulties after the birth too. I was desperate to start breastfeeding, but that didn't work out - at least not until I was given some guidance by the midwife.*

M: OK. So can I ask you about the baby's father?

F: *Sure. That's my husband, Paul. There's something in his family history I should tell you about, I think. His grandfather and father both had epilepsy - though he hasn't developed it himself. I'm not sure if that means his children have a greater chance of having it or not. Oh, also he has a child from his first marriage and she has Down's syndrome. So he gets a bit anxious when I'm pregnant.*

M: Oh well, that's understandable, of course. We can discuss various testing options if you like. You might want to consider amniocentesis, for instance.

F: *But that carries a risk of miscarriage, doesn't it? I don't want to go for that. I've heard about another test called err…CVS. Is that something to consider?*

M: Well, it's certainly an option. However, that procedure in fact also carries a small increase in the risk of miscarriage. And you'd need to come to a decision fairly soon, because it's normally carried out between weeks…ten and twelve of the pregnancy.

F: *Well, I can tell you straightaway that if there's more risk then I wouldn't consider it. I know my husband will feel the same.*

M: Well that's fair enough. So, is there anything else you'd like to ask me about today?

F: *Nothing urgent. But it'd be good to know more about how to get siblings ready for a new addition to the family. I want to make sure Ella doesn't feel threatened or replaced or anything.*

M: Well, there's a leaflet that many parents find helpful. Here we are - have a look through that.

F: *Ahh, thanks – that's great. I'm sure I'll have lots more questions at our next meeting.*

PAUSE: 10 SECONDS
Extract two. Questions 13 to 24.

You hear a GP talking to a new patient called Mike Royce. For questions 13 to 24, complete the notes with a word or short phrase. You now have thirty seconds to look at the notes.

PAUSE: 30 SECONDS
---***---

F   *Hello. Come on in. You must be Mr Royce. I understand that you've just signed up with the practice.*

M   Yeah that's right, Mike Royce. I've joined this practice because my previous GP retired and he suggested I come here.

F   *Right, and I understand you've got an ongoing medical condition you're worried about. Perhaps you'd like to start by telling me about that. How did it start?*

M   Well, I suppose it started out as a really strong pain in my left knee, in, um, I think it's called the… the medial meniscus. Is that right? It came on whenever I tried to bend the knee more than normal. Then I tripped while climbing some stairs at work and that seemed to make things worse. I started to get these very tender bumps all over the back of the knee. They were very painful, even just lightly touching them. The doctor called them trigger points.

F   *Yeah, that's right. They're called that because pain frequently radiates out from them when touched. And how did that affect you day-to-day?*

M   Well, I went back to work after a week or so, but I was still having knee problems. I couldn't really squat properly or climb ladders – that's important in my job. I'm a painter, you know, and I'm always having to get into awkward positions. Anyway, I kept going back to my old GP explaining that I still had severe pain whenever I tried to bend my knee. He gave me all these exercises to do, and I tried doing them, I really did. I made sure I did gentle stretches before I did anything more energetic, everything really. I tried resting like he told me, I used ice packs when, when it got sore, but nothing really worked.

F   *Right, I see…*

M   But then the doctor decided I might be suffering from tendonitis, so he sent me for some rehab work in the hospital. That actually did seem to work, at least at first.

F   *But I'm guessing not for long.*

M   Right. The problem came back. I kept telling the doctor that my knee still wasn't healed, but it was actually my physiotherapist in the hospital rather than my old GP who noticed that something was wrong with my muscles. He wouldn't say what it was, but I knew something was up. He was doing myofascial release on my hamstrings and I was in agony.

F   *Right, so did…did you go back to your GP?*

M   I did. But he didn't know what I should do about it. So I left feeling completely fed up. That's one of the reasons I decided to come here. I just feel like nobody's taking this seriously. I think it's affecting my life in lots of other ways too. The worry's giving me insomnia for one thing. I don't think I have actual depression, but I certainly suffer from constant anxiety about when it's going to flare up.

F   *Is there anything that you're particularly worried you might have?*

M   Well, I've researched this pain I'm getting. Erm, to be honest, I'm convinced I've got fibromyalgia, not just some simple muscle problem, because I fit most of the symptoms, and I've had pain absolutely everywhere. Look. I've even kept a… a pain diary so that I could track what I did that set it off, you know, the weather, if I was working or not, where it was affecting me, what it felt like. I've figured out from this that it's usually in the same places that I mentioned earlier, plus some newish places too… my shoulders and elbows – and I know that my knee's actually one of the more tender points for it. What do you think?

F   *Look, I must say from what you've told me so far that I'm concerned enough to look into that possibility. So, as a next step, we need to get you seen by a rheumatologist. This is a notoriously difficult condition to diagnose, as I'm sure you're aware, because so many of the symptoms overlap with other conditions too.*

M   I won't be happy to be proved right but I'll certainly be glad to get some answers at long last.

PAUSE: 10 SECONDS
That is the end of Part A. Now, look at Part B.

PAUSE: 5 SECONDS
Part B.

In this part of the test, you'll hear six different extracts. In each extract, you'll hear people talking in a different healthcare setting.

For questions 25 to 30, choose the answer A, B or C which fits best according to what you hear. You'll have time to read each question before you listen. Complete your answers as you listen.

Now look at Question 25. You hear a dietitian talking to a patient. Now read the question.

PAUSE: 15 SECONDS
---***---

F: *So what seems to be the problem?*

M: I feel such a failure. I'm sure people think that if I just tried harder, I could lose weight. Maybe I need more willpower.

F: *Well, firstly, well done for seeking medical help. Actually, being overweight or obese is a medical problem, because being overweight changes how your body works.*

M: Oh, thanks, but I do feel that it's my fault for being this way.

F: *Well, I hear what you say, but please understand that these days, we consider that obesity is a disease, like high blood pressure or asthma. You see, the body's signals to the brain stop working correctly when you're overweight. And, with time, you feel less full, even if you eat the same amount. And when you cut calories, your body tries to use less energy to keep your weight the same.*

PAUSE: 5 SECONDS
Question 26. You hear members of a hospital committee discussing problems in the X-ray department. Now read the question.

PAUSE: 15 SECONDS
---***---

F   *So next on the agenda is the problems in the X-ray department. Nick, would you like to fill us in here?*

M   Well, as you all know, this is a very busy department. Err, so we have four X-ray machines in all, including one in the Fracture and Orthopaedic clinic area, but recently one of the other X-ray machines developed a fault and so we had to apply for authorisation for the purchase of a new tube for it. There's been some kind of hold up with the paperwork, and while we've been waiting, patients are being brought into the Fracture and Orthopaedic area for X-rays there instead, and of course that's causing further congestion.

PAUSE: 5 SECONDS

Question 27. You hear a senior nurse giving feedback to a trainee after a training exercise. Now read the question.

PAUSE: 15 SECONDS

---***---

F   *OK, that went quite well, didn't it? But it took you a while to work out where the CPR board was kept. So what does that tell you about this scenario?*

M   We need to check where things are before doing anything else.

F   *Exactly. And of course it takes a second or two to put the head of the bed down, because you've got to have that part of the bed flat before you slip the board in. I wish there was a quicker way.*

M   So do I put the CPR board under, or would I normally hand it over to somebody else?

F   *It makes no difference as long as it's done.*

PAUSE: 5 SECONDS

Question 28. You hear a trainee nurse asking his senior colleague about the use of anti-embolism socks for a patient. Now read the question.

PAUSE: 15 SECONDS

---***---

M: I noticed that Mrs Jones isn't wearing the usual anti-embolism socks, but I didn't want to ask her why not because she was asleep. Is it because her legs are swollen?

F: *Well, sometimes we don't recommend the socks if there's severe swelling with oedema, but that's not the case here. Mrs Jones was actually given them initially on admission last night, but she told us this morning that her lower legs were feeling numb – she described it as having no feeling. Until we've checked out the reason for that, for example it could be an underlying condition which could damage her arterial circulation, we're reducing the risk of thrombosis by pharmacological means.*

M: Oh, I see.

PAUSE: 5 SECONDS

Question 29. You hear a vet talking about her involvement in the management of the practice where she works. Now read the question.

PAUSE: 15 SECONDS

---***---

F: *At first, when I took over the financial running of the practice, I felt rather thrown in at the deep end. I really needed to know my stuff and be super organised, especially with the number of new drugs and treatments available now, all of which have to be very carefully costed. It keeps me super-busy, but monitoring stocks and so on helps give me*

confidence and allows me to see how everything fits into the overall picture of working as a vet. My manager's more than happy to leave me to run this side of things – he's in overall charge, of course, but I can always go to him if there's a problem. I keep him closely informed of what's happening. He's always pleased if I manage to make savings anywhere.

PAUSE: 5 SECONDS
Question 30. You hear a physiotherapist giving a presentation about a study she's been involved in. Now read the question.

PAUSE: 15 SECONDS
---***---

F: *I'm a physiotherapist, and I'm presenting our poster about constraint induced movement therapy for children suffering from partial paralysis following brain surgery.*

We did a case series of four children, who'd all undergone hemispherectomies. They were admitted to inpatient therapy within two weeks post-op and began therapy two to three weeks post-op. The therapy continued after they were discharged. Our findings were that three of the kids regained excellent function and mobility with ambulation and upper extremity function. One didn't do so well, unfortunately, but he gave up the therapy early on. This type of movement therapy has been used a lot in adult populations following stroke. The findings here promote moving forward with further research on the paediatric or adolescent population, following either hemispherectomy or other surgeries, to help us decide how appropriate this therapy would be for them.

PAUSE: 10 SECONDS
That is the end of Part B. Now, look at Part C.

PAUSE: 5 SECONDS
Part C. In this part of the test, you'll hear two different extracts. In each extract, you'll hear health professionals talking about aspects of their work.

For questions 31 to 42, choose the answer A, B or C which fits best according to what you hear. Complete your answers as you listen.

Now look at extract one.

Extract one. Questions 31 to 36. You hear a sports physiotherapist called Chris Maloney giving a presentation in which he describes treating a high jumper with a knee injury.

You now have 90 seconds to read questions 31 to 36.

PAUSE: 90 SECONDS
---***---

M: Hello. I'm Chris Maloney, a physiotherapist specialising in sports injuries, and I'd like to present a case study to give you an idea of the sort of work I do.

It features a very successful high jumper in her mid-twenties, who was referred to me with severe pain in her right knee – and that's the leg she takes off from when she jumps. What's more, when she'd stepped up her training in preparation for a big competition, the pain worsened, and she'd been forced to pull out of the event. After that, she'd taken several months off training to rest and get treatment from various therapists. To her dismay, however, not only did the pain continue, it actually got worse, meaning she was unable to do any strength training, let alone jump-specific work. By the time I saw her, she was on the verge of giving up, having lost virtually all belief in her ability.

My initial assessment quickly confirmed patellar tendinitis in the affected knee, accompanied by some swelling and significant tenderness over the lower part of the kneecap – this wasn't difficult to diagnose. I also noted that she was slightly overweight for her height and had rather flat feet, but that's not so unusual in high jumpers. Further assessment revealed that the gluteal muscles connecting the hips and thighs were considerably less sturdy than you'd expect in an athlete of this calibre, and both the lateral retinaculum connecting the patella to the femur and the ilio-tibial band – the ligament running down the outside of the thigh – were tight and tender.

As a first stage, I was keen to show I could help by relieving some of the pain. So, I worked at loosening her lateral retinaculum to see how much of the tendon pain was due to inflammation and how much came from restriction of normal patellar movement. This manipulation and massage instantly cleared the pain she'd felt while doing a single-leg dip exercise – where you stand on one leg and bend the knee. This indicated that her tendon pain was most likely due to patello-femoral joint dysfunction – caused by muscle imbalance and poor biomechanics – and not by an active inflammatory process or partial tear in her patellar tendon, so an MRI scan wasn't needed. The treatment continued along similar lines for some weeks, with loosening of the lateral retinaculum and deep-tissue massage of the ilio-tibial band and other muscles.

One option at this point was something called 'taping'. This is a way of reducing pain so that athletes can continue with strength exercises. But it seemed clear from early on that we shouldn't put taping on this patient's patella and tendon until she started jumping again. She was getting pain relief and progress simply from the manual techniques, and taping might've led to problems later on. Athletes often become dependent on tape and other accessories. In other words, instead of aiming for one-hundred percent muscle strength and joint position control, they settle for eighty percent plus artificial support.

The patient also had a specially designed programme of gym activities. Although she needed to restore power to those muscles affected by inflammation and tenderness, the priority was to get her posture and alignment right. She started by doing double-leg squats with her back to a wall in front of a mirror so that she could see whether her feet were arched and if her knees were over her feet. She also did squats whilst squeezing a ball between her knees. There was light leg press work, followed by single-leg stance work – first static, then on wobble-boards, and with elastic resistance. She progressed to moving on and off steps, sometimes holding weights, all the time paying close attention to positioning and muscle and joint alignment.

The next stage was to liaise with the patient's coach. She began running – jogging for stamina and then sprint sessions. Work on power was stepped up gradually and included some weightlifting. After some analysis, we also decided to modify her…her run-up to the high-jump bar. By beginning from a wider position and running in with much less of a curve, there was much less of an impact on the ankle, knees and hip, especially in her right jumping leg. Interestingly, the patient reported that remodelling the run-up felt fresh and motivating and helped to reinforce the sense she had of being a reborn athlete. Once the rehabilitation process was complete, she was able to compete without pain and free of any reliance on taping or knee-strapping.

So, before I go on to ….. [fade]

PAUSE: 10 SECONDS
Now look at extract two.

Extract two. Questions 37 to 42. You hear a clinical psychiatrist called Dr Anthony Gibbens giving a presentation about the value of individual patients' experiences and 'stories' in medicine.

You now have 90 seconds to read questions 37 to 42.

PAUSE: 90 SECONDS
---***---

M: Hello. My name's Anthony Gibbens. I'm a clinical psychiatrist and published author. I'd like to talk about something that's relevant to all medical professionals: the use of narratives in medicine.

Let me begin with a case study, sent to me by a colleague who shares my interest in the subject. The study featured a thirty-year-old man who was hospitalised for severe panic attacks. He was treated with 'narcoanalysis' but, feeling no relief, turned to alcohol and endured years of depression and social isolation. Four decades later, he was back in the psychiatric system, but for the first time he was prescribed the antidepressant, Zoloft. Six weeks later, he was discharged because the panic attacks and depression had disappeared. He lived a full life until his death nineteen years later. If the narrative was striking, it was even more so for its inclusion in a medical journal.

Repeatedly, I've been surprised by the impact that even lightly sketched case histories can have on readers. In my first book, I wrote about personality and how it might change on medication. My second was concerned with theories of intimacy. Readers, however, often used the books for a different purpose: identifying depression. Regularly I received and still receive phone calls, people saying 'My husband's just like X', one figure from a clinical example. Other readers wrote to say that they'd recognised themselves. Seeing that they weren't alone gave them hope. Encouragement is another benefit of case description, familiar to us in an age when everyone's writing their biography.

But this isn't to say that stories are a panacea to issues inherent in treating patients, and there can be disadvantages. Consider my experience prescribing Prozac. When certain patients reported feeling 'better than well' after receiving it, I presented these examples, first in essays for psychiatrists and then in my book, where I surrounded the narrative material with accounts of research. In time, my loosely supported descriptions led others to do controlled trials that confirmed the phenomenon. But doctors hadn't waited for those controlled trials. In advance, the better-than-well hypothesis had served as a tentative fact. Treating depression, colleagues looked out for personality change, even aimed for it, even though this wasn't my intended outcome.

This brings me to my next point. Often the knowledge that informs clinical decisions emerges when you stand back from it, like an impressionist painting. What initially seems like randomly scattered information begins to come together, and what you see is the bigger picture. That's where the true worth of anecdote lies. Beyond its role as illustration, hypothesis builder, and low-level guidance for practice, storytelling can act as a modest counterbalance to a narrow focus on data. If we rely solely on 'evidence', we risk moving toward a monoculture whereby patients and their afflictions become reduced to inanimate objects – a result I'd consider unfortunate, since there are many ways to influence people for the better. It's been my hope that, while we wait for conclusive science, stories will preserve diversity in our theories of mind.

My recent reading of outcome trials of antidepressants has strengthened my suspicion that the line between research and storytelling can be fuzzy. In medicine, randomised trials are rarely large enough to provide guidance on their own. Statisticians amalgamate many studies through a technique called meta-analysis. The first step of the process, deciding which data to include, colours the findings. Effectively, the numbers are narrative. Put simply, evidence-based medicine is judgment-based medicine in which randomised trials are carefully assessed and given their due. I don't think we need to be embarrassed about this. Our substantial formal findings require integration. The danger is in pretending otherwise.

I've long felt isolated in embracing the use of narratives in medicine, which is why I warm to the likelihood of narratives being used to inform future medical judgements. It would be unfortunate if medicine moved fully to squeeze the art out of its science by marginalising the narrative. Stories aren't just better at capturing the 'bigger picture' but the smaller picture too. I'm thinking of the article about the depressed man given the drug Zoloft. The degree of transformation in the patient was just as impressive as the length of observation. No formal research can offer a forty-year lead-in or a nineteen-year follow-up. Few studies report on both symptoms and social progress. Research reduces information about many people; narratives retain the texture of life in all its forms. We need storytelling, which is why I'll keep harping on about it until the message gets through.

PAUSE: 10 SECONDS
That is the end of Part C.

You now have two minutes to check your answers.

PAUSE: 120 SECONDS
That is the end of the Listening test.

Reading sub-test

Answer Key – Part A

READING SUB-TEST – ANSWER KEY

PART A: QUESTIONS 1-20

1	A
2	B
3	A
4	D
5	B
6	C
7	B
8	fine bore
9	water-based lubricant
10	tape
11	(a) syringe
12	15-30 minutes/mins OR fifteen-thirty minutes/mins
13	(turn) on(to) left side
14	(to) x-ray (department) OR (to) radiology
15	(a) feeding pump
16	stretch
17	gastroesophageal reflux
18	6/six Fr/French
19	breathlessness
20	(expressed) breast milk

Reading sub-test

Answer Key – Parts B & C

READING SUB-TEST – ANSWER KEY

PART B: QUESTIONS 1-6

1	A	this should be reported.
2	C	communicate their intentions to others.
3	B	best practice procedures
4	A	if non-disclosure could adversely affect those involved
5	A	act as a reminder of their obligations.
6	C	mild dementia in women can remain undiagnosed.

PART C: QUESTIONS 7-14

7	C	the fact that it is used so extensively.
8	A	can be found everywhere.
9	C	the time from exposure to disease may cause delayed diagnosis.
10	D	the degree of contact with asbestos fibres considered harmful.
11	B	tend to remain in the pulmonary tissue.
12	B	infection control
13	B	may pose a future health threat.
14	C	asbestosis as an ongoing medical issue.

PART C: QUESTIONS 15-22

15	B	He appreciates the reasons behind it.
16	C	busy working people who mean to be compliant.
17	B	They fail to recognise that some medical conditions require ongoing treatment.
18	D	Patients need to be informed about the likelihood of them occurring.
19	A	the long-term feasibility of the central idea
20	C	It sends the wrong message to patients.
21	D	a recommended response to the concerns of patients.
22	A	may ultimately have benefited from her non-compliance.

OCCUPATIONAL ENGLISH TEST

WRITING SUB-TEST: NURSING

SAMPLE RESPONSE: LETTER OF DISCHARGE

Ms Jane Rudik
Community Nurse
Newtown Community Health Centre
Newtown

15 July 2017

Dear Ms Rudik,

Re: Ms Mary Bell

Ms Bell has been an inpatient at Newtown Community Hospital for the past three weeks.

Ms Bell was admitted for stabilisation of her non-insulin dependent diabetes mellitus, for which she has been treated with oral anti-hyperglycaemic agents (glibenclamide 5mg daily; metformin 850mg t.d.s.) for the past 15 years. She has also developed a small ulcer on her left foot, which has responded to antibiotic therapy (Augmentin Duo Forte) and daily saline dressings. She will require ongoing management and monitoring of the wound for complications.

Ms Bell retired from a managerial position at the end of 2016, and has not found it easy to establish a new routine in her retirement. She would benefit from your help in monitoring her medication, blood sugars, alcohol intake and diet. It might also help to introduce her to some ways of expanding her social activities and engaging in some moderate exercise. As her income has decreased since her retirement, she might be encouraged to undertake some income-producing activity. A referral to the community social worker service may be of benefit.

I am sure that you will be able to help her establish an ongoing plan for a healthier and more productive lifestyle for her retirement.

Your sincerely,

Nurse

NURSING

PRACTICE TEST

2

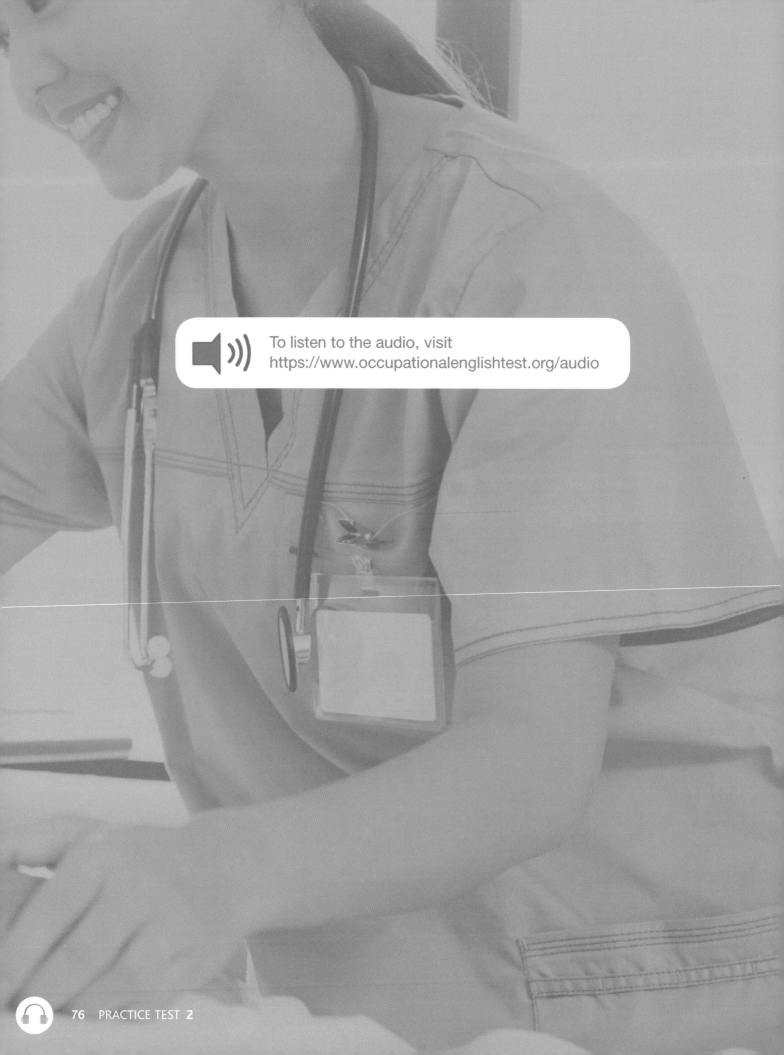

To listen to the audio, visit
https://www.occupationalenglishtest.org/audio

LISTENING SUB-TEST – QUESTION PAPER

CANDIDATE NUMBER:

LAST NAME:

FIRST NAME:

MIDDLE NAMES:

PROFESSION: Candidate details and photo will be printed here.

VENUE:

TEST DATE:

Passport Photo

CANDIDATE DECLARATION

By signing this, you agree not to disclose or use in any way (other than to take the test) or assist any other person to disclose or use any OET test or sub-test content. If you cheat or assist in any cheating, use any unfair practice, break any of the rules or regulations, or ignore any advice or information, you may be disqualified and your results may not be issued at the sole discretion of CBLA. CBLA also reserves its right to take further disciplinary action against you and to pursue any other remedies permitted by law. If a candidate is suspected of and investigated for malpractice, their personal details and details of the investigation may be passed to a third party where required.

CANDIDATE SIGNATURE: _____

TIME: APPROXIMATELY **40 MINUTES**

INSTRUCTIONS TO CANDIDATES

DO NOT open this question paper until you are told to do so.

One mark will be granted for each correct answer.

Answer **ALL** questions. Marks are **NOT** deducted for incorrect answers.

At the end of the test, you will have two minutes to check your answers.

At the end of the test, hand in this **Question Paper.**

You must not remove OET material from the test room.

HOW TO ANSWER THE QUESTIONS

Part A: Write your answers on this **Question Paper** by filling in the blanks. **Example: Patient:** _____ *Ray Sands*

Part B & Part C: Mark your answers on this **Question Paper** by filling in the circle using a 2B pencil. **Example:** Ⓐ
Ⓑ
Ⓒ

www.occupationalenglishtest.org

© Cambridge Boxhill Language Assessment – ABN 51 988 559 414

[CANDIDATE NO.] LISTENING QUESTION PAPER 01/12

Occupational English Test
Listening Test

This test has three parts. In each part you'll hear a number of different extracts. At the start of each extract, you'll hear this sound: --beep—

You'll have time to read the questions before you hear each extract and you'll hear each extract **ONCE ONLY**. Complete your answers as you listen.

At the end of the test you'll have two minutes to check your answers.

Part A

In this part of the test, you'll hear two different extracts. In each extract, a health professional is talking to a patient.

For **questions 1-24**, complete the notes with information you hear.

Now, look at the notes for extract one.

Extract 1: Questions 1-12

You hear a consultant endocrinologist talking to a patient called Sarah Croft. For **questions 1-12**, complete the notes with a word or short phrase.

You now have 30 seconds to look at the notes.

Patient	Sarah Croft
Medical history	• hypertension (recently worsened)
	• 3 years of corticosteroid treatment for **(1)** _____

General symptoms

- gradual weight gain, especially in stomach area
- **(2)** _____ on face: embarrassing
- visible **(3)** _____ between the shoulders
- swollen ankles
- excessive and constant **(4)** _____
- backache
- periods are **(5)** _____
- extreme tiredness

Dermatological symptoms

- tendency to **(6)** _____
- wounds slow to heal, **(7)** _____ on thighs
- face appears red in colour, **(8)** _____ area on neck
- recent development of **(9)** _____

Psychological symptoms

- mildly depressed
- scared by new experience of **(10)** _____
- feels constantly **(11)** _____
- intermittent cognitive difficulties

Recommended tests

- further blood tests
- **(12)** _____ test possibly

Extract 2: Questions 13-24

You hear an anaesthetist talking to a patient called Mary Wilcox prior to an operation. For **questions 13-24**, complete the notes with a word or short phrase.
You now have thirty seconds to look at the notes.

Patient   Mary Wilcox

Current medications

Reason for medication	Medication	Comments
High blood pressure	Thiazide (13) _____	both taken this morning with (14) _____
Heart attack	(15) _____	taken this morning
	(16) _____	stopped taking this 7 days ago

Medical history

- went to GP two years ago feeling **(17)**

  _____ – heart attack subsequently

  diagnosed

- had two **(18)** _____ inserted

Present condition

- alright with **(19)** _____ and walking on

  the flat

- has swelling in one ankle following operation for **(20)**

  _____

- denies **(21)** _____

- reports some **(22)** _____ at night

  (responds to medication)

Concerns expressed

- **(23)** _____ following the procedure

- possible damage to crowns (both are **(24)**

  _____)

That is the end of Part A. Now look at Part B.

Part B

In this part of the test, you'll hear six different extracts. In each extract, you'll hear people talking in a different healthcare setting.

For **questions 25-30**, choose the answer (**A**, **B** or **C**) which fits best according to what you hear. You'll have time to read each question before you listen. Complete your answers as you listen.

Now look at question 25.

25. You hear two trainee doctors doing an activity at a staff training day.

   What does the activity give practice in?

   (A) writing case notes

   (B) prioritising patients

   (C) dealing with consultants

26. You hear a radiographer talking to a patient about her MRI scan.

   What is he doing?

   (A) clarifying the aim of the procedure

   (B) dealing with her particular concerns

   (C) explaining how the equipment works

27. You hear two nurses discussing an article in a nursing journal.

   What do they agree about it?

   (A) It's likely to lead to changes in practice.

   (B) It failed to reach any definite conclusion.

   (C) It confirms what they were already thinking.

28.   You hear two hospital managers talking about a time management course for staff.

They think that few people have shown interest because

(A)   there are so many alternatives on offer.

(B)   they feel it's not relevant to them.

(C)   it hasn't been publicised enough.

29.   You hear an optometrist reporting on some research he's been doing.

The aim of his research was

(A)   to develop nanoparticles for transporting drugs all over the body.

(B)   to find a way of treating infections caused by contact lenses.

(C)   to use contact lenses to administer drugs over time.

30.   You hear a consultant talking to a trainee about a patient's eye condition.

What is the consultant doing?

(A)   explaining why intervention may not be necessary

(B)   suggesting the diagnosis is by no means certain

(C)   describing a possible complication

That is the end of Part B. Now look at Part C.

Part C

In this part of the test, you'll hear two different extracts. In each extract, you'll hear health professionals talking about aspects of their work.

For **questions 31-42**, choose the answer (**A, B** or **C**) which fits best according to what you hear. Complete your answers as you listen.

Now look at extract one.

Extract 1: Questions 31-36

You hear an interview with a neurosurgeon called Dr Ian Marsh who specialises in the treatment of concussion in sport.

You now have 90 seconds to read **questions 31-36**.

31.   Dr Marsh says that one aim of the new guidelines on concussion is

  (A)   to educate young sportspeople in how to avoid getting it.

  (B)   to correct some common misunderstandings about it.

  (C)   to provide a range of specialist advice about it.

32.   Dr Marsh makes the point that someone who has suffered a concussion will

  (A)   be unconscious for varying amounts of time after the event.

  (B)   need a medical examination before doing any further exercise.

  (C)   have to take precautions to avoid the risk of symptoms recurring.

33.   Dr Marsh says returning to sport too early after a concussion is dangerous because

  (A)   a subsequent episode can have a cumulative effect.

  (B)   there is a high risk of fatality in the event of a second one.

  (C)   the brains of younger people need time to return to normal size.

34.   Dr Marsh suggests that the risk of sustaining a concussion in sports

    (A)   lies mainly in the choice of sports played.

    (B)   can be reduced by developing good playing technique.

    (C)   is greater when sports are played in less formal situations.

35.   What is Dr Marsh's view about providing medical support for youth sports events?

    (A)   Some types of sport are risky enough to justify it.

    (B)   The organisers should be capable of dealing with any issues.

    (C)   Certain medical professionals should be encouraged to volunteer.

36.   Dr Marsh thinks that developments in college football in the USA

    (A)   only really address an issue which is particular to that sport.

    (B)   are only likely to benefit the health of professional sports players.

    (C)   are a significant step forward in the prevention of concussion in all sports.

Now look at extract two.

Extract 2: Questions 37-42

You hear a presentation by a consultant cardiologist called Dr Pamela Skelton, who's talking about a research trial called SPRINT which investigated the effects of setting lower blood-pressure targets.

You now have 90 seconds to read **questions 37-42**.

37.   Why was the SPRINT trial stopped before it was due to end?

      (A)   There were conclusive results earlier than expected.

      (B)   The high drop-out rate was likely to invalidate the data.

      (C)   Concerns were raised about possible effects on all participants.

38.   A few participants aged over seventy-five left the trial because

      (A)   there was a negative impact on their daily life.

      (B)   they failed to take the required doses of medication.

      (C)   their health deteriorated due to pre-existing conditions.

39.   A significant feature of measuring blood pressure in the trial was that

      (A)   the highest of three readings was recorded.

      (B)   the patient was alone when it was carried out.

      (C)   it was done manually by the participant at home.

40. How did the SPRINT trial differ from the earlier ACCORD study into blood pressure?

    (A)   SPRINT had fewer participants.

    (B)   SPRINT involved higher-risk patients.

    (C)   SPRINT included patients with diabetes.

41. Dr Skelton's main reservation about the SPRINT trial is that

    (A)   it ignores the wider implications of lowered BP.

    (B)   its results go against the existing body of evidence.

    (C)   it was unduly influenced by pharmaceutical companies.

42. What impact does Dr Skelton think the SPRINT trial will have in the future?

    (A)   It will lead to universally applicable guidelines for BP levels.

    (B)   Increased attention will be given to the effect of lifestyle on BP.

    (C)   GPs will adopt a more active approach to lowering BP in the elderly.

That is the end of Part C.

You now have two minutes to check your answers.

END OF THE LISTENING TEST

OCCUPATIONAL ENGLISH TEST

READING SUB-TEST – TEXT BOOKLET: PART A

CANDIDATE NUMBER:

LAST NAME:

FIRST NAME:

MIDDLE NAMES:

PROFESSION:

VENUE:

TEST DATE:

Candidate details and photo will be printed here.

Passport Photo

CANDIDATE DECLARATION

By signing this, you agree not to disclose or use in any way (other than to take the test) or assist any other person to disclose or use any OET test or sub-test content. If you cheat or assist in any cheating, use any unfair practice, break any of the rules or regulations, or ignore any advice or information, you may be disqualified and your results may not be issued at the sole discretion of CBLA. CBLA also reserves its right to take further disciplinary action against you and to pursue any other remedies permitted by law. If a candidate is suspected of and investigated for malpractice, their personal details and details of the investigation may be passed to a third party where required.

CANDIDATE SIGNATURE: _____

INSTRUCTIONS TO CANDIDATES

You must **NOT** remove OET material from the test room.

www.occupationalenglishtest.org

© Cambridge Boxhill Language Assessment – ABN 51 988 559 414

SAMPLE

Tetanus: Texts

Text A

Tetanus is a severe disease that can result in serious illness and death. Tetanus vaccination protects against the disease.

Tetanus (sometimes called lock-jaw) is a disease caused by the bacteria Clostridium tetani. Toxins made by the bacteria attack a person's nervous system. Although the disease is fairly uncommon, it can be fatal.

Early symptoms of tetanus include:

- Painful muscle contractions that begin in the jaw (lock jaw)
- Rigidity in neck, shoulder and back muscles
- Difficulty swallowing
- Violent generalized muscle spasms
- Convulsions
- Breathing difficulties

A person may have a fever and sometimes develop abnormal heart rhythms. Complications include pneumonia, broken bones (from the muscle spasms), respiratory failure and cardiac arrest.

There is no specific diagnostic laboratory test; diagnosis is made clinically. The spatula test is useful: touching the back of the pharynx with a spatula elicits a bite reflex in tetanus, instead of a gag reflex.

Text B

Tetanus Risk

Tetanus is an acute disease induced by the toxin tetanus bacilli, the spores of which are present in soil.

A TETANUS-PRONE WOUND IS:

- any wound or burn that requires surgical intervention that is delayed for > 6 hours
- any wound or burn at any interval after injury that shows one or more of the following characteristics:
  - a significant degree of tissue damage
  - puncture-type wound particularly where there has been contact with soil or organic matter which is likely to harbour tetanus organisms
- any wound from compound fractures
- any wound containing foreign bodies
- any wound or burn in patients who have systemic sepsis
- any bite wound
- any wound from tooth re-implantation

Intravenous drug users are at greater risk of tetanus. Every opportunity should be taken to ensure that they are fully protected against tetanus. Booster doses should be given if there is any doubt about their immunisation status.

Immunosuppressed patients may not be adequately protected against tetanus, despite having been fully immunised. They should be managed as if they were incompletely immunised.

Text C

Tetanus Immunisation following injuries

Thorough cleaning of the wound is essential irrespective of the immunisation history of the patient, and appropriate antibiotics should be prescribed.

Immunisation Status	Clean Wound	Tetanus-prone wound	
Vaccine		**Vaccine**	**Human Tetanus Immunoglobulin (HTIG)**
Fully immunised[1]	Not required	Not required	Only if high risk[2]
Primary immunisation complete, boosters incomplete but up to date	Not required	Not required	Only if high risk[2]
Primary immunisation incomplete or boosters not up to date	Reinforcing dose and further doses to complete recommended schedule	Reinforcing dose and further doses to complete recommended schedule	Yes (opposite limb to vaccine)
Not immunised or immunisation status not known/uncertain[3]	Immediate dose of vaccine followed by completion of full 5-dose course	Immediate dose of vaccine followed by completion of full 5-dose course	Yes (opposite limb to vaccine)

Notes

1. has received total of 5 doses of vaccine at appropriate intervals
2. heavy contamination with material likely to contain tetanus spores and/or extensive devitalised tissue
3. immunosuppressed patients presenting with a tetanus-prone wound should always be managed as if they were incompletely immunised

Human Tetanus Immunoglobulin (HTIG)

Indications

- – treatment of clinically suspected cases of tetanus
- – prevention of tetanus in high-risk, tetanus-prone wounds

Dose

Available in 1ml ampoules containing 250IU

Prevention Dose	Treatment Dose
250 IU by IM injection[1] Or 500 IU by IM injection[1] if >24 hours since injury/risk of heavy contamination/burns	5,000 – 10,000 IU by IV infusion Or 150 IU/kg by IM injection[1] (given in multiple sites) if IV preparation unavailable

[1] Due to its viscosity, HTIG should be administered slowly, using a 23 gauge needle

Contraindications

- – Confirmed anaphylactic reaction to tetanus containing vaccine
- – Confirmed anaphylactic reaction to neomycin, streptomycin or polymyxin B

Adverse reactions

Local – pain, erythema, induration (Arthus-type reaction)

General – pyrexia, hypotonic-hyporesponsive episode, persistent crying

END OF PART A

THIS TEXT BOOKLET WILL BE COLLECTED

READING SUB-TEST – QUESTION PAPER: PART A

CANDIDATE NUMBER:

LAST NAME:

FIRST NAME:

MIDDLE NAMES:

PROFESSION:

VENUE:

TEST DATE:

Candidate details and photo will be printed here.

Passport Photo

CANDIDATE DECLARATION

By signing this, you agree not to disclose or use in any way (other than to take the test) or assist any other person to disclose or use any OET test or sub-test content. If you cheat or assist in any cheating, use any unfair practice, break any of the rules or regulations, or ignore any advice or information, you may be disqualified and your results may not be issued at the sole discretion of CBLA. CBLA also reserves its right to take further disciplinary action against you and to pursue any other remedies permitted by law. If a candidate is suspected of and investigated for malpractice, their personal details and details of the investigation may be passed to a third party where required.

CANDIDATE SIGNATURE: _____

TIME: 15 MINUTES

INSTRUCTIONS TO CANDIDATES

DO NOT open this **Question Paper** or the **Text Booklet** until you are told to do so.

Write your answers on the spaces provided on this **Question Paper.**

You must answer the questions within the 15-minute time limit.

One mark will be granted for each correct answer.

Answer **ALL** questions. Marks are **NOT** deducted for incorrect answers.

At the end of the 15 minutes, hand in this **Question Paper** and the **Text Booklet.**

DO NOT remove OET material from the test room.

www.occupationalenglishtest.org

© Cambridge Boxhill Language Assessment – ABN 51 988 559 414

[CANDIDATE NO.] READING QUESTION PAPER PART A 01/04

Part A

TIME: 15 minutes

- Look at the four texts, **A-D**, in the separate **Text Booklet**.

- For each question, **1-20**, look through the texts, **A-D**, to find the relevant information.

- Write your answers on the spaces provided in this **Question Paper**.

- Answer all the questions within the 15-minute time limit.

- Your answers should be correctly spelt.

Tetanus: Questions

Questions 1-6

For each question, **1-6**, decide which text (**A**, **B**, **C** or **D**) the information comes from.
You may use any letter more than once.

In which text can you find information about

1	the type of injuries that may lead to tetanus?	_____
2	signs that a patient may have tetanus?	_____
3	how to decide whether a tetanus vaccine is necessary?	_____
4	an alternative name for tetanus?	_____
5	possible side-effects of a particular tetanus medication?	_____
6	other conditions which are associated with tetanus?	_____

Questions 7-13

Complete each of the sentences, **7-13**, with a word or short phrase from one of the texts.
Each answer may include words, numbers or both.

Patients at increased risk of tetanus:

7   If a patient has been touching _____ or earth, they are more susceptible to tetanus.

8   Any _____ lodged in the site of an injury will increase the likelihood of tetanus.

9   Patients with _____ fractures are prone to tetanus.

10   Delaying surgery on an injury or burn by more than _____ increases the probability of tetanus.

11   If a burns patient has been diagnosed with _____ they are more liable to contract tetanus.

12   A patient who is _____ or a regular recreational drug user will be at greater risk of tetanus.

Management of tetanus-prone injuries:

13   Clean the wound thoroughly and prescribe _____ if necessary, followed by tetanus vaccine and HTIG as appropriate.

Questions 14-20

Answer each of the questions, **14-20**, with a word or short phrase from one of the texts. Each answer may include words, numbers or both.

14   Where will a patient suffering from tetanus first experience muscle contractions?

_____

15   What can muscle spasms in tetanus patients sometimes lead to?

_____

16   If you test for tetanus using a spatula, what type of reaction will confirm the condition?

_____

17   How many times will you have to vaccinate a patient who needs a full course of tetanus vaccine?

_____

18   What should you give a drug user if you're uncertain of their vaccination history?

_____

19   What size of needle should you use to inject HTIG?

_____

20   What might a patient who experienced an adverse reaction to HTIG be unable to stop doing?

_____

END OF PART A
THIS QUESTION PAPER WILL BE COLLECTED

READING SUB-TEST – QUESTION PAPER: PARTS B & C

CANDIDATE NUMBER:

LAST NAME:

FIRST NAME:

MIDDLE NAMES:

PROFESSION: Candidate details and photo will be printed here.

VENUE:

TEST DATE:

Passport Photo

CANDIDATE DECLARATION

By signing this, you agree not to disclose or use in any way (other than to take the test) or assist any other person to disclose or use any OET test or sub-test content. If you cheat or assist in any cheating, use any unfair practice, break any of the rules or regulations, or ignore any advice or information, you may be disqualified and your results may not be issued at the sole discretion of CBLA. CBLA also reserves its right to take further disciplinary action against you and to pursue any other remedies permitted by law. If a candidate is suspected of and investigated for malpractice, their personal details and details of the investigation may be passed to a third party where required.

CANDIDATE SIGNATURE: _____

TIME: 45 MINUTES

INSTRUCTIONS TO CANDIDATES

DO NOT open this **Question Paper** until you are told to do so.

One mark will be granted for each correct answer.

Answer **ALL** questions. Marks are **NOT** deducted for incorrect answers.

At the end of the test, hand in this **Question Paper**.

HOW TO ANSWER THE QUESTIONS:

Mark your answers on this **Question Paper** by filling in the circle using a 2B pencil. **Example:**
Ⓐ
Ⓑ
Ⓒ

www.occupationalenglishtest.org

© Cambridge Boxhill Language Assessment – ABN 51 988 559 414

[CANDIDATE NO.] READING QUESTION PAPER PARTS B & C 01/16

Part B

In this part of the test, there are six short extracts relating to the work of health professionals. For **questions 1-6**, choose answer (**A**, **B** or **C**) which you think fits best according to the text.

1. Nursing staff can remove a dressing if

    (A) a member of the surgical team is present.

    (B) there is severe leakage from the wound.

    (C) they believe that the wound has healed.

Post-operative dressings

Dressings are an important component of post-operative wound management. Any dressings applied during surgery have been done in sterile conditions and should ideally be left in place, as stipulated by the surgical team. It is acceptable for initial dressings to be removed prematurely in order to have the wound reviewed and, in certain situations, apply a new dressing. These situations include when the dressing is no longer serving its purpose (i.e. dressing falling off, excessive exudate soaking through the dressing and resulting in a suboptimal wound healing environment) or when a wound complication is suspected.

---

2. As explained in the protocol, the position of the RUM container will ideally

(A) encourage participation in the scheme.

(B) emphasise the value of recycling.

(C) facilitate public access to it.

Unwanted medicine: pharmacy collection protocol

A Returned Unwanted Medicine (RUM) Project approved container will be delivered by the wholesaler to the participating pharmacy.

The container is to be kept in a section of the dispensary or in a room or enclosure in the pharmacy to which the public does not have access. The container may be placed in a visible position, but out of reach of the public, as this will reinforce the message that unwanted prescription drugs can be returned to the pharmacy and that the returned medicines will not be recycled.

Needles, other sharps and liquid cytotoxic products should not be placed in the container, but in one specifically designed for such waste.

---

3. The report mentioned in the memo suggests that

(A) data about patient errors may be incomplete.

(B) errors by hospital staff can often go unreported.

(C) errors in prescriptions pose the greatest threat to patients.

Memo: Report on oral anti-cancer medications
Nurse Unit Managers are directed to review their systems for the administration of oral anti-cancer drugs, and the reporting of drug errors. Serious concerns have been raised in a recent report drawing on a national survey of pharmacists.
Please note the following paragraph quoted from the report:
Incorrect doses of oral anti-cancer medicines can have fatal consequences. Over the previous four years, there were three deaths and 400 patient safety issues involving oral anti-cancer medicines. Half of the reports concerned the wrong dosage, frequency, quantity or duration of oral anti-cancer treatment. Of further concern is that errors on the part of patients may be under-reported. In light of these reports, there is clearly a need for improved systems covering the management of patients receiving oral therapies.

4.   What point does the training manual make about anaesthesia workstations?

(A)   Parts of the equipment have been shown to be vulnerable to failure.

(B)   There are several ways of ensuring that the ventilator is working effectively.

(C)   Monitoring by health professionals is a reliable way to maintain patient safety.

Anaesthesia Workstations

Studies on safety in anaesthesia have documented that human vigilance alone is inadequate to ensure patient safety and have underscored the importance of monitoring devices. These findings are reflected in improved standards for equipment design, guidelines for patient monitoring and reduced malpractice premiums for the use of capnography and pulse oximetry during anaesthesia. Anaesthesia workstations integrate ventilator technology with patient monitors and alarms to help prevent patient injury in the unlikely event of a ventilator failure. Furthermore, since the reservoir bag is part of the circuit during mechanical ventilation, the visible movement of the reservoir bag is confirmation that the ventilator is functioning.

5.   In cases of snakebite, the flying doctor should be aware of

(A)   where to access specific antivenoms.

(B)   the appropriate method for wound cleaning.

(C)   the patients most likely to suffer complications.

Memo to Flying Doctor staff: Antivenoms for snakebite
Before starting treatment: • Do not wash the snakebite site. • If possible, determine the type of snake by using a 'snake-venom detection kit' to test a bite site swab or, in systemic envenoming, the person's urine. If venom detection is not available or has proved negative, seek advice from a poisons information centre. • Testing blood for venom is not reliable. • Assess the degree of envenoming; not all confirmed snakebites will result in systemic envenoming; risk varies with the species of snake. • People with pre-existing renal, hepatic, cardiac or respiratory impairment and those taking anticoagulant or antiplatelet drugs may have an increased risk of serious outcome from snakebite. Children are also especially at increased risk of severe envenoming because of smaller body mass and the likelihood of physical activity immediately after a bite.

6. What was the purpose of the BMTEC forum?

(A) to propose a new way of carrying out cleaning audits

(B) to draw conclusions from the results of cleaning audits

(C) to encourage more groups to undertake cleaning audits

Cleaning Audits
Three rounds of environmental cleaning audits were completed in 2013-2014. Key personnel in each facility were surveyed to assess the understanding of environmental cleaning from the perspective of the nurse unit manager, environmental services manager and the director of clinical governance. Each facility received a report about their environmental cleaning audits and lessons learned from the surveys. Data from the 15 units were also provided to each facility for comparison purposes.
The knowledge and experiences from the audits were shared at the BMTEC Forum in August 2014. This forum allowed environmental services managers, cleaners, nurses and clinical governance to discuss the application of the standards and promote new and improved cleaning practice. The second day of the forum focused on auditor training and technique with the view of enhancing internal environmental cleaning auditing by the participating groups.

Part C

In this part of the test, there are two texts about different aspects of healthcare. For **questions 7-22**, choose the answer (**A**, **B**, **C** or **D**) which you think fits best according to the text.

Text 1: Does homeopathy 'work'?

For many, homeopathy is simply unscientific, but regular users hold a very different view.

Homeopathy works by giving patients very dilute substances that, in larger doses, would cause the very symptoms that need curing. Taking small doses of these substances – derived from plants, animals or minerals – strengthens the body's ability to heal and increases resistance to illness or infection. Or that is the theory. The debate about its effectiveness is nothing new. Recently, Australia's National Health and Medical Research Council (NHMRC) released a paper which found there were 'no health conditions for which there was reliable evidence that homeopathy was effective'. This echoed a report from the UK House of Commons which said that the evidence failed to show a 'credible physiological mode of action' for homeopathic products, and that what data were available showed homeopathic products to be no better than placebo. Yet Australians spend at least $11 million per year on homeopathy.

So what's going on? If Australians – and citizens of many other nations around the world – are voting with their wallets, does this mean homeopathy must be doing something right? 'For me, the crux of the debate is a disconnect between how the scientific and medical community view homeopathy, and what many in the wider community are getting out of it,' says Professor Alex Broom of the University of Queensland. 'The really interesting question is how can we possibly have something that people think works, when to all intents and purposes, from a scientific perspective, it doesn't?'

Part of homeopathy's appeal may lie in the nature of the patient-practitioner consultation. In contrast to a typical 15-minute GP consultation, a first homeopathy consultation might take an hour and a half. 'We don't just look at an individual symptom in isolation. For us, that symptom is part of someone's overall health condition,' says Greg Cope, spokesman for the Australian Homeopathic Association. 'Often we'll have a consultation with someone and find details their GP simply didn't have time to.' Writer Johanna Ashmore is a case in point. She sees her homeopath for a one-hour monthly consultation. 'I feel, if I go and say I've got this health concern, she's going to treat my body to fight it rather than just treat the symptom.'

Most people visit a homeopath after having received a diagnosis from a 'mainstream' practitioner, often because they want an alternative choice to medication, says Greg Cope. 'Generally speaking, for a homeopath, their preference is if someone has a diagnosis from a medical practitioner before starting homeopathic treatment, so it's rare for someone to come and see us with an undiagnosed condition and certainly if they do come undiagnosed, we'd want to refer them on and get that medical evaluation before starting a course of treatment,' he says.

Given that homeopathic medicines are by their very nature incredibly dilute – and, some might argue, diluted beyond all hope of efficacy – they are unlikely to cause any adverse effects, so where's the harm? Professor Paul Glasziou, chair of the NHMRC's Homeopathy Working Committee, says that while financial cost is one harm, potentially more harmful are the non-financial costs associated with missing out on effective treatments. 'If it's just a cold, I'm not too worried. But if it's for a serious illness, you may not be taking disease-modifying treatments, and most worrying is things like HIV which affect not only you, but people around you,' says Glasziou. This is a particular concern with homeopathic vaccines, he says, which jeopardise the 'herd immunity' – the immunity of a significant proportion of the population – which is crucial in containing outbreaks of vaccine-preventable diseases.

The question of a placebo effect inevitably arises, as studies repeatedly seem to suggest that whatever benefits are being derived from homeopathy are more a product of patient faith rather than of any active ingredient of the medications. However, Greg Cope dismisses this argument, pointing out that homeopathy appears to benefit even the sceptics: 'We might see kids first, then perhaps Mum and after a couple of years, Dad will follow and, even though he's only there reluctantly, we get **wonderful outcomes**. This cannot be explained simply by the placebo effect.' As a patient, Johanna Ashmore is aware scientific research does little to support homeopathy but can still see its benefits. 'If seeing my homeopath each month improves my health, I'm happy. I don't care how it works, even if it's all in the mind – I just know that it does.'

But if so many people around the world are placing their faith in homeopathy, despite the evidence against it, Broom questions why homeopathy seeks scientific validation. The problem, as he sees it, lies in the fact that 'if you're going to dance with conventional medicine and say "we want to be proven to be effective in dealing with discrete physiological conditions", then you indeed do have to show efficacy. In my view **this** is not about broader credibility per se, it's about scientific and medical credibility – there's actually quite a lot of cultural credibility surrounding homeopathy within the community but that's not replicated in the scientific literature.'

Text 1: Questions 7-14

7. The two reports mentioned in the first paragraph both concluded that homeopathy

   A   could be harmful if not used appropriately.

   B   merely works on the same basis as the placebo effect.

   C   lacks any form of convincing proof of its value as a treatment.

   D   would require further investigation before it was fully understood.

8. When commenting on the popularity of homeopathy, Professor Broom shows his

   A   surprise at people's willingness to put their trust in it.

   B   frustration at scientists' inability to explain their views on it.

   C   acceptance of the view that the subject may merit further study.

   D   concern over the risks people face when receiving such treatment.

9. Johanna Ashmore's views on homeopathy highlight

   A   how practitioners put their patients at ease.

   B   the key attraction of the approach for patients.

   C   how it suits patients with a range of health problems.

   D   the opportunities to improve patient care which GPs miss.

10. In the fourth paragraph, it is suggested that visits to homeopaths

   A   occasionally depend on a referral from a mainstream doctor.

   B   frequently result from a patient's treatment preferences.

   C   should be preceded by a visit to a relevant specialist.

   D   often reveal previously overlooked medical problems.

11. What particularly concerns Professor Glasziou?

    (A) the risks to patients of relying on homeopathic vaccinations

    (B) the mistaken view that homeopathic treatments can only do good

    (C) the way that homeopathic remedies endanger more than just the user

    (D) the ineffectiveness of homeopathic remedies against even minor illnesses

12. Greg Cope uses the expression '**wonderful outcomes**' to underline

    (A) the ability of homeopathy to defy its scientific critics.

    (B) the value of his patients' belief in the whole process.

    (C) the claim that he has solid proof that homeopathy works.

    (D) the way positive results can be achieved despite people's doubts.

13. From the comments quoted in the sixth paragraph, it is clear that Johanna Ashmore is

    (A) prepared to accept that homeopathy may depend on psychological factors.

    (B) happy to admit that she was uncertain at first about proceeding.

    (C) sceptical about the evidence against homeopathic remedies.

    (D) confident that research will eventually validate homeopathy.

14. What does the word '**this**' in the final paragraph refer to?

    (A) the continuing inability of homeopathy to gain scientific credibility

    (B) the suggestion that the scientific credibility of homeopathy is in doubt

    (C) the idea that there is no need to pursue scientific acceptance for homeopathy

    (D) the motivation behind the desire for homeopathy to gain scientific acceptance

Text 2: Brain-controlled prosthetics

Paralysed from the neck down by a stroke, Cathy Hutchinson stared fixedly at a drinking straw in a bottle on the table in front of her. A cable rose from the top of her head, connecting her to a robot arm, but her gaze never wavered as she mentally guided the robot arm, which was opposite her, to close its grippers around the bottle, then slowly lift the vessel towards her mouth. Only when she finally managed to take a sip did her face relax. This example illustrates the strides being taken in brain-controlled prosthetics. But Hutchinson's focused stare also illustrates the one crucial feature still missing from prosthetics. Her eyes could tell her where the arm was, but she couldn't feel what it was doing.

Prosthetics researchers are now trying to create prosthetics that can 'feel'. It's a **daunting** task: the researchers have managed to read signals from the brain; now they must write information into the nervous system. Touch encompasses a complicated mix of information – everything from the soft prickliness of wool to the slipping of a sweaty soft-drink can. The sensations arise from a host of receptors in the skin, which detect texture, vibration, pain, temperature and shape, as well as from receptors in the muscles, joints and tendons that contribute to 'proprioception' – the sense of where a limb is in space. Prosthetics are being outfitted with sensors that can gather many of these sensations, but the challenge is to get the resulting signals flowing to the correct part of the brain.

For people who have had limbs amputated, the obvious way to achieve that is to route the signals into the remaining nerves in the stump, the part of the limb left after amputation. Ken Horch, a neuroprosthetics researcher, has done just that by threading electrodes into the nerves in stumps then stimulating them with a tiny current, so that patients felt like their fingers were moving or being touched. The technique can even allow patients to distinguish basic features of objects: a man who had lost his lower arms was able to determine the difference between blocks made of wood or foam rubber by using a sensor-equipped prosthetic hand. He correctly identified the objects' size and softness more than twice as often as would have been expected by chance. Information about force and finger position was delivered from the prosthetic to a computer, which prompted stimulation of electrodes implanted in his upper-arm nerves.

As promising as this result was, researchers will probably need to stimulate hundreds or thousands of nerve fibres to create complex sensations, and they'll need to keep the devices working for many years if they are to minimise the number of surgeries required to replace them as they wear out. To get around this, some researchers are instead trying to give patients sensory feedback by touching their skin. The technique was discovered by accident by researcher Todd Kuiken. The idea was to rewire arm nerves that used to serve the hand, for example, to muscles in other parts of the body. When the patient thought about closing his or her hand, the newly targeted muscle would contract and generate an electric signal, driving movement of the prosthetic.

However, this technique won't work for stroke patients like Cathy Hutchinson. So some researchers are skipping directly to the brain. In principle, this should be straightforward. Because signals from specific parts of the body go to specific parts of the brain, scientists should be able to create sensations of touch or proprioception in the limb by directly activating the neurons that normally receive those signals. However, with electrical stimulation, all neurons close to the electrode's tip are activated indiscriminately, so 'even if I had the sharpest needle in the Universe, that could create unintended effects', says Arto Nurmikko, a neuroengineer. For example, an attempt to create sensation in one finger might produce sensation in other parts of the hand as well, he says.

Nurmikko and other researchers are therefore using light, in place of electricity, to activate highly specific groups of neurons and recreate a sense of touch. They trained a monkey to remove its hand from a pad when it vibrated. When the team then stimulated the part of its brain that receives tactile information from the hand with a light source implanted in its skull, the monkey lifted its hand off the pad about 90% of the time. The use of such techniques in humans is still probably 10–20 years away, but it is a promising strategy.

Even if such techniques can be made to work, it's unclear how closely they will approximate natural sensations. Tingles, pokes and vibrations are still **a far cry from** the complicated sensations that we feel when closing a hand over an apple, or running a finger along a table's edge. But patients don't need a perfect sense of touch, says Douglas Weber, a bioengineer. Simply having enough feedback to improve their control of grasp could help people to perform tasks such as picking up a glass of water, he explains. He goes on to say that patients who wear cochlear implants, for example, are often happy to regain enough hearing to hold a phone conversation, even if they're still unable to distinguish musical subtleties.

Text 2: Questions 15-22

15. What do we learn about the experiment Cathy Hutchinson took part in?

   (A) It required intense concentration.

   (B) It failed to achieve what it had set out to do.

   (C) It could be done more quickly given practice.

   (D) It was the first time that it had been attempted.

16. The task facing researchers is described as '**daunting**' because

   (A) signals from the brain can be misunderstood.

   (B) it is hard to link muscle receptors with each other.

   (C) some aspects of touch are too difficult to reproduce.

   (D) the connections between sensors and the brain need to be exact.

17. What is said about the experiment done on the patient in the third paragraph?

   (A) There was statistical evidence that it was successful.

   (B) It enabled the patient to have a wide range of feeling.

   (C) Its success depended on when amputation had taken place.

   (D) It required the use of a specially developed computer program.

18. What drawback does the writer mention in the fourth paragraph?

   (A) The devices have a high failure rate.

   (B) Patients might have to undergo too many operations.

   (C) It would only be possible to create rather simple sensations.

   (D) The research into the new technique hasn't been rigorous enough.

19. What point is made in the fifth paragraph?

(A) Severed nerves may be able to be reconnected.

(B) More research needs to be done on stroke victims.

(C) Scientists' previous ideas about the brain have been overturned.

(D) It is difficult for scientists to pinpoint precise areas with an electrode.

20. What do we learn about the experiment that made use of light?

(A) It can easily be replicated in humans.

(B) It worked as well as could be expected.

(C) It may have more potential than electrical stimulation.

(D) It required more complex surgery than previous experiments.

21. In the final paragraph, the writer uses the phrase '**a far cry from**' to underline

(A) how much more there is to achieve.

(B) how complex experiments have become.

(C) the need to reduce people's expectations.

(D) the differences between types of artificial sensation.

22. Why does Weber give the example of a cochlear implant?

(A) to underline the need for a similar breakthrough in prosthetics

(B) to illustrate the fact that some sensation is better than none

(C) to highlight the advances made in other areas of medicine

(D) to demonstrate the ability of the body to relearn skills

END OF READING TEST
THIS BOOKLET WILL BE COLLECTED

OCCUPATIONAL ENGLISH TEST

WRITING SUB-TEST – TEST BOOKLET

CANDIDATE NUMBER:

LAST NAME:

FIRST NAME:

MIDDLE NAMES:

Candidate details and photo will be printed here.

Passport Photo

PROFESSION:

VENUE:

TEST DATE:

CANDIDATE DECLARATION

By signing this, you agree not to disclose or use in any way (other than to take the test) or assist any other person to disclose or use any OET test or sub-test content. If you cheat or assist in any cheating, use any unfair practice, break any of the rules or regulations, or ignore any advice or information, you may be disqualified and your results may not be issued at the sole discretion of CBLA. CBLA also reserves its right to take further disciplinary action against you and to pursue any other remedies permitted by law. If a candidate is suspected of and investigated for malpractice, their personal details and details of the investigation may be passed to a third party where required.

CANDIDATE SIGNATURE: _____

INSTRUCTIONS TO CANDIDATES

You must write your answer for the Writing sub-test in the **Writing Answer Booklet.**

You must **NOT** remove OET material from the test room.

OCCUPATIONAL ENGLISH TEST

WRITING SUB-TEST: NURSING

TIME ALLOWED: **READING TIME:**   **5 MINUTES**
                            WRITING TIME: **40 MINUTES**

Read the case notes below and complete the writing task which follows.

Notes:

You are a ward nurse in the cardiac unit of Greenville Public Hospital. Your patient, Ms Martin, is due to be discharged tomorrow.

Patient:	Ms Margaret Helen Martin
Address:	23 Third Avenue, Greenville
Age:	81 years old (DOB: 25 July 1935)
Admission date:	15 July 2017

Social/family background:

    Never married, no children
    Lives in own house in Greenville
    Financially independent
    Three siblings (all unwell) and five nieces/nephews living in greater Greenville area
    Contact with family intermittent
    No longer drives
    Has 'meals on wheels' (meal delivery service for elderly) – Mon-Fri (lunch and dinner), orders frozen meals for weekends

Diagnosis: Coronary artery disease (CAD), angina

Treatment: Angioplasty (repeat – first 2008)

Discharge date: <u>16 July 2017</u>, pending cardiologist's report

Medical information:

    Coeliac disease
    Angioplasty 2008
    Anxious about health – tends to focus on health problems
    Coronary artery disease → aspirin, clopidogrel (Plavix)
    Hypertension → metoprolol (Betaloc), ramipril (Tritace)
    Hypercholesterolemia (8.3) → atorvastatin (Lipitor)
    Overweight (BMI 29.5)
    Sedentary (orders groceries over phone to be delivered, neighbour walks dog)
    Family history of coronary heart disease (mother, 2 of 3 brothers)
    Hearing loss – wears hearing aid

Nursing management and progress during hospital stay:

Routine post-operative recovery

Tolerating light diet and fluids

Bruising at catheter insertion site, no signs of infection/bleeding noted post-procedure

Pt anxious about return home, not sure whether she will cope

Discharge plan: **Dietary**

Low-calorie, high-protein, low-cholesterol, gluten-free diet (supervised by dietitian, referred by Dr)

Frequent small meals or snacks

Drink plenty of fluids

Physiotherapy

Daily light exercise (e.g., 15-minute walk, exercise plan monitored by physiotherapist)

No heavy lifting for 12 weeks

Other

Monitor wound site for bruising or infection

Monitor adherence to medication regime

Arrange regular family visits to monitor progress

Anticipated needs of Pt:

Need home visits from community health/district nurse – monitor adherence to post-operative medication, exercise, dietary regime

Regular monitoring by Dr, dietitian, physiotherapist

? Danger of social isolation (infrequent family support)

Writing Task:

Using the information in the case notes, write a letter to the Nurse-in-Charge of the District Nursing Service outlining Ms Martin's situation and anticipated needs following her return home tomorrow. Address the letter to Nurse-in-Charge, District Nursing Service, Greenville Community Health Care Centre, 88 Highton Road, Greenville.

In your answer:

- **Expand the relevant notes into complete sentences**
- **Do not use note form**
- **Use letter format**

The body of the letter should be approximately 180–200 words.

WRITING SUB-TEST – ANSWER BOOKLET

CANDIDATE NUMBER:	
LAST NAME:	
FIRST NAME:	**Passport Photo**
MIDDLE NAMES:	
PROFESSION:	Candidate details and photo will be printed here.
VENUE:	
TEST DATE:	

CANDIDATE DECLARATION

By signing this, you agree not to disclose or use in any way (other than to take the test) or assist any other person to disclose or use any OET test or sub-test content. If you cheat or assist in any cheating, use any unfair practice, break any of the rules or regulations, or ignore any advice or information, you may be disqualified and your results may not be issued at the sole discretion of CBLA. CBLA also reserves its right to take further disciplinary action against you and to pursue any other remedies permitted by law. If a candidate is suspected of and investigated for malpractice, their personal details and details of the investigation may be passed to a third party where required.

CANDIDATE SIGNATURE: _____

TIME ALLOWED
READING TIME: 5 MINUTES
WRITING TIME: 40 MINUTES

INSTRUCTIONS TO CANDIDATES

1. **Reading time: 5 minutes**
   During this time you may study the writing task and notes. You **MUST NOT** write, highlight, underline or make any notes.

2. **Writing time: 40 minutes**

3. Use the back page for notes and rough draft only. Notes and rough draft will **NOT** be marked.

   Please write your answer clearly on page 1 and page 2.

   Cross out anything you **DO NOT** want the examiner to consider.

4. You must write your answer for the Writing sub-test in this **Answer Booklet** using **pen or pencil**.

5. You must **NOT** remove OET material from the test room.

www.occupationalenglishtest.org

© Cambridge Boxhill Language Assessment – ABN 51 988 559 414

[CANDIDATE NO.] WRITING SUB-TEST ANSWER BOOKLET 01/04

Please record your answer on this page.

(Only answers on Page 1 and Page 2 will be marked.)

_____
_____
_____
_____
_____
_____
_____
_____
_____
_____
_____
_____
_____
_____
_____
_____
_____
_____
_____
_____
_____
_____
_____
_____
_____
_____
_____
_____
_____

OET Writing sub-test – Answer booklet   1

Please record your answer on this page.

(Only answers on Page 1 and Page 2 will be marked.)

_____

_____

_____

_____

_____

_____

_____

_____

_____

_____

_____

_____

_____

_____

_____

_____

_____

_____

_____

_____

_____

_____

_____

_____

_____

_____

_____

_____

OET Writing sub-test – Answer booklet 2

Space for notes and rough draft. Only your answers on Page 1 and Page 2 will be marked.

SAMPLE

OCCUPATIONAL ENGLISH TEST

SPEAKING SUB-TEST

CANDIDATE NUMBER:

LAST NAME:

FIRST NAME:

MIDDLE NAMES:

PROFESSION: Your details and photo will be printed here.

VENUE:

TEST DATE:

Passport Photo

CANDIDATE DECLARATION

By signing this, you agree not to disclose or use in any way (other than to take the test) or assist any other person to disclose or use any OET test or sub-test content. If you cheat or assist in any cheating, use any unfair practice, break any of the rules or regulations, or ignore any advice or information, you may be disqualified and your results may not be issued at the sole discretion of CBLA. CBLA also reserves its right to take further disciplinary action against you and to pursue any other remedies permitted by law. If a candidate is suspected of and investigated for malpractice, their personal details and details of the investigation may be passed to a third party where required.

CANDIDATE SIGNATURE: _____

INSTRUCTION TO CANDIDATES

Please confirm with the Interlocutor that your roleplay card number and colour match the Interlocutor card before you begin.

Interlocutor to complete only

ID No: _____   Passport: ☐   National ID: ☐   Alternative ID approved: ☐

Speaking sub-test:

ID document sighted? ☐   Photo match? ☐   Signature match? ☐   Did not attend? ☐

Interlocutor name: _____

Interlocutor signature: _____

[CANDIDATE NO.] SPEAKING SUB-TEST 01/04

OET Sample role-play

ROLEPLAYER CARD NO. 1	NURSING

SETTING	Emergency Department, Local Hospital
PATIENT	You are 35. You were involved in a car accident earlier today and are suffering from whiplash and a headache. You are feeling sorry for yourself and are impatient to be better.
TASK	• Be confused that you have been kept in hospital for so long, given there are no signs of broken bones, cuts or bruises. • Ask why you are being given medication. • Stress that you want to get better in the shortest time possible. Ask if physiotherapy will shorten the recovery period. • Ask about the length of the treatment. How long will it be before you are better? • Ask if there is anything else you need to know. • Ask if there could be 'after effects' or on-going problems as a result of your accident.

Sample role-play

OET Sample role-play

CANDIDATE CARD NO. 1	NURSING

SETTING	Emergency Department, Local Hospital
NURSE	This 35-year-old patient was involved in a car accident earlier today and is now suffering from a headache and whiplash (an injury to the cervical spine). He/she is being kept in the hospital for observation but is expected to be discharged later in the day.
TASK	• Find out what the patient thinks are the reasons why he/she is being kept in the hospital. • Advise the patient on the reason for taking and continuing to take medication, and ways of managing the pain once he/she returns home (e.g., with heat/ice, analgesics, a collar, etc.). • Discuss the best care practices for after the patient leaves the hospital. Describe the benefits of consulting a physiotherapist about exercise and relaxation exercises to loosen up the joints. • Explain that you cannot be sure how long the patient will take to recover fully. • Stress the importance of complying with the treatment and exercise program. • Stress the importance of seeking medical advice if there is any increased pain or discomfort, nausea, vomiting, or vision problems.

Sample role-play

ROLEPLAYER CARD NO. 2   NURSING

SETTING   Community Health Centre

CARER   You are visiting your local health centre to obtain information about your mother's most recent health report. Your mother is now eighty years old and is becoming somewhat forgetful. She is a very independent person and does not like your interfering in her personal affairs. However, she told you recently that when she had her three-monthly check-up, the doctor said her cholesterol level was fairly high. The purpose of your visit is to learn more about cholesterol and how best to reduce it.

TASK

- If the nurse doesn't explain it, find out what cholesterol is.

- Ask what the doctor meant by a fairly high level of cholesterol. Explain that you are concerned that her condition could develop into something worse.

- Ask what the nurse considers your mother's cholesterol level should be.

- Ask for advice about what your mother should do to lower her cholesterol level.

© Cambridge Boxhill Language Assessment   Sample role-play

CANDIDATE CARD NO. 2   NURSING

SETTING   Community Health Centre

NURSE   The son/daughter of an eighty-year-old woman has come to ask for information about cholesterol. He/she wants information about his/her mother's current cholesterol level and how best to reduce it.

TASK

- Find out what the son/daughter already knows about cholesterol.
- Inform your visitor about what cholesterol is (fat-like material present in the blood and most tissues) and about types of cholesterol (high density lipoproteins (HDL) – good, low density lipoproteins (LDL) – bad).
- Tactfully explain that if the fatty deposits are lodged in the arteries, this can lead to heart disease or stroke.

- Explain what the doctor meant by a fairly high level of cholesterol (i.e., elevated above 5.5 mmols/litre in the blood).
- Advise your visitor about how his/her mother can best deal with her cholesterol (e.g., avoid saturated fats and eat more fibre, etc.).

© Cambridge Boxhill Language Assessment   Sample role-play

Listening sub-test

ANSWER KEY – Parts A, B & C

LISTENING SUB-TEST – ANSWER KEY

PART A: QUESTIONS 1-12

1   asthma

2   hair (growth)

3   hump

4   sweating / perspiration / diaphoresis

5   (so) infrequent (now)

6   (easily) bruise

7   stretch marks / striae

8   dark / darkened

9   acne (vulgaris)

10   mood swings

11   irritable

12   saliva

PART A: QUESTIONS 13-24

13   lisinopril

14   (some) water

15   aspirin

16   clopidogrel

17   (a bit) breathless

18   stents

19   (going up/going down/up and down) stairs

20   varicose veins

21   (having) palpitations

22   heartburn / (acid) reflux

23   pain

24   central incisors

LISTENING SUB-TEST – ANSWER KEY

PART B: QUESTIONS 25-30

25	B	prioritising patients
26	B	dealing with her particular concerns
27	A	It's likely to lead to changes in practice.
28	B	they feel it's not relevant to them.
29	C	to use contact lenses to administer drugs over time.
30	A	explaining why intervention may not be necessary

PART C: QUESTIONS 31-36

31	C	to provide a range of specialist advice about it.
32	C	have to take precautions to avoid the risk of symptoms recurring.
33	A	a subsequent episode can have a cumulative effect.
34	A	lies mainly in the choice of sports played.
35	B	The organisers should be capable of dealing with any issues.
36	A	only really address an issue which is particular to that sport.

PART C: QUESTIONS 37-42

37	A	There were conclusive results earlier than expected.
38	C	their health deteriorated due to pre-existing conditions.
39	B	the patient was alone when it was carried out.
40	B	SPRINT involved higher-risk patients.
41	B	its results go against the existing body of evidence.
42	C	GPs will adopt a more active approach to lowering BP in the elderly.

——

END OF KEY

Listening sub-test

Audio Script – Practice test 2

This test has three parts. In each part you'll hear a number of different extracts. At the start of each extract, you'll hear this sound: ---***---.

You'll have time to read the questions before you hear each extract and you'll hear each extract ONCE only. Complete your answers as you listen.

At the end of the test, you'll have two minutes to check your answers.

Part A. In this part of the test, you'll hear two different extracts. In each extract, a health professional is talking to a patient. For questions 1 to 24, complete the notes with information you hear. Now, look at the notes for extract one.

PAUSE: 5 SECONDS
Extract one. Questions 1 to 12.

You hear a consultant endocrinologist talking to a patient called Sarah Croft. For questions 1 to 12, complete the notes with a word or short phrase. You now have thirty seconds to look at the notes.

PAUSE: 30 SECONDS
---***---

M: Good morning, Mrs Croft. I see your GP has referred you to me …

F: Yes.

M: OK … I've got some notes here with his referral letter, but it'd be helpful if you could tell me in your own words the sort of problems you've been experiencing?

F: *OK, well, I've had high blood pressure for several years, but these last few months…that's tending to get worse. I've been on corticosteroids too these last three years or so, and that's a result of the fact that I've suffered from asthma since my teens.*

M: I see. But I understand you've developed several other problems recently?

F: *Oh yeah – as you can see, my stomach is huge – I've put on a lot of weight and it seems to be concentrated there. And, oh dear, I don't know what's happened to my face! All this hair which has appeared – it's…so embarrassing. And something else which I didn't notice at first, but which other people have pointed out to me – here, see? In between my shoulders, ah yeah, is this, well, I can only describe it as a hump. That really bothers me too.*

M: Yes – I can see, erm...

F: *And look at my ankles… they're swollen too. Something else which has got really bad is that I'm always sweating so much – even in cold weather.   No amount of anti-perspirant seems to help.*

M: That must be difficult. Erm, and any aches or pains?

F: *Well, my…my back tends to ache a bit, but I take ibuprofen which helps. My periods used to be painful in the past, but, to be honest, they're so infrequent now that the pain really isn't a problem any more. I often feel tired though, in fact…like really tired.*

M: And what about your skin?

F:	Oh yeah… it seems to bruise at the slightest thing. And I've noticed that if I get a cut or a scratch or something, it takes ages to heal. And something else I've spotted on my thighs, see here… is these stretch marks. Ah yes, they're quite noticeable because they're a real purple colour. My face has changed too – I used to have quite pale skin, but, as you can see it's quite red now. And it looks, well, puffy – I mean it never used to look like that.

M:	OK… so there's been quite a change.

F:	Oh, definitely. And if you look, here, on my neck – the skin's gone dark. Really odd. I don't know what's happening – and, though I never really had it before, I've now got acne into the bargain!

M:	Ahh tt must all be distressing. I…I can appreciate that this is having an effect on you. Erm, have you noticed your general mood changing at all?

F:	Well, it's enough to get anyone down really – and, yes, I do feel a bit depressed. But the frightening thing is that I've started getting mood swings. I've never had them before. I mean, one minute I'm laughing and the next I'm crying – and.. and I don't know why. It's quite alarming.

M:	Anything else?

F:	Well I confess I feel, well…irritable all the time. Everything seems to get on my nerves! And I can't seem to concentrate like I used to, you know – I find it hard sometimes to do stuff in my head like working out a sum, or remembering names and things. I… I just hope that you can help find out what's wrong with me.

M:	Well, I'm sure we will. Now, I see you've already had some blood tests, but I'll need to do one or two more. You've had a urine test to look at your blood sugar, so I probably won't need to repeat that. We may do a saliva test, depending on the bloods.

F:	OK, I see. And how long will everything take, I mean before we know what's causing the problems?

M:	Well, I'm afraid it can all take some time as diagnosis can be quite complicated and we may need to (FADE)

PAUSE: 10 SECONDS
Extract two. Questions 13 to 24.

You hear an anaesthetist talking to a patient called Mary Wilcox prior to an operation. For questions 13 to 24, complete the notes with a word or short phrase. You now have thirty seconds to look at the notes.

PAUSE: 30 SECONDS
---***---

M	So, Mrs. Wilcox, you tell me you've had high blood pressure, so are you taking any medications for that?

F	Yes, erm… a blue one and a white one

M	And do you know the names of the tablets?

F	Yes, so one's thiazide.

M	OK

F	and the other one's lisinopril.
M	Perfect, thank you that's very helpful. And have you had them this morning?
F	Yes, that's what the nurse told me at the pre-assessment, yes, so is that all right? Just with some water. I usually have them before breakfast but she said no food at all this morning.
M	Excellent. And apart from the high blood pressure do you have any other medical problems at all?
F	Err… Yes, I take some blood-thinning drugs because I had a small heart attack a bit ago, so I'm taking aspirin and… at the pre-assessment they said to keep on with them, so I had one this morning like I usually do. They told me to stop the other one … err, I can't remember the name …
M	Ahh… Warfarin?
F	No, it begins with c… err… clop…clopidogrel. Err... they told me to stop it a week before the operation. Seven days.
M	Fantastic
F	So I stopped last Tuesday.
M	Great. Now, tell me a bit more about this heart attack. How long ago was that?
F	Err… two years ago. My GP picked up on it.
M	Did that all go …
F	Yes, err… pretty good
M	And why did you go to your GP, were you having chest pains?
F	Err… they weren't chest pains, they were … I was just getting a bit breathless and it was difficult for me to tell what was going on but, err…Dr Scott picked up on it when I went to see him and he sent me to the cardiology team.
M	Right. Did they say you'd had a heart attack?
F	Yes, they told me I'd had a small one and so I had some stents put in … a couple of them.
M	And since they were done…
F	Yes, I've been better you know, I… err I don't feel so tired all the time
M	OK. And what can you do in terms of exercising?
F	Well I can do anything … anything really.
M	Mmm and, tell me what you can do.
F	Well we have stairs at home and we don't have a loo on the ground floor, it's on the first floor, so I'm up and down a few times a day.
M	And walking on the flat's fine?
F	Yes, that's OK.
M	Any problems with your ankles swelling?
F	Well this one it swells up if I've been standing. Alright, I had my veins done, my varicose veins. But, err the other one's alright. I sprained it quite badly last year but it's fine now.

M	Right. Erm, can I just ask you a few other questions about your heart.
F	*Sure*
M	Have you ever had any palpitations at all? When your heart goes boom boom boom.
F	*No*
M	You've never experienced any of those?
F	*Well no… no. Not really. I mean if… if I run my heart beats a bit faster but that's normal isn't it.*
M	Sure. Erm, anything else … any digestive problems?
F	*No … well if I have a heavy meal late at night, like if… if I have pastry or something, I sometimes wake up in the night feeling a bit erm… like heartburn, erm… but if I take an anti-acid it's fine.*
M	Right. So in general you sound to be in pretty good shape. Hmm now in a minute I'll tell you about exactly what type of anaesthesia we'll be using. But, first of all is there anything you'd like to ask me … do you have any concerns about anything?
F	*Erm, well I suppose the main thing is after the operation, err, when I wake up… Erm I mean will I be in a lot of pain when I come round?*
M	No, you'll be given morphine during the procedure and that will still be working when you wake up, and then when that wears off you'll be given something else. There'll be someone keeping an eye on you.
F	*OK. Ohh… Err and the other thing is, Err I've heard that if you have crowns in your mouth they can get damaged if they put in an air tube.*
M	Well, it's unlikely but we'll take special care. So which teeth are we talking about?
F	*Err, these two.*
M	OK the two central incisors. And do you have any other teeth with crowns or implants.
F	*No.*
M	OK. So what we have planned for you is …[fade]

PAUSE: 10 SECONDS
That is the end of Part A. Now, look at Part B.

PAUSE: 5 SECONDS
Part B. In this part of the test, you'll hear six different extracts. In each extract, you'll hear people talking in a different healthcare setting.

For questions 25 to 30, choose the answer A, B or C which fits best according to what you hear. You'll have time to read each question before you listen. Complete your answers as you listen.

Now look at Question 25. You hear two trainee doctors doing an activity at a staff training day. Now read the question.

M   So what did the trainer say we have to do?

F   *Well, we've got to look through these case notes – ten sets in total – and decide which of the patients should be referred to the consultant as a matter of urgency, and which can wait.*

M   Oh right. And did I hear him say there's a limited number you can refer?

F   *Not exactly. He said that we should put them in rank order according to the severity of the symptoms and other factors evident from the case notes. Once we've agreed on our list, we have to go and compare with another pair of trainees.*

M   OK. Let's get started then.

PAUSE: 5 SECONDS

Question 26. You hear a radiographer talking to a patient about her MRI scan. Now read the question.

PAUSE: 15 SECONDS

---***---

M   Come in, come in. Mrs Brown, isn't it? My name's Ted and I'm going to be doing your MRI scan today. Now, can you get up on the table for me?

F   *You know, I'm really claustrophobic.*

M   Mm, well, this is a new piece of equipment. The diameter's much larger, so it should make it a little more comfortable for you. You'll also have this call bell, so if you need me at any point during the test you squeeze that, OK?

F   *OK.*

M   Now your scan's only going to take about 15 minutes. Are you OK with that?

F   *I am.*

M   OK. Let's get started then.

PAUSE: 5 SECONDS

Question 27. You hear two nurses discussing an article in a nursing journal. Now read the question.

PAUSE: 15 SECONDS

---***---

F: *Did you see the article about research on strokes and sight problems in the latest Nursing magazine?*

M: Yes, I found it interesting that there's quite such a high degree of visual impairment after a stroke.

F: Yeah, but I think I could've told them that without an expensive research study.

M: Well, you need evidence to get progress in how people are treated. And now there'll be a push for all stroke patients to have eye assessments as a matter of course.

F: It certainly makes a pretty solid case for that. Especially as there's plenty that can be done to help people if early screening diagnoses an issue.

M: Absolutely.

F: I was just sorry the article didn't provide more detail about the type of sight problems that are most common after a stroke.

M: Well there's a reference to where the whole study's been published - so you could always find out there.

PAUSE: 5 SECONDS

Question 28. You hear two hospital managers talking about a time management course for staff. Now read the question.

PAUSE: 15 SECONDS

---***---

M   The uptake for the course in time management for staff has been disappointing, hasn't it?

F   It has – but I'm not exactly sure why, because everyone seems to know about it. And we asked for it to be changed from a four-hour session to two two-hour slots to make it easier for nurses to be released from their wards. But apparently that wasn't possible because it has to be done a certain way.

M   Yeah, I'm not convinced that was the problem anyway. I think once staff become aware of what it's aiming to do, and how it fits together with other initiatives, there might be more interest.

F   Yeah. There certainly is a need, even if the staff themselves don't actually realise it at present.

PAUSE: 5 SECONDS
Question 29. You hear an optometrist reporting on some research he's been doing. Now read the question.

PAUSE: 15 SECONDS
---***---

M: I specialise in dealing with fungal eye infections. At present, treatment involves giving eye drops every hour for at least two weeks. I wanted to improve this process, by designing a system capable of releasing anti-fungal drugs onto the eye over an extended period. Contact lenses are perfect for this, as their hydrogel structure has the ability to uptake and release drugs, and their placement on the eye ensures the drug gets released directly to the cornea. In order to make a contact lens provide drugs over a sustained period, I've modified the lens. I've also used nanoparticles for packaging the drugs. So, I've managed to create a system capable of delivering an anti-fungal drug called Nanomycin for up to four hours. I now hope to increase this, and use this system with other drugs.

PAUSE: 5 SECONDS
Question 30. You hear a consultant talking to a trainee about a patient's eye condition. Now read the question.

PAUSE: 15 SECONDS
---***---

M   Have we got Mrs Kent's notes?

F   Yes, they're here. She's coming in today for possible laser surgery for her retinopathy, isn't she?

M   Well, depending on results – and from the look of these pictures we took last time, there's been a slow improvement, so we'll talk to her and perhaps hold off for the time being – unless her condition's worsened, 'cos it can in some cases.

F   So what's the cause?

M   Well, we know a leak of fluid behind the retina causes the distorted vision which sufferers get, but not why that occurs. There may be a link with stress, and also steroid use, but the jury's still out, I'm afraid.

PAUSE: 10 SECONDS
That is the end of Part B. Now, look at Part C.

PAUSE: 5 SECONDS
Part C. In this part of the test, you'll hear two different extracts. In each extract, you'll hear health professionals talking about aspects of their work.

For questions 31 to 42, choose the answer A, B or C which fits best according to what you hear. Complete your answers as you listen.

Now look at extract one.

Extract one. Questions 31 to 36. You hear an interview with a neurosurgeon called Dr Ian Marsh who specialises in the treatment of concussion in sport.

You now have 90 seconds to read questions 31 to 36.

PAUSE: 90 SECONDS
---***---

F: My guest today is Dr Ian Marsh, a specialist in the treatment of concussion in sport and a co-author on a new set of guidelines. So, Dr Marsh, what's the aim of these new guidelines?

M: Well the aim was really to provide a resource, not for the top-level professional sports people, but for parents, teachers and coaches of young people playing sport. The guidelines basically offer some expert information from a GP, an emergency physician, and myself as a neurosurgeon, about what the condition is, also how to identify the symptoms and how to manage it. If any of your listeners have ever had a concussion doing sports, you'll know how frightening it can be. It's confusing and painful, and difficult sometimes for teachers, parents, or whoever to work out if someone with concussion is okay. I mean… we hope to remedy that.

F: And how do we know when someone is suffering from concussion?

M: Well, obviously, if the person's actually knocked out – it's clear. But not all patients actually lose consciousness. Often following a hard knock to the head, they become disorientated or experience headaches, nausea or vomiting. These are signs of concussion and they may clear initially, but then return when the individual actually undertakes further physical activity; right, when they start to train, say. So, it can actually take quite a while for things to really clear up. The essence of it is that people shouldn't start playing again until those warning signs have completely subsided.

F: *Yes, and you say that waiting anything less than fourteen days after all the symptoms have cleared would be too early to return?*

M: Yeah, that's right. If they go back too early, they risk a second concussion and, as we know from professional athletes, they may have to give up their sport if they have too many concussions. Right, so it's better, particularly in a young person with a developing brain, to allow all of the symptoms to settle, and only then return to play — well usually return to train first, then return to play after that. It used to be thought that receiving another concussion, could lead to severe brain swelling, and that could be fatal or at least involve a visit to the emergency room. I think the evidence is fairly slim for that. What we do know though is that the compounding effect of having one concussion followed by another seems to be more severe than just the one. So it's always better to let the brain recover fully before playing again.

F: *Right, so who's at the highest risk of sports concussion?*

M: Well, actually a concussion can happen whenever anyone receives a blow to the head. Usually it's a sort of twisting blow, not a straight-on blow. But, obviously people playing sports like rugby - where there's bodily contact – stand more chance of being at the receiving end of such a blow. But having said that, it's just as likely to affect kids kicking a ball around a park as it is to affect top professional players in big matches.

F: *Do you think that youth sports need specialist concussion doctors on hand? Like the professionals do?*

M: There's always a risk and we know that it happens from time to time, but I mean most games — even the most dangerous ones — are without incident at all. I think people who are involved in running youth sports, whether they be referees, coaches, or parents, can be made aware of how to manage concussion, the signs that they need to look out for, and maybe the warnings of something more serious, so that they can take the appropriate actions. But I think always having a doctor on the sidelines where young people are playing is just an over-reaction.

F: *In the USA, college football is big business. They're trialling helmet sensors and impact sensors. Do you think that's something we need everywhere?*

M: Well, I don't think it'll come to that. I think there are two scenarios here. The first is one where a concussion's a one-off event following a significant blow to the head. Right, the second's quite different and involves Chronic Traumatic Encephalopathy. This comes about particularly in American Football, where players use their helmets and heads almost like weapons. That type of repeated impact seems to add up over the player's career. That's something we've heard being discussed, mostly in the USA. Naturally there's interest generally in protecting players, particularly in the professional levels of sport, but I see that as a different matter to the management of concussion itself.

PAUSE: 10 SECONDS

Now look at extract two.

Extract two. Questions 37 to 42. You hear a presentation by a consultant cardiologist called Dr Pamela Skelton, who's talking about a research trial called SPRINT which investigated the effects of setting lower blood-pressure targets.

You now have 90 seconds to read questions 37 to 42.

PAUSE: 90 SECONDS

---***---

F: *Hello - I'm Dr Pamela Skelton, Consultant Cardiologist at this hospital, and I'm talking about the recent SPRINT study into the effects of setting lower blood-pressure targets, which in turn affects the advice and medication which patients are given. I'm going to describe the patients who were selected, how the trial was conducted and the implications of its results for us all as health professionals.*

First – the trial itself. It involved over nine-thousand hypertensive participants, aged fifty-plus, most of whom were on blood-pressure medication. They were randomly assigned to one of two groups – one with a goal of less than one-hundred-and-twenty millimetres systolic BP, the other with a goal of less than one-hundred-and-forty millimetres, the traditional standard. The intention was to follow these patients for five years, factoring in the usual drop-out rate. As it turned out, however, the trial was stopped after just three years thanks to an all-cause mortality reduction of nearly thirty percent for the one-hundred-and-twenty group, which was definitive and shocking - but wonderful. As I mentioned, the participants were over-fifties and it goes without saying that as people age, they develop more diseases and health problems as a matter of course. But there was a specific group of over-seventy-fives who did just as well as younger patients.

Before the trial, some medics referred to the natural stiffening of the arteries with ageing, suggesting that a hundred-and-twenty was too low a target for the over-seventy-fives, risking an increase of dizzy spells which would affect general wellbeing. But this concern turned out to be unfounded. Others thought there'd be a failure to take the number of tablets needed to reach a BP of a hundred-and-twenty, especially among older participants. Again, this wasn't an issue - the average needed was just three per day. The over-seventy-fives, already on various drugs, didn't object to extra medication. Participants from this age group who didn't finish the trial were taken out because some conditions, which were already present, worsened; for example in some cases obesity levels rose too high.

To manage their blood pressure, participants were given standard drugs – nothing experimental, just drugs that are readily available and low-cost. Another key factor was that blood pressure was measured in a very specific way. Rather than give patients an arm cuff for at-home twenty-four-hour ambulatory monitoring, an automated machine was used at the hospital. This took three separate readings and averaged them. Also, readings were taken while staff were out of the room to avoid what's called 'white coat syndrome' in patients.

Now, some of you may be familiar with the ACCORD study into blood pressure levels several years ago, which in some respects was similar to SPRINT. There are some differences, though. For example, ACCORD was about half the size of SPRINT, and unlike SPRINT, the ACCORD study allowed diabetic patients to take part. Despite this, in general, the ACCORD participants were rather lower risk than those in the SPRINT trial – probably because of the slightly lower average age. The ACCORD trial didn't show a statistically significant benefit for overall cardiovascular outcomes, but there was a clear forty percent reduction in strokes – even though that was a secondary outcome.

So, to summarise, the SPRINT trial seems to support a hundred-and-twenty as a recommended blood-pressure target. This is doubtless a landmark study and, importantly, one which was sponsored by government rather than by the interests of the pharmaceutical corporations. I recommend a note of caution though, as SPRINT does contradict previous findings. The Cochrane View in 2011, for example, said that lowering to under a hundred and-forty didn't produce a change in the risk of death overall. However, we must bear in mind that Cochrane was looking retrospectively at trials which weren't actually focused on the same particular issue. So it's worth doing a full and systematic evaluation, to see where the SPRINT trial fits in with what we already know.

It's interesting that a few GPs have already been working with older patients to hit lower blood- pressure goals, and the new data will doubtless encourage greater take-up of this more interventionist line of attack.   But the SPRINT results don't mean that everyone with hypertension should be dropping to under a hundred-and-twenty. Plus, to achieve those lower levels, it's unlikely that lifestyle changes alone would be enough, it could well require several anti-hypertensive drugs as well. There remain some unanswered questions, of course - for example whether other groups, like those with a lower heart-attack risk, need to keep their blood pressure that low. So, while SPRINT can help guide doctors' decisions about some patients, it doesn't mean that a new universal standard for blood pressure is in order. Instead, it's a good reason for everyone to discuss with their doctor, their own ideal and particular target.

PAUSE: 10 SECONDS
That is the end of Part C.

You now have two minutes to check your answers.

PAUSE: 120 SECONDS
That is the end of the Listening test.

Reading sub-test

Answer Key – Part A

PART A: QUESTIONS 1-20

1	B
2	A
3	C
4	A
5	D
6	A
7	organic matter
8	foreign bodies
9	compound
10	6/six hours
11	systemic sepsis
12	immuno(-)suppressed
13	antibiotics
14	(in) (the) jaw
15	broken bones
16	(a) bite reflex
17	5/five (times)
18	(a) booster dose OR booster doses
19	twenty-three/23 gauge
20	crying

Reading sub-test

Answer Key – Parts B & C

READING SUB-TEST – ANSWER KEY

PART B: QUESTIONS 1-6

1	B	there is severe leakage from the wound.
2	A	encourage participation in the scheme.
3	A	data about patient errors may be incomplete.
4	B	There are several ways of ensuring that the ventilator is working effectively.
5	C	the patients most likely to suffer complications.
6	B	to draw conclusions from the results of cleaning audits

PART C: QUESTIONS 7-14

7	C	lacks any form of convincing proof of its value as a treatment.
8	A	surprise at people's willingness to put their trust in it.
9	B	the key attraction of the approach for patients.
10	B	frequently result from a patient's treatment preferences.
11	C	the way that homeopathic remedies endanger more than just the user
12	D	the way positive results can be achieved despite people's doubts.
13	A	prepared to accept that homeopathy may depend on psychological factors.
14	D	the motivation behind the desire for homeopathy to gain scientific acceptance

PART C: QUESTIONS 15-22

15	A	It required intense concentration.
16	D	the connections between sensors and the brain need to be exact.
17	A	There was statistical evidence that it was successful.
18	B	Patients might have to undergo too many operations.
19	D	It is difficult for scientists to pinpoint precise areas with an electrode.
20	C	It may have more potential than electrical stimulation.
21	A	how much more there is to achieve.
22	B	to illustrate the fact that some sensation is better than none

OCCUPATIONAL ENGLISH TEST

WRITING SUB-TEST: NURSING

SAMPLE RESPONSE: LETTER

Nurse-in-Charge
District Nursing Service
Greenville Community Health Care Centre
88 Highton Road
Greenville

15 July 2017

Re: Ms Margaret Helen Martin
    DOB: 25 July 1935
    23 Third Avenue, Greenville

Dear Nurse,

Ms Margaret Martin is due for discharge from our hospital tomorrow, after the successful performance of an angioplasty today.

Ms Martin is 81 years old and has an established personal and family history of heart disease. In addition, she suffers from coeliac disease, and has reduced hearing, for which she wears a hearing aid.

Ms Martin is overweight (BMI 29.5) and sedentary. She is anxious about her return home and about her health in general. She does not independently cook for herself and currently has meals delivered. Ms Martin may need support for the implementation of a routine to maintain her remaining function and independence. Dietary and physiotherapy programs have been devised and will be supported by her dietitian and physiotherapist.

Ms Martin has never married, is financially independent, and lives in her own home. Although she has a number of family members living nearby, their support is irregular, and Ms Martin may be at risk of social isolation. Your support in this regard would be appreciated.

Please arrange regular home nursing support for Ms Martin. She has some bruising at the catheter insertion site that will need monitoring for infection or bleeding. It is important to ensure Ms Martin adheres to her medication program.

Yours faithfully,

Ward Nurse

NURSING

PRACTICE TEST  3

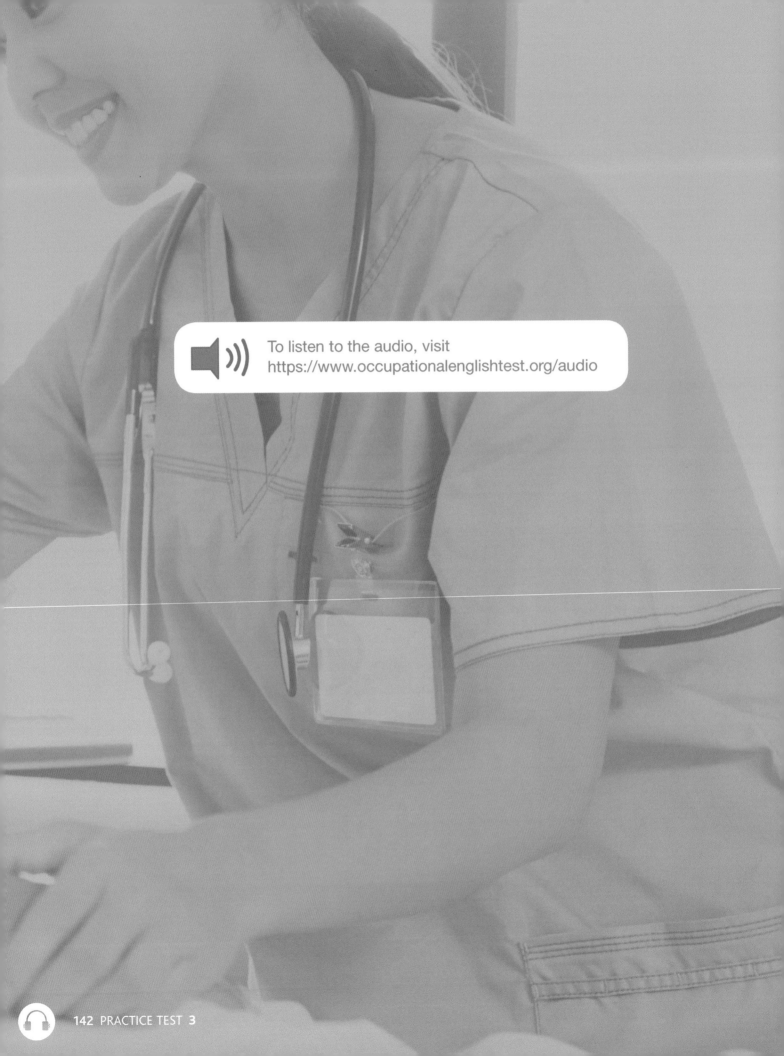

To listen to the audio, visit
https://www.occupationalenglishtest.org/audio

LISTENING SUB-TEST – QUESTION PAPER

CANDIDATE NUMBER:

LAST NAME:

FIRST NAME:

MIDDLE NAMES:

PROFESSION: Candidate details and photo will be printed here.

VENUE:

TEST DATE:

Passport Photo

CANDIDATE DECLARATION

By signing this, you agree not to disclose or use in any way (other than to take the test) or assist any other person to disclose or use any OET test or sub-test content. If you cheat or assist in any cheating, use any unfair practice, break any of the rules or regulations, or ignore any advice or information, you may be disqualified and your results may not be issued at the sole discretion of CBLA. CBLA also reserves its right to take further disciplinary action against you and to pursue any other remedies permitted by law. If a candidate is suspected of and investigated for malpractice, their personal details and details of the investigation may be passed to a third party where required.

CANDIDATE SIGNATURE: _____

TIME: APPROXIMATELY **40 MINUTES**

INSTRUCTIONS TO CANDIDATES

DO NOT open this question paper until you are told to do so.

One mark will be granted for each correct answer.

Answer **ALL** questions. Marks are **NOT** deducted for incorrect answers.

At the end of the test, you will have two minutes to check your answers.

At the end of the test, hand in this **Question Paper.**

You must not remove OET material from the test room.

HOW TO ANSWER THE QUESTIONS

Part A: Write your answers on this **Question Paper** by filling in the blanks. **Example: Patient:** _____ Ray Sands

Part B & Part C: Mark your answers on this **Question Paper** by filling in the circle using a 2B pencil. **Example:** Ⓐ
Ⓑ
Ⓒ

www.occupationalenglishtest.org

© Cambridge Boxhill Language Assessment – ABN 51 988 559 414

[CANDIDATE NO.] LISTENING QUESTION PAPER 01/12

Occupational English Test
Listening Test

This test has three parts. In each part you'll hear a number of different extracts. At the start of each extract, you'll hear this sound: --beep—

You'll have time to read the questions before you hear each extract and you'll hear each extract **ONCE ONLY**. Complete your answers as you listen.

At the end of the test you'll have two minutes to check your answers.

Part A

In this part of the test, you'll hear two different extracts. In each extract, a health professional is talking to a patient.

For **questions 1-24**, complete the notes with information you hear.

Now, look at the notes for extract one.

Extract 1: Questions 1-12

You hear a pulmonologist talking to a patient called Robert Miller. For **questions 1-12**, complete the notes with a word or short phrase.

You now have 30 seconds to look at the notes.

Patient	Robert Miller

Symptoms

- tiredness
- persistent **(1)** _____ cough
- SOB
- weight loss described as **(2)** _____ in nature.
- fingertips appear **(3)** _____
- nails feel relatively **(4)** _____

Background details

- previously employed as a **(5)** _____ (20 yrs)
- now employed as a **(6)** _____
- no longer able to play golf
- keeps pigeons as a hobby

Medical history

- last year diagnosed with hypertension
- current prescription of **(7)** _____
- **(8)** _____ sounds in chest reported by GP
- father suffered from **(9)** _____

Previous tests

- **(10)** _____ six months ago
- chest x-ray one month ago

Future actions

- **(11)** _____ test
- CT scan
- prescription of **(12)** _____ (possibly)

Extract 2: Questions 13-24

You hear an eye specialist talking to a patient called Jasmine Burton, who has recently undergone eye surgery. For **questions 13-24**, complete the notes with a word or short phrase.

You now have thirty seconds to look at the notes.

Patient	Jasmine Burton

Patient history

- suffers from **(13)** _____ astigmatism
- also has **(14)** _____ (so surgery under general anaesthetic)
- eye problems may result from a lack of **(15)** _____
- sight problems mean **(16)** _____ isn't an option for her
- reports some slowness to **(17)** _____
- has poor perception of **(18)** _____
- works as a **(19)** _____
  - reports having no issues at work
- eyes checked every few years

Surgery

- **(20)** _____ in right eye first noted three years ago
- February this year - had surgery
- some capsular **(21)** _____ noted post-operatively
- examination showed no sign of a **(22)** _____
  - follow up appointment in 6 months

Presenting with

- reported increase in number of **(23)** _____
- increased sensitivity to **(24)** _____

That is the end of Part A. Now look at Part B.

Part B

In this part of the test, you'll hear six different extracts. In each extract, you'll hear people talking in a different healthcare setting.

For **questions 25-30**, choose the answer (**A**, **B** or **C**) which fits best according to what you hear. You'll have time to read each question before you listen. Complete your answers as you listen.

Now look at question 25.

25. You hear a nurse briefing a colleague at the end of her shift.

   What does the colleague have to do for the patient tonight?

   (**A**)   remove her saline drip

   (**B**)   arrange for more tests

   (**C**)   monitor her blood pressure

26. You hear part of a hospital management meeting where a concern is being discussed.

   What is the committee concerned about?

   (**A**)   poor response to recruitment drives

   (**B**)   difficulties in retaining suitable staff

   (**C**)   relatively high staff absence rates

27. You hear a GP and his practice nurse discussing a vaccination programme.

   They agree that the practice should

   (**A**)   make sure patients are aware of it.

   (**B**)   organise it more effectively than in the past.

   (**C**)   prepare to cope with an increasing demand for it.

28. You hear two hospital nurses discussing the assessment of a patient on their ward.

What is the problem?

(A) The patient's documentation has been sent to the wrong place.

(B) Nobody has taken responsibility for assessing the patient.

(C) The duty doctor was unable to locate the patient.

29. You hear the beginning of a training session for dental students.

The trainer is explaining that the session will

(A) focus on aspects of dental hygiene.

(B) expand upon what they studied previously.

(C) introduce them to a completely new technique.

30. You hear two nurses discussing the treatment of a patient with a kidney infection.

What is the female nurse doing?

(A) emphasising the urgency of a procedure

(B) suggesting how to overcome a difficulty

(C) warning him about a possible problem

That is the end of Part B. Now look at Part C.

Part C

In this part of the test, you'll hear two different extracts. In each extract, you'll hear health professionals talking about aspects of their work.

For **questions 31-42**, choose the answer (**A, B** or **C**) which fits best according to what you hear. Complete your answers as you listen.

Now look at extract one.

Extract 1: Questions 31-36

You hear a geriatrician called Dr Clare Cox giving a presentation on the subject of end-of-life care for people with dementia.

You now have 90 seconds to read **questions 31-36**.

31.   What problem does Dr Cox identify concerning dementia patients?

(A)   They can often make unrealistic demands on their carers.

(B)   Their condition can develop in a number of different ways.

(C)   The type of care that they may require is extremely costly.

32.   Why did *Dementia Australia* decide to examine the issue of end-of-life dementia care?

(A)   There was a lack of reliable information on it.

(B)   The number of stories about poor care made it urgent.

(C)   There were enough data on which to base an effective care plan.

33.   For Dr Cox, the initial results of the dementia survey reveal that palliative care

(A)   was working more effectively than people had thought.

(B)   was more widely available than some users imagined.

(C)   was viewed negatively by medical professionals.

34. Dr Cox says that lack of knowledge of the law by care professionals

  (A)   proves that family members should help make pain management decisions.

  (B)   could be resulting in a surprisingly high number of premature deaths.

  (C)   may lead to dementia patients experiencing unnecessary distress.

35. Dr Cox thinks that the statistics she quotes on refusing treatment

  (A)   illustrate a gap in current medical education programmes.

  (B)   show how patients' wishes are too often misunderstood by carers.

  (C)   demonstrate the particular difficulties presented by dementia patients.

36. Dr Cox makes the point that end-of-life planning is desirable because

  (A)   it reduces the complexity of certain care decisions.

  (B)   it avoids carers having to speculate about a patient's wishes.

  (C)   it ensures that everyone receives the best possible quality of care.

Now look at extract two.

Extract 2: Questions 37-42

You hear a hospital doctor called Dr Keith Gardiner giving a presentation about some research he's done on the subject of staff-patient communication.

You now have 90 seconds to read **questions 37-42**.

37.   Dr Gardiner first became interested in staff-patient communication after

(A)   experiencing poor communication as an in-patient.

(B)   observing the effects of poor communication on a patient.

(C)   analysing patient feedback data on the subject of communication.

38.   What point does Dr Gardiner make about a typical admission to hospital?

(A)   The information given can overwhelm patients.

(B)   Patients often feel unable to communicate effectively.

(C)   Filling in detailed paperwork can be stressful for patients.

39.   Dr Gardiner uses an example of poor communication to illustrate the point that

(A)   patients should be consulted about the desirability of a hospital stay.

(B)   specialists need to be informed if there are any mental health issues.

(C)   relatives' knowledge of a patient's condition shouldn't be taken for granted.

40. Dr Gardiner explains that a survey conducted among in-patients about communication

    (A)   measured the difference between their expectations and their actual experience.

    (B)   asked their opinion about all aspects of the service they received.

    (C)   included questions on how frequently they visited the hospital.

41. One common complaint arising from Dr Gardner's survey concerned

    (A)   a lack of privacy for patients receiving sensitive information.

    (B)   the over-use of unclear medical terminology with patients.

    (C)   a tendency not to address patients in a respectful way.

42. How does Dr Gardiner feel about the results of the survey?

    (A)   surprised by one response from patients

    (B)   reassured by the level of patient care identified

    (C)   worried that unforeseen problems were highlighted

That is the end of Part C.

You now have two minutes to check your answers.

END OF THE LISTENING TEST

READING SUB-TEST – TEXT BOOKLET: PART A

CANDIDATE NUMBER:

LAST NAME:

FIRST NAME:

MIDDLE NAMES:

PROFESSION:

VENUE:

TEST DATE:

Candidate details and photo will be printed here.

Passport Photo

CANDIDATE DECLARATION

By signing this, you agree not to disclose or use in any way (other than to take the test) or assist any other person to disclose or use any OET test or sub-test content. If you cheat or assist in any cheating, use any unfair practice, break any of the rules or regulations, or ignore any advice or information, you may be disqualified and your results may not be issued at the sole discretion of CBLA. CBLA also reserves its right to take further disciplinary action against you and to pursue any other remedies permitted by law. If a candidate is suspected of and investigated for malpractice, their personal details and details of the investigation may be passed to a third party where required.

CANDIDATE SIGNATURE: _____

INSTRUCTIONS TO CANDIDATES

You must **NOT** remove OET material from the test room.

Necrotizing Fasciitis (NF): Texts

Text A

Necrotizing fasciitis (NF) is a severe, rare, potentially lethal soft tissue infection that develops in the scrotum and perineum, the abdominal wall, or the extremities. The infection progresses rapidly, and septic shock may ensue; hence, the mortality rate is high (median mortality 32.2%). NF is classified into four types, depending on microbiological findings.

Table 1

Classification of responsible pathogens according to type of infection

Microbiological type	Pathogens	Site of infection	Co-morbidities
Type 1 (polymicrobial)	Obligate and facultative anaerobes	Trunk and perineum	Diabetes mellitus
Type 2 (monomicrobial)	Beta-hemolytic streptococcus A	Limbs	
Type 3	*Clostridium* species Gram-negative bacteria Vibrios spp. Aeromonas hydrophila	Limbs, trunk and perineum	Trauma Seafood consumption (for *Aeromonas*)
Type 4	*Candida* spp. Zygomycetes	Limbs, trunk, perineum	Immuno-suppression

Text B

Antibiotic treatment for NF

Type 1

- Initial treatment includes ampicillin or ampicillin–sulbactam combined with metronidazole or clindamycin.
- Broad gram-negative coverage is necessary as an initial empirical therapy for patients who have recently been treated with antibiotics, or been hospitalized. In such cases, antibiotics such as ampicillin–sulbactam, piperacillin–tazobactam, ticarcillin–clavulanate acid, third or fourth generation cephalosporins, or carbapenems are used, and at a higher dosage.

Type 2

- First or second generation of cephalosporins are used for the coverage of methicillin-sensitive Staphylococcus aureus (MSSA).
- MRSA tends to be covered by vancomycin, or daptomycin and linezolid in cases where S. aureus is resistant to vancomycin.

Type 3

- NF should be managed with clindamycin and penicillin, which kill the Clostridium species.
- If Vibrio infection is suspected, the early use of tetracyclines (including doxycycline and minocycline) and third-generation cephalosporins is crucial for the survival of the patient, since these antibiotics have been shown to reduce the mortality rate drastically.

Type 4

- Can be treated with amphotericin B or fluoroconazoles, but the results of this treatment are generally disappointing.

Antibiotics should be administered for up to 5 days after local signs and symptoms have resolved. The mean duration of antibiotic therapy for NF is 4–6 weeks.

Text C

Supportive care in an ICU is critical to NF survival. This involves fluid resuscitation, cardiac monitoring, aggressive wound care, and adequate nutritional support. Patients with NF are in a catabolic state and require increased caloric intake to combat infection. This can be delivered orally or via nasogastric tube, peg tube, or intravenous hyperalimentation. This should begin immediately (within the first 24 hours of hospitalization). Prompt and aggressive support has been shown to lower complication rates. Baseline and repeated monitoring of albumin, prealbumin, transferrin, blood urea nitrogen, and triglycerides should be performed to ensure the patient is receiving adequate nutrition.

Wound care is also an important concern. Advanced wound dressings have replaced wet-to-dry dressings. These dressings promote granulation tissue formation and speed healing. Advanced wound dressings may lend to healing or prepare the wound bed for grafting. A healthy wound bed increases the chances of split-thickness skin graft take. Vacuum-assisted closure (VAC) was recently reported to be effective in a patient whose cardiac status was too precarious to undergo a long surgical reconstruction operation. With the VAC., the patient's wound decreased in size, and the VAC was thought to aid in local management of infection and improve granulation tissue.

Text D

Advice to give the patient before discharge

- Help arrange the patient's aftercare, including home health care and instruction regarding wound management, social services to promote adjustment to lifestyle changes and financial concerns, and physical therapy sessions to help rebuild strength and promote the return to optimal physical health.

- The life-threatening nature of NF, scarring caused by the disease, and in some cases the need for limb amputation can alter the patient's attitude and viewpoint, so be sure to take a holistic approach when dealing with the patient and family.

Remind the diabetic patient to

- control blood glucose levels, keeping the glycated haemoglobin (HbAlc) level to 7% or less.
- keep needles capped until use and not to reuse needles.
- clean the skin thoroughly before blood glucose testing or insulin in¬jection, and to use alcohol pads to clean the area afterward.

END OF PART A

THIS TEXT BOOKLET WILL BE COLLECTED

OCCUPATIONAL ENGLISH TEST

READING SUB-TEST – QUESTION PAPER: PART A

CANDIDATE NUMBER:

LAST NAME:

FIRST NAME:

MIDDLE NAMES:

PROFESSION:

VENUE:

TEST DATE:

Candidate details and photo will be printed here.

Passport Photo

CANDIDATE DECLARATION

By signing this, you agree not to disclose or use in any way (other than to take the test) or assist any other person to disclose or use any OET test or sub-test content. If you cheat or assist in any cheating, use any unfair practice, break any of the rules or regulations, or ignore any advice or information, you may be disqualified and your results may not be issued at the sole discretion of CBLA. CBLA also reserves its right to take further disciplinary action against you and to pursue any other remedies permitted by law. If a candidate is suspected of and investigated for malpractice, their personal details and details of the investigation may be passed to a third party where required.

CANDIDATE SIGNATURE: _____

TIME: 15 MINUTES

INSTRUCTIONS TO CANDIDATES

DO NOT open this **Question Paper** or the **Text Booklet** until you are told to do so.

Write your answers on the spaces provided on this **Question Paper.**

You must answer the questions within the 15-minute time limit.

One mark will be granted for each correct answer.

Answer **ALL** questions. Marks are **NOT** deducted for incorrect answers.

At the end of the 15 minutes, hand in this **Question Paper** and the **Text Booklet.**

DO NOT remove OET material from the test room.

Part A

TIME: 15 minutes

- Look at the four texts, **A-D**, in the separate **Text Booklet**.

- For each question, **1-20**, look through the texts, **A-D**, to find the relevant information.

- Write your answers on the spaces provided in this **Question Paper**.

- Answer all the questions within the 15-minute time limit.

- Your answers should be correctly spelt.

Necrotizing Fasciitis (NF): Questions

Questions 1-7

For each question, **1-7**, decide which text (**A**, **B**, **C** or **D**) the information comes from. You may use any letter more than once.

In which text can you find information about

1   the drug treatment required?   _____

2   which parts of the body can be affected?   _____

3   the various ways calories can be introduced?   _____

4   who to contact to help the patient after they leave hospital?   _____

5   what kind of dressing to use?   _____

6   how long to give drug therapy to the patient?   _____

7   what advice to give the patient regarding needle use?   _____

Questions 8-14

Answer each of the questions, **8-14**, with a word or short phrase from one of the texts. Each answer may include words, numbers or both.

8   Which two drugs can you use to treat the clostridium species of pathogen?

_____

9   Which common metabolic condition may occur with NF?

_____

10   What complication can a patient suffer from if NF isn't treated quickly enough?

_____

11   What procedure can you use with a wound if the patient can't be operated on?

_____

12   What should the patient be told to use to clean an injection site?

_____

13   Which two drugs can be used if you can't use vancomycin?

_____

14   What kind of infection should you use tetracyclines for?

_____

Questions 15-20

Complete each of the sentences, **15-20**, with a word or short phrase from one of the texts. Each answer may include words, numbers or both.

15   The average proportion of patients who die as a result of contracting NF is

_____.

16   Patients who have eaten _____ may be infected with Aeromonas hydrophilia.

17   Patients with Type 2 infection usually present with infected

_____.

18   Type 1 NF is also known as _____.

19   The patient needs to be aware of the need to keep glycated haemoglobin levels lower than _____.

20   The patient will need a course of _____ to regain fitness levels after returning home.

END OF PART A
THIS QUESTION PAPER WILL BE COLLECTED

READING SUB-TEST – QUESTION PAPER: PARTS B & C

CANDIDATE NUMBER:

LAST NAME:

FIRST NAME:

MIDDLE NAMES:

PROFESSION:

VENUE:

TEST DATE:

Candidate details and photo will be printed here.

Passport Photo

TIME: 45 MINUTES

INSTRUCTIONS TO CANDIDATES

DO NOT open this **Question Paper** until you are told to do so.

One mark will be granted for each correct answer.

Answer **ALL** questions. Marks are **NOT** deducted for incorrect answers.

At the end of the test, hand in this **Question Paper**.

HOW TO ANSWER THE QUESTIONS:

Mark your answers on this **Question Paper** by filling in the circle using a 2B pencil. **Example:** Ⓐ
Ⓑ
Ⓒ

Part B

In this part of the test, there are six short extracts relating to the work of health professionals. For **questions 1-6**, choose answer (**A**, **B** or **C**) which you think fits best according to the text.

1. The policy document tells us that

    (A) stop dates aren't relevant in all circumstances.

    (B) anyone using EPMA can disregard the request for a stop date.

    (C) prescribers must know in advance of prescribing what the stop date should be.

Prescribing stop dates

Prescribers should write a review date or a stop date on the electronic prescribing system EPMA or the medicine chart for each antimicrobial agent prescribed. On the EPMA, there is a forced entry for stop dates on oral antimicrobials. There is not a forced stop date on EPMA for IV antimicrobial treatment – if the prescriber knows how long the course of IV should be, then the stop date can be filled in. If not known, then a review should be added to the additional information, e.g. 'review after 48 hrs'. If the prescriber decides treatment needs to continue beyond the stop date or course length indicated, then it is their responsibility to amend the chart. In critical care, it has been agreed that the routine use of review/stop dates on the charts is not always appropriate.

2. The guidelines inform us that personalised equipment for radiotherapy

(A) is advisable for all patients.

(B) improves precision during radiation.

(C) needs to be tested at the first consultation.

Guidelines: Radiotherapy Simulation Planning Appointment

The initial appointment may also be referred to as the Simulation Appointment. During this appointment you will discuss your patient's medical history and treatment options, and agree on a radiotherapy treatment plan. The first step is usually to take a CT scan of the area requiring treatment. The patient will meet the radiation oncologist, their registrar and radiation therapists. A decision will be made regarding the best and most comfortable position for treatment, and this will be replicated daily for the duration of the treatment. Depending on the area of the body to be treated, personalised equipment such as a face mask may be used to stabilise the patient's position. This equipment helps keep the patient comfortable and still during the treatment and makes the treatment more accurate.

3.   The purpose of these instructions is to explain how to

(A)   monitor an ECG reading.

(B)   position electrodes correctly.

(C)   handle an animal during an ECG procedure.

CT200CV Veterinarian Electrocardiograph User Manual

Animal connections

Good electrode connection is the most important factor in recording a high quality ECG. By following a few basic steps, consistent, clean recordings can be achieved.

1. Shave a patch on each forelimb of the animal at the contact site.

2. Clean the electrode sites with an alcohol swab or sterilising agent.

3. Attach clips to the ECG leads.

4. Place a small amount of ECG electrode gel on the metal electrode of the limb strap or adapter clip.

5. Pinch skin on animal and place clips on the shaved skin area of the animal being tested. The animal must be kept still.

6. Check the LCD display for a constant heart reading.

7. If there is no heart reading, you have a contact problem with one or more of the leads.

8. Recheck the leads and reapply the clips to the shaven skin of the animal.

4.   The group known as 'impatient patients' are more likely to continue with a course of prescribed medication if

(A)   their treatment can be completed over a reduced period of time.

(B)   it is possible to link their treatment with a financial advantage.

(C)   its short-term benefits are explained to them.

Medication adherence and impatient patients

A recent article addressed the behaviour of people who have a 'taste for the present rather than the future'. It proposed that these so-called 'impatient patients' are unlikely to adhere to medications that require use over an extended period. The article proposes that, an 'impatience genotype' exists and that assessing these patients' view of the future while stressing the immediate advantages of adherence may improve adherence rates more than emphasizing potentially distant complications. The authors suggest that rather than attempting to change the character of those who are 'impatient', it may be wise to ascertain the patient's individual priorities, particularly as they relate to immediate gains. For example, while advising an 'impatient' patient with diabetes, stressing improvement in visual acuity rather than avoidance of retinopathy may result in greater medication adherence rates. Additionally, linking the cost of frequently changing prescription lenses when visual acuity fluctuates with glycemic levels may sometimes provide the patient with an immediate financial motivation for improving adherence.

5.   The memo reminds nursing staff to avoid

Ⓐ   x-raying a patient unless pH readings exceed 5.5.

Ⓑ   the use of a particular method of testing pH levels.

Ⓒ   reliance on pH testing in patients taking acid-inhibiting medication.

Checking the position of a nasogastric tube
It is essential to confirm the position of the tube in the stomach by one of the following: • Testing pH of aspirate: gastric placement is indicated by a pH of less than 4, but may increase to between pH 4-6 if the patient is receiving acid-inhibiting drugs. Blue litmus paper is insufficiently sensitive to adequately distinguish between levels of acidity of aspirate. • X-rays: will only confirm position at the time the X-ray is carried out. The tube may have moved by the time the patient has returned to the ward. In the absence of a positive aspirate test, where pH readings are more than 5.5, or in a patient who is unconscious or on a ventilator, an X-ray must be obtained to confirm the initial position of the nasogastric tube.

6. This extract informs us that

(A) the amount of oxytocin given will depend on how the patient reacts.

(B) the patient will go into labour as soon as oxytocin is administered.

(C) the staff should inspect the oxytocin pump before use.

Extract from guidelines: Oxytocin

1 Oxytocin Dosage and Administration

Parenteral drug products should be inspected visually for particulate matter and discoloration prior to administration, whenever solution and container permit. Dosage of Oxytocin is determined by the uterine response. The dosage information below is based upon various regimens and indications in general use.

1.1 Induction or Stimulation of Labour

Intravenous infusion (drip method) is the only acceptable method of administration for the induction or stimulation of labour. Accurate control of the rate of infusion flow is essential. An infusion pump or other such device and frequent monitoring of strength of contractions and foetal heart rate are necessary for the safe administration of Oxytocin for the induction or stimulation of labour. If uterine contractions become too powerful, the infusion can be abruptly stopped, and oxytocic stimulation of the uterine musculature will soon wane.

Part C

In this part of the test, there are two texts about different aspects of healthcare. For **questions 7-22**, choose the answer (**A**, **B**, **C** or **D**) which you think fits best according to the text.

Text 1: Phobia pills

An irrational fear, or phobia, can cause the heart to pound and the pulse to race. It can lead to a full-blown panic attack – and yet the sufferer is not in any real peril. All it takes is a glimpse of, for example, a spider's web for the mind and body to race into panicked overdrive. These fears are difficult to conquer, largely because, although there are no treatment guidelines specifically about phobias, the traditional way of helping the sufferer is to expose them to the fear numerous times. Through the cumulative effect of these experiences, sufferers should eventually feel an increasing sense of control over their phobia. For some people, the process is too protracted, but there may be a short cut. Drugs that work to boost learning may help someone with a phobia to 'detrain' their brain, losing the fearful associations that fuel the panic.

The brain's extraordinary ability to store new memories and forge associations is so well celebrated that its **dark side** is often disregarded. A feeling of contentment is easily evoked when we see a photo of loved ones, though the memory may sometimes be more idealised than exact. In the case of a phobia, however, a nasty experience with, say, spiders, that once triggered a panicked reaction, leads the feelings to resurge whenever the relevant cue is seen again. The current approach is exposure therapy, which uses a process called extinction learning. This involves people being gradually exposed to whatever triggers their phobia until they feel at ease with it. As the individual becomes more comfortable with each situation, the brain automatically creates a new memory – one that links the cue with reduced feelings of anxiety, rather than the sensations that mark the onset of a panic attack.

Unfortunately, while it is relatively easy to create a fear-based memory, expunging that fear is more complicated. Each exposure trial will involve a certain degree of distress in the patient, and although the process is carefully managed throughout to limit this, some psychotherapists have concluded that the treatment is unethical. Neuroscientists have been looking for new ways to speed up extinction learning **for that same reason**.

One such avenue is the use of 'cognitive enhancers' such as a drug called D-cycloserine or DCS. DCS slots into part of the brain's 'NMDA receptor' and seems to modulate the neurons' ability to adjust their signalling in response to events. This tuning of a neuron's firing is thought to be one of the key ways the brain stores memories, and, at very low doses, DCS appears to boost that process, improving our ability to learn. In 2004, a team from Emory University in Atlanta, USA, tested whether DCS could also help people with phobias. A pilot trial was conducted on 28 people undergoing specific exposure therapy for acrophobia – a fear of heights. Results showed that those given a small amount of DCS alongside their regular therapy were able to reduce their phobia to a greater extent than those given a placebo. Since then, other groups have replicated the finding in further trials.

For people undergoing exposure therapy, achieving just one of the steps on the long journey to overcoming their fears requires considerable perseverance, says Cristian Sirbu, a behavioural scientist and psychologist. Thanks to improvement being so slow, patients – often already anxious – tend to feel they have failed. But Sirbu thinks that DCS may make it possible to tackle the problem in a single 3-hour session, which is enough for the patient to make real headway and to leave with a feeling of satisfaction. However, some people have misgivings about this approach, claiming that as it doesn't directly undo the fearful response which is deep-seated in the memory, there is a very real risk of relapse.

Rather than simply attempting to overlay the fearful associations with new ones, Merel Kindt at the University of Amsterdam is instead trying to alter the associations at source. Kindt's studies into anxiety disorders are based on the idea that memories are not only vulnerable to alteration when they're first laid down, but, of key importance, also at later retrieval. This allows for memories to be 'updated', and these amended memories are re-consolidated by the effect of proteins which alter synaptic responses, thereby maintaining the strength of feeling associated with the original memory. Kindt's team has produced encouraging results with arachnophobic patients by giving them propranolol, a well-known and well-tolerated beta-blocker drug, while they looked at spiders. This blocked the effects of norepinephrine in the brain, disrupting the way the memory was put back into storage after being retrieved, as part of the process of reconsolidation. Participants reported that while they still don't like spiders, they were able to approach them. Kindt reports that the benefit was still there three months after the test ended.

Text 1: Questions 7-14

7. In the first paragraph, the writer says that conventional management of phobias can be problematic because of

(A) the lasting psychological effects of the treatment.

(B) the time required to identify the cause of the phobia.

(C) the limited choice of therapies available to professionals.

(D) the need for the phobia to be confronted repeatedly over time.

8. In the second paragraph, the writer uses the phrase '**dark side**' to reinforce the idea that

(A) memories of agreeable events tend to be inaccurate.

(B) positive memories can be negatively distorted over time.

(C) unhappy memories are often more detailed than happy ones.

(D) unpleasant memories are aroused in response to certain prompts.

9. In the second paragraph, extinction learning is explained as a process which

(A) makes use of an innate function of the brain.

(B) encourages patients to analyse their particular fears.

(C) shows patients how to react when having a panic attack.

(D) focuses on a previously little-understood part of the brain.

10. What does the phrase '**for that same reason**' refer to?

(A) the anxiety that patients feel during therapy

(B) complaints from patients who feel unsupported

(C) the conflicting ethical concerns of neuroscientists

(D) psychotherapists who take on unsuitable patients

11.   In the fourth paragraph, we learn that the drug called DCS

(A)   is unsafe to use except in small quantities.

(B)   helps to control only certain types of phobias.

(C)   affects how neurons in the brain react to stimuli.

(D)   increases the emotional impact of certain events.

12.   In the fifth paragraph, some critics believe that one drawback of using DCS is that

(A)   its benefits are likely to be of limited duration.

(B)   it is only helpful for certain types of personality.

(C)   few patients are likely to complete the course of treatment.

(D)   patients feel discouraged by their apparent lack of progress.

13.   In the final paragraph, we learn that Kindt's studies into anxiety disorders focused on how

(A)   proteins can affect memory retrieval.

(B)   memories are superimposed on each other.

(C)   negative memories can be reduced in frequency.

(D)   the emotional force of a memory is naturally retained.

14.   The writer suggests that propranolol may

(A)   not offer a permanent solution for patients' phobias.

(B)   increase patients' tolerance of key triggers.

(C)   produce some beneficial side-effects.

(D)   be inappropriate for certain phobias.

Text 2: Challenging medical thinking on placebos

Dr Damien Finniss, Associate Professor at Sydney University's Pain Management and Research Institute, was previously a physiotherapist. He regularly treated football players during training sessions using therapeutic ultrasound. 'One particular session', Finniss explains, 'I treated five or six athletes. I'd treat them for five or ten minutes and they'd say, "I feel much better" and run back onto the field. But at the end of the session, I realised the ultrasound wasn't on.' It was a light bulb moment that set Finniss on the path to becoming a leading researcher on the placebo effect.

Used to treat depression, psoriasis and Parkinson's, to name but a few, placebos have an image problem among medics. For years, the thinking has been that a placebo is useless unless the doctor convinces the patient that it's a genuine treatment – problematic for a profession that promotes informed consent. However, a new study casts doubt on this assumption and, along with a swathe of research showing some remarkable results with placebos, raises questions about whether they should now enter the mainstream as legitimate prescription items. The study examined five trials in which participants were told they were getting a placebo, and the conclusion was that doing so honestly can work.

'If the evidence is there, I don't see the harm in openly administering a placebo,' says Ben Colagiuri, a researcher at the University of Sydney. Colagiuri recently published a meta-analysis of thirteen studies which concluded that placebo sleeping pills, whose genuine counterparts **notch up** nearly three million prescriptions in Australia annually, significantly improve sleep quality. The use of placebos could therefore reduce medical costs and the burden of disease in terms of adverse reactions.

But the placebo effect isn't just about fake treatments. It's about raising patients' expectations of a positive result; something which also occurs with real drugs. Finniss cites the 'open-hidden' effect, whereby an analgesic can be twice as effective if the patient knows they're getting it, compared to receiving it unknowingly. 'Treatment is always part medical and part ritual,' says Finniss. This includes the austere consulting room and even the doctor's clothing. But behind the performance of healing is some strong science. Simply believing an analgesic will work activates the same brain regions as the genuine drug. 'Part of the outcome of what we do is the way we interact with patients,' says Finniss.

That interaction is also the focus of Colagiuri's research. He's looking into the 'nocebo' effect, when a patient's pessimism about a treatment becomes self-fulfilling. 'If you give a placebo, and warn only 50% of the patients about side effects, those you warn report more side effects,' says Colagiuri. He's aiming to reverse that by exploiting the psychology of food packaging. Products are labelled '98% fat-free' rather than '2% fat' because positive reference to the word 'fat' puts consumers off. Colagiuri is deploying similar tactics. A drug with a 30% chance of causing a side effect can be reframed as having a 70% chance of not causing it. 'You're giving the same information, but framing it a way that minimises negative expectations,' says Colagiuri.

There is also a body of research showing that a placebo can produce a genuine biological response that could affect the disease process itself. <u>It</u> can be traced back to a study from the 1970s, when psychologist Robert Ader was trying to condition taste-aversion in rats. He gave them a saccharine drink whilst simultaneously injecting Cytoxan, an immune-suppressant which causes nausea. The rats learned to hate the drink due to the nausea. But as Ader continued giving it to them, without Cytoxan, they began to die from infection. Their immune system had 'learned' to fail by repeated pairing of the drink with Cytoxan. Professor Andrea Evers of Leiden University is running a study that capitalises on this conditioning effect and may benefit patients with rheumatoid arthritis, which causes the immune system to attack the joints. Evers' patients are given the immunosuppressant methotrexate, but instead of always receiving the same dose, they get a higher dose followed by a lower one. The theory is that the higher dose will cause the body to link the medication with a damped-down immune system. The lower dose will then work because the body has 'learned' to curb immunity as a placebo response to taking the drug. Evers hopes it will mean effective drug regimes that use lower doses with fewer side effects.

The medical profession, however, remains less than enthusiastic about placebos. 'I'm one of two researchers in the country who speak on placebos, and I've been invited to lecture at just one university,' says Finniss. According to Charlotte Blease, a philosopher of science, this antipathy may go to the core of what it means to be a doctor. 'Medical education is largely about biomedical facts. 'Softer' sciences, such as psychology, get marginalised because it's the hard stuff that's associated with what it means to be a doctor.' The result, says Blease, is a large, placebo-shaped hole in the medical curriculum. 'There's a great deal of medical illiteracy about the placebo effect ... it's the science behind the art of medicine. Doctors need training in that.'

Text 2: Questions 15-22

15. A football training session sparked Dr Finniss' interest in the placebo effect because

(A) he saw for himself how it could work in practice.

(B) he took the opportunity to try out a theory about it.

(C) he made a discovery about how it works with groups.

(D) he realised he was more interested in research than treatment.

16. The writer suggests that doctors should be more willing to prescribe placebos now because

(A) research indicates that they are effective even without deceit.

(B) recent studies are more reliable than those conducted in the past.

(C) they have been accepted as a treatment by many in the profession.

(D) they have been shown to relieve symptoms in a wide range of conditions.

17. What is suggested about sleeping pills by the use of the verb '**notch up**'?

(A) they may have negative results

(B) they could easily be replaced

(C) they are extremely effective

(D) they are very widely used

18. What point does the writer make in the fourth paragraph?

(A) The way a treatment is presented is significant even if it is a placebo.

(B) The method by which a drug is administered is more important than its content.

(C) The theatrical side of medicine should not be allowed to detract from the science.

(D) The outcome of a placebo treatment is affected by whether the doctor believes in it.

19. In researching side effects, Colagiuri aims to

(A) discover whether placebos can cause them.

(B) reduce the number of people who experience them.

(C) make information about them more accessible to patients.

(D) investigate whether pessimistic patients are more likely to suffer from them.

20. What does the word '**it**' in the sixth paragraph refer to?

(A) a placebo treatment

(B) the disease process itself

(C) a growing body of research

(D) a genuine biological response

21. What does the writer tell us about Ader's and Evers' studies?

(A) Both involve gradually reducing the dosage of a drug.

(B) Evers is exploiting a response which Ader discovered by chance.

(C) Both examine the side effects caused by immunosuppressant drugs.

(D) Evers is investigating whether the human immune system reacts to placebos as Ader's rats did.

22. According to Charlotte Blease, placebos are omitted from medical training because

(A) there are so many practical subjects which need to be covered.

(B) those who train doctors do not believe that they work.

(C) they can be administered without specialist training.

(D) their effect is more psychological than physical.

END OF READING TEST
THIS BOOKLET WILL BE COLLECTED

OCCUPATIONAL ENGLISH TEST

WRITING SUB-TEST – TEST BOOKLET

CANDIDATE NUMBER:

LAST NAME:

FIRST NAME:

MIDDLE NAMES:

PROFESSION:

VENUE:

TEST DATE:

Candidate details and photo will be printed here.

Passport Photo

CANDIDATE DECLARATION

By signing this, you agree not to disclose or use in any way (other than to take the test) or assist any other person to disclose or use any OET test or sub-test content. If you cheat or assist in any cheating, use any unfair practice, break any of the rules or regulations, or ignore any advice or information, you may be disqualified and your results may not be issued at the sole discretion of CBLA. CBLA also reserves its right to take further disciplinary action against you and to pursue any other remedies permitted by law. If a candidate is suspected of and investigated for malpractice, their personal details and details of the investigation may be passed to a third party where required.

CANDIDATE SIGNATURE: _____

INSTRUCTIONS TO CANDIDATES

You must write your answer for the Writing sub-test in the **Writing Answer Booklet.**

You must **NOT** remove OET material from the test room.

www.occupationalenglishtest.org

© Cambridge Boxhill Language Assessment – ABN 51 988 559 414

[CANDIDATE NO.] WRITING SUB-TEST TEST BOOKLET 01/04

OCCUPATIONAL ENGLISH TEST

WRITING SUB-TEST: NURSING

TIME ALLOWED: **READING TIME:** 5 MINUTES
WRITING TIME: 40 MINUTES

Read the case notes below and complete the writing task which follows.

Notes:

You are a Registered Nurse preparing Mrs Jasmine Thompson's discharge. Mrs Thompson has had a right total shoulder replacement. She is to be discharged home today with assistance from 'In-Home Nursing Service'.

Patient: Mrs Jasmine Thompson

Address: 73 White Road, Bayview

DOB: 01.07.1942

Age: 75

Social/Family background:

    Lives in single-storey house with large garden

    Utilises cleaning services once a month

    Widow. 1 daughter – lives in Bayview. 1 son – married with 2 children, lives in Stillwater.

    Daughter will stay with mother for 1 month post-surgery

Medical history: R humerus fracture – 1997

    Osteoarthritis – R shoulder which has not responded to conservative treatment

    Chronic R shoulder pain – ↓ movement and ability to carry out activities of daily living (ADL)

Current medications:

    Voltaren 50mg daily (ceased 14 days pre-operatively)
    Panadeine Forte (codeine/paracetamol) 30/500mg x 2, 6hrly p.r.n.

Admission diagnosis:
    R shoulder osteoarthritis

Medical treatment record:
    11.07.17   R Total shoulder replacement (TSR)

Medical progress: Post-op R shoulder X-rays – confirm position of TSR

    Post-op exercise regime – compliant with physiotherapy

    Post-op bloods – within normal limits

    Post-op pain management – analgesia, cold compress R shoulder

    R shoulder wound – clean & dry, drain site – clean & dry

    15.07.17   Plan for discharge home with daughter today – home nurse to assist at home

Nursing management:

Observations – T, P, R, BP (all within normal range)

Neurovascular observations – colour, warmth, movement, sensation

Oral analgesia

Wound care and observations

Cold compress/shoulder-brace 4 hours per day

ADL assistance as required

Physiotherapy management:

Exercises as per TSR protocol – Neck range of movement exercises

Elbow and hand ROM exercises

Pendular shoulder exercises

Cryo cuff (cold compress) 4 hours per day

Discharge education

Follow-up physiotherapy outpatients appointments

Referral to community hydrotherapy

Discharge plan:
- Patient discharge education – Post TSR:
  - R arm sling for 4 weeks
  - Strictly no lifting for 4 weeks
  - Physiotherapy outpatients x 2 per week, plus hydrotherapy x 1 per week
- 10 days post-op – staples removal, follow-up appointment in Orthopaedic Joint Replacement Outpatient Department
- Orthopaedic Joint Replacement Nurse Specialist contactable by calling hospital, Mon-Fri for any concerns
- Referral to 'In-Home Nursing Service' – assist with showering, administration of LMWH (Clexane) subcutaneous for 4 days as DVT (deep vein thrombosis) prophylaxis

Writing Task:

Using the information given in the case notes, write a letter of referral to Ms Roberts, a home nurse, informing her of the patient's situation and requesting appropriate care. Address the letter to Ms Nita Roberts, In-Home Nursing Service, 79 Beachside Street, Bayview.

In your answer:
- **Expand the relevant notes into complete sentences**
- **Do _not_ use note form**
- **Use letter format**

The body of the letter should be approximately 180–200 words.

WRITING SUB-TEST – ANSWER BOOKLET

CANDIDATE NUMBER:	
LAST NAME:	
FIRST NAME:	
MIDDLE NAMES:	**Passport Photo**
PROFESSION:	Candidate details and photo will be printed here.
VENUE:	
TEST DATE:	

CANDIDATE DECLARATION

By signing this, you agree not to disclose or use in any way (other than to take the test) or assist any other person to disclose or use any OET test or sub-test content. If you cheat or assist in any cheating, use any unfair practice, break any of the rules or regulations, or ignore any advice or information, you may be disqualified and your results may not be issued at the sole discretion of CBLA. CBLA also reserves its right to take further disciplinary action against you and to pursue any other remedies permitted by law. If a candidate is suspected of and investigated for malpractice, their personal details and details of the investigation may be passed to a third party where required.

CANDIDATE SIGNATURE: _____

TIME ALLOWED
READING TIME: 5 MINUTES
WRITING TIME: 40 MINUTES

INSTRUCTIONS TO CANDIDATES

1. **Reading time: 5 minutes**
   During this time you may study the writing task and notes. You **MUST NOT** write, highlight, underline or make any notes.

2. **Writing time: 40 minutes**

3. Use the back page for notes and rough draft only. Notes and rough draft will **NOT** be marked.

   Please write your answer clearly on page 1 and page 2.

   Cross out anything you **DO NOT** want the examiner to consider.

4. You must write your answer for the Writing sub-test in this **Answer Booklet** using **pen or pencil**.

5. You must **NOT** remove OET material from the test room.

www.occupationalenglishtest.org
© Cambridge Boxhill Language Assessment – ABN 51 988 559 414

[CANDIDATE NO.] WRITING SUB-TEST ANSWER BOOKLET 01/04

Please record your answer on this page.

(Only answers on Page 1 and Page 2 will be marked.)

_____

_____

_____

_____

_____

_____

_____

_____

_____

_____

_____

_____

_____

_____

_____

_____

_____

_____

_____

_____

_____

_____

_____

_____

_____

_____

OET Writing sub-test – Answer booklet   1

Please record your answer on this page.

(Only answers on Page 1 and Page 2 will be marked.)

_____

_____

_____

_____

_____

_____

_____

_____

_____

_____

_____

_____

_____

_____

_____

_____

_____

_____

_____

_____

_____

_____

_____

_____

_____

_____

_____

_____

_____

_____

_____

OET Writing sub-test – Answer booklet   2

Space for notes and rough draft. Only your answers on Page 1 and Page 2 will be marked.

SPEAKING SUB-TEST

CANDIDATE NUMBER:

LAST NAME:

FIRST NAME:

MIDDLE NAMES:

PROFESSION: Your details and photo will be printed here.

VENUE:

TEST DATE:

Passport Photo

CANDIDATE DECLARATION

By signing this, you agree not to disclose or use in any way (other than to take the test) or assist any other person to disclose or use any OET test or sub-test content. If you cheat or assist in any cheating, use any unfair practice, break any of the rules or regulations, or ignore any advice or information, you may be disqualified and your results may not be issued at the sole discretion of CBLA. CBLA also reserves its right to take further disciplinary action against you and to pursue any other remedies permitted by law. If a candidate is suspected of and investigated for malpractice, their personal details and details of the investigation may be passed to a third party where required.

CANDIDATE SIGNATURE: _____

INSTRUCTION TO CANDIDATES

Please confirm with the Interlocutor that your roleplay card number and colour match the Interlocutor card before you begin.

Interlocutor to complete only

ID No: _____ Passport: ☐   National ID: ☐   Alternative ID approved: ☐

Speaking sub-test:

ID document sighted? ☐   Photo match? ☐   Signature match? ☐   Did not attend? ☐

Interlocutor name: _____

Interlocutor signature: _____

OET Sample role-play

ROLEPLAYER CARD NO. 1	NURSING

SETTING	Hospital Ward
PATIENT	Last night, following an acute attack of asthma, your family brought you into the emergency department of your local hospital for treatment. You have never had an asthma attack prior to this one. Currently you are being held in the hospital for observation purposes. You anticipate that you will be discharged from hospital within 2-3 hours and you suddenly realise not only that you have had a fright, but that you know little about asthma, e.g., what causes it, how it is treated, and possible long-term effects.
TASK	• Express concern about your condition. • Find out about asthma, its causes and how it can be treated. You have heard stories about people dying from asthma attacks. • Be anxious about the proposal to use a Ventolin inhaler – people have told you about its misuse. • Ask about your long-term prospects now that you have had an asthma attack and been held in hospital overnight for observation.

© Cambridge Boxhill Language Assessment

Sample role-play

OET Sample role-play

CANDIDATE CARD NO. 1	NURSING

SETTING	Hospital Ward
NURSE	This patient was brought into the emergency department of your hospital late last night suffering from an acute asthma attack. He/she is currently being held for observation. The patient has had a fright and is very concerned about his/her condition.
TASK	• Find out how the patient is feeling and if they have any questions about asthma. • Explain what asthma is (e.g., a chronic disease of the airways, etc.). • Discuss the causes, such as environmental factors and an inherited predisposition. • Explain the treatment, for example, a Ventolin (salbutamol) inhaler, and how to use such an inhaler. • Discuss the prognosis for asthma patients. • Deal with the patient's anxiety about the problem, emphasising that asthma can be controlled.

© Cambridge Boxhill Language Assessment

Sample role-play

ROLEPLAYER CARD NO. 2	NURSING

SETTING — Reception Centre at a Public Hospital

CARER — You are visiting a nearby public hospital with your 81-year-old father. Your father has recently been diagnosed as suffering from kidney failure. As a consequence, he is to undergo a tri-weekly dialysis program. Today is 'day one' of your father's dialysis treatment and, while you are waiting for him to have his personal details taken by the charge nurse, you decide to ask another nurse, who is on the reception desk, for information about your father's medical condition and the proposed treatment.

TASK
- You don't know anything about dialysis, so you would like some detailed information about your father's condition. What does kidney failure really mean?
- You would like to know more about what is involved in dialysis. What is it exactly? Why does your father have to come three times a week?
- Ask if the dialysis will improve your father's current medical condition.
- Ask if the dialysis treatment is painful and if there are any side effects.
- Explain that your father is 81 years old, then ask what could happen were he to decide not to continue his treatment.

© Cambridge Boxhill Language Assessment   Sample role-play

OET Sample role-play

CANDIDATE CARD NO. 2	NURSING

SETTING — Reception Centre at a Public Hospital

NURSE — You are working at the reception desk of a public hospital. The son/daughter of an 81-year-old man, who has recently been diagnosed as suffering from kidney failure and who is to undergo a tri-weekly dialysis program, has approached you to ask questions about his/her father's medical condition and the proposed treatment.

TASK
- Find out what the son/daughter already knows about dialysis.
- Explain what kidney failure is. Explain that the kidneys are no longer working, and what this means.
- Describe what dialysis is (e.g., machine which cleans the blood, etc.).
- Explain why his/her father's treatment is to happen three times a week.
- Explain that his/her father's medical condition is unlikely to improve (i.e., it is very unlikely his kidneys will start working again).
- Give details about whether the treatment is painful or has any side effects (e.g., fatigue, low blood pressure, muscle cramps, etc.).
- Tactfully warn what could happen if his/her father decided not to continue with his dialysis treatment (e.g., the patient will become very ill, etc.).

© Cambridge Boxhill Language Assessment   Sample role-play

Listening sub-test

ANSWER KEY – Parts A, B & C

LISTENING SUB-TEST – ANSWER KEY

PART A: QUESTIONS 1-12

1   dry

2   (very) gradual

3   swollen / bulging (out)

4   soft

5   farm labourer

6   (night) security guard

7   beta blockers

8   crackling (accept: cracking)/ crep / crepitation

9   (bad) eczema

10   echocardiogram / cardiac echo / echo

11   arterial blood gas / ABG

12   corticosteroids

PART A: QUESTIONS 13-24

13   myopic / short(-)sighted / near(-)sighted

14   nystagmus / (a) flicker(ing)

15   pigment (in eye)

16   driving

17   focus

18   distance

19   (hotel) receptionist

20   cataract (developed)

21   opacity / clouding

22   detached retina / retina(l) detachment

23   (eye) floaters

24   glare / bright lights

LISTENING SUB-TEST – ANSWER KEY

PART B: QUESTIONS 25-30

25	A	remove her saline drip
26	C	relatively high staff absence rates
27	C	prepare to cope with an increasing demand for it.
28	B	Nobody has taken responsibility for assessing the patient.
29	B	expand upon what they studied previously.
30	C	warning him about a possible problem

PART C: QUESTIONS 31-36

31	B	Their condition can develop in a number of different ways.
32	A	There was a lack of reliable information on it.
33	B	was more widely available than some users imagined.
34	C	may lead to dementia patients experiencing unnecessary distress.
35	A	illustrate a gap in current medical education programmes.
36	B	it avoids carers having to speculate about a patient's wishes.

PART C: QUESTIONS 37-42

37	B	observing the effects of poor communication on a patient.
38	A	The information given can overwhelm patients.
39	C	relatives' knowledge of a patient's condition shouldn't be taken for granted.
40	A	measured the difference between their expectations and their actual experience.
41	B	the over-use of unclear medical terminology with patients.
42	A	surprised by one response from patients

———

END OF KEY

Listening sub-test

Audio Script – Practice test 3

This test has three parts. In each part you'll hear a number of different extracts. At the start of each extract, you'll hear this sound: ---***---.

You'll have time to read the questions before you hear each extract and you'll hear each extract ONCE only. Complete your answers as you listen.

At the end of the test, you'll have two minutes to check your answers.

Part A. In this part of the test, you'll hear two different extracts. In each extract, a health professional is talking to a patient. For questions 1 to 24, complete the notes with information you hear. Now, look at the notes for extract one.

PAUSE: 5 SECONDS
Extract one. Questions 1 to 12.

You hear a consultant endocrinologist talking to a patient called Sarah Croft. For questions 1 to 12, complete the notes with a word or short phrase. You now have thirty seconds to look at the notes.

PAUSE: 30 SECONDS
---***---

You hear a pulmonologist talking to a patient called Robert Miller. For questions 1 to 12, complete the notes with a word or short phrase. You now have thirty seconds to look at the notes.

PAUSE: 30 SECONDS
---***---

F   Good morning, Mr Miller. Now, looking at your notes, I see you've been having a few problems recently. Could you tell me a little about what's been happening, in your own words?

M   *Well, yeah – it's a combination of things really. To kick-off, I feel pretty tired most of the time – just haven't got the energy I used to have. And I've got this cough – it's there all the time and it feels dry – I mean, I'm not coughing up phlegm or blood or anything like that. But the worst thing, which really bothers me, is that I'm so short of breath – even if I'm just getting dressed in the morning or going up a few steps, I have to stop 'cos I get breathless so quickly. And I've lost quite a bit of weight, too – I mean, I didn't notice at first cos it was very gradual. But all in all, I'm about ten kilos lighter than I was six months ago. I've not been dieting or anything – I, I love my food!*

F   OK. And, well have you noticed anything else?

M   *Yeah – just take a look at my fingers. The tips look swollen, don't they – and it's the same with my toes, which are bulging out at the end too. It's weird. And my nails – I don't understand it – they've become soft. They're not hard like they used to be. Look….*

F   Erm, OK … I see what you mean. And tell me a little about yourself…. Umm what do you do for a living?

M   *Well, till recently, I worked as a farm labourer. Did it for about twenty years in total. It was hard physical graft, and it finally got to the stage where I just couldn't cope with it any more. It really took it out of me. So, this last couple of years, I've been a security guard, working nights at a local DIY warehouse. It's a bit boring, and the late shifts took a bit of getting used to, but it's OK.*

F	And, erm, are you finding it less physically demanding?
M	*That's right. I just haven't got the stamina now for anything else – in fact, I've even had to give up my golf. Can't manage it any more. Any spare time now goes on looking after my pigeons – I've done that since I was a teenager.*
F	Oh very nice. And, erm, what about your medical history. Now, I see you were diagnosed with hypertension last year, and you're taking beta blockers at the moment for that.
M	*That's right. My GP said it'd help. Something the GP also said, when I saw him about my breathing problems, was that he heard what he called 'crackling' noises in my chest. I can't hear them, but he could - through the stethoscope.*
F	OK. And is there any family history of breathing or lung problems, or any serious illnesses that you know of?
M	*I don't think so. My mother was always healthy, but my dad developed bad eczema as an adult. I remember the red patches on his hands and face. But he didn't have any lung problems as far as I know.*
F	Right, and… well looking at your previous tests, you were diagnosed with hypertension about 6 months ago, you had…
M	*Oh yeah, erm… an echocardiogram, you know, to check my heart… and a chest x-ray about four weeks ago after I saw my GP. That came back OK as far as I know.*
F	I see.
M	*I'm not keen on hospitals, to be honest. Am I going to need to have lots more tests?*
F	Well, I'm going to suggest you have what's called an arterial blood gas test. This will let us check how well your lungs are working – how they move oxygen into your blood and remove carbon dioxide from it.
M	*OK.*
F	And, I'm also going to order a CT scan. Now, this'll be more revealing than the chest x-ray you had. And I may then prescribe a course of corticosteroids. This will depend on what the tests show up. Now, I'd start you on a relatively low dose and then we'll … [fade]

PAUSE: 10 SECONDS
Extract two. Questions 13 to 24.

You hear an eye specialist talking to a patient called Jasmine Burton, who has recently undergone eye surgery. For questions 13 to 24, complete the notes with a word or short phrase. You now have thirty seconds to look at the notes.

PAUSE: 30 SECONDS
---***---

M:	I've got your notes here Mrs Burton, but as we're meeting for the first time, could you begin by telling me a little about your eyesight and the treatment you've had over the years. Erm, did you wear glasses as a child, for example?
F:	*Ahh yes, since I was about seven. My parents were concerned by the way I held a book when I was reading so they took me to an optometrist. He told them I had some kind of astigmatism.*

M: Am I right in assuming that's myopic rather than hyperopic?

F: *Well yes, I'm near-sighted...if that's what you mean.*

M: That's right. Some people actually have mixed astigmatism - they're far-sighted in one eye and near in the other.

F: *Oh well, that's not me. And, as well as my astigmatism, as you've probably noticed, my eyes flicker. I'm not aware of it myself but other people comment on it sometimes. I think you call it... nystagmus. It meant that, when I had my eye surgery, they preferred to use a general rather than a local anaesthetic.*

M: OK, so did anyone ever tell you what they thought might have caused the condition?

F: *Well, I was once told that my generally poor eyesight is most probably down to the fact that I don't have enough pigment in the eye. On the whole, my eyes have never really caused me any significant difficulties, however. I've always had to wear glasses, so that's a part of life now. I suppose...the only thing is that driving's always been out of the question. I'd never have passed the sight part of the test. That's probably a good thing because it takes me some time to focus, which could make me pretty dangerous if I was ever behind the wheel of a car.*

M: Yes, indeed.

F: *Also I'm useless at sports like tennis - I think that's because I'm...I'm poor at judging the distance between myself and the ball. That was a pain as a teenager, but I've never particularly wanted to play since then. And I've hardly had any issues at work because of my sight. I'm a receptionist in a hotel and I've never had any difficulty reading computer screens or anything fortunately.*

M: You've...You've had your eyes regularly checked throughout your life presumably?

F: *Yeah that's right. Every couple of years. My prescription's changed a little over time - but not that much. Though I certainly couldn't manage without reading glasses these days. About three years ago, I was told a cataract was developing in my right eye. It was a few years before they decided to remove it – that was this February – and it all went very smoothly.*

M: Good, and you... you were pleased with the result?

F: *Yeah I was, yeah, thrilled. If only all our failing parts could be replaced so easily! However, when I had the routine check-up a couple of weeks after the operation, I was told there was some clouding...err opacity, I think was the word they used - in the capsule containing the new lens. It's a bit disappointing. They could clear it with a laser if it gets to be a real problem...erm, but my flicker makes that rather a risky option. I knew that there's a greater chance of developing a detached retina after a cataract op...but I'm glad to say they found there wasn't any evidence of that in my case. All they did was make an appointment for me to be checked out again in six months-time. But they said I should get in touch if I felt concerned about my eyes.*

M: And is that what brings you here today?

F: *Yeah, because I am bothered about a couple of things. So, firstly I've noticed more floaters than usual. I don't know if that's something to worry about or not. Erm, more annoying is the fact that I'm much more troubled by glare than I used to be. So I wanted to ask your opinion on that.*

M: OK, well let's start by having .....[fade]

PAUSE: 10 SECONDS
That is the end of Part A. Now, look at Part B.

PAUSE: 5 SECONDS

Part B. In this part of the test, you'll hear six different extracts. In each extract, you'll hear people talking in a different healthcare setting.

For questions 25 to 30, choose the answer A, B or C which fits best according to what you hear. You'll have time to read each question before you listen. Complete your answers as you listen.

Now look at Question 25. You hear a nurse briefing a colleague at the end of her shift. Now read the question.

PAUSE: 15 SECONDS
---***---

F   OK, so the next thing is about Suzie Williams in bed three.

M   Right.

F   She's been admitted for chest pain to rule out MI. So far she had an EKG which was OK, and the first set of cardiac enzymes and troponins are negative. When she came in, her blood pressure was elevated a little, like one eighty two over ninety five, but she was given losartan and at six o'clock it was one forty two over eighty two. She was also dehydrated so we started her on IV fluids, D5 half-normal saline running at a hundred and twenty five millilitres. That can go until midnight and then it can be disconnected. She's scheduled for a stress test tomorrow and some more enzyme tests. OK?

M   OK.

PAUSE: 5 SECONDS
Question 26. You hear part of a hospital management meeting where a concern is being discussed. Now read the question.

PAUSE: 15 SECONDS
---***---

M   Now I'll hand over to Jenny, who has a few words to say about staffing. Jenny?

F   Thanks. Now, if we compare ourselves to other hospitals of the same size, in other regions, we're actually recording lower rates of staff turnover. That's just as well given the challenges filling vacant positions across the sector. Where we do compare unfavourably is in the number of days lost to sick leave. That's making it hard to maintain full cover on the wards, and we all know the costs of that. As a matter of urgency then, HR are looking into the worst affected areas to understand the reasons behind it and to see if there's anything we can do to help and support the staff involved.

PAUSE: 5 SECONDS
Question 27. You hear a GP and his practice nurse discussing a vaccination programme. Now read the question.

M: *It's coming up to that time of year when we have to start preparing for the flu vaccination programme.*

F: Yes, we usually do it at the start of next month, don't we?

M: *That's right. If you remember last year we hired a local hall and did as many people as we could in one afternoon.*

F: Yes, I'd just started working here then. It was a hectic couple of hours but it worked pretty well, don't you think?

M: *Sure, but there's been so much publicity recently about how sensible it is to get the jab that I suspect we'll have a lot more people coming along this year.*

F: So we better think about taking on an agency nurse perhaps to lend an extra hand.

M: *OK. Let's run that by the practice manager. And she might have some other suggestions too.*

PAUSE: 5 SECONDS

Question 28. You hear two hospital nurses discussing the assessment of a patient on their ward. Now read the question.

PAUSE: 15 SECONDS

---***---

M   The bed manager just rang. He wants us to clear three spaces in the ward. Today.

F   *Oh it's never-ending! Let's see what we can do. There's no one ready to be discharged. But we could try chasing referrals for Mr Davison to the community hospital for rehab. Where are his notes?*

M   Yes, but has he had his assessment yet?

F   *They were all away at that conference yesterday and the day before. I think he'll have slipped through the net.*

M: But Doctor Ammat's already got him medically stable and signed off. So he should   be the next one to move on.

F   *Well I'd get him there as quickly as possible before they give the place to somebody else.*

M   I'll phone them straight away.

PAUSE: 5 SECONDS

Question 29. You hear the beginning of a training session for dental students. Now read the question.

PAUSE: 15 SECONDS

---***---

F   *This is session number four, which is going to include, again, impression-taking. We've created the crown impression of tooth number 30, we also took care of an inlay preparation. So today*

we're going to stay on that side with our impression-taking. We're going to make a duplicate of what we've already done. And our attention to detail is now going up another notch.

When I take an impression of a tooth that I've created in the mouth, I naturally have to take care of the saliva, the blood, the gum tissue… We're not going to cover all that today. You'll hit that next semester. What we are going to cover are the dynamics of your impression, the margins, the proximal contacts, the bite and the occlusion. We're going to capture all that in one impression.

PAUSE: 5 SECONDS
Question 30. You hear two nurses discussing the treatment of a patient with a kidney infection. Now read the question.

PAUSE: 15 SECONDS
---***---

M   I can't see the results of Mr Roberts' last blood test to check creatinine levels. Did you do the last one?

F   *No, not me. Let's see. Ah, here it is. The last test was four hours ago and results show a level of thirty eight, so it's still well below normal. We'd better do one when he wakes up, as it might have changed. The patient's not keen on needles though. I had a real job last night trying to convince him it was necessary. Not the easiest of patients, if you're happy to have a go.*

M   OK. My turn, I reckon.

PAUSE: 10 SECONDS
That is the end of Part B. Now, look at Part C.

PAUSE: 5 SECONDS

Part C. In this part of the test, you'll hear two different extracts. In each extract, you'll hear health professionals talking about aspects of their work.

For questions 31 to 42, choose the answer A, B or C which fits best according to what you hear. Complete your answers as you listen.

Now look at extract one.

Extract one. Questions 31 to 36. You hear a geriatrician called Dr Clare Cox giving a presentation on the subject of end-of-life care for people with dementia.

You now have 90 seconds to read questions 31 to 36.

PAUSE: 90 SECONDS
---***---

F: My name's Dr Clare Cox. I'm a geriatrician specialising in palliative care. My topic today is an increasingly important issue: end-of-life care for dementia patients.

    The care of dementia patients presents certain problems. Dementia is a terminal illness and is the third highest cause of death in Australia. But dementia is different from other such conditions. It has an unpredictable trajectory and there can be difficult issues around patients' mental capacity, decision-making and communication. But, in spite of an equal need for palliative care services, dementia patients don't always fit the traditional model of such care. Families often suffer distress because they feel unable to ensure that their loved one's wishes are being respected, or just don't know what that person wanted because the discussion wasn't held early enough. There is, therefore, a clear need for well-funded, patient-centred palliative dementia care that's available when and where it's needed.

I do a lot of work with Dementia Australia – an organisation which represents the needs of Australians living with all types of dementia, and of their families and carers. It also campaigns on dementia issues and funds research.

Dementia Australia decided it was the right time to examine the issue of end-of-life dementia care, from the perspective of the consumer as well as from that of the healthcare professional. It's a timely initiative. We have plenty of anecdotal evidence, but not enough hard facts about what's going wrong and why the system's failing. But the current situation isn't all bad. Despite the issues I've mentioned, I've heard some wonderful examples of how palliative care has made a big difference to people's lives. Things can obviously go badly wrong if this isn't handled well, but in the right circumstances people with dementia can reach the end of their lives peacefully and with dignity.

Dementia Australia commissioned researchers to conduct a survey on the end-of-life issues affecting dementia patients. The survey covered both care professionals, that's doctors, nurses and others working with dementia patients, as well as family-member carers. The interest was overwhelming with more than a thousand responses from around Australia. But what do the results tell us? Well, the initial results confirmed what we've heard about access to appropriate end-of-life care. It was obvious immediately that there was a striking gap between the perceptions of care professionals, and family-member carers about end-of-life dementia care. For instance, while fifty-eight per cent of family-member carers said that they didn't have access to palliative care specialists, and sixty-eight per cent didn't have access to hospices, three-quarters of care professionals indicated that people with dementia in their area do in fact have access to palliative care. This begs the question of whether consumers – that is patients and family-member carers – might not be aware of services that are available.

Another notable finding of the survey was that care professionals often lack knowledge of the legal issues surrounding end-of-life care. Some reports indicate that care professionals are at times reluctant to use pain medications such as morphine because of concerns about hastening a patient's death. However, access to appropriate pain relief is considered to be a fundamental human right, even if death is earlier as a secondary effect of medication. Our survey found that twenty-seven per cent of care professionals were unsure about this, or didn't believe that patients are legally entitled to adequate pain control, if it might hasten death. So perhaps it isn't surprising then, that a quarter of former family-member carers felt that pain wasn't adequately managed in end-of-life care.

This lack of awareness extends beyond pain management. The statistics on refusing treatment were particularly shocking. Almost a third of care professionals were unaware that people have the right to refuse food and hydration, and one in ten also thought refusal of antibiotics wasn't an option for patients in end-of-life care. How can we ever achieve consumer empowerment and consumer-directed care if the professionals are so ill informed? There's a clear need for greater information and training on patient rights, yet over a third of care professionals said they hadn't received any such training at all.

It's obvious that end-of-life care planning is desirable. Discussing and documenting preferences is clearly the best way of minimising the burden of decision-making on carers, and ensuring patients' wishes are respected. Advance care planning is essentially an insurance policy that helps to protect our patients in case they lose their decision-making capacity. Even though a patient might believe that loved ones will have their best interests at heart, the evidence shows that such people aren't that good at knowing what decisions those they love would make on complex matters such as infection control and hydration.

So, before I go on to …..[fade]

PAUSE: 10 SECONDS

Now look at extract two.

Extract two. Questions 37 to 42. You hear a hospital doctor called Dr Keith Gardiner giving a presentation about some research he's done on the subject of staff-patient communication.

You now have 90 seconds to read questions 37 to 42.

PAUSE: 90 SECONDS
---***---

M: Good morning. My name's Dr Keith Gardiner, and I'd like to talk to you today about some research I've been involved in, concerning something that affects all health professionals – staff-patient communication.

Now, firstly, let me reassure you that in feedback, patients seem positive about the way information is communicated to them. But I recently decided to explore the issue in more detail when I was in a hospital with a patient and witnessed for myself what can result when a health care professional assumes they've made themselves clear to a patient, when in fact they've been anything but. Luckily, I've had very few complaints made against members of my team, but the potential is certainly there.

So first, let's start by looking at a typical hospital admission for an in-patient, and the first communication they have about any procedures they are to undergo. On arrival, a patient will complete necessary paperwork. Various staff will talk to them about their treatment during their stay, which is designed to reduce patient anxiety. However, from some patients' point of view, this interaction can seem very complex and difficult to take in, especially at a time when they're not at their best physically or mentally. So it's doubly important to check that any communication has been understood.

Now, to illustrate what I'm talking about, let's take a hypothetical situation. I often use this because it highlights the potential consequences of poor communication. A man in his eighties is admitted to hospital, despite his protestations, with ongoing severe back pain. On investigation, it's found his cancer has spread. The outlook is poor - and further compounded by his becoming depressed and refusing to eat while in hospital. A feeding tube is inserted, a procedure which the patient complies with, but which his family members query. The doctor on duty updates them, assuming they're aware of the severity of the patient's condition – when in fact no such prognosis has been shared with them. An extreme case, but a plausible one, nevertheless.

In order to find out exactly what in-patients felt about the service they were receiving in this hospital, we conducted a patient survey. The questions were carefully targeted to capture patients' opinions about the effectiveness of the communication they'd been involved in during their stay. The survey questioned patients on both what they had expected prior to admission, and what their stay was really like. These two scores were then used to calculate what's called a 'gap' score. The survey also included questions to measure the patients' behavioural intention – that is, how willing they would be to return to the hospital for treatment. Patients completed the survey themselves, and results were then processed with the help of medical students.

Now, the survey produced some interesting data about communication, including both praise and complaints. Clearly in a hospital situation, staff are dealing with confidential and sensitive information, which must be communicated in private – a situation which can be difficult to achieve in a large and busy hospital. However, we scored highly on that point. And we were also pleased to note that staff did manage to communicate in a manner that treated patients with dignity and respect. Of course, staff also have to ensure patients fully understand what's been said to them. And this last point's where we received the most negative feedback. Both patients and relatives noted a tendency for professionals to resort to the use of jargon, and complex terms when explaining both diagnoses and procedures, which left some patients confused. However, patients were generally satisfied with the information about any follow-up treatment provided after discharge.

Also, once we'd sifted through all the results, a clear pattern began to emerge regarding the care given by nurses, which I found particularly interesting. I'd assumed that having a number of different nurses attending to a patient during their stay was a good thing, because you need enough staff to cover the various shifts, and attend to patients' needs. What I certainly hadn't expected, though, was for patients to say they felt their recovery was faster when they had to communicate with only a small number of nurses - in other words when they were surrounded by familiar faces. The findings aren't conclusive, and more investigative work needs to be done on a bigger sample – but it's certainly food for thought.

PAUSE: 10 SECONDS
That is the end of Part C.

You now have two minutes to check your answers.

PAUSE: 120 SECONDS
That is the end of the Listening test.

Reading sub-test

Answer Key – Part A

READING SUB-TEST – ANSWER KEY

PART A: QUESTIONS 1-20

1	B
2	A
3	C
4	D
5	C
6	B
7	D
8	clindamycin (and) penicillin
9	diabetes mellitus
10	septic shock
11	VAC/ vacuum-assisted closure
12	alcohol pads
13	daptomycin (and) linezolid
14	vibrio (infection)
15	32.2%
16	seafood
17	limbs
18	polymicrobial
19	7%
20	physical therapy

Reading sub-test

Answer Key – Parts B & C

READING SUB-TEST – ANSWER KEY

PART B: QUESTIONS 1-6

1	A	stop dates aren't relevant in all circumstances.
2	B	improves precision during radiation.
3	B	position electrodes correctly.
4	C	its short-term benefits are explained to them.
5	B	the use of a particular method of testing pH levels.
6	A	the amount of oxytocin given will depend on how the patient reacts.

PART C: QUESTIONS 7-14

7	D	the need for the phobia to be confronted repeatedly over time.
8	D	unpleasant memories are aroused in response to certain prompts.
9	A	makes use of an innate function of the brain.
10	A	the anxiety that patients feel during therapy
11	C	affects how neurons in the brain react to stimuli.
12	A	its benefits are likely to be of limited duration.
13	D	the emotional force of a memory is naturally retained.
14	B	increase patients' tolerance of key triggers.

PART C: QUESTIONS 15-22

15	A	he saw for himself how it could work in practice.
16	A	research indicates that they are effective even without deceit.
17	D	they are very widely used
18	A	The way a treatment is presented is significant even if it is a placebo.
19	B	reduce the number of people who experience them.
20	C	a growing body of research
21	B	Evers is exploiting a response which Ader discovered by chance.
22	D	their effect is more psychological than physical.

OCCUPATIONAL ENGLISH TEST

WRITING SUB-TEST: NURSING

SAMPLE RESPONSE: LETTER OF REFERRAL

Ms Nita Roberts
In-Home Nursing Service
79 Beachside Street
Bayview

15 July 2017

Dear Ms Roberts,

Re: Mrs Jasmine Thompson
    73 White Road, Bayview
    DOB: 01.07.1942

I would be most grateful if you could manage home care for Mrs Thompson, who is being discharged today after a total right shoulder replacement, following admission to the hospital for right shoulder osteoarthritis. Her daughter will stay with her for one month in her single-storey house once she has been discharged.

Mrs Thompson's post-operative phase was largely uneventful. She has been compliant with her physiotherapy exercise regime and her post-operative bloods remain in normal limits. Post-operative pain was managed with analgesia and a cold compress for four hours each day.

On discharge, the patient was educated in post-operative care: she will wear a right arm sling for four weeks, and will require physiotherapy in the outpatient's clinic twice a week, and hydrotherapy once a week. She is not to do any lifting for four weeks.

Mrs Thompson will require assistance with showering and administration of her prescription Clexane injection, which is to be administered for four days as DVT prophylaxis.

In ten days, her staples are scheduled to be removed with a follow-up appointment in the Orthopaedic Joint Replacement Outpatient Department. In case any issues arise, the nurse specialist can be contacted by calling the hospital during the week.

Do not hesitate to contact me if you require additional assistance.

Sincerely,

Nurse

How we assess writing

Your letter is assessed against five criteria:

» **Overall task fulfilment**
including the overall impression of the performance and whether the response is of the required length

» **Appropriateness of language**
including the use of appropriate register and tone in the response, and whether it is organised appropriately

» **Comprehension of stimulus**
including whether the response shows you have understood the situation and provided relevant rather than unnecessary information to your reader

» **Control of linguistic features (grammar and cohesion)**
how effectively you communicate using the grammatical structures and cohesive devices of English

» **Control of presentation features (spelling, punctuation and layout)**
how these areas affect the message you want to communicate

Overall task fulfilment

» Write enough so the assessors have a sufficient sample of your writing – the task requires approximately 180-200 words in the body of the letter.

» Don't write too much – you may need to select content carefully to keep to the required word count.

» Use your own words as much as possible – don't simply copy sections from the case notes.

» Avoid using a 'formulaic' response – if you include elements that do not fit the task, it indicates a lack of flexibility in your writing.

» Don't include information that the intended reader clearly knows already (e.g., if you are replying to a colleague who has referred a patient to you).

Appropriateness of language

» Organise the information clearly – the sequence of information in the case notes may not be the most appropriate sequence of information for your letter.

» Highlight the main purpose of your letter at the start – this provides the context for the information you include.

» Be clear about the level of urgency for the communication.

» Always keep in mind the reason for writing – don't just summarise the case notes provided.

» Focus on important information and minimise incidental detail.

» If it will help, be explicit about the organisation of your letter: e.g., 'First I will outline the problems the patient has, then I will make some suggestions for his treatment'.

» Consider using dates and other time references (e.g., three months later, last week, a year ago, etc.) to give a clear sequence of events where necessary.

» Remember that all professional letters are written in a relatively formal style.

» Avoid informal language, slang, colloquialisms and spoken idioms unless you are sure this is appropriate (e.g., use 'Thank you' rather than 'Thanks a lot').

» Avoid SMS texting abbreviations in a formal letter (e.g., use 'you' not 'u').

» Give the correct salutation: if you are told the recipient's name and title, use them.

» Show awareness of your audience by choosing appropriate words and phrases: if you are writing to another professional, you may use technical terms and, possibly, abbreviations; if you are writing to a parent or a group of lay people, use non-technical terms and explain carefully.

Comprehension of stimulus

» Demonstrate in your response that you have understood the case notes fully.

» Be clear what the most relevant issues for the reader are.

» Don't let the main issue become hidden by including too much supporting detail.

» Show clearly the connections between information in the case notes if these are made; however, do not add information that is not given in the notes (e.g., your suggested diagnosis), particularly if the reason for the letter is to get an expert opinion.

» Take relevant information from the case notes and transform it to fit the task set.

» If the stimulus material includes questions that require an answer in your response, be explicit about this – don't 'hide' the relevant information in a general summary of the notes provided.

Control of linguistic features (grammar and cohesion)

» Show that you can use language accurately and flexibly in your writing.

» Make sure you demonstrate a range of language structures – use complex sentences as well as simple ones.

» Split a long sentence into two or three sentences if you feel you are losing control of it.

» Review areas of grammar to ensure you convey your intended meaning accurately – particular areas to focus on might include*:

  • articles – a/an, the (e.g., 'She had an operation.', 'on the internet')

  • countable and uncountable nouns (e.g., some evidence, an opinion, an asthma attack)

  • verb forms used to indicate past time and the relationship between events in the past and now (past simple, present perfect, past perfect)

  • adverbs that give time references (e.g., 'two months previously' is different from 'two months ago')

  • prepositions following other words (e.g., 'Thank you very much ~~to see~~ for seeing …', 'sensitivity ~~of~~ to pressure', 'my examination ~~on~~ of the patient', 'diagnosed with cancer')

  • passive forms (e.g., '~~He involved in an accident.~~' for 'He was involved in an accident.')

» Use connecting words and phrases ('connectives') to link ideas together clearly (e.g., however, therefore, subsequently, etc.).

» Create a mental checklist of problems that you have with grammar and go through this when you review your response towards the end of the test; particular areas to focus on might include:

  • number agreement, e.g. 'The test result shows that …', 'There is no evidence …', 'He lives …', 'one of the side effects'

  • complete sentences, i.e., the main clause includes 'subject and verb', e.g., 'On examination showed that …' should be 'Examination showed that …' or 'On examination, it was found that …'

  • gender agreement, e.g. 'Mr Jones and ~~her~~ his daughter'

  • tense agreement, e.g., 'Examination on 15 May 2006 revealed she ~~is~~ was overweight.' [creating confusion over whether she is still overweight at the time of writing]

* In the following list, a line through text indicates inaccurate grammar.

Control of presentation features (spelling, punctuation and layout)

» Take care with the placement of commas and full stops:

  • Make sure there are enough – separating ideas into sentences.

  • Make sure there are not too many – keeping elements of the text meaningfully connected together.

» Leave a blank line between paragraphs to show clearly the overall structure of the letter.

» Don't write on every other line – this does not assist the reader particularly.

» Check for spelling mistakes and for spelling consistency through your writing (e.g., with a patient's name).

» Remember that many of the words you write are also in the case notes – check that the spelling you use is the same.

» Be consistent in your spelling: alternative spelling conventions (e.g., American or British English) are acceptable as long as your use is consistent.

» Don't use symbols and abbreviations in formal letters.

» Avoid creating any negative impact on your reader through the presentation of the letter.

» Use a clear layout to avoid any miscommunication.

» Make sure poor handwriting does not confuse the reader over spelling and meaning.

» Write legibly so the assessor can grade your response fairly using the set criteria.

» Candidates are assessed on their ability to:

  • Select, transform and organise information in the case notes into a coherently structured letter

  • Include relevant information to:

    – explain the patient's condition, history and reason for referral,

    – explain a problematic situation, OR

    – outline drug information

  • Use appropriate conventions of letter format (including addressee's details, date, opening and closing moves)

  • Use register, tone and vocabulary appropriate to the professional context

  • Show adequate control of a range of grammatical structures and cohesive devices

  • Show adequate control of spelling and punctuation

How we assess Speaking

OET is a test of English language, not a test of professional knowledge.

The whole Speaking sub-test is audio recorded and the audio recording is assessed. The assessment is given on the candidate's performance in the two role-plays only (not the warm-up conversation).

The candidate's speaking performance is assessed by two qualified assessors who have been trained in OET assessment procedures.

The Speaking sub-test recordings are assessed in Melbourne, Australia. All recordings are double marked.

Important: The interlocutor is trained to ensure the structure of the Speaking sub-test is consistent for each candidate. The interlocutor also uses detailed information on his/her role-play card. The interlocutor DOES NOT assess the candidate.

Rationale

An important part of a health professional's role is the ability to communicate effectively in speech with his/her patients or clients. The role-plays allow the candidate to take his/her professional role and demonstrate the ability to deal with common workplace situations. These situations may include elements of tension which are a normal part of the real-life context, for example, anxious or angry patients, patients who misunderstand their situation, etc.

The two role-plays, each with a different scenario, provide two separate opportunities for the candidate to demonstrate spoken proficiency, therefore giving a broad view of the candidate's spoken skills.

Role-play tasks are designed to give candidates opportunities to demonstrate their language ability, for example, to:

» negotiate meaning with the interlocutor who is playing the role of the patient (e.g., reassure a worried patient, clarify a medical explanation, manage an upset patient, etc.).

» explain medical conditions/treatments and terminology in an accessible way.

» rephrase ideas and opinions in different ways to try and convince a patient.

» ask and answer questions to and from the patient.

» engage with a variety of patient types (different ages, personalities, different health concerns, etc.).

The candidate's performance in the two role-plays is assessed against linguistic criteria and clinical communication criteria:

Linguistic Criteria (6 marks each)

1. Intelligibility
2. Fluency
3. Appropriateness
4. Resources of Grammar and Expression

Clinical Communication Criteria (3 marks each)

1. Relationship building
2. Understanding and incorporating the patient's perspective
3. Providing structure
4. Information gathering
5. Information giving

Linguistic Criteria

NOTE: The following extracts are examples only. Assessors are carefully trained to assess candidates' sustained performance across both role-plays.

1. Intelligibility

This criterion assesses how well a candidate's speech can be heard and understood. It concerns the impact of such features of speech as pronunciation, rhythm, stress, intonation, pitch and accent on the listener.

Assessors will use this criterion to evaluate the candidate's production of comprehensible speech.

A strong proficiency candidate will:

» use natural flow of speech, giving stress to particular words within sentences to emphasise meaning, e.g., 'I'm unable to do THOSE tests in THIS clinic'.

» use natural flow of speech, giving correct stress to syllables within words so that they are identifiable to the listener, e.g., 'I will reCORD your results'. 'This is an accurate REcord of your results'.

» show control of intonation (voice falling or rising) and stress (appropriate force, length, emphasis or loudness) to enhance meaning and strengthen the communication he/she is wanting to provide.

» pronounce words clearly, for example:

1. consonants at the end of words or syllables (e.g., 'head', 'weakness').
2. consonants that distinguish different meanings of similar words (e.g., 'worry', 'worries', 'worried').
3. consonant sounds at the beginning of words (e.g., /v/ as in '**v**omit', /b/ '**b**ill' versus /p/ '**p**ill').
4. syllables within words (e.g., 'dang(er)ous', 'a coup(le) of days').
5. clear initial consonant blends 'problem', 'bleeding'.
6. word stress in longer words (e.g., 'PAINkiller' not 'painKILLer', 'HOSpital' not 'hosPItal').
7. vowel sounds (/əʊ/ 'n**o**te' versus /ɒ/ 'n**o**t').

» minimise any intrusive sounds, rhythm and accent which may be influenced by his/her mother tongue.

» show the ability to link words together naturally. For example, there are often no 'spaces' between words in phrases like, 'in_about_an_hour'.

Now, look at the following examples. Examples 1 and 2 demonstrate HIGH and LOW performances respectively. Some key points are highlighted in each example in relation to the criterion: Intelligibility.

Example 1

HIGHER — LOWER

" ... I **think** you can **find_**a few friends who **regularly** go for_a_walk; ↘ you can **start** with_them. ↘ And if_you **reduce** smoking and cut_the amount of **coffee** you drink_a_ day, it would **help_**your **blood** pressure level. ↘ **Start_**to drink more **water** and do some **exercise**, your **blood** pressure will be **better** in_a month. ↘ "

Comment

Prosodic features (stress, intonation ↘ and rhythm) are used efficiently. The speech is easily understood even though the evidence of the first language is present. Certain words are linked_together naturally.

Example 2

HIGHER — LOWER

"
Wrong		Correct
in**ju**ry	=>	**in**jury
se**vere**	=>	se**ve**re
inf**lu**ence	=>	**in**fluence
"

Comment

Issues with non-standard word level stress and incorrectly pronounced vowels interfere with the listener's ability to understand all information. This affects 'Intelligibility'.

"
- ... er... she injured her spine (pronounced as 'spʌn')... is a very important... organ...

  [sp/aɪ/n]
- .. may be several months, she can't mobilise (pronounced as 'mobjuːlaiz') herself...

  [moub/ə/laiz] "

Comment

Vowels are not pronounced correctly, which confuses the patient. The vowel sound in 'spine' [sp/aɪ/n] is not the same as the vowel in 'spun' [sp/ʌ/n], but should be pronounced as [sp/aɪ/n]. The vowel sound in 'mobilise' [moubə laiz] is not the same as the vowel in 'bureaucrat' [bjuːrəkræt], but should be pronounced as [moubə laiz].

2. Fluency

This criterion assesses how well a candidate's speech is delivered in terms of rate and flow of speech.

Assessors will use this criterion to evaluate the degree to which a candidate is able to speak continuously, evenly and smoothly – without excessive hesitation, repetition, self-correction or use of 'fillers'.

A strong proficiency candidate will:

» maintain a natural speed to make it easier for the listener to follow the message (not too slow, not too fast).

» use even speech (not broken up into fragments) and limit hesitations or speaking in 'bursts' of language.

» avoid overusing sounds (e.g., 'err', 'um', 'ah') and words (e.g., 'OK', 'yes') to fill in gaps.

» use a smoother flow of speech, stressing syllables appropriately and linking words/syllables together.

» use pauses appropriately, for example:

1. to make his/her meaning clear, e.g., for emphasis.

2. to separate clearly the points he/she is making.

3. to think about what he/she is going to say next.

» avoid restarting sentences or repeating words and phrases as he/she corrects himself/herself.

Look at the following examples. Examples 1 and 2 demonstrate HIGH and LOW performances respectively. Some key points are described on each example in relation to the criterion: Fluency.

Example 1

HIGHER
LOWER

"... I think you can find a few friends who regularly go for a walk; you can start with them...(omission)... .

Start to drink more water and do some exercise, your blood pressure will be better in a month."

Comment

The flow of the speech is good, not too fast or not too slow.

The speech is even and hesitation is rarely evident.

There is little use of 'fillers' (e.g., 'err', 'um', 'OK', etc.).

Restarting sentences is rare.

Example 2

HIGHER
LOWER

- That is a common concerned from some patients...because they don't know any...don't know more... don't know many medications... something like that...

- You can also give her some... ~~give~~ [let] her inhaler some steams...she can inhaler the steam... That can make her ~~to breath~~ easily...
  [breathe]

Comment

There is some hesitation that affects fluency.

This candidate often pauses during his/her speech while he/she prepares what to say next.

This 'breaking up' of the message can affect the listener trying to decode it. This affects 'Fluency'.

How to improve

Try to work on a smoother delivery without so many false starts and reformations.

3. Appropriateness

This criterion assesses how well a candidate uses language, register and tone that are appropriate to the situation and the patient.

Assessors will use this criterion to evaluate the degree to which the individual words, grammar and style of speech the candidate selects are appropriate to the particular situation and context.

A strong proficiency candidate will:

» use suitable, professional language.

» use appropriate paraphrasing and re-wording if necessary to explain, in simple terms, technical procedures or medical conditions to a patient who may have little knowledge of these.

» adapt their style and tone to suit the particular situation of the role-play, e.g., giving bad news versus giving positive news or using language suitable for talking to an older person versus a younger person.

» respond appropriately to what the 'patient' says during the role-plays, e.g., the candidate's responses are logically linked with the patient's questions or concerns.

» use language that might reflect the professionalism a health practitioner might require when dealing with patients, e.g., not overly-familiar or informal.

» demonstrate that he/she has the language skills to deal well with complicated situations, e.g., complaints, difficult patients, patients who need convincing, etc.

» use appropriate phrases that are suited to common functions found in medical exchanges, e.g., to 'reassure', 'encourage', 'be supportive', 'explain', etc.

» show awareness of the patient's sensitivities to the condition or information the candidate gives.

Now, look at the following examples. Examples 1 and 2 demonstrate HIGH and LOW performances respectively. Some key points are described on each example in relation to the criterion: Appropriateness.

Example 1

HIGHER
LOWER

" ... What do you think is easier or better for you? Where do you want to start? Do you want to start with ... your eating habit? "

" ... and you do not need to do some intensive fitness activities. I think it's enough if you start with walking for half an hour everyday. "

Comment

This candidate uses a good strategy to convince the unwilling patient (e.g., using questions rather than imperative forms to encourage the patient).

An appropriate tone is used to encourage the patient.

Example 2

HIGHER
LOWER

"
effective
• If...she doesn't get treatment ~~effectively~~...
it may ~~be worsen~~...
get worse   is not
• <u>As far as we know</u>, the antibiotic ~~doesn't~~
really helpful for viral infections... "

Comment

The misuse of natural phrases and expressions is affecting 'Appropriateness'. The underlined phrase indicates considerable doubt, whereas antibiotics definitely do not work for viral infections.

"
an
• If you don't keep eye on this disease...you
go
might ~~get~~ blind unfortunately. But if you
checking
keep ~~to do~~ your blood sugar level and to
an   your
keep eye on diet... "

Comment

At times the message is interrupted by word choice errors. This affects 'Appropriateness'.

How to improve

Take care with phrases that can be easily confused. Meaning breaks down if the phrase is only partially correct.

4. Resources of Grammar and Expression

This criterion assesses the level and extent of the candidate's grammar and vocabulary resources and their appropriate use.

Assessors will use this criterion to evaluate the range and accuracy of the language resources the candidate has applied in the performance to convey clear meaning.

A strong proficiency candidate will:

» use appropriate structures to make what he/she is saying coherent, for example, outlining options or choices to a patient (e.g., 'There are several options you can consider. Firstly, in the short term, …').

» show flexibility by using different phrases to communicate the same idea, if necessary, to make it clearer.

» form questions correctly, particularly those questions that are often used in health professional/patient dialogues (e.g., 'How long have you been experiencing this?', 'When did the symptoms start?').

» minimise grammatical inaccuracy to enhance communicative effectiveness.

» use more complex structures and expressions confidently (e.g., idiomatic speech, sentences with multiple clauses, etc.), i.e., not just a series of simple utterances.

» use a wide variety of grammatical structures and vocabulary that reflects the depth and range of their linguistic resources.

» show accurate control of grammatical features including, for example:

  1. correct word order (e.g., 'She broke her tooth' not 'She tooth her broke').

  2. correct use of pronouns/relative pronouns (e.g., 'Tell her it's ok if she (not he) waits then comes back to see me when she (not he) feels better').

  3. correct word choice (e.g., 'Your daughter is breathing more rapidly/repeatedly/regularly' (all have different meanings)).

  4. not omitting words that could affect clear meaning (e.g., 'I recommend that you consider several options including crown, fillings and inlays' not 'I recommend about crown, filling, inlay').

  5. correct use of prepositions (e.g., 'I can explain to you about asthma' not 'I can explain you about asthma').

  6. correct use of articles (e.g., 'A form is completed and then given to the Pharmacist' not 'Form is completed and then given to Pharmacist').

  7. use correct word form (e.g., 'Smoking is dangerous for your health' not 'Smoking is danger for your health').

  8. correct use of countable and uncountable expressions (e.g., 'not many side effects' not 'not much side effects').

  9. use appropriate structures to convey information about time and the sequence of past or future events (e.g., 'We have X-rayed your arm and the results will be available today/next week' not 'We X-ray your arm and the results available').

Now, look at the following examples. Examples 1 and 2 demonstrate HIGH and LOW performances respectively. Some key points are described on each example in relation to the criterion: Resources of Grammar and Expression.

Example 1

HIGHER

LOWER

" ... You have two options. The first option is, you're going to have medication, which would be the last solution. The second option, the better option I think, is changing your lifestyle. You do not need to change everything in your life, but you need to make it better... "

Comment

The available options for the patient are outlined in a coherent manner (e.g., 'You have two options. First...').

The number of errors are not intrusive.

Information is given in a confident manner.

Different structures are used to communicate the same idea effectively (e.g., '...is changing your lifestyle. You do not need to change everything...').

Example 2

HIGHER

LOWER

" • No, I'm not forcing, this is option... you

• If you have some pain, try not to use an it too much because I will put some dressing...' on it "

Comment

Many sentences are incomplete. Watch out for pronouns such as 'you', 'it' and prepositions such as 'put something on (something)'.

" You need to be free of infections. What you can do is to take some cleaning gloves every time and <u>do something</u> with clean clothes <u>and something like that</u>... "

Comment

Many simple words are used repetitively, affecting "Resources of Grammar and Expression'. In the above example, 'something' is overused, indicating gaps in vocabulary.

How to improve
Be more specific with word choice.

OET Speaking clinical communication criteria

A: Indicators of relationship building

A1	Initiating the interaction appropriately (greeting, introductions)	Initiating the interview appropriately helps establish rapport and a supportive environment. Initiation involves greeting the patient, introducing yourself, clarifying the patient's name and clarifying your role in their care. The nature of the interview can be explained and if necessary negotiated.
A2	Demonstrating an attentive and respectful attitude	Throughout the interview, demonstrating attentiveness and respect establishes trust with the patient, lays down the foundation for a collaborative relationship and ensures that the patient understands your motivation to help. Examples of such behaviour would include attending to the patient's comfort, asking permission and consent to proceed, and being sensitive to potentially embarrassing or distressing matters.
A3	Demonstrating a non-judgemental approach	Accepting the patient's perspective and views reassuringly and non-judgementally without initial rebuttal is a key component of relationship building. A judgemental response to patients' ideas and concerns devalues their contributions. A non-judgemental response would include accepting the patient's perspective and acknowledging the legitimacy of the patient to hold their own views and feelings.
A4	Showing empathy for feelings/ predicament/ emotional state	Empathy is one of the key skills of building the relationship. Empathy involves the understanding and sensitive appreciation of another person's predicament or feelings and the communication of that understanding back to the patient in a supportive way. This can be achieved through both non-verbal and verbal behaviours. Even with audio alone, some non-verbal behaviours such as the use of silence and appropriate voice tone in response to a patient's expression of feelings can be observed. Verbal empathy makes this more explicit by specifically naming and appreciating the patient's emotions or predicament.

B: Indicators of understanding & incorporating the patient's perspective

B1	Eliciting and exploring patient's ideas/concerns/ expectations	Understanding the patient's perspective is a key component of patient-centred health care. Each patient has a unique experience of sickness that includes the feelings, thoughts, concerns and effect on life that any episode of sickness induces. Patients may either volunteer this spontaneously (as direct statements or cues) or in response to health professionals' enquiries.
B2	Picking up patient's cues	Patients are generally eager to tell us about their own thoughts and feelings but often do so indirectly through verbal hints or changes in non-verbal behaviour (such as vocal cues including hesitation or change in volume). Picking up these cues is essential for exploring both the biomedical and the patient's perspectives. Some of the techniques for picking up cues would include echoing, i.e. repeating back what has just been said and either adding emphasis where appropriate or turning the echoed statement into a question, e.g. *"Something could be done…?"* . Another possibility is more overtly checking out statements or hints, e.g. *"I sense that you are not happy with the explanations you've been given in the past"*
B3	Relating explanations to elicited ideas/concerns/ expectations	One of the key reasons for discovering the patient's perspective is to incorporate this into explanations often in the later aspects of the interview. If the explanation does not address the patient's individual ideas, concerns and expectations, then recall, understanding and satisfaction suffer as the patient is still worrying about their still unaddressed concerns

C: Indicators of providing structure

C1	Sequencing the interview purposefully and logically	It is the responsibility of the health professional to maintain a logical sequence apparent to the patient as the interview unfolds. An ordered approach to organisation helps both professional and patient in efficient and accurate data gathering and information-giving. This needs to be balanced with the need to be patient-centred and follow the patient's needs. Flexibility and logical sequencing need to be thoughtfully combined.
		It is more obvious when sequencing is inadequate: the health professional will meander aimlessly or jump around between segments of the interview making the patient unclear as to the point of specific lines of enquiry.
C2	Signposting changes in topic	Signposting is a key skill in enabling patients to understand the structure of the interview by making the organisation overt: not only the health professional but also the patient needs to understand where the interview is going and why. A signposting statement introduces and draws attention to what we are about to say.
		For instance, it is helpful to use a signposting statement to introduce a summary. Signposting can also be used to make the progression from one section to another and explain the rationale for the next section.
C3	Using organising techniques in explanations	A variety of skills help to organise explanations in a way that leads particularly to increased patient recall and understanding. Skills include:
		categorisation in which the health professional informs the patient about which categories of information are to be provided
		labelling in which important points are explicitly labelled by the health professional. This can be achieved by using emphatic phrases or adverb intensifiers
		chunking in which information is delivered in chunks with clear gaps in between sections before proceeding
		repetition and summary of important points

D: Indicators for information-gathering

D1	Facilitating patient's narrative with active listening techniques, minimising interruption	Listening to the patient's narrative, particularly at the beginning of an interview, enables the health professional to more efficiently discover the story, hear the patient's perspective, appear supportive and interested and pick up cues to patients' feelings. Interruption of the narrative has the opposite effect and in particular generally leads to a predominantly biomedical history, omitting the patient's perspective. Observable skills of active listening techniques include: **A.** the use of silence and pausing **B.** verbal encouragement such as *um, uh-huh, I see* **C.** echoing and repetition such as "*chest pain?*" or "*not coping?*" **D.** paraphrasing and interpretation such as "*Are you thinking that when John gets even more ill, you won't be strong enough to nurse him at home by yourself?*"
D2	Using initially open questions, appropriately moving to closed questions	Understanding how to intentionally choose between open and closed questioning styles at different points in the interview is of key importance. An effective health professional uses open questioning techniques first to obtain a picture of the problem from the patient's perspective. Later, the approach becomes more focused with increasingly specific though still open questions and eventually closed questions to elicit additional details that the patient may have omitted. The use of open questioning techniques is critical at the beginning of the exploration of any problem and the most common mistake is to move to closed questioning too quickly. Closed questions are questions for which a specific and often one word answer is elicited. These responses are often "*yes/no*". *Open questioning techniques* in contrast are designed to introduce an area of enquiry without unduly shaping or focusing the content of the response. They still direct the patient to a specific area but allow the patient more discretion in their answer, suggesting to the patient that elaboration is both appropriate and welcome.
D3	NOT using compound questions/ leading questions	A compound question is when more than one question is asked without allowing time to answer. It confuses the patient about what information is wanted, and introduces uncertainty about which of the questions asked the eventual reply relates to. An example would be "*have you ever had chest pain or felt short of breath?*" A leading question includes an assumption in the question which makes it more difficult for the respondent to contradict the assumption. e.g., "*You've lost weight, haven't you? or "you haven't had any ankle swelling?*"

| D4 | Clarifying statements which are vague or need amplification | Clarifying statements which are vague or need further amplification is a vital information gathering skill. After an initial response to an open ended question, health professionals may need to prompt patients for more precision, clarity or completeness. Often patients' statements can have two (or more) possible meanings: it is important to ascertain which one is intended. |
| D5 | Summarising information to encourage correction/ invite further information | Summarising is the deliberate step of making an explicit verbal summary to the patient of the information gathered so far and is one of the most important of all information gathering skills. Used periodically throughout the interview, it helps with two significant tasks – ensuring accuracy and facilitating the patient's further responses. |

E: Indicators for information-giving

E1	Establishing initially what patient already knows	One key interactive approach to giving information to patients involves assessing their prior knowledge. This allows you to determine at what level to pitch information, how much and what information the patient needs, and the degree to which your view of the problem differs from that of the patient.
E2	Pausing periodically when giving information, using response to guide next steps	This approach, often called chunking and checking, is a vital skill throughout the information-giving phase of the interview. Here, the health professional gives information in small pieces, pausing and checking for understanding before proceeding and being guided by the patient's reactions to see what information is required next. This technique is a vital component of assessing the patient's overall information needs: if you give information in small chunks and give patients ample opportunity to contribute, they will respond with clear signals about both the amount and type of information they still require.
E3	Encouraging patient to contribute reactions/ feelings	A further element of effective information giving is providing opportunities to the patient to ask questions, seek clarification or express doubts. Health professionals have to be very explicit here: many patients are reluctant to express what is on the tip of their tongue and are extremely hesitant to ask the doctor questions. Unless positively invited to do so, they may leave the consultation with their questions unanswered and a reduced understanding and commitment to plans.
E4	Checking whether patient has understood information	Checking the patient has understood the information given is an important step in ensuring accuracy of information transfer. This can be done by asking "*does that make sense?*" although many patients will say yes when they mean no to avoid looking stupid. A more effective method is to use patient restatement, i.e. asking the patient to repeat back to the doctor what has been discussed to ensure that their understanding is the same
E5	Discovering what further information patient needs	Deliberately asking the patient what other information would be helpful enables the health professional to directly discover areas to address which the health professional might not have considered. It is difficult to guess each patient's individual needs and asking directly is an obvious way to prevent the omission of important information.

Useful language

Greeting Introduction

» Good morning/afternoon/evening.
» Nice to see you (again).
» How are you today?

» My name is Dr .../I'm Dr ...
» Thanks for coming to see me today.
» Pleased to meet you (response to patient's introduction).

Getting information

Starting the interview:

» What brings you along here today?
» What brought you here today?
» What seems to be the trouble/problem?
» How can I help you?
» What can I do for you?
» What seems to be bothering you?

Asking about location of the problem:

» Where is the sensation?
» Can you tell me where it hurts?
» Where do you feel sore?
» Where does it feel sore?
» Which part of the/your body is affected?
» Show me where the pain is.
» Tell me where the pain is.

Asking about duration:

» When did it start?
» How long have you had it?
» How long have you been feeling like this?
» How often has this been occurring?
» How long have you been suffering from this problem?
» When did the problem start?

Asking about severity of pain or type of pain:

» Is the pain dull or sharp?
» What is the pain like?
» Could you describe the pain?
» How severe is the pain?
» Does it disturb you at night?
» Does it feel numb?
» Does it occur all of the time or just now and again?

Questioning

To clarify/to get details:

» Have you had any...?
» Does the discomfort appear to be brought on by anything in particular?
» What do you do when you get the pain?
» Do you ever get pain at night?

» Does anything special make it worse?
» Does anything seem to bring it on/aggravate the problem?
» Is there anything that seems to relieve this?

Prescribing

Tests, medicine, treatment:

» I think we would start with...

» I will give you a prescription for...

» I will give you a referral for...

» I'll write a referral letter to...

» I'm going to ask you to fill a prescription for...

» We'll run some tests to see...

Check understanding

» Do you have any questions?

» Have you ever heard of ...?

Reassurance

» I can understand your concerns, but...

» I'm sure you won't have any more trouble...

» Don't worry, it'll go away by itself/in a few days/with some rest...

» Rest assured, this is quite common...

» There is nothing to be overly concerned about.

Feedback

Respond to patient's questions:

» Were there any other questions?

» Does this sound ok/ like an acceptable plan?

Advising Suggesting

» What I think we'll do is ...

» What I suggest you do is ...

» It is worthwhile...

» I advise you...

» We could make a time to follow up on that.

» It's a good idea to ...

Leave-taking

Pleasure to meet you.

» Nice to meet you, ...

» Let's leave it there.

» All the best, ...

» I'll see you next time/soon.

» Thanks very much for coming to see me.

Notes

Printed in Germany
by Amazon Distribution
GmbH, Leipzig

Aug 19

PE CAM 2018

OET

OCCUPATIONAL ENGLISH TEST

NURSING

Official OET Practice Book 1

Contents

An overview of OET

About OET

OET is an international English language test that assesses the language proficiency of healthcare professionals seeking to register and practise in an English-speaking environment. It provides a validated, reliable assessment of all four language skills – listening, reading, writing and speaking – with the emphasis on communication in healthcare professional settings.

OET tests candidates from the following 12 health professions: Dentistry, Dietetics, Medicine, Nursing, Occupational Therapy, Optometry, Pharmacy, Physiotherapy, Podiatry, Radiography, Speech Pathology and Veterinary Science.

Candidates are encouraged to prepare thoroughly for their OET test.

Language proficiency and test taking skills

For more information about OET including the latest test dates and a complete list of test locations and preparation providers, as well as access to our free test preparation package Start for Success, visit the OET website: **www.occupationalenglishtest.org**

About the test

OET assesses listening, reading, writing and speaking.

There is a separate sub-test for each skill area. The Listening and Reading sub-tests are designed to assess the ability to understand spoken and written English in contexts related to general health and medicine. The sub-tests for Listening and Reading are common to all professions.

The Writing and Speaking sub-tests are specific to each profession and are designed to assess the ability to use English appropriately in the relevant professional context.

Sub-test (duration)	Content	Shows candidates can:
Listening (45 minutes)	3 tasks Common to all 12 professions	follow and understand a range of health-related spoken materials such as patient consultations and lectures.
Reading (60 minutes)	3 tasks Common to all 12 professions	read and understand different types of text on health-related subjects.
Writing (45 minutes)	1 task Specific to each profession	write a letter in a clear and accurate way which is relevant for the reader.
Speaking (20 minutes)	2 tasks Specific to each profession	effectively communicate in a real-life context through the use of role plays.

Listening sub-test

The Listening sub-test consists of three parts, and a total of 42 question items. You will hear each recording once and are expected to write your answers while listening. All three parts take 45 minutes to complete. The Listening sub-test has the following structure:

Part A – consultation extracts

Part A assesses your ability to identify specific information during a consultation. You will listen to two five-minute health professional-patient consultations and you will complete the health professional's notes using the information you hear.

Part B – short workplace extracts

Part B assesses your ability to identify the detail, gist, opinion or purpose of short extracts from the healthcare workplace. You will listen to six one-minute extracts (e.g. team briefings, handovers, or health professional-patient dialogues) and you will answer one multiple-choice question for each extract.

Part C – presentation extracts

Part C assesses your ability to follow a recorded presentation or interview on a range of accessible healthcare topics. You will listen to two different five-minute extracts and you will answer six multiple-choice questions for each extract.

Reading sub-test

The Reading sub-test consists of three parts, with a total of 42 question items. You are given 60 minutes to complete all three parts (15 minutes for Part A and 45 minutes for Part B and Part C). The Reading sub-test has the following structure:

Part A – expeditious reading task

Part A assesses your ability to locate specific information from four short texts in a quick and efficient manner. The four short texts relate to a single healthcare topic, and you must answer 20 questions in the allocated time period. The 20 questions consist of matching, sentence completion and short answer questions.

Part B and Part C – careful reading tasks

Part B assesses your ability to identify the detail, gist or purpose of six short texts sourced from the healthcare workplace (100-150 words each). The texts might consist of extracts from policy documents, hospital guidelines, manuals or internal communications, such as email or memos. For each text, there is one three-option multiple-choice question.

Part C assesses your ability to identify detailed meaning and opinion in two texts on a topic of interest to healthcare professionals (800 words each). For each text, you must answer eight four-option multiple choice questions.

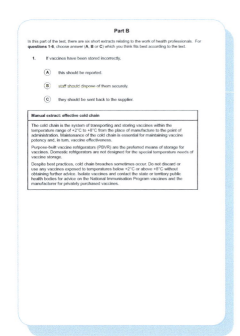

Writing sub-test

The Writing sub-test consists of one profession specific task based on a typical workplace situation. The writing test takes 45 minutes to complete - 40 minutes to write your letter and 5 minutes at the start to read the case notes on which to base you writing. The Writing sub-test has the following structure:

The task is to write a letter, usually a referral letter but sometimes a different type of letter such as a letter of transfer or discharge.

Along with the task instructions, you will receive stimulus material (case notes and/or other related documentation) which includes information to use in your response.

Speaking sub-test

The Speaking sub-test consists of two profession specific role-plays and is delivered individually. It takes around 20 minutes to complete. In each role-play, you take your professional role (for example, as a nurse or as a pharmacist) while the interlocutor plays a patient, a client, or a patient's relative or carer. For veterinary science, the interlocutor is the owner or carer of the animal. The Speaking sub-test has the following structure:

In each Speaking test, your identity and profession are checked by the interlocutor and there is a short warm-up conversation about your professional background. Then the role-plays are introduced one by one and you have 3 minutes to prepare for each. The role-plays take about five minutes each.

You receive information for each role-play on a card that you keep while you do the role-play. The card explains the situation and what you are required to do. You may write notes on the card if you want. If you have any questions about the content of the role-play or how a role-play works, you can ask them during the preparation time.

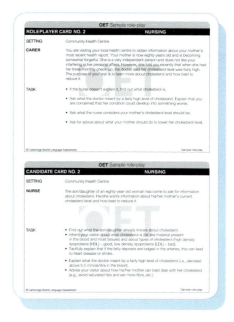

The role-plays are based on typical workplace situations and reflect the demands made on a health professional in those situations. The interlocutor follows a script so that the Speaking test structure is similar for each candidate. The interlocutor also has detailed information to use in each role-play. Different role-plays are used for different candidates at the same test administration.

How the test is scored

You will receive your results in the form of a score on a scale from 0 to 500 for each of the four sub-tests:

OET Results table

OET results to August 2018	OET score from September 2018	OET band descriptors	IELTS equivalent band score
A	500 490 480 470 460 450	Can communicate very fluently and effectively with patients and health professionals using appropriate register, tone and lexis. Shows complete understanding of any kind of written or spoken language.	8.0 - 9.0
B	440 430 420 410 400 390 380 370 360 350	Can communicate effectively with patients and health professionals using appropriate register, tone and lexis, with only occasional inaccuracies and hesitations. Shows good understanding in a range of clinical contexts.	7.0 – 7.5
C+	340 330 320 310 300		6.5
C	290 280 270 260 250 240 230 220 210 200	Can maintain the interaction in a relevant healthcare environment despite occasional errors and lapses, and follow standard spoken language normally encountered in his/her field of specialisation.	5.5 – 6.0
D	190 180 170 160 150 140 130 120 110 100	Can maintain some interaction and understand straightforward factual information in his/her field of specialisation, but may ask for clarification. Frequent errors, inaccuracies and mis-or overuse of technical language can cause strain in communication.	Less than 5.5
E	90 80 70 60 50 40 30 20 10 0	Can manage simple interaction on familiar topics and understand the main point in short, simple messages, provided he/she can ask for clarification. High density of errors and mis- or overuse of technical language can cause significant strain and breakdowns in communication.	

Test taker's guide to OET

Listening

Part A

Remember, in **Part A** you listen to a recording of 2 consultations between a health professional and a patient (dialogue). You take notes while you listen. This part of the test usually lasts around 15 minutes. Before you attempt the Practice Test, consider some important tips below.

Do

» Use the sub-headings to guide you .

» Give specific rather than general information from the recording.

Don't

» Jump ahead or back: the gaps follow the sequence of the recording.

» Write full sentences: a word or short phrase is sufficient.

» Don't waste valuable time using an eraser to correct a mistake if you make one. Simply cross out any words you don't want the person marking your paper to accept; this takes a lot less time and you will not be penalised.

Part B

Remember, in **Part B** you listen to six recorded extracts from the healthcare workplace. You answer one multiple-choice question for each extract. This part of the test usually lasts around 10 minutes.

Do

» Read the contextual information for each extract to understand the interaction you will hear.

» Read through each question carefully.

» Mark your answers on this Question Paper by filling in the circle using a 2B pencil.

Don't

» Select your answer until you have heard the whole extract.

» Fill in more than one circle on the Question Paper as the scanner will not be able to recognise your answer and you will not receive any marks for that question.

Part C

Remember, in **Part C** you listen to 2 recordings of a recorded presentation or interview on a health-related issue. You will answer six multiple-choice questions for each recording while you listen. This part of the test usually lasts around 15 minutes. Before you attempt the Practice Test, consider some important tips below.

Do

» Read through each question carefully.

» Mark your answers on this Question Paper by filling in the circle using a 2B pencil.

Don't

» Wait for key words in the question or answer options to be said in the recording. The speaker(s) will often use synonyms of the words you read.

» Fill in more than one circle on the Question Paper as the scanner will not be able to recognise your answer and you will not receive any marks for that question.

General

» Have a spare pen or pencil ready just in case.

» Stay relaxed and receptive – ready to listen.

» Focus on listening and understanding then recording your answer.

» Demonstrate that you have understood the recording (as well as heard it).

» Take a sample test under test conditions beforehand so you know what it feels like.

» Don't be distracted by what is going on around you (e.g., sneezing, a nervous candidate at the next desk)

» When the recording starts, use the time allowed to look through the questions carefully, scanning the headings and questions so you know what to listen out for.

» Use common abbreviations and symbols.

» Write clearly; don't make it difficult for the assessor to read your responses as you may not get all the marks you could.

» Don't lose your place during the test; remain focused on each question.

Checking at the end

» Think twice about going back to change something – it may be better to leave what you wrote the first time if you are not sure.

» Don't leave any blanks; have a guess at the answer.

Developing your listening skills

» You should practise listening to English delivered at natural speed in a variety of voices and contexts. Learners who do this regularly are more confident at extracting key information and gist meaning, even when they are not able to decode every single word or phrase. Make sure you are exposed to speakers of different ages and backgrounds, and to the language of different contexts (e.g., informal discussions, formal lectures, etc.).

» Although it is useful to practise exam techniques by using exam materials and course books, you should also use real-life sources to develop your listening skills. You can find a variety of authentic sources for free on the internet, particularly in the form of training videos and professional development talks.

» Practise dealing with listening texts in a variety of ways. For example, you can listen to a text once for the gist, and produce a summary of the main ideas or attitudes expressed by the speakers. You can then listen to the same text a second time in order to retrieve specific information or to focus on useful language.

» At a high level in OET Listening, it is not enough to be able to pick out particular words or specific details. You need to be able to understand the overall meaning of what the speakers are saying. It is important to practise following a speaker's line of argument and identifying his/her opinion or attitude.

What to expect in the test

» The instructions for each task are given on the question paper, and you will also hear them on the recording. They give you information about the topic and the speakers, and tell you about the type of task you have to do.

» There is a pause before each section to give you time to read through and think about the questions. Use the time to familiarise yourself with the task and start to predict what you are likely to hear.

» Use the task on the paper to guide you through the recording as you answer the questions.

Reading

Part A

Remember, in **Part A** you locate specific information from four short texts related to a single healthcare topic. You have 15 minutes to answer 20 questions. Before you attempt the Practice Test, consider some important tips below.

Do

» Keep the Text Booklet open in front of you so that you can see all the texts and the answer booklet at the same time. You need to be able to move between the different texts quickly and easily.

» Use the headings and layout of the short texts to get a quick initial idea of the type of information they contain and how they are organised. This will help you select which text you need for each section of the test.

» For short answer and sentence completion questions, use the statement to find out what type of information you need and decide which of the short texts is likely to contain that information. Then navigate to the relevant part of the text.

» Use correct spelling: incorrectly spelt answers do not receive any marks. You may use either British or American spelling variations (e.g. anemia and anaemia are both acceptable).

Don't

» The answers for Part A need to be consistent with the information of the texts. It is not a good strategy to use your professional background knowledge to answer Part A and avoid skimming and scanning the text.

» Use words with similar meaning to words in the texts. These words are known as synonyms.

» Waste valuable time using an eraser to correct a mistake if you make one. You may, for example, accidentally include an extra word or write the wrong word in the wrong space. Simply cross out any words you don't want the assessor marking your paper to accept; this takes a lot less time and you will not be penalised.

» Begin Part A by simply reading all texts from beginning to end as this will waste valuable time. Use the questions to guide you to which text to read first.

Part B

Remember, in **Part B** you answer one multiple-choice question about six short texts sourced from the healthcare workplace. The combined time for Parts B and C is 45 minutes. Before you attempt the Practice Test, consider some important tips below.

Do

» Read the contextual information for each text to help you understand the purpose and audience of the content.

» Read each answer option carefully and scan the text for evidence to support this option being correct or incorrect.

» Manage your time carefully. You should aim to spend the majority of the 45 minutes on Part C.

» Mark your answers on this Question Paper by filling in the circle using a 2B pencil.

Don't

» Read each text before reading the questions. You need to be efficient with your time: read the answer options and then focus on the text.

» Be distracted by unfamiliar vocabulary. Use the surrounding words to approximate the meaning and continue to search for the answer. Questions can often be answered without understanding all the vocabulary.

» Fill in more than one circle on the Question Paper as the scanner will not be able to recognise your answer and you will not receive any marks for that question.

Part C

Remember, in **Part C** you answer eight multiple-choice questions on each of two texts which are about a topic of interest to healthcare professionals. The combined time for Parts B and C is 45 minutes. Before you attempt the Practice Test, consider some important points below.

Do

- » There are no thematic links between the two texts. Focus on one text at a time rather than moving backwards and forwards between them.
- » Manage your time carefully. Allow enough time for both Part C texts as the reading skills it requires are quite considered and detailed.
- » Read each question carefully, looking out for key words.
- » Consider each of the options and explain to yourself what makes each one right or wrong.
- » If you are unsure about a question, consider moving on and coming back to it later.
- » Mark your answers on this Question Paper by filling in the circle using a 2B pencil.

Don't

- » Get stuck on one question – keep going and come back to it at the end when you have answered all other questions. Marks are not deducted for incorrect answers.
- » Fill in more than one circle on the Question Paper as the scanner will not be able to recognise your answer and you will not receive any marks for that question.

General

- » Have a spare pen and pencil ready just in case.
- » Bring and use a soft (2B) pencil. Remember you cannot use a pen to answer the multiple-choice questions for Parts B and C. It is a good idea to bring one or two extra 2B pencils as spares or a small pencil sharpener.
- » Note how the text is organised (e.g., with sub-headings, tables/diagrams etc.).
- » Write on the texts if it helps you (e.g., underlining key words and phrases etc.) but don't make it more difficult for you to read by adding too many marks.
- » When checking at the end, don't make any last-minute changes unless you are sure.

Developing your reading skills

- » You should practise reading a variety of text types in English so that you become familiar with a wide range of language and organisational features. Candidates who do this regularly are more confident at understanding the overall function and message of texts and at following a line of argument in a text.
- » Although it is useful to practise exam techniques by using exam materials and course books, you should also use real-life sources to develop your reading skills. Following up on your own professional or personal interests is a good way to increase your exposure to different types of texts.
- » Practise dealing with texts in a variety of ways. For example, you could read a text once for the gist, and produce a summary of the main ideas or attitudes expressed by the writers. You could then read the same text a second time in order to retrieve specific information or to focus on useful language.
- » At a high level in OET Reading, it is not enough to be able to pick out particular words or specific details. You need to be able to understand the overall meaning of the text. It is important to practise following a writer's line of argument as well as identifying specific pieces of information.
- » Take the sample test under test conditions beforehand so you know what it feels like. For Part A, set yourself a strict time limit of 15 minutes. For Part B, set your timer for 45 minutes.

What to expect in the test

» The instructions for each task are given on the question paper. They give you information about the topic and the texts, and tell you about the type of task you have to do.

» You will complete the Reading sub-test in two parts. First you will be given the Text Booklet and the Answer Booklet for Part A. When the 15 minutes for Part A have finished, these will be collected from you. You will then be given the Text Booklet for Parts B & C.

» You will not be able to go back to Part A, even if you finish Parts B & C early. Leave yourself enough time in each Part to check your answers.

» You may write your answers in either **pen** or **pencil** for Part A.

Writing

Do

» Take time to understand the task requirements.

» Use your own words to paraphrase or summarise longer pieces of information from the case notes.

» Make sure you understand the situation described in the case notes.

» Think about how best to organise your letter before you start writing.

» Use the space provided to plan your letter (though a draft is not compulsory).

» Use the five minutes' reading time effectively to understand the task set

- What is your role?
- Who is your audience (the intended reader)?
- What is the current situation?
- How urgent is the current situation?
- What is the main point you must communicate to the reader?
- What supporting information is necessary to give to the reader?
- What background information is useful to the reader?
- What information is unnecessary for the reader? Why is it unnecessary?

» Explain the current situation at the start of the letter (e.g., perhaps an emergency situation).

» Use the names and address given.

» Set out the names, address, date and other information to start the letter clearly.

» As you write, indicate each new paragraph clearly, perhaps by leaving a blank line.

Don't

» Include everything from the case notes – select information relevant to the task.

» Simply copy chunks of text from the case notes.

» Write notes or numbered points.

General

» Have a spare pen and pencil ready, just in case.

» Fill in the cover pages for the task booklet and the answer booklet correctly.

» Fill in your personal information on the answer sheet correctly.

» Take a sample test under test conditions beforehand so you know what it feels like.

» Practise writing clearly if you have poor handwriting.

» Write clearly and legibly.

Checking at the end

» Make sure your letter communicates what you intend.

» Make sure you meet the basic task requirements:

- length of the body of the text approximately 180–200 words
- full sentences, not note form
- appropriate letter format.

» Check for any simple grammar and spelling errors that you may have made.

» If a page is messy, use clear marks (e.g., arrows, numbers) to show the sequence in which the parts of your text should be read.

» Cross out clearly anything you do not want the assessors to read.

Speaking

Do

Candidates should use the prompts/notes on the role-play card to guide them through the role-play:

» What is your role?

» What role is your interlocutor playing – patient, parent/son/daughter, carer?

» Where is the conversation taking place?

» What is the current situation?

» How urgent is the situation?

» What background information are you given about the patient and the situation?

» What are you required to do?

» What is the main purpose of the conversation (e.g., explain, find out, reassure, persuade etc.)?

» What other elements of the situation do you know about (e.g., the patient appears nervous or angry, you don't have much time etc.)?

» What information do you need to give the patient (remember, though, this is not a test of your professional skills)?

Don't

» Rely on scripted or rehearsed phrases during the test. Many of these phrases will not be appropriate for certain role-plays.

» Speak about topics not related to the role-play. Your focus should be on what's on your role-play card.

Information about role-play cards

Candidates will have an opportunity to read through the role-play card before starting each role-play. Both role-play cards are laid out in a similar way. At the top of the role-play card is information about the setting (i.e. where the conversation is taking place). Candidates receive information on each role-play card, which he/she keeps while doing the role-play. Candidates may write notes on the role-play card if they want to.

The role-play card explains the situation and what candidates are required to do. If candidates have any questions about the content of the role-play or how a role-play works, they may ask for clarification before starting.

The top paragraph contains background information about the patient and his/her situation. It will be made clear if the interlocutor is taking on the role of the patient or somebody talking on behalf of the patient (i.e., the patient's carer, parent, etc.). The bottom half of the role-play card contains information to assist candidates in what they need to mention during the role-play. Each role-play card contains approximately 100-150 words (prompts/notes to guide candidates during the role-play).

The Speaking sub-test is in three parts:

1. Warm-up conversation (this is not assessed)

- » format of the test explained
- » candidate helped to relax
- » questions asked about areas of professional interest, previous work experience, future plans, etc.

2. First role-play (assessed)

- » candidate handed role-play card
- » candidate has 2-3 minutes to prepare
- » candidate can ask questions to clarify before role-play starts
- » role-play is conducted (approximately 5 minutes)

3. Second role-play (assessed)

- » above procedure is repeated using a different role-play

Using the Speaking practice tests

- » Copy the role-play.
- » Ask a friend or colleague to play the role of the patient (or patient's carer, etc.).
- » Take the role of the health professional.
- » Ask another friend or colleague to observe the role-play and give you feedback on your performance.
- » Read the information on the role-play card carefully.
- » You have to deal with the case details as outlined on the role-play card by asking and answering questions put to you by the patient or client.
- » Speak as naturally as possible.
- » Remember it is important to be interested in the welfare of the patient and to reassure the patient or relation of the patient that the treatment being proposed is appropriate.
- » Keep to the time limit of 5 minutes (approximate) for each role-play.
- » Ask the friend or colleague who observed for comments and feedback.

NURSING

PRACTICE TEST
1

To listen to the audio, visit
https://www.occupationalenglishtest.org/audio

LISTENING SUB-TEST – QUESTION PAPER

CANDIDATE NUMBER:	
LAST NAME:	
FIRST NAME:	
MIDDLE NAMES:	**Passport Photo**
PROFESSION:	Candidate details and photo will be printed here.
VENUE:	
TEST DATE:	

CANDIDATE DECLARATION

By signing this, you agree not to disclose or use in any way (other than to take the test) or assist any other person to disclose or use any OET test or sub-test content. If you cheat or assist in any cheating, use any unfair practice, break any of the rules or regulations, or ignore any advice or information, you may be disqualified and your results may not be issued at the sole discretion of CBLA. CBLA also reserves its right to take further disciplinary action against you and to pursue any other remedies permitted by law. If a candidate is suspected of and investigated for malpractice, their personal details and details of the investigation may be passed to a third party where required.

CANDIDATE SIGNATURE: _____

TIME: APPROXIMATELY **40 MINUTES**

INSTRUCTIONS TO CANDIDATES

DO NOT open this question paper until you are told to do so.

One mark will be granted for each correct answer.

Answer **ALL** questions. Marks are **NOT** deducted for incorrect answers.

At the end of the test, you will have two minutes to check your answers.

At the end of the test, hand in this **Question Paper**.

You must not remove OET material from the test room.

HOW TO ANSWER THE QUESTIONS

Part A: Write your answers on this **Question Paper** by filling in the blanks. **Example: Patient:** _____ *Ray Sands*

Part B & Part C: Mark your answers on this **Question Paper** by filling in the circle using a 2B pencil. **Example:** Ⓐ
Ⓑ
Ⓒ

www.occupationalenglishtest.org

© Cambridge Boxhill Language Assessment – ABN 51 988 559 414

[CANDIDATE NO.] LISTENING QUESTION PAPER 01/12

Occupational English Test

Listening Test

This test has three parts. In each part you'll hear a number of different extracts. At the start of each extract, you'll hear this sound: --beep—

You'll have time to read the questions before you hear each extract and you'll hear each extract **ONCE ONLY**. Complete your answers as you listen.

At the end of the test you'll have two minutes to check your answers.

Part A

In this part of the test, you'll hear two different extracts. In each extract, a health professional is talking to a patient.

For **questions 1-24**, complete the notes with information you hear.

Now, look at the notes for extract one.

Extract 1: Questions 1-12

You hear an obstetrician talking to a patient called Melissa Gordon. For **questions 1-12**, complete the notes with a word or short phrase.

You now have 30 seconds to look at the notes.

Patient	Melissa Gordon

- works as a **(1)**

Medical history

- has occasional **(2)**

- is allergic to **(3)**

- has a **(4)** _____ diet

- non-smoker

- this will be her second child

- needed **(5)** _____ treatment before first pregnancy

- first baby presented as **(6)** _____

    - **(7)** _____ required during intervention

- after giving birth, had problems with **(8)**

    – helped by midwife

Baby's father

- family history of **(9)** _____

- child from previous marriage has **(10)**

    _____

Points raised

- not keen on amniocentesis

- enquired about the possibility of **(11)**

    _____ testing

- provided her with a leaflet on preparing **(12)**

    _____ for new baby

Extract 2: Questions 13-24

You hear a GP talking to a new patient called Mike Royce. For **questions 13-24**, complete the notes with a word or short phrase.

You now have thirty seconds to look at the notes.

Patient   Mike Royce

                         New patient transferring from another practice

Description of initial symptoms

- severe left knee pain in **(13)** _____ area

- worsened after an accident at work

- developed **(14)** _____ on back of knee
  (described as trigger points.)

Impact on daily life
- unable to **(15)** _____ while working
  (house painter)

- problems climbing ladders

Initial treatment
- exercise programme including

  - stretching exercises

  - rest

- **(16)** _____ for pain

Developments in condition

- GP suspected **(17)** _____

- prescribed hospital-based rehabilitation

- temporary improvement noted

Current condition	• muscular problem diagnosed by **(18)** _____
	– was performing treatment on **(19)** _____
	• experiencing insomnia and **(20)** _____
	• suspects **(21)** _____ (own research)
	• has recorded experiences in **(22)** _____
	• beginning to experience pain in both **(23)** _____

Suggested course of action

    • recommend referral to **(24)** _____

That is the end of Part A. Now look at Part B.

Part B

In this part of the test, you'll hear six different extracts. In each extract, you'll hear people talking in a different healthcare setting.

For **questions 25-30**, choose the answer (**A**, **B** or **C**) which fits best according to what you hear. You'll have time to read each question before you listen. Complete your answers as you listen.

Now look at question 25.

25.   You hear a dietitian talking to a patient.

           What is she doing?

              A   correcting the patient's misconception about obesity

              B   describing the link between obesity and other diseases

              C   stressing the need for a positive strategy aimed at weight loss

26.   You hear members of a hospital committee discussing problems in the X-ray department.

           The problems are due to a delay in

              A   buying a replacement machine.

              B   getting approval for a repair to a machine.

              C   identifying a problem with a particular machine.

27.   You hear a senior nurse giving feedback to a trainee after a training exercise.

           The trainee accepts that he failed to

              A   locate the CPR board quickly enough.

              B   deal with the CPR board on his own.

              C   install the CPR board correctly.

28. You hear a trainee nurse asking his senior colleague about the use of anti-embolism socks (AES) for a patient.

The patient isn't wearing the socks because

(A) she's suffering from arterial disease in her legs.

(B) there is sensory loss in her legs.

(C) her legs are too swollen.

29. You hear a vet talking about her involvement in the management of the practice where she works.

How does she feel about her role?

(A) She accepts that it's become surprisingly complex.

(B) She wishes her boss took more interest in the finances.

(C) She values the greater understanding it gives her of her work.

30. You hear a physiotherapist giving a presentation about a study she's been involved in.

She suggests that her findings are of particular interest because of

(A) the age of the subjects.

(B) the type of disorder involved.

(C) the length of time covered by the study.

That is the end of Part B. Now look at Part C.

Part C

In this part of the test, you'll hear two different extracts. In each extract, you'll hear health professionals talking about aspects of their work.

For **questions 31-42**, choose the answer (**A, B** or **C**) which fits best according to what you hear. Complete your answers as you listen.

Now look at extract one.

Extract 1: Questions 31-36

You hear a sports physiotherapist called Chris Maloney giving a presentation in which he describes treating a high jumper with a knee injury.

You now have 90 seconds to read **questions 31-36**.

31. When Chris first met the patient, he found out that

   (A) she was considering retirement from her sport.

   (B) her state of mind had aggravated the pain in her knee.

   (C) she had ignored professional advice previously offered to her.

32. During his assessment of the patient's knee, Chris decided that

   (A) her body type wasn't naturally suited to her sport.

   (B) the pain she felt was mainly located in one place.

   (C) some key muscles weren't strong enough.

33. In the first stage of his treatment, Chris

   (A) was careful to explain his methods in detail.

   (B) soon discovered what was causing the problem.

   (C) used evidence from MRI scans to inform his approach.

34. Why did Chris decide against the practice known as 'taping'?

   (A) The patient was reluctant to use it.

   (B) It might give a false sense of security.

   (C) The treatment was succeeding without it.

35. In the patient's gym work, Chris's main concern was to ensure that she

(A) tried out a wide range of fitness exercises.

(B) focussed on applying the correct techniques.

(C) was capable of managing her own training regime.

36. Why was the patient's run-up technique changed?

(A) to enable her to gain more speed before take off

(B) to reduce the stress placed on her take-off leg

(C) to reinforce the break from her old mindset

Now look at extract two.

Extract 2: Questions 37-42

You hear a clinical psychiatrist called Dr Anthony Gibbens giving a presentation about the value of individual patients' experiences and 'stories' in medicine.

You now have 90 seconds to read **questions 37-42**.

37. What impressed Dr Gibbens about the case study that was sent to him?

(A) where it was originally published

(B) how controversial its contents were

(C) his colleague's reasons for sending it to him

38. Dr Gibbens has noticed that people who read his books

(A) gain insights into their mental health problems.

(B) see an improvement in personal relationships.

(C) benefit from a subtle change in behaviour.

39. What disadvantage of doctors using patients' stories does Dr Gibbens identify?

    (A) evidence-based research being disregarded

    (B) patients being encouraged to self-diagnose

    (C) a tendency to jump to conclusions

40. In Dr Gibbens' opinion, why should patients' stories inform medical practice?

    (A) They provide an insight not gained from numbers alone.

    (B) They prove useful when testing new theories.

    (C) They are more accessible than statistics.

41. How does Dr Gibbens feel about randomised medical trials?

    (A) He questions the reliability of the method.

    (B) He is suspicious of the way data are selected for them.

    (C) He is doubtful of their value when used independently.

42. When talking about the use of narratives in medicine in the future, Dr Gibbens reveals

    (A) his determination that they should be used to inform research.

    (B) his commitment to making them more widely accepted.

    (C) his optimism that they will be published more widely.

That is the end of Part C.

You now have two minutes to check your answers.

END OF THE LISTENING TEST

CANDIDATE NUMBER:

LAST NAME:

FIRST NAME:

MIDDLE NAMES:

PROFESSION:

VENUE:

TEST DATE:

Candidate details and photo will be printed here.

Passport Photo

CANDIDATE SIGNATURE: _____

INSTRUCTIONS TO CANDIDATES

You must **NOT** remove OET material from the test room.

www.occupationalenglishtest.org

© Cambridge Boxhill Language Assessment – ABN 51 988 559 414

[CANDIDATE NO.] READING TEXT BOOKLET PART A 01/04

The use of feeding tubes in paediatrics: Texts

Text A

Paediatric nasogastric tube use

Nasogastric is the most common route for enteral feeding. It is particularly useful in the short term, and when it is necessary to avoid a surgical procedure to insert a gastrostomy device. However, in the long term, gastrostomy feeding may be more suitable.

Issues associated with paediatric nasogastric tube feeding include:

- The procedure for inserting the tube is traumatic for the majority of children.
- The tube is very noticeable.
- Patients are likely to pull out the tube making regular re-insertion necessary.
- Aspiration, if the tube is incorrectly placed.
- Increased risk of gastro-esophageal reflux with prolonged use.
- Damage to the skin on the face.

Text B

Inserting the nasogastric tube

All tubes must be radio opaque throughout their length and have externally visible markings.

1. Wide bore:
    - for short-term use only.
    - should be changed every seven days.
    - range of sizes for paediatric use is 6 Fr to 10 Fr.

2. Fine bore:
    - for long-term use.
    - should be changed every 30 days.

In general, tube sizes of 6 Fr are used for standard feeds, and 7-10 Fr for higher density and fibre feeds. Tubes come in a range of lengths, usually 55cm, 75cm or 85cm.

Wash and dry hands thoroughly. Place all the equipment needed on a clean tray.

- Find the most appropriate position for the child, depending on age and/or ability to co-operate. Older children may be able to sit upright with head support. Younger children may sit on a parent's lap. Infants may be wrapped in a sheet or blanket.
- Check the tube is intact then stretch it to remove any shape retained from being packaged.
- Measure from the tip of the nose to the bottom of the ear lobe, then from the ear lobe to xiphisternum. The length of tube can be marked with indelible pen or a note taken of the measurement marks on the tube (for neonates: measure from the nose to ear and then to the halfway point between xiphisternum and umbilicus).
- Lubricate the end of the tube using a water-based lubricant.
- Gently pass the tube into the child's nostril, advancing it along the floor of the nasopharynx to the oropharynx. Ask the child to swallow a little water, or offer a younger child their soother, to assist passage of the tube down the oesophagus. Never advance the tube against resistance.
- If the child shows signs of breathlessness or severe coughing, remove the tube immediately.
- Lightly secure the tube with tape until the position has been checked.

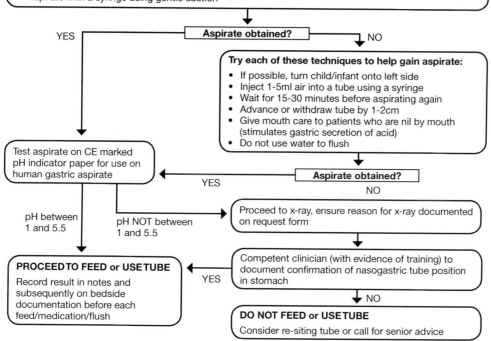

- Estimate NEX measurement (Place exit port of tube at tio of nose. Extend tube to earlobe, and then to xiphistemum)
- Insert fully radio-opaque nasogastric tube for feeding (follow manufacturer's instructions for insertion)
- Confirm and document secured NEX measurement
- Aspirate with a syringe using gentle suction

Aspirate obtained?

YES ← → NO

Try each of these techniques to help gain aspirate:
- If possible, turn child/infant onto left side
- Inject 1-5ml air into a tube using a syringe
- Wait for 15-30 minutes before aspirating again
- Advance or withdraw tube by 1-2cm
- Give mouth care to patients who are nil by mouth (stimulates gastric secretion of acid)
- Do not use water to flush

Aspirate obtained?

YES NO

Test aspirate on CE marked pH indicator paper for use on human gastric aspirate

pH between 1 and 5.5   pH NOT between 1 and 5.5

Proceed to x-ray, ensure reason for x-ray documented on request form

PROCEED TO FEED or USE TUBE

Record result in notes and subsequently on bedside documentation before each feed/medication/flush

YES Competent clinician (with evidence of training) to document confirmation of nasogastric tube position in stomach

NO

DO NOT FEED or USE TUBE

Consider re-siting tube or call for senior advice

A pH of between 1 and 5.5 is reliable confirmation that the tube is not in the lung, however, it does not confirm gastric placement. If this is any concern, the patient should proceed to x-ray in order to confirm tube position.

Where pH readings fall between 5 and 6 it is recommended that a second competent person checks the reading or retests.

Text D

Administering feeds/fluid via a feeding tube

Feeds are ordered through a referral to the dietitian.

When feeding directly into the small bowel, feeds must be delivered continuously via a feeding pump. The small bowel cannot hold large volumes of feed.

Feed bottles must be changed every six hours, or every four hours for expressed breast milk.

Under no circumstances should the feed be decanted from the container in which it is sent up from the special feeds unit.

All feeds should be monitored and recorded hourly using a fluid balance chart.

If oral feeding is appropriate, this must also be recorded.

The child should be measured and weighed before feeding commences and then twice weekly.

The use of this feeding method should be re-assessed, evaluated and recorded daily.

END OF PART A
THIS TEXT BOOKLET WILL BE COLLECTED

READING SUB-TEST – QUESTION PAPER: PART A

CANDIDATE NUMBER:

LAST NAME:

FIRST NAME:

MIDDLE NAMES:

PROFESSION:

VENUE:

TEST DATE:

Candidate details and photo will be printed here.

Passport Photo

CANDIDATE DECLARATION

By signing this, you agree not to disclose or use in any way (other than to take the test) or assist any other person to disclose or use any OET test or sub-test content. If you cheat or assist in any cheating, use any unfair practice, break any of the rules or regulations, or ignore any advice or information, you may be disqualified and your results may not be issued at the sole discretion of CBLA. CBLA also reserves its right to take further disciplinary action against you and to pursue any other remedies permitted by law. If a candidate is suspected of and investigated for malpractice, their personal details and details of the investigation may be passed to a third party where required.

CANDIDATE SIGNATURE: _____

TIME: 15 MINUTES

INSTRUCTIONS TO CANDIDATES

DO NOT open this **Question Paper** or the **Text Booklet** until you are told to do so.

Write your answers on the spaces provided on this **Question Paper.**

You must answer the questions within the 15-minute time limit.

One mark will be granted for each correct answer.

Answer **ALL** questions. Marks are **NOT** deducted for incorrect answers.

At the end of the 15 minutes, hand in this **Question Paper** and the **Text Booklet.**

DO NOT remove OET material from the test room.

www.occupationalenglishtest.org

© Cambridge Boxhill Language Assessment – ABN 51 988 559 414

[CANDIDATE NO.] READING QUESTION PAPER PART A 01/04

Part A

TIME: 15 minutes

- Look at the four texts, **A-D**, in the separate **Text Booklet**.

- For each question, **1-20**, look through the texts, **A-D**, to find the relevant information.

- Write your answers on the spaces provided in this **Question Paper**.

- Answer all the questions within the 15-minute time limit.

- Your answers should be correctly spelt.

The use of feeding tubes in paediatrics: Questions

Questions 1-7

For each question, **1-7**, decide which text (**A**, **B**, **C** or **D**) the information comes from.
You may use any letter more than once.

In which text can you find information about

1	the risks of feeding a child via a nasogastric tube?	_____
2	calculating the length of tube that will be required for a patient?	_____
3	when alternative forms of feeding may be more appropriate than nasogastric?	_____
4	who to consult over a patient's liquid food requirements?	_____
5	the outward appearance of the tubes?	_____
6	knowing when it is safe to go ahead with the use of a tube for feeding?	_____
7	how regularly different kinds of tubes need replacing?	_____

Questions 8-15

Answer each of the questions, **8-15**, with a word or short phrase from one of the texts. Each answer may include words, numbers or both.

8   What type of tube should you use for patients who need nasogastric feeding for an

extended period?

_____

9   What should you apply to a feeding tube to make it easier to insert?

_____

10   What should you use to keep the tube in place temporarily?

_____

11   What equipment should you use initially to aspirate a feeding tube?

_____

12   If initial aspiration of the feeding tube is unsuccessful, how long should you wait before trying again?

_____

13   How should you position a patient during a second attempt to obtain aspirate?

_____

14   If aspirate exceeds pH 5.5, where should you take the patient to confirm the position of the tube?

_____

15   What device allows for the delivery of feeds via the small bowel?

_____

Questions 16-20

Complete each of the sentences, **16-20**, with a word or short phrase from one of the texts. Each answer may include words, numbers or both.

16   If a feeding tube isn't straight when you unwrap it, you should

_____ it.

17   Patients are more likely to experience _____ if they need long-term feeding via a tube.

18   If you need to give the patient a standard liquid feed, the tube to use is

_____ in size.

19   You must take out the feeding tube at once if the patient is coughing badly or is

experiencing _____ .

20   If a child is receiving _____ via a feeding tube, you should replace the feed bottle after four hours.

END OF PART A

THIS QUESTION PAPER WILL BE COLLECTED

READING SUB-TEST – QUESTION PAPER: PARTS B & C

CANDIDATE NUMBER:

LAST NAME:

FIRST NAME:

MIDDLE NAMES:

Candidate details and photo will be printed here.

Passport Photo

PROFESSION:

VENUE:

TEST DATE:

CANDIDATE SIGNATURE: _____

TIME: 45 MINUTES

INSTRUCTIONS TO CANDIDATES

DO NOT open this **Question Paper** until you are told to do so.

One mark will be granted for each correct answer.

Answer **ALL** questions. Marks are **NOT** deducted for incorrect answers.

At the end of the test, hand in this **Question Paper**.

HOW TO ANSWER THE QUESTIONS:

Mark your answers on this **Question Paper** by filling in the circle using a 2B pencil. **Example:** Ⓐ
Ⓑ
Ⓒ

Part B

In this part of the test, there are six short extracts relating to the work of health professionals. For **questions 1-6**, choose answer (**A**, **B** or **C**) which you think fits best according to the text.

1. If vaccines have been stored incorrectly,

    (**A**)   this should be reported.

    (**B**)   staff should dispose of them securely.

    (**C**)   they should be sent back to the supplier.

Manual extract: effective cold chain

The cold chain is the system of transporting and storing vaccines within the temperature range of +2°C to +8°C from the place of manufacture to the point of administration. Maintenance of the cold chain is essential for maintaining vaccine potency and, in turn, vaccine effectiveness.

Purpose-built vaccine refrigerators (PBVR) are the preferred means of storage for vaccines. Domestic refrigerators are not designed for the special temperature needs of vaccine storage.

Despite best practices, cold chain breaches sometimes occur. Do not discard or use any vaccines exposed to temperatures below +2°C or above +8°C without obtaining further advice. Isolate vaccines and contact the state or territory public health bodies for advice on the National Immunisation Program vaccines and the manufacturer for privately purchased vaccines.

---

2. According to the extract, prior to making a home visit, nurses must

    (A)   record the time they leave the practice.

    (B)   refill their bag with necessary items.

    (C)   communicate their intentions to others.

Nurse home visit guidelines

When the nurse is ready to depart, he/she must advise a minimum of two staff members that he/she is commencing home visits, with one staff member responsible for logging the nurse's movements. More than one person must be made aware of the nurse's movements; failure to do so could result in the breakdown of communication and increased risk to the nurse and/or practice.

On return to the practice, the nurse will immediately advise staff members of his/her return. This time will be documented on the patient visit list, and then scanned and filed by administration staff. The nurse will then attend to any specimens, cold chain requirements, restocking of the nurse kit and biohazardous waste.

3. What is being described in this section of the guidelines?

(A) changes in procedures

(B) best practice procedures

(C) exceptions to the procedures

Guidelines for dealing with hospital waste
All biological waste must be carefully stored and disposed of safely. Contaminated materials such as blood bags, dirty dressings and disposable needles are also potentially hazardous and must be treated accordingly. If biological waste and contaminated materials are not disposed of properly, staff and members of the community could be exposed to infectious material and become infected. It is essential for the hospital to have protocols for dealing with biological waste and contaminated materials. All staff must be familiar with them and follow them.
The disposal of biohazardous materials is time-consuming and expensive, so it is important to separate out non-contaminated waste such as paper, packaging and non-sterile materials. Make separate disposal containers available where waste is created so that staff can sort the waste as it is being discarded.

4. When is it acceptable for a health professional to pass on confidential information given by a patient?

(A) if non-disclosure could adversely affect those involved

(B) if the patient's treatment might otherwise be compromised

(C) if the health professional would otherwise be breaking the law

---

Extract from guidelines: Patient Confidentiality

Where a patient objects to information being shared with other health professionals involved in their care, you should explain how disclosure would benefit the continuity and quality of care. If their decision has implications for the proposed treatment, it will be necessary to inform the patient of this. Ultimately if they refuse, you must respect their decision, even if it means that for reasons of safety you must limit your treatment options. You should record their decision within their clinical notes.

It may be in the public interest to disclose information received in confidence without consent, for example, information about a serious crime. It is important that confidentiality may only be broken in this way in exceptional circumstances and then only after careful consideration. This means you can justify your actions and point out the possible harm to the patient or other interested parties if you hadn't disclosed the information. Theft, fraud or damage to property would generally not warrant a breach of confidence.

---

5. The purpose of the email to practitioners about infection control obligations is to

(A) act as a reminder of their obligations.

(B) respond to a specific query they have raised.

(C) announce a change in regulations affecting them.

Email from Dental Board of Australia

Dear Practitioner,

You may be aware of the recent media and public interest in standards of infection control in dental practice. As regulators of the profession, we are concerned that there has been doubt among registered dental practitioners about these essential standards.

Registered dental practitioners must comply with the National Board's Guidelines on infection control. The guidelines list the reference material that you must have access to and comply with, including the National Health and Medical Research Council's (NHMRC) Guidelines for the prevention and control of infection in healthcare.

We believe that most dental practitioners consistently comply with these guidelines and implement appropriate infection control protocols. However, the consequences for non-compliance with appropriate infection control measures will be significant for you and also for your patients and the community.

6.   The results of the study described in the memo may explain why

    (A)   superior communication skills may protect women from dementia.

    (B)   female dementia sufferers have better verbal skills.

    (C)   mild dementia in women can remain undiagnosed.

Memo to staff: Women and Dementia

Please read this extract from a recent research paper

Women's superior verbal skills could work against them when it comes to recognizing Alzheimer's disease. A new study looked at more than 1300 men and women divided into three groups: one group comprised patients with amnestic mild cognitive impairment; the second group included patients with Alzheimer's dementia; and the final group included healthy controls. The researchers measured glucose metabolic rates with PET scans. Participants were then given immediate and delayed verbal recall tests.

Women with either no, mild or moderate problems performed better than men on the verbal memory tests. There was no difference in those with advanced Alzheimer's.

Because verbal memory scores are used for diagnosing Alzheimer's, some women may be further along in their disease before they are diagnosed. This suggests the need to have an increased index of suspicion when evaluating women with memory problems.

Part C

In this part of the test, there are two texts about different aspects of healthcare. For **questions 7-22**, choose the answer (**A**, **B**, **C** or **D**) which you think fits best according to the text.

Text 1: Asbestosis

Asbestos is a naturally occurring mineral that has been linked to human lung disease. It has been used in a huge number of products due to its high tensile strength, relative resistance to acid and temperature, and its varying textures and degrees of flexibility. It does not evaporate, dissolve, burn or undergo significant reactions with other chemicals. Because of the widespread use of asbestos, its fibres are **ubiquitous** in the environment. Building insulation materials manufactured since 1975 should no longer contain asbestos; however, products made or stockpiled before this time remain in many homes. Indoor air may become contaminated with fibres released from building materials, especially if they are damaged or crumbling.

One of the three types of asbestos-related diseases is asbestosis, a process of lung tissue scarring caused by asbestos fibres. The symptoms of asbestosis usually include slowly progressing shortness of breath and cough, often 20 to 40 years after exposure. Breathlessness advances throughout the disease, even without further asbestos inhalation. This fact is highlighted in the case of a 67-year-old retired plumber. He was on ramipril to treat his hypertension and developed a persistent dry cough, which his doctor presumed to be an ACE inhibitor induced cough. The ramipril was changed to losartan. The patient had never smoked and did not have a history of asthma or COPD. His cough worsened and he complained of breathlessness on exertion. In view of this history and the fact that he was a non-smoker, he was referred for a chest X-ray and to the local respiratory physician. His doctor was surprised to learn that the patient had asbestosis, diagnosed by a high-resolution CT scan. The patient then began legal proceedings to claim compensation as he had worked in a dockyard 25 years previously, during which time he was exposed to asbestos.

There are two major groups of asbestos fibres, the amphibole and chrysotile fibres. The amphiboles are much more likely to cause cancer of the lining of the lung (mesothelioma) and scarring of the lining of the lung (pleural fibrosis). Either group of fibres can cause disease of the lung, such as asbestosis. The risk of developing asbestos-related lung cancer varies between fibre types. Studies of groups of patients exposed to chrysotile fibres show only a moderate increase in risk. On the other hand, exposure to amphibole fibres or to both types of fibres increases the risk of lung cancer two-fold. Although the Occupational Safety and Health Administration (OSHA) has a standard for workplace exposure to asbestos (0.2 fibres/ millilitre of air), there is debate over what constitutes a safe level of exposure. While some believe asbestos-related disease is a 'threshold phenomenon', which requires a certain level of exposure for disease to occur, others believe there is no safe level of asbestos.

Depending on their shape and size, asbestos fibres deposit in different areas of the lung. Fibres less than 3mm easily move into the lung tissue and the lining surrounding the lung. Long fibres, greater than 5mm cannot be completely broken down by scavenger cells (macrophages) and become lodged in the lung tissue, causing inflammation. Substances damaging to the lungs are then released by cells that are responding to the foreign asbestos material. The persistence of these long fibres in the lung tissue and the resulting inflammation seem to initiate the process of cancer formation. As inflammation and damage to tissue around the asbestos fibres continues, the resulting scarring can extend from the small airways to the larger airways and the tiny air sacs (alveoli) at the end of the airways.

There is no cure for asbestosis. Treatments focus on a patient's ability to breathe. Medications like bronchodilators, aspirin and antibiotics are often prescribed and such treatments as oxygen therapy and postural drainage may be recommended. If symptoms are so severe that medications don't work, surgery may be recommended to remove scar tissue. Patients with asbestosis, like others with chronic lung disease, are at a higher risk of serious infections that take advantage of diseased or scarred lung tissue, so prevention and rapid treatment is vital. Flu and pneumococcal vaccinations are a part of routine care for these patients. Patients with progressive disease may be given corticosteroids and cyclophosphamide with limited improvement.

Chrysotile is the only form of asbestos that is currently in production today. Despite their association with lung cancer, chrysotile products are still used in 60 countries, according to the industry-sponsored Asbestos Institute. Although the asbestos industry proclaims the 'safety' of chrysotile fibres, which are now imbedded in less friable and 'dusty' products, little is known about the long term effects of these products because of the long delay in the development of disease. In spite of their potential health risks, the durability and cheapness of these products continue to attract commercial applications. Asbestosis remains a significant clinical problem even after marked reductions in on-the-job exposure to asbestos. Again, **this** is due to the long period of time between exposure and the onset of disease.

Text 1: Questions 7-14

7.   The writer suggests that the potential for harm from asbestos is increased by

      (A)   a change in the method of manufacture.

      (B)   the way it reacts with other substances.

      (C)   the fact that it is used so extensively.

      (D)   its presence in recently constructed buildings.

8.   The word 'ubiquitous' in paragraph one suggests that asbestos fibres

      (A)   can be found everywhere.

      (B)   may last for a long time.

      (C)   have an unchanging nature.

      (D)   are a natural substance.

9.   The case study of the 67-year-old man is given to show that

      (A)   smoking is unrelated to a diagnosis of asbestosis.

      (B)   doctors should be able to diagnose asbestosis earlier.

      (C)   the time from exposure to disease may cause delayed diagnosis.

      (D)   patients must provide full employment history details to their doctors.

10.   In the third paragraph, the writer highlights the disagreement about

      (A)   the relative safety of the two types of asbestos fibres.

      (B)   the impact of types of fibres on disease development.

      (C)   the results of studies into the levels of risk of fibre types.

      (D)   the degree of contact with asbestos fibres considered harmful.

11. In the fourth paragraph, the writer points out that longer asbestos fibres

   (A)   can travel as far as the alveoli.

   (B)   tend to remain in the pulmonary tissue.

   (C)   release substances causing inflammation.

   (D)   mount a defence against the body's macrophages.

12. What is highlighted as an important component of patient management?

   (A)   the use of corticosteroids

   (B)   infection control

   (C)   early intervention

   (D)   excision of scarred tissue

13. The writer states that products made from chrysotile

   (A)   have restricted application.

   (B)   may pose a future health threat.

   (C)   enjoy approval by the regulatory bodies.

   (D)   are safer than earlier asbestos-containing products.

14. In the final paragraph, the word 'this' refers to

   (A)   the interval from asbestos exposure to disease.

   (B)   the decreased use of asbestos in workplaces.

   (C)   asbestosis as an ongoing medical issue.

   (D)   occupational exposure to asbestos.

Text 2: Medication non-compliance

A US doctor gives his views on a new program

An important component of a patient's history and physical examination is the question of 'medication compliance,' the term used by physicians to designate whether, or not, a patient is taking his or her medications. Many a hospital chart bears the notorious comment 'Patient has a history of non-compliance.' Now, under a new experimental program in Philadelphia, USA, patients are being paid to take their medications. The concept makes sense in theory - failure to comply is one of the most common reasons that patients are readmitted to hospital shortly after being discharged.

Compliant patients take their medications because they want to live as long as possible; some simply do so because they're responsible, conscientious individuals by nature. But the hustle and bustle of daily life and employment often get in the way of taking medications, especially those that are timed inconveniently or in frequent doses, even for such well-intentioned patients. For the elderly and the mentally or physically impaired, US insurance companies will often pay for a daily visit by a nurse, to ensure a patient gets at least one set of the most vital pills. But other patients are left to fend for themselves, and it is not uncommon these days for patients to be taking a considerable number of vital pills daily.

Some patients have not been properly educated about the importance of their medications in layman's terms. They have told me, for instance, that they don't have high blood pressure because they were once prescribed a high blood pressure pill – in essence, they view an antihypertensive as an antibiotic that can be used as short-term treatment for a short-term problem. Others have told me that they never had a heart attack because they were taken to the cardiac catheterization lab and 'fixed.' As physicians we are responsible for making sure patients understand their own medical history and their own medications.

Not uncommonly patients will say, 'I googled it the other day, and there was a long list of side effects.' But a simple conversation with the patient at this juncture can easily change their perspective. As with many things in medicine, it's all about risks versus benefits – that's what we as physicians are trained to analyse. And patients can rest assured that we'll monitor them closely for side effects and address any that are unpleasant, either by treating them or by trying a different medication.

But to return to the program in Philadelphia, my firm belief is that if patients don't have strong enough incentives to take their medications so they can live longer, healthier lives, then the long-term benefits of providing a financial incentive are likely to be minimal. At the outset, the rewards may be substantial enough to elicit a response. But one isolated system or patient study is not an accurate depiction of the real-life scenario: patients will have to be taking these medications for decades.

Although a simple financial incentives program has its appeal, its complications abound. What's worse, it seems to be saying to society: as physicians, we tell our patients that not only do we work to care for them, but we'll now pay them to take better care of themselves. And by the way, for all you medication-compliant patients out there, you can have the inherent reward of a longer, healthier life, but we're not going to bother sending you money. This seems like some sort of implied punishment.

But more generally, what advice can be given to doctors with non-compliant patients? Dr John Steiner has written a paper on the matter: 'Be compassionate,' he urges doctors. 'Understand what a complicated balancing act it is for patients.' He's surely right **on that score**. Doctors and patients need to work together to figure out what is reasonable and realistic, prioritizing which measures are most important. For one patient, taking the diabetes pills might be more crucial than trying to quit smoking. For another, treating depression is more critical than treating cholesterol. 'Improving compliance is a team sport,' Dr Steiner adds. 'Input from nurses, care managers, social workers and pharmacists is critical.'

When discussing the complicated nuances of compliance with my students, I give the example of my grandmother. A thrifty, no-nonsense woman, she routinely sliced all the cholesterol and heart disease pills her doctor prescribed in half, taking only half the dose. If I questioned this, she'd wave me off with, 'What do those doctors know, anyway?' Sadly, she died suddenly, aged 87, most likely of a massive heart attack. Had she taken her medicines at the appropriate doses, she might have survived it. But then maybe she'd have died a more painful death from some other ailment. Her biggest fear had always been ending up dependent in a nursing home, and by luck or design, she was able to avoid that. Perhaps there was some wisdom in her 'non-compliance.'

Text 2: Questions 15-22

15. In the first paragraph, what is the writer's attitude towards the new programme?

- (A) He doubts that it is correctly named.
- (B) He appreciates the reasons behind it.
- (C) He is sceptical about whether it can work.
- (D) He is more enthusiastic than some other doctors.

16. In the second paragraph, the writer suggests that one category of non-compliance is

- (A) elderly patients who are given occasional assistance.
- (B) patients who are over-prescribed with a certain drug.
- (C) busy working people who mean to be compliant.
- (D) people who are by nature wary of taking pills.

17. What problem with some patients is described in the third paragraph?

- (A) They forget which prescribed medication is for which of their conditions.
- (B) They fail to recognise that some medical conditions require ongoing treatment.
- (C) They don't understand their treatment even when it's explained in simple terms.
- (D) They believe that taking some prescribed pills means they don't need to take others.

18. What does the writer say about side effects to medication?

- (A) Doctors need to have better plans in place if they develop.
- (B) There is too much misleading information about them online.
- (C) Fear of them can waste a lot of unnecessary consultation time.
- (D) Patients need to be informed about the likelihood of them occurring.

19. In the fifth paragraph, what is the writer's reservation about the Philadelphia program?

  (A) the long-term feasibility of the central idea

  (B) the size of the financial incentives offered

  (C) the types of medication that were targeted

  (D) the particular sample chosen to participate

20. What objection to the program does the writer make in the sixth paragraph?

  (A) It will be counter-productive.

  (B) It will place heavy demands on doctors.

  (C) It sends the wrong message to patients.

  (D) It is a simplistic idea that falls down on its details.

21. The expression '**on that score**' in the seventh paragraph refers to

  (A) a complex solution to patients' problems.

  (B) a co-operative attitude amongst medical staff.

  (C) a realistic assessment of why something happens.

  (D) a recommended response to the concerns of patients.

22. The writer suggests that his grandmother

  (A) may ultimately have benefited from her non-compliance.

  (B) would have appreciated closer medical supervision.

  (C) might have underestimated how ill she was.

  (D) should have followed her doctor's advice.

END OF READING TEST
THIS BOOKLET WILL BE COLLECTED

OCCUPATIONAL ENGLISH TEST

WRITING SUB-TEST – TEST BOOKLET

CANDIDATE NUMBER:

LAST NAME:

FIRST NAME:

MIDDLE NAMES:

PROFESSION: Candidate details and photo will be printed here.

VENUE:

TEST DATE:

Passport Photo

CANDIDATE SIGNATURE: _____

INSTRUCTIONS TO CANDIDATES

You must write your answer for the Writing sub-test in the **Writing Answer Booklet.**

You must **NOT** remove OET material from the test room.

www.occupationalenglishtest.org

© Cambridge Boxhill Language Assessment – ABN 51 988 559 414

[CANDIDATE NO.] WRITING SUB-TEST TEST BOOKLET 01/04

OCCUPATIONAL ENGLISH TEST

WRITING SUB-TEST: **NURSING**

TIME ALLOWED: **READING TIME: 5 MINUTES**
                    WRITING TIME: 40 MINUTES

Read the case notes below and complete the writing task which follows.

Notes:

You are a registered nurse working at Newtown Community Hospital. Your patient, Ms Mary Bell, is being discharged today.

Patient:	Mary Bell (Ms)
Age:	66 Years
Marital status:	Single
Family:	Nil
First admitted:	24 June 2018, Newtown Community Hospital
Discharge:	15 July 2018
Diagnosis:	Unstable diabetes mellitus
	Small infected (left) foot ulcer
Medical history:	Non-insulin-dependent diabetes mellitus – 15 years
Medications:	Glibenclamide (Glimel) 5mg daily
	Metformin (Diabex) 850mg t.d.s.
	Amoxycillin/clavulanate (Augmentin Duo Forte) 875/125mg orally, b.d.

Social/family background: Retired at 65 from managerial position 2017

Lives alone in own four-bedroom home

Income: small pension – much lower than pre-retirement income

Reports no relatives or close friends

Reports no outside interests

Since retirement alcohol intake has increased and dietary quality has decreased

Periodic problems with self-administration of hypoglycaemic medication

Nursing management and progress:

Medical hypoglycaemic agent (glibenclamide) to continue

Antibiotic therapy (Augmentin Duo Forte) for review at completion of current course

Ulcer daily saline dressing, monitor wound margins, observe for signs of complications, review healing progress, etc.

Discharge plan:	Monitor medication compliance, blood sugar levels, alcohol intake, diet
	Encourage moderate exercise programme
	Suggest establishment of income-producing activity
	Encourage establishment of social activities
	Prepare a letter to the community nurse, emphasising the need for an overall life-style plan, and suggesting involvement of community social worker service

Writing Task:

Using the information given in the case notes, write a letter of discharge to Ms Jane Rudik, the community nurse at Newtown Community Health Centre, informing her about the patient's condition and her medical and social needs. Address your letter to Ms Jane Rudik, Community Nurse, Newtown Community Health Centre, Newtown.

In your answer:

- **Expand the relevant notes into complete sentences**
- **Do not use note form**
- **Use letter format**

The body of the letter should be approximately 180–200 words.

WRITING SUB-TEST – ANSWER BOOKLET

CANDIDATE NUMBER:

LAST NAME:

FIRST NAME:

MIDDLE NAMES:

PROFESSION:

VENUE:

TEST DATE:

Candidate details and photo will be printed here.

Passport Photo

CANDIDATE DECLARATION

By signing this, you agree not to disclose or use in any way (other than to take the test) or assist any other person to disclose or use any OET test or sub-test content. If you cheat or assist in any cheating, use any unfair practice, break any of the rules or regulations, or ignore any advice or information, you may be disqualified and your results may not be issued at the sole discretion of CBLA. CBLA also reserves its right to take further disciplinary action against you and to pursue any other remedies permitted by law. If a candidate is suspected of and investigated for malpractice, their personal details and details of the investigation may be passed to a third party where required.

CANDIDATE SIGNATURE: _____

TIME ALLOWED
READING TIME: 5 MINUTES
WRITING TIME: 40 MINUTES

INSTRUCTIONS TO CANDIDATES

1. **Reading time: 5 minutes**
   During this time you may study the writing task and notes. You **MUST NOT** write, highlight, underline or make any notes.

2. **Writing time: 40 minutes**

3. Use the back page for notes and rough draft only. Notes and rough draft will **NOT** be marked.

   Please write your answer clearly on page 1 and page 2.

   Cross out anything you **DO NOT** want the examiner to consider.

4. You must write your answer for the Writing sub-test in this **Answer Booklet** using **pen or pencil**.

5. You must **NOT** remove OET material from the test room.

www.occupationalenglishtest.org
© Cambridge Boxhill Language Assessment – ABN 51 988 559 414

[CANDIDATE NO.] WRITING SUB-TEST ANSWER BOOKLET 01/04

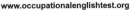

Please record your answer on this page.

(Only answers on Page 1 and Page 2 will be marked.)

_____

_____

_____

_____

_____

_____

_____

_____

_____

_____

_____

_____

_____

_____

_____

_____

_____

_____

_____

_____

_____

_____

_____

_____

_____

_____

_____

_____

_____

_____

_____

OET Writing sub-test – Answer booklet   1

Please record your answer on this page.

(Only answers on Page 1 and Page 2 will be marked.)

_____

_____

_____

_____

_____

_____

_____

_____

_____

_____

_____

_____

_____

_____

_____

_____

_____

_____

_____

_____

_____

_____

_____

_____

_____

_____

_____

_____

_____

_____

OET Writing sub-test – Answer booklet   2

Space for notes and rough draft. Only your answers on Page 1 and Page 2 will be marked.

SPEAKING SUB-TEST

CANDIDATE NUMBER:	
LAST NAME:	
FIRST NAME:	
MIDDLE NAMES:	**Passport Photo**
PROFESSION:	Your details and photo will be printed here.
VENUE:	
TEST DATE:	

CANDIDATE DECLARATION

By signing this, you agree not to disclose or use in any way (other than to take the test) or assist any other person to disclose or use any OET test or sub-test content. If you cheat or assist in any cheating, use any unfair practice, break any of the rules or regulations, or ignore any advice or information, you may be disqualified and your results may not be issued at the sole discretion of CBLA. CBLA also reserves its right to take further disciplinary action against you and to pursue any other remedies permitted by law. If a candidate is suspected of and investigated for malpractice, their personal details and details of the investigation may be passed to a third party where required.

CANDIDATE SIGNATURE: _____

INSTRUCTION TO CANDIDATES

Please confirm with the Interlocutor that your roleplay card number and colour match the Interlocutor card before you begin.

Interlocutor to complete only

ID No: _____ Passport: ☐ National ID: ☐ Alternative ID approved: ☐

Speaking sub-test:

ID document sighted? ☐   Photo match? ☐   Signature match? ☐   Did not attend? ☐

Interlocutor name: _____

Interlocutor signature: _____

 54 PRACTICE TEST **1**

ROLEPLAYER CARD NO. 1   **NURSING**

SETTING   Hospital Casualty Ward

PATIENT   You are in hospital following a road accident. You are not seriously injured, but have lost blood and have been told that you need a blood transfusion. You have no idea what the procedure will involve. You are anxious about the procedure and the danger of receiving infected blood. You have read that patients have contracted HIV through blood transfusions.

TASK

- You are anxious and upset. Express your fear of contracting HIV. Respond to the nurse's reassurances accordingly.

- Seek an explanation from the nurse about the procedure and the risks involved.

- Eventually agree to have the transfusion.

       Sample role-play

CANDIDATE CARD NO. 1   **NURSING**

SETTING   Hospital Casualty Ward

NURSE   The patient is in hospital following a road accident. The patient's condition is stable but he/she has lost blood and needs a blood transfusion. The patient does not understand what will happen. The patient is anxious about the procedure.

TASK

- Find out about the patient's concerns.

- Reassure the patient that the possibility of infection is very small (as care is taken to screen donors and test donated blood for possible infection).

- Explain the procedure for a blood transfusion (e.g., sterile conditions, new syringes, nurses watch closely, etc.).

- Stress that the patient really needs the transfusion in order to recover fully.

       Sample role-play

ROLEPLAYER CARD NO. 2   NURSING

SETTING   Community Health Centre

PARENT   Your six-year-old son has just cut a finger on his right hand with a kitchen knife that
                   was left on the kitchen bench. The finger won't stop bleeding, and you are
                   panicking about it. Your child is afraid of doctors and you have to weigh this
                   consideration against your concern about his finger. You are also worried about
                   possible scarring.

TASK
- Outline what happened. Explain that the cut looks deep to you, your child is in
  pain and you are very worried. Shouldn't your son have stitches?
- Convey your anxiety and uncertainty to the nurse. Ask how long the finger will
  take to heal and if it will be scarred for a long time. Ask when your son, who is
  right-handed, will be able to use this hand properly again.
- Ask the nurse what to do about your son's finger.
- If the question of your responsibility for the injury comes up, be defensive. You're
  a busy person and can't spend every minute of your day watching him.

CANDIDATE CARD NO. 2   NURSING

SETTING   Community Health Centre

NURSE   This parent's six-year-old son has cut his finger, which is bleeding freely. You
                   examine the cut, which is not too serious, and you don't think he needs stitches.

TASK
- Find out how the cut happened.

- Reassure the parent. Answer his/her questions about length of time for healing,
  any scarring, whether stitches are necessary, etc.

- Explain how to clean, apply antiseptic, and dress the cut suitably. Point out the
  need to keep the finger clean and dry.

- Warn the parent about keeping sharp implements out of reach. Be tactful in
  giving advice.

Listening sub-test
ANSWER KEY – Parts A, B & C

LISTENING SUB-TEST – ANSWER KEY

PART A: QUESTIONS 1-12

1. (computer) programmer

2. asthma (attacks)

3. penicillin

4. vegetarian

5. fertility

6. breech

7. forceps / forcipes

8. breastfeeding

9. epilepsy

10. Down syndrome / DS / DNS / Down's (syndrome)

11. CVS / chronic vill(o)us sampling

12. sibling(s) / brothers and/or sisters

PART A: QUESTIONS 13-24

13. medial meniscus OR medial

14. (very tender/tender/painful) bumps

15. squat (properly) / bend (his) knee

16. (used) ice pack(s)

17. tendonitis

18. (hospital) physio(therapist) / physio(therapist) (in the hospital)

19. hamstring(s)

20. (constant) anxiety

21. fibromyalgia

22. (a pain/pain) diary

23. (his) shoulders and elbows / (his) elbows and shoulders

24. rheumatologist

PART B: QUESTIONS 25-30

25. A correcting patient's misconception about obesity

26. B getting approval for a repair to a machine.

27. A locate the CPR board quickly enough.

28. B there is sensory loss in her legs.

29. C She values the greater understanding it gives her of her work.

30. A the age of the subjects.

PART C: QUESTIONS 31-36

31. A she was considering retirement from her sport.

32. C some key muscles weren't strong enough.

33. B soon discovered what was causing the problem.

34. C The treatment was succeeding without it.

35. B focussed on applying the correct techniques.

36. B to reduce the stress placed on her take-off leg

PART C: QUESTIONS 37-42

37. A where it was originally published

38. A gain insights into their mental health problems.

39. C a tendency to jump to conclusions

40. A They provide an insight not gained from numbers alone.

41. C He is doubtful of their value when used independently.

42. B his commitment to making them more widely accepted.

___

END OF KEY

Listening sub-test

Audio Script – Practice test 1

This test has three parts. In each part you'll hear a number of different extracts. At the start of each extract, you'll hear this sound: ---***---.

You'll have time to read the questions before you hear each extract and you'll hear each extract ONCE only. Complete your answers as you listen.

At the end of the test, you'll have two minutes to check your answers.

Part A. In this part of the test, you'll hear two different extracts. In each extract, a health professional is talking to a patient. For questions 1 to 24, complete the notes with information you hear. Now, look at the notes for extract one.

PAUSE: 5 SECONDS
Extract one. Questions 1 to 12.

You hear an obstetrician talking to a patient called Melissa Gordon. For questions 1 to 12, complete the notes with a word or short phrase. You now have thirty seconds to look at the notes.

PAUSE: 30 SECONDS

---***---

M: So, this first meeting, Mrs Gordon, is mainly a chance for you and I to get to know each other. I'll ask you about your medical history and this is also an opportunity for you to ask me any questions that you've got at this point.

F: *Sure.*

M: So, some background. What kind of work do you do?

F: *I have a job at an engineering company. I'm a computer programmer. I currently do four days a week, but I hope to reduce that to three after my maternity leave.*

M: Ahh, excellent. So tell me about your medical health? Do you have any conditions I should know about?

F: *Well err, I have asthma attacks but they don't happen often. I lost about ten kilos and that's certainly helped. I have an inhaler but I hardly ever use it. Oh, I should also let you know that I come out in terrible hives if I take penicillin, but not other things - I'm fine if I eat nuts, for example. I have a fairly healthy lifestyle. I'm a vegetarian and I've never smoked.*

M: Good.

F: *I'm afraid I don't go to the gym or anything, but I walk to work and err… generally keep active.*

M: Ahh that's good. So is this your first pregnancy?

F: *No, I have a daughter called Ella – she's three now.*

M: Ahh…and did everything go smoothly that time?

F: *There were no major problems during the pregnancy itself. But it took me quite a time to fall pregnant - the first time. After having various tests, I was given some fertility drugs. Ohh what were they called? It's on the tip of my tongue. Ahm, never mind. It'll come back to me. This time, though, I didn't need any help.*

M: It's no problem. What about labour last time around?

F: That was a nightmare…though everything - thank goodness - worked out in the end. It was a breech birth. It looked as if I might have to have a caesarean, and I really didn't want that. I was pleased I managed without an epidural too. They had to use forceps to get Ella out but I didn't need any stitches, so that was OK. Unfortunately, though, I had some difficulties after the birth too. I was desperate to start breastfeeding, but that didn't work out - at least not until I was given some guidance by the midwife.

M: OK. So can I ask you about the baby's father?

F: Sure. That's my husband, Paul. There's something in his family history I should tell you about, I think. His grandfather and father both had epilepsy - though he hasn't developed it himself. I'm not sure if that means his children have a greater chance of having it or not. Oh, also he has a child from his first marriage and she has Down's syndrome. So he gets a bit anxious when I'm pregnant.

M: Oh well, that's understandable, of course. We can discuss various testing options if you like. You might want to consider amniocentesis, for instance.

F: But that carries a risk of miscarriage, doesn't it? I don't want to go for that. I've heard about another test called err…CVS. Is that something to consider?

M: Well, it's certainly an option. However, that procedure in fact also carries a small increase in the risk of miscarriage. And you'd need to come to a decision fairly soon, because it's normally carried out between weeks…ten and twelve of the pregnancy.

F: Well, I can tell you straightaway that if there's more risk then I wouldn't consider it. I know my husband will feel the same.

M: Well that's fair enough. So, is there anything else you'd like to ask me about today?

F: Nothing urgent. But it'd be good to know more about how to get siblings ready for a new addition to the family. I want to make sure Ella doesn't feel threatened or replaced or anything.

M: Well, there's a leaflet that many parents find helpful. Here we are - have a look through that.

F: Ahh, thanks – that's great. I'm sure I'll have lots more questions at our next meeting.

PAUSE: 10 SECONDS
Extract two. Questions 13 to 24.

You hear a GP talking to a new patient called Mike Royce. For questions 13 to 24, complete the notes with a word or short phrase. You now have thirty seconds to look at the notes.

PAUSE: 30 SECONDS
---***---

F   Hello. Come on in. You must be Mr Royce. I understand that you've just signed up with the practice.

M   Yeah that's right, Mike Royce. I've joined this practice because my previous GP retired and he suggested I come here.

F   Right, and I understand you've got an ongoing medical condition you're worried about. Perhaps you'd like to start by telling me about that. How did it start?

M	Well, I suppose it started out as a really strong pain in my left knee, in, um, I think it's called the... the medial meniscus. Is that right? It came on whenever I tried to bend the knee more than normal. Then I tripped while climbing some stairs at work and that seemed to make things worse. I started to get these very tender bumps all over the back of the knee. They were very painful, even just lightly touching them. The doctor called them trigger points.
F	*Yeah, that's right. They're called that because pain frequently radiates out from them when touched. And how did that affect you day-to-day?*
M	Well, I went back to work after a week or so, but I was still having knee problems. I couldn't really squat properly or climb ladders – that's important in my job. I'm a painter, you know, and I'm always having to get into awkward positions. Anyway, I kept going back to my old GP explaining that I still had severe pain whenever I tried to bend my knee. He gave me all these exercises to do, and I tried doing them, I really did. I made sure I did gentle stretches before I did anything more energetic, everything really. I tried resting like he told me, I used ice packs when, when it got sore, but nothing really worked.
F	*Right, I see...*
M	But then the doctor decided I might be suffering from tendonitis, so he sent me for some rehab work in the hospital. That actually did seem to work, at least at first.
F	*But I'm guessing not for long.*
M	Right. The problem came back. I kept telling the doctor that my knee still wasn't healed, but it was actually my physiotherapist in the hospital rather than my old GP who noticed that something was wrong with my muscles. He wouldn't say what it was, but I knew something was up. He was doing myofascial release on my hamstrings and I was in agony.
F	*Right, so did...did you go back to your GP?*
M	I did. But he didn't know what I should do about it. So I left feeling completely fed up. That's one of the reasons I decided to come here. I just feel like nobody's taking this seriously. I think it's affecting my life in lots of other ways too. The worry's giving me insomnia for one thing. I don't think I have actual depression, but I certainly suffer from constant anxiety about when it's going to flare up.
F	*Is there anything that you're particularly worried you might have?*
M	Well, I've researched this pain I'm getting. Erm, to be honest, I'm convinced I've got fibromyalgia, not just some simple muscle problem, because I fit most of the symptoms, and I've had pain absolutely everywhere. Look. I've even kept a... a pain diary so that I could track what I did that set it off, you know, the weather, if I was working or not, where it was affecting me, what it felt like. I've figured out from this that it's usually in the same places that I mentioned earlier, plus some newish places too... my shoulders and elbows – and I know that my knee's actually one of the more tender points for it. What do you think?
F	*Look, I must say from what you've told me so far that I'm concerned enough to look into that possibility. So, as a next step, we need to get you seen by a rheumatologist. This is a notoriously difficult condition to diagnose, as I'm sure you're aware, because so many of the symptoms overlap with other conditions too.*
M	I won't be happy to be proved right but I'll certainly be glad to get some answers at long last.

PAUSE: 10 SECONDS
That is the end of Part A. Now, look at Part B.

PAUSE: 5 SECONDS

Part B.

In this part of the test, you'll hear six different extracts. In each extract, you'll hear people talking in a different healthcare setting.

For questions 25 to 30, choose the answer A, B or C which fits best according to what you hear. You'll have time to read each question before you listen. Complete your answers as you listen.

Now look at Question 25. You hear a dietitian talking to a patient. Now read the question.

PAUSE: 15 SECONDS

---***---

F: *So what seems to be the problem?*

M: I feel such a failure. I'm sure people think that if I just tried harder, I could lose weight. Maybe I need more willpower.

F: *Well, firstly, well done for seeking medical help. Actually, being overweight or obese is a medical problem, because being overweight changes how your body works.*

M: Oh, thanks, but I do feel that it's my fault for being this way.

F: *Well, I hear what you say, but please understand that these days, we consider that obesity is a disease, like high blood pressure or asthma. You see, the body's signals to the brain stop working correctly when you're overweight. And, with time, you feel less full, even if you eat the same amount. And when you cut calories, your body tries to use less energy to keep your weight the same.*

PAUSE: 5 SECONDS

Question 26. You hear members of a hospital committee discussing problems in the X-ray department. Now read the question.

PAUSE: 15 SECONDS

---***---

F   *So next on the agenda is the problems in the X-ray department. Nick, would you like to fill us in here?*

M   Well, as you all know, this is a very busy department. Err, so we have four X-ray machines in all, including one in the Fracture and Orthopaedic clinic area, but recently one of the other X-ray machines developed a fault and so we had to apply for authorisation for the purchase of a new tube for it. There's been some kind of hold up with the paperwork, and while we've been waiting, patients are being brought into the Fracture and Orthopaedic area for X-rays there instead, and of course that's causing further congestion.

PAUSE: 5 SECONDS

Question 27. You hear a senior nurse giving feedback to a trainee after a training exercise. Now read the question.

PAUSE: 15 SECONDS

---***---

F   *OK, that went quite well, didn't it? But it took you a while to work out where the CPR board was kept. So what does that tell you about this scenario?*

M   We need to check where things are before doing anything else.

F   *Exactly. And of course it takes a second or two to put the head of the bed down, because you've got to have that part of the bed flat before you slip the board in. I wish there was a quicker way.*

M   So do I put the CPR board under, or would I normally hand it over to somebody else?

F   *It makes no difference as long as it's done.*

PAUSE: 5 SECONDS
Question 28. You hear a trainee nurse asking his senior colleague about the use of anti-embolism socks for a patient. Now read the question.

PAUSE: 15 SECONDS
---***---

M: I noticed that Mrs Jones isn't wearing the usual anti-embolism socks, but I didn't want to ask her why not because she was asleep. Is it because her legs are swollen?

F: *Well, sometimes we don't recommend the socks if there's severe swelling with oedema, but that's not the case here. Mrs Jones was actually given them initially on admission last night, but she told us this morning that her lower legs were feeling numb – she described it as having no feeling. Until we've checked out the reason for that, for example it could be an underlying condition which could damage her arterial circulation, we're reducing the risk of thrombosis by pharmacological means.*

M: Oh, I see.

PAUSE: 5 SECONDS
Question 29. You hear a vet talking about her involvement in the management of the practice where she works. Now read the question.

PAUSE: 15 SECONDS
---***---

F: *At first, when I took over the financial running of the practice, I felt rather thrown in at the deep end. I really needed to know my stuff and be super organised, especially with the number of new drugs and treatments available now, all of which have to be very carefully costed. It keeps me super-busy, but monitoring stocks and so on helps give me confidence and allows me to see how everything fits into the overall picture of working as a vet. My manager's more than happy to leave me to run this side of things – he's in overall charge, of course, but I can always go to him if there's a problem. I keep him closely informed of what's happening. He's always pleased if I manage to make savings anywhere.*

PAUSE: 5 SECONDS
Question 30. You hear a physiotherapist giving a presentation about a study she's been involved in. Now read the question.

F: *I'm a physiotherapist, and I'm presenting our poster about constraint induced movement therapy for children suffering from partial paralysis following brain surgery.*

We did a case series of four children, who'd all undergone hemispherectomies. They were admitted to inpatient therapy within two weeks post-op and began therapy two to three weeks post-op. The therapy continued after they were discharged. Our findings were that three of the kids regained excellent function and mobility with ambulation and upper extremity function. One didn't do so well, unfortunately, but he gave up the therapy early on. This type of movement therapy has been used a lot in adult populations following stroke. The findings here promote moving forward with further research on the paediatric or adolescent population, following either hemispherectomy or other surgeries, to help us decide how appropriate this therapy would be for them.

PAUSE: 10 SECONDS

That is the end of Part B. Now, look at Part C.

PAUSE: 5 SECONDS

Part C. In this part of the test, you'll hear two different extracts. In each extract, you'll hear health professionals talking about aspects of their work.

For questions 31 to 42, choose the answer A, B or C which fits best according to what you hear. Complete your answers as you listen.

Now look at extract one.

Extract one. Questions 31 to 36. You hear a sports physiotherapist called Chris Maloney giving a presentation in which he describes treating a high jumper with a knee injury.

You now have 90 seconds to read questions 31 to 36.

PAUSE: 90 SECONDS

---***---

M: Hello. I'm Chris Maloney, a physiotherapist specialising in sports injuries, and I'd like to present a case study to give you an idea of the sort of work I do.

It features a very successful high jumper in her mid-twenties, who was referred to me with severe pain in her right knee – and that's the leg she takes off from when she jumps. What's more, when she'd stepped up her training in preparation for a big competition, the pain worsened, and she'd been forced to pull out of the event. After that, she'd taken several months off training to rest and get treatment from various therapists. To her dismay, however, not only did the pain continue, it actually got worse, meaning she was unable to do any strength training, let alone jump-specific work. By the time I saw her, she was on the verge of giving up, having lost virtually all belief in her ability.

My initial assessment quickly confirmed patellar tendinitis in the affected knee, accompanied by some swelling and significant tenderness over the lower part of the kneecap – this wasn't difficult to diagnose. I also noted that she was slightly overweight for her height and had rather flat feet, but that's not so unusual in high jumpers. Further assessment revealed that the gluteal muscles connecting the hips and thighs were considerably less sturdy than you'd expect in an athlete of this calibre, and both the lateral retinaculum connecting the patella to the femur and the ilio-tibial band – the ligament running down the outside of the thigh – were tight and tender.

As a first stage, I was keen to show I could help by relieving some of the pain. So, I worked at loosening her lateral retinaculum to see how much of the tendon pain was due to inflammation and how much came from restriction of normal patellar movement. This manipulation and massage instantly cleared the pain she'd felt while doing a single-leg dip exercise – where you stand on one leg and bend the knee. This indicated that her tendon pain was most likely due to patello-femoral joint dysfunction – caused by muscle imbalance and poor biomechanics – and not by an active inflammatory process or partial tear in her patellar tendon, so an MRI scan wasn't needed. The treatment continued along similar lines for some weeks, with loosening of the lateral retinaculum and deep-tissue massage of the ilio-tibial band and other muscles.

One option at this point was something called 'taping'. This is a way of reducing pain so that athletes can continue with strength exercises. But it seemed clear from early on that we shouldn't put taping on this patient's patella and tendon until she started jumping again. She was getting pain relief and progress simply from the manual techniques, and taping might've led to problems later on. Athletes often become dependent on tape and other accessories. In other words, instead of aiming for one-hundred percent muscle strength and joint position control, they settle for eighty percent plus artificial support.

The patient also had a specially designed programme of gym activities. Although she needed to restore power to those muscles affected by inflammation and tenderness, the priority was to get her posture and alignment right. She started by doing double-leg squats with her back to a wall in front of a mirror so that she could see whether her feet were arched and if her knees were over her feet. She also did squats whilst squeezing a ball between her knees. There was light leg press work, followed by single-leg stance work – first static, then on wobble-boards, and with elastic resistance. She progressed to moving on and off steps, sometimes holding weights, all the time paying close attention to positioning and muscle and joint alignment.

The next stage was to liaise with the patient's coach. She began running – jogging for stamina and then sprint sessions. Work on power was stepped up gradually and included some weightlifting. After some analysis, we also decided to modify her…her run-up to the high-jump bar. By beginning from a wider position and running in with much less of a curve, there was much less of an impact on the ankle, knees and hip, especially in her right jumping leg. Interestingly, the patient reported that remodelling the run-up felt fresh and motivating and helped to reinforce the sense she had of being a reborn athlete. Once the rehabilitation process was complete, she was able to compete without pain and free of any reliance on taping or knee-strapping.

So, before I go on to ….. [fade]

PAUSE: 10 SECONDS
Now look at extract two.

Extract two. Questions 37 to 42. You hear a clinical psychiatrist called Dr Anthony Gibbens giving a presentation about the value of individual patients' experiences and 'stories' in medicine.

You now have 90 seconds to read questions 37 to 42.

PAUSE: 90 SECONDS
---***---

M: Hello. My name's Anthony Gibbens. I'm a clinical psychiatrist and published author. I'd like to talk about something that's relevant to all medical professionals: the use of narratives in medicine.

Let me begin with a case study, sent to me by a colleague who shares my interest in the subject. The study featured a thirty-year-old man who was hospitalised for severe panic attacks. He was treated with 'narcoanalysis' but, feeling no relief, turned to alcohol and endured years of depression and social isolation. Four decades later, he was back in the psychiatric system, but for the first time he was prescribed the antidepressant, Zoloft. Six weeks later, he was discharged because the panic attacks and depression had disappeared. He lived a full life until his death nineteen years later. If the narrative was striking, it was even more so for its inclusion in a medical journal.

Repeatedly, I've been surprised by the impact that even lightly sketched case histories can have on readers. In my first book, I wrote about personality and how it might change on medication. My second was concerned with theories of intimacy. Readers, however, often used the books for a different purpose: identifying depression. Regularly I received and still receive phone calls, people saying 'My husband's just like X', one figure from a clinical example. Other readers wrote to say that they'd recognised themselves. Seeing that they weren't alone gave them hope. Encouragement is another benefit of case description, familiar to us in an age when everyone's writing their biography.

But this isn't to say that stories are a panacea to issues inherent in treating patients, and there can be disadvantages. Consider my experience prescribing Prozac. When certain patients reported feeling 'better than well' after receiving it, I presented these examples, first in essays for psychiatrists and then in my book, where I surrounded the narrative material with accounts of research. In time, my loosely supported descriptions led others to do controlled trials that confirmed the phenomenon. But doctors hadn't waited for those controlled trials. In advance, the better-than-well hypothesis had served as a tentative fact. Treating depression, colleagues looked out for personality change, even aimed for it, even though this wasn't my intended outcome.

This brings me to my next point. Often the knowledge that informs clinical decisions emerges when you stand back from it, like an impressionist painting. What initially seems like randomly scattered information begins to come together, and what you see is the bigger picture. That's where the true worth of anecdote lies. Beyond its role as illustration, hypothesis builder, and low-level guidance for practice, storytelling can act as a modest counterbalance to a narrow focus on data. If we rely solely on 'evidence', we risk moving toward a monoculture whereby patients and their afflictions become reduced to inanimate objects – a result I'd consider unfortunate, since there are many ways to influence people for the better. It's been my hope that, while we wait for conclusive science, stories will preserve diversity in our theories of mind.

My recent reading of outcome trials of antidepressants has strengthened my suspicion that the line between research and storytelling can be fuzzy. In medicine, randomised trials are rarely large enough to provide guidance on their own. Statisticians amalgamate many studies through a technique called meta-analysis. The first step of the process, deciding which data to include, colours the findings. Effectively, the numbers are narrative. Put simply, evidence-based medicine is judgment-based medicine in which randomised trials are carefully assessed and given their due. I don't think we need to be embarrassed about this. Our substantial formal findings require integration. The danger is in pretending otherwise.

I've long felt isolated in embracing the use of narratives in medicine, which is why I warm to the likelihood of narratives being used to inform future medical judgements. It would be unfortunate if medicine moved fully to squeeze the art out of its science by marginalising the narrative. Stories aren't just better at capturing the 'bigger picture' but the smaller picture too. I'm thinking of the article about the depressed man given the drug Zoloft. The degree of transformation in the patient was just as impressive as the length of observation. No formal research can offer a forty-year lead-in or a nineteen-year follow-up. Few studies report on both symptoms and social progress. Research reduces information about many people; narratives retain the texture of life in all its forms. We need storytelling, which is why I'll keep harping on about it until the message gets through.

PAUSE: 10 SECONDS
That is the end of Part C.

You now have two minutes to check your answers.

PAUSE: 120 SECONDS
That is the end of the Listening test.

Reading sub-test

Answer Key – Part A

READING SUB-TEST – ANSWER KEY

PART A: QUESTIONS 1-20

1	A
2	B
3	A
4	D
5	B
6	C
7	B
8	fine bore
9	water-based lubricant
10	tape
11	(a) syringe
12	15-30 minutes/mins OR fifteen-thirty minutes/mins
13	(turn) on(to) left side
14	(to) x-ray (department) OR (to) radiology
15	(a) feeding pump
16	stretch
17	gastroesophageal reflux
18	6/six Fr/French
19	breathlessness
20	(expressed) breast milk

Reading sub-test

Answer Key – Parts B & C

READING SUB-TEST – ANSWER KEY

PART B: QUESTIONS 1-6

1	A	this should be reported.
2	C	communicate their intentions to others.
3	B	best practice procedures
4	A	if non-disclosure could adversely affect those involved
5	A	act as a reminder of their obligations.
6	C	mild dementia in women can remain undiagnosed.

PART C: QUESTIONS 7-14

7	C	the fact that it is used so extensively.
8	A	can be found everywhere.
9	C	the time from exposure to disease may cause delayed diagnosis.
10	D	the degree of contact with asbestos fibres considered harmful.
11	B	tend to remain in the pulmonary tissue.
12	B	infection control
13	B	may pose a future health threat.
14	C	asbestosis as an ongoing medical issue.

PART C: QUESTIONS 15-22

15	B	He appreciates the reasons behind it.
16	C	busy working people who mean to be compliant.
17	B	They fail to recognise that some medical conditions require ongoing treatment.
18	D	Patients need to be informed about the likelihood of them occurring.
19	A	the long-term feasibility of the central idea
20	C	It sends the wrong message to patients.
21	D	a recommended response to the concerns of patients.
22	A	may ultimately have benefited from her non-compliance.

OCCUPATIONAL ENGLISH TEST

WRITING SUB-TEST: NURSING

SAMPLE RESPONSE: LETTER OF DISCHARGE

Ms Jane Rudik
Community Nurse
Newtown Community Health Centre
Newtown

15 July 2018

Dear Ms Rudik,

Re: Ms Mary Bell. 66 years of age.

Thank you for continuing the care of Ms Bell after her discharge from Newtown Community Hospital today. She was admitted due to unstable diabetes mellitus and a minor infected ulcer on her left foot.

Ms Bell is a Type 2 diabetic of 15 years. Her occasional problems with self-administering medication, combined with poor dietary habits and a recent increase in alcohol consumption is the likely cause of her admission on 24 June 2018.

Currently, Ms Bell takes Metformin 850mg t.d.s., Glimel 5mg daily and Augmentin Duo Forte 875/125mg orally, b.d., the latter needing review upon completion of her current course.

Having recently retired in 2017, Ms Bell survives on a small pension. Therefore, encouragement to begin supplementing this with an additional form of income would be beneficial. In addition, she requires your ongoing support for lifestyle changes including dietary adjustment and a decrease of her alcohol intake. Monitoring of her medication compliance and blood sugar levels, as well as encouragement for social activities and an exercise programme are highly recommended. A community social worker could prove invaluable during this time.

Your monitoring of her wound and ongoing management of her condition is greatly appreciated.

Please do not hesitate to contact me if you require further information.

Yours sincerely,

Nurse

NURSING

PRACTICE TEST 2

To listen to the audio, visit
https://www.occupationalenglishtest.org/audio

OCCUPATIONAL ENGLISH TEST

LISTENING SUB-TEST – QUESTION PAPER

CANDIDATE NUMBER:

LAST NAME:

FIRST NAME:

MIDDLE NAMES:

PROFESSION: Candidate details and photo will be printed here.

VENUE:

TEST DATE:

Passport Photo

CANDIDATE DECLARATION

By signing this, you agree not to disclose or use in any way (other than to take the test) or assist any other person to disclose or use any OET test or sub-test content. If you cheat or assist in any cheating, use any unfair practice, break any of the rules or regulations, or ignore any advice or information, you may be disqualified and your results may not be issued at the sole discretion of CBLA. CBLA also reserves its right to take further disciplinary action against you and to pursue any other remedies permitted by law. If a candidate is suspected of and investigated for malpractice, their personal details and details of the investigation may be passed to a third party where required.

CANDIDATE SIGNATURE: _____

TIME: APPROXIMATELY **40 MINUTES**

INSTRUCTIONS TO CANDIDATES

DO NOT open this question paper until you are told to do so.

One mark will be granted for each correct answer.

Answer **ALL** questions. Marks are **NOT** deducted for incorrect answers.

At the end of the test, you will have two minutes to check your answers.

At the end of the test, hand in this **Question Paper**.

You must not remove OET material from the test room.

HOW TO ANSWER THE QUESTIONS

Part A: Write your answers on this **Question Paper** by filling in the blanks. **Example: Patient:** _____ *Ray Sands*

Part B & Part C: Mark your answers on this **Question Paper** by filling in the circle using a 2B pencil. **Example:** Ⓐ

Ⓑ
Ⓒ

Occupational English Test
Listening Test

This test has three parts. In each part you'll hear a number of different extracts. At the start of each extract, you'll hear this sound: --beep—

You'll have time to read the questions before you hear each extract and you'll hear each extract **ONCE ONLY**. Complete your answers as you listen.

At the end of the test you'll have two minutes to check your answers.

Part A

In this part of the test, you'll hear two different extracts. In each extract, a health professional is talking to a patient.

For **questions 1-24**, complete the notes with information you hear.

Now, look at the notes for extract one.

Extract 1: Questions 1-12

You hear a consultant endocrinologist talking to a patient called Sarah Croft. For **questions 1-12**, complete the notes with a word or short phrase.

You now have 30 seconds to look at the notes.

Patient   Sarah Croft

Medical history
- hypertension (recently worsened)
- 3 years of corticosteroid treatment for **(1)** _____

General symptoms

- gradual weight gain, especially in stomach area
- **(2)** _____ on face: embarrassing
- visible **(3)** _____ between the shoulders
- swollen ankles
- excessive and constant **(4)** _____
- backache
- periods are **(5)** _____
- extreme tiredness

Dermatological symptoms

- tendency to **(6)** _____
- wounds slow to heal, **(7)** _____ on thighs
- face appears red in colour, **(8)** _____ area on neck
- recent development of **(9)** _____

Psychological symptoms

- mildly depressed

- scared by new experience of **(10)** _____

- feels constantly **(11)** _____

- intermittent cognitive difficulties

Recommended tests

- further blood tests

- **(12)** _____ test possibly

Extract 2: Questions 13-24

You hear an anaesthetist talking to a patient called Mary Wilcox prior to an operation. For **questions 13-24**, complete the notes with a word or short phrase.
You now have thirty seconds to look at the notes.

Patient Mary Wilcox

Current medications

Reason for medication	Medication	Comments
High blood pressure	Thiazide	both taken this morning with (14) _____
	(13) _____	
Heart attack	(15) _____	taken this morning
	(16) _____	stopped taking this 7 days ago

Medical history

- went to GP two years ago feeling **(17)**

  _____ – heart attack subsequently

  diagnosed

- had two **(18)** _____ inserted

Present condition

- alright with **(19)** _____ and walking on

  the flat

- has swelling in one ankle following operation for **(20)**

  _____

- denies **(21)** _____

- reports some **(22)** _____ at night

  (responds to medication)

Concerns expressed

- **(23)** _____ following the procedure

- possible damage to crowns (both are **(24)**

  _____)

That is the end of Part A. Now look at Part B.

Part B

In this part of the test, you'll hear six different extracts. In each extract, you'll hear people talking in a different healthcare setting.

For **questions 25-30**, choose the answer (**A**, **B** or **C**) which fits best according to what you hear. You'll have time to read each question before you listen. Complete your answers as you listen.

Now look at question 25.

25.   You hear two trainee doctors doing an activity at a staff training day.

What does the activity give practice in?

(**A**)   writing case notes

(**B**)   prioritising patients

(**C**)   dealing with consultants

26.   You hear a radiographer talking to a patient about her MRI scan.

What is he doing?

(**A**)   clarifying the aim of the procedure

(**B**)   dealing with her particular concerns

(**C**)   explaining how the equipment works

27.   You hear two nurses discussing an article in a nursing journal.

What do they agree about it?

(**A**)   It's likely to lead to changes in practice.

(**B**)   It failed to reach any definite conclusion.

(**C**)   It confirms what they were already thinking.

28. You hear two hospital managers talking about a time management course for staff.

They think that few people have shown interest because

(A) there are so many alternatives on offer.

(B) they feel it's not relevant to them.

(C) it hasn't been publicised enough.

29. You hear an optometrist reporting on some research he's been doing.

The aim of his research was

(A) to develop nanoparticles for transporting drugs all over the body.

(B) to find a way of treating infections caused by contact lenses.

(C) to use contact lenses to administer drugs over time.

30. You hear a consultant talking to a trainee about a patient's eye condition.

What is the consultant doing?

(A) explaining why intervention may not be necessary

(B) suggesting the diagnosis is by no means certain

(C) describing a possible complication

That is the end of Part B. Now look at Part C.

Part C

In this part of the test, you'll hear two different extracts. In each extract, you'll hear health professionals talking about aspects of their work.

For **questions 31-42**, choose the answer (**A, B** or **C**) which fits best according to what you hear. Complete your answers as you listen.

Now look at extract one.

Extract 1: Questions 31-36

You hear an interview with a neurosurgeon called Dr Ian Marsh who specialises in the treatment of concussion in sport.

You now have 90 seconds to read **questions 31-36**.

31.   Dr Marsh says that one aim of the new guidelines on concussion is

   (A)   to educate young sportspeople in how to avoid getting it.

   (B)   to correct some common misunderstandings about it.

   (C)   to provide a range of specialist advice about it.

32.   Dr Marsh makes the point that someone who has suffered a concussion will

   (A)   be unconscious for varying amounts of time after the event.

   (B)   need a medical examination before doing any further exercise.

   (C)   have to take precautions to avoid the risk of symptoms recurring.

33.   Dr Marsh says returning to sport too early after a concussion is dangerous because

   (A)   a subsequent episode can have a cumulative effect.

   (B)   there is a high risk of fatality in the event of a second one.

   (C)   the brains of younger people need time to return to normal size.

34. Dr Marsh suggests that the risk of sustaining a concussion in sports

    (A)   lies mainly in the choice of sports played.

    (B)   can be reduced by developing good playing technique.

    (C)   is greater when sports are played in less formal situations.

35. What is Dr Marsh's view about providing medical support for youth sports events?

    (A)   Some types of sport are risky enough to justify it.

    (B)   The organisers should be capable of dealing with any issues.

    (C)   Certain medical professionals should be encouraged to volunteer.

36. Dr Marsh thinks that developments in college football in the USA

    (A)   only really address an issue which is particular to that sport.

    (B)   are only likely to benefit the health of professional sports players.

    (C)   are a significant step forward in the prevention of concussion in all sports.

Now look at extract two.

Extract 2: Questions 37-42

You hear a presentation by a consultant cardiologist called Dr Pamela Skelton, who's talking about a research trial called SPRINT which investigated the effects of setting lower blood-pressure targets.

You now have 90 seconds to read **questions 37-42**.

37.   Why was the SPRINT trial stopped before it was due to end?

      (A)   There were conclusive results earlier than expected.

      (B)   The high drop-out rate was likely to invalidate the data.

      (C)   Concerns were raised about possible effects on all participants.

38.   A few participants aged over seventy-five left the trial because

      (A)   there was a negative impact on their daily life.

      (B)   they failed to take the required doses of medication.

      (C)   their health deteriorated due to pre-existing conditions.

39.   A significant feature of measuring blood pressure in the trial was that

      (A)   the highest of three readings was recorded.

      (B)   the patient was alone when it was carried out.

      (C)   it was done manually by the participant at home.

40. How did the SPRINT trial differ from the earlier ACCORD study into blood pressure?

(A) SPRINT had fewer participants.

(B) SPRINT involved higher-risk patients.

(C) SPRINT included patients with diabetes.

41. Dr Skelton's main reservation about the SPRINT trial is that

(A) it ignores the wider implications of lowered BP.

(B) its results go against the existing body of evidence.

(C) it was unduly influenced by pharmaceutical companies.

42. What impact does Dr Skelton think the SPRINT trial will have in the future?

(A) It will lead to universally applicable guidelines for BP levels.

(B) Increased attention will be given to the effect of lifestyle on BP.

(C) GPs will adopt a more active approach to lowering BP in the elderly.

That is the end of Part C.

You now have two minutes to check your answers.

END OF THE LISTENING TEST

READING SUB-TEST – TEXT BOOKLET: PART A

CANDIDATE NUMBER:

LAST NAME:

FIRST NAME:

MIDDLE NAMES:

PROFESSION:

VENUE:

TEST DATE:

Candidate details and photo will be printed here.

Passport Photo

CANDIDATE SIGNATURE: _____

INSTRUCTIONS TO CANDIDATES

You must **NOT** remove OET material from the test room.

www.occupationalenglishtest.org

© Cambridge Boxhill Language Assessment – ABN 51 988 559 414

[CANDIDATE NO.] READING TEXT BOOKLET PART A 01/04

Tetanus: Texts

Text A

Tetanus is a severe disease that can result in serious illness and death. Tetanus vaccination protects against the disease.

Tetanus (sometimes called lock-jaw) is a disease caused by the bacteria Clostridium tetani. Toxins made by the bacteria attack a person's nervous system. Although the disease is fairly uncommon, it can be fatal.

Early symptoms of tetanus include:

- Painful muscle contractions that begin in the jaw (lock jaw)
- Rigidity in neck, shoulder and back muscles
- Difficulty swallowing
- Violent generalized muscle spasms
- Convulsions
- Breathing difficulties

A person may have a fever and sometimes develop abnormal heart rhythms. Complications include pneumonia, broken bones (from the muscle spasms), respiratory failure and cardiac arrest.

There is no specific diagnostic laboratory test; diagnosis is made clinically. The spatula test is useful: touching the back of the pharynx with a spatula elicits a bite reflex in tetanus, instead of a gag reflex.

Text B

Tetanus Risk

Tetanus is an acute disease induced by the toxin tetanus bacilli, the spores of which are present in soil.

A TETANUS-PRONE WOUND IS:

- any wound or burn that requires surgical intervention that is delayed for > 6 hours
- any wound or burn at any interval after injury that shows one or more of the following characteristics:
    - a significant degree of tissue damage
    - puncture-type wound particularly where there has been contact with soil or organic matter which is likely to harbour tetanus organisms
- any wound from compound fractures
- any wound containing foreign bodies
- any wound or burn in patients who have systemic sepsis
- any bite wound
- any wound from tooth re-implantation

Intravenous drug users are at greater risk of tetanus. Every opportunity should be taken to ensure that they are fully protected against tetanus. Booster doses should be given if there is any doubt about their immunisation status.

Immunosuppressed patients may not be adequately protected against tetanus, despite having been fully immunised. They should be managed as if they were incompletely immunised.

Text C

Tetanus Immunisation following injuries

Thorough cleaning of the wound is essential irrespective of the immunisation history of the patient, and appropriate antibiotics should be prescribed.

Immunisation Status	Clean Wound	Tetanus-prone wound	
Vaccine		Vaccine	Human Tetanus Immunoglobulin (HTIG)
Fully immunised[1]	Not required	Not required	Only if high risk[2]
Primary immunisation complete, boosters incomplete but up to date	Not required	Not required	Only if high risk[2]
Primary immunisation incomplete or boosters not up to date	Reinforcing dose and further doses to complete recommended schedule	Reinforcing dose and further doses to complete recommended schedule	Yes (opposite limb to vaccine)
Not immunised or immunisation status not known/uncertain[3]	Immediate dose of vaccine followed by completion of full 5-dose course	Immediate dose of vaccine followed by completion of full 5-dose course	Yes (opposite limb to vaccine)

Notes

1. has received total of 5 doses of vaccine at appropriate intervals

2. heavy contamination with material likely to contain tetanus spores and/or extensive devitalised tissue

3. immunosuppressed patients presenting with a tetanus-prone wound should always be managed as if they were incompletely immunised

Text D

Human Tetanus Immunoglobulin (HTIG)

Indications

- treatment of clinically suspected cases of tetanus
- prevention of tetanus in high-risk, tetanus-prone wounds

Dose

Available in 1ml ampoules containing 250IU

Prevention Dose	Treatment Dose
250 IU by IM injection[1] Or 500 IU by IM injection[1] if >24 hours since injury/risk of heavy contamination/burns	5,000 – 10,000 IU by IV infusion Or 150 IU/kg by IM injection[1] (given in multiple sites) if IV preparation unavailable

[1] Due to its viscosity, HTIG should be administered slowly, using a 23 gauge needle

Contraindications

- Confirmed anaphylactic reaction to tetanus containing vaccine
- Confirmed anaphylactic reaction to neomycin, streptomycin or polymyxin B

Adverse reactions

Local – pain, erythema, induration (Arthus-type reaction)

General – pyrexia, hypotonic-hyporesponsive episode, persistent crying

END OF PART A

THIS TEXT BOOKLET WILL BE COLLECTED

OCCUPATIONAL ENGLISH TEST

READING SUB-TEST – QUESTION PAPER: PART A

TIME: 15 MINUTES

INSTRUCTIONS TO CANDIDATES

DO NOT open this **Question Paper** or the **Text Booklet** until you are told to do so.

Write your answers on the spaces provided on this **Question Paper.**

You must answer the questions within the 15-minute time limit.

One mark will be granted for each correct answer.

Answer **ALL** questions. Marks are **NOT** deducted for incorrect answers.

At the end of the 15 minutes, hand in this **Question Paper** and the **Text Booklet.**

DO NOT remove OET material from the test room.

Part A

TIME: 15 minutes

- Look at the four texts, **A-D**, in the separate **Text Booklet**.

- For each question, **1-20**, look through the texts, **A-D**, to find the relevant information.

- Write your answers on the spaces provided in this **Question Paper**.

- Answer all the questions within the 15-minute time limit.

- Your answers should be correctly spelt.

Tetanus: Questions

Questions 1-6

For each question, **1-6**, decide which text (**A, B, C** or **D**) the information comes from.
You may use any letter more than once.

In which text can you find information about

1	the type of injuries that may lead to tetanus?	_____
2	signs that a patient may have tetanus?	_____
3	how to decide whether a tetanus vaccine is necessary?	_____
4	an alternative name for tetanus?	_____
5	possible side-effects of a particular tetanus medication?	_____
6	other conditions which are associated with tetanus?	_____

Questions 7-13

Complete each of the sentences, **7-13**, with a word or short phrase from one of the texts.
Each answer may include words, numbers or both.

Patients at increased risk of tetanus:

7   If a patient has been touching _____ or earth, they are more susceptible to tetanus.

8   Any _____ lodged in the site of an injury will increase the likelihood of tetanus.

9   Patients with _____ fractures are prone to tetanus.

10   Delaying surgery on an injury or burn by more than _____ increases the probability of tetanus.

11   If a burns patient has been diagnosed with _____ they are more liable to contract tetanus.

12   A patient who is ___ _____ or a regular recreational drug user will be at greater risk of tetanus.

Management of tetanus-prone injuries:

13   Clean the wound thoroughly and prescribe _____ if necessary, followed by tetanus vaccine and HTIG as appropriate.

Questions 14-20

Answer each of the questions, **14-20**, with a word or short phrase from one of the texts. Each answer may include words, numbers or both.

14   Where will a patient suffering from tetanus first experience muscle contractions?

_____

15   What can muscle spasms in tetanus patients sometimes lead to?

_____

16   If you test for tetanus using a spatula, what type of reaction will confirm the condition?

_____

17   How many times will you have to vaccinate a patient who needs a full course of tetanus vaccine?

_____

18   What should you give a drug user if you're uncertain of their vaccination history?

_____

19   What size of needle should you use to inject HTIG?

_____

20   What might a patient who experienced an adverse reaction to HTIG be unable to stop doing?

_____

END OF PART A
THIS QUESTION PAPER WILL BE COLLECTED

READING SUB-TEST – QUESTION PAPER: PARTS B & C

CANDIDATE NUMBER:

LAST NAME:

FIRST NAME:

MIDDLE NAMES:

PROFESSION:

Candidate details and photo will be printed here.

VENUE:

TEST DATE:

Passport Photo

CANDIDATE DECLARATION

By signing this, you agree not to disclose or use in any way (other than to take the test) or assist any other person to disclose or use any OET test or sub-test content. If you cheat or assist in any cheating, use any unfair practice, break any of the rules or regulations, or ignore any advice or information, you may be disqualified and your results may not be issued at the sole discretion of CBLA. CBLA also reserves its right to take further disciplinary action against you and to pursue any other remedies permitted by law. If a candidate is suspected of and investigated for malpractice, their personal details and details of the investigation may be passed to a third party where required.

CANDIDATE SIGNATURE: _____

TIME: 45 MINUTES

INSTRUCTIONS TO CANDIDATES

DO NOT open this **Question Paper** until you are told to do so.

One mark will be granted for each correct answer.

Answer **ALL** questions. Marks are **NOT** deducted for incorrect answers.

At the end of the test, hand in this **Question Paper**.

HOW TO ANSWER THE QUESTIONS:

Mark your answers on this **Question Paper** by filling in the circle using a 2B pencil. **Example:** Ⓐ
Ⓑ
Ⓒ

Part B

In this part of the test, there are six short extracts relating to the work of health professionals. For **questions 1-6**, choose answer (**A, B** or **C**) which you think fits best according to the text.

1.   Nursing staff can remove a dressing if

   (**A**)   a member of the surgical team is present.

   (**B**)   there is severe leakage from the wound.

   (**C**)   they believe that the wound has healed.

Post-operative dressings

Dressings are an important component of post-operative wound management. Any dressings applied during surgery have been done in sterile conditions and should ideally be left in place, as stipulated by the surgical team. It is acceptable for initial dressings to be removed prematurely in order to have the wound reviewed and, in certain situations, apply a new dressing. These situations include when the dressing is no longer serving its purpose (i.e. dressing falling off, excessive exudate soaking through the dressing and resulting in a suboptimal wound healing environment) or when a wound complication is suspected.

---

2.   As explained in the protocol, the position of the RUM container will ideally

(A)   encourage participation in the scheme.

(B)   emphasise the value of recycling.

(C)   facilitate public access to it.

Unwanted medicine: pharmacy collection protocol

A Returned Unwanted Medicine (RUM) Project approved container will be delivered by the wholesaler to the participating pharmacy.

The container is to be kept in a section of the dispensary or in a room or enclosure in the pharmacy to which the public does not have access. The container may be placed in a visible position, but out of reach of the public, as this will reinforce the message that unwanted prescription drugs can be returned to the pharmacy and that the returned medicines will not be recycled.

Needles, other sharps and liquid cytotoxic products should not be placed in the container, but in one specifically designed for such waste.

---

3. The report mentioned in the memo suggests that

(A)   data about patient errors may be incomplete.

(B)   errors by hospital staff can often go unreported.

(C)   errors in prescriptions pose the greatest threat to patients.

Memo: Report on oral anti-cancer medications
Nurse Unit Managers are directed to review their systems for the administration of oral anti-cancer drugs, and the reporting of drug errors. Serious concerns have been raised in a recent report drawing on a national survey of pharmacists. Please note the following paragraph quoted from the report: Incorrect doses of oral anti-cancer medicines can have fatal consequences. Over the previous four years, there were three deaths and 400 patient safety issues involving oral anti-cancer medicines. Half of the reports concerned the wrong dosage, frequency, quantity or duration of oral anti-cancer treatment. Of further concern is that errors on the part of patients may be under-reported. In light of these reports, there is clearly a need for improved systems covering the management of patients receiving oral therapies.

4. What point does the training manual make about anaesthesia workstations?

(A) Parts of the equipment have been shown to be vulnerable to failure.

(B) There are several ways of ensuring that the ventilator is working effectively.

(C) Monitoring by health professionals is a reliable way to maintain patient safety.

Anaesthesia Workstations

Studies on safety in anaesthesia have documented that human vigilance alone is inadequate to ensure patient safety and have underscored the importance of monitoring devices. These findings are reflected in improved standards for equipment design, guidelines for patient monitoring and reduced malpractice premiums for the use of capnography and pulse oximetry during anaesthesia. Anaesthesia workstations integrate ventilator technology with patient monitors and alarms to help prevent patient injury in the unlikely event of a ventilator failure. Furthermore, since the reservoir bag is part of the circuit during mechanical ventilation, the visible movement of the reservoir bag is confirmation that the ventilator is functioning.

5.   In cases of snakebite, the flying doctor should be aware of

(A)   where to access specific antivenoms.

(B)   the appropriate method for wound cleaning.

(C)   the patients most likely to suffer complications.

Memo to Flying Doctor staff: Antivenoms for snakebite

Before starting treatment:

- Do not wash the snakebite site.
- If possible, determine the type of snake by using a 'snake-venom detection kit' to test a bite site swab or, in systemic envenoming, the person's urine. If venom detection is not available or has proved negative, seek advice from a poisons information centre.
- Testing blood for venom is not reliable.
- Assess the degree of envenoming; not all confirmed snakebites will result in systemic envenoming; risk varies with the species of snake.
- People with pre-existing renal, hepatic, cardiac or respiratory impairment and those taking anticoagulant or antiplatelet drugs may have an increased risk of serious outcome from snakebite. Children are also especially at increased risk of severe envenoming because of smaller body mass and the likelihood of physical activity immediately after a bite.

6.   What was the purpose of the BMTEC forum?

(A)   to propose a new way of carrying out cleaning audits

(B)   to draw conclusions from the results of cleaning audits

(C)   to encourage more groups to undertake cleaning audits

Cleaning Audits
Three rounds of environmental cleaning audits were completed in 2013-2014. Key personnel in each facility were surveyed to assess the understanding of environmental cleaning from the perspective of the nurse unit manager, environmental services manager and the director of clinical governance. Each facility received a report about their environmental cleaning audits and lessons learned from the surveys. Data from the 15 units were also provided to each facility for comparison purposes.   The knowledge and experiences from the audits were shared at the BMTEC Forum in August 2014. This forum allowed environmental services managers, cleaners, nurses and clinical governance to discuss the application of the standards and promote new and improved cleaning practice. The second day of the forum focused on auditor training and technique with the view of enhancing internal environmental cleaning auditing by the participating groups.

Part C

In this part of the test, there are two texts about different aspects of healthcare. For **questions 7-22**, choose the answer (**A**, **B**, **C** or **D**) which you think fits best according to the text.

Text 1: Does homeopathy 'work'?

For many, homeopathy is simply unscientific, but regular users hold a very different view.

Homeopathy works by giving patients very dilute substances that, in larger doses, would cause the very symptoms that need curing. Taking small doses of these substances – derived from plants, animals or minerals – strengthens the body's ability to heal and increases resistance to illness or infection. Or that is the theory. The debate about its effectiveness is nothing new. Recently, Australia's National Health and Medical Research Council (NHMRC) released a paper which found there were 'no health conditions for which there was reliable evidence that homeopathy was effective'. This echoed a report from the UK House of Commons which said that the evidence failed to show a 'credible physiological mode of action' for homeopathic products, and that what data were available showed homeopathic products to be no better than placebo. Yet Australians spend at least $11 million per year on homeopathy.

So what's going on? If Australians – and citizens of many other nations around the world – are voting with their wallets, does this mean homeopathy must be doing something right? 'For me, the crux of the debate is a disconnect between how the scientific and medical community view homeopathy, and what many in the wider community are getting out of it,' says Professor Alex Broom of the University of Queensland. 'The really interesting question is how can we possibly have something that people think works, when to all intents and purposes, from a scientific perspective, it doesn't?'

Part of homeopathy's appeal may lie in the nature of the patient-practitioner consultation. In contrast to a typical 15-minute GP consultation, a first homeopathy consultation might take an hour and a half. 'We don't just look at an individual symptom in isolation. For us, that symptom is part of someone's overall health condition,' says Greg Cope, spokesman for the Australian Homeopathic Association. 'Often we'll have a consultation with someone and find details their GP simply didn't have time to.' Writer Johanna Ashmore is a case in point. She sees her homeopath for a one-hour monthly consultation. 'I feel, if I go and say I've got this health concern, she's going to treat my body to fight it rather than just treat the symptom.'

Most people visit a homeopath after having received a diagnosis from a 'mainstream' practitioner, often because they want an alternative choice to medication, says Greg Cope. 'Generally speaking, for a homeopath, their preference is if someone has a diagnosis from a medical practitioner before starting homeopathic treatment, so it's rare for someone to come and see us with an undiagnosed condition and certainly if they do come undiagnosed, we'd want to refer them on and get that medical evaluation before starting a course of treatment,' he says.

Given that homeopathic medicines are by their very nature incredibly dilute – and, some might argue, diluted beyond all hope of efficacy – they are unlikely to cause any adverse effects, so where's the harm? Professor Paul Glasziou, chair of the NHMRC's Homeopathy Working Committee, says that while financial cost is one harm, potentially more harmful are the non-financial costs associated with missing out on effective treatments. 'If it's just a cold, I'm not too worried. But if it's for a serious illness, you may not be taking disease-modifying treatments, and most worrying is things like HIV which affect not only you, but people around you,' says Glasziou. This is a particular concern with homeopathic vaccines, he says, which jeopardise the 'herd immunity' – the immunity of a significant proportion of the population – which is crucial in containing outbreaks of vaccine-preventable diseases.

The question of a placebo effect inevitably arises, as studies repeatedly seem to suggest that whatever benefits are being derived from homeopathy are more a product of patient faith rather than of any active ingredient of the medications. However, Greg Cope dismisses this argument, pointing out that homeopathy appears to benefit even the sceptics: 'We might see kids first, then perhaps Mum and after a couple of years, Dad will follow and, even though he's only there reluctantly, we get **wonderful outcomes**. This cannot be explained simply by the placebo effect.' As a patient, Johanna Ashmore is aware scientific research does little to support homeopathy but can still see its benefits. 'If seeing my homeopath each month improves my health, I'm happy. I don't care how it works, even if it's all in the mind – I just know that it does.'

But if so many people around the world are placing their faith in homeopathy, despite the evidence against it, Broom questions why homeopathy seeks scientific validation. The problem, as he sees it, lies in the fact that 'if you're going to dance with conventional medicine and say "we want to be proven to be effective in dealing with discrete physiological conditions", then you indeed do have to show efficacy. In my view **this** is not about broader credibility per se, it's about scientific and medical credibility – there's actually quite a lot of cultural credibility surrounding homeopathy within the community but that's not replicated in the scientific literature.'

Text 1: Questions 7-14

7.   The two reports mentioned in the first paragraph both concluded that homeopathy

(A)   could be harmful if not used appropriately.

(B)   merely works on the same basis as the placebo effect.

(C)   lacks any form of convincing proof of its value as a treatment.

(D)   would require further investigation before it was fully understood.

8.   When commenting on the popularity of homeopathy, Professor Broom shows his

(A)   surprise at people's willingness to put their trust in it.

(B)   frustration at scientists' inability to explain their views on it.

(C)   acceptance of the view that the subject may merit further study.

(D)   concern over the risks people face when receiving such treatment.

9.   Johanna Ashmore's views on homeopathy highlight

(A)   how practitioners put their patients at ease.

(B)   the key attraction of the approach for patients.

(C)   how it suits patients with a range of health problems.

(D)   the opportunities to improve patient care which GPs miss.

10.   In the fourth paragraph, it is suggested that visits to homeopaths

(A)   occasionally depend on a referral from a mainstream doctor.

(B)   frequently result from a patient's treatment preferences.

(C)   should be preceded by a visit to a relevant specialist.

(D)   often reveal previously overlooked medical problems.

11. What particularly concerns Professor Glasziou?

    (A)   the risks to patients of relying on homeopathic vaccinations

    (B)   the mistaken view that homeopathic treatments can only do good

    (C)   the way that homeopathic remedies endanger more than just the user

    (D)   the ineffectiveness of homeopathic remedies against even minor illnesses

12. Greg Cope uses the expression '**wonderful outcomes**' to underline

    (A)   the ability of homeopathy to defy its scientific critics.

    (B)   the value of his patients' belief in the whole process.

    (C)   the claim that he has solid proof that homeopathy works.

    (D)   the way positive results can be achieved despite people's doubts.

13. From the comments quoted in the sixth paragraph, it is clear that Johanna Ashmore is

    (A)   prepared to accept that homeopathy may depend on psychological factors.

    (B)   happy to admit that she was uncertain at first about proceeding.

    (C)   sceptical about the evidence against homeopathic remedies.

    (D)   confident that research will eventually validate homeopathy.

14. What does the word '**this**' in the final paragraph refer to?

    (A)   the continuing inability of homeopathy to gain scientific credibility

    (B)   the suggestion that the scientific credibility of homeopathy is in doubt

    (C)   the idea that there is no need to pursue scientific acceptance for homeopathy

    (D)   the motivation behind the desire for homeopathy to gain scientific acceptance

Text 2: Brain-controlled prosthetics

Paralysed from the neck down by a stroke, Cathy Hutchinson stared fixedly at a drinking straw in a bottle on the table in front of her. A cable rose from the top of her head, connecting her to a robot arm, but her gaze never wavered as she mentally guided the robot arm, which was opposite her, to close its grippers around the bottle, then slowly lift the vessel towards her mouth. Only when she finally managed to take a sip did her face relax. This example illustrates the strides being taken in brain-controlled prosthetics. But Hutchinson's focused stare also illustrates the one crucial feature still missing from prosthetics. Her eyes could tell her where the arm was, but she couldn't feel what it was doing.

Prosthetics researchers are now trying to create prosthetics that can 'feel'. It's a **daunting** task: the researchers have managed to read signals from the brain; now they must write information into the nervous system. Touch encompasses a complicated mix of information – everything from the soft prickliness of wool to the slipping of a sweaty soft-drink can. The sensations arise from a host of receptors in the skin, which detect texture, vibration, pain, temperature and shape, as well as from receptors in the muscles, joints and tendons that contribute to 'proprioception' – the sense of where a limb is in space. Prosthetics are being outfitted with sensors that can gather many of these sensations, but the challenge is to get the resulting signals flowing to the correct part of the brain.

For people who have had limbs amputated, the obvious way to achieve that is to route the signals into the remaining nerves in the stump, the part of the limb left after amputation. Ken Horch, a neuroprosthetics researcher, has done just that by threading electrodes into the nerves in stumps then stimulating them with a tiny current, so that patients felt like their fingers were moving or being touched. The technique can even allow patients to distinguish basic features of objects: a man who had lost his lower arms was able to determine the difference between blocks made of wood or foam rubber by using a sensor-equipped prosthetic hand. He correctly identified the objects' size and softness more than twice as often as would have been expected by chance. Information about force and finger position was delivered from the prosthetic to a computer, which prompted stimulation of electrodes implanted in his upper-arm nerves.

As promising as this result was, researchers will probably need to stimulate hundreds or thousands of nerve fibres to create complex sensations, and they'll need to keep the devices working for many years if they are to minimise the number of surgeries required to replace them as they wear out. To get around this, some researchers are instead trying to give patients sensory feedback by touching their skin. The technique was discovered by accident by researcher Todd Kuiken. The idea was to rewire arm nerves that used to serve the hand, for example, to muscles in other parts of the body. When the patient thought about closing his or her hand, the newly targeted muscle would contract and generate an electric signal, driving movement of the prosthetic.

However, this technique won't work for stroke patients like Cathy Hutchinson. So some researchers are skipping directly to the brain. In principle, this should be straightforward. Because signals from specific parts of the body go to specific parts of the brain, scientists should be able to create sensations of touch or proprioception in the limb by directly activating the neurons that normally receive those signals. However, with electrical stimulation, all neurons close to the electrode's tip are activated indiscriminately, so 'even if I had the sharpest needle in the Universe, that could create unintended effects', says Arto Nurmikko, a neuroengineer. For example, an attempt to create sensation in one finger might produce sensation in other parts of the hand as well, he says.

Nurmikko and other researchers are therefore using light, in place of electricity, to activate highly specific groups of neurons and recreate a sense of touch. They trained a monkey to remove its hand from a pad when it vibrated. When the team then stimulated the part of its brain that receives tactile information from the hand with a light source implanted in its skull, the monkey lifted its hand off the pad about 90% of the time. The use of such techniques in humans is still probably 10–20 years away, but it is a promising strategy.

Even if such techniques can be made to work, it's unclear how closely they will approximate natural sensations. Tingles, pokes and vibrations are still **a far cry from** the complicated sensations that we feel when closing a hand over an apple, or running a finger along a table's edge. But patients don't need a perfect sense of touch, says Douglas Weber, a bioengineer. Simply having enough feedback to improve their control of grasp could help people to perform tasks such as picking up a glass of water, he explains. He goes on to say that patients who wear cochlear implants, for example, are often happy to regain enough hearing to hold a phone conversation, even if they're still unable to distinguish musical subtleties.

Text 2: Questions 15-22

15. What do we learn about the experiment Cathy Hutchinson took part in?

    (A) It required intense concentration.

    (B) It failed to achieve what it had set out to do.

    (C) It could be done more quickly given practice.

    (D) It was the first time that it had been attempted.

16. The task facing researchers is described as '**daunting**' because

    (A) signals from the brain can be misunderstood.

    (B) it is hard to link muscle receptors with each other.

    (C) some aspects of touch are too difficult to reproduce.

    (D) the connections between sensors and the brain need to be exact.

17. What is said about the experiment done on the patient in the third paragraph?

    (A) There was statistical evidence that it was successful.

    (B) It enabled the patient to have a wide range of feeling.

    (C) Its success depended on when amputation had taken place.

    (D) It required the use of a specially developed computer program.

18. What drawback does the writer mention in the fourth paragraph?

    (A) The devices have a high failure rate.

    (B) Patients might have to undergo too many operations.

    (C) It would only be possible to create rather simple sensations.

    (D) The research into the new technique hasn't been rigorous enough.

19. What point is made in the fifth paragraph?

    (A) Severed nerves may be able to be reconnected.

    (B) More research needs to be done on stroke victims.

    (C) Scientists' previous ideas about the brain have been overturned.

    (D) It is difficult for scientists to pinpoint precise areas with an electrode.

20. What do we learn about the experiment that made use of light?

    (A) It can easily be replicated in humans.

    (B) It worked as well as could be expected.

    (C) It may have more potential than electrical stimulation.

    (D) It required more complex surgery than previous experiments.

21. In the final paragraph, the writer uses the phrase '**a far cry from**' to underline

    (A) how much more there is to achieve.

    (B) how complex experiments have become.

    (C) the need to reduce people's expectations.

    (D) the differences between types of artificial sensation.

22. Why does Weber give the example of a cochlear implant?

    (A) to underline the need for a similar breakthrough in prosthetics

    (B) to illustrate the fact that some sensation is better than none

    (C) to highlight the advances made in other areas of medicine

    (D) to demonstrate the ability of the body to relearn skills

END OF READING TEST
THIS BOOKLET WILL BE COLLECTED

WRITING SUB-TEST – TEST BOOKLET

CANDIDATE NUMBER:	
LAST NAME:	
FIRST NAME:	
MIDDLE NAMES:	Passport Photo
PROFESSION:	Candidate details and photo will be printed here.
VENUE:	
TEST DATE:	

CANDIDATE SIGNATURE: _____

INSTRUCTIONS TO CANDIDATES

You must write your answer for the Writing sub-test in the **Writing Answer Booklet.**

You must **NOT** remove OET material from the test room.

OCCUPATIONAL ENGLISH TEST

WRITING SUB-TEST: NURSING

TIME ALLOWED: **READING TIME:**   **5 MINUTES**
                     WRITING TIME: **40 MINUTES**

Read the case notes below and complete the writing task which follows.

Notes:

You are a ward nurse in the cardiac unit of Greenville Public Hospital. Your patient, Ms Martin, is due to be discharged tomorrow.

Patient:	Ms Margaret Helen Martin
Address:	23 Third Avenue, Greenville
Age:	82 years old (DOB: 25 July 1935)
Admission date:	15 July 2018

Social/family background:
> Never married, no children
> Lives in own house in Greenville
> Financially independent
> Three siblings (all unwell) and five nieces/nephews living in greater Greenville area
> Contact with family intermittent
> No longer drives
> Has 'meals on wheels' (meal delivery service for elderly) – Mon-Fri (lunch and dinner), orders frozen meals for weekends

Diagnosis: Coronary artery disease (CAD), angina

Treatment: Angioplasty (repeat – first 2008)

Discharge date: 16 July 2018, pending cardiologist's report

Medical information:
> Coeliac disease
> Angioplasty 2008
> Anxious about health – tends to focus on health problems
> Coronary artery disease → aspirin, clopidogrel (Plavix)
> Hypertension → metoprolol (Betaloc), ramipril (Tritace)
> Hypercholesterolemia (8.3) → atorvastatin (Lipitor)
> Overweight (BMI 29.5)
> Sedentary (orders groceries over phone to be delivered, neighbour walks dog)
> Family history of coronary heart disease (mother, 2 of 3 brothers)
> Hearing loss – wears hearing aid

Nursing management and progress during hospital stay:

    Routine post-operative recovery

    Tolerating light diet and fluids

    Bruising at catheter insertion site, no signs of infection/bleeding noted post-procedure

    Pt anxious about return home, not sure whether she will cope

Discharge plan: **Dietary**

    Low-calorie, high-protein, low-cholesterol, gluten-free diet (supervised by dietitian, referred by Dr)

    Frequent small meals or snacks

    Drink plenty of fluids

    Physiotherapy

    Daily light exercise (e.g., 15-minute walk, exercise plan monitored by physiotherapist)

    No heavy lifting for 12 weeks

    Other

    Monitor wound site for bruising or infection

    Monitor adherence to medication regime

    Arrange regular family visits to monitor progress

Anticipated needs of Pt:

    Need home visits from community health/district nurse – monitor adherence to post-operative medication, exercise, dietary regime

    Regular monitoring by Dr, dietitian, physiotherapist

    ? Danger of social isolation (infrequent family support)

Writing Task:

Using the information in the case notes, write a letter to the Nurse-in-Charge of the District Nursing Service outlining Ms Martin's situation and anticipated needs following her return home tomorrow. Address the letter to Nurse-in-Charge, District Nursing Service, Greenville Community Health Care Centre, 88 Highton Road, Greenville.

In your answer:

- **Expand the relevant notes into complete sentences**
- **Do <u>not</u> use note form**
- **Use letter format**

The body of the letter should be approximately 180–200 words.

OCCUPATIONAL ENGLISH TEST

WRITING SUB-TEST – ANSWER BOOKLET

CANDIDATE NUMBER:

LAST NAME:

FIRST NAME:

MIDDLE NAMES:

PROFESSION: Candidate details and photo will be printed here.

VENUE:

TEST DATE:

Passport Photo

CANDIDATE DECLARATION

By signing this, you agree not to disclose or use in any way (other than to take the test) or assist any other person to disclose or use any OET test or sub-test content. If you cheat or assist in any cheating, use any unfair practice, break any of the rules or regulations, or ignore any advice or information, you may be disqualified and your results may not be issued at the sole discretion of CBLA. CBLA also reserves its right to take further disciplinary action against you and to pursue any other remedies permitted by law. If a candidate is suspected of and investigated for malpractice, their personal details and details of the investigation may be passed to a third party where required.

CANDIDATE SIGNATURE: _____

TIME ALLOWED
READING TIME: 5 MINUTES
WRITING TIME: 40 MINUTES

INSTRUCTIONS TO CANDIDATES

1. **Reading time: 5 minutes**
   During this time you may study the writing task and notes. You **MUST NOT** write, highlight, underline or make any notes.

2. **Writing time: 40 minutes**

3. Use the back page for notes and rough draft only. Notes and rough draft will **NOT** be marked.

   Please write your answer clearly on page 1 and page 2.

   Cross out anything you **DO NOT** want the examiner to consider.

4. You must write your answer for the Writing sub-test in this **Answer Booklet** using **pen or pencil**.

5. You must **NOT** remove OET material from the test room.

www.occupationalenglishtest.org
© Cambridge Boxhill Language Assessment – ABN 51 988 559 414

[CANDIDATE NO.] WRITING SUB-TEST ANSWER BOOKLET 01/04

Please record your answer on this page.

(Only answers on Page 1 and Page 2 will be marked.)

_____

_____

_____

_____

_____

_____

_____

_____

_____

_____

_____

_____

_____

_____

_____

_____

_____

_____

_____

_____

_____

_____

_____

_____

_____

_____

_____

_____

OET Writing sub-test – Answer booklet   1

Please record your answer on this page.

(Only answers on Page 1 and Page 2 will be marked.)

_____

_____

_____

_____

_____

_____

_____

_____

_____

_____

_____

_____

_____

_____

_____

_____

_____

_____

_____

_____

_____

_____

_____

_____

_____

_____

_____

_____

_____

_____

_____

_____

OET Writing sub-test – Answer booklet 2

Space for notes and rough draft. Only your answers on Page 1 and Page 2 will be marked.

SPEAKING SUB-TEST

CANDIDATE NUMBER:

LAST NAME:

FIRST NAME:

MIDDLE NAMES:

PROFESSION:

VENUE:

TEST DATE:

Your details and photo will be printed here.

Passport Photo

CANDIDATE DECLARATION

By signing this, you agree not to disclose or use in any way (other than to take the test) or assist any other person to disclose or use any OET test or sub-test content. If you cheat or assist in any cheating, use any unfair practice, break any of the rules or regulations, or ignore any advice or information, you may be disqualified and your results may not be issued at the sole discretion of CBLA. CBLA also reserves its right to take further disciplinary action against you and to pursue any other remedies permitted by law. If a candidate is suspected of and investigated for malpractice, their personal details and details of the investigation may be passed to a third party where required.

CANDIDATE SIGNATURE: _____

INSTRUCTION TO CANDIDATES

Please confirm with the Interlocutor that your roleplay card number and colour match the Interlocutor card before you begin.

Interlocutor to complete only

ID No: _____   Passport: ☐   National ID: ☐   Alternative ID approved: ☐

Speaking sub-test:

ID document sighted? ☐   Photo match? ☐   Signature match? ☐   Did not attend? ☐

Interlocutor name: _____

Interlocutor signature: _____

ROLEPLAYER CARD NO. 1   **NURSING**

SETTING   Emergency Department, Local Hospital

PATIENT   You are 35. You were involved in a car accident earlier today and are suffering from whiplash and a headache. You are feeling sorry for yourself and are impatient to be better.

TASK
- Be confused that you have been kept in hospital for so long, given there are no signs of broken bones, cuts or bruises.
- Ask why you are being given medication.
- Stress that you want to get better in the shortest time possible. Ask if physiotherapy will shorten the recovery period.
- Ask about the length of the treatment. How long will it be before you are better?
- Ask if there is anything else you need to know.
- Ask if there could be 'after effects' or on-going problems as a result of your accident.

Sample role-play

CANDIDATE CARD NO. 1   **NURSING**

SETTING   Emergency Department, Local Hospital

NURSE   This 35-year-old patient was involved in a car accident earlier today and is now suffering from a headache and whiplash (an injury to the cervical spine). He/she is being kept in the hospital for observation but is expected to be discharged later in the day.

TASK
- Find out what the patient thinks are the reasons why he/she is being kept in the hospital.
- Advise the patient on the reason for taking and continuing to take medication, and ways of managing the pain once he/she returns home (e.g., with heat/ice, analgesics, a collar, etc.).
- Discuss the best care practices for after the patient leaves the hospital. Describe the benefits of consulting a physiotherapist about exercise and relaxation exercises to loosen up the joints.
- Explain that you cannot be sure how long the patient will take to recover fully.
- Stress the importance of complying with the treatment and exercise program.
- Stress the importance of seeking medical advice if there is any increased pain or discomfort, nausea, vomiting, or vision problems.

Sample role-play

ROLEPLAYER CARD NO. 2	NURSING

SETTING   Community Health Centre

CARER   You are visiting your local health centre to obtain information about your mother's most recent health report. Your mother is now eighty years old and is becoming somewhat forgetful. She is a very independent person and does not like your interfering in her personal affairs. However, she told you recently that when she had her three-monthly check-up, the doctor said her cholesterol level was fairly high. The purpose of your visit is to learn more about cholesterol and how best to reduce it.

TASK
- If the nurse doesn't explain it, find out what cholesterol is.

- Ask what the doctor meant by a fairly high level of cholesterol. Explain that you are concerned that her condition could develop into something worse.

- Ask what the nurse considers your mother's cholesterol level should be.

- Ask for advice about what your mother should do to lower her cholesterol level.

      Sample role-play

CANDIDATE CARD NO. 2	NURSING

SETTING   Community Health Centre

NURSE   The son/daughter of an eighty-year-old woman has come to ask for information about cholesterol. He/she wants information about his/her mother's current cholesterol level and how best to reduce it.

TASK
- Find out what the son/daughter already knows about cholesterol.
- Inform your visitor about what cholesterol is (fat-like material present in the blood and most tissues) and about types of cholesterol (high density lipoproteins (HDL) – good, low density lipoproteins (LDL) – bad).
- Tactfully explain that if the fatty deposits are lodged in the arteries, this can lead to heart disease or stroke.

- Explain what the doctor meant by a fairly high level of cholesterol (i.e., elevated above 5.5 mmols/litre in the blood).
- Advise your visitor about how his/her mother can best deal with her cholesterol (e.g., avoid saturated fats and eat more fibre, etc.).

      Sample role-play

Listening sub-test

ANSWER KEY – Parts A, B & C

LISTENING SUB-TEST – ANSWER KEY

PART A: QUESTIONS 1-12

1 asthma

2 hair (growth)

3 hump

4 sweating / perspiration / diaphoresis

5 (so) infrequent (now)

6 (easily) bruise

7 stretch marks / striae

8 dark / darkened

9 acne (vulgaris)

10 mood swings

11 irritable

12 saliva

PART A: QUESTIONS 13-24

13 lisinopril

14 (some) water

15 aspirin

16 clopidogrel

17 (a bit) breathless

18 stents

19 (going up/going down/up and down) stairs

20 varicose veins

21 (having) palpitations

22 heartburn / (acid) reflux

23 pain

24 central incisors

LISTENING SUB-TEST – ANSWER KEY

PART B: QUESTIONS 25-30

25	B	prioritising patients
26	B	dealing with her particular concerns
27	A	It's likely to lead to changes in practice.
28	B	they feel it's not relevant to them.
29	C	to use contact lenses to administer drugs over time.
30	A	explaining why intervention may not be necessary

PART C: QUESTIONS 31-36

31	C	to provide a range of specialist advice about it.
32	C	have to take precautions to avoid the risk of symptoms recurring.
33	A	a subsequent episode can have a cumulative effect.
34	A	lies mainly in the choice of sports played.
35	B	The organisers should be capable of dealing with any issues.
36	A	only really address an issue which is particular to that sport.

PART C: QUESTIONS 37-42

37	A	There were conclusive results earlier than expected.
38	C	their health deteriorated due to pre-existing conditions.
39	B	the patient was alone when it was carried out.
40	B	SPRINT involved higher-risk patients.
41	B	its results go against the existing body of evidence.
42	C	GPs will adopt a more active approach to lowering BP in the elderly.

END OF KEY

Listening sub-test

Audio Script – Practice test 2

This test has three parts. In each part you'll hear a number of different extracts. At the start of each extract, you'll hear this sound: ---***---.

You'll have time to read the questions before you hear each extract and you'll hear each extract ONCE only. Complete your answers as you listen.

At the end of the test, you'll have two minutes to check your answers.

Part A. In this part of the test, you'll hear two different extracts. In each extract, a health professional is talking to a patient. For questions 1 to 24, complete the notes with information you hear. Now, look at the notes for extract one.

PAUSE: 5 SECONDS
Extract one. Questions 1 to 12.

You hear a consultant endocrinologist talking to a patient called Sarah Croft. For questions 1 to 12, complete the notes with a word or short phrase. You now have thirty seconds to look at the notes.

PAUSE: 30 SECONDS
---***---

M: Good morning, Mrs Croft. I see your GP has referred you to me …

F: Yes.

M: OK … I've got some notes here with his referral letter, but it'd be helpful if you could tell me in your own words the sort of problems you've been experiencing?

F: OK, well, I've had high blood pressure for several years, but these last few months…that's tending to get worse. I've been on corticosteroids too these last three years or so, and that's a result of the fact that I've suffered from asthma since my teens.

M: I see. But I understand you've developed several other problems recently?

F: Oh yeah – as you can see, my stomach is huge – I've put on a lot of weight and it seems to be concentrated there. And, oh dear, I don't know what's happened to my face! All this hair which has appeared – it's…so embarrassing. And something else which I didn't notice at first, but which other people have pointed out to me – here, see? In between my shoulders, ah yeah, is this, well, I can only describe it as a hump. That really bothers me too.

M: Yes – I can see, erm...

F: And look at my ankles… they're swollen too. Something else which has got really bad is that I'm always sweating so much – even in cold weather.   No amount of anti-perspirant seems to help.

M: That must be difficult. Erm, and any aches or pains?

F: Well, my…my back tends to ache a bit, but I take ibuprofen which helps. My periods used to be painful in the past, but, to be honest, they're so infrequent now that the pain really isn't a problem any more. I often feel tired though, in fact…like really tired.

M: And what about your skin?

F: Oh yeah… it seems to bruise at the slightest thing. And I've noticed that if I get a cut or a scratch or something, it takes ages to heal. And something else I've spotted on my thighs, see here…is these stretch marks. Ah yes, they're quite noticeable because they're a real purple colour. My face has changed too – I used to have quite pale skin, but, as you can see it's quite red now. And it looks, well, puffy – I mean it never used to look like that.

M: OK… so there's been quite a change.

F: Oh, definitely. And if you look, here, on my neck – the skin's gone dark. Really odd. I don't know what's happening – and, though I never really had it before, I've now got acne into the bargain!

M: Ahh tt must all be distressing. I…I can appreciate that this is having an effect on you. Erm, have you noticed your general mood changing at all?

F: Well, it's enough to get anyone down really – and, yes, I do feel a bit depressed. But the frightening thing is that I've started getting mood swings. I've never had them before. I mean, one minute I'm laughing and the next I'm crying – and.. and I don't know why. It's quite alarming.

M: Anything else?

F: Well I confess I feel, well…irritable all the time. Everything seems to get on my nerves! And I can't seem to concentrate like I used to, you know – I find it hard sometimes to do stuff in my head like working out a sum, or remembering names and things. I… I just hope that you can help find out what's wrong with me.

M: Well, I'm sure we will. Now, I see you've already had some blood tests, but I'll need to do one or two more. You've had a urine test to look at your blood sugar, so I probably won't need to repeat that. We may do a saliva test, depending on the bloods.

F: OK, I see. And how long will everything take, I mean before we know what's causing the problems?

M: Well, I'm afraid it can all take some time as diagnosis can be quite complicated and we may need to (FADE)

PAUSE: 10 SECONDS
Extract two. Questions 13 to 24.

You hear an anaesthetist talking to a patient called Mary Wilcox prior to an operation. For questions 13 to 24, complete the notes with a word or short phrase. You now have thirty seconds to look at the notes.

PAUSE: 30 SECONDS
---***---

M   So, Mrs. Wilcox, you tell me you've had high blood pressure, so are you taking any medications for that?

F   Yes, erm… a blue one and a white one

M   And do you know the names of the tablets?

F   Yes, so one's thiazide.

M   OK

F   and the other one's lisinopril.

M   Perfect, thank you that's very helpful. And have you had them this morning?

F Yes, that's what the nurse told me at the pre-assessment, yes, so is that all right? Just with some water. I usually have them before breakfast but she said no food at all this morning.

M Excellent. And apart from the high blood pressure do you have any other medical problems at all?

F Err… Yes, I take some blood-thinning drugs because I had a small heart attack a bit ago, so I'm taking aspirin and… at the pre-assessment they said to keep on with them, so I had one this morning like I usually do. They told me to stop the other one … err, I can't remember the name …

M Ahh… Warfarin?

F No, it begins with c… err… clop…clopidogrel. Err… they told me to stop it a week before the operation. Seven days.

M Fantastic

F So I stopped last Tuesday.

M Great. Now, tell me a bit more about this heart attack. How long ago was that?

F Err… two years ago. My GP picked up on it.

M Did that all go …

F Yes, err… pretty good

M And why did you go to your GP, were you having chest pains?

F Err… they weren't chest pains, they were … I was just getting a bit breathless and it was difficult for me to tell what was going on but, err…Dr Scott picked up on it when I went to see him and he sent me to the cardiology team.

M Right. Did they say you'd had a heart attack?

F Yes, they told me I'd had a small one and so I had some stents put in … a couple of them.

M And since they were done…

F Yes, I've been better you know, I… err I don't feel so tired all the time

M OK. And what can you do in terms of exercising?

F Well I can do anything … anything really.

M Mmm and, tell me what you can do.

F Well we have stairs at home and we don't have a loo on the ground floor, it's on the first floor, so I'm up and down a few times a day.

M And walking on the flat's fine?

F Yes, that's OK.

M Any problems with your ankles swelling?

F Well this one it swells up if I've been standing. Alright, I had my veins done, my varicose veins. But, err the other one's alright. I sprained it quite badly last year but it's fine now.

M Right. Erm, can I just ask you a few other questions about your heart.

F	Sure
M	Have you ever had any palpitations at all? When your heart goes boom boom boom.
F	*No*
M	You've never experienced any of those?
F	*Well no… no. Not really. I mean if… if I run my heart beats a bit faster but that's normal isn't it.*
M	Sure. Erm, anything else … any digestive problems?
F	*No … well if I have a heavy meal late at night, like if… if I have pastry or something, I sometimes wake up in the night feeling a bit erm… like heartburn, erm… but if I take an anti-acid it's fine.*
M	Right. So in general you sound to be in pretty good shape. Hmm now in a minute I'll tell you about exactly what type of anaesthesia we'll be using. But, first of all is there anything you'd like to ask me … do you have any concerns about anything?
F	*Erm, well I suppose the main thing is after the operation, err, when I wake up… Erm I mean will I be in a lot of pain when I come round?*
M	No, you'll be given morphine during the procedure and that will still be working when you wake up, and then when that wears off you'll be given something else. There'll be someone keeping an eye on you.
F	*OK. Ohh… Err and the other thing is, Err I've heard that if you have crowns in your mouth they can get damaged if they put in an air tube.*
M	Well, it's unlikely but we'll take special care. So which teeth are we talking about?
F	*Err, these two.*
M	OK the two central incisors. And do you have any other teeth with crowns or implants.
F	*No.*
M	OK. So what we have planned for you is …[fade]

PAUSE: 10 SECONDS
That is the end of Part A. Now, look at Part B.

PAUSE: 5 SECONDS
Part B. In this part of the test, you'll hear six different extracts. In each extract, you'll hear people talking in a different healthcare setting.

For questions 25 to 30, choose the answer A, B or C which fits best according to what you hear. You'll have time to read each question before you listen. Complete your answers as you listen.

Now look at Question 25. You hear two trainee doctors doing an activity at a staff training day. Now read the question.

PAUSE: 15 SECONDS
---***---

M	So what did the trainer say we have to do?

F   Well, we've got to look through these case notes – ten sets in total – and decide which of the patients should be referred to the consultant as a matter of urgency, and which can wait.

M   Oh right. And did I hear him say there's a limited number you can refer?

F   Not exactly. He said that we should put them in rank order according to the severity of the symptoms and other factors evident from the case notes. Once we've agreed on our list, we have to go and compare with another pair of trainees.

M   OK. Let's get started then.

PAUSE: 5 SECONDS
Question 26. You hear a radiographer talking to a patient about her MRI scan. Now read the question.

PAUSE: 15 SECONDS
---***---

M   Come in, come in. Mrs Brown, isn't it? My name's Ted and I'm going to be doing your MRI scan today. Now, can you get up on the table for me?

F   *You know, I'm really claustrophobic.*

M   Mm, well, this is a new piece of equipment. The diameter's much larger, so it should make it a little more comfortable for you. You'll also have this call bell, so if you need me at any point during the test you squeeze that, OK?

F   *OK.*

M   Now your scan's only going to take about 15 minutes. Are you OK with that?

F   *I am.*

M   OK. Let's get started then.

PAUSE: 5 SECONDS

Question 27. You hear two nurses discussing an article in a nursing journal. Now read the question.

PAUSE: 15 SECONDS
---***---

F: *Did you see the article about research on strokes and sight problems in the latest Nursing magazine?*

M: Yes, I found it interesting that there's quite such a high degree of visual impairment after a stroke.

F: *Yeah, but I think I could've told them that without an expensive research study.*

M: Well, you need evidence to get progress in how people are treated. And now there'll be a push for all stroke patients to have eye assessments as a matter of course.

F: *It certainly makes a pretty solid case for that. Especially as there's plenty that can be done to help people if early screening diagnoses an issue.*

M: Absolutely.

F: *I was just sorry the article didn't provide more detail about the type of sight problems that are most common after a stroke.*

M: Well there's a reference to where the whole study's been published - so you could always find out there.

PAUSE: 5 SECONDS

Question 28. You hear two hospital managers talking about a time management course for staff. Now read the question.

PAUSE: 15 SECONDS

---***---

M The uptake for the course in time management for staff has been disappointing, hasn't it?

F *It has – but I'm not exactly sure why, because everyone seems to know about it. And we asked for it to be changed from a four-hour session to two two-hour slots to make it easier for nurses to be released from their wards. But apparently that wasn't possible because it has to be done a certain way.*

M Yeah, I'm not convinced that was the problem anyway. I think once staff become aware of what it's aiming to do, and how it fits together with other initiatives, there might be more interest.

F *Yeah. There certainly is a need, even if the staff themselves don't actually realise it at present.*

PAUSE: 5 SECONDS
Question 29. You hear an optometrist reporting on some research he's been doing. Now read the question.

PAUSE: 15 SECONDS
---***---

M: I specialise in dealing with fungal eye infections. At present, treatment involves giving eye drops every hour for at least two weeks. I wanted to improve this process, by designing a system capable of releasing anti-fungal drugs onto the eye over an extended period. Contact lenses are perfect for this, as their hydrogel structure has the ability to uptake and release drugs, and their placement on the eye ensures the drug gets released directly to the cornea. In order to make a contact lens provide drugs over a sustained period, I've modified the lens. I've also used nanoparticles for packaging the drugs. So, I've managed to create a system capable of delivering an anti-fungal drug called Nanomycin for up to four hours. I now hope to increase this, and use this system with other drugs.

PAUSE: 5 SECONDS
Question 30. You hear a consultant talking to a trainee about a patient's eye condition. Now read the question.

PAUSE: 15 SECONDS
---***---

M Have we got Mrs Kent's notes?

F *Yes, they're here. She's coming in today for possible laser surgery for her retinopathy, isn't she?*

M Well, depending on results – and from the look of these pictures we took last time, there's been a slow improvement, so we'll talk to her and perhaps hold off for the time being – unless her condition's worsened, 'cos it can in some cases.

F *So what's the cause?*

M Well, we know a leak of fluid behind the retina causes the distorted vision which sufferers get, but not why that occurs. There may be a link with stress, and also steroid use, but the jury's still out, I'm afraid.

PAUSE: 10 SECONDS
That is the end of Part B. Now, look at Part C.

PAUSE: 5 SECONDS
Part C. In this part of the test, you'll hear two different extracts. In each extract, you'll hear health professionals talking about aspects of their work.

For questions 31 to 42, choose the answer A, B or C which fits best according to what you hear. Complete your answers as you listen.

Now look at extract one.

Extract one. Questions 31 to 36. You hear an interview with a neurosurgeon called Dr Ian Marsh who specialises in the treatment of concussion in sport.

You now have 90 seconds to read questions 31 to 36.

PAUSE: 90 SECONDS
---***---

F: *My guest today is Dr Ian Marsh, a specialist in the treatment of concussion in sport and a co-author on a new set of guidelines. So, Dr Marsh, what's the aim of these new guidelines?*

M: Well the aim was really to provide a resource, not for the top-level professional sports people, but for parents, teachers and coaches of young people playing sport. The guidelines basically offer some expert information from a GP, an emergency physician, and myself as a neurosurgeon, about what the condition is, also how to identify the symptoms and how to manage it. If any of your listeners have ever had a concussion doing sports, you'll know how frightening it can be. It's confusing and painful, and difficult sometimes for teachers, parents, or whoever to work out if someone with concussion is okay. I mean… we hope to remedy that.

F: *And how do we know when someone is suffering from concussion?*

M: Well, obviously, if the person's actually knocked out – it's clear. But not all patients actually lose consciousness. Often following a hard knock to the head, they become disorientated or experience headaches, nausea or vomiting. These are signs of concussion and they may clear initially, but then return when the individual actually undertakes further physical activity; right, when they start to train, say. So, it can actually take quite a while for things to really clear up. The essence of it is that people shouldn't start playing again until those warning signs have completely subsided.

F: *Yes, and you say that waiting anything less than fourteen days after all the symptoms have cleared would be too early to return?*

M: Yeah, that's right. If they go back too early, they risk a second concussion and, as we know from professional athletes, they may have to give up their sport if they have too many concussions. Right, so it's better, particularly in a young person with a developing brain, to allow all of the symptoms to settle, and only then return to play — well usually return to train first, then return to play after that. It used to be thought that receiving another concussion, could lead to severe brain swelling, and that could be fatal or at least involve a visit to the emergency room. I think the evidence is fairly slim for that. What we do know though is that the compounding effect of having one concussion followed by another seems to be more severe than just the one. So it's always better to let the brain recover fully before playing again.

F: *Right, so who's at the highest risk of sports concussion?*

M: Well, actually a concussion can happen whenever anyone receives a blow to the head. Usually it's a sort of twisting blow, not a straight-on blow. But, obviously people playing sports like rugby - where there's bodily contact – stand more chance of being at the receiving end of such a blow. But having said that, it's just as likely to affect kids kicking a ball around a park as it is to affect top professional players in big matches.

F: *Do you think that youth sports need specialist concussion doctors on hand? Like the professionals do?*

M: There's always a risk and we know that it happens from time to time, but I mean most games — even the most dangerous ones — are without incident at all. I think people who are involved in running youth sports, whether they be referees, coaches, or parents, can be made aware of how to manage concussion, the signs that they need to look out for, and maybe the warnings of something more serious, so that they can take the appropriate actions. But I think always having a doctor on the sidelines where young people are playing is just an over-reaction.

F: *In the USA, college football is big business. They're trialling helmet sensors and impact sensors. Do you think that's something we need everywhere?*

M: Well, I don't think it'll come to that. I think there are two scenarios here. The first is one where a concussion's a one-off event following a significant blow to the head. Right, the second's quite different and involves Chronic Traumatic Encephalopathy. This comes about particularly in American Football, where players use their helmets and heads almost like weapons. That type of repeated impact seems to add up over the player's career. That's something we've heard being discussed, mostly in the USA. Naturally there's interest generally in protecting players, particularly in the professional levels of sport, but I see that as a different matter to the management of concussion itself.

PAUSE: 10 SECONDS
Now look at extract two.

Extract two. Questions 37 to 42. You hear a presentation by a consultant cardiologist called Dr Pamela Skelton, who's talking about a research trial called SPRINT which investigated the effects of setting lower blood-pressure targets.

You now have 90 seconds to read questions 37 to 42.

PAUSE: 90 SECONDS
---***---

F: Hello - I'm Dr Pamela Skelton, Consultant Cardiologist at this hospital, and I'm talking about the recent SPRINT study into the effects of setting lower blood-pressure targets, which in turn affects the advice and medication which patients are given. I'm going to describe the patients who were selected, how the trial was conducted and the implications of its results for us all as health professionals.

First – the trial itself. It involved over nine-thousand hypertensive participants, aged fifty-plus, most of whom were on blood-pressure medication. They were randomly assigned to one of two groups – one with a goal of less than one-hundred-and-twenty millimetres systolic BP, the other with a goal of less than one-hundred-and-forty millimetres, the traditional standard. The intention was to follow these patients for five years, factoring in the usual drop-out rate. As it turned out, however, the trial was stopped after just three years thanks to an all-cause mortality reduction of nearly thirty percent for the one-hundred-and-twenty group, which was definitive and shocking - but wonderful. As I mentioned, the participants were over-fifties and it goes without saying that as people age, they develop more diseases and health problems as a matter of course. But there was a specific group of over-seventy-fives who did just as well as younger patients.

Before the trial, some medics referred to the natural stiffening of the arteries with ageing, suggesting that a hundred-and-twenty was too low a target for the over-seventy-fives, risking an increase of dizzy spells which would affect general wellbeing. But this concern turned out to be unfounded. Others thought there'd be a failure to take the number of tablets needed to reach a BP of a hundred-and-twenty, especially among older participants. Again, this wasn't an issue - the average needed was just three per day. The over-seventy-fives, already on various drugs, didn't object to extra medication. Participants from this age group who didn't finish the trial were taken out because some conditions, which were already present, worsened; for example in some cases obesity levels rose too high.

To manage their blood pressure, participants were given standard drugs – nothing experimental, just drugs that are readily available and low-cost. Another key factor was that blood pressure was measured in a very specific way. Rather than give patients an arm cuff for at-home twenty-four-hour ambulatory monitoring, an automated machine was used at the hospital. This took three separate readings and averaged them. Also, readings were taken while staff were out of the room to avoid what's called 'white coat syndrome' in patients.

Now, some of you may be familiar with the ACCORD study into blood pressure levels several years ago, which in some respects was similar to SPRINT. There are some differences, though. For example, ACCORD was about half the size of SPRINT, and unlike SPRINT, the ACCORD study allowed diabetic patients to take part. Despite this, in general, the ACCORD participants were rather lower risk than those in the SPRINT trial – probably because of the slightly lower average age. The ACCORD trial didn't show a statistically significant benefit for overall cardiovascular outcomes, but there was a clear forty percent reduction in strokes – even though that was a secondary outcome.

So, to summarise, the SPRINT trial seems to support a hundred-and-twenty as a recommended blood-pressure target. This is doubtless a landmark study and, importantly, one which was sponsored by government rather than by the interests of the pharmaceutical corporations. I recommend a note of caution though, as SPRINT does contradict previous findings. The Cochrane View in 2011, for example, said that lowering to under a hundred and-forty didn't produce a change in the risk of death overall. However, we must bear in mind that Cochrane was looking retrospectively at trials which weren't actually focused on the same particular issue. So it's worth doing a full and systematic evaluation, to see where the SPRINT trial fits in with what we already know.

It's interesting that a few GPs have already been working with older patients to hit lower blood- pressure goals, and the new data will doubtless encourage greater take-up of this more interventionist line of attack.   But the SPRINT results don't mean that everyone with hypertension should be dropping to under a hundred-and-twenty. Plus, to achieve those lower levels, it's unlikely that lifestyle changes alone would be enough, it could well require several anti-hypertensive drugs as well. There remain some unanswered questions, of course - for example whether other groups, like those with a lower heart-attack risk, need to keep their blood pressure that low. So, while SPRINT can help guide doctors' decisions about some patients, it doesn't mean that a new universal standard for blood pressure is in order. Instead, it's a good reason for everyone to discuss with their doctor, their own ideal and particular target.

PAUSE: 10 SECONDS
That is the end of Part C.

You now have two minutes to check your answers.

PAUSE: 120 SECONDS
That is the end of the Listening test.

Reading sub-test

Answer Key – Part A

READING SUB-TEST – ANSWER KEY

PART A: QUESTIONS 1-20

1	B
2	A
3	C
4	A
5	D
6	A
7	organic matter
8	foreign bodies
9	compound
10	6/six hours
11	systemic sepsis
12	immuno(-)suppressed
13	antibiotics
14	(in) (the) jaw
15	broken bones
16	(a) bite reflex
17	5/five (times)
18	(a) booster dose OR booster doses
19	twenty-three/23 gauge
20	crying

Reading sub-test

Answer Key – Parts B & C

READING SUB-TEST – ANSWER KEY

PART B: QUESTIONS 1-6

1	B	there is severe leakage from the wound.
2	A	encourage participation in the scheme.
3	A	data about patient errors may be incomplete.
4	B	There are several ways of ensuring that the ventilator is working effectively.
5	C	the patients most likely to suffer complications.
6	B	to draw conclusions from the results of cleaning audits

PART C: QUESTIONS 7-14

7	C	lacks any form of convincing proof of its value as a treatment.
8	A	surprise at people's willingness to put their trust in it.
9	B	the key attraction of the approach for patients.
10	B	frequently result from a patient's treatment preferences.
11	C	the way that homeopathic remedies endanger more than just the user
12	D	the way positive results can be achieved despite people's doubts.
13	A	prepared to accept that homeopathy may depend on psychological factors.
14	D	the motivation behind the desire for homeopathy to gain scientific acceptance

PART C: QUESTIONS 15-22

15	A	It required intense concentration.
16	D	the connections between sensors and the brain need to be exact.
17	A	There was statistical evidence that it was successful.
18	B	Patients might have to undergo too many operations.
19	D	It is difficult for scientists to pinpoint precise areas with an electrode.
20	C	It may have more potential than electrical stimulation.
21	A	how much more there is to achieve.
22	B	to illustrate the fact that some sensation is better than none

OCCUPATIONAL ENGLISH TEST

WRITING SUB-TEST: NURSING

SAMPLE RESPONSE: LETTER

Nurse-in-Charge
District Nursing Service
Greenville Community Health Care Centre
88 Highton Road
Greenville

15 July 2018

Re: Ms Margaret Helen Martin. DOB: 25 July 1935

Dear Nurse-in-Charge,

Ms Martin requires the assistance of a community nurse following a successful angioplasty today for her coronary artery disease and angina. She is due to be discharged tomorrow.

Ms Martin is overweight with a BMI of 29.5, a contributing factor of which is her sedentary lifestyle. She rarely leaves her home or interacts socially, which could potentially lead to isolation. She also has coeliac disease.

Her current medications include aspirin and Plavix for her CAD, Betaloc and Tritace for hypertension, and Lipitor for hypercholesterolemia. Monitoring of medication adherence is highly recommended.

Ms Martin feels she may not be able to cope at home alone, therefore, encouraging regular family visits is essential and may help prevent any feeling of isolation. She has been instructed not to lift heavy items for 12 weeks but will receive support from her physiotherapist in terms of a daily exercise programme. She currently receives weekly meals on wheels and will receive supervision from a dietitian to help maintain good dietary habits. Her doctor will also be involved in monitoring her adjustment to home life. Nevertheless, assistance from your community nurse is required to monitor her exercise and dietary habits as well as the bruising of her catheter insertion site and any potential infection.

If you require further information, please do not hesitate to contact me.

Yours sincerely,

Ward Nurse

NURSING

PRACTICE TEST 3

To listen to the audio, visit
https://www.occupationalenglishtest.org/audio

LISTENING SUB-TEST – QUESTION PAPER

CANDIDATE NUMBER:

LAST NAME:

FIRST NAME:

MIDDLE NAMES:

PROFESSION:

Candidate details and photo will be printed here.

VENUE:

TEST DATE:

Passport Photo

CANDIDATE DECLARATION

By signing this, you agree not to disclose or use in any way (other than to take the test) or assist any other person to disclose or use any OET test or sub-test content. If you cheat or assist in any cheating, use any unfair practice, break any of the rules or regulations, or ignore any advice or information, you may be disqualified and your results may not be issued at the sole discretion of CBLA. CBLA also reserves its right to take further disciplinary action against you and to pursue any other remedies permitted by law. If a candidate is suspected of and investigated for malpractice, their personal details and details of the investigation may be passed to a third party where required.

CANDIDATE SIGNATURE: _____

TIME: APPROXIMATELY **40 MINUTES**

INSTRUCTIONS TO CANDIDATES

DO NOT open this question paper until you are told to do so.

One mark will be granted for each correct answer.

Answer **ALL** questions. Marks are **NOT** deducted for incorrect answers.

At the end of the test, you will have two minutes to check your answers.

At the end of the test, hand in this **Question Paper.**

You must not remove OET material from the test room.

HOW TO ANSWER THE QUESTIONS

Part A: Write your answers on this **Question Paper** by filling in the blanks. **Example: Patient:** _____ *Ray Sands*

Part B & Part C: Mark your answers on this **Question Paper** by filling in the circle using a 2B pencil. **Example:** Ⓐ
Ⓑ
Ⓒ

Occupational English Test
Listening Test

This test has three parts. In each part you'll hear a number of different extracts. At the start of each extract, you'll hear this sound: --beep—

You'll have time to read the questions before you hear each extract and you'll hear each extract **ONCE ONLY**. Complete your answers as you listen.

At the end of the test you'll have two minutes to check your answers.

Part A

In this part of the test, you'll hear two different extracts. In each extract, a health professional is talking to a patient.

For **questions 1-24**, complete the notes with information you hear.

Now, look at the notes for extract one.

Extract 1: Questions 1-12

You hear a pulmonologist talking to a patient called Robert Miller. For **questions 1-12**, complete the notes with a word or short phrase.

You now have 30 seconds to look at the notes.

Patient	Robert Miller

Symptoms

- tiredness
- persistent **(1)** _____ cough
- SOB
- weight loss described as **(2)** _____ in nature.
- fingertips appear **(3)** _____
- nails feel relatively **(4)** _____

Background details

- previously employed as a **(5)** _____ (20 yrs)
- now employed as a **(6)** _____
- no longer able to play golf
- keeps pigeons as a hobby

Medical history

- last year diagnosed with hypertension
- current prescription of **(7)** _____
- **(8)** _____ sounds in chest reported by GP
- father suffered from **(9)** _____

Previous tests

- **(10)** _____ six months ago
- chest x-ray one month ago

Future actions

- **(11)** _____ test
- CT scan
- prescription of **(12)** _____ (possibly)

Extract 2: Questions 13-24

You hear an eye specialist talking to a patient called Jasmine Burton, who has recently undergone eye surgery. For **questions 13-24**, complete the notes with a word or short phrase.

You now have thirty seconds to look at the notes.

Patient   Jasmine Burton

Patient history

- suffers from **(13)** _____ astigmatism

- also has **(14)** _____ (so surgery under general anaesthetic)

- eye problems may result from a lack of **(15)** _____

- sight problems mean **(16)** _____ isn't an option for her

- reports some slowness to **(17)** _____

- has poor perception of **(18)** _____

- works as a **(19)** _____
  - reports having no issues at work

- eyes checked every few years

Surgery

- **(20)** _____ in right eye first noted three years ago

- February this year - had surgery

- some capsular **(21)** _____ noted post-operatively

- examination showed no sign of a **(22)** _____
  - follow up appointment in 6 months

Presenting with

- reported increase in number of **(23)** _____

- increased sensitivity to **(24)** _____

That is the end of Part A. Now look at Part B.

Part B

In this part of the test, you'll hear six different extracts. In each extract, you'll hear people talking in a different healthcare setting.

For **questions 25-30**, choose the answer (**A**, **B** or **C**) which fits best according to what you hear. You'll have time to read each question before you listen. Complete your answers as you listen.

Now look at question 25.

25. You hear a nurse briefing a colleague at the end of her shift.

    What does the colleague have to do for the patient tonight?

    Ⓐ   remove her saline drip

    Ⓑ   arrange for more tests

    Ⓒ   monitor her blood pressure

26. You hear part of a hospital management meeting where a concern is being discussed.

    What is the committee concerned about?

    Ⓐ   poor response to recruitment drives

    Ⓑ   difficulties in retaining suitable staff

    Ⓒ   relatively high staff absence rates

27. You hear a GP and his practice nurse discussing a vaccination programme.

    They agree that the practice should

    Ⓐ   make sure patients are aware of it.

    Ⓑ   organise it more effectively than in the past.

    Ⓒ   prepare to cope with an increasing demand for it.

28. You hear two hospital nurses discussing the assessment of a patient on their ward.

What is the problem?

- (A) The patient's documentation has been sent to the wrong place.
- (B) Nobody has taken responsibility for assessing the patient.
- (C) The duty doctor was unable to locate the patient.

29. You hear the beginning of a training session for dental students.

The trainer is explaining that the session will

- (A) focus on aspects of dental hygiene.
- (B) expand upon what they studied previously.
- (C) introduce them to a completely new technique.

30. You hear two nurses discussing the treatment of a patient with a kidney infection.

What is the female nurse doing?

- (A) emphasising the urgency of a procedure
- (B) suggesting how to overcome a difficulty
- (C) warning him about a possible problem

That is the end of Part B. Now look at Part C.

Part C

In this part of the test, you'll hear two different extracts. In each extract, you'll hear health professionals talking about aspects of their work.

For **questions 31-42**, choose the answer (**A, B** or **C**) which fits best according to what you hear. Complete your answers as you listen.

Now look at extract one.

Extract 1: Questions 31-36

You hear a geriatrician called Dr Clare Cox giving a presentation on the subject of end-of-life care for people with dementia.

You now have 90 seconds to read **questions 31-36**.

31. What problem does Dr Cox identify concerning dementia patients?

  (A) They can often make unrealistic demands on their carers.

  (B) Their condition can develop in a number of different ways.

  (C) The type of care that they may require is extremely costly.

32. Why did *Dementia Australia* decide to examine the issue of end-of-life dementia care?

  (A) There was a lack of reliable information on it.

  (B) The number of stories about poor care made it urgent.

  (C) There were enough data on which to base an effective care plan.

33. For Dr Cox, the initial results of the dementia survey reveal that palliative care

  (A) was working more effectively than people had thought.

  (B) was more widely available than some users imagined.

  (C) was viewed negatively by medical professionals.

34. Dr Cox says that lack of knowledge of the law by care professionals

(A) proves that family members should help make pain management decisions.

(B) could be resulting in a surprisingly high number of premature deaths.

(C) may lead to dementia patients experiencing unnecessary distress.

35. Dr Cox thinks that the statistics she quotes on refusing treatment

(A) illustrate a gap in current medical education programmes.

(B) show how patients' wishes are too often misunderstood by carers.

(C) demonstrate the particular difficulties presented by dementia patients.

36. Dr Cox makes the point that end-of-life planning is desirable because

(A) it reduces the complexity of certain care decisions.

(B) it avoids carers having to speculate about a patient's wishes.

(C) it ensures that everyone receives the best possible quality of care.

Now look at extract two.

Extract 2: Questions 37-42

You hear a hospital doctor called Dr Keith Gardiner giving a presentation about some research he's done on the subject of staff-patient communication.

You now have 90 seconds to read **questions 37-42**.

37.　　Dr Gardiner first became interested in staff-patient communication after

　　　　(**A**)　　experiencing poor communication as an in-patient.

　　　　(**B**)　　observing the effects of poor communication on a patient.

　　　　(**C**)　　analysing patient feedback data on the subject of communication.

38.　　What point does Dr Gardiner make about a typical admission to hospital?

　　　　(**A**)　　The information given can overwhelm patients.

　　　　(**B**)　　Patients often feel unable to communicate effectively.

　　　　(**C**)　　Filling in detailed paperwork can be stressful for patients.

39.　　Dr Gardiner uses an example of poor communication to illustrate the point that

　　　　(**A**)　　patients should be consulted about the desirability of a hospital stay.

　　　　(**B**)　　specialists need to be informed if there are any mental health issues.

　　　　(**C**)　　relatives' knowledge of a patient's condition shouldn't be taken for granted.

40. Dr Gardiner explains that a survey conducted among in-patients about communication

    (A) measured the difference between their expectations and their actual experience.

    (B) asked their opinion about all aspects of the service they received.

    (C) included questions on how frequently they visited the hospital.

41. One common complaint arising from Dr Gardner's survey concerned

    (A) a lack of privacy for patients receiving sensitive information.

    (B) the over-use of unclear medical terminology with patients.

    (C) a tendency not to address patients in a respectful way.

42. How does Dr Gardiner feel about the results of the survey?

    (A) surprised by one response from patients

    (B) reassured by the level of patient care identified

    (C) worried that unforeseen problems were highlighted

That is the end of Part C.

You now have two minutes to check your answers.

END OF THE LISTENING TEST

READING SUB-TEST – TEXT BOOKLET: PART A

CANDIDATE NUMBER:

LAST NAME:

FIRST NAME:

MIDDLE NAMES:

PROFESSION:

VENUE:

TEST DATE:

Candidate details and photo will be printed here.

Passport Photo

CANDIDATE SIGNATURE: _____

INSTRUCTIONS TO CANDIDATES

You must **NOT** remove OET material from the test room.

www.occupationalenglishtest.org

© Cambridge Boxhill Language Assessment – ABN 51 988 559 414

[CANDIDATE NO.] READING TEXT BOOKLET PART A 01/04

Necrotizing Fasciitis (NF): Texts

Text A

Necrotizing fasciitis (NF) is a severe, rare, potentially lethal soft tissue infection that develops in the scrotum and perineum, the abdominal wall, or the extremities. The infection progresses rapidly, and septic shock may ensue; hence, the mortality rate is high (median mortality 32.2%). NF is classified into four types, depending on microbiological findings.

Table 1

Classification of responsible pathogens according to type of infection

Microbiological type	Pathogens	Site of infection	Co-morbidities
Type 1 (polymicrobial)	Obligate and facultative anaerobes	Trunk and perineum	Diabetes mellitus
Type 2 (monomicrobial)	Beta-hemolytic streptococcus A	Limbs	
Type 3	Clostridium species Gram-negative bacteria Vibrios spp. Aeromonas hydrophila	Limbs, trunk and perineum	Trauma Seafood consumption (for Aeromonas)
Type 4	Candida spp. Zygomycetes	Limbs, trunk, perineum	Immuno-suppression

Text B

Antibiotic treatment for NF

Type 1

- Initial treatment includes ampicillin or ampicillin–sulbactam combined with metronidazole or clindamycin.
- Broad gram-negative coverage is necessary as an initial empirical therapy for patients who have recently been treated with antibiotics, or been hospitalized. In such cases, antibiotics such as ampicillin–sulbactam, piperacillin–tazobactam, ticarcillin–clavulanate acid, third or fourth generation cephalosporins, or carbapenems are used, and at a higher dosage.

Type 2

- First or second generation of cephalosporins are used for the coverage of methicillin-sensitive Staphylococcus aureus (MSSA).
- MRSA tends to be covered by vancomycin, or daptomycin and linezolid in cases where S. aureus is resistant to vancomycin.

Type 3

- NF should be managed with clindamycin and penicillin, which kill the Clostridium species.
- If Vibrio infection is suspected, the early use of tetracyclines (including doxycycline and minocycline) and third-generation cephalosporins is crucial for the survival of the patient, since these antibiotics have been shown to reduce the mortality rate drastically.

Type 4

- Can be treated with amphotericin B or fluoroconazoles, but the results of this treatment are generally disappointing.

Antibiotics should be administered for up to 5 days after local signs and symptoms have resolved. The mean duration of antibiotic therapy for NF is 4–6 weeks.

Text C

Supportive care in an ICU is critical to NF survival. This involves fluid resuscitation, cardiac monitoring, aggressive wound care, and adequate nutritional support. Patients with NF are in a catabolic state and require increased caloric intake to combat infection. This can be delivered orally or via nasogastric tube, peg tube, or intravenous hyperalimentation. This should begin immediately (within the first 24 hours of hospitalization). Prompt and aggressive support has been shown to lower complication rates. Baseline and repeated monitoring of albumin, prealbumin, transferrin, blood urea nitrogen, and triglycerides should be performed to ensure the patient is receiving adequate nutrition.

Wound care is also an important concern. Advanced wound dressings have replaced wet-to-dry dressings. These dressings promote granulation tissue formation and speed healing. Advanced wound dressings may lend to healing or prepare the wound bed for grafting. A healthy wound bed increases the chances of split-thickness skin graft take. Vacuum-assisted closure (VAC) was recently reported to be effective in a patient whose cardiac status was too precarious to undergo a long surgical reconstruction operation. With the VAC., the patient's wound decreased in size, and the VAC was thought to aid in local management of infection and improve granulation tissue.

Text D

Advice to give the patient before discharge

- Help arrange the patient's aftercare, including home health care and instruction regarding wound management, social services to promote adjustment to lifestyle changes and financial concerns, and physical therapy sessions to help rebuild strength and promote the return to optimal physical health.

- The life-threatening nature of NF, scarring caused by the disease, and in some cases the need for limb amputation can alter the patient's attitude and viewpoint, so be sure to take a holistic approach when dealing with the patient and family.

Remind the diabetic patient to

- control blood glucose levels, keeping the glycated haemoglobin (HbAlc) level to 7% or less.
- keep needles capped until use and not to reuse needles.
- clean the skin thoroughly before blood glucose testing or insulin in¬jection, and to use alcohol pads to clean the area afterward.

END OF PART A

THIS TEXT BOOKLET WILL BE COLLECTED

READING SUB-TEST – QUESTION PAPER: PART A

CANDIDATE NUMBER:

LAST NAME:

FIRST NAME:

MIDDLE NAMES:

PROFESSION: Candidate details and photo will be printed here.

VENUE:

TEST DATE:

Passport Photo

CANDIDATE DECLARATION

By signing this, you agree not to disclose or use in any way (other than to take the test) or assist any other person to disclose or use any OET test or sub-test content. If you cheat or assist in any cheating, use any unfair practice, break any of the rules or regulations, or ignore any advice or information, you may be disqualified and your results may not be issued at the sole discretion of CBLA. CBLA also reserves its right to take further disciplinary action against you and to pursue any other remedies permitted by law. If a candidate is suspected of and investigated for malpractice, their personal details and details of the investigation may be passed to a third party where required.

CANDIDATE SIGNATURE: _____

TIME: 15 MINUTES

INSTRUCTIONS TO CANDIDATES

DO NOT open this **Question Paper** or the **Text Booklet** until you are told to do so.

Write your answers on the spaces provided on this **Question Paper.**

You must answer the questions within the 15-minute time limit.

One mark will be granted for each correct answer.

Answer **ALL** questions. Marks are **NOT** deducted for incorrect answers.

At the end of the 15 minutes, hand in this **Question Paper** and the **Text Booklet.**

DO NOT remove OET material from the test room.

www.occupationalenglishtest.org

© Cambridge Boxhill Language Assessment – ABN 51 988 559 414

[CANDIDATE NO.] READING QUESTION PAPER PART A 01/04

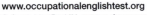

Part A

- Look at the four texts, **A-D**, in the separate **Text Booklet**.

- For each question, **1-20**, look through the texts, **A-D**, to find the relevant information.

- Write your answers on the spaces provided in this **Question Paper**.

- Answer all the questions within the 15-minute time limit.

- Your answers should be correctly spelt.

Necrotizing Fasciitis (NF): Questions

Questions 1-7

For each question, **1-7**, decide which text (**A**, **B**, **C** or **D**) the information comes from. You may use any letter more than once.

In which text can you find information about

1 the drug treatment required? _____

2 which parts of the body can be affected? _____

3 the various ways calories can be introduced? _____

4 who to contact to help the patient after they leave hospital? _____

5 what kind of dressing to use? _____

6 how long to give drug therapy to the patient? _____

7 what advice to give the patient regarding needle use? _____

Questions 8-14

Answer each of the questions, **8-14**, with a word or short phrase from one of the texts. Each answer may include words, numbers or both.

8 Which two drugs can you use to treat the clostridium species of pathogen?

_____

9 Which common metabolic condition may occur with NF?

_____

10 What complication can a patient suffer from if NF isn't treated quickly enough?

_____

11 What procedure can you use with a wound if the patient can't be operated on?

_____

12   What should the patient be told to use to clean an injection site?

_____

13   Which two drugs can be used if you can't use vancomycin?

_____

14   What kind of infection should you use tetracyclines for?

_____

Questions 15-20

Complete each of the sentences, **15-20**, with a word or short phrase from one of the texts. Each answer may include words, numbers or both.

15   The average proportion of patients who die as a result of contracting NF is

_____.

16   Patients who have eaten _____ may be infected with Aeromonas hydrophilia.

17   Patients with Type 2 infection usually present with infected

_____.

18   Type 1 NF is also known as _____.

19   The patient needs to be aware of the need to keep glycated haemoglobin levels lower than _____.

20   The patient will need a course of _____ to regain fitness levels after returning home.

END OF PART A
THIS QUESTION PAPER WILL BE COLLECTED

READING SUB-TEST – QUESTION PAPER: PARTS B & C

CANDIDATE NUMBER:

LAST NAME:

FIRST NAME:

MIDDLE NAMES:

PROFESSION:

VENUE:

TEST DATE:

Candidate details and photo will be printed here.

Passport Photo

TIME: 45 MINUTES

INSTRUCTIONS TO CANDIDATES

DO NOT open this **Question Paper** until you are told to do so.

One mark will be granted for each correct answer.

Answer **ALL** questions. Marks are **NOT** deducted for incorrect answers.

At the end of the test, hand in this **Question Paper**.

HOW TO ANSWER THE QUESTIONS:

Mark your answers on this **Question Paper** by filling in the circle using a 2B pencil. **Example:** Ⓐ
Ⓑ
Ⓒ

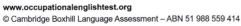

Part B

In this part of the test, there are six short extracts relating to the work of health professionals. For **questions 1-6**, choose answer (**A, B** or **C**) which you think fits best according to the text.

1. The policy document tells us that

   (A) stop dates aren't relevant in all circumstances.

   (B) anyone using EPMA can disregard the request for a stop date.

   (C) prescribers must know in advance of prescribing what the stop date should be.

Prescribing stop dates

Prescribers should write a review date or a stop date on the electronic prescribing system EPMA or the medicine chart for each antimicrobial agent prescribed. On the EPMA, there is a forced entry for stop dates on oral antimicrobials. There is not a forced stop date on EPMA for IV antimicrobial treatment – if the prescriber knows how long the course of IV should be, then the stop date can be filled in. If not known, then a review should be added to the additional information, e.g. 'review after 48 hrs'. If the prescriber decides treatment needs to continue beyond the stop date or course length indicated, then it is their responsibility to amend the chart. In critical care, it has been agreed that the routine use of review/stop dates on the charts is not always appropriate.

---

2. The guidelines inform us that personalised equipment for radiotherapy

(A)   is advisable for all patients.

(B)   improves precision during radiation.

(C)   needs to be tested at the first consultation.

Guidelines: Radiotherapy Simulation Planning Appointment

The initial appointment may also be referred to as the Simulation Appointment. During this appointment you will discuss your patient's medical history and treatment options, and agree on a radiotherapy treatment plan. The first step is usually to take a CT scan of the area requiring treatment. The patient will meet the radiation oncologist, their registrar and radiation therapists. A decision will be made regarding the best and most comfortable position for treatment, and this will be replicated daily for the duration of the treatment. Depending on the area of the body to be treated, personalised equipment such as a face mask may be used to stabilise the patient's position. This equipment helps keep the patient comfortable and still during the treatment and makes the treatment more accurate.

---

3. The purpose of these instructions is to explain how to

    (A)   monitor an ECG reading.

    (B)   position electrodes correctly.

    (C)   handle an animal during an ECG procedure.

CT200CV Veterinarian Electrocardiograph User Manual

Animal connections

Good electrode connection is the most important factor in recording a high quality ECG. By following a few basic steps, consistent, clean recordings can be achieved.

1. Shave a patch on each forelimb of the animal at the contact site.

2. Clean the electrode sites with an alcohol swab or sterilising agent.

3. Attach clips to the ECG leads.

4. Place a small amount of ECG electrode gel on the metal electrode of the limb strap or adapter clip.

5. Pinch skin on animal and place clips on the shaved skin area of the animal being tested. The animal must be kept still.

6. Check the LCD display for a constant heart reading.

7. If there is no heart reading, you have a contact problem with one or more of the leads.

8. Recheck the leads and reapply the clips to the shaven skin of the animal.

4. The group known as 'impatient patients' are more likely to continue with a course of prescribed medication if

(A) their treatment can be completed over a reduced period of time.

(B) it is possible to link their treatment with a financial advantage.

(C) its short-term benefits are explained to them.

Medication adherence and impatient patients

A recent article addressed the behaviour of people who have a 'taste for the present rather than the future'. It proposed that these so-called 'impatient patients' are unlikely to adhere to medications that require use over an extended period. The article proposes that, an 'impatience genotype' exists and that assessing these patients' view of the future while stressing the immediate advantages of adherence may improve adherence rates more than emphasizing potentially distant complications. The authors suggest that rather than attempting to change the character of those who are 'impatient', it may be wise to ascertain the patient's individual priorities, particularly as they relate to immediate gains. For example, while advising an 'impatient' patient with diabetes, stressing improvement in visual acuity rather than avoidance of retinopathy may result in greater medication adherence rates. Additionally, linking the cost of frequently changing prescription lenses when visual acuity fluctuates with glycemic levels may sometimes provide the patient with an immediate financial motivation for improving adherence.

5. The memo reminds nursing staff to avoid

    (A)   x-raying a patient unless pH readings exceed 5.5.

    (B)   the use of a particular method of testing pH levels.

    (C)   reliance on pH testing in patients taking acid-inhibiting medication.

Checking the position of a nasogastric tube

It is essential to confirm the position of the tube in the stomach by one of the following:

- Testing pH of aspirate: gastric placement is indicated by a pH of less than 4, but may increase to between pH 4-6 if the patient is receiving acid-inhibiting drugs. Blue litmus paper is insufficiently sensitive to adequately distinguish between levels of acidity of aspirate.
- X-rays: will only confirm position at the time the X-ray is carried out. The tube may have moved by the time the patient has returned to the ward. In the absence of a positive aspirate test, where pH readings are more than 5.5, or in a patient who is unconscious or on a ventilator, an X-ray must be obtained to confirm the initial position of the nasogastric tube.

6. This extract informs us that

    (A)   the amount of oxytocin given will depend on how the patient reacts.

    (B)   the patient will go into labour as soon as oxytocin is administered.

    (C)   the staff should inspect the oxytocin pump before use.

Extract from guidelines: Oxytocin

1   Oxytocin Dosage and Administration

Parenteral drug products should be inspected visually for particulate matter and discoloration prior to administration, whenever solution and container permit. Dosage of Oxytocin is determined by the uterine response. The dosage information below is based upon various regimens and indications in general use.

1.1   Induction or Stimulation of Labour

Intravenous infusion (drip method) is the only acceptable method of administration for the induction or stimulation of labour. Accurate control of the rate of infusion flow is essential. An infusion pump or other such device and frequent monitoring of strength of contractions and foetal heart rate are necessary for the safe administration of Oxytocin for the induction or stimulation of labour. If uterine contractions become too powerful, the infusion can be abruptly stopped, and oxytocic stimulation of the uterine musculature will soon wane.

Part C

In this part of the test, there are two texts about different aspects of healthcare. For **questions 7-22**, choose the answer (**A**, **B**, **C** or **D**) which you think fits best according to the text.

Text 1: Phobia pills

An irrational fear, or phobia, can cause the heart to pound and the pulse to race. It can lead to a full-blown panic attack – and yet the sufferer is not in any real peril. All it takes is a glimpse of, for example, a spider's web for the mind and body to race into panicked overdrive. These fears are difficult to conquer, largely because, although there are no treatment guidelines specifically about phobias, the traditional way of helping the sufferer is to expose them to the fear numerous times. Through the cumulative effect of these experiences, sufferers should eventually feel an increasing sense of control over their phobia. For some people, the process is too protracted, but there may be a short cut. Drugs that work to boost learning may help someone with a phobia to 'detrain' their brain, losing the fearful associations that fuel the panic.

The brain's extraordinary ability to store new memories and forge associations is so well celebrated that its **dark side** is often disregarded. A feeling of contentment is easily evoked when we see a photo of loved ones, though the memory may sometimes be more idealised than exact. In the case of a phobia, however, a nasty experience with, say, spiders, that once triggered a panicked reaction, leads the feelings to resurge whenever the relevant cue is seen again. The current approach is exposure therapy, which uses a process called extinction learning. This involves people being gradually exposed to whatever triggers their phobia until they feel at ease with it. As the individual becomes more comfortable with each situation, the brain automatically creates a new memory – one that links the cue with reduced feelings of anxiety, rather than the sensations that mark the onset of a panic attack.

Unfortunately, while it is relatively easy to create a fear-based memory, expunging that fear is more complicated. Each exposure trial will involve a certain degree of distress in the patient, and although the process is carefully managed throughout to limit this, some psychotherapists have concluded that the treatment is unethical. Neuroscientists have been looking for new ways to speed up extinction learning **for that same reason**.

One such avenue is the use of 'cognitive enhancers' such as a drug called D-cycloserine or DCS. DCS slots into part of the brain's 'NMDA receptor' and seems to modulate the neurons' ability to adjust their signalling in response to events. This tuning of a neuron's firing is thought to be one of the key ways the brain stores memories, and, at very low doses, DCS appears to boost that process, improving our ability to learn. In 2004, a team from Emory University in Atlanta, USA, tested whether DCS could also help people with phobias. A pilot trial was conducted on 28 people undergoing specific exposure therapy for acrophobia – a fear of heights. Results showed that those given a small amount of DCS alongside their regular therapy were able to reduce their phobia to a greater extent than those given a placebo. Since then, other groups have replicated the finding in further trials.

For people undergoing exposure therapy, achieving just one of the steps on the long journey to overcoming their fears requires considerable perseverance, says Cristian Sirbu, a behavioural scientist and psychologist. Thanks to improvement being so slow, patients – often already anxious – tend to feel they have failed. But Sirbu thinks that DCS may make it possible to tackle the problem in a single 3-hour session, which is enough for the patient to make real headway and to leave with a feeling of satisfaction. However, some people have misgivings about this approach, claiming that as it doesn't directly undo the fearful response which is deep-seated in the memory, there is a very real risk of relapse.

Rather than simply attempting to overlay the fearful associations with new ones, Merel Kindt at the University of Amsterdam is instead trying to alter the associations at source. Kindt's studies into anxiety disorders are based on the idea that memories are not only vulnerable to alteration when they're first laid down, but, of key importance, also at later retrieval. This allows for memories to be 'updated', and these amended memories are re-consolidated by the effect of proteins which alter synaptic responses, thereby maintaining the strength of feeling associated with the original memory. Kindt's team has produced encouraging results with arachnophobic patients by giving them propranolol, a well-known and well-tolerated beta-blocker drug, while they looked at spiders. This blocked the effects of norepinephrine in the brain, disrupting the way the memory was put back into storage after being retrieved, as part of the process of reconsolidation. Participants reported that while they still don't like spiders, they were able to approach them. Kindt reports that the benefit was still there three months after the test ended.

Text 1: Questions 7-14

7. In the first paragraph, the writer says that conventional management of phobias can be problematic because of

(A) the lasting psychological effects of the treatment.

(B) the time required to identify the cause of the phobia.

(C) the limited choice of therapies available to professionals.

(D) the need for the phobia to be confronted repeatedly over time.

8. In the second paragraph, the writer uses the phrase '**dark side**' to reinforce the idea that

(A) memories of agreeable events tend to be inaccurate.

(B) positive memories can be negatively distorted over time.

(C) unhappy memories are often more detailed than happy ones.

(D) unpleasant memories are aroused in response to certain prompts.

9. In the second paragraph, extinction learning is explained as a process which

(A) makes use of an innate function of the brain.

(B) encourages patients to analyse their particular fears.

(C) shows patients how to react when having a panic attack.

(D) focuses on a previously little-understood part of the brain.

10. What does the phrase '**for that same reason**' refer to?

(A) the anxiety that patients feel during therapy

(B) complaints from patients who feel unsupported

(C) the conflicting ethical concerns of neuroscientists

(D) psychotherapists who take on unsuitable patients

11. In the fourth paragraph, we learn that the drug called DCS

    (A)   is unsafe to use except in small quantities.

    (B)   helps to control only certain types of phobias.

    (C)   affects how neurons in the brain react to stimuli.

    (D)   increases the emotional impact of certain events.

12. In the fifth paragraph, some critics believe that one drawback of using DCS is that

    (A)   its benefits are likely to be of limited duration.

    (B)   it is only helpful for certain types of personality.

    (C)   few patients are likely to complete the course of treatment.

    (D)   patients feel discouraged by their apparent lack of progress.

13. In the final paragraph, we learn that Kindt's studies into anxiety disorders focused on how

    (A)   proteins can affect memory retrieval.

    (B)   memories are superimposed on each other.

    (C)   negative memories can be reduced in frequency.

    (D)   the emotional force of a memory is naturally retained.

14. The writer suggests that propranolol may

    (A)   not offer a permanent solution for patients' phobias.

    (B)   increase patients' tolerance of key triggers.

    (C)   produce some beneficial side-effects.

    (D)   be inappropriate for certain phobias.

Text 2: Challenging medical thinking on placebos

Dr Damien Finniss, Associate Professor at Sydney University's Pain Management and Research Institute, was previously a physiotherapist. He regularly treated football players during training sessions using therapeutic ultrasound. 'One particular session', Finniss explains, 'I treated five or six athletes. I'd treat them for five or ten minutes and they'd say, "I feel much better" and run back onto the field. But at the end of the session, I realised the ultrasound wasn't on.' It was a light bulb moment that set Finniss on the path to becoming a leading researcher on the placebo effect.

Used to treat depression, psoriasis and Parkinson's, to name but a few, placebos have an image problem among medics. For years, the thinking has been that a placebo is useless unless the doctor convinces the patient that it's a genuine treatment – problematic for a profession that promotes informed consent. However, a new study casts doubt on this assumption and, along with a swathe of research showing some remarkable results with placebos, raises questions about whether they should now enter the mainstream as legitimate prescription items. The study examined five trials in which participants were told they were getting a placebo, and the conclusion was that doing so honestly can work.

'If the evidence is there, I don't see the harm in openly administering a placebo,' says Ben Colagiuri, a researcher at the University of Sydney. Colagiuri recently published a meta-analysis of thirteen studies which concluded that placebo sleeping pills, whose genuine counterparts **notch up** nearly three million prescriptions in Australia annually, significantly improve sleep quality. The use of placebos could therefore reduce medical costs and the burden of disease in terms of adverse reactions.

But the placebo effect isn't just about fake treatments. It's about raising patients' expectations of a positive result; something which also occurs with real drugs. Finniss cites the 'open-hidden' effect, whereby an analgesic can be twice as effective if the patient knows they're getting it, compared to receiving it unknowingly. 'Treatment is always part medical and part ritual,' says Finniss. This includes the austere consulting room and even the doctor's clothing. But behind the performance of healing is some strong science. Simply believing an analgesic will work activates the same brain regions as the genuine drug. 'Part of the outcome of what we do is the way we interact with patients,' says Finniss.

That interaction is also the focus of Colagiuri's research. He's looking into the 'nocebo' effect, when a patient's pessimism about a treatment becomes self-fulfilling. 'If you give a placebo, and warn only 50% of the patients about side effects, those you warn report more side effects,' says Colagiuri. He's aiming to reverse that by exploiting the psychology of food packaging. Products are labelled '98% fat-free' rather than '2% fat' because positive reference to the word 'fat' puts consumers off. Colagiuri is deploying similar tactics. A drug with a 30% chance of causing a side effect can be reframed as having a 70% chance of not causing it. 'You're giving the same information, but framing it a way that minimises negative expectations,' says Colagiuri.

There is also a body of research showing that a placebo can produce a genuine biological response that could affect the disease process itself. It can be traced back to a study from the 1970s, when psychologist Robert Ader was trying to condition taste-aversion in rats. He gave them a saccharine drink whilst simultaneously injecting Cytoxan, an immune-suppressant which causes nausea. The rats learned to hate the drink due to the nausea. But as Ader continued giving it to them, without Cytoxan, they began to die from infection. Their immune system had 'learned' to fail by repeated pairing of the drink with Cytoxan. Professor Andrea Evers of Leiden University is running a study that capitalises on this conditioning effect and may benefit patients with rheumatoid arthritis, which causes the immune system to attack the joints. Evers' patients are given the immunosuppressant methotrexate, but instead of always receiving the same dose, they get a higher dose followed by a lower one. The theory is that the higher dose will cause the body to link the medication with a damped-down immune system. The lower dose will then work because the body has 'learned' to curb immunity as a placebo response to taking the drug. Evers hopes it will mean effective drug regimes that use lower doses with fewer side effects.

The medical profession, however, remains less than enthusiastic about placebos. 'I'm one of two researchers in the country who speak on placebos, and I've been invited to lecture at just one university,' says Finniss. According to Charlotte Blease, a philosopher of science, this antipathy may go to the core of what it means to be a doctor. 'Medical education is largely about biomedical facts. 'Softer' sciences, such as psychology, get marginalised because it's the hard stuff that's associated with what it means to be a doctor.' The result, says Blease, is a large, placebo-shaped hole in the medical curriculum. 'There's a great deal of medical illiteracy about the placebo effect ... it's the science behind the art of medicine. Doctors need training in that.'

Text 2: Questions 15-22

15. A football training session sparked Dr Finniss' interest in the placebo effect because

- (A) he saw for himself how it could work in practice.
- (B) he took the opportunity to try out a theory about it.
- (C) he made a discovery about how it works with groups.
- (D) he realised he was more interested in research than treatment.

16. The writer suggests that doctors should be more willing to prescribe placebos now because

- (A) research indicates that they are effective even without deceit.
- (B) recent studies are more reliable than those conducted in the past.
- (C) they have been accepted as a treatment by many in the profession.
- (D) they have been shown to relieve symptoms in a wide range of conditions.

17. What is suggested about sleeping pills by the use of the verb '**notch up**'?

- (A) they may have negative results
- (B) they could easily be replaced
- (C) they are extremely effective
- (D) they are very widely used

18. What point does the writer make in the fourth paragraph?

- (A) The way a treatment is presented is significant even if it is a placebo.
- (B) The method by which a drug is administered is more important than its content.
- (C) The theatrical side of medicine should not be allowed to detract from the science.
- (D) The outcome of a placebo treatment is affected by whether the doctor believes in it.

19. In researching side effects, Colagiuri aims to

  (A) discover whether placebos can cause them.

  (B) reduce the number of people who experience them.

  (C) make information about them more accessible to patients.

  (D) investigate whether pessimistic patients are more likely to suffer from them.

20. What does the word '**it**' in the sixth paragraph refer to?

  (A) a placebo treatment

  (B) the disease process itself

  (C) a growing body of research

  (D) a genuine biological response

21. What does the writer tell us about Ader's and Evers' studies?

  (A) Both involve gradually reducing the dosage of a drug.

  (B) Evers is exploiting a response which Ader discovered by chance.

  (C) Both examine the side effects caused by immunosuppressant drugs.

  (D) Evers is investigating whether the human immune system reacts to placebos as Ader's rats did.

22. According to Charlotte Blease, placebos are omitted from medical training because

  (A) there are so many practical subjects which need to be covered.

  (B) those who train doctors do not believe that they work.

  (C) they can be administered without specialist training.

  (D) their effect is more psychological than physical.

END OF READING TEST
THIS BOOKLET WILL BE COLLECTED

OCCUPATIONAL ENGLISH TEST

WRITING SUB-TEST – TEST BOOKLET

CANDIDATE NUMBER:

LAST NAME:

FIRST NAME:

MIDDLE NAMES:

PROFESSION:

VENUE:

TEST DATE:

Candidate details and photo will be printed here.

Passport Photo

CANDIDATE DECLARATION

By signing this, you agree not to disclose or use in any way (other than to take the test) or assist any other person to disclose or use any OET test or sub-test content. If you cheat or assist in any cheating, use any unfair practice, break any of the rules or regulations, or ignore any advice or information, you may be disqualified and your results may not be issued at the sole discretion of CBLA. CBLA also reserves its right to take further disciplinary action against you and to pursue any other remedies permitted by law. If a candidate is suspected of and investigated for malpractice, their personal details and details of the investigation may be passed to a third party where required.

CANDIDATE SIGNATURE: _____

INSTRUCTIONS TO CANDIDATES

You must write your answer for the Writing sub-test in the **Writing Answer Booklet.**

You must **NOT** remove OET material from the test room.

www.occupationalenglishtest.org

© Cambridge Boxhill Language Assessment – ABN 51 988 559 414

[CANDIDATE NO.] WRITING SUB-TEST TEST BOOKLET 01/04

OCCUPATIONAL ENGLISH TEST

WRITING SUB-TEST: NURSING

TIME ALLOWED: **READING TIME:** 5 MINUTES
WRITING TIME: 40 MINUTES

Read the case notes below and complete the writing task which follows.

Notes:

You are a Registered Nurse preparing Mrs Jasmine Thompson's discharge. Mrs Thompson has had a right total shoulder replacement. She is to be discharged home today with assistance from 'In-Home Nursing Service'.

Patient: Mrs Jasmine Thompson

Address: 73 White Road, Bayview

DOB: 01.07.1942

Age: 76

Social/Family background:
Lives in single-storey house with large garden

Utilises cleaning services once a month

Widow. 1 daughter – lives in Bayview. 1 son – married with 2 children, lives in Stillwater.

Daughter will stay with mother for 1 month post-surgery

Medical history: R humerus fracture – 1997

Osteoarthritis – R shoulder which has not responded to conservative treatment

Chronic R shoulder pain – ↓ movement and ability to carry out activities of daily living (ADL)

Current medications:
Voltaren 50mg daily (ceased 14 days pre-operatively)
Panadeine Forte (codeine/paracetamol) 30/500mg x 2, 6hrly
p.r.n. LMWH (Clexane)

Admission diagnosis:
R shoulder osteoarthritis

Medical treatment record:
<u>11.07.18</u> R Total shoulder replacement (TSR)

Medical progress: Post-op R shoulder X-rays – confirm position of TSR

Post-op exercise regime – compliant with physiotherapy

Post-op bloods – within normal limits

Post-op pain management – analgesia, cold compress R shoulder

R shoulder wound – clean & dry, drain site – clean & dry

<u>15.07.18</u> Plan for discharge home with daughter today – home nurse to assist at home

Nursing management:

Observations – T, P, R, BP (all within normal range)

Neurovascular observations – colour, warmth, movement, sensation

Oral analgesia

Wound care and observations

Cold compress/shoulder-brace 4 hours per day

ADL assistance as required

Physiotherapy management:

Exercises as per TSR protocol – Neck range of movement exercises
Elbow and hand ROM exercises
Pendular shoulder exercises

Cryo cuff (cold compress) 4 hours per day

Discharge education

Follow-up physiotherapy outpatients appointments

Referral to community hydrotherapy

Discharge plan:
- Patient discharge education – Post TSR:
  - R arm sling for 4 weeks
  - Strictly no lifting for 4 weeks
  - Physiotherapy outpatients x 2 per week, plus hydrotherapy x 1 per week
- 10 days post-op – staples removal, follow-up appointment in Orthopaedic Joint Replacement Outpatient Department
- Orthopaedic Joint Replacement Nurse Specialist contactable by calling hospital, Mon-Fri for any concerns
- Referral to 'In-Home Nursing Service' – assist with showering, administration of LMWH (Clexane) subcutaneous for 4 days as DVT (deep vein thrombosis) prophylaxis

Writing Task:

Using the information given in the case notes, write a letter of referral to Ms Roberts, a home nurse, informing her of the patient's situation and requesting appropriate care. Address the letter to Ms Nita Roberts, In-Home Nursing Service, 79 Beachside Street, Bayview.

In your answer:
- **Expand the relevant notes into complete sentences**
- **Do not use note form**
- **Use letter format**

The body of the letter should be approximately 180–200 words.

OCCUPATIONAL ENGLISH TEST

WRITING SUB-TEST – ANSWER BOOKLET

CANDIDATE NUMBER:

LAST NAME:

FIRST NAME:

MIDDLE NAMES:

Candidate details and photo will be printed here.

Passport Photo

PROFESSION:

VENUE:

TEST DATE:

CANDIDATE DECLARATION

By signing this, you agree not to disclose or use in any way (other than to take the test) or assist any other person to disclose or use any OET test or sub-test content. If you cheat or assist in any cheating, use any unfair practice, break any of the rules or regulations, or ignore any advice or information, you may be disqualified and your results may not be issued at the sole discretion of CBLA. CBLA also reserves its right to take further disciplinary action against you and to pursue any other remedies permitted by law. If a candidate is suspected of and investigated for malpractice, their personal details and details of the investigation may be passed to a third party where required.

CANDIDATE SIGNATURE: _____

TIME ALLOWED
READING TIME: 5 MINUTES
WRITING TIME: 40 MINUTES

INSTRUCTIONS TO CANDIDATES

1. **Reading time: 5 minutes**
    During this time you may study the writing task and notes. You **MUST NOT** write, highlight, underline or make any notes.

2. **Writing time: 40 minutes**

3. Use the back page for notes and rough draft only. Notes and rough draft will **NOT** be marked.

    Please write your answer clearly on page 1 and page 2.

    Cross out anything you **DO NOT** want the examiner to consider.

4. You must write your answer for the Writing sub-test in this **Answer Booklet** using **pen or pencil**.

5. You must **NOT** remove OET material from the test room.

www.occupationalenglishtest.org
© Cambridge Boxhill Language Assessment – ABN 51 988 559 414

[CANDIDATE NO.] WRITING SUB-TEST ANSWER BOOKLET 01/04

Please record your answer on this page.

(Only answers on Page 1 and Page 2 will be marked.)

_____
_____
_____
_____
_____
_____
_____
_____
_____
_____
_____
_____
_____
_____
_____
_____
_____
_____
_____
_____
_____
_____
_____
_____
_____
_____
_____
_____
_____
_____
_____
_____
_____

OET Writing sub-test – Answer booklet   1

Please record your answer on this page.

(Only answers on Page 1 and Page 2 will be marked.)

_____

_____

_____

_____

_____

_____

_____

_____

_____

_____

_____

_____

_____

_____

_____

_____

_____

_____

_____

_____

_____

_____

_____

_____

_____

_____

_____

_____

_____

OET Writing sub-test – Answer booklet   2

Space for notes and rough draft. Only your answers on Page 1 and Page 2 will be marked.

SPEAKING SUB-TEST

CANDIDATE NUMBER:

LAST NAME:

FIRST NAME:

MIDDLE NAMES:

PROFESSION: Your details and photo will be printed here.

VENUE:

TEST DATE:

Passport Photo

CANDIDATE DECLARATION

By signing this, you agree not to disclose or use in any way (other than to take the test) or assist any other person to disclose or use any OET test or sub-test content. If you cheat or assist in any cheating, use any unfair practice, break any of the rules or regulations, or ignore any advice or information, you may be disqualified and your results may not be issued at the sole discretion of CBLA. CBLA also reserves its right to take further disciplinary action against you and to pursue any other remedies permitted by law. If a candidate is suspected of and investigated for malpractice, their personal details and details of the investigation may be passed to a third party where required.

CANDIDATE SIGNATURE: _____

INSTRUCTION TO CANDIDATES

Please confirm with the Interlocutor that your roleplay card number and colour match the Interlocutor card before you begin.

Interlocutor to complete only

ID No: _____   Passport: ☐   National ID: ☐   Alternative ID approved: ☐

Speaking sub-test:

ID document sighted? ☐   Photo match? ☐   Signature match? ☐   Did not attend? ☐

Interlocutor name: _____

Interlocutor signature: _____

www.occupationalenglishtest.org
© Cambridge Boxhill Language Assessment – ABN 51 988 559 414

[CANDIDATE NO.] SPEAKING SUB-TEST 01/04

OET Sample role-play

ROLEPLAYER CARD NO. 1	NURSING

SETTING Hospital Ward

PATIENT Last night, following an acute attack of asthma, your family brought you into the emergency department of your local hospital for treatment. You have never had an asthma attack prior to this one. Currently you are being held in the hospital for observation purposes. You anticipate that you will be discharged from hospital within 2-3 hours and you suddenly realise not only that you have had a fright, but that you know little about asthma, e.g., what causes it, how it is treated, and possible long-term effects.

TASK

- Express concern about your condition.

- Find out about asthma, its causes and how it can be treated. You have heard stories about people dying from asthma attacks.

- Be anxious about the proposal to use a Ventolin inhaler – people have told you about its misuse.

- Ask about your long-term prospects now that you have had an asthma attack and been held in hospital overnight for observation.

Sample role-play

OET Sample role-play

CANDIDATE CARD NO. 1	NURSING

SETTING Hospital Ward

NURSE This patient was brought into the emergency department of your hospital late last night suffering from an acute asthma attack. He/she is currently being held for observation. The patient has had a fright and is very concerned about his/her condition.

TASK

- Find out how the patient is feeling and if they have any questions about asthma.
- Explain what asthma is (e.g., a chronic disease of the airways, etc.).
- Discuss the causes, such as environmental factors and an inherited predisposition.
- Explain the treatment, for example, a Ventolin (salbutamol) inhaler, and how to use such an inhaler.
- Discuss the prognosis for asthma patients.
- Deal with the patient's anxiety about the problem, emphasising that asthma can be controlled.

Sample role-play

ROLEPLAYER CARD NO. 2   NURSING

SETTING	Reception Centre at a Public Hospital
CARER	You are visiting a nearby public hospital with your 81-year-old father. Your father has recently been diagnosed as suffering from kidney failure. As a consequence, he is to undergo a tri-weekly dialysis program. Today is 'day one' of your father's dialysis treatment and, while you are waiting for him to have his personal details taken by the charge nurse, you decide to ask another nurse, who is on the reception desk, for information about your father's medical condition and the proposed treatment.

TASK

- You don't know anything about dialysis, so you would like some detailed information about your father's condition. What does kidney failure really mean?
- You would like to know more about what is involved in dialysis. What is it exactly? Why does your father have to come three times a week?
- Ask if the dialysis will improve your father's current medical condition.
- Ask if the dialysis treatment is painful and if there are any side effects.
- Explain that your father is 81 years old, then ask what could happen were he to decide not to continue his treatment.

     Sample role-play

CANDIDATE CARD NO. 2   NURSING

SETTING	Reception Centre at a Public Hospital
NURSE	You are working at the reception desk of a public hospital. The son/daughter of an 81-year-old man, who has recently been diagnosed as suffering from kidney failure and who is to undergo a tri-weekly dialysis program, has approached you to ask questions about his/her father's medical condition and the proposed treatment.

TASK

- Find out what the son/daughter already knows about dialysis.
- Explain what kidney failure is. Explain that the kidneys are no longer working, and what this means.
- Describe what dialysis is (e.g., machine which cleans the blood, etc.).
- Explain why his/her father's treatment is to happen three times a week.
- Explain that his/her father's medical condition is unlikely to improve (i.e., it is very unlikely his kidneys will start working again).
- Give details about whether the treatment is painful or has any side effects (e.g., fatigue, low blood pressure, muscle cramps, etc.).
- Tactfully warn what could happen if his/her father decided not to continue with his dialysis treatment (e.g., the patient will become very ill, etc.).

     Sample role-play

Listening sub-test

ANSWER KEY – Parts A, B & C

LISTENING SUB-TEST – ANSWER KEY

PART A: QUESTIONS 1-12

1 dry

2 (very) gradual

3 swollen / bulging (out)

4 soft

5 farm labourer

6 (night) security guard

7 beta blockers

8 crackling (accept: cracking)/ crep / crepitation

9 (bad) eczema

10 echocardiogram / cardiac echo / echo

11 arterial blood gas / ABG

12 corticosteroids

PART A: QUESTIONS 13-24

13 myopic / short(-)sighted / near(-)sighted

14 nystagmus / (a) flicker(ing)

15 pigment (in eye)

16 driving

17 focus

18 distance

19 (hotel) receptionist

20 cataract (developed)

21 opacity / clouding

22 detached retina / retina(l) detachment

23 (eye) floaters

24 glare / bright lights

LISTENING SUB-TEST – ANSWER KEY

PART B: QUESTIONS 25-30

25	A	remove her saline drip
26	C	relatively high staff absence rates
27	C	prepare to cope with an increasing demand for it.
28	B	Nobody has taken responsibility for assessing the patient.
29	B	expand upon what they studied previously.
30	C	warning him about a possible problem

PART C: QUESTIONS 31-36

31	B	Their condition can develop in a number of different ways.
32	A	There was a lack of reliable information on it.
33	B	was more widely available than some users imagined.
34	C	may lead to dementia patients experiencing unnecessary distress.
35	A	illustrate a gap in current medical education programmes.
36	B	it avoids carers having to speculate about a patient's wishes.

PART C: QUESTIONS 37-42

37	B	observing the effects of poor communication on a patient.
38	A	The information given can overwhelm patients.
39	C	relatives' knowledge of a patient's condition shouldn't be taken for granted.
40	A	measured the difference between their expectations and their actual experience.
41	B	the over-use of unclear medical terminology with patients.
42	A	surprised by one response from patients

END OF KEY

Listening sub-test

Audio Script – Practice test 3

This test has three parts. In each part you'll hear a number of different extracts. At the start of each extract, you'll hear this sound: ---***---.

You'll have time to read the questions before you hear each extract and you'll hear each extract ONCE only. Complete your answers as you listen.

At the end of the test, you'll have two minutes to check your answers.

Part A. In this part of the test, you'll hear two different extracts. In each extract, a health professional is talking to a patient. For questions 1 to 24, complete the notes with information you hear. Now, look at the notes for extract one.

PAUSE: 5 SECONDS
Extract one. Questions 1 to 12.

You hear a consultant endocrinologist talking to a patient called Sarah Croft. For questions 1 to 12, complete the notes with a word or short phrase. You now have thirty seconds to look at the notes.

PAUSE: 30 SECONDS
---***---

You hear a pulmonologist talking to a patient called Robert Miller. For questions 1 to 12, complete the notes with a word or short phrase. You now have thirty seconds to look at the notes.

PAUSE: 30 SECONDS
---***---

F Good morning, Mr Miller. Now, looking at your notes, I see you've been having a few problems recently. Could you tell me a little about what's been happening, in your own words?

M Well, yeah – it's a combination of things really. To kick-off, I feel pretty tired most of the time – just haven't got the energy I used to have. And I've got this cough – it's there all the time and it feels dry – I mean, I'm not coughing up phlegm or blood or anything like that. But the worst thing, which really bothers me, is that I'm so short of breath – even if I'm just getting dressed in the morning or going up a few steps, I have to stop 'cos I get breathless so quickly. And I've lost quite a bit of weight, too – I mean, I didn't notice at first cos it was very gradual. But all in all, I'm about ten kilos lighter than I was six months ago. I've not been dieting or anything – I, I love my food!

F OK. And, well have you noticed anything else?

M Yeah – just take a look at my fingers. The tips look swollen, don't they – and it's the same with my toes, which are bulging out at the end too. It's weird. And my nails – I don't understand it – they've become soft. They're not hard like they used to be. Look....

F Erm, OK ... I see what you mean. And tell me a little about yourself.... Umm what do you do for a living?

M Well, till recently, I worked as a farm labourer. Did it for about twenty years in total. It was hard physical graft, and it finally got to the stage where I just couldn't cope with it any more. It really took it out of me. So, this last couple of years, I've been a security guard, working nights at a local DIY warehouse. It's a bit boring, and the late shifts took a bit of getting used to, but it's OK.

F   And, erm, are you finding it less physically demanding?

M   *That's right. I just haven't got the stamina now for anything else – in fact, I've even had to give up my golf. Can't manage it any more. Any spare time now goes on looking after my pigeons – I've done that since I was a teenager.*

F   Oh very nice. And, erm, what about your medical history. Now, I see you were diagnosed with hypertension last year, and you're taking beta blockers at the moment for that.

M   *That's right. My GP said it'd help. Something the GP also said, when I saw him about my breathing problems, was that he heard what he called 'crackling' noises in my chest. I can't hear them, but he could - through the stethoscope.*

F   OK. And is there any family history of breathing or lung problems, or any serious illnesses that you know of?

M   *I don't think so. My mother was always healthy, but my dad developed bad eczema as an adult. I remember the red patches on his hands and face. But he didn't have any lung problems as far as I know.*

F   Right, and… well looking at your previous tests, you were diagnosed with hypertension about 6 months ago, you had…

M   *Oh yeah, erm… an echocardiogram, you know, to check my heart… and a chest x-ray about four weeks ago after I saw my GP. That came back OK as far as I know.*

F   I see.

M   *I'm not keen on hospitals, to be honest. Am I going to need to have lots more tests?*

F   Well, I'm going to suggest you have what's called an arterial blood gas test. This will let us check how well your lungs are working – how they move oxygen into your blood and remove carbon dioxide from it.

M   *OK.*

F   And, I'm also going to order a CT scan. Now, this'll be more revealing than the chest x-ray you had. And I may then prescribe a course of corticosteroids. This will depend on what the tests show up. Now, I'd start you on a relatively low dose and then we'll … [fade]

PAUSE: 10 SECONDS
Extract two. Questions 13 to 24.

You hear an eye specialist talking to a patient called Jasmine Burton, who has recently undergone eye surgery. For questions 13 to 24, complete the notes with a word or short phrase. You now have thirty seconds to look at the notes.

PAUSE: 30 SECONDS
---***---

M: I've got your notes here Mrs Burton, but as we're meeting for the first time, could you begin by telling me a little about your eyesight and the treatment you've had over the years. Erm, did you wear glasses as a child, for example?

F: *Ahh yes, since I was about seven. My parents were concerned by the way I held a book when I was reading so they took me to an optometrist. He told them I had some kind of astigmatism.*

M: Am I right in assuming that's myopic rather than hyperopic?

F: *Well yes, I'm near-sighted...if that's what you mean.*

M: That's right. Some people actually have mixed astigmatism - they're far-sighted in one eye and near in the other.

F: *Oh well, that's not me. And, as well as my astigmatism, as you've probably noticed, my eyes flicker. I'm not aware of it myself but other people comment on it sometimes. I think you call it...nystagmus. It meant that, when I had my eye surgery, they preferred to use a general rather than a local anaesthetic.*

M: OK, so did anyone ever tell you what they thought might have caused the condition?

F: *Well, I was once told that my generally poor eyesight is most probably down to the fact that I don't have enough pigment in the eye. On the whole, my eyes have never really caused me any significant difficulties, however. I've always had to wear glasses, so that's a part of life now. I suppose...the only thing is that driving's always been out of the question. I'd never have passed the sight part of the test. That's probably a good thing because it takes me some time to focus, which could make me pretty dangerous if I was ever behind the wheel of a car.*

M: Yes, indeed.

F: *Also I'm useless at sports like tennis - I think that's because I'm...I'm poor at judging the distance between myself and the ball. That was a pain as a teenager, but I've never particularly wanted to play since then. And I've hardly had any issues at work because of my sight. I'm a receptionist in a hotel and I've never had any difficulty reading computer screens or anything fortunately.*

M: You've...You've had your eyes regularly checked throughout your life presumably?

F: *Yeah that's right. Every couple of years. My prescription's changed a little over time - but not that much. Though I certainly couldn't manage without reading glasses these days. About three years ago, I was told a cataract was developing in my right eye. It was a few years before they decided to remove it – that was this February – and it all went very smoothly.*

M: Good, and you... you were pleased with the result?

F: *Yeah I was, yeah, thrilled. If only all our failing parts could be replaced so easily! However, when I had the routine check-up a couple of weeks after the operation, I was told there was some clouding...err opacity, I think was the word they used - in the capsule containing the new lens. It's a bit disappointing. They could clear it with a laser if it gets to be a real problem...erm, but my flicker makes that rather a risky option. I knew that there's a greater chance of developing a detached retina after a cataract op...but I'm glad to say they found there wasn't any evidence of that in my case. All they did was make an appointment for me to be checked out again in six months-time. But they said I should get in touch if I felt concerned about my eyes.*

M: And is that what brings you here today?

F: *Yeah, because I am bothered about a couple of things. So, firstly I've noticed more floaters than usual. I don't know if that's something to worry about or not. Erm, more annoying is the fact that I'm much more troubled by glare than I used to be. So I wanted to ask your opinion on that.*

M: OK, well let's start by having .....[fade]

PAUSE: 10 SECONDS

That is the end of Part A. Now, look at Part B.

PAUSE: 5 SECONDS

Part B. In this part of the test, you'll hear six different extracts. In each extract, you'll hear people talking in a different healthcare setting.

For questions 25 to 30, choose the answer A, B or C which fits best according to what you hear. You'll have time to read each question before you listen. Complete your answers as you listen.

Now look at Question 25. You hear a nurse briefing a colleague at the end of her shift. Now read the question.

PAUSE: 15 SECONDS

---***---

F   OK, so the next thing is about Suzie Williams in bed three.

M   Right.

F   She's been admitted for chest pain to rule out MI. So far she had an EKG which was OK, and the first set of cardiac enzymes and troponins are negative. When she came in, her blood pressure was elevated a little, like one eighty two over ninety five, but she was given losartan and at six o'clock it was one forty two over eighty two. She was also dehydrated so we started her on IV fluids, D5 half-normal saline running at a hundred and twenty five millilitres. That can go until midnight and then it can be disconnected. She's scheduled for a stress test tomorrow and some more enzyme tests. OK?

M   OK.

PAUSE: 5 SECONDS

Question 26. You hear part of a hospital management meeting where a concern is being discussed. Now read the question.

PAUSE: 15 SECONDS

---***---

M   Now I'll hand over to Jenny, who has a few words to say about staffing. Jenny?

F   Thanks. Now, if we compare ourselves to other hospitals of the same size, in other regions, we're actually recording lower rates of staff turnover. That's just as well given the challenges filling vacant positions across the sector. Where we do compare unfavourably is in the number of days lost to sick leave. That's making it hard to maintain full cover on the wards, and we all know the costs of that. As a matter of urgency then, HR are looking into the worst affected areas to understand the reasons behind it and to see if there's anything we can do to help and support the staff involved.

PAUSE: 5 SECONDS

Question 27. You hear a GP and his practice nurse discussing a vaccination programme. Now read the question.

PAUSE: 15 SECONDS

---***---

M: It's coming up to that time of year when we have to start preparing for the flu vaccination programme.

F: Yes, we usually do it at the start of next month, don't we?

M: That's right. If you remember last year we hired a local hall and did as many people as we could in one afternoon.

F: Yes, I'd just started working here then. It was a hectic couple of hours but it worked pretty well, don't you think?

M: Sure, but there's been so much publicity recently about how sensible it is to get the jab that I suspect we'll have a lot more people coming along this year.

F: So we better think about taking on an agency nurse perhaps to lend an extra hand.

M: OK. Let's run that by the practice manager. And she might have some other suggestions too.

PAUSE: 5 SECONDS
Question 28. You hear two hospital nurses discussing the assessment of a patient on their ward. Now read the question.

PAUSE: 15 SECONDS

---***---

M The bed manager just rang. He wants us to clear three spaces in the ward. Today.

F Oh it's never-ending! Let's see what we can do. There's no one ready to be discharged. But we could try chasing referrals for Mr Davison to the community hospital for rehab. Where are his notes?

M Yes, but has he had his assessment yet?

F They were all away at that conference yesterday and the day before. I think he'll have slipped through the net.

M: But Doctor Ammat's already got him medically stable and signed off. So he should   be the next one to move on.

F Well I'd get him there as quickly as possible before they give the place to somebody else.

M I'll phone them straight away.

PAUSE: 5 SECONDS
Question 29. You hear the beginning of a training session for dental students. Now read the question.

PAUSE: 15 SECONDS

---***---

F This is session number four, which is going to include, again, impression-taking. We've created the crown impression of tooth number 30, we also took care of an inlay preparation. So today we're going to stay on that side with our impression-taking. We're going to make a duplicate of what we've already done. And our attention to detail is now going up another notch.

When I take an impression of a tooth that I've created in the mouth, I naturally have to take care of the saliva, the blood, the gum tissue… We're not going to cover all that today. You'll hit that next semester. What we are going to cover are the dynamics of your impression, the margins, the proximal contacts, the bite and the occlusion. We're going to capture all that in one impression.

PAUSE: 5 SECONDS

Question 30. You hear two nurses discussing the treatment of a patient with a kidney infection. Now read the question.

PAUSE: 15 SECONDS

---***---

M   I can't see the results of Mr Roberts' last blood test to check creatinine levels. Did you do the last one?

F   *No, not me. Let's see. Ah, here it is. The last test was four hours ago and results show a level of thirty eight, so it's still well below normal. We'd better do one when he wakes up, as it might have changed. The patient's not keen on needles though. I had a real job last night trying to convince him it was necessary. Not the easiest of patients, if you're happy to have*
a go.

M   OK. My turn, I reckon.

PAUSE: 10 SECONDS

That is the end of Part B. Now, look at Part C.

PAUSE: 5 SECONDS

Part C. In this part of the test, you'll hear two different extracts. In each extract, you'll hear health professionals talking about aspects of their work.

For questions 31 to 42, choose the answer A, B or C which fits best according to what you hear. Complete your answers as you listen.

Now look at extract one.

Extract one. Questions 31 to 36. You hear a geriatrician called Dr Clare Cox giving a presentation on the subject of end-of-life care for people with dementia.

You now have 90 seconds to read questions 31 to 36.

PAUSE: 90 SECONDS

---***---

F: My name's Dr Clare Cox. I'm a geriatrician specialising in palliative care. My topic today is an increasingly important issue: end-of-life care for dementia patients.

     The care of dementia patients presents certain problems. Dementia is a terminal illness and is the third highest cause of death in Australia. But dementia is different from other such conditions. It has an unpredictable trajectory and there can be difficult issues around patients' mental capacity, decision-making and communication. But, in spite of an equal need for palliative care services, dementia patients don't always fit the traditional model of such care. Families often suffer distress because they feel unable to ensure that their loved one's wishes are being respected, or just don't know what that person wanted because the discussion wasn't held early enough. There is, therefore, a clear need for well-funded, patient-centred palliative dementia care that's available when and where it's needed.

I do a lot of work with Dementia Australia – an organisation which represents the needs of Australians living with all types of dementia, and of their families and carers. It also campaigns on dementia issues and funds research.

Dementia Australia decided it was the right time to examine the issue of end-of-life dementia care, from the perspective of the consumer as well as from that of the healthcare professional. It's a timely initiative. We have plenty of anecdotal evidence, but not enough hard facts about what's going wrong and why the system's failing. But the current situation isn't all bad. Despite the issues I've mentioned, I've heard some wonderful examples of how palliative care has made a big difference to people's lives. Things can obviously go badly wrong if this isn't handled well, but in the right circumstances people with dementia can reach the end of their lives peacefully and with dignity.

Dementia Australia commissioned researchers to conduct a survey on the end-of-life issues affecting dementia patients. The survey covered both care professionals, that's doctors, nurses and others working with dementia patients, as well as family-member carers. The interest was overwhelming with more than a thousand responses from around Australia. But what do the results tell us? Well, the initial results confirmed what we've heard about access to appropriate end-of-life care. It was obvious immediately that there was a striking gap between the perceptions of care professionals, and family-member carers about end-of-life dementia care. For instance, while fifty-eight per cent of family-member carers said that they didn't have access to palliative care specialists, and sixty-eight per cent didn't have access to hospices, three-quarters of care professionals indicated that people with dementia in their area do in fact have access to palliative care. This begs the question of whether consumers – that is patients and family-member carers – might not be aware of services that are available.

Another notable finding of the survey was that care professionals often lack knowledge of the legal issues surrounding end-of-life care. Some reports indicate that care professionals are at times reluctant to use pain medications such as morphine because of concerns about hastening a patient's death. However, access to appropriate pain relief is considered to be a fundamental human right, even if death is earlier as a secondary effect of medication. Our survey found that twenty-seven per cent of care professionals were unsure about this, or didn't believe that patients are legally entitled to adequate pain control, if it might hasten death. So perhaps it isn't surprising then, that a quarter of former family-member carers felt that pain wasn't adequately managed in end-of-life care.

This lack of awareness extends beyond pain management. The statistics on refusing treatment were particularly shocking. Almost a third of care professionals were unaware that people have the right to refuse food and hydration, and one in ten also thought refusal of antibiotics wasn't an option for patients in end-of-life care. How can we ever achieve consumer empowerment and consumer-directed care if the professionals are so ill informed? There's a clear need for greater information and training on patient rights, yet over a third of care professionals said they hadn't received any such training at all.

It's obvious that end-of-life care planning is desirable. Discussing and documenting preferences is clearly the best way of minimising the burden of decision-making on carers, and ensuring patients' wishes are respected. Advance care planning is essentially an insurance policy that helps to protect our patients in case they lose their decision-making capacity. Even though a patient might believe that loved ones will have their best interests at heart, the evidence shows that such people aren't that good at knowing what decisions those they love would make on complex matters such as infection control and hydration.

So, before I go on to …..[fade]

PAUSE: 10 SECONDS

Now look at extract two.

Extract two. Questions 37 to 42. You hear a hospital doctor called Dr Keith Gardiner giving a presentation about some research he's done on the subject of staff-patient communication.

You now have 90 seconds to read questions 37 to 42.

PAUSE: 90 SECONDS
---***---

M: Good morning. My name's Dr Keith Gardiner, and I'd like to talk to you today about some research I've been involved in, concerning something that affects all health professionals – staff-patient communication.

Now, firstly, let me reassure you that in feedback, patients seem positive about the way information is communicated to them. But I recently decided to explore the issue in more detail when I was in a hospital with a patient and witnessed for myself what can result when a health care professional assumes they've made themselves clear to a patient, when in fact they've been anything but. Luckily, I've had very few complaints made against members of my team, but the potential is certainly there.

So first, let's start by looking at a typical hospital admission for an in-patient, and the first communication they have about any procedures they are to undergo. On arrival, a patient will complete necessary paperwork. Various staff will talk to them about their treatment during their stay, which is designed to reduce patient anxiety. However, from some patients' point of view, this interaction can seem very complex and difficult to take in, especially at a time when they're not at their best physically or mentally. So it's doubly important to check that any communication has been understood.

Now, to illustrate what I'm talking about, let's take a hypothetical situation. I often use this because it highlights the potential consequences of poor communication. A man in his eighties is admitted to hospital, despite his protestations, with ongoing severe back pain. On investigation, it's found his cancer has spread. The outlook is poor - and further compounded by his becoming depressed and refusing to eat while in hospital. A feeding tube is inserted, a procedure which the patient complies with, but which his family members query. The doctor on duty updates them, assuming they're aware of the severity of the patient's condition – when in fact no such prognosis has been shared with them. An extreme case, but a plausible one, nevertheless.

In order to find out exactly what in-patients felt about the service they were receiving in this hospital, we conducted a patient survey. The questions were carefully targeted to capture patients' opinions about the effectiveness of the communication they'd been involved in during their stay. The survey questioned patients on both what they had expected prior to admission, and what their stay was really like. These two scores were then used to calculate what's called a 'gap' score. The survey also included questions to measure the patients' behavioural intention – that is, how willing they would be to return to the hospital for treatment. Patients completed the survey themselves, and results were then processed with the help of medical students.

Now, the survey produced some interesting data about communication, including both praise and complaints. Clearly in a hospital situation, staff are dealing with confidential and sensitive information, which must be communicated in private – a situation which can be difficult to achieve in a large and busy hospital. However, we scored highly on that point. And we were also pleased to note that staff did manage to communicate in a manner that treated patients with dignity and respect. Of course, staff also have to ensure patients fully understand what's been said to them. And this last point's where we received the most negative feedback. Both patients and relatives noted a tendency for professionals to resort to the use of jargon, and complex terms when explaining both diagnoses and procedures, which left some patients confused. However, patients were generally satisfied with the information about any follow-up treatment provided after discharge.

Also, once we'd sifted through all the results, a clear pattern began to emerge regarding the care given by nurses, which I found particularly interesting. I'd assumed that having a number of different nurses attending to a patient during their stay was a good thing, because you need enough staff to cover the various shifts, and attend to patients' needs. What I certainly hadn't expected, though, was for patients to say they felt their recovery was faster when they had to communicate with only a small number of nurses - in other words when they were surrounded by familiar faces. The findings aren't conclusive, and more investigative work needs to be done on a bigger sample – but it's certainly food for thought.

PAUSE: 10 SECONDS
That is the end of Part C.

You now have two minutes to check your answers.

PAUSE: 120 SECONDS
That is the end of the Listening test.

OCCUPATIONAL ENGLISH TEST

Reading sub-test

Answer Key – Part A

READING SUB-TEST – ANSWER KEY

PART A: QUESTIONS 1-20

1	B
2	A
3	C
4	D
5	C
6	B
7	D
8	clindamycin (and) penicillin
9	diabetes mellitus
10	septic shock
11	VAC/ vacuum-assisted closure
12	alcohol pads
13	daptomycin (and) linezolid
14	vibrio (infection)
15	32.2%
16	seafood
17	limbs
18	polymicrobial
19	7%
20	physical therapy

Reading sub-test

Answer Key – Parts B & C

READING SUB-TEST – ANSWER KEY

PART B: QUESTIONS 1-6

1	A	stop dates aren't relevant in all circumstances.
2	B	improves precision during radiation.
3	B	position electrodes correctly.
4	C	its short-term benefits are explained to them.
5	B	the use of a particular method of testing pH levels.
6	A	the amount of oxytocin given will depend on how the patient reacts.

PART C: QUESTIONS 7-14

7	D	the need for the phobia to be confronted repeatedly over time.
8	D	unpleasant memories are aroused in response to certain prompts.
9	A	makes use of an innate function of the brain.
10	A	the anxiety that patients feel during therapy
11	C	affects how neurons in the brain react to stimuli.
12	A	its benefits are likely to be of limited duration.
13	D	the emotional force of a memory is naturally retained.
14	B	increase patients' tolerance of key triggers.

PART C: QUESTIONS 15-22

15	A	he saw for himself how it could work in practice.
16	A	research indicates that they are effective even without deceit.
17	D	they are very widely used
18	A	The way a treatment is presented is significant even if it is a placebo.
19	B	reduce the number of people who experience them.
20	C	a growing body of research
21	B	Evers is exploiting a response which Ader discovered by chance.
22	D	their effect is more psychological than physical.

OCCUPATIONAL ENGLISH TEST

WRITING SUB-TEST: NURSING

SAMPLE RESPONSE: LETTER OF REFERRAL

Ms Nita Roberts
In-Home Nursing Service
79 Beachside Street
Bayview

15 July 2018

Re: Mrs Jasmine Thompson. DOB: 01/07/1942.

Dear Ms Roberts,

Thank you for accepting Mrs Thompson into your care. She underwent a successful right total shoulder replacement on 11/07/18 after a long history of osteoarthritis which affected her ability to perform her daily activities. She will be discharged today with her daughter who will live with Mrs Thompson for a period of one month. Nevertheless, she will require your assistance.

Mrs Thompson currently takes Panadeine Forte as required for pain relief and LMWH (Clexane). Her wound and drain site remain clean and dry. She has been very compliant with her physiotherapy regimen and has received post-operative education regarding care after her surgery.

Mrs Thompson has been instructed to refrain from any lifting for 4 weeks while her arm remains in a sling. She is required to participate in physiotherapy twice per week and hydrotherapy once per week at the outpatient clinic. She also has a follow-up appointment on Day 10 after her operation at the Orthopaedic Joint Replacement Outpatients Department where she will have her staples removed.

Please assist Mrs Thompson with showering and the administration of Clexane subcutaneously for 4 days to help prevent DVT. For any concerns, please contact either myself or the Orthopaedic Joint Replacement Nurse Specialist by calling the hospital.

Yours sincerely,

Registered Nurse

How we assess Writing

OET is a test of English language, not a test of professional knowledge.

The candidate's writing performance in the single writing task is assessed by two qualified assessors who have been trained in OET assessment procedures.

The Writing task responses are assessed in Melbourne, Australia. All responses are double marked.

Subject matter experts for each profession are involved in the test writing process and identify the key relevant information from the case notes which must be included in responses for the reader to be adequately informed. The assessors are language experts trained to assess how this information is communicated.

Rationale

In the healthcare workplace, professionals are expected to be able to communicate with colleagues, peers and patients clearly and effectively. The Writing task allows candidates to demonstrate the ability to communicate information about a healthcare scenario in written form.

The case notes provided in the Writing task present candidates with authentic stimulus material from which to demonstrate their communicative writing proficiency.

The written letter task is designed to give candidates opportunities to demonstrate their communicative language ability in ways that are valued in the healthcare context.

For example, that they can:

» summarise information about a patient or healthcare situation to provide the reader with the salient points.

» select and prioritise information which is relevant to the reader.

» make requests for action to ensure continuity of care.

» communicate information using appropriate formality and language as would be expected from someone working in the healthcare field.

The candidate's performance in the written task is assessed against 6 criteria:

1. Purpose (3 marks)
2. Content
3. Conciseness & Clarity
4. Genre & Style   (7 marks each)
5. Organisation & Layout
6. Language

Your letter is assessed against six criteria:

» **Purpose:** Whether the purpose of the letter is immediately apparent to the reader and sufficiently expanded in the course of the letter.

» **Content:** Whether all the necessary information is included and is accurate for the reader.

» **Conciseness & Clarity:** Whether unnecessary information is omitted so that the letter is an effective summary for the reader.

» **Genre & Style:** Whether the register, tone and use of abbreviations are appropriate for the reader.

» **Organisation & Layout:** Whether the letter is organised and well laid out for the reader.

» **Language:** Whether the accuracy of the grammar, vocabulary, spelling and punctuation communicates the necessary information to the reader.

Purpose

» Clearly explain the main purpose of your letter early in the document, within the first paragraph when appropriate – this provides the context for the information you include.

» Clearly expand on the purpose within the letter – this assists the reader to understand what is required of them.

» Be clear about the level of urgency for the communication.

Content

» Always keep in mind the reason for writing – don't just summarise the case notes provided.

» Focus on important information and minimise incidental detail.

» Demonstrate in your response that you have understood the case notes fully.

» Be clear what the most relevant issues for the reader are.

» Don't let the main issue become hidden by including too much supporting detail.

» Show clearly the connections between information in the case notes if these are made; however, do not add information that is not given in the notes (e.g., your suggested diagnosis), particularly if the reason for the letter is to get an expert opinion.

» Take relevant information from the case notes and transform it to fit the task set.

» If the stimulus material includes questions that require an answer in your response, be explicit about this – don't 'hide' the relevant information in a general summary of the notes provided.

» Write enough so the reader would be accurately informed of the situation.

Conciseness & Clarity

» Avoid writing too much –if you select the case notes carefully, you will naturally end up within the guided word limit.

» Avoid using a 'formulaic' response – if you include elements that do not fit the task, it indicates a lack of flexibility in your writing.

» Don't include information that the intended reader clearly knows already (e.g., if you are replying to a colleague who has referred a patient to you).

» Don't include information that the reader will not need to provide continued care (e.g. medical history that is not relevant to the current situation).

» Use your own words to clearly summarise the case notes to keep information concise for the reader.

Genre & Style

» Remember that all professional letters are written in a relatively formal style.

» Avoid informal language, slang, colloquialisms and spoken idioms unless you are sure this is appropriate (e.g., use 'Thank you' rather than 'Thanks a lot').

» Avoid SMS texting abbreviations in a formal letter (e.g., use 'you' not 'u').

» Give the correct salutation: if you are told the recipient's name and title, use them.

» Show awareness of your audience by choosing appropriate words and phrases: if you are writing to another healthcare professional in the same medical discipline, you may use technical terms and, possibly, abbreviations. If you are writing to a parent or a group of lay people, use non-technical terms and explain carefully.

» Avoid judgemental or opinionated language. Clinical/factual language sounds more professional.

» Use short forms appropriately

  • Don't use symbols in formal letters.

  • Be judicious with your use of abbreviations. Use them minimally where a colleague would understand them but do not overuse so that the tone of your letter becomes informal.

» Use statements rather than questions to make requests (e.g. 'A second opinion would be appreciated' rather than 'Please can you provide a second opinion?') to explain action you want the reader to take.

» Prioritise the patient or the treatment over who provided or authorised this treatment in the appropriate context (e.g., 'IV Morphine was commenced post-operatively' rather than 'I commenced the patient on IV Morphine post-operatively').

» Refer to the patient by name not as 'the patient' or 'the client' to make your letter personalized and to sound polite. For children aged 16 years or younger, using their first name only is often appropriate following the initial introduction.

» Remember brackets are not a common feature of formal writing and can often be replaced by a pair of commas or embedded within the sentence (e.g. 'have not responded to migraine treatments: dark room, sleep and ice' rather than 'have not responded to migraine treatments [dark room, sleep and ice]').

» Close the letter using an appropriately formal salutation (e.g. 'Yours sincerely' or 'Yours faithfully' rather than 'Kind regards').

Organisation & Layout

» Organise the information clearly – the sequence of information in the case notes may not be the most appropriate sequence of information for your letter.

» Consider using dates and other time references (e.g., three months later, last week, a year ago, etc.) to give a clear sequence of events where necessary.

» Think about your reader; writing about related information in the same paragraph is much clearer to understand

» Use connecting words and phrases ('connectives') to link ideas together clearly (e.g., however, therefore, subsequently, etc.).

» Use a clear layout to avoid any miscommunication: leave a blank line between paragraphs to show clearly the overall structure of the letter.

» Avoid creating any negative impact on your reader through the presentation of the letter: don't write on every other line – this does not assist the reader particularly.

» There is no need to include the patient's address as a separate part of your letter, you are not assessed on this.

Language

» Show that you can use language accurately and flexibly in your writing.

» Use language naturally – complex as well as simple sentences, a variety of tenses – to help your reader clearly understand the content.

» Split a long sentence into two or three sentences if you feel you are losing control of it.

» Review areas of grammar to ensure you convey your intended meaning accurately – particular areas to focus on might include*:

  • articles – a/an, the (e.g., 'She had an operation.', 'on the Internet')

  • countable and uncountable nouns (e.g., some evidence, an opinion, an asthma attack)

  • verb forms used to indicate past time and the relationship between events in the past and now (past simple, present perfect, past perfect)

  • adverbs that give time references (e.g., 'two months previously' is different from 'two months ago')

  • prepositions following other words (e.g., 'Thank you very much ~~to see~~ for seeing ...', 'sensitivity ~~of~~ to pressure', 'my examination ~~on~~ of the patient', 'diagnosed with cancer')

  • passive forms (e.g., '~~He involved in an accident.~~' for 'He was involved in an accident.')

» Take care with the placement of commas and full stops:

  • Make sure there are enough – separating ideas into sentences.

  • Make sure there are not too many – keeping elements of the text meaningfully connected together.

  • Use as part of titles, dates and salutations if you prefer or omit if this is your personal style.

How we assess Speaking

OET is a test of English language, not a test of professional knowledge.

The whole Speaking sub-test is audio recorded and the audio recording is assessed. The assessment is given on the candidate's performance in the two role-plays only (not the warm-up conversation).

The candidate's speaking performance is assessed by two qualified assessors who have been trained in OET assessment procedures.

The Speaking sub-test recordings are assessed in Melbourne, Australia. All recordings are double marked.

Important: The interlocutor is trained to ensure the structure of the Speaking sub-test is consistent for each candidate. The interlocutor also uses detailed information on his/her role-play card. The interlocutor DOES NOT assess the candidate.

Rationale

An important part of a health professional's role is the ability to communicate effectively in speech with his/her patients or clients. The role-plays allow the candidate to take his/her professional role and demonstrate the ability to deal with common workplace situations. These situations may include elements of tension which are a normal part of the real-life context, for example, anxious or angry patients, patients who misunderstand their situation, etc.

The two role-plays, each with a different scenario, provide two separate opportunities for the candidate to demonstrate spoken proficiency, therefore giving a broad view of the candidate's spoken skills.

Role-play tasks are designed to give candidates opportunities to demonstrate their language ability, for example, to:

» negotiate meaning with the interlocutor who is playing the role of the patient (e.g., reassure a worried patient, clarify a medical explanation, manage an upset patient, etc.).

» explain medical conditions/treatments and terminology in an accessible way.

» rephrase ideas and opinions in different ways to try and convince a patient.

» ask and answer questions to and from the patient.

» engage with a variety of patient types (different ages, personalities, different health concerns, etc.).

The candidate's performance in the two role-plays is assessed against linguistic criteria and clinical communication criteria:

Linguistic Criteria (6 marks each)

7. Intelligibility
8. Fluency
9. Appropriateness
10. Resources of Grammar and Expression

Clinical Communication Criteria (3 marks each)

1. Relationship building
2. Understanding and incorporating the patient's perspective
3. Providing structure
4. Information gathering
5. Information giving

Linguistic criteria

NOTE: The following extracts are examples only. Assessors are carefully trained to assess candidates' sustained performance across both role-plays.

1. Intelligibility

> *This criterion assesses how well a candidate's speech can be heard and understood. It concerns the impact of such features of speech as pronunciation, rhythm, stress, intonation, pitch and accent on the listener.*

Assessors will use this criterion to evaluate the candidate's production of comprehensible speech.

A strong proficiency candidate will:

» use natural flow of speech, giving stress to particular words within sentences to emphasise meaning, e.g., 'I'm unable to do THOSE tests in THIS clinic'.

» use natural flow of speech, giving correct stress to syllables within words so that they are identifiable to the listener, e.g., 'I will reCORD your results'. 'This is an accurate REcord of your results'.

» show control of intonation (voice falling or rising) and stress (appropriate force, length, emphasis or loudness) to enhance meaning and strengthen the communication he/she is wanting to provide.

» pronounce words clearly, for example:

  1. consonants at the end of words or syllables (e.g., 'head', 'weakness').
  2. consonants that distinguish different meanings of similar words (e.g., 'worry', 'worries', 'worried').
  3. consonant sounds at the beginning of words (e.g., /v/ as in '**v**omit', /b/ '**b**ill' versus /p/ '**p**ill').
  4. syllables within words (e.g., 'dang(er)ous', 'a coup(le) of days').
  5. clear initial consonant blends 'problem', 'bleeding'.
  6. word stress in longer words (e.g., 'PAINkiller' not 'painKILLer', 'HOSpital' not 'hosPItal').
  7. vowel sounds (/əʊ/ 'n**o**te' versus /ɒ/ 'n**o**t').

» minimise any intrusive sounds, rhythm and accent which may be influenced by his/her mother tongue.

» show the ability to link words together naturally. For example, there are often no 'spaces' between words in phrases like, 'in_about_an_hour'.

Now, look at the following examples. Examples 1 and 2 demonstrate HIGH and LOW performances respectively. Some key points are highlighted in each example in relation to the criterion: Intelligibility.

Example 1

HIGHER
LOWER

"
... I **think** you can **find**_a few friends who

regularly go for_a_**walk**; ↘ you can **start**

with_them. ↘ And if_you **reduce** smoking

and cut_the amount of **coffee** you **drink**_a_

day, it would **help**_your **blood** pressure

level. ↘ **Start**_to drink more **water** and do

some **exercise**, your **blood** pressure will be

better in_a month. ↘
"

Comment

Prosodic features (stress, intonation ↘ and rhythm) are used efficiently. The speech is easily understood even though the evidence of the first language is present. Certain words are linked_together naturally.

Example 2

HIGHER
LOWER

"
Wrong		Correct
in**ju**ry	=>	in**j**ury
se**ve**re	=>	seve**r**e
infl**u**ence	=>	i**n**fluence
"

Comment

Issues with non-standard word level stress and incorrectly pronounced vowels interfere with the listener's ability to understand all information. This affects 'Intelligibility'.

"
• ... er... she injured her spine (pronounced as 'spʌn')... is a very important... organ...

[sp/aɪ/n]

• .. may be several months, she can't mobilise (pronounced as 'mobju:laiz') herself...

[moub/ə/laiz]
"

Comment

Vowels are not pronounced correctly, which confuses the patient. The vowel sound in 'spine' [sp/aɪ/n] is not the same as the vowel in 'spun' [sp/ʌ/n], but should be pronounced as [sp/aɪ/n]. The vowel sound in 'mobilise' [moubəlaiz] is not the same as the vowel in 'bureaucrat' [bju:rəkræt], but should be pronounced as [moubəlaiz].

2. Fluency

This criterion assesses how well a candidate's speech is delivered in terms of rate and flow of speech.

Assessors will use this criterion to evaluate the degree to which a candidate is able to speak continuously, evenly and smoothly – without excessive hesitation, repetition, self-correction or use of 'fillers'.

A strong proficiency candidate will:

» maintain a natural speed to make it easier for the listener to follow the message (not too slow, not too fast).

» use even speech (not broken up into fragments) and limit hesitations or speaking in 'bursts' of language.

» avoid overusing sounds (e.g., 'err', 'um', 'ah') and words (e.g., 'OK', 'yes') to fill in gaps.

» use a smoother flow of speech, stressing syllables appropriately and linking words/syllables together.

» use pauses appropriately, for example:

   1. to make his/her meaning clear, e.g., for emphasis.

   2. to separate clearly the points he/she is making.

   3. to think about what he/she is going to say next.

» avoid restarting sentences or repeating words and phrases as he/she corrects himself/herself.

Look at the following examples. Examples 1 and 2 demonstrate HIGH and LOW performances respectively. Some key points are described on each example in relation to the criterion: Fluency.

Example 1

HIGHER
LOWER

" ... I think you can find a few friends who regularly go for a walk; you can start with them...(omission)... .

Start to drink more water and do some exercise, your blood pressure will be better in a month. "

Comment

The flow of the speech is good, not too fast or not too slow.

The speech is even and hesitation is rarely evident.

There is little use of 'fillers' (e.g., 'err', 'um', 'OK', etc.).

Restarting sentences is rare.

Example 2

HIGHER
LOWER

- That is a common concerned from some patients...because they don't know any...don't know more... don't know many medications...something like that...

let

- You can also give her some... ~~give~~ her inhaler some steams...she can inhaler the steam... That can make her ~~to breath~~ easily...

breathe

Comment

There is some hesitation that affects fluency.

This candidate often pauses during his/her speech while he/she prepares what to say next.

This 'breaking up' of the message can affect the listener trying to decode it. This affects 'Fluency'.

How to improve

Try to work on a smoother delivery without so many false starts and reformations.

3. Appropriateness

This criterion assesses how well a candidate uses language, register and tone that are appropriate to the situation and the patient.

Assessors will use this criterion to evaluate the degree to which the individual words, grammar and style of speech the candidate selects are appropriate to the particular situation and context.

A strong proficiency candidate will:

» use suitable, professional language.

» use appropriate paraphrasing and re-wording if necessary to explain, in simple terms, technical procedures or medical conditions to a patient who may have little knowledge of these.

» adapt their style and tone to suit the particular situation of the role-play, e.g., giving bad news versus giving positive news or using language suitable for talking to an older person versus a younger person.

» respond appropriately to what the 'patient' says during the role-plays, e.g., the candidate's responses are logically linked with the patient's questions or concerns.

» use language that might reflect the professionalism a health practitioner might require when dealing with patients, e.g., not overly-familiar or informal.

» demonstrate that he/she has the language skills to deal well with complicated situations, e.g., complaints, difficult patients, patients who need convincing, etc.

» use appropriate phrases that are suited to common functions found in medical exchanges, e.g., to 'reassure', 'encourage', 'be supportive', 'explain', etc.

» show awareness of the patient's sensitivities to the condition or information the candidate gives.

Now, look at the following examples. Examples 1 and 2 demonstrate HIGH and LOW performances respectively. Some key points are described on each example in relation to the criterion: Appropriateness.

Example 1

HIGHER — **LOWER**

" ... What do you think is easier or better for you? Where do you want to start? Do you want to start with ... your eating habit? "

" ... and you do not need to do some intensive fitness activities. I think it's enough if you start with walking for half an hour everyday. "

Comment

This candidate uses a good strategy to convince the unwilling patient (e.g., using questions rather than imperative forms to encourage the patient).

An appropriate tone is used to encourage the patient.

Example 2

HIGHER — **LOWER**

"
- If...she doesn't get treatment ~~effectively~~... [effective]
it may ~~be worsen~~... [get worse]
- As far as we know, the antibiotic ~~doesn't~~ [is not] really helpful for viral infections... "

Comment

The misuse of natural phrases and expressions is affecting 'Appropriateness'. The underlined phrase indicates considerable doubt, whereas antibiotics definitely do not work for viral infections.

"
- If you don't keep [an] eye on this disease...you might ~~get~~ [go] blind unfortunately. But if you keep ~~to do~~ [checking] your blood sugar level and to keep [an] eye [your] on diet... "

Comment

At times the message is interrupted by word choice errors. This affects 'Appropriateness'.

How to improve

Take care with phrases that can be easily confused. Meaning breaks down if the phrase is only partially correct.

4. Resources of grammar and expression

This criterion assesses the level and extent of the candidate's grammar and vocabulary resources and their appropriate use.

Assessors will use this criterion to evaluate the range and accuracy of the language resources the candidate has applied in the performance to convey clear meaning.

A strong proficiency candidate will:

» use appropriate structures to make what he/she is saying coherent, for example, outlining options or choices to a patient (e.g., 'There are several options you can consider. Firstly, in the short term, …').

» show flexibility by using different phrases to communicate the same idea, if necessary, to make it clearer.

» form questions correctly, particularly those questions that are often used in health professional/patient dialogues (e.g., 'How long have you been experiencing this?', 'When did the symptoms start?').

» minimise grammatical inaccuracy to enhance communicative effectiveness.

» use more complex structures and expressions confidently (e.g., idiomatic speech, sentences with multiple clauses, etc.), i.e., not just a series of simple utterances.

» use a wide variety of grammatical structures and vocabulary that reflects the depth and range of their linguistic resources.

» show accurate control of grammatical features including, for example:

1. correct word order (e.g., 'She broke her tooth' not 'She tooth her broke').

2. correct use of pronouns/relative pronouns (e.g., 'Tell her it's ok if she (not he) waits then comes back to see me when she (not he) feels better').

3. correct word choice (e.g., 'Your daughter is breathing more rapidly/repeatedly/regularly' (all have different meanings)).

4. not omitting words that could affect clear meaning (e.g., 'I recommend that you consider several options including crown, fillings and inlays' not 'I recommend about crown, filling, inlay').

5. correct use of prepositions (e.g., 'I can explain to you about asthma' not 'I can explain you about asthma').

6. correct use of articles (e.g., 'A form is completed and then given to the Pharmacist' not 'Form is completed and then given to Pharmacist').

7. use correct word form (e.g., 'Smoking is dangerous for your health' not 'Smoking is danger for your health').

8. correct use of countable and uncountable expressions (e.g., 'not many side effects' not 'not much side effects').

9. use appropriate structures to convey information about time and the sequence of past or future events (e.g., 'We have X-rayed your arm and the results will be available today/next week' not 'We X-ray your arm and the results available').

Now, look at the following examples. Examples 1 and 2 demonstrate HIGH and LOW performances respectively. Some key points are described on each example in relation to the criterion: Resources of Grammar and Expression.

Example 1

HIGHER
LOWER

" ... You have two options. The first option is, you're going to have medication, which would be the last solution. The second option, the better option I think, is changing your lifestyle. You do not need to change everything in your life, but you need to make it better... "

Comment

The available options for the patient are outlined in a coherent manner (e.g., 'You have two options. First...').

The number of errors are not intrusive.

Information is given in a confident manner.

Different structures are used to communicate the same idea effectively (e.g., '...is changing your lifestyle. You do not need to change everything...').

Example 2

HIGHER
LOWER

" • No, I'm not forcing, this is option...
• If you have some pain, try not to use too much because I will put some dressing...'

you

an

it

on it "

Comment

Many sentences are incomplete. Watch out for pronouns such as 'you', 'it' and prepositions such as 'put something on (something)'.

" You need to be free of infections. What you can do is to take some cleaning gloves every time and <u>do something</u> with clean clothes <u>and something like that</u>... "

Comment

Many simple words are used repetitively, affecting "Resources of Grammar and Expression". In the above example, 'something' is overused, indicating gaps in vocabulary.

How to improve
Be more specific with word choice.

OET Speaking clinical communication criteria

A: Indicators of relationship building

A1	Initiating the interaction appropriately (greeting, introductions)	Initiating the interview appropriately helps establish rapport and a supportive environment. Initiation involves greeting the patient, introducing yourself, clarifying the patient's name and clarifying your role in their care. The nature of the interview can be explained and if necessary negotiated.
A2	Demonstrating an attentive and respectful attitude	Throughout the interview, demonstrating attentiveness and respect establishes trust with the patient, lays down the foundation for a collaborative relationship and ensures that the patient understands your motivation to help. Examples of such behaviour would include attending to the patient's comfort, asking permission and consent to proceed, and being sensitive to potentially embarrassing or distressing matters.
A3	Demonstrating a non-judgemental approach	Accepting the patient's perspective and views reassuringly and non-judgementally without initial rebuttal is a key component of relationship building. A judgemental response to patients' ideas and concerns devalues their contributions. A non-judgemental response would include accepting the patient's perspective and acknowledging the legitimacy of the patient to hold their own views and feelings.
A4	Showing empathy for feelings/ predicament/ emotional state	Empathy is one of the key skills of building the relationship. Empathy involves the understanding and sensitive appreciation of another person's predicament or feelings and the communication of that understanding back to the patient in a supportive way. This can be achieved through both non-verbal and verbal behaviours. Even with audio alone, some non-verbal behaviours such as the use of silence and appropriate voice tone in response to a patient's expression of feelings can be observed. Verbal empathy makes this more explicit by specifically naming and appreciating the patient's emotions or predicament.

B: Indicators of understanding and incorporating the patient's perspective

B1	Eliciting and exploring patient's ideas/concerns/expectations	Understanding the patient's perspective is a key component of patient-centred health care. Each patient has a unique experience of sickness that includes the feelings, thoughts, concerns and effect on life that any episode of sickness induces. Patients may either volunteer this spontaneously (as direct statements or cues) or in response to health professionals' enquiries.
B2	Picking up patient's cues	Patients are generally eager to tell us about their own thoughts and feelings but often do so indirectly through verbal hints or changes in non-verbal behaviour (such as vocal cues including hesitation or change in volume). Picking up these cues is essential for exploring both the biomedical and the patient's perspectives.
		Some of the techniques for picking up cues would include echoing, i.e. repeating back what has just been said and either adding emphasis where appropriate or turning the echoed statement into a question, e.g. "*Something could be done...?*" . Another possibility is more overtly checking out statements or hints, e.g. "*I sense that you are not happy with the explanations you've been given in the past*"
B3	Relating explanations to elicited ideas/concerns/ expectations	One of the key reasons for discovering the patient's perspective is to incorporate this into explanations often in the later aspects of the interview. If the explanation does not address the patient's individual ideas, concerns and expectations, then recall, understanding and satisfaction suffer as the patient is still worrying about their still unaddressed concerns

C: Indicators of providing structure

C1	Sequencing the interview purposefully and logically	It is the responsibility of the health professional to maintain a logical sequence apparent to the patient as the interview unfolds. An ordered approach to organisation helps both professional and patient in efficient and accurate data gathering and information-giving. This needs to be balanced with the need to be patient-centred and follow the patient's needs. Flexibility and logical sequencing need to be thoughtfully combined. It is more obvious when sequencing is inadequate: the health professional will meander aimlessly or jump around between segments of the interview making the patient unclear as to the point of specific lines of enquiry.
C2	Signposting changes in topic	Signposting is a key skill in enabling patients to understand the structure of the interview by making the organisation overt: not only the health professional but also the patient needs to understand where the interview is going and why. A signposting statement introduces and draws attention to what we are about to say. For instance, it is helpful to use a signposting statement to introduce a summary. Signposting can also be used to make the progression from one section to another and explain the rationale for the next section.
C3	Using organising techniques in explanations	A variety of skills help to organise explanations in a way that leads particularly to increased patient recall and understanding. Skills include: categorisation in which the health professional informs the patient about which categories of information are to be provided labelling in which important points are explicitly labelled by the health professional. This can be achieved by using emphatic phrases or adverb intensifiers chunking in which information is delivered in chunks with clear gaps in between sections before proceeding repetition and summary of important points

D: Indicators for information-gathering

D1	Facilitating patient's narrative with active listening techniques, minimising interruption	Listening to the patient's narrative, particularly at the beginning of an interview, enables the health professional to more efficiently discover the story, hear the patient's perspective, appear supportive and interested and pick up cues to patients' feelings. Interruption of the narrative has the opposite effect and in particular generally leads to a predominantly biomedical history, omitting the patient's perspective. Observable skills of active listening techniques include: **A.** the use of silence and pausing **B.** verbal encouragement such as *um, uh-huh, I see* **C.** echoing and repetition such as "*chest pain?*" or "*not coping?*" **D.** paraphrasing and interpretation such as "*Are you thinking that when John gets even more ill, you won't be strong enough to nurse him at home by yourself?*"
D2	Using initially open questions, appropriately moving to closed questions	Understanding how to intentionally choose between open and closed questioning styles at different points in the interview is of key importance. An effective health professional uses open questioning techniques first to obtain a picture of the problem from the patient's perspective. Later, the approach becomes more focused with increasingly specific though still open questions and eventually closed questions to elicit additional details that the patient may have omitted. The use of open questioning techniques is critical at the beginning of the exploration of any problem and the most common mistake is to move to closed questioning too quickly. Closed questions are questions for which a specific and often one word answer is elicited. These responses are often "*yes/no*". *Open questioning techniques* in contrast are designed to introduce an area of enquiry without unduly shaping or focusing the content of the response. They still direct the patient to a specific area but allow the patient more discretion in their answer, suggesting to the patient that elaboration is both appropriate and welcome.
D3	NOT using compound questions/ leading questions	A compound question is when more than one question is asked without allowing time to answer. It confuses the patient about what information is wanted, and introduces uncertainty about which of the questions asked the eventual reply relates to. An example would be "*have you ever had chest pain or felt short of breath?*" A leading question includes an assumption in the question which makes it more difficult for the respondent to contradict the assumption. e.g., "*You've lost weight, haven't you?* or "*you haven't had any ankle swelling?*"

| D4 | Clarifying statements which are vague or need amplification | Clarifying statements which are vague or need further amplification is a vital information gathering skill. After an initial response to an open ended question, health professionals may need to prompt patients for more precision, clarity or completeness. Often patients' statements can have two (or more) possible meanings: it is important to ascertain which one is intended. |
| D5 | Summarising information to encourage correction/ invite further information | Summarising is the deliberate step of making an explicit verbal summary to the patient of the information gathered so far and is one of the most important of all information gathering skills. Used periodically throughout the interview, it helps with two significant tasks – ensuring accuracy and facilitating the patient's further responses. |

E: Indicators for information-giving

E1	Establishing initially what patient already knows	One key interactive approach to giving information to patients involves assessing their prior knowledge. This allows you to determine at what level to pitch information, how much and what information the patient needs, and the degree to which your view of the problem differs from that of the patient.
E2	Pausing periodically when giving information, using response to guide next steps	This approach, often called chunking and checking, is a vital skill throughout the information-giving phase of the interview. Here, the health professional gives information in small pieces, pausing and checking for understanding before proceeding and being guided by the patient's reactions to see what information is required next. This technique is a vital component of assessing the patient's overall information needs: if you give information in small chunks and give patients ample opportunity to contribute, they will respond with clear signals about both the amount and type of information they still require.
E3	Encouraging patient to contribute reactions/ feelings	A further element of effective information giving is providing opportunities to the patient to ask questions, seek clarification or express doubts. Health professionals have to be very explicit here: many patients are reluctant to express what is on the tip of their tongue and are extremely hesitant to ask the doctor questions. Unless positively invited to do so, they may leave the consultation with their questions unanswered and a reduced understanding and commitment to plans.
E4	Checking whether patient has understood information	Checking the patient has understood the information given is an important step in ensuring accuracy of information transfer. This can be done by asking "*does that make sense?*" although many patients will say yes when they mean no to avoid looking stupid. A more effective method is to use patient restatement, i.e. asking the patient to repeat back to the doctor what has been discussed to ensure that their understanding is the same
E5	Discovering what further information patient needs	Deliberately asking the patient what other information would be helpful enables the health professional to directly discover areas to address which the health professional might not have considered. It is difficult to guess each patient's individual needs and asking directly is an obvious way to prevent the omission of important information.

Useful language

Greeting Introduction

- » Good morning/afternoon/evening.
- » Nice to see you (again).
- » How are you today?
- » My name is Dr .../I'm Dr ...
- » Thanks for coming to see me today.
- » Pleased to meet you (response to patient's introduction).

Getting information

Starting the interview:

- » What brings you along here today?
- » What brought you here today?
- » What seems to be the trouble/problem?
- » How can I help you?
- » What can I do for you?
- » What seems to be bothering you?

Asking about location of the problem:

- » Where is the sensation?
- » Can you tell me where it hurts?
- » Where do you feel sore?
- » Where does it feel sore?
- » Which part of the/your body is affected?
- » Show me where the pain is.
- » Tell me where the pain is.

Asking about duration:

- » When did it start?
- » How long have you had it?
- » How long have you been feeling like this?
- » How often has this been occurring?
- » How long have you been suffering from this problem?
- » When did the problem start?

Asking about severity of pain or type of pain:

- » Is the pain dull or sharp?
- » What is the pain like?
- » Could you describe the pain?
- » How severe is the pain?
- » Does it disturb you at night?
- » Does it feel numb?
- » Does it occur all of the time or just now and again?

Questioning

To clarify/to get details:

- » Have you had any...?
- » Does the discomfort appear to be brought on by anything in particular?
- » What do you do when you get the pain?
- » Do you ever get pain at night?
- » Does anything special make it worse?
- » Does anything seem to bring it on/aggravate the problem?
- » Is there anything that seems to relieve this?

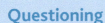

Prescribing

Tests, medicine, treatment:

» I think we would start with...
» I will give you a prescription for...
» I will give you a referral for...
» I'll write a referral letter to...
» I'm going to ask you to fill a prescription for...
» We'll run some tests to see...

Check understanding

» Do you have any questions?
» Have you ever heard of ...?

Reassurance

» I can understand your concerns, but...
» I'm sure you won't have any more trouble...
» Don't worry, it'll go away by itself/in a few days/with some rest...
» Rest assured, this is quite common...
» There is nothing to be overly concerned about.

Feedback

Respond to patient's questions:

» Were there any other questions?
» Does this sound ok/ like an acceptable plan?

Advising Suggesting

» What I think we'll do is ...
» What I suggest you do is ...
» It is worthwhile...
» I advise you...
» We could make a time to follow up on that.
» It's a good idea to ...

Leave-taking

Pleasure to meet you.

» Nice to meet you, ...
» Let's leave it there.
» All the best, ...
» I'll see you next time/soon.

» Thanks very much for coming to see me.

Notes

26439524R00126

Printed in Great Britain
by Amazon